D1311336

Microsoft® Visual C#® 2008 Comprehensive

An Introduction to Object-Oriented Programming

Microsoft® Visual C#® 2008 Comprehensive

An Introduction to Object-Oriented Programming

Joyce Farrell

Australia • Brazil • Japan • Korea • Mexico • Singapore • Spain • United Kingdom • United States

Microsoft® Visual C#® 2008 Comprehensive: An Introduction to Object-Oriented Programming
Joyce Farrell

Executive Editor: Marie Lee

Acquisitions Editor: Amy Jollymore

Managing Editor: Tricia Coia

Developmental Editor: Dan Seiter

Editorial Assistant: Julia Leroux-Lindsey

Marketing Manager: Bryant Chrzan

Content Project Manager: Heather Furrow

Art Director: Marissa Falco

Cover Designer: Bruce Bond

Cover Photo: © iStockphoto.com/4x6

Manufacturing Coordinator: Julio Esperas

Proofreader: Andrea Schein

Indexer: Alexandra Nickerson

Compositor: International Typesetting and Composition

© 2010 Course Technology, Cengage Learning

ALL RIGHTS RESERVED. No part of this work covered by the copyright herein may be reproduced, transmitted, stored or used in any form or by any means—graphic, electronic, or mechanical, including but not limited to photocopying, recording, scanning, digitizing, taping, Web distribution, information networks, or information storage and retrieval systems, except as permitted under Section 107 or 108 of the 1976 United States Copyright Act—without the prior written permission of the publisher.

For product information and technology assistance, contact us at
Cengage Learning Customer & Sales Support, 1-800-354-9706
For permission to use material from this text or product,
submit all requests online at **www.cengage.com/permissions**
Further permissions questions can be e-mailed to
permissionrequest@cengage.com

Microsoft® is a registered trademark of the Microsoft Corporation.

ISBN-13: 978-0-495-80643-1

ISBN-10: 0-495-80643-9

Course Technology
25 Thomson Place
Boston, MA 02210
USA

Cengage Learning is a leading provider of customized learning solutions with office locations around the globe, including Singapore, the United Kingdom, Australia, Mexico, Brazil, and Japan. Locate your local office at:
international.cengage.com/region

Cengage Learning products are represented in Canada by Nelson Education, Ltd.

For your lifelong learning solutions, visit **www.course.cengage.com**

Visit our corporate Web site at **www.cengage.com**

Some of the product names and company names used in this book have been used for identification purposes only and may be trademarks or registered trademarks of their respective manufacturers and sellers.

Course Technology, a part of Cengage Learning, reserves the right to revise this publication and make changes from time to time in its content without notice.

Printed in The United States of America
2 3 4 5 6 7 12 11 10

BRIEF CONTENTS

BRIEF CONTENTS

CONTENTS

CONTENTS

CONTENTS

PREFACE

Microsoft Visual C# 2008 Comprehensive: An Introduction to Object-Oriented Programming provides the beginning programmer with a guide to developing programs in C#, a language created by the Microsoft Corporation as part of the .NET Framework and Visual Studio platform. The .NET Framework contains a wealth of libraries for developing applications for the Windows family of operating systems. With C#, you can build small, reusable components that are well suited to twenty-first century Web-based programming applications. Although similar to Java and C++, many features of C# make it easier to learn and ideal for the beginning programmer. You can program in C# using a simple text editor and the command prompt, or you can manipulate program components using Visual Studio's sophisticated Integrated Development Environment. This book provides you with the tools to use both techniques.

This textbook assumes that you have little or no programming experience. The writing is nontechnical and emphasizes good programming practices. The examples are business examples; they do not assume mathematical background beyond high school business math. Additionally, the examples illustrate one or two major points; they do not contain so many features that you become lost following irrelevant or extraneous details. This book provides you with a solid background in good object-oriented programming techniques and introduces you to object-oriented terminology using clear, familiar language.

ORGANIZATION AND COVERAGE

Microsoft Visual C# 2008 Comprehensive: An Introduction to Object-Oriented Programming presents C# programming concepts, enforcing good style, logical thinking, and the object-oriented paradigm. Chapter 1 introduces you to the language by letting you create working C# programs using both the simple command line and the Visual Studio environment. In Chapter 2 you learn about data and how to input, store, and output data in C#. In Chapters 3, 4, and 5, you learn about the classic programming structures and how to implement them: making selections, looping, and manipulating arrays. Chapter 6 provides a thorough study of methods, including passing parameters into and out of methods and overloading them.

Chapter 7 introduces the object-oriented concepts of classes, objects, data hiding, constructors, and destructors. After completing Chapters 8 and 9, you will be thoroughly grounded in the object-oriented concepts of inheritance and exception handling, and you will be able to take advantage of both features in your C# programs. Chapters 10 and 11 introduce you to GUI objects. You will learn about controls, how to set their properties, and how to make attractive, useful, graphical, and interactive programs. Chapter 12 takes you further into the intricacies of handling events in your interactive GUI programs. In Chapter 13, you learn to save data to and retrieve data from files. In Chapter 14, you learn how to interact with databases in C# programs—an increasingly valuable skill in the information-driven business world. C# 3.0 supports LINQ (Language Integrated Query) statements, which allow you to integrate SQL-like queries into C# programs. Chapter 14 provides you with the fundamentals of this important technology.

Chapters 15 through 20 explore advanced topics that will allow you to produce more sophisticated C# applications and learn concepts you can apply to other object-oriented languages. Chapter 15 covers multithreading—the ability to execute different logical paths concurrently. Chapter 16 provides tools that allow you to create exciting programs by adding graphics and multimedia.

Chapters 17 and 18 introduce the Windows Presentation Foundation (WPF). The WPF is a presentation system included in the Microsoft.NET Framework that allows developers to build impressive and eye-catching Windows client applications using both markup and traditional programming code. These chapters provide a solid foundation in both skills.

Chapters 19 and 20 teach you about dynamic data structures and generics. Dynamic data structures allow sophisticated manipulations like those provided by linked lists, stacks, and queues. Generics allow the programmer to create reusable code that works with any data type. These chapters include the best of the old and the new; although they provide background in advanced computer science topics that are applicable to all object-oriented languages, they also explain features introduced in the most current version of C#.

FEATURES

Microsoft Visual C# 2008 Comprehensive: An Introduction to Object-Oriented Programming is a superior textbook because it also includes the following features:

- *C# 3.0 in Visual Studio 2008*—This edition is written and tested using the latest version of C#.
- *Objectives*—Each chapter begins with a list of objectives so you know the topics that will be presented in the chapter. In addition to providing a quick reference to topics covered, this feature provides a useful study aid.
- *Notes*—These tips provide additional information—for example, an alternative method of performing a procedure, another term for a concept, background information on a technique, or a common error to avoid.
- *Figures*—Each chapter contains many figures. Code figures are most frequently 25 lines or shorter, illustrating one concept at a time. Frequently placed screen shots show exactly how program output appears. In this edition, all C# keywords that appear in figures are blue to help them stand out from programmer-created identifiers.
- *Summaries*—Following each chapter is a summary that recaps the programming concepts and techniques covered in the chapter. This feature helps you to check your understanding of the main points in each chapter.
- *Key Terms*—Each chapter includes a list of newly introduced vocabulary, shown in the order of appearance in the text. The list of key terms provides a mini-review of the major concepts in the chapter.
- *You Do It*—In each chapter, step-by-step exercises help the student create multiple working programs that emphasize the logic a programmer uses in choosing statements. This section enables students to achieve success on their own—even students in online or distance learning classes.
- *Two Truths and a Lie*—These true-false mini-quizzes appear throughout each chapter, with answers provided. The quiz contains three statements from the preceding section of text—two true and one false. Over the years, students have requested answers to problems, but we have hesitated to distribute them in case instructors want to use problems as assignments or test questions. These true-false

mini-quizzes provide students with immediate feedback as they read, without "giving away" answers to the existing multiple-choice and programming problem questions.

- *Review Questions*—Each chapter contains 20 multiple-choice questions that provide a review of the key concepts in the chapter.
- *Exercises*—Each chapter concludes with meaningful programming exercises that provide additional practice of the skills and concepts you learned in the chapter. These exercises increase in difficulty and allow you to explore logical programming concepts.
- *Debugging Exercises*—Each chapter contains four programs that contain syntax and/or logical errors that you fix. Completing these exercises provides valuable experience in locating errors, interpreting code written by others, and observing how another programmer has approached a problem.
- *Glossary*—This edition includes a glossary that contains definitions for all key terms in the book, presented in alphabetical order.
- *Up for Discussion*—Each chapter concludes with a few thought-provoking questions that concern programming in general or C# in particular. The questions can be used to start classroom or online discussions, or to develop and encourage research, writing, and language skills.
- *Program code*—The Student Disk provides code for each full program presented in the chapter figures. Providing the code on disk allows students to run it, view the results for themselves, and experiment with multiple input values. Having the code on disk also enables students to experiment with the code without a lot of typing.
- *Quality*—Every program example and exercise in the book was tested by the author using Visual Studio 2008 Express Edition, and then tested again by a Quality Assurance team using Visual Studio 2008 Professional Edition, the most recent version available.

TEACHING TOOLS

The following supplemental materials are available when this book is used in a classroom setting. All of the instructor resources for this book are provided to the instructor on a single CD-ROM.

- *Electronic Instructor's Manual*—The Instructor's Manual that accompanies this textbook includes additional instructional material to assist in class preparation, including teaching tips, quick quizzes, class discussion topics, and additional projects.
- *ExamView®*—This textbook is accompanied by ExamView, a powerful testing software package that allows instructors to create and administer printed, computer (LAN-based), and Internet exams. ExamView includes hundreds of questions that correspond to the topics covered in this text, enabling students to generate detailed study guides that include page references for further review. The computer-based and Internet testing components allow students to take exams at their computers, and save the instructor time by grading each exam automatically.
- *PowerPoint Presentations*—This book comes with Microsoft PowerPoint slides for each chapter. These slides are included as a teaching aid for classroom presentation; teachers can make them available on the network for chapter review, or print them for classroom distribution. Instructors can add their own slides for additional topics they introduce to the class.
- *Solution Files*—Password-protected solutions to all Review Questions, end-of-chapter programming exercises, debugging exercises, Up For Discussion questions, and You Do It exercises are provided on the Instructor Resources CD-ROM and on the Course Technology Web site at *www.course.com*.

- *Distance Learning*—Course Technology is proud to present online test banks in WebCT and Blackboard to provide the most complete and dynamic learning experience possible. Instructors are encouraged to make the most of the course, both online and offline. For more information on how to access the online test bank, contact your local Course Technology sales representative.

ACKNOWLEDGMENTS

I would like to thank all of the people who helped to make this book a reality, especially Dan Seiter, the developmental editor, who once again worked against multiple, aggressive deadlines to make this book into a superior instructional tool. Thanks also to Tricia Coia, managing editor; Amy Jollymore, acquisitions editor; and Heather Furrow, content project manager. The Quality Assurance team, including Chris Scriver and Serge Palladino, was instrumental in making this an excellent textbook. I am grateful to be able to work with so many fine people who are dedicated to producing top-quality instructional materials.

I am also grateful to the many reviewers who provided helpful comments and encouragement during this book's development:

- Albert Arnold, Ozarks Technical Community College
- Kevin Bayer, Central Georgia Technical College
- I-Ping Chu, DePaul University
- Dr. Barbara Doyle, Jacksonville University
- Jean Evans, Brevard Community College
- Valerie Frear, Daytona Beach Community College
- Dan Guilmette, Cochise College
- Phil Jalowiec, Maricopa County Community College
- Matthew McCaskill, Brevard Community College
- John Morack, Waukesha County Technical College
- Richard Mowe, St. Cloud State University
- Von Plessner, Northwest State Community College
- Paul Rosenberg, DePaul University
- Dolly Samson, Hawaii Pacific University
- Phil Sciame, Dominican College
- Jo Ann Smith, Harper College
- John Stryker, Oakton Community College
- James Toalu, Chancellor University
- Paul Turnage, Schoolcraft College
- Matt Weisfeld, Cuyahoga Community College
- Judi Zaplatynsky, Harper College
- Lhoucine Zerrouki, Renton Technical College

Thanks, too, to my husband, Geoff, for his constant support and encouragement. Finally, this book is dedicated to my goddaughter Robin.

Joyce Farrell

READ THIS BEFORE YOU BEGIN

TO THE USER

To complete the exercises in this book, you will need data files that have been created specifically for the book. Your instructor will provide the data files to you. You also can obtain the files electronically from the Course Technology Web site by connecting to *www.course.com* and then searching for this book title. Note that you can use a computer in your school lab or your own computer to complete the exercises in this book.

The data files for this book are organized such that the examples and exercises are divided into folders named Chapter.*xx*, where *xx* is the chapter number. You can save these files in the same folders unless specifically instructed to do otherwise in the chapter.

USING YOUR OWN COMPUTER

To use your own computer to complete the steps and exercises, you will need the following:

- » *Software*—Microsoft Visual C# 2008 Express Edition or Professional Edition, including the Microsoft .NET Framework. If your book came with a copy of the software, you may install it on your computer and use it to complete the material.
- » *Hardware*—*Minimum*: 1.6-GHz CPU, 192 MB of RAM, 1024 × 768 display, 5400-RPM hard disk. *Recommended*: At least a 2.2-GHz CPU, at least 384 MB of RAM, 1280 × 1024 display, at least a 7200-RPM hard disk. *On Windows Vista*: 2.4-GHz CPU, 768 MB of RAM, 1.3 GB available disk space for full installation.
- » *Operating system*—Windows Vista or XP.
- » *Data files*—You will not be able to complete the exercises in this book using your own computer unless you have the data files. You can get the data files from your instructor, or you can obtain them electronically from the Course Technology Web site by connecting to *www.course.com* and searching for this book title.

TO THE INSTRUCTOR

To complete all the exercises and chapters in this book, your users must work with a set of data files. These files are included on the Instructor Resources CD. You can also obtain these files electronically through the Course Technology Web site at *www.course.com*. Follow the instructions in the Help file to copy the user files to your server or stand-alone computer. You can view the Help file using a text editor such as WordPad or Notepad.

Once the files are copied, you can make copies for the users yourself or tell them where to find the files so they can make their own copies.

LICENSE TO USE DATA FILES

You are granted a license to copy the files that accompany this book to any computer or computer network used by people who have purchased this book.

CHAPTERONE

1

A FIRST PROGRAM USING C#

In this chapter you will:

- Learn about programming
- Explore object-oriented programming concepts
- Learn about the C# programming language
- Write a C# program that produces output
- Learn how to select identifiers to use within your programs
- Add comments to a C# program
- Eliminate the reference to `Out` by using the `System` namespace
- Write and compile a C# program using the command prompt and using Visual Studio
- Learn alternate ways to write the `Main()` method

Programming a computer is an interesting, challenging, fun, and sometimes frustrating task. It requires you to be precise and careful as well as creative. If you do this, you will find that learning a new programming language expands your horizons.

As new programming languages are developed and introduced, your job becomes easier and more difficult at the same time. Programming becomes easier because built-in capabilities are added to every new language that is developed, and tasks that might have taken you weeks or months to develop 20 years ago are now included in the language so you can add them to a program with a few keystrokes. Programming becomes more difficult for the same reason—new languages have so many features that you must devote a significant amount of time to learning them.

C# (pronounced "C Sharp") is a relatively new language that provides you with a wide range of options and features. As you work through this book, you will master many of them, one step at a time. If this is your first programming experience, you will learn new ways to approach and solve problems and to think logically. If you know how to program but are new to C#, you will be impressed by its capabilities.

In this chapter, you will learn about the background of programming that led to the development of C#, and you will write and execute your first C# programs.

PROGRAMMING

A computer **program** is a set of instructions that you write to tell a computer what to do. Internally, computers are constructed from circuitry that consists of small on/off switches; the most basic circuitry-level language that computers use to control the operation of those switches is called **machine language**. Machine language is expressed as a series of 1s and 0s—1s represent switches that are on, and 0s represent switches that are off. If programmers had to write computer programs using machine language, they would have to keep track of the hundreds of thousands of 1s and 0s involved in programming any worthwhile task. Not only would writing a program be a time-consuming and difficult task, but modifying programs, understanding others' programs, and locating errors within programs all would be cumbersome. Additionally, the number and location of switches vary from computer to computer, which means you would need to customize a machine-language program for every type of machine on which the program had to run.

Fortunately, programming has evolved into an easier task because of the development of high-level programming languages. A **high-level programming language** allows you to use a vocabulary of reasonable terms such as "read," "write," or "add" instead of the sequence of on/off switches that perform these tasks. High-level languages also allow you to assign reasonable names to areas of computer memory; you can use names such as "`hoursWorked`" or "`payRate`," rather than having to remember the memory locations (switch numbers) of those values.

Each high-level language has its own **syntax**, or rules of the language. For example, to produce output, you might use the verb "print" in one language and "write" in another. All languages have a specific, limited vocabulary, along with a set of rules for using that vocabulary. Programmers use a computer program called a **compiler** to translate their high-level language statements into machine code. The compiler issues an error message each time a programmer commits a **syntax error**—that is, each time the programmer uses the language incorrectly. Subsequently, the programmer can correct the error and attempt another translation by compiling the program again. The program can be completely translated to machine language only when all syntax errors have been corrected. When you learn a computer programming language such as C#, C++, Visual Basic, or Java, you really are learning the vocabulary and syntax rules for that language.

»NOTE In some languages, such as BASIC, the language translator is called an interpreter. In others, such as assembly language, it is called an assembler. These translators operate in different fashions, but the ultimate goal of each is to translate the higher-level language into machine language.

In addition to learning the correct syntax for a particular language, a programmer must understand computer programming logic. The **logic** behind any program involves executing the various statements and procedures in the correct order to produce the desired results. For example, you might be able to execute perfect individual notes on a musical instrument, but if you do not execute them in the proper order (or execute a B-flat when an F-sharp was expected), no one will enjoy your performance. Similarly, you might be able to use a computer language's syntax correctly, but be unable to execute a logically constructed, workable program. Examples of logical errors include multiplying two values when you should divide them, or attempting to calculate a paycheck before obtaining the appropriate payroll data.

»NOTE Programmers call some logical errors **semantic errors.** For example, if you misspell a programming language word, you commit a syntax error, but if you use a correct word in the wrong context, you commit a semantic error.

To achieve a working program that accomplishes the tasks it is meant to accomplish, you must remove all syntax and logical errors from the program. This process is called **debugging** the program.

»NOTE Since the early days of computer programming, program errors have been called "bugs." The term is often said to have originated from an actual moth that was discovered trapped in the circuitry of a computer at Harvard University in 1945. Actually, the term "bug" was in use prior to 1945 to mean trouble with any electrical apparatus; even during Thomas Edison's life, it meant an "industrial defect." In any case, the process of finding and correcting program errors has come to be known as debugging.

»TWO TRUTHS AND A LIE: PROGRAMMING

Two of the following statements are true, and one is false. Identify the false statement and explain why it is false.

1. A high-level programming language allows you to use a vocabulary of reasonable terms such as "read," "write," or "add" instead of the sequence of on/off switches that perform these tasks.
2. Each high-level programming language has its own syntax, or rules of the language.
3. Programmers use a computer program called a compiler to translate machine code into a high-level language they can understand.

The false statement is #3. Programmers use a computer program called a compiler to translate their high-level language statements into machine code.

OBJECT-ORIENTED PROGRAMMING

Two popular approaches to writing computer programs are procedural programming and object-oriented programming.

When you write a **procedural program**, you use your knowledge of a programming language to create and name computer memory locations that can hold values, and you write a series of steps or operations to manipulate those values. The named computer memory locations are called **variables** because they hold values that might vary. In programming languages, a variable is referenced by using a one-word name (an **identifier**) with no embedded spaces. For example, a company's payroll program might contain a variable named `payRate`. The memory location referenced by the name `payRate` might contain different values at different times. For instance, an organization's payroll program might contain a different value for `payRate` for each of 100 employees. Additionally, a single employee's `payRate` variable might contain different values before or after a raise or before or after surpassing 40 work hours in one week. During the execution of the payroll program, each value stored under the name `payRate` might have many operations performed on it—for example, reading it from an input device, multiplying it by another variable representing hours worked, and printing it on paper.

»NOTE When programmers do not capitalize the first letter of an identifier but do capitalize each new word, as in `payRate`, they call the style **camel casing**, because the identifier appears to have a hump in the middle. When programmers adopt the style of capitalizing the first letter of all new words in an identifier, even the first one, as in `PayRate`, they call the style **Pascal casing**. Most C# programmers use camel casing when creating variable names, but this convention is not required to produce a workable program.

»NOTE Depending on the programming language, methods are sometimes called *procedures*, *subroutines*, or *functions*. In C#, the preferred term is *methods*.

For convenience, the individual operations used in a computer program often are grouped into logical units called **procedures** or **methods**. For example, a series of four or five comparisons and calculations that together determine an employee's federal tax withholding value might be grouped as a method named `CalculateFederalWithholding()`. A procedural program defines the variable memory locations, then **calls** or **invokes** a series of procedures to input, manipulate, and output the values stored in those locations. A single procedural program often contains hundreds of variables and thousands of procedure calls.

»NOTE In C#, methods conventionally are named using Pascal casing, and all method names are followed by a set of parentheses. When you pronounce a method name, you ignore the parentheses. When this book refers to a method, the name will be followed with parentheses. This practice helps distinguish method names from variable and class names.

Object-oriented programming is an extension of procedural programming. Object-oriented programs contain variables, methods, and six other features:

- » Objects
- » Classes
- » Encapsulation

» Interfaces
» Polymorphism
» Inheritance

»NOTE Although procedural and object-oriented programming techniques are somewhat similar, they raise different concerns in the design and development phase that occurs before programs are written.

The components called **objects** are similar to concrete objects in the real world. You create objects that contain their own variables and methods, and then you manipulate those objects to achieve a desired result. Writing object-oriented programs involves both creating objects and creating applications that use those objects.

If you've ever used a computer that has a command-line operating system (such as DOS), and if you've used a GUI (a graphical user interface, such as Microsoft Windows), then you already have an idea of the difference between procedural and object-oriented programs. If you want to move several files from a CD to a hard disk, you can accomplish the task using either a typed command at a prompt or command line (as in DOS), or using a mouse in a graphical environment (as in Windows). The difference lies in whether you issue a series of sequential commands to move the files (in DOS) or drag icons representing the files from one screen location to another (in Windows). You can move the files using either operating system, but the GUI system allows you to simulate the way you would move their real-world paper counterparts. In other words, the GUI system allows you to treat files as objects.

»NOTE The **command line** is the line on which you type a command in a system that uses a text interface. The **command prompt** is a request for input that appears at the beginning of the command line. In DOS, the command prompt indicates the disk drive and optional path, and ends with >.

Objects in both the real world and in object-oriented programming are made up of attributes and methods. The **attributes** of an object represent its characteristics. For example, some of your `Automobile`'s attributes are its make, model, year, and purchase price. Other attributes describe whether the `Automobile` is currently running, its gear, its speed, and whether it is dirty. All `Automobile`s possess the same attributes, but not the same values, or **states**, for those attributes. For example, some `Automobile`s currently are running, but some are not. The value of an attribute can change over time; for example, some `Automobile`s are running now, but will not be running in the future. Therefore, the states of an `Automobile` are variable. Similarly, your `Dog` has attributes that include its breed, name, age, and shot status (that is, whether its shots are current); the states for a particular dog might be "Labrador retriever", "Murphy", "7", and "yes".

»NOTE Programmers also call the values of an object's attributes the **properties** of the object. The **state of an object** is the collective value of all its attributes at any point in time.

A **class** is a category of objects or a type of object. A class describes the attributes and methods of every object that is an **instance**, or example, of that class. For example, `Automobile` is a class whose objects have a year, make, model, color, and current running status. Your 2005 red Chevrolet is an instance of the class that is made up of all `Automobile`s; so is my supervisor's 2009 black Porsche. Your Collie named Bosco is an instance of the class that is made up of all Dogs; so is my Labrador named Murphy. Thinking of items as instances of a class allows you to apply your general knowledge of the class to its individual members. The particular instances of these objects contain all of the attributes that their general category contains; only the states of those attributes vary. If your friend purchases an Automobile, you know it has some model name; if your friend gets a Dog, you know it has some breed. You probably don't know the current state of the Automobile's speed or exact contents of the Dog's shots, but you do know that those attributes exist for the Automobile and Dog classes. Similarly, in a GUI operating environment, you expect each window you open to have specific, consistent attributes, such as a menu bar and a title bar, because each window includes these attributes as a member of the general class of GUI windows.

NOTE By convention, programmers using C# begin their class names with an uppercase letter. Thus, the class that defines the attributes and methods of an automobile would probably be named Automobile, and the class that contains dogs would probably be named Dog. However, following this convention is not required to produce a workable program.

Besides attributes, objects possess methods that they use to accomplish tasks, including changing attributes and discovering the values of attributes. Automobiles, for example, have methods for moving forward and backward. They also can be filled with gasoline or be washed; both are methods that change some of an Automobile's attributes. Methods also exist for ascertaining the status of certain attributes, such as the current speed of an Automobile and the status of its gas tank. Similarly, a Dog can walk or run, eat, and get a bath, and there are methods for determining whether it needs a walk, food, or a bath. GUI operating system components, such as windows, can be maximized, minimized, and dragged; depending on the component, they can also have their color or font style altered.

Like procedural programs, object-oriented programs have variables (attributes) and procedures (methods), but the attributes and methods are encapsulated into objects that are then used much like real-world objects. **Encapsulation** is the technique of packaging an object's attributes and methods into a cohesive unit that can be used as an undivided entity. Programmers sometimes refer to encapsulation as using a "**black box**," a device you use without regard for the internal mechanisms. If an object's methods are well written, the user is unaware of the low-level details of how the methods are executed; in such a case, the user must understand only the **interface** or interaction between the method and object. For example, if you can fill your Automobile with gasoline, it is because you understand the interface between the gas pump nozzle and the vehicle's gas tank opening. You don't need to understand how the pump works or where the gas tank is located inside your vehicle. If you can read your speedometer, it does not matter how the display figure is calculated. In fact, if someone produces a new, more accurate speedometer and inserts it into your Automobile, you don't have to know or care how it operates, as long as the interface remains the same as the previous one. The same principles apply to well-constructed objects used in object-oriented programs.

Object-oriented programming languages support two other distinguishing features in addition to organizing objects as members of classes. One feature, **polymorphism**, describes the ability to create methods that act appropriately depending on the context. For example, you are able to "fill" both a Dog and an Automobile, but you do so by very different means. A friend would have no trouble understanding your meaning if you said "I need to fill my Automobile" and distinguishing that process from the process of "filling" your `Dog`, your `BankAccount`, or your `AppointmentCalendar`. Older, non-object-oriented languages could not make such distinctions, but object-oriented languages can.

Object-oriented languages also support inheritance. **Inheritance** provides the ability to extend a class so as to create a more specific class. The more specific class contains all the attributes and methods of the more general class and usually contains new attributes or methods as well. For example, if you have created a `Dog` class, you might then create a more specific class named `ShowDog`. Each instance of the `ShowDog` class would contain all the attributes and methods of a `Dog`, along with additional methods or attributes. For example, a `ShowDog` might require an attribute to hold the number of ribbons won and a method for entering a dog show. Using polymorphism, you might need to specialize the `Dog`'s methods to be appropriate for a `ShowDog`. For example, the fill method might be different (perhaps using more expensive food). The advantage of inheritance is that when you need a class such as `ShowDog`, you often can extend an existing class, thereby saving a lot of time and work.

»TWO TRUTHS AND A LIE: OBJECT-ORIENTED PROGRAMMING

1. Procedural programs use variables and tasks that are grouped into methods or procedures.
2. Object-oriented programming languages do not support variables or methods, but they do contain objects and classes.
3. In object-oriented programming, a class is a category of objects or a type of object, and each object is an instance of a class.

The false answer is #2. Object-oriented programs contain variables and methods just as procedural programs do.

THE C# PROGRAMMING LANGUAGE

The **C# programming language** was developed as an object-oriented and component-oriented language. It is part of Microsoft Visual Studio 2008, a package designed for developing applications that run on Windows computers. Unlike other programming languages, C# allows every piece of data to be treated as an object and to employ the principles of object-oriented programming. C# provides constructs for creating components with properties, methods, and events, making it an ideal language for twenty-first-century programming, where building small, reusable components is more important than building huge, stand-alone applications.

C# contains a GUI interface that makes it similar to Visual Basic. C# is considered more concise than Visual Basic, and is modeled after the C++ programming language, but some of the most difficult features to understand in C++ have been eliminated in C#. For example, pointers are not used in C#, object destructors and forward declarations are not needed, and using `#include` files is not necessary. Multiple inheritance, which causes many C++ programming errors, is not allowed in C#.

»NOTE Technically, you can use pointers in C#, but only in a mode called unsafe, which is rarely used.

C# is very similar to Java, because Java was also based on C++. In Java, simple data types are not objects; therefore, they do not work with built-in methods. In C#, every piece of data is an object, providing all data with the functionality of true objects. Additionally, in Java, simple parameters (also called primitive parameters) must be passed by value, which means a copy must be made of any data that is sent to a method for alteration, and the copy must be sent back to the original object. C# provides the convenience of passing primitive parameters by reference, which means the actual object can be altered by a method without a copy being passed back. If you have not programmed before, the difference between C# and other languages means little to you. However, experienced programmers will appreciate the thought that the developers of C# put into its features.

»NOTE Microsoft Corporation refers to the current version of C# as C# 3.5. You can find Microsoft's C# specifications at *msdn.microsoft.com/vcsharp/programming/language*.

»NOTE **Primitive data** is simple data, such as a number, as opposed to complex data, such as an `Employee`, a `BankAccount`, or an `Automobile`. In Chapter 2, you will learn about C#'s simple data types—those that are intrinsic to the language. In Chapter 7, you will create complex objects that are composed of primitive data types.

»NOTE The C# programming language was standardized in 2002 by Ecma International. You can read or download this set of standards at *www.ecma-international.org/publication/standards/Ecma-334.htm*.

»TWO TRUTHS AND A LIE: THE C# PROGRAMMING LANGUAGE

1. The C# programming language was developed as an object-oriented and component-oriented language.
2. C# contains several features that make it similar to other languages such as Java and Visual Basic.
3. C# contains many advanced features, so the C++ programming language was created as a simpler version of the language.

The false statement is #3. C# is modeled after the C++ programming language, but some of the most difficult features to understand in C++ have been eliminated in C#.

WRITING A C# PROGRAM THAT PRODUCES OUTPUT

At first glance, even the simplest C# program involves a fair amount of confusing syntax. Consider the simple program in Figure 1-1. This program is written on seven lines, and its only task is to display "This is my first C# program" on the screen.

»NOTE Some words appear in blue in Figure 1-1. These are C# keywords. A complete list of keywords appears in Table 1-1.

```
public class FirstClass
{
   public static void Main()
   {
      System.Console.Out.WriteLine("This is my first C# program");
   }
}
```

Figure 1-1 `FirstClass` console application

The statement that does the actual work in this program is in the middle of the figure:

```
System.Console.Out.WriteLine("This is my first C# program");
```

The statement ends with a semicolon because all C# statements do.

The text "This is my first C# program" is a **literal string** of characters—that is, a series of characters that will be used exactly as entered. Any literal string in C# appears between double quotation marks.

The string "This is my first C# program" appears within parentheses because the string is an argument to a method, and arguments to methods always appear within parentheses. **Arguments** represent information that a method needs to perform its task. For example, if making an appointment with a dentist's office was a C# method, you would write the following:

```
MakeAppointment("September 10", "2 p.m.");
```

Accepting and processing a dental appointment is a method that consists of a set of standard procedures. However, each appointment requires different information—the date and time—and this information can be considered the arguments of the `MakeAppointment()` method. If you make an appointment for September 10 at 2 p.m., you expect different results than if you make one for September 9 at 8 a.m. or December 25 at midnight. Likewise, if you pass the argument "Happy Holidays" to a method, you will expect different results than if you pass the argument "This is my first C# program."

»NOTE The words *argument* and *parameter* are closely related. An argument is the expression used when you call or invoke a method, while a **parameter** is an object or reference that is declared in a method definition, where the method instructions are written. You will learn more about the terms *call* and *invoke* in Chapter 6. Do not worry if you do not understand arguments and parameters at this point; their uses will become clearer when you write methods in Chapter 6.

»NOTE Although a string can be an argument to a method, not all arguments are strings. In this book, you will see and write methods that accept many other types of data.

Within the statement `System.Console.Out.WriteLine("This is my first C# program");`, the method to which you are passing the argument string "This is my first C# program" is named `WriteLine()`. The **`WriteLine()` method** displays output on the screen and positions the cursor on the next line, where additional output might be displayed subsequently.

»NOTE In C#, you usually refer to method names by including their parentheses, as in `WriteLine()`. This practice makes it easy for you to distinguish method names from variable names.

»NOTE The **`Write()` method** is very similar to the `WriteLine()` method. With `WriteLine()`, the cursor is moved to the following line after the message is displayed. With `Write()`, the cursor does not advance to a new line; it remains on the same line as the output.

»NOTE The C# programming language is case sensitive. Thus, the object named `Out` is a completely different object than one named `out`, `OUT`, or `oUt`.

Within the statement `System.Console.Out.WriteLine("This is my first C# program");`, `Out` is an object. The `Out` object represents the screen on the terminal or computer where you are working. Of course, not all objects have a `WriteLine()` method (for instance, you can't write a line to a computer's mouse, your `Automobile`, or your `Dog`), but the creators of C# assumed that you frequently would want to display output on the screen at your terminal. For this reason, the `Out` object was created and endowed with the method named `WriteLine()`. Soon, you will create your own C# objects and endow them with your own methods.

Within the statement `System.Console.Out.WriteLine("This is my first C# program");`, `Console` is a class. It defines the attributes of a collection of similar "`Console`" objects, just as the `Dog` class defines the attributes of a collection of similar `Dog` objects. One of the `Console` objects is `Out`. (You might guess that another `Console` object is `In`, which represents the keyboard.)

»NOTE You will create your own namespaces in Chapter 3.

Within the statement `System.Console.Out.WriteLine("This is my first C# program");`, `System` is a namespace. A **namespace** is a scheme or mechanism that provides a way to group similar classes. To organize your classes, you can (and will) create your own namespaces. The **`System` namespace**, which is built into your C# compiler, holds commonly used classes.

»NOTE An advantage to using Visual Studio is that all of its languages use the same namespaces. In other words, everything you learn about any namespace in C# is knowledge you can transfer to Visual C++ and Visual Basic.

The dots (periods) in the statement `System.Console.Out.WriteLine("This is my first C# program");` are used to separate the names of the namespace, class, object, and method. You will use this same namespace-dot-class-dot-object-dot-method format repeatedly in your C# programs.

In the `FirstClass` class in Figure 1-1, the statement `System.Console.Out.WriteLine ("This is my first C# program");` appears within a method named `Main()`. Every method in C# contains a header and a body. A **method header** includes the method name and information about what will pass into and be returned from a method. The **method body** of every method is contained within a pair of curly braces ({ }) and includes all the instructions executed by the method. The program in Figure 1-1 includes only one statement between the curly braces of the `Main()` method. Soon, you will write methods with many more statements. In Figure 1-1, the statement within the `Main()` method (the `WriteLine()` statement) is indented within the curly braces. Although the C# compiler does not require such indentation, it is conventional and clearly shows that the `WriteLine()` statement lies within the `Main()` method.

For every opening curly brace ({) in a C# program, there must be a corresponding closing curly brace (}). The precise position of the opening and closing curly braces is not important to the compiler. For example, the method in Figure 1-2 executes exactly the same way as the one shown in Figure 1-1. The only difference is in the amount of whitespace used in the method. In general, whitespace is optional in C#. **Whitespace** is any combination of spaces, tabs, and carriage returns (blank lines). You use whitespace to organize your program code and make it easier to read; it does not affect your program. Usually, vertically aligning each pair of opening and closing curly braces and indenting the contents between them, as in Figure 1-1, makes your code easier to read than the format shown in Figure 1-2.

```
public static void Main(){System.Console.Out.WriteLine
("This is my first C# program");}
```

Figure 1-2 A `Main()` method with little whitespace

The method header for the `Main()` method contains four words. Three of these words are **keywords**—predefined and reserved identifiers that have special meaning to the compiler. In the method header `public static void Main()`, the word `public` is an access modifier. When used in a method header, an **access modifier** defines the circumstances under which the method can be accessed. As opposed to cases in which a method is **`private`**, the access modifier **`public`** indicates that other classes may use this method.

»NOTE If you do not use an access modifier within a method header, then by default the method is `private`. Other classes cannot use a `private` method. You will learn more about public and private access modifiers in Chapter 7.

In the English language, the word *static* means "showing little change" or "stationary." In C#, the reserved keyword **`static`** has a related meaning. It indicates that the `Main()` method will be executed through a class—not by a variety of objects. It means that you do not need to create an object of type `FirstClass` to use the `Main()` method defined within `FirstClass`. In C#, you will create many nonstatic methods within classes that are executed by objects. For example, you might create a `display()` method in an `Automobile` class that you use to display an `Automobile`'s attributes. If you create 100 `Automobile` objects, the `display()` method will operate differently and appropriately for each object, displaying different makes, models, and colors of `Automobiles`. (Programmers would say a nonstatic method is "invoked" by each instance of the object.) However, a `static` method does not require an object to be used to invoke it. Only one version of the `static Main()` method for `FirstClass` will ever be executed. Of course, other classes eventually might have their own, different `Main()` methods. You will learn the mechanics of how `static` and nonstatic methods differ in Chapter 4.

In English, the word *void* means empty. When the keyword **`void`** is used in the `Main()` method header, it does not indicate that the `Main()` method is empty, but rather that the method does not return any value when called. This doesn't mean that `Main()` doesn't produce output—it does. Instead, it means the `Main()` method does not send any value back to any method that calls it. You will learn more about return values when you study methods in greater detail in Chapter 3.

In the method header, the name of the method is `Main()`. All C# applications must include a method named `Main()`, and most C# applications will have additional methods with other names. When you execute a C# application, the `Main()` method always executes first.

»NOTE You will write many C# *classes* that do not contain a `Main()` method. However, all executable *applications* (runnable programs) must contain a `Main()` method.

»NOTE You also can write the `Main()` method header as `public static int Main()`, `public static void Main(string[] args)`, or `public static int Main(string[] args)`. You will learn more about these alternative forms of `Main()` at the end of this chapter.

»TWO TRUTHS AND A LIE: WRITING A C# PROGRAM THAT PRODUCES OUTPUT

1. Strings are information that methods need to perform their tasks.
2. The `WriteLine()` method displays output on the screen and positions the cursor on the next line, where additional output might be displayed.
3. Many methods such as `WriteLine()` have been created for you because the creators of C# assumed you would need them frequently.

The false statement is #1. Strings are literal values represented between quotation marks. Arguments represent information that a method needs to perform its task. Although an argument might be a string, not all arguments are strings.

SELECTING IDENTIFIERS

Every method that you use within a C# program must be part of a class. To create a class, you use a class header and curly braces in much the same way you use a header and braces for a method within a class. When you write `public class FirstClass`, you are defining a class named `FirstClass`. A class name does not have to contain the word "Class" as `FirstClass` does. You can define a C# class using any identifier you need, as long as it meets the following requirements:

»NOTE In this book, all identifiers begin with a letter.

»NOTE An identifier with an @ prefix is a **verbatim identifier**.

- » An identifier must begin with an underscore, the at sign (@), or a letter. (Letters include foreign-alphabet letters such as Π and Ω, which are contained in the set of characters known as Unicode.)
- » An identifier can contain only letters or digits, not special characters such as #, $, or &.
- » An identifier cannot be a C# reserved keyword, such as `public` or `class`. Table 1-1 provides a complete list of reserved keywords. (Actually, you can use a keyword as an identifier if you precede it with an "at" sign, as in `@class`. This feature allows you to use code written in other languages that do not have the same set of reserved keywords. However, when you write original C# programs, you should not use the keywords as identifiers.)

abstract	float	return
as	for	sbyte
base	foreach	sealed
bool	goto	short
break	if	sizeof
byte	implicit	stackalloc
case	in	static
catch	int	string
char	interface	struct
checked	internal	switch
class	is	this
const	lock	throw
continue	long	true
decimal	namespace	try
default	new	typeof
delegate	null	uint
do	object	ulong
double	operator	unchecked
else	out	unsafe
enum	override	ushort
event	params	using
explicit	private	virtual
extern	protected	void
false	public	volatile
finally	readonly	while
fixed	ref	

Table 1-1 C# reserved keywords

NOTE The following identifiers have special meaning in C# but are not keywords: add, alias, get, global, partial, remove, set, value, where, and yield. For clarity, you should avoid using these words as your own identifiers.

A programming standard in C# is to begin class names with an uppercase letter and use other uppercase letters as needed to improve readability. Table 1-2 lists some valid and conventional class names you might use when creating classes in C#. Table 1-3 lists some class names that are valid, but unconventional; Table 1-4 lists some illegal class names.

NOTE
You should follow established conventions for C# so that other programmers can interpret and follow your programs. This book uses established C# programming conventions.

Class Name	Description
`Employee`	Begins with an uppercase letter
`FirstClass`	Begins with an uppercase letter, contains no spaces, and has an initial uppercase letter that indicates the start of the second word
`PushButtonControl`	Begins with an uppercase letter, contains no spaces, and has an initial uppercase letter that indicates the start of all subsequent words
`Budget2010`	Begins with an uppercase letter and contains no spaces

Table 1-2 Some valid and conventional class names in C#

Class Name	Description
`employee`	Begins with a lowercase letter
`First_Class`	Although legal, the underscore is not commonly used to indicate new words
`Pushbuttoncontrol`	No uppercase characters are used to indicate the start of a new word, making the name difficult to read
`BUDGET2010`	Appears with all uppercase letters
`Public`	Although this identifier is legal because it is different from the keyword `public`, which begins with a lowercase "p," the similarity could cause confusion

Table 1-3 Some unconventional (though legal) class names in C#

Class Name	Description
`an employee`	Space character is illegal
`Push Button Control`	Space characters are illegal
`class`	"class" is a reserved word
`2011Budget`	Class names cannot begin with a digit
`phone#`	The # symbol is not allowed; identifiers consist of letters and digits

Table 1-4 Some illegal class names in C#

In Figure 1-1, the line `public class FirstClass` contains the keyword `class`, which identifies `FirstClass` as a class. The reserved word `public` is an access modifier. Similar to the way an access modifier describes a method's accessibility, when used with a class, the access modifier defines the circumstances under which the class can be accessed; `public` access is the most liberal type of access.

The simple program shown in Figure 1-1 has many pieces to remember. For now, you can use the program shown in Figure 1-3 as a shell, where you replace the identifier `AnyLegalClassName` with any legal class name, and the line `/*********/` with any statements that you want to execute.

```
public class AnyLegalClassName
{
    public static void Main()
    {
        /*********/;
    }
}
```

Figure 1-3 Shell program

»TWO TRUTHS AND A LIE: SELECTING IDENTIFIERS

1. In C#, an identifier must begin with an underscore, the at sign (@), or an uppercase letter.
2. An identifier can contain only letters or digits, not special characters such as #, $, or &.
3. An identifier cannot be a C# reserved keyword.

The false statement is #1. In C#, an identifier must begin with an underscore, the at sign (@), or a letter. There is no requirement that the initial letter be capitalized, although in C#, it is a convention that the initial letter of a class name is capitalized.

ADDING COMMENTS TO A PROGRAM

As you can see, even the simplest C# program takes several lines of code and contains somewhat perplexing syntax. Large programs that perform many tasks include much more code. As you write longer programs, it becomes increasingly difficult to remember why you included steps and how you intended to use particular variables. **Program comments** are nonexecuting statements that you add to document a program. Programmers use comments to leave notes for themselves and for others who might read their programs in the future.

»NOTE As you work through this book, you should add comments as the first few lines of every program file. The comments should contain your name, the date, and the name of the program. Your instructor might want you to include additional comments.

Comments also can be useful when you are developing a program. If a program is not performing as expected, you can **comment out** various statements and subsequently run the program to observe the effect. When you comment out a statement, you turn it into a comment so that the compiler will ignore it. This approach helps you pinpoint the location of errant statements in malfunctioning programs.

There are three types of comments in C#:

- **Line comments** start with two forward slashes (//) and continue to the end of the current line. Line comments can appear on a line by themselves, or at the end of a line following executable code.
- **Block comments** start with a forward slash and an asterisk (/*) and end with an asterisk and a forward slash (*/). Block comments can appear on a line by themselves, on a line before executable code, or after executable code. When a comment is long, block comments can extend across as many lines as needed.
- C# also supports a special type of comment used to create documentation from within a program. These comments, called **XML-documentation format comments**, use a special set of tags within angle brackets (< >). (XML stands for Extensible Markup Language.) You will learn more about this type of comment as you continue your study of C#.

NOTE The forward slash (/) and the backslash (\) characters often are confused, but they are distinct characters. You cannot use them interchangeably.

Figure 1-4 shows how comments can be used in code. The program covers 12 lines of type, yet only seven are part of the executable C# program, and the only line that actually *does* anything is the shaded one that displays "Message".

```
public class ClassWithOneExecutingLine
/* This class has only one line that executes */
{
   public static void Main()
   {
      // The next line writes the message
      System.Console.Out.WriteLine("Message");   // Comment
   }
/* This program serves
   to demonstrate that a program
   can "look" a lot longer than it really is */
}
```

Figure 1-4 Using comments within a program

»TWO TRUTHS AND A LIE: ADDING COMMENTS TO A PROGRAM

1. Line comments start with two forward slashes (//) and end with two backslashes (\\).
2. Block comments can extend across as many lines as needed.
3. XML-documentation format comments use a special set of tags within angle brackets (< >).

The false statement is #1. Line comments start with two forward slashes (//) and continue to the end of the current line.

ELIMINATING THE REFERENCE TO `Out` BY USING THE `System` NAMESPACE

A program can contain as many statements as you want. For example, the program in Figure 1-5 produces the three lines of output shown in Figure 1-6. A semicolon separates each program statement.

```
public class ThreeLines
{
   public static void Main()
   {
      System.Console.Out.WriteLine("Line one");
      System.Console.Out.WriteLine("Line two");
      System.Console.Out.WriteLine("Line three");
   }
}
```

Figure 1-5 A program that produces three lines of output

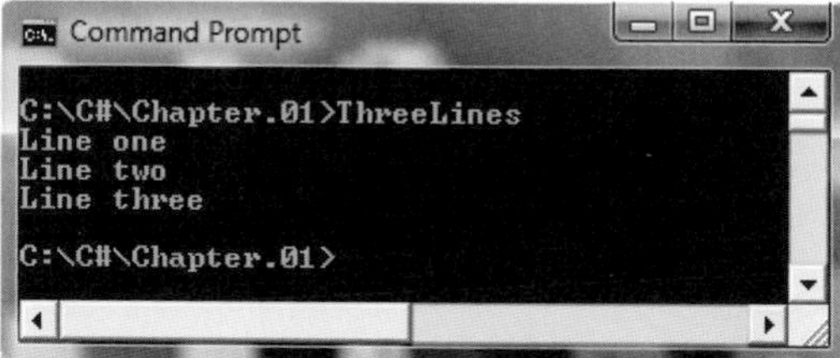

Figure 1-6 Output of `ThreeLines` program

The program in Figure 1-5 shows a lot of repeated code—the phrase `System.Console.Out.WriteLine` appears three times. When you use the name of the object `Out`, you are indicating the console screen. However, `Out` is the default output object. That is, if you write `System.Console.WriteLine("Hi");` without specifying a `Console` object, the message "Hi" goes to the default `Console` object, which is `Out`. Most C# programmers usually use the `WriteLine()` method without specifying the `Out` object.

When you need to repeatedly use a class from the same namespace, you can shorten the statements you type by using a clause that indicates a namespace where the class can be found. You use a namespace with a **`using` clause**, or **`using` directive**, as shown in the shaded statement in the program in Figure 1-7. If you type `using System;` prior to the class definition, the compiler knows to use the `System` namespace when it encounters the `Console` class. The output of the program in Figure 1-7 is identical to that in Figure 1-5, in which `System` and `Out` were both repeated with each `WriteLine()` statement.

```
using System;
public class ThreeLines
{
   public static void Main()
   {
      Console.WriteLine("Line one");
      Console.WriteLine("Line two");
      Console.WriteLine("Line three");
   }
}
```

Figure 1-7 A program that produces three lines of output with a `using System` clause and no explicit reference to the `Out` object

NOT RECOMMENDED: USING AN ALIAS

At this point, the clever programmer will say, "I'll shorten my typing tasks even further by typing `using System.Console;` at the top of my programs, and producing output with statements like `WriteLine("Hi");`." However, `using` cannot be used with a class name like `System.Console`—only with a namespace name like `System`. Another option is to assign an alias to a class with a `using` clause. An **alias** is an alternative name for a class. You might assign one as a convenience when a fully qualified class name is very long. For example, Figure 1-8 shows a program that uses an alias for `System.Console` (see shaded statement). The lines of code within the program are shorter, but more difficult for another programmer to read. In general, and especially while you are learning C#, you should avoid using aliases if your intention is simply to reduce typing.

```
using SC = System.Console;
public class ThreeLines
{
   public static void Main()
   {
      SC.WriteLine("Line one");
      SC.WriteLine("Line two");
      SC.WriteLine("Line three");
   }
}
```

»DON'T DO IT

This alias is not conventional and makes the program harder for other programmers to understand.

Figure 1-8 Using an alias for `System.Console`—a technique that is not recommended

TWO TRUTHS AND A LIE: ELIMINATING THE REFERENCE TO `Out` BY USING THE `System` NAMESPACE

1. Most C# programmers usually use the `WriteLine()` method without specifying the `Out` object.
2. You use a namespace with a `using` clause, or `using` directive, to shorten statements when you need to repeatedly use a class from the same namespace.
3. Whenever possible, you should use aliases to make your programs as concise as you can.

The false statement is #3. You might assign an alias as a convenience when a fully qualified class name is very long. However, using an alias makes your programs more difficult for other programmers to read. In general, and especially while you are learning C#, avoid using aliases if your intention is simply to reduce typing.

WRITING AND COMPILING A C# PROGRAM

After you write and save a program, two more steps must be performed before you can view the program output:

1. You must compile the program you wrote (called the **source code**) into **intermediate language (IL)**.
2. The C# **just in time (JIT)** compiler must translate the intermediate code into executable code.

NOTE When you compile a C# program, you translate your source code into intermediate language. The JIT compiler converts IL instructions into native code at the last moment, and appropriately for each different type of computer on which the code might eventually be executed. In other words, the same set of IL can be JIT-compiled and executed on any supported architecture.

NOTE Some developers say that languages like C# are "semi-compiled." That is, instead of being translated i mmediately from source code to their final executable versions, programs are compiled into an intermediate version that is later translated into the correct executable statements for the machine on which the program is running.

You can perform these steps from the command line or within the Integrated Development Environment (IDE) that comes with Visual Studio. Both methods produce the same results; the one you use is a matter of preference. You might prefer the simplicity of the command line because you do not work with multiple menus and views. Additionally, if you want to pass command-line arguments to a program, you must compile from the command line. On the other hand, many programmers prefer using the IDE because it provides features such as color-coded keywords and automatic statement completion.

COMPILING CODE FROM THE COMMAND PROMPT

To compile your source code from the command line, you first locate the command prompt. For example, in Windows Vista, you click Start, All Programs, Accessories, and Command

Prompt. As shown in Figure 1-9, you type `csc` at the command prompt, followed by the name of the file that contains the source code. The command `csc` stands for "C Sharp compiler." For example, to compile a file named ThreeLines.cs, you would type `csc ThreeLines.cs` and then press the Enter key. One of three outcomes will occur:

- You receive an operating system error message such as "Bad command or file name" or "csc is not recognized as an internal or external command, operable program or batch file".
- You receive one or more program language error messages.
- You receive no error messages (only a copyright statement from Microsoft), indicating that the program has compiled successfully.

```
C:\>csc ThreeLines.cs
Microsoft (R) Visual C# 2008 Compiler Beta 2 version 3.05.20706.1
for Microsoft (R) .NET Framework version 3.5
Copyright (C) Microsoft Corporation. All rights reserved.

error CS2001: Source file 'ThreeLines.cs' could not be found
fatal error CS2008: No inputs specified

C:\>
```

Figure 1-9 Attempt to compile a program from the root directory at the command line, and error message received

If you receive an operating system message such as "csc is not recognized . . . ," or "Source file . . . could not be found," it may mean that:

- You misspelled the command `csc`.
- You misspelled the filename.
- You forgot to include the extension .cs with the filename.
- You didn't use the correct case. If your filename is ThreeLines.cs, then `csc threelines.cs` will not compile.
- You are not within the correct subdirectory or folder on your command line. For example, Figure 1-9 shows the `csc` command typed in the root directory of the C drive. If the ThreeLines.cs file is stored in a folder on the C drive, then the command shown will not work.
- The C# compiler was not installed properly.
- You need to set a path command.

To set a path command, you must locate the C# compiler on your hard disk. To locate the C# compiler whose name is csc.exe, use one of the following techniques:

- In either Vista or Windows XP, double-click Computer (or My Computer), double-click the C drive, double-click the Windows folder, double-click the Microsoft.NET folder, double-click the Framework folder, double-click the v3.5 folder, and confirm that csc.exe is a program listed there. C# should be installed in this location if the program was installed using the default options.

- If the compiler can't be found in the default location, click Start in Vista, click Search, click the button to the right of Advanced Search, and then click the list box next to Location. From the drop-down list, click OS (C:) or the name of your local hard drive. Check the box next to "Include non-indexed, hidden, and system files." In the Name dialog box, type csc.exe, then click Search.
- If the compiler can't be found in the default location, click Start in Windows XP, click Search, and choose All Files or Folders to look for the file named csc.exe.
- If your search fails to find csc.exe, you need to obtain and install a copy of the C# compiler. For more information, visit *http://msdn2.microsoft.com/en-us/vcsharp/default.aspx.*

If you do find the csc.exe file, type `path =` at the command line, followed by the complete path name that describes where csc.exe is stored; then try to compile the `ThreeLines` program again. For example, if C# was stored in the default location, you might type the following:

```
path = c:\Windows\Microsoft.NET\Framework\v3.5
```

Press Enter. Next, type `csc ThreeLines.cs` and press Enter again.

NOTE In Windows XP, you also can change the path command if you are the System Administrator on the local computer. Click Start, click Control Panel, and then double-click System. In Vista, click Advanced system settings, then click Continue. In either Vista or Windows XP, click Environment Variables on the Advanced tab, then scroll through the list of variables for the path command. If it is there, click it and click Edit; if not, click New. Either way, type the new path variable value in the dialog box that appears. Then click OK twice and close the System Properties window.

If you receive a programming language error message, it means that the source code contains one or more syntax errors. A syntax error occurs when you introduce typing errors into your program. For example, if the first line of your program begins with "Public" (with an uppercase *P*), you will get an error message such as "`A namespace does not directly contain members such as fields or methods`" after compiling the program, because the compiler won't recognize `ThreeLines` as a class with a `Main()` method. If this problem occurs, you must reopen the text file that contains the source code, make the necessary corrections, save the file, and compile it again.

NOTE The C# compiler issues warnings as well as errors. A warning is less serious than an error; it means that the compiler has determined you have done something unusual, but not illegal. If you have purposely introduced a warning situation to test a program, then you can ignore the warning. Usually, however, you should treat a warning message just as you would an error message and attempt to remedy the situation.

If you receive no error messages after compiling the code, then the program compiled successfully and a file with the same name as the source code—but with an .exe extension—is created and saved in the same folder as the program text file. For example, if ThreeLines.cs compiles successfully, then a file named ThreeLines.exe is created.

To run the program from the command line, you simply type the program name—for example, `ThreeLines`. You can also type the full filename, ThreeLines.exe, but it is not necessary to include the extension.

COMPILING CODE FROM WITHIN THE VISUAL STUDIO IDE

As an alternative to using the command line, you can compile and write your program within the Visual Studio IDE. This approach has several advantages:

- Some of the code you need is already created for you.
- The code is displayed in color, so you can more easily identify parts of your program. Reserved words appear in blue, comments in green, and identifiers in black.
- If error messages appear when you compile your program, you can double-click an error message and the cursor will move to the line of code that contains the error.
- Other debugging tools are available. You will become more familiar with these tools as you develop more sophisticated programs.

Figure 1-10 shows a program written in the editor of the Visual Studio IDE. You can see that the environment looks like a word processor, containing menu options such as File, Edit, and Help, and buttons with icons representing options such as Save, Copy, and Paste. You will learn about some of these options later in this chapter and continue to learn about more of them as you work with C# in the IDE.

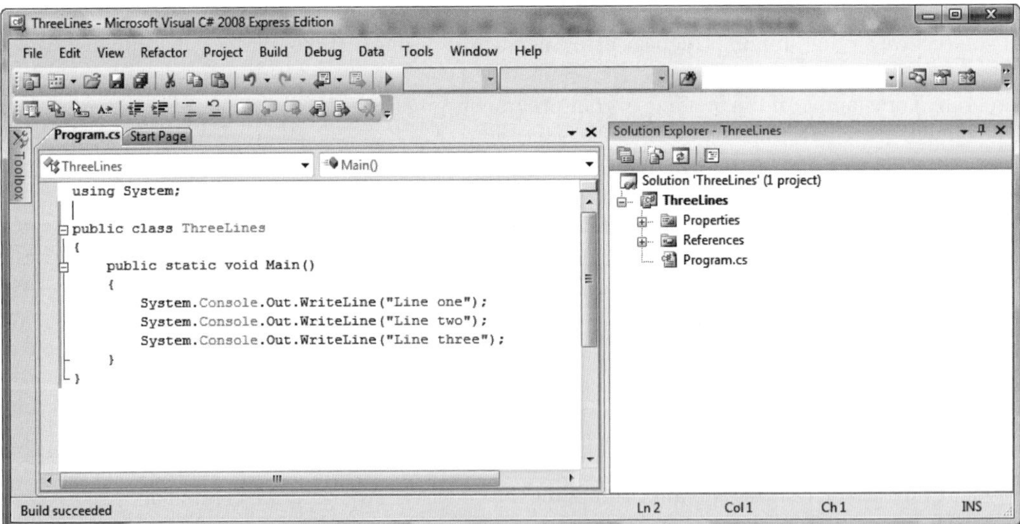

Figure 1-10 `ThreeLines` program as it appears in Visual Studio Express Edition

»TWO TRUTHS AND A LIE: WRITING AND COMPILING A C# PROGRAM

1. After you write and save a program, you must compile it into intermediate language and then the C# just in time (JIT) compiler must translate the intermediate code into executable code.
2. You can compile and execute a C# program from the command line or within the Integrated Development Environment (IDE) that comes with Visual Studio.
3. Many programmers prefer to compile their programs from the command line because it provides features such as color-coded keywords and automatic statement completion.

The false statement is #3. Programmers who prefer the command line prefer its simplicity. Programmers who prefer the Visual Studio IDE prefer the color-coded keywords and automatic statement completion.

ALTERNATE WAYS TO WRITE A `Main()` METHOD

Figures 1-8 and 1-10 show a `Main()` method with the following header:

```
public static void Main()
```

Using the return type `void` and listing nothing between the parentheses that follow `Main` is just one way to write a `Main()` method header in a program. (However, it is the first way listed in the C# documentation, and it is the convention that this book uses.)

Figure 1-11 shows an alternate way to write the `Main()` method header in the `ThreeLines` class. The shaded phrase `string[] args` is a parameter to the `Main()` method. A **`string`** is a data type that can hold a series of characters. The square brackets indicate that you can include a list or array of those strings. In Figure 1-11, `args` is a programmer-chosen name for the memory location where the list of `strings` is stored. Although you can use any

»NOTE In Chapter 6, you will create other methods that can accept parameters.

```
using System;
public class ThreeLines
{
   public static void Main(string[] args)
   {
      Console.WriteLine("Line one");
      Console.WriteLine("Line two");
      Console.WriteLine("Line three");
   }
}
```

Figure 1-11 A `Main()` method with a `string[] args` parameter

»NOTE You will learn more about the `string` data type in Chapter 2. You will learn more about how to use command-line arguments in Chapter 5 when you study arrays.

identifier, `args` is traditional. Use this format for the `Main()` method header if you need to access command-line arguments passed in to your application. For example, if you issued the following command, then the `strings` "yes", "no", and "maybe" would be stored at the memory location named `args`:

```
cs ThreeLines yes, no, maybe
```

NOTE In particular, Java programmers might prefer the version of `Main()` that includes the `string[] args` parameter because, conventionally, they write their main methods with the same parameter.

Even if you do not need access to command-line arguments, you can still use the version of the `Main()` method header that references them. You should use this form for your `Main()` method headers if your instructor at school or supervisor at work indicates you should follow this convention.

Some programmers prefer to write the `ThreeLines` class `Main()` method as shown in Figure 1-12. The shaded keyword `int` replaces `void` in the method header, indicating that the method returns an integer value. If you use this form of method header, then the last statement in the `Main()` method must be a return statement that returns an integer. By convention, a return value of 0 means an application ended without error. The value might be used by your operating system or another program that uses your program.

```
using System;
public class ThreeLines
{
   public static int Main(string[] args)
   {
      Console.WriteLine("Line one");
      Console.WriteLine("Line two");
      Console.WriteLine("Line three");
      return 0;
   }
}
```

Figure 1-12 A `Main()` method with an `int` return type

NOTE You will learn more about the `int` data type in Chapter 2. You will learn more about how to return values from methods in Chapter 6.

NOTE In particular, C++ programmers might prefer the version of `Main()` that returns an `int` because, conventionally, they write their main methods with an `int` return type.

Even if you do not need to use a return value from a `Main()` method, you can still use the version of the `Main()` method header that uses a return value. You should use this form for your `Main()` method headers if your instructor at school or supervisor at work indicates you should follow this convention.

»TWO TRUTHS AND A LIE: ALTERNATE WAYS TO WRITE A `Main()` METHOD

1. In C#, a `Main()` method header can be written `public static void Main()`.
2. In C#, a `Main()` method header can be written `public static void Main(string[] args)`.
3. In C#, a `Main()` method header can be written `public static int main(string args)`.

The false statement is #3. In C#, a `Main()` method header can be written as shown in either of the first two examples, or as `public static int Main(string[] args)`. That is, `Main()` must be capitalized and `string` must be followed by a pair of square brackets.

YOU DO IT

Now that you understand the basic framework of a program written in C#, you are ready to enter your first C# program into a text editor so you can compile and execute it. It is a tradition among programmers that the first program you write in any language produces "Hello, world!" as its output. You will create such a program now. To create a C# program, you can use the editor that is included as part of the Microsoft Visual Studio IDE. (The C# compiler, other language compilers, and many development tools also are contained in the IDE, which is where you build, test, and debug your C# application.) Alternatively, you can use any text editor. There are advantages to using the C# editor to write your programs, but using a plain text editor is simpler when you are getting started.

ENTERING A PROGRAM INTO AN EDITOR

To write your first C# program:

1. Start any text editor, such as Notepad, and open a new document, if necessary.
2. Type the class header **public class Hello**. In this example, the class name is `Hello`.
3. Press the **Enter** key and type the class-opening curly brace **{**. Press **Enter** again to start a new line.
4. Type three spaces to indent, and write the `Main()` method header:

   `public static void Main()`

   Press **Enter** to start a new line.
5. Type three spaces to indent, type **{**, and then press **Enter**.

6. Type six spaces so the next statement will be indented within the curly braces of the `Main()` method. Type the one executing statement in this program:

   `System.Console.Out.WriteLine("Hello, world!");`

7. Press **Enter**, type three spaces, type a closing curly brace for the `Main()` method, press **Enter**, and type a closing curly brace for the class. Your code should look like Figure 1-13.

```
public class Hello
{
   public static void Main()
   {
      System.Console.Out.WriteLine("Hello, world!");
   }
}
```

Figure 1-13 The `Hello` class

8. Choose a location that is meaningful to you to save your program. For example, you might create a folder named C# on your hard drive. Within that folder, you might create a folder named Chapter.01 in which you will store all the examples and exercises in this chapter. If you are working in a school lab, you might be assigned a storage location of your school's server, or you might prefer to store your examples on a USB drive or other portable storage media. Save the program as **Hello.cs**. It is important that the file extension be .cs, which stands for *C Sharp*. If the file has a different extension, the compiler for C# will not recognize the program as a C# program.

NOTE Many text editors attach their own filename extension (such as .txt or .doc) to a saved file. Double-check your saved file to ensure that it does not have a double extension (as in Hello.cs.txt). If the file has a double extension, rename it. If you type quotes surrounding a filename (as in "Hello.cs"), most editors will save the file as you specify, without adding their own extension. If you use a word-processing program as your editor, select the option to save the file as a plain text file.

COMPILING AND EXECUTING A PROGRAM FROM THE COMMAND LINE

To compile and execute your `Hello` program from the command line:

1. Go to the command prompt on your system. For example, in Vista or Windows XP, click **Start**, click **All Programs**, click **Accessories**, and click **Command Prompt**. Change the current directory to the name of the folder that holds your program.

   If your command prompt indicates a path other than the one you want, you can type `cd\` and then press Enter to return to the root directory. You can then type `cd` to change the path to the one where your program resides. For example, if you stored your program file in a folder named Chapter.01 within a folder named C#, then you can type the following:

   ```
   cd C#\Chapter.01
   ```

   The command `cd` is short for *change directory*.

2. Type the command that compiles your program:

   ```
   csc Hello.cs
   ```

   If you receive no error messages and the prompt returns, it means that the compile operation was successful, that a file named Hello.exe has been created, and that you can execute the program. If you do receive error messages, check every character of the program you typed to make sure it matches Figure 1-13. Remember, C# is case sensitive, so all casing must match exactly. When you have corrected the errors, repeat this step to compile the program again.

3. You can verify that a file named Hello.exe was created in several ways:
   - At the command prompt, type **dir** to view a directory of the files stored in the current folder. Both Hello.cs and Hello.exe should appear in the list. See Figure 1-14.

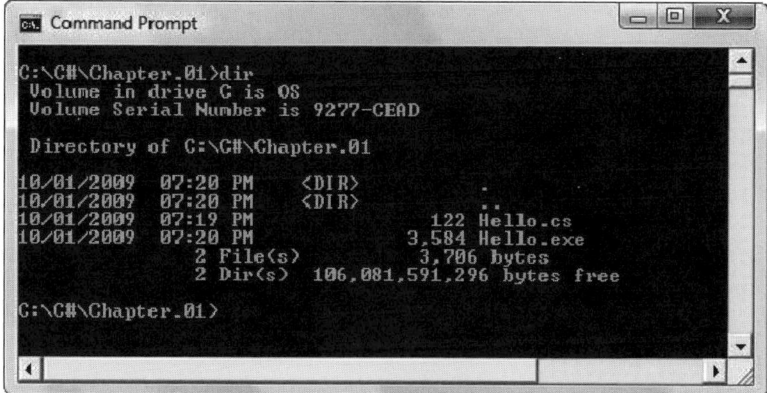

Figure 1-14 Directory of Chapter.01 folder after compiling Hello.cs

   - Use Windows Explorer to view the contents of the Chapter.01 folder, verifying that two Hello files are listed.
   - Double-click the **My Computer** icon, find and double-click the **Chapter.01** folder, and verify that two Hello files are listed.

4. At the command prompt, type **Hello**, which is the name of the program (the name of the executable file), and then press **Enter**. Alternatively, you can type the full filename **Hello.exe**, but typing the .exe extension isn't necessary. The output should look like Figure 1-15.

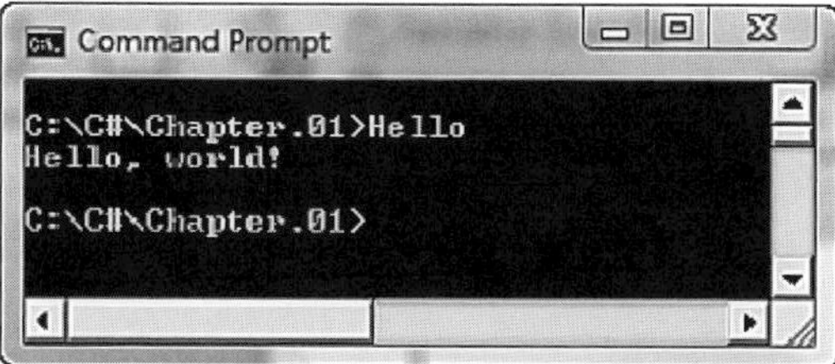

Figure 1-15 Output of the `Hello` application

NOTE You can use the `/out` compiler option between the `csc` command and the name of the .cs file to indicate the name of the output file. For example, if you type `csc /out:Hello.exe Hello.cs`, you create an output file named Hello.exe. By default, the name of the output file is the same as the name of the .cs file. Usually, this is your intention, so most often you omit the `/out` option. You will learn to add other options to the command line in Chapter 3.

COMPILING AND EXECUTING A PROGRAM USING THE VISUAL STUDIO IDE

Next, you will use the C# compiler environment to compile and execute the same `Hello` program you ran from the command line.

To compile and execute the `Hello` program in the Visual Studio IDE:

1. Within the text editor you used to write the `Hello` program, select the entire program text. In Notepad, for example, you can highlight all the lines of text with your mouse (or press **Ctrl+A**). Next, copy the text to the Clipboard for temporary storage by clicking **Edit** on the menu bar and then clicking **Copy** (or by pressing **Ctrl+C**). You'll paste the text in a few steps.
2. Open Visual Studio. If there is a shortcut icon on your desktop, you can double-click it. Alternatively, in Vista or Windows XP, you can click the **Start** button and then click **All Programs**. Then you can click **Microsoft Visual C# 2008 Express Edition**.

NOTE The instructions and screen images in this chapter assume you are using the Express Edition of C#. If you are using the Professional Edition, some screen elements will have minor differences. For example, in the Professional Edition, you open Visual Studio by clicking **Microsoft Visual Studio 2008**. Also, when you are working in Visual Studio, the title bar looks different.

3. On the Start Page, click **File** on the menu bar, then click **New Project**, as shown in Figure 1-16.

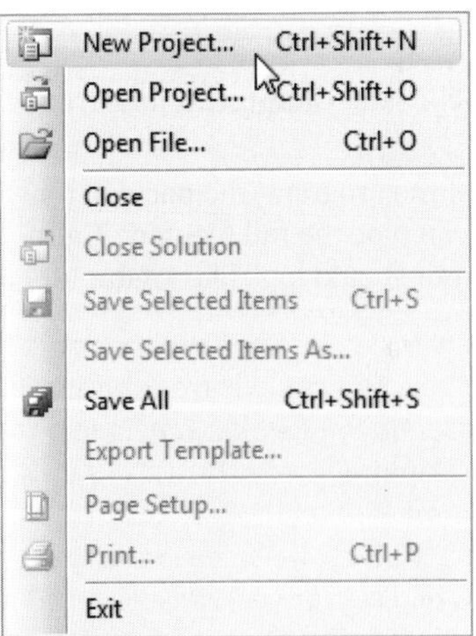

Figure 1-16 Selecting a new project

4. In the New Project window, click **Console Application**. Enter **Hello** as the name for this project (see Figure 1-17). Click **OK**. Visual C# creates a new folder for your project named after the project title.

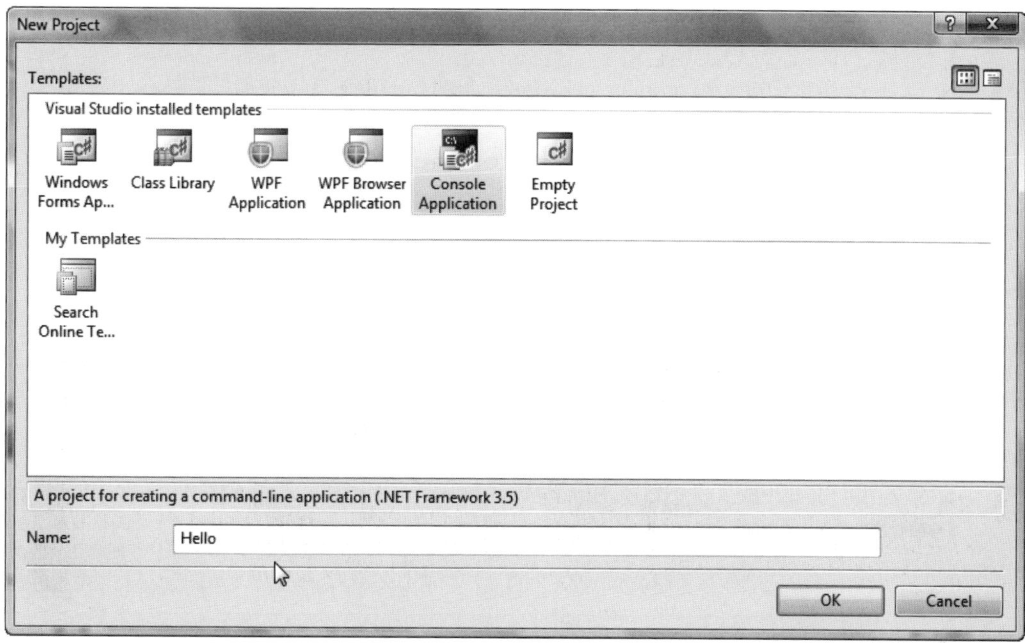

Figure 1-17 Entering the project name

> **NOTE** In Visual Studio Professional 2008, you click **Visual C#** under Project types and then click **Console Application** under Templates.

5. The `Hello` application editing window appears, as shown in Figure 1-18. A lot of code is already written for you in this window, including some `using` statements, a namespace named `Hello`, a class named `Program`, and a `Main()` method. You could leave the class header, `Main()` method header, and other features, and just add the specific statements you need. You would save a lot of typing and prevent typographical errors. But in this case, you have already written a functioning `Hello` program, so you will replace the prewritten code with your `Hello` code. Select all the code in the editor window by highlighting it with your mouse (or by pressing **Ctrl+A**). Then press **Delete**. Paste the previously copied `Hello` program into the editor by pressing **Ctrl+V** (or by clicking **Edit** on the menu bar and then clicking **Paste**).

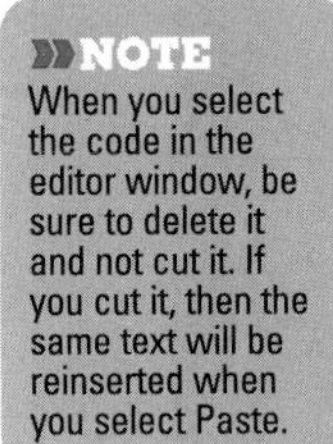

NOTE
When you select the code in the editor window, be sure to delete it and not cut it. If you cut it, then the same text will be reinserted when you select Paste.

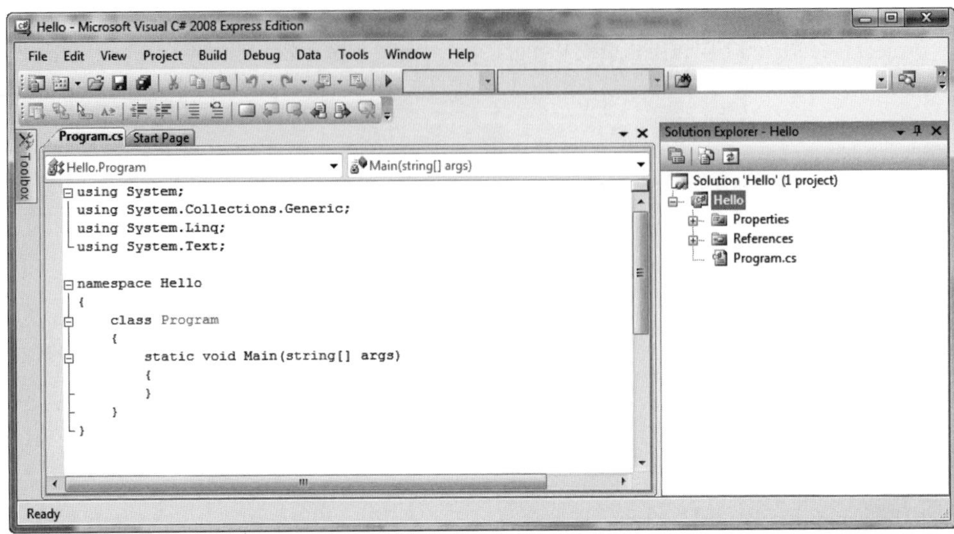

Figure 1-18 The `Hello` application editing window

6. Save the file by clicking **File** on the menu bar and then clicking **Save Hello**, or by clicking the **Save** button on the toolbar. Your screen looks like Figure 1-19.

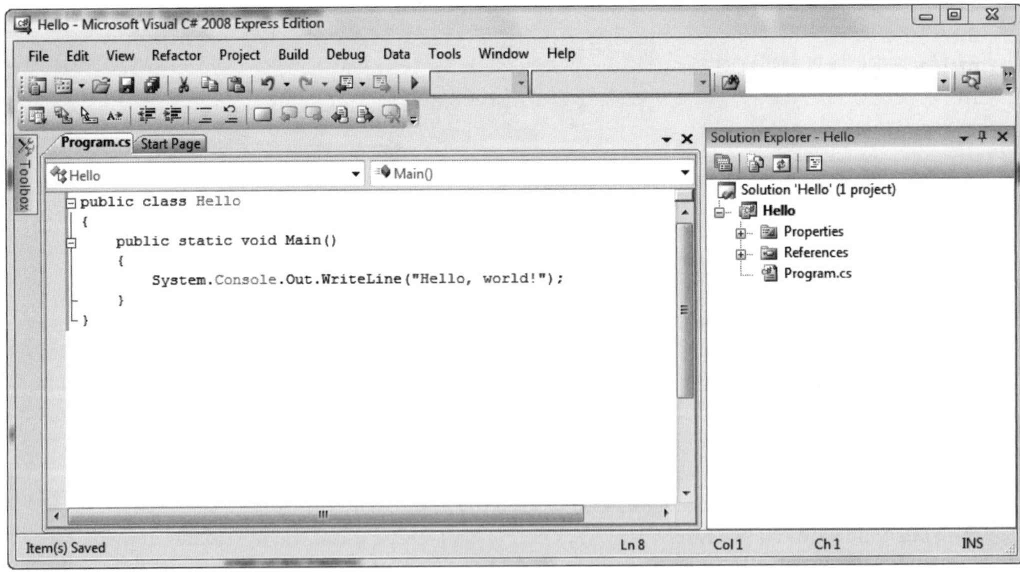

Figure 1-19 The `Hello` application in the IDE

»NOTE The tab that contains Program.cs does not contain an asterisk if your program has been saved. As soon as you change even one character in the editor, an asterisk appears in the Program.cs tab, indicating that a change has been made but not yet saved.

7. To compile the program, click **Build** on the menu bar and then click **Build Solution**. (Alternatively, you can press **F6**.) You should receive no error messages, and the words "Build succeeded" should appear near the lower-left edge of the window.
8. Click **Debug** on the menu bar and then click **Start Without Debugging**. Figure 1-20 shows the output; you see "Hello, world!" followed by the message "Press any key to continue". Press any key to dismiss the output screen.

»NOTE If the output appears but quickly disappears before you can read it, you can add a statement to the program to hold the output screen until you press Enter. Position your insertion point at the end of the `WriteLine()` statement, press Enter to insert a new line, and type `System.Console.ReadLine();`. Then build and start the program again.

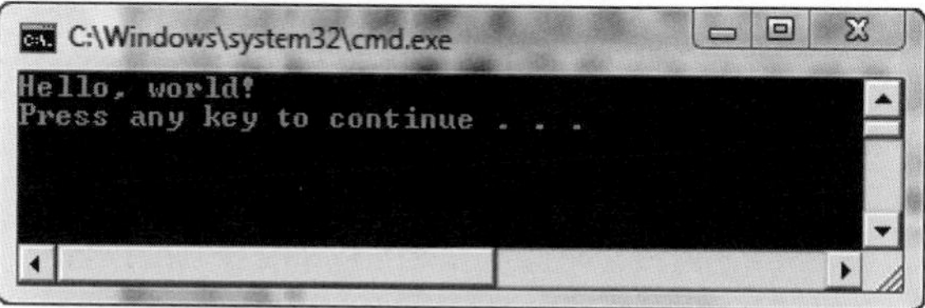

Figure 1-20 Output of the `Hello` application in Visual Studio

9. Close Visual Studio by clicking **File** on the menu bar and then clicking **Exit**, or by clicking the **Close** box in the upper-right corner of the Visual Studio window. When you receive a message "Do you want to save or discard changes to the current solution?", click **Save**. In the Save Project window, you can select a folder location to save the project, as shown in Figure 1-21.

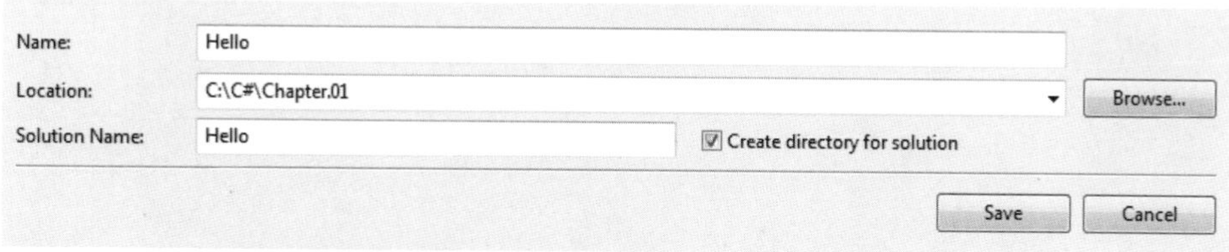

Figure 1-21 The Save Project window

10. When you create a C# program using an editor such as Notepad and compiling with the `csc` command, only two files are created—Hello.cs and Hello.exe. When you create a C# program using the Visual Studio editor, many additional files are created. You can view their filenames in several ways:
    - » At the command prompt, type **dir** to view a directory of the files stored in the folder where you saved the project (for example, your Chapter.01 folder). Within the folder, a

new folder named Hello has been created. Type the command **cd Hello** to change the current path to include this new folder, then type **dir** again. You see another folder named Hello. Type **cd Hello** again, and **dir** again. Figure 1-22 shows the output using this method; it shows several folders and files.

» Double-click the **Computer** icon (or My Computer in Windows XP), find and double-click the correct drive, select the **C#** folder and the **Chapter.01** folder (or the path you are using), double-click the **Hello** folder, and view the contents. Double-click the second **Hello** folder and view the contents there too. Figure 1-23 shows the second Hello folder contents.

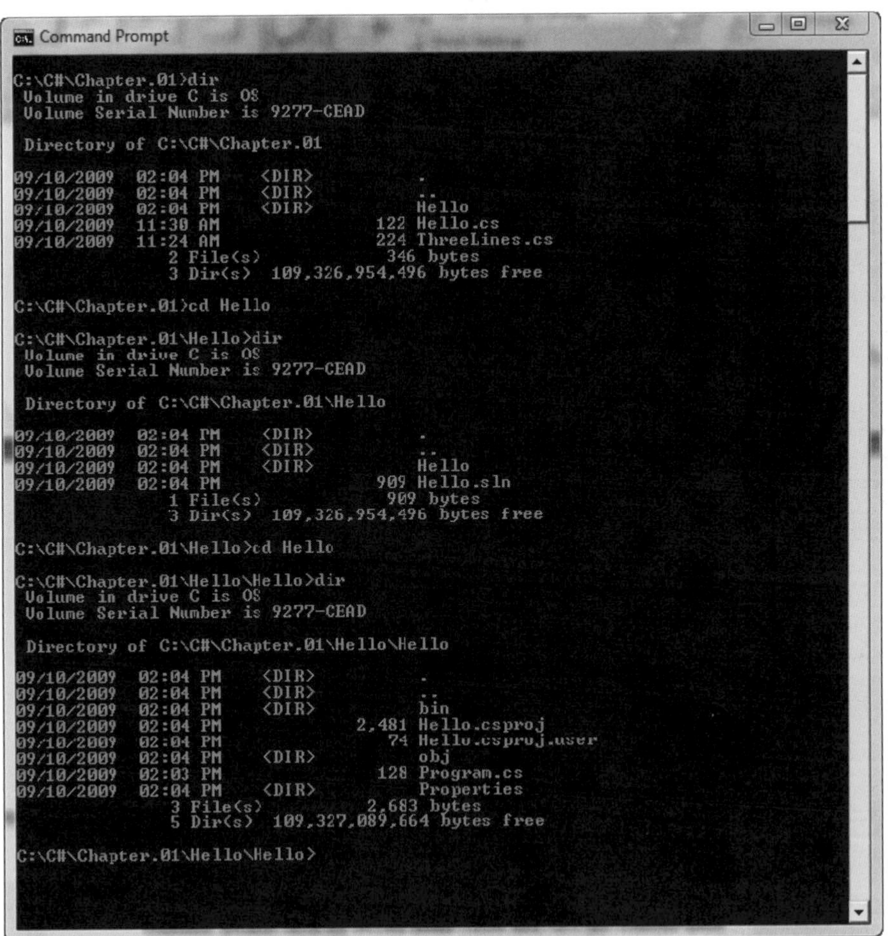

Figure 1-22 Directory listing for Hello folder

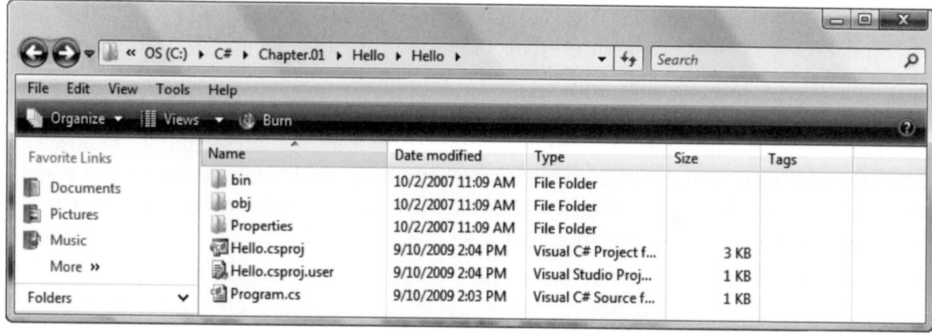

Figure 1-23 Contents of the C#/Chapter.01/Hello/Hello folder

» Use Windows Explorer to view the contents of the Hello folders within the Chapter.01 folder. In Vista, click **Start**, **All Programs**, **Accessories**, and **Windows Explorer**. Then, in the left panel, select **Desktop** and **Computer**. The remaining navigation steps are the same as using **Computer** from the desktop in the last bullet.

The innermost Hello folder contains a bin folder, an obj folder, a Properties folder, and additional files. If you explore further, you will find that the bin folder contains Debug and Release folders, which include additional files. Using the Visual Studio editor to compile your programs creates a lot of overhead. These additional files become important as you create more sophisticated C# projects. For now, while you learn C# syntax, using the command line to compile programs is simpler.

» **NOTE** If you are using a version of Visual Studio other than 2008 Express, your folder configuration might be slightly different.

» **NOTE** If you followed the earlier instructions on compiling a program from the command line, and you used the same folder when using the IDE, you will see the additional Hello.cs and Hello.exe files in your folder. These files will have an earlier time stamp than the files you just created. If you were to execute a new program from within Visual Studio without saving and executing it from the command line first, you would not see these two additional files.

DECIDING WHICH METHOD TO USE

When you write, compile, and execute a C# program, you can use either the command line or the Visual Studio IDE. You would never need to use both. You might prefer using an editor with which you are already familiar (such as Notepad) and compiling from the command line because only two files are generated, saving disk space.

On the other hand, the IDE provides many useful features, such as automatic statement completion. For example, if you type `System` and a dot, then a list of choices is displayed, and you can click `Console` instead of typing it. Similarly, after the dot that follows `Console`, a list of choices is displayed from which you can select `Out`. Additionally, in the IDE, words are displayed using different colors based on their category; for example, one color is used for C#-reserved words and a different color for literal strings. It is also easier to correct many errors using the IDE. When compiler errors or warnings are issued, you can double-click the message, and the cursor jumps to the location in the code where the error was detected.

Another advantage to learning the IDE is that if you use another programming language in Visual Studio (C++ or Visual Basic), the environment will already be familiar to you.

The C# language works the same way, no matter what method you use to compile your programs. Everything you learn in the next chapters about input, output, decision making, loops, and arrays will work the same way, regardless of the compilation technique you use. You can use just one technique, or compile some programs in each environment as the mood strikes you. You can also mix and match techniques if you prefer. For example, you can use an editor you like to compose your programs, then paste them into the IDE to execute them.

Although any program can be written using either compilation technique, when you write graphical user interface (GUI) applications that use existing objects such as message boxes and buttons, you will find that the extensive amount of code automatically generated by the IDE is very helpful. For the first nine chapters of this book, you are encouraged to use whichever compilation technique you prefer. In Chapter 10, you will be encouraged to use the IDE to take advantage of its many time-saving features.

ADDING COMMENTS TO A PROGRAM

To add comments to your program:

1. If you prefer compiling programs from the command line, then open the **Hello.cs** file in your text editor. If you prefer compiling programs from within Visual Studio, then open Visual Studio, click **File**, click **Open Project**, browse for the correct folder, double-click the **Hello** folder, and then double-click the **Hello** file. In the Solution Explorer at the side of the screen, double-click **Hello.cs**, as shown in Figure 1-24.

»NOTE In Visual Studio Professional, you click **File**, point to Open, and click **Project/Solution**.

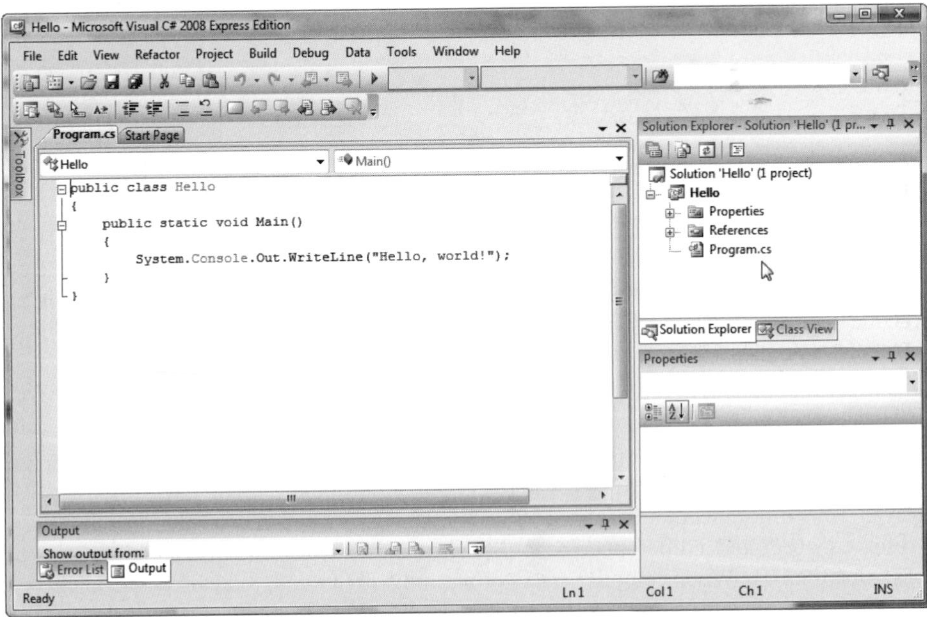

Figure 1-24 Visual C# and the Solution Explorer window

»NOTE If you do not see the Solution Explorer window in Visual Studio, click the Solution Explorer icon on the toolbar (shown at right). Alternatively, from the main menu, choose **View** and then **Solution Explorer**. The Solution Explorer displays the various files that make up a project.

2. Position your cursor at the top of the file, press **Enter** to insert a new line, press the **Up** arrow key to go to that line, and then type the following comments at the top of the file. Press **Enter** after typing each line. Insert your name and today's date where indicated.

```
// Filename Hello.cs
// Written by <your name>
// Written on <today's date>
```

3. Scroll to the line that reads `public static void Main()` and press **Enter** to start a new line. Then press the **Up** arrow; in the new blank line, aligned with the start of the `Main()` method header, type the following block comment in the program:

```
/*  This program demonstrates the use of
the WriteLine() method to print the
message Hello, world!   */
```

4. Save the file, replacing the old Hello.cs file with this new, commented version.
5. If you prefer to compile programs from the command line, type **csc Hello.cs** at the command line. When the program compiles successfully, execute it with the command **Hello**. If you prefer compiling and executing programs from within Visual Studio, click **Debug** and **Start Without Debugging**. Adding program comments makes no difference in the execution of the program.

CHAPTER SUMMARY

» A computer program is a set of instructions that you write to tell a computer what to do. Programmers write their programs, then use a compiler to translate their high-level language statements into intermediate language and machine code. A program works correctly when both its syntax and logic are correct.

» Procedural programming involves creating computer memory locations, called variables, and sets of operations, called methods. In object-oriented programming, you envision program components as objects that are similar to concrete objects in the real world; then you manipulate the objects to achieve a desired result. Objects exist as members of classes and are made up of states and methods.

» The C# programming language was developed as an object-oriented and component-oriented language. It contains many features similar to those in Visual Basic, Java, and C++.

» To write a C# program that produces a line of console output, you must pass a literal string as an argument to the `System.Console.Out.WriteLine()` method. `System` is a namespace, `Console` is a class, and `Out` is an object. The `WriteLine()` method call appears within the `Main()` method of a class you create.

- You can define a C# class or variable by using any name or identifier that begins with an underscore or a letter, contains only letters or digits, and is not a C#-reserved keyword.
- Program comments are nonexecuting statements that you add to document a program or to disable statements when you test a program. There are three types of comments in C#: line comments that start with two forward slashes (//) and continue to the end of the current line, block comments that start with a forward slash and an asterisk (/*) and end with an asterisk and a forward slash (*/), and XML-documentation comments.
- When you need to repeatedly use a class from the same namespace, you can shorten the statements you type by using a clause that indicates a namespace where the class can be found.
- To create a C# program, you can use the Microsoft Visual Studio environment. You can also use any text editor, such as Notepad, WordPad, or any word-processing program. After you write and save a program, you must compile the source code into intermediate and machine language.
- You have multiple options for writing the `Main()` method header; the format you use depends on your need for command-line arguments and the conventions you prefer in your working environment.

KEY TERMS

A computer **program** is a set of instructions that you write to tell a computer what to do.

Machine language is the most basic circuitry-level language.

A **high-level programming language** allows you to use a vocabulary of reasonable terms such as "read," "write," or "add" instead of the sequence of on/off switches that perform these tasks.

A language's **syntax** is its set of rules.

A **compiler** is a computer program that translates high-level language statements into machine code.

A **syntax error** is an error that occurs when a programming language is used incorrectly.

The **logic** behind any program involves executing the various statements and methods in the correct order to produce the desired results.

Semantic errors are the type of logical errors that occur when you use a correct word in the wrong context.

Debugging a program is the process of removing all syntax and logical errors from the program.

A **procedural program** is created by writing a series of steps or operations to manipulate values.

Variables are named computer memory locations that hold values that might vary.

An **identifier** is the name of a program component such as a variable, class, or method.

Camel casing is a style of creating identifiers in which the first letter is not capitalized, but each new word is.

Pascal casing is a style of creating identifiers in which the first letter of all new words in a variable name, even the first one, is capitalized.

Procedures or **methods** are compartmentalized program units that accomplish tasks.

A program **calls** or **invokes** methods.

Object-oriented programming is a programming technique that features objects, classes, encapsulation, interfaces, polymorphism, and inheritance.

Objects are program elements that are instances of a class.

The **command line** is the line on which you type a command in a system that uses a text interface.

The **command prompt** is a request for input that appears at the beginning of the command line.

The **attributes** of an object represent its characteristics.

The **states** of an object are the values of its attributes.

The **properties** of an object are its values.

The **state of an object** is the collective value of all its attributes at any point in time.

A **class** is a category of objects or a type of object.

Each object is an **instance** of a class.

Encapsulation is the technique of packaging an object's attributes and methods into a cohesive unit that can be used as an undivided entity.

A **black box** is a device you use without regard for the internal mechanisms.

An **interface** is the interaction between a method and an object.

Polymorphism is the ability to create methods that act appropriately depending on the context.

Inheritance is the ability to extend a class so as to create a more specific class that contains all the attributes and methods of a more general class; the extended class usually contains new attributes or methods as well.

The **C# programming language** was developed as an object-oriented and component-oriented language. It exists as part of Visual Studio 2008, a package used for developing applications for the Windows family of operating systems.

Primitive data is simple data, such as a number.

A **literal string** of characters is a series of characters that is used exactly as entered.

An **argument** or a **parameter** to a method represents information that a method needs to perform its task. An argument is the expression used when you call a method, while a parameter is an object or reference that is declared in a method definition; that is, where the method instructions are written.

The **WriteLine() method** displays a line of output on the screen, positions the cursor on the next line, and waits for additional output.

The **Write() method** displays a line of output on the screen, but the cursor does not advance to a new line; it remains on the same line as the output.

A **namespace** is a scheme that provides a way to group similar classes.

The **System namespace**, which is built into your C# compiler, holds commonly used classes.

A **method header** includes the method name and information about what will pass into and be returned from a method.

The **method body** of every method is contained within a pair of curly braces ({ }) and includes all the instructions executed by the method.

Whitespace is any combination of spaces, tabs, and carriage returns (blank lines). You use whitespace to organize your program code and make it easier to read.

Keywords are predefined and reserved identifiers that have special meaning to the compiler.

An **access modifier** defines the circumstances under which a method or class can be accessed; `public` access is the most liberal type of access.

In a method header, **public** is an access modifier that indicates other classes may use the method.

In a method header, **private** is an access modifier that indicates other classes may not use the method.

The reserved keyword **static** indicates that a method will be executed through a class and not by an object.

In a method header, the keyword **void** indicates that the method does not return any value when called.

A **verbatim identifier** is an identifier with an @ prefix.

Program comments are nonexecuting statements that you add to document a program.

When you **comment out** a statement, you turn it into a comment so that the compiler will not execute its command.

Line comments start with two forward slashes (//) and continue to the end of the current line. Line comments can appear on a line by themselves, or at the end of a line following executable code.

Block comments start with a forward slash and an asterisk (/*) and end with an asterisk and a forward slash (*/). Block comments can appear on a line by themselves, on a line before executable code, or after executable code. They can also extend across as many lines as needed.

XML-documentation format comments use a special set of tags within angle brackets to create documentation from within a program.

You use a namespace with a **using clause**, or **using directive**.

An **alias** is an alternative name for a class.

Source code is the statements you write when you create a program.

Intermediate language (IL) is the language into which source code statements are compiled.

The C# **just in time (JIT)** compiler translates intermediate code into executable code.

A **`string`** is a data type that can hold a series of characters.

REVIEW QUESTIONS

1. A computer program written as a series of on and off switches is written in __________.

   a. machine language
   b. a low-level language
   c. a high-level language
   d. a compiled language

2. A program that translates high-level programs into intermediate or machine code is a(n) __________.

   a. mangler
   b. compiler
   c. analyst
   d. logician

3. The grammar and spelling rules of a programming language constitute its __________.

   a. logic
   b. variables
   c. syntax
   d. vortex

4. Variables are __________.

   a. procedures
   b. named memory locations
   c. grammar rules
   d. operations

5. Programs in which you create and use objects that have attributes similar to their real-world counterparts are known as __________ programs.

   a. procedural
   b. logical
   c. authentic
   d. object-oriented

6. Which of the following pairs is an example of a class and an object, in that order?

   a. robin and bird
   b. chair and desk
   c. university and Harvard
   d. oak and tree

7. The technique of packaging an object's attributes into a cohesive unit that can be used as an undivided entity is ________.

   a. inheritance
   b. encapsulation
   c. polymorphism
   d. interfacing

8. Of the following languages, which is least similar to C#?

   a. Java
   b. Visual Basic
   c. C++
   d. COBOL

9. A series of characters that appears within double quotation marks is a(n) ________.

   a. parameter
   b. interface
   c. argument
   d. literal string

10. The C# method that prints a line of output on the screen and then positions the cursor on the next line is ________.

    a. `WriteLine()`
    b. `PrintLine()`
    c. `DisplayLine()`
    d. `OutLine()`

11. Which of the following is an object?

    a. `System`
    b. `Console`
    c. `Out`
    d. `WriteLine`

12. In C#, a scheme that groups similar classes is a(n) ________.

    a. superclass
    b. method
    c. namespace
    d. identifier

13. Every method in C# contains a ________.

    a. header and a body
    b. header and a footer
    c. variable and a class
    d. class and an object

14. Which of the following is a method?

    a. `namespace`
    b. `public`
    c. `Main()`
    d. `static`

15. Which of the following statements is true?

    a. An identifier must begin with an underscore.
    b. An identifier can contain digits.
    c. An identifier must be no more than 16 characters long.
    d. An identifier can contain only lowercase letters.

16. Which of the following identifiers is not legal in C#?
    - a. `per cent increase`
    - b. `annualReview`
    - c. `HTML`
    - d. `alternativetaxcredit`

17. The text of a program you write is called ________ .
    - a. object code
    - b. source code
    - c. machine language
    - d. executable documentation

18. Programming errors such as using incorrect punctuation or misspelling words are collectively known as ________ errors.
    - a. syntax
    - b. logical
    - c. executable
    - d. fatal

19. A comment in the form `/* this is a comment */` is a(n) ________ .
    - a. XML comment
    - b. block comment
    - c. executable comment
    - d. line comment

20. If a programmer inserts `using System;` at the top of a C# program, which of the following can the programmer use as an alternative to `System.Console.Out.WriteLine("Hello");`?
    - a. `System("Hello");`
    - b. `WriteLine("Hello");`
    - c. `Console.WriteLine("Hello");`
    - d. `Console.Out("Hello");`

EXERCISES

1. Indicate whether each of the following C# programming language identifiers is legal or illegal.
    - a. `WeeklySales`
    - b. `last character`
    - c. `class`
    - d. `MathClass`
    - e. `myfirstinitial`
    - f. `phone#`
    - g. `abcdefghijklmnop`
    - h. `23jordan`
    - i. `my_code`
    - j. `90210`
    - k. `year2008Budget`
    - l. `abfSorority`

2. Name at least three attributes that might be appropriate for each of the following classes:
    - a. `TelevisionSet`
    - b. `EmployeePaycheck`
    - c. `PatientMedicalRecord`

3. Name a class to which each of these objects might belong:

    a. your red bicycle
    b. Albert Einstein
    c. last month's credit card bill

4. Write, compile, and test a program that displays your first name on the screen. Save the program as **Name.cs**.

5. Write, compile, and test a program that displays your full name, street address, and city and state on three separate lines on the screen. Save the program as **Address.cs**.

6. Write, compile, and test a program that displays your favorite quotation on the screen. Include the name of the person to whom the quote is attributed. Use as many display lines as you feel are appropriate. Save the program as **Quotation.cs**.

7. Write, compile, and test a program that displays a pattern similar to the following on the screen:

```
   X
  XXX
 XXXXX
XXXXXXX
   X
```

    Save the program as **Tree.cs**.

8. Write a program that displays your initials in a pattern on the screen. Compose each initial with six lines of smaller initials, as in the following example:

```
     J    FFFFFF
     J    F
     J    FFF
     J    F
J    J    F
JJJJJJ    F
```

    Save the program as **Initials.cs**.

9. From 1925 through 1963, Burma Shave advertising signs appeared next to highways all across the United States. There were always four or five signs in a row containing pieces of a rhyme, followed by a final sign that read "Burma Shave." For example, one set of signs that has been preserved by the Smithsonian Institution reads as follows:

```
Shaving brushes
You'll soon see 'em
On a shelf
In some museum
Burma Shave
```

Find a classic Burma Shave rhyme on the Web and write a program that displays it. Save the program as **BurmaShave.cs**.

DEBUGGING EXERCISES

Each of the following files in the Chapter.01 folder on your Student Disk has syntax and/or logical errors. In each case, determine the problem and fix the program. After you correct the errors, save each file using the same filename preceded with "Fixed". For example, DebugOne1.cs will become FixedDebugOne1.cs.

a. DebugOne1.cs
b. DebugOne2.cs
c. DebugOne3.cs
d. DebugOne4.cs

UP FOR DISCUSSION

1. Using an Internet search engine, find at least three definitions for *object-oriented programming*. (Try searching with and without the hyphen in *object-oriented*.) Compare the definitions and compile them into one "best" definition.
2. What is the difference between a compiler and an interpreter? What programming languages use each? Under what conditions would you prefer to use one over the other?
3. What is the image of the computer programmer in popular culture? Is the image different in books than in TV shows and movies? Would you like a programmer image for yourself, and if so, which one?

CHAPTER TWO

2

USING DATA

In this chapter you will:

Learn about declaring variables
Display variable values
Learn about the integral data types
Learn about floating-point data types
Format floating-point values
Use standard binary arithmetic operators
Use shortcut arithmetic operators
Learn about the `bool` data type
Learn about numeric type conversion
Learn about the `char` data type
Learn about the `string` data type
Define named constants
Accept console input

In Chapter 1, you learned about programming in general and the C# programming language in particular. You wrote, compiled, and ran a C# program that produces output. In this chapter, you build on your basic C# programming skills by learning how to manipulate data, including variables, data types, and constants. As you will see, using variables makes writing computer programs worth the effort.

DECLARING VARIABLES

You can categorize data as variable or constant. A data item is **constant** when it cannot be changed after a program is compiled—in other words, when it cannot vary. For example, if you use the number 347 within a C# program, then 347 is a constant, and every time you execute the program, the value 347 will be used. You can refer to the number 347 as a **literal constant**, because its value is taken literally at each use.

>> **NOTE** You will learn to create named constants later in this chapter.

On the other hand, when you want a value to be able to change, you can create a variable. A **variable** is a named location in computer memory that can hold different values at different points in time. For example, if you create a variable named `heatingBill` and include it in a C# program, `heatingBill` might contain the value 347, or it might contain 200. Different values might be used when the program is executed multiple times, or different values might even be used at different times during the same execution of the program. Because you can use a variable to hold `heatingBill` within a utility company's billing system, you can write one set of instructions to compute `heatingBill`, yet use different `heatingBill` values for thousands of utility customers during one execution of the program.

Whether it is stored as a constant or in a variable, each data item you use in a C# program has a data type. A **data type** describes the format and size of (amount of memory occupied by) a data item. C# provides for 14 basic or **intrinsic types** of data, as shown in Table 2-1. Of these built-in data types, the ones most commonly used are `int`, `double`, `char`, `string`, and `bool`. Each C# intrinsic type is an **alias**, or other name for, a class in the `System` namespace.

>> **NOTE** You learned about the `System` namespace in Chapter 1.

Type	System Type	Bytes	Description	Largest Value	Smallest Value
`byte`	Byte	1	Unsigned byte	255	0
`sbyte`	Sbyte	1	Signed byte	127	–128
`short`	Int16	2	Signed short	32,767	–32,768
`ushort`	UInt16	2	Unsigned short	65,535	0
`int`	Int32	4	Signed integer	2,147,483,647	–2,147,483,648
`uint`	UInt32	4	Unsigned integer	4,294,967,295	0
`long`	Int64	8	Signed long integer	Approximately 9×10^{18}	Approximately -9×10^{18}
`ulong`	UInt64	8	Unsigned long integer	Approximately 18×10^{18}	0
`float`	Single	4	Floating-point	Approximately 3.4×10^{38}	Approximately -3.4×10^{38}
`double`	Double	8	Double-precision floating-point	Approximately 1.8×10^{308}	Approximately -1.8×10^{308}
`decimal`	Decimal	16	Fixed precision number	Approximately 7.9×10^{28}	Approximately -7.9×10^{28}
`string`	String	NA	Unicode string	NA	NA
`char`	Char	2	Unicode character	0xFFFF	0x0000
`bool`	Boolean	1	Boolean value (true or false)	NA	NA

Table 2-1 C# data types

»**NOTE** The highest `char` value, 0xFFFF, represents the character in which every bit is turned on. The lowest value, 0x0000, represents the character in which every bit is turned off. Any value that begins with "0x" represents a hexadecimal, or base 16, value.

»**NOTE** For any two `string`s, the one with the higher Unicode character value in an earlier position is considered higher. For example, "AAB" is higher than "AAA". The `string` type has no true minimum. However, you can think of the empty string "" as being the lowest.

»**NOTE** Although the `bool` type has no true maximum or minimum, you can think of `true` as the highest and `false` as the lowest.

You name variables using the same rules for identifiers as you use for class names. Basically, variable names must start with a letter, cannot include embedded spaces, and cannot be a reserved keyword. You must declare all variables you want to use in a program. A **variable declaration** is the statement that names a variable and reserves storage for it; it includes:

- The data type that the variable will store
- The identifier that is the variable's name
- An optional assignment operator and assigned value when you want a variable to contain an initial value
- An ending semicolon

NOTE Variable names usually begin with lowercase letters to distinguish them from class names. You should follow this convention when naming your variables. However, variable names *can* begin with either an uppercase or lowercase letter.

NOTE You learned the rules for creating identifiers in Chapter 1. The C# reserved keywords are listed in Table 1-1 in Chapter 1.

For example, the variable declaration `int myAge = 25;` declares a variable of type `int` named `myAge` and assigns it an initial value of 25. In other words, four bytes of memory are reserved with the name `myAge` and the value 25 is stored there. The declaration is a complete statement that ends in a semicolon. The equal sign (=) is the **assignment operator**; any value to the right of the assignment operator is assigned to, or taken on by, the variable to the left. An assignment made when a variable is declared is an **initialization**; an assignment made later is simply an **assignment**. Thus, `int myAge = 25;` initializes `myAge` to 25, and a subsequent statement, such as `myAge = 42;`, assigns a new value to the variable. Note that the expression `25 = myAge;` is illegal because assignment always takes place from right to left. By definition, a constant cannot be altered, so it is illegal to place one (such as 25) on the left side of an assignment operator.

NOTE The assignment operator means "is assigned the value of the following expression." In other words, the statement `myAge = 25` can be read as "`myAge` is assigned the value of the following expression: 25".

NOTE The number 32 in the name `System.Int32` represents the number of bits of storage allowed for the data type. There are 8 bits in a byte, and an `int` occupies 4 bytes.

Instead of using a name from the Type column of Table 2-1, you can use the fully qualified type name from the `System` namespace that is listed in the System Type column. For example, instead of using the type name `int`, you can use the full name `System.Int32`. It's better to use the shorter alias `int`, however, for several reasons:

- The shorter alias is easier to type and read.
- The shorter alias resembles type names used in other languages such as Java and C++.
- Other C# programmers expect the shorter type names.

The variable declaration `int myAge;` declares a variable of type `int` named `myAge`, but no value is assigned at the time of creation. You can make an assignment later in the program, but you cannot use the variable in an arithmetic expression or display the value of the variable until you assign a value to it.

You can declare multiple variables of the same type in separate statements on different lines. For example, the following statements declare two variables. The first variable is named `myAge` and its value is 25. The second variable is named `yourAge` and its value is 19.

```
int myAge = 25;
int yourAge = 19;
```

You also can declare two variables of the same type in a single statement by using the type once and separating the variable declarations with a comma, as shown in the following statement:

```
int myAge = 25, yourAge = 19;
```

Some programmers prefer to use the data type once and break the declaration across multiple lines, as in the following example:

```
int myAge = 25,
    yourAge = 19;
```

NOTE When a statement occupies more than one line, it is easier to read if lines after the first one are indented a few spaces. This book follows that convention.

NOTE A statement and a line of code are not synonymous. In C#, a statement might occupy multiple lines or a single line might contain multiple statements. Every statement ends with a semicolon.

When you declare multiple variables of the same type, a comma separates the variable names and a single semicolon appears at the end of the declaration statement, no matter how many lines the declaration occupies. However, when declaring variables of different types, you must use a separate statement for each type. The following statements declare two variables of type `int` (`myAge` and `yourAge`) and two variables of type `double` (`mySalary` and `yourSalary`), without assigning initial values to any of them:

```
int myAge, yourAge;
double mySalary, yourSalary;
```

Similarly, the following statements declare two `int`s and two `double`s, assigning values to two of the four named variables:

```
int     numCarsIOwn = 2,
        numCarsYouOwn;
double  myCarsMpg,
        yourCarsMpg = 31.5;
```

»TWO TRUTHS AND A LIE: DECLARING VARIABLES

1. A constant cannot be changed after a program is compiled, but a variable can be changed.
2. A data type describes the format and size of a data item.
3. A variable declaration is the statement that names a variable and assigns a value to it.

The false statement is #3. A variable declaration names a variable and reserves storage for it; it includes the data type that the variable will store, and an identifier. An assignment operator and assigned value can be included, but they are not required.

DISPLAYING VARIABLE VALUES

»NOTE You first used the `WriteLine()` method to display strings in Chapter 1.

You can display variable values by using the variable name within a `WriteLine()` method call. For example, Figure 2-1 shows a C# program that displays the value of the variable `someMoney`. Figure 2-2 shows the output of the program.

```
using System;
public class DisplaySomeMoney
{
   public static void Main()
   {
      double someMoney = 39.45;
      Console.WriteLine(someMoney);
   }
}
```

Figure 2-1 Program that displays a variable value

Figure 2-2 Output of `DisplaySomeMoney` program

The output shown in Figure 2-2 is rather stark—just a number with no explanation. The program in Figure 2-3 adds some explanation to the output; the result is shown in Figure 2-4. This program uses the `Write()` method to display the string "The money is $" before displaying the value of `someMoney`. Because the program uses `Write()` instead of `WriteLine()`, the second output appears on the same line as the first output.

```
using System;
public class DisplaySomeMoney2
{
   public static void Main()
   {
      double someMoney = 39.45;
      Console.Write("The money is $");
      Console.WriteLine(someMoney);
   }
}
```

Figure 2-3 Program that displays a string and a variable value

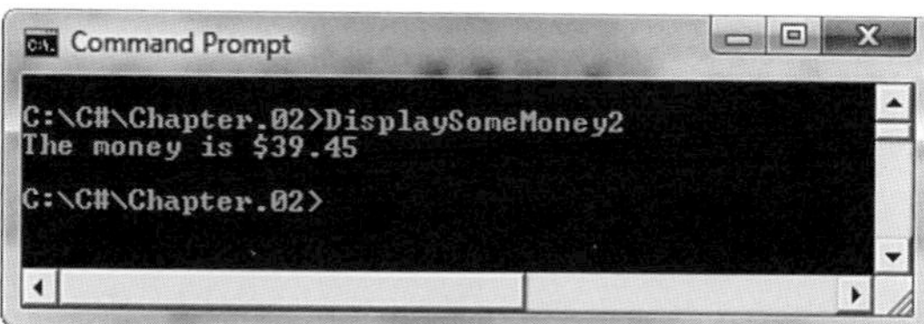

Figure 2-4 Output of `DisplaySomeMoney2` program

If you want to display several strings and several variables, you can end up with quite a few `Write()` and `WriteLine()` statements. To make producing output easier, you can combine strings and variable values into a single `Write()` or `WriteLine()` statement by using a format string. A **format string** is a string of characters that optionally contains fixed text and contains one or more format items or placeholders for variable values. A **placeholder** consists of a pair of curly braces containing a number that indicates the desired variable's position in a list that follows the string. The first position is always position 0. For example, if you remove the `Write()` and `WriteLine()` statements from the program in Figure 2-3 and replace them with the shaded statement in Figure 2-5, the program produces the output

```
using System;
public class DisplaySomeMoney3
{
   public static void Main()
   {
      double someMoney = 39.45;
      Console.WriteLine("The money is ${0} exactly",
         someMoney);
   }
}
```

Figure 2-5 Using a format string

shown in Figure 2-6. The placeholder {0} holds a position into which the value of `someMoney` is inserted. Because `someMoney` is the first variable after the format string (as well as the only variable), its position is 0.

Figure 2-6 Output produced using format string

To display two variables within a single call to `Write()` or `WriteLine()`, you can use a statement like the following:

```
Console.WriteLine("The money is {0} and my age is {1}",
      someMoney, myAge);
```

The number within the curly braces in the format string must be less than the number of values you list after the format string. In other words, if you list six values to be displayed, valid format position numbers are 0 through 5. You do not have to use the positions in order. For example, you can choose to display the value in position 2, then 1, then 0. You also can display a specific value multiple times. For example, if `someMoney` has been assigned the value 439.75, the following code produces the output shown in Figure 2-7:

```
Console.WriteLine("I have ${0}. ${0}!! ${0}!!",
     someMoney);
```

»NOTE When C# program statements become lengthy, you might want to split them into multiple lines in your editor. However, you cannot split a statement in the middle of a string.

Figure 2-7 Displaying the same value multiple times

When you use a series of `WriteLine()` statements to display a list of variable values, the values are not right-aligned as you normally expect numbers to be. For example, the following code produces the output shown in Figure 2-8:

```
int num1 = 4, num2 = 56, num3 = 789;
Console.WriteLine("{0}", num1);
Console.WriteLine("{0}", num2);
Console.WriteLine("{0}", num3);
```

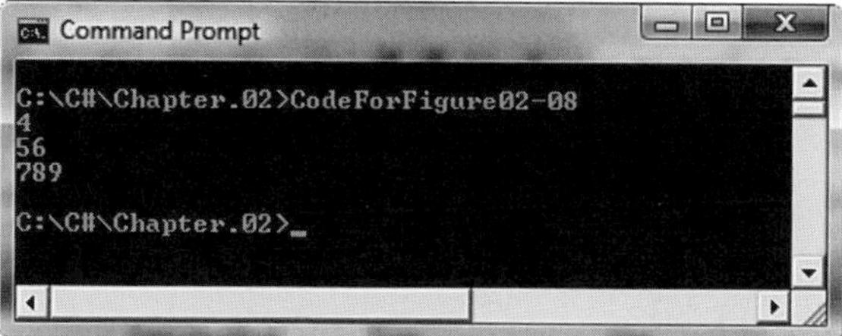

Figure 2-8 Displaying values with different numbers of digits without using field sizes

If you use a second number within the curly braces in a number format, you can specify alignment and field size. For example, the following code produces the output shown in Figure 2-9. The output created by each `WriteLine()` statement is right-aligned in a field that is five characters wide.

```
int num1 = 4, num2 = 56, num3 = 789;
Console.WriteLine("{0, 5}", num1);
Console.WriteLine("{0, 5}", num2);
Console.WriteLine("{0, 5}", num3);
```

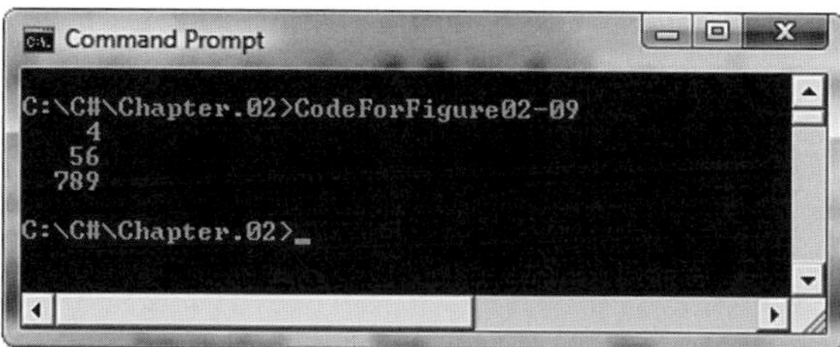

Figure 2-9 Displaying values with different numbers of digits using field sizes

NOTE By default, numbers are right-aligned in their fields. If you use a negative value for the field size in a `Write()` or `WriteLine()` statement, the value displayed will be left-aligned in the field.

When you include a format string in a `Console.WriteLine()` statement, you cannot extend the string across multiple lines by pressing Enter. Instead, you can **concatenate** (join together in a chain) multiple strings into a single entity using a plus sign (+). For example, the following two statements produce identical results. In the second, the format string is broken into two parts and concatenated.

```
Console.WriteLine("I have ${0}. ${0} is a lot.",
    someMoney);
Console.WriteLine("I have ${0}. " +
    "${0} is a lot. ", someMoney);
```

»NOTE In this example, the + could go at the end of the first code line or the beginning of the second one. If the + is placed at the end of the first line, someone reading your code is more likely to notice that the statement is not yet complete. Because of the limitations of this book's page width, you will see examples of concatenation frequently in program code.

»TWO TRUTHS AND A LIE: DISPLAYING VARIABLE VALUES

1. Assuming `number` and `answer` are legally declared variables, then the following statement is valid:

```
Console.WriteLine("{1}{2}", number, answer);
```

2. Assuming `number` and `answer` are legally declared variables, then the following statement is valid:

```
Console.WriteLine("{1}{1}{0}", number, answer);
```

3. Assuming `number` and `answer` are legally declared variables, then the following statement is valid:

```
Console.WriteLine("{0}{1}{1}{0}", number, answer);
```

The false statement is #1. When two values are available for display, the position number between any pair of curly braces in the format string must be 0 or 1.

USING THE INTEGRAL DATA TYPES

»NOTE You first learned about Unicode in Chapter 1; you examine it further later in this chapter.

In C#, nine data types are considered **integral data types**—that is, types that store whole numbers. The nine types are **`byte`**, **`sbyte`**, **`short`**, **`ushort`**, **`int`**, **`uint`**, **`long`**, **`ulong`**, and **`char`**. The first eight always represent whole numbers, and the ninth type, `char`, is used for characters like 'A' or 'a'. Actually, you can think of all nine types as numbers because every Unicode character, including the letters of the alphabet and punctuation marks, can be represented as a number. For example, the character 'A' is stored within your computer as a 65. Because you more commonly think of the `char` type as holding alphabetic characters instead of their numeric equivalents, the `char` type will be discussed in its own section later in this chapter.

The most basic of the other eight integral types is `int`. You use variables of type `int` to store (or hold) **integers**, or whole numbers. An `int` uses four bytes of memory and can hold any whole number value ranging from 2,147,483,647 down to -2,147,483,648. If you want to save memory and know you need only a small value, you can use one of the shorter integer types—`byte`, `sbyte` (which stands for signed byte), `short` (short `int`), or `ushort` (unsigned short `int`). For example, a payroll program might contain a variable named `numberOfDependents` that is declared as type `byte`, because `numberOfDependents` will never need to hold a negative value or a value exceeding 255; for that reason, you can allocate just one byte of storage to hold the value.

»NOTE When you declare variables, you always make a judgment about which type to use. If you use a type that is too large, you waste storage. If you use a type that is too small, your program won't compile. Many programmers simply use `int` for most whole numbers.

When you assign a value to any numeric variable, you do not use any commas; you type only digits. You can also type a plus or minus sign to indicate a positive or negative integer. For example, to initialize a variable named `annualSalary`, you might write the following:

```
int annualSalary = 20000;
```

»TWO TRUTHS AND A LIE: USING THE INTEGRAL DATA TYPES

1. C# supports nine integral data types, including the most basic one, `int`.
2. Every Unicode character, including the letters of the alphabet and punctuation marks, can be represented as a number.
3. When you assign a value to any numeric variable, it is optional to use commas for values in the thousands.

The false answer is # 3. When you assign a value to a numeric variable, you do not use commas, but you can type a plus or minus sign to indicate a positive or negative integer.

USING FLOATING-POINT DATA TYPES

A **floating-point** number is one that contains decimal positions. C# supports three floating-point data types: `float`, `double`, and `decimal`. A **`float`** data type can hold as many as seven significant digits of accuracy. A **`double`** data type can hold 15 or 16 significant digits of accuracy. A value's number of **significant digits** specifies the mathematical accuracy of the value. For example, a `double` given the value 123456789.987654321 will appear as 123456789.987654 because it is accurate to only the fifteenth digit (the sixth digit to the right of the decimal point). Compared to `float`s and `double`s, the **`decimal`** type has a greater precision and a smaller range, which makes it suitable for financial and monetary calculations. For example, a `decimal` given the value 123456789.987654321 will appear as 123456789.987654321 (notice that it is accurate to the rightmost digit). A `decimal` cannot hold as large a value as a `double` can, but the `decimal` will be more accurate to more decimal places.

Just as an integer constant such as 178 is an `int` by default, a floating-point number constant such as 18.23 is a `double` by default. To explicitly store a constant as a `float`, you place an *F* after the number, as in the following:

```
float pocketChange = 4.87F;
```

You can use either a lowercase or uppercase *F*. You can also place a *D* (or *d*) after a floating-point value to indicate that it is a `double`; even without the *D*, however, it will be stored as a `double` by default. To explicitly store a value as a `decimal`, use an *M* (or *m*) after the number. (*M* stands for monetary; *D* can't be used for `decimal`s because it indicates `double`.)

If you store a value that is too large in a floating-point variable, you will see output expressed in **scientific notation**. Values expressed in scientific notation include an *E* (for exponent). For example, if you declare `float f = 1234567890f;`, the value will appear as 1.234568E9, meaning that the numeric constant you used is approximately 1.234568 times 10 to the ninth power, or 1.234568 with the decimal point moved nine positions to the right.

»TWO TRUTHS AND A LIE: USING FLOATING-POINT DATA TYPES

1. A floating-point number is one in which the decimal point varies each time you reference it.
2. C# supports three floating-point data types: `float`, `double`, and `decimal`.
3. To explicitly store a constant as a `float`, you may place an *F* after the number, but to store a constant as a `double` you need no special designation.

The false statement is #1. A floating-point number is one that contains decimal positions.

FORMATTING FLOATING-POINT VALUES

By default, C# always displays floating-point numbers in the most concise way it can while maintaining the correct value. For example, if you declare a variable and display it as in the following statements, the output will appear as "The amount is 14".

```
double myMoney = 14.00;
Console.WriteLine("The amount is {0}", myMoney);
```

The two zeros to the right of the decimal point in the value will not appear because they add no mathematical information. To see the decimal places, you can convert the floating-point value to a string using a standard numeric format string.

Standard numeric format strings are strings of characters expressed within double quotation marks that indicate a format for output. They take the form *X0*, where *X* is the format specifier and *0* is the precision specifier. The **format specifier** can be one of nine built-in format characters that define the most commonly used numeric format types. The **precision specifier** controls the number of significant digits or zeros to the right of the decimal point. Table 2-2 lists the nine format specifiers.

You can use a format specifier with the `ToString()` method to convert a number into a string that has the desired format. For example, you can use the *F* format specifier to insert a decimal point to the right of a number that does not contain digits to the right of the decimal point, followed by the number of zeros indicated by the precision specifier. (If no precision

Format Character	Description	Default Format (if no precision is given)
C or c	Currency	$XX,XXX.XX ($XX,XXX.XX)
D or d	Decimal	[-]XXXXXXX
E or e	Scientific (exponential)	[-]X.XXXXXXE+xxx [-]X.XXXXXXe+xxx [-]X.XXXXXXE-xxx [-]X.XXXXXXe-xxx
F or f	Fixed-point	[-]XXXXXXX.XX
G or g	General	Variable; either with decimal places or scientific
N or n	Number	[-]XX,XXX.XX
P or p	Percent	Represents a numeric value as a percentage
R or r	Round trip	Ensures that numbers converted to strings will have the same values when they are converted back into numbers
X or x	Hexadecimal	Minimum hexadecimal (base 16) representation

Table 2-2 Format specifiers

specifier is supplied, two zeros are inserted.) For example, the first `WriteLine()` statement in the following code produces 123.00, and the second produces 123.000:

```
double someMoney = 123;
string moneyString;
moneyString = someMoney.ToString("F");
Console.WriteLine(moneyString);
moneyString = someMoney.ToString("F3");
Console.WriteLine(moneyString);
```

» **NOTE** You will learn more about strings later in this chapter.

» **NOTE** You will learn more about creating and using methods in Chapter 6.

You use *C* as the format specifier when you want to represent a number as a currency value. Currency values appear with a dollar sign and appropriate commas as well as the desired number of decimal places, and negative values appear within parentheses. The integer you use following the *C* indicates the number of decimal places. If you do not provide a value for the number of decimal places, then two digits are shown after the decimal separator by default. For example, both of the following `WriteLine()` statements produce $456,789.00:

```
double moneyValue = 456789;
string conversion;
conversion = moneyValue.ToString("C");
```

```
Console.WriteLine(conversion);
conversion = moneyValue.ToString("C2");
Console.WriteLine(conversion);
```

»NOTE Currency appears with a dollar sign and commas in the English culture. A **culture** is a set of rules that determines how culturally dependent values such as money and dates are formatted. You can change a program's culture by using the `CultureInfoClass`. The .NET framework supports more than 200 culture settings, such as Japanese, French, Urdu, and Sanskrit.

To display a numeric value as a formatted string, you do not have to create a separate string object. You also can make the conversion in a single statement; for example, the following code displays $12,345.00:

```
double payAmount = 12345;
Console.WriteLine(payAmount.ToString("c2"));
```

»TWO TRUTHS AND A LIE: FORMATTING FLOATING-POINT VALUES

1. If `gpa` contains the value 4, then the value of `gpa.ToString("F")` is "4.00".
2. If `gpa` contains the value 4, then the value of `gpa.ToString("F")` is the same as `gpa.ToString("F0")`.
3. If `gpa` contains the value 4, then the value of `gpa.ToString("C")` is "$4.00".

The false statement is #2. If `gpa` contains the value 4, then the value of `gpa.ToString("F")` is the same as `gpa.ToString("F2")`.

USING THE STANDARD BINARY ARITHMETIC OPERATORS

»NOTE Several shortcut arithmetic operators will be discussed in the next section.

Table 2-3 describes the five most commonly used binary arithmetic operators. You use these operators to manipulate values in your programs. The operators are called **binary operators** because you use two arguments with each—one value to the left of the operator and another value to the right of it. The values that operators use in expressions are called **operands**; binary operators are surrounded by two operands.

Operator	Description	Example
+	Addition	45 + 2: the result is 47
–	Subtraction	45 – 2: the result is 43
*	Multiplication	45 * 2: the result is 90
/	Division	45 / 2: the result is 22 (not 22.5)
%	Remainder (modulus)	45 % 2: the result is 1 (that is, 45 / 2 = 22 with a remainder of 1)

Table 2-3 Binary arithmetic operators

The operators / and % deserve special consideration. When you divide two integers using the / operator, whether they are integer constants or integer variables, the result is an integer; in other words, any fractional part of the result is lost. For example, the result of 45 / 2 is 22, not 22.5. When you use the remainder (modulus) operator with two integers, the result is an integer with the value of the remainder after division takes place—so the result of 45 % 2 is 1 because 2 "goes into" 45 twenty-two times with a remainder of 1.

»NOTE In older languages, such as assembler, you had to perform division before you could take a remainder. In C#, you do not need to perform a division operation before you can perform a remainder operation. In other words, a remainder operation can stand alone.

»NOTE Even though you define a result variable as a floating-point type, integer division still results in an integer. For example, the statement `double d = 7 / 2;` results in `d` holding 3, not 3.5, because the expression on the right is evaluated as integer-by-integer division before the assignment takes place. If you want the result to hold 3.5, at least one of the operands in the calculation must be a floating-point number, or else you must perform a cast. You will learn about casting later in this chapter.

»NOTE As with `int`s, you can add, subtract, multiply, and divide with floating-point numbers. Unlike with `int`s, however, you cannot perform modulus operations with such numbers. (Floating-point division results in a floating-point answer, so there is no remainder.)

When you combine mathematical operations in a single statement, you must understand **operator precedence**, or the rules that determine the order in which parts of a mathematical expression are evaluated. Multiplication, division, and remainder always take place prior to addition or subtraction in an expression. For example, the following expression results in 14:

```
int result = 2 + 3 * 4;
```

The result is 14 because the multiplication operation (3 * 4) occurs before adding 2. You can override normal operator precedence by putting the operation that should be performed first in parentheses. The following statement results in 20 because the addition within parentheses takes place first:

```
int result = (2 + 3) * 4;
```

In this statement, an intermediate result (5) is calculated before it is multiplied by 4.

»NOTE Operator precedence is also called **order of operation**. A closely linked term is **associativity**, which specifies the order in which a sequence of operations with the same precedence are evaluated. Appendix A contains a chart that describes the precedence and associativity of every C# operator.

»NOTE You can use parentheses in an arithmetic expression even if they do not alter the default order of operation. You can do so to make your intentions clearer to other programmers who read your programs, and so they do not have to rely on their memory of operator precedence.

»TWO TRUTHS AND A LIE: USING THE STANDARD BINARY ARITHMETIC OPERATORS

1. The value of 26 % 4 * 3 is 18.
2. The value of 4 / 3 + 2 is 3.
3. The value of 5 + 6 / 4 is 6.

The false statement is #1. The value of 26 % 4 * 3 is 6. The value of the first part of the expression, 26 % 4, is 2, because 2 is the remainder when 4 is divided into 26. Then 2 * 3 is 6.

USING SHORTCUT ARITHMETIC OPERATORS

Increasing the value held in a variable is a common programming task. Assume that you have declared a variable named `counter` that counts the number of times an event has occurred. Each time the event occurs, you want to execute a statement such as the following:

```
counter = counter + 1;
```

This type of statement looks incorrect to an algebra student, but the equal sign (=) is not used to compare values in C#; it is used to assign values. The statement `counter = counter + 1;` says "Take the value of `counter`, add 1 to it, and assign the result to `counter`."

Because increasing the value of a variable is so common, C# provides several shortcut ways to count and accumulate. The following two statements are identical in meaning:

```
counter += 1;
counter = counter + 1;
```

The `+=` operator is the **add and assign operator**; it adds the operand on the right to the operand on the left and assigns the result to the operand on the left in one step. Similarly, the following statement increases `bankBal` by a rate stored in `interestRate`:

```
bankBal += bankBal * interestRate;
```

Besides the shortcut operator +=, you can use –=, *=, and /=. Each of these operators is used to perform an operation and assign the result in one step. For example:

- » `balanceDue -= payment` subtracts a payment from `balanceDue` and assigns the result to `balanceDue`.
- » `rate *= 100` multiplies `rate` by 100. For example, it converts a fractional value stored in `rate`, such as 0.27, to a whole number, such as 27.
- » `payment /= 12` changes a payment value from an annual amount to a monthly amount due.

NOTE You cannot place spaces between the two symbols used in any of the shortcut arithmetic operators. Spaces surrounding the operators are optional.

When you want to increase a variable's value by exactly 1, you can use either of two other shortcut operators—the **prefix increment operator** and the **postfix increment operator**. To use a prefix increment operator, you type two plus signs before the variable name. For example, these statements result in `someValue` holding 7:

```
int someValue = 6;
++someValue;
```

The variable `someValue` holds 1 more than it held before the ++ operator was applied. To use a postfix ++, you type two plus signs just after a variable name. Executing the following statements results in `anotherValue` holding 57:

```
int anotherValue = 56;
anotherValue++;
```

You can use the prefix ++ and postfix ++ with variables, but not with constants. An expression such as ++84 is illegal because 84 is constant and must always remain as 84. However, you can create a variable as in `int val = 84;`, and then write `++val` or `val++` to increase the variable's value to 85.

The prefix and postfix increment operators are **unary operators** because you use them with one operand. Most arithmetic operators, like those used for addition and multiplication, are binary operators that operate on two operands.

When you only want to increase a variable's value by 1, there is no apparent difference between using the prefix and postfix increment operators. However, these operators function differently. When you use the prefix ++, the result is calculated and stored, and then the variable is used. For example, in the following code, both `b` and `c` end up holding 5. The `WriteLine()` statement displays "5 5". In this example, 4 is assigned to `b`, then `b` becomes 5, and then 5 is assigned to `c`.

```
b = 4;
c = ++b;
Console.WriteLine("{0} {1}", b, c);
```

In contrast, when you use the postfix ++, the variable is used, and then the result is calculated and stored. For example, in the second line of the following code, 4 is assigned to `c`; then, *after* the assignment, `b` is increased and takes the value 5.

```
b = 4;
c = b++;
Console.WriteLine("{0} {1}", b, c);
```

This last `WriteLine()` statement displays "5 4". In other words, if `b = 4`, then the value of `b++` is also 4, and that value is assigned to `c`. However, after the 4 is assigned to `c`, `b` is increased to 5.

Besides the prefix and postfix increment operators, you can use a prefix or postfix **decrement operator** (--) that reduces a variable's value by 1. For example, if `s` and `t` are both assigned the value 34, then the expression `--s` has the value 33 and the expression `t--` has the value 34, but `t` then becomes 33.

»TWO TRUTHS AND A LIE: USING SHORTCUT ARITHMETIC OPERATORS

1. If `price` is 4 and `tax` is 5, then the value of `++price + tax` is 10.
2. If `price` is 4 and `tax` is 5, then the value of `price++ * tax` is 25.
3. If `price` is 4 and `tax` is 5, then the value of `price - tax++` is -1.

The false statement is #2. If `price` is 4 and `tax` is 5, then the value of the expression `price++ * tax` is 20. The value of the expression `price++` is only 4 when it is multiplied by `tax`, although after the operation occurs, the value of `price` becomes 5. The value of `++price * tax` would be 25.

USING THE `bool` DATA TYPE

Boolean logic is based on true-or-false comparisons. An `int` variable can hold millions of different values at different times, but a **Boolean variable** can hold only one of two values—true or false. You declare a Boolean variable by using type **`bool`**. The following statements declare and assign appropriate values to two `bool` variables:

```
bool isItMonday = false;
bool areYouTired = true;
```

»NOTE If you begin a `bool` variable name with a form of the verb "to be" or "to do," such as "is" or "are," then you can more easily recognize the identifiers as Boolean variables when you encounter them within your programs.

»NOTE When you use "Boolean" as an adjective, as in "Boolean variable," you usually begin with an uppercase B because the data type is named for Sir George Boole, the founder of symbolic logic, who lived from 1815 to 1864. The C# data type `bool`, however, begins with a lowercase "b."

You also can assign values based on the result of comparisons to Boolean variables. A **comparison operator** compares two items; an expression containing a comparison operator has a Boolean value. Table 2-4 describes the six comparison operators that C# supports.

Operator	Description	`true` Example	`false` Example
<	Less than	3 < 8	8 < 3
>	Greater than	4 > 2	2 > 4
==	Equal to	7 == 7	3 == 9
<=	Less than or equal to	5 <=5	8 <= 6
>=	Greater than or equal to	7 >= 3	1 >= 2
!=	Not equal to	5 != 6	3 != 3

Table 2-4 Comparison operators

When you use any of the operators that require two keystrokes (==, <=, >=, or !=), you cannot place any whitespace between the two symbols.

Legal (but somewhat useless) declaration statements might include the following, which compare two values directly:

```
bool isSixBigger = 6 > 5;   // Value stored would be true
bool isSevenSmallerOrEqual = 7 <= 4;
   // Value stored would be false
```

Using Boolean values is more meaningful when you use variables (that have been assigned values) rather than constants in the comparisons, as in the following examples:

```
bool doesEmployeeReceiveOvertime = hoursWorked > 40;
bool isEmployeeInHighTaxBracket = annualIncome > 100000;
```

In the first statement, the `hoursWorked` variable is compared to a constant value of 40. If the `hoursWorked` variable holds a value less than or equal to 40, then the expression is evaluated as false. In the second statement, the `annualIncome` variable value must be greater than 100000 for the expression to be true.

»NOTE Boolean variables become more useful after you learn to make decisions within C# programs. You learn about decision making in Chapter 3.

»NOTE When you display a `bool` variable's value with `Console.WriteLine()`, the displayed value is `True` or `False`. However, the values within your programs are `true` and `false`.

»TWO TRUTHS AND A LIE: USING THE `bool` DATA TYPE

1. If `rate` is 7.5 and `min` is 7, then the value of `rate >= min` is `false`.
2. If `rate` is 7.5 and `min` is 7, then the value of `rate < min` is `false`.
3. If `rate` is 7.5 and `min` is 7, then the value of `rate == min` is `false`.

The false statement is #1. If `rate` is 7.5 and `min` is 7, then the value of `rate >= min is true`.

UNDERSTANDING NUMERIC TYPE CONVERSION

When you perform arithmetic with variables or constants of the same type, the result of the arithmetic retains the same type. For example, when you divide two `int`s, the result is an `int`; when you subtract two `double`s, the result is a `double`. Often, however, you need to perform mathematical operations on different types. For example, in the following code, you multiply an `int` by a `double`:

```
int hoursWorked = 36;
double payRate = 12.35;
double grossPay = hoursWorked * payRate;
```

When you perform arithmetic operations with operands of dissimilar types, C# chooses a **unifying type** for the result and **implicitly** (or automatically) converts nonconforming operands to the unifying type, which is the type with the higher **type precedence**. The conversion is called an **implicit cast**—the automatic transformation that occurs when a value is assigned to a type with higher precedence.

For example, if you multiply an `int` and a `double`, the result is implicitly a `double`. This requirement means the result must be stored in a `double`; if you attempt to assign the result to an `int`, you will receive a compiler error message like the one shown in Figure 2-10.

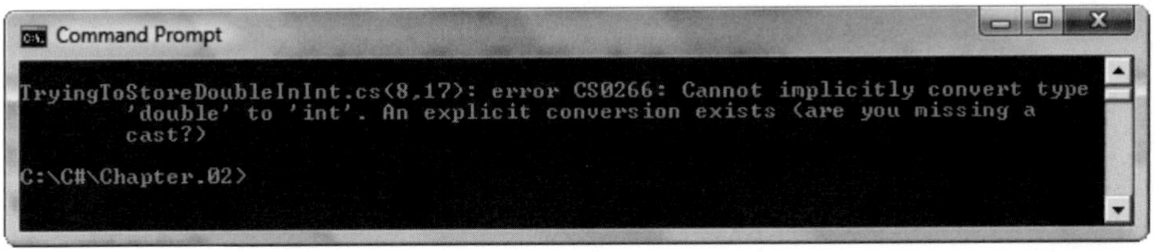

```
Command Prompt
TryingToStoreDoubleInInt.cs(8,17): error CS0266: Cannot implicitly convert type
        'double' to 'int'. An explicit conversion exists (are you missing a
        cast?)

C:\C#\Chapter.02>
```

Figure 2-10 Error message received when trying to compile a program that attempts to store a `double` in an `int`

The implicit numeric conversions are:

- » From `sbyte` to `short`, `int`, `long`, `float`, `double`, or `decimal`
- » From `byte` to `short`, `ushort`, `int`, `uint`, `long`, `ulong`, `float`, `double`, or `decimal`
- » From `short` to `int`, `long`, `float`, `double`, or `decimal`
- » From `ushort` to `int`, `uint`, `long`, `ulong`, `float`, `double`, or `decimal`
- » From `int` to `long`, `float`, `double`, or `decimal`
- » From `uint` to `long`, `ulong`, `float`, `double`, or `decimal`
- » From `long` to `float`, `double`, or `decimal`
- » From `ulong` to `float`, `double`, or `decimal`
- » From `char` to `ushort`, `int`, `uint`, `long`, `ulong`, `float`, `double`, or `decimal`
- » From `float` to `double`

»NOTE Implicit conversions are not always the result of arithmetic calculations; simple assignments often result in implicit conversions. For example, if `money` is declared as a `double`, then the following statement implicitly converts the integer 15 to a `double`:

```
money = 15;
```

»NOTE A constant expression of type `int`, such as 25, can be converted to `sbyte`, `byte`, `short`, `ushort`, `uint`, or `ulong`. For example, `sbyte age = 19;` is legal. However, you must make sure that the value of the constant expression is within the range of the destination type, or the program will not compile.

»NOTE Conversions from `int`, `uint`, or `long` to `float` and from `long` to `double` may cause a loss of precision, but will never cause a loss of magnitude.

The error message in Figure 2-10 asks "are you missing a cast?" You may **explicitly** (or purposefully) override the unifying type imposed by C# by performing an explicit cast. An **explicit cast** involves placing the desired result type in parentheses followed by the variable or constant to be cast. For example, two explicit casts are performed in the following code:

```
double bankBalance = 189.66;
float weeklyBudget = (float) bankBalance / 4;
      // weeklyBudget is 47.415, one-fourth of bankBalance
int dollars = (int) weeklyBudget;
      // dollars is 47, the integer part of weeklyBudget
```

The value of `bankBalance / 4` is implicitly a `double` because a `double` divided by an `int` produces a `double`. The `double` result is then converted to a `float` before it is stored in `weeklyBudget`, and the `float` value `weeklyBudget` is converted to an `int` before it is stored in `dollars`. When the `float` value is converted to an `int`, the decimal-place values are lost.

»NOTE It is easy to lose data when performing a cast. For example, the largest `byte` value is 255, and the largest `int` value is 2,147,483,647, so the following statements produce distorted results:

```
int anOkayInt = 345;
byte aBadByte = (byte)anOkayInt;
```

»NOTE If you attempt to store 256 in a `byte`, you will receive an error message unless you place the statement in a section of code preceded by the keyword `unchecked`, which tells the compiler not to check for invalid data. If you use the unchecked mode and store 256 in a byte, the results will look the same as storing 0; if you store 257, the result will appear as 1. You will see 89 when you store 345 in a `byte` variable and display the results, because the value 89 is exactly 256 less than 345.

»TWO TRUTHS AND A LIE: UNDERSTANDING NUMERIC TYPE CONVERSION

1. If `deptNum` is an `int` with a value of 10, then `double answer = deptNum` is a valid statement.
2. If `deptNum` is an `int` with a value of 10, and `answer` is a `double` with a value of 4, then `deptNum = answer` is a valid statement.
3. If `deptNum` is an `int` with a value of 10, and `answer` is a `double` with a value of 4, then `double answer = (int) value` is a valid statement.

The false statement is #2. If `deptNum` is an `int` with a value of 10, and `answer` is a `double` with a value of 4, then `deptNum = answer` is invalid because a `double` cannot be implicitly converted to an `int`.

USING THE char DATA TYPE

You use the **char** data type to hold any single character. You place constant character values within single quotation marks because the computer stores characters and integers differently. For example, the following statements are both legal:

```
char aCharValue = '9';
int aNumValue = 9;
```

However, the following statements are both illegal:

```
char aCharValue = 9;
int aNumValue = '9';
```

A number can be a character, in which case it must be enclosed in single quotation marks and declared as a char type. An alphabetic letter, however, cannot be stored in a numeric type variable. The following code shows how you can store several characters using the char data type:

```
char myInitial = 'J';
char percentSign = '%';
char numThatIsAChar = '9';
```

NOTE A variable of type char can hold only one character. To store a string of characters, such as a person's name, you must use a string. You will learn about strings later in this chapter.

You can store any character—including nonprinting characters such as a backspace or a tab—in a char variable. To store these characters, you use two symbols in an **escape sequence**, which always begins with a backslash. The pair of symbols represents a single character. For example, the following code stores a backspace character and a tab character in the char variables aBackspaceChar and aTabChar, respectively:

```
char aBackspaceChar = '\b';
char aTabChar = '\t';
```

In the preceding code, the escape sequence indicates a unique value for each character—a backspace or tab instead of the letter *b* or *t*. Table 2-5 describes some common escape sequences that are used in C#.

The characters used in C# are represented in **Unicode**, which is a 16-bit coding scheme for characters. For example, the letter *A* actually is stored in computer memory as a set of 16 zeros and ones—namely, 0000 0000 0100 0001. (The spaces are inserted here after every set of four digits for readability.) Because 16-bit numbers are difficult to read, programmers often use a shorthand notation called **hexadecimal**, or **base 16**. In hexadecimal shorthand, 0000 becomes 0, 0100 becomes 4, and 0001 becomes 1. Thus, the letter *A* is represented in hexadecimal as 0041. You tell the compiler to treat the four-digit hexadecimal 0041 as a single

Escape Sequence	Character Name
`\'`	Single quotation mark
`\"`	Double quotation mark
`\\`	Backslash
`\0`	Null
`\a`	Alert
`\b`	Backspace
`\f`	Form feed
`\n`	Newline
`\r`	Carriage return
`\t`	Horizontal tab
`\v`	Vertical tab

Table 2-5 Common escape sequences

character by preceding it with the `\u` escape sequence. Therefore, there are two ways to store the character *A*:

```
char letter = 'A';
char letter = '\u0041';
```

»NOTE For more information about Unicode, go to *www.unicode.org*.

The second option, using hexadecimal, obviously is more difficult and confusing than the first option, so it is not recommended that you store letters of the alphabet using the hexadecimal method. However, you can produce some interesting values using the Unicode format, and so you should know how to use it. For example, letters from foreign alphabets that use characters instead of letters (Greek, Hebrew, Chinese, and so on) and other special symbols (foreign currency symbols, mathematical symbols, geometric shapes, and so on) are not available on a standard keyboard, but they are available in Unicode.

»TWO TRUTHS AND A LIE: USING THE `char` DATA TYPE

1. The following statement is legal in C#:

   `char department = '5';`

2. The following statement is legal in C#:

   `char department = '\f';`

3. The following statement is legal in C#:

   `char department = '32';`

The false statement is #3. Only a single character can appear between single quotes, with the exception of escape sequence characters such as '\t' and '\f'. In these cases, a single character is created using two symbols.

USING THE string DATA TYPE

In C#, you use the **string** data type to hold a series of characters. The value of a string is always expressed within double quotation marks. For example, the following statement declares a string named firstName and assigns "Jane" to it:

```
string firstName = "Jane";
```

When you assign a literal (such as "Jane") to a string, you can compare the string to another string using the == and != operators in the same ways that you compare numeric or character variables. For example, the program in Figure 2-11 declares three string variables. Figure 2-12 shows the results: strings that contain "Amy" and "Amy" are considered equal, but strings that contain "Amy" and "Matthew" are not.

```
using System;
public class CompareNames1
{
   public static void Main()
   {
      string name1 = "Amy";
      string name2 = "Amy";
      string name3 = "Matthew";
      Console.WriteLine("compare {0} to {1}: {2}",
         name1, name2, name1 == name2);
      Console.WriteLine("compare {0} to {1}: {2}",
         name1, name3, name1 == name3);
   }
}
```

Figure 2-11 Program that compares two strings using == operator (not recommended)

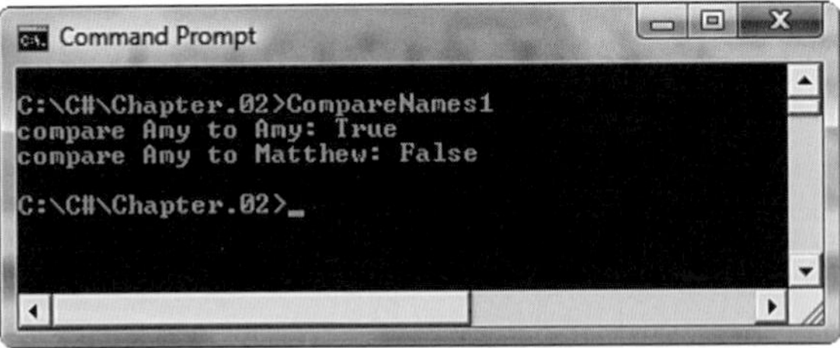

Figure 2-12 Output of CompareNames1 program

»NOTE Later in this chapter, you learn how to allow a user to enter data into a program from the keyboard.

Besides the == comparison operator, you can use several prewritten methods to compare strings. The advantage to using these other methods is that other classes you eventually will create use methods with the same names to compare their objects.

You can compare strings with any of the following methods: Equals(), Compare(), and CompareTo().

The String class **Equals()** method requires two string arguments that you place within its parentheses, separated by a comma. As when you use the == operator, the Equals() method returns true or false.

The **Compare()** method also requires two string arguments, but it returns an integer. When it returns 0, the two strings are equivalent; when it returns a positive number, the first string is greater than the second; and when it returns a negative value, the first string is less than the second. A string is considered equal to, greater than, or less than another string **lexically**, which in the case of letter values means alphabetically. That is, when you compare two strings, you compare each character in turn from left to right. If each Unicode value is the same, then the strings are equivalent. If any corresponding character values are different, the string that has the greater Unicode value earlier in the string is considered greater.

The **CompareTo()** method uses a string, a dot, and the method name. The string to compare to is placed within parentheses. Like the Compare() method, it returns a 0 when the compared strings are equal, a negative number if the first string is less, and a positive number if the second string (the one in parentheses) is less. Figure 2-13 shows a program

```
using System;
public class CompareTwoNames
{
   public static void Main()
   {
      string name1 = "Amy";
      string name2 = "Amy";
      string name3 = "Matthew";
      Console.WriteLine("Using Equals() method");
      Console.WriteLine("   compare {0} to {1}: {2}",
         name1, name2, String.Equals(name1, name2));
      Console.WriteLine("   compare {0} to {1}: {2}",
         name1, name3, String.Equals(name1, name3));
      Console.WriteLine("Using Compare() method");
      Console.WriteLine("   compare {0} to {1}: {2}",
         name1, name2, String.Compare(name1, name2));
      Console.WriteLine("   compare {0} to {1}: {2}",
         name1, name3, String.CompareTo(name1, name3));
      Console.WriteLine("Using CompareTo() method");
      Console.WriteLine("   compare {0} to {1}: {2}",
         name1, name2, name1.CompareTo(name2));
      Console.WriteLine("   compare {0} to {1}: {2}",
         name1, name3, name1.CompareTo(name3));
   }
}
```

Figure 2-13 Program that compares two strings using three methods

that makes several comparisons using the three methods; in each case the method name is shaded. Figure 2-14 shows the program's output.

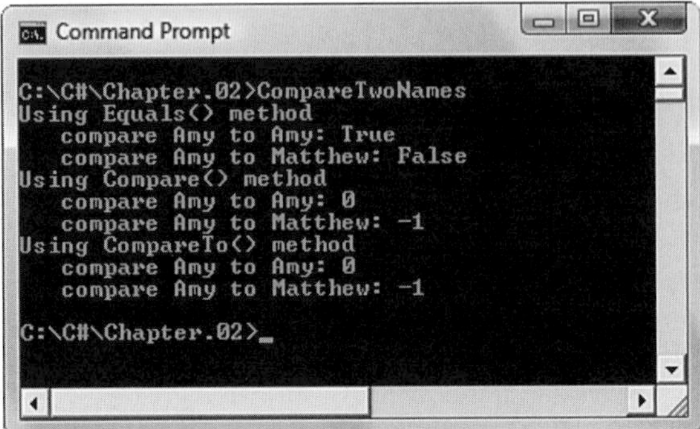

Command Prompt
C:\C#\Chapter.02>CompareTwoNames
Using Equals() method
compare Amy to Amy: True
compare Amy to Matthew: False
Using Compare() method
compare Amy to Amy: 0
compare Amy to Matthew: -1
Using CompareTo() method
compare Amy to Amy: 0
compare Amy to Matthew: -1
C:\C#\Chapter.02>_

Figure 2-14 Output of `CompareTwoNames` program

»NOTE The `Equals()`, `Compare()`, and `CompareTo()` methods are case sensitive. In other words, "Amy" does not equal "amy". In Unicode, the decimal value of each uppercase letter is exactly 32 less than its lowercase equivalent. For example, the decimal value of a Unicode 'a' is 97 and the value of 'A' is 65.

»NOTE In C#, a string is **immutable**. That is, a string's value is not actually modified when you assign a new value to it. For example, when you write `name = "Amy";` followed by `name = "Donald";`, the first literal string of characters "Amy" still exists in computer memory, but the `name` variable no longer refers to the string's memory address. The situation is different than with numbers; when you assign a new value to a numeric variable, the value at the named memory address actually changes.

»NOTE In Chapter 7, you will learn how to write your own `CompareTo()` methods for classes you create.

»NOTE Another useful string method is **`StartsWith()`**. In the `CompareTwoNames` program, the expression `name3.StartsWith("Ma")` would be true.

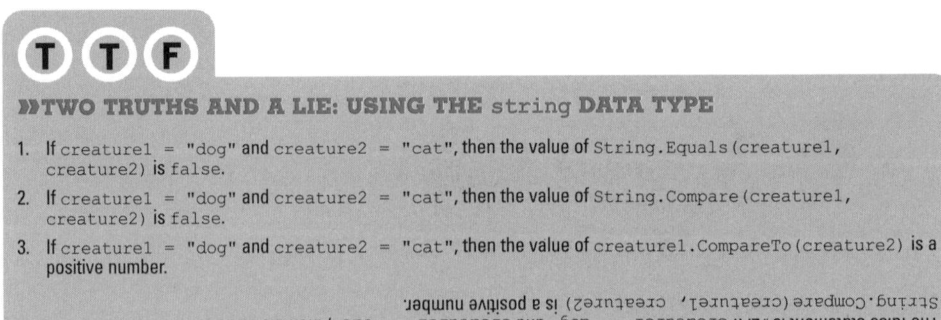

»TWO TRUTHS AND A LIE: USING THE `string` DATA TYPE

1. If `creature1 = "dog"` and `creature2 = "cat"`, then the value of `String.Equals(creature1, creature2)` is `false`.
2. If `creature1 = "dog"` and `creature2 = "cat"`, then the value of `String.Compare(creature1, creature2)` is `false`.
3. If `creature1 = "dog"` and `creature2 = "cat"`, then the value of `creature1.CompareTo(creature2)` is a positive number.

The false statement is #2. If `creature1 = "dog"` and `creature2 = "cat"`, then the value of `String.Compare(creature1, creature2)` is a positive number.

DEFINING NAMED CONSTANTS

By definition, a variable's value can vary, or change. Sometimes you want to create a **named constant** (often called simply a constant), an identifier for a memory location whose contents cannot change. You create a named constant similarly to the way you create a named variable, but by using the keyword `const`. Although there is no requirement to do so, programmers usually name constants using all uppercase letters, inserting underscores for readability. This convention makes constant names stand out so that the reader is less likely to confuse them with changeable variable names. For example, the following declares a constant named `TAX_RATE` that is assigned a value of 0.06:

```
const double TAX_RATE = 0.06;
```

You must assign a value to a constant when you create it. You can use a constant just as you would use a variable of the same type—for example, display it or use it in a mathematical equation—but you cannot assign any new value to it. Figure 2-15 shows a program that uses a `TAX_RATE` constant to calculate the tax on two different-priced items. Figure 2-16 shows the output.

```
using System;
public class SalesTax
{
   public static void Main()
   {
      const double TAX_RATE = .06;
      double itemPrice = 3.99;
      double tax;
      tax = itemPrice * TAX_RATE;
      Console.WriteLine("With {0} tax, a {1} item costs {2} more",
         TAX_RATE, itemPrice.ToString("C"), tax.ToString("C"));
      itemPrice = 145.65;
      tax = itemPrice * TAX_RATE;
      Console.WriteLine("With {0} tax, a {1} item costs {2} more",
         TAX_RATE, itemPrice.ToString("C"), tax.ToString("C"));
   }
}
```

Figure 2-15 `SalesTax` program

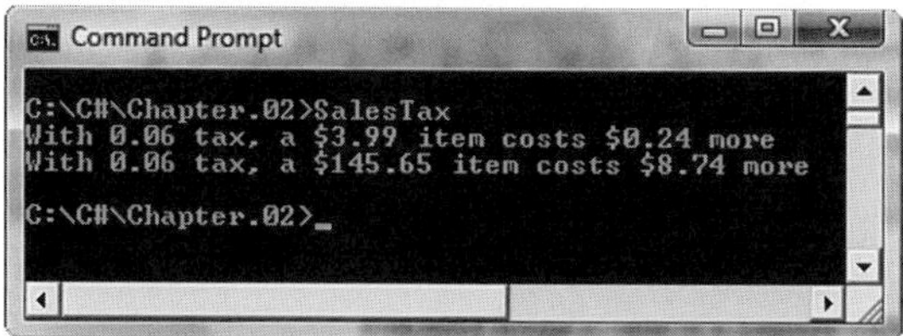

Figure 2-16 Output of `SalesTax` program

It's good programming practice to declare constants for any value that should never change; doing so makes your programs clearer. For example, when you declare a constant `const int INCHES_IN_A_FOOT = 12;` within a program, then you can use a statement such as the following:

```
lengthInInches = lengthInFeet * INCHES_IN_A_FOOT;
```

This statement is **self-documenting**; that is, even without a program comment, it is easy for someone reading your program to tell why you performed the calculation in the way you did.

»TWO TRUTHS AND A LIE: DEFINING NAMED CONSTANTS

1. The following is a valid C# constant:
   `const string FIRST_HEADING = "Progress Report";`
2. The following is a valid C# constant:
   `const int maximumDays = 7;`
3. The following is a valid C# constant:
   `const double COMMISSION_RATE;`

The false answer is #3. A constant must be assigned a value when it is declared. Answer #2 is legal, but not conventional because constants generally are declared using all uppercase characters.

ACCEPTING CONSOLE INPUT

When you write a program in which you assign values to variables and then manipulate those values, the output of the program is always the same. For example, no matter how many times you execute the `SalesTax` program in Figure 2-15, the two tax values are always calculated as $0.24 and $8.74. A more useful program would allow a user to input any price for which the tax could be calculated. A program that allows user input is an **interactive program**.

You can use the **`Console.ReadLine()`** method to accept user input from the keyboard. This method accepts all of the characters entered by a user until the user presses Enter. The characters can be assigned to a `string`. For example, the following statement accepts a user's input and stores it in the variable `myString`:

```
myString = Console.ReadLine();
```

If you want to use the data as a `string`—for example, if the input is a word or a name—then you simply use the variable to which you assigned the value. If you want to use the data as a number, then you must use a `Convert()` method to convert the input `string` to the proper type.

»NOTE The `Console.Read()` method is similar to the `Console.ReadLine()` method. `Console.Read()` reads just one character from the input stream, whereas `Console.ReadLine()` reads every character in the input stream until the user presses the Enter key.

Figure 2-17 shows an interactive program that prompts the user for a price and calculates a 6 percent sales tax. The program displays "Enter the price of an item" on the screen. Such an instruction to the user to enter data is called a **prompt**. After the prompt appears, the `Console.ReadLine()` statement accepts a string of characters and assigns them to the variable `itemPriceAsString`. Before the tax can be calculated, this value must be converted to a number. This conversion is accomplished in the shaded statement. Figure 2-18 shows a typical execution of the program in which the user typed 28.77 as the input value.

```
using System;
public class InteractiveSalesTax
{
   public static void Main()
   {
      const double TAX_RATE = 0.06;
      string itemPriceAsString;
      double itemPrice;
      double total;
      Console.WriteLine("Enter the price of an item");
      itemPriceAsString = Console.ReadLine();
      itemPrice = Convert.ToDouble(itemPriceAsString);
      total = itemPrice * TAX_RATE;
      Console.WriteLine("With a tax rate of {0}, a {1} item " +
         "costs {2} more.", TAX_RATE, itemPrice.ToString("C"),
         total.ToString("C"));
   }
}
```

Figure 2-17 `InteractiveSalesTax` program

Figure 2-18 Typical execution of `InteractiveSalesTax` program

As a shortcut, you can avoid declaring and using the `string itemPriceAsString` in the program in Figure 2-17. Instead, you can accept and convert the input string in one step, as in the following:

```
itemPrice = Convert.ToDouble(Console.ReadLine());
```

Table 2-6 shows `Convert` class methods you can use to change `string`s into more useful data types. The methods use the class types (also called run-time types) in their names. For example, recall from Table 2-1 that the "formal" name for an `int` is `Int32`, so the method you use to convert a `string` to an `int` is named `Convert.ToInt32()`.

Method	Description
`ToBoolean()`	Converts a specified value to an equivalent Boolean value
`ToByte()`	Converts a specified value to an 8-bit unsigned integer
`ToChar()`	Converts a specified value to a Unicode character
`ToDecimal()`	Converts a specified value to a decimal number
`ToDouble()`	Converts a specified value to a double-precision floating-point number
`ToInt16()`	Converts a specified value to a 16-bit signed integer
`ToInt32()`	Converts a specified value to a 32-bit signed integer
`ToInt64()`	Converts a specified value to a 64-bit signed integer
`ToSByte()`	Converts a specified value to an 8-bit signed integer
`ToSingle()`	Converts a specified value to a single-precision floating-point number
`ToString()`	Converts the specified value to its equivalent `String` representation
`ToUInt16()`	Converts a specified value to a 16-bit unsigned integer
`ToUInt32()`	Converts a specified value to a 32-bit unsigned integer
`ToUInt64()`	Converts a specified value to a 64-bit unsigned integer

Table 2-6 Selected `Convert` class methods

»TWO TRUTHS AND A LIE: ACCEPTING CONSOLE INPUT

1. The following is valid:
   `int age = Convert.ToInt(Console.ReadLine());`
2. The following is valid:
   `double payRate = Convert.ToDouble(Console.ReadLine());`
3. The following is valid:
   `char middleInitial = Convert.ToChar(Console.ReadLine());`

The false statement is #1. The method to convert a string to an integer is `ToInt32()`, not `ToInt()`.

YOU DO IT

DECLARING AND USING VARIABLES

In the following steps, you will write a program that declares several integral variables, assigns values to them, and displays the results.

To write a program with integral variables:

1. Open a new file in the text editor you are using to write your C# programs. Create the beginning of a program that will demonstrate variable use. Use the `System` namespace, name the class **DemoVariables**, and type the class-opening curly brace.

```
using System;
public class DemoVariables
{
```

>>NOTE Recall from Chapter 1 that you can write C# programs in any editor with which you are comfortable.

2. In the `Main()` method, declare two variables (an integer and an unsigned integer) and assign values to them.

```
public static void Main()
{
   int anInt = -123;
   uint anUnsignedInt = 567;
```

3. Add a statement to display the two values.

```
Console.WriteLine("The int is {0} and the unsigned int
   is {1}.", anInt, anUnsignedInt);
```

4. Add two closing curly braces—one that closes the `Main()` method, and one that closes the `DemoVariables` class. Align each closing curly brace vertically with the opening brace that is its partner. In other words, the first closing brace aligns with the brace that opens `Main()`, and the second aligns with the brace that opens `DemoVariables`.
5. Save the program as **DemoVariables.cs** and compile it. If you receive any error messages, correct the errors and compile the program again. When the file is error-free, execute the program. The output should look like Figure 2-19.

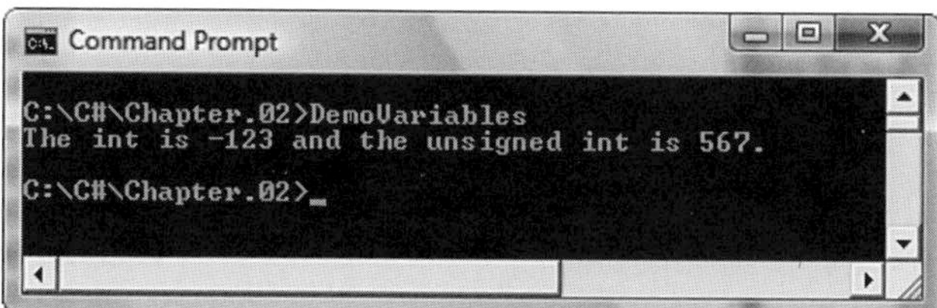

Figure 2-19 Output of `DemoVariables` program

6. Experiment with the program by introducing invalid values for the named variables. For example, change the value of `anUnsignedInt` to **–567** by typing a minus sign in front of the constant value. Compile the program. You receive the following error message:

   Constant value '-567' cannot be converted to a 'uint'.

7. Correct the error either by removing the minus sign or by changing the data type of the variable to **int**, and compile the program again. You should not receive any error messages. Remember to save your program file after you make each change and before you compile.

8. Change the value of `anInt` from –123 to **–123456789000**. When you compile the program, the following error message appears:

   Cannot implicitly convert type 'long' to 'int'.

   The value is a `long` because it is greater than the highest allowed `int` value. Correct the error either by using a lower value or by changing the variable type to **long**, and compile the program again. You should not receive any error messages.

9. Experiment with other changes to the variables. Include some variables of type `short`, `ushort`, `byte`, and `sbyte`, and experiment with their values.

PERFORMING ARITHMETIC

In the following steps, you will add some arithmetic statements to a program.

To use arithmetic statements in a program:

1. Open a new C# program file and enter the following statements to start a program that demonstrates arithmetic operations:

```
using System;
public class DemoVariables2
{
   public static void Main()
   {
```

2. Write a statement that will declare seven integer variables. You will assign initial values to two of the variables; the values for the other five variables will be calculated. Because all of these variables are the same type, you can use a single statement to declare all seven integers. Recall that to do this, you insert commas between variable names and place a single semicolon at the end. You can place line breaks wherever you want for readability. (Alternatively, you could use as many as seven separate declarations.)

```
int value1 = 43, value2 = 10,
        sum, diff, product, quotient, remainder;
```

3. Write the arithmetic statements that calculate the sum of, difference between, product of, quotient of, and remainder of the two assigned variables.

```
sum = value1 + value2;
diff = value1 - value2;
product = value1 * value2;
quotient = value1 / value2;
remainder = value1 % value2;
```

»NOTE Instead of declaring the variables `sum`, `diff`, `product`, `quotient`, and `remainder` and assigning values later, you could declare and assign all of them at once, as in `int sum = value1 + value2;`. The only requirement is that `value1` and `value2` must be assigned values before you can use them in a calculation.

4. Include five `WriteLine()` statements to display the results.

```
Console.WriteLine("The sum of {0} and {1} is {2}",
   value1, value2, sum);
Console.WriteLine("The difference between {0} and {1}" +
   " is {2}", value1, value2, diff);
Console.WriteLine("The product of {0} and {1} is {2}",
   value1, value2, product);
Console.WriteLine("{0} divided by {1} is {2}", value1,
   value2, quotient);
Console.WriteLine("and the remainder is {0}", remainder);
```

5. Add two closing curly braces—one for the `Main()` method and the other for the `DemoVariables2` class.
6. Save the file as **DemoVariables2.cs**. Compile and execute the program. The output should look like Figure 2-20.

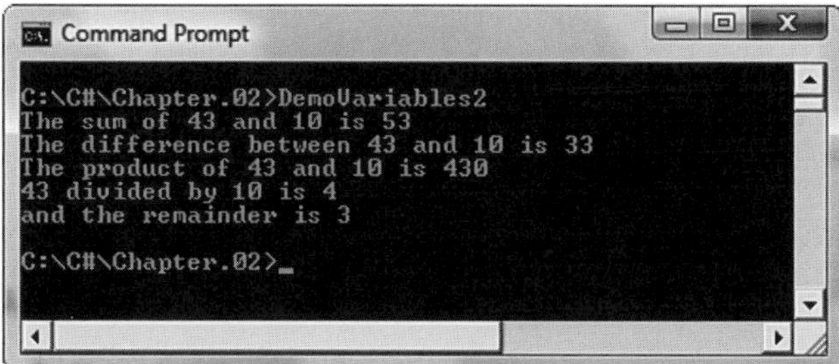

Figure 2-20 Output of `DemoVariables2` program

7. Change the values of the `value1` and `value2` variables, save the program, and compile and run it again. Repeat this process several times. After each execution, analyze the output to make sure you understand the results of the arithmetic operations.

WORKING WITH BOOLEAN VARIABLES

Next, you will write a program that demonstrates how Boolean variables operate.

To write a program that uses Boolean variables:

1. Open a new file in your editor and enter the following code. In the `Main()` method, you declare an integer value, then assign different values to a Boolean variable. Notice that when you declare `value` and `isSixMore`, you assign types. When you reassign values to

these variables later in the program, you do not redeclare them by using a type name. Instead, you simply assign new values to the already declared variables.

```
using System;
public class DemoVariables3
{
   public static void Main()
   {
      int value = 4;
      bool isSixMore = 6 > value;
      Console.WriteLine("When value is {0} isSixMore is {1}",
         value, isSixMore);
      value = 35;
      isSixMore = 6 > value;
      Console.WriteLine("When value is {0} isSixMore is {1}",
         value, isSixMore);
   }
}
```

2. Save the program as **DemoVariables3.cs**. Compile and run the program. The output looks like Figure 2-21.

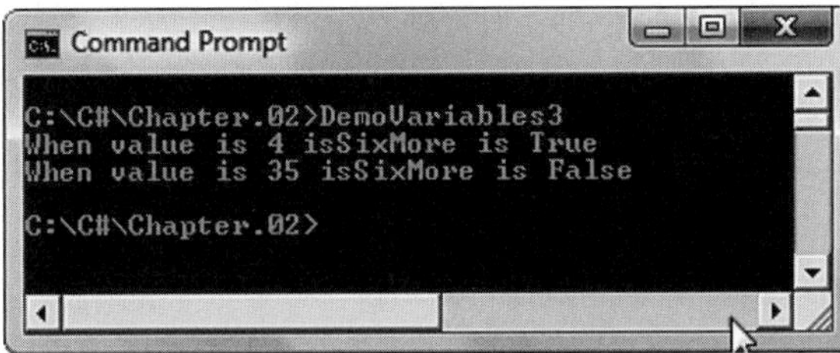

Figure 2-21 Output of `DemoVariables3` program

3. Change the value of the variable named `value` and try to predict the outcome. Run the program to confirm your prediction.

USING ESCAPE SEQUENCES

Next, you will write a short program to demonstrate the use of escape sequences.

To write a program using escape sequences:

1. Open a new file in your text editor and name it **DemoEscapeSequences**.
2. Enter the following code. The three `WriteLine()` statements demonstrate using escape sequences for tabs, a newline, and alerts.

```
using System;
public class DemoEscapeSequences
{
   public static void Main()
   {
```

```
            Console.WriteLine("This line\tcontains two\ttabs");
            Console.WriteLine("This statement\ncontains a new line");
            Console.WriteLine("This statement sounds " +
              "three alerts\a\a\a");
        }
    }
```

3. Save the program as **DemoEscapeSequences.cs**. Compile and test the program. Your output should look like Figure 2-22. Additionally, if your system has speakers and they are on, you should hear three "beep" sounds caused by the three alert characters: '\a'.

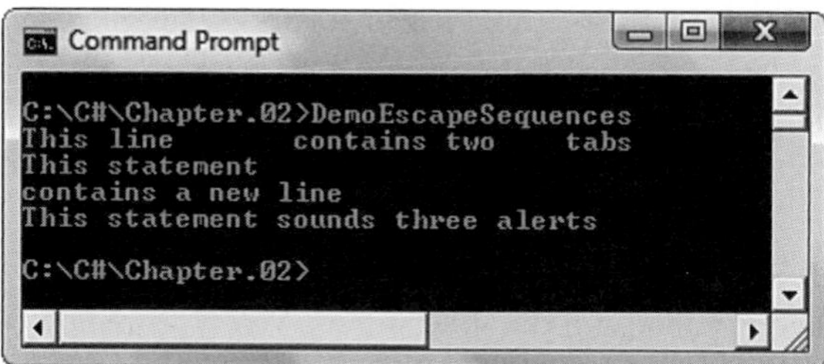

Figure 2-22 Output of `DemoEscapeSequences` program

WRITING A PROGRAM THAT ACCEPTS USER INPUT

In the next steps, you will write an interactive program that allows the user to enter two integer values. The program then calculates and displays their sum.

To write the interactive addition program:

1. Open a new file in your editor. Type the first few lines needed for the `Main()` method of an `InteractiveAddition` class.

```
using System;
public class InteractiveAddition
{
    public static void Main()
    {
```

2. Add variable declarations for two `strings` that will accept the user's input values. Also, declare three integers for the numeric equivalents of the `string` input values and their sum.

```
string name, firstString, secondString;
int first, second, sum;
```

3. Prompt the user for his or her name, accept it into the `name string`, and then display a personalized greeting to the user, along with the prompt for the first integer value.

```
Console.WriteLine("Enter your name");
name = Console.ReadLine();
Console.WriteLine("Hello {0}! Enter the first integer", name);
```

4. Accept the user's input as a `string`, and then convert the input `string` to an integer.

```
firstString = Console.ReadLine();
first = Convert.ToInt32(firstString);
```

5. Add statements that prompt for and accept the second `string` and convert it to an integer.

```
Console.WriteLine("Enter the second integer");
secondString = Console.ReadLine();
second = Convert.ToInt32(secondString);
```

6. Assign the sum of the two integers to the `sum` variable and display all of the values. Add the closing curly brace for the `Main()` method and the closing curly brace for the class.

```
        sum = first + second;
        Console.WriteLine("{0}, the sum of {1} and {2} is {3}",
           name, first, second, sum);
    }
}
```

7. Save the file as **InteractiveAddition.cs**. Compile and run the program. When prompted, supply your name and any integers you want, and confirm that the result appears correctly. Figure 2-23 shows a typical run of the program.

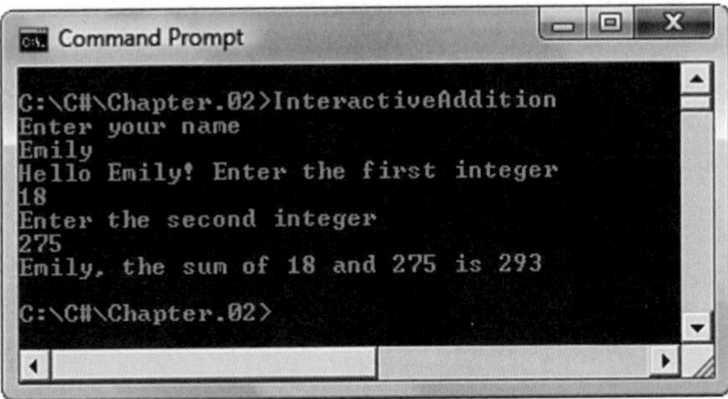

Figure 2-23 Typical execution of `InteractiveAddition` program

CHAPTER SUMMARY

- Data is constant when it cannot be changed after a program is compiled; data is variable when it might change. C# provides for 14 basic built-in types of data. A variable declaration includes a data type, an identifier, an optional assigned value, and a semicolon.
- You can display variable values by using the variable name within a `WriteLine()` or `Write()` method call. To make producing output easier, you can combine strings and variable values into a single `Write()` or `WriteLine()` statement by using a format string.
- In C#, nine data types are considered integral data types—`byte`, `sbyte`, `short`, `ushort`, `int`, `uint`, `long`, `ulong`, and `char`.

- C# supports three floating-point data types: `float`, `double`, and `decimal`. You can perform the mathematical operations of addition, subtraction, multiplication, and division with floating-point data, but not modulus. You can use format and precision specifiers to display floating-point data to a specified number of decimal places.
- You use the binary arithmetic operators +, -, *, /, and % to manipulate values in your programs. When you combine mathematical operations in a single statement, you must understand operator precedence, or the order in which parts of a mathematical expression are evaluated. Multiplication, division, and remainder always take place prior to addition or subtraction in an expression, unless you use parentheses to override the normal precedence.
- Because altering the value of a variable is a common task, C# provides you with several shortcut arithmetic operators. They include the binary operators +=, −=, *=, /=, and the unary prefix and postfix increment (++) and decrement (−−) operators.
- A `bool` variable can hold only one of two values—true or false. C# supports six comparison operators: >, <, >=, <=, ==, and !=. An expression containing a comparison operator has a Boolean value.
- When you perform arithmetic with variables or constants of the same type, the result of the arithmetic retains the same type. When you perform arithmetic operations with operands of different types, C# chooses a unifying type for the result and implicitly converts nonconforming operands to the unifying type. You may explicitly override the unifying type imposed by C# by performing a cast.
- You use the `char` data type to hold any single character. You place constant character values within single quotation marks. You can store any character—including nonprinting characters such as a backspace or a tab—in a `char` variable. To store these characters, you must use an escape sequence, which always begins with a backslash.
- In C#, you use the `string` data type to hold a series of characters. The value of a `string` is always expressed within double quotation marks. Although the == and != comparison operators can be used with `string`s that are assigned literal values, you also can use the `Equals()`, `Compare()`, and `CompareTo()` methods that belong to the `String` class.
- Named constants are program identifiers you cannot change.
- You can use the `Console.ReadLine()` method to accept user input. Often you must use a `Convert` class method to change the input string into a usable data type.

KEY TERMS

A data item is **constant** when it cannot be changed after a program is compiled—in other words, when it cannot vary.

A **literal constant** is a value that is taken literally at each use.

A **variable** is a named location in computer memory that can hold different values at different points in time.

A **data type** describes the format and size of a data item.

Intrinsic types of data are basic types; C# provides 14 intrinsic types.

An **alias** is another name for something.

A **variable declaration** is the statement that names a variable; it includes the data type that the variable will store, an identifier that is the variable's name, an optional assignment operator and assigned value when you want a variable to contain an initial value, and an ending semicolon.

The **assignment operator** is the equal sign (=); any value to the right of the assignment operator is assigned to, or taken on by, the variable to the left.

An **initialization** is an assignment made when a variable is declared.

An **assignment** is a statement that provides a variable with a value.

A **format string** is a string of characters that contains one or more placeholders for variable values.

A **placeholder** in a format string consists of a pair of curly braces containing a number that indicates the desired variable's position in a list that follows the string.

To **concatenate** strings is to join them together in a chain.

Integral data types are those that store whole numbers.

The nine integral types are **`byte`**, **`sbyte`**, **`short`**, **`ushort`**, **`int`**, **`uint`**, **`long`**, **`ulong`**, and **`char`**. The first eight always represent whole numbers, and the ninth type, `char`, is used for characters like 'A' or 'a'.

Integers are whole numbers.

A **floating-point** number is one that contains decimal positions.

A **`float`** data type can hold a floating-point number with as many as seven significant digits of accuracy.

A **`double`** data type can hold a floating-point number with 15 or 16 significant digits of accuracy.

A value's number of **significant digits** specifies the mathematical accuracy of the value.

The **`decimal`** data type is a floating-point type that has a greater precision and a smaller range than a `float` or `double`, which makes it suitable for financial and monetary calculations.

Values expressed in **scientific notation** include an *E* (for exponent).

Standard numeric format strings are strings of characters expressed within double quotation marks that indicate a format for output.

The **format specifier** in a format string can be one of nine built-in format characters that define the most commonly used numeric format types.

The **precision specifier** in a format string controls the number of significant digits or zeros to the right of the decimal point.

A **culture** is a set of rules that determines how culturally dependent values such as money and dates are formatted.

Binary operators use two arguments—one value to the left of the operator and another value to the right of it.

Operands are the values that operators use in expressions.

Operator precedence determines the order in which parts of a mathematical expression are evaluated.

Operator precedence is also called **order of operation**.

Associativity specifies the order in which a sequence of operations with the same precedence are evaluated.

The **add and assign operator** (+=) adds the operand on the right to the operand on the left and assigns it to the operand on the left in one step.

The **prefix increment operator** (++ before a variable) increases the variable's value by 1 and then evaluates it.

The **postfix increment operator** (++ after a variable) evaluates a variable and then adds 1 to it.

Unary operators are operators used with one operand.

The **decrement operator** (--) reduces a variable's value by 1. There is a prefix and a postfix version.

A **Boolean variable** can hold only one of two values—true or false.

The `bool` data type holds a Boolean value.

A **comparison operator** compares two items; an expression containing a comparison operator has a Boolean value.

A **unifying type** is the type chosen for an arithmetic result when operands are of dissimilar types.

Implicitly means automatically.

Type precedence is a hierarchy of data types used to determine the unifying type in arithmetic expressions containing dissimilar data types.

An **implicit cast** is the automatic transformation that occurs when a value is assigned to a type with higher precedence.

Explicitly means purposefully.

An **explicit cast** purposefully assigns a value to a different data type; it involves placing the desired result type in parentheses followed by the variable or constant to be cast.

The `char` data type can hold any single character.

An **escape sequence** is two symbols beginning with a backslash that represent a nonprinting character such as a tab.

Unicode is a 16-bit coding scheme for characters.

Hexadecimal, or **base 16**, is a mathematical system that uses 16 symbols to represent numbers.

The **string** data type is used to hold a series of characters.

The String class **Equals()** method determines if two strings have the same value; it requires two string arguments that you place within its parentheses, separated by a comma.

The **Compare()** method requires two string arguments. When it returns 0, the two strings are equivalent; when it returns a positive number, the first string is greater than the second; and when it returns a negative value, the first string is less than the second.

Lexically means alphabetically.

The **CompareTo()** method uses a string, a dot, and the method name. When it returns 0, the two strings are equivalent; when it returns a positive number, the first string is greater than the second; and when it returns a negative value, the first string is less than the second.

In C#, a string is **immutable**, or unchangeable. That is, a string's value is not actually modified when you assign a new value to it; instead, the string refers to a new memory location.

The **StartsWith()** method is used with a string and a dot, and its parentheses contain another string. It returns true if the first string starts with the characters contained in the second string.

A **named constant** (often called simply a constant) is an identifier whose contents cannot change.

A **self-documenting** program element is one that is self-explanatory.

An **interactive program** is one that allows user input.

The **Console.ReadLine()** method accepts user input from the keyboard.

A **prompt** is an instruction to the user to enter data.

REVIEW QUESTIONS

1. When you use a number such as 45 in a C# program, the number is a ________ .

   a. literal constant
   b. figurative constant
   c. literal variable
   d. figurative variable

2. A variable declaration must contain all of the following *except* a(n) ________ .

   a. data type
   b. identifier
   c. assigned value
   d. ending semicolon

3. Which of the following is true of variable declarations?

   a. Two variables of the same type can be declared in the same statement.
   b. Two variables of different types can be declared in the same statement.
   c. Two variables of the same type must be declared in the same statement.
   d. Two variables of the same type cannot coexist in a program.

4. Assume you have two variables declared as `int var1 = 3;` and `int var2 = 8;`. Which of the following would display *838*?

   a. `Console.WriteLine("{0}{1}{2}", var1, var2);`

   b. `Console.WriteLine("{0}{1}{0}", var1, var2);`

   c. `Console.WriteLine("{0}{1}{2}", var2, var1);`

   d. `Console.WriteLine("{0}{1}{0}", var2, var1);`

5. Assume you have a variable declared as `int var1 = 3;`. Which of the following would display *X 3X*?

   a. `Console.WriteLine("X{0}X", var1);`

   b. `Console.WriteLine("X{0,2}X", var1);`

   c. `Console.WriteLine("X{2,0}X", var1);`

   d. `Console.WriteLine("X{0}{2}", var1);`

6. Assume you have a variable declared as `int var1 = 3;`. What is the value of `22 % var1`?

   a. 0 c. 7

   b. 1 d. 21

7. Assume you have a variable declared as `int var1 = 3;`. What is the value of `22 / var1`?

   a. 1 c. 7.333

   b. 7 d. 21

8. What is the value of the expression `4 + 2 * 3`?

   a. 0 c. 18

   b. 10 d. 36

9. Assume you have a variable declared as `int var1 = 3;`. If `var2 = ++var1`, what is the value of `var2`?

   a. 2 c. 4

   b. 3 d. 5

10. Assume you have a variable declared as `int var1 = 3;`. If `var2 = var1++`, what is the value of `var2`?

   a. 2 c. 4

   b. 3 d. 5

11. A variable that can hold the two values `true` and `false` is of type ________.

    a. `int` c. `char`

    b. `bool` d. `double`

12. Which of the following is *not* a C# comparison operator?

    a. => c. ==

    b. != d. <

13. What is the value of the expression `6 >= 7`?

    a. 0 c. true

    b. 1 d. false

14. Which of the following C# types *cannot* contain floating-point numbers?

    a. `float` c. `decimal`

    b. `double` d. `int`

15. Assume you have declared a variable as `double hourly = 13.00;`. What will the statement `Console.WriteLine(hourly);` display?

    a. 13 c. 13.00

    b. 13.0 d. 13.000000

16. Assume you have declared a variable as `double salary = 45000.00;`. Which of the following will display *$45,000*?

    a. `Console.WriteLine(salary.toString("f"));`

    b. `Console.WriteLine(salary.toString("c"));`

    c. `Console.WriteLine(salary);`

    d. two of these

17. When you perform arithmetic operations with operands of different types, such as adding an `int` and a `float`, ________.

    a. C# chooses a unifying type for the result c. you must provide a cast

    b. you must choose a unifying type for the result d. you receive an error message

18. Unicode is ________.

    a. an object-oriented language c. a 16-bit coding scheme

    b. a subset of the C# language d. another term for hexadecimal

19. Which of the following declares a variable that can hold the word *computer*?

    a. `string device = 'computer';` c. `char device = 'computer';`

    b. `string device = "computer";` d. `char device = "computer";`

20. Which of the following compares two string variables named `string1` and `string2` to determine if their contents are equal?

    a. `string1 = string2`
    b. `string1 == string2`
    c. `Equals.String(string1,string2)`
    d. Two of the above

EXERCISES

1. What is the numeric value of each of the following expressions, as evaluated by the C# programming language?

    a. 4 + 2 * 3
    b. 6 / 4 * 7
    c. 16 / 2 + 14 / 2
    d. 18 / 2
    e. 17 / 2
    f. 32 / 5
    g. 14 % 2
    h. 15 % 2
    i. 28 % 5
    j. 28 % 4 * 3 + 1
    k. (2 + 6) * 4
    l. 20 / (4 + 1)

2. What is the value of each of the following Boolean expressions?

    a. 5 > 2
    b. 6 <= 18
    c. 49 >= 49
    d. 2 == 3
    e. 2 + 6 == 7
    f. 3 + 7 <= 10
    g. 3 != 9
    h. 12 != 12
    i. –2 != 2
    j. 2 + 5 * 3 ==21

3. Are any of the following expressions illegal? For the legal expressions, what is the numeric value of each statement, as evaluated by the C# programming language?

    a. 2.2 * 1.4
    b. 6.78 – 2
    c. 24.0 / 6.0
    d. 7.0 % 3.0
    e. 9 % 2.0

4. Choose the best data type for each of the following, so that no memory storage is wasted. Give an example of a typical value that would be held by the variable and explain why you chose the type you did.

    a. your age
    b. the U.S. national debt
    c. your shoe size
    d. your middle initial

5. In this chapter you learned that although a `double` and a `decimal` both hold floating-point numbers, a `double` can hold a larger value. Write a C# program that declares two variables—a `double` and a `decimal`. Experiment by assigning the same constant value to

each variable so that the assignment to the `double` is legal but the assignment to the `decimal` is not. In other words, when you leave the `decimal` assignment statement in the program, an error message should be generated that indicates the value is outside the range of the type `decimal`, but when you comment out the `decimal` assignment, the program should compile correctly. Save the program as **DoubleDecimalTest.cs**.

6. Write a C# program that declares variables to represent the length and width of a room in feet. Assign appropriate values to the variables, such as `length = 15` and `width = 25`. Compute and display the floor space of the room in square feet (area = length * width). As output, do not display only a value; instead, display explanatory text with the value, such as *`The floor space is 375 square feet.`* Save the program as **Room.cs**.

7. Write a C# program that declares variables to represent the length and width of a room in feet and the price of carpeting *per square foot* in dollars and cents. Assign appropriate values to the variables. Compute and display, with explanatory text, the cost of carpeting the room. Save the program as **Carpet.cs**.

8. Write a program that declares variables to represent the length and width of a room in feet and the price of carpeting *per square yard* in dollars and cents. Assign the value 25 to the `length` variable and the value 42 to the `width` variable. Compute and display the cost of carpeting the room. (*Hint:* There are nine square feet in one square yard.) Save the program as **Yards.cs**.

9. Write a program that declares a `minutes` variable to represent minutes worked on a job, and assign a value to it. Display the value in hours and minutes. For example, 197 minutes becomes 3 hours and 17 minutes. Save the program as **HoursAndMinutes.cs**.

10. Write a program that declares four variables to hold the number of eggs produced in a month by each of four chickens, and assign a value to each variable. Sum the eggs, then display the total in dozens and eggs. For example, a total of 127 eggs is 10 dozen and 7 eggs. Save the program as **Eggs.cs**.

11. Modify the `Eggs` program in Exercise 10 so it prompts the user for and accepts a number of eggs for each chicken. Save the program as **EggsInteractive.cs**.

12. Write a program that declares five variables to hold scores for five tests you have taken, and assign a value to each variable. Display the average of the test scores to two decimal places. Save the program as **Tests.cs**.

13. Modify the `Tests` program in Exercise 12 so it accepts five test scores from a user. Save the program as **TestsInteractive.cs**.

14. Write a program that declares two variables to hold the names of two of your friends, and assign a value to each variable. Display the result of using the `String.Compare()` method with your friends' names. Save the program as **TwoFriends.cs**.

15. Modify the `TwoFriends` program in Exercise 14 so it accepts your friends' names from the keyboard. Save the program as **TwoFriendsInteractive.cs**.

16. Write a program that prompts the user for a name, Social Security number, hourly pay rate, and number of hours worked. In an attractive format (similar to Figure 2-24), display all the input data as well as the following:

    » Gross pay, defined as hourly pay rate times hours worked

    » Federal withholding tax, defined as 15% of the gross pay

    » State withholding tax, defined as 5% of the gross pay

    » Net pay, defined as gross pay minus taxes

    Save the program as **Payroll.cs**.

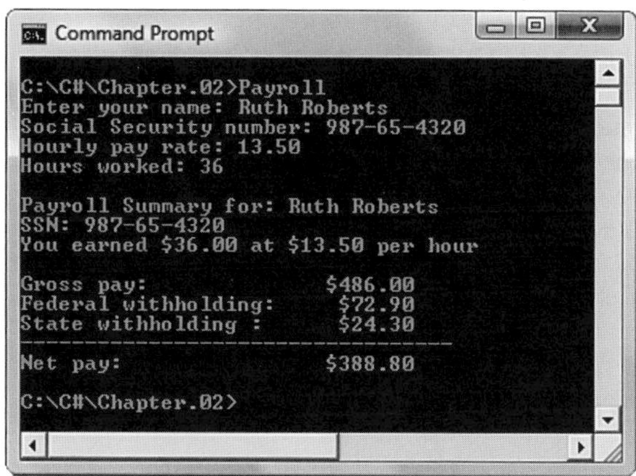

Figure 2-24 Typical execution of `Payroll` program

17. Write a program for the Magic Blender Company. The program prompts the user for a name, street address, city, state, zip code, and quantity of blenders ordered at $39.95 each. In an attractive format (similar to Figure 2-25), display all the input data as well as the following:

    » Amount due before tax, defined as number ordered times price each

    » Sales tax, defined as 7% of the amount due

    » Net due, defined as amount due before tax, plus tax

    Save the program as **OrderReceipt.cs**.

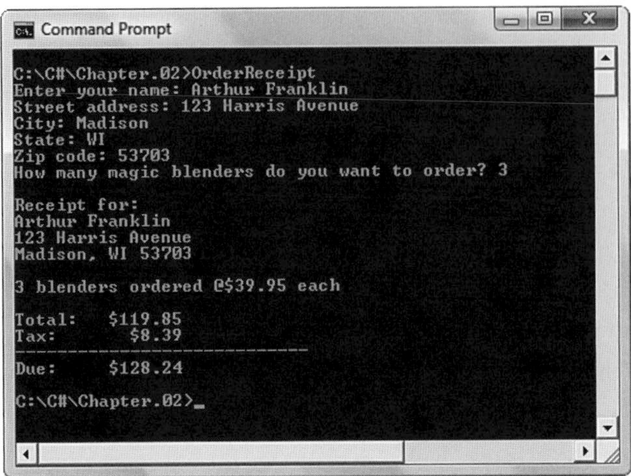

Figure 2-25 Typical execution of `OrderReceipt` program

DEBUGGING EXERCISES

Each of the following files in the Chapter.02 folder on your Student Disk has syntax and/or logical errors. In each case, determine the problem and fix the program. After you correct the errors, save each file using the same filename preceded with "Fixed". For example, DebugTwo1.cs will become FixedDebugTwo1.cs.

a. DebugTwo1.cs
b. DebugTwo2.cs
c. DebugTwo3.cs
d. DebugTwo4.cs

UP FOR DISCUSSION

1. What advantages are there to requiring variables to have a data type?
2. Some programmers use a system called Hungarian notation when naming their variables. What is Hungarian notation, and why do many object-oriented programmers feel it is not a valuable style to use?
3. Computers can perform millions of arithmetic calculations in an hour. How can we possibly know the results are correct?

CHAPTERTHREE

3

MAKING DECISIONS

In this chapter you will:

Understand logic-planning tools and decision making
Learn how to make decisions using the `if` statement
Learn how to make decisions using the `if-else` statement
Use compound expressions in `if` statements
Make decisions using the `switch` statement
Use the conditional operator
Use the NOT operator
Learn to avoid common errors when making decisions

A major reason that computer programs seem so powerful is their ability to make decisions. Programs that decide which travel route will afford the best weather conditions, which Web site will provide the closest match to search criteria, or which recommended medical treatment has the highest probability of success all rely on a program's decision making. In this chapter you will learn to make decisions in C# programs.

UNDERSTANDING LOGIC-PLANNING TOOLS AND DECISION MAKING

»NOTE You learned the difference between a program's logic and its syntax in Chapter 1.

When computer programmers write programs, they rarely just sit down at a keyboard and begin typing. Programmers must plan the complex portions of programs using paper and pencil. Programmers often use **pseudocode**, a tool that helps them plan a program's logic by writing plain English statements. Using pseudocode requires that you write down the steps needed to accomplish a given task. You write pseudocode in everyday language, not the syntax used in a programming language. In fact, a task you write in pseudocode does not have to be computer-related. If you have ever written a list of directions to your house—for example, (1) go west on Algonquin Road, (2) turn left on Roselle Road, (3) enter expressway heading east, and so on—you have written pseudocode. A **flowchart** is similar to pseudocode, but you write the steps in diagram form, as a series of shapes connected by arrows.

Some programmers use a variety of shapes to represent different tasks in their flowcharts, but you can draw simple flowcharts that express very complex situations using just rectangles and diamonds. You use a rectangle to represent any unconditional step and a diamond to represent any decision. For example, Figure 3-1 shows a flowchart and pseudocode describing

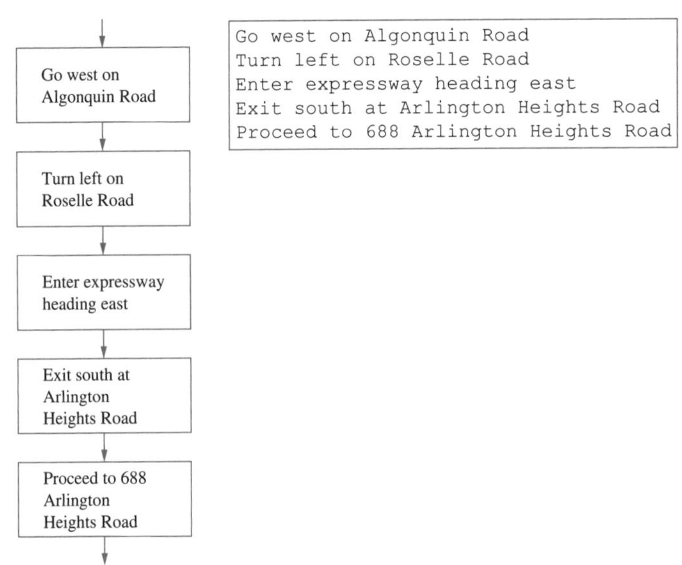


```
Go west on Algonquin Road
Turn left on Roselle Road
Enter expressway heading east
Exit south at Arlington Heights Road
Proceed to 688 Arlington Heights Road
```

Figure 3-1 Flowchart and pseudocode of a series of sequential steps

driving directions to a friend's house. Notice how the actions illustrated in the flowchart and the pseudocode statements correspond. The logic in Figure 3-1 is an example of a logical structure called a **sequence structure**—one step follows another unconditionally. A sequence structure might contain any number of steps, but when one task follows another with no chance to branch away or skip a step, you are using a sequence.

Sometimes, logical steps do not follow in an unconditional sequence—some tasks might or might not occur based on decisions you make. Flowchart creators use diamond shapes to indicate alternative courses of action, which are drawn starting from the sides of the diamonds. Figure 3-2 shows a flowchart describing directions in which the execution of some steps depends on decisions.

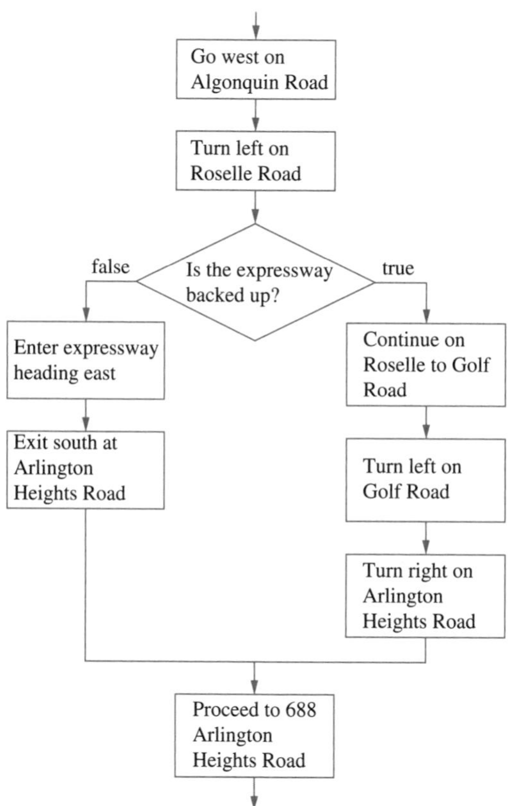

Figure 3-2 Flowchart including a decision

Figure 3-2 shows a **decision structure**—one that involves choosing between alternative courses of action based on some value within a program. For example, the program that produces your paycheck can make decisions about the proper amount to withhold for taxes, the program that guides a missile can alter its course, and a program that monitors your blood pressure during surgery can determine when to sound an alarm. Making decisions is what makes computer programs seem "smart."

When reduced to their most basic form, all computer decisions are yes-or-no decisions. That is, the answer to every computer question is "yes" or "no" (or "true" or "false," or "on" or "off"). This is because computer circuitry consists of millions of tiny switches that are either "on" or "off," and the result of every decision sets one of these switches in memory. The values `true` and `false` are Boolean values; every computer decision results in a Boolean value. Thus, internally, a program you write never asks, for example, "What number did the user enter?" Instead, the decisions might be "Did the user enter a 1?" "If not, did the user enter a 2?" "If not, did the user enter a 3?"

»TWO TRUTHS AND A LIE: UNDERSTANDING DECISION MAKING

1. A sequence structure has three or more alternative logical paths.
2. A decision structure involves choosing between alternative courses of action based on some value within a program.
3. When reduced to their most basic form, all computer decisions are yes-or-no decisions.

The false statement is #1. In a sequence structure, one step follows another unconditionally.

MAKING DECISIONS USING THE `if` STATEMENT

The `if` and `if-else` statements are the two most commonly used decision-making statements in C#. You use an **`if` statement** to make a single-alternative decision. In other words, you use an `if` statement to determine whether an action will occur. The `if` statement takes the following form:

```
if(expression)
     statement;
```

where *expression* represents any C# expression that can be evaluated as `true` or `false` and *statement* represents the action that will take place if the expression evaluates as `true`. You must place the `if` statement's evaluated expression between parentheses.

»NOTE You learned about Boolean expressions and the `bool` data type in Chapter 2. Table 2-4 summarizes how you use the comparison operators.

Usable expressions in an `if` statement include Boolean expressions such as `amount > 5` and `month == "May"` as well as the value of `bool` variables such as `isValidIDNumber`. If the expression evaluates as `true`, then the statement executes. Whether the expression evaluates as `true` or `false`, the program continues with the next statement following the complete `if` statement.

NOTE Often, programmers mistakenly use a single equal sign rather than the double equal sign when attempting to determine equivalency. For example, the expression `number = HIGH` does not compare `number` to `HIGH`. Instead, it attempts to assign the value `HIGH` to the `number` variable. When it is part of an `if` statement, this assignment is illegal.

NOTE The only condition under which the assignment operator would work as part of an `if` statement is when the assignment is made to a `bool` variable. For example, suppose a dating-service program has defined two `bool` variables—`doesSheSmoke` and `doesHeSmoke`. Suppose you want to match smokers only with other smokers. The statement that uses a single = sign, `if(doesSheSmoke = doesHeSmoke)...`, compiles. However, it does not compare smoking preferences. Instead, it assigns the second value to the first, then makes the decision based on the single resulting value.

NOTE In some programming languages, such as C++, nonzero numbers evaluate as `true` and 0 evaluates as `false`. In C#, only Boolean expressions evaluate as `true` and `false`.

For example, the code segment written and diagrammed in Figure 3-3 displays "A" and "B" when `number` holds a value less than 5. The expression `number < 5` evaluates as `true`, so the statement that displays "A" executes. Then the independent statement that displays "B" executes.

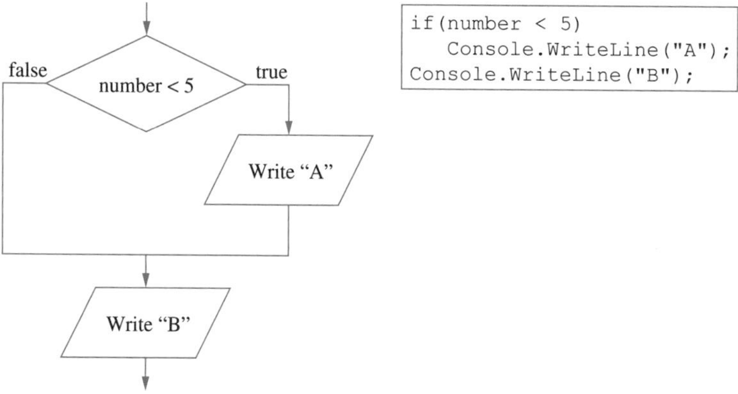


```
if(number < 5)
   Console.WriteLine("A");
Console.WriteLine("B");
```

NOTE You can leave a space between the keyword `if` and the opening parenthesis if you think that format is easier to read.

Figure 3-3 Flowchart and code including a typical `if` statement followed by a separate statement

When an evaluated expression is `false`, the rest of the statement does not execute. For example, when `number` is 5 or greater in Figure 3-3, only "B" is displayed. Because the expression `number < 5` is `false`, the statement that displays "A" never executes.

In Figure 3-3, notice there is no semicolon at the end of the line that contains `if(number < 5)`. The statement does not end at that point; it ends after `Console.WriteLine("A");`. If you incorrectly insert a semicolon at the end of `if(number < 5)`, then the statement says,

"If `number` is less than 5, do nothing; then, no matter what the value of `number` is, print 'A'". Figure 3-4 shows the flowchart logic that matches the code when a semicolon is placed at the end of the `if` expression.

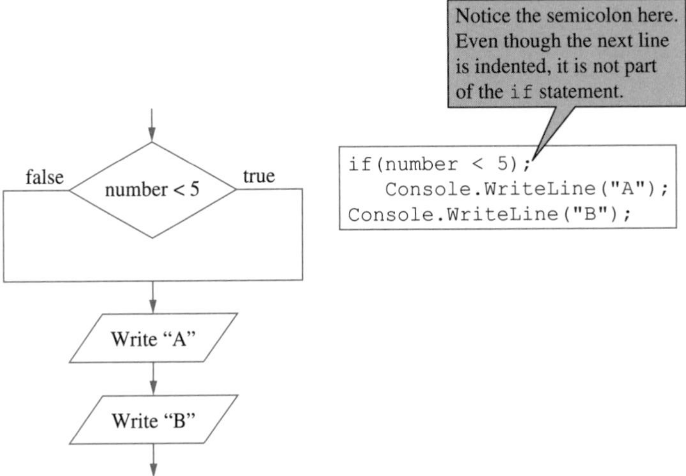

Figure 3-4 Flowchart and code including an `if` statement with a semicolon following the `if` expression

Although it is customary, and good style, to indent any statement that executes when an `if` Boolean expression evaluates as `true`, the C# compiler does not pay any attention to the indentation. Each of the following `if` statements displays "A" when `number` is less than 5. The first shows an `if` written on a single line; the second shows an `if` on two lines but with no indentation. The third uses conventional indentation.

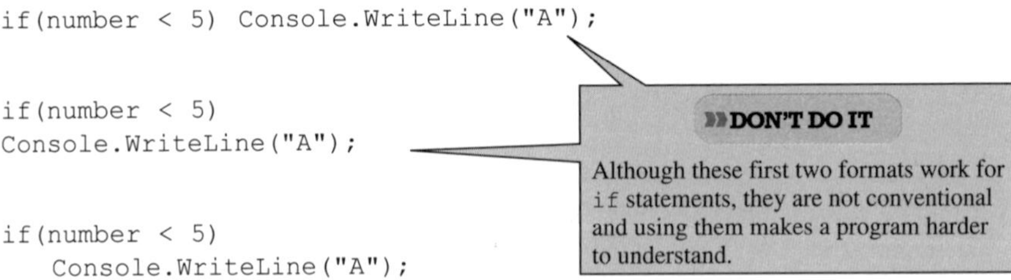

When you want to execute two or more statements conditionally, you must place the statements within a block. A **block** is a collection of one or more statements contained within a pair of

curly braces. For example, the code segment written and diagrammed in Figure 3-5 displays both "C" and "D" when `number` is less than 5, and it displays neither when `number` is not less than 5.

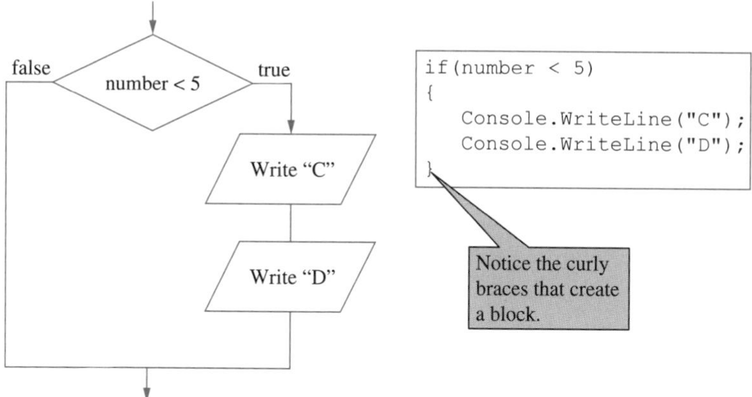

Figure 3-5 Flowchart and code including a typical `if` statement containing a block

Indenting alone does not cause multiple statements to depend on the evaluation of a Boolean expression in an `if`. For multiple statements to depend on an `if`, they must be blocked with braces. For example, Figure 3-6 shows two statements that are indented below an `if` expression. When you glance at the code, it might first appear that both statements depend on the `if`; in fact, however, only the first one does, as shown in the flowchart, because the statements are not blocked.

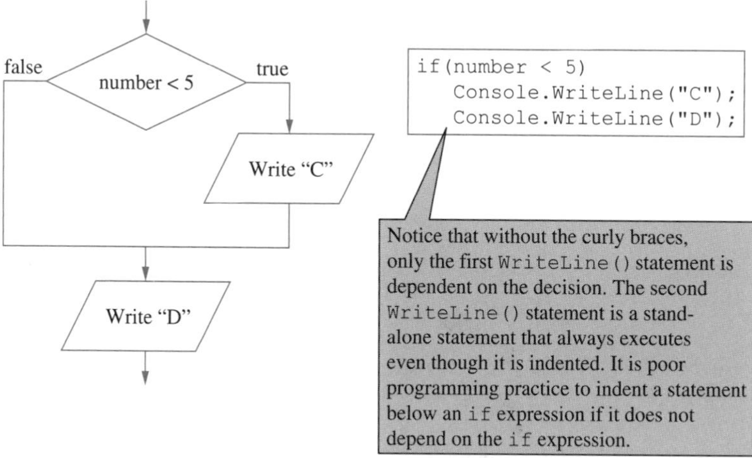

Figure 3-6 Flowchart and code including an `if` statement that is missing curly braces or that has inappropriate indenting

>>NOTE When you create a block using curly braces, you do not have to place multiple statements within it. It is perfectly legal to block a single statement. Blocking a single statement can be a useful technique to help prevent future errors. When a program later is modified to include multiple statements that depend on the `if`, it is easy to forget to add curly braces. You will naturally place the additional statements within the block if the braces are already in place.

>>NOTE It also is legal to create a block that contains no statements. You usually do so only when starting to write a program, as a reminder to yourself to add statements later.

You can place any number of statements within the block contained by the curly braces, including another `if` statement. Of course, if the second `if` statement is the only statement that depends on the `if`, then no braces are required. Figure 3-7 shows the logic for a **nested `if`** statement—one in which one decision structure is contained within another. With a nested `if` statement, a second `if`'s Boolean expression is tested only when the first `if`'s Boolean expression evaluates as `true`.

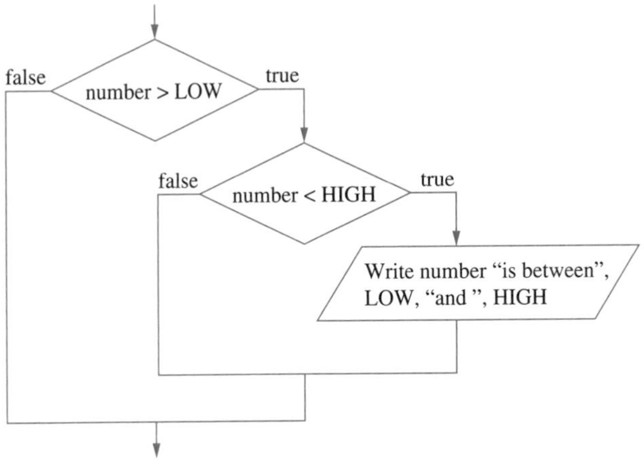


```
if(number > LOW)
   if(number < HIGH)
      Console.WriteLine("{0} is between {1} and {2}",
         number, LOW, HIGH);
```

Figure 3-7 Flowchart and code showing the logic of a nested `if`

Figure 3-8 shows a program that contains the logic. When a user enters a number greater than 5 in the program in Figure 3-8, the first `if` expression evaluates as `true` and the `if`

```
using System;
public class NestedDecision
{
   public static void Main()
   {
      const int HIGH = 10, LOW = 5;
      string numberString;
      int number;
      Console.Write("Enter an integer ");
      numberString = Console.ReadLine();
      number = Convert.ToInt32(numberString);
       if(number > LOW)
          if(number < HIGH)
            Console.WriteLine("{0} is between {1} and {2}",
               number, LOW, HIGH);
   }
}
```

Figure 3-8 Program using nested `if`

statement that tests whether the number is less than 10 executes. When the second `if` evaluates as `true`, the `Console.WriteLine()` statement executes. However, if the second `if` is `false`, no output occurs. When the user enters a number less than or equal to 5, the first `if` expression is `false` and the second `if` expression is never tested, and again no output occurs. Figure 3-9 shows the output after the program is executed three times using three different input values. Notice that when the value input by the user is not between 5 and 10, no output message appears; the message is displayed only when both `if` expressions are `true`.

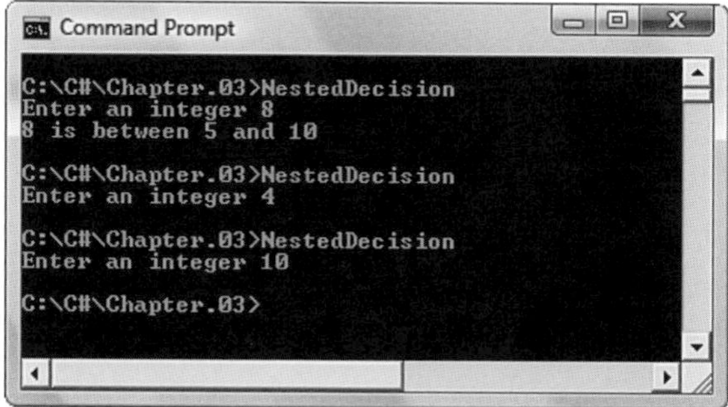

Figure 3-9 Output of three executions of the `NestedDecision` program

»TWO TRUTHS AND A LIE: MAKING DECISIONS USING THE `if` STATEMENT

1. In C#, you must place an `if` statement's evaluated expression between parentheses.
2. In C#, for multiple statements to depend on an `if`, they must be indented.
3. In C#, you can place one `if` statement within a block that depends on another `if` statement.

The false statement is #2. Indenting alone does not cause multiple statements to depend on the evaluation of a Boolean expression in an `if`. For multiple statements to depend on an `if`, they must be blocked with braces.

MAKING DECISIONS USING THE `if-else` STATEMENT

> **»NOTE** You can code an `if` without an `else`, but it is illegal to code an `else` without an `if`.

Some decisions you make are **dual-alternative decisions**; they have two possible resulting actions. If you want to perform one action when a Boolean expression evaluates as `true` and an alternate action when it evaluates as `false`, you can use an **`if-else` statement**. The `if-else` statement takes the following form:

```
if(expression)
   statement1;
else
   statement2;
```

For example, Figure 3-10 shows the logic for an `if-else` statement, and Figure 3-11 shows a program that contains the statement. With every execution of the program,

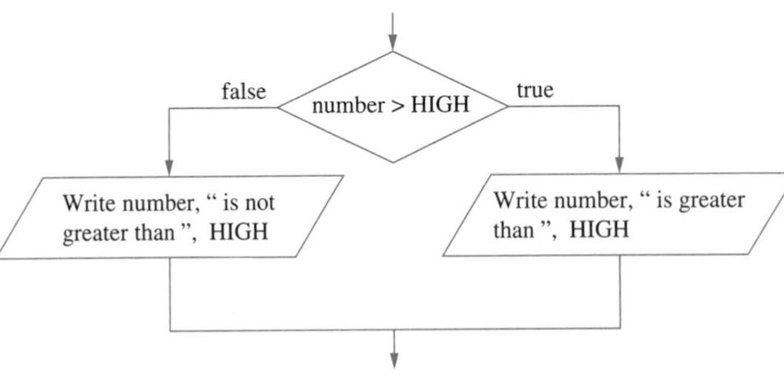


```
if(number > HIGH)
   Console.WriteLine("{0} is greater than {1}",
      number, HIGH);
else
   Console.WriteLine("{0} is not greater than {1}",
      number, HIGH);
```

Figure 3-10 Flowchart and code showing the logic of a dual-alternative `if-else` statement

```
using System;
public class IfElseDecision
{
    public static void Main()
    {
        const int HIGH = 10;
        string numberString;
        int number;
        Console.Write("Enter an integer ");
        numberString = Console.ReadLine();
        number = Convert.ToInt32(numberString);
        if(number > HIGH)
           Console.WriteLine("{0} is greater than {1}",
              number, HIGH);
        else
           Console.WriteLine("{0} is not greater than {1}",
              number, HIGH);
    }
}
```

Figure 3-11 Program with a dual-alternative `if-else` statement

one or the other of the two `WriteLine()` statements executes. Figure 3-12 shows two executions of the program.

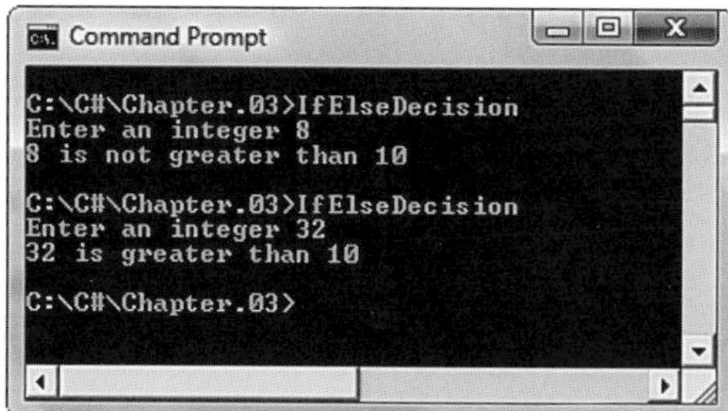

Figure 3-12 Output of two executions of the `IfElseDecision` program

»NOTE The indentation shown in the `if-else` example in Figure 3-11 is not required, but is standard. You vertically align the keyword `if` with the keyword `else`, and then indent the action statements that depend on the evaluation.

»NOTE Just as you can block several statements so they all execute when an expression within an `if` is `true`, you can block multiple statements after an `else` so that they will all execute when the evaluated expression is `false`.

When `if-else` statements are nested, each `else` always is paired with the most recent unpaired `if`. For example, in the following code, the `else` is paired with the second `if`.

```
if(saleAmount > 1000)
    if(saleAmount < 2000)
       bonus = 100;
    else
       bonus = 50;
```

In this example, the following bonuses are assigned:

» If `saleAmount` is between $1000 and $2000, `bonus` is $100 because both evaluated expressions are `true`.

» If `saleAmount` is $2000 or more, `bonus` is $50 because the first evaluated expression is `true` and the second one is `false`.

» If `saleAmount` is $1000 or less, `bonus` is unassigned because the first evaluated expression is `false` and there is no corresponding `else`.

»TWO TRUTHS AND A LIE: MAKING DECISIONS USING THE `if-else` STATEMENT

1. Dual-alternative decisions have two possible outcomes.
2. In an `if-else` statement, a semicolon is always the last character typed before the `else`.
3. When `if-else` statements are nested, the first `if` always is paired with the first `else`.

The false statement is #3. When `if-else` statements are nested, each `else` always is paired with the most recent unpaired `if`.

USING COMPOUND EXPRESSIONS IN `if` STATEMENTS

In many programming situations you encounter, you need to make multiple decisions. For example, suppose a specific college scholarship is available:

» If your high school class rank is higher than 75 percent

» And if your grade-point average is higher than 3.0

» And if you are a state resident

» Or if you are a resident of a cooperating state

» Or if one of your parents went to the college

No matter how many decisions must be made, you can decide on the scholarship eligibility for any student by using a series of `if` statements to test the appropriate variables. For convenience and clarity, however, you can combine multiple decisions into a single `if` statement using a combination of AND and OR operators.

USING THE CONDITIONAL AND OPERATOR

As an alternative to nested `if` statements, you can use the **conditional AND operator** (or simply the **AND operator**) within a Boolean expression to determine whether two expressions are both `true`. The AND operator is written as two ampersands (`&&`). For example, the two code samples shown in Figure 3-13 work exactly the same way. The `age` variable is tested, and if it is greater than or equal to 0 and less than 120, a message prints to explain that the value is valid.

```
// using &&
 if(age >= 0 && age < 120)
   Console.WriteLine("Age is valid");
// using nested ifs
 if(age >= 0)
    if(age < 120)
      Console.WriteLine("Age is valid");
```

Figure 3-13 Comparing using the AND operator and nested `if` statements

You are never required to use the AND operator, because nested `if` statements achieve the same result, but using the AND operator often makes your code more concise, less error-prone, and easier to understand.

It is important to note that when you use the AND operator, you must include a complete Boolean expression on each side of the `&&` operator. If you want to set a bonus to $400 when a `saleAmount` is both over $1000 and under $5000, the correct statement is as follows:

```
if(saleAmount > 1000 && saleAmount < 5000)
   bonus = 400;
```

The following statement is incorrect and will not compile:

```
if(saleAmount > 1000 && < 5000)
   bonus = 400;
```

»DON'T DO IT

5000 is not a Boolean expression (it is a numeric constant), so this statement is invalid.

The statement is invalid because the numeric expression `< 5000` is used on the right side of the AND expression, and `< 5000` is not a complete Boolean expression.

NOTE For clarity, many programmers prefer to surround each Boolean expression that is part of a compound Boolean expression with its own set of parentheses. For example:

```
if((saleAmount > 1000) && (saleAmount < 5000))
   bonus = 400;
```

Use this format if it is clearer to you.

The expressions in each part of an AND expression are evaluated only as much as necessary to determine whether the entire expression is `true` or `false`. This feature is called **short-circuit evaluation**. With the AND operator, both Boolean expressions must be `true` before the action in the statement can occur. If the first expression is `false`, the second expression is never evaluated, because its value does not matter. For example, if `a` is not greater than `LIMIT` in the following `if` statement, then the evaluation is complete because there is no need to evaluate whether `b` is greater than `LIMIT`.

```
if(a > LIMIT && b > LIMIT)
   Console.WriteLine("Both are greater than LIMIT");
```

USING THE CONDITIONAL OR OPERATOR

You can use the **conditional OR operator** (or simply the **OR operator**) when you want some action to occur even if only one of two conditions is `true`. The OR operator is written as ||. For example, if you want to print a message indicating an invalid age when the variable is less than 0 or is 120 or greater, you can use either code sample in Figure 3-14.

NOTE You create the OR operator by using two vertical pipes. On most keyboards, the pipe is found above the backslash key; typing it requires that you also hold down the Shift key.

```
// using ||
 if(age < 0 || age >= 120)
    Console.WriteLine("Age is not valid");
// using nested ifs
 if(age < 0)
    Console.WriteLine("Age is not valid");
 else
    if(age >= 120)
       Console.WriteLine("Age is not valid");
```

Figure 3-14 Using the OR operator or nested `if` statements

NOTE A common use of the OR operator is to decide to take action whether a character variable is uppercase or lowercase. For example, in the following decision, any subsequent action occurs whether the selection variable holds an uppercase or lowercase 'A':

```
if(selection == 'A' || selection == 'a')...
```

When the OR operator is used in an `if` statement, only one of the two Boolean expressions in the tested expression needs to be `true` for the resulting action to occur. As with the AND operator, this feature is called short-circuit evaluation. When you use the OR operator and the first Boolean expression is `true`, the second expression is never evaluated, because it doesn't matter whether it is `true` or `false`.

USING THE LOGICAL AND AND OR OPERATORS

The **Boolean logical AND** (&) and **Boolean logical inclusive OR** (|) operators work just like their `&&` and `||` (*conditional* AND and OR) counterparts, except they do not support short-circuit evaluation. That is, they always evaluate both sides of the expression, no matter what the first evaluation is. This can lead to a **side effect**, or unintended consequence. For example, in the following statement that uses `&&`, if `salesAmountForYear` is not at least $10000, the first half of the expression is `false`, so the second half of the Boolean expression is never evaluated and `yearsOfService` is not increased.

```
if(salesAmountForYear >= 10000 && ++yearsOfService > 10)
   bonus = 200;
```

On the other hand, when a single & is used and `salesAmountForYear` is not at least 10000, then even though the first half of the expression is `false`, the second half is still evaluated, and `yearsOfService` is increased:

```
if(salesAmountForYear >= 10000 & ++yearsOfService > 10)
   bonus = 200;
```

Because the first half of the expression is `false`, the entire evaluation is `false`, and, as with `&&`, `bonus` is still not set to 200. However, a side effect has occurred: `yearsOfService` is incremented.

In general, you should avoid writing expressions that contain side effects. If you want `yearsOfService` to increase no matter what the `salesAmountForYear` is, then you should increase it in a stand-alone statement.

COMBINING AND AND OR OPERATORS

You can combine as many AND and OR operators in an expression as you need. For example, when three conditions must be `true` before performing an action, you can use an expression such as `if(a && b && c)`. When you combine AND and OR operators within the same Boolean expression, the AND operators take precedence, meaning their Boolean values are evaluated first.

For example, consider a program that determines whether a movie theater patron can purchase a discounted ticket. Assume discounts are allowed for children (age 12 and younger) and for senior citizens (age 65 and older) who attend G-rated movies. The following code looks reasonable, but it produces incorrect results because the `&&` evaluates before the `||`.

```
if(age <= 12 || age >= 65 && rating == 'G')
   Console.WriteLine("Discount applies");
```

For example, assume a movie patron is 10 years old and the movie rating is 'R'. The patron should not receive a discount (or be allowed to see the movie!). However, within the `if` statement above, the expression `age >= 65 && rating == 'G'` evaluates first. It is `false`, so the `if` becomes the equivalent of `if(age <= 12 || false)`. Because `age <= 12` is `true`, the `if` becomes the equivalent of `if(true || false)`, which evaluates as `true`, and the statement "Discount applies" incorrectly displays.

You can use parentheses to correct the logic and force the expression `age <= 12 || age >= 65` to evaluate first, as shown in the following code.

```
if((age <= 12 || age >= 65) && rating == 'G')
   Console.WriteLine("Discount applies");
```

With the added parentheses, if `age` is 12 or less OR 65 or greater, the expression is evaluated as `if(true && rating == 'G')`. When the `age` value qualifies a patron for a discount, then the `rating` value must also be acceptable. Figure 3-15 shows the `if` within a complete program; note that the discount age limits now are represented as named constants. Figure 3-16 shows the execution before the parentheses

```
using System;
public class MovieDiscount
{
   public static void Main()
   {
      int age = 10;
      char rating = 'R';
      const int CHILD_AGE = 12;
      const int SENIOR_AGE = 65;
      Console.WriteLine("When age is {0} and rating is {1}",
         age, rating);
      if((age <= CHILD_AGE || age >= SENIOR_AGE) && rating == 'G')
         Console.WriteLine("Discount applies");
      else
         Console.WriteLine("Full price");
   }
}
```

Figure 3-15 Movie ticket discount program using parentheses to alter precedence of Boolean evaluations

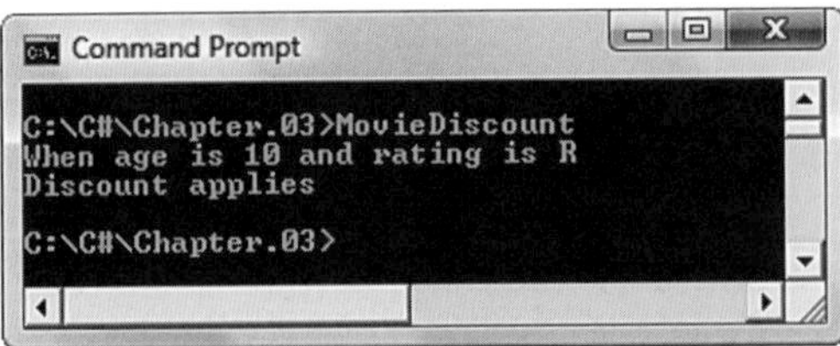

Figure 3-16 Incorrect results when `MovieDiscount` program is executed without added parentheses

were added to the `if` statement, and Figure 3-17 shows the output after the inclusion of the parentheses.

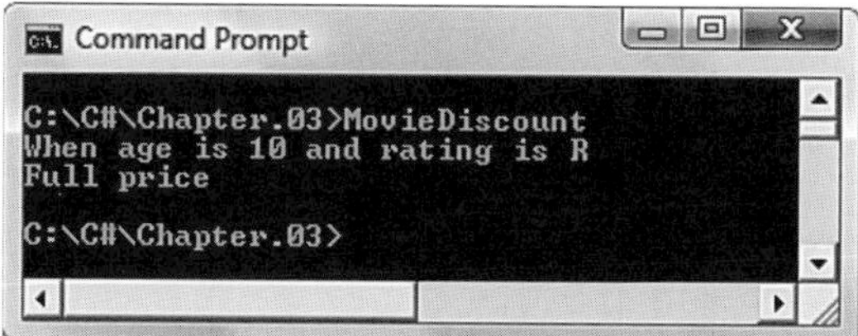

Figure 3-17 Correct results when parentheses are added to `MovieDiscount` program

»NOTE You can use parentheses for clarity even when they are not required. For example, the following expressions both evaluate `a && b` first:

```
a && b || c
(a && b) || c
```

If the version with parentheses makes your intentions clearer, you should use it.

»NOTE In Chapter 2, you controlled arithmetic operator precedence by using parentheses. Appendix A describes the precedence of every C# operator. For example, in Appendix A you can see that the comparison operators <= and >= have higher precedence than both `&&` and `||`.

»TWO TRUTHS AND A LIE: USING COMPOUND EXPRESSIONS IN `if` STATEMENTS

1. If `a` is `true` and `b` and `c` are `false`, then the value of `b && c || a` is `true`.
2. If `d` is `true` and `e` and `f` are `false`, then the value of `e || d && f` is `true`.
3. If `g` is `true` and `h` and `i` are `false`, then the value of `g || h && i` is `true`.

The false statement is #2. If `d` is `true` and `e` and `f` are `false`, then the value of `e || d && f` is `false`. Because you evaluate `&&` before `||`, first `d && f` is evaluated and found to be `false`, then `e || false` is evaluated and found to be `false`.

MAKING DECISIONS USING THE switch STATEMENT

By nesting a series of if and else statements, you can choose from any number of alternatives. For example, suppose you want to print different strings based on a student's class year. Figure 3-18 shows the logic using nested if statements. The program segment tests the year variable four times and executes one of four statements, or displays an error message.

```
if(year == 1)
   Console.WriteLine("Freshman");
else
   if(year == 2)
      Console.WriteLine("Sophomore");
   else
      if(year == 3)
         Console.WriteLine("Junior");
      else
         if(year == 4)
            Console.WriteLine("Senior");
         else
            Console.WriteLine("Invalid year");
```

Figure 3-18 Executing multiple alternatives using a series of if statements

An alternative to the series of nested if statements in Figure 3-18 is to use the switch structure (see Figure 3-19). The **switch structure** tests a single variable against a series of exact

```
switch(year)
{
   case 1:
      Console.WriteLine("Freshman");
      break;
   case 2:
      Console.WriteLine("Sophomore");
      break;
   case 3:
      Console.WriteLine("Junior");
      break;
   case 4:
      Console.WriteLine("Senior");
      break;
   default:
      Console.WriteLine("Invalid year");
      break;
}
```

Figure 3-19 Executing multiple alternatives using a switch statement

matches. The switch structure in Figure 3-19 is easier to read and interpret than the series of nested if statements in Figure 3-18. The if statements would become harder to read if additional choices were required and if multiple statements had to execute in each case. These additional choices and statements might also make it easier to make mistakes.

»NOTE The switch statement is not as flexible as the if because you can test only one variable, and it must be tested for equality.

The switch structure uses four new keywords:

- The keyword **switch** starts the structure and is followed immediately by a test expression (called the **switch expression**) enclosed in parentheses.
- The keyword **case** is followed by one of the possible values that might equal the switch expression. A colon follows the value. The entire expression—for example, case 1:—is a case label. A **case label** identifies a course of action in a switch structure. Most switch structures contain several case labels.
- The keyword **break** usually terminates a switch structure at the end of each case. Although other statements can end a case, break is the most commonly used.
- The keyword **default** optionally is used prior to any action that should occur if the test expression does not match any case.

»NOTE Besides break, you can use a return statement or a throw statement to end a case. You learn about return statements in Chapter 6 and throw statements in Chapter 9.

»NOTE You are not required to list the case label values in ascending order, as shown in Figure 3-19. It is most efficient to list the most common case first, instead of the case with the lowest value. Often, the default case is the most common.

The switch structure shown in Figure 3-19 begins by evaluating the year variable shown in the switch statement. If year is equal to the first case label value, which is 1, then the statement that displays "Freshman" will execute. The break statement causes a bypass of the rest of the switch structure, and execution continues with any statement after the closing curly brace of the switch structure.

If the year variable is not equivalent to the first case label value of 1, then the next case label value is compared, and so on. If the year variable does not contain the same value as any of the case label expressions, then the default statement or statements execute.

In C#, an error occurs if you reach the end point of the statement list of a switch section. For example, the following code is not allowed, because when the year value is 1, "Freshman" is displayed, and the code reaches the end of the case.

```
switch(year)
{
   case 1:
      Console.WriteLine("Freshman");
   case 2:
      Console.WriteLine("Sophomore");
      break;
}
```

»DON'T DO IT
This code is invalid because the end of the case is reached after "Freshman" is displayed.

Not allowing code to reach the end of a case is known as the "no fall through rule" because in other programming languages, such as Java and C++, this syntax would be allowed; when year equals 1, both "Freshman" and "Sophomore" would be displayed. Falling through to the next case is not allowed in C#; the most common way to avoid this error is to use a break statement at the end of each case.

NOTE The **governing type** of a switch statement is established by the switch expression. The governing type can be sbyte, byte, short, ushort, int, uint, long, ulong, char, string, or an enum type. An **enum** is an enumeration—a programmer-defined type that declares a set of constants. You will use enumerations in Chapter 11.

A switch does not need to contain a default case. If the test expression in a switch does not match any of the case label values, and there is no default value, then the program simply continues with the next executable statement. However, it is good programming practice to include a default label in a switch structure; that way, you provide for actions when your data does not match any case. The default label does not have to appear last, although usually it does.

You can use multiple labels to govern a list of statements. For example, in the code in Figure 3-20, "Upperclass" is displayed whether the year value is 3 or 4.

NOTE You receive a compiler error if two or more case label values in a switch statement are the same.

```
switch(year)
{
   case 1:
      Console.WriteLine("Freshman");
      break;
   case 2:
      Console.WriteLine("Sophomore");
      break;
   case 3:
   case 4:
      Console.WriteLine("Upperclass");
      break;
   default:
      Console.WriteLine("Invalid year");
      break;
}
```

Cases 3 and 4 are both "Upperclass".

Figure 3-20 Example switch structure using multiple labels to execute a single statement block

You are never required to use a switch structure; you can always achieve the same results with nested if statements. The switch structure is simply a convenience you can use when there are several alternative courses of action depending on a match with a variable. Additionally, it makes sense to use a switch only when there are a reasonable number of specific matching values to be tested. For example, if every sale amount from $1 to $500 requires a 5 percent commission, it is not reasonable to test every possible dollar amount using the following code:

```
switch(saleAmount)
{
    case 1:
        commRate = .05;
        break;
    case 2:
        commRate = .05;
        break;
    case 3:
        commRate = .05;
        break;
// ...and so on for several hundred more cases
```

With 500 different dollar values resulting in the same commission, one test—`if(saleAmount <= 500)`—is far more reasonable than listing 500 separate cases.

»TWO TRUTHS AND A LIE: MAKING DECISIONS USING THE switch STATEMENT

1. In a `switch` statement, the keyword `case` is followed by one of the possible values that might equal the `switch` expression, and a colon follows the value.
2. The keyword `break` always terminates a `switch` structure at the end of each `case`.
3. A `switch` statement does not need to contain a `default` case.

The false statement is #2. The keyword `break` usually terminates a `switch` structure at the end of each `case`, but other statements can end a `case`.

USING THE CONDITIONAL OPERATOR

The **conditional operator** is used as an abbreviated version of the `if-else` statement; it requires three expressions separated with a question mark and a colon. Like the `switch` structure, you never are required to use the conditional operator. Rather, it is simply a convenient shortcut, especially when you want to use the result immediately as an expression. The syntax of the conditional operator is:

```
testExpression ? trueResult : falseResult;
```

»NOTE Unary operators use one operand; binary operators use two. The conditional operator ?: is **ternary** because it requires three arguments: a test expression and `true` and `false` result expressions. The conditional operator is the only ternary operator in C#.

The first expression, `testExpression`, is evaluated as `true` or `false`. If it is `true`, then the entire conditional expression takes on the value of the expression following the question mark (`trueResult`). If the value of the `testExpression` is `false`, then the entire expression takes on the value of `falseResult`. For example, consider the following statement:

```
biggerNum = (a > b) ? a : b;
```

This statement evaluates `a > b`. If `a` is greater than `b`, then the entire conditional expression takes the value of `a`, which then is assigned to `biggerNum`. If `a` is not greater than `b`, then the expression assumes the value of `b`, and `b` is assigned to `biggerNum`.

The conditional operator is most often used when you want to use the result as an expression without creating an intermediate variable. For example, suppose an income tax program has declared `doubles` for tax owed when calculated using a standard formula and when calculated using an alternative minimum-tax formula. A taxpayer is required to make a quarterly payment that is one-fourth of the larger of the two values. A usable statement might be as follows:

```
double payment = ((altMinTax > stdTax) ? altMinTax : stdTax) / 4;
```

This code provides the same results as the following:

```
double payment;
if(altMinTax > stdTax)
   payment = altMinTax / 4;
else
   payment = stdTax / 4;
```

As another example, a conditional operator can be used directly in an output statement such as the following:

```
Console.WriteLine((testScore >= 60) ? "Pass" : "Fail");
```

Conditional expressions are frequently more difficult to read than `if-else` statements, but they can be used in places where `if-else` statements cannot.

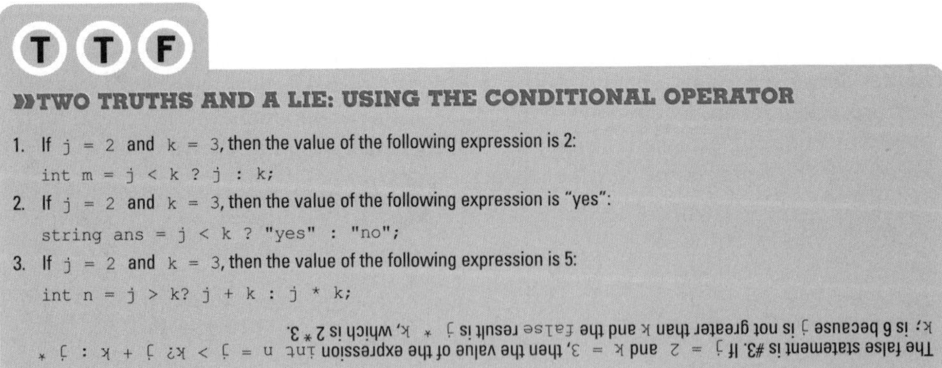

T T F

»TWO TRUTHS AND A LIE: USING THE CONDITIONAL OPERATOR

1. If `j = 2` and `k = 3`, then the value of the following expression is 2:
   `int m = j < k ? j : k;`
2. If `j = 2` and `k = 3`, then the value of the following expression is "yes":
   `string ans = j < k ? "yes" : "no";`
3. If `j = 2` and `k = 3`, then the value of the following expression is 5:
   `int n = j > k? j + k : j * k;`

The false statement is #3. If `j = 2` and `k = 3`, then the value of the expression `int n = j > k? j + k : j * k;` is 6 because `j` is not greater than `k` and the `false` result is `j * k`, which is 2 * 3.

USING THE NOT OPERATOR

You use the **NOT operator**, which is written as an exclamation point (!), to negate the result of any Boolean expression. Any expression that evaluates as `true` becomes `false` when preceded by the NOT operator, and any `false` expression preceded by the NOT operator becomes `true`.

For example, suppose a monthly car insurance premium is $200 if the driver is younger than age 26 and $125 if the driver is age 26 or older. Each of the following `if` statements (which have been placed on single lines for convenience) correctly assigns the premium values.

```
if(age < 26) premium = 200;    else premium = 125;
if(!(age < 26)) premium = 125;    else premium = 200;
if(age >= 26) premium = 125;    else premium = 200;
if(!(age >= 26)) premium = 200;    else premium = 125;
```

The statements with the NOT operator are somewhat more difficult to read, particularly because they require the double set of parentheses, but the result is the same in each case. Using the NOT operator is clearer when the value of a Boolean variable is tested. For example, a variable initialized as `bool oldEnough = (age >= 25);` can become part of the relatively easy-to-read expression `if(!oldEnough)....`

>>**NOTE** The NOT operator has higher precedence than the AND and OR operators. For example, suppose you have declared two Boolean variables named `ageOverMinimum` and `ticketsUnderMinimum`. The following expressions are evaluated in the same way:

```
ageOverMinimum && !ticketsUnderMinimum
ageOverMinimum && (!ticketsUnderMinimum)
```

>>**NOTE** Augustus de Morgan was a 19th-century mathematician who originally observed the following:

`!(a && b)` is equivalent to `!a || !b`

`!(a || b)` is equivalent to `!(a && b)`

>>TWO TRUTHS AND A LIE: USING THE NOT OPERATOR

1. Assume `p`, `q`, and `r` are all Boolean variables that have been assigned the value `true`. After the following statement executes, the value of `p` is still `true`.

   `p = !q || r;`

2. Assume `p`, `q`, and `r` are all Boolean variables that have been assigned the value `true`. After the following statement executes, the value of `p` is still `true`.

   `p = !(!q && !r);`

3. Assume `p`, `q`, and `r` are all Boolean variables that have been assigned the value `true`. After the following statement executes, the value of `p` is still `true`.

   `p = !(q || !r);`

The false statement is #3. If `p`, `q`, and `r` are all Boolean variables that have been assigned the value `true`, then after `p = !(q || !r);` executes, the value of `p` is `false`. First `q` is evaluated as `true`, so the entire expression within the parentheses is `true`. The leading NOT operator reverses that result to `false` and assigns it to `p`.

AVOIDING COMMON ERRORS WHEN MAKING DECISIONS

New programmers frequently make errors when they first learn to make decisions. As you have seen, the most frequent errors include the following:

- Using the assignment operator instead of the comparison operator when testing for equality
- Inserting a semicolon after the Boolean expression in an `if` statement instead of after the entire statement is completed
- Failing to block a set of statements with curly braces when several statements depend on the `if` or the `else` statement
- Failing to include a complete Boolean expression on each side of an `&&` or `||` operator in an `if` statement

In this section, you will learn to avoid other types of errors with `if` statements. Programmers often make errors at the following times:

- When performing a range check incorrectly or inefficiently
- When using the wrong operator with AND and OR
- Using NOT incorrectly

PERFORMING ACCURATE AND EFFICIENT RANGE CHECKS

When new programmers must make a range check, they often introduce incorrect or inefficient code into their programs. A **range check** is a series of `if` statements that determine whether a value falls within a specified range. Consider a situation in which salespeople can receive one of three possible commission rates based on their sales. For example, a sale totaling $1000 or more earns the salesperson an 8% commission, a sale totaling $500 through $999 earns 6% of the sale amount, and any sale totaling $499 or less earns 5%. Using three separate `if` statements to test single Boolean expressions might result in some incorrect commission assignments. For example, examine the following code:

```
if(saleAmount >= 1000)
  commissionRate = 0.08;
if(saleAmount >= 500)
  commissionRate = 0.06;
if(saleAmount <= 499)
  commissionRate = 0.05;
```

DON'T DO IT

Although it was not the programmer's intention, both of the first two `if` statements are true for any `saleAmount` greater than or equal to 1000.

NOTE In this example, `saleAmount` is assumed to be an integer. As long as you are dealing with whole dollar amounts, the expression `if(saleAmount >= 1000)` can be expressed just as well as `if(saleAmount > 999)`. If `saleAmount` was a floating-point variable, the preceding code would fail to assign a commission rate for sales from $499.01 through $499.99.

Using this code, if a `saleAmount` is $5000, the first `if` statement executes. The Boolean expression `(saleAmount >= 1000)` evaluates as `true`, and 0.08 is correctly assigned to `commissionRate`. However, when a `saleAmount` is $5000, the next `if` expression, `(saleAmount >= 500)`, also evaluates as `true`, so the `commissionRate`, which was 8%, is incorrectly reset to 6%.

A partial solution to this problem is to use an `else` statement following the `if(saleAmount >= 1000)` expression:

```
if(saleAmount >= 1000)
   commissionRate = 0.08;
else if(saleAmount >= 500)
   commissionRate = 0.06;
else if(saleAmount <= 499)
   commissionRate = 0.05;
```

»DON'T DO IT

If the logic reaches this point, the expression is always true, so it is a waste of time to make this decision.

»NOTE The last two logical tests in this code are sometimes called `else-if` statements because each `else` and its subsequent `if` are placed on the same line. When the `else-if` format is used to test multiple cases, programmers frequently forego the traditional indentation and align each `else-if` with the others.

With this code, when the `saleAmount` is $5000, the expression `(saleAmount >= 1000)` is `true` and the `commissionRate` becomes 8%; then the entire `if` structure ends. When the `saleAmount` is not greater than or equal to $1000 (for example, $800), the first `if` expression is `false` and the `else` statement executes and correctly sets the `commissionRate` to 6%.

This version of the code works, but it is somewhat inefficient. When the `saleAmount` is any amount that is at least $500, either the first `if` sets `commissionRate` to 8% for amounts of at least $1000, or its `else` sets `commissionRate` to 6% for amounts of at least $500. In either of these two cases, the Boolean value tested in the next statement, `if(saleAmount <= 499)`, is always `false`. After you know that the `saleAmount` is not at least $500, rather than asking `if(saleAmount <= 499)`, it's easier and more efficient to use an `else`. If the `saleAmount` is not at least $1000 and is also not at least $500, it must by default be less than or equal to $499. The improved code is as follows:

```
if(saleAmount >= 1000)
   commissionRate = 0.08;
else if(saleAmount >= 500)
   commissionRate = 0.06;
else commissionRate = 0.05;
```

In other words, because this example uses three commission rates, two boundaries should be checked. If there were four rates, there would be three boundaries, and so on.

Within a nested `if-else`, it is most efficient to ask the most likely question first. In other words, if you know that most `saleAmount` values are over $1000, compare `saleAmount` to that value first. That way, you most frequently avoid asking multiple questions. If, however, you know that most `saleAmounts` are small, you should ask `if(saleAmount < 500)` first.

USING AND AND OR APPROPRIATELY

Beginning programmers often use the AND operator when they mean to use OR, and often use OR when they should use AND. Part of the problem lies in the way we use the English language. For example, your boss might request, "Print an error message when an employee's hourly pay rate is under $5.65 and when an employee's hourly pay rate is over $60." Because your boss used the word "and" in the request, you might be tempted to write a program statement like the following:

```
if(payRate < 5.65 && payRate > 60)
  Console.WriteLine("Error in pay rate");
```

»DON'T DO IT
This expression can never be true.

However, as a single variable, no `payRate` value can ever be both below 5.65 and over 60 at the same time, so the print statement can never execute, no matter what value the `payRate` has. In this case, you must write the following statement to print the error message under the correct circumstances:

```
if(payRate < 5.65 || payRate > 60)
   Console.WriteLine("Error in pay rate");
```

Similarly, your boss might request, "Print the names of those employees in departments 1 and 2." Because the boss used the word "and" in the request, you might be tempted to write the following:

```
if(department == 1 && department == 2)
  Console.WriteLine("Name is: {0}", name);
```

»DON'T DO IT
This expression can never be true.

However, the variable `department` can never contain both a 1 and a 2 at the same time, so no employee name will ever be printed, no matter what department the employee is in.

USING NOT CORRECTLY

Whenever you use negatives, it is easy to make logical mistakes. For example, suppose your boss says, "Make sure if the sales code is not 'A' or 'B', the customer gets a 10% discount. You might be tempted to code the following:

```
if(salesCode != 'A' || salesCode != 'B')
   discount = 0.10;
```

»DON'T DO IT
This expression can never be true.

However, this logic will result in every customer receiving the 10% discount because every `salesCode` is either not 'A' or not 'B'. For example, a `salesCode` of 'A' is not 'B'. The statement above is always `true`. The correct statement is either one of the following:

```
if(salesCode != 'A' && salesCode != 'B')
   discount = 0.10;
if(!(salesCode == 'A' || salesCode == 'B'))
   discount = 0.10;
```

In the first example, if the `salesCode` is not 'A' and it also is not 'B', then the discount is applied correctly. In the second example, if the `salesCode` is 'A' or 'B', the inner Boolean expression is `true`, and the NOT operator (!) changes the evaluation to `false`, not applying the discount for 'A' or 'B' sales. You also could avoid the confusing negative situation by asking questions in a positive way, as in the following:

```
if(salesCode == 'A' || salesCode == 'B')
   discount = 0;
else
   discount = 0.10;
```

»TWO TRUTHS AND A LIE: AVOIDING COMMON ERRORS WHEN MAKING DECISIONS

1. If you want to display "OK" when `userEntry` is 12 and when it is 13, then the following is a usable C# statement:

```
if(userEntry == 12 && userEntry == 13)
   Console.WriteLine("OK");
```

2. If you want to display "OK" when `userEntry` is 20 or when `highestScore` is at least 70, then the following is a usable C# statement:

```
if(userEntry == 20 || highestScore >= 70)
   Console.WriteLine("OK");
```

3. If you want to display "OK" when `userEntry` is anything other than 99 or 100, then the following is a usable C# statement:

```
if(userEntry != 99 && userEntry != 100)
   Console.WriteLine("OK");
```

The false statement is #1. If you want to display "OK" when `userEntry` is 12 and when it is 13, then you want to display it when it is either 12 or 13 because it cannot be both simultaneously. The expression `userEntry == 12 && userEntry == 13` can never be true. The correct Boolean expression is `userEntry == 12 || userEntry == 13`.

YOU DO IT

USING if-else STATEMENTS

In the next steps, you will write a program that requires using multiple, nested `if-else` statements to accomplish its goal—determining whether any of the three integers entered by a user are equal.

To create a program that uses nested `if-else` statements:

1. Open a new text file and write the first lines necessary for a `CompareThreeNumbers` class.

```
using System;
public class CompareThreeNumbers
{
```

2. Begin a `Main()` method by declaring a string for input and three integers that will hold the input values.

```
public static void Main()
{
   string numberString;
   int num1, num2, num3;
```

3. Add the statements that retrieve the three integers from the user and assign them to the appropriate variables.

```
      Console.Write("Enter an integer ");
      numberString = Console.ReadLine();
      num1 = Convert.ToInt32(numberString);
      Console.Write("Enter an integer ");
      numberString = Console.ReadLine();
      num2 = Convert.ToInt32(numberString);
      Console.Write("Enter an integer ");
      numberString = Console.ReadLine();
      num3 = Convert.ToInt32(numberString);
```

»NOTE In Chapter 6, you will learn to write methods, avoiding repetitive code like that shown here.

4. If the first number and the second number are equal, there are two possibilities: either the first is also equal to the third, in which case all three numbers are equal, or the first is not equal to the third, in which case only the first two numbers are equal. Insert the following code:

```
if(num1 == num2)
   if(num1 == num3)
      Console.WriteLine("All three numbers are equal");
   else
      Console.WriteLine("First two are equal");
```

5. If the first two numbers are not equal, but the first and third are equal, print an appropriate message. For clarity, the `else` should vertically align under `if(num1 == num2)`.

```
else
   if(num1 == num3)
      Console.WriteLine("First and last are equal");
```

6. When `num1` and `num2` are not equal, and `num1` and `num3` are not equal, but `num2` and `num3` are equal, display an appropriate message. For clarity, the `else` should vertically align under `if(num1 == num3)`.

```
   else
      if(num2 == num3)
         Console.WriteLine("Last two are equal");
```

7. Finally, if none of the pairs (`num1` and `num2`, `num1` and `num3`, or `num2` and `num3`) is equal, display an appropriate message. For clarity, the `else` should vertically align under `if(num2 == num3)`.

```
else
   Console.WriteLine
      ("No two numbers are equal");
```

8. Add a closing curly brace for the `Main()` method and a closing curly brace for the class.
9. Save the file as **CompareThreeNumbers.cs**. Compile the program, then execute it several times, providing different combinations of equal and nonequal integers when prompted. Figure 3-21 shows several executions of the program.

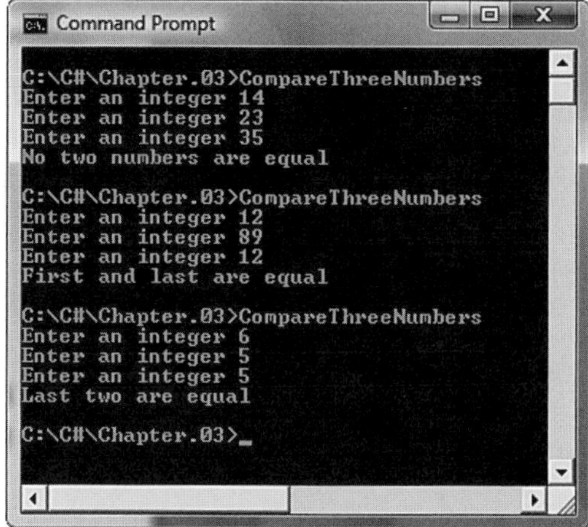

Figure 3-21 Several executions of the `CompareThreeNumbers` program

USING AND AND OR LOGIC

In the next steps, you will create an interactive program that allows you to test AND and OR logic for yourself. The program decides whether a delivery charge applies to a shipment. If the customer lives in Zone 1 or Zone 2, then shipping is free, as long as the order contains fewer than 10 boxes. If the customer lives in another zone or if the order is too large, then a delivery charge applies. First, you will create a program with incorrect logic; then you will fix it to demonstrate correct use of parentheses when combining ANDs and ORs.

To create the delivery charge program:

1. Open a new file in your text editor and enter the first few lines of the program. Define constants for `ZONE1`, `ZONE2`, and the `LOWQUANTITY` limit, as well as variables to hold the customer's input string, which will be converted to the zone and number of boxes in the shipment.

```
using System;
public class DemoORAndANDWrongLogic
{
   public static void Main()
   {
```

```
const int ZONE1 = 1, ZONE2 = 2;
const int LOWQUANTITY = 10;
string inputString;
int quantity;
int deliveryZone;
```

2. Enter statements that describe the delivery charge criteria to the user and accept keyboard values for the customer's delivery zone and shipment size.

```
Console.WriteLine("Delivery is free for zone {0} or {1}",
   ZONE1, ZONE2);
Console.WriteLine("when the number of boxes is less than {0}",
   LOWQUANTITY);
Console.WriteLine("Enter delivery zone ");
inputString = Console.ReadLine();
deliveryZone = Convert.ToInt32(inputString);
Console.WriteLine
   ("Enter the number of boxes in the shipment");
inputString = Console.ReadLine();
quantity = Convert.ToInt32(inputString);
```

3. Write a compound `if` statement that appears to test whether the customer lives in Zone 1 or 2 and has a shipment consisting of fewer than 10 boxes.

```
if(deliveryZone == ZONE1 || deliveryZone == ZONE2    &&
   quantity < LOWQUANTITY)
        Console.WriteLine("Delivery is free");
else
   Console.WriteLine("A delivery charge applies");
```

4. Add closing curly braces for the `Main()` method and for the class, and save the file as **DemoORAndANDWrongLogic.cs**. Compile and execute the program. Enter values for the zone and shipment size. The program appears to run correctly until you enter a shipment for Zone 1 that exceeds nine boxes. Such a shipment should not be free, but the output indicates that it is. Figure 3-22 shows the output.

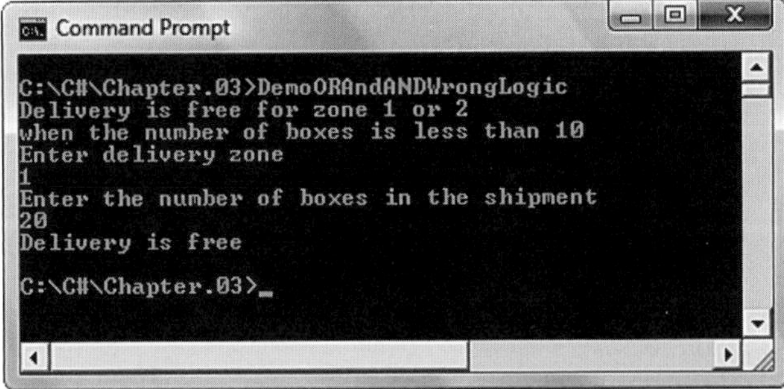

Figure 3-22 Sample execution of `DemoORAndANDWrongLogic` program

5. To remedy the problem, insert parentheses around the expression `deliveryZone == ZONE1 || deliveryZone == ZONE2` within the `if` statement in the `Main()` method. Change the class name to `DemoORAndAND` (removing *WrongLogic*). Save the new version of the program as **DemoORAndAND.cs**. When you compile and execute this version of the program, every combination of zone and quantity values should work correctly. Figure 3-23 shows the output for a Zone 1 delivery of 20 boxes.

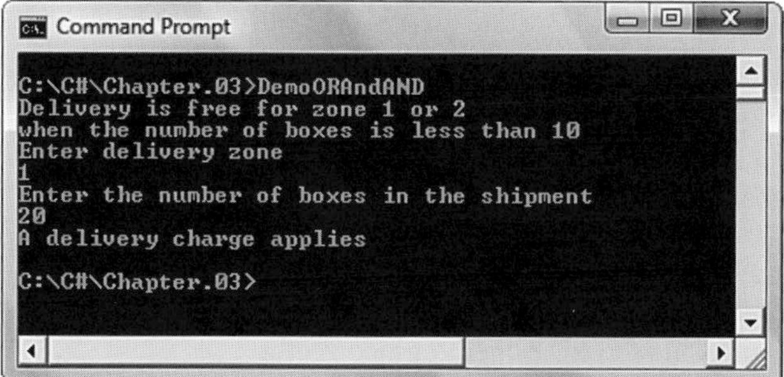

Figure 3-23 Output of `DemoORAndAND` program when user enters 1 and 20

CHAPTER SUMMARY

- A flowchart is a pictorial tool that helps you understand a program's logic. A decision structure is one that involves choosing between alternative courses of action based on some value within a program.
- You use an `if` statement to make a single-alternative decision. The `if` statement takes the form `if(expression) statement;`. When you want to execute multiple statements conditionally, you can place the statements within a block defined by curly braces.
- When you make a dual-alternative decision, you can use an `if-else` statement. The `if-else` statement takes the following form:

```
if(expression) statement1;
else statement2;
```

  Just as you can block several statements so they all execute when an expression within an `if` is `true`, you can block multiple statements after an `else` so they all execute when the evaluated expression is `false`.
- You can use the conditional AND operator (or simply the AND operator) within a Boolean expression to determine whether two expressions are both `true`. The AND operator is written as two ampersands (`&&`). When you use the AND operator, you must include a complete Boolean expression on each side of the `&&` operator.

- You can use the conditional OR operator (or simply the OR operator) when you want some action to occur when one or both of two conditions are `true`. The OR operator is written as `||`.
- When you combine AND and OR operators within the same Boolean expression without parentheses, the AND operators take precedence, meaning their Boolean values are evaluated first.
- The `switch` statement tests a single variable against a series of exact matches.
- The conditional operator is used as an abbreviated version of the `if-else` statement. It requires three expressions separated with a question mark and a colon.
- You use the NOT operator, which is written as an exclamation point (!), to negate the result of any Boolean expression.
- Common errors when making decisions include using the assignment operator instead of the comparison operator, inserting a semicolon after the Boolean expression in an `if` statement, failing to block a set of statements when they should be blocked, failing to include a complete Boolean expression on each side of an `&&` or `||` operator in an `if` statement, performing a range check incorrectly or inefficiently, using the wrong operator with AND and OR, and using the NOT operator incorrectly.

KEY TERMS

Pseudocode is a tool that helps programmers plan a program's logic by writing plain English statements.

A **flowchart** is a tool that helps programmers plan a program's logic by writing program steps in diagram form, as a series of shapes connected by arrows.

A **sequence structure** is a unit of program logic in which one step follows another unconditionally.

A **decision structure** is a unit of program logic that involves choosing between alternative courses of action based on some value.

An **`if` statement** is used to make a single-alternative decision.

A **block** is a collection of one or more statements contained within a pair of curly braces.

A **nested `if`** statement is one in which one decision structure is contained within another.

Dual-alternative decisions have two possible outcomes.

An **`if-else` statement** performs a dual-alternative decision.

The **conditional AND operator** (or simply the **AND operator**) determines whether two expressions are both `true`; it is written using two ampersands (`&&`).

Short-circuit evaluation is the C# feature in which parts of an AND or OR expression are evaluated only as far as necessary to determine whether the entire expression is `true` or `false`.

The **conditional OR operator** (or simply the **OR operator**) determines whether at least one of two conditions is `true`; it is written using two pipes (`||`).

The **Boolean logical AND** operator determines whether two expressions are both `true`; it is written using a single ampersand (&). Unlike the conditional AND operator, it does not use short-circuit evaluation.

The **Boolean logical inclusive OR** operator determines whether at least one of two conditions is `true`; it is written using a single pipe (|). Unlike the conditional OR operator, it does not use short-circuit evaluation.

A **side effect** is an unintended consequence.

The **`switch` structure** tests a single variable against a series of exact matches.

The keyword **`switch`** starts a `switch` structure.

The **`switch` expression** is a condition in a `switch` statement enclosed in parentheses.

The keyword **`case`** in a `switch` structure is followed by one of the possible values that might equal the `switch` expression.

A **`case` label** identifies a course of action in a `switch` structure.

The keyword **`break`** optionally terminates a `switch` structure at the end of each `case`.

The keyword **`default`** optionally is used prior to any action that should occur if the test expression in a `case` structure does not match any `case`.

The **governing type** of a `switch` statement is established by the `switch` expression. The governing type can be `sbyte`, `byte`, `short`, `ushort`, `int`, `uint`, `long`, `ulong`, `char`, `string`, or `enum`.

An **`enum`** is an enumeration—a programmer-defined type that declares a set of constants.

The **conditional operator** is used as an abbreviated version of the `if-else` statement; it requires three expressions separated by a question mark and a colon.

A **ternary** operator requires three arguments.

The **NOT operator** (!) negates the result of any Boolean expression.

A **range check** is a series of `if` statements that determine whether a value falls within a specified range.

REVIEW QUESTIONS

1. What is the output of the following code segment?

```
int a = 3, b = 4;
if(a == b)
   Console.Write("Black ");
   Console.WriteLine("White");
```

a. Black
b. White
c. Black White
d. nothing

2. What is the output of the following code segment?

```
int a = 3, b = 4;
if(a < b)
{
   Console.Write("Black ");
   Console.WriteLine("White");
}
```

a. Black
b. White
c. Black White
d. nothing

3. What is the output of the following code segment?

```
int a = 3, b = 4;
if(a > b)
   Console.Write("Black ");
else
   Console.WriteLine("White");
```

a. Black
b. White
c. Black White
d. nothing

4. If the following code segment compiles correctly, what do you know about the variable x?

```
if(x) Console.WriteLine("OK");
```

a. x is an integer variable
b. x is a Boolean variable
c. x is greater than 0
d. none of these

5. What is the output of the following code segment?

```
int c = 6, d = 12;
if(c > d);
   Console.Write("Green ");
   Console.WriteLine("Yellow");
```

a. Green
b. Yellow
c. Green Yellow
d. nothing

6. What is the output of the following code segment?

```
int c = 6, d = 12;
if(c < d)
   if(c > 8)
      Console.Write("Green");
   else
      Console.Write("Yellow");
else
   Console.Write("Blue");
```

a. Green
b. Yellow
c. Blue
d. nothing

7. What is the output of the following code segment?

```
int e = 5, f = 10;
if(e < f && f < 0)
   Console.Write("Red ");
else
   Console.Write("Orange");
```

a. Red
b. Orange
c. Red Orange
d. nothing

8. What is the output of the following code segment?

```
int e = 5, f = 10;
if(e < f || f < 0)
   Console.Write("Red ");
else
   Console.Write("Orange");
```

a. Red
b. Orange
c. Red Orange
d. nothing

9. Which of the following expressions is equivalent to the following code segment?

```
if(g > h)
   if(g < k)
      Console.Write("Brown");
```

a. `if(g > h && g < k) Console.Write("Brown");`
b. `if(g > h && < k) Console.Write("Brown");`
c. `if(g > h || g < k) Console.Write("Brown");`
d. two of these

10. Which of the following expressions assigns `true` to a Boolean variable named `isIDValid` when the `idNumber` is greater than 1000, less than or equal to 9999, or equal to 123456?

a. `isIDValid = (idNumber > 1000 && idNumber <= 9999 && idNumber == 123456)`
b. `isIDValid = (idNumber > 1000 && idNumber <= 9999 || idNumber == 123456)`
c. `isIDValid = ((idNumber > 1000 && idNumber <= 9999) || idNumber == 123456)`
d. two of these

11. Which of the following expressions is equivalent to `a || b && c || d`?

    a. `a && b || c && d`

    b. `(a || b) && (c || d)`

    c. `a || (b && c) || d`

    d. two of these

12. How many `case` labels would a `switch` statement require to be equivalent to the following `if` statement?

```
if(v == 1)
   Console.WriteLine("one");
else
   Console.WriteLine("two");
```

    a. zero

    b. one

    c. two

    d. impossible to tell

13. Falling through a `switch case` is most often prevented by using the ________.

    a. `break` statement

    b. `default` statement

    c. `case` statement

    d. `end` statement

14. If the test expression in a `switch` does not match any of the `case` values, and there is no `default` value, then ________.

    a. a compiler error occurs

    b. a run-time error occurs

    c. the program continues with the next executable statement

    d. the expression is incremented and the `case` values are tested again

15. Which of the following is equivalent to the statement `if(m == 0) d = 0 ; else d = 1;`?

    a. `? m == 0 : d = 0, d = 1;`

    b. `m? d = 0; d = 1;`

    c. `m == 0 ; d = 0; d = 1?`

    d. `m == 0 ? d = 0 : d = 1;`

16. Which of the following C# expressions is equivalent to `a < b && b < c`?

    a. `c > b > a`

    b. `a < b && c >= b`

    c. `!(b <= a) && b < c`

    d. two of these

17. Which of the following C# expressions means, "If `itemNumber` is not 8 or 9, add `TAX` to `price`"?

a.
```
if(itemNumber != 8 || itemNumber != 9)
      price = price + TAX;
```

b.
```
if(itemNumber != 8 && itemNumber != 9)
      price = price + TAX;
```

c.
```
if(itemNumber != 8 && != 9)
      price = price + TAX;
```

d. two of these

18. Which of the following C# expressions means, "If `itemNumber` is 1 or 2 and `quantity` is 12 or more, add `TAX` to `price`"?

a.
```
if(itemNumber = 1 || itemNumber = 2 && quantity >= 12)
      price = price + TAX;
```

b.
```
if(itemNumber == 1 || itemNumber == 2 || quantity >= 12)
      price = price + TAX;
```

c.
```
if(itemNumber == 1 && itemNumber == 2 && quantity >= 12)
      price = price + TAX;
```

d. none of these

19. Which of the following C# expressions means, "If `itemNumber` is 5 and `zone` is 1 or 3, add `TAX` to `price`"?

a.
```
if(itemNumber == 5 && zone == 1 || zone == 3)
      price = price + TAX;
```

b.
```
if(itemNumber == 5 && (zone == 1 || zone == 3))
      price = price + TAX;
```

c.
```
if(itemNumber == 5 && (zone == 1 || 3))
      price = price + TAX;
```

d. two of these

20. Which of the following C# expressions means, "If `itemNumber` is not 100, add `TAX` to `price`"?

a.
```
if(itemNumber != 100)
      price = price + TAX;
```

b.
```
if(!(itemNumber == 100)
      price = price + TAX;
```

c.
```
if(!(itemNumber <100) && !(itemNumber > 100)
      price = price + TAX;
```

d. all of these

EXERCISES

1. Write a program that prompts the user for an hourly pay rate. If the value entered is less than $5.65, display an error message. Save the program as **CheckLowRate.cs**.

2. Write a program that prompts a user for an hourly pay rate. If the value entered is less than $5.65 or greater than $49.99, display an error message. Save the program as **CheckLowAndHighRate.cs**.

3. Write a program that prompts a user for an hourly pay rate. If the user enters values less than $5.65 or greater than $49.99, prompt the user again. If the user enters an invalid value again, display an appropriate error message. If the user enters a valid value on either the first or second attempt, display the pay rate as well as the weekly rate, which is calculated as 40 times the hourly rate. Save the program as **EnsureValidPayRate.cs**.

4. Write a program for a furniture company. Ask the user to choose *P* for pine, *O* for oak, or *M* for mahogany. Show the price of a table manufactured with the chosen wood. Pine tables cost $100, oak tables cost $225, and mahogany tables cost $310. (If the user enters something other than *P*, *O*, or *M*, set the price to 0.) Save the program as **Furniture.cs**.

5. Write a program for a college's admissions office. The user enters a numeric high school grade point average (for example, 3.2) and an admission test score. Print the message "Accept" if the student meets either of the following requirements:

   » A grade point average of 3.0 or higher and an admission test score of at least 60

   » A grade point average of less than 3.0 and an admission test score of at least 80

   If the student does not meet either of the qualification criteria, print "Reject". Save the program as **Admission.cs**.

6. Write a program that prompts the user for an hourly pay rate and hours worked. Compute gross pay (hours times pay rate), withholding tax, and net pay (gross pay minus withholding tax). Withholding tax is computed as a percentage of gross pay based on the following:

Gross Pay	**Withholding Percentage**
Up to and including 300.00	10%
300.01 and up	12%

   Save the program as **Payroll.cs**.

7. Write a program that allows the user to enter two integers and a character. If the character is *A*, add the two integers. If it is *S*, subtract the second integer from the first. If it is *M*, multiply the integers. Display the results of the arithmetic. Save the file as **Calculate.cs**.

8. a. Write an application for a lawn-mowing service. The lawn-mowing season lasts 20 weeks. The weekly fee for mowing a lot under 400 square feet is $25. The fee for a lot that is 400 square feet or more, but under 600 square feet, is $35 per week. The fee for a lot that is 600 square feet or over is $50 per week. Prompt the user for the length and width of a lawn, and then print the weekly mowing fee, as well as the total fee for the 20-week season. Save the file as **Lawn.cs**.

   b. To the `Lawn` application you created in Exercise 8a, add a prompt that asks the user whether the customer wants to pay (1) once, (2) twice, or (3) 20 times per year. If the user enters 1 for once, the fee for the season is simply the seasonal total. If the customer requests two payments, each payment is half the seasonal fee plus a $5 service charge. If the user requests 20 separate payments, add a $3 service charge per week. Display the number of payments the customer must make, each payment amount, and the total for the season. Save the file as **Lawn2.cs**.

9. Write an application that asks a user to enter an IQ score. If the score is a number less than 0 or greater than 200, issue an error message; otherwise, issue an "above average", "average", or "below average" message for scores over, at, or under 100, respectively. Save the file as **IQ.cs**.

DEBUGGING EXERCISES

Each of the following files in the Chapter.03 folder on your Student Disk has syntax and/or logical errors. In each case, determine the problem and fix the program. After you correct the errors, save each file using the same filename preceded with *Fixed*. For example, save DebugThree1.cs as **FixedDebugThree1.cs**.

a. DebugThree1.cs

b. DebugThree2.cs

c. DebugThree3.cs

d. DebugThree4.cs

UP FOR DISCUSSION

1. In this chapter, you learned how computer programs make decisions. Insurance companies use programs to make decisions about your insurability as well as the rates you will be charged for health and life insurance policies. For example, certain preexisting conditions may raise your insurance premiums considerably. Is it ethical for insurance companies to access your health records and then make insurance decisions about you?

2. Job applications are sometimes screened by software that makes decisions about a candidate's suitability based on keywords in the applications. For example, when a help-wanted ad lists "management experience," the presence of those exact words might determine which résumés are chosen for further scrutiny. Is such screening fair to applicants?
3. Medical facilities often have more patients waiting for organ transplants than there are available organs. Suppose you have been asked to write a computer program that selects which of several candidates should receive an available organ. What data would you want on file to use in your program, and what decisions would you make based on the data? What data do you think others might use that you would not use?

CHAPTER FOUR

4

LOOPING

In this chapter you will:

- Learn about the loop structure
- Learn how to create loops using the `while` statement
- Learn how to create loops using the `for` statement
- Learn how to create loops using the `do` statement
- Use nested loops
- Accumulate totals
- Understand how to improve loop performance

In Chapter 3, you learned how computers make decisions. Looping allows a program to repeat tasks based on a decision. For example, programs that produce thousands of paychecks or invoices rely on the ability to loop to repeat instructions. Likewise, programs that repeatedly prompt you for a valid credit card number or for the correct answer to a tutorial question require the ability to loop to do their jobs efficiently. In this chapter, you will learn to create loops in C# programs.

LEARNING ABOUT THE LOOP STRUCTURE

> **NOTE** One execution of any loop is called an **iteration**.

If making decisions is what makes programs seem smart, looping is what makes programs seem powerful. A **loop** is a structure that allows repeated execution of a block of statements. Within a looping structure, a Boolean expression is evaluated. If it is `true`, a block of statements called the **loop body** executes, and the Boolean expression is evaluated again. As long as the expression is `true`, the statements in the loop body continue to execute. When the Boolean evaluation is `false`, the loop ends. Figure 4-1 shows a diagram of the logic of a loop.

> **NOTE** Recall from Chapter 3 that a block of statements might be a single statement with or without curly braces, or it might be multiple statements with curly braces.

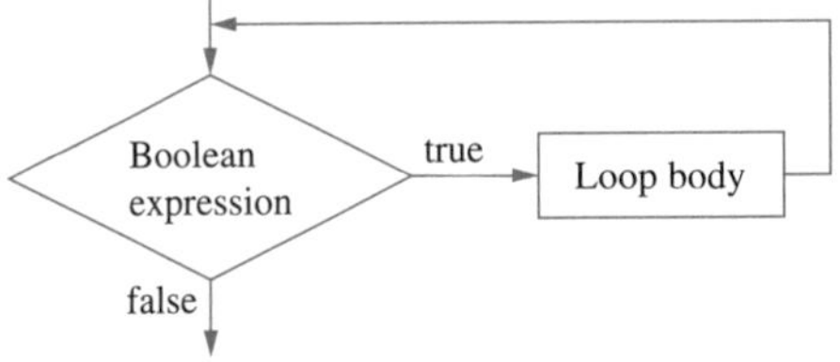

Figure 4-1 Flowchart of a loop structure

In C#, you can use several mechanisms to create loops. In this chapter, you will learn to use three types of loops:

- A `while` loop, in which the loop-controlling Boolean expression is the first statement in the loop
- A `for` loop, which is usually used as a concise format in which to execute loops
- A `do` loop (or `do-while` loop), in which the loop-controlling Boolean expression is the last statement in the loop

TWO TRUTHS AND A LIE: LEARNING ABOUT THE LOOP STRUCTURE

1. A loop is a structure that allows repeated execution of a block of statements.
2. In a loop, when a tested expression is `true`, the loop ends.
3. In a `while` loop, a loop-controlling Boolean expression is the first statement.

The false statement is #2. A loop continues while a tested expression is `true` and ends when it is `false`.

USING THE while LOOP

You can use a **while loop** to execute a body of statements continuously as long as some condition continues to be true. A while loop consists of the keyword while, followed by a Boolean expression within parentheses, followed by the body of the loop. The body can be a single statement or a block of statements surrounded by curly braces.

>NOTE The evaluated Boolean expression in a while statement can be a compound expression that uses ANDs and ORs (just as within an if statement).

For example, the following code shows an integer declaration followed by a loop that causes the message "Hello" to display (theoretically) forever because there is no code to end the loop. A loop that never ends is called an **infinite loop**.

```
int number = 1;
while (number > 0)
   Console.WriteLine("Hello");
```

In this loop, the expression number > 0 evaluates as true, and "Hello" is displayed. The expression number > 0 evaluates as true again and "Hello" is displayed again. Because nothing ever alters the value of number, the loop runs forever, evaluating the same Boolean expression and repeatedly printing "Hello" (as long as computer memory and hardware allow).

>NOTE An infinite loop does not actually execute infinitely. All programs run with the help of computer memory and hardware, both of which have finite capacities.

>NOTE It is always a bad idea to write an infinite loop, although even experienced programmers write them by accident. If you ever find yourself in the midst of executing an infinite loop, you can break out by holding down the Ctrl key and pressing the C key or the Break (Pause) key.

To make a while loop end correctly, three separate actions should occur:

- A variable, the **loop control variable**, is initialized (before entering the loop).
- The loop control variable is tested in the while expression.
- The body of the while statement must take some action that alters the value of the loop control variable (so that the while expression eventually evaluates as false).

For example, Figure 4-2 shows the logic for a loop that displays "Hello" four times. The variable number is initialized to 1 and a constant, LIMIT, is initialized to 5. The variable is less

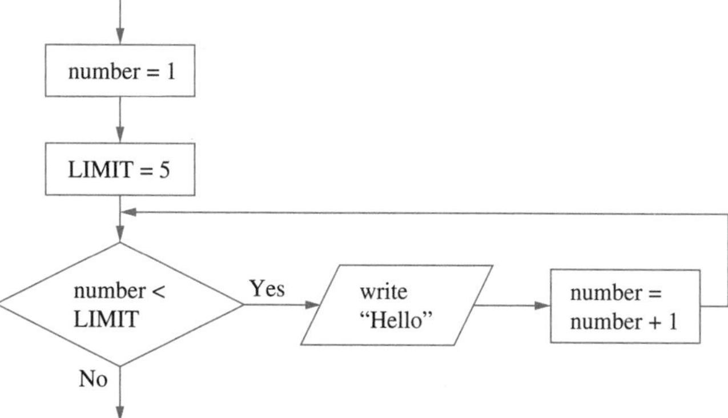

Figure 4-2 Flowchart for the logic of a while loop whose body executes four times

than LIMIT, and so the loop body executes. The loop body shown in Figure 4-2 contains two statements. The first prints "Hello" and the second adds 1 to number. The next time number is evaluated, its value is 2, which is still less than LIMIT, so the loop body executes again. "Hello" prints a third time and the number becomes 4, then "Hello" prints a fourth time and the number becomes 5. Now when the expression number < LIMIT evaluates, it is false, so the loop ends. If there were any subsequent statements following the while loop's closing curly brace, they would execute after the loop was finished.

Figure 4-3 shows a C# program that uses the same logic as diagrammed in Figure 4-2. After the declarations, the shaded while expression compares number to LIMIT. The two statements that execute each time the Boolean expression is true are blocked using a pair of curly braces. Figure 4-4 shows the output.

```
using System;
public class FourHellos
{
   public static void Main()
   {
      int number = 1;
      const int LIMIT = 5;
      while(number < LIMIT)
      {
         Console.WriteLine("Hello");
         number = number + 1;
      }
   }
}
```

Figure 4-3 A program that contains a while loop whose body executes four times

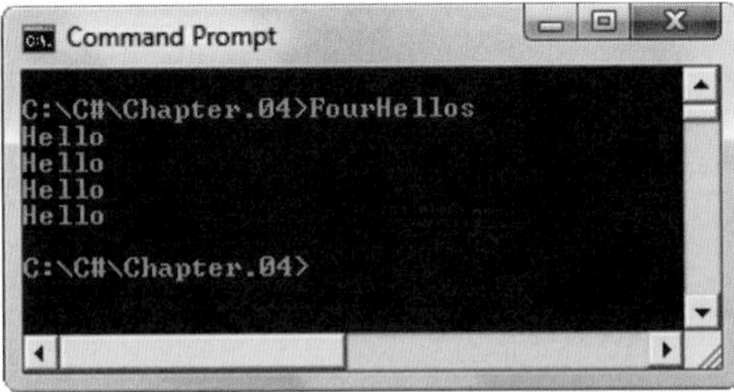

Figure 4-4 Output of FourHellos program

NOTE To an algebra student, a statement such as number = number + 1; looks wrong—a value can never be one more than itself. In C# (and many other programming languages), however, the expression number = number + 1; isn't a mathematical equation; rather, it is a programming language statement that takes the value of number, adds 1 to it, and assigns the new value back into number. Recall from Chapter 2 that you also can use a shortcut operator to increase the value of a variable by 1. Instead of number = number + 1, you could achieve the same final result by writing number++, ++number, or number += 1.

The curly braces surrounding the body of the `while` loop in Figure 4-3 are important. If they are omitted, the `while` loop ends at the end of the "Hello" statement. Adding 1 to `number` would no longer be part of the loop body, so an infinite loop would be created. Even if the statement `number = number + 1;` was indented under the `while` statement, it would not be part of the loop without the surrounding curly braces. Figure 4-5 shows the incorrect logic that would result from omitting the curly braces.

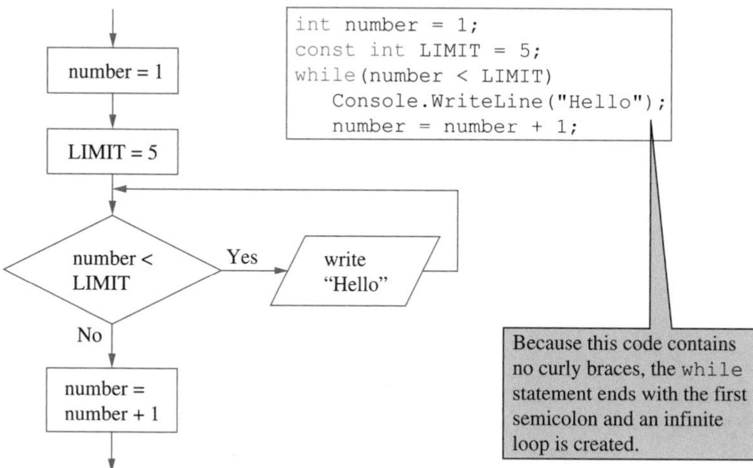

number = 1
LIMIT = 5
number < LIMIT
Yes
write "Hello"
No
number = number + 1
int number = 1;
const int LIMIT = 5;
while(number < LIMIT)
Console.WriteLine("Hello");
number = number + 1;
Because this code contains no curly braces, the while statement ends with the first semicolon and an infinite loop is created.

Figure 4-5 Incorrect logic when curly braces are omitted from the loop in the `FourHellos` program

Also, if a semicolon is mistakenly placed at the end of the partial statement, as in Figure 4-6, then the loop is also infinite. This loop has an **empty body**, or a body with no statements in it. In this case, `number` is initialized to 1, the Boolean expression `number < LIMIT` evaluates, and because it is `true`, the loop body is entered. Because the loop body is empty, ending at the semicolon, no action takes place, and the Boolean expression evaluates again. It is still `true` (nothing has changed), so the empty body is entered again, and the infinite loop continues. The program can never progress to either the statement that displays "Hello" or the statement that increases the value of `number`. The fact that these two statements are blocked using curly braces has no effect because of the incorrectly placed semicolon.

Within a correctly functioning loop's body, you can change the value of the loop control variable in a number of ways. Many loop control variable values are altered by **incrementing**, or adding to them, as in Figures 4-2 and 4-3. Other loops are controlled by reducing, or **decrementing**, a variable and testing whether the value remains greater than some benchmark value. A loop for which the number of iterations is predetermined is called a **definite loop** or **counted loop**. Often, the value of a loop control variable is not altered by arithmetic, but instead is altered by user input. For example, perhaps you want to continue performing some task while the user indicates a desire to continue. In that case, you do not know when you write the program whether the loop will be executed two times, 200 times, or not at all. This type of loop is an **indefinite loop**.

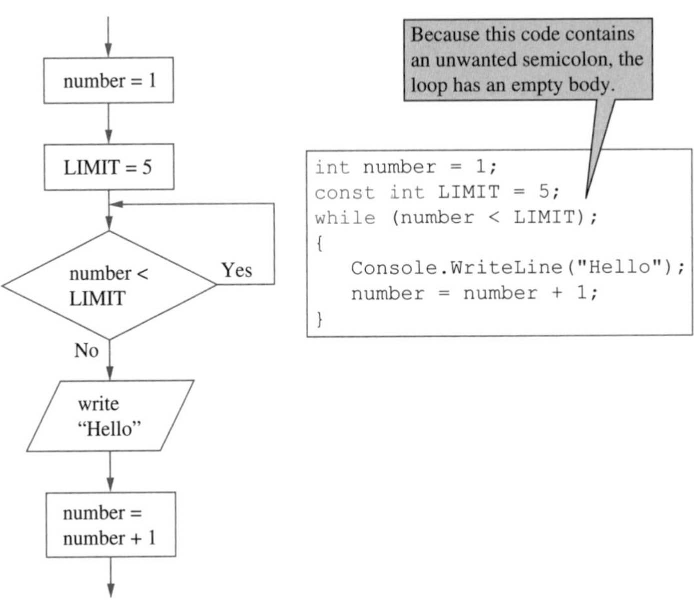
number = 1
LIMIT = 5
number < LIMIT
Yes
No
write "Hello"
number = number + 1
Because this code contains an unwanted semicolon, the loop has an empty body.
int number = 1;
const int LIMIT = 5;
while (number < LIMIT);
{
Console.WriteLine("Hello");
number = number + 1;
}

Figure 4-6 Incorrect logic when an unwanted semicolon is mistakenly added to the loop in the `FourHellos` program

Consider a program that displays a bank balance and asks if the user wants to see what the balance will be after one year of interest has accumulated. Each time the user indicates she wants to continue, an increased balance appears. When the user finally indicates she has had enough, the program ends. The program appears in Figure 4-7, and a typical execution appears in Figure 4-8.

> **»NOTE** The program shown in Figure 4-7 continues to display bank balances while the response is *Y*. It could also be written to display while the response is not *N*, as in `while (response != 'N')....` A value such as `'Y'` or `'N'` that a user must supply to stop a loop is called a **sentinel value**.

The program shown in Figure 4-7 contains two variables and a constant that are involved in the looping process: a bank balance, an interest rate, and a response. The `response` is the loop control variable. It is initialized when the program asks the user, "Do you want to see your balance?" and reads the response. The loop control variable is tested with `while(response == 'Y')`. If the user types any response other than *Y*, then the loop body never executes; instead, the next statement to execute is the display of "Have a nice day!". However, if the user enters *Y*, then all five statements within the loop body execute. The current balance is displayed, and the program increases the balance by the interest rate value; this value will not be displayed unless the user requests another loop repetition. Within the loop, the program prompts the user and reads in a new value for `response`. This is the statement that potentially alters the loop control variable. The loop ends with

```
using System;
public class LoopingBankBal
{
   public static void Main()
   {
      double bankBal = 1000;
      const double INT_RATE = 0.04;
      string inputString;
      char response;
      Console.Write("Do you want to see your balance? Y or N ...");
      inputString = Console.ReadLine();
      response = Convert.ToChar(inputString);
      while(response == 'Y')
      {
         Console.WriteLine("Bank balance is {0}", bankBal.ToString("C"));
         bankBal = bankBal + bankBal * INT_RATE;
         Console.Write("Do you want to see next year's balance? Y or N ...");
         inputString = Console.ReadLine();
         response = Convert.ToChar(inputString);
      }
      Console.WriteLine("Have a nice day!");
   }
}
```

Figure 4-7 `LoopingBankBal` program

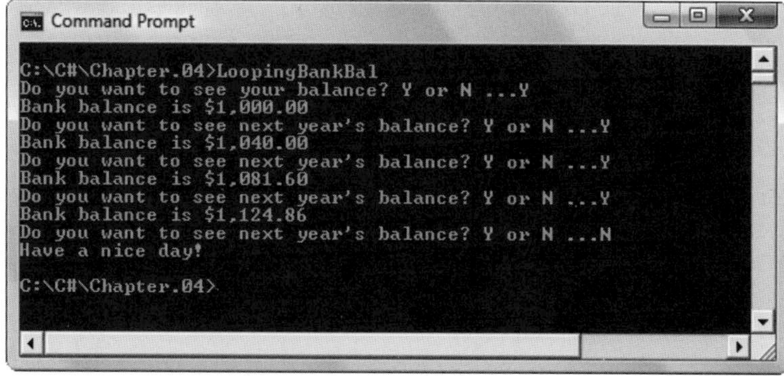

Figure 4-8 Typical execution of the `LoopingBankBal` program

a closing curly brace, and program control returns to the top of the loop, where the Boolean expression in the `while` loop is tested again. If the user typed *Y* at the last prompt, then the loop is entered and the increased `bankBal` value that was calculated during the last loop cycle is finally displayed.

»NOTE In C#, character data is case sensitive. If a program tests `response == 'Y'`, a user response of *y* will result in a `false` evaluation. Beware of the pitfall of writing a loop similar to `while(response != 'Y' || response != 'y')...` to test both for uppercase and lowercase versions of the response. Every character is either not 'Y' or not 'y', even 'Y' and 'y'. The correct loop begins with `while(response != 'Y' && response != 'y')....`

»TWO TRUTHS AND A LIE: USING THE `while` LOOP

1. To make a `while` loop that executes correctly, a loop control variable is initialized before entering the loop.
2. To make a `while` loop that executes correctly, the loop control variable is tested in the `while` expression.
3. To make a `while` loop that executes correctly, the body of the `while` statement must never alter the value of the loop control variable.

The false statement is #3. To make a `while` loop that executes correctly, the body of the `while` statement must take some action that alters the value of the loop control variable.

USING THE `for` LOOP

Each time the `LoopingBankBal` program in Figure 4-7 executes, the user might continue the loop a different number of times, which makes it an indefinite loop. You can use a `while` loop for either definite or indefinite loops. To write either type of `while` loop, you initialize a loop control variable, and as long as its test expression is `true`, you continue to execute the body of the `while` loop. To avoid an infinite loop, the body of the `while` loop must contain a statement that alters the loop control variable.

Because you need definite loops so frequently when you write programs, C# provides a shorthand way to create such a loop. This shorthand structure is called a **`for` loop**. With a `for` loop, you can indicate the starting value for the loop control variable, the test condition that controls loop entry, and the expression that alters the loop control variable, all in one convenient place.

You begin a `for` statement with the keyword `for` followed by a set of parentheses. Within the parentheses are three sections separated by exactly two semicolons. The three sections are usually used for:

- » Initializing the loop control variable
- » Testing the loop control variable
- » Updating the loop control variable

»NOTE The amount by which a loop control variable increases or decreases on each cycle through the loop is often called the **step value**. That's because in the BASIC programming language, the keyword `STEP` was actually used in `for` loops.

The body of the `for` statement follows the parentheses. As with an `if` or a `while` statement, you can use a single statement as the body of a `for` loop, or you can use a block of statements enclosed in curly braces. The `while` and `for` statements shown in Figure 4-9 produce the same output—the integers 1 through 10.

Within the parentheses of the `for` statement shown in Figure 4-9, the initialization section prior to the first semicolon sets a variable named `x` to 1. The program will execute this statement once, no matter how many times the body of the `for` loop eventually executes.

```
// Declare loop control variable and limit
int x;
const int LIMIT = 10

// Using a while loop to display 1 through 10
x = 1;
while(x <= LIMIT)
{
   Console.WriteLine(x);
   ++x;
}

// Using a for loop to display 1 through 10
for(x = 1; x <= LIMIT; ++x)
   Console.WriteLine(x);
```

Figure 4-9 Printing integers 1 through 10 with `while` and `for` loops

After the initialization expression executes, program control passes to the middle, or test, section of the `for` statement. If the Boolean expression found there evaluates to `true`, then the body of the `for` loop is entered. In the program segment shown in Figure 4-9, `x` is initialized to 1, so when `x <= LIMIT` is tested, it evaluates to `true` and the loop body prints the value of `x`.

After the loop body executes, the final one-third of the `for` expression (the update section) executes, and `x` increases to 2. Following the third section, program control returns to the second (test) section, where `x` is compared to `LIMIT` a second time. Because the value of `x` is 2, it is still less than or equal to `LIMIT`, so the body of the `for` loop executes. The value of `x` is displayed. Then the third, altering portion of the `for` statement executes again. The variable `x` increases to 3, and the `for` loop continues.

Eventually, when `x` is *not* less than or equal to `LIMIT` (after 1 through 10 have printed), the `for` loop ends, and the program continues with any statements that follow the `for` loop.

Although the three sections of the `for` loop are most commonly used for initializing, testing, and incrementing, you can also perform other tasks:

» You can initialize more than one variable by placing commas between the separate statements, as in the following:

```
for(g = 0, h = 1; g < 6; ++g)
```

» You can declare a new variable, as in the following:

```
for(int k = 0; k < 5; ++k)
```

» In this example, `k` is declared to be an `int` and is initialized to 0. This technique is used frequently when the variable exists only to control the loop and for no other purpose. When a variable is declared inside a loop, as `k` is in this example, it can be referenced only for the duration of the loop body; then it is **out of scope**, which means it is not usable because it has ceased to exist.

- You can perform more than one test by evaluating compound conditions, as in the following:

  ```
  for(g = 0; g < 3 && h > 1; ++g)
  ```

- You can decrement or perform some other task at the end of the loop's execution, as in:

  ```
  for(g = 5; g >= 1; --g)
  ```

- You can perform multiple tasks at the end of the loop's execution, as in:

  ```
  for(g = 0; g < 5; ++g, ++h)
  ```

- You can leave one or more portions of the `for` expression empty, although the two semicolons are still required as placeholders to separate the three sections.

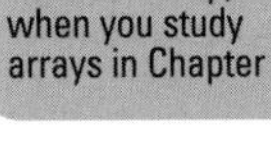

NOTE You will learn about a similar loop, the `foreach` loop, when you study arrays in Chapter 5.

Generally, you should use the `for` loop for its intended purpose, which is a shorthand way of programming a definite loop.

Just as with a decision or a `while` loop, statements in a `for` loop can be blocked. For example, the following loop displays "Hello" and "Goodbye" four times each:

```
const int TIMES = 4;
for(int var = 0; var < TIMES; ++var)
{
   Console.WriteLine("Hello");
   Console.WriteLine("Goodbye");
}
```

Without the curly braces in this code, "Hello" would be displayed four times, but "Goodbye" would be displayed only once.

TWO TRUTHS AND A LIE: USING THE `for` LOOP

1. The following statement displays the numbers 3 through 6:

   ```
   for(int x = 3; x <= 6; ++x)
      Console.WriteLine(x);
   ```

2. The following statement displays the numbers 4 through 9:

   ```
   for(int x = 3; x < 9; ++x)
      Console.WriteLine(x + 1);
   ```

3. The following statement displays the numbers 5 through 12:

   ```
   for(int x = 5; x < 12; ++x)
      Console.WriteLine(x);
   ```

The false statement is #3. That loop only displays the numbers 5 through 11, because when x is 12, the loop body is not entered.

USING THE do LOOP

With each of the loops you have learned about so far, the loop body might execute many times, but it is also possible that the loop will not execute at all. For example, recall the bank balance program that displays compound interest, part of which is shown in Figure 4-10. The loop begins by testing the value of `response`. If the user has not entered *Y*, the loop body never executes. The `while` loop checks a value at the "top" of the loop before the body has a chance to execute.

```
Console.Write("Do you want to see your balance? Y or N ...");
inputString = Console.ReadLine();
response = Convert.ToChar(inputString);
while(response == 'Y')
{
   Console.WriteLine("Bank balance is {0}", bankBal.ToString("C"));
   bankBal = bankBal + bankBal * INT_RATE;
   Console.Write("Do you want to see next year's balance? Y or N ...");
   inputString = Console.ReadLine();
   response = Convert.ToChar(inputString);
}
```

Figure 4-10 Part of the bank balance program using a `while` loop

Sometimes you might need a loop body to execute at least one time. If so, you want to write a loop that checks at the "bottom" of the loop after the first iteration. The **do loop** checks the bottom of the loop after one repetition has occurred. Figure 4-11 shows a diagram of the structure of a do loop.

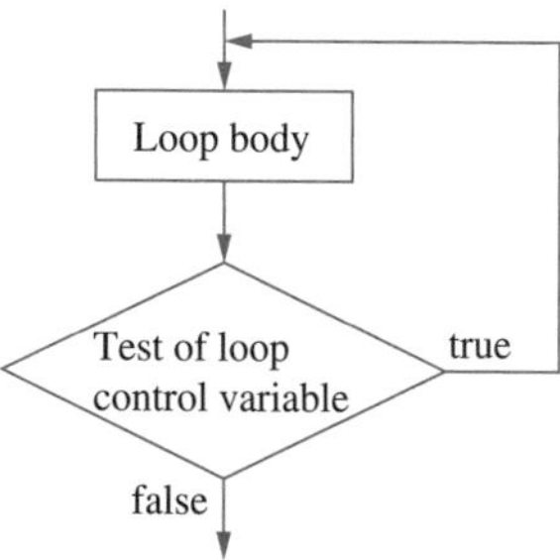

Figure 4-11 Flowchart of a do loop

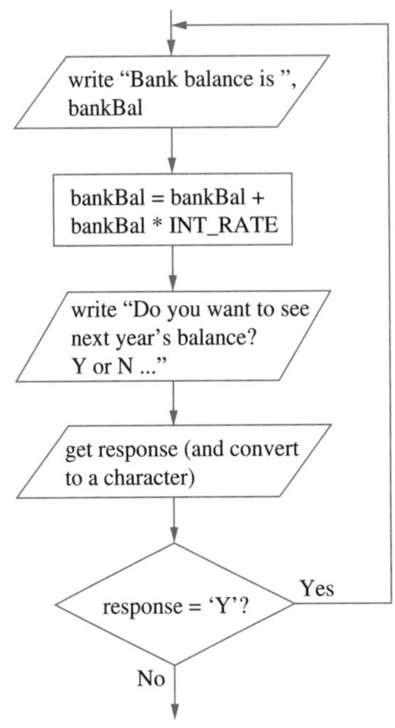


```
do
{
   Console.WriteLine("Bank balance is {0}", bankBal.ToString("C"));
   bankBal = bankBal + bankBal * INT_RATE;
   Console.Write("Do you want to see next year's balance? Y or N ...");
   inputString = Console.ReadLineGetChar();
   response = Convert.ToChar(inputString);
}  while(response == 'Y');
```

With the do loop, the loop control variable is tested after the loop body has executed one time.

Figure 4-12 Part of the bank balance program using a do loop

Figure 4-12 shows the logic for a do loop in a bank balance program, along with the C# code. The loop starts with the keyword do. The body of the loop follows and is contained within curly braces. Within the loop, the next balance is calculated and the user is prompted for a response. The Boolean expression that controls loop execution is written using a while statement, placed after the loop body. The bankBal variable is output the first time before the user has any option of responding. At the end of the loop, the user is prompted, "Do you want to see next year's balance? Y or N . . . ". Now the user has the option of seeing more balances, but the first view of the balance was unavoidable. The user's response is checked at the bottom of the loop. If it is *Y*, then the loop repeats.

»NOTE In a `do` loop, as a matter of style, many programmers prefer to align the `while` expression with the `do` keyword that starts the loop. Others feel that placing the `while` expression on its own line increases the chances that readers might misinterpret the line as the start of its own `while` statement instead of marking the end of a `do` statement.

In any situation where you want to loop, you never are required to use a `do` loop. Within the bank balance example, you could unconditionally display the bank balance once, prompt the user, and then start a `while` loop that might not be entered. However, when you know you want to perform some task at least one time, the `do` loop is convenient.

»NOTE A `while` loop is a **pretest loop**—one in which the loop control variable is tested before the loop body executes. The `do-while` loop is a **posttest loop**—one in which the loop control variable is tested after the loop body executes.

»TWO TRUTHS AND A LIE: USING THE `do` LOOP

1. The `do` loop checks the bottom of the loop after one repetition has occurred.
2. The Boolean expression that controls `do` loop execution is written using a `do` statement, placed after the loop body.
3. You never are required to use a `do` loop; you can always substitute one execution of the body statements followed by a `while` loop.

The false statement is #2. The Boolean expression that controls `do` loop execution is written using a `while` statement, placed after the loop body.

USING NESTED LOOPS

Just as `if` statements can be nested, so can loop statements. You can place a `while` loop within a `while` loop, a `for` loop within a `for` loop, a `while` loop within a `for` loop, or any other combination. When loops are nested, each pair contains an **inner loop** and an **outer loop**. The inner loop must be entirely contained within the outer loop; loops can never overlap. Figure 4-13 shows a diagram in which the shaded loop is nested within another loop; the shaded area is the inner loop as well as the body of the outer loop.

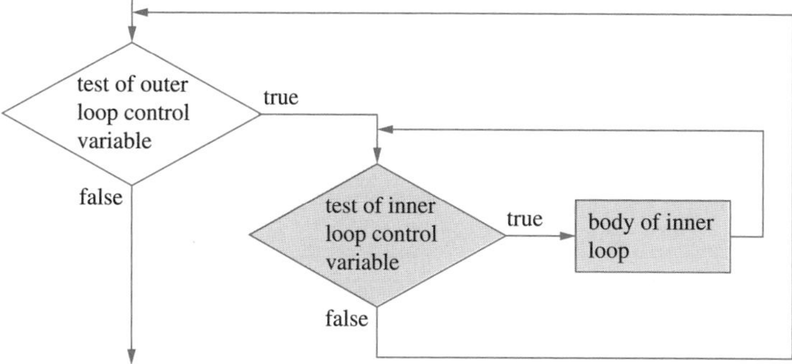

Figure 4-13 Nested loops

Suppose you want to display future bank balances for different years at a variety of interest rates. Figure 4-14 shows an application that contains an outer loop controlled by interest rates (starting with the first shaded statement in the figure) and an inner loop controlled by years (starting with the second shaded statement). The application displays annually compounded interest on $1000 at 4%, 6%, and 8% interest rates for 1 through 5 years. Figure 4-15 shows the output.

When you use a loop within a loop, you should always think of the outer loop as the all-encompassing loop. When you describe the task at hand, you often use the word “each” to refer to the inner loop. For example, if you wanted to print balances for different

```
using System;
public class LoopingBankBal2
{
   public static void Main()
   {
      double bankBal;
      double rate;
      int year;
      const double START_BAL = 1000;
      const double START_INT = 0.04;
      const double INT_INCREASE = 0.02;
      const double LAST_INT = 0.08;
      const int END_YEAR = 5;
      for(rate = START_INT; rate <= LAST_INT; rate += INT_INCREASE)
      {
         bankBal = START_BAL;
         Console.WriteLine("Starting bank balance is {0}",
             bankBal.ToString("C"));
         Console.WriteLine("  Interest Rate: {0}",
             rate.ToString("P"));
         for(year = 1; year <= END_YEAR; ++year)
         {
            bankBal = bankBal + bankBal * rate;
            Console.WriteLine("   After year {0}, bank balance is {1}",
                year, bankBal.ToString("C"));
         }
      }
   }
}
```

Figure 4-14 The `LoopingBankBal2` program

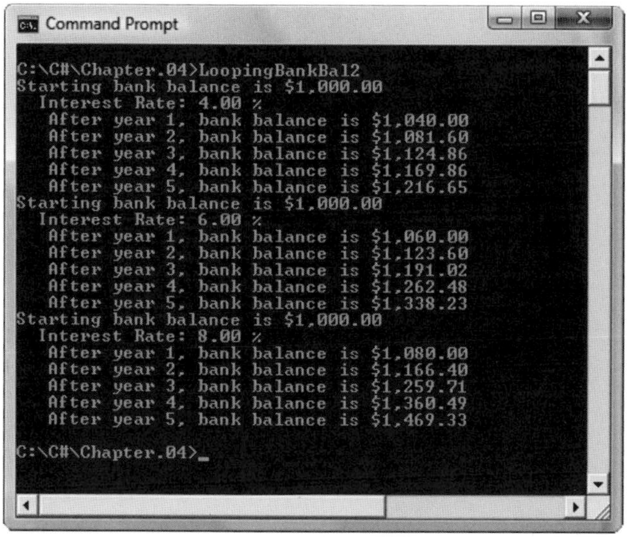

```
C:\C#\Chapter.04>LoopingBankBal2
Starting bank balance is $1,000.00
  Interest Rate: 4.00 %
   After year 1, bank balance is $1,040.00
   After year 2, bank balance is $1,081.60
   After year 3, bank balance is $1,124.86
   After year 4, bank balance is $1,169.86
   After year 5, bank balance is $1,216.65
Starting bank balance is $1,000.00
  Interest Rate: 6.00 %
   After year 1, bank balance is $1,060.00
   After year 2, bank balance is $1,123.60
   After year 3, bank balance is $1,191.02
   After year 4, bank balance is $1,262.48
   After year 5, bank balance is $1,338.23
Starting bank balance is $1,000.00
  Interest Rate: 8.00 %
   After year 1, bank balance is $1,080.00
   After year 2, bank balance is $1,166.40
   After year 3, bank balance is $1,259.71
   After year 4, bank balance is $1,360.49
   After year 5, bank balance is $1,469.33

C:\C#\Chapter.04>_
```

Figure 4-15 Output of the `LoopingBankBal2` program

interest rates each year for 10 years, you could appropriately initialize some constants as follows:

```
const double RATE1 = 0.03;
const double RATE2= 0.07
const double RATE_INCREASE = 0.01
const int END_YEAR = 10;
```

Then you could use the following nested `for` loops:

```
for(rate = RATE1; rate <= RATE2; rate += RATE_INCREASE)
   for(year = 1; year <= END_YEAR; ++year)
      Console.WriteLine(bankBal + bankBal * rate);
```

However, if you wanted to print balances for years 1 through 10 for each possible interest rate, you would use the following:

```
for(year = 1; year <= END_YEAR; ++year)
   for(rate = RATE1; rate <= RATE2; rate += RATE_INCREASE)
      Console.WriteLine(bankBal + bankBal * rate);
```

In both of these examples, the same 50 values would be displayed—five different interest rates for 10 years. However, in the first example, balances for years 1 through 10 would display "within" each interest rate, and in the second example, each balance for each interest rate would display "within" each year, 1 through 10. In other words, in the first example, the first 10 amounts to display would be annual values using a rate of 0.03, and in the second example, the first five amounts to display would be based on different interest values in the first year.

»TWO TRUTHS AND A LIE: USING NESTED LOOPS

1. The body of the following loop executes six times:

```
for(a = 1; a < 4; ++a)
   for(b = 2; b < 3; ++b)
```

2. The body of the following loop executes four times:

```
for(c = 1; c < 3; ++c)
   for(d = 1; d < 3; ++d)
```

3. The body of the following loop executes 15 times:

```
for(e = 1; e <= 5; ++e)
   for(f = 2; f <= 4; ++f)
```

The false statement is #1. That loop executes only three times. First, `a = 1`, and it is less than 4, so the inner loop executes. In the inner loop, `b` is 2 and it is less than 3, so the loop body executes a second time. Then `a` becomes 3, and it is still less than 4, so the inner loop executes a third time. Then `a` becomes 4, and it is no longer less than 4, so the outer loop is done.

ACCUMULATING TOTALS

Many computer programs display totals. When you receive a credit card or telephone service bill, you are usually provided with individual transaction details, but you are most interested in the total bill. Similarly, some programs total the number of credit hours generated by college students, the gross payroll for all employees of a company, or the total accounts receivable value for an organization. These totals are **accumulated**—that is, gathered together and added into a final sum by processing individual records one at a time in a loop.

Figure 4-16 shows an example of an interactive program that accumulates the user's total purchases. The program prompts the user to enter a purchase price or 0 to quit. While the user continues to enter nonzero values, the amounts are added to a total. With each pass through the loop, the total is calculated to be its current amount plus the new purchase amount. After the user enters the loop-terminating 0, the accumulated total can be displayed. Figure 4-17 shows a typical program execution.

In the application in Figure 4-16, it is very important that the `total` variable used for accumulation is initialized to 0. When it is not, the program will not compile. When `total` is not initialized, it might hold any value. The value could be 0 by chance, but it also could be any other value that happens to be located at the memory address of `total`. (For example, by chance, it could hold 1000 and your total would end up $1000 too high.) An unknown value like this is known as **garbage**. The C# compiler prevents you from seeing an incorrect total by requiring you to provide a starting value; C# will not use the garbage value that happens to be stored at an uninitialized memory location.

```
using System;
public class TotalPurchase
{
   public static void Main()
   {
      double purchase;
      double total = 0;
      string inputString;
      const double QUIT = 0;
      Console.WriteLine("Enter purchase amount ");
      inputString = Console.ReadLine();
      purchase = Convert.ToDouble(inputString);
      while(purchase != QUIT)
      {
         total += purchase;
         Console.WriteLine("Enter next purchase amount, or " +
            QUIT + " to quit ");
         inputString = Console.ReadLine();
         purchase = Convert.ToDouble(inputString);
      }
      Console.WriteLine("Your total is {0}", total.ToString("C"));
   }
}
```

Figure 4-16 An application that accumulates total purchases entered by the user

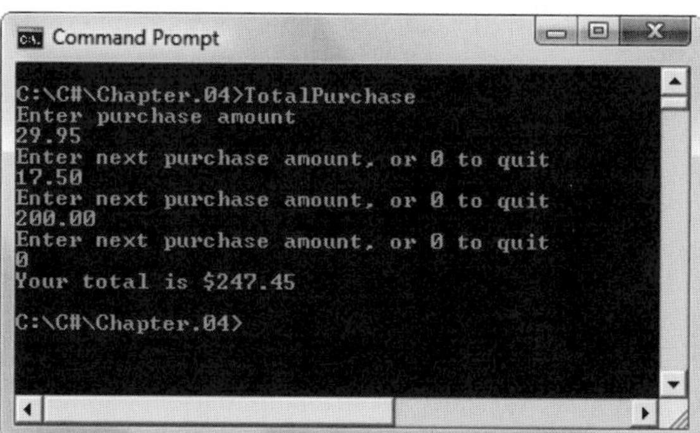

Figure 4-17 Typical execution of the `TotalPurchase` program

NOTE In the application in Figure 4-16, the `total` variable must be initialized to 0, but the `purchase` variable is uninitialized. Many programmers would say it makes no sense to initialize this variable because no matter what starting value you provide, the value can be changed by the first input statement before the variable is ever used. As a matter of style, this book will not initialize a variable if the initialization value is never used; doing so might mislead you into thinking the starting value had some purpose.

»TWO TRUTHS AND A LIE: ACCUMULATING TOTALS

1. When totals are accumulated, 1 is added to a variable that represents the total.
2. A variable used to hold a total must be set to 0 before it is used to accumulate a total.
3. The C# compiler will not allow you to accumulate totals in an uninitialized variable.

The false answer is #1. When totals are accumulated, any value might be added to a variable that represents the total. For example, if you total 10 test scores, then each score is added. If you add only 1 to a total variable on each cycle through a loop, then you are counting rather than accumulating a total.

IMPROVING LOOP PERFORMANCE

Whether you decide to use a `while`, `for`, or `do-while` loop in an application, you can improve loop performance by making sure the loop does not include unnecessary operations or statements. For example, suppose a loop should execute while `x` is less than the sum of two integers, `a` and `b`. The loop could be written as:

```
while (x < a + b)
   // loop body
```

If this loop executes 1000 times, then the expression `a + b` is calculated 1000 times. Instead, if you use the following code, the results are the same, but the arithmetic is performed only once:

```
int sum = a + b;
while(x < sum)
   // loop body
```

Of course, if `a` or `b` is altered in the loop body, then a new sum must be calculated with every loop iteration. However, if the sum of `a` and `b` is fixed prior to the start of the loop, then writing the code the second way is far more efficient.

As another example, suppose you need a temporary variable within a loop to use for some calculation. The loop could be written as follows:

```
while x < LIMIT)
{
   int tempTotal = a + b;
   // more statements here
}
```

When you declare a variable like `tempTotal` within a loop, it exists only for the duration of the loop; that is, it exists only until the loop's closing brace. Each time the loop executes, the variable is recreated. A more efficient solution is to declare the variable outside of the loop, as follows:

```
int tempTotal;
while x < LIMIT)
{
    tempTotal = a + b;
    // more statements here
}
```

It is more efficient to declare this variable outside the loop than to redeclare it on every loop iteration.

As you continue to study programming, you will discover many situations in which you can make your programs more efficient. You should always be on the lookout for ways to improve program performance.

»TWO TRUTHS AND A LIE: IMPROVING LOOP PERFORMANCE

1. You can improve loop performance by making sure the loop does not include unnecessary operations or statements.
2. You can improve loop performance by declaring temporary variables outside of a loop instead of continuously redeclaring them.
3. You can improve loop performance by omitting the initialization of the loop control variable.

The false answer is #3. A loop control variable must be initialized for every loop.

YOU DO IT

USING A `while` LOOP

In the next steps, you will write a program that continuously prompts the user for a valid ID number until the user enters an ID that is acceptable. For this application, assume that a valid ID number must be between 1000 and 9999 inclusive.

To create an application that verifies an ID number:

1. Open a new file in your text editor and enter the beginning of the program. It begins by declaring variables for an ID number, the user's input, and constant values for the highest and lowest acceptable ID numbers.

```
using System;
public class ValidID
{
    public static void Main()
    {
        int idNum;
        string input;
        const int LOW = 1000;
        const int HIGH = 9999;
```

2. Add code to prompt the user for an ID number and to then convert it to an integer.

```
Console.Write("Enter an ID number: ");
input = Console.ReadLine();
idNum = Convert.ToInt32(input);
```

3. Create a loop that continues while the entered ID number is out of range. While the number is invalid, explain valid ID parameters and reprompt the user, converting the input to an integer.

```
while(idNum < LOW || idNum > HIGH)
{
   Console.WriteLine("{0} is an invalid ID number", idNum);
   Console.Write("ID numbers must be ");
   Console.WriteLine("between {0} and {1} inclusive",
      LOW, HIGH);
   Console.Write("Enter an ID number: ");
   input = Console.ReadLine();
   idNum = Convert.ToInt32(input);
}
```

4. When the user eventually enters a valid ID number, the loop ends. Display a message and add closing curly braces for the `Main()` method and for the class.

```
      Console.WriteLine("ID number {0} is valid", idNum);
   }
}
```

5. Save the file as **ValidID.cs**. Compile and execute the program. A typical execution during which the user makes several invalid entries is shown in Figure 4-18.

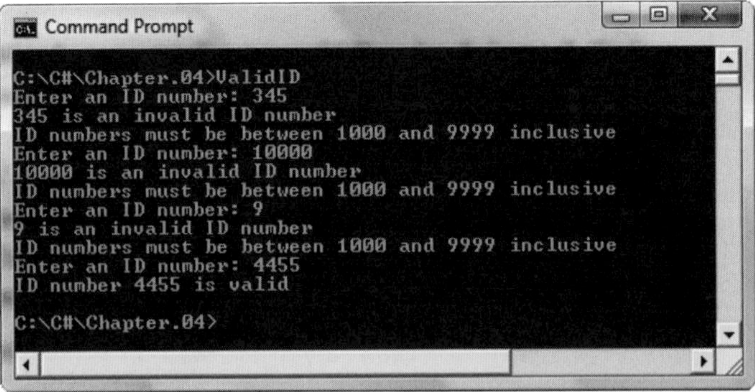

Figure 4-18 Typical execution of `ValidID` program

USING `for` LOOPS

In the next steps, you will write a program that creates a tipping table. Restaurant patrons can use this table to approximate the correct tip for meal prices from $10 to $100, at tipping percentage rates from 10 percent to 25 percent. The program uses several loops.

To create the tipping table:

1. Open a new file in your text editor and enter the beginning of the program. It begins by declaring variables to use for the price of a dinner, a tip percentage rate, and the amount of the tip.

```
using System;
public class TippingTable
{
   public static void Main()
   {
      double dinnerPrice = 10.00;
      double tipRate;
      double tip;
```

2. Next, create some constants. Every tip from 10% through 25% will be computed in 5% intervals, so declare those values as `LOWRATE`, `MAXRATE`, and `TIPSTEP`. Tips will be calculated on dinner prices up to $100.00 in $10.00 intervals, so declare those constants too.

```
      const double LOWRATE = 0.10;
      const double MAXRATE = 0.25;
      const double TIPSTEP = 0.05;
      const double MAXDINNER = 100.00;
      const double DINNERSTEP = 10.00;
```

3. To create a heading for the table, display "Price". (For alignment, insert three spaces after the quotes and before the *P* in *Price.*) On the same line, use a loop that displays every tip rate from `LOWRATE` through `MAXRATE` in increments of `TIPSTEP`. In other words, the tip rates are 0.10, 0.15, 0.20, and 0.25. Complete the heading for the table using a `WriteLine()` statement that advances the cursor to the next line of output and a `WriteLine()` statement that displays a dashed line.

```
Console.Write("   Price");
for(tipRate = LOWRATE; tipRate <= MAXRATE; tipRate += TIPSTEP)
   Console.Write("{0, 8}",tipRate.ToString("F"));
Console.WriteLine();
Console.WriteLine
("----------------------------------------");
const int NUM_DASHES = 40;
for(int x = 0; x < NUM_DASHES; ++x)
    Console.Write("-");
Console.WriteLine();
```

NOTE Recall that within a `for` loop, the expression before the first semicolon executes once, the middle expression is tested, the loop body executes, and then the expression to the right of the second semicolon executes. In other words, `TIPSTEP` is not added to `tipRate` until after the `tipRate` displays on each cycle through the loop.

NOTE As an alternative to typing 40 dashes in the `WriteLine()` statement, you could use the following loop to display a single dash 40 times. When the 40 dashes are completed, use `WriteLine()` to advance the cursor to a new line.

4. Reset `tipRate` to 0.10. You must reset the rate because after the last loop, the rate will have been increased to greater than 0.25.

```
tipRate = LOWRATE;
```

5. Create a nested loop that continues while the `dinnerPrice` remains 100.00 (`MAXDINNER`) or less. Each iteration of this loop displays one row of the tip table. Within this loop, display the `dinnerPrice`, then loop to display four tips while the `tipRate` varies from 0.10 through 0.25. At the end of the loop, increase the `dinnerPrice` by 10.00, reset the `tipRate` to 0.10 so it is ready for the next row, and write a new line to advance the cursor.

```
while(dinnerPrice <= MAXDINNER)
{
    Console.Write("{0, 8}", dinnerPrice.ToString("C"));
    while(tipRate <= MAXRATE)
    {
        tip = dinnerPrice * tipRate;
        Console.Write("{0, 8}",tip.ToString("F"));
        tipRate += 0.05;
    }
    dinnerPrice += DINNERSTEP;
    tipRate = LOWRATE;
    Console.WriteLine();
}
```

NOTE Recall that the {0, 8} format string in the `Write()` statements displays the first argument in fields that are eight characters wide. You learned about format strings in Chapter 2.

6. Add two closing curly braces—one for the `Main()` method and one for the class.
7. Save the file as **TippingTable.cs**. Compile and execute the program. The output looks like Figure 4-19.

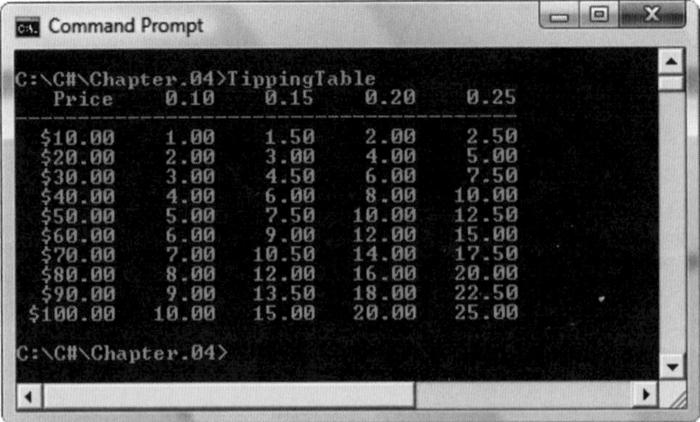

Figure 4-19 Output of `TippingTable` program

»NOTE In the exercises at the end of this chapter, you will be instructed to make an interactive version of the `TippingTable` program in which many of the values are input by the user instead of being coded into the program as unnamed constants.

CHAPTER SUMMARY

- A loop is a structure that allows repeated execution of a block of statements. Within a looping structure, a Boolean expression is evaluated. As long as it is `true`, a block of statements called the loop body executes and the Boolean expression is evaluated again.
- You can use a `while` loop to execute a body of statements continuously while some condition continues to be `true`. A `while` loop consists of the keyword `while`, followed by a Boolean expression within parentheses, followed by the body of the loop, which can be a single statement or a block of statements surrounded by curly braces.
- When you use a `for` statement, you can indicate the starting value for the loop control variable, the test condition that controls loop entry, and the expression that alters the loop control variable, all in one convenient place. You begin a `for` statement with the keyword `for`, followed by a set of parentheses. Within the parentheses are three sections that are separated by exactly two semicolons. The three sections are typically used to initialize, test, and update the loop control variable.
- The `do` loop checks the bottom of the loop after one repetition has occurred.
- You can nest any combination of loops to achieve desired results.
- In computer programs, totals frequently are accumulated—that is, gathered together and added into a final sum by processing individual records one at a time in a loop.
- You can improve loop performance by making sure the loop does not include unnecessary operations or statements.

KEY TERMS

A **loop** is a structure that allows repeated execution of a block of statements.

A **loop body** is the block of statements executed in a loop.

An **iteration** is one execution of any loop.

A **`while` loop** executes a body of statements continuously while some condition continues to be `true`; it uses the keyword `while`.

An **infinite loop** is one that (theoretically) never ends.

A **loop control variable** determines whether loop execution will continue.

An **empty body** has no statements in it.

Incrementing a variable means adding a value to it. (Specifically, the term often means to add 1 to a variable.)

Decrementing a variable means subtracting a value from it. (Specifically, the term often means to subtract 1 from a variable.)

In a **definite loop**, the number of iterations is predetermined.

A **counted loop** is a definite loop.

In an **indefinite loop**, the number of iterations is not predetermined.

A **sentinel value** is one that a user must supply to stop a loop.

A **`for` loop** contains the starting value for the loop control variable, the test condition that controls loop entry, and the expression that alters the loop control variable, all in one statement.

A **step value** is the amount by which a loop control variable is altered, especially in a `for` loop.

When a variable is **out of scope**, it is not usable because it has ceased to exist.

The **`do` loop** checks the bottom of the loop after one repetition has occurred.

In a **pretest loop**, the loop control variable is tested before the loop body executes.

In a **posttest loop**, the loop control variable is tested after the loop body executes.

An **inner loop** is the loop in a pair of nested loops that is entirely contained within another loop.

An **outer loop** is the loop in a pair of nested loops that contains another loop.

Accumulated totals are added into a final sum by processing individual records one at a time in a loop.

An unknown memory value is known as **garbage**.

REVIEW QUESTIONS

1. A structure that allows repeated execution of a block of statements is a(n) ______.

   a. selection
   b. loop
   c. sequence
   d. array

2. The body of a `while` loop can consist of ______.

   a. a single statement
   b. a block of statements within curly braces
   c. either a or b
   d. neither a nor b

3. A loop that never ends is called a(n) ______ loop.

   a. `while`
   b. `for`
   c. counted
   d. infinite

4. Which of the following is not required of a loop control variable in a correctly working loop?
   a. It is initialized before the loop starts.
   b. It is tested.
   c. It is reset to its initial value before the loop ends.
   d. It is altered in the loop body.

5. A `while` loop with an empty body contains no ________ .
   a. loop control variable
   b. statements
   c. curly braces
   d. test within the parentheses of the `while` statement

6. A loop for which you do not know the number of iterations is a(n) ________ .
   a. definite loop
   b. indefinite loop
   c. counted loop
   d. `for` loop

7. What is the major advantage of using a `for` loop instead of a `while` loop?
   a. With a `for` loop, it is impossible to create an infinite loop.
   b. It is the only way to achieve an indefinite loop.
   c. Unlike with a `while` loop, the execution of multiple statements can depend on the test condition.
   d. The loop control variable is initialized, tested, and altered all in one place.

8. A `for` loop statement must contain ________ .
   a. two semicolons
   b. three commas
   c. four dots
   d. five pipes

9. In a `for` statement, the section before the first semicolon executes ________ .
   a. once
   b. once prior to each loop iteration
   c. once after each loop iteration
   d. one less time than the initial loop control variable value

10. The three sections of the `for` loop are most commonly used for ________ the loop control variable.
    a. testing, printing, and incrementing
    b. initializing, testing, and incrementing
    c. incrementing, selecting, and testing
    d. initializing, converting, and displaying

11. Which loop is most convenient to use if the loop body must always execute at least once?

    a. a `do` loop
    b. a `while` loop
    c. a `for` loop
    d. an `if` loop

12. The loop control variable is checked at the bottom of which kind of loop?

    a. a `while` loop
    b. a `do` loop
    c. a `for` loop
    d. all of the above

13. A `for` loop is an example of a(n) ________ loop.

    a. untested
    b. pretest
    c. posttest
    d. infinite

14. A `while` loop is an example of a(n) ________ loop.

    a. untested
    b. pretest
    c. posttest
    d. infinite

15. When a loop is placed within another loop, the loops are said to be ________.

    a. infinite
    b. bubbled
    c. nested
    d. overlapping

16. What does the following code segment display?

```
a = 1;
while (a < 5);
{
   Console.Write("{0} ", a);
   ++a;
}
```

    a. 1 2 3 4
    b. 1
    c. 4
    d. nothing

17. What is the output of the following code segment?

```
s = 1;
while (s < 4)
   ++s;
   Console.Write(" {0}", s);
```

    a. 1
    b. 4
    c. 1 2 3 4
    d. 2 3 4

18. What is the output of the following code segment?

```
j = 5;
while(j > 0)
{
     Console.Write("{0} ", j);
     j--;
}
```

a. 0   c. 5 4 3 2 1

b. 5   d. 5 4 3 2 1 0

19. What does the following code segment display?

```
for(f = 0; f < 3; ++f);
    Console.Write("{0} ", f);
```

a. 0   c. 3

b. 0 1 2   d. nothing

20. What does the following code segment display?

```
for(t = 0; t < 3; ++t)
    Console.Write("{0} ", t);
```

a. 0   c. 0 1 2

b. 0 1   d. 0 1 2 3

EXERCISES

1. Write a program that allows the user to enter any number of integer values continuously (in any order) until the user enters 999. Display the sum of the values entered, not including 999. Save the file as **Sum.cs**.

2. Write a program that asks the user to type a vowel from the keyboard. If the character entered is a vowel, display "OK"; if it is not a vowel, display an error message. Be sure to allow both uppercase and lowercase vowels. The program continues until the user types '!'. Save the file as **GetVowel.cs**.

3. Write a program that prompts a user for an hourly pay rate. While the user enters values less than $5.65 or greater than $49.99, continue to prompt the user. Save the program as **EnsureValidPayRateLoop.cs**.

4. Three salespeople work at Sunshine Hot Tubs—Andrea, Brittany, and Eric. Write a program that prompts the user for a salesperson's initial ('A', 'B', or 'E'). While the user does not type 'Z', continue by prompting for the amount of a sale the salesperson

made. Calculate the salesperson's commission as 10 percent of the sale amount, and add the commission to a running total for that salesperson. After the user types 'Z' for an initial, display each salesperson's total commission earned. Save the file as **TubSales.cs**.

5. Display a multiplication table that shows the product of every integer from 1 through 10 multiplied by every integer from 1 through 10. Save the file as **MultiplicationTable.cs**.
6. Write a program that prints all even numbers from 2 to 100, inclusive. Save the file as **EvenNums.cs**.
7. Write a program that prints every integer value from 1 to 20, along with its squared value. Save the file as **TableOfSquares.cs**.
8. Write a program that sums the integers from 1 to 50. Save the file as **Sum50.cs**.
9. Write a program that prints every perfect number from 1 through 1000. A number is perfect if it equals the sum of all the smaller positive integers that divide evenly into it. For example, 6 is perfect because 1, 2, and 3 divide evenly into it and their sum is 6. Save the file as **Perfect.cs**.
10. In the "You Do It" section of this chapter, you created a tipping table for patrons to use when analyzing their restaurant bills. Modify the program so that each of the following values is obtained from user input:
    - The lowest tipping percentage
    - The highest tipping percentage
    - The lowest possible restaurant bill
    - The highest restaurant bill

    Save the file as **TippingTable2.cs**.

DEBUGGING EXERCISES

Each of the following files in the Chapter.04 folder on your Student Disk has syntax and/or logical errors. In each case, determine the problem and fix the program. After you correct the errors, save each file using the same filename preceded with *Fixed*. For example, save DebugFour1.cs as **FixedDebugFour1.cs**.

a. DebugFour1.cs

b. DebugFour2.cs

c. DebugFour3.cs

d. DebugFour4.cs

UP FOR DISCUSSION

1. Suppose you wrote a program that you suspect is in an infinite loop because it keeps running for several minutes with no output and without ending. What would you add to your program to help you discover the origin of the problem?
2. Suppose that every employee in your organization has a seven-digit logon ID number for retrieving personal information, some of which might be sensitive in nature. For example, each employee has access to his own salary data and insurance claim information, but not to the information of others. Writing a loop would be useful to guess every combination of seven digits in an ID. Are there any circumstances in which you should try to guess another employee's ID number?

CHAPTER FIVE

5

USING ARRAYS

In this chapter you will:

Declare an array and assign values to array elements
Initialize an array
Use subscripts to access array elements
Use the `Length` property
Use `foreach` to control array access
Search an array to find an exact match
Search an array to find a range match
Use the `BinarySearch()` method
Use the `Sort()` and `Reverse()` methods
Use multidimensional arrays

Storing values in variables provides programs with flexibility—a program that uses variables to replace constants can manipulate different values each time the program executes. When you add loops to your programs, the same variable can hold different values during successive cycles through the loop within the same program execution. This ability makes the program even more flexible. Learning to use the data structure known as an array provides you with further flexibility—you can store multiple values in adjacent memory locations and access them by varying a value that indicates which of the stored values you want to use. In this chapter, you will learn to create and manage C# arrays.

DECLARING AN ARRAY AND ASSIGNING VALUES TO ARRAY ELEMENTS

Sometimes, storing just one value in memory at a time isn't adequate. For example, a sales manager who supervises 20 employees might want to determine whether each employee has produced sales above or below the average amount. When you enter the first employee's sales figure into a program, you can't determine whether it is above or below average, because you won't know the average until you have entered all 20 figures. You might plan to assign 20 sales figures to 20 separate variables, each with a unique name, then sum and average them. That process is awkward and unwieldy, however—you need 20 prompts, 20 read statements using 20 separate storage locations (in other words, 20 separate variable names), and 20 addition statements. This method might work for 20 salespeople, but what if you have 30, 40, or 10,000 salespeople?

A superior approach is to assign the sales value to the same variable in 20 successive iterations through a loop that contains one prompt, one read statement, and one addition statement. Unfortunately, when you read in the sales value for the second employee, that data item replaces the figure for the first employee, and the first employee's value is no longer available to compare to the average of all 20 values. When the data-entry loop finishes, the only sales value left in memory is the last one entered.

The best solution to this problem is to create an array. An **array** is a list of data items that all have the same data type and the same name. (As you will learn shortly, each item in the list is distinguished from the others by an index.) You declare an array variable in the same way as you declare any other variable, but you insert a pair of square brackets after the type. For example, to declare an array of `double` values to hold sales figures for salespeople, you write the following:

```
double[] sales;
```

»NOTE In some programming languages, such as C++ and Java, you also can declare an array variable by placing the square brackets after the array name, as in `double sales[];`. This format is illegal in C#.

After you create an array variable, you still need to create the actual array. Declaring an array and actually reserving memory space for it are two distinct processes. To reserve memory locations for 20 `sales` objects, you declare the array variable with the following two statements:

```
double[] sales;
sales = new double[20];
```

The keyword **new** is also known as the **new operator**; it is used to create objects. In this case, it creates 20 separate `sales`. You also can declare and create an array in one statement, such as the following:

```
double[] sales = new double[20];
```

NOTE You will learn about creating other objects using the `new` operator in Chapter 6.

NOTE You can change the size of an array associated with an identifier, if necessary. For example, if you declare `int[] array;`, you can assign five elements later with `array = new int[5];`; later in the program, you might alter the array size to 100 with `array = new int[100];`. Still later, you could alter it again to be either larger or smaller. Most other programming languages do not provide this capability. If you resize an array in this manner, the same identifier refers to a new array in memory and all the values are set to 0.

The statement `double[] sales = new double[20];` reserves 20 memory locations for 20 `sales` objects. Each object in an array is an **array element**. You can distinguish each element from the others in an array with a subscript. A **subscript** (also called an **index**) is an integer contained within square brackets that indicates the position of one of an array's elements. In C#, an array's elements are numbered beginning with 0, so you can legally use any subscript from 0 through 19 when working with an array that has 20 elements. In other words, the first `sales` array element is `sales[0]` and the last `sales` element is `sales[19]`. Figure 5-1 shows how the array of 20 sales figures appears in computer memory. The figure assumes that the array begins at memory address 20000. Because a `double` takes eight bytes of storage, each element of the array is stored in succession at an address that is eight bytes higher than the previous one.

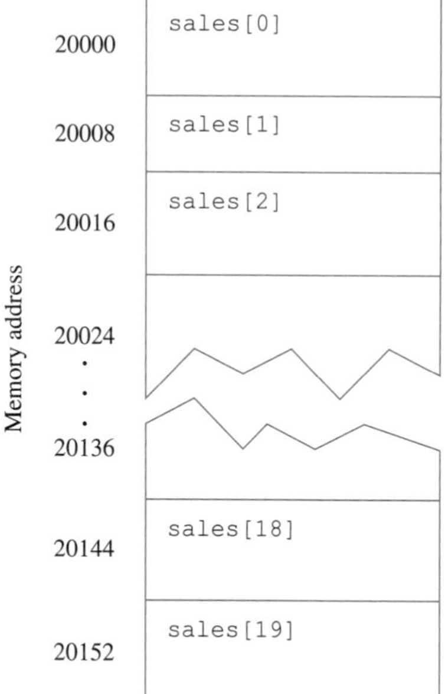

Figure 5-1 An array of 20 `sales` items in memory

NOTE In C#, an array subscript must be an integer. For example, no array contains an element with a subscript of 1.5.

NOTE The first element in an array is sometimes called the "zeroth element."

»NOTE When you instantiate an array, you cannot choose its location in memory any more than you can choose the location of any other variable. However, you do know that after the first array element, the subsequent elements will follow immediately.

»NOTE Some other languages, such as COBOL, BASIC, and Visual Basic, use parentheses rather than square brackets to refer to individual array elements. By using brackets, the creators of C# made it easier for you to distinguish arrays from methods. Like C#, C++ and Java also use brackets surrounding array subscripts.

A common mistake is to forget that the first element in an array is element 0, especially if you know another programming language in which the first array element is element 1. Making this mistake means you will be "off by one" in your use of any array.

»NOTE If you are "off by one" but still using a valid subscript when accessing an array element, your program will produce incorrect output. If you are "off by one" so that your subscript becomes larger than the highest value allowed, you will cause a program error.

»NOTE To remember that array elements begin with element 0, it might be helpful to think of the first array element as being "zero elements away from" the beginning of the array, the second element as being "one element away from" the beginning of the array, and so on.

»NOTE An array subscript can be an expression, as long as the expression evaluates to an integer. For example, if `x` and `y` are integers and their sum is at least 0 but less than the size of an array named `array`, then it is legal to refer to `array[x + y]`.

When you work with any individual array element, you treat it no differently than you treat a single variable of the same type. For example, to assign a value to the first `sales` in an array, you use a simple assignment statement, such as the following:

```
sales[0] = 2100.00;
```

To print the value of the last `sales` in a 20-element array, you write:

```
Console.WriteLine(sales[19]);
```

»TWO TRUTHS AND A LIE: DECLARING AN ARRAY AND ASSIGNING VALUES TO ARRAY ELEMENTS

1. To reserve memory locations for 10 `testScore` objects, you can use the following statement:
   ```
   int[] testScore = new int[9];
   ```
2. To assign 90 to the third element in a 10-element array named `testScore`, you can use the following statement:
   ```
   testScore[2] = 90;
   ```
3. To assign 60 to the last element in a 10-element array named `testScore`, you can use the following statement:
   ```
   testScore[9] = 60;
   ```

The false statement is #1. To reserve memory locations for 10 `testScore` objects, you must use 10 within the second set of square braces. The 10 elements will use the subscripts 0 through 9.

INITIALIZING AN ARRAY

In C#, arrays are objects. When you instantiate an array, you are creating a specific instance of a class named `System.Array`. When you declare objects, their numeric fields initialize to 0, character fields are set to '\u0000' or `null`, and `bool` fields are set to `false`. For example, when you initialize an array with a statement such as the following, each of the five elements of `someNums` has a value of 0 because `someNums` is a numeric array object:

>> **NOTE** You learned about the notation '\u0000' in Chapter 2.

```
int[] someNums = new int[5];
```

You already know how to assign a different value to a single element of an array, as in `someNums[0] = 46;`. You also can assign nondefault values to array elements upon creation. To initialize an array to nondefault values, you use a list of values that are separated by commas and enclosed within curly braces. For example, if you want to create an array named `myScores` and store five test scores within the array, you can use any of the following declarations:

```
int[] myScores = new int[5] {100, 76, 88, 100, 90};
int[] myScores = new int[] {100, 76, 88, 100, 90};
int[] myScores = {100, 76, 88, 100, 90};
```

>> **NOTE** You first learned the term *instance* in Chapter 1. You will understand classes and their instances more thoroughly after you complete Chapter 7.

The list of values provided for an array is an **initializer list**. When you initialize an array by providing a size and an initializer list, as in the first example, the stated size and number of list elements must match. However, when you initialize an array by giving it values upon creation, you are not required to give the array a size, as shown in the second example; in that case, the size is assigned based on the number of values in the initializing list. The third example shows that when you initialize an array, you do not need to use the keyword `new` and repeat the type; instead, new memory is assigned based on the stated array type and the length of the list of provided values. Use the form of array initialization that is clearest to you.

>> **NOTE** When you use curly braces at the end of a block of code, you do not follow the closing curly brace with a semicolon. Conversely, when you use curly braces to enclose a list of array values, you must complete the statement with a semicolon.

>> **NOTE** Programmers who have used other languages such as C++ and Java might expect that when an initialization list is shorter than the number of declared array elements, the "extra" elements will be set to default values. This is not the case in C#; if you declare a size, then you must list a value for each element.

»TWO TRUTHS AND A LIE: INITIALIZING AN ARRAY

1. The following statement creates an array named `purchases` and stores four values within the array:
```
double[] purchases = new [4] {23.55, 99.20, 4.67, 9.99};
```
2. The following statement creates an array named `purchases` and stores four values within the array:
```
double[] purchases = new double[] {23.55, 99.20, 4.67, 9.99};
```
3. The following statement creates an array named `purchases` and stores four values within the array:
```
double[] purchases = {23.55, 99.20, 4.67, 9.99};
```

The false statement is #1. If you chose to use the keyword `new` after the assignment operator when initializing an array, then you must include the data type, as in the following:
```
double[] purchases = new double[4] {23.55, 99.20, 4.67, 9.99};
```
Inserting the size within the brackets that follow `new` and the data type, as in #2, is optional. C# counts the number of initializers for you and uses that value.

USING SUBSCRIPTS TO ACCESS ARRAY ELEMENTS

If you treat each array element as an individual entity, there isn't much of an advantage to declaring an array over declaring individual variables. The power of arrays becomes apparent when you use subscripts that are variables rather than constant values.

For example, when you declare an array of five integers, such as the following, you often want to perform the same operation on each array element:

```
int[] myScores = {100, 76, 88, 100, 90};
```

To increase each array element by 3, for example, you can write the following five statements:

```
myScores[0] += 3;
myScores[1] += 3;
myScores[2] += 3;
myScores[3] += 3;
myScores[4] += 3;
```

With five array elements, this task is manageable. However, you can shorten the task by using a variable as the subscript. Then you can use a loop to perform arithmetic on each element in the array. For example:

```
for(int sub = 0; sub < 5; ++sub)
   myScores[sub] += 3;
```

The variable `sub` is declared and initialized to 0, then compared to 5. Because it is less than 5, the loop executes and `myScores[0]` increases by 3. The variable `sub` is incremented and becomes 1, which is still less than 5, so when the loop executes again, `myScores[1]` increases by 3, and so on. A process that took five statements now takes only one. Additionally, if the array had 100 elements, the first method of individually increasing the array values by 3 would require 95 additional statements. The only change required using the `for` loop would be to compare `sub` to 100 instead of 5.

>> **NOTE** New array users sometimes think there is a permanent connection between a variable used as a subscript and the array with which it is used, but that is not the case. For example, if you vary `sub` from 0 to 10 to fill an array, you do not need to use `sub` later when displaying the array elements—either the same variable or a different variable can be used as a subscript elsewhere in the program.

>>TWO TRUTHS AND A LIE: USING SUBSCRIPTS TO ACCESS ARRAY ELEMENTS

1. Assume you have declared an array of six `double`s named `balances`. The following statement displays all the elements:

```
for(int index = 0; index < 6; ++index)
   Console.WriteLine(balances[index]);
```

2. Assume you have declared an array of eight `double`s named `prices`. The following statement subtracts 2 from each element:

```
for(double pr = 0; pr < 8; ++pr)
   prices[pr] -= 2;
```

3. Assume you have declared an array of four `string`s named `titles`. The following statement displays each element in reverse order:

```
for(int whichOne = 3; whichOne >= 0; --whichOne)
   Console.WriteLine(titles[whichOne]);
```

The false statement is #2. You can only use an `int` as the subscript to an array, and this example attempts to use a `double`.

USING THE `Length` PROPERTY

When you work with array elements, you must ensure that the subscript you use remains in the range of 0 through one less than the array's length. If you declare an array with five elements and use a subscript that is negative or more than 4, you will receive the error message "IndexOutOfRangeException" when you run the program. This message means the index, or subscript, does not hold a value that legally can access an array element. When you declare an array of five integers, as in the following example, you can access all five elements by coding the number 5 explicitly within the middle expression in the `for` statement. The example displays all five scores, each separated by a space.

```
int[] myScores = {100, 75, 88, 100, 90};
for(int sub = 0; sub < 5; ++sub)
   Console.WriteLine("{0} ", myScores[sub]);
```

>> **NOTE** You will learn about the term `Exception` in `IndexOutOfRangeException` in Chapter 9.

If you use this code and then modify your program to hold more or fewer array elements, you must remember to change the comparison in the display loop as well as every other reference to the array size within the program. Many text editors have a "find and replace" feature that lets you change (for example) all of the 5s either simultaneously or one by one. However, you must be careful not to change 5s that have nothing to do with the array; for example, do not change the 5 in 75 inadvertently—it is the second listed value in the `myScores` array and has nothing to do with the array size. As another example, the program might also have a stored interest rate variable holding 5 percent, and you would not want to alter that value. A better technique is to use a named constant that holds the array size and use it to control any loops, as in the following:

```
int[] myScores = {100, 75, 88, 100, 90};
const int MY_ARRAYS_LENGTH = 5;
for(sub = 0; sub < MY_ARRAYS_LENGTH; ++sub)
   Console.WriteLine("{0} ", myScores[sub]);
```

That way, if you change the size of the array and the value of the `MY_ARRAYS_LENGTH` constant, the loop always will use the correct maximum length. However, even this approach has a drawback, because when you change the number of elements in the array declaration, you also must remember to change the value of the named constant.

> **»NOTE**
> An array's `Length` is a read-only property—you cannot assign it a new value. It is capitalized, like all property identifiers. You will create property identifiers for your own classes in Chapter 7.

The superior approach is to use a value that is automatically altered when you change the number of elements in an array declaration. Because every array automatically is a member of the class **`System.Array`**, you can use the fields and methods that are part of the `System.Array` class with any array you create. The **`Length` property** is a member of the `System.Array` class and automatically holds an array's length. Instead of creating your own variable or constant, it is most efficient to use this property, which always updates to reflect any changes you make to your array's size. The following segment of code displays "Array size is 5" and subsequently displays the array's contents:

> **»NOTE**
> In C#, every string also has a built-in `Length` property. For example, if `string name = "Chloe"`, then `name.Length` is 5.

```
int[] myScores = {100, 76, 88, 100, 90};
Console.WriteLine("Array size is {0}", myScores.Length);
for(int x = 0; x < myScores.Length; ++x)
   Console.WriteLine(myScores[x]);
```

»TWO TRUTHS AND A LIE: USING THE `Length` PROPERTY

1. The following code displays 3:

```
int[] array = {1, 2, 3};
Console.WriteLine(array.Length);
```

2. The following code displays 3:

```
int[] array = {1, 2, 3};
Console.WriteLine(array[array.Length - 1]);
```

3. The following code displays 3:

```
int[] array = {1, 2, 3};
Console.WriteLine(array[array.Length] - 1);
```

The false statement is #3. When you declare an array with three elements, then the value of the array's `Length` property is 3. It is illegal to access element 3 of the array because the legitimate subscripts are only 0, 1, and 2.

USING `foreach` TO CONTROL ARRAY ACCESS

You can easily navigate through arrays using a `for` or `while` loop that varies a subscript from 0 to `Array.Length` – 1. C# also supports a **foreach statement** that you can use to cycle through every array element without using a subscript. With the `foreach` statement, you provide a temporary **iteration variable** that automatically holds each array value in turn.

For example, the following code prints each element in the `payRate` array in sequence:

```
double[] payRate = {6.00, 7.35, 8.12, 12.45, 22.22};
foreach(double money in payRate)
   Console.WriteLine("{0}", money.ToString("C"));
```

The variable `money` is declared as a `double` within the `foreach` statement. During the execution of the loop, `money` holds each `payRate` value in turn—first, `payRate[0]`, then `payRate[1]`, and so on. As a simple variable, `money` does not require a subscript, making it easier to work with.

The `foreach` statement is used only under certain circumstances:

» You typically use `foreach` only when you want to access every array element; to access only selected array elements, you must manipulate subscripts using some other technique—for example, using a `for` loop or `while` loop.

» The `foreach` iteration variable is read-only—that is, you cannot assign a value to it. If you want to assign a value to array elements, you must use a different type of loop.

»TWO TRUTHS AND A LIE: USING `foreach` TO CONTROL ARRAY ACCESS

1. The `foreach` statement is used to cycle through every element in an array without using a subscript.
2. With the `foreach` statement, you declare a temporary iteration variable that automatically holds each array subscript in turn.
3. You cannot assign a value to the `foreach` iteration variable.

The false statement is #2. With the `foreach` statement, you declare a temporary iteration variable that automatically holds each array value in turn, not each subscript.

SEARCHING AN ARRAY FOR AN EXACT MATCH

When you want to determine whether some variable holds one of many possible valid values, one option is to use a series of `if` statements to compare the variable to a series of valid values. For example, suppose that a company manufactures 10 items. When a customer places an order for an item, you need to determine whether the item number is valid. If valid item numbers are sequential, say 101 through 110, then the following simple `if` statement that uses a logical AND operator can verify the order number and set a Boolean field to `true`:

```
if(itemOrdered >= 101 && itemOrdered <= 110)
   isValidItem = true;
```

If the valid item numbers are nonsequential, however—for example, 101, 108, 201, 213, 266, 304, and so on—you must code the following deeply nested `if` statement or a lengthy OR comparison to determine the validity of an item number:

```
if(itemOrdered == 101)
   isValidItem = true;
else if(itemOrdered == 108)
   isValidItem = true;
else if(itemOrdered == 201)
   isValidItem = true;
// and so on
```

USING A `for` LOOP TO SEARCH AN ARRAY

Instead of creating a long series of `if` statements, a more elegant solution is to compare the `itemOrdered` variable to a list of values in an array. You can initialize the array with the valid values by using the following statement:

```
int[] validValues = {101, 108, 201, 213, 266, 304, 311,
       409, 411, 412};
```

»NOTE You might prefer to declare the `validValues` array as a constant because presumably, the valid item numbers should not change during program execution. In C# you must use the keywords `static` and `readonly` prior to the constant declaration. To keep these examples simple, all arrays in this chapter are declared as variable arrays.

Next, you can use a `for` statement to loop through the array and set a Boolean variable to `true` when a match is found:

»NOTE In place of the `for` loop, you could use a `foreach` loop.

```
for(int x = 0; x < validValues.Length; ++x)
   if(itemOrdered == validValues[x])
      isValidItem = true;
```

This simple `for` loop replaces the long series of `if` statements. What's more, if a company carries 1000 items instead of 10, then the list of valid items in the array must be altered, but the `for` statement does not change at all. As an added bonus, if you set up another array as a **parallel array** with the same number of elements and corresponding data, you can use the same subscript to access additional information. For example, if the 10 items your company carries have 10 different prices, then you can set up any array to hold those prices as follows:

```
double[] prices = {0.89, 1.23, 3.50, 0.69...}; // and so on
```

The prices must appear in the same order as their corresponding item numbers in the `validValues` array. Now the same `for` loop that finds the valid item number also finds the price, as shown in the program in Figure 5-2. In other words, if the item number is found in the second position in the `validValues` array, then you can find the correct price in the

```
using System;
public class FindPriceWithForLoop
{
   public static void Main()
   {
     int[] validValues = {101,  108,   201,  213,  266,
        304,   311,  409,  411,  412};
     double[] prices =   {0.89, 1.23, 3.50, 0.69, 5.79,
        3.19, 0.99, 0.89, 1.26, 8.00};
     int itemOrdered;
     double itemPrice = 0;
     bool isValidItem = false;
     Console.Write("Please enter an item ");
     itemOrdered = Convert.ToInt32(Console.ReadLine());
     for(int x = 0; x < validValues.Length; ++x)
     {
        if(itemOrdered == validValues[x])
        {
           isValidItem = true;
           itemPrice = prices[x];
        }
     }
     if(isValidItem)
        Console.WriteLine("Price is {0}", itemPrice);
     else
        Console.WriteLine("Sorry - item not found");
   }
}
```

Figure 5-2 The `FindPriceWithForLoop` program

second position in the `prices` array. In the program in Figure 5-2, the variable used as a subscript, `x`, is set to 0 and the Boolean variable `isValidItem` is `false`. In the shaded portion of the figure, while the subscript remains smaller than the length of the array of valid item numbers, the subscript is continuously increased so that subsequent array values can be tested. When a match between the user's item and an item in the array is found, `isValidItem` is set to `true` and the price of the item is stored in `itemPrice`.

»NOTE If you initialize parallel arrays, it is convenient to use spacing so that the corresponding values visually align on the screen or printed page.

Figure 5-3 shows two typical program executions.

Within the code shown in Figure 5-2, you compare every `itemOrdered` with each of the 10 `validValues`. Even when an `itemOrdered` is equivalent to the first value in the `validValues`

»NOTE In the fourth statement of the `Main()` method in Figure 5-2, `itemPrice` is set to 0. Setting this variable is required, because its value is later altered only if an item number match is found in the `validValues` array. When C# determines that a variable's value is only set depending on an `if` statement, C# will not allow you to display the variable, because the compiler assumes the variable might not have been set to a valid value.

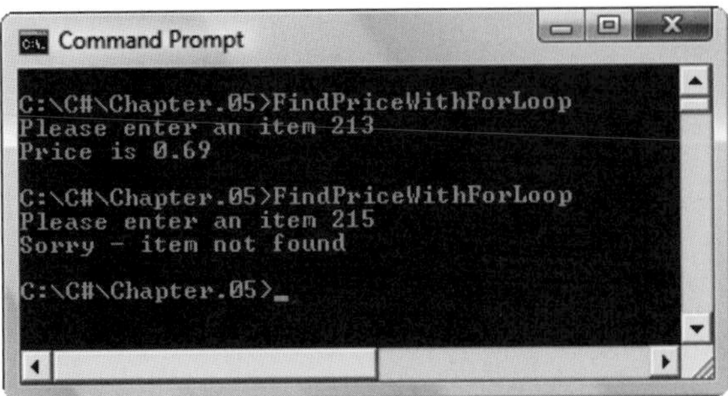

Figure 5-3 Two typical executions of the `FindPriceWithForLoop` program

> **NOTE** In an array with many possible matches, it is most efficient to place the most common items first, so they are matched right away. For example, if item 311 is ordered most often, place 311 first in the `validValues` array and its price ($0.99) first in the `prices` array.

array (101), you always make nine additional cycles through the array. On each of these nine additional iterations, the comparison between `itemOrdered` and `validValues[x]` is always `false`. As soon as a match for an `itemOrdered` is found, it is most efficient to break out of the `for` loop early. An easy way to accomplish this task is to set `x` to a high value within the block of statements executed when a match is found. Then, after a match, the `for` loop will not execute again because the limiting comparison (`x < validValues.Length`) will have been surpassed. The following code shows this approach:

```
for(int x = 0; x < validValues.Length; ++x)
{
    if(itemOrdered == validValues[x])
    {
        isValidItem = true;
        itemPrice = prices[x];
        x = validValues.Length;
             // break out of loop when you find a match
    }
}
```

Instead of the statement that sets `x` to `validValues.Length` when a match is found, you could remove that statement and change the comparison in the middle section of the `for` statement to a compound statement, as follows:

```
for(int x = 0; x < validValues.Length && !isValidItem; ++x)...
```

As another alternative, you could remove the statement that sets `x` to `validValues.Length` and place a `break` statement within the loop in its place. Some programmers disapprove of exiting a `for` loop early, whether by setting a variable's value or by using a `break` statement. They argue that programs are easier to debug and maintain if each program segment has only one entry and one exit point. If you (or your instructor) agree with this philosophy, then you can select an approach that uses a `while` statement, as described next.

> **NOTE** Although parallel arrays can be very useful, they also can increase the likelihood of mistakes. Any time you make a change to one array, you must remember to make the corresponding change in its parallel array. As you continue to study C#, you will learn superior ways to correlate data items. For example, Chapter 7 explains how you can encapsulate corresponding data items in objects and create arrays of objects.

USING A while LOOP TO SEARCH AN ARRAY

As an alternative to using a `for` or `foreach` loop to search an array, you can use a `while` loop to search for a match. Using this approach, you set a subscript to 0 and, while the `itemOrdered` is not equal to a value in the array, increase the subscript and keep looking. You search only while the subscript remains lower than the number of elements in the array. If the subscript increases to match `validValues.Length`, then you never found a match in the 10-element array. If the loop ends before the subscript reaches `validValues.Length`, then you found a match and the correct price can be assigned to the `itemPrice` variable. Figure 5-4 shows a program that uses this approach.

```
using System;
public class FindPriceWithWhileLoop
{
   public static void Main()
   {
      int x;
      string inputString;
      int itemOrdered;
      double itemPrice = 0;
      bool isValidItem = false;
      int[] validValues = {101,  108,   201,  213,  266,
         304,   311,  409,  411,  412};
      double[] prices =   {0.89, 1.23, 3.50, 0.69, 5.79,
        3.19,  0.99, 0.89, 1.26, 8.00};
      Console.Write("Enter item number ");
      inputString = Console.ReadLine();
      itemOrdered = Convert.ToInt32(inputString);
      x = 0;
      while(x < validValues.Length &&
         itemOrdered != validValues[x])
            ++x;
      if(x != validValues.Length)
      {
         isValidItem = true;
         itemPrice = prices[x];
      }
      if(isValidItem)
         Console.WriteLine("Item {0} sells for {1}",
            itemOrdered, itemPrice.ToString("C"));
      else
         Console.WriteLine("No such item as {0}",
            itemOrdered);
   }
}
```

Figure 5-4 The `FindPriceWithWhileLoop` program that searches with a `while` loop

In the application in Figure 5-4, the variable used as a subscript, `x`, is set to 0 and the Boolean variable `isValidItem` is `false`. In the shaded portion of the figure, while the subscript remains smaller than the length of the array of valid item numbers, and while the user's requested item does not match a valid item, the subscript is increased so that subsequent array values can be tested. The `while` loop ends when a match is found or the array tests have been exhausted, whichever comes first. When the loop ends, if `x` is not equal to the size of the array, then a valid item has been found and its price can be retrieved from the `prices` array. Figure 5-5 shows two executions of the program. In the first execution, a match is found; in the second, an invalid item number is entered, so no match is found.

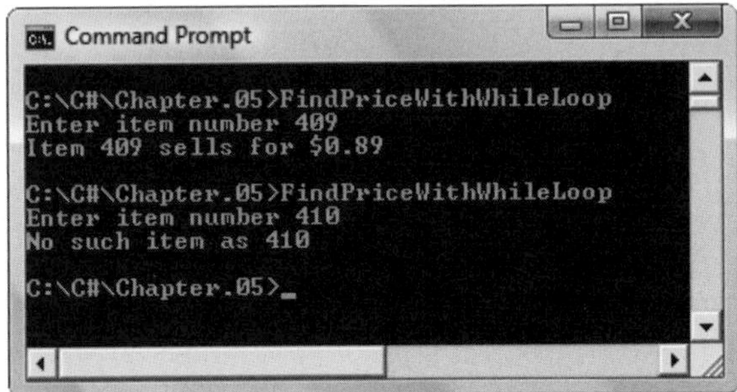

Figure 5-5 Two executions of the `FindPriceWithWhileLoop` application

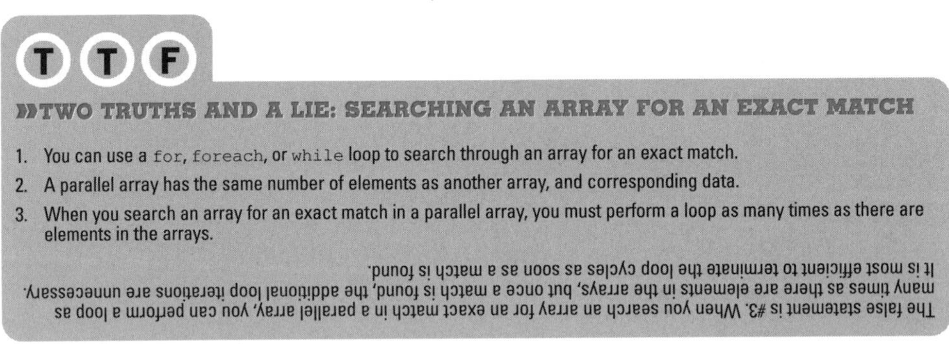

»TWO TRUTHS AND A LIE: SEARCHING AN ARRAY FOR AN EXACT MATCH

1. You can use a `for`, `foreach`, or `while` loop to search through an array for an exact match.
2. A parallel array has the same number of elements as another array, and corresponding data.
3. When you search an array for an exact match in a parallel array, you must perform a loop as many times as there are elements in the arrays.

The false statement is #3. When you search an array for an exact match in a parallel array, you can perform a loop as many times as there are elements in the arrays, but once a match is found, the additional loop iterations are unnecessary. It is most efficient to terminate the loop cycles as soon as a match is found.

SEARCHING AN ARRAY FOR A RANGE MATCH

Searching an array for an exact match is not always practical. For example, suppose your mail-order company gives customer discounts based on the quantity of items ordered. Perhaps no discount is given for any order of fewer than a dozen items, but increasing discounts are available for orders of increasing quantities, as shown in Figure 5-6.

Total Quantity Ordered	Discount (%)
1 to 12	None
13 to 49	10
50 to 99	14
100 to 199	18
200 or more	20

Figure 5-6 Discount table for a mail-order company

One awkward, impractical option is to create a single array to store the discount rates. You could use a variable named `numOfItems` as a subscript to the array, but the array would need hundreds of entries, such as the following:

```
double[] discount = {0, 0, 0, 0, 0, 0, 0, 0, 0, 0,
     0, 0, 0, 0.10, 0.10, 0.10 ...}; // and so on
```

When `numOfItems` is 3, for example, then `discount[numOfItems]` or `discount[3]` is 0. When `numOfItems` is 14, then `discount[numOfItems]` or `discount[14]` is 0.10. Because a customer might order thousands of items, the array would need to be ridiculously large.

»NOTE Notice that 13 zeroes are listed in the discount array in this example. The first array element has a 0 subscript (and a 0 discount for 0 items). The next 12 discounts (1 through 12 items) also have 0 discounts.

A better option is to create parallel arrays. One array will hold the five discount rates, and the other array will hold five discount range limits. Then you can perform a **range match** by determining the pair of limiting values between which a customer's order falls. The Total Quantity Ordered column in Figure 5-6 shows five ranges. If you use only the first figure in each range, then you can create an array that holds five low limits:

```
int[] discountRangeLowLimit = {1, 13, 50, 100, 200};
```

A parallel array will hold the five discount rates:

```
double[] discount = {0, 0.10, 0.14, 0.18, 0.20};
```

Then, starting at the last `discountRangeLowLimit` array element, for any `numOfItems` greater than or equal to `discountRangeLowLimit[4]`, the appropriate discount is `discount[4]`. In other words, for any `numOfItems` less than `discountRangeLowLimit[4]`, you should decrement the subscript and look in a lower range. Figure 5-7 shows the code.

```
// assume numOfItems is a declared integer for which a user
// has input a value
int[] discountRangeLowLimit = {1,    13,    50,   100,   200};
double[] discount =           {0, 0.10, 0.14, 0.18, 0.20};
double customerDiscount;
int sub = discountRangeLowLimit.Length - 1;
while(sub >= 0 && numOfItems < discountRangeLowLimit[sub])
   --sub;
customerDiscount = discount[sub];
```

Figure 5-7 Searching an array of ranges

> **»NOTE**
> In the search in Figure 5-7, either `discountRangeLowLimit.Length - 1` or `discount.Length - 1` could have been used to initialize `sub`.

As an alternate approach to the range-checking logic in Figure 5-7, you can choose to create an array that contains the upper limit of each range, such as the following:

```
int[] discountRangeUpperLimit = {12, 49, 99, 199, 9999999};
```

Then the logic can be written to compare `numOfItems` to each range limit until the correct range is located, as follows:

```
int sub = 0;
while(sub < discountRangeUpperLimit.Length && numOfItems >
    discountRangeUpperLimit[sub])
        ++sub;
customerDiscount = discount[sub];
```

In this example, `sub` is initialized to 0. While it remains within array bounds, and while `numOfItems` is more than each upper-range limit, `sub` is increased. In other words, if `numOfItems` is 3, the `while` expression is false on the first loop iteration, the loop ends, `sub` remains 0, and the customer discount is the first discount. However, if `numOfItems` is 30, then the `while` expression is true on the first loop iteration, `sub` becomes 1, the `while` expression is false on the second iteration, and the second discount is used. In this example, the last `discountRangeUpperLimit` array value is 9999999. This very high value was used with the assumption that no `numOfItems` would ever exceed it. As with many issues in programming, multiple correct approaches frequently exist for the same problem.

»TWO TRUTHS AND A LIE: SEARCHING AN ARRAY FOR A RANGE MATCH

1. A practical solution to creating an array with which to perform a range check is to design the array to hold the lowest value in each range.
2. A practical solution to creating an array with which to perform a range check is to design the array to hold the highest value in each range.
3. A practical solution to creating an array with which to perform a range check is to design the array to hold the average value in each range.

The false statement is #3. It would be impractical to design an array with average range values to use in a program that should check ranges.

USING THE `BinarySearch()` METHOD

> **»NOTE**
> You already have used many built-in C# methods such as `WriteLine()` and `ReadLine()`. You will learn to write your own methods in Chapter 6.

You have already learned that because every array in C# automatically is a member of the `System.Array` class, you can use the `Length` property. Additionally, the `System.Array` class contains a variety of useful, built-in methods.

The **`BinarySearch()` method** finds a requested value in a sorted array. Instead of employing the logic you used to find a match in the last section, you can take advantage of this built-in method to locate a value within an array, as long as the array items are organized in ascending order.

»NOTE A binary search is one in which a sorted list of objects is split in half repeatedly as the search gets closer and closer to a match. Perhaps you have played a guessing game, trying to guess a number from 1 to 100. If you asked, "Is it less than 50?," then continued to narrow your guesses upon hearing each subsequent answer, then you have performed a binary search.

Figure 5-8 shows a program that declares an array of integer `idNumbers` arranged in ascending order. The program prompts a user for a value, converts it to an integer, and, rather than using a loop to examine each array element and compare it to the entered value, simply passes the array and the entered value to the `BinarySearch()` method in the shaded statement. The method returns –1 if the value is not found in the array; otherwise, it returns the array position of the sought value. Figure 5-9 shows two executions of this program.

»NOTE The `BinarySearch()` method takes two arguments—the array name and the value for which to search. In Chapter 1 you learned that arguments represent information that a method needs to perform its task. When methods require multiple arguments, they are separated by commas. For example, when you have used the `Console.WriteLine()` method, you have passed a format string and values to be displayed, all separated by commas.

```
using System;
public class BinarySearchDemo
{
   public static void Main()
   {
      int[] idNumbers = {122, 167, 204, 219, 345};
      int x;
      string entryString;
      int entryId;
      Console.Write("Enter an Employee ID ");
      entryString = Console.ReadLine();
      entryId = Convert.ToInt32(entryString);
      x = Array.BinarySearch(idNumbers, entryId);
      if(x < 0)
         Console.WriteLine("ID {0} not found", entryId);
      else
         Console.WriteLine("ID {0} found at position {1} ",
            entryId, x);
   }
}
```

Figure 5-8 `BinarySearchDemo` program

When you use the following statement, you send a string to the `Write()` method:

```
Console.Write("Enter an Employee ID ");
```

When you use the following statement, you get a value back from the `ReadLine()` method:

```
entryString = Console.ReadLine();
```

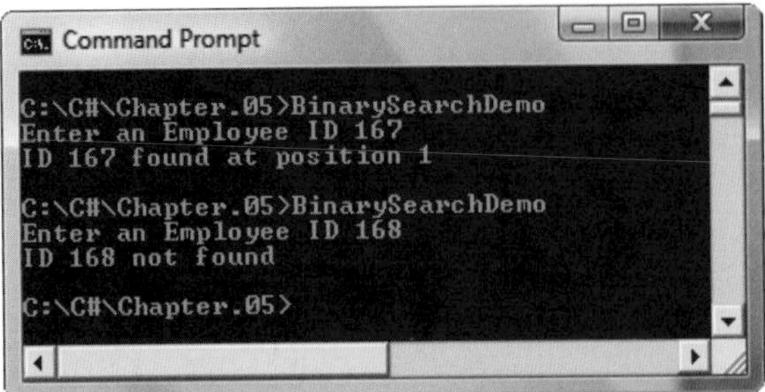

Figure 5-9 Two executions of the `BinarySearchDemo` program

In Figure 5-8, the following single statement both sends a value to a method and gets a value back:

```
x = Array.BinarySearch(idNumbers, entryId);
```

The statement calls the method that performs the search, returning a -1 or the position where `entryId` was found; that value is then stored in `x`. This single line of code is easier to write, less prone to error, and easier to understand than writing a loop to cycle through the `idNumbers` array looking for a match. Still, it is worthwhile to understand how to perform the search without the `BinarySearch()` method, as you learned while studying parallel arrays. You will need to use that technique under the following conditions, when the `BinarySearch()` method proves inadequate:

- If your array items are not arranged in ascending order, the `BinarySearch()` method does not work correctly.
- If your array holds duplicate values and you want to find all of them, the `BinarySearch()` method doesn't work—it can return only one value, so it returns the position of the first matching value it finds (which is not necessarily the first instance of the value in the array).
- If you want to find a range match rather than an exact match, the `BinarySearch()` method does not work.

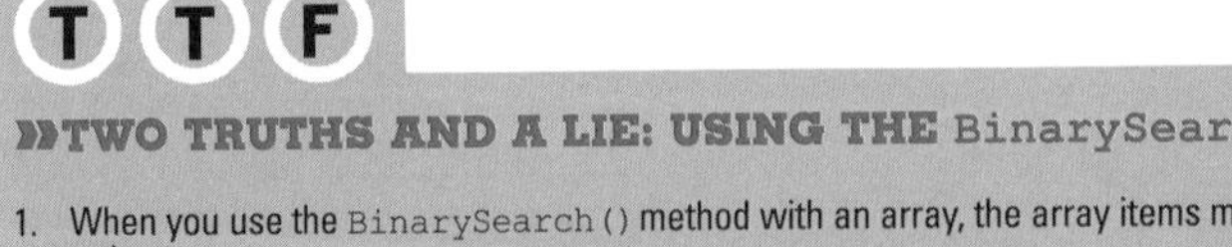

T T F

»TWO TRUTHS AND A LIE: USING THE `BinarySearch()` METHOD

1. When you use the `BinarySearch()` method with an array, the array items must first be organized in ascending order.
2. The `BinarySearch()` method requires three arguments—the name of an array, a value for which you want to search, and a code that indicates whether the array has been presorted.
3. The `BinarySearch()` method returns –1 if the search value is not found in the array; otherwise, it returns the array position of the sought value.

The false statement is #2. The `BinarySearch()` method requires two arguments—the name of an array and a value for which you want to search. The array items must be sorted in ascending order for the method to work correctly.

USING THE Sort() AND Reverse() METHODS

The System.Array class contains other useful methods you can use to manipulate your arrays. As with the BinarySearch() method, you could write all of these methods yourself. C# provides them as a convenience, however.

The **Sort() method** arranges array items in ascending order. Ascending order is lowest to highest; it works numerically for number types and alphabetically for characters and strings. To use the method, you pass the array name to Array.Sort(), and the element positions within the array are rearranged appropriately. Figure 5-10 shows a program that sorts an array of strings; Figure 5-11 shows its execution.

```
using System;
public class SortArray
{
   public static void Main()
   {
      string[] names = {"Olive", "Patty",
         "Richard", "Ned", "Mindy"};
      int x;
      Array.Sort(names);
      for(x = 0; x < names.Length; ++x)
         Console.WriteLine(names[x]);
   }
}
```

Figure 5-10 SortArray program

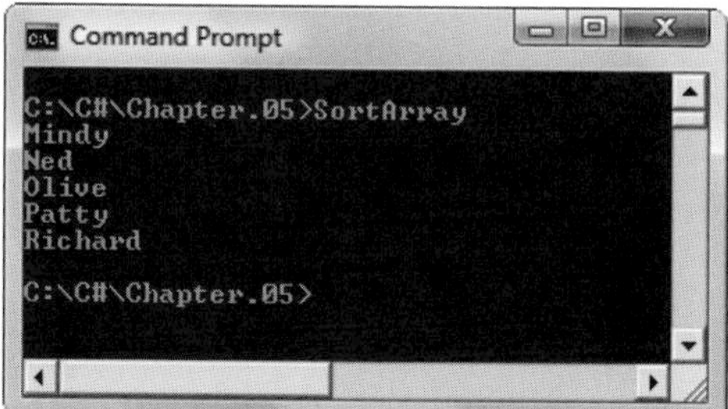

Figure 5-11 Execution of SortArray program

NOTE Because the BinarySearch() method requires that array elements be sorted in order, the Sort() method is often used in conjunction with it.

NOTE When you Reverse() an array that contains an odd number of elements, the middle element will remain in its original location.

The **Reverse() method** reverses the order of items in an array. In other words, for any array, the element that starts in position 0 is relocated to position Length - 1, the element that starts in position 1 is relocated to position Length - 2, and so on until the element that starts in position Length - 1 is relocated to position 0. You call the Reverse() method the same

>> **NOTE**
>
> The `Reverse()` method does not sort array elements; it only rearranges their positions to the opposite order.

way you call the `Sort()` method—you simply pass the array name to the method. Figure 5-12 shows a program that uses `Reverse()` with an array of strings, and Figure 5-13 shows its execution.

```
using System;
public class ReverseArray
{
   public static void Main()
   {
      string[] names = {"Zach", "Rose", "Wendy", "Marcia"};
      int x;
      Array.Reverse(names);
      for(x = 0; x < names.Length; ++x)
         Console.WriteLine(names[x]);
   }
}
```

Figure 5-12 `ReverseArray` program

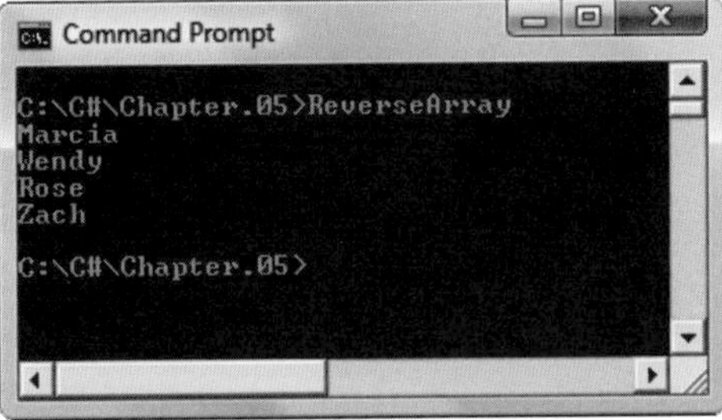

Figure 5-13 Execution of `ReverseArray` program

>>TWO TRUTHS AND A LIE: USING THE `Sort()` AND `Reverse()` METHODS

1. The `Array.Sort()` and `Array.Reverse()` methods are similar in that both belong to the `Array` class.
2. The `Array.Sort()` and `Array.Reverse()` methods are similar in that both require a single argument.
3. The `Array.Sort()` and `Array.Reverse()` methods are different in that one places items in ascending order and the other places them in descending order.

The false statement is #3. The `Array.Sort()` method places items in ascending order, but the `Array.Reverse()` method simply reverses the existing order of any array whether it was presorted or not.

USING MULTIDIMENSIONAL ARRAYS

When you declare an array such as `double[] sales = new double[20];`, you can envision the declared integers as a column of numbers in memory, as shown at the beginning of this chapter in Figure 5-1. In other words, you can picture the 20 declared numbers stacked one on top of the next. An array that you can picture as a column of values, and whose elements you can access using a single subscript, is a **one-dimensional** or **single-dimensional array**.

NOTE You can think of the single dimension of a single-dimensional array as the height of the array.

C# also supports **multidimensional arrays**—those that require multiple subscripts to access the array elements. The most commonly used multidimensional arrays are two-dimensional arrays that are rectangular. **Two-dimensional arrays** have two or more columns of values for each row, as shown in Figure 5-14. In a **rectangular array**, each row has the same number of columns. You must use two subscripts when you access an element in a two-dimensional array. When mathematicians use a two-dimensional array, they often call it a **matrix** or a **table**; you might have used a two-dimensional array called a spreadsheet.

sales[0, 0]	sales[0, 1]	sales[0, 2]	sales[0, 3]
sales[1, 0]	sales[1, 1]	sales[1, 2]	sales[1, 3]
sales[2, 0]	sales[2, 1]	sales[2, 2]	sales[2, 3]

Figure 5-14 View of a rectangular, two-dimensional array in memory

NOTE You can think of the two dimensions of a two-dimensional array as height and width.

NOTE You might want to create a `sales` array with two dimensions as shown in Figure 5-14 if, for example, each row represented a category of items sold, and each column represented a salesperson who sold them.

When you declare a one-dimensional array, you type a single, empty set of square brackets after the array type, and you use a single subscript in a set of square brackets when reserving memory. To declare a two-dimensional array, you type a comma in the square brackets after the array type, and you use two subscripts, separated by a comma in brackets, when reserving memory. For example, the array in Figure 5-14 can be declared as the following, creating an array named `saleFigures` that holds three rows and four columns:

```
double[ , ]sales = new double[3, 4];
```

NOTE When you declare a two-dimensional array, spaces surrounding the comma within the square brackets are optional.

Just as with a one-dimensional array, if you do not provide values for the elements in a two-dimensional numerical array, the values are set to the default value for the data type (zero for numeric data). You can assign other values to the array elements later. For example, the following statement assigns the value 14.00 to the element of the `sales` array that is in the first column of the first row:

```
sales[0, 0] = 14.00;
```

Alternatively, you can initialize a two-dimensional array with values when it is created. For example, the following code assigns values to `sales` when it is created:

```
double[ , ] sales = {{14.00, 15.00, 16.00, 17.00},
                     {21.99, 34.55, 67.88, 31.99},
                     {12.03, 55.55, 32.89,  1.17}};
```

»NOTE You do not need to place each row of values that initializes a two-dimensional array on its own line. However, doing so makes the positions of values easier to understand.

The `sales` array contains three rows and four columns. You contain the entire set of values within a pair of curly braces. The first row of the array holds the four `doubles` 14.00, 15.00, 16.00, and 17.00. Notice that these four values are placed within their own inner set of curly braces to indicate that they constitute one row, or the first row, which is row 0. Similarly, the next four values make up the second row (row 1), which you reference with the subscript 1. The value of `sales[0, 0]` is 14.00. The value of `sales[0, 1]` is 15.00. The value of `sales[2, 3]` is 1.17. The first value within the brackets following the array name always refers to the row; the second value, after the comma, refers to the column.

As an example of how useful two-dimensional arrays can be, assume you own an apartment building with four floors—a basement, which you refer to as floor zero, and three other floors numbered one, two, and three. In addition, each of the floors has studio (with no bedroom), one-, and two-bedroom apartments. The monthly rent for each type of apartment is different, and the rent is higher for apartments with more bedrooms. Table 5-1 shows the rental amounts.

Floor	Zero Bedrooms	One Bedroom	Two Bedrooms
0	400	450	510
1	500	560	630
2	625	676	740
3	1000	1250	1600

Table 5-1 Rents charged (in dollars)

To determine a tenant's rent, you need to know two pieces of information: the floor on which the tenant rents an apartment and the number of bedrooms in the apartment. Within a C# program, you can declare an array of rents using the following code:

```
int[ , ] rents = { {400, 450, 510},
                   {500, 560, 630},
                   {625, 676, 740},
                   {1000, 1250, 1600} };
```

Assume you declare two integers to hold the floor number and bedroom count, as in the following statement:

```
int floor, bedrooms;
```

Then any tenant's rent can be referred to as `rents[floor, bedrooms]`.

Figure 5-15 shows a complete program that uses a rectangular, two-dimensional array to hold rent values. Figure 5-16 shows a typical execution.

```
using System;
public class Rents
{
   public static void Main()
   {
      int[ , ] rents = { {400, 450, 510},
                         {500, 560, 630},
                         {625, 676, 740},
                         {1000, 1250, 1600} };
      int floor;
      int bedrooms;
      string inputString;
      Console.Write("Enter the floor on which you want to live ");
      inputString = Console.ReadLine();
      floor = Convert.ToInt32(inputString);
      Console.Write("Enter the number of bedrooms you need ");
      inputString = Console.ReadLine();
      bedrooms = Convert.ToInt32(inputString);
      Console.WriteLine("The rent is {0}",
         rents[floor, bedrooms]);
   }
}
```

Figure 5-15 The `Rents` program

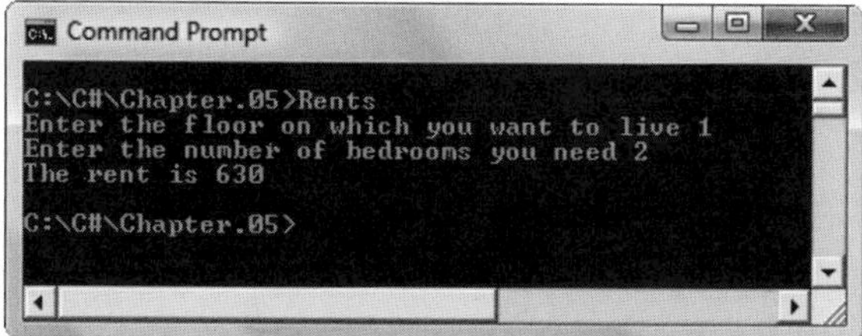

Figure 5-16 Typical execution of the `Rents` program

C# supports arrays with more than two dimensions. For example, if you own a multistory apartment building with different numbers of bedrooms available in apartments on each floor, you can use a two-dimensional array to store the rental fees. If you own several apartment buildings, you might want to employ a third dimension to store the building number. Suppose you want to store rents for four buildings that have three floors each and that each hold two types of apartments. Figure 5-17 shows how you might define such an array.

```
int[ , , ] rents = { { {400, 500}, {450, 550}, {500, 550}},
                     { {510, 610}, {710, 810}, {910, 1010}},
                     { {525, 625}, {725, 825}, {925, 1025}},
                     { {850, 950}, {1050, 1150}, {1250, 1350}}};
```

Figure 5-17 A three-dimensional array definition

The empty brackets that follow the data type contain two commas, showing that the array supports three dimensions. A set of curly braces surrounds all the data. Four inner sets of braces surround the data for each floor. In this example, each row of values represents a building (0 through 3). Then 12 sets of innermost brackets surround the values for each floor—first a zero-bedroom apartment and then a one-bedroom apartment.

Using the three-dimensional array in Figure 5-17, an expression such as `rents[building, floor, bedrooms]` refers to a specific rent figure for a building whose number is stored in the `building` variable and whose floor and bedroom numbers are stored in the `floor` and `bedrooms` variables. Specifically, `rents[3, 1, 0]` refers to a studio (zero-bedroom) apartment on the first floor of building 3 ($1050 in Figure 5-17). When you are programming in C#, you can use four, five, or more dimensions in an array. As long as you can keep track of the order of the variables needed as subscripts, and as long as you don't exhaust your computer's memory, C# lets you create arrays of any size.

C# also supports jagged arrays. A **jagged array** is a one-dimensional array in which each element is another array. The major difference between jagged and rectangular arrays is that in jagged arrays, each row can be a different length.

For example, consider an application in which you want to store train ticket prices for each stop along five different routes. Suppose some of the routes have as many as 10 stops and others have as few as two. Each of the five routes could be represented by a row in a multidimensional array. Then you would have two logical choices for the columns:

» You could create a rectangular, two-dimensional array, allowing 10 columns for each row. In some of the rows, as many as eight of the columns would be empty, because some routes have only two stops.

» You could create a jagged two-dimensional array, allowing a different number of columns for each row. Figure 5-18 shows how you could implement this option.

```
double [][] tickets = {
   new double[] {5.50, 6.75, 7.95, 9.00, 12.00,
      13.00, 14.50, 17.00, 19.00, 20.25},
   new double[] {5.00, 6.00},
   new double[] {7.50, 9.00, 9.95, 12.00, 13.00, 14.00},
   new double[] {3.50, 6.45, 9.95, 10.00, 12.75},
   new double[] {15.00, 16.00} };
```

Figure 5-18 A jagged, two-dimensional array

The array in Figure 5-18 contains five separate one-dimensional arrays. Two square brackets are used following the data type. Then, within the array, each row needs its own `new` operator and data type. To refer to a jagged array element, you use two sets of brackets after the array name—for example, `tickets[route][stop]`. In Figure 5-18, the value of `tickets[0][0]` is 5.50, the value of `tickets[0][1]` is 6.75, and the value of `tickets[0][2]` is 7.95. The value of `tickets[1][0]` is 5.00, and the value of `tickets[1][1]` is 6.00. Referring to `tickets[1][2]` is invalid because there is no column 2 in the second row (that is, there are only two stops, not three, on the second train route).

»TWO TRUTHS AND A LIE: USING MULTIDIMENSIONAL ARRAYS

1. A rectangular array has the same number of columns as rows.
2. The following array contains two rows and three columns:

```
int[ , ] departments = {{12, 54, 16},
                        {22, 44, 47}};
```

3. A jagged array is a one-dimensional array in which each element is another array.

The false statement is #1. In a rectangular array, each row has the same number of columns, but there is no requirement that the numbers of rows and columns be the same.

YOU DO IT

CREATING AND USING AN ARRAY

In the next steps, you will create a small array to see how arrays are used. The array will hold salaries for four categories of employees.

To create a program that uses an array:

1. Open a new text file in your text editor.
2. Begin the class that will demonstrate array use by typing the following:

```
using System;
public class ArrayDemo1
{
   public static void Main()
   {
```

3. Declare and create an array that can hold four `double` values by typing:

```
double[] payRate;
payRate = new double[4];
```

4. One by one, assign four values to the four pay rate array elements by typing:

```
payRate[0] = 6.00;
payRate[1] = 7.35;
payRate[2] = 8.12;
payRate[3] = 12.45;
```

5. To confirm that the four values have been assigned, print the pay rates, one by one, using the following code:

```
Console.WriteLine("Pay rate {0} is {1}",
   0, payRate[0].ToString("C"));
Console.WriteLine("Pay rate {0} is {1}",
   1, payRate[1].ToString("C"));
Console.WriteLine("Pay rate {0} is {1}",
   2, payRate[2].ToString("C"));
Console.WriteLine("Pay rate {0} is {1}",
   3, payRate[3].ToString("C"));
```

6. Add the two closing curly brackets that end the `Main()` method and the `ArrayDemo1` class.
7. Save the program as **ArrayDemo1.cs**.
8. Compile and run the program. The program's output appears in Figure 5-19.

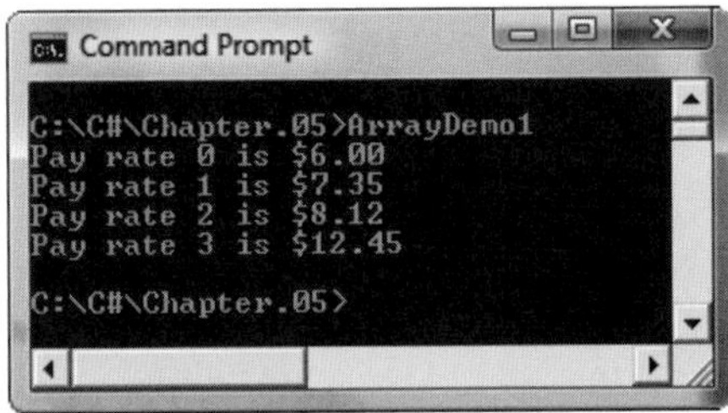

Figure 5-19 Output of `ArrayDemo1` program

INITIALIZING AN ARRAY

Next, you will alter your `ArrayDemo1` program to initialize the array of `double`s, rather than declaring the array in one step and assigning values later.

To initialize an array of `doubles`:

1. Open the **ArrayDemo1.cs** file in your text editor and immediately save it as **ArrayDemo2.cs**. Change the class name from `ArrayDemo1` to **`ArrayDemo2`**.
2. Delete the first six statements within the `Main()` method; these statements declare the array, instantiate it, and assign four values. Replace them with a single statement that accomplishes the same tasks:

```
double[] payRate = {6.00, 7.35, 8.12, 12.45};
```

3. Save, compile, and execute the program. The output looks the same as in Figure 5-19.

USING A `for` LOOP WITH AN ARRAY

Next, you will modify the `ArrayDemo2` program to use a `for` loop with the array.

To use a `for` loop with an array:

1. Open the **ArrayDemo2.cs** file in your text editor and immediately save it as **ArrayDemo3.cs**. Change the class name to **`ArrayDemo3`**.

2. Delete the four `WriteLine()` statements that print the four array values and replace them with the following `for` loop:

```
for(int x = 0; x < 4; ++x)
   Console.WriteLine("Pay rate {0} is {1}",
      x, payRate[x].ToString("C"));
```

   In this version of the statement, as `x` varies from 0 through 3, the value of `x` and the value of `payRate[x]` are both displayed.

3. Save, compile, and run the program. Again, the output is the same as in Figure 5-19.

USING THE `Length` PROPERTY WITH AN ARRAY

Next, you will modify the `ArrayDemo3` program to use the `Length` property. By doing so, no changes will be necessary to the `for` loop if you change the array size later—the `Length` field will automatically be updated to hold the current size of the array.

To use the `Length` property:

1. Open the **ArrayDemo3.cs** file in your text editor and immediately save it as **ArrayDemo4.cs**. Change the class name to **`ArrayDemo4`**.
2. Within the `for` statement that prints the array elements, change the 4 to **`payRate.Length`**.
3. Save, compile, and execute the program. The output is the same as in Figure 5-19.
4. At the end of the list of pay rates, insert a comma and a new, fifth rate of **22.22**.
5. Save the program, then compile and execute it again. The output looks like Figure 5-20. Even though you only added a new pay rate without making any other adjustments to the program, all five pay rates print correctly because C# adjusted the `Length` property.

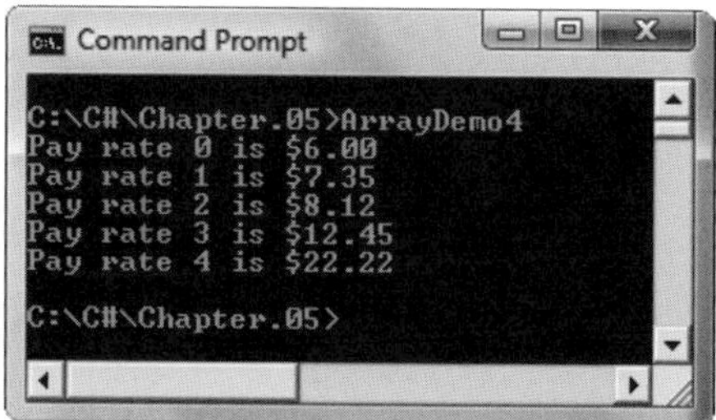

Figure 5-20 Output of `ArrayDemo4` program

USING THE `Sort()` AND `Reverse()` METHODS

In the next steps you will create an array of integers and use the `Sort()` and `Reverse()` methods to manipulate it.

To use the `Sort()` and `Reverse()` methods:

1. Open a new file in your text editor.
2. Type the beginning of a class named `MyTestScores` that includes an array of eight integer test scores, an integer you will use as a subscript, and a string that will hold user-entered data.

```
using System;
public class MyTestScores
{
   public static void Main()
   {
      int[] scores = new int[8];
      int x;
      string inputString;
```

>> **NOTE**
> The program displays `x + 1` with each `score[x]` because, although array elements are numbered starting with 0, people usually count items starting with 1.

3. Add a loop that prompts the user, accepts a test score, converts the score to an integer, and stores it as the appropriate element of the `scores` array.

```
for(x = 0; x < scores.Length; ++x)
{
   Console.Write("Enter your score on test {0} ", x + 1);
   inputString = Console.ReadLine();
   scores[x] = Convert.ToInt32(inputString);
}
```

>> **NOTE**
> You learned to set display field sizes when you learned about format strings in Chapter 2.

4. Add a statement that creates a dashed line to visually separate the input from the output. Display "Scores in original order:", then use a loop to display each score in a field that is six characters wide.

```
Console.WriteLine("\n-------------------------------");
Console.WriteLine("Scores in original order:");
for(x = 0; x < scores.Length; ++x)
    Console.Write("{0, 6}", scores[x]);
```

5. Add another dashed line for visual separation, then pass the `scores` array to the `Array.Sort()` method. Print "Scores in sorted order:", then use a loop to display each of the newly sorted scores.

```
Console.WriteLine("\n-------------------------------");
Array.Sort(scores);
Console.WriteLine("Scores in sorted order:");
for(x = 0; x < scores.Length; ++x)
    Console.Write("{0, 6}", scores[x]);
```

6. Add one more dashed line, reverse the array elements by passing `scores` to the `Array.Reverse()` method, display "Scores in reverse order:", and show the rearranged scores.

```
Console.WriteLine("\n-------------------------------");
Array.Reverse(scores);
Console.WriteLine("Scores in reverse order:");
for(x = 0; x < scores.Length; ++x)
    Console.Write("{0, 6}", scores[x]);
```

7. Add two closing curly braces—one for the `Main()` method and one for the class. Save the file as **MyTestScores.cs**. Compile and execute the program. Figure 5-21 shows a typical execution of the program. The user-entered scores are not in order, but after the call to the `Sort()` method, they appear in ascending order. After the call to the `Reverse()` method, they appear in descending order.

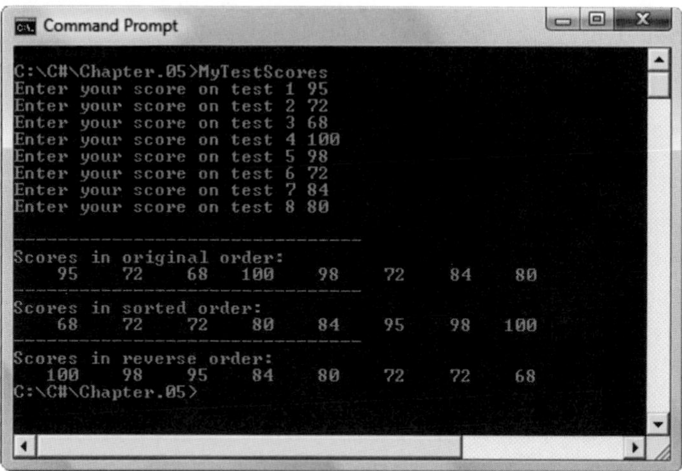

Figure 5-21 Typical execution of `MyTestScores` program

USING A CONSTANT FORMAT STRING

In the `MyTestScores` application, you repeatedly use the format string `"{0, 6}"` in the `Write()` statements to display each score in a field of size 6. Throughout this book, when a constant value has been used repeatedly, you have seen examples that employ a named constant. The advantage of creating a named constant to represent the format string in this program is that you can reformat the output's appearance in the future just by changing one line of code. Next, you will modify the `MyTestScores` class so the format string used for output can be easily modified.

To modify `MyTestScores` to use a constant format string for output:

1. Open the `MyTestScores` application in your text editor. Change the class name to **`MyTestScoresWithConstantFormat`** and immediately save the file as **MyTestScoresWithConstantFormat.cs**.
2. At the end of the existing list of declared variables, add a constant declaration as follows:

```
const string FORMAT = "{0, 6}";
```

3. Replace each occurrence of `"{0, 6}"` in the program with **`FORMAT`**. (With the addition of the constant format string in Step 2, these occurrences should be at lines 18, 23, and 28.) Make sure you replace all eight characters, including the existing quotation marks.

4. Save the file and execute the program. The output is identical to the output in Figure 5-21.
5. Modify the declaration of the `FORMAT` constant to the following:

```
const string FORMAT = "{0, 9}";
```

6. Save and execute the program. The output looks like Figure 5-22. By changing one character, you have consistently altered the output throughout the program. Whenever possible, you should consider how constants might help expedite future program modifications.

```
C:\C#\Chapter.05>MyTestScoresWithConstantFormat
Enter your score on test 1 95
Enter your score on test 2 72
Enter your score on test 3 68
Enter your score on test 4 100
Enter your score on test 5 98
Enter your score on test 6 72
Enter your score on test 7 84
Enter your score on test 8 80
------------------------------
Scores in original order:
       95       72       68      100       98       72       84       80
------------------------------
Scores in sorted order:
       68       72       72       80       84       95       98      100
------------------------------
Scores in reverse order:
      100       98       95       84       80       72       72       68
C:\C#\Chapter.05>
```

Figure 5-22 Typical execution of `MyTestScoresWithConstantFormat` program

NOTE If it makes more sense to your application, you could define a constant integer such as `const int SIZE = 6;`, and then create a format string with a statement such as `string format = "{0, " + SIZE + "}";`. In this case, `SIZE` would be constant, but `format` would be required to be a variable.

CHAPTER SUMMARY

» An array is a list of data items, all of which have the same type and the same name, but are distinguished from each other using a subscript or index. You declare an array variable by inserting a pair of square brackets after the type. You reserve memory for an array by using the keyword `new`. A subscript (also called an index) is an integer contained within square brackets that indicates one of an array's variables, or elements. Any array's elements are numbered 0 through one less than the array's length.

» In C#, arrays are objects of a class named `System.Array`. An array's fields are initialized to default values. To initialize an array to nondefault values, you use a list of values that are separated by commas and enclosed within curly braces.

» The power of arrays becomes apparent when you begin to use subscripts that are variables rather than constant values, and when you use loops to process array elements.

- When you work with array elements, you must ensure that the subscript you use remains in the range of 0 through `length - 1`. You can use the `Length` property, which is a member of the `System.Array` class, to automatically hold an array's length.
- You can use the `foreach` statement to cycle through every array element without using subscripts. With the `foreach` statement, you provide a temporary variable that automatically holds each array value in turn.
- When you want to determine whether some variable holds one of many possible valid values, you can compare the variable to a list of values in an array. If you set up a parallel array with the same number of elements and corresponding data, you can use the same subscript to access additional information.
- You can create parallel arrays to more easily perform a range match.
- The `BinarySearch()` method finds a requested value in a sorted array. The method returns –1 if the value is not found in the array; otherwise, it returns the array position of the sought value. You cannot use the `BinarySearch()` method if your array items are not arranged in ascending order, if the array holds duplicate values and you want to find all of them, or if you want to find a range match rather than an exact match.
- The `Sort()` method arranges array items in ascending order. The `Reverse()` method reverses the order of items in an array.
- C# supports multidimensional arrays—those that require multiple subscripts to access the array elements. The most commonly used multidimensional arrays are two-dimensional arrays that are rectangular. Two-dimensional arrays have two or more columns of values for each row. In a rectangular array, each row has the same number of columns. C# also supports jagged arrays, which are arrays of arrays.

KEY TERMS

An **array** is a list of data items that all have the same data type and the same name, but are distinguished from each other by a subscript or index.

The keyword **`new`** is also known as the **`new` operator**; it is used to create objects.

Each object in an array is an **array element**.

A **subscript** (also called an **index**) is an integer contained within square brackets that indicates the position of one of an array's elements.

An **initializer list** is the list of values provided for an array.

The class **`System.Array`** defines fields and methods that belong to every array.

The **`Length` property** is a member of the `System.Array` class that automatically holds an array's length.

The **`foreach` statement** is used to cycle through every array element without using a subscript.

A temporary **iteration variable** holds each array value in turn in a `foreach` statement.

A **parallel array** has the same number of elements as another array and corresponding data.

A **range match** determines the pair of limiting values between which a value falls.

The **`BinarySearch()` method** finds a requested value in a sorted array.

The **`Sort()` method** arranges array items in ascending order.

The **`Reverse()` method** reverses the order of items in an array.

A **one-dimensional** or **single-dimensional array** is an array whose elements you can access using a single subscript.

Multidimensional arrays require multiple subscripts to access the array elements.

Two-dimensional arrays have two or more columns of values for each row.

In a **rectangular array**, each row has the same number of columns.

When mathematicians use a two-dimensional array, they often call it a **matrix** or a **table**.

A **jagged array** is a one-dimensional array in which each element is another array.

REVIEW QUESTIONS

1. In an array, every element has the same ________ .

   a. subscript
   b. data type
   c. memory location
   d. all of the above

2. The operator used to create objects is ________ .

   a. =
   b. +=
   c. `new`
   d. `create`

3. Which of the following correctly declares an array of four integers?

   a. `int array[4];`
   b. `int[] array = 4;`
   c. `int[4] array;`
   d. `int[] array = new int[4];`

4. The value placed within square brackets after an array name is ________ .

   a. a subscript
   b. an index
   c. always an integer
   d. all of these

5. If you define an array to contain seven elements, then the highest array subscript you can use is ________ .

   a. 5
   b. 6
   c. 7
   d. 8

6. Initializing an array is ________ in C#.

   a. required
   b. optional
   c. difficult
   d. prohibited

7. When you declare an array of six `double` elements but provide no initialization values, the value of the first element is ________.

   a. 0.0　　c. 5.0

   b. 1.0　　d. unknown

8. Which of the following correctly declares an array of four integers?

   a. `int[] ages = new int[4] {20, 30, 40, 50};`

   b. `int[] ages = new int[] {20, 30, 40, 50};`

   c. `int[] ages = {20, 30, 40, 50};`

   d. all of these

9. When an `ages` array is correctly initialized using the values `{20, 30, 40, 50}`, as in Question 8, then the value of `ages[1]` is ________.

   a. 0　　c. 30

   b. 20　　d. undefined

10. When an `ages` array is correctly initialized using the values `{20, 30, 40, 50}`, as in Question 8, then the value of `ages[4]` is ________.

    a. 0　　c. 50

    b. 4　　d. undefined

11. When you declare an array as `int[] temperature = {0, 32, 50, 90, 212, 451};`, the value of `temperature.Length` is ________.

    a. 5　　c. 7

    b. 6　　d. unknown

12. Which of the following doubles every value in a 10-element integer array named `amount`?

    a. `for(int x = 9; x >= 0; --x) amount[x] *= 2;`

    b. `foreach(int number in amount) number *= 2;`

    c. both of these

    d. neither of these

13. Which of the following adds 10 to every value in a 15-element integer array named `points`?

    a. `for(int sub = 0; sub > 15; ++sub) points[sub] += 10;`

    b. `foreach(int sub in points) points += 10;`

    c. both of these

    d. neither of these

14. Two arrays that store related information in corresponding element positions are ________ .

    a. analogous arrays
    b. polymorphic arrays
    c. relative arrays
    d. parallel arrays

15. Assume an array is defined as `int[] nums = {2, 3, 4, 5};`. Which of the following would display the values in the array in reverse?

    a. `for(int x = 4; x > 0; --x) Console.Write(nums[x]);`
    b. `for(int x = 3; x >= 0; --x) Console.Write(nums[x]);`
    c. `for(int x = 3; x > 0; --x) Console.Write(nums[x]);`
    d. `for(int x = 4; x >= 0; --x) Console.Write(nums[x]);`

16. Assume an array is defined as `int[] nums = {7, 15, 23, 5};`. Which of the following would place the values in the array in descending numeric order?

    a. `Array.Sort(nums);`
    b. `Array.Reverse(nums);`
    c. `Array.Sort(nums); Array.Reverse(nums);`
    d. `Array.Reverse(nums); Array.Sort(nums);`

17. Which of the following traits do the `BinarySearch()` and `Sort()` methods have in common?

    a. Both methods take a single argument that must be an array.
    b. Both methods belong to the `System.Array` class.
    c. The array that each method uses must be in ascending order.
    d. They both operate on arrays made up of simple data types but not class objects.

18. If you use the `BinarySearch()` method and the object you seek is not found in the array, ________ .

    a. an error message is displayed
    b. a zero is returned
    c. the value `false` is returned
    d. a negative value is returned

19. The `BinarySearch()` method is inadequate when ________ .

    a. array items are in ascending order
    b. the array holds duplicate values and you want to find them all
    c. you want to find an exact match for a value
    d. array items are not numeric

20. Which of the following declares an integer array that contains eight rows and five columns?

    a. `int[8, 5] num = new int[ , ];`

    b. `int [8][5] num = new int[];`

    c. `int [ , ] num = new int[5, 8];`

    d. `int [ , ] num = new int[8, 5];`

EXERCISES

1. Write a program containing an array that holds five integers. Assign values to the integers. Display the integers from first to last, and then display them from last to first. Save the program as **IntegerList.cs**.

2. Write a program for a package delivery service. The program contains an array that holds the 10 zip codes to which the company delivers packages. Prompt a user to enter a zip code and display a message indicating whether the zip code is one to which the company delivers. Save the program as **CheckZips.cs**.

3. Write another program for the package delivery service in Exercise 2. The program should again use an array that holds the 10 zip codes to which the company delivers packages. Create a parallel array containing 10 delivery charges that differ for each zip code. Prompt a user to enter a zip code and then display either a message indicating the price of delivery to that zip code or a message indicating that the company does not deliver to the requested zip code. Save the program as **DeliveryCharges.cs**.

4. The Chat-A-While phone company provides service to six area codes and charges the following per-minute rates for phone calls:

Area Code	Per-Minute Rate ($)
262	0.07
414	0.10
608	0.05
715	0.16
815	0.24
920	0.14

   Write a program that allows a user to enter an area code and the length of time for a call in minutes, then display the total cost of the call. Save the program as **ChatAWhile.cs**.

5. The Whippet Bus Company charges prices for tickets based on distance traveled, as follows:

Distance (miles)	Ticket Price ($)
0–99	25.00
100–299	40.00
300–499	55.00
500 and farther	70.00

   Write a program that allows a user to enter a trip distance. The output is the ticket price. Save the program as **WhippetBus.cs**.

6. a. Write a program that prompts the user to make a choice for a pizza size—*S*, *M*, *L*, or *X*—and then displays the price as $6.99, $8.99, $12.50, or $15.00, respectively. Save the program as **PizzaPrices.cs**.

   b. Modify the `PizzaPrices` program so that the following discounts apply: no discount for one pizza, 10% for two pizzas, 15% for three or four pizzas, and 20% for five or more pizzas. Display a full accounting of the transaction, similar to that shown in Figure 5-23. Save the program as **PizzaPrices2.cs**.

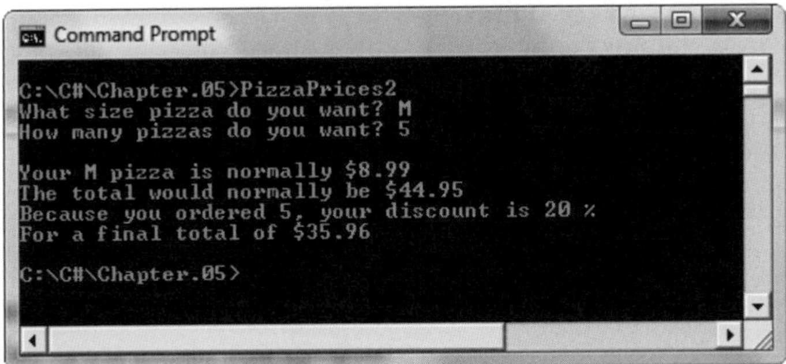

Figure 5-23 Typical execution of `PizzaPrices2` program

7. Write a program that computes commissions for automobile salespeople based on the value of the car. Salespeople receive 5 percent of the sale price for any car sold for up to and including $15,000; 7 percent for any car over $15,000 up to and including $24,000; and 10 percent of the sale price of any car over $24,000. Write a program that allows a user to enter a car price. The output is the salesperson's commission. Save the program as **Commission.cs**.

8. Create an array that stores 20 prices. Prompt a user to enter 20 values, then display the sum of the values. Next, display all values of less than $5.00. Finally, calculate the average of the prices, and display all values that are higher than the calculated average. Save the program as **Prices.cs**.

9. The Tiny Tots Tee-Ball league has 12 players who have jersey numbers 0 through 11. The coach wants a program into which he can type a player's number and the number of bases the player got in a turn at bat (a number 0 through 4). Write a program that allows the coach to continually enter the values until 999 is entered. Store the statistics in a two-dimensional array. At the end of a data-entry session, display each player's number and the number of 0-base, 1-base, 2-base, 3-base, and 4-base turns the player had. Display a separate count of the number of data-entry errors the coach makes (a player number greater than 11 or a number of bases greater than 4). The output should look similar to Figure 5-24. Save the program as **TeeBall.cs**.

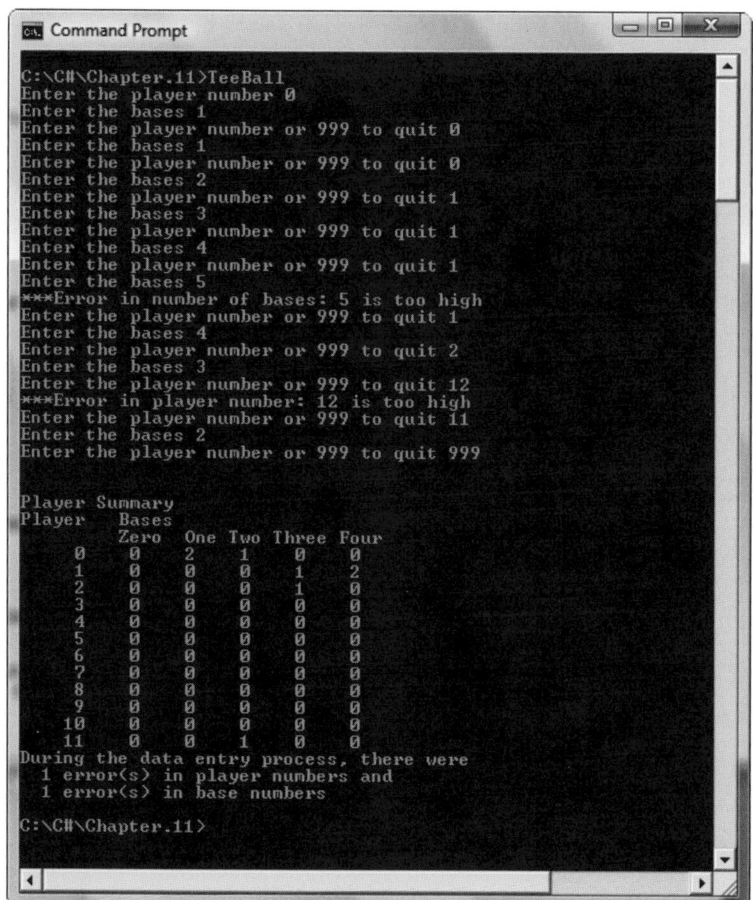

Figure 5-24 Typical execution of `TeeBall` program

DEBUGGING EXERCISES

Each of the following files in the Chapter.05 folder on your Student Disk has syntax and/or logical errors. In each case, determine the problem and fix the program. After you correct the errors, save each file using the same filename preceded with *Fixed*. For example, DebugFive01.cs will become FixedDebugFive01.cs.

a. DebugFive01.cs
b. DebugFive02.cs
c. DebugFive03.cs
d. DebugFive04.cs

UP FOR DISCUSSION

1. A train schedule is an everyday, real-life example of an array. Think of at least four more.
2. This chapter discusses sorting data. Suppose you are hired by a large hospital to write a program that displays lists of potential organ recipients. The hospital's doctors will consult this list if they have an organ that can be transplanted. You are instructed to sort potential recipients by last name and display them sequentially in alphabetical order. If more than 10 patients are waiting for a particular organ, the first 10 patients are displayed; the user can either select one of these or move on to view the next set of 10 patients. You worry that this system gives an unfair advantage to patients with last names that start with A, B, C, and D. Should you write and install the program? If you do not, many transplant opportunities will be missed while the hospital searches for another programmer to write the program.
3. This chapter discusses sorting data. Suppose your supervisor asks you to create a report that lists all employees sorted by salary. Suppose you also know that your employer will use this report to lay off the highest-paid employee in each department. Would you agree to write the program? Instead, what if the report's purpose was to list the worst performer in each department in terms of sales? What if the report grouped employees by gender? What if the report grouped employees by race? Suppose your supervisor asks you to sort employees by the dollar value of medical insurance claims they have in a year, and you fear the employer will use the report to eliminate workers who are driving up the organization's medical insurance costs. Do you agree to write the program even if you know that the purpose of the report is to eliminate workers?

CHAPTER SIX

6

USING METHODS

In this chapter you will:

- Learn about methods
- Write methods with no parameters and no return value
- Learn about implementation hiding
- Write methods that require a single argument
- Write methods that require multiple arguments
- Write a method that returns a value
- Pass an array to a method
- Use reference parameters, output parameters, and parameter arrays with methods
- Overload methods
- Learn how to avoid ambiguous methods

In the first five chapters of this book, you learned to create C# programs containing `Main()` methods that declare variables, accept input, perform arithmetic, and produce output. You learned to add decisions, loops, and arrays to your programs. As your programs grow in complexity, their `Main()` methods will contain many additional statements. Rather than creating increasingly long `Main()` methods, most programmers prefer to modularize their programs, placing instructions in smaller "packages" called methods. In this chapter, you learn to create many types of C# methods. You will gain the ability to send data to these methods and to receive information back from them.

UNDERSTANDING METHODS

A **method** is an encapsulated series of statements that carry out a task. Any class can contain an unlimited number of methods. So far, you have written classes that contain a `Main()` method, but no others. Your `Main()` methods have **invoked**, or **called**, other methods; that is, your program used a method's name and the method performed a job for the class. For example, you have created many programs that call the `WriteLine()` and `ReadLine()` methods. When you used arrays in Chapter 5, you learned how to use the `BinarySearch()`, `Sort()`, and `Reverse()` methods. The methods you have used were written for you; you only had to call them to have them work.

»NOTE You first learned the term "argument" in Chapter 1.

»NOTE Methods are similar to the procedures, functions, and subroutines used in other programming languages.

For example, consider the simple `HelloClass` program shown in Figure 6-1. The `Main()` method contains a statement that calls the `Console.WriteLine()` method. You can identify method names because they always are followed by a set of parentheses. Depending on the method, there might be an argument within the parentheses. The call to the `WriteLine()` method within the `HelloClass` program in Figure 6-1 contains the string argument "Hello". The simplest methods you can invoke don't require any arguments.

```
using System;
public class HelloClass
{
   public static void Main()
   {
      Console.WriteLine("Hello");
   }
}
```

Figure 6-1 The `HelloClass` program

»NOTE In the `HelloClass` program in Figure 6-1, `Main()` is a **calling method**—one that calls another. The `WriteLine()` method is a **called method**.

When you call the `WriteLine()` method within the `HelloClass` program in Figure 6-1, you use a method that has already been created for you. Because the creators of C# knew you would often want to write a message to the output screen, they created a method you could call to accomplish that task. This method takes care of all the hardware details of producing a message on the output device; you simply call the method and pass the desired message to it. The creators of C# were able to anticipate many of the methods you would need for your programs; you will continue to use many of these methods throughout this book. However, your programs often will require custom methods that the creators of C# could not have expected. In this chapter, you will learn to write your own custom methods.

»TWO TRUTHS AND A LIE: UNDERSTANDING METHODS

1. A method is an encapsulated series of statements that carry out a task.
2. Any class can contain an unlimited number of methods.
3. All the methods your programs will use have been written for you and stored in files.

The false statement is #3. As you write programs, you will want to write many of your own custom methods.

WRITING METHODS WITH NO PARAMETERS AND NO RETURN VALUE

The output of the program in Figure 6-1 is simply the word “Hello”. Suppose you want to add three more lines of output to display a standard welcoming message when users execute your program. Of course, you can add three new `WriteLine()` statements to the existing program, but you also can create a method to display the three new lines.

There are two major reasons to create a method instead of adding three lines to the existing program:

- If you add a method call instead of three new lines, the `Main()` method will remain short and easy to follow. The `Main()` method will contain just one new statement that calls a method rather than three separate `WriteLine()` statements.
- More importantly, a method is easily *reusable*. After you create the welcoming method, you can use it in any program. In other words, you do the work once, and then you can use the method many times.

»NOTE When you place code in a callable method instead of repeating the same code at several points in a program, you are avoiding **code bloat**—a colorful term that describes unnecessarily long or repetitive statements.

In C#, a method must include:

- A **method declaration**, which is also known as a **method header** or **method definition**
- An opening curly brace
- A **method body**, which is a block of statements that carry out the method's work
- A closing curly brace

The method declaration defines the rules for using the method; it contains:

- » Optional declared accessibility
- » An optional `static` modifier
- » The return type for the method
- » The method name, or identifier
- » An opening parenthesis
- » An optional list of method parameters (you separate the parameters with commas if there is more than one)
- » A closing parenthesis

»NOTE A method is always accessible by other methods in the same class.

The optional declared **accessibility** for a method sets limits as to how other methods can use your method; it can be any of the following:

- » **Public access**, which you select by including a `public` modifier in the member declaration. This modifier allows unlimited access to a method.
- » **Protected internal access**, which you select by including both a `protected` and an `internal` modifier in the member declaration. This modifier limits method access to the containing program, the containing class, or types derived from the containing class.
- » **Protected access**, which you select by including a `protected` modifier in the member declaration. This modifier limits method access to the containing class or types derived from the containing class.
- » **Internal access**, which you select by including an `internal` modifier in the member declaration. This modifier limits method access to the containing class or program.
- » **Private access**, which you select by including a `private` modifier in the member declaration. This modifier limits method access to the containing class.

»NOTE You will learn about protected access and what it means to derive types in Chapter 8.

Table 6-1 summarizes where a method is accessible, depending on its accessibility modifier. If you do not provide an accessibility modifier for a method, it is `private` by default. As you study C#, deciding which access modifier to choose will become clearer. For example, when you begin to create your own class objects, you usually will provide them with `public` methods, but sometimes you will make methods `private`. For now, all the methods you create will be `public`.

Declared accessibility	Containing classes	Derived classes	Containing programs	All classes
`public`	Yes	Yes	Yes	Yes
`protected internal`	Yes	Yes	Yes	No
`protected`	Yes	Yes	No	No
`internal`	Yes	No	Yes	No
`private`	Yes	No	No	No

Table 6-1 Summary of method accessibility

Additionally, you can declare a method to be **static** or **nonstatic**. If you use the keyword modifier `static`, you indicate that a method can be called without referring to an object. Instead, you refer to the class. If you do not indicate that a method is `static`, it is nonstatic by default and can only be used in conjunction with an object. When you begin to create your own class objects in Chapter 7, you will write many nonstatic methods and your understanding of the use of these terms will become clearer. For now, all methods you create will be `static`.

Every method has a **return type**, indicating what kind of value the method will return to any other method that calls it. If a method does not return a value, its return type is `void`. A method's return type is known more succinctly as a **method's type**. Later in this chapter, you will create methods that return values; for now, the methods will be `void` methods.

>>NOTE When a method's return type is `void`, most C# programmers do not end the method with a `return` statement. However, you can end a `void` method with the following statement that indicates nothing is returned:

```
return;
```

>>NOTE You have used a return value from the `ReadLine()` method when you have written a statement such as `inputString = Console.ReadLine();`.

Every method has a name that must be a legal C# identifier; that is, it must not contain spaces and must begin with a letter of the alphabet or an underscore.

Every method name is followed by a set of parentheses. Sometimes these parentheses contain parameters, but in the simplest methods, the parentheses are empty.

In summary, the first methods you write will be `public`, `static`, and `void` and will have empty parameter lists. Therefore, you can write the `WelcomeMessage()` method as it is shown in Figure 6-2. According to its declaration, it is `public` and `static`. It returns nothing, so its return type is `void`. Its identifier is `WelcomeMessage`, and it receives nothing, so its parentheses are empty. Its body, consisting of three `WriteLine()` statements, appears within curly braces.

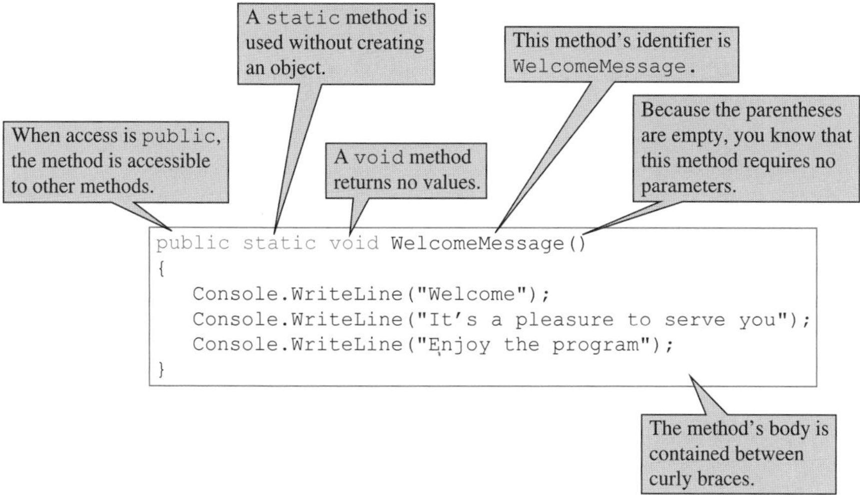

Figure 6-2 The `WelcomeMessage()` method

You can place any statements you want within a method body, and you can declare variables within a method. When a variable is declared within a method, it is known only from that point to the end of the method. The area in which a variable is known is its **scope**.

NOTE
In Chapter 4 you learned that when a method ceases to exist, it is *out of scope*.

You can place a method in its own file, as you will learn in the next section. You also can place a method within the file of a program that will use it, but you cannot place a method within any other method. Figure 6-3 shows the two locations where you can place the `WelcomeMessage()` method within the `HelloClass` program file—before the `Main()` method header or after the `Main()` method's closing brace.

```
using System;
public class HelloClass
{
   // The WelcomeMessage() method could go here
   public static void Main()
   {
      Console.WriteLine("Hello");
   }
   // Alternatively, the WelcomeMessage() method could go here
   // But it cannot go in both places
}
```

Figure 6-3 Placement of methods

If a `Main()` method calls the `WelcomeMessage()` method, then you simply use the `WelcomeMessage()` method's name as a statement within the body of the `Main()` method. Figure 6-4 shows the complete program with the method call shaded, and Figure 6-5 shows the output.

```
using System;
public class HelloClass
{
   public static void Main()
   {
      WelcomeMessage();
      Console.WriteLine("Hello");
   }
   public static void WelcomeMessage()
   {
      Console.WriteLine("Welcome");
      Console.WriteLine("It's a pleasure to serve you");
      Console.WriteLine("Enjoy the program");
   }
}
```

Figure 6-4 `HelloClass` program with `Main()` method calling the `WelcomeMessage()` method

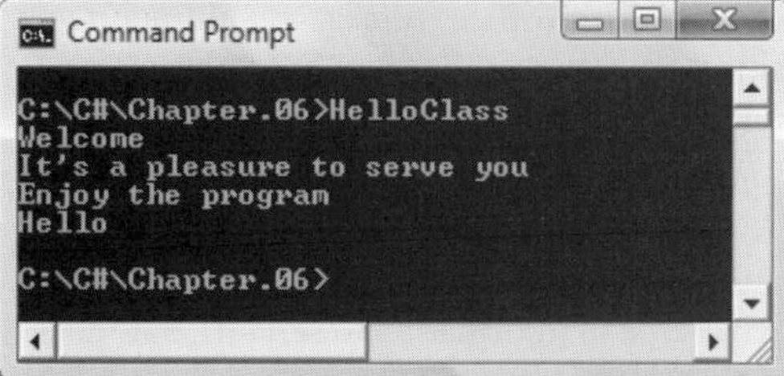

Figure 6-5 Output of `HelloClass` program

When the `Main()` method executes, it calls the `WelcomeMessage()` method, then it prints "Hello". Because the `Main()` method calls the `WelcomeMessage()` method before it prints "Hello", the three lines that make up the welcome message appear first in the output.

»NOTE Each of two different classes can have its own method named `WelcomeMessage()`. Such a method in the second class would be entirely distinct from the identically named method in the first class.

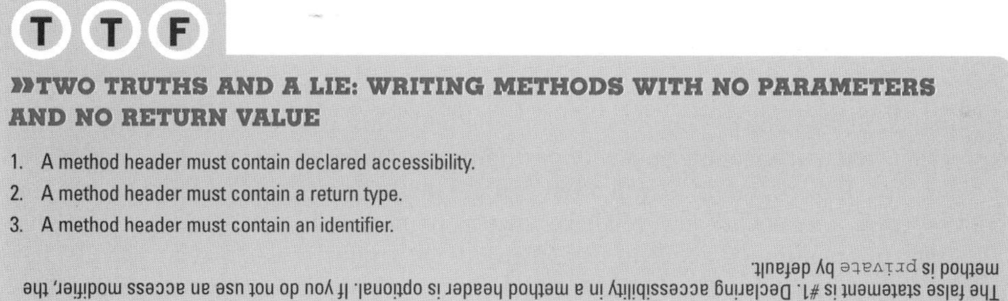

»TWO TRUTHS AND A LIE: WRITING METHODS WITH NO PARAMETERS AND NO RETURN VALUE

1. A method header must contain declared accessibility.
2. A method header must contain a return type.
3. A method header must contain an identifier.

The false statement is #1. Declaring accessibility in a method header is optional. If you do not use an access modifier, the method is `private` by default.

HIDING IMPLEMENTATION

An important principle of object-oriented programming is the notion of **implementation hiding**—keeping the details of a method's operations hidden. When you make a request to a method, you don't need to know the details of how the method is implemented. For example, when you make a dental appointment, you do not need to know how the appointment is actually recorded at the dental office—perhaps it is written in a book, marked on a large chalkboard, or entered into a computerized database. The implementation details are of no concern to you as a client, and if the dental office changes its methods from one year to the next, the change does not affect your use of the appointment method. Your only concern is the way you **interface** or interact with the dental office, not how the office records appointments. Similarly, if you use a thermostat to raise the temperature in your apartment or house, you do not need to know whether the heat is generated by natural gas, electricity, solar energy, or a hamster on a wheel. As long as you receive heat, the implementation details can remain hidden.

The same is true with well-written program methods; the invoking program or method must know the name of the method it is using (and what type of information to send it), but the program does not need to know how the method works. Later, you can substitute a new, improved method for the old one, and if the interface to the method does not change, you won't need to make any changes in programs that invoke the method.

>> **NOTE** Hidden implementation methods often are said to exist in a black box. A **black box** is any device you can use without knowing how it works internally.

>> **NOTE** A method that uses another is called a **client** of the second method.

For example, suppose you rewrite the `WelcomeMessage()` method as shown in Figure 6-6. The method is constructed differently from the one with the identical name shown in Figure 6-2—the new method uses two statements instead of three, uses a `Write()` method for a portion of its output instead of all `WriteLine()` methods, and uses two newline escape sequences ('\n'). Nevertheless, if you substitute the new version for the old one, any program that uses the method does not need to be altered, and the output is identical.

```
public static void WelcomeMessage()
{
   Console.Write("Welcome\nIt's a pleasure ");
   Console.WriteLine("to serve you\nEnjoy the program");
}
```

Figure 6-6 Alternate `WelcomeMessage()` method

>> **NOTE** You first learned about escape sequences in Chapter 2. Table 2-5 provides a list of commonly used escape sequences.

You should not alter the `WelcomeMessage()` method arbitrarily. However, as you learn to program, you will encounter many opportunities to substitute an improved method for an older, less efficient one. Also, you often will use methods written by others or that you "borrow" from other applications you have written. To more easily incorporate methods into a program, it is common practice to store methods (or groups of associated methods) in their own classes and files. Then you can add them into any application that uses them. The resulting compound program is called a **multifile assembly**. As you learn more about C#, you might prefer to take this approach with your own programs. For now, for simplicity, methods will be contained in the same file as any other methods that use them.

>> **NOTE** Details on creating a multifile assembly are provided in Appendix B.

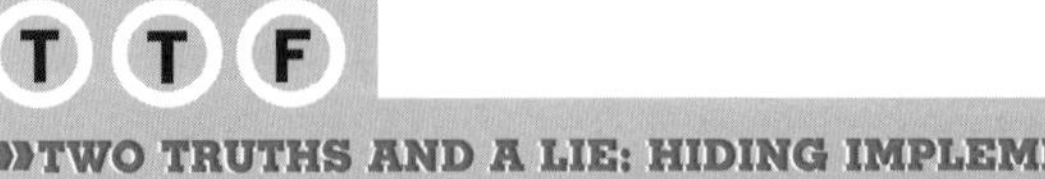

>>TWO TRUTHS AND A LIE: HIDING IMPLEMENTATION

1. When you call a method, you must know the method's identifier.
2. When you call a method, you must know what type of information to send it.
3. When you call a method, you must know how the method works.

The false statement is #3. You do not need to know how a method is implemented in order to use it.

WRITING METHODS THAT REQUIRE A SINGLE ARGUMENT

Some methods require additional information. If a method could not receive arguments, then you would have to write an infinite number of methods to cover every possible situation. For example, when you make a dental appointment, you do not need to employ a different method for every date of the year at every possible time of day. Rather, you can supply the date and time as information to the method, and no matter what date and time you supply, the method is carried out in the same manner. If you design a method to triple numeric values, it makes sense that you can supply the `Triple()` method with an argument representing the value to be tripled, rather than having to develop a `Triple1()` method, a `Triple2()` method, and so on.

»NOTE In Chapter 1, you learned that arguments are passed into methods in the method call. A data item accepted by a method in its header is a parameter.

»NOTE You already have used a method to which you supplied a wide variety of parameters. At any call, the `System.WriteLine()` method can receive any one of an infinite number of strings as a parameter—"Hello", "Goodbye", and so on. No matter what message you send to the `WriteLine()` method, the message will be displayed correctly.

When you write the declaration for a method that can receive a parameter, you need to include the following items within the method declaration parentheses:

» The type of the parameter
» A local identifier (name) for the parameter

For example, consider a `public` method named `DisplaySalesTax()`, which displays the result of multiplying a value that represents a selling price by 7%. The method header for a usable `DisplaySalesTax()` method could be the following:

```
public static void DisplaySalesTax(double saleAmount)
```

You can think of the parentheses in a method declaration as a funnel into the method—data parameters listed there are "dropping in" to the method.

The parameter `double saleAmount` within the parentheses indicates that the `DisplaySalesTax()` method will receive a value of type `double`. Within the method, the value will be known as `saleAmount`. Figure 6-7 shows a complete method.

```
public static void DisplaySalesTax(double saleAmount)
{
   double tax;
   const double RATE = 0.07;
   tax = saleAmount * RATE;
   Console.WriteLine("The tax on {0} is {1}",
      saleAmount, tax.ToString("C"));
}
```

Figure 6-7 The `DisplaySalesTax()` method

»NOTE Within the DisplaySalesTax() method, you must use the format string and ToString() method if you want figures to display to exactly two decimal positions. You learned how to display values to a fixed number of decimal places in Chapter 2; recall that using the fixed format with no number defaults to two decimal places.

You create the DisplaySalesTax() method as a void method (it has a void return type) because you do not need it to return any value to any method that uses it—its only function is to receive the saleAmount value, multiply it by 0.07, and then display the result. You create it as a static method because you do not want to create an object with which to use it.

Within a program, you can call the DisplaySalesTax() method by using the method's name, and, within parentheses, an argument that is either a constant value or a variable. Thus, both of the following calls to the DisplaySalesTax() method invoke it correctly:

```
double myPurchase = 12.99;
DisplaySalesTax(12.99);
DisplaySalesTax(myPurchase);
```

»NOTE A variable is local to a method when it is declared within that method.

You can call the DisplaySalesTax() method any number of times, with a different constant or variable argument each time. The value of each of these arguments becomes known as saleAmount within the method. The identifier saleAmount holds any double value passed into the method. Interestingly, if the argument in the method call is a variable, it might possess the same identifier as saleAmount or a different one, such as myPurchase. The identifier saleAmount is simply the name the value "goes by" while being used within the method, no matter what name it goes by in the calling program. That is, the variable saleAmount is a **local variable** to the DisplaySalesTax() method. The variable saleAmount is also an example of a **formal parameter**, a parameter within a method header that accepts a value. In contrast, arguments within a method *call* often are referred to as **actual parameters**.

»NOTE The variable saleAmount is also an example of a value parameter, or a parameter that receives a copy of the value passed to it. You will learn more about value parameters as well as other types of parameters later in this chapter.

If a programmer changes the way in which the tax value is calculated—for example, by coding one of the following—programs that use the DisplaySalesTax() method will not be affected and will not need to be modified:

```
tax = saleAmount * 7 / 100;
tax = 0.07 * saleAmount;
tax = RATE * saleAmount;
```

Each of these statements computes tax as 7% of saleAmount. No matter how the tax is calculated, a calling program passes a value into the DisplaySalesTax() method, and a calculated result appears on the screen.

Figure 6-8 shows a complete program called `UseTaxMethod`. It uses the `DisplaySalesTax()` method twice, first with a variable argument, and then with a constant argument. The program's output appears in Figure 6-9.

```
using System;
public class UseTaxMethod
{
   public static void Main()
   {
      double myPurchase = 12.99;
      DisplaySalesTax(myPurchase);
      DisplaySalesTax(35.67);
   }
   public static void DisplaySalesTax(double saleAmount)
   {
      double tax;
      const double RATE = 0.07;
      tax = saleAmount * RATE;
      Console.WriteLine("The tax on {0} is {1}",
         saleAmount.ToString("C"), tax.ToString("C"));
   }
}
```

Figure 6-8 Complete program using the `DisplaySalesTax()` method two times

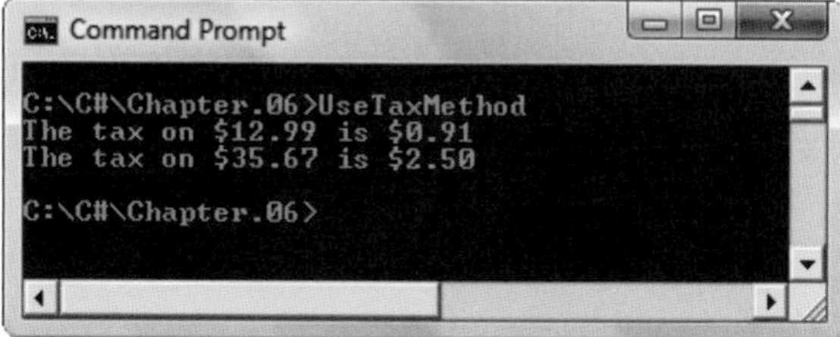

Figure 6-9 Output of the `UseTaxMethod` program

NOTE Now that you have seen how to write methods that accept an argument, you might guess that when you write `Console.WriteLine("Hello");`, the header for the called method is similar to `public void WriteLine(string s)`. You might not know the parameter name the creators of C# have chosen, but you do know the method's return type, name, and parameter type. (If you use the IntelliSense feature of Visual Studio, you can discover the parameter name. See Appendix C for more details.)

»TWO TRUTHS AND A LIE: WRITING METHODS THAT REQUIRE A SINGLE ARGUMENT

1. When you write the declaration for a method that can receive a parameter, you need to include the parameter's data type within the method header.
2. When you write the declaration for a method that can receive a parameter, you need to include the identifier of the argument that will be sent to the method within the method header.
3. When you write the declaration for a method that can receive a parameter, you need to include a local identifier for the parameter within the method header.

The false statement is #2. When you write the definition for a method, you include the data type and a local parameter name within the parentheses of the method header, but you do not include the name of any argument that will be sent from a calling method. After all, the method might be invoked any number of times with any number of different arguments.

WRITING METHODS THAT REQUIRE MULTIPLE ARGUMENTS

A method can require more than one argument. You can pass multiple arguments to a method by listing the arguments within the call to the method and separating them with commas. For example, rather than creating a `DisplaySalesTax()` method that multiplies an amount by 0.07, you might prefer to create a more flexible method to which you can pass two values—the value on which the tax is calculated and the tax percentage by which it should be multiplied. Figure 6-10 shows a method that uses two such arguments.

```
public static void DisplaySalesTax(double saleAmount, double taxRate)
{
    double tax;
    tax = saleAmount * taxRate;
    Console.WriteLine("The tax on {0} at {1} is {2}",
        saleAmount.ToString("C"),
        taxRate.ToString("P"), tax.ToString("C"));
}
```

Figure 6-10 The `DisplaySalesTax()` method that takes two arguments

In Figure 6-10, two parameters (`double saleAmount` and `double taxRate`) appear within the parentheses in the method header. A comma separates the parameters, and each parameter requires its own named type (in this case, both parameters are of type `double`) and an identifier. When you pass values to the method in a statement such as `DisplaySalesTax(myPurchase, localRate);`, the first value passed will be referenced as `saleAmount` within the method, and the second value passed will be referenced as `taxRate`. Therefore, it is very important that arguments be passed to a method in the correct order. The following call results in output stating that "The tax on $200.00 is $20.00":

```
DisplaySalesTax(200.00, 0.10);
```

However, the following call results in output stating that "The tax on $0.10 is $20.00", which is clearly incorrect.

```
DisplaySalesTax(0.10, 200.00);
```

»NOTE A declaration for a method that receives two or more arguments must list the type for each parameter separately, even if the parameters have the *same* type.

»NOTE If two method parameters are of the same type—for example, two `doubles`—passing arguments to a method in the wrong order results in a logical error. If a method expects parameters of diverse types, then passing arguments in reverse order constitutes a syntax error.

Figure 6-11 shows a complete program that calls the `DisplaySalesTax()` method two times. Figure 6-12 shows the output.

```
using System;
public class UseTaxMethod2
{
   public static void Main()
   {
      double myPurchase = 239.11;
      double myRate = 0.10;
      DisplaySalesTax(myPurchase, myRate);
      DisplaySalesTax(16.55, 0.02);
   }
   public static void DisplaySalesTax(double saleAmount,
      double taxRate)
   {
      double tax;
      tax = saleAmount * taxRate;
      Console.WriteLine("The tax on {0} at {1} is {2}",
         saleAmount.ToString("C"),
         taxRate.ToString("P"), tax.ToString("C"));
   }
}
```

Figure 6-11 The `UseTaxMethod2` program

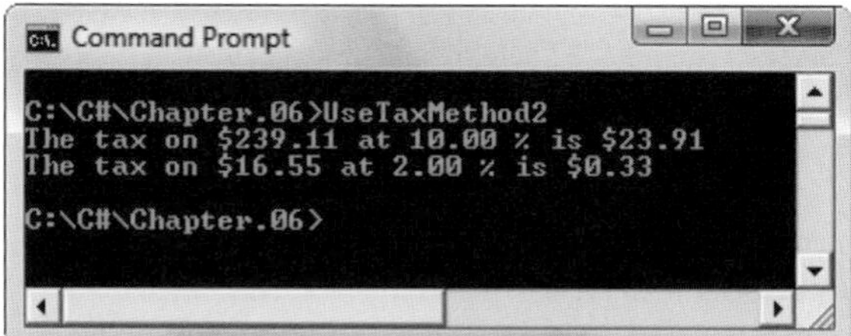

Figure 6-12 Output of the `UseTaxMethod2` program

You can write a method to take any number of parameters in any order. When you call the method, however, the arguments you send to it must match (in both number and type) the parameters listed in the method declaration. Thus, a method to compute an automobile salesperson's commission might require arguments such as an integer value of a sold car, a `double` percentage commission rate, and a character code for the vehicle type. The correct method will execute only when three arguments of the correct types are sent in the correct order.

»TWO TRUTHS AND A LIE: WRITING METHODS THAT REQUIRE MULTIPLE ARGUMENTS

1. The following is a usable C# method header:
   `public static void MyMethod(double amt, sum)`
2. The following is a usable C# method header:
   `private void MyMethod2(int x, double y)`
3. The following is a usable C# method header:
   `static void MyMethod3(int id, string name, double rate)`

The false statement is #1. In a method header, each parameter must have a data type, even if the data types for all the parameters are the same. The header in #2 does not contain the keyword `static`, but that is optional. Likewise, the header in #3 does not contain an accessibility indicator, but that is optional also.

WRITING A METHOD THAT RETURNS A VALUE

A method can return, at most, one value to a method that calls it. The return type for a method can be any type used in the C# programming language, which includes the basic built-in types `int`, `double`, `char`, and so on, as well as class types (including class types you create). Of course, a method also can return nothing, in which case the return type is `void`.

»NOTE In addition to the primitive types, a method can return a class type. If a class named `BankLoan` exists, a method might return an instance of a `BankLoan` as in `public BankLoan ApprovalProcess()`. In other words, a method can return anything from a simple `int` to a complicated `BankLoan` object that contains 20 data fields. You will create classes like `BankLoan` in Chapter 7.

For example, the declaration for the `WelcomeMessage()` method shown in Figure 6-2 is:

```
public static void WelcomeMessage()
```

This method is `public` and returns no value, so it is of type `void`. A method that returns `true` or `false` depending on whether an employee worked overtime hours might be defined as:

```
public bool IsOvertimeEarned()
```

This method is `public` and returns a `bool` value, so it is of type `bool`.

Suppose you want to create a method to accept the hours an employee worked and the hourly pay rate, and to return a calculated gross pay value. The header for this method could be:

```
public static double CalcPay(double hours, double rate)
```

Figure 6-13 shows this method.

```
public static double CalcPay(double hours, double rate)
{
    double gross;
    gross = hours * rate;
    return gross;
}
```

Figure 6-13 The `CalcPay()` method

Notice the return type `double` in the method header. Also notice the `return` statement, which is the last statement within the method. A **`return` statement** causes a value to be sent back to the calling method; in the `CalcPay()` method, the value stored in `gross` is sent back to any method that calls the `CalcPay()` method. The data type used in a method's `return` statement must be the same as the return type declared in the method's header.

If a method returns a value and you call the method, you typically will want to use the returned value, although you are not required to use it. For example, when you invoke the `CalcPay()` method, you might want to assign the value to a `double` variable named `grossPay`, as in the following statement:

```
grossPay = CalcPay(myHours, myRate);
```

The `CalcPay()` method returns a `double`, so it is appropriate to assign the returned value to a `double` variable. Figure 6-14 shows a program that uses the `CalcPay()` method in the shaded statement, and Figure 6-15 shows the output.

Instead of storing a method's returned value in a variable, you can use it directly, as in either of the following statements:

```
Console.WriteLine("My gross pay is {0}",
    CalcPay(myHours, myRate).ToString("C"));
double tax = CalcPay(myHours, myRate) * TAX_RATE;
```

In the first statement, the call to the `CalcPay()` method is made from within the `WriteLine()` method call. In the second, `CalcPay()`'s returned value is used in an arithmetic statement. Because `CalcPay()` returns a `double`, you can use the method call `CalcPay()` in the same way you would use any `double` value. The method call `CalcPay()` has a `double` value in the same way a `double` variable has a `double` value.

```
using System;
public class UseCalcPay
{
   public static void Main()
   {
      double myHours = 37.5;
      double myRate = 12.75;
      double grossPay;
      grossPay = CalcPay(myHours, myRate);
      Console.WriteLine("I worked {0} hours at {1} per hour",
         myHours, myRate);
      Console.WriteLine("My gross pay is {0}",
         grossPay.ToString("C"));
   }
   public static double CalcPay(double hours, double rate)
   {
      double gross;
      gross = hours * rate;
      return gross;
   }
}
```

Figure 6-14 Program using the `CalcPay()` method

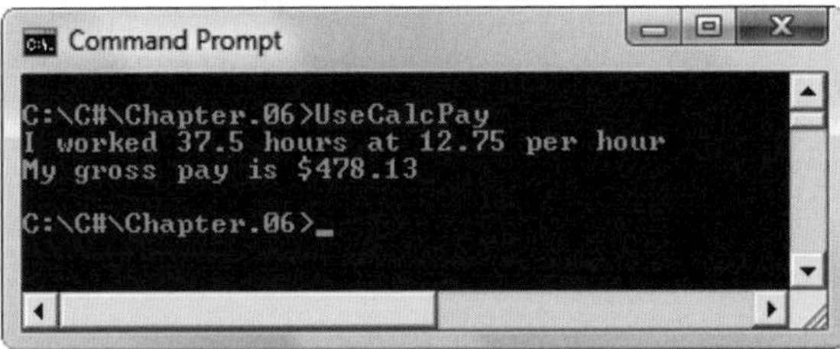

Figure 6-15 Output of `UseCalcPay` program

As an additional example, suppose you have a method named `GetPrice()` whose header is as follows:

```
double GetPrice(int itemNumber)
```

The method accepts an integer item number and returns its price. Further suppose that you want to ask the user to enter an item number from the keyboard so you can pass it to the `GetPrice()` method. You can get the value from the user, store it in a string, convert the string to an integer, pass the integer to the `GetPrice()` method, and store the returned value in a variable named `price` in four or five separate statements, or you can write the following:

```
price = GetPrice(Convert.ToInt32(Console.ReadLine));
```

This statement contains a method call to `ReadLine()` within a method call to `Convert.ToInt32()`, within a method call to `GetPrice()`. When method calls are placed inside other method calls, the calls are **nested method calls**. When you write a statement with three nested method calls like the previous statement, the innermost method executes first. Its return value is then used as an argument to the intermediate method, and its return value is used as an argument to the outer method. There is no limit to how "deep" you can go with nested method calls.

»NOTE Now that you have seen how to write methods that accept arguments, you might guess that the method header for the `Console.ReadLine()` method is `public static string ReadLine()`. You know the method returns a `string`, and you know it takes no parameters.

»TWO TRUTHS AND A LIE: WRITING A METHOD THAT RETURNS A VALUE

1. A method can return, at most, one value to a method that calls it.
2. The data type used in a method's `return` statement must be the same as the return type declared in the method's header.
3. If a method returns a value and you call the method, you must store the value in a variable that has the same data type as the method's parameter.

The false statement is #3. If a method returns a value and you call the method, you typically will want to use the returned value, but you are not required to use it. Furthermore, if you do store the returned value in a variable, that variable must be the same data type as the method's return value, not its parameter's value.

PASSING AN ARRAY TO A METHOD

In Chapter 5, you learned that you can declare an array to create a list of elements, and that you can use any individual array element in the same manner as you would use any single variable of the same type. That is, suppose you declare an integer array as follows:

```
int[] someNums = new int[12];
```

You can subsequently print `someNums[0]` or add one to `someNums[1]`, just as you would for any integer. Similarly, you can pass a single array element to a method in exactly the same manner as you would pass a variable.

```
using System;
public class PassArrayElement
{
   public static void Main()
   {
      int[] someNums = {10, 12, 22, 35};
      int x;
      Console.Write("\nAt beginning of Main() method...");
      for(x = 0; x < someNums.Length; ++x)
         Console.Write("{0, 6}", someNums[x]);
      Console.WriteLine();
      for(x = 0; x < someNums.Length; ++x)
         MethodGetsOneInt(someNums[x]);
      Console.Write("At end of Main() method.........");
      for(x = 0; x < someNums.Length; ++x)
         Console.Write("{0, 6}", someNums[x]);
   }
   public static void MethodGetsOneInt(int oneVal)
   {
      Console.Write("In MethodGetsOneInt() {0}", oneVal);
      oneVal = 999;
      Console.WriteLine("     After change {0}", oneVal);
   }
}
```

Figure 6-16 `PassArrayElement` program

Consider the program shown in Figure 6-16. This program creates an array of four integers and prints them. Next, the program calls a method named `MethodGetsOneInt()` four times, passing each of the array elements in turn. The method prints the passed value, changes the number to 999, and then prints the number again. Finally, back in the `Main()` method, the four numbers print again. Figure 6-17 shows the output.

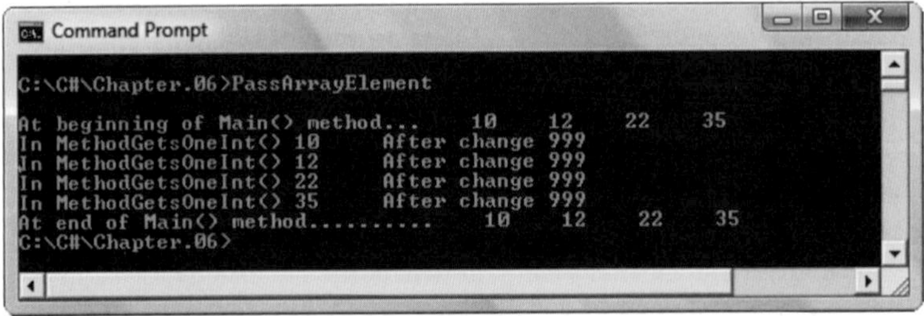

Figure 6-17 Output of `PassArrayElement` program

As you can see in Figure 6-17, the program displays the four original values, then passes each to the `MethodGetsOneInt()` method, where it is displayed and then changed to 999. After the method executes four times, the `Main()` method displays the four values again, showing that they are unchanged by the assignments within `MethodGetsOneInt()`. The `oneVal` variable is local to the `MethodGetsOneInt()` method; therefore, any changes to variables passed into the method are not permanent and are not reflected in the array declared in the `Main()` program. Each `oneVal` variable in the `MethodGetsOneInt()` method holds only a copy of the array element passed into the method, and the `oneVal` variable holding the assigned value of 999 exists only while the `MethodGetsOneInt()` method is executing.

Instead of passing a single array element to a method, you can pass an entire array as a parameter. You indicate that a method parameter must be an array by placing square brackets after the data type in the method's parameter list. When you pass an array to a method, changes you make to array elements within the method are permanent; that is, they are reflected in the original array that was sent to the method. Arrays, like all objects but unlike built-in types, are **passed by reference**; that is, the method receives the actual memory address of the array and has access to the actual values in the array elements.

NOTE You already have seen that methods can alter arrays passed to them. When you use the `Sort()` and `Reverse()` methods, the methods change the array contents.

NOTE You can create and pass an unnamed array to a method in a single step. For example, you can write the following:

```
MethodThatAcceptsArray(new int[] {45, 67, 89});
```

The program shown in Figure 6-18 creates an array of four integers. After the integers are printed, the entire array is passed to a method named `MethodGetsArray()` in the shaded statement. Within the method header, the parameter is declared as an array by using square brackets after the parameter type. Within the method, the numbers are printed, which shows that they retain their values from `Main()` upon entering the method, but then the value 888 is assigned to each number. Even though `MethodGetsArray()` is a `void` method (meaning that nothing is returned to the `Main()` method), when the program prints the array for the second time within the `Main()` method, all of the values have been changed to 888, as you can see in Figure 6-19. Because arrays are passed by reference, the `MethodGetsArray()` method "knows" the address of the array declared in `Main()` and makes its changes directly to the original array that was declared in the `Main()` method.

You can pass a multidimensional array to a method by indicating the appropriate number of dimensions after the data type in the method header. For example, the following method headers accept two-dimensional arrays of `int`s and `double`s, respectively:

```
public static void displayScores(int[,]scoresArray)
public static boolean areAllPricesHigh(double[,] prices)
```

NOTE Recall that in Chapter 5 you learned how two-dimensional arrays are stored in computer memory.

With jagged arrays, you can insert the appropriate number of square brackets after the data type in the method header. For example, the following method headers accept jagged arrays of `int`s and `double`s, respectively:

```
public static void displayIDs(int[][] idArray)
public static double computeTotal(double[][] prices)
```

```
using System;
public class PassEntireArray
{
   public static void Main()
   {
      int[] someNums = {10, 12, 22, 35};
      int x;
      Console.Write("\nAt beginning of Main() method...");
      for(x = 0; x < someNums.Length; ++x)
         Console.Write("{0, 6}", someNums[x]);
      Console.WriteLine();
      MethodGetsArray(someNums);
      Console.Write("At end of Main() method.........");
      for(x = 0; x < someNums.Length; ++x)
         Console.Write("{0, 6}", someNums[x]);
   }
   public static void MethodGetsArray(int[] vals)
   {
      int x;
      Console.Write("In MethodGetsArray() ");
      for(x = 0; x < vals.Length; ++x)
         Console.Write(" {0}", vals[x]);
      Console.WriteLine();
      for(x = 0; x < vals.Length; ++x)
         vals[x] = 888;
      Console.Write("After change");
      for(x = 0; x < vals.Length; ++x)
         Console.Write(" {0}", vals[x]);
      Console.WriteLine();
   }
}
```

Figure 6-18 `PassEntireArray` program

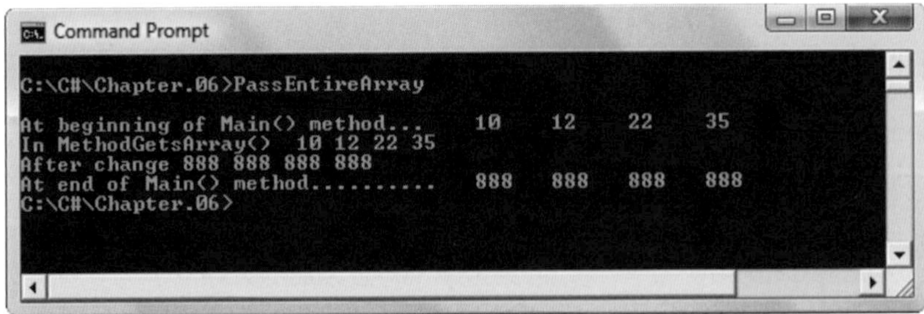

Figure 6-19 Output of the `PassEntireArray` program

In each case, notice that the brackets that define the array in the method header are empty. There is no need to insert numbers into the brackets because each passed array name is a starting memory address. The way you manipulate subscripts within the method determines how rows and columns are accessed.

»NOTE The size of each dimension of a multidimensional array can be accessed using the `GetLength()` method. For example, `scoresArray.GetLength(0)` returns the value of the first dimension of `scoresArray`.

»TWO TRUTHS AND A LIE: PASSING AN ARRAY TO A METHOD

1. You indicate that a method parameter can be an array element by placing a data type and identifier in the method's parameter list.
2. You indicate that a method parameter must be an array by placing parentheses after the data type in the method's parameter list.
3. Arrays are passed by reference; that is, the method receives the actual memory address of the array and has access to the actual values in the array elements.

The false statement is #2. You indicate that a method parameter must be an array by placing square brackets after the data type in the method's parameter list.

USING `ref`, `out`, AND `params` PARAMETERS WITHIN METHODS

In C#, you can write methods with four kinds of formal parameters listed within the parentheses in the method header. These four types are:

- » Value parameters, which are declared without any modifiers
- » Reference parameters, which are declared with the `ref` modifier
- » Output parameters, which are declared with the `out` modifier
- » Parameter arrays, which are declared with the `params` modifier

USING VALUE PARAMETERS

So far, all of the method parameters you have created (except arrays) have been value parameters. When you use a **value parameter** in a method header, you indicate the parameter's type and name, and the method receives a copy of the value passed to it. This copy—the formal parameter—is stored at a different memory address than the variable that was used as the parameter in the method call—the actual parameter. In other words, the actual parameter and the formal parameter refer to two separate memory locations, and any change to the formal parameter value within the method has no effect on the actual parameter value back in the calling method. Changes to value parameters never affect the original argument in the calling method.

NOTE Using a real-world analogy, you know that people with the same name living in different places are not the same person. Changes in the life of Jane Doe in Maine, such as a raise or a department transfer, have no effect on Jane Doe in Vermont. The same is true of like-named variables located in different methods.

Figure 6-20 shows a program that declares a variable named `var`, assigns 4 to it, prints it, and passes it to a method that accepts a value parameter. The method assigns a new value, 777, to the formal, passed parameter and prints it. When control returns to the `Main()` method, the value of `var` remains 4. Changing the value of `var` within the `MethodWithValueParam()` method has no effect on `var` in `Main()`. Even though both methods contain a variable named `var`, they represent two separate variables, each with its own memory location. Figure 6-21 shows the output.

```
using System;
public class ParameterDemo1
{
   public static void Main()
   {
      int var = 4;
      Console.WriteLine("In Main var is {0}", var);
      MethodWithValueParam(var);
      Console.WriteLine("In Main var is {0}", var);
   }
   public static void MethodWithValueParam(int var)
   {
      var = 777;
      Console.WriteLine("In MethodWithValueParam, param is {0}", var);
   }
}
```

Figure 6-20 Program calling method with a value parameter

NOTE A variable that is used as an argument to a method with a value parameter must have a value assigned to it. If it does not, the program will not compile.

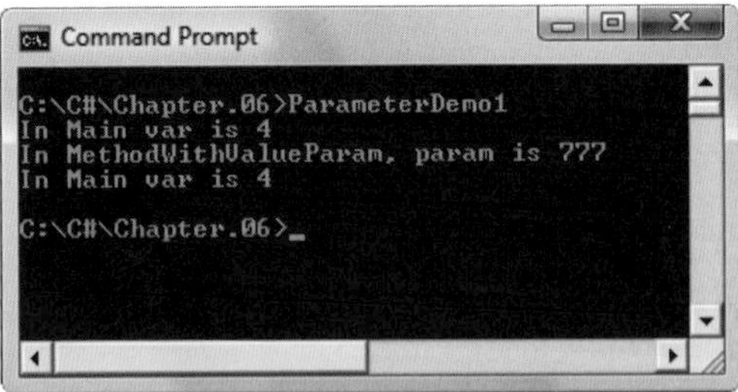

Figure 6-21 Output of `ParameterDemo1` program

NOTE Programmers say that a value parameter is used for "in" parameter passing—that is, values for these parameters go into a method, but modifications to them do not come "out."

In the `MethodWithValueParam()` method, it makes no difference whether you use the name `var` as the `Main()` method's actual parameter or use some other name. In either case, the passed and received variables occupy separate memory locations.

USING REFERENCE AND OUTPUT PARAMETERS

On occasion, you might want a method to be able to alter a value you pass to it. In that case, you can use a reference parameter or an output parameter. Both **reference** and **output parameters** have memory addresses that are passed to a method, allowing it to alter the original variables. Reference and output parameters differ as follows:

- » When you declare a reference parameter in a method header, the parameter must have been assigned a value; in other words, in the calling method, any argument must be a constant or a variable with an assigned value.
- » When you use an output parameter, it need not contain an original value. However, an output parameter must receive a value before the method ends.

Neither reference nor output parameters occupy their own memory locations. Rather, both reference and output parameters act as **aliases**, or pseudonyms (other names), for the same memory location occupied by the original passed variable. You use the keyword `ref` as a modifier to indicate a reference parameter and the keyword `out` as a modifier to indicate an output parameter.

»NOTE Using an alias for a variable is similar to using an alias for a person. Jane Doe might be known as "Ms. Doe" at work but "Sissy" at home. Both names refer to the same person.

Figure 6-22 shows a `Main()` program that calls a `MethodWithRefParam()` method. The `Main()` method declares a variable, displays its value, and then passes the variable to the `MethodWithRefParam()` method in the shaded statement. The modifier `ref` precedes the variable name `var` in both the method call and the method header. The method's parameter `myParam` holds the memory address of `var`, making `myParam` an alias for `var`. When the

```
using System;
public class ParameterDemo2
{
   public static void Main()
   {
      int var = 4;
      Console.WriteLine("In Main var is {0}", var);
      MethodWithRefParam(ref var);   // notice use of ref
      Console.WriteLine("In Main var is {0}", var);
   }
   public static void MethodWithRefParam(ref int myParam)
      // notice use of ref
   {
      myParam = 888;
      Console.WriteLine("In MethodWithRefParam, myParam is {0}",
         myParam);
   }
}
```

Figure 6-22 Program calling method with a reference parameter

method changes the value of myParam, the change persists in the var variable within Main(). Figure 6-23 shows the output of the program.

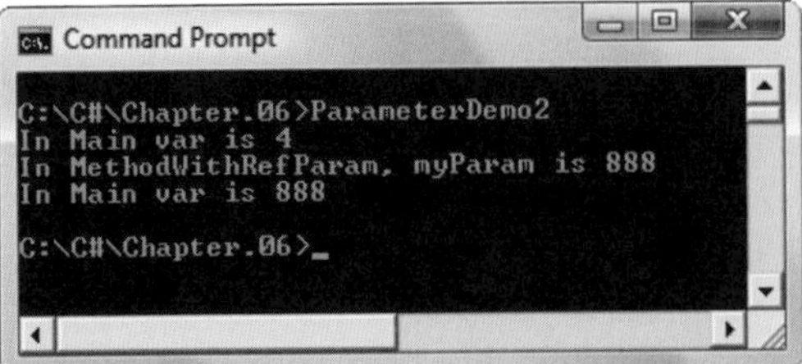

Figure 6-23 Output of ParameterDemo2 program

In the header for the MethodWithRefParam() method, it makes no difference whether you use the same name as the Main() method's passed variable (var) or some other name, such as myParam. In either case, the passed and received variables occupy the same memory location—the address of one is the address of the other.

When you use a reference parameter, the passed variable must have an assigned value. Using an output parameter is convenient when the passed variable doesn't have a value yet. For example, the program in Figure 6-24 uses InputMethod() to obtain values for two parameters. The

```
using System;
public class InputMethodDemo
{
   public static void Main()
   {
      int first, second;
      InputMethod(out first, out second); // notice use of out
      Console.WriteLine("After InputMethod first is {0}", first);
      Console.WriteLine("and second is {0}", second);
   }
   public static void InputMethod(out int one, out int two)
      // notice use of out
   {
      string s1, s2;
      Console.Write("Enter first integer ");
      s1 = Console.ReadLine();
      Console.Write("Enter second integer ");
      s2 = Console.ReadLine();
      one = Convert.ToInt32(s1);
      two = Convert.ToInt32(s2);
   }
}
```

Figure 6-24 InputMethodDemo program

parameters that are sent in the shaded statement get their values from the method, so it makes sense to provide them with no values going in. Instead, they acquire values in the method and retain the values coming out. Figure 6-25 shows a typical execution of the program.

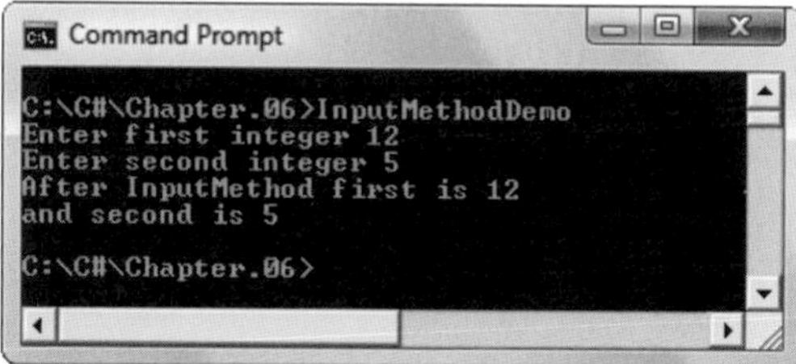

Figure 6-25 Output of `InputMethodDemo` program

In summary, when you need a method to alter a single value, you have two options:

- » You can send a value parameter to a method, alter the local version of the variable within the method, return the altered value, and assign the return value to the original variable back in the calling method.
- » You can send a reference or output parameter and alter the original value from within the method.

A major advantage to using reference or output parameters exists when you want a method to change multiple variables. A method can have only a single return type and can return at most only one value. By using reference or output parameters to a method, you can change multiple values.

»NOTE As with simple parameters, you can use `out` or `ref` when passing an array to a method. You do so when you want the method to create a new array by using the location of the named array in the calling method. For example, assume a `Main()` method declares an array without assigning any values or using the `new` operator to assign memory, as in:

```
double[] payRate;
```

Then you can pass the array to a method with the header:

```
AssignValues(out double[] money);
```

You do so by using the statement:

```
AssignValues(out payRate);
```

Within the `AssignValues()` method, you can initialize the array as `money = new double[6];`, thereby creating a new array.

USING PARAMETER ARRAYS

When you don't know how many arguments you might eventually send to a method, you can declare a **parameter array**—a local array declared within the method header by using the keyword **`params`**. Such a method accepts any number of arguments.

For example, a method with the following header accepts an array of strings:

```
public static void DisplayStrings(params string[] people)
```

In the call to this method, you can use one, two, or any other number of strings as actual parameters; within the method, they will be treated as an array. Figure 6-26 shows a program that calls `DisplayStrings()` three times—once with one string argument, once with three string arguments, and once with an array of strings. In each case, the method works correctly, treating the passed strings as an array and displaying them appropriately. Figure 6-27 shows the output.

```
using System;
public class ParamsDemo
{
   public static void Main()
   {
      string[] names = {"Mark", "Paulette", "Carol", "James"};
      DisplayStrings("Ginger");
      DisplayStrings("George", "Maria", "Thomas");
      DisplayStrings(names);
   }
   public static void DisplayStrings(params string[] people)
   {
      foreach(string person in people)
         Console.Write("{0} ", person);
      Console.WriteLine("\n----------------");
   }
}
```

Figure 6-26 `ParamsDemo` program

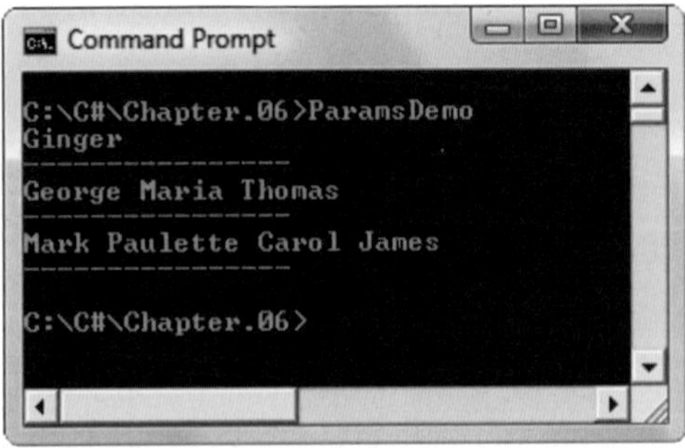

Figure 6-27 Output of `ParamsDemo` program

»NOTE You could create an even more flexible method by using a method header such as `Display(params Object[] things)`. Then the passed parameters could be any type—strings, integers, other classes, and so on. The method could be implemented as follows:

```
public static void Display(params Object[] things)
{
    foreach(Object obj in things)
        Console.Write("{0} ", obj);
    Console.WriteLine("\n--------------")
}
```

All data types are `Objects`; you will learn more about the `Object` class in Chapter 7.

»NOTE No additional parameters are permitted after the `params` keyword in a method declaration, and only one `params` keyword is permitted in a method declaration.

»TWO TRUTHS AND A LIE: USING `ref`, `out`, AND `params` PARAMETERS WITHIN METHODS

1. A value parameter is declared without a modifier and receives a copy of the argument passed in; the argument must have been assigned a value.
2. A reference parameter is declared with the `ref` modifier, receives a memory address, and the argument passed in must have been assigned a value.
3. An output parameter is declared with the `out` modifier, receives a memory address, and the argument passed in must not have been assigned a value.

The false statement is #3. When you use an output parameter, it need not contain an original value, but it can have one. However, an output parameter must receive a value before the method ends.

OVERLOADING METHODS

Overloading involves using one term to indicate diverse meanings. When you use the English language, you frequently overload words. When you say "open the door," "open your eyes," and "open a computer file," you describe three very different actions that use different methods and produce different results. However, anyone who speaks English fluently has no trouble comprehending your meaning because the verb "open" is understood in the context of the noun that follows it.

»NOTE Overloading a method is an example of polymorphism—the ability of a method to act appropriately depending on the context. You first learned the term *polymorphism* in Chapter 1.

»NOTE Some C# operators are overloaded. For example, a + between two values indicates addition, but a single + to the left of a value means the value is positive. The + sign has different meanings based on the arguments used with it. In Chapter 7, you will learn how to overload operators to make them mean what you want with your own classes.

»NOTE
A method's name and parameter list constitute the method's **signature.**

When you overload a C# method, you write multiple methods with a shared name. The compiler understands your meaning based on the arguments you use with the method. For example, suppose you create a method to display a `string` surrounded by a border. The method receives a `string` and uses the `string Length` property to determine how many asterisks to use to construct a border around the `string`. Figure 6-28 shows the method.

»NOTE
In Chapter 5 you learned that arrays and `string`s both automatically acquire a `Length` property upon creation.

```
public static void DisplayWithBorder(string word)
{
    const int EXTRA_STARS = 4;
    const string SYMBOL = "*";
    int size = word.Length + EXTRA_STARS;
    int x;
    for(x = 0; x < size; ++x)
       Console.Write(SYMBOL);
    Console.WriteLine();
    Console.WriteLine(SYMBOL + " " + word + " " + SYMBOL);
    for(x = 0; x < size; ++x)
       Console.Write(SYMBOL);
    Console.WriteLine("\n\n");
}
```

Figure 6-28 The `DisplayWithBorder()` method with a `string` parameter

When a program calls the `DisplayWithBorder()` method and passes a `string` value, as in `DisplayWithBorder("Ed")`, the method calculates a size as the length of the string plus 4, and then draws that many symbols on a single line. The method then displays a symbol, a space, the string, another space, and another symbol on the next line. The method ends by again displaying a row of symbols and some blank lines. Figure 6-29 shows a sample program that uses the method, and Figure 6-30 shows the output.

Suppose you are so pleased with the output of the `DisplayWithBorder()` method that you want to use something similar to display your company's weekly sales goal figure. The problem is that the weekly sales goal amount is stored as an integer, and so it cannot be passed to the existing method. You can take one of several approaches:

- » You can convert the integer sales goal to a `string` and use the existing method. This is an acceptable approach, but it requires that you remember to write an extra step in any program in which you display an integer using the border.
- » You can create a new method with a unique name such as `DisplayWithBorderUsingInt()` and use it to accept an integer parameter. The drawback to this approach is that you must remember different method names when you use different data types.

```
using System;
public class BorderDemo1
{
   public static void Main()
   {
      DisplayWithBorder("Ed");
      DisplayWithBorder("Theodore");
      DisplayWithBorder("Jennifer Ann");
   }
   public static void DisplayWithBorder(string word)
   {
      const int EXTRA_STARS = 4;
      const string SYMBOL = "*";
      int size = word.Length + EXTRA_STARS;
      int x;
      for(x = 0; x < size; ++x)
         Console.Write(SYMBOL);
      Console.WriteLine();
      Console.WriteLine(SYMBOL + " " + word + " " + SYMBOL);
      for(x = 0; x < size; ++x)
         Console.Write(SYMBOL);
      Console.WriteLine("\n\n");
   }
}
```

Figure 6-29 The `BorderDemo1` program

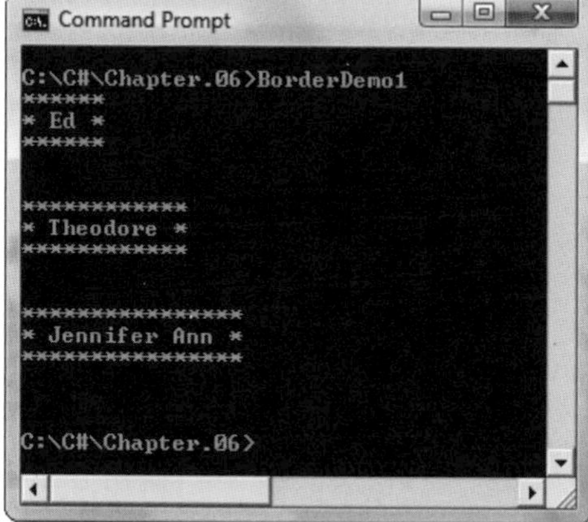

Figure 6-30 Output of the `BorderDemo1` program

» You can overload the `DisplayWithBorder()` method. Overloading methods involves writing multiple methods with the same name, but with different parameter types. For example, in addition to the `DisplayWithBorder()` method shown in Figure 6-28, you could use the method shown in Figure 6-31.

```
public static void DisplayWithBorder(int number)
{
   const int EXTRA_STARS = 4;
   const string SYMBOL = "*";
   int size = EXTRA_STARS + 1;
   int leftOver = number;
   int x;
   while(leftOver >= 10)
   {
      leftOver = leftOver / 10;
      ++size;
   }
   for(x = 0; x < size; ++x)
      Console.Write(SYMBOL);
   Console.WriteLine();
   Console.WriteLine(SYMBOL + " " + number + " " + SYMBOL);
   for(x = 0; x < size; ++x)
      Console.Write(SYMBOL);
   Console.WriteLine("\n\n");
}
```

Figure 6-31 The `DisplayWithBorder()` method with an integer parameter

In the version of the `DisplayWithBorder()` method in Figure 6-31, the parameter is an `int`. The method used to determine how many asterisks to display is to discover the number of digits in the parameter by repeatedly dividing by 10. For example, when the argument to the method is 456, `leftOver` is initialized to 456. Because it is at least 10, it is divided by 10, giving 45, and `size` is increased to 2. Then 45 is divided by 10, giving 4, and `size` is increased to 3. Because 4 is not at least 10, the loop ends, and the program has determined that the parameter contains three digits. The rest of the method executes like the original version that accepts a `string` parameter.

»NOTE The `DisplayWithBorder()` method does not work correctly if a negative integer is passed to it because the negative sign occupies an additional display space. To rectify the problem, you could modify the method to add an extra symbol to the border when a negative argument is passed in, or you could force all negative numbers to be their positive equivalent.

If both versions of `DisplayWithBorder()` are included in a program and you call the method using a `string`, as in `DisplayWithBorder("Ed")`, the first version of the method shown in Figure 6-28 executes. If you use an integer as the argument in the call to `DisplayWithBorder()`, as in `DisplayWithBorder(456)`, then the method shown in Figure 6-31 executes. Figure 6-32 shows a program that demonstrates several method calls, and Figure 6-33 shows the output.

```
using System;
public class BorderDemo2
{
   public static void Main()
   {
      DisplayWithBorder("Ed");
      DisplayWithBorder(3);
      DisplayWithBorder(456);
      DisplayWithBorder(897654);
      DisplayWithBorder("Veronica");
   }
   public static void DisplayWithBorder(string word)
   {
      const int EXTRA_STARS = 4;
      const string SYMBOL = "*";
      int size = word.Length + EXTRA_STARS;
      int x;
      for(x = 0; x < size; ++x)
         Console.Write(SYMBOL);
      Console.WriteLine();
      Console.WriteLine(SYMBOL + " " + word + " " + SYMBOL);
      for(x = 0; x < size; ++x)
         Console.Write(SYMBOL);
      Console.WriteLine("\n\n");
   }
   public static void DisplayWithBorder(int number)
   {
      const int EXTRA_STARS = 4;
      const string SYMBOL = "*";
      int size = EXTRA_STARS + 1;
      int leftOver = number;
      int x;
      while(leftOver >= 10)
      {
         leftOver = leftOver / 10;
         ++size;
      }
      for(x = 0; x < size; ++x)
         Console.Write(SYMBOL);
      Console.WriteLine();
      Console.WriteLine(SYMBOL + " " + number + " " + SYMBOL);
      for(x = 0; x < size; ++x)
         Console.Write(SYMBOL);
      Console.WriteLine("\n\n");
   }
}
```

Figure 6-32 The `BorderDemo2` program

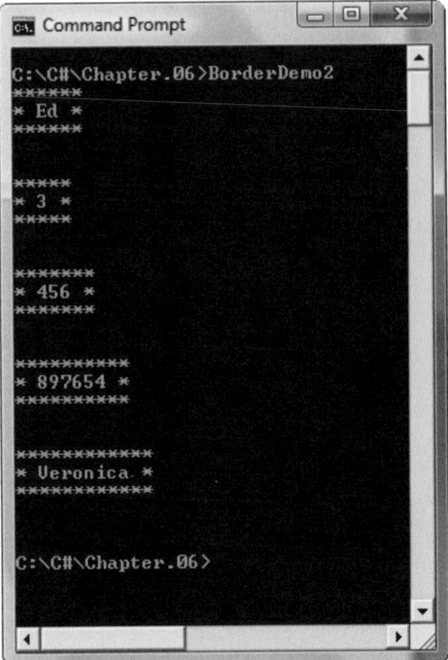

Figure 6-33 Output of the `BorderDemo2` program

Methods are overloaded correctly when they have the same identifier but their parameter types are different. For example, you could write several methods with the same identifier and one could accept an `int`, another two `int`s, and another three `int`s. A fourth version could accept an `int` followed by a `double` and another could accept a `double` followed by an `int`. Yet another version could accept no parameters. The parameter identifiers in overloaded methods do not matter; it is only the method identifier and parameter list types that cause a method to be overloaded.

Instead of overloading methods, you can choose to use methods with different names to accept the diverse data types, and you can place a decision within your program to determine which version of the method to call. However, it is more convenient to use one method name and then let the compiler determine which method to use. Overloading a method also makes it more convenient for other programmers to use your method in the future. Frequently, you create overloaded methods in your classes not because you need them immediately, but because you know client programs might need multiple versions in the future, and it is easier for programmers to remember one reasonable name for tasks that are functionally identical except for parameter types.

»NOTE In this book you have seen the `Console.WriteLine()` method used with a string parameter, a numeric parameter, and with no parameter. You have also seen it used with several parameters when you use a format string along with several variables. Therefore, you know `Console.WriteLine()` is an overloaded method.

»TWO TRUTHS AND A LIE: OVERLOADING METHODS

1. The following methods are overloaded:

```
public static void MethodA(int a)
public static void MethodA(double b)
```

2. The following methods are overloaded:

```
public static void MethodC(int c)
public static void MethodD(int c)
```

3. The following methods are overloaded:

```
public static void MethodE(int e)
public static void MethodE(int e, int f)
```

The false answer is #2. Overloaded methods must have the same name, but different parameter lists.

AVOIDING AMBIGUOUS METHODS

When you overload a method, you run the risk of creating **ambiguous** methods—a situation in which the compiler cannot determine which method to use. Every time you call a method, the compiler decides whether a suitable method exists; if so, the method executes, and if not, you receive an error message.

For example, suppose you write two versions of a simple method, as in the program in Figure 6-34. The class contains two versions of a method named `SimpleMethod()`—one that takes a `double` and `int`, and one that takes an `int` and a `double`.

```
using System;
public class AmbiguousMethods
{
   public static void Main()
   {
      int iNum = 20;
      double dNum = 4.5;
      SimpleMethod(iNum, dNum);   // calls first version
      SimpleMethod(dNum, iNum);   // calls second version
      SimpleMethod(iNum, iNum);   // error! Call is ambiguous.
   }
   public static void SimpleMethod(int i, double d)
   {
       Console.WriteLine("Method receives int and double");
   }
   public static void SimpleMethod(double d, int i)
   {
       Console.WriteLine("Method receives double and int");
   }
}
```

Figure 6-34 Program containing ambiguous method call

»NOTE In Chapter 2 you learned that when an `int` is promoted to a `double`, the process is called an *implicit conversion*.

In the `Main()` method in Figure 6-34, a call to `SimpleMethod()` with an integer argument first and a `double` argument second executes the first version of the method, and a call to `SimpleMethod()` with a `double` argument first and an integer argument second executes the second version of the method. With each of these calls, the compiler can find an exact match for the arguments you send. However, if you call `SimpleMethod()` using two integer arguments, as in the shaded statement, an ambiguous situation arises because there is no exact match for the method call. Because the first integer could be promoted to a `double` (matching the second version of the overloaded method), or the second integer could be promoted to a `double` (matching the first version), the compiler does not know which version of `SimpleMethod()` to use, and the program will not compile or execute. Figure 6-35 shows the error message that is generated.

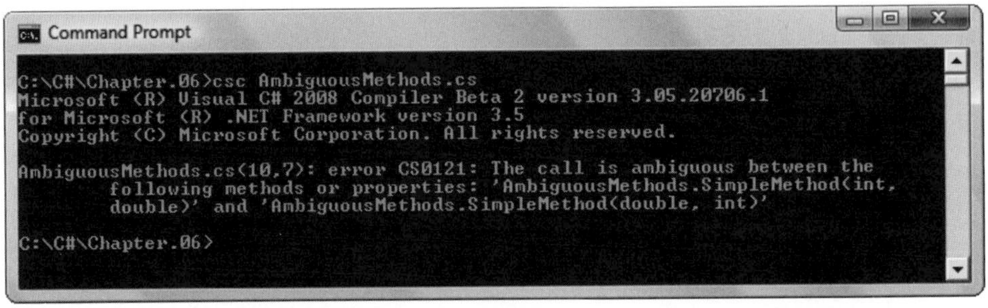

```
Command Prompt

C:\C#\Chapter.06>csc AmbiguousMethods.cs
Microsoft (R) Visual C# 2008 Compiler Beta 2 version 3.05.20706.1
for Microsoft (R) .NET Framework version 3.5
Copyright (C) Microsoft Corporation. All rights reserved.

AmbiguousMethods.cs(10,7): error CS0121: The call is ambiguous between the
        following methods or properties: 'AmbiguousMethods.SimpleMethod(int,
        double)' and 'AmbiguousMethods.SimpleMethod(double, int)'

C:\C#\Chapter.06>
```

Figure 6-35 Error message generated by ambiguous method call

»NOTE An overloaded method is not ambiguous on its own—it becomes ambiguous only if you create an ambiguous situation. A program with potentially ambiguous methods will run without problems if you make no ambiguous method calls. For example, if you remove the `SimpleMethod()` call that contains two integers from the program in Figure 6-34, the program runs as expected.

»NOTE If you remove one of the versions of `SimpleMethod()` from the program in Figure 6-34, then the method call that uses two integer arguments would work, because one of the integers could be promoted to a `double`.

Methods can be overloaded correctly by providing different parameter lists for methods with the same name. Methods with identical names that have identical parameter lists but different return types are not overloaded—they are illegal. For example, the following two methods cannot coexist within a program:

```
public static int AMethod(int x)
public static void AMethod(int x)
```

The compiler determines which of several versions of a method to call based on parameter lists. When the method call `AMethod(17);` is made, the compiler will not know which method to execute because both possibilities take an integer argument. Similarly, the following method could not coexist with either of the previous versions:

```
public static void AMethod(int someNumber)
```

Even though this method uses a different local identifier for the passed value, its parameter list is still the same to the compiler—a single integer.

»TWO TRUTHS AND A LIE: AVOIDING AMBIGUOUS METHODS

1. The following methods are potentially ambiguous:
```
public static int Method1(int g)
public static int Method1(int g, int h)
```
2. The following methods are potentially ambiguous:
```
public static double Method2(int j)
public static void Method2(int k)
```
3. The following methods are potentially ambiguous:
```
public static void Method3(string m)
public static string Method3(string n)
```

The false answer is #1. Those methods are not ambiguous because they have different parameter lists. Their matching return types do not cause ambiguity.

YOU DO IT

CALLING A METHOD

To write a program in which a `Main()` method calls another method that displays a company's logo:

1. Open a new file in your text editor. Enter the statement that uses the `System` namespace, then type the class header for the `DemoLogo` class and type the class-opening curly brace.
```
using System;
public class DemoLogo
{
```
2. Type the `Main()` method for the `DemoLogo` class. This method prints a line, then calls the `PrintCompanyLogo()` method.
```
public static void Main()
{
   Console.Write("Our company is ");
   PrintCompanyLogo();
}
```
3. Add a method that prints a two-line logo for a company.
```
public static void PrintCompanyLogo()
{
   Console.WriteLine("See Sharp Optical");
   Console.WriteLine("We prize your eyes");
}
```

4. Add the closing curly brace for the class (}), then save the file as **DemoLogo.cs**.
5. Compile and execute the program. The output should look like Figure 6-36.

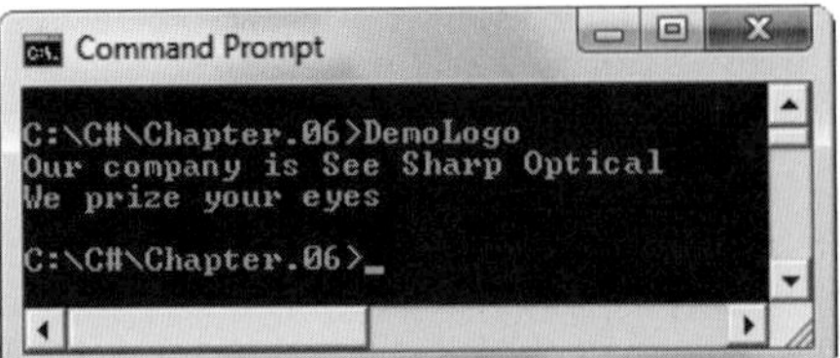

Figure 6-36 Output of `DemoLogo` program

WRITING A METHOD THAT RECEIVES PARAMETERS AND RETURNS A VALUE

Next, you will write a method named `CalcPhoneCallPrice()` that both receives parameters and returns a value. The purpose of the method is to take the length of a phone call in minutes and the rate charged per minute, and to then calculate the price of a call, assuming each call includes a 25-cent connection charge in addition to the per-minute charge. After writing the `CalcPhoneCallPrice()` method, you will write a `Main()` method that calls the `CalcPhoneCallPrice()` method using four different sets of data as arguments.

To create a class containing a method that receives two parameters and returns a value:

1. Open your text editor and type the **`using System;`** statement.
2. Add the class header for **`public class PhoneCall`** and an opening curly brace.
3. Type the following `CalcPhoneCallPrice()` method. It receives an integer and a `double` as parameters. The fee for a call is calculated as 0.25 plus the minutes times the rate per minute. The method returns the phone call fee to the calling method.

```
public static double CalcPhoneCallPrice(int minutes,
   double rate)
{
   const double BASE_FEE = 0.25;
   double callFee;
   callFee = BASE_FEE + minutes * rate;
   return callFee;
}
```

4. Add the `Main()` method header for the `PhoneCall` class. Begin the method by declaring two arrays; one contains two call lengths and the other contains two rates. You will use all the possible combinations of call lengths and rates to test the `CalcPhoneCallPrice()` method. Also, declare a `double` named `priceOfCall` that will hold the result of a calculated call price.

```
public static void Main()
{
   int[] callLength = {2, 5};
   double[] rate = {0.03, 0.12};
   double priceOfCall;
```

5. Add a statement that prints column headings under which you can list combinations of call lengths, rates, and prices. The three column headings are right-aligned, each in a field 10 characters wide.

```
Console.WriteLine("{0, 10}{1, 10}{2, 10}",
   "Minutes", "Rate", "Price");
```

6. Add a pair of nested loops that, in turn, passes each `callLength` and each `rate` to the `CalcPhoneCallPrice()` method. As each pair is passed, the result is stored in the `priceOfCall` variable, and the details are displayed. Using the nested loops allows you to pass each combination of call time and rate so that multiple possibilities for the values can be tested conveniently.

```
for(int x = 0; x < callLength.Length; ++x)
   for(int y = 0; y < rate.Length; ++y)
   {
      priceOfCall = CalcPhoneCallPrice(callLength[x],
         rate[y]);
      Console.WriteLine("{0, 10}{1, 10}{2, 10}",
         callLength[x], rate[y],
         priceOfCall.ToString("C"));
   }
```

7. Add a closing curly brace for the `Main()` method and another for the `PhoneCall` class.
8. Save the file as **PhoneCall.cs**. Compile and run the program. The output looks like Figure 6-37. It shows how a single method can produce a variety of results when you use different values for the arguments.

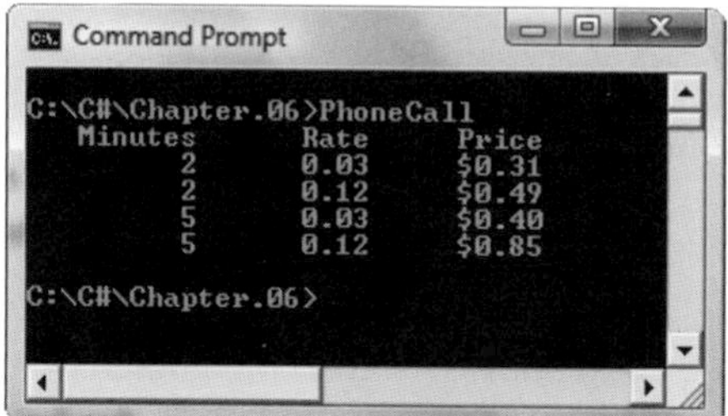

Figure 6-37 Output of the `PhoneCall` program

USING REFERENCE PARAMETERS

You use reference parameters when you want a method to have access to the memory address of arguments in a calling method. For example, suppose you have two values and you want to exchange them (or swap them), making each equal to the value of the other. Because you want to change two values, a method that accepts copies of arguments will not work—a method can return, at most, one value. Therefore, you can use reference parameters to provide your method with the actual addresses of the values you want to change.

To write a program that uses a method to swap two values:

1. Open your editor and begin the `SwapProgram` as follows:

```
using System;
public class SwapProgram
{
   public static void Main()
   {
```

2. Declare two integers and display their values. Call the `Swap()` method and pass in the addresses of the two variables to swap. Because the parameters already have assigned values, and because you want to alter those values in `Main()`, you can use reference parameters. After the method call, display the two values again. Add the closing curly brace for the `Main()` method.

```
      int first = 34, second = 712;
      Console.Write("Before swap first is {0}", first);
      Console.WriteLine(" and second is {0}", second);
      Swap(ref first, ref second);
      Console.Write("After swap first is {0}", first);
      Console.WriteLine(" and second is {0}", second);
   }
```

3. Create the `Swap()` method as shown. You can swap two values by storing the first value in a temporary variable, then assigning the second value to the first variable. At this point, both variables hold the value originally held by the second variable. When you assign the temporary variable's value to the second variable, the two values are reversed.

```
   public static void Swap(ref int one, ref int two)
   {
      int temp;
      temp = one;
      one = two;
      two = temp;
   }
```

4. Add the closing curly brace for the class. Save the file as **SwapProgram.cs**. Compile and execute the program. Figure 6-38 shows the output.

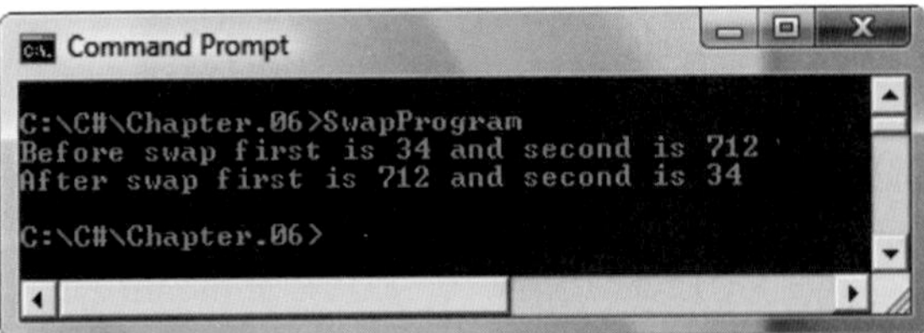

Figure 6-38 Output of `SwapProgram` program

NOTE You might want to use a module like `Swap()` as part of a larger program in which you verify, for example, that a higher value is displayed before a lower one; you would include the call to `Swap()` as part of a decision whose body executes only when a first value is less than a second one.

OVERLOADING METHODS

In the next steps you will overload a method that correctly triples an integer or a string, depending on how you call the method.

1. Open a new file in your text editor. Create a method that triples and displays an integer parameter as follows:

```
public static void Triple(int num)
{
    const int THREE = 3;
    Console.WriteLine("{0} times {1} is {2}\n",
       num, THREE, num * THREE);
}
```

2. Create a second method with the same name that takes a string parameter. Assume you want to define tripling a message as printing it three times, separated by tabs.

```
public static void Triple(string message)
{
    Console.WriteLine("{0}\t{0}\t{0}\n", message);
}
```

3. Position your cursor at the top of the file and add a `using` statement, class header, and opening curly brace so the overloaded `Triple()` methods will be contained in a class named `OverloadedTriples`.

```
using System;
public class OverloadedTriples
{
```

4. Position your cursor at the bottom of the file and add the closing curly brace for the `OverloadedTriples` class.

5. Position your cursor after the opening curly brace for the class. On a new line, insert a `Main()` method that declares an integer and a string and, in turn, passes each to the appropriate `Triple()` method.

```
public static void Main()
{
    int num = 20;
    string message = "Go team!";
    Triple(num);
    Triple(message);
}
```

6. Save the file as **OverloadedTriples.cs**. Compile and execute the program. Figure 6-39 shows the output. Even though the same method name is used in the two method calls, the appropriate overloaded method executes each time.

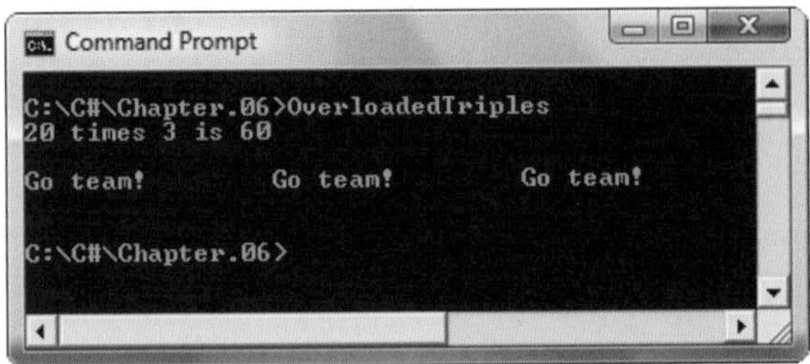

Figure 6-39 Output of `OverloadedTriples` program

CHAPTER SUMMARY

- » A method is a series of statements that carry out a task. Any class can contain an unlimited number of methods.
- » You write methods to make programs easier to understand and so that you can easily reuse them. In C#, a method must include a method declaration, an opening curly brace, a method body, and a closing curly brace. The method declaration defines the rules for using the method; it contains an optional declared accessibility, an optional `static` modifier, a return type for the method, an identifier, and an optional list of method parameters between parentheses.
- » Object-oriented programs hide their methods' implementation. A client method uses an interface to work with the method. To more easily incorporate methods into a program, it is common practice to store methods (or groups of associated methods) in their own classes and files, but methods can also be contained in the same file as the methods that use them.
- » Some methods require passed-in information called arguments or parameters. When you write the declaration for a method that can receive a parameter, you need to include the type of parameter and a local identifier for it within the method declaration parentheses. A variable declared in a method header is a formal parameter, and an argument within a method call is an actual parameter.
- » You can pass multiple arguments to a method by listing the arguments within the parentheses in the call to the method and separating them with commas. You can write a method to take any number of parameters in any order. When you call the method, however, the arguments you send to it must match in both number and type with the parameters listed in the method declaration.
- » The return type for a method can be any type used in the C# programming language, which includes the basic built-in types `int`, `double`, `char`, and so on, as well as class types (including class types you create). A method also can return nothing, in which case the return type is `void`. A method's return type is known more succinctly as a method's type. When a `return` statement includes a value, the value is sent back to the calling method.

» You can pass an array as a parameter to a method. You indicate that a method parameter is an array by placing square brackets after the data type in the method's parameter list. When you pass an array to a method, changes you make to array elements within the method are permanent; that is, they are reflected in the original array that was sent to the method. Arrays, like all objects but unlike built-in types, are passed by reference; that is, the method receives the actual memory address of the array and has access to the actual values in the array elements.

» In C#, you can write methods with four kinds of formal parameters listed within the parentheses in the method header: value parameters, which are declared without any modifiers; reference parameters, which are declared with the `ref` modifier; output parameters, which are declared with the `out` modifier; and parameter arrays, which are declared with the `params` modifier. A major advantage to using reference or output parameters exists when you want a method to change multiple variables. When you don't know how many arguments you might eventually send to a method, you can declare a local array within the method header by using the keyword `params`. Such a method accepts any number of arguments.

» When you overload a C# method, you write multiple methods with a shared name but different argument lists. The compiler understands your meaning based on the combination of arguments you use with the method.

» When you overload a method, you run the risk of creating an ambiguous situation—one in which the compiler cannot determine which method to use. Methods can be overloaded correctly by providing different parameter lists for methods with the same name.

KEY TERMS

A **method** is an encapsulated series of statements that carry out a task.

Methods are **invoked**, or **called**, by other methods.

A **calling method** calls another method.

A method invoked by another is a **called method**.

Code bloat is a term that describes unnecessarily long or repetitive program statements.

A **method declaration** is a **method header** or **method definition**.

A **method body** is a block of statements that carry out a method's work.

The optional declared **accessibility** for a method sets limits as to whether and how other methods can use your method.

Public access is a level of method accessibility that allows unlimited access to a method.

Protected internal access is a level of method accessibility that limits method access to the containing program, containing class, or types derived from the containing class.

Protected access is a level of method accessibility that limits method access to the containing class or types derived from the containing class.

Internal access is a level of method accessibility that limits method access to the containing class or program.

Private access is a level of method accessibility that limits method access to the containing class.

A **static** method can be called without referring to an object.

A **nonstatic** method requires an object reference.

A **return type** indicates what kind of value a method will return to any other method that calls it.

A **method's type** is its return type.

A variable's **scope** is the area where it is known and can be used.

Implementation hiding means keeping the details of a method's operations hidden.

To **interface** with a system is to interact with it.

A **black box** is any device you can use without knowing how it works internally.

A **client** of a method is a method that uses it.

A **multifile assembly** is a group of files containing methods that work together to create an application.

A **local variable** is one that is declared in the current method.

A **formal parameter** is a parameter within a method header that accepts a value.

Actual parameters are arguments within a method call.

A **`return` statement** causes a value to be sent back from a method to its calling method.

Nested method calls are method calls placed inside other method calls.

When data is **passed by reference** to a method, the method receives the memory address of the argument passed to it.

When you use a **value parameter** in a method header, you indicate the parameter's type and name, and the method receives a copy of the value passed to it.

When you use a **reference parameter** to a method, the parameter must have been assigned a value before you use it in the method call, and the method receives the parameter's address.

When you use an **output parameter**, it need not contain an original value, and the method receives the parameter's address.

Aliases are alternate names or pseudonyms.

A **parameter array** is a local array declared within a method header.

The keyword **`params`** is used to declare a local array in a method so the method can receive any number of arguments.

Overloading involves using one term to indicate diverse meanings. When you overload a C# method, you write multiple methods with the same name but different parameter lists.

A method's **signature** is composed of its name and parameter list.

Ambiguous methods are overloaded methods for which the compiler cannot determine which one to use.

REVIEW QUESTIONS

1. At most, a class can contain ________ method(s).

   a. 0
   b. 1
   c. 2
   d. any number of

2. What is the most important reason for creating methods within a program?

   a. Methods are easily reusable.
   b. Because all methods must be stored in the same class, they are easy to find.
   c. The `Main()` method becomes more detailed.
   d. All of these are true.

3. In C#, a method must include all of the following *except* a ________ .

   a. method declaration
   b. parameter list
   c. body
   d. closing curly brace

4. A method declaration must contain ________ .

   a. a statement of purpose
   b. declared accessibility
   c. the static modifier
   d. a return type

5. If you use the keyword modifier `static` in a method header, you indicate that the method ________ .

   a. can be called without referring to an object
   b. cannot be copied
   c. cannot be overloaded
   d. can be ambiguous

6. When you write the method declaration for a method that can receive a parameter, you need to include all of the following items *except* ________ .

   a. a pair of parentheses
   b. the type of the parameter
   c. a local name for the parameter
   d. an initial value for the parameter

7. Suppose you have declared a variable as `int myAge = 21;`. Which of the following is a legal call to a method with the declaration `public static void AMethod(int num)`?

   a. `AMethod(int 55);`
   b. `AMethod(myAge);`
   c. `AMethod(int myAge);`
   d. `AMethod();`

8. Suppose you have declared a method named `public static void CalculatePay(double rate)`. Which is true of a method that calls the `CalculatePay()` method?

   a. The calling method must contain a declared `double` named `rate`.

   b. The calling method might contain a declared `double` named `rate`.

   c. The calling method cannot contain a declared `double` named `rate`.

   d. The calling method can contain no declared `double` variables.

9. In the method call `PrintTheData(double salary);`, `salary` is the ________ parameter.

   a. formal
   b. actual
   c. proposed
   d. preferred

10. A program contains the method call `PrintTheData(salary);`. In the method definition, the name of the formal parameter must be ________ .

    a. `salary`

    b. any legal identifier other than `salary`

    c. any legal identifier

    d. omitted

11. What is a correct declaration for a method that receives two `double` arguments and calculates the difference between them?

    a.
    ```
    public static void CalcDifference(double price1,
        price2)
    ```

    b.
    ```
    public static void CalcDifference(double price1,
        double price2)
    ```

    c.
    ```
    public static void CalcDifference(double price1,
        double anotherPrice)
    ```

    d. Two of these are correct.

12. A method is declared as `double CalcPay(int hoursWorked)`. Suppose you write a `Main()` method containing `int hours = 35;` and `double pay;`. Which of the following represents a correct way to call the `CalcPay()` method from the `Main()` method?

    a. `hours = CalcPay();`
    b. `hours = CalcPay(pay);`
    c. `pay = CalcPay(hoursWorked);`
    d. `pay = CalcPay(hours);`

13. Which is *not* a type of method parameter in C#?

    a. value
    b. reference
    c. forensic
    d. output

14. Which type of method parameter receives the address of the variable passed in?

a. a value parameter
b. a reference parameter
c. an output parameter
d. two of the above

15. Assume you declare a variable as `int x = 100;` and correctly pass it to a method with the declaration `public static void IncreaseValue(ref int x)`. There is a single statement within the `IncreaseValue()` method: `x = x + 25;`. Back in the `Main()` method, after the method call, what is the value of `x`?

a. 100
b. 125
c. It is impossible to tell.
d. The program will not run.

16. Assume you declare a variable as `int x = 100;` and correctly pass it to a method with the declaration `public static void IncreaseValue(int x)`. There is a single statement within the `IncreaseValue()` method: `x = x + 25;`. Back in the `Main()` method, after the method call, what is the value of `x`?

a. 100
b. 125
c. It is impossible to tell.
d. The program will not run.

17. What is the difference between a reference parameter and an output parameter?

a. A reference parameter receives a memory address; an output parameter does not.
b. A reference parameter occupies a unique memory address; an output parameter does not.
c. A reference parameter must have an initial value; an output parameter need not.
d. A reference parameter need not have an initial value; an output parameter must.

18. Methods are ambiguous when they ________ .

a. are overloaded
b. are written in a confusing manner
c. are indistinguishable to the compiler
d. have the same parameter type as their return type

19. Which of the following pairs of method declarations represent correctly overloaded methods?

a.
```
public static void MethodA(int a)
public static void MethodA(int b, double c)
```
b.
```
public static void MethodB(double d)
public static void MethodB()
```
c.
```
public static double MethodC(int e)
public static double MethodD(int f)
```
d. Two of these are correctly overloaded methods.

20. Which of the following pairs of method declarations represent correctly overloaded methods?

    a. `public static void Method(int a)`
    `public static void Method(int b)`

    b. `public static void Method(double d)`
    `public static int Method()`

    c. `public static double Method(int e)`
    `public static int Method(int f)`

    d. Two of these are correctly overloaded methods.

EXERCISES

1. a. Create a class named `Numbers` whose `Main()` method holds two integer variables. Assign values to the variables. Within the class, create two methods, `Sum()` and `Difference()`, that compute the sum of and difference between the values of the two variables, respectively. Each method should perform the computation and display the results. In turn, call each of the two methods from `Main()`, passing the values of the two integer variables. Save the program as **Numbers.cs**.

   b. Add a method named `Product()` to the `Numbers` class. This method should compute the multiplication product of two integers, but not display the answer. Instead, it should return the answer to the calling `Main()` method, which displays the answer. Save the program as **Numbers2.cs**.

2. a. Create a class named `InchesToFeet`. Its `Main()` method holds an integer variable named `inches` to which you will assign a value. Create a method to which you pass `inches`. The method displays `inches` in feet and inches. For example, 67 inches is 5 feet 7 inches. Save the program as **InchesToFeet.cs**.

   b. Add a second method to the `InchesToFeet` class. This method displays a passed argument as yards, feet, and inches. For example, 67 inches is 1 yard, 2 feet, and 7 inches. Add a statement to the `Main()` method so that after it calls the method to convert inches to feet and inches, it passes the same variable to the new method to convert the same value to yards, feet, and inches. Save the program as **InchesToYards.cs**.

3. Create a class named `Monogram`. Its `Main()` method holds six character variables that hold your first, middle, and last initials, and a friend's first, middle, and last initials, respectively. Create a method named `DisplayMonogram()` to which you pass three initials. The method displays the initials surrounded by two asterisks on each side and with periods following each initial, as shown in the following example:

```
** J. M. F. **
```

   Within the `Main()` method, call the `DisplayMonogram()` method twice—once using your initials and once using your friend's initials. Save the program as **Monogram.cs**.

4. Create a class named `Exponent`. Its `Main()` method prompts the user for an integer value and, in turn, passes the value to a method that squares the number and to a method that cubes the number. The `Main()` method prints the results returned from each of the other methods. Save the program as **Exponent.cs**.

5. Create a class named `Square`. In the `Main()` method, declare an integer and prompt the user for a value. Display the value of the integer, then pass it to a method that accepts the value as a reference parameter and prints its square (the number times itself). In `Main()`, print the value again, proving that the original argument to the method was altered. Save the program as **Square.cs**.

6. a. Create a class named `Reverse3`. Within its `Main()` method, declare three integers named `firstInt`, `middleInt`, and `lastInt`. Assign values to the variables, display them, and then pass them to a method that places the first value in the `lastInt` variable and the last value in the `firstInt` variable. In the `Main()` method, display the three variables again, demonstrating that their positions have been reversed. Save the program as **Reverse3.cs**.

   b. Create a new class named `Reverse4`, which contains a method that reverses the positions of four variables. Write a `Main()` method that demonstrates the method works correctly. Save the program as **Reverse4.cs**.

7. Create a class named `Area`. Include three overloaded methods that compute the area of a rectangle when two dimensions are passed to it. One method takes two integers as parameters, one takes two `double`s, and the third takes an integer and a `double`. Write a `Main()` method that demonstrates each method works correctly. Save the program as **Area.cs**.

8. Create a class named `ComputeWeeklySalary`. Include two overloaded methods—one that accepts an annual salary as an integer and one that accepts an annual salary as a `double`. Each method should calculate and display a weekly salary, assuming 52 weeks in a year. Include a `Main()` method that demonstrates both overloaded methods work correctly. Save the program as **ComputeWeeklySalary.cs**.

9. Create a class named `TaxCalculation`. Include two overloaded methods—one that accepts a price and a tax rate expressed as `double`s (for example, 79.95 and 0.06, where 0.06 represents 6%), and one that accepts a price as a `double` and a tax rate as an integer (for example, 79.95 and 6, where 6 also represents 6%). Include a `Main()` method that demonstrates each method calculates the same tax amount appropriately. Save the program as **TaxCalculation.cs**.

10. Write an application that contains a method that calculates the conversion of any amount of money into the fewest bills; it calculates the number of 20s, 10s, 5s, and 1s needed. Create a `Main()` method that prompts the user for an integer number of dollars, uses the conversion method, and then displays the monetary breakdown. Save the program as **`Dollars.cs`**.

11. The `InputMethod()` in the `InputMethodDemo` program in Figure 6-24 contains repetitive code that prompts the user and retrieves integer values. Rewrite the program so the `InputMethod()` calls another method to do the work. The rewritten `InputMethod()` will need to contain only two statements:

```
one = DataEntry("first");
two = DataEntry("second");
```

    Save the new program as **InputMethodDemo2.cs**.

12. Create a method named `Sum()` that accepts any number of integer parameters and displays their sum. Write a `Main()` method that demonstrates the `Sum()` method works correctly when passed one, three, five, or an array of 10 integers. Save the program as **UsingSum.cs**.

DEBUGGING EXERCISES

Each of the following files in the Chapter.06 folder on your Student Disk has syntax and/or logical errors. In each case, determine the problem and fix the program. After you correct the errors, save each file using the same filename preceded with *Fixed*. For example, DebugSix1.cs will become FixedDebugSix1.cs.

a. DebugSix1.cs
b. DebugSix2.cs
c. DebugSix3.cs
d. DebugSix4.cs

UP FOR DISCUSSION

1. One of the advantages to writing a program that is subdivided into methods is that such a structure allows different programmers to write separate methods, thus dividing the work. Would you prefer to write a large program by yourself, or to work on a team in which each programmer produces one or more modules? Why?
2. In this chapter, you learned that hidden implementations are often said to exist in a black box. What are the advantages to this approach in both programming and real life? Are there any disadvantages?

CHAPTER SEVEN

7

USING CLASSES AND OBJECTS

In this chapter you will:

Learn about class concepts
Create classes from which objects can be instantiated
Create objects
Create properties, including auto-implemented properties
Learn useful techniques for storing and organizing classes
Learn about using `public` fields and `private` methods
Learn about the `this` reference
Write constructors and use them
Pass objects to methods
Use object initializers
Overload operators
Declare an array of objects and use the `Sort()` and `BinarySearch()` methods with them
Write destructors

Much of your understanding of the world comes from your ability to categorize objects and events into classes. As a young child, you learned the concept of "animal" long before you knew the word. Your first encounter with an animal might have been with the family dog, a neighbor's cat, or a goat at a petting zoo. As you developed speech, you might have used the same term for all of these creatures, gleefully shouting "Doggie!" as your parents pointed out cows, horses, and sheep in picture books or along the roadside on drives in the country. As you grew more sophisticated, you learned to distinguish dogs from cows; still later, you learned to distinguish breeds. Your understanding of the class "animal" helps you see the similarities between dogs and cows, and your understanding of the class "dog" helps you see the similarities between a Great Dane and a Chihuahua. Understanding classes gives you a framework for categorizing new experiences. You might not know the term "okapi," but when you learn it's an animal, you begin to develop a concept of what an okapi might be like.

Classes are also the basic building blocks of object-oriented programming. You already understand that differences exist among the `Double`, `Int32`, and `Float` classes, yet you also understand that items that are members of these classes possess similarities—they are all data types, you can perform arithmetic with all of them, they all can be converted to strings, and so on. Understanding classes enables you to see similarities in objects and increases your understanding of the programming process. In this chapter, you will discover how C# handles classes, learn to create your own classes, and learn to construct objects that are members of those classes.

UNDERSTANDING CLASS CONCEPTS

When you write programs in C#, you create two distinct types of classes:

» Classes that are only application programs with a `Main()` method. These classes can contain other methods that the `Main()` method calls.

» Classes from which you instantiate objects; these classes can contain a `Main()` method, but it is not required.

All of the classes you have created so far in this book have been applications with a `Main()` method that executes when you run the program in which it resides. Many classes do not contain a `Main()` method; instead, you use these classes to create objects.

»NOTE In C#, an application you write to use other classes is a class itself.

When you think in an object-oriented manner, everything is an object, and every object is a member of a class. You can think of any inanimate physical item as an object—your desk, your computer, and your house are all called "objects" in everyday conversation. You can think of living things as objects, too—your houseplant, your pet fish, and your sister are objects. Events also are objects—the stock purchase you made, the mortgage closing you attended, or a graduation party in your honor are all objects.

»NOTE Object-oriented programmers also use the term *is-a* when describing inheritance. You will learn about inheritance in Chapter 8.

Everything is an object, and every object is a member of a more general class. Your desk is a member of the class that includes all desks, and your pet fish is a member of the class that contains all fish. An object-oriented programmer would say that your desk is an instance of the `Desk` class and your fish is an instance of the `Fish` class. These statements represent **is-a relationships** because you can say, "My oak desk with the scratch on top *is a* `Desk` and my goldfish named Moby *is a* `Fish`." The difference between a class and an object parallels the difference between abstract and concrete. An object is an **instantiation** of a class; an object is one tangible example of a class. Your goldfish, my guppy, and the zoo's shark each constitute one instantiation of the `Fish` class.

The concept of a class is useful because of its reusability. Objects receive their attributes from classes. For example, if you invite me to a graduation party, I automatically know many things about the object (the party). I assume there will be a starting time, a number of guests, some quantity of food, and some nature of gifts. I understand parties because of my previous knowledge of the `Party` class, of which all parties are members. I don't know the number of guests or the date or time of this particular party, but I understand that because all parties have a date and time, then this one must as well. Similarly, even though every stock purchase is unique, each must have a dollar amount and a number of shares. All objects have predictable attributes because they are members of certain classes.

The data components of a class often are called its **instance variables**. Also, object attributes often are called **fields** to help distinguish them from other variables you might use. The set of contents of an object's instance variables also are known as its **state**. For example, the current state of a particular party is 8 p.m. and Friday; the state of a particular stock purchase is $10 and five shares.

In addition to their attributes, objects have methods associated with them, and every object that is an instance of a class possesses the same methods. For example, at some point you might want to issue invitations for a party. You might name the method `IssueInvitations()`, and it might display some text as well as the values of the party's date and time fields. Your graduation party, then, might possess the identifier `myGraduationParty`. As a member of the `Party` class, it might have data members for the date and time, like all parties, and it might have a method to issue invitations. When you use the method, you might want to be able to send an argument to `IssueInvitations()` that indicates how many copies to print. When you think of an object and its methods, it's as though you can send a message to the object to direct it to accomplish some task—you can tell the party object named `myGraduationParty` to print the number of invitations you request. Even though `yourAnniversaryParty` also is a member of the `Party` class, and even though it also has an `IssueInvitations()` method, you will send a different argument value to `yourAnniversaryParty`'s `IssueInvitations()` method than I send to `myGraduationParty`'s corresponding method. Within any object-oriented program, you continuously make requests to objects' methods, often including arguments as part of those requests.

When you program in C#, you frequently create classes from which objects will be instantiated (or other programmers create them for you). You also write applications to use the objects, along with their data and methods. Often, you will write programs that use classes created by others, as you have used the `Console` class; similarly, you might create a class that other programmers will use to instantiate objects within their own programs. A program or class that instantiates objects of another prewritten class is a **class client** or **class user**.

»TWO TRUTHS AND A LIE: UNDERSTANDING CLASS CONCEPTS

1. C# classes always contain a `Main()` method.
2. An object is an instantiation of a class.
3. The data components of a class often are its instance variables.

The false answer is #1. C# applications always contain a `Main()` method, but some classes do not if they are not meant to be run as programs.

CREATING A CLASS FROM WHICH OBJECTS CAN BE INSTANTIATED

> **»NOTE** You will learn other optional components you can add to a class definition as you continue to study C#.

When you create a class, you must assign a name to it, and you must determine what data and methods will be part of the class. For example, suppose you decide to create a class named `Employee`. One instance variable of `Employee` might be an employee number, and one necessary method might display a welcome message to new employees. To begin, you create a **class header** or **class definition** that describes the class. It contains three parts:

1. An optional access modifier
2. The keyword `class`
3. Any legal identifier you choose for the name of your class

For example, a header for an `Employee` class is `internal class Employee`. The keyword `internal` is an example of a **class access modifier**. You can declare a class to be one of the following:

- **`public`**, meaning access to the class is not limited.
- **`protected`**, meaning access to the class is limited to the class and to any classes derived from the class. (You will learn about deriving classes in Chapter 8.)
- **`internal`**, meaning access is limited to the assembly (a group of code modules compiled together) to which the class belongs.
- **`private`**, meaning access is limited to another class to which the class belongs. In other words, a class can be `private` if it is contained within another class, and only the containing class should have access to the `private` class.

Note that `private` and `protected` classes have limited uses. Furthermore, when you declare a class using a namespace, you only can declare it to be `public` or `internal`. For now, you will use either the `public` or `internal` modifier with your classes. If you do not explicitly include an access specifier, class access is `internal` by default. Because most classes you create will have `internal` access, typing an access specifier is often unnecessary.

> **»NOTE** You first learned about namespaces in Chapter 1.

In addition to the class header, classes you create must have a class body enclosed between curly braces. Figure 7-1 shows a shell for an `Employee` class.

```
class Employee
{
   // Instance variables and methods go here
}
```

Figure 7-1 `Employee` class shell

CREATING INSTANCE VARIABLES AND METHODS

When you create a class, you define both its attributes and its methods. You declare the class's instance variables, which are the attributes or fields, within the curly braces using the same syntax you use to declare other variables—you provide a type and an identifier. When you create an instance variable, you create an attribute to hold a value that describes a feature of every object of that class. For example, within the `Employee` class, you can declare an integer ID number; when you create `Employee` objects, each will have its own `idNumber`. You can define the ID number simply as `int idNumber;`. However, programmers frequently include an access modifier for each of the class fields and declare the `idNumber` as `private int idNumber;`. Figure 7-2 shows an `Employee` class that contains the `idNumber` field.

NOTE If you do not provide an access specifier for a class field, its access is `private` by default.

```
class Employee
{
   private int idNumber;
}
```

Figure 7-2 `Employee` class containing `idNumber` field

The allowable field modifiers are `new`, `public`, `protected`, `internal`, `private`, `static`, `readonly`, and `volatile`. Most class fields are `private`, which provides the highest level of security. Identifying a field as `private` means that no other class can access the field's values, and only methods of the same class will be allowed to set, get, or otherwise use the field. Using `private` fields within classes is an example of **information hiding**, a feature found in all object-oriented languages. You see cases of information hiding in real-life objects every day. For instance, you cannot see into your automobile's gas tank to determine how full it is. Instead, you use a gauge on the dashboard to provide you with the necessary information. Similarly, data fields are frequently `private` in object-oriented programming, but their contents are accessed through `public` methods. The `private` data of a class should be changed or manipulated only by its own methods, not by methods that belong to other classes.

NOTE A benefit of information hiding is the ability to validate data. A method that sets a variable's value can ensure that the value falls within a specified range. For example, perhaps an `Employee`'s salary should not be below the federal minimum wage, or a department number should not be negative or greater than 10.

In contrast to a class's private data fields, most class methods are not usually private; they are public. The resulting private data/public method arrangement provides a means to control outside access to your data—only a class's nonprivate methods can be used to access a class's private data. The situation is similar to having a "public" receptionist who controls the messages passed in and out of your private office. The way in which the nonprivate methods are written controls how you will use the private data.

For example, one method you need for an Employee class that contains an idNumber is the method to display the employee's welcoming message to company clients. A reasonable name for this method is WelcomeMessage(), and its declaration is public void WelcomeMessage(), because it will have public access and return nothing. Figure 7-3 shows the Employee class with the addition of the WelcomeMessage() method.

```
class Employee
{
   private int idNumber;
   public void WelcomeMessage()
   {
       Console.WriteLine("Welcome from Employee #{0}", idNumber);
       Console.WriteLine("How can I help you?");
   }
}
```

Figure 7-3 Employee class with idNumber field and WelcomeMessage() method

NOTE You can call class (static) methods without creating an instance of the class. Instance methods require an instantiated object; class methods do not.

Notice that the WelcomeMessage() method does not employ the static modifier, unlike many other methods you have created. The keyword static is used for class-wide methods, but not for instance methods that "belong" to objects. If you are creating a program with a Main() method that you will execute to perform some task, then many of your methods will be static. You can call the static methods from within Main() without creating an object. However, if you are creating a class from which objects will be instantiated, most methods will probably be nonstatic, as you will be associating the methods with individual objects and their data. Methods used with object instantiations are called **instance methods**. Each time the WelcomeMessage() instance method is used in the class in Figure 7-3, it will display an idNumber for a specific object. In other words, the method will work appropriately for each object instance.

NOTE The Employee class in Figure 7-3 is not a program that will run; it contains no Main() method. Rather, it simply describes what Employee objects will have (an idNumber) and be able to do (display a greeting) when you write a program that contains one or more Employee objects.

NOTE A class can contain other classes as data members. For example, you might create a class named Date that contains a month, day, and year, and add two Date fields to an Employee class to hold the Employee's birth date and hire date. Using an object within another object is known as **composition**. The relationship created is also called a **has-a relationship** because one class "has an" instance of another.

»TWO TRUTHS AND A LIE: CREATING A CLASS FROM WHICH OBJECTS CAN BE INSTANTIATED

1. A class header always contains the keyword `class`.
2. When you create a class, you define both its attributes and its methods.
3. Most class fields and methods are `private`.

The false statement is #3. Most class fields are `private`, but most class methods are `public`.

CREATING OBJECTS

Declaring a class does not create any actual objects. A class is just an abstract description of what an object will be like if any objects are ever actually instantiated. Just as you might understand all the characteristics of an item you intend to manufacture long before the first item rolls off the assembly line, you can create a class with fields and methods long before you instantiate any objects that are members of that class.

> **»NOTE** You can think of a class declaration as similar to a blueprint for building a new house or a recipe for baking a cake. In other words, it is a plan that exists before any objects are created.

A two-step process creates an object that is an instance of a class. First, you supply a type and an identifier, just as when you declare any variable. Second, you create the object, which includes allocating computer memory for it. For example, you might define an integer as `int someValue;` and you might define an `Employee` as `Employee myAssistant;`, where `myAssistant` could be any legal identifier you choose to represent an `Employee`.

> **»NOTE** Every object name is a reference—that is, a computer memory location where the fields for the object reside.

When you declare an integer as `int myInteger;`, you notify the compiler that an integer named `myInteger` will exist, and computer memory automatically is reserved for it at the same time—the exact amount of computer memory depends on the declared data type. When you declare the `myAssistant` instance of the `Employee` class, you are notifying the compiler that you will use the identifier `myAssistant`. However, you are not yet setting aside computer memory in which the `Employee` named `myAssistant` can be stored—that is done only for the built-in, predefined types. To allocate the needed memory and instantiate the object, you must use the `new` operator.

> **»NOTE** In Chapter 5, you used the `new` operator when setting aside memory for arrays.

Defining an `Employee` object named `myAssistant` requires two steps—you must declare a reference to the object and then you must use the statement that actually sets aside enough memory to hold `myAssistant`, as in the following:

```
Employee myAssistant;
myAssistant = new Employee();
```

You also can declare and reserve memory for `myAssistant` in one statement, as in the following:

```
Employee myAssistant = new Employee();
```

In this statement, `Employee` is the object's type (as well as its class), and `myAssistant` is the name of the object. The equal sign is the assignment operator, so a value is being assigned to `myAssistant`. The `new` operator is allocating a new, unused portion of computer memory for `myAssistant`. The value being assigned to `myAssistant` is a memory address at which it will be located. You need not be concerned with the actual memory address—when you refer to `myAssistant`, the compiler will locate it at the appropriate address for you.

»NOTE Because the identifiers for objects are references to their memory addresses, you can call any class a **reference type**—in other words, a type that refers to a specific memory location. A reference type is a type that holds an address, as opposed to the predefined types such as `int`, `double`, and `char`, which are **value types**.

»NOTE You also can use the `new` operator for simple data types. For example, to declare an integer variable `x`, you can write the following:

```
int x = new int();
```

However, programmers usually use the simpler form:

```
int x;
```

With the first form, `x` is initialized to 0. With the second form, `x` holds no usable starting value.

In the statement `Employee myAssistant = new Employee();`, the last portion of the statement after the `new` operator, `Employee()`, looks suspiciously like a method name with its parentheses. In fact, it is the name of a method that constructs an `Employee` object. `Employee()` is a constructor. You will write your own constructors later in this chapter. For now, note that when you don't write a constructor for a class, C# writes one for you, and the name of the constructor is always the same as the name of the class whose objects it constructs.

After an object has been instantiated, its public members (usually its methods) can be accessed using the object's identifier, a dot, and a method call. For example, if you declare an `Employee` named `myAssistant`, you can access `myAssistant`'s `WelcomeMessage()` method with the following statement:

```
myAssistant.WelcomeMessage();
```

»NOTE The statement `myAssistant.WelcomeMessage()` would be illegal if `WelcomeMessage()` was a `static` method. The method can be used with an `Employee` object only because it is nonstatic.

No class client (for example, a `Main()` method) can access `myAssistant`'s `idNumber` directly; the only way a client can access the `private` data is by sending a message through one of the object's `public` methods. Because the `WelcomeMessage()` method is part of the same class as `idNumber`, and because `WelcomeMessage()` is `public`, a `Main()` method can use the method that displays the `idNumber`. Figure 7-4 shows a class named `CreateEmployee` whose `Main()` method declares an `Employee` and displays the `Employee`'s welcome message. Figure 7-5 shows the execution of the program.

```
using System;
public class CreateEmployee
{
    public static void Main()
    {
        Employee myAssistant = new Employee();
        myAssistant.WelcomeMessage();
    }
}
```

Figure 7-4 The `CreateEmployee` program

Figure 7-5 Output of the `CreateEmployee` program

In the output in Figure 7-5, the `Employee`'s ID number is 0. By default, all unassigned numeric fields in an object are initialized to 0. When you compile the program in Figure 7-4, you receive a warning message:

```
Field 'Employee.idNumber' is never assigned to, and will always have
its default value 0.
```

Of course, usually you want to provide a different value for each `Employee`'s `idNumber` field. To accomplish this, you can create properties.

»TWO TRUTHS AND A LIE: CREATING OBJECTS

1. Declaring a class creates one object of a new data type.
2. After you declare a class, you must use the `new` operator to allocate memory for an object of that class and to instantiate it.
3. After an object has been instantiated, its public members can be accessed using the object's identifier, a dot, and a method call.

The false statement is #1. Declaring a class does not create any actual objects; the declaration only describes what an object of that class will be.

CREATING PROPERTIES

Frequently, methods you call with an object are used to alter the states of its fields. For example, you might want to set or change the date or time of a party. If the `Party` class contained a `string` field named `partyDate`, you could write a method such as `SetDate()` to set a party's date, similar to the following method:

```
public void SetDate(string date)
{
   partyDate = date;
}
```

Then, you could call the method with a statement like the following:

```
myGraduationParty.SetDate("May 12");
```

Although this technique would work, and might be used in other programming languages, C# programmers more often create a property to perform this task. A **property** is a member of a class that provides access to a field of a class; properties define how fields will be set and retrieved. Properties have **accessors** that specify the statements that execute when a class's fields are accessed. Specifically, properties contain **`set` accessors** for setting an object's fields and **`get` accessors** for retrieving the stored values. When you create properties, the syntax in your client programs becomes more natural and easier to understand.

Figure 7-6 shows an `Employee` class in which a property has been defined in the shaded area. The property is `IdNumber`. A property declaration resembles a variable declaration; it contains an

```
class Employee
{
   private int idNumber;
   public int IdNumber
   {
      get
      {
         return idNumber;
      }
      set
      {
         idNumber = value;
      }
   }
   public void WelcomeMessage()
   {
      Console.WriteLine("Welcome from Employee #{0}", IdNumber);
      Console.WriteLine("How can I help you?");
   }
}
```

Figure 7-6 `Employee` class with defined property

NOTE C# programmers refer to properties as "smart fields."

NOTE When a property has a `set` accessor, programmers say the property can be "written to." When it has a `get` accessor, programmers say the property can be "read from."

NOTE It is important to pay attention to capitalization so you can distinguish a field from a property.

NOTE When a property has only a `get` accessor (and not a `set` accessor), it is a **read-only property**.

NOTE In C#, the `get` and `set` accessors often are called the **getter** and the **setter**, respectively.

access modifier, a data type, and an identifier. It also resembles a method in that it is followed by curly braces that contain statements. By convention, a property identifier is the same as the field it manipulates, except the first letter is capitalized. Following the property identifier, you define accessors between curly braces. The `IdNumber` property in Figure 7-6 contains both `get` and `set` accessors; a property declaration can contain a `get` accessor, a `set` accessor, or both.

»NOTE In the altered `WelcomeMessage()` method in Figure 7-6, the `IdNumber` property is displayed. Alternately, this method could continue to use the `idNumber` field (as in Figure 7-3) because the method is a member of the same class as the field. Programmers are divided on whether a method of a class should use a field or a property to access its own methods. One popular position is that if `get` and `set` accessors are well-designed, they should be used everywhere, even from within the class. Sometimes, you want a field to be read-only, so you do not create a `set` accessor. In such a case, you can use the field (with the lowercase initial by convention) within class methods.

»NOTE Be careful with capitalization in properties. For example, within a `get` accessor for `IdNumber`, if you return `IdNumber` instead of `idNumber`, you initiate an infinite loop—the property continuously accesses itself.

»NOTE Throughout this book you have seen keywords displayed in blue in the program figures. The words "`get`" and "`set`" are not C# keywords—for example, you could declare a variable named `get` within a C# program. However, within a property, `get` and `set` have special meanings and are not allowed to be declared as identifiers there. In the Visual Studio Integrated Development Environment, the words `get` and `set` appear in blue within properties, but in black elsewhere. The figures in this book follow the same convention.

Each accessor in a property looks like a method, except no parentheses are included in the identifier. A `set` accessor acts like a method that accepts a parameter and assigns it to a variable. However, it is not a method and you do not use parentheses with it. A `get` accessor returns the value of the field associated with the property, but you do not code a `return` type; the `return` type of a `get` accessor is implicitly the type of the property in which it is contained.

»NOTE Identifiers that act like keywords in specific circumstances are **contextual keywords.** C# has six contextual keywords: `get`, `set`, `value`, `partial`, `where`, and `yield`.

When you use `set` and `get` accessors in a method, you do not use the words "set" or "get." Instead, to set a value, you use the assignment operator (=), and to get a value, you simply use the property name. For example, if you declare an `Employee` named `myChef`, you can assign an `IdNumber` as simply as you would a variable, as in the following:

```
Employee myChef = new Employee();
myChef.IdNumber = 2345;
```

In the second statement, the `IdNumber` property is set to 2345. The value to the right of the equal sign is sent to the `set` accessor as an implicit parameter named `value`. (An **implicit parameter** is one that is undeclared and that gets its value automatically.) In the statement `myChef.IdNumber = 2345;`, the constant 2345 is sent to the `set` accessor, where it becomes the value of `value`. Within the `set` accessor, `value` is assigned to the class field `idNumber`. The `idNumber` field could not have been set directly from `Main()` because it is `private`; however, the `IdNumber` property can be set through its `set` accessor because the property is `public`.

Writing a get accessor allows you to use a property like you would a simple variable. For example, a declared Employee's ID number can be displayed with the following:

```
Console.WriteLine("ID number is {0}", myChef.IdNumber);
```

The expression myChef.idNumber (using the field name that starts with a lowercase *i*) would not be allowed in a client program because idNumber is private; however, the public get accessor of the property allows myChef.IdNumber to be displayed. Figure 7-7 shows a complete application that uses the modified class in Figure 7-6. Figure 7-8 shows the output.

```
using System;
public class CreateEmployee2
{
   public static void Main()
   {
       Employee myChef = new Employee();
       myChef.IdNumber = 2345;
       Console.WriteLine("ID number is {0}",
          myChef.IdNumber);
       myChef.WelcomeMessage();
   }
}
```

Figure 7-7 The CreateEmployee2 application that uses the Employee class containing a property

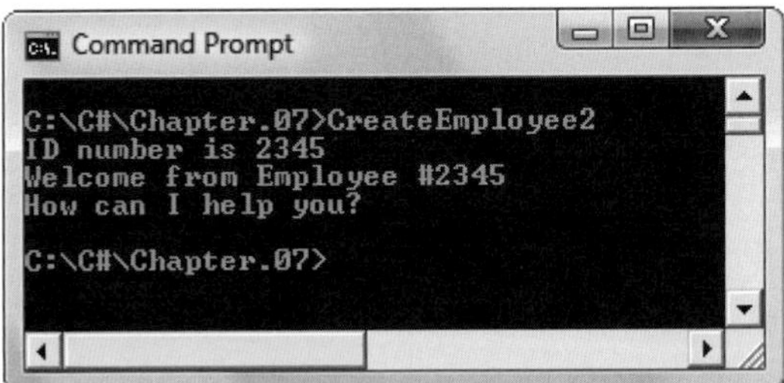

Figure 7-8 Output of the CreateEmployee2 application

At this point, declaring get and set accessors that do nothing except retrieve a value from a field or assign a value to one might seem like a lot of work for very little payoff. After all, if a class field was public instead of private, you would just use it directly and avoid the work of creating the property. However, it is conventional (and consistent with object-oriented principles) to make class fields private and allow accessors to manipulate them only as you deem appropriate. Keeping data hidden is an important feature of object-oriented programming, as is controlling how data values are set and used. Additionally, you can customize accessors to suit the restrictions you want to impose on how some class fields are retrieved and accessed. For example, you could write a set accessor that restricts ID numbers within the Employee class as follows:

```
set
{
    if(value < 500)
        idNumber = value;
    else
        idNumber = 500;
}
```

This set accessor would ensure that an Employee idNumber would never be greater than 500. If clients had direct access to a private idNumber field, you could not control what values could be assigned there, but when you write a custom set accessor for your class, you gain full control over the allowed data values.

USING AUTO-IMPLEMENTED PROPERTIES

Although you can include any number of custom statements within the get and set accessors in a property, the most frequent scenario is that a set accessor simply assigns a value to the appropriate class field, and the get accessor simply returns the field value. Because the code in get and set accessors frequently is standard as well as brief, programmers sometimes take one of several shorthand approaches to writing properties.

For example, instead of writing an IdNumber property using 11 code lines as in Figure 7-6, a programmer might write the property on five lines, as follows:

```
public int IdNumber
{
    get{return idNumber;}
    set{idNumber = value;}
}
```

This format does not eliminate any of the characters typed in the original version of the property; it only eliminates some of the white space, placing each accessor on a single line.

Other programmers choose an even more condensed form and write the entire property on one line as:

```
public int IdNumber {get{return idNumber;} set{idNumber = value;}}
```

An even more concise format is new to C# 3.0. In this version, you can write a property as follows:

```
public int IdNumber {get; set;}
```

A property written in this format is an **auto-implemented property**—the property's implementation (its set of working statements) is created for you automatically with the assumption that the set accessor should simply assign a value to the appropriate field, and the get accessor should simply return the field. You cannot use an auto-implemented property if you need to include customized statements within one of your accessors (such as placing restrictions on an assigned value), and you can only declare an auto-implemented property when you use both get and set.

Conveniently, when you use an auto-implemented property, you do not need to declare the field that corresponds to the property (although you still can do so). For example, Figure 7-9 shows an `Employee` class in which no specialized code is needed for the properties for what would ordinarily be declared as `idNumber` and `salary` fields. In this class, only the properties are declared using auto-implemented properties. The figure also contains a short program that uses the class, and Figure 7-10 shows the output. Auto-implemented properties provide a convenient shortcut when you need both a `get` and `set` but no specialized statements are needed.

```
using System;
public class CreateEmployeeWithAutoImplementedProperty
{
   public static void Main()
   {
      Employee aWorker = new Employee();
      aWorker.IdNumber = 3872;
      aWorker.Salary = 22.11;
      Console.WriteLine("Employee #{0} makes {1}",
         aWorker.IdNumber, aWorker.Salary.ToString("C"));
   }
}
public class Employee
{
   public int IdNumber {get; set;}
   public double Salary {get; set;}
}
```

Figure 7-9 An `Employee` class with no declared fields and auto-implemented properties, and a program that uses them

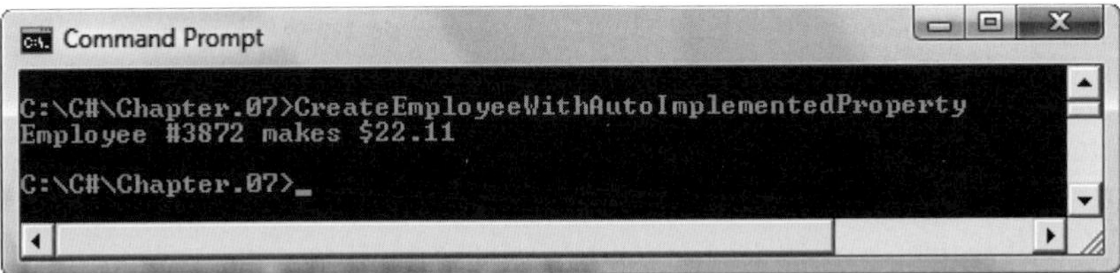

Figure 7-10 Output of the `CreateEmployeeWithAutoImplementedProperty` application

NOTE If you want to create a read-only property using auto-implemented accessors, you can make the `set` accessor private, as in the following:

```
public int IdNumber {get; private set};
```

Using this technique, the `IdNumber` property cannot be set by any statement in another class. If you use this technique, most likely you want to explicitly declare an `idNumber` field that can be set from within the class, possibly by a constructor.

»TWO TRUTHS AND A LIE: CREATING PROPERTIES

1. A property is a member of a class that defines how fields will be set and retrieved.
2. Properties contain `set` accessors for retrieving an object's fields and `get` accessors for setting the stored values.
3. You can create auto-implemented properties when you want a field's `set` accessor to assign a value to the appropriate class field, and a field's `get` accessor simply to return the field value.

The false statement is #2. Properties contain `set` accessors for setting an object's fields and `get` accessors for retrieving the stored values.

STORING AND ORGANIZING YOUR CLASSES

When you create a class that describes objects to be instantiated, and another class that instantiates those objects, you physically can contain the two classes within a single file or place each class in its own file.

By placing both classes within the same file, you typically reduce development time and simplify the compilation process. When you first develop classes, you are likely to introduce both syntax and logical errors into each file you use. By placing your classes in the same file, you reduce the time needed to navigate through multiple files and to check issues such as consistent spelling of variable and method names and consistent use of data types. Also, when you compile only a single file, the sources of any error messages you receive are easier to locate.

There are also advantages to placing classes in separate files. One advantage is simply organization. Just as you can arrange all your nuts, bolts, and nails in the various drawers of a hardware storage cabinet and then find a quarter-inch bolt when you need it, containing each class in its own file makes the classes more manageable and easier to locate. More importantly, when a class resides within its own file, the class is easier to reuse within additional programs you create in the future.

Most classes you create will have more than a few data fields and property definitions for each field. For example, a typical `Employee` class would contain more than an `idNumber` field—a few of the many possibilities include `firstName`, `lastName`, `address`, `phoneNumber`, `salary`, `departmentNumber`, `hireDate`, `numberOfDependents`, and so on. Although there is no requirement to do so, most programmers place data fields in some logical order at the beginning of a class. For example, the `idNumber` field is most likely used as a unique identifier for each `Employee` (which database users often call a **primary key**), so it makes sense to list the employee ID number first in the class. An employee's last name and first name "go together," so it makes sense to store these two `Employee` components adjacently. Despite these common-sense rules, you have a lot of flexibility in how you position data fields within any class.

>> **NOTE** A unique identifier must have no duplicates within an application. In other words, although an organization might have many employees with the last name "Johnson" or a salary of 400.00, only one employee will have ID number 128. For that reason, if you were designing a professional `Employee` class, you might choose to make the ID number property read-only and to allow assignment only at construction using a formula that provides a unique number, or perhaps accessing a file of available numbers.

Additionally, if you define properties for each data field as well as a few methods, quite a lot of code is required. Finding your way through the list of fields, properties, and methods can become a formidable task. For ease in locating class methods and properties, many programmers prefer to store them in alphabetical order. Another logical organization scheme is to store all properties first, in the same order as their corresponding data fields, followed by other methods. Any of these organizational techniques can produce usable classes and workable programs, but your organization or instructor might have a preference for how to assemble class members.

An additional aid to keeping your classes organized is to use comments liberally. For example, comments can be used to separate functional areas within a class and to describe the purposes of methods.

>> **NOTE** Although good program comments are crucial to creating understandable code, they have been left out of many examples in this book to save space. Your programs should contain many comments that identify your program components and explain the purpose and structure of your methods.

>> **NOTE** Although good comments can help others to understand your programs, they are no substitute for clear, appropriate identifiers.

>>TWO TRUTHS AND A LIE: STORING AND ORGANIZING YOUR CLASSES

1. You can contain two classes in the same file.
2. Within a class you must place all properties first.
3. You can store class methods and properties in any order that makes sense for your class.

The false statement is #2. You can place properties first within a class, but there is no requirement to do so. Most programmers place data fields in some logical order at the beginning of a class, followed by properties and methods.

UNUSUAL USE: public FIELDS AND private METHODS

Most of the time, class data fields are `private` and class methods are `public`. This technique ensures that data will be used and changed only in the ways provided in your accessors. Novice programmers might make a data field `public` to avoid having to create a property containing `get` and `set` accessors. For example, Figure 7-11 shows a `Desk` class that contains two `public` fields. Because the fields are `public`, no `get` or `set` accessors are needed. The program that instantiates a `Desk` can set and retrieve the values in the fields without "bothering" with the accessors that would be needed if the fields were `private`. Although it is easy to work with, the `Desk` class in Figure 7-11 violates a basic principle of object-oriented programming. That is, data should be hidden when at all possible, and access to it should be controlled by well-designed accessors.

```
using System;
class Desk
{
   public string wood;
   public int drawers;
}
public class TestDesk
{
   public static void Main()
   {
      Desk myDesk = new Desk();
      myDesk.wood = "mahogany";   // notice wood and drawers
      myDesk.drawers = 4;         // are accessed directly
      Console.WriteLine("My {0} desk has {1} drawers",
         myDesk.wood, myDesk.drawers);
   }
}
```

»DON'T DO IT

Making these fields public is NOT a recommended technique.

Figure 7-11 Poorly designed `Desk` class with program that instantiates a `Desk`

Although `private` fields and `public` methods and accessors are the norm, occasionally you need to create `public` fields or `private` methods. Consider the `Carpet` class shown in Figure 7-12. Although it contains several `private` data fields, this class also contains one `public` data field (shaded). Following the three `public` property declarations, one `private` method is defined (also shaded).

```
class Carpet
{
   public const string MOTTO = "Our carpets are quality-made";
   private int length;
   private int width;
   private int area;
   public int Length
   {
      get
      {
         return length;
      }
      set
      {
         length = value;
         CalcArea();
      }
   }
   public int Width
   {
      get
      {
         return width;
      }
      set
      {
         width = value;
         CalcArea();
      }
   }
   public int Area
   {
      get
      {
        return area;
      }
   }
   private void CalcArea()
   {
      area = Length * Width;
   }
}
```

Figure 7-12 The `Carpet` class

»NOTE In the `Carpet` class, the `Area` property does not contain a `set` accessor because no outside program is allowed to set the area. Instead, it is calculated whenever `width` or `length` changes.

For example, you can create a `public` data field when you want all objects of a class to contain the same value. When you create `Carpet` objects from the class in Figure 7-12, each `Carpet` will have its own `length`, `width`, and `area`, but all `Carpet` objects will have the same `MOTTO`. The field `MOTTO` is preceded by the keyword `const`, meaning `MOTTO` is constant. That is, no program can change its value. When you define a named constant within a class, it is always `static`. That is, the field belongs to the entire class, not to any particular instance of the class. When you create a `static` field, only one copy is stored for the entire class, no matter how many objects you instantiate. On the other hand, multiple copies of nonstatic fields exist—one for each object instantiated. When you use a constant field, you use the class name rather than an object name. The class name is followed by a dot and the constant name, as in `Carpet.MOTTO`.

»NOTE Throughout this book, you have been using `static` to describe the `Main()` method of a class. You do not need to create an object of any class that contains a `Main()` method to be able to use `Main()`.

»NOTE You learned to create named constants in Chapter 2, and learned that identifiers of named constants such as `MOTTO` conventionally are capitalized. Some built-in C# classes contain useful named constants, such as `Math.PI`, which contains the value of pi. You do not create a `Math` object to use `PI`; therefore, you know it is `static`.

Figure 7-13 shows a program that instantiates and uses a `Carpet` object, and Figure 7-14 shows the results when the program executes. Notice that, although the write statements require an object to use `Width`, `Length`, and `Area`, `MOTTO` is referenced using the class name only.

```
using System;
public class TestCarpet
{
   public static void Main()
   {
      Carpet aRug = new Carpet();
      aRug.Width = 12;
      aRug.Length = 14;
      Console.Write("The {0} X {1} carpet ", aRug.Width, aRug.Length);
      Console.WriteLine("has an area of {0}", aRug.Area);
      Console.WriteLine("Our motto is: {0}", Carpet.MOTTO);
   }
}
```

Figure 7-13 The `TestCarpet` class

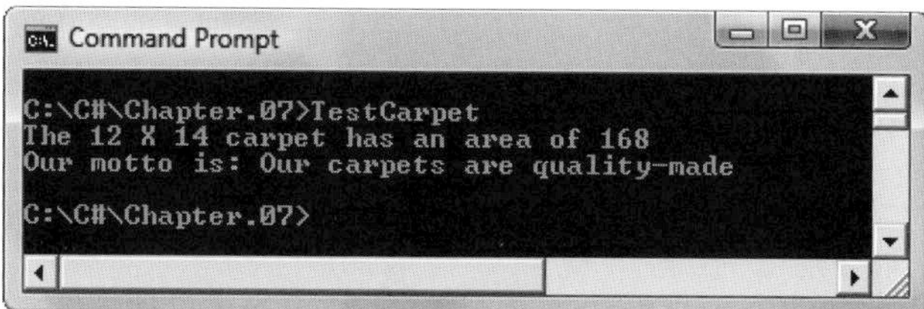

Figure 7-14 Output of the `TestCarpet` program

The `Carpet` class contains one private method named `CalcArea()`. As you examine the code in the `TestCarpet` class in Figure 7-13, notice that `Width` and `Length` are set using an assignment operator, but `Area` is not. The `TestCarpet` class can make assignments to `Width` and `Length` because these properties are `public`. However, you would not want a client program to assign a value to `Area` because the assigned value might not agree with the `Width` and `Length` values. Therefore, the `Area` property is a read-only property—it does not contain a `set` accessor, and no assignments by clients are allowed. Instead, whenever the `Width` or `Length` properties are set, the `private CalcArea()` method is called from the accessor. The `CalcArea()` method is defined as `private` because there is no reason for a client class like `TestCarpet` to call `CalcArea()`. The `Carpet` class's own accessors should call `CalcArea()` only after a valid value has been assigned to the `length` or `width` field. You create a method to be `private` when it should be called only by other methods or accessors within the class and not by outside classes.

»NOTE Programmers probably create `private` methods more frequently than they create `public` data fields. Some programmers feel that the best style is to use `public` methods that are nothing but a list of method calls with descriptive names. Then, the methods that actually do the work are all `private`.

»TWO TRUTHS AND A LIE: UNUSUAL USE: `public` FIELDS AND `private` METHODS

1. Good object-oriented techniques require that data should usually be hidden and access to it should be controlled by well-designed accessors.
2. Although `private` fields, methods, and accessors are the norm, occasionally you need to create `public` versions of them.
3. When you define a named constant within a class, it is always `static`; that is, the field belongs to the entire class, not to any particular instance of the class.

The false statement is #2. Although `private` fields and `public` methods and accessors are the norm, occasionally you need to create `public` fields or `private` methods.

UNDERSTANDING THE `this` REFERENCE

After you create a class, you might eventually create thousands of objects from that class. When you create each object, you provide storage for each of the object's instance variables. For example, Figure 7-15 shows part of a `Book` class that contains only three fields, a property for the title field, and an advertising message method. When you declare several `Book` objects, as in the following statements, each `Book` object requires separate memory locations for its `title`, `numPages`, and `price`:

```
Book myBook = new Book();
Book yourBook = new Book();
```

```
class Book
{
   private string title;
   private int numPages;
   private double price;
   public string Title
   {
      get
      {
         return title;
      }
      set
      {
         title = value;
      }
   }
   public void AdvertisingMessage()
   {
      Console.WriteLine("Buy it now: {0}", Title);
   }
}
```

Figure 7-15 Partially developed `Book` class

>> **NOTE** A fully developed `Book` class would most likely contain properties for the other data fields. This version excludes those properties to keep the example short.

>> **NOTE** When you compile the `Book` class, you receive warnings that the `numPages` and `price` fields are never used. The omission was purposeful for this demonstration program.

Storing a single `Book` object requires allocating storage space for three separate fields; the storage requirements for `Book` objects used by a library or retail bookstore would be far more considerable, but necessary—each `Book` must be able to "hold" its own data, including publisher, date published, author, ISBN, and so on. If each `Book` object also required its own copy of each property and method contained in the class, the storage requirements would multiply. It makes sense that each `Book` needs space to store its unique title and other data, but because every `Book` uses the same methods, storing multiple copies is wasteful and unnecessary.

>> **NOTE** An object's non-static fields are "instance variables" because there is a stored version for each object instance.

Fortunately, each `Book` object does not need to store its own copy of each property and method. Whether you make the method call `myBook.AdvertisingMessage()` or `yourBook.AdvertisingMessage()`, you access the same `AdvertisingMessage()` method. However, there must be a difference between the two method calls, because each displays a different title in its message. The difference lies in an implicit, or invisible, reference that is passed to every instance method and property accessor. The implicitly passed reference is the **`this` reference**. When you call the method `myBook.AdvertisingMessage()`, you automatically pass the `this` reference to the method so the method knows which instance of `Book` to use.

>> **NOTE** Only nonstatic methods receive a `this` reference. Nonstatic methods are instance methods—they can work differently and appropriately for each object—so it makes sense that they receive a `this` reference.

You can explicitly refer to the this reference within an instance method or property, as shown in Figure 7-16. When you refer to Title (or title) within a Book class method or accessor, you are referring to the title field of "this" Book—the Book whose name you used in the method call—perhaps myBook or yourBook. Using the shaded keywords in Figure 7-16 is not required; the version of the methods shown in Figure 7-15 (where this was implied but not written explicitly) works just as well. Figure 7-17 shows an application that uses the Book class, and Figure 7-18 shows the output.

```
class Book
{
   private string title;
   private int numPages;
   private double price;
   public string Title
   {
     get
     {
        return this.title;
     }
     set
     {
        this.title = value;
     }
   }
   public void AdvertisingMessage()
   {
      Console.WriteLine("Buy it now: {0}", this.Title);
   }
}
```

Figure 7-16 Book class with methods explicitly using this references

```
using System;
public class CreateTwoBooks
{
   public static void Main()
   {
      Book myBook = new Book();
      Book yourBook = new Book();
      myBook.Title = "Silas Marner";
      yourBook.Title = "The Time Traveler's Wife";
      myBook.AdvertisingMessage();
      yourBook.AdvertisingMessage();
   }
}
```

Figure 7-17 Program that declares two Book objects

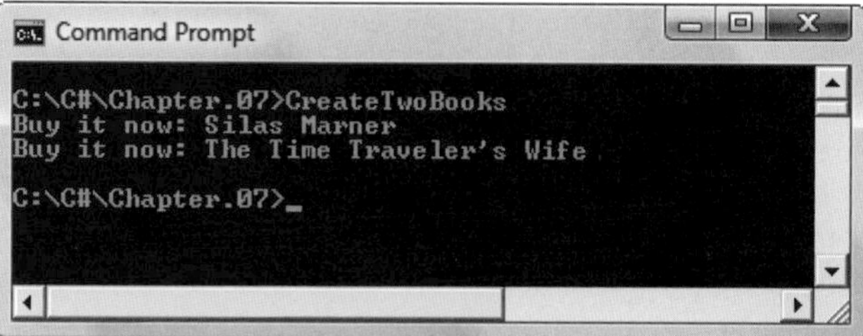

Figure 7-18 Output of `CreateTwoBooks` program

The `Book` class in Figure 7-16 worked without adding the references to `this`. However, you should be aware that the `this` reference is always there, working behind the scenes, even if you do not code it. Sometimes, you may want to include the `this` reference within a method for clarity, so the reader has no doubt when you are referring to a class instance variable.

»NOTE On occasion, you might need to explicitly code the `this` reference. You will see some examples later in this chapter after you learn about constructors.

»TWO TRUTHS AND A LIE: UNDERSTANDING THE `this` REFERENCE

1. An implicit, or invisible, `this` reference is passed to every instance method and property accessor in a class; instance methods and properties are nonstatic.
2. You can explicitly refer to the `this` reference within an instance method or property.
3. Although the `this` reference exists in every instance method, you can never refer to it within a method.

The false statement is #3. Sometimes, you may want to include the `this` reference within a method for clarity, so the reader has no doubt when you are referring to a class instance variable.

UNDERSTANDING CONSTRUCTORS

When you create a class such as `Employee` and instantiate an object with a statement such as `Employee aWorker = new Employee();`, you are actually calling a method named `Employee()` that is provided by C#. A **constructor** is a method that instantiates (creates an instance of) an object. Every class you create is automatically supplied with a `public` constructor with no parameters. A constructor without parameters is a class's **default constructor**. The constructor named `Employee()` establishes one `Employee` with the identifier `aWorker`, and provides the following initial values to the `Employee`'s data fields:

- Numeric fields are set to 0 (zero).
- Character fields are set to '\0'.
- Boolean fields are set to `false`.
- References, such as `string` fields or any other object fields, are set to `null` (or empty).

»NOTE You will learn to create constructors with parameters in the next section of this chapter.

»NOTE The value of an object initialized with a default constructor is known as the **default value of the object**.

»NOTE The term *default constructor* is not just used for a class's automatically supplied constructor; it is used for any constructor that takes no parameters.

If you do not want an Employee's fields to hold these default values, or if you want to perform additional tasks when you create an Employee, you can write your own constructor to replace the automatically supplied version. Any constructor you write must have the same name as its class, and constructors cannot have a return type. For example, if you create an Employee class that contains a Salary property, and you want every new Employee object to have a salary of 300.00, you could write the constructor for the Employee class that appears in Figure 7-19. Any instantiated Employee will have a default salary value of 300.00.

```
Employee()
{
   Salary = 300.00;
}
```

Figure 7-19 Employee class constructor that initializes the Salary property

»NOTE The constructor in Figure 7-19 assumes a Salary property has been defined with a set accessor. If there is no set accessor, but there is a salary field, then the assignment could be salary = 300;.

You can write any statement in a constructor. Although you usually would have no reason to do so, you could print a message from within a constructor or perform any other task. The most common constructor task is to initialize fields.

PASSING PARAMETERS TO CONSTRUCTORS

You can create a constructor to ensure that all objects of a class are initialized with the same values in their data fields. After construction, you might change the value in an individual object's fields by using the appropriate set accessors in its properties. Alternatively, you might create objects that hold unique field values right from the start by writing constructors to which you pass one or more parameters. You then can use the parameter values to set properties or fields for individual object instantiations. For example, consider an Employee class with two data fields, a constructor, and an auto-implemented property, as shown in Figure 7-20. Its constructor assigns 999 to each potentially instantiated Employee's idNumber. Any time an Employee object is created using a statement such as Employee partTimeWorker = new Employee();, even if no other data-assigning methods are ever used, you are ensured that the Employee's idNumber holds a default value. The partTimeWorker Employee object, like all Employees, will have an initial idNumber of 999.

»NOTE Using this technique would cause all employees to have the same ID number, which usually is contrary to the purpose of an ID number.

```
public class Employee
{
   private int idNumber;
   private double salary;
   public Employee()
   {
      IdNumber = 999;
   }
   public int IdNumber {get; set;}
   //  Other class members can go here
}
```

Figure 7-20 `Employee` class with a parameterless constructor

The constructor in Figure 7-20 is a **parameterless constructor**—one that takes no arguments. As an alternative, you might choose to create `Employees` with initial `idNumber` fields that differ for each `Employee`. To accomplish this task within a constructor, you can pass an employee number to the constructor. Figure 7-21 shows an `Employee` constructor that receives a parameter. With this constructor, an integer is passed in using a statement such as the following:

```
Employee partTimeWorker = new Employee(876);
```

When the constructor executes, the integer used as the actual parameter within the method call is passed to `Employee()` and assigned to the `Employee`'s `idNumber`.

»NOTE A class can contain only one parameterless constructor: the default constructor.

```
public Employee(int empID)
{
   IdNumber = empID;
}
```

Figure 7-21 `Employee` constructor with parameter

»NOTE Suppose you want the parameter to the `Employee` class constructor to have the identifier `idNumber`. Further, suppose you want the `Employee` class to contain a read-only property for `idNumber`; that is, there is no `set` accessor for `IdNumber`. Then you would write the constructor as follows:

```
public Employee(int idNumber)
{
   this.idNumber = idNumber);
}
```

»NOTE The `idNumber` value on the right of the assignment operator would refer to the constructor parameter, but `this.idNumber` on the left of the assignment statement refers to the current object's `idNumber` field.

NOTE You learned the meaning of *ambiguity* and how to avoid it in Chapter 6.

NOTE If you create class constructors but do not create a parameterless version, then the class does not have a default constructor.

OVERLOADING CONSTRUCTORS

If you create a class from which you can instantiate objects, C# automatically provides a default constructor. As soon as you create your own constructor, whether it has parameters or not, you no longer have access to the automatically created version. However, if you want a class to have both parameter and parameterless versions of a constructor, you can create them. Like any other C# methods, constructors can be overloaded. You can write as many constructors for a class as you want, as long as their argument lists do not cause ambiguity. For example, the `Employee` class in Figure 7-22 contains four constructors. The `Main()` method within the `CreateSomeEmployees` class in Figure 7-23 shows how different types of `Employees` might be instantiated. Notice that one version of the `Employee` constructor—the one that supports a character parameter—doesn't even use the parameter; sometimes you might create a constructor with a specific parameter type simply to force that constructor to be the version that executes. The output of the `CreateSomeEmployees` program is shown in Figure 7-24.

```
public class Employee
{
   public int IdNumber {get; set;}
   public double Salary {get; set;}
   public Employee()
   {
      IdNumber = 999;
      Salary = 0;
   }
   public Employee(int empId)
   {
      IdNumber = empId;
      Salary = 0;
   }
   public Employee(int empId, double sal)
   {
      IdNumber = empId;
      Salary = sal;
   }
   public Employee(char code)
   {
      IdNumber = 111;
      Salary = 100000;
   }
}
```

This parameterless constructor is the class's default constructor.

Figure 7-22 `Employee` class with four constructors

NOTE In Figure 7-22, fields could have been declared for `idNumber` and `salary`, but they have been omitted because they are not necessary when auto-implemented properties are declared and the field names are not required by any other methods.

```
using System;
public class CreateSomeEmployees
{
   public static void Main()
   {
      Employee aWorker = new Employee();
      Employee anotherWorker = new Employee(234);
      Employee theBoss = new Employee('A');
      Console.WriteLine("{0,4}{1,14}", aWorker.IdNumber,
         aWorker.Salary.ToString("C"));
      Console.WriteLine("{0,4}{1,14}", anotherWorker.IdNumber,
         anotherWorker.Salary.ToString("C"));
      Console.WriteLine("{0,4}{1,14}", theBoss.IdNumber,
         theBoss.Salary.ToString("C"));
   }
}
```

Figure 7-23 `CreateSomeEmployees` program

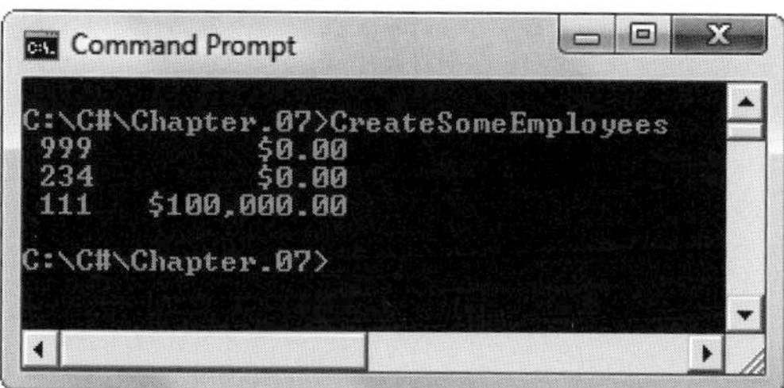

Figure 7-24 Output of `CreateSomeEmployees` program

Most likely, a single application would not use all four constructors of the `Employee` class. More likely, each application that uses the class would use only one or two constructors. You create a class with multiple constructors to provide flexibility for your clients. For example, some clients might choose to construct `Employee` objects with just ID numbers, and others might prefer to construct them with ID numbers and salaries.

USING CONSTRUCTOR INITIALIZERS

The `Employee` class in Figure 7-22 contains four constructors, and each constructor initializes the same two fields. In a fully developed class used by a company, many more fields would be initialized, creating a lot of duplicated code. Besides the original extra work of writing the repetitive statements in these constructors, even more extra work will be required when the class is modified in the future. For example, if your organization institutes a new employee ID number format that requires a specific number of digits, then each constructor will have to be modified. Besides the extra work to modify each constructor, it is possible that one or more of the constructor versions will be overlooked, introducing errors into the programs that are clients of the class.

As an alternative to repeating code in the constructors, you can use a constructor initializer. A **constructor initializer** is a clause that indicates another instance of a class constructor should be executed before any statements in the current constructor body. Figure 7-25 shows a new version of the `Employee` class using constructor initializers in three of the four overloaded constructor versions.

```
public class Employee
{
    public int IdNumber {get; set;}
    public double Salary {get; set;}
    public Employee() : this(999, 0)
    {
    }
    public Employee(int empId) : this(empId, 0)
    {
    }
    public Employee(int empId, double sal)
    {
        IdNumber = empId;
        Salary = sal;
    }
    public Employee(char code) : this(111, 100000)
    {
    }
}
```

Figure 7-25 `Employee` class with constructor initializers

In the three shaded clauses in Figure 7-25, the `this` reference is used to mean "the constructor for this object being constructed." For example, when a client calls the parameterless `Employee` constructor, 999 and 0 are passed to the two-parameter constructor. There, they become `empId` and `sal`, parameters that are assigned to the `IdNumber` and `Salary` properties. If there were statements within the parameterless constructor, they would then execute; however, in this class, there is no reason for additional statements. Similarly, if a client uses the constructor version that accepts only an ID number, that parameter and a 0 for salary are passed to the two-parameter constructor. The only time just one version of the constructor executes is when a client uses both an ID number and a salary as constructor arguments. In the future, if additional statements needed to be added to the class (for example, a decision that ensures an ID number was at least five digits at construction), the decision would be added only to the two-parameter version of the constructor, and all the other versions could use it.

»TWO TRUTHS AND A LIE: UNDERSTANDING CONSTRUCTORS

1. Every class you create is automatically supplied with a `public` constructor with no parameters.
2. If you write a constructor for a class, you do not have a default constructor for the class.
3. Any constructor you write must have the same name as its class, and constructors cannot have a return type.

The false statement is #2. If you write a parameterless constructor for a class, it becomes the default constructor, and you lose the automatically supplied version. If you write only constructors that require parameters, then the class no longer contains a default constructor.

PASSING OBJECTS TO METHODS

You can pass objects to methods just as you can simple data types. For example, the `CreateSomeEmployees` application in Figure 7-23 can be rewritten as shown in Figure 7-26. In this version, instead of repeating the details of the `WriteLine()` method, the statement can be placed in its own method, and each `Employee` object can be passed into it, in turn. The output of the program in Figure 7-27 is identical to the output shown in Figure 7-24.

```
using System;
public class CreateSomeEmployees2
{
   public static void Main()
   {
      Employee aWorker = new Employee();
      Employee anotherWorker = new Employee(234);
      Employee theBoss = new Employee('A');
      WriteEmployeeData(aWorker);
      WriteEmployeeData(anotherWorker);
      WriteEmployeeData(theBoss);
   }
   public static void WriteEmployeeData(Employee emp)
   {
      Console.WriteLine("{0,4}{1,14}", emp.IdNumber, emp.Salary.ToString("C"));
   }
}
```

Figure 7-26 `CreateSomeEmployees2` program

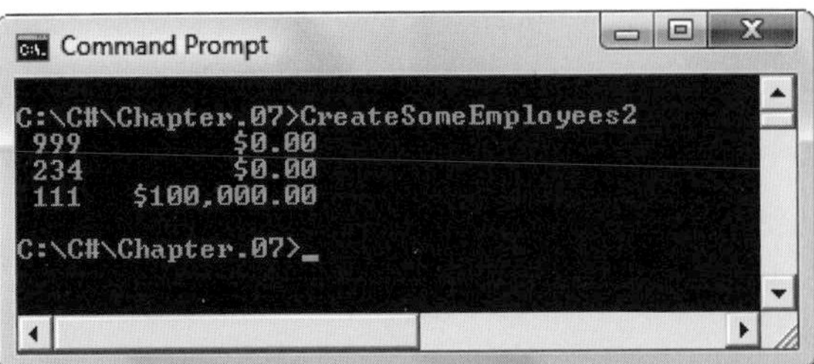

Figure 7-27 Output of `CreateSomeEmployees2` program

When you pass an object to a method, you pass a reference. Therefore, any change made to an object parameter in a method also affects the object used as an argument in the calling method.

»TWO TRUTHS AND A LIE: PASSING OBJECTS TO METHODS

1. You can pass objects to methods just as you can pass simple data types.
2. When you pass an object to a method, you pass a copy of the object used as an argument in the calling statement.
3. Any change made to an object parameter in a method also affects the object used as an argument in the calling method.

The false statement is #2. When you pass an object to a method, you pass a reference. That is, you pass the memory address of the object.

USING OBJECT INITIALIZERS

An **object initializer** allows you to assign values to any accessible members or properties of a class at the time of instantiation without calling a constructor with parameters. For example, assuming an `Employee` class has been created with a public `IdNumber` property and a parameterless constructor, you can write an object initializer as follows:

```
Employee aWorker = new Employee {IdNumber = 101};
```

In this statement, 101 is assigned to the `aWorker` object's `IdNumber` property. The assignment is made within a pair of curly braces; no parentheses are used with the class name. When this statement executes, the parameterless, default constructor for the class is executed first, and then the object initializer assignment is made.

> **»NOTE** Object initializers are a new feature in C# 3.0.

For example, Figure 7-28 shows an `Employee` class that contains properties for `IdNumber` and `Salary` and a default constructor that assigns a value to `Salary`. For demonstration purposes, the constructor displays the current object's ID number and salary. Figure 7-29 shows a program that instantiates one `Employee` object and displays its value, and Figure 7-30 shows the output. When the object is created in the shaded statement in Figure 7-29, the constructor executes,

```
class Employee
{
   public int IdNumber {get; set;}
   public double Salary {get; set;}
   public Employee()
   {
      Salary = 99.99;
      Console.WriteLine("Employee #{0} created. Salary is {1}.",
         IdNumber, Salary);
   }
}
```

Figure 7-28 `Employee` class with default constructor that assigns `Salary` and displays data

```
using System;
public class DemoObjectInitializer
{
   public static void Main()
   {
      Employee aWorker = new Employee {IdNumber = 101};
      Console.WriteLine("Employee #{0} exists. Salary is {1}.",
         aWorker.IdNumber, aWorker.Salary);
   }
}
```

Figure 7-29 `DemoObjectInitializer` program

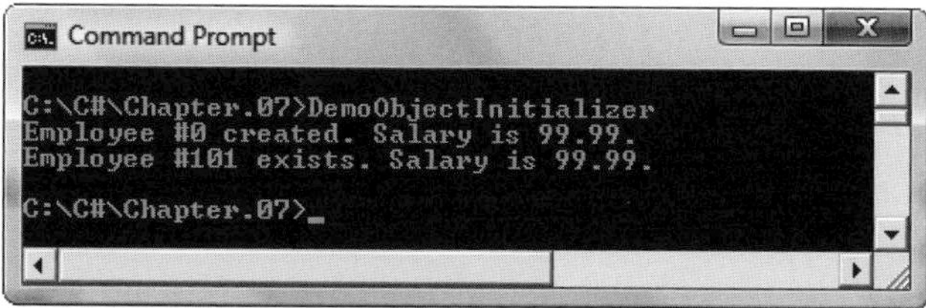

Figure 7-30 Output of `DemoObjectInitializer` program

assigns 99.99 to `Salary`, and displays the first line of output in Figure 7-30, showing `IdNumber` is still 0. After the object is constructed in the `Main()` method in Figure 7-29, the next output line is displayed, showing that the assignment of the ID number occurred after construction.

For you to use object initializers, a class must have a default constructor. That is, you must not have created any constructors, or you must have created one that requires no parameters.

Multiple assignments can be made with an object initializer by separating them with commas, as in the following:

```
Employee myAssistant = new Employee {IdNumber = 202, Salary = 25.00};
```

This single code line has the same results as the following three statements:

```
Employee myAssistant = new Employee();
myAssistant.IdNumber = 202;
myAssistant.Salary = 25.00;
```

Using object initializers allows you to create multiple objects with different initial assignments without having to provide multiple constructors to cover every possible situation. Additionally, using object initializers allows you to create objects with different starting values for different properties of the same data type. For example, consider a class like the `Box` class in Figure 7-31 that contains multiple properties of the same type. The constructor sets the `Height`, `Width`, and `Depth` properties to 1. You could write a constructor that accepts an integer parameter to be assigned to `Height` (using the default value 1 for the other dimensions), but then you could not write an additional overloaded constructor that accepts an integer parameter to be assigned to `Width` because the constructors would be ambiguous. However, by using object initializers, you can create objects to which you assign the properties you want. Figure 7-32 shows a program that declares three `Box` objects, each with a different assigned dimension, and Figure 7-33 shows the output, which demonstrates that each property was assigned appropriately.

```
class Box
{
   public int Height {get; set;}
   public int Width {get; set;}
   public int Depth {get; set;}
   public Box()
   {
      Height = 1;
      Width = 1;
      Depth = 1;
   }
}
```

Figure 7-31 The `Box` class

```
using System;
public class DemoObjectInitializer2
{
   public static void Main()
   {
     Box box1 = new Box {Height = 3};
     Box box2 = new Box {Width = 15};
     Box box3 = new Box {Depth = 268};
     DisplayDimensions(1, box1);
     DisplayDimensions(2, box2);
     DisplayDimensions(3, box3);
   }
   public static void DisplayDimensions(int num, Box box)
   {
      Console.WriteLine("Box {0}: Height: {1} Width: {2} Depth: {3}",
        num, box.Height, box.Width, box.Depth);
   }
}
```

Figure 7-32 The `DemoObjectInitializer2` program

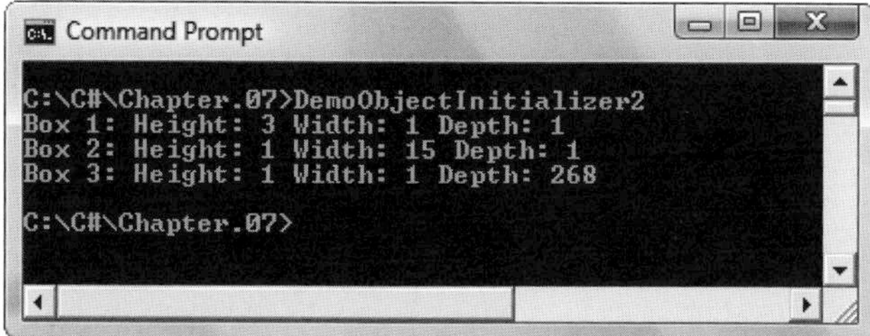

Figure 7-33 Output of the `DemoObjectInitializer2` program

>>**NOTE** Object initializers have additional uses in LINQ statements. You will learn about LINQ in Chapter 14.

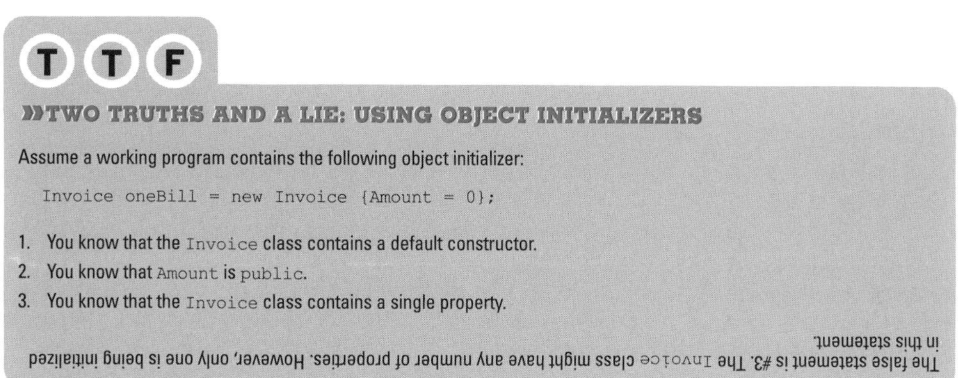

T T F

>>TWO TRUTHS AND A LIE: USING OBJECT INITIALIZERS

Assume a working program contains the following object initializer:

```
Invoice oneBill = new Invoice {Amount = 0};
```

1. You know that the `Invoice` class contains a default constructor.
2. You know that `Amount` is `public`.
3. You know that the `Invoice` class contains a single property.

The false statement is #3. The `Invoice` class might have any number of properties. However, only one is being initialized in this statement.

» NOTE
In Chapter 6 you learned that when a language feature such as the plus sign has multiple meanings depending on the context, it is overloaded and demonstrates polymorphism.

OVERLOADING OPERATORS

C# operators are the symbols you use to perform operations on objects. You have used many operators, including arithmetic operators (such as + and –) and logical operators (such as == and <). Separate actions can result from what seems to be the same operation or command. This occurs frequently in all computer programming languages, not just object-oriented languages. For example, in most programming languages and applications such as spreadsheets and databases, the + operator has a variety of meanings. A few of them include:

- » Alone before a value (called unary form), + indicates a positive value, as in the expression `+7`.
- » Between two integers (called binary form), + indicates integer addition, as in the expression `5 + 9`.
- » Between two floating-point numbers (also called binary form), + indicates floating-point addition, as in the expression `6.4 + 2.1`.

Expressing a value as positive is a different operation from using the + operator to perform arithmetic, so + is overloaded several times in that it can take one or two arguments and have a different meaning in each case. It also can take different operand types—you use a + to add two `int`s, two `double`s, an `int` and a `double`, and a variety of other combinations. Each use results in different actions behind the scenes.

» NOTE In addition to overloading, compilers often need to perform coercion, or implicit casting, when the + symbol is used with mixed arithmetic. For example, when an integer and floating-point number are added in C#, the integer is coerced into a floating-point number before the appropriate addition code executes. You learned about casting in Chapter 2.

Just as it is convenient to use a + between both integers and `double`s to add them, it also can be convenient to use a + between objects, such as `Employee`s or `Book`s, to add them. To be able to use arithmetic symbols with your own objects, you must overload the symbols.

C# operators are classified as unary or binary, depending on whether they take one or two arguments, respectively. The rules for overloading are shown in the following list:

- » The overloadable unary operators are:

```
+ - ! ~ ++ -- true false
```

» NOTE Although `true` and `false` are not used explicitly as operators in expressions, they are considered operators in Boolean expressions and in expressions involving the conditional operator and conditional logical operators.

- » The overloadable binary operators are:

```
+ - * / % & | ^ == != > < >= <=
```

- » You cannot overload the following operators:

```
= && || ?? ?: checked unchecked new typeof as is
```

» You cannot overload an operator for a built-in data type. For example, you cannot change the meaning of + between two ints.
» When a binary operator is overloaded and it has a corresponding assignment operator, it is also overloaded. For example, if you overload +, then += is automatically overloaded too.
» Some operators must be overloaded in pairs. For example, when you overload ==, you also must overload !=, and when you overload >, you also must overload <.

» NOTE You are already familiar with about half of these operators. You will learn more about the rest as you continue to study C#.

» NOTE When you overload ==, you also receive warnings about methods in the Object class. You will learn about this class in Chapter 8; you should not attempt to overload == until you have studied that chapter.

You have used many of the operators listed above. If you want to include these operators in your own classes, you must decide what the operator will mean in your class. When you do, you write statements in a method to carry out your meaning. The method has a return type and arguments just like other methods, but its identifier is required to be followed by the operator being overloaded; for example, operator+() or operator*().

» NOTE For an overloaded unary operator, the method has the following format:
type operator *overloadable-operator* (*type identifier*)

» NOTE For an overloaded binary operator, the method has the following format:
type operator *overloadable-operator* (*type identifier, type operand*)

For example, suppose you create a Book class in which each object has a title, number of pages, and a price. Further assume that, as a publisher, you have decided to "add" Books together. That is, you want to take two existing Books and combine them into one. Assume you want the new book to have the following characteristics:

» The new title is a combination of the old titles, joined by the word "and."
» The number of pages in the new book is equal to the sum of the pages in the original Books.
» Instead of charging twice as much for a new Book, you have decided to charge the price of the more expensive of the two original Books, plus $10.

A different publisher might have decided that "adding Books" means something different—for example, an added Book might have a fixed new price of $29.99. The statements you write in your operator+() method depend on how you define adding for your class. You could write an ordinary method to perform these tasks, but you could also overload the + operator to mean "add two Books." Figure 7-34 shows a Book class. (This class actually is an expanded version of the Book class in Figure 7-15, modified to use auto-implemented properties and to add the operator+() method.) This class has properties for each field and a shaded operator+() method.

```
class Book
{
   public Book(string title, int pages, double price)
   {
      Title = title;
      NumPages = pages;
      Price = price;
   }
   public static Book operator+(Book first, Book second)
   {
      const double EXTRA = 10.00;
      string newTitle = first.Title + " and " +
         second.Title;
      int newPages = first.NumPages + second.NumPages;
      double newPrice;
      if(first.Price > second.Price)
         newPrice = first.Price + EXTRA;
      else
         newPrice = second.Price + EXTRA;
      return(new Book(newTitle, newPages, newPrice));
   }
   public string Title {get; set;}
   public int NumPages {get; set;}
   public double Price {get; set;}
}
```

Figure 7-34 `Book` class with overloaded + operator

The `operator+()` method in Figure 7-34 is declared to be `public` (so that class clients can use it) and `static`, which is required. The return type is `Book` because the addition of two `Book`s is defined to be a new `Book` with different values from either of the originals. You could overload the + operator so that when two `Book`s are added they return some other type, but it is most common to make the addition of two objects result in an "answer" of the same type.

The two parameters in the `operator+()` method in the `Book` class are both `Book`s. Therefore, when you eventually call this method, the data types on both sides of the + sign will be `Book`s. For example, you could write other methods that add a `Book` and an `Employee`, or a `Book` and a `double`.

> **»NOTE**
> Notice that the + between the `string`s in creating the new `Book` title is itself an overloaded operator; concatenating strings is a different operation from adding `int`s or `double`s.

Within the `operator+()` method, the statements perform the following tasks:

- » A constant is declared to hold the extra price used in creating a new `Book` from two existing ones.
- » A new string is created and assigned the first parameter `Book`'s title, plus the `string` `" and "`, plus the second parameter `Book`'s title.

» A new integer is declared and assigned the sum of the number of pages in each of the parameter Books.

» A new double is declared and assigned the value of the more expensive original Book plus $10.00.

» Within the return statement, a new anonymous Book is created (an anonymous object is one without an identifier) using the new title, page number, and price, and returned to the calling method. (Instead of an anonymous Book, it would have been perfectly acceptable to use two statements—the first one creating a named Book with the same arguments, and the second one returning the named Book.)

»NOTE It is possible to rewrite the operator+() method in the Book class in Figure 7-34 so that all the work is done in the return statement. For example:

```
public static Book operator+(Book first, Book second)
{
   const double EXTRA = 10.00;
   return(new Book(first.Title + " and " + second.Title,
      first.NumPages + second.NumPages,
      first.Price > second.Price ? first.Price + EXTRA :
         second.Price + EXTRA));
}
```

```
using System;
public class AddBooks
{
   public static void Main()
   {
      Book book1 = new Book("Silas Marner", 350, 15.95);
      Book book2 = new Book("Moby Dick", 250, 16.00);
      Book book3;
      book3 = book1 + book2;
      Console.WriteLine("The new book is \"{0}\"", book3.Title);
      Console.WriteLine("It has {0} pages and costs {1}",
         book3.NumPages, book3.Price.ToString("C"));
   }
}
```

Figure 7-35 The AddBooks program

Figure 7-35 shows a client program that can use the + operator in the Book class. It first declares three Books; then, in the shaded statement, it adds two Books together and assigns the result to the third. When book1 and book2 are added, the operator+() method is called automatically because the + sign is used in the code. The returned Book is assigned to book3, which is then displayed. Figure 7-36 shows the results.

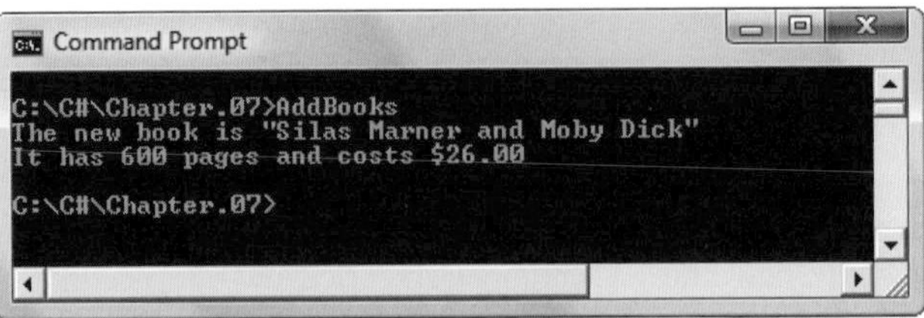

Figure 7-36 Output of the `AddBooks` program

NOTE Because each addition operation returns a `Book`, it is possible to chain addition in a statement such as `collection = book1 + book2 + book3;` (assuming all the variables have been declared to be `Book` objects). In this example, `book1` and `book2` would be added, returning a temporary `Book`. Then the temporary `Book` and `book3` would be added, returning a different temporary `Book` that would be assigned to `collection`.

In the `Book` class, it took many statements to overload the operator; however, in the client class, just typing a + between objects allows a programmer to use the objects and operator intuitively. You could write any statements you wanted within the operator method. However, for clarity, you should write statements that intuitively have the same meaning as the common use of the operator. For example, although you could overload the `operator*()` method to display a `Book`'s title and price instead of performing multiplication, it would be a bad programming technique.

NOTE When you overload an operator in a class, at least one argument to the method must be a member of the class. In other words, within the `Book` class, you can overload `operator*()` to multiply a `Book` by an integer, but you cannot overload `operator*()` to multiply a `double` by an integer.

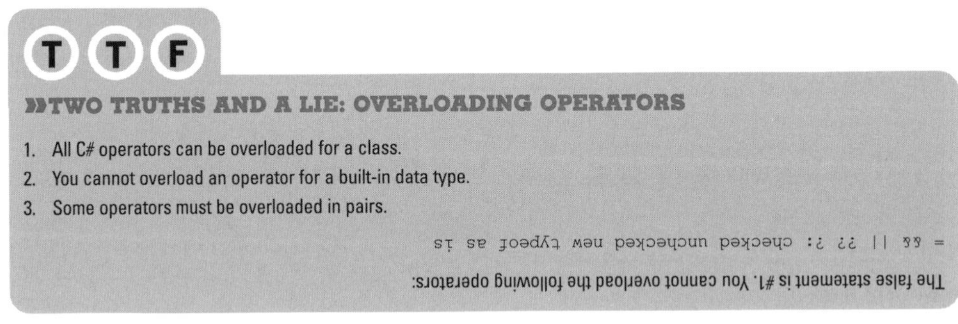

TWO TRUTHS AND A LIE: OVERLOADING OPERATORS

1. All C# operators can be overloaded for a class.
2. You cannot overload an operator for a built-in data type.
3. Some operators must be overloaded in pairs.

The false statement is #1. You cannot overload the following operators: `= && || ?? ?: checked unchecked new typeof as is`

DECLARING AN ARRAY OF OBJECTS

Just as you can declare arrays of integers or `double`s, you can declare arrays that hold elements of any type, including objects. For example, Figure 7-37 shows an abbreviated `Employee` class that contains just one property named `IdNumber`, which gets and sets an implied `idNumber` field.

```
class Employee
{
   public int IdNumber {get; set;}
}
```

Figure 7-37 A simple `Employee` class

Of course, you also can create separate `Employee` objects with unique names, such as in the following statement:

```
Employee painter, electrician, plumber;
```

For many programs, however, it is far more convenient to create an array of `Employee` objects. An array named `empArray` that holds seven `Employee` objects is defined by the following:

```
Employee[] empArray = new Employee[7];
```

This statement reserves enough computer memory for the references to seven `Employee` objects named `empArray[0]` through `empArray[6]`. It does not actually construct those `Employees`; instead, you must call the seven individual constructors to do so. Because the `Employee` class in Figure 7-37 contains a default constructor that requires no arguments, the following loop calls the constructor seven times:

```
for(int x = 0; x < empArray.Length; ++x)
   empArray[x] = new Employee();
```

As `x` varies from 0 through 6, each of the seven `empArray` objects is constructed.

»NOTE When you create an array from a value type, such as `int` or `char`, the array holds the actual values. When you create an array from a reference type, such as a class you create, then the array holds the memory addresses of the objects. In other words, the array "refers to" the objects instead of containing the objects.

»NOTE You can create an array of objects and provide default values to the elements' constructors in one step. For example, if an `Inventory` class contains a constructor that requires an integer argument, you can declare an array of `Inventory` objects by writing the following:

```
Inventory[] items = {new Inventory(123), new
   Inventory(345), new Inventory(678)};
```

To use a method that belongs to an object that is part of an array, you insert the appropriate subscript notation after the array name and before the dot-method. For example, to set all seven `Employee IdNumber` properties to 999, you can write the following:

```
for(int x = 0; x < empArray.Length; ++x)
   empArray[x].IdNumber = 999;
```

USING THE `Sort()` AND `BinarySearch()` METHODS WITH ARRAYS OF OBJECTS

In Chapter 6, you learned about using the `System.Array` class's built-in `BinarySearch()` and `Sort()` methods with simple data types such as `int`, `double`, and `string`. The `Sort()` method accepts an array parameter and arranges its elements in descending order. The `BinarySearch()` method accepts a sorted array and a value that it attempts to match in the array.

>> **NOTE** You learned about the built-in data type class names in Chapter 2; they are summarized in Table 2-1.

A complication arises when you consider searching or sorting arrays of objects you create. When you create and sort an array of simple data items, there is only one type of value to consider, and the order is based on the Unicode value of that item. The classes that support simple data items each contain a method named **`CompareTo()`**, which provides the details of how the basic data types compare to each other. In other words, they define comparisons such as "2 is more than 1" and "B is more than A." The `Sort()` and `BinarySearch()` methods use the `CompareTo()` method for the current type of data being sorted. In other words, `Sort()` uses the `Int32` version of `CompareTo()` when sorting integers and the `Char` version of `CompareTo()` when sorting characters.

>> **NOTE** You have been using the `String` class (and its `string` alias) throughout this book. The class also contains a `CompareTo()` method that you first used in Chapter 2.

>> **NOTE** You first learned about polymorphism in Chapter 1.

When you create a class that contains many fields, however, you must tell the compiler which field to use when making comparisons. For example, you logically might sort an organization's `Employee` objects by ID number, salary, department number, last name, hire date, or any field contained in the class. To tell C# which field to use for placing `Employee` objects in order, you must create an interface. An **interface** is a collection of abstract methods (and perhaps other members) that can be used by any class, as long as the class provides a definition to override the interface's do-nothing, or abstract, method definitions. When a method **overrides** another, it takes precedence over the method, hiding the original version. In other words, the methods in an interface are empty, and any class that uses them must contain a new version that provides the details. Interfaces define named behaviors that classes must implement, so that all classes can use the same method names but use them appropriately for the class. In this way, interfaces provide for polymorphism—the ability of different objects to use the same method names but act appropriately based on the context.

>> **NOTE** When a method overrides another, it has the same signature as the method it overrides. When methods are overloaded, they have different signatures. You learned about method signatures in Chapter 6. You will learn more about overriding methods and abstract methods and classes in Chapter 8.

>> **NOTE** C# supports many interfaces. You can identify an interface name by its initial letter I.

C# contains an **`IComparable` interface,** which contains the definition for the `CompareTo()` method that compares one object to another and returns an integer. Figure 7-38 shows the definition of `IComparable`. The `CompareTo()` method accepts an `Object`, but does not contain any statements; you must provide an implementation for this method in classes you create if you want the objects to be comparable.

```
interface IComparable
{
   int CompareTo(Object o);
}
```

Figure 7-38 The `IComparable` interface

When you create a class whose members you predict clients will want to compare:

» You must include a single colon and the interface name `IComparable` after the class name.

» You must write a method that contains the following header:

```
int IComparable.CompareTo(Object o)
```

»NOTE `Object` is a class—the most generic of all classes. Every `Employee` object you create is not only an `Employee`, but also an `Object`. (This concept is similar to "every banana is a fruit" or "every collie is a dog.") By using the type `Object` as a parameter, the `CompareTo()` method can accept anything. You will learn more about the `Object` class in Chapter 8.

To work correctly in methods such as `BinarySearch()` and `Sort()`, the `CompareTo()` method you create for your class must return an integer value. Table 7-1 shows the return values that every version of `CompareTo()` should provide.

Return Value	Meaning
Negative	This instance is less than the compared object.
Zero	This instance is equal to the compared object.
Positive	This instance is greater than the compared object.

Table 7-1 Return values of `IComparable.CompareTo()` method

When you create a class that contains an `IComparable.CompareTo()` method, the method is an instance method and receives a `this` reference to the object used to call it. A second object is passed to the method; within the method, you first must convert, or cast, the passed object to the same type as the calling object's class, and then compare the corresponding fields you want from the `this` object and the passed object. For example, Figure 7-39 shows an `Employee` class that contains a shaded `CompareTo()` method and compares `Employee` objects based on the contents of their `idNumber` fields.

»NOTE You first learned about casting in Chapter 2.

```
class Employee : IComparable
{
   public int IdNumber {get; set;}
   public double Salary {get; set;}
   int IComparable.CompareTo(Object o)
   {
      int returnVal;
      Employee temp = (Employee)o;
      if(this.IdNumber > temp.IdNumber)
         returnVal = 1;
      else
         if(this.IdNumber < temp.IdNumber)
            returnVal = -1;
         else
            returnVal = 0;
      return returnVal;
   }
}
```

Figure 7-39 `Employee` class using `IComparable` interface

The `Employee` class in Figure 7-39 uses a colon and `IComparable` in its class header to indicate an interface. The shaded method is an instance method; that is, it "belongs" to an `Employee` object. When another `Employee` is passed in as `Object o`, it is cast as an `Employee` and stored in the `temp` variable. The `idNumber` values of the `this` Employee and the passed `Employee` are compared, and one of three integer values is returned.

For example, if you declare two `Employee` objects named `worker1` and `worker2`, you can use the following statement:

```
int answer = worker1.CompareTo(worker2);
```

> **NOTE** The controlling "`this`" object in an instance method is the **invoking object**.

Within the `CompareTo()` method in the `Employee` class, `worker1` would be "`this`" `Employee`—the controlling `Employee` in the method. The `temp` `Employee` would be `worker2`. If, for example, `worker1` had a higher ID number than `worker2`, the value of `answer` would be 1.

Figure 7-40 shows a program that uses the `Employee` class. The program declares an array of five `Employee` objects with different ID numbers and salaries; the ID numbers are purposely out of order to demonstrate that the `Sort()` method works correctly. The program also declares a `seekEmp` object with an ID number of 222. The program sorts the array, displays the sorted elements, then finds the array element that matches the `seekEmp` object. Figure 7-41 shows the program execution.

```
using System;
public class ComparableEmployeeArray
{
   public static void Main()
   {
      Employee[] empArray = new Employee[5];
      int x;
      for(x = 0; x < empArray.Length; ++x)
         empArray[x] = new Employee();
      empArray[0].IdNumber = 333;
      empArray[1].IdNumber = 444;
      empArray[2].IdNumber = 555;
      empArray[3].IdNumber = 111;
      empArray[4].IdNumber = 222;
      Employee seekEmp = new Employee();
      seekEmp.IdNumber = 222;
      Array.Sort(empArray);
      Console.WriteLine("Sorted employees:");
      for(x = 0; x < empArray.Length; ++x)
         Console.WriteLine("Employee #{0}: {1} {2}",
            x, empArray[x].IdNumber,
            empArray[x].Salary.ToString("C"));
      x = Array.BinarySearch(empArray, seekEmp);
      Console.WriteLine("Employee #{0} was found at position {1}",
         seekEmp.IdNumber, x);
   }
}
```

Figure 7-40 `ComparableEmployeeArray` program

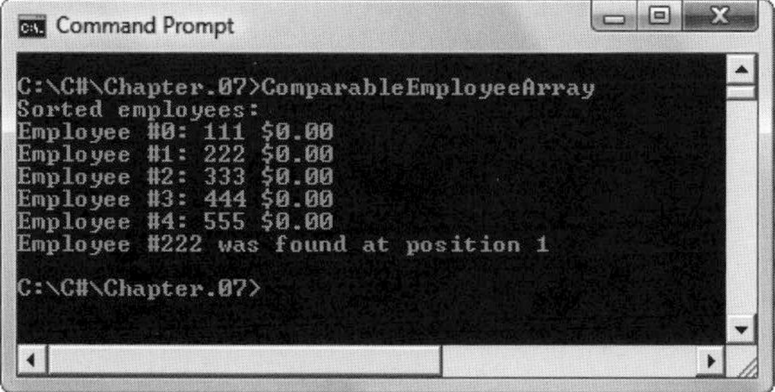

Figure 7-41 Output of `ComparableEmployeeArray` program

Notice that the `seekEmp` object matches the `Employee` in the second array position based on the `idNumber` only—not the salary—because the `CompareTo()` method in the `Employee` class uses only `idNumber` values and not salaries to make comparisons. You *could* have written code that requires both the `idNumber` and `salary` values to match before returning a positive number.

»TWO TRUTHS AND A LIE: DECLARING AN ARRAY OF OBJECTS

Assume a working program contains the following array declaration:

```
BankAccount[] acctArray = new BankAccount[500];
```

1. This statement reserves enough computer memory for 500 `BankAccount` objects.
2. This statement constructs 500 `BankAccount` objects.
3. The valid subscripts for `acctArray` are 0 through 499.

The false statement is #2. This statement declares 500 `BankAccount` objects but does not actually construct those objects; to do so, you must call the 500 individual constructors.

UNDERSTANDING DESTRUCTORS

> **»NOTE** You learned about an object's scope in Chapter 6.

A **destructor** contains the actions you require when an instance of a class is destroyed. Most often, an instance of a class is destroyed when it goes out of scope. As with constructors, if you do not explicitly create a destructor for a class, C# automatically provides one.

To explicitly declare a destructor, you use an identifier that consists of a tilde (~) followed by the class name. You cannot provide any parameters to a destructor; it must have an empty argument list. As a consequence, destructors cannot be overloaded; a class can have at most one destructor. Like a constructor, a destructor has no return type.

Figure 7-42 shows an `Employee` class that contains only one property (`IdNumber`), a constructor, and a (shaded) destructor. When you execute the `Main()` method in the `DemoEmployeeDestructor` class in Figure 7-43, you instantiate two `Employee` objects, each with its own `idNumber` value. When the `Main()` method ends, the two `Employee` objects go out of scope, and the destructor for each object is called. Figure 7-44 shows the output.

```
class Employee
{
   public int IdNumber {get; set;}
   public Employee(int empID)
   {
      IdNumber = empID;
      Console.WriteLine("Employee object {0} created", IdNumber);
   }
   ~Employee()
   {
      Console.WriteLine("Employee object {0} destroyed!", IdNumber);
   }
}
```

Figure 7-42 `Employee` class with destructor

```
using System;
public class DemoEmployeeDestructor
{
   public static void Main()
   {
      Employee aWorker = new Employee(101);
      Employee anotherWorker = new Employee(202);
   }
}
```

Figure 7-43 `DemoEmployeeDestructor` program

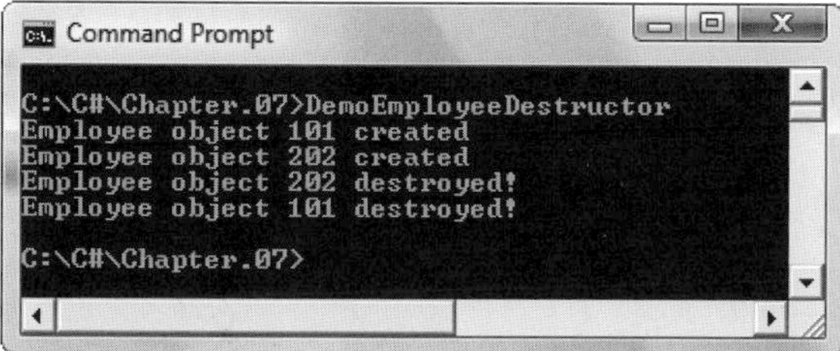

Figure 7-44 Output of `DemoEmployeeDestructor` program

The program in Figure 7-43 never explicitly calls the `Employee` class destructor, yet you can see from the output that the destructor executes twice. Destructors are invoked automatically; you cannot explicitly call one. Interestingly, the last object created is the first object destroyed; the same relationship would hold true no matter how many objects the program instantiated.

For now, you have little reason to create a destructor except to demonstrate how it is called automatically. Later, when you write more sophisticated C# programs that work with files, databases, or large quantities of computer memory, you might want to perform specific clean-up or close-down tasks when an object goes out of scope. Then you will place appropriate instructions within a destructor.

»NOTE An instance of a class becomes eligible for destruction when it is no longer possible for any code to use it—that is, when it goes out of scope. The actual execution of an object's destructor might occur at any time after the object becomes eligible for destruction.

»TWO TRUTHS AND A LIE: UNDERSTANDING DESTRUCTORS

1. To explicitly declare a destructor, you use an identifier that consists of a tilde (~) followed by the class name.
2. You cannot provide any parameters to a destructor; it must have an empty argument list.
3. The return type for a destructor is always `void`.

The false statement is #3. Like a constructor, a destructor has no return type.

YOU DO IT

CREATING A CLASS AND OBJECTS

In this section, you will create a `Student` class and instantiate objects from it. This class contains an ID number, last name, and grade point average for the `Student`. It also contains properties that get and set each of these fields. You will also pass each `Student` object to a method.

To create a `Student` class:

1. Open a new file in your text editor. Begin the `Student` class by declaring the class name, inserting an opening curly brace, and declaring three `private` fields that will hold an ID number, last name, and grade point average, as follows:

```
class Student
{
   private int idNumber;
   private string lastName;
   private double gradePointAverage;
```

2. Add two constants that represent the highest and lowest possible values for a grade point average.

```
public const double HIGHEST_GPA = 4.0;
public const double LOWEST_GPA = 0.0;
```

3. Add two properties that get and set `idNumber` and `lastName`. By convention, properties have an identifier that is the same as the field they service, except they start with a capital letter.

```
public int IdNumber
{
   get
   {
      return idNumber;
   }
   set
   {
      idNumber = value;
   }
}
public string LastName
{
   get
   {
      return lastName;
   }
   set
   {
      lastName = value;
   }
}
```

4. Add the following `set` accessor in the property for the `gradePointAverage` field. It sets limits on the value assigned, assigning 0 if the value is out of range.

```
public double GradePointAverage
{
   get
   {
      return gradePointAverage;
   }
   set
   {
      if(value >= LOWEST_GPA && value <= HIGHEST_GPA)
         gradePointAverage = value;
      else
         gradePointAverage = LOWEST_GPA;
   }
}
```

5. Add a closing curly brace for the class. Save the file as **Student.cs**.

6. Open a new file in your text editor and begin a program that creates two `Student` objects, assigns some values, and displays the `Students`.

```
using System;
public class CreateStudents
{
```

7. Add a `Main()` method that declares two `Students`. Assign field values, including one "illegal" value—a grade point average that is too high.

```
public static void Main()
{
   Student first = new Student();
   Student second = new Student();
   first.IdNumber = 123;
   first.LastName = "Anderson";
   first.GradePointAverage = 3.5;
   second.IdNumber = 789;
   second.LastName = "Daniels";
   second.GradePointAverage = 4.1;
```

8. Instead of creating similar `WriteLine()` statements to display the two `Students`, call a method with each `Student`. You will create the method to accept a `Student` argument in the next step. Add a closing curly brace for the `Main()` method.

```
   Display(first);
   Display(second);
}
```

NOTE
Recall from Chapter 2 that field contents are left aligned when you use a minus sign before the field size. Also recall that the "F1" argument to the `ToString()` method causes the value to be displayed to one decimal place.

9. Write the `Display()` method so that the passed-in `Student`'s `IdNumber`, `LastName`, and `GradePointAverage` are displayed and aligned. Add a closing curly brace for the class.

```
    public static void Display(Student stu)
    {
        Console.WriteLine("{0,5}{1,-10}{2,6}",
            stu.IdNumber, stu.LastName,
            stu.GradePointAverage.ToString("F1"));
    }
}
```

10. Save the file as **CreateStudents.cs**.
11. You can choose to create a multifile assembly, as described in Appendix B; or, for convenience, you can combine the two files into one. Either way, compile the files and execute the program. Figure 7-45 shows the output. Each `Student` has unique data values and uses the same `Display()` method. Notice how the second `Student`'s grade point average was forced to 0 by the `set` accessor in the property for the field.

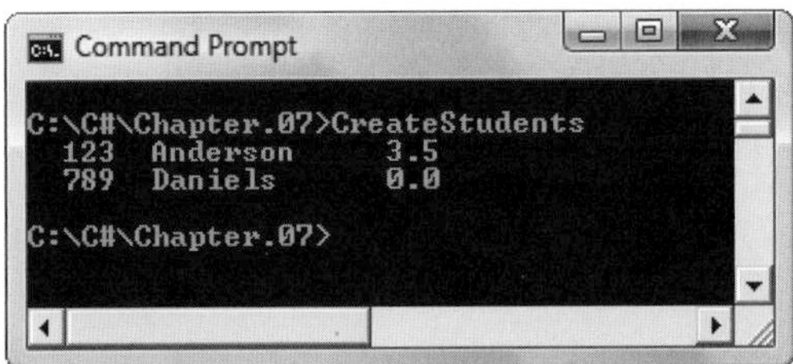

Figure 7-45 Output of `CreateStudents` program

USING AUTO-IMPLEMENTED PROPERTIES

When a property's `get` accessor simply returns the corresponding field's value, and its `set` accessor simply assigns a value to the appropriate field, you can reduce the code in your classes by using auto-implemented properties. In the `Student` class, both `IdNumber` and `LastName` are candidates for this shortcut, so you can replace the full versions of these properties with their auto-implemented versions. The `GradePointAverage` property cannot take advantage of auto-implementation because additional code is required for the property to fulfill its intended function.

To include auto-implemented properties in the `Student` class:

1. Open the file that contains the `Student` class if it is not still open on your screen. Remove the properties for `IdNumber` and `LastName` and replace them with these auto-implemented versions:

```
public int IdNumber {get; set;}
public string LastName {get; set;}
```

2. Save the file and recompile it. Execute the `CreateStudents` program. The output is the same as when the program used the original version of the `Student` class in Figure 7-45.

ADDING OVERLOADED CONSTRUCTORS TO A CLASS

Frequently, you create constructors for a class so that fields will hold initial values when objects are instantiated. You can overload constructors by writing multiple versions with different parameter lists; you often want to do this so that different clients can use your class in the way that suits them best.

To add overloaded constructors to the `Student` class:

1. Open the file that contains the `Student` class if it is not still open on your screen. Just before the closing curly brace for the `Student` class, add the following constructor. It takes three parameters and assigns them to the appropriate fields:

```
public Student(int id, string name, double gpa)
{
    IdNumber = id;
    LastName = name;
    GradePointAverage = gpa;
}
```

2. Add a second parameterless constructor. It calls the first constructor, passing 0 for the ID number, "XXX" for the name, and 0.0 for the grade point average. Its body is empty.

```
public Student() : this(0, "XXX", 0.0)
{
}
```

3. Save the file.

4. Open the **CreateStudents.cs** file and immediately save it as **CreateStudents2.cs**. Change the class name to `CreateStudents2`. If you previously included a copy of the `Student` class within this file, replace the `Student` class with the new version to which you just added constructors.

5. After the existing declarations of the `Student` objects, add two more declarations. With one, use three arguments, but with the other, do not use any.

```
Student third = new Student(456, "Marco", 2.4);
Student fourth = new Student();
```

6. At the end of the `Main()` method, just after the two existing calls to the `Display()` method, add two more calls using the new objects.

```
Display(third);
Display(fourth);
```

7. Save the file, then compile and execute it. The output looks like Figure 7-46. All four objects are displayed. The first two have had values assigned to them after declaration, but the third and fourth ones obtained their values from their constructors.

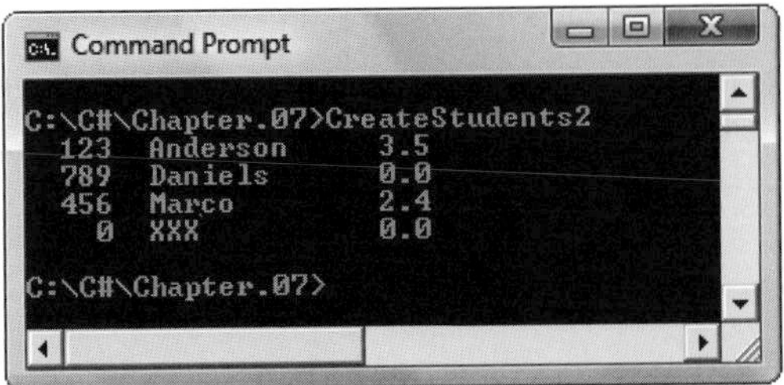

Figure 7-46 Output of `CreateStudents2` program

CREATING AN ARRAY OF OBJECTS

Just like variables of the built-in, primitive data types, objects you create can be stored in arrays. In the next steps, you will create an array of `Student` objects. You will prompt the user for data to fill the array, and you will sort the array by student ID number before displaying all the data.

To create and use an array of objects:

1. Open the **CreateStudents2.cs** file and immediately save it as **CreateStudents3.cs**. Change the class name to **CreateStudents3**.

2. Delete all the existing statements in the `Main()` method, leaving the opening and closing curly braces. Between the braces, declare an array of eight `Student` objects. Also declare a variable to use as an array subscript and declare three variables that will temporarily hold a user's input data before `Student` objects are constructed.

```
Student[] student = new Student[8];
int x;
int id;
string name;
double gpa;
```

3. In a loop, call a `GetData()` method (which you will write shortly); send it `out` arguments so that you can retrieve values for variables that will hold an ID number, name, and grade point average. Then, in turn, send these three values to the `Student` constructor for each of the eight `Student` objects.

```
for(x = 0; x < student.Length; ++x)
{
   GetData(out id, out name, out gpa);
   student[x] = new Student(id, name, gpa);
}
```

4. Call the `Array.Sort()` method, sending it the student array. Then, one object at a time in a loop, call the `Display()` method that you wrote in a previous set of steps.

```
Array.Sort(student);
Console.WriteLine("Sorted List:");
for(x = 0; x < student.Length; ++x)
   Display(student[x]);
```

5. Write the GetData() method. Its parameters are out parameters so that their values will be known to the calling method. The method simply prompts the user for each data item, reads it, and converts it to the appropriate type, if necessary.

```
public static void GetData(out int id, out string name,
   out double gpa)
   {
      string inString;
      Console.Write("Please enter student ID number ");
      inString = Console.ReadLine();
      id = Convert.ToInt32(inString);
      Console.Write("Please enter last name for " +
         "student {0} ", id);
      name = Console.ReadLine();
      Console.Write("Please enter grade point average ");
      inString = Console.ReadLine();
      gpa = Convert.ToDouble(inString);
   }
```

6. Copy the existing Student class to the bottom of the current file, if necessary. After the class header, add a colon and **IComparable** so that objects of the class can be sorted.

```
public class Student : IComparable
```

7. Just before the closing curly brace for the Student class, add the IComparable.CompareTo() method that is required for the objects of the class to be sortable. The method will sort Student objects based on their ID numbers, so it returns 1, –1, or 0 based on IdNumber property comparisons. The method accepts an object that is cast to a Student object. If the IdNumber of the controlling Student object is greater than the argument's IdNumber, then the return value is set to 1. If the IdNumber of the controlling Student object is less than the argument's IdNumber, then the return value is –1. Otherwise, the return value is 0.

```
int IComparable.CompareTo(Object o)
{
   int returnVal;
   Student temp = (Student)o;
   if(this.IdNumber > temp.IdNumber)
      returnVal = 1;
   else
      if(this.IdNumber < temp.IdNumber)
         returnVal = -1;
      else
         returnVal = 0;
   return returnVal;
}
```

8. Save the file (as CreateStudents3.cs) and compile and execute it. When prompted, enter any student IDs, names, and grade point averages you choose. The objects will be sorted and displayed. Figure 7-47 shows a typical execution. After the Student array is sorted, the Student objects appear in idNumber order.

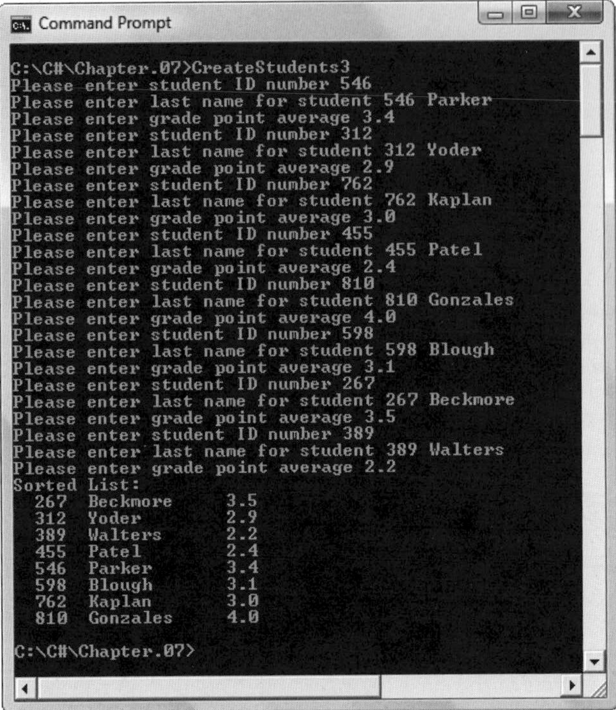

Figure 7-47 Typical execution of `CreateStudents3` program

CHAPTER SUMMARY

- When you write programs in C#, you create classes that are only programs with a `Main()` method and classes from which you instantiate objects. The data components of a class are its instance variables. Object attributes often are called fields to help distinguish them from other variables you might use. In addition to their attributes, objects have methods associated with them, and every object that is an instance of a class is assumed to possess the same methods. A program or class that instantiates objects of another prewritten class is a class client or class user.
- When you create a class, you must assign a name to it and determine what data and methods will be part of the class. A class header or class definition contains an optional access modifier, the keyword `class`, and any legal identifier you choose for the name of your class. In addition to the class header, classes you create must have a class body enclosed between curly braces.
- When you create a class, you define both its attributes and its methods. You usually declare instance variables to be `private` and instance methods to be `public`.

- When you create an object that is an instance of a class, you supply a type and an identifier, and you allocate computer memory for that object using the `new` operator. After an object has been instantiated, its `public` methods can be accessed using the object's identifier, a dot, and a method call.
- A property is a member of a class that provides access to a field of a class; properties define how fields will be set and retrieved. Properties have `set` accessors for setting an object's fields and `get` accessors for retrieving the stored values. When you create properties, the syntax in your client programs becomes more natural and easier to understand. As a shortcut, you can create an auto-implemented property when a field's `set` accessor should simply assign a value to the appropriate field, and when its `get` accessor should simply return the field.
- When you create a class that describes objects to be instantiated and another class that instantiates those objects, you can contain the two classes within a single file or place each class in its own file. A class can contain many fields and methods. Although there is no requirement to do so, most programmers place data fields in some logical order at the beginning of a class. For ease in locating class methods and properties, many programmers prefer to store them in alphabetical order. Another logical organization scheme is to store all properties first, in the same order as their corresponding data fields, followed by other methods. An additional aid to keeping your classes organized is to use comments liberally.
- Most of the time, class data fields are `private` and class methods are `public`. This technique ensures that data will be used and changed only in the ways provided in your accessors. Occasionally, however, you need to create `public` fields or `private` methods. For example, you can create a `public` data field when you want all objects of a class to contain the same value. You create a method to be `private` when it should be called only by other methods or accessors within the class and not by outside classes.
- Each instantiation of a class accesses the same copy of its methods. This is possible because an implicit reference, the `this` reference, is passed to every instance method and property accessor. You can explicitly refer to the `this` reference within an instance method or property, but usually you are not required to do so.
- A constructor is a method that instantiates (creates an instance of) an object. Every class you create is automatically supplied with a `public` constructor with no parameters. You can write your own constructor to replace the automatically supplied version. Any constructor you write must have the same name as its class, and constructors cannot have a return type.
- You can pass one or more arguments to a constructor. Frequently you do so to initialize fields.
- An object initializer allows you to assign values to any accessible members or properties of a class at the time of instantiation without calling a constructor with parameters. Using object initializers allows you to create multiple objects with different initial assignments without having to provide multiple constructors to cover every possible situation. Additionally, using object initializers allows you to create objects with different starting values for different properties of the same data type.

- Like any other C# methods, constructors can be overloaded. You can write as many constructors for a class as you want, as long as their argument lists do not cause ambiguity.
- A constructor initializer is a clause that indicates another instance of a class constructor should be executed before any statements in the current constructor body.
- You can pass objects to methods just as you can simple data types.
- You can overload operators to use with objects by writing a method to carry out your meaning. The method has a return type and arguments just like other methods, but its identifier is required to be followed by the operator being overloaded—for example, `operator+()` or `operator*()`. When you overload an operator, you should write statements that intuitively have the same meaning as the common use of the operator.
- Just as you can declare arrays of integers or `double`s, you can declare arrays that hold elements of any type, including objects. After you declare an array of objects, you must call a constructor for each object. To use a method that belongs to an object that is part of an array, you insert the appropriate subscript notation after the array name and before the dot-method.
- When you create a class that contains many fields, you must tell the compiler which field to use when making comparisons by using an interface—a collection of methods (and perhaps other members) that can be used by any class, as long as the class provides a definition to override the interface's do-nothing, or abstract, method definitions. C# contains an interface named `IComparable`, which in turn contains the definition for the `CompareTo()` method that compares one object to another and returns an integer. You must override this definition in classes you create if you want the objects to be comparable.
- A destructor contains the actions you require when an instance of a class is destroyed. If you do not explicitly create a destructor for a class, C# automatically provides one. To explicitly declare a destructor, you use an identifier that consists of a tilde (~) followed by the class name. You cannot provide any parameters to a destructor; a class can have at most one destructor.

KEY TERMS

Is-a relationships describe object-class relationships.

An **instantiation** of a class is a created object.

The **instance variables** of a class are the data components that exist separately for each instantiation.

Fields are instance variables within a class.

An object's **state** is the set of contents of its fields.

A **class client** or **class user** is a program or class that instantiates objects of another prewritten class.

A **class header** or **class definition** describes a class; it contains an optional access modifier, the keyword `class`, and any legal identifier for the name of the class.

A **class access modifier** describes access to a class.

The **`public`** class access modifier means access to the class is not limited.

The **`protected`** class access modifier means access to the class is limited to the class and to any classes derived from the class.

The **`internal`** class access modifier means access is limited to the assembly to which the class belongs.

The **`private`** class access modifier means access is limited to another class to which the class belongs. In other words, a class can be `private` if it is contained within another class, and only the containing class should have access to the `private` class.

Information hiding is a feature found in all object-oriented languages, in which a class's data is private and changed or manipulated only by its own methods.

Instance methods are methods that are used with object instantiations.

Composition is the technique of using an object within another object.

The relationship created using composition is called a **has-a relationship** because one class "has an" instance of another.

A **reference type** is a type that holds a memory address.

Value types hold a value; they are predefined types such as `int`, `double`, and `char`.

A **property** is a member of a class that provides access to a field of a class; properties define how fields will be set and retrieved.

Accessors in properties specify how a class's fields are accessed.

An object's fields are assigned by **`set` accessors** that allow use of the assignment operator with a property name.

An object's fields are accessed by **`get` accessors** that allow retrieval of a field value by using a property name.

A **read-only property** has only a `get` accessor, and not a `set` accessor.

The **getter** is another term for a class property's `get` accessor.

The **setter** is another term for a class property's `set` accessor.

Contextual keywords are identifiers that act like keywords in specific circumstances.

An **implicit parameter** is undeclared and gets its value automatically.

An **auto-implemented property** is one in which the code within the accessors is created automatically. The only action in the `set` accessor is to assign a value to the associated field, and the only action in the `get` accessor is to return the associated field value.

A **primary key** is a field that uniquely identifies a record; the term is often used in databases.

The **`this` reference** is the reference to an object that is implicitly passed to an instance method of its class.

A **constructor** is a method that instantiates (creates an instance of) an object.

A **default constructor** is an automatically supplied parameterless constructor.

The **default value of an object** is the value initialized with a default constructor.

A **parameterless constructor** is one that takes no arguments.

A **constructor initializer** is a clause that indicates another instance of a class constructor should be executed before any statements in the current constructor body.

An **object initializer** allows you to assign values to any accessible members or properties of a class at the time of instantiation without calling a constructor with parameters.

The **`CompareTo()` method** of the `IComparable` interface compares one object to another and returns an integer.

An **interface** is a collection of abstract methods (and perhaps other members) that can be used by any class, as long as the class provides a definition to override the interface's do-nothing, or abstract, method definitions.

When a method **overrides** another, it takes precedence over the method, hiding the original version.

The **`IComparable` interface** contains the definition for the `CompareTo()` method.

An instance method's **invoking object** is the object referenced by `this`.

A **destructor** contains the actions you require when an instance of a class is destroyed.

REVIEW QUESTIONS

1. An object is a(n) ________ of a class.

   a. child　　c. instantiation

   b. institution　　d. relative

2. A class header or class definition can contain all of the following *except* ________ .

   a. an optional access modifier　　c. an identifier

   b. the keyword `class`　　d. initial field values

3. Most class fields are created with the ________ modifier.

   a. `public`　　c. `new`

   b. `protected`　　d. `private`

4. Most class methods are created with the ________ modifier.

   a. `public`　　c. `new`

   b. `protected`　　d. `private`

5. Instance methods that belong to individual objects are ________ `static` methods.

   a. always　　c. occasionally

   b. usually　　d. never

6. To allocate memory for an object instantiation, you must use the ________ operator.

   a. `mem` c. `new`

   b. `alloc` d. `instant`

7. Assume you have created a class named `MyClass`. The header of the `MyClass` constructor can be ________ .

   a. `public void MyClass()`

   b. `public MyClassConstructor()`

   c. Either of these can be the constructor header.

   d. Neither of these can be the constructor header.

8. Assume you have created a class named `MyClass`. The header of the `MyClass` constructor can be ________ .

   a. `public MyClass()`

   b. `public MyClass (double d)`

   c. Either of these can be the constructor header.

   d. Neither of these can be the constructor header.

9. Assume you have created a class named `DemoCar`. Within the `Main()` method of this class, you instantiate a `Car` object named `myCar` and the following statement executes correctly:

```
Console.WriteLine("The Car gets {0} miles per gallon",
   myCar.ComputeMpg());
```

   Within the `Car` class, the `ComputeMpg()` method must be ________ .

   a. `public` and `static` c. `private` and `static`

   b. `public` and nonstatic d. `private` and nonstatic

10. Assume you have created a class named `TermPaper` that contains a character field named `letterGrade`. You also have created a property for the field. Which of the following cannot be true?

    a. The property name is `letterGrade`.

    b. The property is read-only.

    c. The property contains a `set` accessor that does not allow a grade lower than 'C'.

    d. The property does not contain a `get` accessor.

11. A `this` reference is ________ .

    a. implicitly passed to nonstatic methods

    b. implicitly passed to `static` methods

    c. explicitly passed to nonstatic methods

    d. explicitly passed to `static` methods

12. When you use an instance variable within a class's nonstatic methods, you ________ explicitly refer to the method's `this` reference.

    a. must
    b. can
    c. cannot
    d. should (even though it is not required)

13. A class's default constructor ________ .

    a. sets numeric fields to 0
    b. is parameterless
    c. both of these
    d. none of these

14. Assume you have created a class named `Chair` with a constructor defined as `Chair(int height)`. Which of the following overloaded constructors could coexist with the `Chair` constructor without ambiguity?

    a. `Chair(int legs)`
    b. `Chair(int height, int legs)`
    c. both of these
    d. none of these

15. Which of the following statements correctly instantiates a `House` object if the `House` class contains a single constructor with the declaration `House(int bedrooms, double price)`?

    a. `House myHouse = new House();`
    b. `House myHouse = new House(3, 125000.00);`
    c. `House myHouse = House(4, 200,000.00);`
    d. two of these

16. You explicitly call a destructor ________ .

    a. when you are finished using an object
    b. when an object goes out of scope
    c. when a class is destroyed
    d. You cannot explicitly call a destructor.

17. In a program that creates five object instances of a class, the constructor executes ________ time(s) and the destructor executes ________ time(s).

    a. one; one
    b. one; five
    c. five; one
    d. five; five

18. Suppose you declare a class named `Furniture` that contains a `string` field named `woodType` and a conventionally named property with a `get` accessor. When you declare an array of 200 `Furniture` objects named `myChairs`, which of the following accesses the last `Furniture` object's wood type?

    a. `Furniture.Get(woodType[199])`

    b. `myChairs[199].WoodType()`

    c. `myChairs.WoodType[199]`

    d. `myChairs[199].WoodType`

19. What is a collection of methods (and perhaps other members) that can be used by any class, as long as the class provides a definition to override the collection's do-nothing, or abstract, definitions?

    a. a superclass

    b. a polymorph

    c. a perimeter

    d. an interface

20. When you create a class whose members clients are likely to want to compare using the `Array.Sort()` or `Array.BinarySearch()` method, you must ________ .

    a. include at least one numeric field within the class

    b. write a `CompareTo()` method for the class

    c. be careful not to override the existing `IComparable.CompareTo()` method

    d. Two of these are true.

EXERCISES

1. Create a class named `Pizza`. Data fields include a string for toppings (such as pepperoni), an integer for diameter in inches (such as 12), and a `double` for price (such as 13.99). Include properties to get and set values for each of these fields. Create a class named `TestPizza` that instantiates one `Pizza` object and demonstrates the use of the `Pizza` `set` and `get` accessors. Save this class as **TestPizza.cs**.

2. Create a class named `HousePlant`. A `HousePlant` has fields for a name (for example, "Philodendron"), a price (for example, 29.99), and a value indicating whether the plant has been fed in the last month (for example, `true`). Include properties that contain `get` and `set` accessors for each field. Create a class named `DisplayHousePlants` that instantiates three `HousePlant` objects. Demonstrate the use of each property for each object. Save the file as **DisplayHousePlants.cs**.

3. Create a class named `Circle` with fields named `radius`, `area`, and `diameter`. Include a constructor that sets the radius to 1. Also include `public` properties for each field. The `Radius` property should have `get` and `set` accessors, but `Area` and `Diameter`

should be read-only. The `set` accessor for the radius should also provide values for the `diameter` and `area`. (The diameter of a circle is twice its radius; the area is pi multiplied by the square of the radius. You can use the public `Math` class property `Math.PI` for the value of pi.) Create a class named `TestCircles` whose `Main()` method declares three `Circle` objects. Assign a small radius value to one `Circle` and assign a larger radius value to another `Circle`. Do not assign a value to the radius of the third circle; instead, retain the value assigned at construction. Display the radius, diameter, and area for each `Circle`. (Display the area to two decimal places.) Save the program as **TestCircles.cs**.

4. Create a class named `Square` that contains fields for area and the length of a side and whose constructor requires a parameter for the length of one side of a `Square`. The constructor assigns its parameter to the length of the `Square`'s side field and calls a `private` method that computes the area field. Also include read-only properties to get a `Square`'s side and area. Create a class named `DemoSquares` that instantiates an array of 10 `Square` objects with sides that have values of 1 through 10. Display the values for each `Square`. Save the class as **DemoSquares.cs**.

5. Create a class named `GirlScout` that contains fields for a `GirlScout`'s name, troop number, and dues owed. Include a constant `static` field that contains the last words of the `GirlScout` motto ("to obey the Girl Scout law"). Include overloaded constructors that allow you to set all three nonstatic `GirlScout` fields to default values or to parameter values. Also include properties for each field. Create a class named `DemoScouts` that instantiates two `GirlScout` objects and displays their values. Create one object to use the default constructor and the other to use the constructor that requires arguments. Also display the `GirlScout` motto. Save the class as **DemoScouts.cs**.

6. a. Create a class named `Taxpayer`. Data fields for `Taxpayer` objects include the Social Security number (use a `string` for the type, but do not use dashes within the Social Security number), the yearly gross income, and the tax owed. Include a property with `get` and `set` accessors for the first two data fields, but make the tax owed a read-only property. The tax should be calculated whenever the income is set. Assume the tax is 15% of income for incomes under $30,000 and 28% for incomes that are $30,000 or higher. Write a program that declares an array of 10 `Taxpayer` objects. Prompt the user for data for each object and display the 10 objects. Save the program as **TaxPayerDemo.cs**.

   b. Modify the `Taxpayer` class so its objects are comparable to each other based on tax owed. Modify the `TaxPayerDemo` application so that after the 10 objects are displayed, they are sorted in order by the amount of tax owed; then display the objects again. Save the program as **TaxPayerDemo2.cs**.

7. Create a class named `Car` with fields that hold a vehicle ID number, make, model, color, and value for a `Car` object. Include appropriate properties for each field. Write a `DisplayFleet()` method that accepts any number of `Car` objects, displays their values, and displays the total value of all `Car` objects passed to the method. Write a `Main()` method that declares five `Car` objects and assigns values to each, then calls

`DisplayFleet()` three times—passing three, four, and five `Car` objects in successive calls. Save the program as **CarsDemo.cs**.

8. a. Create a class named `School` that contains fields for the `School` name and number of students enrolled and properties for each field. Also, include an `IComparable.CompareTo()` method so that `School` objects can be sorted by enrollment. Write a program that allows a user to enter information about five `School` objects. Display the `School` objects in order of enrollment size from smallest to largest `School`. Save the program as **SchoolsDemo.cs**.

   b. Modify the program created in Exercise 8a so that after the `School` objects are displayed in order, the program prompts the user to enter a minimum enrollment figure. Display all `School` objects that have an enrollment at least as large as the entered value. Save the program as **SchoolMinEnroll.cs**.

9. a. Create a class named `Friend`. Its fields include a `Friend`'s name, phone number, and three integer fields that together represent the `Friend`'s birthday—month, day, and year. Write a program that declares an array of eight `Friend` objects and prompts the user to enter data about eight friends. Display the `Friend` objects in alphabetical order by first name. Save the program as **FriendList.cs**.

   b. Modify the program created in Exercise 9a so that after the list of `Friend` objects is displayed, the program prompts the user for a specific `Friend`'s name and the program returns the `Friend`'s phone number and birthday. Display an appropriate message if the friend the user requests is not found. Save the program as **FriendBirthday.cs**.

   c. Modify the program in Exercise 9b so that after the requested `Friend`'s birthday displays, the program also displays a list of every `Friend` who has a birthday in the same month. Save the program as **AllFriendsInSameMonth.cs**.

10. a. Design a `Job` class for Harold's Home Services. The class contains four data fields—`Job` description (for example, "wash windows"), time in hours to complete the `Job` (for example, 3.5), per-hour rate charged for the `Job` (for example, $25.00), and total fee for the `Job` (hourly rate times hours). Include properties to get and set each field except the total fee—that field will be read-only, and its value is calculated each time either the hourly fee or the number of hours is set. Overload the + operator so that two `Jobs` can be added. The sum of two `Jobs` is a new `Job` containing the descriptions of both original `Jobs` (joined by "and"), the sum of the time in hours for the original `Jobs`, and the average of the hourly rate for the original `Jobs`. Write a `Main()` function that demonstrates all the methods work correctly. Save the file as **DemoJobs.cs**.

    b. Harold has realized that his method for computing the fee for combined jobs is not fair. For example, consider the following:

    » His fee for painting a house is $100 per hour. If a job takes 10 hours, he earns $1000.

    » His fee for dog walking is $10 per hour. If a job takes 1 hour, he earns $10.

    » If he combines the two jobs and works a total of 11 hours, he earns only the average rate of $55 per hour, or $605.

Devise an improved, weighted method for calculating Harold's fees for combined `Jobs` and include it in the overloaded `operator+()` method. Write a `Main()` function that demonstrates all the methods in the class work correctly. Save the file as **DemoJobs2.cs**.

11. a. Create a `Fraction` class with fields that hold a whole number, a numerator, and a denominator. In addition:

    » Create properties for each field. The `set` accessor for the denominator should not allow a 0 value; the value defaults to 1.

    » Add three constructors. One takes three parameters for a whole number, numerator, and denominator. Another accepts two parameters for the numerator and denominator; when this constructor is used, the whole number value is 0. The last constructor is parameterless; it sets the whole number and numerator to 0 and the denominator to 1. (After construction, `Fractions` do not have to be reduced to proper form. For example, even though 3/9 could be reduced to 1/3, your constructors do not have to perform this task.)

    » Add a `Reduce()` method that reduces a `Fraction` if it is in improper form. For example, 2/4 should be reduced to 1/2.

    » Add an `operator+()` method that adds two `Fractions`. To add two fractions, first eliminate any whole number part of the value. For example, 2 1/4 becomes 9/4 and 1 3/5 becomes 8/5. Find a common denominator and convert the fractions to it. For example, when adding 9/4 and 8/5, you can convert them to 45/20 and 32/20. Then you can add the numerators, giving 77/20. Finally, call the `Reduce()` method to reduce the result, restoring any whole number value so the fractional part of the number is less than 1. For example, 77/20 becomes 3 17/20.

    » Include a function that returns a `string` that contains a `Fraction` in the usual display format—the whole number, a space, the numerator, a slash (/), and a denominator. When the whole number is 0, just the `Fraction` part of the value should be displayed (for example, `1/2` instead of `0 1/2`). If the numerator is 0, just the whole number should display (for example, `2` instead of `2 0/3`).

    Write a `Main()` method that instantiates several `Fractions` and demonstrate that all the methods work correctly. Save the program as **FractionDemo.cs**.

    b. Add an `operator*()` method to the `Fraction` class created in Exercise 11a so that it correctly multiplies two `Fractions`. The result should be in proper, reduced format. Demonstrate that the method works correctly. Save the program as **FractionDemo2.cs**.

    c. Create an array of four `Fractions`. Prompt the user for values for each. Display every possible combination of addition results and every possible combination of multiplication results for each `Fraction` pair (that is, each type will have 16 results). Figure 7-48 shows a sample execution. Save the program as **FractionDemo3.cs**.

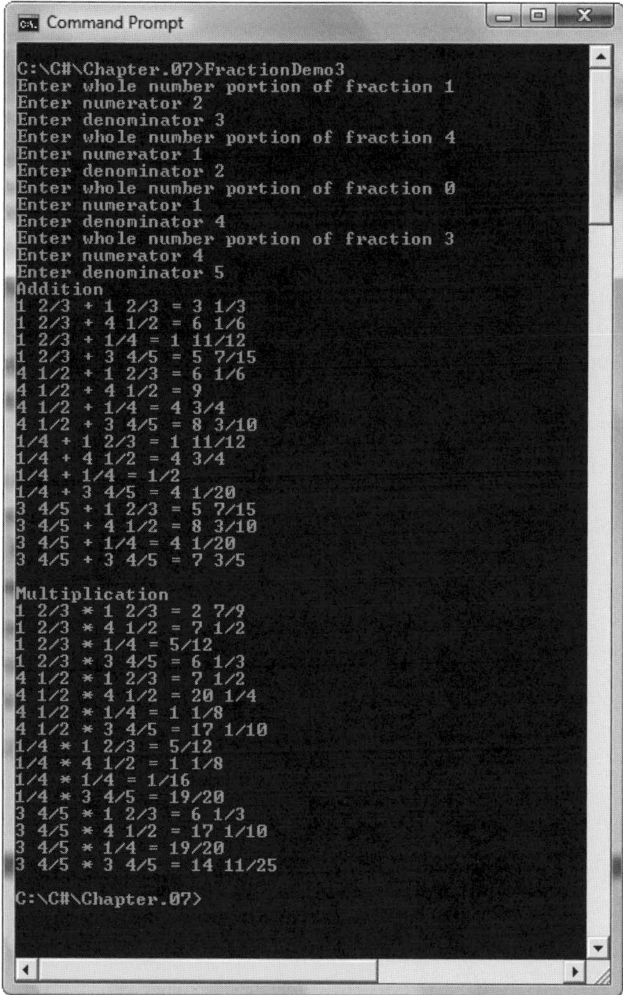

Figure 7-48 Sample execution of `FractionDemo3` program

DEBUGGING EXERCISES

Each of the following files saved in the Chapter.07 folder on your Student Disk has syntax and/or logical errors. In each case, determine the problem and fix the program. After you correct the errors, save each file using the same filename preceded with "Fixed." For example, DebugSeven1.cs will become FixedDebugSeven1.cs.

a. DebugSeven1.cs
b. DebugSeven2.cs
c. DebugSeven3.cs
d. DebugSeven4.cs

UP FOR DISCUSSION

1. In this chapter, you learned that instance data and methods belong to objects (which are class members), but that static data and methods belong to a class as a whole. Consider the real-life class named `StateInTheUnitedStates`. Name some real-life attributes of this class that are static attributes and instance attributes. Create another example of a real-life class and discuss what its static and instance members might be.

» NOTE
The first computerized payroll system produced checks for the employees of Lyons Bakeries in England in February 1954.

2. Fifty or 60 years ago, most people's paychecks were produced by hand; now your check is probably printed by a computer, or not printed at all but deposited into an account electronically. Thirty-five years ago, most grocery store checkers keyed item prices into a cash register; now your items are probably scanned. Police officers used to direct traffic at many major urban intersections; now the traffic flow is often computer controlled. Would any other tasks that are currently performed by people be better handled by a computer? Are there any tasks that you hope never become computerized?

» NOTE
On June 26, 1974, a checkout clerk in Ohio was the first to scan a grocery item's bar code—a ten-pack of Juicy Fruit gum.

3. If you are completing all the programming exercises at the ends of the chapters in this book, you can see how much work goes into a full-blown professional program. How would you feel if someone copied your work without compensating you? Investigate the magnitude of software piracy in our society. What are the penalties for illegally copying software? Are there circumstances under which it is acceptable to copy a program? If a friend asked you to make a copy of a program for him, would you? What do you suggest we do about this problem, if anything?

CHAPTER EIGHT

8

INTRODUCTION TO INHERITANCE

In this chapter you will:

- Learn about the concept of inheritance
- Learn inheritance terminology
- Extend classes
- Use the `protected` access specifier
- Override base class methods
- Access base class methods from a derived class
- Understand how a derived class object "is an" instance of the base class
- Learn about the `Object` class
- Work with base class constructors
- Create and use abstract classes
- Create and use interfaces
- Use extension methods
- Understand the benefits of inheritance

Understanding classes helps you organize objects in real life. Understanding inheritance helps you organize them more precisely. If you have never heard of a Braford, for example, you would have a hard time forming a picture of one in your mind. When you learn that a Braford is an animal, you gain some understanding of what it must be like. That understanding grows when you learn it is a mammal, and the understanding is almost complete when you learn it is a cow. When you learn that a Braford is a cow, you understand it has many characteristics that are common to all cows. To identify a Braford, you must learn only relatively minor details—its color or markings, for example. Most of a Braford's characteristics, however, derive from its membership in a particular hierarchy of classes: animal, mammal, and cow.

All object-oriented programming languages make use of inheritance for the same reasons—to organize the objects programs use, and to make new objects easier to understand based on your knowledge of their inherited traits. In this chapter, you will learn to make use of inheritance with your C# objects.

UNDERSTANDING THE CONCEPT OF INHERITANCE

»NOTE
You first learned about inheritance in Chapter 1.

Inheritance is the principle that you can apply your knowledge of a general category to more specific objects. You are familiar with the concept of inheritance from all sorts of situations. When you use the term *inheritance,* you might think of genetic inheritance. You know from biology that your blood type and eye color are the products of inherited genes. You can say that many other facts about you (your attributes) are inherited. Similarly, you often can attribute your behaviors to inheritance; for example, the way you handle money might be similar to the way your grandmother handles it, and your gait might be the same as your father's—so your methods are inherited, too.

You also might choose to have plants and animals based on their inherited attributes. You plant impatiens next to your house because they thrive in the shade; you adopt a poodle because you know poodles don't shed. Every plant and pet has slightly different characteristics, but within a species, you can count on many consistent inherited attributes and behaviors. In other words, you can reuse the knowledge you gain about general categories and apply it to more specific categories. Similarly, the classes you create in object-oriented programming languages can inherit data and methods from existing classes. When you create a class by making it inherit from another class, you are provided with data fields and methods automatically; you can reuse fields and methods that are already written and tested.

You already know how to create classes and how to instantiate objects that are members of those classes. For example, consider the `Employee` class in Figure 8-1. The class contains two data fields, `empNum` and `empSal`, as well as properties that contain accessors for each field and a method that creates an `Employee` greeting.

```
public class Employee
{
   private int empNum;
   private double empSal;
   public int EmpNum {get; set;}
   public double EmpSal {get; set;}
   public string GetGreeting()
   {
      string greeting = "Hello. I am employee #" + EmpNum;
      return greeting;
   }
}
```

Figure 8-1 An `Employee` class

NOTE As you learned in Chapter 7, you are not required to declare `empNum` and `empSal` in the `Employee` class because their declarations are assumed by the property declarations when you use auto-implemented properties. When you use this `Employee` class in a program, you will receive two warnings that these fields are never used. You can safely ignore these warnings.

After you create the `Employee` class, you can create specific `Employee` objects, as in the following:

```
Employee receptionist = new Employee();
Employee deliveryPerson = new Employee();
```

These `Employee` objects can eventually possess different numbers and salaries, but because they are `Employee` objects, you know that each possesses *some* number and salary.

Suppose you hire a new type of `Employee` who earns a commission as well as a salary. You can create a class with a name such as `CommissionEmployee`, and provide this class with three fields (`empNum`, `empSal`, and `commissionRate`), three properties (with accessors to get and set each of the three fields), and a greeting method. However, this work would duplicate much of the work that you already have done for the `Employee` class. The wise and efficient alternative is to create the class `CommissionEmployee` so it inherits all the attributes and methods of `Employee`. Then, you can add just the single field and property with two accessors that are additions within `CommissionEmployee` objects. Figure 8-2 depicts these relationships.

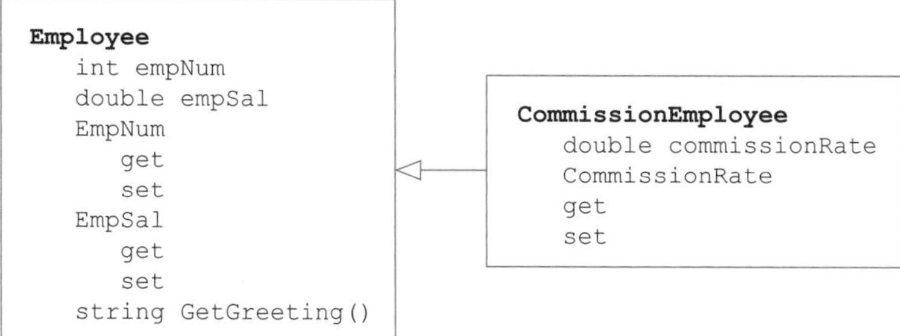

Figure 8-2 `CommissionEmployee` inherits from `Employee`

>>**NOTE** The left-pointing arrow in Figure 8-2 indicates that the class on the right inherits from the one on the left. Using an arrow in this way is conventional in **Unified Modeling Language (UML) diagrams**, which are graphical tools that programmers and analysts use to describe systems.

When you use inheritance to create the `CommissionEmployee` class, you acquire the following benefits:

- You save time, because you need not recreate the `Employee` fields, properties, and methods.
- You reduce the chance of errors, because the `Employee` properties and methods have already been used and tested.
- You make it easier for anyone who has used the `Employee` class to understand the `CommissionEmployee` class because such users can concentrate on the new features only.

The ability to use inheritance makes programs easier to write, easier to understand, and less prone to errors. Imagine that besides `CommissionEmployee`, you want to create several other specific `Employee` classes (perhaps `PartTimeEmployee`, including a field for hours worked, or `DismissedEmployee`, including a reason for dismissal). By using inheritance, you can develop each new class correctly and more quickly.

>>**NOTE** In part, the concept of class inheritance is useful because it makes class code reusable. However, you do not use inheritance simply to save work. When properly used, inheritance always involves a general-to-specific relationship.

>>TWO TRUTHS AND A LIE: UNDERSTANDING THE CONCEPT OF INHERITANCE

1. When you use inheritance to create a class, you save time because you can copy and paste fields, properties, and methods that have already been created for the original class.
2. When you use inheritance to create a class, you reduce the chance of errors because the original class's properties and methods have already been used and tested.
3. When you use inheritance to create a class, you make it easier for anyone who has used the original class to understand the new class because such users can concentrate on the new features.

The false statement is #1. When you use inheritance to create a class, you save time because you need not recreate fields, properties, and methods that have already been created for the original class. You do not copy these class members; you inherit them.

UNDERSTANDING INHERITANCE TERMINOLOGY

A class that is used as a basis for inheritance, like `Employee`, is called a **base class**. When you create a class that inherits from a base class (such as `CommissionEmployee`), it is a **derived class** or **extended class**. When presented with two classes that have a parent-child relationship, you can tell which class is the base class and which is the derived class by using the two classes in a sentence with the phrase "is a." A derived class always "is a" case or instance of the more general base class. For example, a `Tree` class may be a base class to an `Evergreen` class. Every `Evergreen` "is a" `Tree`; however, it is not true that every `Tree` is an `Evergreen`. Thus, `Tree` is the base class and `Evergreen` is the derived class. Similarly, a `CommissionEmployee` "is an" `Employee`—not always the other way around—so `Employee` is the base class and `CommissionEmployee` is derived.

You can use the terms **superclass** and **subclass** as synonyms for base class and derived class. Thus, `Evergreen` can be called a subclass of the `Tree` superclass. You also can use the terms **parent class** and **child class**. A `CommissionEmployee` is a child to the `Employee` parent. Use the pair of terms with which you are most comfortable; all of these terms will be used interchangeably in this book.

As an alternative way to discover which of two classes is the base class and which is the derived class, you can try saying the two class names together (although this technique might not work with every superclass-subclass pair). When people say their names together in the English language, they state the more specific name before the all-encompassing family name, such as "Ginny Kroening." Similarly, with classes, the order that "makes more sense" is the child-parent order. Thus, because "Evergreen Tree" makes more sense than "Tree Evergreen," you can deduce that `Evergreen` is the child class.

>> **NOTE** It also is convenient to think of a derived class as building upon its base class by providing the "adjectives" or additional descriptive terms for the "noun." Frequently, the names of derived classes are formed in this way, as in `CommissionEmployee`.

Finally, you usually can distinguish base classes from their derived classes by size. Although it is not required, a derived class is generally larger than a base class, in the sense that it usually has additional fields and methods. A subclass description may look small, but any subclass contains all of its superclass's fields and methods as well as its own more specific fields and methods.

>> **NOTE** Do not think of a subclass as a "subset" of another class—in other words, possessing only parts of its superclass. In fact, a derived class usually contains more than its parent.

A derived class can be further extended. In other words, a subclass can have a child of its own. For example, after you create a `Tree` class and derive `Evergreen`, you might derive a `Spruce` class from `Evergreen`. Similarly, a `Poodle` class might derive from `Dog`, `Dog` from `DomesticPet`, and `DomesticPet` from `Animal`. The entire list of parent classes from which a child class is derived constitutes the **ancestors** of the subclass.

>> **NOTE** After you create the `Spruce` class, you might be ready to create `Spruce` objects. For example, you might create `theTreeInMyBackYard`, or you might create an array of 1000 `Spruce` objects for a tree farm.

Inheritance is **transitive**, which means a child inherits all the members of all its ancestors. In other words, when you declare a `Spruce` object, it contains all the attributes and methods of both an `Evergreen` and a `Tree`. As you work with C#, you will encounter many examples of such transitive chains of inheritance.

>> **NOTE** When you create your own transitive inheritance chains, you want to place fields and methods at their most general level. In other words, a method named `Grow()` rightfully belongs in a `Tree` class, whereas `LeavesTurnColor()` does not, because the method applies to only some of the `Tree` child classes. Similarly, a `LeavesTurnColor()` method would be better located in a `Deciduous` class than separately within the `Oak` or `Maple` child class.

>> **NOTE** In math, a transitive relationship occurs when something that is true for a and b and for b and c is also true for a and c. For example, equality is transitive. If a = b and b = c, then a = c. In inheritance, the term implies that when something is true for the parent, it is also true for the child.

>>TWO TRUTHS AND A LIE: UNDERSTANDING INHERITANCE TERMINOLOGY

1. The terms *superclass* and *parent class* both mean the same thing as *base class*.
2. A derived class is generally smaller than a base class.
3. A child class inherits all the members of all its ancestors.

The false statement is #2. A derived class is generally larger than a base class, in the sense that it usually has additional fields and methods.

EXTENDING CLASSES

When you create a class that is an extension or child of another class, you use a single colon between the derived class name and its base class name. For example, the following class header creates a subclass-superclass relationship between `CommissionEmployee` and `Employee`.

```
public class CommissionEmployee : Employee
```

Each `CommissionEmployee` object automatically contains the data fields and methods of the base class; you then can add new fields and methods to the new derived class. Figure 8-3 shows a `CommissionEmployee` class.

```
public class CommissionEmployee : Employee
{
   private double commissionRate;
   public double CommissionRate {get; set;}
}
```

Figure 8-3 `CommissionEmployee` class

The CommissionEmployee class in Figure 8-3 contains three fields: empNum and empSal, inherited from Employee, and commissionRate, which is defined within the CommissionEmployee class. Similarly, the CommissionEmployee class contains three properties and a method—two properties and the method are inherited from Employee, and one property is defined within CommissionEmployee itself. When you write a program that instantiates an object using the following statement, then you can use any of the next statements to set field values for the salesperson:

```
CommissionEmployee salesperson = new CommissionEmployee();
salesperson.EmpNum = 234;
salesperson.EmpSal = Convert.ToDouble(Console.ReadLine());
salesperson.CommissionRate = 0.07;
```

The salesperson object has access to all three set accessors (two from its parent and one from its own class) because it is both a CommissionEmployee and an Employee. Similarly, the object has access to three get accessors and the GetGreeting() method. Figure 8-4 shows a Main() method that declares Employee and CommissionEmployee objects and shows all the properties and methods that can be used with each. Figure 8-5 shows the program output.

```
using System;
public class DemoEmployees
{
   public static void Main()
   {
      Employee clerk = new Employee();
      CommissionEmployee salesperson = new CommissionEmployee();
      clerk.EmpNum = 123;
      clerk.EmpSal = 30000.00;
      salesperson.EmpNum = 234;
      salesperson.EmpSal = 20000;
      salesperson.CommissionRate = 0.07;
      Console.WriteLine("\n" + clerk.GetGreeting());
      Console.WriteLine("Clerk #{0} makes {1} per year",
         clerk.EmpNum,
         clerk.EmpSal.ToString("C"));
      Console.WriteLine("\n" + salesperson.GetGreeting());
      Console.WriteLine("Salesperson #{0} makes {1} per year",
         salesperson.EmpNum,
         salesperson.EmpSal.ToString("C"));
      Console.WriteLine("...plus {0} commission on all sales",
         salesperson.CommissionRate.ToString("P"));
   }
}
```

Figure 8-4 DemoEmployees class that declares Employee and CommissionEmployee objects

```
C:\C#\Chapter.08>DemoEmployees

Hello. I am employee #123
Clerk #123 makes $30,000.00 per year

Hello. I am employee #234
Salesperson #234 makes $20,000.00 per year
...plus 7.00 % commission on all sales

C:\C#\Chapter.08>
```

Figure 8-5 Output of the `DemoEmployees` program

Inheritance works only in one direction: A child inherits from a parent—not the other way around. If a program instantiates an `Employee` object as in the following statement, the `Employee` object does *not* have access to the `CommissionEmployee` properties or methods.

```
Employee clerk = new Employee();
clerk.CommissionRate = 0.1;
```

»DON'T DO IT
This statement is invalid—`Employee` objects don't have a `CommissionRate`.

»NOTE As with doctors, it is convenient to think of derived classes as *specialists*. That is, their fields and methods are more specialized than those of the base class.

`Employee` is the parent class, and `clerk` is an object of the parent class. It makes sense that a parent class object does not have access to its child's data and methods. When you create the parent class, you do not know how many future child classes might be created, or what their data or methods might look like. In addition, child classes are more specific. A `HeartSurgeon` class and an `Obstetrician` class are children of a `Doctor` class. You do not expect all members of the general parent class `Doctor` to have the `HeartSurgeon`'s `RepairValve()` method or the `Obstetrician`'s `DeliverBaby()` method. However, `HeartSurgeon` and `Obstetrician` objects have access to the more general `Doctor` methods `TakeBloodPressure()` and `BillPatients()`.

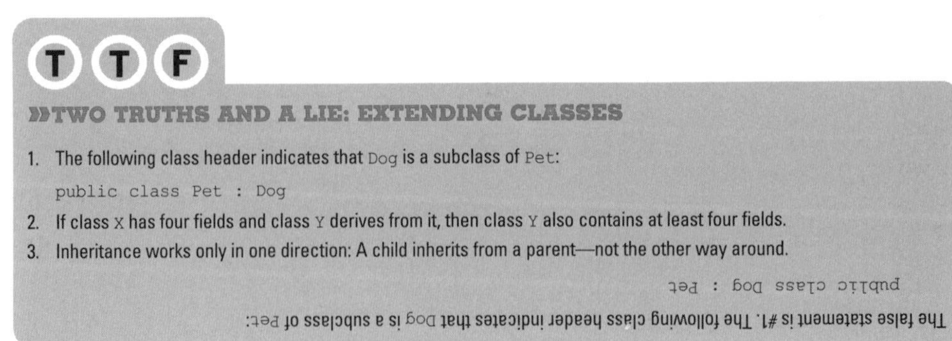

»TWO TRUTHS AND A LIE: EXTENDING CLASSES

1. The following class header indicates that `Dog` is a subclass of `Pet`:

   `public class Pet : Dog`

2. If class `X` has four fields and class `Y` derives from it, then class `Y` also contains at least four fields.
3. Inheritance works only in one direction: A child inherits from a parent—not the other way around.

The false statement is #1. The following class header indicates that `Dog` is a subclass of `Pet`:

`public class Dog : Pet`

USING THE protected ACCESS SPECIFIER

The Employee class in Figure 8-1 is a typical C# class in that its data fields are private and its properties and methods are public. In Chapter 7, you learned that this scheme provides for information hiding—protecting your private data from alteration by methods outside the data's own class. When a program is a client of the Employee class (that is, it instantiates an Employee object), the client cannot alter the data in any private field directly. For example, when you write a Main() method that creates an Employee named clerk, you cannot change the Employee's empNum or empSal directly using a statement such as clerk.empNum = 2222;. Instead, you must use the EmpNum property to set the empNum field of the clerk object.

When you use information hiding, you are assured that your data will be altered only by the properties and methods you choose and only in ways that you can control. If outside classes could alter an Employee's private fields, then the fields could be assigned values that the Employee class couldn't control. In such a case, the principle of information hiding would be destroyed, causing the behavior of the object to be unpredictable.

Any derived class you create, such as CommissionEmployee, inherits all the data and methods of its base class. However, even though a child of Employee has empNum and empSal fields, the CommissionEmployee methods cannot alter or use those private fields directly. If you could use private data outside of its class, the principle of information hiding would be destroyed. If you intend the Employee class data field empNum to be private, then you don't want any outside classes using the field. If a new class could simply extend your Employee class and "get to" its data fields without "going through the proper channels," then information hiding would not be operating.

On some occasions, you do want to access parent class data from within a child class. For example, suppose that the Employee class EmpSal property set accessor has been written so that no Employee's salary is ever set to less than 15000, as follows:

```
set
{
    if(value < 15000)
        empSal = 15000;
    else
        empSal = value;
}
```

»NOTE In this example, you probably would prefer to use a named constant for the value 15000.

Also assume that a CommissionEmployee draws commission only and no regular salary; that is, when you set a CommissionEmployee's commissionRate field, the empSal should become 0. You would write the CommissionEmployee class CommissionRate property set accessor as follows:

```
set
{
    commissionRate = value;
    EmpSal = 0;
}
```

Using this implementation, when you create a CommissionEmployee object and set its CommissionRate, 0 is sent to the set accessor for the Employee class EmpSal property. There, because the value of the salary is less than 15000, the salary is forced to 15000 even though you want it to be 0.

An alternative is to rewrite the set accessor for the CommissionRate property in the CommissionEmployee class as follows:

```
set
{
    commissionRate = value;
    empSal = 0;
}
```

In this set accessor, you bypass the parent class's EmpSal set accessor and directly use the empSal field. However, when you include this accessor in a program and compile it, you receive an error message: "Employee.empSal is inaccessible due to its protection level". In other words, Employee.empSal is private, and no other class can access it. So, in summary:

- Using the public set accessor in the parent class does not work because of the minimum salary requirement.
- Using the private field in the parent class does not work because it is inaccessible.
- Making the parent class field public would work, but doing so would violate the principle of information hiding.

Fortunately, there is a fourth option. If you want a derived class property or method to be able to access empSal, then it cannot be private. However, if you don't want other, nonchild classes to access the field, then it cannot be public. The solution is to create the empSal field using the modifier protected, which provides you with an intermediate level of security between public and private access. A **protected** data field or method can be used within its own class or in any classes extended from that class, but it cannot be used by "outside" classes. In other words, protected members can be used "within the family"—by a class and its descendants.

Figure 8-6 shows how you can declare empSal as protected within the Employee class so that it becomes legal to access it directly within the CommissionRate set accessor of the CommissionEmployee derived class. Figure 8-7 shows a program that instantiates a CommissionEmployee object, and Figure 8-8 shows the output. Notice that the CommissionEmployee's salary initially is set to 20000 in the program, but the salary becomes 0 when the CommissionRate is set later.

NOTE If you set the salesperson's CommissionRate first in the DemoSalesperson program, then set EmpSal to a nonzero value, empSal will not be reduced to 0. If your intention is to always create CommissionEmployees with salaries of 0, then the EmpSal property should also be overridden in the derived class.

```
public class Employee
{
   private int empNum;
   protected double empSal;
   public int EmpNum {get; set;}
   public double EmpSal
   {
      get
      {
         return empSal;
      }
      set
      {
         if(value < 15000)
            empSal = 15000;
         else
            empSal = value;
      }
   }
   public string GetGreeting()
   {
      string greeting = "Hello. I am employee #" + EmpNum;
      return greeting;
   }
}
public class CommissionEmployee : Employee
{
   private double commissionRate;
   public double CommissionRate
   {
      get
      {
         return commissionRate;
      }
      set
      {
         commissionRate = value;
         empSal = 0;
      }
   }
}
```

The protected `empSal` field is accessible in the child class.

Figure 8-6 `Employee` class with a `protected` field and `CommissionEmployee` class

```
using System;
public class DemoSalesperson
{
    public static void Main()
    {
        CommissionEmployee salesperson = new CommissionEmployee();
        salesperson.EmpNum = 345;
        salesperson.EmpSal = 20000;
        salesperson.CommissionRate = 0.07;
        Console.WriteLine("Salesperson #{0} makes {1} per year",
            salesperson.EmpNum,
            salesperson.EmpSal.ToString("C"));
        Console.WriteLine("...plus {0} commission on all sales",
            salesperson.CommissionRate.ToString("P"));
    }
}
```

Figure 8-7 The `DemoSalesperson` program

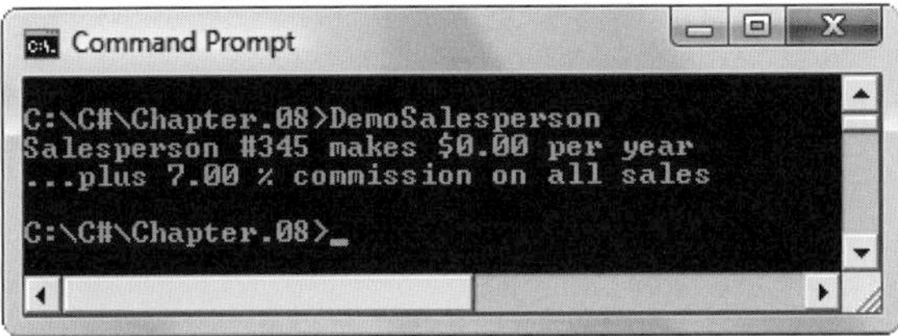

Figure 8-8 Output of the `DemoSalesperson` program

>>**NOTE** Classes that depend on field names from parent classes are said to be **fragile** because they are prone to errors—that is, they are easy to "break."

Using the `protected` access modifier for a field can be convenient, and it also improves program performance a little by using a field directly instead of "going through" property accessors. Also, using the `protected` access modifier is occasionally necessary. However, `protected` data members should be used sparingly. Whenever possible, the principle of information hiding should be observed, and even child classes should have to go through accessors to "get to" their parent's private data. When child classes are allowed direct access to a parent's fields, the likelihood of future errors increases.

>>TWO TRUTHS AND A LIE: USING THE `protected` ACCESS SPECIFIER

1. A child class does not possess the private members of its parent.
2. A child class cannot use the private members of its parent.
3. A child class can use the protected members of its parent, but outside classes cannot.

The false statement is #1. A child class possesses the private members of its parent, but cannot use them directly.

OVERRIDING BASE CLASS METHODS

When you create a derived class by extending an existing class, the new derived class contains data and methods that were defined in the original base class. Sometimes, the superclass fields, properties, and methods are not entirely appropriate for the subclass objects.

For example, suppose you have created a `Student` class as shown in Figure 8-9. `Students` have `names`, `credits` for which they are enrolled, and `tuition` amounts. You can set a `Student's` `name` and `credits` by using the `set` accessors in the `Name` and `Credits` properties, but you cannot set a `Student's` `tuition` directly because there is no `set` accessor for the `Tuition` property. Instead, `tuition` is calculated based on a standard `RATE` (of $55.75) for each `credit` that the `Student` takes.

```
class Student
{
   private const double RATE = 55.75;
   private string name;
   protected int credits;
   protected double tuition;
   public string Name {get; set;}
   public int Credits
   {
      get
      {
         return credits;
      }
      set
      {
          credits = value;
          tuition = credits * RATE;
      }
   }
   public double Tuition
   {
      get
      {
         return tuition;
      }
   }
}
```

Figure 8-9 The `Student` class

»NOTE In Figure 8-9, the `Student` fields that hold `credits` and `tuition` are declared as `protected` because a child class will use them.

Suppose you derive a subclass from `Student` called `ScholarshipStudent`. A `ScholarshipStudent` has a `name`, `credits`, and `tuition`, but the tuition is not calculated in the same way as it is for a `Student`; instead, `tuition` for a `ScholarshipStudent` should be set to 0. You want to use the `Credits` property to set a `ScholarshipStudent's` `credits`, but

»NOTE You first learned about polymorphism in Chapter 1.

you want the property to behave differently than the parent class `Student`'s `Credits` property. Using the same method or property name to indicate different implementations is called polymorphism. The word *polymorphism* means "many forms;" it means that many forms of action take place, even though you use the same name to describe the action. In other words, there are many forms of the same method depending on the object associated with the word.

The English language provides many examples of polymorphism:

- A race is *run* differently than a business.
- A chess game is *played* differently than a guitar.
- A door is *opened* differently than a bank account.

You understand each use of these English verbs based on the context in which it is used. In a similar way, C# understands your use of the same method name based on the type of object associated with it. Figure 8-10 shows a `ScholarshipStudent` class. As a child of `Student`, a `ScholarshipStudent` possesses all the attributes, properties, and methods of a `Student`, but its `Credits` property behaves differently.

```
class ScholarshipStudent : Student
{
    new public int Credits
    {
        set
        {
            credits = value;
            tuition = 0;
        }
    }
}
```

Figure 8-10 The `ScholarshipStudent` class

In the child `ScholarshipStudent` class in Figure 8-10, the `Credits` property is declared as `new` (see shading) because it has the same header as a property in its parent class—it overrides and **hides** its counterpart in the parent class. (You could do the same thing with methods.) If you omit `new`, the program will still operate correctly, but you will receive a warning that you are hiding an inherited member with the same name in the base class. Using the keyword `new` eliminates the warning and makes your intentions clear. When you use the `Name` property with a `ScholarshipStudent` object, a program uses the parent class property `Name`; it is not hidden. However, when you use `Credits` to set a value for a `ScholarshipStudent` object, the program uses the new, overriding property from its own class.

» **NOTE** If `credits` and `tuition` had been declared as `private` within the `Student` class, then `ScholarshipStudent` would not be able to use them.

Figure 8-11 shows a program that uses `Student` and `ScholarshipStudent` objects. Even though each object assigns the `Credits` property the same number of credit hours (in the two shaded statements), the calculated `tuition` values are different because each object uses a different version of the `Credits` property. Figure 8-12 shows the execution of the program.

»NOTE
A superclass member that is not hidden by the derived class is **visible** in the derived class.

```
using System;
class DemoStudents
{
   public static void Main()
   {
      Student payingStudent = new Student();
      ScholarshipStudent freeStudent = new ScholarshipStudent();
      payingStudent.Name = "Megan";
      payingStudent.Credits = 15;
      freeStudent.Name = "Luke";
      freeStudent.Credits = 15;
      Console.WriteLine("{0}'s tuition is {1}",
         payingStudent.Name,
         payingStudent.Tuition.ToString("C"));
      Console.WriteLine("{0}'s tuition is {1}",
         freeStudent.Name,
         freeStudent.Tuition.ToString("C"));
   }
}
```

Figure 8-11 The `DemoStudents` program

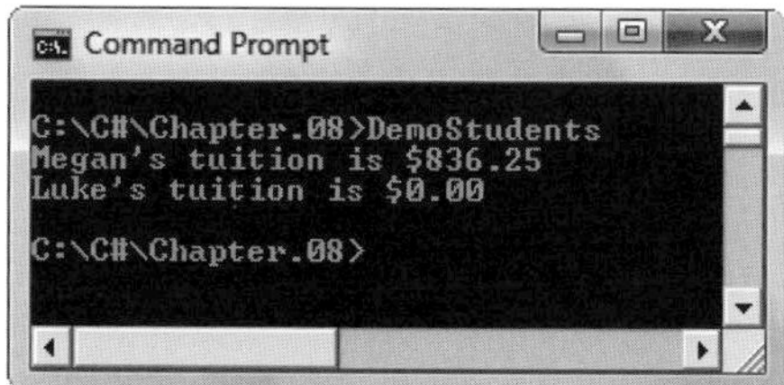

Figure 8-12 Output of the `DemoStudents` program

If a base class and a derived class have methods with the same names but different argument lists, then the derived class method does not override the base class method; instead, it overloads it. For example, if a base class contains a method with the header `public void Display()`, and its child contains a method with the header `public void Display(string s)`, then the child class would have access to both methods.

»NOTE
You learned about overloading methods in Chapter 3.

»TWO TRUTHS AND A LIE: OVERRIDING BASE CLASS METHODS

1. When you override a parent class method in a child class, the methods have the same name.
2. When you override a parent class method in a child class, the methods have the same parameter list.
3. When you override a parent class method in a child class, and you use the child class method, the parent class method executes first, followed by the child class method.

The false statement is #3. When you override a parent class method in a child class and then use the child class method, the child class method executes instead of the parent class version.

ACCESSING BASE CLASS METHODS FROM A DERIVED CLASS

A derived class can contain a method with the same name and arguments as a method in its parent class; when this happens, using the derived class method overrides the parent class method. In some situations, you might want to use the parent class method within a subclass. If so, you can use the keyword `base` to access the parent class method. For example, recall the `GetGreeting()` method that appears in the `Employee` class in Figure 8-6. If its child, `CommissionEmployee`, also contains a `GetGreeting()` method, as shown in Figure 8-13,

```
public class CommissionEmployee : Employee
{
   private double commissionRate;
   public double CommissionRate
   {
      get
      {
         return commissionRate;
      }
      set
      {
         commissionRate = value;
         empSal = 0;
      }
   }
   new public string GetGreeting()
   {
      string greeting = base.GetGreeting();
      greeting += "\nI work on commission.";
      return greeting;
   }
}
```

Figure 8-13 The `CommissionEmployee` class with a `GetGreeting()` method

then within the `CommissionEmployee` class you can call `base.GetGreeting()` to access the base class version of the method. Figure 8-14 shows an application that uses the method with a `CommissionEmployee` object. Figure 8-15 shows the output.

```
using System;
public class DemoSalesperson2
{
   public static void Main()
   {
      CommissionEmployee salesperson = new CommissionEmployee();
      salesperson.EmpNum = 345;
      Console.WriteLine(salesperson.GetGreeting());
   }
}
```

Figure 8-14 The `DemoSalesperson2` program

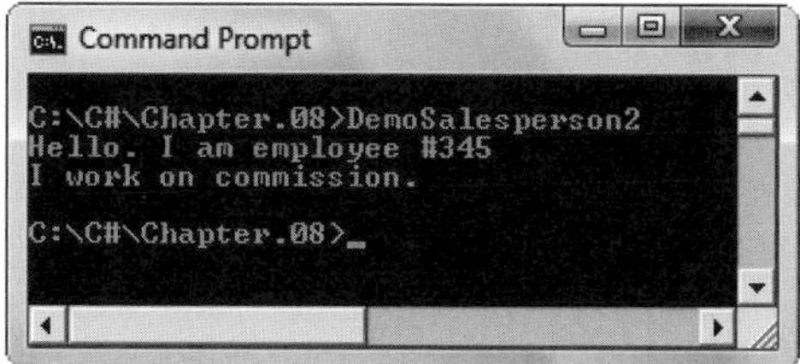

Figure 8-15 Output of the `DemoSalesperson2` program

In Figure 8-13, the child class method uses the keyword `new` to eliminate a compiler warning. Then, within the `GetGreeting()` method, the parent's version is called. The returned string is stored in the `greeting` variable, and then an "I work on commission." statement is added to it before the complete message is returned to the calling program. By overriding the base class method in the child class, the duplicate typing to create the first part of the message was eliminated. Additionally, if the first part of the message is altered in the future, it will be altered in only one place—in the base class.

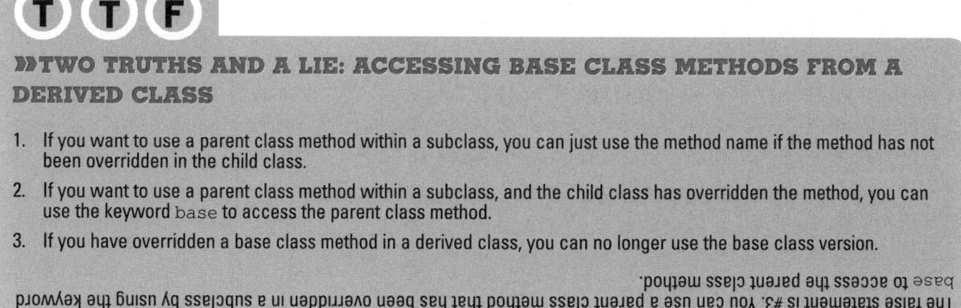

T T F

»TWO TRUTHS AND A LIE: ACCESSING BASE CLASS METHODS FROM A DERIVED CLASS

1. If you want to use a parent class method within a subclass, you can just use the method name if the method has not been overridden in the child class.
2. If you want to use a parent class method within a subclass, and the child class has overridden the method, you can use the keyword `base` to access the parent class method.
3. If you have overridden a base class method in a derived class, you can no longer use the base class version.

The false statement is #3. You can use a parent class method that has been overridden in a subclass by using the keyword `base` to access the parent class method.

UNDERSTANDING HOW A DERIVED CLASS OBJECT "IS AN" INSTANCE OF THE BASE CLASS

Every derived class object "is a" specific instance of both the derived class and the base class. In other words, `myCar` "is a" `Car` as well as a `Vehicle`, and `myDog` "is a" `Dog` as well as a `Mammal`. You can assign a derived class object to an object of any of its superclass types. When you do, C# makes an **implicit conversion** from derived class to base class.

»NOTE C# also makes implicit conversions when casting one data type to another. For example, in the statement `double money = 10;`, the value 10 is implicitly converted (or cast) to a double.

»NOTE When a derived class object is assigned to its ancestor's data type, the conversion can more specifically be called an **implicit reference conversion**. This term is more accurate because it emphasizes the difference between numerical conversions and reference objects. When you assign a derived class object to a base class type, the object is treated as though it had only the characteristics defined in the base class.

For example, when a `CommissionEmployee` class inherits from `Employee`, an object of either type can be passed to a method that accepts an `Employee` parameter. In Figure 8-16, an `Employee` is passed to `DisplayGreeting()` in the first shaded statement, and a `CommissionEmployee` is passed in the second shaded statement. Each is referred to as `emp` within the method, and each is used correctly, as shown in Figure 8-17.

```
using System;
public class DemoSalesperson3
{
   public static void Main()
   {
      Employee clerk = new Employee();
      CommissionEmployee salesperson = new CommissionEmployee();
      clerk.EmpNum = 234;
      salesperson.EmpNum = 345;
      DisplayGreeting(clerk);
      DisplayGreeting(salesperson);
   }
   public static void DisplayGreeting(Employee emp)
   {
      Console.WriteLine("Hi there from #" + emp.EmpNum);
      Console.WriteLine(emp.GetGreeting());
   }
}
```

Figure 8-16 The `DemoSalesperson3` program

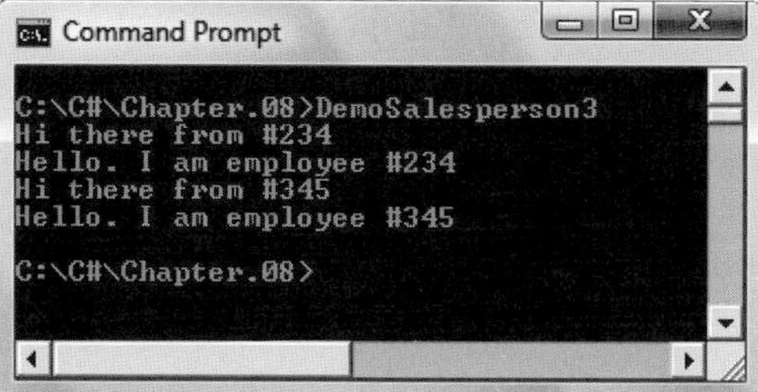

Figure 8-17 Output of the `DemoSalesperson3` program

>> **NOTE** In C#, you can use either `new` or `override` when defining a derived class member that has the same name as a base class member. When you write a statement such as `ScholarshipStudent s1 = new ScholarshipStudent();`, you won't notice the difference. However, if you use `new` when defining the derived class `Credits` property and write a statement such as `Student s2 = new ScholarshipStudent();`, then `s2.Credits` accesses the base class property. On the other hand, if you use `override` when defining `Credits` in the derived class, then `s2.Credits` uses the derived class property.

>> **NOTE** You cannot use both `new` and `override` on the same member because they have mutually exclusive meanings. Using `new` creates a `new` member with the same name and causes the original member to become hidden. Using `override` extends the implementation for an inherited member.

>>TWO TRUTHS AND A LIE: UNDERSTANDING HOW A DERIVED CLASS OBJECT "IS AN" INSTANCE OF THE BASE CLASS

1. You can assign a derived class object to an object of any of its superclass types.
2. You can assign a base class object to an object of any of its derived types.
3. An implicit conversion from one type to another is an automatic conversion.

The false statement is #2. You can assign a derived class object to an object of any of its superclass types, but not the other way around.

USING THE `Object` CLASS

Every class you create in C# derives from a single class named `System.Object`. In other words, the **`object`** (or `Object`) class type in the `System` namespace is the ultimate base class for all other types. The keyword `object` is an alias for the `System.Object` class. You can use the lowercase and uppercase versions of the class interchangeably.

>> **NOTE** When you create a class such as `Employee`, you usually use the header `class Employee`, which implicitly, or automatically, descends from the `Object` class. Alternatively, you could use the header `class Employee : Object` to explicitly show the name of the base class, but you have not seen this format in this book, and it would be extremely unusual to see such a format in a C# program.

Because every class descends from `Object`, every object "is an" `Object`. As proof, you can write a method that accepts an argument of type `Object`; it will accept arguments of any type. Figure 8-18 shows a program that declares three objects—a `Student`, a `ScholarshipStudent`, and an `Employee`. Even though these types possess different attributes and methods (and one type, `Employee`, has nothing in common with the other two), each type can serve as an argument to the `DisplayObjectMessage()` because each type "is an" `Object`. Figure 8-19 shows the execution of the program.

```
using System;
class DiverseObjects
{
   public static void Main()
   {
      Student payingStudent = new Student();
      ScholarshipStudent freeStudent = new ScholarshipStudent();
      Employee clerk = new Employee();
      Console.Write("Using Student: ");
      DisplayObjectMessage(payingStudent);
      Console.Write("Using ScholarshipStudent: ");
      DisplayObjectMessage(freeStudent);
      Console.Write("Using Employee: ");
      DisplayObjectMessage(clerk);
   }
   public static void DisplayObjectMessage(Object o)
   {
      Console.WriteLine("Method successfully called");
   }
}
```

Figure 8-18 `DiverseObjects` program

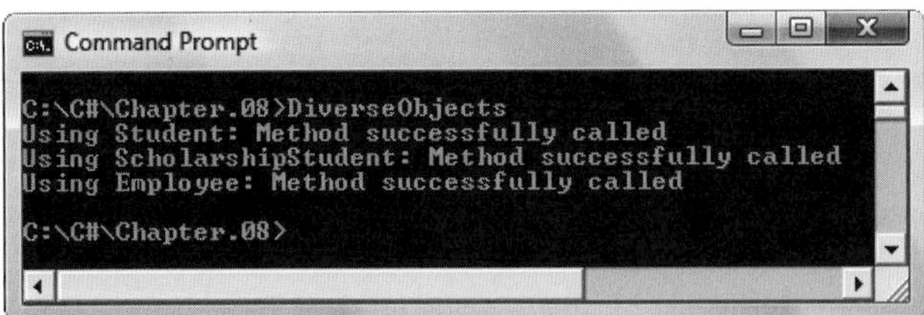

Figure 8-19 Output of the `DiverseObjects` program

When you create any child class, it inherits all the methods of its parent. Because all classes inherit from the `Object` class, all classes inherit the `Object` class methods. The

Object class contains a constructor, a destructor, and four public instance methods, as summarized in Table 8-1.

Method	Explanation
Equals()	Determines whether two Object instances are equal
GetHashCode()	Gets a unique code for each object; useful in certain sorting and data management tasks
GetType()	Returns the type, or class, of an object
ToString()	Returns a String that represents the object

Table 8-1 The four public instance methods of the Object class

»NOTE The Object class contains other nonpublic and noninstance (static) methods in addition to the four methods listed in Table 8-1. The C# documentation provides more details on these methods.

USING THE Object CLASS'S GetType() METHOD

The GetType() method returns an object's type, or class. For example, if you have created an Employee object named someWorker, then the following statement displays Employee:

```
Console.WriteLine(someWorker.GetType());
```

»NOTE If an object's class is defined in a namespace, then GetType() returns a string composed of the namespace, a dot, and the class name.

USING THE Object CLASS'S ToString() METHOD

The Object class methods are not very useful as they stand. For example, when you use the Object class's ToString() method with an object you create, it simply returns a string that holds the name of the class, just as GetType() does. That is, if someWorker is an Employee, then the following statement displays Employee:

```
Console.WriteLine(someWorker.ToString());
```

When you create a class such as Employee, you should override the Object class's ToString() method with your own, more useful version—perhaps one that returns an Employee's ID number, name, or combination of the two. Of course, you could create a differently named method to do the same thing—perhaps GetEmployeeIdentification() or ConvertEmployeeToString(). However, by naming your class method ToString(), you make the class easier for others to understand and use. Programmers know the ToString() method works with every object; when they use it with your objects, you can provide a useful set of information. Additionally, many C# built-in classes use the ToString() method; if you have named your method conventionally, those classes will use your version because it is more helpful than the generic one.

For example, you might create an Employee class ToString() method, as shown in Figure 8-20. This method assumes that EmpNum and Name are Employee properties with get accessors. The returned string will have a value such as "Employee: 234 Johnson".

»NOTE A class's ToString() method is often a useful debugging aid.

```
public override string ToString()
{
   return(getType() + ": " + EmpNum + " " + Name);
}
```

Figure 8-20 An Employee class ToString() method

»NOTE You have been using overloaded versions of the ToString() method to format numeric output since Chapter 2.

USING THE Object CLASS'S Equals() METHOD AND GetHashCode() METHOD

The Object class's Equals() method returns true if two Objects have the same memory address—that is, if one object is a reference to the other and both are literally the same object. For example, you might write the following:

```
if oneObject.Equals(anotherObject)...
```

»NOTE The Equals() method compares objects for reference equality. **Reference equality** occurs when two reference type objects refer to the same object.

Like the ToString() method, this method might not be useful to you in its original form. For example, you might prefer to think of two Employee objects as equal if their ID numbers or names are equal. You might want to override the Equals() method for any class you create if you anticipate that class clients will want to compare objects based on any of their field values.

If you overload the Equals() method, it should meet the following requirements by convention:

- Its header should be as follows (you can use any identifier for the Object parameter):
  ```
  public override bool Equals(Object o)
  ```
- It should return false if the argument is null.
- It should return true if an object is compared to itself.
- It should return true only if both of the following are true:
  ```
  oneObject.Equals(anotherObject)
  anotherObject.Equals(oneObject)
  ```
- If oneObject.Equals(anotherObject) returns true and oneObject.Equals(aThirdObject) returns true, then anotherObject.Equals(aThirdObject) should also be true.

When you override the Equals() method, you should also override the GetHashCode() method, because Equals() uses GetHashCode() and two objects that are considered equal should have the same hash code. A **hash code** is a number that should uniquely identify an object; you might use hash codes in some advanced C# applications. For example,

Figure 8-21 shows an application that declares two `Employee`s from a class in which the `GetHashCode()` method has not been overridden. The output in Figure 8-22 shows a unique number for each object. (The number, however, is meaningless to you.) If you choose to override the `GetHashCode()` method, you should write this method so it returns a unique integer for every object—an `Employee` number, for example.

NOTE In cooking, hash is a dish that is created by combining ingredients. The term *hash code* derives from the fact that the code is sometimes created by mixing some of an object's data.

NOTE A hash code is sometimes called a "fingerprint" for an object because it uniquely identifies the object. In C#, the default implementation of the `GetHashCode()` method does not guarantee unique return values for different objects. However, if `GetHashCode()` is explicitly implemented in a derived class, it must return a unique hash code.

```
using System;
public class TestHashCode
{
   public static void Main()
   {
      Employee first = new Employee();
      Employee second = new Employee();
      Console.WriteLine(first.GetHashCode());
      Console.WriteLine(second.GetHashCode());
   }
}
```

Figure 8-21 `TestHashCode` program

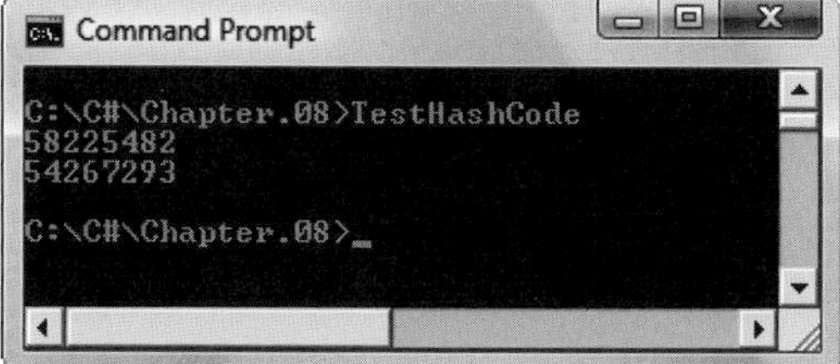

Figure 8-22 Output of the `TestHashCode` program

NOTE You first used the `Equals()` method to compare `String` objects in Chapter 2. When you use `Equals()` with `String`s, you use the `String` class's `Equals()` method that compares `String` contents as opposed to `String` addresses. In other words, the `Object` class's `Equals()` method has already been overridden in the `String` class.

NOTE In Chapter 7, you learned to overload operators. If you overload == or != for a class, you will receive warning messages if you do not also override both the `Equals()` and `GetHashCode()` methods.

NOTE Although you can write an `Equals()` method for a class without overriding `GetHashCode()`, you receive a warning message. See the C# documentation for information on the `HashTable` class.

When you create an `Equals()` method to override the one in the `Object` class, the parameter must be an `Object`. For example, if you consider `Employee` objects equal when the `EmpNum` properties are equal, then an `Employee` class `Equals()` method might be created as follows:

```
public override bool Equals(Object e)
{
    bool equal;
    Employee temp = (Employee)e;
    if(EmpNum == temp.EmpNum)
      equal = true;
    else
      equal = false;
    return equal;
}
```

In the shaded second statement in the method, the `Object` argument is cast to an `Employee` so the `Employee`'s `EmpNum` can be compared. If you did not perform the cast, and tried to make the comparison with `o.EmpNum`, the method would not compile because an `Object` does not have an `EmpNum`.

An even better alternative is to ensure that compared objects are the same type before making any other decisions. For example, the `Equals()` method in Figure 8-23 uses the `GetType()` method with both the `this` object and the parameter before proceeding. If compared objects are not the same type, then the `Equals()` method should return `false`.

```
public override bool Equals(Object e)
{
    bool equal;
    if(this.GetType() != e.GetType())
       equal = false;
    else
    {
       Employee temp = (Employee)e;
       if(EmpNum == temp.EmpNum)
          equal = true;
       else
          equal = false;
     }
    return equal;
}
```

Figure 8-23 An `Equals()` method for the `Employee` class

»TWO TRUTHS AND A LIE: USING THE `Object` CLASS

1. The `Object` class contains a method named `GetType()` that returns an object's type, or class.
2. If you do not override the `ToString()` method for a class, it returns the value of all the strings within the class.
3. The `Object` class's `Equals()` method returns `true` if two `Objects` have the same memory address—that is, if one object is a reference to the other and both are literally the same object.

The false statement is #2. If you do not override the `ToString()` method for a class, it returns a string that holds the name of the class.

WORKING WITH BASE CLASS CONSTRUCTORS

When you create any object, you are calling a class constructor method that has the same name as the class itself; for example:

```
SomeClass anObject = new SomeClass();
```

When you instantiate an object that is a member of a derived class, you call both the constructor for the base class and the constructor for the extended, derived class. When you create any derived class object, the base class constructor must execute first; only then does the derived class constructor execute.

»NOTE When you create any object, you call its constructor and the `Object` constructor because all classes are derived from `Object`. So, when you create a base class and a derived class, and instantiate a derived class object, you call three constructors: one from the `Object` class, one from the base class, and one from the derived class.

In the examples of inheritance you have seen so far in this chapter, each class contained default constructors, so their execution was transparent. However, you should realize that when you create a subclass, both the base and derived constructors execute. For example, consider the abbreviated `Employee` and `CommissionEmployee` classes in Figure 8-24. `Employee` contains just two fields and a constructor; `CommissionEmployee` descends from `Employee` and contains a constructor as well. The `DemoSalesperson4` program in Figure 8-25 contains just one statement; it instantiates a `CommissionEmployee`. The output in Figure 8-26 shows that this one statement causes both constructors to execute.

Of course, most constructors perform many more tasks than printing a message to inform you that they exist. When constructors initialize variables, you usually want the base class constructor to initialize the data fields that originate in the base class. The derived class constructor needs to initialize only the data fields that are specific to the derived class.

```
public class Employee
{
   private int empNum;
   protected double empSal;
   public Employee()
   {
      Console.WriteLine("Employee constructed");
   }
}
public class CommissionEmployee : Employee
{
   private double commissionRate;
   public CommissionEmployee()
   {
      Console.WriteLine("CommissionEmployee constructed");
   }
}
```

Figure 8-24 `Employee` and `CommissionEmployee` classes with parameterless constructors

```
using System;
public class DemoSalesperson4
{
   public static void Main()
   {
      CommissionEmployee salesperson = new CommissionEmployee();
   }
}
```

Figure 8-25 The `DemoSalesperson4` program

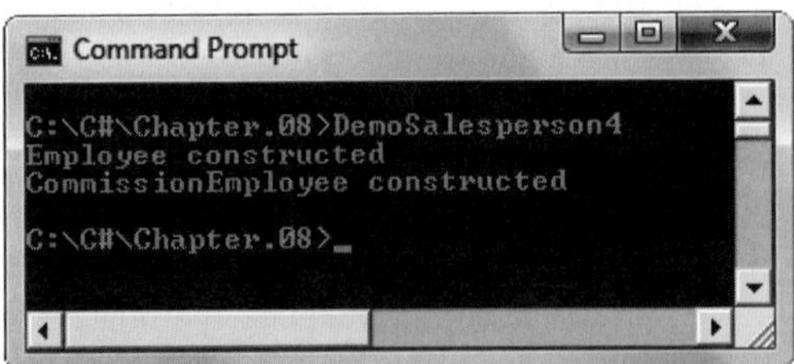

Figure 8-26 Output of the `DemoSalesperson4` program

USING BASE CLASS CONSTRUCTORS THAT REQUIRE ARGUMENTS

When you create a class and do not provide a constructor, C# automatically supplies one that never requires arguments. When you write your own constructor for a class, you replace the automatically supplied version. Depending on your needs, the constructor you create for a class might require arguments. When you use a class as a base class and the class has a constructor that requires arguments, then you must make sure that any derived classes provide the base class constructor with what it needs.

»NOTE Don't forget that a class can have many overloaded constructors. As soon as you create at least one constructor for a class, you can no longer use the automatic version.

When a base class constructor requires arguments, you must include a constructor for each derived class you create. Your derived class constructor can contain any number of statements; however, within the header of the constructor, you must provide values for any arguments required by the base class constructor. Even if you have no other reason for creating a derived class constructor, you must write the derived class constructor so it can call its parent's constructor.

The format of the portion of the constructor header that calls a base class constructor is `base(list of arguments)`. The keyword **base** always refers to the superclass of the class in which you use it. For example, if you create an `Employee` class with a constructor that requires two arguments—an integer and a string—and you create a `CommissionEmployee` class that is a subclass of `Employee`, then the following code shows a valid constructor for `CommissionEmployee`:

```
public CommissionEmployee() : base(1234, "XXXX")
{
      // Other statements can go here
}
```

In this example, the `CommissionEmployee` constructor requires no arguments, but it passes two arguments to its base class constructor. Every `CommissionEmployee` passes 1234 and "XXXX" to the `Employee` constructor. A different `CommissionEmployee` constructor might require arguments; then it could pass the appropriate arguments on to the base class constructor, as in the following example:

»NOTE Although it seems as though you should be able to use the base class constructor name to call the base class constructor, C# does not allow you to do so. You must use the keyword `base`.

```
public CommissionEmployee(int id, string name) : base(id, name)
{
   // Other statements can go here
}
```

Yet another `CommissionEmployee` constructor might require three or more arguments. Some arguments might be passed to the base class constructor, and some might be used within `CommissionEmployee`. Consider the following example:

```
public CommissionEmployee(int id, string name, double rate) :
    base(id, name) // two parameters passed to base constructor
{
      CommissionRate = rate;
      // rate is used within child constructor
      // Other statements can go here
}
```

»TWO TRUTHS AND A LIE: WORKING WITH BASE CLASS CONSTRUCTORS

1. When you create any derived class object, the base class constructor executes first, followed by the derived class constructor.
2. When a base class constructor requires arguments, you must include a constructor for each derived class you create.
3. When a derived class's constructor requires arguments, all of the arguments must be passed to the base class constructor.

The false statement is #3. When a derived class's constructor requires arguments, all of the arguments might be needed in the derived class, or perhaps all must be passed to the base class constructor. It also might be possible that some arguments are passed to the base class constructor and others are used within the derived class constructor.

CREATING AND USING ABSTRACT CLASSES

Creating classes is easier after you understand the concept of inheritance. When you create a child class, it inherits all the general attributes you need; you must create only the new, more specific attributes required by the child class. For example, a `Painter` and a `Sculptor` are more specific than an `Artist`. They inherit all the general attributes of `Artists`, but you must add the attributes and methods that are specific to `Painter` and `Sculptor`.

Another way to think about a superclass is to notice that it contains the features shared by its subclasses. The derived classes are more specific examples of the base class type; they add features to the shared, general features. Conversely, when you examine a derived class, you notice that its parent is more general. Sometimes you create a parent class to be so general that you never intend to create any specific instances of the class. For example, you might never create "just" an `Artist`; each `Artist` is more specifically a `Painter`, `Sculptor`, `Illustrator`, and so on. A class that you create only to extend from, but not to instantiate from, is an abstract class. An **abstract class** is one from which you cannot create concrete objects, but from which you can inherit. You use the keyword `abstract` when you declare an abstract class.

> **»NOTE** Nonabstract classes from which objects *can* be instantiated are called **concrete** classes.

> **»NOTE** If you attempt to instantiate an object from an abstract class, you will receive a compiler error message.

Abstract classes are like regular classes in that they can contain data fields and methods. The difference is that you cannot create instances of abstract classes by using the `new` operator. Rather, you create abstract classes simply to provide a base class from which other objects may be derived. Abstract classes usually contain abstract methods, although methods are not required. An **abstract method** has no method statements; any class derived from a class that contains an abstract method must override the abstract method by providing a body (an implementation) for it. (Alternatively, the derived class can declare the method to be abstract; in that case, the derived class's children must implement the method.)

> **»NOTE** An abstract method is a virtual method. A **virtual method** is one whose behavior is determined by the implementation in a child class.

When you create an abstract method, you provide the keyword `abstract` and the intended method type, name, and arguments, but you do not provide statements within the method; you do not even supply curly braces. When you create a derived class that inherits an abstract method from a parent, you must use the keyword **`override`** in the method header and provide the actions, or implementation, for the inherited method within the derived class. In other words, you are required to code a derived class method to override the empty base class method that is inherited.

For example, suppose you want to create classes to represent different animals. You can create a generic, abstract class named `Animal` so you can provide generic data fields, such as the animal's name, only once. An `Animal` is generic, but each specific `Animal`, such as `Dog` or `Cat`, makes a unique sound that differs from `Animal` to `Animal`. If you code an abstract `Speak()` method in the abstract `Animal` class, then you require all future `Animal` derived classes to override the `Speak()` method and provide an implementation that is specific to the derived class. Figure 8-27 shows an abstract `Animal` class that contains a data field for the name, a constructor that assigns a name, a `Name` property, and an abstract `Speak()` method.

```
abstract class Animal
{
   protected string name;
   public Animal(string name)
   {
      this.name = name;
   }
   public string Name
   {
      get
      {
         return name;
      }
   }
   public abstract string Speak();
}
```

Figure 8-27 `Animal` class

The `Animal` class in Figure 8-27 is declared to be `abstract`. (The keyword is shaded.) You cannot place a statement such as `Animal myPet = new Animal("Murphy");` within a program, because the program will not compile. Because `Animal` is an `abstract` class, no `Animal` objects can exist.

You create an abstract class like `Animal` so that you can extend it. For example, you can create `Dog` and `Cat` classes as shown in Figure 8-28. Because the `Animal` class contains a constructor that requires a `string` argument, both `Dog` and `Cat` must contain constructors that provide `string` arguments for their base class.

The `Dog` and `Cat` constructors perform no tasks other than passing out the name to the `Animal` constructor. The overriding `Speak()` methods within `Dog` and `Cat` are required because the `abstract` parent `Animal` class contains an `abstract Speak()` method. The

»NOTE You can create an `abstract` class with no `abstract` methods, but you cannot create an `abstract` method outside of an `abstract` class.

```
class Dog : Animal
{
   public Dog(string name) : base(name)
   {
   }
   public override string Speak()
   {
      return "woof";
   }
}
class Cat : Animal
{
   public Cat(string name) : base(name)
   {
   }
   public override string Speak()
   {
      return "meow";
   }
}
```

Figure 8-28 Dog and Cat classes

keyword override (shaded) is required in the method header. You can code any statements you want within the Dog and Cat class Speak() methods, but the Speak() methods must exist.

Figure 8-29 shows a program that implements Dog and Cat objects, and Figure 8-30 shows the output. Speak() operates polymorphically; that is, each object acts appropriately using the correct Speak() method.

```
using System;
class DemoAnimals
{
   public static void Main()
   {
      Dog spot = new Dog("Spot");
      Cat puff = new Cat("Puff");
      Console.WriteLine(spot.Name + " says " + spot.Speak());
      Console.WriteLine(puff.Name + " says " + puff.Speak());
   }
}
```

Figure 8-29 DemoAnimals program

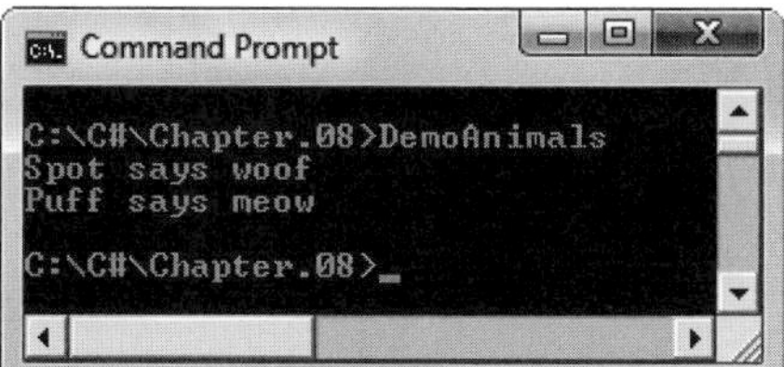

Figure 8-30 Output of the `DemoAnimals` program

»TWO TRUTHS AND A LIE: CREATING AND USING ABSTRACT CLASSES

1. An abstract class is one from which you cannot create concrete objects.
2. Unlike regular classes, abstract classes cannot contain methods.
3. When a base class contains an abstract method, its descendants must override it or declare it to be abstract.

The false statement is #2. Abstract classes are like regular classes in that they can contain data fields and methods. The difference is that you cannot create instances of abstract classes by using the `new` operator. Rather, you create abstract classes simply to provide a base class from which other objects may be derived.

CREATING AND USING INTERFACES

Some object-oriented programming languages, notably C++, allow a subclass to inherit from more than one parent class. For example, you might create an `Employee` class that contains data fields pertaining to each employee in your organization. You also might create a `Product` class that holds information about each product your organization manufactures. When you create a `Patent` class for each product for which your company holds a patent, you might want to include product information as well as information about the employee who was responsible for the invention. In this situation, it would be convenient to inherit fields and methods from both the `Product` and `Employee` classes. The ability to inherit from more than one class is called **multiple inheritance**.

Multiple inheritance is a difficult concept, and programmers encounter many problems when they use it. For example, variables and methods in the parent classes may have identical names, creating a conflict when the child class uses one of the names. Additionally, as you already have learned, a child class constructor must call its parent class constructor. When two or more parents exist, this becomes a more complicated task: To which class should `base` refer when a child class has multiple parents?

For all of these reasons, multiple inheritance is prohibited in C#. However, C# does provide an alternative to multiple inheritance, known as an interface. Much like an abstract class, an **interface** is a collection of methods (and perhaps other members) that can be used by any

»NOTE You first learned about interfaces in Chapter 7 when you used the `IComparable` interface.

class as long as the class provides a definition to override the interface's abstract definitions. Within an abstract class, some methods can be abstract, while others need not be. Within an interface, all methods are abstract.

You create an interface much as you create an abstract class definition, except that you use the keyword `interface` instead of `abstract class`. For example, suppose you create an `IWork` interface as shown in Figure 8-31. For simplicity, the `IWork` interface contains a single method named `Work()`.

NOTE Although not required, in C# it is customary to start interface names with an uppercase "I". Other languages follow different conventions. Interface names frequently end with "able".

```
public interface IWork
{
   string Work();
}
```

Figure 8-31 The `IWork` interface

When any class implements `IWork`, it must also include a `Work()` method that returns a `string`. Figure 8-32 shows two classes that implement `IWork`: the `Employee` class and the `Animal` class. Because each implements `IWork`, each must declare a `Work()` method. The `Employee` class implements `Work()` to return the "I do my job" `string`. The abstract `Animal` class defines `Work()` as an abstract method, meaning that descendants of `Animal` must implement `Work()`. Figure 8-32 also shows two child classes of `Animal`: `Dog` and `Cat`. Note how `Work()` is defined differently for each.

```
class Employee : IWork
{
   private string name;
   public Employee(string name)
   {
       Name = name;
   }
   public string Name {get; set;}
   public string Work()
   {
      return "I do my job";
   }
}
```

Figure 8-32 `Employee`, `Animal`, `Cat`, and `Dog` classes with the `IWork` interface (*continued*)

```
abstract class Animal : IWork
{
   protected string name;
   public Animal(string name)
   {
      Name = name;
   }
   public string Name
   {
      get
      {
         return name;
      }
      set
      {
         name = value;
      }
   }
   public abstract string Work();
}
class Dog : Animal
{
   public Dog(string name) : base(name)
   {
   }
   public override string Work()
   {
      return "I watch the house";
   }
}
class Cat : Animal
{
   public Cat(string name) : base(name)
   {
   }
   public override string Work()
   {
      return "I catch mice";
   }
}
```

Figure 8-32 (*continued*)

When you create a program that instantiates an `Employee`, a `Dog`, or a `Cat`, as in the `DemoWorking` program in Figure 8-33, each object type knows how to "`Work()`" appropriately. Figure 8-34 shows the output.

```
using System;
class DemoWorking
{
   public static void Main()
   {
      Employee bob = new Employee("Bob");
      Dog spot = new Dog("Spot");
      Cat puff = new Cat("Puff");
      Console.WriteLine(bob.Name + " says " + bob.Work());
      Console.WriteLine(spot.Name + " says " + spot.Work());
      Console.WriteLine(puff.Name + " says " + puff.Work());
   }
}
```

Figure 8-33 `DemoWorking` program

Figure 8-34 Output of the `DemoWorking` program

Abstract classes and interfaces are similar in that you cannot instantiate concrete objects from either one. Abstract classes differ from interfaces in that abstract classes can contain nonabstract methods, but all methods within an interface must be abstract. A class can inherit from only one base class (whether abstract or not), but it can implement any number of interfaces. For example, if you want to create a `Child` that inherits from a `Parent` class and implements two interfaces, `IWork` and `IPlay`, you would define the class name and list the base class and interfaces separated by commas:

```
class Child : Parent, IWork, IPlay
```

> **NOTE** You can think of an interface as a contract. A class that implements an interface must abide by the rules of the contract.

You implement an existing interface because you want a class to be able to use a method that already exists in other applications. For example, suppose you have created a `Payroll` application that uses the `Work()` method in the interface class. Also suppose you create a new class named `BusDriver`. If `BusDriver` implements the `IWork` interface, then `BusDriver` objects can be used by the existing `Payroll` program. As another example, suppose you have written a game program that uses an `IAttack` interface with methods that determine how and when an object can attack. When you create new classes such as `MarsAlien`, `Vampire`, and `CivilWarSoldier`, and each implements the interface, you can define how each one attacks and how each type of object can be added to the game.

Beginning programmers sometimes find it difficult to decide when to create an abstract base class and when to create an interface. Typically, you create an abstract class when you want to provide some data or methods that derived classes can inherit, but you want the subclasses to override some specific methods that you declare to be `abstract`. You create an interface when you want derived classes to override every method. Use a base class when the class you want to create "is a" subtype of another class; use an interface when the class you want to create will act like the interface.

Interfaces provide you with a way to exhibit polymorphic behavior. If diverse classes implement the same interface in unique ways, then you can treat each class type in the same way using the same language. When various classes use the same interface, you know the names of the methods that are available with those classes, and C# classes adopt a more uniform functionality; this consistency helps you to understand new classes you encounter more easily. If you know, for example, the method names contained in the `IWork` interface, and you see that a class implements `IWork`, you have a head start in understanding how the class functions.

»NOTE Now that you understand how to construct your own interfaces, you will benefit from rereading the section describing the `IComparable` interface in Chapter 7.

»TWO TRUTHS AND A LIE: CREATING AND USING INTERFACES

1. An interface is a collection of methods (and perhaps other members) that can be used by any class as long as the class provides a definition to override the interface's abstract definitions.
2. Abstract classes and interfaces differ in that all methods in abstract classes must be abstract, but interfaces can contain nonabstract methods.
3. A class can inherit from only one base class, but it can implement any number of interfaces.

The false statement is #2. Abstract classes and interfaces are similar in that you cannot instantiate concrete objects from either one. However, they differ in that abstract classes can contain nonabstract methods, but all methods within an interface must be abstract.

USING EXTENSION METHODS

When you write C# programs you constantly use classes, some that you ha… …tten yourself and many more that have been written by others. Sometimes you migh… …class had an additional method that would be useful to you. If you created the c… …lass, you have two options:

» You could revise the existing class, including the ne… …ethod.

» You could derive a child class from the existing… …ovide it with a new method.

Sometimes, however, classes you use were c… …rs, and you might not be allowed to either revise or extend them. Of course … …ce an entirely new class that includes

»NOTE Extension methods are a new feature in C# 3.0.

>> **NOTE** Programmers sometimes define their classes as sealed. A **sealed** class cannot be extended.

>> **NOTE** In Chapter 2 you learned that each C# intrinsic type, such as `int`, is an alias for a class in the `System` namespace, such as `Int32`.

your new method, but that would duplicate a lot of the work already done when the first class was created. In these cases, the best option is to write an extension method. **Extension methods** are methods you can write to add to any type.

For example, you have used the prewritten `Int32` class throughout this book to declare integers. Suppose you work for a company that frequently uses customer account numbers, and that the company has decided to add an extra digit to each account number. For simplicity, assume all account numbers are two digits and that the new, third number should be the rightmost digit in the sum of the first two digits. You could handle this problem by creating a class named `AccountNumber`, including a method to produce the extra digit, and redefining every instance of a customer's account number in your applications as an `AccountNumber` object. However, if you already have a lot of applications that define the account number as an integer, you might prefer to create an extension method that extends the `Int32` class.

>> **NOTE** When organizations append extra digits to account numbers, the extra digits are called check digits. **Check digits** help assure that all the digits in account numbers and other numbers are entered correctly. Check digits are calculated using different formulas. If a digit used to calculate the check digit is incorrect, then the resulting check digit is probably incorrect as well.

Figure 8-35 contains a method that extends the `Int32` class. The first parameter in an extension method specifies the type extended and must begin with the keyword `this`. For example, the first (and in this case, only) parameter in the `GetCheckDigit()` method is `this int num`, as shown in the shaded portion of the figure. Extension methods must be static methods. Within the `GetCheckDigit()` method in Figure 8-35, the first digit is extracted from the two-digit account number by dividing by 10 and taking the resulting whole number, and the second digit is extracting by taking the remainder. Those two digits are added, and the last digit of that sum is returned from the method. For example, if 49 is passed into the method, `first` becomes 4, `second` becomes 9, and `third` becomes the last digit of 13, or 3. Then the original number (49) is multiplied by 10 and added to the third digit, resulting in 493.

```
public static int GetCheckDigit(this int num)
{
    int first = num / 10;
    int second = num % 10;
    int third = (first + second) % 10;
    int result = num * 10 + third;
    return result;
}
```

Figure 8-35 The GetCheck… …xtension method

When you write an extensio…
DemoExtensionMethod prog… …it must be stored in a static class. For example, the
in the first shaded statement and… …e 8-36 shows an application that is declared static
…ension method in the second shaded statement.

and when an object can attack. When you create new classes such as `MarsAlien`, `Vampire`, and `CivilWarSoldier`, and each implements the interface, you can define how each one attacks and how each type of object can be added to the game.

Beginning programmers sometimes find it difficult to decide when to create an abstract base class and when to create an interface. Typically, you create an abstract class when you want to provide some data or methods that derived classes can inherit, but you want the subclasses to override some specific methods that you declare to be `abstract`. You create an interface when you want derived classes to override every method. Use a base class when the class you want to create "is a" subtype of another class; use an interface when the class you want to create will act like the interface.

Interfaces provide you with a way to exhibit polymorphic behavior. If diverse classes implement the same interface in unique ways, then you can treat each class type in the same way using the same language. When various classes use the same interface, you know the names of the methods that are available with those classes, and C# classes adopt a more uniform functionality; this consistency helps you to understand new classes you encounter more easily. If you know, for example, the method names contained in the `IWork` interface, and you see that a class implements `IWork`, you have a head start in understanding how the class functions.

» **NOTE**
Now that you understand how to construct your own interfaces, you will benefit from rereading the section describing the `IComparable` interface in Chapter 7.

» TWO TRUTHS AND A LIE: CREATING AND USING INTERFACES

1. An interface is a collection of methods (and perhaps other members) that can be used by any class as long as the class provides a definition to override the interface's abstract definitions.
2. Abstract classes and interfaces differ in that all methods in abstract classes must be abstract, but interfaces can contain nonabstract methods.
3. A class can inherit from only one base class, but it can implement any number of interfaces.

The false statement is #2. Abstract classes and interfaces are similar in that you cannot instantiate concrete objects from either one. However, they differ in that abstract classes can contain nonabstract methods, but all methods within an interface must be abstract.

USING EXTENSION METHODS

When you write C# programs you constantly use classes, some that you have written yourself and many more that have been written by others. Sometimes you might wish a class had an additional method that would be useful to you. If you created the original class, you have two options:

» You could revise the existing class, including the new useful method.

» You could derive a child class from the existing class and provide it with a new method.

» **NOTE**
Extension methods are a new feature in C# 3.0.

Sometimes, however, classes you use were created by others, and you might not be allowed to either revise or extend them. Of course, you could create an entirely new class that includes

>> **NOTE** Programmers sometimes define their classes as sealed. A **sealed** class cannot be extended.

>> **NOTE** In Chapter 2 you learned that each C# intrinsic type, such as `int`, is an alias for a class in the `System` namespace, such as `Int32`.

your new method, but that would duplicate a lot of the work already done when the first class was created. In these cases, the best option is to write an extension method. **Extension methods** are methods you can write to add to any type.

For example, you have used the prewritten `Int32` class throughout this book to declare integers. Suppose you work for a company that frequently uses customer account numbers, and that the company has decided to add an extra digit to each account number. For simplicity, assume all account numbers are two digits and that the new, third number should be the rightmost digit in the sum of the first two digits. You could handle this problem by creating a class named `AccountNumber`, including a method to produce the extra digit, and redefining every instance of a customer's account number in your applications as an `AccountNumber` object. However, if you already have a lot of applications that define the account number as an integer, you might prefer to create an extension method that extends the `Int32` class.

>> **NOTE** When organizations append extra digits to account numbers, the extra digits are called check digits. **Check digits** help assure that all the digits in account numbers and other numbers are entered correctly. Check digits are calculated using different formulas. If a digit used to calculate the check digit is incorrect, then the resulting check digit is probably incorrect as well.

Figure 8-35 contains a method that extends the `Int32` class. The first parameter in an extension method specifies the type extended and must begin with the keyword `this`. For example, the first (and in this case, only) parameter in the `GetCheckDigit()` method is `this int num`, as shown in the shaded portion of the figure. Extension methods must be static methods. Within the `GetCheckDigit()` method in Figure 8-35, the first digit is extracted from the two-digit account number by dividing by 10 and taking the resulting whole number, and the second digit is extracting by taking the remainder. Those two digits are added, and the last digit of that sum is returned from the method. For example, if 49 is passed into the method, `first` becomes 4, `second` becomes 9, and `third` becomes the last digit of 13, or 3. Then the original number (49) is multiplied by 10 and added to the third digit, resulting in 493.

```
public static int GetCheckDigit(this int num)
{
   int first = num / 10;
   int second = num % 10;
   int third = (first + second) % 10;
   int result = num * 10 + third;
   return result;
}
```

Figure 8-35 The `GetCheckDigit()` extension method

When you write an extension method, it must be stored in a static class. For example, the `DemoExtensionMethod` program in Figure 8-36 shows an application that is declared static in the first shaded statement and uses the extension method in the second shaded statement.

The static method GetCheckDigit() is used as if it were an instance method of the Int32 class; in other words, it is attached to an Int32 object with a dot, just as instance methods are when used with objects. No arguments are passed to the GetCheckDigit() method explicitly from the DemoExtensionMethod class. The parameter in the method is implied, just as these references are always implied in instance methods. Figure 8-37 shows the execution of the program.

```
using System;
static class DemoExtensionMethod
{
    public static void Main()
    {
        int acctNum = 49;
        int revisedAcctNum = acctNum.GetCheckDigit();
        Console.WriteLine("Original account number was {0}",
           acctNum);
        Console.WriteLine("Revised account number is {0}",
           revisedAcctNum);
    }
    public static int GetCheckDigit(this int num)
    {
        int first = num / 10;
        int second = num % 10;
        int third = (first + second) % 10;
        int result = num * 10 + third;
        return result;
    }
}
```

Figure 8-36 The DemoExtensionMethod application

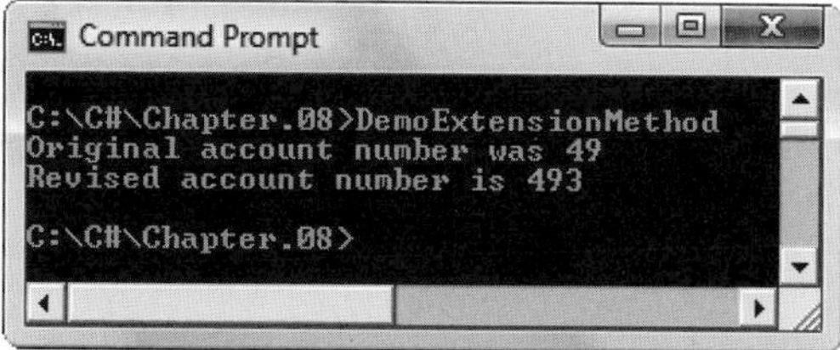

Figure 8-37 Execution of the DemoExtensionMethod application

You can create extension methods for your own classes in the same way one was created for the Int32 class in this example. Just like other outside methods, and unlike ordinary class instance methods, extension methods cannot access any private members of classes they extend. Furthermore, if a class contains an instance method with the same signature as an extension method, the instance method takes priority and will be the one that executes.

»TWO TRUTHS AND A LIE: USING EXTENSION METHODS

1. The first parameter in an extension method specifies the type extended and must begin with the keyword `this`.
2. Extension methods must be static methods.
3. When you write an extension method, it must be stored within the class to which it refers, along with the class's other instance methods.

The false statement is #3. Although you use an extension method like an instance method, any extension method you write must be stored in a static class.

RECAPPING THE BENEFITS OF USING INHERITANCE

When an automobile company designs a new car model, it does not build every component from scratch. The car might include a new feature—for example, some model contained the first air bag—but many of a new car's features are simply modifications of existing features. The manufacturer might create a larger gas tank or a more comfortable seat, but these new features still possess many of the properties of their predecessors from older models. Most features of new car models are not even modified; instead, existing components, such as air filters and windshield wipers, are included on the new model without any changes.

Similarly, you can create powerful computer programs more easily if many of their components are used either "as is" or with slight modifications. Inheritance does not enable you to write any programs that you could not write if inheritance did not exist; you *could* create every part of a program from scratch, but reusing existing classes and interfaces makes your job easier.

You already have used many "as is" classes, such as `Console`, `Int32`, and `String`. Using these classes made it easier to write programs than if you had to invent the classes yourself. Now that you have learned about inheritance, you can extend existing classes as well as just use them. When you create a useful, extendable base class, you and other future programmers gain several advantages:

- » Derived class creators save development time because much of the code that is needed for the class already has been written.
- » Derived class creators save testing time because the base class code already has been tested and probably used in a variety of situations. In other words, the base class code is reliable.

» Programmers who create or use new derived classes already understand how the base class works, so the time it takes to learn the new class features is reduced.

» When you create a derived class in C#, the base class source code is not changed. Thus, the base class maintains its integrity.

»NOTE Classes that are not intended to be instantiated and that contain only `static` members are declared as `static` classes. You cannot extend `static` classes. For example, `System.Console` is a static class.

When you think about classes, you need to think about the commonalities between them, and then you can create base classes from which to inherit. You might even be rewarded professionally when you see your own superclasses extended by others in the future.

»TWO TRUTHS AND A LIE: RECAPPING THE BENEFITS OF USING INHERITANCE

1. Inheritance enables you to create powerful computer programs more easily.
2. Without inheritance, you *could* create every part of a program from scratch, but reusing existing classes and interfaces makes your job easier.
3. Inheritance is frequently inefficient because base class code is seldom reliable when extended to a derived class.

The false statement is #3. Derived class creators save testing time because the base class code already has been tested and probably used in a variety of situations. In other words, the base class code is reliable.

YOU DO IT

In this section, you will create a working example of inheritance. You will create this example in four parts:

1. You will create a general `BankLoan` class that holds data pertaining to a bank loan—a loan number, a customer name, and the amount borrowed.
2. After you create the general `BankLoan` class, you will write a program to instantiate and use a `BankLoan` object.
3. You will create a more specific `CarLoan` derived class that inherits the attributes of the `BankLoan` class but adds information about the automobile that serves as collateral for the loan.
4. You will modify the `BankLoan` demonstration program to add a `CarLoan` object and demonstrate its use.

To create the `BankLoan` class:

1. Open a new file in your text editor, then enter the following first few lines for a `BankLoan` class. The class will host three data fields—the loan number, the last name of the customer, and the value of the loan.

```
public class BankLoan
{
   private int loanNumber;
   private string lastName;
   private double loanAmount;
```

2. Add a property with `get` and `set` accessors for each of the three data fields.

```
   public int LoanNumber {get; set;}
   public string LastName {get; set;}
   public double LoanAmount {get; set;}
```

3. Add a closing curly brace for the class. Save the file as **DemoBankLoan.cs**. Compile the file and correct any errors other than the one error you expect, which tells you that the program does not define an entry point. The message means that you cannot execute the file because it doesn't contain a class with a `Main()` method yet.

4. At the top of the file, enter the following code to add a `DemoBankLoan` class that contains a `Main()` method. The class declares a `BankLoan` object and shows how to set each field and display the results.

```
using System;
public class DemoBankLoan
{
   public static void Main()
   {
      BankLoan aLoan = new BankLoan();
      aLoan.LoanNumber = 2239;
      aLoan.LastName = "Mitchell";
      aLoan.LoanAmount = 1000.00;
      Console.WriteLine("Loan #{0} for {1} is for {2}",
         aLoan.LoanNumber, aLoan.LastName,
         aLoan.LoanAmount.ToString("C2"));
   }
}
```

5. Save the file, then compile the program. (You can safely ignore warnings about fields that are not used.) Execute the program. The output looks like Figure 8-38. There is nothing unusual about this class or how it operates; it is similar to many you saw in Chapter 7.

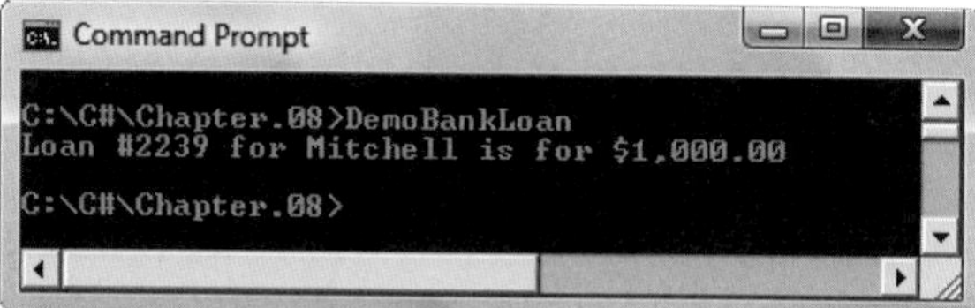

Figure 8-38 Output of the `DemoBankLoan` program

EXTENDING A CLASS

Next, you will create a class named `CarLoan`. A `CarLoan` "is a" type of `BankLoan`. As such, it has all the attributes of a `BankLoan`, but it also has the year and make of the car that the customer is using as collateral for the loan. Therefore, `CarLoan` is a subclass of `BankLoan`.

To create the `CarLoan` class that extends the `BankLoan` class:

1. Save the DemoBankLoan.cs file as **DemoCarLoan.cs**. Change the `DemoBankLoan` class name to **`DemoCarLoan`**. Position your cursor after the closing brace for the `BankLoan` class, press **Enter** to start a new line, and begin the definition of the `CarLoan` class. It extends `BankLoan` and contains two fields: `year` and `make`.

```
class CarLoan : BankLoan
{
   private int year;
   private string make;
```

2. Include properties for the fields you created in Step 1.

```
   public int Year {get; set;}
   public string Make {get; set;}
```

3. Add a closing curly brace for the class. Save the program, compile it, and correct any errors.

4. Modify the `DemoBankLoan` class to include a `CarLoan` object. First, change the name of the class from `DemoBankLoan` to **`DemoCarLoan`**.

5. Within the `Main()` method, just after the declaration of the `BankLoan` object, declare a `CarLoan` as follows:

```
CarLoan aCarLoan = new CarLoan();
```

6. After the three property assignments for the `BankLoan` object, insert five assignment statements for the `CarLoan` object.

```
aCarLoan.LoanNumber = 3358;
aCarLoan.LastName = "Jansen";
aCarLoan.LoanAmount = 20000.00;
aCarLoan.Make = "Ford";
aCarLoan.Year = 2005;
```

7. Following the `WriteLine()` statement that displays the `BankLoan` object data, insert two `WriteLine()` statements that display the `CarLoan` object's data.

```
Console.WriteLine("Loan #{0} for {1} is for {2}",
   aCarLoan.LoanNumber, aCarLoan.LastName,
   aCarLoan.LoanAmount.ToString("C2"));
Console.WriteLine("Loan #{0} is for a {1} {2}",
   aCarLoan.LoanNumber, aCarLoan.Year,
   aCarLoan.Make);
```

8. Save the program, then compile and execute it. The output looks like Figure 8-39. The `CarLoan` object correctly uses its own fields and properties as well as those of the parent `BankLoan` class.

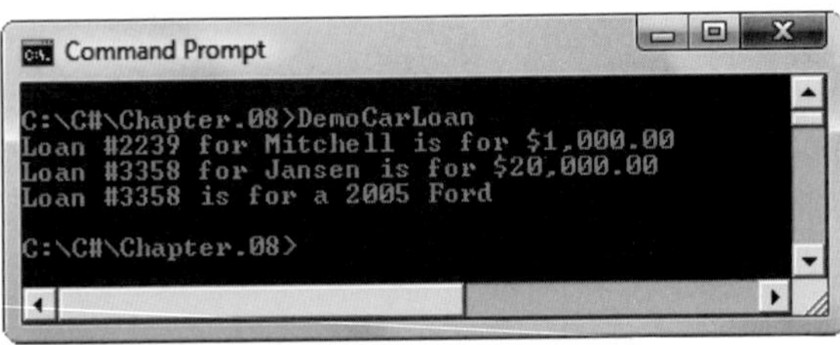

Figure 8-39 Output of the `DemoCarLoan` program

USING BASE CLASS MEMBERS IN A DERIVED CLASS

In the previous sections, you created `BankLoan()` and `CarLoan()` classes and objects. Suppose the bank adopts new rules as follows:

- » No regular loan will be made for less than $5000.
- » No car loan will be made for any car older than model year 2006.
- » Although `BankLoan`s might have larger loan numbers, `CarLoan`s will have loan numbers that are no more than three digits. If a larger loan number is provided, the program will use only the last three digits for the loan number.

To implement the new `CarLoan` rules:

1. Open the DemoCarLoan.cs file and immediately save it as **DemoCarLoan2.cs**. Also change the class name from `DemoCarLoan` to **`DemoCarLoan2`**.

2. Within the `BankLoan` class, add a new constant that represents the minimum loan value.

```
public const double MINIMUM_LOAN = 5000;
```

3. Replace the auto-implemented property for `LoanAmount` in the `BankLoan` class with standard `get` and `set` accessors as follows. This change ensures that no loan is made for less than the minimum allowed value.

```
public double LoanAmount
{
    set
    {
        if(value < MINIMUM_LOAN)
           loanAmount = MINIMUM_LOAN;
        else
           loanAmount = value;
    }
    get
    {
        return loanAmount;
    }
}
```

4. Within the `BankLoan` class, change the access modifier of `loanAmount` from `private` to **`protected`**. You do so to enable the `CarLoan` child class to change the `loanAmount` to 0 if a car year is older than 2006. If the child class had to use the `public` property to change the loan value, the value would become equal to `MINIMUM_LOAN` instead of 0.
5. Within the `CarLoan` class, add two new constants to hold the earliest year for which car loans will be given and the lowest allowed loan number.

```
private const int EARLIEST_YEAR = 2006;
private const int LOWEST_INVALID_NUM = 1000;
```

6. Also within the `CarLoan` class, replace the existing auto-implemented `Year` property with one that contains coded `get` and `set` accessors. The `Year` property `set` accessor not only sets the `year` field, it sets `loanAmount` to 0 when a car's year is less than 2006.

```
public int Year
{
    set
    {
        if(value < EARLIEST_YEAR)
        {
           year = value;
           loanAmount = 0;
        }
        else
           year = value;
    }
    get
    {
        return year;
    }
}
```

If `loanAmount` was `private` in the parent `BankLoan` class, you would not be able to set its value in the child `CarLoan` class, as you do here. You could use the `public` property

LoanAmount to set the value, but the parent class set accessor would force the value to 5000.

7. Suppose there are unique rules for issuing loan numbers for cars. Within the CarLoan class, just before the closing curly brace, change the inherited LoanNumber property to accommodate the new rules. If a car loan number is three digits or fewer, pass it on to the base class property. If not, obtain the last three digits by calculating the remainder when the loan number is divided by 1000 and pass the new number to the base class property. Add the following property after the definition of the Make property.

```
public new int LoanNumber
{
    get
    {
        return base.LoanNumber;
    }
    set
    {
        if(value < LOWEST_INVALID_NUM)
           base.LoanNumber = value;
        else
           base.LoanNumber = value % LOWEST_INVALID_NUM;
    }
}
```

If you did not use the keyword base to access the LoanNumber property within the CarLoan class, you would be telling this version of the LoanNumber property to call itself. Although the program would compile, it would run continuously in an infinite loop until it ran out of memory and issued an error message.

>> **NOTE**
> A method that calls itself is a **recursive** method. Recursive methods are sometimes useful, but they are not in this case.

8. Save the file. Compile it and correct any errors. When you execute the program, the output looks like Figure 8-40. Compare the output to Figure 8-39. Notice that the $1000 bank loan has been forced to $5000. Also notice that the car loan number has been shortened to three digits and the value of the loan is $0 because of the age of the car.

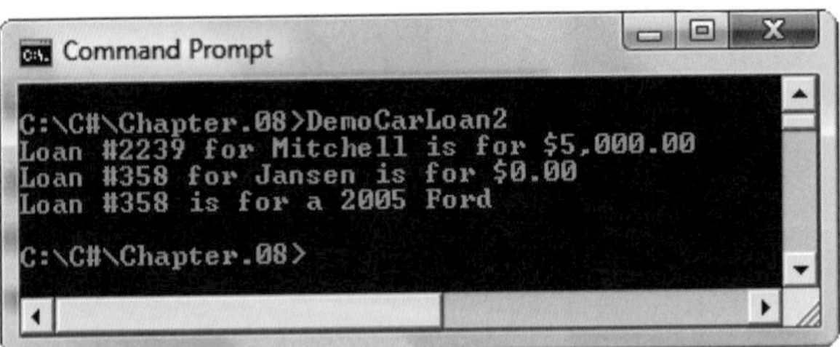

Figure 8-40 Output of the DemoCarLoan2 program

9. Change the assigned values within the `DemoCarLoan2` class to combinations of early and late years and valid and invalid loan numbers. After each change, save the program, compile and execute it, and confirm that the program operates as expected.

ADDING CONSTRUCTORS TO BASE AND DERIVED CLASSES

When a base class contains only constructors that require parameters, then any derived classes must provide for the base class constructor. In the next steps, you will add constructors to the `BankLoan` and `CarLoan` classes and demonstrate that they work as expected.

To add constructors to the classes:

1. Open the `DemoCarLoan2` program and change the class name to `DemoCarLoan3`. Save the file as **DemoCarLoan3.cs**.
2. In the `BankLoan` class, just after the declaration of the fields and constants, add a constructor that requires values for all the `BankLoan`'s fields and assigns them to the properties:

```
public BankLoan(int num, string name, double amount)
{
    LoanNumber = num;
    LastName = name;
    LoanAmount = amount;
}
```

3. In the `CarLoan` class, just after the declaration of the fields and constants, add a constructor that takes five parameters. It passes three of the parameters to the base class constructor and uses the other two to assign values to the properties that are unique to the child class.

```
public CarLoan(int num, string name, double amount,
    int year, string make) : base(num, name, amount)
{
    Year = year;
    Make = make;
}
```

4. In the `Main()` method of the `DemoCarLoan3` class, remove the existing declarations for `aLoan` and `aCarLoan` and replace them with two declarations that use the arguments passed to the constructors.

```
BankLoan aLoan = new BankLoan(333, "Hanson", 7000.00);
CarLoan aCarLoan = new CarLoan(444, "Carlisle", 30000.00,
     2009, "BMW");
```

5. Remove the eight statements that assigned values to the `BankLoan` and `CarLoan`, but retain the `Console.WriteLine()` statements that display the values.
6. Save the program, then compile and execute it. The output looks like Figure 8-41. Both constructors work as expected. The `CarLoan` constructor has called its parent's constructor to set the necessary fields before executing its own unique statements.

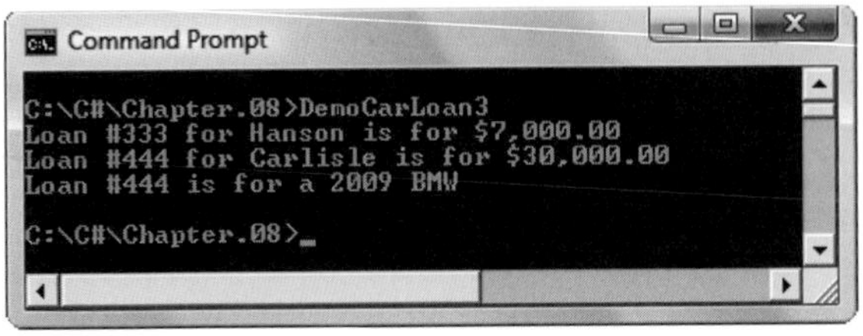

```
Command Prompt
C:\C#\Chapter.08>DemoCarLoan3
Loan #333 for Hanson is for $7,000.00
Loan #444 for Carlisle is for $30,000.00
Loan #444 is for a 2009 BMW

C:\C#\Chapter.08>_
```

Figure 8-41 Output of the `DemoCarLoan3` program

CHAPTER SUMMARY

- Inheritance is the principle that you can apply your knowledge of a general category to more specific objects. The classes you create in object-oriented programming languages can inherit data and methods from existing classes. The ability to use inheritance makes programs easier to write, easier to understand, and less prone to errors.
- A class that is used as a basis for inheritance is called a base class. When you create a class that inherits from a base class, it is called a derived class or extended class. A derived class always "is a" case or instance of the more general base class. You can use the terms *superclass* and *parent class* as synonyms for base class, and the terms *subclass* and *child class* as synonyms for derived class.
- When you create a class that is an extension or child of another class, you use a single colon between the derived class name and its base class name. The child class inherits all the methods and fields of its parent. Inheritance works only in one direction—a child inherits from a parent, but not the other way around.
- If you could use private data outside of its class, the principle of information hiding would be destroyed. On some occasions, however, you want to access parent class data from within a derived class. For those occasions, you declare parent class fields using the keyword `protected`, which provides you with an intermediate level of security between `public` and `private` access.
- You can declare a child class method with the same name and argument list as a method within its parent class. When you do so, you override the parent class method and allow your class objects to exhibit polymorphic behavior. You can use the keyword `new` or `override` with the derived class method.
- When a derived class overrides a parent class method but you want to access the parent class version of the method, you can use the keyword `base`.
- Every derived class object "is a" specific instance of both the derived class and the base class. Therefore, you can assign a derived class object to an object of any of its base class types. When you do so, C# makes an implicit conversion from derived class to base class.

» Every class you create in C# derives from a single class named `System.Object`. Because all classes inherit from the `Object` class, all classes inherit the `Object` class methods. The `Object` class contains four `public` instance methods: `Equals()`, `GetHashCode()`, `GetType()`, and `ToString()`.

» When you instantiate an object that is a member of a subclass, you actually call two constructors: the constructor for the base class and the constructor for the extended, derived class. When you create any derived class object, the base class constructor must execute first; only then does the derived class constructor execute.

» When you use a class as a base class and the class has a constructor that requires arguments, then within the header of the derived class constructor you must provide values for any arguments required by the base class constructor. Even if you have no other reason for creating a derived class constructor, you must write the subclass constructor so it can call its parent's constructor.

» An abstract class is one from which you cannot create concrete objects, but from which you can inherit. Usually, abstract classes contain abstract methods; an abstract method has no method statements. Any class derived from a class that contains an abstract method must override the abstract method by providing a body (an implementation) for it.

» C# provides an alternative to multiple inheritance, known as an interface. Much like an abstract class, an interface is a collection of methods (and perhaps other members) that can be used by any class as long as the class provides a definition to override the interface's abstract definitions. Within an abstract class, some methods can be abstract, while others need not be. Within an interface, all methods are abstract. A class can inherit from only one abstract base class, but it can implement any number of interfaces.

» Extension methods are methods you can write to add to any type. They are static methods, but they operate like instance methods. Their parameter lists begin with the keyword `this` and the data type being extended.

KEY TERMS

Inheritance is the application of your knowledge of a general category to more specific objects.

Unified Modeling Language (UML) diagrams are graphical tools that programmers and analysts use to describe systems.

A **base class** is a class that is used as a basis for inheritance.

A **derived class** or **extended class** is one that has inherited from a base class.

A **superclass** is a base class.

A **subclass** is a derived class.

A **parent class** is a base class.

A **child class** is a derived class.

The **ancestors** of a derived class are all the superclasses from which the subclass is derived.

Inheritance is **transitive**, which means that a child inherits all the members of all its ancestors.

Using the keyword **`protected`** provides you with an intermediate level of security between `public` and `private` access. A `protected` data field or method can be used within its own class or in any classes extended from that class, but it cannot be used by "outside" classes.

Classes that depend on field names from parent classes are said to be **fragile** because they are prone to errors—that is, they are easy to "break."

A derived class member that overrides a parent class member **hides** it.

A base class member that is not hidden by the derived class is **visible** in the derived class.

An **implicit conversion** occurs when a type is automatically converted to another upon assignment.

An **implicit reference conversion** occurs when a derived class object is assigned to its ancestor's data type.

The **`object`** (or `Object`) class type in the `System` namespace is the ultimate base class for all other types.

Reference equality occurs when two reference type objects refer to the same object.

A **hash code** is a number that should uniquely identify an object.

The keyword **`base`** always refers to the superclass of the class in which you use it.

An **abstract class** is one from which you cannot create concrete objects, but from which you can inherit.

Concrete classes are nonabstract classes from which objects can be instantiated.

An **abstract method** has no method statements; any class derived from a class that contains an abstract method must override the abstract method by providing a body (an implementation) for it.

The keyword **`override`** is used in method headers when you create a derived class that inherits an abstract method from a parent.

A **virtual method** is one whose behavior is determined by the implementation in a child class.

Multiple inheritance is the ability to inherit from more than one class.

An **interface** is a collection of abstract methods (and perhaps other members) that can be used by any class as long as the class provides a definition to override the interface's abstract definitions.

Extension methods are static methods that act like instance methods. You can write extension methods to add to any type.

A **sealed** class cannot be extended.

A **check digit** is a digit calculated from a formula and appended to a number to help verify the accuracy of the other digits in the number.

A method that calls itself is a **recursive** method.

REVIEW QUESTIONS

1. The principle that you can apply your knowledge of a general category to more specific objects is ________.

   a. polymorphism
   b. encapsulation
   c. inheritance
   d. structure

2. Which of the following is *not* a benefit of using inheritance when creating a new class?

   a. You save time, because you need not create fields and methods that already exist in a parent class.
   b. You reduce the chance of errors, because the parent class methods have already been used and tested.
   c. You make it easier for anyone who has used the parent class to understand the new class because the programmer can concentrate on the new features.
   d. You save computer memory because when you create objects of the new class, storage is not required for parent class fields.

3. A child class is also called a(n) ________.

   a. extended class
   b. base class
   c. superclass
   d. delineated class

4. Assuming that the following classes are well named, which of the following is a parent class of `House`?

   a. `Apartment`
   b. `Building`
   c. `Victorian`
   d. `myHouse`

5. A derived class usually contains ________ than its parent.

   a. more fields and methods
   b. the same number of fields but fewer methods
   c. fewer fields but more methods
   d. fewer fields and methods

6. When you create a class that is an extension or child of another class, you use a(n) ________ between the derived class name and its base class name.

   a. ampersand
   b. colon
   c. dot
   d. hyphen

7. A base class named `Garden` contains a private field `width` and a property `public int Width` that contains `get` and `set` accessors. A child class named `VegetableGarden`

does not contain a `Width` property. When you write a class in which you declare an object as follows, what statement can you use to access the `VegetableGarden`'s `width`?

```
VegetableGarden myGarden = new VegetableGarden();
```

a. `myGarden.Width`

b. `myGarden.base.Width`

c. `VegetableGarden.Width`

d. You cannot use `Width` with a `VegetableGarden` object.

8. When a parent class contains a `private` data field, the field is ________ the child class.

   a. hidden in

   b. not a member of

   c. directly accessible in

   d. `public` in

9. When a base class and a derived class contain a method with the same name and argument list, and you call the method using a derived class object, ________.

   a. you receive an error message

   b. the base class version overrides the derived class version

   c. the derived class version overrides the base class version

   d. both method versions execute

10. Which of the following is an English-language form of polymorphism?

    a. seeing a therapist and seeing the point

    b. moving friends with a compelling story and moving friends to a new apartment

    c. both of these

    d. neither of these

11. When base and derived classes contain a method with the same name and argument list, you can use the base class method within the derived class by using the keyword ________ before the method name.

    a. `new`

    b. `override`

    c. `base`

    d. `super`

12. In a program that declares a derived class object, you ________ assign it to an object of its base class type.

    a. can

    b. cannot

    c. must

    d. should not

13. The ultimate base class for all other class types is __________.

a. `Base`

b. `Super`

c. `Parent`

d. `Object`

14. All of the following are `Object` class methods *except* __________.

a. `ToString()`

b. `Equals()`

c. `Print()`

d. `GetHashCode()`

15. When you create any derived class object, __________.

a. the base class and derived class constructors execute simultaneously

b. the base class constructor must execute first; then the derived class constructor executes

c. the derived class constructor must execute first; then the base class constructor executes

d. neither the base class nor the derived class constructor executes

16. When a base class constructor requires arguments, then each derived class __________.

a. must include a constructor

b. must include a constructor that requires arguments

c. must include two or more constructors

d. must not include a constructor

17. When you create an abstract class, __________.

a. you can inherit from it

b. you can create concrete objects from it

c. both of these are true

d. neither of these is true

18. When you create an abstract method, you provide __________.

a. the keyword `abstract`

b. curly braces

c. method statements

d. all of these

19. Within an interface, __________.

a. no methods can be `abstract`

b. some methods might be `abstract`

c. some, but not all, methods must be `abstract`

d. all methods must be `abstract`

20. Abstract classes and interfaces are similar in that ________.
    a. you can instantiate concrete objects from both
    b. you cannot instantiate concrete objects from either one
    c. all methods in both must be `abstract`
    d. neither can contain nonabstract methods

EXERCISES

1. Create a class named `Game` that contains a string with the name of the `Game` and an integer that holds the maximum number of players. Include properties with `get` and `set` accessors for each field. Also, include a `ToString()` `Game` method that overrides the `Object` class's `ToString()` method and returns a string that contains the name of the class (using `GetType()`), the name of the `Game`, and the number of players. Create a child class named `GameWithTimeLimit` that includes an integer time limit in minutes and a property that contains `get` and `set` accessors for the field. Write a program that instantiates an object of each class and demonstrates all the methods. Save the file as **GameDemo.cs**.

2. Create a class named `Tape` that includes fields for length and width in inches and properties for each field. Also include a `ToString()` method that returns a string constructed from the return value of the object's `GetType()` method and the values of the length and width fields. Derive two subclasses—`VideoCassetteTape` and `AdhesiveTape`. The `VideoCassetteTape` class includes an integer field to hold playing time in minutes and a property for the field. The `AdhesiveTape` class includes an integer field that holds a stickiness factor—a value from 1 to 10—and a property for the field. Write a program that instantiates one object of each of the three classes, and demonstrate that all of each class's methods work correctly. Be sure to use valid and invalid values when testing the numbers you can use to set the `AdhesiveTape` class stickiness factor. Save the file as **TapeDemo.cs**.

3. a. Create a class named `Order` that performs order processing of a single item that sells for $19.95 each. The class has four variable fields: order number, customer name, quantity ordered, and total price. Create a constructor that requires parameters for all the fields except total price. Include `public` `get` and `set` accessors for each field except the total price field; that field is calculated as quantity ordered times unit price (19.95) whenever the quantity is set, so it needs only a `get` accessor. Also create the following for the class:

    » An `Equals()` method that determines two `Orders` are equal if they have the same order number

    » A `GetHashCode()` method that returns the order number

    » A `ToString()` method that returns a string containing all order information

    Write an application that declares a few `Order` objects and sets their values, making sure to create at least two with the same order number. Display the string from the

ToString() method for each order. Write a method that compares two orders at a time and displays a message if they are equal. Send the Orders you created to the method two at a time and display the results. Save the file as **OrderDemo.cs.**

b. Using the Order class you created in Exercise 3a, write a new application that creates an array of five Orders. Prompt the user for values for each Order. Do not allow duplicate order numbers; force the user to reenter the order when a duplicate order number is entered. When five valid orders have been entered, display them all, plus a total of all orders. Save the program as **OrderDemo2.cs**.

c. Create a ShippedOrder class that derives from Order. A ShippedOrder has a $4.00 shipping fee (no matter how many items are ordered). Override any methods in the parent class as necessary. Write a new application that creates an array of five ShippedOrders. Prompt the user for values for each, and do not allow duplicate order numbers; force the user to reenter the order when a duplicate order number is entered. When five valid orders have been entered, display them all, plus a total of all orders. Save the program as **OrderDemo3.cs**.

d. Make any necessary modifications to the ShippedOrder class so that it can be sorted by order number. Modify the OrderDemo3 application so the displayed orders have been sorted. Save the application as **OrderDemo4.cs**.

4. a. Create a class named Book that includes fields for the International Standard Book Number (ISBN), title, author, and price. Include properties for each field. (An ISBN is a unique number assigned to each published book.) Create a child class named TextBook that includes a grade level and a CoffeeTableBook child class that contains no additional fields. In the child classes, override the accessor that sets a Book's price so that TextBooks must be priced between $20.00 and $80.00, inclusive, and CoffeeTableBooks must be priced between $35.00 and $100.00, inclusive. Write a program that creates a few objects of each type and demonstrate that all of the methods and properties work correctly. Be sure to use valid and invalid values when testing the child class properties. Save the file as **BookDemo.cs**.

b. In the Book class you created in Exercise 4a, overload the Object class Equals() method to consider two Books equal if they have the same ISBN. Create a program that declares three Books; two should have the same ISBN and one should have a different one. Demonstrate that the Equals() method works correctly to compare the Books. Save the program as **BookDemo2.cs**.

c. Write an application that declares two Book objects and uses an extension method named DisplayTitleAndAuthor() with each. The method displays a Book's title, the word "by", and the author's name. Save the program as **BookDemo3.cs**.

5. a. Create a Patient class for the Wrightstown Hospital Billing Department. Include a patient ID number, name, age, and amount due to the hospital. Include properties and any other methods you need. Override the ToString() method to return all the details for a patient. Write an application that prompts the user for data for five

`Patients`. Sort them in patient ID number order and display them all, including a total amount owed. Save the program as **PatientDemo.cs**.

b. Using the `Patient` class as a base, derive an `InsuredPatient` class. An `InsuredPatient` contains all the data of a `Patient`, plus fields to hold an insurance company name and the percentage of the hospital bill the insurance company will pay. Insurance payments are based on the following table:

Insurance Company	Portion of bill paid by insurance (%)
Wrightstown Mutual	80
Red Umbrella	60
All other companies	25

Create an array of five `InsuredPatient` objects. Prompt the user for all the patient data, plus the name of the insurance company; the insurance company `set` accessor determines the percentage paid. Override the parent class `ToString()` method to include the name of the insurance company, the percent paid, and the amount due after the insurance has been applied to the bill. Sort all the records in ID number order and display them with a total amount due from all insured patients. Save the program as **PatientDemo2.cs**.

c. Write an application that uses an extension method for the `Patient` class. The method computes and returns a `Patient`'s quarterly insurance payment (one-fourth of the annual premium). The application should allow the user to enter data for five `Patients` and then display all the `Patient` data for each, including the quarterly payment. Save the program as **PatientDemo3.cs**.

6. Create an abstract class called `GeometricFigure`. Each figure includes a height, a width, and an area. Provide `get` and `set` accessors for each field except for area; the area is computed and is read-only. Include an abstract method called `ComputeArea()` that computes the area of the `GeometricFigure`. Create three additional classes:

   » A `Rectangle` is a `GeometricFigure` whose area is determined by multiplying width by height.

   » A `Square` is a `Rectangle` in which the width and height are the same. Provide a constructor that accepts both height and width, forcing them to be equal if they are not. Provide a second constructor that accepts just one dimension and uses it for both height and width. The `Square` class uses the `Rectangle`'s `ComputeArea()` method.

   » A `Triangle` is a `GeometricFigure` whose area is determined by multiplying the width by half the height.

Create an application that demonstrates creating objects of each class. After each is created, pass it to a method that accepts a `GeometricFigure` argument in which the figure's data is displayed. Change some dimensions of some of the figures and pass each to the display method again. Save the program as **ShapesDemo.cs**.

7. Create an interface named `IRecoverable`. It contains a single method named `Recover()`. Create classes named `Patient`, `Furniture`, and `Football`; each of these classes implements `IRecoverable`. Create each class's `Recover()` method to display an appropriate message. For example, the `Patient`'s `Recover()` method might display "I am getting better." Write a program that declares an object of each of the three types and uses its `Recover()` method. Save the file as **RecoveringDemo.cs**.

8. Create an interface named `ITurnable`. It contains a single method named `Turn()`. Create classes named `Page`, `Corner`, `Pancake`, and `Leaf`; each of these classes implements `ITurnable`. Create each class's `Turn()` method to display an appropriate message. For example, the `Page`'s `Turn()` method might display "You turn a page in a book." Write a program that declares an object of each of the four types and uses its `Turn()` method. Save the file as **TurningDemo.cs**.

9. Create an abstract class named `Salesperson`. Fields include first and last names; the `Salesperson` constructor requires both these values. Include properties for the fields. Include a method that returns a string that holds the `Salesperson`'s full name—the first and last names separated by a space. Then perform the following tasks:
   - Create two child classes of `Salesperson`: `RealEstateSalesperson` and `GirlScout`. The `RealEstateSalesperson` class contains fields for total value sold in dollars and total commission earned (both of which are initialized to 0), and a commission rate field required by the class constructor. The `GirlScout` class includes a field to hold the number of boxes of cookies sold, which is initialized to 0. Include properties for every field.
   - Create an interface named `ISell` that contains two methods: `SalesSpeech()` and `MakeSale()`. In each `RealEstateSalesperson` and `GirlScout` class, implement `SalesSpeech()` to display an appropriate one- or two-sentence sales speech that the objects of the class could use. In the `RealEstateSalesperson` class, implement the `MakeSale()` method to accept an integer dollar value for a house, add the value to the `RealEstateSalesperson`'s total value sold, and compute the total commission earned. In the `GirlScout` class, implement the `MakeSale()` method to accept an integer representing the number of boxes of cookies sold and add it to the total field.
   - Write a program that instantiates a `RealEstateSalesperson` object and a `GirlScout` object. Demonstrate the `SalesSpeech()` method with each object, then use the `MakeSale()` method two or three times with each object. Display the final contents of each object's data fields. Save the file as **SalespersonDemo.cs**.

DEBUGGING EXERCISES

Each of the following files in the Chapter.08 folder on your Student Disk has syntax and/or logical errors. In each case, determine the problem and fix the program. After you correct the errors, save each file using the same filename preceded with *Fixed*. For example, DebugEight01.cs will become FixedDebugEight01.cs.

a. DebugEight01.cs
b. DebugEight02.cs
c. DebugEight03.cs
d. DebugEight04.cs

UP FOR DISCUSSION

1. In this chapter, you learned the difference between `public`, `private`, and `protected` class members. Why are some programmers opposed to classifying class members as `protected`? Do you agree with them?
2. Playing computer games has been shown to increase the level of dopamine in the human brain. High levels of this substance are associated with addiction to drugs. Suppose you work for a company that manufactures games and it decides to research how its games can produce more dopamine in the brains of players. Would you support the company's decision?
3. If you are completing all the programming exercises at the ends of the chapters in this book, you know that it takes a lot of time to write and test programs that work. Professional programs require even more hours of work. In the workplace, programs frequently must be completed by strict deadlines—for example, a tax-calculating program must be completed by year's end, or an advertising Web site must be completed by the launch of the product. Programmers often find themselves working into the evenings or weekends to complete rush projects at work. How would you feel about having to do this? What types of compensation would make the extra hours worthwhile for you?
4. Suppose your organization asks you to develop a code of ethics for the Information Technology Department. What would you include?

CHAPTER NINE

9

EXCEPTION HANDLING

In this chapter you will:

- Learn about exceptions and the `Exception` class
- Purposely generate a `SystemException`
- Learn about traditional error-handling methods
- Learn about object-oriented exception-handling methods
- Use the `Exception` class's `ToString()` method and `Message` property
- Catch multiple `Exceptions`
- Use the `finally` block
- Handle an `Exception` with a loop
- Throw an `Exception`
- Trace `Exceptions` through the call stack
- Create your own `Exception` classes
- Rethrow `Exceptions`

While visiting Web sites, you have probably seen an unexpected and cryptic message that announces an error and then shuts down your browser immediately. Perhaps something similar has happened to you while using a piece of application software. Certainly, if you have worked your way through all of the programming exercises in this book, you have encountered such errors while running your own programs. When a program just stops, it is aggravating, especially when you lose data you have typed and the program error message seems to indicate the program "knows" exactly what is wrong. You might grumble, "If it knows what is wrong, why doesn't it just fix it?" In this chapter, you will learn how to handle these unexpected error conditions so your programs can be more user-friendly than those that simply shut down in the face of errors.

UNDERSTANDING EXCEPTIONS

An **exception** is any error condition or unexpected behavior in an executing program. The programs you write can generate many types of potential exceptions, including when:

- Your program asks for user input, but the user enters invalid data.
- The program attempts to divide a value by zero.
- You attempt to access an array with a subscript that is too large or too small.
- You calculate a value that is too large for the answer's variable type.

These errors are called exceptions because presumably, they are not usual occurrences; they are "exceptional." The object-oriented techniques used to manage such errors make up the group of methods known as **exception handling**.

»NOTE Managing exceptions involves an oxymoron; you must expect the unexpected.

In C#, all exceptions are objects that are instances of the `Exception` class or one of its derived classes. An exception condition generates an object that encapsulates information about the error. Like all other classes in the C# programming language, the `Exception` class is a descendant of the `Object` class. The `Exception` class has several descendant classes of its own, many with unusual names such as `CodeDomSerializerException`, `SUDSParserException`, and `SoapException`. Others have names that are more easily understood, such as `IOException` (for input and output errors), `InvalidPrinterException` (for when a user requests an invalid printer), and `PathTooLongException` (used when the path to a file contains more characters than a system allows). C# has more than 100 defined `Exceptions`; Table 9-1 lists just a few to give you an idea of the wide variety of circumstances they cover.

»NOTE Errors you discover when compiling a program are not exceptions; only execution-time errors are called exceptions.

Most exceptions you will use derive from three classes:

»NOTE Table 9-1 uses the term "thrown," which is explained later in this chapter.

- The predefined Common Language Runtime exception classes derived from `SystemException`
- The user-defined application exception classes you derive from `ApplicationException`
- The `Exception` class, which is the parent of `SystemException` and `ApplicationException`

Class	Description
`System.ArgumentException`	Thrown when one of the arguments provided to a method is not valid
`System.ArithmeticException`	Thrown for errors in an arithmetic, casting, or conversion operation
`System.ArrayTypeMismatchException`	Thrown when an attempt is made to store an element of the wrong type within an array
`System.Data.OperationAbortedException`	Thrown when an ongoing operation is aborted by the user
`System.Drawing.Printing.InvalidPrinterException`	Thrown when you try to access a printer using printer settings that are not valid
`System.FormatException`	Thrown when the format of an argument does not meet the parameter specifications of the invoked method
`System.IndexOutOfRangeException`	Thrown when an attempt is made to access an element of an array with an index that is outside the bounds of the array; this class cannot be inherited
`System.InvalidCastException`	Thrown for an invalid casting or explicit conversion
`System.InvalidOperationException`	Thrown when a method call is invalid for the object's current state
`System.IO.InvalidDataException`	Thrown when a data stream is in an invalid format
`System.IO.IOException`	Thrown when an I/O error occurs
`System.MemberAccessException`	Thrown when an attempt to access a class member fails
`System.NotImplementedException`	Thrown when a requested method or operation is not implemented
`System.NullReferenceException`	Thrown when there is an attempt to dereference a null object reference
`System.OperationCanceledException`	Thrown in a thread upon cancellation of an operation that the thread was executing
`System.OutOfMemoryException`	Thrown when there is not enough memory to continue the execution of a program
`System.RankException`	Thrown when an array with the wrong number of dimensions is passed to a method
`System.StackOverflowException`	Thrown when the execution stack overflows because it contains too many nested method calls; this class cannot be inherited

Table 9-1 Selected C# `Exception`s

NOTE Microsoft previously advised that you should create your own custom exceptions from the `ApplicationException` class. They have revised their thinking because in practice, they have not found the approach to be of significant value. For updates, visit *http://msdn2.microsoft.com*.

TWO TRUTHS AND A LIE: UNDERSTANDING EXCEPTIONS

1. An exception is any error condition or unexpected behavior in an executing program.
2. The object-oriented techniques used to manage errors make up the group of methods known as behavior management.
3. In C#, all exceptions are objects that are members of the `Exception` class or one of its derived classes.

The false statement is #2. The object-oriented techniques used to manage errors make up the group of methods known as exception handling.

PURPOSELY GENERATING A SystemException

You can deliberately generate a `SystemException` by forcing a program to contain an error. As an example, in every programming language, it is illegal to divide a value by zero because the operation is mathematically undefined. Consider the `MilesPerGallon` program in Figure 9-1. It is a simple program that prompts a user for two values and divides them. If the user enters nonzero integers, the program runs correctly and without incident. However, if the user enters 0 when prompted to enter gallons, division by 0 takes place and an error is generated. Figure 9-2 shows two executions of the program.

```
using System;
public class MilesPerGallon
{
   public static void Main()
   {
      int milesDriven;
      int gallonsOfGas;
      int mpg;
      Console.Write("Enter miles driven ");
      milesDriven = Convert.ToInt32(Console.ReadLine());
      Console.Write("Enter gallons of gas purchased ");
      gallonsOfGas = Convert.ToInt32(Console.ReadLine());
      mpg = milesDriven / gallonsOfGas;
      Console.WriteLine("You got {0} miles per gallon", mpg);
   }
}
```

Figure 9-1 `MilesPerGallon` program

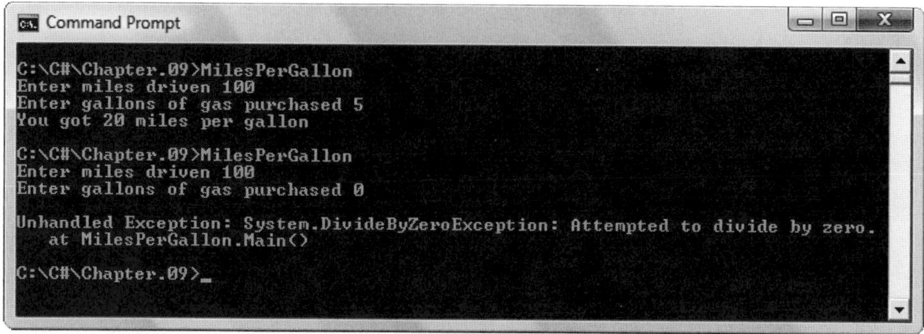
```
C:\C#\Chapter.09>MilesPerGallon
Enter miles driven 100
Enter gallons of gas purchased 5
You got 20 miles per gallon

C:\C#\Chapter.09>MilesPerGallon
Enter miles driven 100
Enter gallons of gas purchased 0

Unhandled Exception: System.DivideByZeroException: Attempted to divide by zero.
   at MilesPerGallon.Main()

C:\C#\Chapter.09>_
```

Figure 9-2 Two executions of `MilesPerGallon` program

» NOTE When the user enters a 0 for gallons in the `MilesPerGallon` program, a dialog box reports that the application has stopped working and needs to close. Because this error is intentional for demonstration purposes, you can ignore the message by clicking Close program.

In the first execution of the `MilesPerGallon` program in Figure 9-1, the user entered two usable integers, and division was carried out successfully. However, in the second execution, the user entered 0 for gallons of gas, and the error message indicates that an unhandled exception named `System.DivideByZeroException` was created. The message gives further information ("Attempted to divide by zero."), and shows the method where the exception occurred—in `MilesPerGallon.Main()`.

» NOTE The `DivideByZeroException` object was generated automatically by C#. It is an instance of the `DivideByZeroException` class that has four ancestors. It is a child of the `ArithmeticException` class, which descends from the `SystemException` class. The `SystemException` class derives from the `Exception` class, which is a child of the `Object` class.

Just because an exception occurs and an `Exception` object is created, you don't necessarily have to deal with it. In the `MilesPerGallon` class, you simply let the offending program terminate; that's why the error message in Figure 9-2 indicates that the `Exception` is "Unhandled." However, the termination of the program is abrupt and unforgiving. When a program divides two numbers, or even performs a more trivial task like playing a game, the user might be annoyed if the program ends abruptly. If the program is used for air-traffic control or to monitor a patient's vital statistics during surgery, an abrupt conclusion could be disastrous. Object-oriented error-handling techniques provide more elegant solutions than simply shutting down.

» NOTE Programs that can handle exceptions appropriately are said to be more fault tolerant and robust than those that do not. **Fault-tolerant** applications are designed so that they continue to operate, possibly at a reduced level, when some part of the system fails. **Robustness** represents the degree to which a system is resilient to stress, maintaining correct functioning.

»NOTE With exception handling, a program can continue after dealing with a problem. This is especially important in mission-critical applications. The term **mission critical** refers to any process that is crucial to an organization.

»TWO TRUTHS AND A LIE: PURPOSELY GENERATING A `SystemException`

1. You can deliberately generate a `SystemException` by forcing a program to contain an error.
2. A program might automatically generate a `System.DivideByZeroException`.
3. In C#, when an exception occurs and an `Exception` object is created, you must employ a specific set of exception-handling techniques in order to manage the problem.

The false answer is #3. Just because an exception occurs and an `Exception` object is created, you don't necessarily have to deal with it.

UNDERSTANDING TRADITIONAL ERROR-HANDLING METHODS

Programmers had to deal with error conditions long before object-oriented methods were conceived. For example, dividing by zero is an avoidable error for which programmers always have had to plan. If you simply check a variable's value with an `if` statement before attempting to divide it into another number, you can prevent the creation of an `Exception` object. For example, the following code uses a traditional, non-object-oriented method to check a variable to prevent division by zero:

```
if(gallonsOfGas != 0)
   mpg = milesDriven / gallonsOfGas;
else
   mpg = 0;
```

This code successfully prevents division by zero, but it does not really "handle an exception" because no `Exception` class object is created. The example code illustrates a perfectly legal and reasonable method of preventing division by zero, and it represents the most efficient method of handling the error if you think it will be a frequent problem. Because a program that contains this code does not have to instantiate an `Exception` object every time the user enters a 0 for the value of `gallonsOfGas`, the program saves time and computer memory. (Programmers say this program has little "overhead.") On the other hand, if you think dividing by zero will be infrequent—that is, the *exception* to the rule—then the decision will execute many times when it is not needed. In other words, if a user enters 0 for `gallonsOfGas` in only one case out of 1000, then the `if` statement is executed unnecessarily 999 times. In that case, it is more efficient to eliminate the `if` test and instantiate an `Exception` object when needed.

»NOTE The creators of C# define "infrequent" as an event that happens less than 30 percent of the time. That is, if you think an error will occur in less than 30 percent of all program executions, create an `Exception`; if you think the error will occur more often, use traditional error checking. Of course, your boss or instructor might prefer a different percentage.

»NOTE Exception handling is critical in operations that are prone to failure. For example, when you attempt to connect to a remote server, the connection might be down.

»TWO TRUTHS AND A LIE: UNDERSTANDING TRADITIONAL ERROR-HANDLING METHODS

1. Before object-oriented methods were conceived, programmers had no way of handling unexpected conditions.
2. A program that handles potential errors by using `if` statements often saves time and computer memory over one that uses exception-handling methods.
3. Exception handling is most appropriate when an error is expected to occur infrequently.

The false statement is #1. Programmers had to deal with error conditions long before object-oriented methods were conceived.

UNDERSTANDING OBJECT-ORIENTED EXCEPTION-HANDLING METHODS

In object-oriented terminology, you "try" a procedure that may not complete correctly. A method that detects an error condition or `Exception` "throws" an `Exception`, and the block of code that processes the error "catches" the `Exception`.

When you write a block of code in which something can go wrong, you can place the code in a **`try` block,** which consists of the following elements:

» The keyword `try`
» A pair of curly braces containing statements that might cause `Exceptions`

You must code at least one `catch` block or `finally` block immediately following a `try` block. (You will learn about `finally` blocks later in this chapter.) Each **`catch` block** can "catch" one type of `Exception`. You create a `catch` block by typing the following elements:

» The keyword `catch`
» Parentheses containing an `Exception` type, and optionally, a name for an instance of the `Exception` type
» A pair of curly braces containing statements that deal with the error condition

Figure 9-3 shows the general format of a `try...catch` pair. The placeholder `XxxException` represents the `Exception` class or any of its more specific subclasses. If an `Exception` occurs during the execution of the `try` block, then the statements in the `catch` block will execute. If no `Exception` occurs within the `try` block, then the `catch` block will not execute. Either way, the statements following the `catch` block execute normally.

```
try
{
    // Statements including some that might cause an Exception
}
catch(XxxException anExceptionInstance)
{
    // Do something about it
}
// Statements here execute whether there was an Exception or not
```

Figure 9-3 General form of a `try...catch` pair

NOTE As `XxxException` implies, `Exception` classes typically are created using `Exception` as the second half of the name, as in `SystemException` and `ApplicationException`. The compiler does not require this naming convention, but the convention does make `Exception` descendants easier to identify.

Any one of the statements you place within the `try` block in Figure 9-3 might throw an `Exception`. If one is thrown, it goes to the `catch` block, in which its local identifier is `anExceptionInstance`. A `catch` block looks a lot like a method named `catch()`, which takes an argument that is an instance of `XxxException`. However, it is not a method; it has no return type and you can't call it directly.

NOTE Some programmers refer to a `catch` block as a `catch` *clause.*

For example, Figure 9-4 contains a program in which the statements that prompt for, accept, and use `gallonsOfGas` are encased in a `try` block. Figure 9-5 shows two executions of the program. In the first execution, a usable value is entered for `gallonsOfGas` and the program operates normally, bypassing the `catch` block. In the second execution, however, the user enters 0 for `gallonsOfGas`. When division is attempted, an `Exception` object is automatically created and thrown. The `catch` block catches it, where it becomes known as `e`. The statements in the `catch` block set `mpg` to 0 and display a message. Whether the `catch` block executes or not, the final `WriteLine()` statement that follows the `catch` block's closing curly brace executes.

NOTE When you compile the program in Figure 9-4, you receive a warning that `e` is declared but never used. You can declare a variable to hold the thrown `Exception`, but you do not want to use it in this example, so you can safely ignore the warning. If you do not want to use the caught `Exception` object within a `catch` block, then you do not have to provide an instance name for it. For example, in Figure 9-4, the `catch` clause could begin as follows:

```
catch(Exception)
```

In later examples in this chapter, the `Exception` object will be used to provide information. In those cases, it is required to have an identifier.

```
using System;
public class MilesPerGallon2
{
   public static void Main()
   {
      int milesDriven;
      int gallonsOfGas;
      int mpg;
      try
      {
         Console.Write("Enter miles driven ");
         milesDriven = Convert.ToInt32(Console.ReadLine());
         Console.Write("Enter gallons of gas purchased ");
         gallonsOfGas = Convert.ToInt32(Console.ReadLine());
         mpg = milesDriven / gallonsOfGas;
      }
      catch(Exception e)
      {
         mpg = 0;
         Console.WriteLine("You attempted to divide by zero!");
      }
      Console.WriteLine("You got {0} miles per gallon", mpg);
   }
}
```

Figure 9-4 `MilesPerGallon2` program

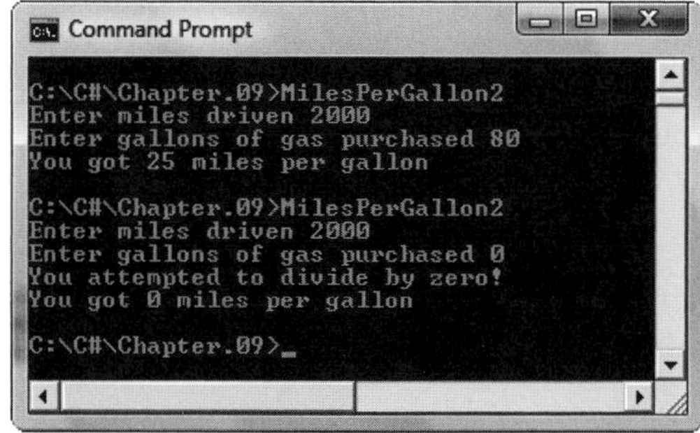

Figure 9-5 Two executions of `MilesPerGallon2` program

In the `MilesPerGallon2` program, you could catch a more specific `DivideByZeroException` object instead of catching an `Exception` object. You will employ this technique later in the chapter. If you are working on a professional project, Microsoft recommends that you never use the general `Exception` class in a `catch` block.

»NOTE In the application in Figure 9-4, the source of the exception and the `catch` block reside in the same method. Later in this chapter, you will learn that exceptions and their corresponding `catch` blocks frequently reside in separate methods.

»TWO TRUTHS AND A LIE: UNDERSTANDING OBJECT-ORIENTED EXCEPTION-HANDLING METHODS

1. Using object-oriented techniques, when you write a block of code in which something can go wrong, you can place the code in a `try` block.
2. If an `Exception` occurs within a `try` block, then the `catch` block that follows it will not execute.
3. If a `catch` block executes, then an `Exception` must have been thrown.

The false statement is #2. If an `Exception` occurs within a `try` block, then the `catch` block that follows it executes. If no `Exception` occurs within a `try` block, then the `catch` block that follows it will not execute.

USING THE `Exception` CLASS'S `ToString()` METHOD AND `Message` PROPERTY

When the `MilesPerGallon2` program prints the error message ("You attempted to divide by zero!"), you actually cannot confirm from the message that division by zero was the source of the error. In reality, any `Exception` generated from within the `try` block in the program would be caught by the `catch` block in the method because the argument in the `catch` block is an `Exception`.

Instead of writing your own message, you can use the `ToString()` method that every `Exception` inherits from the `Object` class. The `Exception` class overrides `ToString()` to provide a descriptive error message so a user can receive precise information about the nature of any `Exception` that is thrown. For example, Figure 9-6 shows a `MilesPerGallon3` program. The only changes from the `MilesPerGallon2` program are shaded: the name of the class and the message that is displayed when an `Exception` is thrown. In this example, the `ToString()` method is used with the caught `Exception e`. Figure 9-7 shows an execution of the program in which the user enters 0 for `gallonsOfGas`.

»NOTE You learned about overriding the `Object` class `ToString()` method in Chapter 8.

The error message displayed in Figure 9-7 ("System.DivideByZeroException: Attempted to divide by zero.") is the same message that appeared in Figure 9-2 when you provided no exception handling. Therefore, you can assume that the operating system uses the same `ToString()` method you can use when displaying information about an `Exception`. In the program in which you provided no exception handling, execution simply stopped; in this one, execution continues and the final output statement is displayed whether the user's input was usable or not. Programmers would say this second version ended more "elegantly."

```
using System;
public class MilesPerGallon3
{
   public static void Main()
   {
      int milesDriven;
      int gallonsOfGas;
      int mpg;
      try
      {
         Console.Write("Enter miles driven ");
         milesDriven = Convert.ToInt32(Console.ReadLine());
         Console.Write("Enter gallons of gas purchased ");
         gallonsOfGas = Convert.ToInt32(Console.ReadLine());
         mpg = milesDriven / gallonsOfGas;
      }
      catch(Exception e)
      {
         mpg = 0;
         Console.WriteLine(e.ToString());
      }
      Console.WriteLine("You got {0} miles per gallon", mpg);
   }
}
```

Figure 9-6 `MilesPerGallon3` program

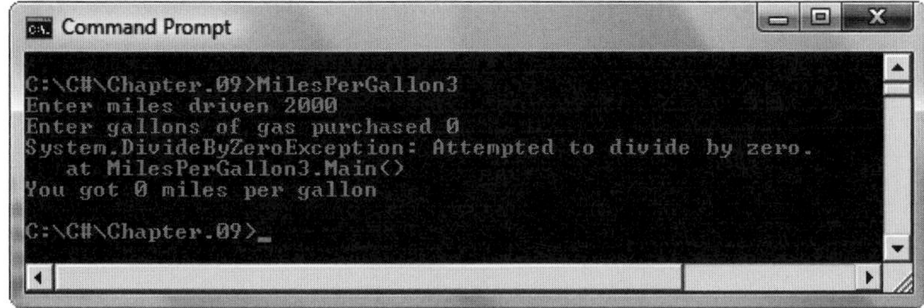

Figure 9-7 Execution of `MilesPerGallon3` program

The `Exception` class also contains a property named `Message` that contains useful information about an `Exception`. For example, the program in Figure 9-8 contains just two shaded changes from the `MilesPerGallon3` program: the class name and the use of the `Message` property in the statement that displays the error message in the `catch` block. The program produces the output shown in Figure 9-9. The value of `e.Message` is a `string` that is identical to the second part of the value returned by the `ToString()` method. You can guess that the `DivideByZeroException` class's `ToString()` method used in `MilesPerGallon3` constructs its string from two parts: the return value of the `getType()` method (that indicates the name of the class) and the return value from the `Message` property.

```
using System;
public class MilesPerGallon4
{
   public static void Main()
   {
      int milesDriven;
      int gallonsOfGas;
      int mpg;
      try
      {
         Console.Write("Enter miles driven ");
         milesDriven = Convert.ToInt32(Console.ReadLine());
         Console.Write("Enter gallons of gas purchased ");
         gallonsOfGas = Convert.ToInt32(Console.ReadLine());
         mpg = milesDriven / gallonsOfGas;
      }
      catch(Exception e)
      {
         mpg = 0;
         Console.WriteLine(e.Message);
      }
      Console.WriteLine("You got {0} miles per gallon", mpg);
   }
}
```

Figure 9-8 `MilesPerGallon4` program

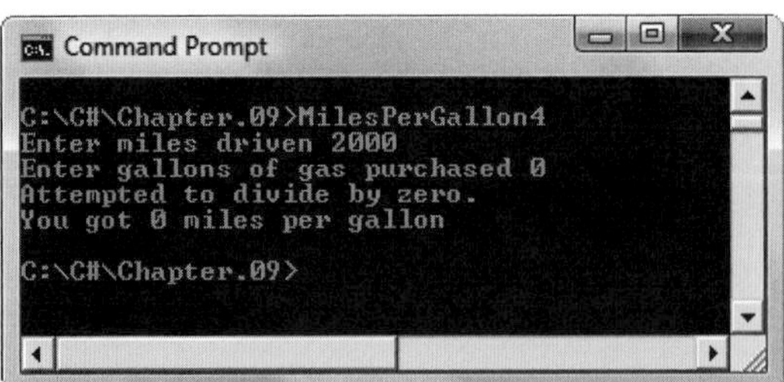

Figure 9-9 Execution of `MilesPerGallon4` program

»TWO TRUTHS AND A LIE: USING THE `Exception` CLASS'S `ToString()` METHOD AND `Message` PROPERTY

1. Any `Exception` generated from within a `try` block in a program will be caught by a `catch` block that has an `Exception` type argument.
2. The `Exception` class overrides the `Object` class `Description()` method to provide a descriptive error message so a user can receive precise information about the nature of any `Exception` that is thrown.
3. The `Exception` class contains a property named `Message` that contains useful information about an `Exception`.

The false statement is #2. The `Exception` class overrides the `Object` class `ToString()` method to provide a descriptive error message so a user can receive precise information about the nature of any `Exception` that is thrown.

CATCHING MULTIPLE `Exception`S

You can place as many statements as you need within a `try` block, and you can catch as many different `Exceptions` as you want. If you `try` more than one statement, only the first error-generating statement throws an `Exception`. As soon as the `Exception` occurs, the logic transfers to the `catch` block, which leaves the rest of the statements in the `try` block unexecuted.

When multiple `catch` blocks are present, they are examined in sequence until a match is found for the `Exception` that occurred. The matching `catch` block then executes, and each remaining `catch` block is bypassed.

For example, consider the program in Figure 9-10. The `Main()` method in the `TwoErrors` class potentially throws two types of `Exceptions`—a `DivideByZeroException` and an `IndexOutOfRangeException`. (An `IndexOutOfRangeException` occurs when an array subscript is not within the allowed range. In the `TwoErrors` program, the array has only three elements, but 13 is used as a subscript.)

The `TwoErrors` class declares three integers and an integer array with three elements. In the `Main()` method, the `try` block executes, and at the first statement within the `try` block, an `Exception` occurs because the `denom` in the division problem is zero. The `try` block is abandoned, and control transfers to the first `catch` block. Division by zero causes a `DivideByZeroException`, and because the first `catch` block receives that type of `Exception`, the message "In first catch block" appears along with the `Message` value of the `Exception`. In this example, the second `try` statement is never attempted, and the second `catch` block is skipped. Figure 9-11 shows the output.

If you reverse the two statements within the `try` block in the `TwoErrors` program, the process changes. If you use the following `try` block, the division by zero does not take place because the invalid array access throws an `Exception` first:

```
try
{
   result = array[num]; // New first try
   result = num / denom; // Old first try
}
```

```
using System;
public class TwoErrors
{
   public static void Main()
   {
      int num = 13, denom = 0, result;
      int[] array = {22, 33, 44};
      try
      {
         result = num / denom; // First try
         result = array[num]; // Second try
      }
      catch(DivideByZeroException error)
      {
         Console.WriteLine("In first catch block: ");
         Console.WriteLine(error.Message);
      }
      catch(IndexOutOfRangeException error)
      {
         Console.WriteLine("In second catch block: ");
         Console.WriteLine(error.Message);
      }
   }
}
```

Figure 9-10 `TwoErrors` program with two `catch` blocks

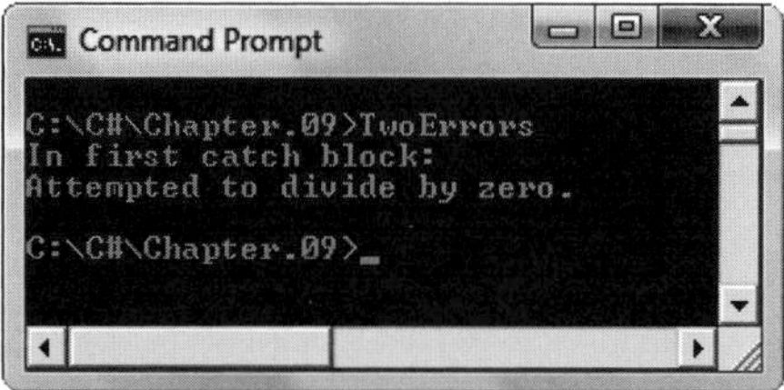

Figure 9-11 Output of `TwoErrors` program

The new first statement within the `try` block attempts to access element 13 of a three-element array, so it throws an `IndexOutOfRangeException`. The `try` block is abandoned, and the first `catch` block is examined and found unsuitable because the `Exception` is of the wrong type—it is not a `DivideByZeroException` object. The program logic proceeds to the second `catch` block, whose `IndexOutOfRangeException` argument type is a match for the thrown `Exception`. The message "In second catch block" and the `Exception`'s `Message` value are therefore displayed. Figure 9-12 shows the output.

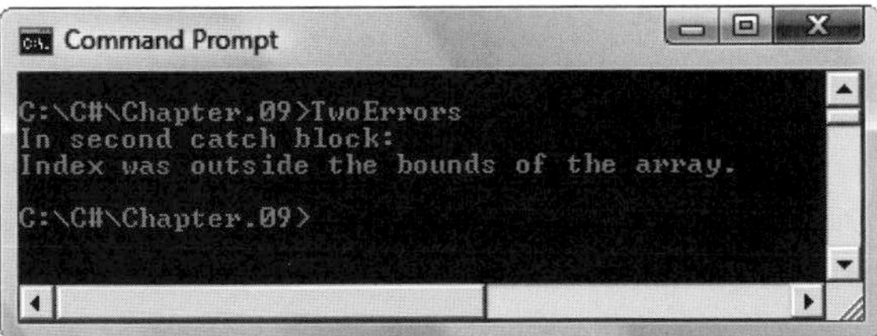

Figure 9-12 Output of `TwoErrors` program when the positions of the statements in the `try` block are reversed

Sometimes you want to execute the same code, no matter which `Exception` type occurs. For example, in the `TwoErrors` program in Figure 9-10, each of the two `catch` blocks prints a unique message. Instead, you might want both the `DivideByZeroException catch` block and the `IndexOutOfRangeException catch` block to simply use the thrown `Exception`'s `Message` field. Because both `DivideByZeroException`s and `IndexOutOfRangeException`s are subclasses of `Exception`, you can rewrite the `TwoErrors` class as shown in Figure 9-13 and include only one `Exception catch` block that catches any type of `Exception`.

```
using System;
public class TwoErrors2
{
   public static void Main()
   {
      int num = 13, denom = 0, result;
      int[] array = {22, 33, 44};
      try
      {
         result = num / denom; // First try
         result = array[num]; // Second try
      }
      catch(Exception error)
      {
         Console.WriteLine(error.Message);
      }
   }
}
```

Figure 9-13 `TwoErrors2` class with one `catch` block

NOTE As an alternative to using a single `catch` block for multiple `Exception` types that require the same action, as in Figure 9-13, you could create the class to have separate `catch` blocks, each of which calls the same method that contains the action.

The catch block in Figure 9-13 accepts a more generic Exception type than either of the potentially error-causing try statements throw, so the generic catch block can act as a "catch-all" block. That is, when either a division arithmetic error or an array error occurs, the thrown error is "promoted" to an Exception error in the catch block. Through inheritance, DivideByZeroExceptions and IndexOutOfRangeExceptions are Exceptions.

»NOTE As stated earlier, Microsoft recommends that a catch block should not handle general Exceptions. They say that if you cannot predict all possible causes of an exception and ensure that malicious code cannot exploit the resulting application state, you should allow the application to terminate instead of handling the exception.

Although a block of code can throw any number of Exception types, many developers believe that it is poor style for a block or method to throw more than three or four types. If it does, one of the following conditions might be true:

- Perhaps the code block or method is trying to accomplish too many diverse tasks and should be broken up into smaller blocks or methods.
- Perhaps the Exception types thrown are too specific and should be generalized, as they are in the TwoErrors2 program in Figure 9-13. As another example, both DivideByZeroExceptions and OverflowExceptions (which occur in some situations when an arithmetic answer is too large) are children of the ArithmeticException class (which, in turn, is a child of the Exception class). If a method throws both subclass Exception types, and you want (for example) to set a result to 0 in either case, then catching one superclass Exception type is sufficient and clearer.

When you list multiple catch blocks following a try block, you must be careful that some catch blocks don't become unreachable. **Unreachable** blocks contain statements that can never execute under any circumstances because the program logic "can't get there." For example, if successive catch blocks catch a DivideByZeroException and an "ordinary" Exception, then DivideByZeroException errors will cause the first catch to execute and other Exceptions will "fall through" to the more general Exception catch. However, if you reverse the sequence of the catch blocks (so the catch block that catches the more general Exception objects comes first), then you indicate that even DivideByZeroExceptions should be caught by the Exception catch. The DivideByZeroException catch block is unreachable because the more general Exception catch block is in its way, and therefore the class will not compile. Figure 9-14 shows a program in which the second catch block is not reachable, and Figure 9-15 shows the error message generated when you try to compile this program.

»NOTE Programmers also call unreachable code **dead code.**

```
using System;
public class UnreachableCatch
{
   public static void Main()
   {
      int num = 13, denom = 0, result;
      try
      {
         result = num / denom;
      }
      catch(Exception error)
      {
         Console.WriteLine(error.Message);
      }
      catch(DivideByZeroException error)
      {
         Console.WriteLine(error.Message);
      }
   }
}
```

Figure 9-14 Program with unreachable `catch` block

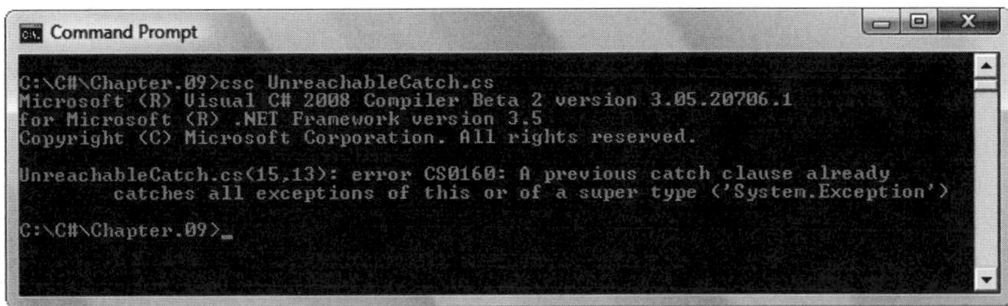

Figure 9-15 Compiler message generated by `UnreachableCatch` program

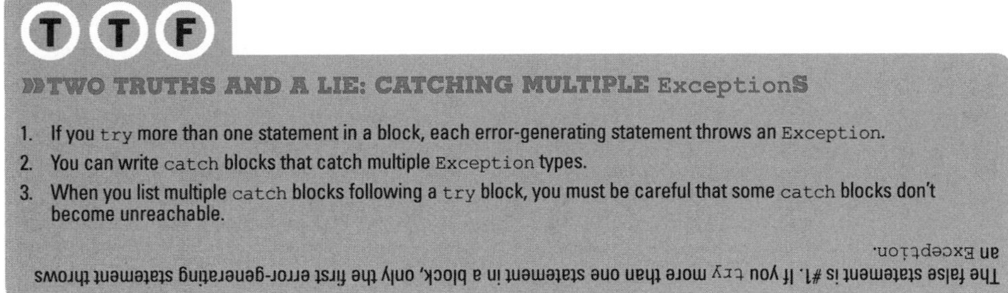

»TWO TRUTHS AND A LIE: CATCHING MULTIPLE Exceptions

1. If you `try` more than one statement in a block, each error-generating statement throws an `Exception`.
2. You can write `catch` blocks that catch multiple `Exception` types.
3. When you list multiple `catch` blocks following a `try` block, you must be careful that some `catch` blocks don't become unreachable.

The false statement is #1. If you `try` more than one statement in a block, only the first error-generating statement throws an `Exception`.

USING THE finally BLOCK

When you have actions to perform at the end of a try...catch sequence, you can use a **finally block**, which executes whether the try block identifies any Exceptions or not. Typically, you use the finally block to perform clean-up tasks that must occur, regardless of whether any errors occurred or were caught. Figure 9-16 shows the format of a try...catch sequence that uses a finally block.

```
try
{
   // Statements that might cause an Exception
}
catch(SomeException anExceptionInstance)
{
   // What to do about it
}
finally
{
   // Statements here execute
   // whether an Exception occurred or not
}
```

Figure 9-16 General form of a try...catch block with a finally block

At first glance, it seems as though the finally block serves no purpose. When a try block works without error, control passes to the statements that come after the catch block. Additionally, if the try code fails and throws an Exception that is caught, then the catch block executes, and control again passes to any statements that are coded after the catch block. Therefore, it seems as though the statements after the catch block always execute, so there is no need to place any statement within a special finally block. However, the last set of statements after the catch might never execute for at least two reasons:

- An Exception for which you did not plan might occur.
- The try or catch block might contain a statement that quits the application.

NOTE You can quit an application with a statement such as Environment.Exit(0);. The Environment.Exit() method is part of the System namespace. It terminates a program and passes the argument (which can be any integer) to the operating system. You also might exit a catch block with a break statement or a return statement. You encountered break statements when you learned about the switch statement in Chapter 3. You learned about return statements and how they return values from methods in Chapter 6.

The possibility exists that your try block might throw an Exception for which you did not provide a catch. After all, Exceptions occur all the time without your handling them, as you saw in the first MilesPerGallon program at the beginning of this chapter. In case of an unhandled Exception, program execution stops immediately, sending the error to the operating system for handling and abandoning the current method. Likewise, if the `try` block contains an exit statement, execution stops immediately. When you include a `finally` block, you are assured that its enclosed statements will execute before the program is abandoned, even if the method concludes prematurely.

For example, the `finally` block is used frequently with file input and output to ensure that open files are closed. You will learn more about writing to and reading from data files in Chapter 13. For now, however, consider the format shown in Figure 9-17, which represents part of the logic for a typical file-handling program. The `catch` block was written to catch an `IOException`, which is the type of exception automatically generated if there is a problem opening a file, reading data from a file, or writing to a file.

```
try
{
   // Open the file
   // Read the file
   // Place the file data in an array
   // Calculate an average from the data
   // Display the average
}
catch(IOException e)
{
   // Issue an error message
   // Exit
}
finally
{
   // If the file is open, close it
}
```

Figure 9-17 Pseudocode that tries reading a file and handles an `Exception`

The pseudocode in Figure 9-17 handles any file problems. However, because the application uses an array (see the statement "Place the file data in an array"), an uncaught `Exception` could occur when using the array or performing the division, even though the file opened successfully. In such an event, you would want to close the file before proceeding. By using the `finally` block, you ensure that the file is closed, because the code in the `finally` block executes before the uncaught exception returns control to the operating system. The code in the `finally` block executes no matter which of the following outcomes of the `try` block occurs:

- The `try` ends normally.
- The `catch` executes.
- The `try` ends abnormally and the `catch` does not execute. For example, an `Exception` might cause the method to abandon prematurely—perhaps the array is not large enough to hold the data, or calculating the average results in division by 0. These `Exceptions` do not allow the `try` block to finish, nor do they cause the `catch` block to execute.

NOTE If an application might throw several types of exceptions, you can try some code, catch the possible exception, try some more code, catch the possible exception, and so on. Usually, however, the superior approach is to try all the statements that might throw exceptions, then include all the needed `catch` blocks and an optional `finally` block. This is the approach shown in Figure 9-17, and it usually results in logic that is easier to follow.

You often can avoid using a `finally` block, but you would need repetitious code. For example, instead of using the `finally` block in the pseudocode in Figure 9-17, you could insert the statement "If the file is open, close it" as both the last statement in the `try` block and the second-to-last statement in the `catch` block, just before the program exits. However, writing code just once in a `finally` block is clearer and less prone to error.

NOTE Java and C++ provide `try` and `catch` blocks. Java also provides a `finally` block, but C++ does not.

NOTE Many well-designed programs that try code do not include any `catch` blocks; instead, they contain only `try-finally` pairs. The `finally` block is used to release resources that other applications might be waiting for, such as database connections.

TWO TRUTHS AND A LIE: USING THE `finally` BLOCK

1. When a `finally` block follows a `try` block, it executes whether the `try` block identifies any `Exception`s or not.
2. Typically, you use a `finally` block to perform clean-up tasks that must occur after an `Exception` has been thrown and caught.
3. Statements that follow a `try-catch` pair might never execute because an unplanned `Exception` might occur, or the `try` or `catch` block might contain a statement that quits the application.

The false statement is #2. Typically, you use a `finally` block to perform clean-up tasks that must occur, regardless of whether any errors occurred or were caught.

HANDLING AN `Exception` WITH A LOOP

Different programs require different ways of handling `Exception`s. In some programs you write, you simply want to display an error message when an `Exception` occurs. In others, you want to remedy the situation the same way every time, such as setting a result to 0. In yet others, you want to keep trying the offending code until it is correct. In these cases, you can place a `try...catch` block within a loop that continues to execute until the code is successful.

As an example, consider the `HandlingAFormatException` program in Figure 9-18. This program asks a user to input an integer value that will be used as a sports team player's number. A Boolean variable named `isGoodNumber` is initialized to `false`; this variable controls the data entry loop that will continue to execute until the variable's value becomes `true`.

```
using System;
public class HandlingAFormatException
{
   public static void Main()
   {
      int playerNumber = 0;
      string strNumber;
      bool isGoodNumber = false;
      while(!isGoodNumber)
      {
         try
         {
            Console.Write("Enter player's number ");
            strNumber = Console.ReadLine();
            playerNumber = Convert.ToInt32(strNumber);
            isGoodNumber = true;
         }
         catch(FormatException fe)
         {
            Console.WriteLine(fe.Message +
               " Player's number should be an integer.");
         }
      }
      Console.WriteLine("Player's number is " + playerNumber);
   }
}
```

Figure 9-18 `HandlingAFormatException` program

Within the `try` block in Figure 9-18, a `string` value is read from the keyboard and then converted to an integer. However, when users enter values from the keyboard, they don't always enter the correct value types. For example, instead of an integer, a user might enter a floating-point number or a non-numeric character. Any keyboard data will successfully be accepted into a string, but only strings containing all digits (or a + or - sign) will successfully be converted to integers. If the user enters a noninteger, the `Convert.ToInt32()` method throws a `FormatException` and execution continues with the `catch` block at the bottom of the loop. The program "gets past" the `Convert.ToInt32()` method only when the user enters an integer and the `ToInt32()` method is successful. Only then will `isGoodNumber` change to `true`, ending the loop when the `while` statement executes. Figure 9-19 shows a typical execution of the program in which the user enters invalid data twice before "getting it right." Trying and catching the `Exception` in a loop ensures that the input data will be the correct type before the program proceeds.

```
Command Prompt

C:\C#\Chapter.09>HandlingAFormatException
Enter player's number 7.3
Input string was not in a correct format. Player's number should be an integer.
Enter player's number seven
Input string was not in a correct format. Player's number should be an integer.
Enter player's number 7
Player's number is 7

C:\C#\Chapter.09>_
```

Figure 9-19 Typical execution of `HandlingAFormatException` program

NOTE In the `HandlingAFormatException` program, the `Convert.ToInt32()` method fails when a floating-point value is entered. If you use the `Convert.ToDouble()` method, it would not throw an `Exception` if you attempted to convert an integer, because an integer can be automatically promoted to a `double`.

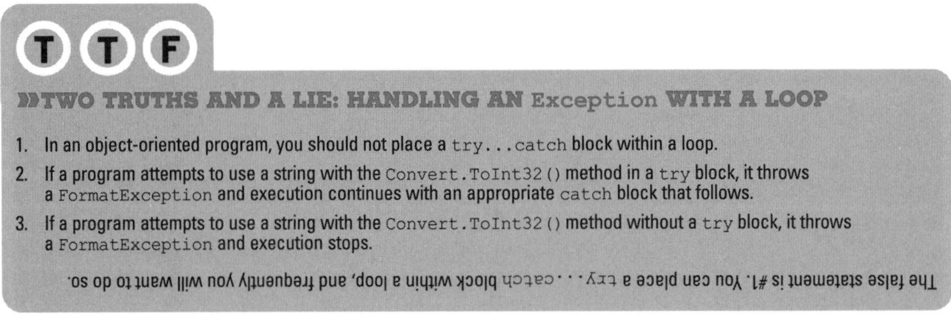

TWO TRUTHS AND A LIE: HANDLING AN `Exception` WITH A LOOP

1. In an object-oriented program, you should not place a `try...catch` block within a loop.
2. If a program attempts to use a string with the `Convert.ToInt32()` method in a `try` block, it throws a `FormatException` and execution continues with an appropriate `catch` block that follows.
3. If a program attempts to use a string with the `Convert.ToInt32()` method without a `try` block, it throws a `FormatException` and execution stops.

The false statement is #1. You can place a `try...catch` block within a loop, and frequently you will want to do so.

THROWING `Exception`S BETWEEN METHODS

An advantage of using object-oriented exception-handling techniques is the ability to deal with `Exceptions` appropriately as you decide how to handle them. When methods from other classes throw `Exceptions`, they don't have to catch them; instead, your calling program can catch them, and you can decide what to do. For example, in the `HandlingAFormatException` program in Figure 9-18, the Convert.ToInt32() method threw an Exception when the user entered a noninteger value, but the Convert.ToInt32() method did not catch the Exception. Instead, the HandlingAFormatException program caught it and handled it by placing the catch in a loop, forcing the user to reenter a value. A different program might force the playerNumber to a default value, or it might display an error message and quit the program. This flexibility is an advantage when you need to create specific reactions to thrown Exceptions.

When a method you write throws an Exception, the same method can catch the Exception, although it is not required, and in most object-oriented programs, it does not. Often, you don't want a method to handle its own Exception. In many cases, you want the method to check for errors, but you do not want to require a method to handle an error if it finds one. An advantage to object-oriented exception handling is that you gain the ability to appropriately deal with Exceptions in each client program. Just as a police officer can deal with a speeding driver differently depending on circumstances, you can react to Exceptions specifically for your current purposes.

When you design classes containing methods that have statements that might throw Exceptions, you most frequently should create the methods so they throw the Exception, but not handle it. Handling an Exception should be left to the client—the program that uses your class—so the Exception can be handled in an appropriate way for the application.

For example, consider the very brief PriceList class in Figure 9-20. The class contains a list of prices and a single method that displays one price based on a parameter subscript value. Because the DisplayPrice() method uses an array, an IndexOutOfRangeException might be thrown. However, the DisplayPrice() method does not handle the potential Exception.

```
public class PriceList
{
   private static double[] price = {15.99, 27.88, 34.56, 45.89};
   public static void DisplayPrice(int item)
   {
      Console.WriteLine("The price is " +
         price[item].ToString("C"));
   }
}
```

Figure 9-20 The PriceList class

Figure 9-21 shows an application that uses the DisplayPrice() method. It calls the method in a try block and handles an IndexOutOfRangeException by displaying a price of $0. Figure 9-22 shows the output when a user enters an invalid item number.

```
using System;
public class PriceListApplication1
{
   public static void Main()
   {
      int item;
      try
      {
         Console.Write("Enter an item number from 0 through 3 ");
         item = Convert.ToInt32(Console.ReadLine());
         PriceList.DisplayPrice(item);
      }
      catch(IndexOutOfRangeException e)
      {
         Console.WriteLine(e.Message + " The price is $0");
      }
   }
}
```

Figure 9-21 The `PriceListApplication1` program

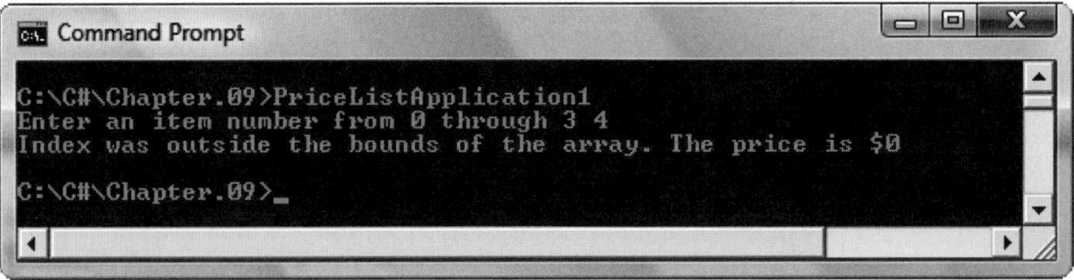

Figure 9-22 Output of `PriceListApplication1` program when user enters invalid item number

Figure 9-23 shows a different application that uses the same `PriceList` class, but handles the exception differently. In this case, the program author wanted the user to keep responding until a correct entry was made. Because the `DisplayPrice()` method in the `PriceList` class was written to throw an `Exception` but not handle it, the programmer of `PriceListApplication2` could handle the `Exception` in a totally different manner from the way it was handled in `PriceListApplication1`. Figure 9-24 shows a typical execution of this program.

```
using System;
public class PriceListApplication2
{
   public static void Main()
   {
      int item = 0;
      bool isGoodItem = false;
      while(!isGoodItem)
      {
         try
         {
            Console.Write("Enter an item number from " +
               "0 through 3 ");
            item = Convert.ToInt32(Console.ReadLine());
            PriceList.DisplayPrice(item);
            isGoodItem = true;
         }
         catch(IndexOutOfRangeException e)
         {
            Console.WriteLine("You must enter a number less " +
               "than 4");
            Console.WriteLine("Please reenter item number ");
         }
      }
      Console.WriteLine("Thank you");
   }
}
```

Figure 9-23 The `PriceListApplication2` program

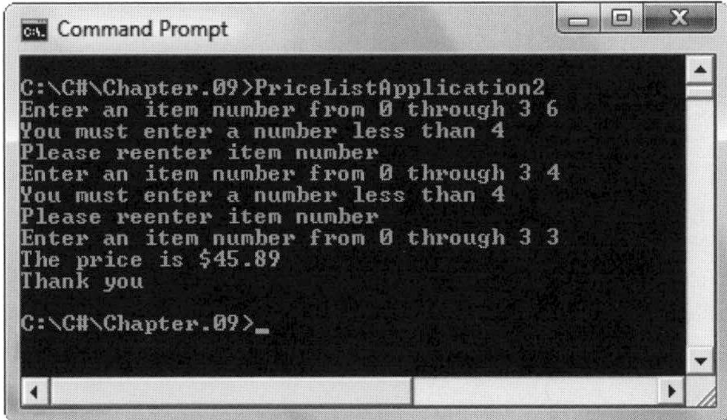

Figure 9-24 Output of `PriceListApplication2` program when user enters invalid item number several times

»TWO TRUTHS AND A LIE: THROWING `Exception`S BETWEEN METHODS

1. When methods from other classes throw `Exception`s, they don't have to catch them; instead, your calling program can catch them, and you can decide what to do.
2. Often, you don't want a method to handle its own `Exception`; in many cases, you want the method to check for errors, but you do not want to require a method to handle an error if it finds one.
3. When you design classes containing methods that have statements that might throw `Exception`s, you should make sure your class handles each `Exception` appropriately.

The false statement is #3. When you design classes containing methods that have statements that might throw `Exception`s, you most frequently should create the methods so they throw the `Exception`, but not handle it.

TRACING `Exception`S THROUGH THE CALL STACK

When one method calls another, the computer's operating system must keep track of where the method call came from, and program control must return to the calling method when the called method is complete. For example, if `MethodA()` calls `MethodB()`, the operating system has to "remember" to return to `MethodA()` when `MethodB()` ends. Similarly, if `MethodB()` calls `MethodC()`, then while `MethodC()` is executing, the computer needs to "remember" that it will return to `MethodB()` and eventually to `MethodA()`. The memory location where the computer stores the list of locations to which the system must return is known as the **call stack**.

If a method throws an `Exception` and the same method does not catch it, then the `Exception` is thrown to the next method "up" the call stack; in other words, it is thrown to the method that called the offending method. Consider this sequence of events:

1. `MethodA()` calls `MethodB()`.
2. `MethodB()` calls `MethodC()`.
3. `MethodC()` throws an `Exception`.
4. C# looks first for a `catch` block in `MethodC()`.
5. If none exists, then C# looks for the same thing in `MethodB()`.
6. If `MethodB()` does not have a `catch` block for the `Exception`, then C# looks to `MethodA()`.
7. If `MethodA()` doesn't catch the `Exception`, then the program terminates and the operating system displays an error message.

This system of passing `Exception`s through the chain of calling methods has great advantages because it allows your methods to handle `Exception`s more appropriately. However, a program that uses several classes has the disadvantage of making it very difficult for the programmer to locate the original source of an `Exception`.

You already have used the Message property to obtain information about an Exception. Another useful Exception property is the StackTrace property. When you catch an Exception, you can print the value of StackTrace to display a list of methods in the call stack so you can determine the location of the Exception.

The StackTrace property can be a useful debugging tool. When your program stops abruptly, it is helpful to discover in which method the Exception occurred. Often, you do not want to display a StackTrace property in a finished program; the typical end user has no interest in the cryptic messages that would be printed. However, while you are developing a program, using StackTrace can help you diagnose your program's problems.

A CASE STUDY: USING StackTrace

As an example of when StackTrace can be useful, consider the Tax class in Figure 9-25. Suppose your company has created or purchased this class to make it easy to calculate tax rates on products sold. For simplicity, assume that only two tax rates are in effect—6% for sales of $20 or less and 7% for sales over $20. The Tax class would be useful for any programmer who wrote a program involving product sales, except for one flaw: in the shaded statement, the subscript is erroneously set to 2 instead of 1 for the higher tax rate. If this subscript is used with the taxRate array in the next statement, it will be out of bounds.

```
public class Tax
{
   private static double[] taxRate = {0.06, 0.07};
   private static double CUTOFF = 20.00;
   public static double DetermineTaxRate(double price)
   {
      int subscript;
      double rate;
      if(price <= CUTOFF)
         subscript = 0;
      else
         subscript = 2;
      rate = taxRate[subscript];
      return rate;
   }
}
```

Figure 9-25 The Tax class

Assume your company has also created a revised PriceList class, as shown in Figure 9-26. This class is similar to the one in Figure 9-20, except that it includes a tax calculation in the shaded statement.

```
public class PriceList
{
   private static double[] price = {15.99, 27.88, 34.56, 45.89};
   public static void DisplayPrice(int item)
   {
      double tax;
      double total;
      double pr;
      pr = price[item];
      tax = pr * Tax.DetermineTaxRate(pr);
      total = pr + tax;
      Console.WriteLine("The total price is " +
         total.ToString("C"));
   }
}
```

Figure 9-26 `PriceList` class that includes call to the `Tax` class method `DetermineTaxRate()`

Suppose you write the application shown in Figure 9-27. Your application is similar to the price list applications earlier in this chapter, including a call to `PriceList.DisplayPrice()`. As in `PriceListApplication1` and `PriceListApplication2`, your new program tries the data entry and display statement and then catches an exception. When you run the program using what you know to be a good item number, as in Figure 9-28, you are surprised to see the shaded "Error!" message you have coded in the `catch` block. In the earlier examples that used `PriceList.DisplayPrice()`, using an item number 1 would have resulted in a successful program execution.

```
using System;
public class PriceListApplication3
{
   public static void Main()
   {
      int item;
      try
      {
         Console.Write("Enter an item number from 0 through 3 ");
         item = Convert.ToInt32(Console.ReadLine());
         PriceList.DisplayPrice(item);
      }
      catch(Exception e)
      {
         Console.WriteLine("Error!");
      }
   }
}
```

Figure 9-27 `PriceListApplication3` class

```
C:\C#\Chapter.09>PriceListApplication3
Enter an item number from 0 through 3 1
Error!

C:\C#\Chapter.09>_
```

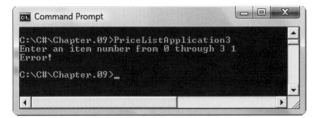

Figure 9-28 Execution of `PriceListApplication3` program when user enters 1 for item number

To attempt to discover what caused the "Error!" message, you can replace the statement that writes it as follows:

```
Console.WriteLine(e.Message);
```

However, when you execute the program with this modification, you receive the output in Figure 9-29, indicating that the index is out of the bounds of the array. You are puzzled because you know 1 is a valid item number for the price array, and it should not be considered out of bounds.

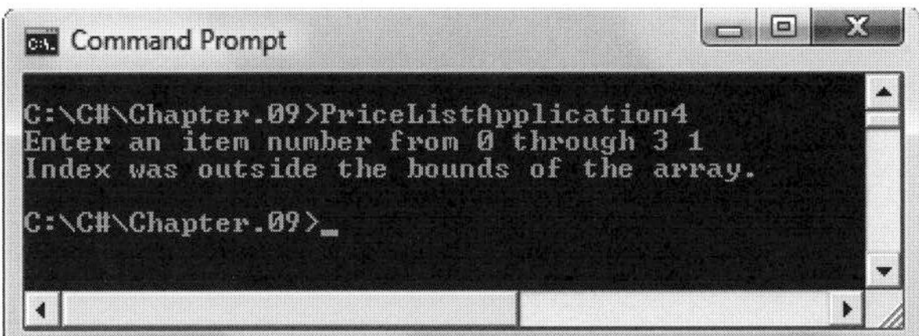

Figure 9-29 Execution of `PriceListApplication4` program in which `e.Message` is displayed in the `catch` block

Finally, you decide to replace the `catch` block statement with a `StackTrace` call, as follows:

```
Console.WriteLine(e.StackTrace);
```

The output is shown in Figure 9-30. You can see from the list of methods that the error in your application came from `PriceList.DisplayPrice()`, which in turn came from `Tax.DetermineTaxRate()`. You had not even considered that the `Tax` class could have been the source of the problem. If you work in a small organization, you can look at the code yourself and fix it. If you work in a larger organization or you purchased the class from an outside vendor, you can contact the programmer who created the class for assistance.

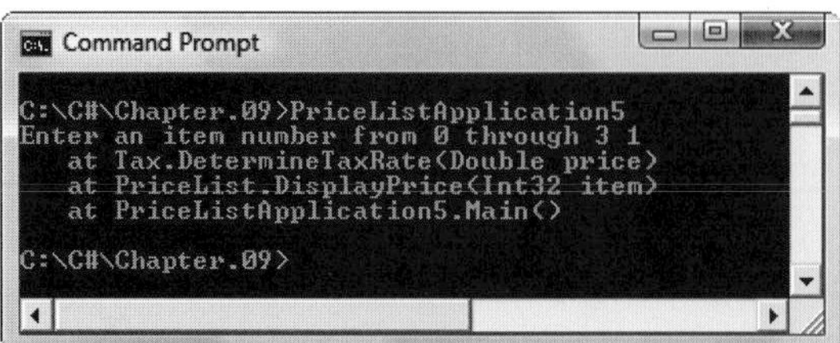

Figure 9-30 Execution of `PriceListApplication5` program in which `e.StackTrace` is displayed in the `catch` block

The classes in this example were small to help you easily follow the discussion. However, a full-blown application might have many more classes that contain many more methods, and so using `StackTrace` would become increasingly beneficial.

»NOTE You might find it useful to locate `StackTrace` calls strategically throughout a program while testing it and then remove them or comment them out when the program is complete.

»TWO TRUTHS AND A LIE: TRACING `Exception`S THROUGH THE CALL STACK

1. The memory location where the computer stores the list of locations to which the system must return after a series of method calls is known as the stack trace.
2. If a method throws an `Exception` and the same method does not catch it, then the `Exception` is thrown to the method that called the offending method.
3. When you catch an `Exception`, you can print the value of `StackTrace` to display a list of methods in the call stack so you can determine the location of the `Exception`.

The false statement is #1. The memory location where the computer stores the list of locations to which the system must return after a series of method calls is known as the call stack.

CREATING YOUR OWN `Exception` CLASSES

C# provides more than 100 categories of `Exception`s that you can throw in your programs. However, C#'s creators could not predict every condition that might be an `Exception` in the programs you write. For example, you might want to declare an `Exception` when your bank balance is negative or when an outside party attempts to access your e-mail account. Most organizations have specific rules for exceptional data, such as "an employee number must not exceed three digits" or "an hourly salary must not be less than the legal minimum wage." Of course, you can handle these potential error situations with `if` statements, but you also can create your own `Exception`s.

To create your own `Exception` that you can throw, you can extend the `ApplicationException` class, which is a subclass of `Exception`, or you can extend `Exception`. As you saw earlier in the chapter, Microsoft's advice on this matter has changed over time. Although you might see extensions of `ApplicationException` in classes written by others, the current advice is to simply derive your own classes from `Exception`. Either approach will produce workable programs.

Figure 9-31 shows a NegativeBalanceException class that extends Exception. This class passes an appropriate string message to its parent's constructor. If you create an Exception and display its Message property, you will see the message "Error in the application." When the NegativeBalanceException constructor passes the string "Bank balance is negative." to its parent's constructor, the Message property will hold this more descriptive message.

>> NOTE
The C# documentation recommends that you create all Exception messages to be grammatically correct, complete sentences ending in a period.

```
public class NegativeBalanceException : Exception
{
   private static string msg = "Bank balance is negative. ";
   public NegativeBalanceException() : base(msg)
   {
   }
}
```

Figure 9-31 The NegativeBalanceException class

When you create a BankAccount class like the one shown in Figure 9-32, you can create the Balance property set accessor to throw a NegativeBalanceException when a client attempts to set the balance to be negative.

```
public class BankAccount
{
   private int accountNum;
   private double balance;
   public int AccountNum {get; set;}
   public double Balance
   {
      get
      {
         return balance;
      }
      set
      {
         if(value < 0)
         {
            NegativeBalanceException nbe =
               new NegativeBalanceException();
            throw(nbe);
         }
         balance = value;
      }
   }
}
```

Figure 9-32 The BankAccount class

NOTE Instead of creating the `nbe` object in the `SetBalance()` method in Figure 9-32, you could code the following statement, which creates and throws an anonymous `NegativeBalanceException` in a single step:

```
throw(new NegativeBalanceException());
```

Figure 9-33 shows a program that attempts to set a `BankAccount` balance to a negative value in the shaded statement. When the `BankAccount` class's `SetBalance()` method throws the `NegativeBalanceException`, the `catch` block in the `TryBankAccount` program executes, displaying both the `NegativeBalanceException` `Message` and the value of `StackTrace`. Figure 9-34 shows the output.

```
using System;
public class TryBankAccount
{
   public static void Main()
   {
      BankAccount acct = new BankAccount();
      try
      {
         acct.AccountNum = 1234;
         acct.Balance = -1000;
      }
      catch(NegativeBalanceException e)
      {
         Console.WriteLine(e.Message);
         Console.WriteLine(e.StackTrace);
      }
   }
}
```

Figure 9-33 The `TryBankAccount` program

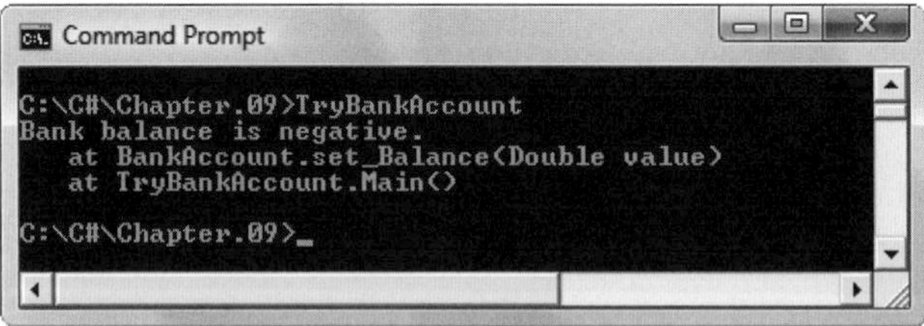

Figure 9-34 Output of `TryBankAccount` program

NOTE In Figure 9-34, notice that the `set` accessor for the `Balance` property is known internally as `set_Balance`. You can guess that the `set` accessor for the `AccountNum` property is known as `set_AccountNum`.

In C#, you can't throw an object unless it is an `Exception` or a descendant of the `Exception` class. In other words, you cannot throw a `double` or a `BankAccount`. However, you can throw any type of `Exception` at any time, not just `Exception`s of your own creation. For example, within any program you can code any of the following:

```
throw(new ApplicationException());
throw(new IndexOutOfRangeException());
throw(new Exception());
```

Of course, you should not throw an `IndexOutOfRangeException` when you encounter division by 0 or data of an incorrect type; you should use it only when an index (subscript) is too high or too low. However, if a built-in `Exception` type is appropriate and suits your needs, you should use it. You should not create an excessive number of special `Exception` types for your classes, especially if the C# development environment already contains an `Exception` that accurately describes the error. Extra `Exception` types add a level of complexity for other programmers who will use your classes. Nevertheless, when appropriate, creating a specialized `Exception` class is an elegant way for you to take care of error situations. They provide you with the capability of separating your error code from the usual, nonexceptional sequence of events. They also allow for errors to be passed up the stack and traced.

»NOTE The `StackTrace` begins at the point where an `Exception` is thrown, not where it is created. This consideration makes a difference when you create an `Exception` and throw it from two different methods.

»NOTE `Exception`s can be particularly useful when you throw them from constructors. Constructors do not have a return type, so they have no other way to send information back to the calling method.

»TWO TRUTHS AND A LIE: CREATING YOUR OWN `Exception` CLASSES

1. To create your own `Exception` that you can throw, you can extend the `ApplicationException` class or the `Exception` class.
2. In C#, you can throw any object you create if it is appropriate for the application.
3. You can throw any type of `Exception` at any time—both those that are already created as part of C# and those of your own creation.

The false statement is #2. In C#, you can't throw an object unless it is an `Exception` or a descendant of the `Exception` class.

RETHROWING AN `Exception`

When you write a method that catches an `Exception`, your method does not have to handle the `Exception`. Instead, you might choose to **rethrow the `Exception`** to the method that called your method. Then you can let the calling method handle the problem. Within a `catch` block, you can rethrow the `Exception` that was caught by using the keyword `throw` with no object after it. For example, Figure 9-35 shows a class that contains four methods. In this program, the following sequence of events takes place:

1. The `Main()` method calls `MethodA()`.
2. `MethodA()` calls `MethodB()`.
3. `MethodB()` calls `MethodC()`.

```
using System;
public class ReThrow
{
   public static void Main()
   {
      try
      {
         Console.WriteLine("Trying in Main() method");
         MethodA();
      }
      catch(Exception ae)
      {
         Console.Write("Caught in Main() method -- ");
         Console.WriteLine(ae.Message);
      }
      Console.WriteLine("Main() method is done");
   }
   public static void MethodA()
   {
      try
      {
         Console.WriteLine("Trying in method A");
         MethodB();
      }
      catch(Exception)
      {
         Console.WriteLine("Caught in method A");
         throw;
      }
   }
   public static void MethodB()
   {
      try
      {
         Console.WriteLine("Trying in method B");
         MethodC();
      }
      catch(Exception)
      {
         Console.WriteLine("Caught in method B");
         throw;
      }
   }
   public static void MethodC()
   {
      Console.WriteLine("In method C");
      throw(new Exception("This came from method C"));
   }
}
```

Figure 9-35 The `ReThrow` program

4. `MethodC()` throws an `Exception`.
5. When `MethodB()` catches the `Exception`, it does not handle the `Exception`; instead, it throws the `Exception` back to `MethodA()`.
6. `MethodA()` catches the `Exception`, but does not handle it either. Instead, `MethodA()` throws the `Exception` back to the `Main()` method.
7. The `Exception` is caught in the `Main()` method, where the message that was created in `MethodC()` is finally displayed.

Figure 9-36 shows the execution of the program.

>> **NOTE** If you name the `Exception` argument to the `catch` block in the preceding figure (for example, `catch(Exception e)`), then you should use that identifier in the `throw` statement at the end of the block (for example, `throw e;`).

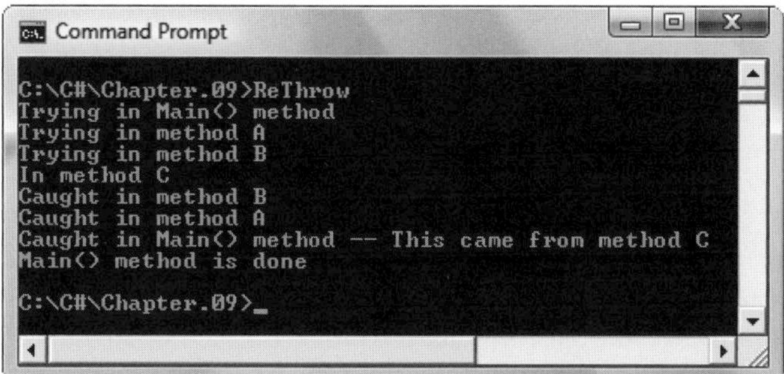

Figure 9-36 Execution of the `ReThrow` program

>> TWO TRUTHS AND A LIE: RETHROWING AN `Exception`

1. When you write a method that catches an `Exception`, your method must handle the `Exception`.
2. When a method catches an `Exception`, you can rethrow it to a method that called the method.
3. Within a `catch` block, you can rethrow a caught `Exception` by using the keyword `throw` with no object after it.

The false statement is #1. When you write a method that catches an `Exception`, your method does not have to handle the `Exception`.

YOU DO IT

PURPOSELY CAUSING ExceptionS

C# generates SystemExceptions automatically under many circumstances. In the next steps, you will purposely generate a SystemException by executing a program that provides multiple opportunities for Exceptions.

To create a program that purposely generates Exceptions:

1. Open a new file in your text editor and type the following program, which allows you to generate several different Exceptions.

```
using System;
public class ExceptionsOnPurpose
{
   public static void Main()
   {
      int answer;
      int result;
      int zero = 0;
      Console.Write("Enter an integer ");
      answer = Convert.ToInt32(Console.ReadLine());
      result = answer / zero;
      Console.WriteLine("The answer is " + answer);
   }
}
```

»NOTE You would never write a program that purposely divides by zero; you do so here to demonstrate C#'s Exception-generating capabilities.

2. The variable zero cannot be defined as a constant; if it is, the program will not compile. As a variable, the compiler "trusts" that a legitimate value will be provided for it before division occurs (although in this case, the trust was not warranted). Save the program as **ExceptionsOnPurpose.cs**. Compile the program.
3. Execute the program several times using different values and observe the results. Depending on your operating system, two windows might appear with each execution. The first says that Windows is collecting more information about the problem. This window is soon replaced with the one shown in Figure 9-37, which repeats that ExceptionsOnPurpose.exe has stopped working. If you were executing a professional application, you might be notified of a solution. Because you created this exception on purpose, just click the **Close program** button.

Figure 9-38 shows three executions of the program during which the user typed the following:

- **seven**—This generates a System.FormatException, which occurs when the program tries to convert the input value to an integer, because letters are not allowed in integers.
- **7.7**—This also generates a System.FormatException because the decimal point is not allowed in an integer.
- **7**—This does not generate a System.FormatException, but instead causes a System.DivideByZero exception when the result is calculated.

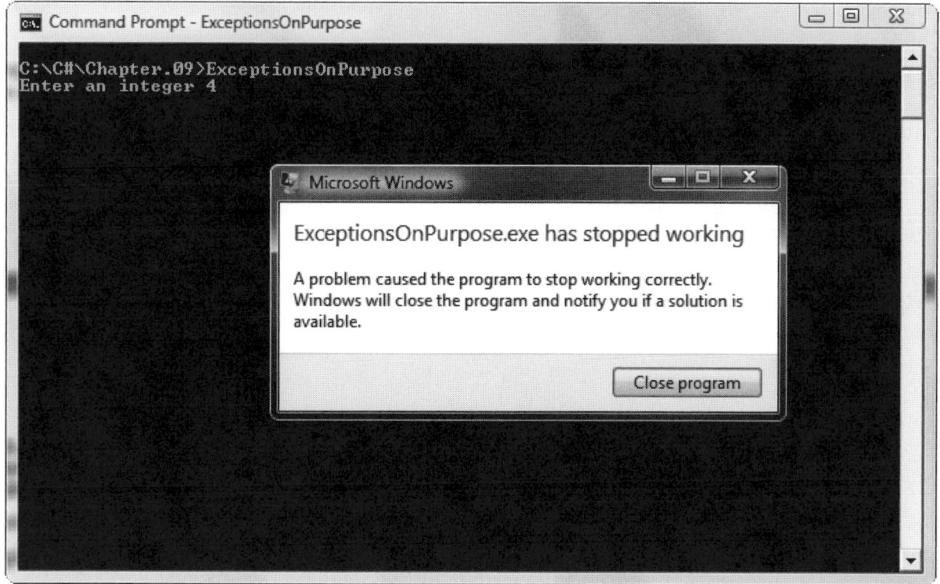

Figure 9-37 Error report window generated by an unhandled `Exception`

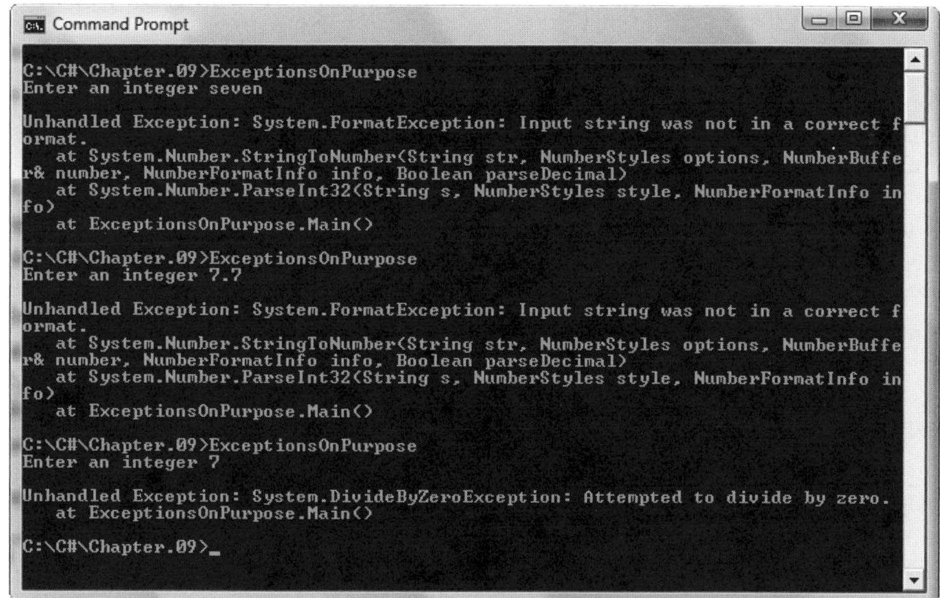

Figure 9-38 Error messages generated by successive executions of `ExceptionsOnPurpose` program

HANDLING ExceptionS

You can handle Exceptions by placing them in a try block and then catching any Exceptions that are thrown from it.

To add a try...catch block to your application:

1. Open the ExceptionsOnPurpose.cs file if it is not still open. Change the class name to **ExceptionsOnPurpose2** and immediately save the file as **ExceptionsOnPurpose2.cs**.

2. In the Main() method, after the three variable declarations, enclose the next three statements in a try block as follows:

```
try
{
    Console.Write("Enter an integer ");
    answer = Convert.ToInt32(Console.ReadLine());
    result = answer / zero;
}
```

3. Following the try block (but before the statement that displays the answer), add a catch block that catches any thrown Exception and displays its Message property.

```
catch(Exception e)
{
    Console.WriteLine(e.Message);
}
```

4. Save the program and compile it. You should receive a compiler error that indicates that answer is an unassigned local variable. This error occurs at the last line of the program where answer is displayed. In the first version of this program, no such message appeared. However, now that the assignment to answer is within the try block, the compiler understands that an Exception might be thrown before a valid value is assigned to answer. To eliminate this problem, initialize answer at its declaration.

```
int answer = 0;
```

5. Compile and execute the program again. Figure 9-39 shows three executions. The values typed by the user are the same as in Figure 9-38. However, the results are different in several significant ways:

   » No error message window appears (as in Figure 9-37).

   » The error messages displayed are cleaner and “friendlier” than the automatically generated versions in Figure 9-38.

   » The program ends normally in each case, with the answer value displayed in a user-friendly manner.

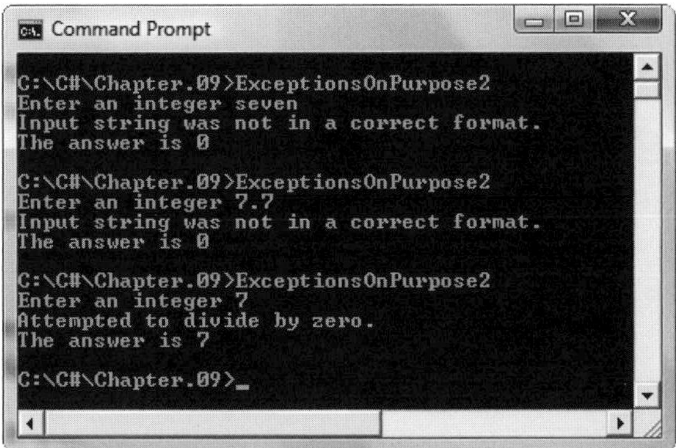

Figure 9-39 Error messages generated by successive executions of `ExceptionsOnPurpose2` program

CATCHING VARIOUS `Exception` TYPES

When you want appropriate actions to occur for various `Exception`s, you can provide multiple `catch` blocks.

To provide multiple `catch` blocks for the `ExceptionsOnPurpose` program:

1. Open the ExceptionsOnPurpose2.cs file if it is not still open. Change the class name to **`ExceptionsOnPurpose3`** and immediately save the file as **ExceptionsOnPurpose3.cs**.
2. Replace the existing generic `catch` block with two `catch` blocks. (The statement that displays the answer still follows these `catch` blocks.) The first catches any `FormatException` and displays a short message. The second catches a `DivideByZeroException` and displays a much longer message.

```
catch(FormatException e)
{
     Console.WriteLine("You did not enter an integer");
}
catch(DivideByZeroException e)
{
   Console.WriteLine("This is not your fault.");
   Console.WriteLine("You entered the integer correctly.");
   Console.WriteLine("The program divides by zero.");
}
```

3. Save the program and compile it. When you execute the program and enter an invalid integer, the first `catch` block executes. When you enter an integer so that the program can proceed to the statement that divides by 0, the second `catch` block executes. Figure 9-40 shows two typical executions of the program.

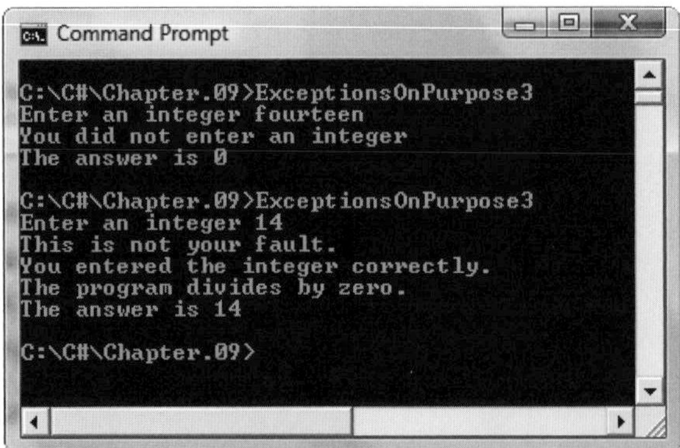

Figure 9-40 Error messages generated by successive executions of `ExceptionsOnPurpose3` program

CHAPTER SUMMARY

- An exception is any error condition or unexpected behavior in an executing program; the object-oriented techniques used to manage such errors make up the group of methods known as exception handling. In C#, all exceptions are objects that are members of the `Exception` class or one of its derived classes. Most exceptions you will use are derived from three classes: `SystemException`, `ApplicationException`, and their parent `Exception`.
- You can purposely generate a `SystemException` by forcing a program to contain an error. Although you are not required to handle `Exception`s, you can use object-oriented techniques to provide elegant error-handling solutions.
- When you think an error will occur frequently, it is most efficient to handle it in the traditional way, with `if` statements. If an error will occur infrequently, it is more efficient to instantiate an `Exception` object when needed.
- In object-oriented terminology, you "try" a procedure that may not complete correctly. A method that detects an error condition or `Exception` "throws" an `Exception`, and the block of code that processes the error "catches" the `Exception`. You must include at least one `catch` block or `finally` block immediately following a `try` block.
- Every `Exception` object contains a `ToString()` method and a `Message` property that contains useful information about the `Exception`.
- You can place as many statements as you need within a `try` block, and you can `catch` as many different `Exception`s as you want. If you `try` more than one statement, only the first error-generating statement will throw an `Exception`. When multiple `catch` blocks are present, they are examined in sequence until a match is found for the `Exception` that occurred. When you list multiple `catch` blocks after a `try` block, you must be careful about their order, or some `catch` blocks might become unreachable.
- When you have actions to perform at the end of a `try...catch` sequence, you can use a `finally` block.

- When you want to keep trying a block of code until some value or state within a program is correct, you can place a `try...catch` block within a loop.
- When methods throw `Exception`s, they don't have to catch them; instead, the program that calls a method that throws an `Exception` can catch it and determine what to do. For the best software design, you should create your classes to throw any `Exception`s so that various application programs can catch them and handle them appropriately.
- If a method throws an `Exception` and does not catch it, then the `Exception` is thrown to the method that called the offending method. When you catch an `Exception`, you can print the value of the `StackTrace` property to display a list of methods in the call stack, allowing you to determine the location of the `Exception`.
- To create your own `Exception` that you can throw, you can extend the `ApplicationException` class or the `Exception` class. The current advice is to extend `Exception`.
- When you write a method that catches an `Exception`, your method does not have to handle the `Exception`. Instead, you might choose to rethrow the `Exception` to the method that called your method and let that method handle it.

KEY TERMS

An **exception** is any error condition or unexpected behavior in an executing program.

Exception handling is the set of object-oriented techniques used to manage unexpected errors.

Fault-tolerant applications are designed so that they continue to operate, possibly at a reduced level, when some part of the system fails.

Robustness represents the degree to which a system is resilient to stress, maintaining correct functioning even in the presence of errors.

The term **mission critical** refers to any process that is crucial to an organization.

A **`try` block** contains code that might create exceptions you want to handle.

A **`catch` block** can catch one type of `Exception`.

Unreachable blocks contain statements that can never execute under any circumstances because the program logic "can't get there."

Dead code is unreachable code.

A **`finally` block** can follow a `try` block; code within one executes whether the `try` block identifies any `Exception`s or not.

The **call stack** is the memory location where the computer stores the list of locations to which the system must return after method calls.

A method can catch an `Exception` and **rethrow the `Exception`** instead of handling it.

REVIEW QUESTIONS

1. Any error condition or unexpected behavior in an executing program is known as an ________ .

   a. exception
   b. anomaly
   c. exclusion
   d. omission

2. Which of the following is *not* treated as a C# `Exception`?

   a. Your program asks the user to input a number, but the user enters a character.
   b. You attempt to execute a C# program, but the C# compiler has not been installed.
   c. You attempt to access an array with a subscript that is too large.
   d. You calculate a value that is too large for the answer's variable type.

3. Most exceptions you will use derive from three classes: ________ .

   a. `Object`, `ObjectException`, and `ObjectApplicationException`
   b. `Exception`, `SystemException`, and `ApplicationException`
   c. `FormatException`, `ApplicationException`, and `IOException`
   d. `SystemException`, `IOException`, and `FormatException`

4. `Exception`s can be ________ .

   a. generated automatically by C#
   b. created by a program
   c. both of these
   d. neither of these

5. When a program creates an `Exception`, you ________ .

   a. must handle it
   b. can handle it
   c. must not handle it
   d. none of these; programs cannot create `Exceptions`

6. Without using object-oriented techniques, ________ .

   a. there are no error situations
   b. you cannot manage error situations
   c. you can manage error situations, but with great difficulty
   d. you can manage error situations

7. In object-oriented terminology, you ________ a procedure that may not complete correctly.

   a. circumvent
   b. attempt
   c. catch
   d. try

8. In object-oriented terminology, a method that detects an error condition ________ an `Exception`.

   a. throws
   b. catches
   c. tries
   d. unearths

9. When you write a block of code in which something can go wrong, you can place the code in a ________ block.

   a. `catch`
   b. `blind`
   c. `system`
   d. `try`

10. A `catch` block executes when its `try` block ________ .

    a. completes
    b. throws any `Exception`
    c. throws an `Exception` of an acceptable type
    d. completes without throwing anything

11. Which of the following `catch` blocks will catch any `Exception`?

    a. `catch(Any e){}`
    b. `catch(Exception e){}`
    c. `catch(e)`
    d. All of the above will catch any `Exception`.

12. Which of the following is valid within a `catch` block with the header `catch(Exception error)`?

    a. `Console.WriteLine(error.ToString());`
    b. `Console.WriteLine(error.Message);`
    c. `return(error.ToString());`
    d. two of these

13. You can place ________ statement(s) within a `try` block.

    a. zero
    b. one
    c. two
    d. any number of

14. How many `catch` blocks might follow a `try` block within the same method?

    a. only one

    b. any number as long as it is greater than zero

    c. any number as long as it is greater than one

    d. any number, including zero or one

15. Consider the following `try` block. If `x` is 15, what is the value of `a` when this code completes?

```
try
{
    a = 99;
    if(x > 10)
        throw(new Exception());
    a = 0;
    ++a;
}
```

    a. 0
    b. 1
    c. 99
    d. undefined

16. Consider the following `catch` blocks. The variable `b` has been initialized to 0. If a `DivideByZeroException` occurs in a `try` block just before this `catch` block, what is the value of `b` when this code completes?

```
catch(DivideByZeroException e)
{
    ++b;
}
catch(Exception e)
{
    ++b;
}
```

    a. 0
    b. 1
    c. 2
    d. 3

17. Consider the following `catch` blocks. The variable `c` has been initialized to 0. If an `IndexOutOfRangeException` occurs in a `try` block just before this `catch` block, what is the value of `c` when this code completes?

```
catch(IndexOutOfRangeException e)
{
      ++c;
}
catch(Exception e)
{
      ++c;
}
finally
{
      ++c;
}
```

a. 0

b. 1

c. 2

d. 3

18. If your program throws an `IndexOutOfRangeException` and the only available `catch` block catches an `Exception`, ________.

    a. an `IndexOutOfRangeException catch` block is generated automatically

    b. the `Exception catch` block executes

    c. the `catch` block is bypassed

    d. an `Exception` is thrown to the operating system

19. When you design your own classes that might cause `Exceptions`, and other classes will use your classes as clients, you should usually create your methods to ________.

    a. neither throw nor handle `Exceptions`

    b. throw `Exceptions` but not handle them

    c. handle `Exceptions` but not throw them

    d. both throw and handle `Exceptions`

20. When you create an `Exception` of your own, you should extend the ________ class.

    a. `SystemException`

    b. `PersonalException`

    c. `OverloadedException`

    d. `Exception`

EXERCISES

1. Write a program in which you declare an array of five integers and store five values in the array. Write a `try` block in which you place a loop that attempts to access each element of the array, incrementing a subscript from 0 to 10. Create a `catch` block that catches the eventual `IndexOutOfRangeException`; within the block, display "Now you've gone too far." on the screen. Save the file as **GoTooFar.cs**.

2. a. The `Convert.ToInt32()` method requires a string argument that can be converted to an `int`. Write a program in which you prompt the user for a stock number and quantity ordered. Accept the strings the user enters and convert them to integers. Catch the `Exception` that is thrown when the user enters noninteger data for either field. Within the `catch` block, display an error message and set both the stock number and quantity values to 0. Save the file as **PlacingOrder.cs**.

   b. Modify the `PlacingOrder` application so that data entry is performed in a `DataEntry()` function that accepts a string parameter to use as a prompt. The function prompts the user, reads a value from the keyboard, attempts to convert it to an integer, and then returns the integer. If an `Exception` is encountered, the function should return 0. Save the file as **PlacingOrder2.cs**.

3. `ArgumentException` is an existing class that derives from `Exception`; you use it when one or more of a method's arguments do not fall within an expected range. Create a class named `CarInsurance` containing variables that can hold a driver's age and state of residence. Within the class, create a method that accepts the two input values and calculates a premium. The premium base price is $100 for residents of Illinois (IL) and $50 for residents of Wisconsin (WI). Additionally, each driver pays $3 times the value of 100 minus his or her age. If the driver is younger than 16, older than 80, or not a resident of IL or WI, throw an `ArgumentException` from the method. In the `Main()` method of the `CarInsurance` class, try code that prompts the user for each value. If the user does not enter a numeric value for age, catch a `FormatException` and display an error message. Call the method that calculates the premium and `catch` the potential `ArgumentException` object. Save the file as **CarInsurance.cs**.

4. The `Math` class contains a static method named `Sqrt()` that accepts a `double` and returns the parameter's square root. Write a program that declares two `doubles`: `number` and `sqrt`. Accept an input value for `number` from the user. Handle the `FormatException` that is thrown if the input value cannot be converted to a `double` by displaying the message "The input should be a number." and setting the `sqrt` variable to 0. If no `FormatException` is thrown, test the input number's value. If it is negative, throw a `new ApplicationException` to which you pass the message "Number can't be negative." and again set `sqrt` to 0. If `number` is not negative, pass it to the `Math.Sqrt()` method, returning the square root to the `sqrt` variable. As the last program statement, display the value of `sqrt`. Save the file as **FindSquareRoot.cs**.

5. a. Create an `Employee` class with two fields: `IDNum` and `hourlyWage`. The `Employee` constructor requires values for both fields. Upon construction, throw an `ArgumentException` if the `hourlyWage` is less than 6.00 or more than 50.00. Write a program that establishes, one at a time, at least three `Employees` with `hourlyWages` that are above, below, and within the allowed range. Immediately after each instantiation attempt, handle any thrown `Exceptions` by displaying an error message. Save the file as **EmployeeExceptionDemo.cs**.

b. Using the `Employee` class created in Exercise 5a, write an application that creates an array of five `Employees`. Prompt the user for values for each field for each `Employee`. If the user enters improper or invalid data, handle any exceptions that are thrown by setting the `Employee`'s ID number to 999 and the `Employee`'s pay rate to the $6.00 minimum. At the end of the program, display all the entered, and possibly corrected, records. Save the file as **EmployeeExceptionDemo2.cs**.

6. a. The Peterman Publishing Company has decided that no published book should cost more than 10 cents per page. Create a `BookException` class whose constructor requires three arguments: a `string Book` title, a `double` price, and an `int` number of pages. Create an error message that is passed to the `Exception` class constructor for the `Message` property when a `Book` does not meet the price-to-pages ratio. For example, an error message might be:

```
For Goodnight Moon, ratio is invalid.
...Price is $12.99 for 25 pages.
```

Create a `Book` class that contains fields for title, author, price, and number of pages. Include properties for each field. Throw a `BookException` if a client program tries to construct a `Book` object for which the price is more than 10 cents per page. Create a program that creates at least four `Book` objects—some where the ratio is acceptable and others where it is not. Catch any thrown exceptions and display the `BookException Message`. Save the file as **BookExceptionDemo.cs**.

b. Using the `Book` class created in Exercise 6a, write an application that creates an array of five `Books`. Prompt the user for values for each `Book`. To handle any exceptions that are thrown because of improper or invalid data entered by the user, set the `Book`'s price to the maximum 10 cents per page. At the end of the program, display all the entered, and possibly corrected, records. Save the file as **BookExceptionDemo2.cs**.

DEBUGGING EXERCISES

Each of the following files in the Chapter.09 folder on your Student Disk has syntax and/or logical errors. In each case, determine the problem and fix the program. After you correct the errors, save each file using the same filename preceded with *Fixed*. For example, DebugNine1.cs will become FixedDebugNine1.cs.

a. DebugNine1.cs

b. DebugNine2.cs

c. DebugNine3.cs

d. DebugNine4.cs

UP FOR DISCUSSION

1. What do the terms *syntactic sugar* and *syntactic salt* mean? From your knowledge of the C# programming language, list as many syntactic sugar and salt features as you can.
2. Have you ever been victimized by a computer error? For example, were you ever incorrectly denied credit, billed for something you did not purchase, or assigned an incorrect grade in a course? How did you resolve the problem? On the Web, find the most outrageous story you can involving a computer error.
3. Search the Web for information about educational video games in which historical simulations are presented in an effort to teach students about history. For example, Civilization IV is a game in which players control a society as it progresses through time. Do you believe such games are useful to history students? Does the knowledge gained warrant the hours it takes to master the games? Do the makers of the games have any obligations to present history factually? Do they have a right to penalize players who choose options of which the game writers disapprove (such as using nuclear weapons or allowing slavery)? Do game creators have the right to create characters who possess negative stereotypical traits—for example, a person of a specific nationality portrayed as being stupid, weak, or evil? Would you like to take a history course that uses such games?

CHAPTERTEN

10

USING GUI OBJECTS AND THE VISUAL STUDIO IDE

In this chapter you will:

Create a MessageBox
Add functionality to MessageBox buttons
Create a Form
Create a Form that is a program's main window
Place a Button on a Window
Use the Visual Studio IDE to design a Form
Learn about the code created by the IDE
Add functionality to a Button on a Form
Use Visual Studio Help

Using the knowledge you have gained so far in this book, you can write many useful C# applications that can accept input, produce output, perform arithmetic, make decisions, handle exceptions, and so on. You also can create classes and instantiate objects from those classes by using the fundamental object-oriented principles of encapsulation, polymorphism, and inheritance. You can create a virtually infinite number of applications that will solve users' problems and provide services for them.

» NOTE
GUI is pronounced "gooey."

Unfortunately, your applications look dull. When you execute the programs you have written so far, input is accepted from a lackluster command prompt, and output is displayed in the same way. Most modern applications, and certainly most programs you have used on the Internet, use visually pleasing graphic objects to interact with users. These **graphical user interface (GUI)** objects include the buttons, check boxes, and toolbars you are used to controlling with a mouse when you interact with Windows-type programs. You can apply everything you have learned about C# classes and methods to the GUI objects that are built into the .NET environment so you can use Visual Studio to create your own interactive GUI applications.

The programs you have written have also been relatively small. When you start to use graphical objects in your programs, the program size quickly can become daunting. So far, you may have been using a simple text editor, such as Notepad, to write your C# programs. If so, it is time to explore the tools in the Visual Studio integrated development environment (IDE). These tools automatically create much of the code you need to develop appealing and attention-grabbing GUI programs. Of course, if you do not understand the C# code that the tools create, you cannot say you have mastered the C# programming language. In this chapter, you will build some graphical objects "by hand." Then, after you understand the details, you will create the same objects by using the IDE.

CREATING A `MessageBox`

A **`MessageBox`** is a GUI object that can contain text, buttons, and symbols that inform and instruct a user. You cannot create a new instance of the `MessageBox` class because its constructor is not `public`. Instead, you use the `static` class method `Show()` to display a `MessageBox`. The `MessageBox` class contains 12 overloaded versions of the `Show()` method; the simplest version accepts a string argument that is displayed within the `MessageBox`. Figure 10-1 shows a program that uses the `MessageBox.Show()` method with the string argument "Hello!". The program must contain the statement `using System.Windows.Forms;` to include the `MessageBox` class. Figure 10-2 shows the output.

» NOTE You could remove the statement `using System.Windows.Forms;` from the program in Figure 10-1 and change the `Show()` statement to its full version: `System.Windows.Forms.MessageBox.Show("Hello!");`. You first learned about the `using` statement in Chapter 1 when you shortened `System.Console.Out.WriteLine()` to `Console.WriteLine();`.

NOTE Including the statement that uses the `System.Windows.Forms` namespace provides you with access to many `Form` features in addition to the `MessageBox`. You will use many of these features as you work through the exercises in the next few chapters.

```
using System;
using System.Windows.Forms;
public class MessageBox1
{
   public static void Main()
   {
      MessageBox.Show("Hello!");
   }
}
```

Figure 10-1 Program that displays a `MessageBox`

Figure 10-2 Output of `MessageBox1` program

The `MessageBox` in Figure 10-2 is similar to those you have used in many Windows programs. It contains a title bar at the top, a Close button in the upper-right corner, the message "Hello!", and an OK button. When the user clicks either the Close button or the OK button, the `MessageBox` disappears. Because the .NET framework contains the `MessageBox` class, you do not have to design these standard `MessageBox` features and capabilities yourself when you write a program. Instead, you can simply use the `MessageBox` class and concentrate on the message you want to convey within the `MessageBox`. Besides saving development time, the built-in `MessageBox` makes your programs look and feel like others your users usually see.

Besides a `string`, you can pass additional arguments to the `MessageBox.Show()` method. You pass these arguments when you want to display a caption in a `MessageBox`'s title bar or add buttons and an icon. Table 10-1 summarizes the features of six of the 12 versions of the `MessageBox.Show()` method. (The other six versions correspond to the table entries, with the addition of naming a component in front of which you want the `MessageBox` to display.) When you use any version of the `Show()` method, you must provide values in the correct order for each argument listed in the table.

Argument to `MessageBox.Show()`	Explanation
`string`	Displays a message box with the specified text
`string, string`	Displays a message box with the specified text and caption
`string, string, MessageBoxButtons`	Displays a message box with specified text, caption, and buttons
`string, string, MessageBoxButtons, MessageBoxIcon`	Displays a message box with specified text, caption, buttons, and icon
`string, string, MessageBoxButtons, MessageBoxIcon, MessageBoxDefaultButton`	Displays a message box with the specified text, caption, buttons, icon, and default button
`string, string, MessageBoxButtons, MessageBoxIcon, MessageBoxDefaultButton, MessageBoxOptions`	Displays a message box with the specified text, caption, buttons, icon, default button, and options

Table 10-1 Arguments used with the `MessageBox.Show()` method

For example, the program in Figure 10-3 uses two `string` arguments with the `MessageBox.Show()` method. Figure 10-4 shows the execution; notice that the second `string` argument passed to the `Show()` method in the program appears in the title bar of the `MessageBox`.

```
using System;
using System.Windows.Forms;
public class MessageBox2
{
   public static void Main()
   {
      MessageBox.Show("Hello!", "MessageBox2");
   }
}
```

Figure 10-3 Using two `string` parameters with `MessageBox.Show()`

Figure 10-4 Output of `MessageBox2` program

Besides `string` parameters, the `MessageBox.Show()` method can also accept `MessageBoxButtons`, `MessageBoxIcon`, `MessageBoxDefaultButton`, and `MessageBoxOptions` parameters. Tables 10-2 through 10-5 describe all of the possible values for each of the arguments you can send to `MessageBox.Show()`. Using different combinations of these arguments provides you with a wide variety of appearances for your `MessageBox` objects.

>> **NOTE** The `MessageBoxOptions` values are not used frequently. They are listed in Table 10-5 but are not used in this chapter.

Member Name	Description
`AbortRetryIgnore`	The message box contains Abort, Retry, and Ignore buttons
`OK`	The message box contains an OK button
`OKCancel`	The message box contains OK and Cancel buttons
`RetryCancel`	The message box contains Retry and Cancel buttons
`YesNo`	The message box contains Yes and No buttons
`YesNoCancel`	The message box contains Yes, No, and Cancel buttons

Table 10-2 `MessageBoxButtons` values

NOTE The description of each `MessageBoxIcon` value contains a typical representation of the symbol. The actual graphic displayed is a function of the operating system in which the program is running.

Member Name	Description
`Asterisk`	The message box contains a lowercase letter *i* in a circle (the result is the same as `Information`)
`Error`	The message box contains a white *X* in a circle with a red background
`Exclamation`	The message box contains an exclamation point in a triangle with a yellow background (the result is the same as `Warning`)
`Hand`	The message box contains a white *X* in a circle with a red background (the result is the same as `Stop`)
`Information`	The message box contains a lowercase letter *i* in a circle
`None`	The message box contains no symbols
`Question`	The message box contains a question mark in a circle
`Stop`	The message box contains a white *X* in a circle with a red background
`Warning`	The message box contains an exclamation point in a triangle with a yellow background

Table 10-3 `MessageBoxIcon` values

Member Name	Description
`Button1`	The first button on the message box is the default button
`Button2`	The second button on the message box is the default button
`Button3`	The third button on the message box is the default button

Table 10-4 `MessageBoxdefaultButton` values

Member Name	Description
`DefaultDesktopOnly`	The message box appears on the active desktop
`RightAlign`	The message box text is right-aligned
`RtlReading`	The message box text is displayed with right-to-left reading order
`ServiceNotification`	The message box appears on the active desktop even if no user is logged on to the computer

Table 10-5 `MessageBoxOptions` values

NOTE You can combine `MessageBoxOptions` values by placing an ampersand (`&`) between them. In Chapter 3, you learned that the single ampersand is the logical AND operator.

Figure 10-5 shows an application that uses a variety of `MessageBox.Show()` options. Figure 10-6 shows how the `MessageBox`es display in sequence.

```
using System;
using System.Windows.Forms;
public class MessageBoxDemo
{
   public static void Main()
   {
      string message = "This is message ";
      string caption = "Message box experiment ";
      int count = 1;
      MessageBox.Show(message + count);
      ++count;
      MessageBox.Show(message + count, caption + count);
      ++count;
      MessageBox.Show(message + count, caption + count,
         MessageBoxButtons.OKCancel);
      ++count;
      MessageBox.Show(message + count, caption + count,
         MessageBoxButtons.RetryCancel, MessageBoxIcon.Warning);
      ++count;
      MessageBox.Show(message + count, caption + count,
         MessageBoxButtons.YesNoCancel,
         MessageBoxIcon.Information,
         MessageBoxDefaultButton.Button3);
   }
}
```

Figure 10-5 `MessageBoxDemo` program

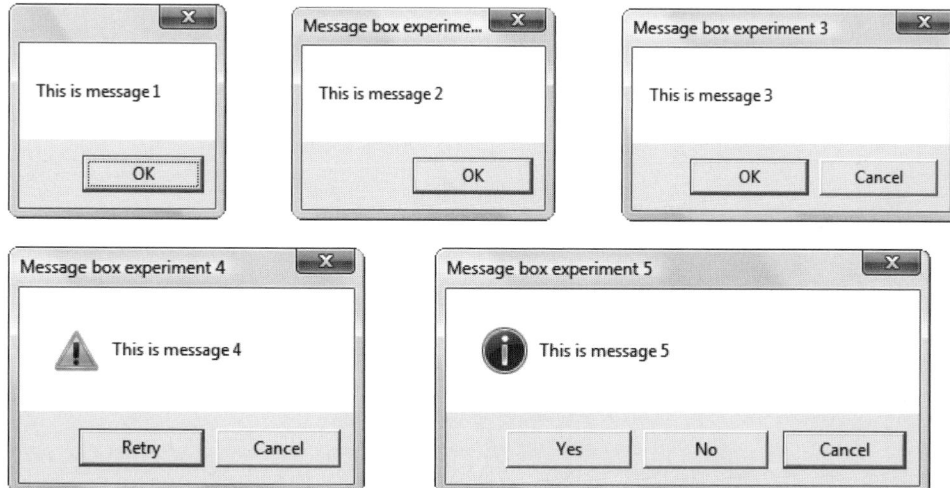

Figure 10-6 Output of `MessageBoxDemo` program

When the first shaded statement in Figure 10-5 executes, the first `MessageBox` in Figure 10-6 appears and a sound is played. The user hears the sound only if the user's system has speakers and they are turned on. This sound calls the user's attention to the `MessageBox`. No caption appears in the first `MessageBox`—just the message "This is message 1". A Close button is available in the upper-right corner. A `MessageBox` is a **modal dialog box**, which means that the program cannot progress until the user dismisses the box. (When you **dismiss** a component, you get rid of it, frequently by pressing its Close button, but in some cases by making some other selection.) When the user clicks OK or Close, the program proceeds; in this case, the second `MessageBox` appears.

The second shaded statement in Figure 10-5 creates a `MessageBox` to which a caption is added. In the second box in Figure 10-6, the message is updated with the new value of `count` , and the `count` is displayed in the caption. This `MessageBox` is automatically wider than the first one to accommodate the title bar caption.

OK and Cancel buttons are added in the third `MessageBox`. The OK button has a darker outline than the Cancel button, which means that the OK button has focus. When a button has **focus**, not only is the user's attention drawn to it visually, but if the user presses the Enter key, the action associated with the button executes, just as it would if the user clicked the button. If you press the Tab key or use the right and left arrow keys on your keyboard, you can change the focus from one button to the other. In this example, whether a user dismisses the third `MessageBox` by pressing the Enter key, closing the box, or clicking one of the two buttons, the fourth `MessageBox` appears.

The fourth `MessageBox` contains Retry and Cancel buttons and the Warning icon—an exclamation point in a triangle. The Warning icon might come with a different sound than a box without a warning. Because you normally would use the Warning icon in a "dangerous" situation, the sound is intended to get the user's attention. For example, you might use the Warning icon if a user leaves a required field blank on an order form or enters a phone number with too few or too many digits.

The last `MessageBox` includes an Information icon and three buttons. When this box appears, the button on the far right has focus because `MessageBoxDefaultButton.Button3` was used as an argument to the `MessageBox.Show()` method.

»TWO TRUTHS AND A LIE: CREATING A `MessageBox`

1. You create a new instance of the `MessageBox` class using the keyword `new` and the `MessageBox` constructor.
2. A `MessageBox` is a modal dialog box, which means a user must dismiss the box before the program continues.
3. When a button has focus and the user presses the Enter key, the action associated with the button executes.

The false statement is #1. You cannot create a new instance of the `MessageBox` class because its constructor is not `public`. Instead, you use the `static` class method `Show()` to display a `MessageBox`.

ADDING FUNCTIONALITY TO MessageBox BUTTONS

MessageBox objects provide an easy way to display information to a user in a GUI format. When you use a MessageBox to display some text you want the user to read, it makes sense to include only an OK button that the user can click after reading the text. Including multiple MessageBoxButtons, all of which dismiss the MessageBox, doesn't make sense. Usually you want to determine users' interactions with a MessageBox's buttons and take appropriate action based on the users' choices. **DialogResult** is an **enumeration**, or list of values in which names are substituted for numeric values. Each value corresponds to a user's potential MessageBox button selection. Table 10-6 contains DialogResult values you can compare to the return value of MessageBox.Show(). The DialogResult member names correspond to the button labels available within a MessageBox.

Member Name	Description
Abort	The dialog box return value is Abort
Cancel	The dialog box return value is Cancel
Ignore	The dialog box return value is Ignore
No	The dialog box return value is No
None	Nothing is returned from the dialog box, which means that the modal dialog box stays open
OK	The dialog box return value is OK
Retry	The dialog box return value is Retry
Yes	The dialog box return value is Yes

Table 10-6 DialogResult values

Figure 10-7 shows a program written for a fast-food restaurant. Its MessageBox asks the user to click Yes or No in response to a standard fast-food question. If the user clicks the Yes button, then the return value of MessageBox.Show() is equivalent to DialogResult.Yes, the choice string is set to "With fries", and the price increases by 0.75; otherwise, the choice string retains its original value "Without fries", and the price remains $3.00. Whatever button the user chooses, a new MessageBox displays the final description and meal price. Figure 10-8 shows the MessageBox that contains the question and two results: the first occurs when the user clicks Yes, and the second occurs when the user clicks No.

```
using System;
using System.Windows.Forms;
public class HamburgerAddition
{
   public static void Main()
   {
      string question = "Do you want fries with that?";
      string caption = "Hamburger addition";
      string choice = "Without fries";
      double price = 3.00;
      const double FRIES_PRICE = 0.75;
      if(MessageBox.Show(question, caption,
         MessageBoxButtons.YesNo, MessageBoxIcon.Question) ==
         DialogResult.Yes)
      {
         choice = "With fries";
         price += FRIES_PRICE;
      }
      MessageBox.Show(choice + "total is " +
         price.ToString("C"));
   }
}
```

Figure 10-7 `HamburgerAddition` program

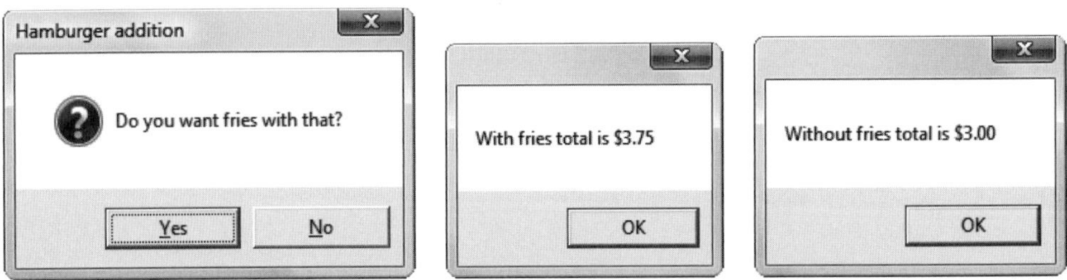

Figure 10-8 `MessageBox` in `HamburgerAddition` program, and results when user clicks Yes and No

NOTE Instead of the long, shaded `if` statement in Figure 10-7, you could create a `DialogResult` object and assign the result of the `MessageBox.Show()` method to it, as in the following code:

```
DialogResult dResult = MessageBox.Show(question, caption,
      MessageBoxButtons.YesNo, MessageBoxIcon.Question);
```

Then the `if` expression becomes simpler:

```
if(dResult = DialogResult.Yes)...
```

Also, when you use this technique, you can reuse `dResult`, comparing it to different values one at a time.

»TWO TRUTHS AND A LIE: ADDING FUNCTIONALITY TO `MessageBox` BUTTONS

1. `DialogResult` is an enumeration, or list of values in which names are substituted for numeric values.
2. `DialogResult` values include `Yes`, `No`, `OK`, and `Cancel`.
3. `MessageBox.Show()` is a `void` method.

The false statement is #3. `MessageBox.Show()` returns a `DialogResult` value that you often want to compare with another value such as `DialogResult`.

CREATING A `Form`

`MessageBox`es offer a large, but not infinite, number of ways to interact with users. They provide information, and several versions can allow a user to select one of two or three button options. However, some applications require more components than a few buttons; for example, they might require an entire grid of buttons, lists of available options from which to select, or text fields in which to type. **`Forms`** provide an interface for collecting, displaying, and delivering such information; they are key components of GUI programs. You can use a `Form` to represent any window you want to display within your application. Although they are not required, you can include **controls** such as text fields, buttons, and check boxes that users can manipulate to interact with a program.

The `Form` class descends from the `Object` class like all other C# classes, but not directly. It is six generations removed from the `Object` class in the following line of descent:

- `Object`
- `MarshalByRefObject`
- `Component`
- `Control`
- `ScrollableControl`
- `ContainerControl`
- `Form`

»NOTE To use a `Form`, you must include the `using` statement at the top of the program file, as shown in Figure 10-9.

You can create an instance of the `Form` class. (This is different from the `MessageBox` class, in which you cannot create an instance but must use the `Show()` method.) Figure 10-9 shows a program that creates the simplest `Form` possible, and Figure 10-10 shows the output.

```
using System.Windows.Forms;
public class CreateForm1
{
    public static void Main()
    {
        Form form1 = new Form();
        form1.ShowDialog();
    }
}
```

Figure 10-9 `CreateForm1` program

Figure 10-10 Output of `CreateForm1` program

NOTE If you use a Microsoft product such as Word and open a new, unnamed document, it is called `Document1`. When you open Excel, the first unnamed spreadsheet is called `Sheet1`. Microsoft uses the same naming convention for `Form`s, `WindowsApplication`s, and other components in the IDE.

In Figure 10-9, the object `form1` is an instance of the `Form` class. The `ShowDialog()` method displays the `Form` as a modal dialog box, so the user must dismiss the box before the program proceeds. The `Form` contains neither a caption nor components, but it does possess a title bar with an icon. You can use your mouse to minimize, restore, resize (by dragging on the `Form`'s borders), and close the `Form`, just as you can with most of the `Form`s you have encountered when you have used programs written by others.

You can change the appearance, size, color, and window management features of a `Form` by setting its properties. The `Form` class contains approximately 100 properties, many of which it inherits from the `Control` class. Table 10-7 lists just some of them. For example, setting the `Text` property allows you to specify the caption of the `Form` in the title bar. The `Size` and `DesktopLocation` properties allow you to define the size and position of the window when it is displayed.

NOTE You have been creating properties for your own classes since Chapter 7. There, you learned that a property is a member of a class that defines how fields will be set and retrieved. When you use controls in a C# project, you are using properties that have already been created by others.

NOTE If you use the Visual Studio .NET Search option, you can find descriptions for all the `Form` class properties. Additionally, if you highlight a property and press F1 or click a property name, you will see a description of the property at the bottom of the Properties window. Not every property you can use with a `Form` appears in the Properties window in the Visual Studio IDE—only the most frequently used are listed.

Member Name	Description
`AcceptButton`	Gets or sets the button on the form that is clicked when the user presses the Enter key
`AllowDrop`	Gets or sets a value indicating whether the control can accept data that the user drags and drops into it
`BackColor`	Gets or sets the background color for this control
`BackgroundImage`	Gets or sets the background image displayed in the control
`Bottom`	Gets the distance between the bottom edge of the control and the top edge of its container's client area
`CancelButton`	Gets or sets the button control that is clicked when the user presses the Esc key
`CanFocus`	Gets a value indicating whether the control can receive focus
`CanSelect`	Gets a value indicating whether the control can be selected
`ContainsFocus`	Gets a value indicating whether the control or one of its child controls currently has the input focus
`ControlBox`	Gets or sets a value indicating whether a control box is displayed in the title bar of the form
`Cursor`	Gets or sets the cursor that is displayed when the user moves the mouse pointer over this control
`DesktopBounds`	Gets or sets the size and location of the form on the Windows desktop
`DesktopLocation`	Gets or sets the location of the form on the Windows desktop
`DialogResult`	Gets or sets the dialog result for the form
`Focused`	Gets a value indicating whether the control has input focus
`Font`	Gets or sets the current font for the control
`ForeColor`	Gets or sets the foreground color of the control
`FormBorderStyle`	Gets or sets the border style of the form
`Height`	Gets or sets the height of the control
`HelpButton`	Gets or sets a value indicating whether a Help button should be displayed in the title bar of the form
`Icon`	Gets or sets the icon for the form
`Left`	Gets or sets the x-coordinate of a control's left edge in pixels
`Location`	Gets or sets the coordinates of the upper-left corner of the control relative to the upper-left corner of its container
`MaximizeBox`	Gets or sets a value indicating whether the Maximize button is displayed in the title bar of the form
`MaximumSize`	Gets the maximum size to which the form can be resized
`Menu`	Gets or sets the main menu that is displayed in the form

Table 10-7 Properties of `Forms` (*continued*)

Member Name	Description
MinimizeBox	Gets or sets a value indicating whether the Minimize button is displayed in the title bar of the form
MinimumSize	Gets the minimum size to which the form can be resized
Modal	Gets a value indicating whether this form is displayed modally
Name	Gets or sets the name of the control
Opacity	Gets or sets the opacity level of the form
Right	Gets the distance between the right edge of the control and the left edge of its container
RightToLeft	Gets or sets whether the alignment of the control's elements is reversed to support locales using right-to-left fonts
ShowInTaskbar	Gets or sets a value indicating whether the form is displayed in the Windows taskbar
Size	Gets or sets the size of the form
StartPosition	Gets or sets the starting position of the form at run time
TabStop	Gets or sets a value indicating whether the user can give the focus to this control using the Tab key
Text	Gets or sets the text associated with this control
Top	Gets or sets the top coordinate of the control
Visible	Gets or sets a value indicating whether the control is visible
Width	Gets or sets the width of the control

Table 10-7 *(continued)*

Figure 10-11 shows a `CreateForm2` class that instantiates a `Form` object and sets several of its properties: a caption and a Help button with a question mark are set in the title bar, and the Minimize and Maximize buttons that usually appear on a `Form` are removed. Figure 10-12 shows the output.

```
using System.Windows.Forms;
public class CreateForm2
{
    public static void Main()
    {
        Form form2 = new Form();
        form2.Text = "This is a Form2 Form";
        form2.HelpButton = true;
        form2.MaximizeBox = false;
        form2.MinimizeBox = false;
        form2.ShowDialog();
    }
}
```

Figure 10-11 `CreateForm2` class

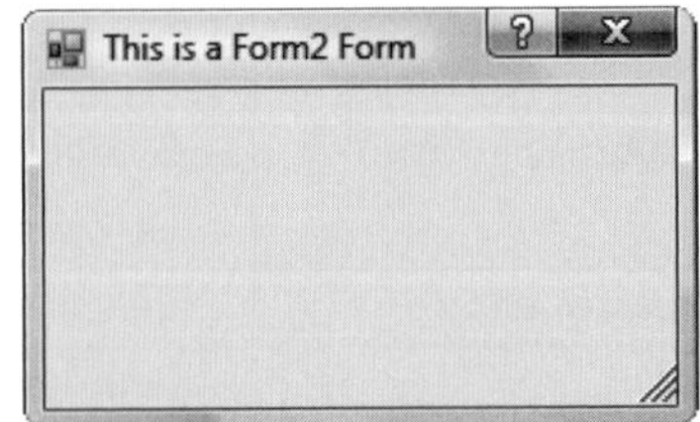

Figure 10-12 Output of `CreateForm2` program

»TWO TRUTHS AND A LIE: CREATING A `Form`

1. You cannot create an instance of the `Form` class because its constructor is private.
2. By default, a `Form` contains neither a caption nor components, but it does possess a title bar with an icon.
3. You can change the appearance, size, color, and window management features of a `Form` by setting its properties.

The false statement is #1. You can create an instance of the `Form` class. This is different from the `MessageBox` class, in which you cannot create an instance but must use the `Show()` method.

CREATING A `Form` THAT IS A PROGRAM'S MAIN WINDOW

You can instantiate a `Form` within an application and use the `ShowDialog()` method to display it, as in Figure 10-11. More frequently, you create a child class from `Form` that becomes the main window of an application. When you create a new main window, you must complete two steps:

» You must derive a new custom class from the base class `System.Windows.Forms.Form`.

» You must write a `Main()` method that calls the `Application.Run()` method, and you must pass an instance of your newly created `Form` class as an argument. This activity starts the program and makes the form visible.

»NOTE Later in this chapter, you will learn to create a `Form` using the Visual Studio IDE. Here, you learn to create one "by hand" so you better understand what the IDE does automatically.

Figure 10-13 shows the simplest program you can write that creates a new main window for a program. The class name is `Window1`; it extends the `Form` class, as you can see by the shaded colon and base class name in the class header.

```
using System.Windows.Forms;
public class Window1 : Form
{
   public static void Main()
   {
      Application.Run(new Window1());
   }
}
```

Figure 10-13 `Window1` class

»NOTE You learned about inheritance and the syntax of using the colon and the base class name in Chapter 8.

»NOTE The statement `Application.Run(new Window1());` creates an unnamed instance of the `Window1` class. Alternatively, you could instantiate a named `Window` object using `Window1 aWindow = new Window();` and then call `Application.Run(aWindow);`. However, because this application never needs to use the name `aWindow`, there is no need to provide the new `Window1` object with a unique identifier.

The `Window1` class in Figure 10-13 contains a single method: a `Main()` method that calls the `Application.Run()` method, passing a new instance of the `Window1` class. Figure 10-14 shows the output. The `Form` created has no title and contains no components, but it has a title bar that displays an icon and Minimize, Restore, and Close buttons in the expected locations.

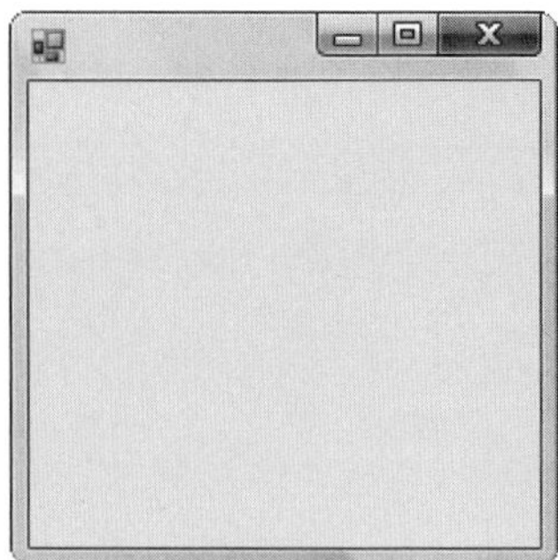

Figure 10-14 Output of `Window1` program

The `Application.Run()` method processes messages from the operating system to the application. Without the call to `Application.Run()`, the program would compile and execute, but the program would end without displaying the window.

When you want to add property settings to a program's main window, you can do so within the class constructor. Figure 10-15 shows a `Window2` class in which the `Size` and `Text` attributes of a `Window` are set. The keyword `this` in the constructor method refers to "this `Form` being constructed"; you could eliminate `this`, and the constructor would work in the same way. To set the `Size` property, you must instantiate a `System.Drawing.Size` object. Its constructor takes two parameters. The first indicates the horizontal size, or width, of a component; the second indicates the vertical size (or height) of a component. Setting the `Size` to `System.Drawing.Size(500, 100)` creates a window that is five times wider than it is tall. The `Text` property supplies the caption that appears in the window's title bar. Figure 10-16 shows the created `Window2` object.

```
using System.Windows.Forms;
public class Window2 : Form
{
   public Window2()
   {
      this.Size = new System.Drawing.Size(500, 100);
      this.Text = "This is a Window2 Object";
   }
   public static void Main()
   {
      Application.Run(new Window2());
   }
}
```

Figure 10-15 `Window2` class

Figure 10-16 Output of `Window2` program

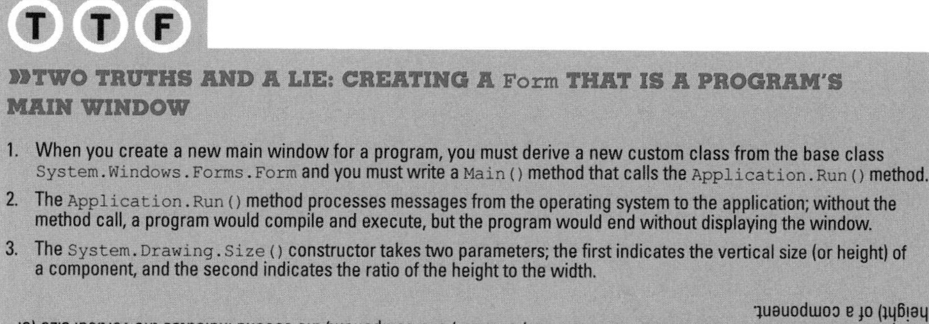

»TWO TRUTHS AND A LIE: CREATING A `Form` THAT IS A PROGRAM'S MAIN WINDOW

1. When you create a new main window for a program, you must derive a new custom class from the base class `System.Windows.Forms.Form` and you must write a `Main()` method that calls the `Application.Run()` method.
2. The `Application.Run()` method processes messages from the operating system to the application; without the method call, a program would compile and execute, but the program would end without displaying the window.
3. The `System.Drawing.Size()` constructor takes two parameters; the first indicates the vertical size (or height) of a component, and the second indicates the ratio of the height to the width.

The false statement is #3. A window's `Size` property uses a `System.Drawing.Size` object whose constructor takes two parameters. The first indicates the horizontal size, or width, of a component; the second indicates the vertical size (or height) of a component.

PLACING A `Button` ON A `Window`

Although it has interesting dimensions, the window in Figure 10-16 is not yet as useful as a `MessageBox`. However, a window is more flexible than a `MessageBox` because you can place manipulatable `Window` controls wherever you like on the surface of the `Window`.

One type of control the user can manipulate is a `Button`. A **`Button`** is a GUI object you can click to cause some action. (Alternatively, you can press the Enter key if the `Button` has focus.) You can create your own `Button` objects by using the `Button` class. This class contains more than 60 properties; two of the most useful are its `Text` and `Location` properties. You use the `Text` property to set a `Button`'s label. You can use the `Location` property to position a `Button` relative to the upper-left corner of the `Form` (or any other `ContainerControl` object) that contains it.

When you set the `Location` property, you instantiate a `System.Drawing.Point` object and supply two integer arguments to its constructor. The first argument represents a number of horizontal pixels to the right of the upper-left corner of a `Form` (or other container). The second argument represents the vertical position down from the top. For example, 0, 0 is the upper-left corner, and 10, 200 is a little to the right but much further down.

Figure 10-17 shows a `WindowWithButton` class that descends from `Form`. The class declares a `Button` named `button1`. The class constructor sets the form size to 300 by 150—a size that is twice as wide as it is tall. The `Form`'s `Text` property is set, as is the `Button`'s `Text` property. The `Button` is located at `Point(25, 50)`, not very far from the `Form`'s left side. Figure 10-18 shows the resulting `Form`—a `Window` with `Text` in the title bar and a clickable `Button` with text.

```
using System.Windows.Forms;
public class WindowWithButton : Form
{
   Button button1 = new Button();
   public WindowWithButton()
   {
      this.Size = new System.Drawing.Size(300, 150);
      this.Text = "Window Object With Button";
      button1.Text = "Press";
      this.Controls.AddRange(new System.Windows.Forms.Control[]
         {this.button1});
      this.button1.Location = new System.Drawing.Point(25, 50);
   }
   public static void Main()
   {
      Application.Run(new WindowWithButton());
   }
}
```

Figure 10-17 `WindowWithButton` class

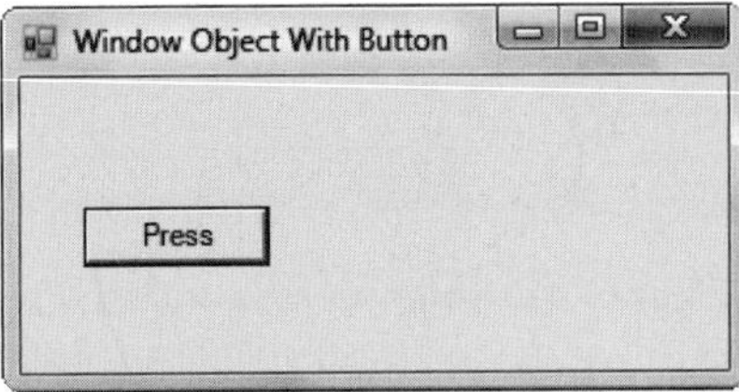

Figure 10-18 Output of `WindowWithButton` program

NOTE In the `WindowWithButton` class, you could leave out the four instances of `this`. For example, the statement `Text = "Window Object With Button";` would work exactly like the one that uses the `this` reference. Figure 10-17 includes the `this` reference for two reasons. First, it helps you understand that "this" object, the `WindowWithButton Form`, has `Text` that is being altered, and not some other component on the `Form`. Second, when you create programs visually using the IDE, as you will do later in this chapter, you will see liberal uses of `this` in the automatically generated code. That's because the IDE cannot predict what identifiers you will use for your components, so it fully qualifies its statements to avoid conflicts.

TWO TRUTHS AND A LIE: PLACING A `Button` ON A `Window`

1. You can use the `Button` class `Text` property to set a `Button`'s label.
2. You use the `Button` class `Location` property to position a `Button` relative to the center of the `Form` that contains it.
3. A `Form` with a `Size` property set to `System.Drawing.Size(200, 400)` is twice as tall as it is wide.

The false statement is #2. The `Button` class `Location` property positions a `Button` relative to the upper-left corner of the `Form` that contains it.

USING THE VISUAL STUDIO IDE TO DESIGN A Form

The window in Figure 10-18 consists of only a Form and a Button, and even though the Button doesn't do anything yet, scores of additional options are available to you. The program in Figure 10-17 sets only two attributes for the Form (Size and Text), yet Table 10-7 shows dozens of additional properties you can set—and that table lists only half the available properties. Likewise, the program in Figure 10-17 sets only two Button properties (Text and Location); by the time you create a full-blown Windows application, you might want to set several more properties for the existing Button, add more Buttons, and set all their properties. You might want to add other components to the window, supplying locations and appropriate actions for each of them as well. Just determining an attractive and useful layout in which to position all the components on your Form would take many lines of code and a lot of trial and error. A simple but fully functional GUI program might require several hundred statements. Therefore, coding such a program can be tedious.

The Visual Studio IDE provides a wealth of tools to help you design Forms. Rather than having to write multiple assignment statements and guess at appropriate component locations, it allows you to use a visual environment for designing your Forms.

»NOTE Chapter 1 contains instructions for creating and running a console application using the IDE. If you have been using the IDE throughout this book to create programs, you are already familiar with many of the menu options. If you have been using a simple text editor instead of the IDE, you might want to return to the "You Do It" section in Chapter 1 and create, compile, and execute a simple console application, just to get used to the IDE. In the "You Do It" section at the end of this chapter, you will create your own Windows application. Note that when you use the IDE to create Windows applications, you choose the Windows Application option instead of Console Application when starting the new project.

»NOTE Designing aesthetically pleasing, functional, and user-friendly Forms is an art; entire books are devoted to the topic.

Figure 10-19 shows the environment in which you can create Windows applications. Some key features in Visual C# include:

- The **main menu**, which includes a File menu from which you open, close, and save projects. It also contains submenus for editing, debugging, and help tasks, among others.
- The **Toolbox tab**, which, when you open it, provides lists of controls you can drag onto a Form so that you can develop programs visually, using a mouse.
- The **Form Designer** and **Code Editor**, which appear in the center of the screen. You can switch back and forth between these two when you want to design an application by dragging components onto the screen or when you want to write or view code statements.
- The **Solution Explorer**, for viewing and managing project files and settings.
- The **Properties window**, for configuring properties and events on controls in your user interface. For example, you can use this window to set the Size property of a Button or the Text property of a Form without writing the necessary C# statements; the IDE will create the statements for you.
- The **output tab** and **error list tab**, which display messages about projects you are running and list any compiler errors in your code.

»NOTE If some of these features are not immediately visible after you start a project in the IDE, you can select them from the View menu.

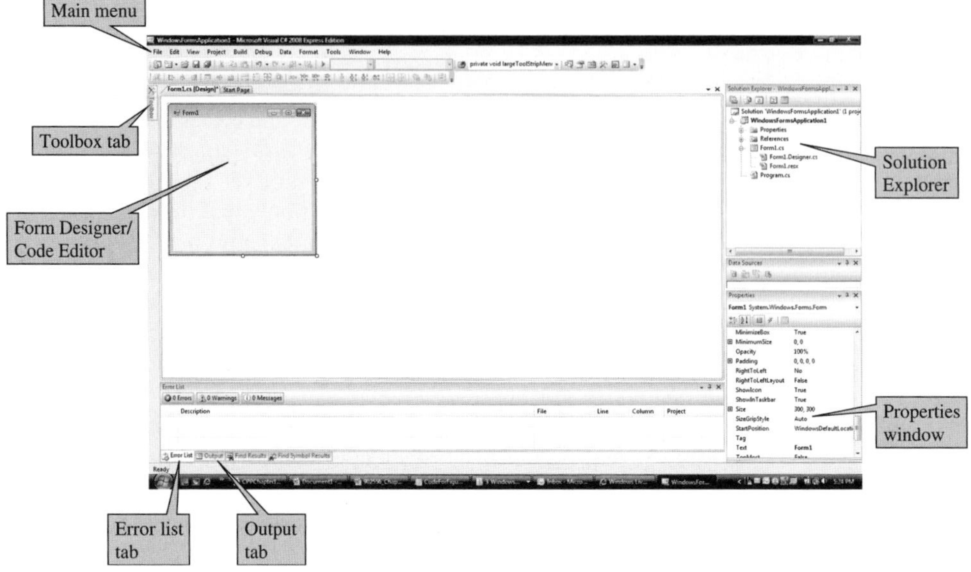

Figure 10-19 Features of the Visual Studio IDE

> **»NOTE** Figure 10-19 shows the environment for C# Express. Your title bar and other features might look slightly different if you are using a different edition of Microsoft Visual Studio.

When you create a Windows Forms project, Visual C# names the project `WindowsFormsApplication1` by default. In Figure 10-19, you see this name in the following locations:

- » In the title bar above the main menu
- » In the title bar of the Solution Explorer
- » In two locations in the Solution Explorer file list

When you create a Windows Forms project, Visual C# adds a form to the project and calls it `Form1`. You can see `Form1` in the following locations in Figure 10-19:

- » On the folder tab at the top of the Form Designer area
- » In the title bar of the form in the Form Designer area
- » In the Solution Explorer file list (with a .cs extension)
- » In the Properties window

The Solution Explorer file list shows the files that are part of the current project. If you expand the Form1.cs node by clicking the small plus sign to the left of it, you see two files that represent the form: Form1.Designer.cs and Form1.resx. As you develop an application, you write your code for the form in the Form1.cs file. The Windows Forms Designer automatically writes code in the Designer.cs file; the code created there implements all the actions that are performed when you drag and drop controls from the Toolbox. The Program.cs file contains the `Main()` method of the program.

NOTE In Visual Studio, a **node** is a box that appears on a vertical tree to the left of a list or a section of code and that can be expanded or condensed. When the node contains a plus (+), clicking it reveals hidden items or code. When the node contains a minus (–), you see all the items in the list (or all the hidden code); clicking the node collapses the list so you can work with a condensed view.

When you select the Toolbox tab, a list of groups of tools appears. The list will automatically close when you move your mouse off the list, or you can pin the Toolbox to the screen by clicking the pushpin icon at the top of the list. Selecting All Windows Forms displays a complete list of available tools; selecting Common Controls displays a smaller list that is a subset of the original one. As shown in Figure 10-20, this list contains many controls—the GUI objects a user can click or manipulate. The list includes controls you probably have seen when using Windows applications—for example, `Button`, `CheckBox`, and `Label`. You can drag these controls onto the `Form`. For example, Figure 10-20 contains a pinned Toolbox and a `Form` onto which a `Button` has been dragged.

NOTE You learn more about controls in Chapter 11.

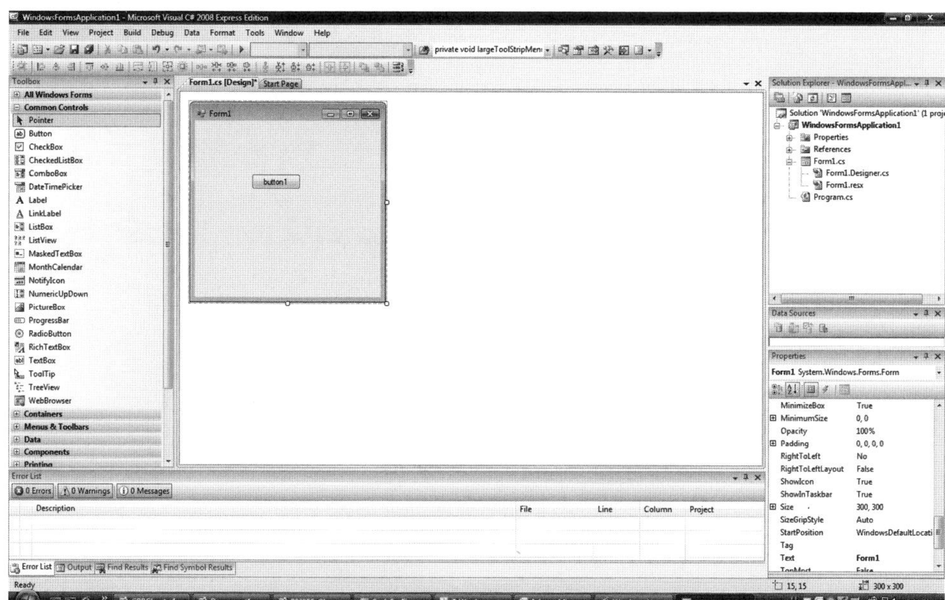

Figure 10-20 The pinned Toolbox and a `Form` with a `Button` in the IDE

NOTE All of the windows in Visual C# can be made dockable or floating, hidden or visible, or can be moved to new locations. To change the behavior of a window, click the down arrow or pushpin icons on the title bar and select from among the available options. You can customize many aspects of the IDE by clicking the Tools menu, then clicking Options.

NOTE In Figure 10-20, notice that the file folder tab for `Form1` now contains an asterisk, which means the file contents have changed since the last time the file was saved.

NOTE You also can view the code by pressing the F7 key on your keyboard or by right-clicking the form and clicking the Code option.

When you select View from the main menu bar and then select Code, the IDE appears as in Figure 10-21. This code (and more that currently is hidden) was automatically generated for you.

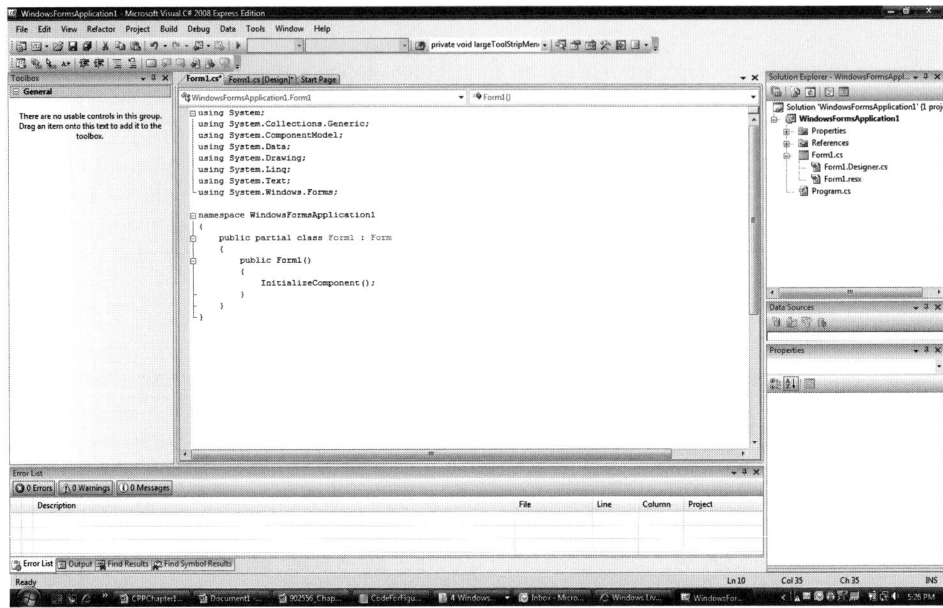

Figure 10-21 Sample code generated by C#

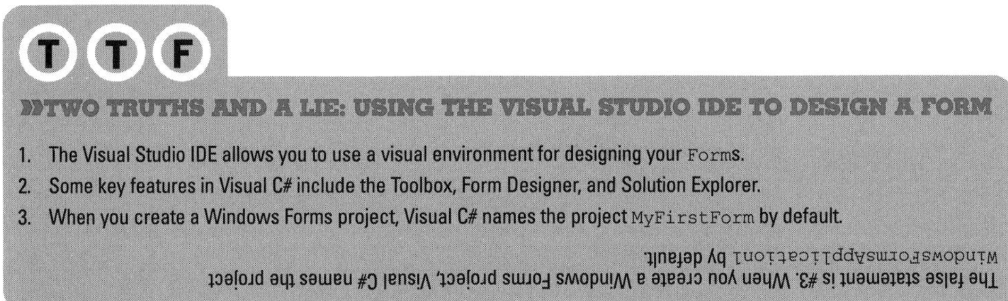

TWO TRUTHS AND A LIE: USING THE VISUAL STUDIO IDE TO DESIGN A FORM

1. The Visual Studio IDE allows you to use a visual environment for designing your `Forms`.
2. Some key features in Visual C# include the Toolbox, Form Designer, and Solution Explorer.
3. When you create a Windows Forms project, Visual C# names the project `MyFirstForm` by default.

The false statement is #3. When you create a Windows Forms project, Visual C# names the project `WindowsFormsApplication1` by default.

UNDERSTANDING THE CODE CREATED BY THE IDE

Using the Visual Studio IDE, it is easy to create elaborate forms with a few keystrokes. However, if you don't understand the code behind the forms you create, you cannot say you have truly mastered the C# language, and you won't be able to troubleshoot problems as easily. Everything you have learned to this point has prepared you to understand the code that underlies a visually designed form. The generated code is simply a collection of C# statements and method calls similar to those you have used throughout this book. When you use the Designer in the IDE to design your forms, you save a lot of typing, which reduces the errors you create. As shown in Figure 10-21, it takes quite a bit of code to create even a simple form with a single button. Examine the code piece by piece.

>> **NOTE** Because the IDE generates so much code automatically, it is often more difficult to find and correct errors in programs created using the IDE than in programs you code by hand.

The code in Figure 10-21 contains a list of `using` statements as follows:

```
using System;
using System.Collections.Generic;
using System.ComponentModel;
using System.Data;
using System.Drawing;
using System.Linq;
using System.Text;
using System.Windows.Forms;
```

You have placed many statements like these within your earlier programs. These statements simply list the namespaces for the classes the program will use.

The next code segment in Figure 10-21 creates a namespace using the name the programmer supplied when this C# Windows project was started: `namespace WindowsFormsApplication1`. You have been using the `System` namespace since Chapter 1. Using the IDE, C# creates a namespace for you. The namespace declaration is followed by an opening curly brace and, several statements later, a closing curly brace.

In Figure 10-21, you can see the declaration of the `Form1` class as follows:

```
public partial class Form1 : Form
{
      public Form1()
      {
           InitializeComponent();
      }
}
```

The name `Form1` was supplied by default; you can change this name using the form's `Name` property if you want. The `Form1` class header shows that the class descends from the `Form` class. The class header is followed by an opening curly brace, and several lines later, the matching closing brace.

>> **NOTE** You should change the IDE's automatically supplied identifiers, such as `Form1`, to more meaningful names. However, many examples in this book show components with their original names so changes are kept to a minimum and you can concentrate on the topic at hand.

The `Form1` class is declared as a `partial` class. As you might imagine, a `partial` class contains only part of the class; the rest is spread among multiple files. (The rest of the class will be discussed shortly.)

>> **NOTE** In Chapter 7, you learned that `partial` is a contextual keyword, like `get` and `set`.

The `Form1` class contains one method—a constructor. It looks like many other constructors you have created: it is `public`, has no `return` type, and has the same name as the class. The

Form1() constructor is parameterless and contains one statement—a call to a method named InitializeComponent().

In Figure 10-21, notice the node for Form1.Designer.cs below Form1.cs. Figure 10-22 shows the IDE after the Form1.Designer.cs icon is selected to reveal more of the partial Form1() class.

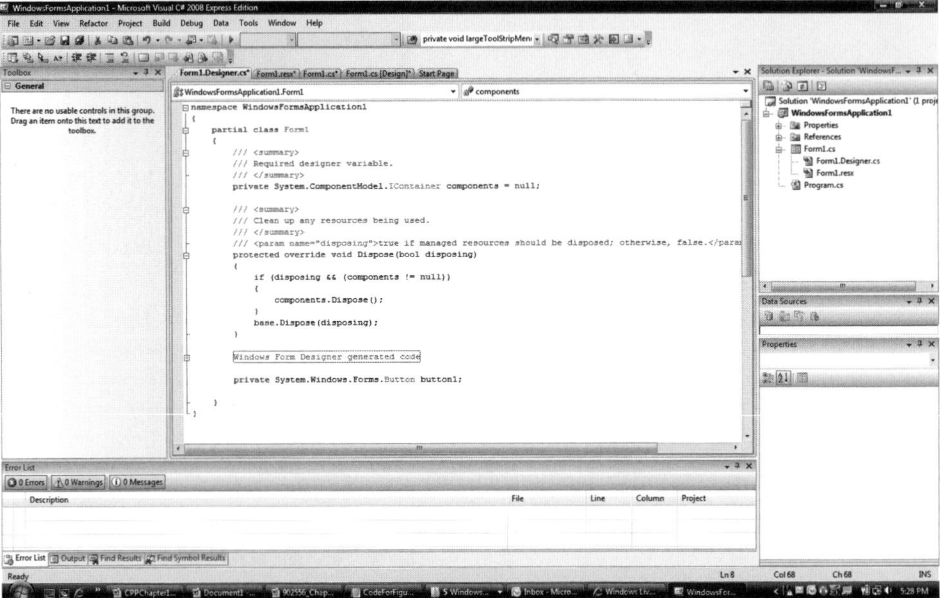

Figure 10-22 Code revealed in the IDE after user double-clicks the Form1.Designer node in the Solution Explorer

The significant parts of the automatically generated code that you can see in Figure 10-22 include:

- » Comments
- » The Dispose() method
- » Object declarations

Other parts of the code that you can reveal (and that you will see in later figures) include:

- » The InitializeComponent() method
- » Preprocessor directives
- » A Main() method

The following sections describe each part of the generated code. Again, you might need to scroll down to see it.

COMMENTS

The code in Figure 10-22 contains many comments, such as the following:

```
/// <summary>
/// Clean up any resources being used.
/// </summary>
```

In other C# programs, you have seen many line comments that begin with two slashes. C# uses three slashes (///) to begin an XML comment. When C# inserts the tag pairs `<summary>` and `</summary>` within the code, it allows the IntelliSense feature in Visual Studio to display additional information about the members contained between the tags. The IntelliSense feature automatically completes statements for you within the Visual Studio IDE.

»NOTE You first learned about XML comments when you learned about block and line comments in Chapter 1. Recall that XML stands for eXtensible Markup Language. To obtain more information, search for XML in the Visual Studio Help facility; it will direct you to several articles that discuss XML.

THE `Dispose()` METHOD

The code created by C# in Figure 10-22 and visible in the IDE includes a method named `Dispose()`, as follows:

```
protected override void Dispose(bool disposing)
{
    if (disposing && (components != null))
    {
       components.Dispose();
    }
    base.Dispose(disposing);
}
```

By now, you should be familiar and comfortable with most of the elements in the method:

- This method is `protected`, meaning any descendants can access it.
- The method header uses the term `override`, meaning it overrides a method with the same name in an interface named `IDisposable`. That interface provides a mechanism for releasing program resources, such as files, that can be used by only one program at a time. This method contains any cleanup activities you need when a `Form` is dismissed. When you write an application that leaves open files or other unfinished business, you might want to add statements to this method. You do not need to understand all the details of the `Dispose()` method in order to create a workable program. C# has created the method for you, and for now, you can let C# take care of the cleanup tasks that are invisible to you.
- The method's return type is `void`, so the method returns nothing to any method that calls it.
- The method accepts a `bool` parameter.
- The method includes an `if` statement and a call to another method that resides in its base class.

OBJECT DECLARATIONS

Within the Form1 class in Figure 10-22, you can see two object declarations:

```
private System.ComponentModel.IContainer components = null;
private System.Windows.Forms.Button button1;
```

The first statement declares an object named components that is used by the designer. The second statement declares an object named button1 . This object declaration was added to the code when the programmer dragged the Button onto the Form's surface. You could change the Button's access from private to public if you liked, but it is defined as private because it will be used only within this class. You also could eliminate the fully qualified System.Windows.Forms.Button class name and replace it with Button because the using statement at the top of the file includes System.Windows.Forms. You also can change the name of button1 to any other legal identifier you choose. However, if you delete button1 in the declaration and replace it with a new name, then you must be sure to change every instance of button1 in the program. The safer, and recommended, alternative is to change button1's Name property in the IDE. (You change it in the Settings box for the Name property, which you can locate in the Properties window of the Designer view. You can see the Properties window in the lower-right corner of Figure 10-19. You will get the opportunity to perform similar steps in the "You Do It" section later in this chapter.) When you change a control's Name property in the Properties window, every reference to the control will be replaced with its new identifier.

> **NOTE** If you change button1 's Name property within the code, switch to Designer view and then double-click the button to switch back to Code view. You will find that every instance of button1 has been changed to the new name you assigned.

When you create more complicated forms that contain additional objects such as Checkboxes, Labels, or more Buttons, more objects will be declared in the code.

THE InitializeComponent() METHOD

A dimmed rectangle with the label "Windows Form Designer generated code" appears just above the button1 declaration in Figure 10-22. To its left is a node with a plus sign (+). If you double-click the box, additional code is exposed, as shown in Figure 10-23. A method named InitializeComponent() occupies most of the newly exposed code.

The InitializeComponent() method contains all of the component initialization tasks. Many of the statements within the method should look familiar to you. These statements reflect the code generated by the properties that have been selected for the Form. For example, the button1.Text and Form this.Text properties contain values like those you would have typed into the code when creating a GUI application "by hand," without using the Visual Studio design environment. Similarly, the following statement sets a drawing size:

```
this.button1.Size = new System.Drawing.Size(75, 23);
```

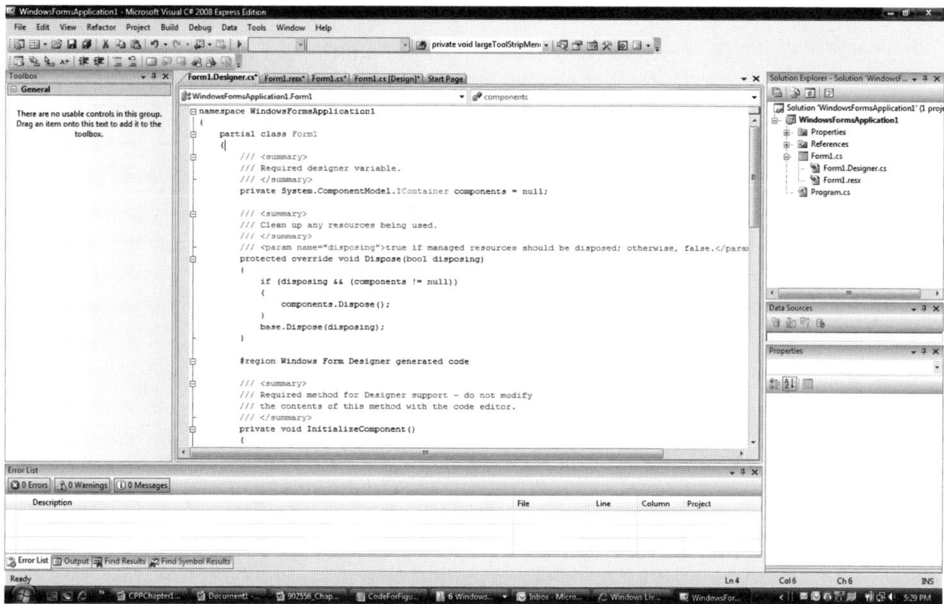

Figure 10-23 The `InitializeComponent()` method

PREPROCESSOR DIRECTIVES

The statements in the code that do not look familiar begin with a pound sign (#). The statements `#region` and `#endregion` are examples of preprocessor directives. **Preprocessor directives** always start with a pound sign (#) and are instructions to a program that executes before the compiler (called the **preprocessor**) to modify the code in some way. Any code placed between the `#region` and `#endregion` directives constitutes a group that can be used by some of the IDE's automated tools.

>> **NOTE**
> You can see the `#region` preprocessor directive in Figure 10-23. You would have to scroll down to see the `#endregion` directive.

For example, the Code Editor treats namespaces, classes, and methods as regions that you can collapse. Collapsing regions provides an outline of your code, hiding the details. Using this feature can make parts of your code easier to find. On the vertical line to the left of the code in the Code Editor, you can click a + to expand code and a – to collapse it. You can make your own collapsible code regions by surrounding sections with `#region` and `#endregion`. The `#region` and `#endregion` statements do not affect the way the code operates; they help you navigate the editor.

>> **NOTE**
> Other preprocessor directives in C# include `#if`, `#else`, `#elif`, `#endif`, `#define`, `#undef`, `#warning`, `#error`, and `#line`.

THE PROJECT'S `Main()` METHOD

At the right side of Figure 10-22, the Solution Explorer screen contains a file named Program.cs. This file contains the `Main()` method for the `WindowsFormsApplication1` application, as shown in Figure 10-24. You can see that the last line of code calls `Application.Run()` for this `Form`, just as you did manually for the `Windows` in Figures 10-13, 10-15, and 10-17 earlier in this chapter.

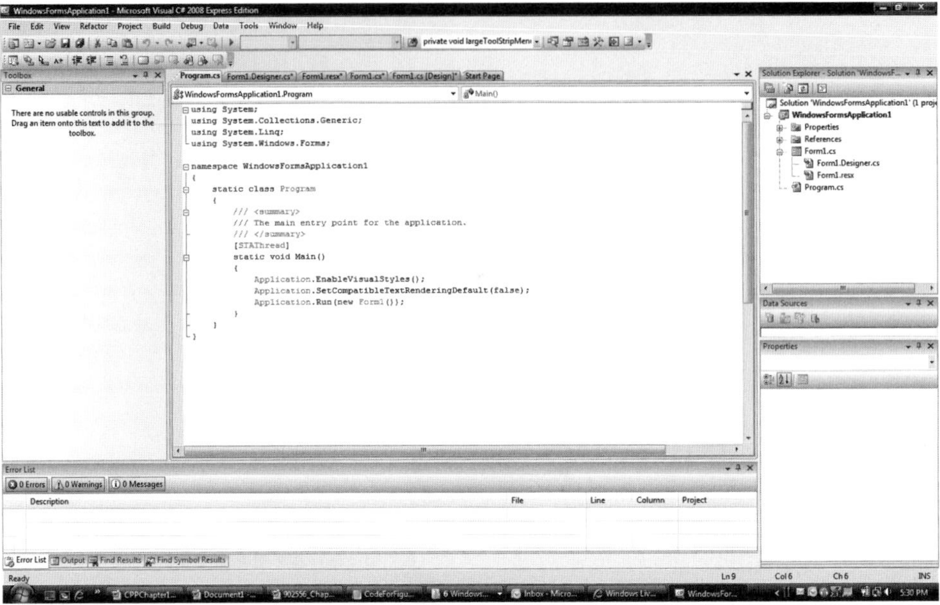

Figure 10-24 Program.cs file

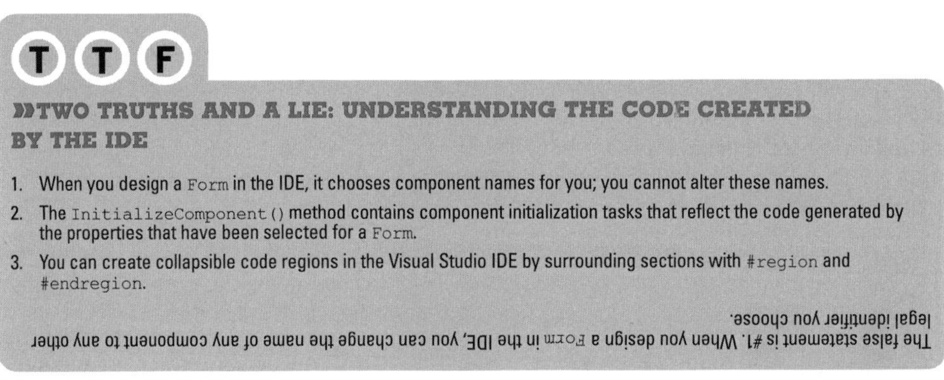

T T F

»TWO TRUTHS AND A LIE: UNDERSTANDING THE CODE CREATED BY THE IDE

1. When you design a `Form` in the IDE, it chooses component names for you; you cannot alter these names.
2. The `InitializeComponent()` method contains component initialization tasks that reflect the code generated by the properties that have been selected for a `Form`.
3. You can create collapsible code regions in the Visual Studio IDE by surrounding sections with `#region` and `#endregion`.

The false statement is #1. When you design a `Form` in the IDE, you can change the name of any component to any other legal identifier you choose.

ADDING FUNCTIONALITY TO A `Button` ON A `Form`

In most cases, it is easier to design a `Form` using the IDE than it is to write by hand all the code a `Form` requires. Adding functionality to a `Button` is particularly easy when you use the IDE. After you have dragged a `Button` onto a `Form`, you can double-click it. Figure 10-25 shows the generated code. The class contains a constructor that performs a single task—it calls the

```
using System.Text;
using System.Windows.Forms;

namespace WindowsFormsApplication1
{
   public partial class Form1 : Form
   {
      public Form1()
      {
          InitializeComponent();
      }

      private void button1_Click(object sender, EventArgs e)
      {

      }
   }
}
```

Figure 10-25 Partial `Form1` class that contains a constructor and `Click()` method

`InitializeComponent()` method. Following the constructor is a shell of a method named `button1_Click()`. In Figure 10-25, you can see that the method is `private` and `void`.

When a user interacts with a GUI object, an **event** is generated that causes the program to perform a task. When a user clicks a `Button`, the action fires a **click event**. This event causes the `Button`'s `Click()` method to execute. You might guess that if you placed a second button on the form, its method would be named `button2_Click()`. You might also guess that if you changed the `Name` property of the `button1` object in the IDE, the name of this method should also change. For example, if you renamed the `Button` `acceptLicenseAgreement`, the name of the method should become:

```
acceptLicenseAgreement_Click()
```

»NOTE Actually, the click event indirectly causes the `Button`'s `Click()` method to execute. Event handler code is operating "behind the scenes."

»NOTE Using a process called refactoring, C# can automatically change a method name when its associated object's name changes. See Appendix C.

»NOTE You are not required to create a `Click()` method for a `Button`. If, for some reason, you did not want to take any action when a user clicked a button, you simply would not include the method in your program. Alternatively, you could create an empty method that contains no statements between its curly braces and thus does nothing. However, these choices would be unusual—you usually place a `Button` on a `Form` because you expect it to be clicked at some point. You will frustrate users if you do not allow your `Controls` to act in expected ways.

You can write any statements you want between the curly braces of the `button1_Click()` method. For example, if you write the following statement, a `MessageBox` will be displayed when the user clicks the `Button`:

```
MessageBox.Show("You clicked the button");
```

»NOTE Chapter 12 describes event handling in detail.

Alternatively, you could declare a string that contains a message and use it within the class (see Figure 10-26).

```
using System.Text;
using System.Windows.Forms;

namespace WindowsFormsApplication1
{
    public partial class Form1 : Form
    {
        const string MESSAGE = "You clicked the button";
        public Form1()
        {
            InitializeComponent();
        }

        private void button1_Click(object sender, EventArgs e)
        {
            MessageBox.Show(MESSAGE);
        }
    }
}
```

Figure 10-26 `Form1` class that contains a declaration

»NOTE In Chapter 11, you will learn to place additional statements within your application's `Click()` methods.

»NOTE If you see a code screen in the IDE, you can return to the visual view of the `Form` by double-clicking Form1.cs in the Solution Explorer panel at the right side of the screen. Alternatively, you can right-click in the Code window and click View Designer.

»TWO TRUTHS AND A LIE: ADDING FUNCTIONALITY TO A `Button` ON A `Form`

1. When a user clicks a `Button`, the action fires a click event that causes the `Button`'s `Click()` method to execute.
2. If a `Button`'s identifier is `myButton`, then the name of its `Click()` method is `myButton.Click()`.
3. You can write any statements you want between the curly braces of a `Button`'s `Click()` method.

The false statement is #2. If a `Button`'s identifier is `myButton`, then the name of its `Click()` method is `myButton_Click()`.

USING VISUAL STUDIO HELP

When you are working with a class that is new to you, such as `Button` or `Form`, no book can answer all of your questions. The ultimate authority on C# classes is the Visual Studio Help documentation. You should use this tool often as you continue to learn about C# in particular and the Visual Studio products in general.

The Help documentation for Visual Studio is in the MSDN Library, which you can install locally on your own computer. It is also available at *http://msdn.microsoft.com/library*. You can install all or part of the library on your machine; the complete MSDN installation is close to 2 GB in size, and includes documentation for many Microsoft technologies besides C#.

There are multiple ways to access Help while working in Visual C#:

- » *F1 Search*—In the Code Editor, you can position the cursor on or just after a keyword or class member and press F1. The Help provided is context-sensitive, which means the screen you see depends on where your cursor is located.
- » *Search*—On the main menu, you can click Help, click Search, and type in a topic.
- » *Index*—You can select Help from the main menu and click Index. The index provides a quick way to locate documents in your local MSDN library. It searches only the index keywords that have been assigned to each document.
- » *Table of Contents*—The MSDN library table of contents shows all the topics in the library in a hierarchical tree structure. It is a useful tool for browsing through the documentation to see what is in the library, and for exploring documents that you might not find through the Index or Search tools. Often, when you find a document using F1, Index, or Search, it is useful to know where the document is located in the table of contents so you can see other related documentation.
- » *How Do I*—How Do I provides a view of MSDN documents called How-to's or Walkthroughs. These documents show you how to perform a specific task.
- » *Dynamic Help*—Dynamic Help provides a way to get information about the IDE. To open the Dynamic Help window, select Help from the main menu, and then click Dynamic Help. Then, when you click a word in the code, help topics are displayed accordingly.

»NOTE
You will learn much more about creating Windows applications using the IDE in the next two chapters.

»TWO TRUTHS AND A LIE: USING VISUAL STUDIO HELP

1. To get help in the Visual Studio IDE, you can position the cursor on or just after a keyword or class member in the Code Editor and press F10.
2. To get help in the Visual Studio IDE, you can click Help on the main menu, click Search, and type in a topic.
3. To get help in the Visual Studio IDE Index, you can select Help from the main menu and click Index.

The false statement is #1. As is the convention with most Microsoft products, you can get help in the Visual Studio IDE by positioning the cursor on or just after a keyword or class member in the Code Editor and pressing F1.

YOU DO IT

CREATING MessageBoxES

In the following steps, you will create GUI objects using the `MessageBox` class, and you will experiment with `MessageBox.Show()` method arguments.

To create MessageBoxes:

>> **NOTE**
> Appendix C contains details about using and getting the most benefit from the Visual C# editor, including why words appear in different colors as you type.

1. Open a new file in your text editor. Enter the first few lines of a program that will instantiate several `MessageBox` objects.

```
using System;
using System.Windows.Forms;
public class MessageBoxExperiment
{
```

2. Add a `Main()` method that declares two constant strings to serve as the `MessageBox` messages and captions.

```
public static void Main()
{
   const string MESSAGE = "Hello";
   const string CAPTION = "Message box experiment";
```

3. Create three `MessageBox` objects. The first has a single string argument that is the `MessageBox`'s message. The second `MessageBox` adds a caption, and the third adds two buttons.

```
MessageBox.Show(MESSAGE);
MessageBox.Show(MESSAGE, CAPTION);
MessageBox.Show(MESSAGE, CAPTION,
   MessageBoxButtons.OKCancel);
```

4. Add two closing curly braces—one for the `Main()` method and one for the class.
5. Save the file as **MessageBoxExperiment.cs**. Compile and execute the program. The first `MessageBox` appears on the left in Figure 10-27. Notice that the string "Hello" appears as the message, but no caption appears in the `MessageBox` title bar. A Close button is available in the upper-right corner of the `MessageBox`. Whether you click **OK** or **Close**, the second `MessageBox` appears, including the caption. Notice that this `MessageBox` is slightly wider than the first one to accommodate the title bar caption.

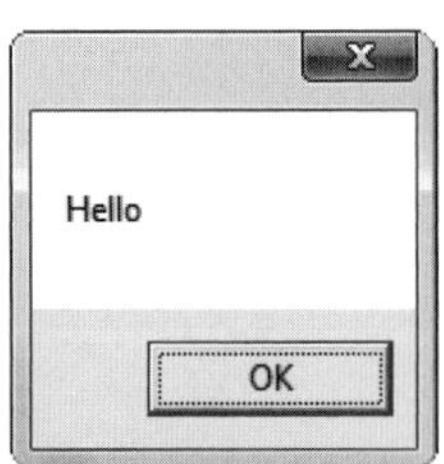

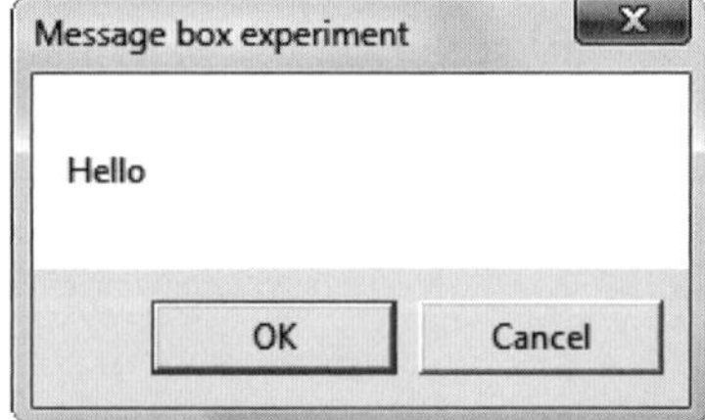

Figure 10-27 The three `MessageBox` objects created by `MessageBoxExperiment`

NOTE After you save the project, select Computer (or My Computer in Windows XP) or Windows Explorer to examine the `MessageBoxExperiment` folder in the directory where you saved the project. You will find multiple files and folders that require much more disk storage space than the simple .exe files for the applications you created without the IDE.

6. Whether you click **OK** or **Close** in the second `MessageBox`, the third `MessageBox` appears; it contains OK and Cancel buttons (see Figure 10-27). The OK button has a darker outline than the Cancel button, which means that the OK button has focus. If you press the Tab key or use the right and left arrow keys on your keyboard, you can change the focus from one button to the other. Whether you dismiss this `MessageBox` by pressing the Enter key, closing the box, or clicking one of the two buttons, the program ends.
7. Run the program several times and experiment by dismissing the `MessageBox`es using the various options (the Enter key, the `Button`s, or the Close button.).

NOTE After you run a program, you must remember to end it by clicking the Close button on the `Form`. If you return to the editor and make changes without closing the `Form`, the next time you attempt to run the program, you will receive an error message indicating that it cannot execute because it is being used by another process.

8. Resave the program as **MessageBoxExperiment2.cs**, then experiment by using different values for the message, caption, `MessageBoxButtons`, `MessageBoxIcon`, `MessageBoxDefaultButton`, and `MessageBoxOptions` for the individual `MessageBox`es.

WORKING WITH THE VISUAL STUDIO IDE

You can most easily understand the Visual Studio environment by using it. In the next steps, you will use the IDE to create a `Form` with a `Button`.

To use the IDE:

1. Open Microsoft Visual C# 2008 Express Edition. You might have a desktop shortcut you can double-click, or you might click **Start** on the taskbar, point to **All Programs**, and then click **Microsoft Visual C# 2008 Express Edition**. If you are using a school network, you might be able to select Visual Studio from the school's computing menu. Figure 10-28 shows the Visual C# Start Page.

NOTE Your steps might differ slightly from the ones listed here if you are using a version of C# other than Microsoft Visual C# 2008 Express Edition.

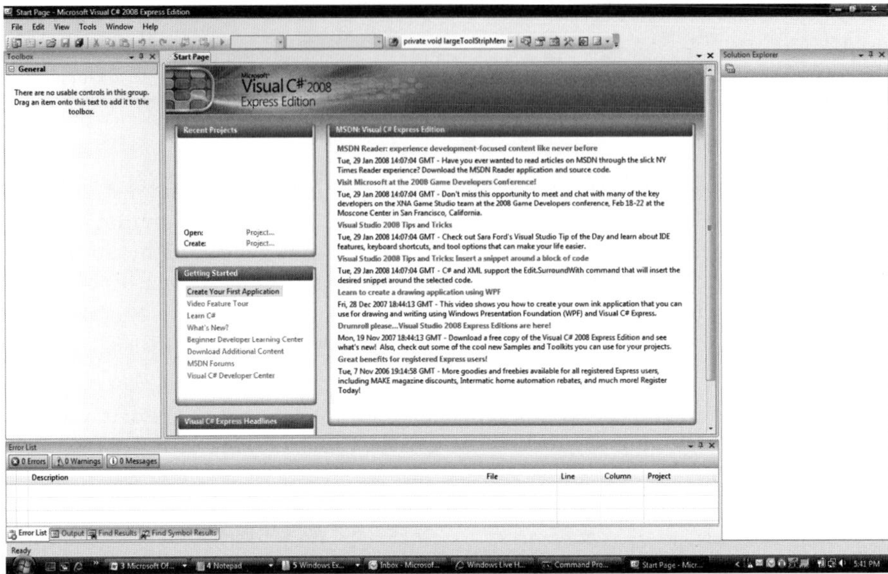

Figure 10-28 Visual C# Start Page

2. Click **File** on the menu bar and click **New Project**, as shown in Figure 10-29.

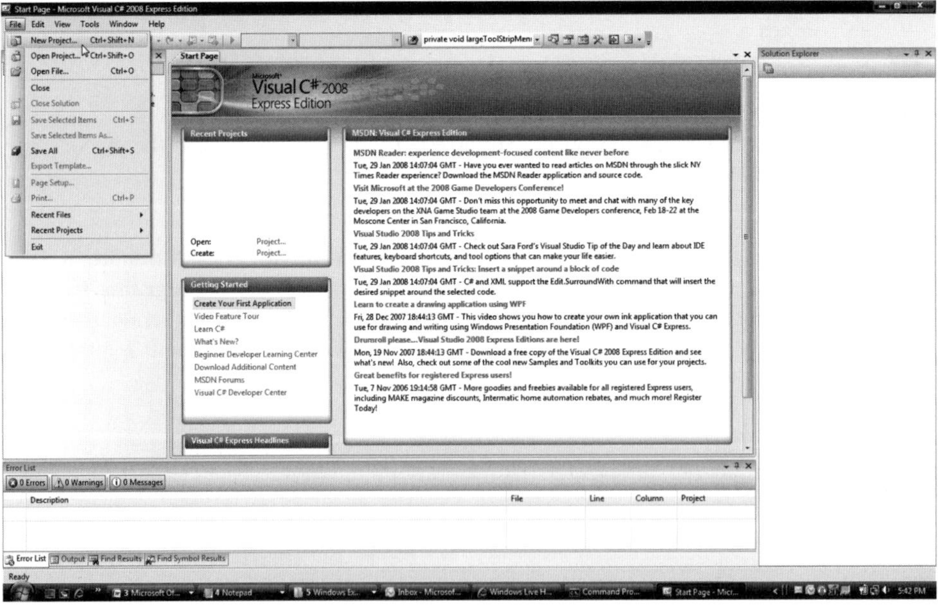

Figure 10-29 Opening a new project

3. A New Project window (see Figure 10-30) appears. Click **Windows Forms Application**. Near the bottom of the New Project window, click in the **Name** text box and replace the default name there (WindowsFormsApplication1) with **WindowCreatedWithIDE** as the name for your application. Figure 10-31 shows the design screen that appears.

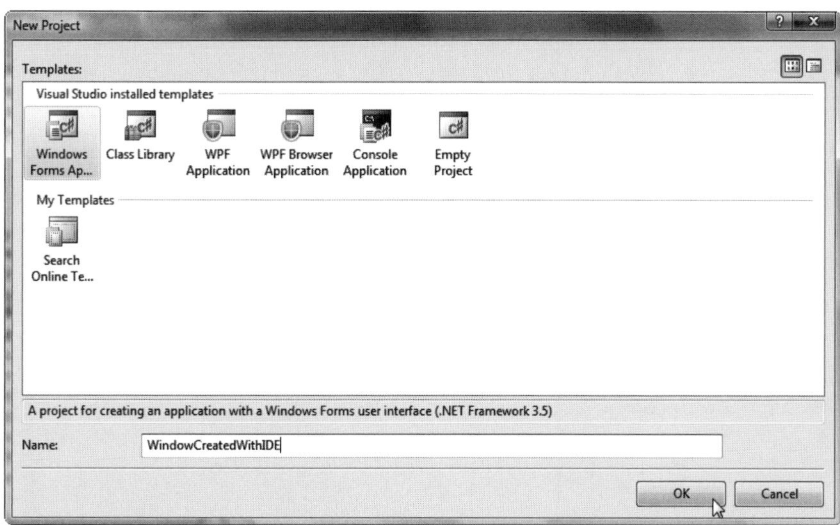

Figure 10-30 The New Project window

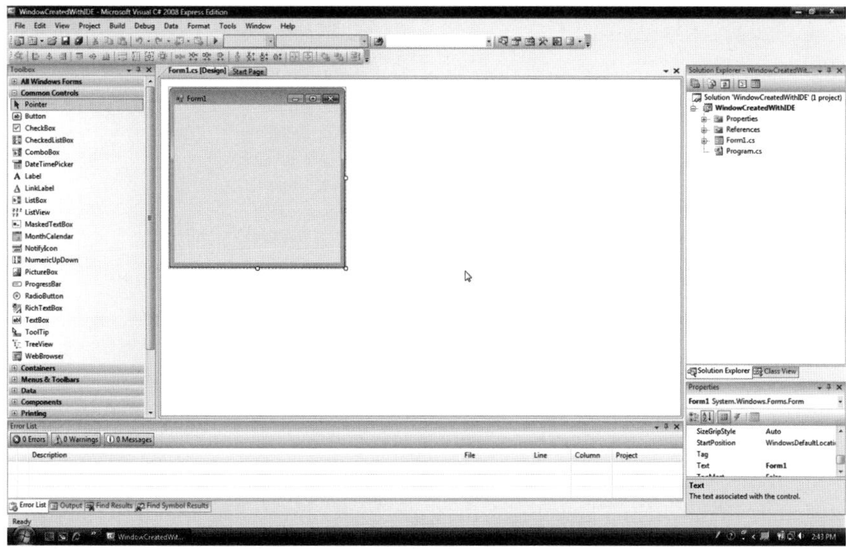

Figure 10-31 The `WindowCreatedWithIDE` project environment

»NOTE If you do not see the Toolbox as shown in Figure 10-31, click the Toolbox tab at the left side of the screen, and then click the pushpin near the top to pin the Toolbox to the screen. Alternatively, you can select View from the main menu bar at the top of the screen and then click Toolbox.

»NOTE If you do not see the Properties window in the lower-right corner of your screen, click the title bar on the `Form`. Alternatively, click View in the main menu and click Properties Window.

4. The text in the title bar of the blank `Form` contains the default name `Form1`. In the Properties window in the lower-right portion of the screen, you can see that the `Text` property is set to `Form1`. Take a moment to scroll through the list in the Properties window, examining the values of other properties of the `Form`. For example, the value of the `Size` property is 300, 300.
5. In the Properties window, click the description **Form1** in the Settings box for the `Text` property. Delete `Form1` and type **My First Form**. Press **Enter**; the title of the `Form` in the center of the screen changes to "My First Form". See Figure 10-32.

Figure 10-32 My First Form window

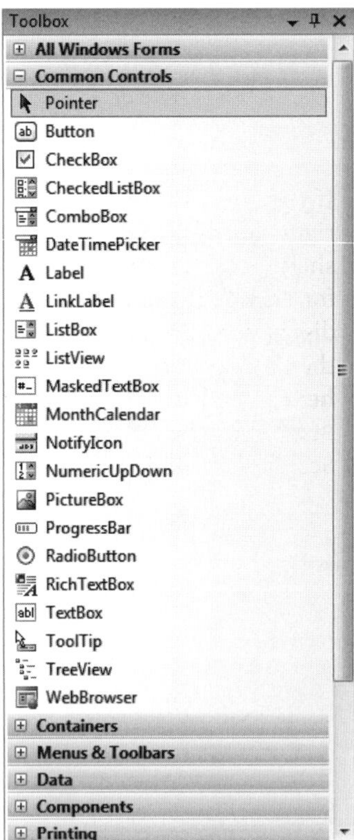

Figure 10-33 The Toolbox

6. Examine the Toolbox on the left side of the screen. Select **Common Controls** if it is not already selected. As shown in Figure 10-33, the Common Controls listed in the Toolbox are components that can be added to a `Form`, including `Pointer`, `Button`, `CheckBox`, and many others.

7. In the Toolbox, click **Button**. As you move your mouse off the Toolbox and onto the form, the mouse pointer changes so that it appears to carry a `Button`. Position your mouse anywhere on the form, then click and drag down and to the right. When you release the mouse button, the `Button` appears on the `Form` and contains the text "button1" (see Figure 10-34). When you click the `Button`, it displays handles that you can drag to resize the `Button`. When you click off the `Button` on the `Form`, the handles disappear.

Figure 10-34 A `Button` on a `Form`

8. If you click the `Form`, the list box on the right side of the screen under Properties shows that you are viewing the properties for `Form1`. If you click the `Button`, the list displays the properties for `button1`. Change the `Text` property of `button1` to **Click here**, then press **Enter**. The text of the `Button` on the `Form` changes to "Click here". See Figure 10-35.

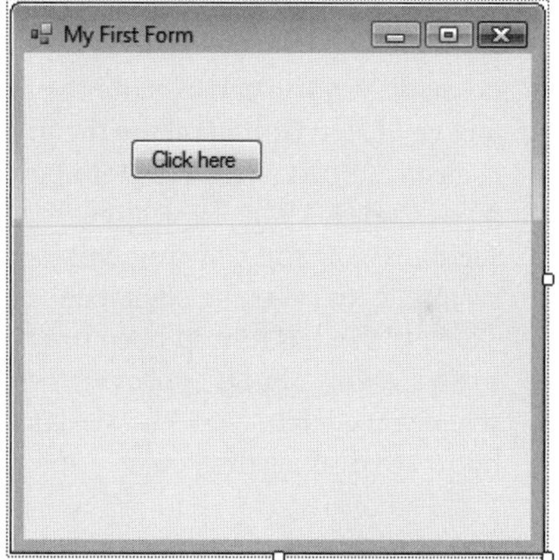

Figure 10-35 A `Button` with changed `Text`

9. Scroll through the other `button1` properties. The value in the Settings box for the `Location` property of the `Button` in Figure 10-35 is 59, 46. Your `Location` property might be different, depending on where you released the `Button` when you dragged it onto the `Form`. Drag the `Button` across the `Form` to a new position. Each time you release your mouse button, the value of the `Form Button`'s `Location` property is updated to reflect the new location. Try to drag the `Button` to location 80, 64. Alternatively, delete the contents of the `Location` property field and type **80, 64**. The `Button` moves to the requested location on the `Form`.

10. Save your form by clicking **File** on the menu bar, then clicking **Save All**. Alternatively, you can click the **Save All** button on the toolbar; its icon is a stack of diskettes. A Save Project dialog box appears, as in Figure 10-36. Confirm that the program name and disk location are correct. (You can click the **Browse** button to choose another storage location, or you can just type in the location.)

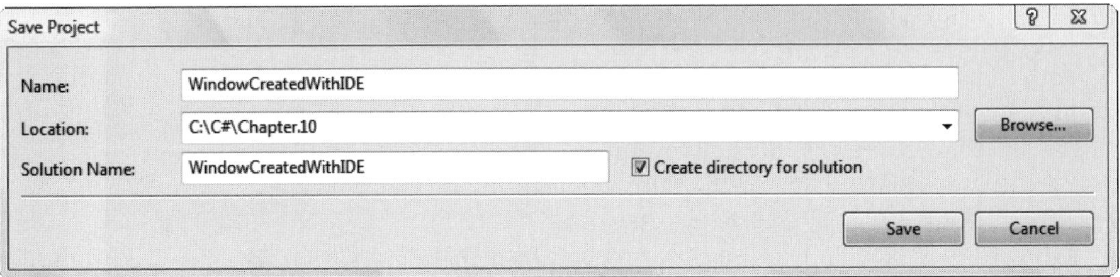

Figure 10-36 The Save Project dialog box

11. Although the `Form` you have designed doesn't do much yet, you can execute the program anyway. Click **Debug** on the menu bar and then click **Start Without Debugging**, or press **Ctrl+F5**. The `Form` appears. (See Figure 10-37.) You can drag, minimize, and restore it, and you can click its `Button`. The `Button` has not yet been programmed to do anything, but it appears to be pressed when you click it. Click the `Form`'s **Close** button to dismiss the `Form`.

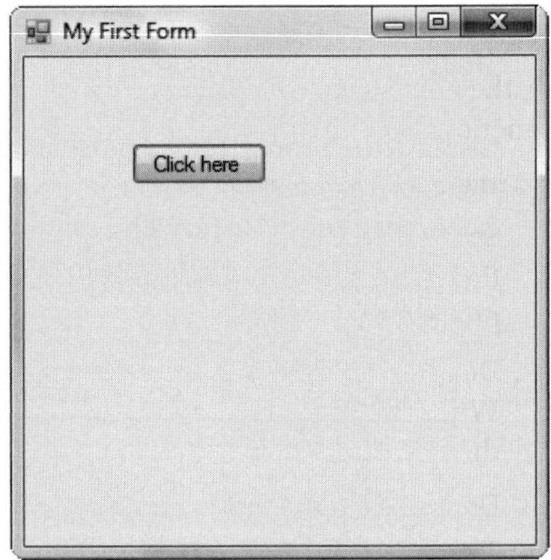

Figure 10-37 My First Form with a "Click here" button

12. Click **View** on the menu bar, click **Code**, and then view some of the code for the `Form`. In the Solution Explorer window at the right of the screen, click **Form1.Designer.cs** and view that code. (You might have to expand the Form1.cs node to see Form1.Designer.cs.) Finally, click **Program.cs** in the Solution Explorer window and view that part of the code. Based on the descriptions of the code presented in this chapter, how many components of the code do you recognize? For example, you should be able to identify comments, method calls, and the `Form1` constructor. Make some modifications to the properties. For example, if you want to change the location of the `Button` on the `Form`, return to Designer View

by choosing **View** on the menu bar and then **Designer**. (You can also click the **Form1.cs [Design]** page tab at the top of the code area.) Click on the Button so its Properties window is displayed in the lower-right corner of the screen. Next, change the Location values in the Properties window.

NOTE Recall that after any changes, an asterisk appears on the tab for Form1.Designer.cs. The asterisk means that changes have been made but not yet saved. When you save the project, the asterisk disappears.

Also experiment by changing the Font, Forecolor, and Text of the Button. Click on the Form so its properties are displayed, and modify its Text and Size . You can preview any changes by clicking the **Form1.Design** tab, or you can save the program and execute it again; the Button 's appearance will be modified.

13. Exit Visual Studio by clicking the **Close** button in the upper-right corner of the screen, or by clicking **File** on the menu bar and then clicking **Exit**. If you have made more changes since the last time you saved, you will be prompted to save again. When you choose **Yes**, the program closes.

PROVIDING FUNCTIONALITY FOR A Button

In the next steps, you will make the Button on the WindowCreatedWithIDE Form functional; it will display a MessageBox when the user clicks it.

To make a Button functional:

1. Start Visual Studio. Click **File** on the menu bar and then click **Open Project**. In the Open Project window, navigate to the folder where you stored the WindowCreatedWithIDE project.
2. Double-click the **WindowCreatedWithIDE** folder. Double-click the **WindowCreatedWithIDE.sln** file. In the Solution Explorer window, double-click the **Form1.cs** entry. The Form you created should appear in Designer View.
3. Double-click the Button on the Form. A new window that contains program code appears, revealing a newly created button1_Click method with no statements:

```
private void button1_Click(object sender, EventArgs e)
{
}
```

4. The method named button1_Click() will contain the code that identifies the actions you want to perform when a user clicks button1. The method receives two arguments—an object named sender and an EventArgs object named e. You will examine these objects more thoroughly in Chapter 11. For now, add some code that will display a MessageBox when the user clicks button1. Place your insertion point between the curly braces of the button1_Click() method, if necessary, and add the following:

```
MessageBox.Show("Thank you");
```

5. Save the file, then run the program by clicking **Debug** on the menu bar and clicking **Start Without Debugging**, or press **Ctrl+F5**. When My First Form appears, click the **Click here** button. The `MessageBox` that contains "Thank you" is displayed, as shown in Figure 10-38.

Figure 10-38 The `MessageBox` displayed after the user clicks the `Button` on My First Form

6. Dismiss the `MessageBox`, then close the `Form`.
7. In the Solution Explorer, click **Form1.Designer.cs** and expand the **Windows Form Designer generated code**. In the twelfth line of the `InitializeComponent()` method, a new statement has been added:

```
this.button1.Click += new System.EventHandler(this.button1_Click);
```

   This statement associates the `button1_Click()` method with the `button1.Click` event that is generated when a user clicks the `button1 Button`. In Chapter 12, you will learn more about events. Fortunately, the IDE allows you to use an event without understanding all the details of how one operates.
8. Select **Save All**, then close the IDE.

ADDING A SECOND `Button` TO A `Form`

`Forms` often contain multiple `Button` objects; a `Form` can contain as many `Buttons` as you need. Because each `Button` has a unique identifier, you can provide unique methods that execute when a user clicks each `Button`.

When you first use the IDE, the generated code appears intimidating. However, it is just C# code. You are already familiar with many of the statements you need to create useful and interesting programs. In the next steps, you will create a form that allows a customer to select one of two `Buttons` that identify two types of pizza—Cheese or Sausage. The form will then display one of two pizza prices—$10 or $12, depending on the user's selection.

1. Start Visual Studio. Click **File** on the menu bar, click **New Project**, and then click **Windows Forms Application**. Change the name of the project to **`WindowWithTwoButtons`**, as shown in Figure 10-39. Click **OK**.

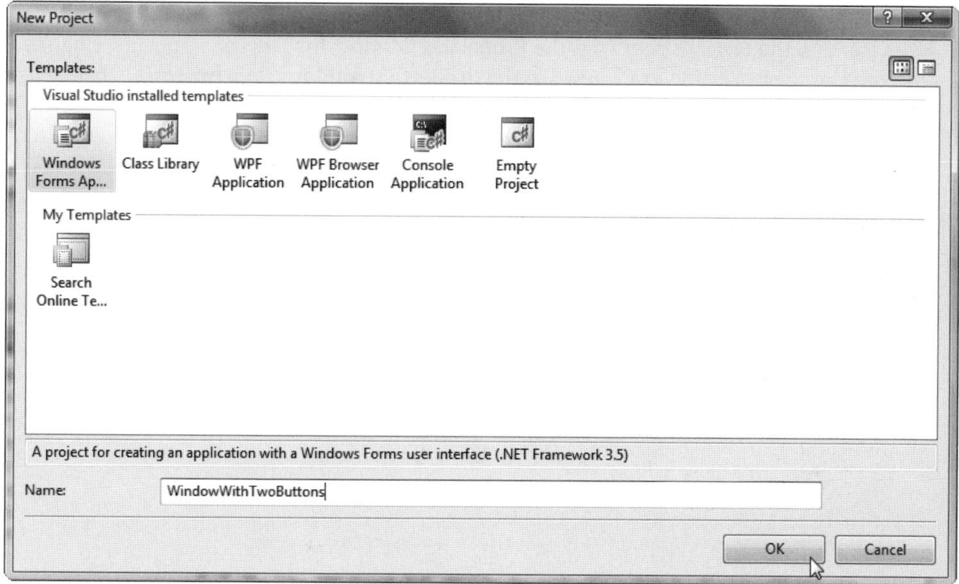

Figure 10-39 Opening a project

2. Click the title bar of the Form Designer that appears. In the `Form`'s Properties window, change the `Text` property of the form from Form1 to **Make a Choice**. When you press **Enter**, "Make a Choice" appears in the `Form`'s title bar. Drag a `Button` onto the `Form`. Release your mouse button to place the `Button` on the `Form`, then drag a second `Button` onto the `Form`. The `Button`s automatically contain text labels `button1` and `button2`, as shown in Figure 10-40.

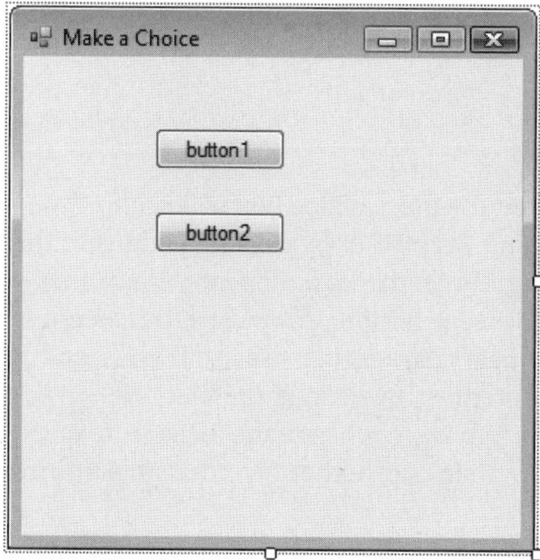

Figure 10-40 Two `Button`s on a `Form`

3. In the Properties window, click the list box and click **button1**. Alternatively, click `button1` on the `Form`. Either way, the Properties window for `button1` appears. Change its `Text` property setting to **Cheese**. In the Properties window, click **button2**. Change its `Text` property to **Sausage**. See Figure 10-41.

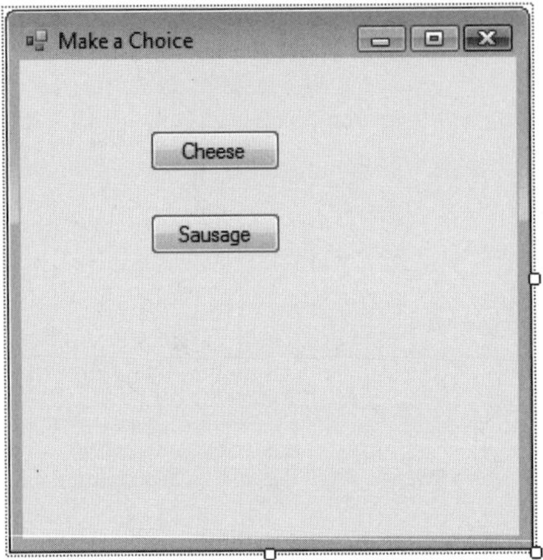

Figure 10-41 Two `Button`s on a `Form` with altered `Text` properties

4. Double-click the **Cheese** button to view the code for the `button1_Click()` method. Between the curly braces, type the following:

```
MessageBox.Show("Price is $10");
```

5. Return to Designer View. Double-click the **Sausage** button. Between the curly braces of the method, add the following:

```
MessageBox.Show("Price is $12");
```

6. Save the file. (If this is the first time you have saved the file, a dialog box will prompt you for a storage location.) Run the program by pressing **Ctrl+F5** or by clicking **Debug** on the menu bar and clicking **Start Without Debugging**. When the `Form` appears, notice that the Cheese button has a darker outline than the Sausage button; this means the Cheese button has focus. When a `Button` has focus, it appears darker than other `Button`s, and you can activate it by clicking it or pressing the Enter key. By default, the first `Button` you place on a `Form` has focus. The user can press the Tab key to change the focus from one `Button` to the next. Experiment with the **Tab** key, then click either `Button` and confirm that the correct price message is displayed.

7. Dismiss the MessageBox and click the other Button. Again, the correct price is displayed. Figure 10-42 shows the result when the user clicks **Sausage**.

Figure 10-42 A MessageBox displayed by the WindowWithTwoButtons project

8. Dismiss the MessageBox and close the Form.
9. If you want, you can experiment with the Size and Location properties of the Buttons. For example, when you dragged them onto the Form, you might not have created the Button objects to be exactly the same size or distance from the top of the Form. Correct this in the Properties window if necessary. Remember to save the project after you make any changes you want to keep.
10. Close Visual Studio.

CHAPTER SUMMARY

» A MessageBox is a GUI object that can contain text, buttons, and icons that inform and instruct a user. You use the static class method Show() to display a MessageBox; the method can accept strings as text or as a title for the MessageBox, and it can also accept arguments for buttons, icons, and other options.

» Usually you want to determine users' interactions with a MessageBox's buttons and take appropriate action based on the users' choices. DialogResult is an enumeration, or list of values, that correspond to a user's potential MessageBox button selections.

» Forms provide an interface for collecting, displaying, and delivering information; they are key components of GUI programs. Forms often contain controls such as text fields, buttons, and check boxes that users can manipulate to interact with a program. You can change the appearance, size, color, and window management features of a Form by setting its properties.

» You can create a child class from Form that becomes the main window of an application. You must derive a new custom class from the base class System.Windows.Forms.Form and write a Main() method that calls the Application.Run() method, passing an instance of your newly created Form class as an argument. This activity starts the program and makes the form visible.

» A window is more flexible than a MessageBox because you can place manipulatable Window controls wherever you like on the surface of the window. For example, you can create Button objects.

» The Visual Studio IDE provides a wealth of tools to help you design Forms. It allows you to use a visual environment rather than having to write multiple assignment statements and guess at appropriate component locations.

- » Using the Visual Studio IDE, it is easy to create elaborate forms with a few keystrokes. The generated code is simply a collection of C# statements. When you use the Designer in the IDE to design your forms, you save a lot of typing, which reduces the errors you create. The IDE creates a `Form` onto which you can drag controls. The generated code contains familiar components such as comments, object declarations, and methods.
- » Adding functionality to a `Button` is particularly easy using the IDE. After you have dragged a `Button` onto a `Form`, you can double-click it to generate a shell method into which you can place statements.
- » The ultimate authority on C# classes is the Visual Studio Help documentation. You should use this tool often as you continue to learn about C# in particular and the Visual Studio products in general. The Help documentation for Visual Studio is in the MSDN Library, which you can install locally on your own computer or view online.

KEY TERMS

A **graphical user interface (GUI)** employs graphical images that the user manipulates. GUI objects include the buttons, check boxes, and toolbars you are used to controlling with a mouse when you interact with Windows-type programs.

A **`MessageBox`** is a GUI object that can contain text, buttons, and icons that inform and instruct a user.

A **modal dialog box** prevents a program from further progress until the user dismisses the box.

When you **dismiss** a component, you get rid of it, frequently by pressing its Close button, but in some cases by making some other selection.

When a button has **focus**, not only is the user's attention drawn to it visually, but if the user presses the Enter key, the action associated with the button executes, just as it would if the user clicked the button.

`DialogResult` is an enumeration that contains a user's potential `MessageBox` button selections.

An **enumeration** is a list of values in which names are substituted for numeric values.

`Forms` provide an interface for collecting, displaying, and delivering information; they are key components of GUI programs.

Controls are GUI components such as text fields, buttons, and check boxes that users can manipulate to interact with a program.

A **`Button`** is a GUI object you can click to cause some action.

The **main menu** of the IDE runs horizontally across the top of the screen; it includes a File menu from which you open, close, and save projects.

The **Toolbox tab** of the IDE contains controls you can drag onto a `Form` so that you can develop programs visually, using a mouse.

The **Form Designer** and **Code Editor** of the IDE appear in the center of the Visual Studio screen. You can switch back and forth between these two when you want to design an application by dragging components onto the screen or you want to write or view code statements.

The **Solution Explorer** of the IDE allows you to view and manage project files and settings.

The **Properties window** of the IDE allows you to configure properties and events on controls in your user interface.

The **output tab** and **error list tab** of the IDE display any compiler errors.

In Visual Studio, a **node** is a box that appears on a vertical tree to the left of a list or a section of code and that can be expanded or condensed.

Preprocessor directives always start with a pound sign (#) and are instructions to the preprocessor to modify the code in some way.

The **preprocessor** is a program that executes before the compiler and looks for preprocessor directives for instructions on how to modify code.

When a user interacts with a GUI object, an **event** is generated that causes the program to perform a task.

When a user clicks a button, the action fires a **click event**.

REVIEW QUESTIONS

1. Which is true of the `MessageBox` class?

   a. You cannot create a new instance of this class.

   b. Its constructor is `public`.

   c. Its methods cannot be overloaded.

   d. Its `Show()` method is not overloaded.

2. A programmer who uses a `MessageBox` must ________ .

   a. determine the message that will appear on the OK button

   b. write the message that will appear in the `MessageBox`

   c. write an overloaded version of the `Show()` method

   d. select an icon to be displayed within the `MessageBox`

3. A programmer can select all of the following for a `MessageBox` except ________ .

   a. a message within it

   b. a caption in its title bar

   c. its default button

   d. its modality

4. A `MessageBox` is modal, meaning ________ .

   a. it can appear in several different styles

   b. the program will not progress until a user dismisses the `MessageBox`

   c. it is always rectangular with a title bar

   d. it appears in the Windows style so that all components have the same look and feel

5. An enumeration is a ________ in a program.
   a. list of values you can use
   b. sum or total of values used
   c. count of the number of values used
   d. list of values that cannot be used

6. Which of the following is not a possible `DialogResult`?
   a. Cancel
   b. OK
   c. End
   d. Retry

7. The `Form` class descends from the ________ class.
   a. `Object`
   b. `Component`
   c. `Control`
   d. all of these

8. The `Form` class differs from the `MessageBox` class in that ________ .
   a. you can create an instance of the `Form` class, but not the `MessageBox` class
   b. you can create an instance of the `MessageBox` class, but not the `Form` class
   c. `Form`s can contain `Button`s, but `MessageBox`es cannot
   d. `MessageBox`es can contain `Button`s, but `Form`s cannot

9. The `Form` class contains ________ properties.
   a. 2
   b. 5
   c. about 100
   d. more than 4000

10. Which of the following is not a `Form` property?
    a. `BackColor`
    b. `DesktopLocation`
    c. `Invisible`
    d. `Size`

11. When you create a new main window, you must ________ .
    a. derive a new custom class from the base class `System.Windows.Forms.Form`
    b. write a `Main()` method that calls the `Application.Run()` method
    c. either a or b, but not both
    d. both a and b

12. When used with a component, the `System.Drawing.Size` constructor takes two parameters representing ________ .
    a. width and height
    b. line thickness and horizontal position
    c. height and degrees of rotation
    d. horizontal position and width

13. A `Form`'s `Controls` are its ________ .
    a. `static` methods
    b. nonstatic methods
    c. manipulatable components
    d. parents

14. For a `Button` to appear to be pressed when a user clicks it, you ________ .
    a. need only to add the `Button` to a `Form`
    b. use the `System.Windows.Forms.Control` class
    c. include a `GUIImplement()` method within your program
    d. write a method named `ClickButton()`

15. The main reason to use the Visual Studio integrated development environment is to ________ .
    a. use methods that are not available when you write code by hand
    b. have access to the Studio's private data types
    c. make programs easier to design
    d. all of these

16. When you begin to create a `Form` using the Visual Studio IDE, the default `Form` name is ________ .
    a. `MyForm`
    b. `IDEForm`
    c. `Form1`
    d. `null`

17. When you design a `Form` using the IDE, ________ .
    a. much less code is generated than when you design a `Form` by hand
    b. the generated code is written in machine language so you cannot read it
    c. you cannot alter the generated code
    d. none of these

18. If you do not like the default name the IDE gives to a `Button`, you should ________ .
    a. change the `Name` property in the code
    b. change the `Name` property in the Properties window in the IDE
    c. either of these
    d. none of these

19. A partial class ________ .
    a. exists as an outline into which you must add statements
    b. is still being written
    c. has been saved, but not yet compiled
    d. is spread among multiple files

20. If a `Form` contains a `Button` named `agreeButton`, then you should code the actions to be performed when the user clicks the `Button` in a method named ________ .
    a. `ButtonClick()`
    b. `Button_Click()`
    c. `agreeButtonClick()`
    d. `agreeButton_Click()`

EXERCISES

1. Write a program that displays a `MessageBox` that contains contact information for your company. Save the program as **Contact.cs**.

2. Write a program for an Internet provider that displays a `MessageBox` asking users whether they want Internet access. If they do not, their total price is $0. If they do, display a second `MessageBox` asking whether they want limited access (at $10.95 per month) or unlimited access (at $19.95 per month). Display the total price in a third `MessageBox`. Save the program as **InternetAccess.cs**.

3. Write a program for an Internet provider that displays a `MessageBox` asking users whether they want to read the company's usage policy. Include a question icon. If the user chooses Yes, display a `MessageBox` that contains a short usage policy. If the user chooses No, display a `MessageBox` reminding the user to read the policy later. If the user chooses Cancel, end the program. Save the program as **Policy.cs**.

4. Write a program that simulates an Internet connection error. Display a `MessageBox` that notifies the user of the error and provide three buttons: Abort, Retry, and Ignore. If the user chooses Retry, display a message indicating that the connection succeeded. If the user chooses Ignore, display a message indicating that the user will work off-line. If the user chooses Abort, end the program. Save the program as **Connection.cs**.

5. Using the Visual Studio IDE, create a `Form` that contains a button labeled “About”. When a user clicks the button, display a `MessageBox` that contains your personal copyright statement for the program. Save the project as **About**.

6. Create a `Form` that contains two buttons for a book publisher. If a user clicks the Paperback button, display a `MessageBox` that contains a book price of $6.99. If the user clicks the Hardback button, display $24.99. Save the project as **Book**.

7. Create a game `Form` that contains six buttons. Display different prizes depending on the button the user selects. Save the project as **Game**.

DEBUGGING EXERCISES

Each of the following files or projects in the Chapter.10 folder on your Student Disk has syntax and/or logical errors. In each case, determine the problem and fix the program. After you correct the errors, save each file or project using the same filename preceded with *Fixed*. For example, the file DebugTen1.cs will become FixedDebugTen1.cs and the project folder for DebugTen3 will become FixedDebugTen3.

a. DebugTen1.cs

b. DebugTen2.cs

c. DebugTen3

d. DebugTen4

»NOTE
Immediately save the two project folders with their new names before you correct their errors.

UP FOR DISCUSSION

1. Think of some practice or position to which you are opposed. For example, you might have objections to organizations on the far right or left politically. Now suppose that such an organization offered you twice your annual salary to create Web sites for them. Would you do it? Is there a price at which you would do it? What if the organization was not so extreme, but featured products you found distasteful? What if the Web site you designed was not objectionable, but the parent company’s policies were objectionable? For example, if you are opposed to smoking, would you design a Web site for a tobacco company? At what price? What if the site just displayed sports scores without promoting smoking directly?
2. Suppose you have learned a lot about programming from your employer. Is it ethical for you to use this knowledge to start your own home-based programming business on the side? Does it matter whether you are in competition for the same clients as your employer? Does it matter whether you use just your programming expertise or whether you also use information about clients’ preferences and needs gathered from your regular job?

CHAPTER ELEVEN

11

USING CONTROLS

In this chapter you will:

Learn about `Controls`
Create a `Form` that contains `Labels`
Set a `Label`'s `Font`
Create a `Form` that contains `LinkLabels`
Add color to a `Form`
Add `CheckBox` and `RadioButton` objects to a `Form`
Add a `PictureBox` to a `Form`
Add `ListBox`, `ComboBox`, and `CheckedListBox` items to a `Form`
Add a `MonthCalendar` and `DateTimePicker` to a `Form`
Work with a `Form`'s layout
Add a `MenuStrip` to a `Form`
Learn to use other controls

In Chapter 10, you learned to create `Forms` by hand using an ordinary text editor and by using the Visual Studio IDE. Both approaches yield the same results, but the IDE provides you with an easy-to-use design environment. Additionally, by examining the IDE-generated program code, you can learn more about code you want to write by hand.

The `Form` and `Button` objects you created in Chapter 10 represent only a tiny fraction of the types of objects that are available to you in C#. When using programs or visiting Internet sites, you have encountered and used many other interactive **widgets**—elements of graphical interfaces that allow you to interact with programs—such as labels, scroll bars, check boxes, and radio buttons. C# has many classes that represent these GUI objects, and the Visual Studio IDE makes it easy to add them to your programs. In this chapter, you will learn to incorporate some of the most common and useful widgets into your programs. Additionally, you will see how these components work in general so you can use other widgets that are not covered in this book or that become available to programmers in future releases of C#.

NOTE GUI components are referred to as *widgets,* which some sources claim is a combination of the terms *window* and *gadgets.* Originally, "widget" comes from the 1924 play "Beggar on Horseback," by George Kaufman and Marc Connelly. In the play, a young composer gets engaged to the daughter of a rich businessman, and foresees spending his life doing pointless work in a bureaucratic big business that manufactures widgets, which represent a useless item whose purpose is never explained.

UNDERSTANDING ControlS

When you design a `Form`, you can place `Buttons` and other controls on the `Form` surface. The **`Control`** class provides the definitions for these GUI objects. `Control` objects such as `Forms` and `Buttons`, like all other objects in C#, ultimately derive from the `Object` class. Figure 11-1 shows where the `Control` class fits into the inheritance hierarchy.

```
System.Object
   System.MarshalByRefObject
      System.ComponentModel.Component
         System.Windows.Forms.Control
            26 Derived classes
```

Figure 11-1 `Control` class inheritance hierarchy

Figure 11-1 shows that all `Controls` are `Objects`, of course. They are also all `MarshalByRefObjects`. (A `MarshalByRefObject` is one you can instantiate on a remote computer so that you can manipulate a reference to the object rather than a local copy of the object.) `Controls` also descend from `Component`. (The **`Component`** class provides containment and cleanup for other objects—inheriting from `Component` allows `Controls` to be contained in objects such as `Forms`, and provides for disposal of `Controls` when they are destroyed. The `Control` class adds visual representation to `Components`.) The `Control` class implements very basic functionality required by classes that appear to the user—in other words, the GUI objects the user sees on the screen. This class handles user input through the keyboard and pointing devices as well as message routing and security. It defines the bounds of a `Control` by determining its position and size.

Table 11-1 shows the 26 direct descendants of `Control` and some commonly used descendants of those classes. It does not show all the descendants that exist; rather, it shows only the descendants covered in this chapter. For example, the `ButtonBase` class is the parent of `Button`, a class you used in Chapter 10. In this chapter, you will use two other `ButtonBase` children—`CheckBox` and `RadioButton`. This chapter cannot cover every `Control` that has been invented; however, after you learn to use some `Controls`, you will find that others work in much the same way. You also can read more about them in the Visual Studio Help documentation.

Class	Commonly Used Descendants
`Microsoft.WindowsCE.Forms.DocumentList`	
`System.Windows.Forms.AxHost`	
`System.Windows.Forms.ButtonBase`	`Button`, `CheckBox`, `RadioButton`
`System.Windows.Forms.DataGrid`	
`System.Windows.Forms.DataGridView`	
`System.Windows.Forms.DateTimePicker`	
`System.Windows.Forms.GroupBox`	
`System.Windows.Forms.Integration.ElementHost`	
`System.Windows.Forms.Label`	`LinkLabel`
`System.Windows.Forms.ListControl`	`ListBox`, `ComboBox`, `CheckedListBox`
`System.Windows.Forms.ListView`	
`System.Windows.Forms.MdiClient`	
`System.Windows.Forms.MonthCalendar`	
`System.Windows.Forms.PictureBox`	
`System.Windows.Forms.PrintPreviewControl`	
`System.Windows.Forms.ProgressBar`	
`System.Windows.Forms.ScrollableControl`	
`System.Windows.Forms.ScrollBar`	
`System.Windows.Forms.Splitter`	
`System.Windows.Forms.StatusBar`	
`System.Windows.Forms.TabControl`	
`System.Windows.Forms.TextBoxBase`	
`System.Windows.Forms.ToolBar`	
`System.Windows.Forms.TrackBar`	
`System.Windows.Forms.TreeView`	
`System.Windows.Forms.WebBrowserBase`	

Table 11-1 Classes derived from `System.Windows.Forms.Control`

Because Controls are all relatives, they share many of the same attributes. Each Control has more than 80 public properties and 20 protected ones. For example, each Control has a Font and a ForeColor that dictate how its text is displayed, and each Control has a Width and Height. Table 11-2 shows just some of the public properties associated with Controls in general; reading through them will give you an idea of the Control attributes that you can change.

Property	Description
AllowDrop	Gets or sets a value indicating whether the control can accept data that the user drags onto it
Anchor	Gets or sets the edges of the container to which a control is bound and determines how a control is resized with its parent
BackColor	Gets or sets the background color for the control
BackgroundImage	Gets or sets the background image displayed in the control
Bottom	Gets the distance, in pixels, between the bottom edge of the control and the top edge of its container's client area
Bounds	Gets or sets the size and location of the control, including its nonclient elements, in pixels, relative to the parent control
CanFocus	Gets a value indicating whether the control can receive focus
CanSelect	Gets a value indicating whether the control can be selected
Capture	Gets or sets a value indicating whether the control has captured the mouse
Container	Gets the IContainer that contains the Component (inherited from Component)
ContainsFocus	Gets a value indicating whether the control or one of its child controls currently has the input focus
Cursor	Gets or sets the cursor that is displayed when the mouse pointer is over the control
Disposing	Gets a value indicating whether the base Control class is in the process of disposing
Dock	Gets or sets which control borders are docked to its parent control and determines how a control is resized with its parent
Enabled	Gets or sets a value indicating whether the control can respond to user interaction
Focused	Gets a value indicating whether the control has input focus
Font	Gets or sets the font of the text displayed by the control
ForeColor	Gets or sets the foreground color of the control
HasChildren	Gets a value indicating whether the control contains one or more child controls
Height	Gets or sets the height of the control

Table 11-2 Selected public Control properties (*continued*)

Property	Description
`IsDisposed`	Gets a value indicating whether the control has been disposed of
`Left`	Gets or sets the distance, in pixels, between the left edge of the control and the left edge of its container's client area
`Location`	Gets or sets the coordinates of the upper-left corner of the control relative to the upper-left corner of its container
`Margin`	Gets or sets the space between controls
`ModifierKeys`	Gets a value indicating which of the modifier keys (Shift, Ctrl, and Alt) is in a pressed state
`MouseButtons`	Gets a value indicating which of the mouse buttons is in a pressed state
`MousePosition`	Gets the position of the mouse cursor in screen coordinates
`Name`	Gets or sets the name of the control
`Parent`	Gets or sets the parent container of the control
`Right`	Gets the distance, in pixels, between the right edge of the control and the left edge of its container's client area
`Size`	Gets or sets the height and width of the control
`TabIndex`	Gets or sets the tab order of the control within its container
`TabStop`	Gets or sets a value indicating whether the user can give focus to the control using the Tab key
`Text`	Gets or sets the text associated with this control
`Top`	Gets or sets the distance, in pixels, between the top edge of the control and the top edge of its container's client area
`TopLevelControl`	Gets the parent control that is not parented by another Windows `Forms` control; typically, this is the outermost `Form` in which the control is contained
`Visible`	Gets or sets a value indicating whether the control and all its parent controls are displayed
`Width`	Gets or sets the width of the control

Table 11-2 (*continued*)

»NOTE The description of each property in Table 11-2 indicates whether the property is read-only; such properties only get values and do not set them.

»NOTE In Chapter 10, you learned about the `Button Control` and how to declare a `Button`. You learned that you could change `Button` properties such as its `Text` either by typing statements or using the Properties window in Visual Studio. All the other `Control`s you learn about in this chapter can be manipulated in the same ways.

»TWO TRUTHS AND A LIE: UNDERSTANDING `Control`S

1. The `Control` class implements basic functionality required by GUI objects that a user sees on the screen.
2. Most `Control`s have `Font` and `ForeColor` properties.
3. Every `Control` has `Width` and `Height` properties.

The false statement is #2. Every `Control` has `Font` and `ForeColor` properties.

CREATING A `Form` WITH `Label`S

A **`Label`** is one of the simplest GUI `Control` objects you can place on a `Form`. The `Label` class descends directly from `Control`. Typically, you use a `Label` to provide descriptive text for another `Control` object (for example, to tell the user what pressing a `Button` will accomplish). You can also use a `Label` to display other text information on a `Form`.

Creating a `Label` is very similar to creating a `Button`. You can manually create a `Label` by using the class name and an identifier and then calling the class constructor. For example:

```
private Label label1;
label1 = new Label();
```

Alternatively, you could use the fully qualified class name and the `this` reference with the `label1` object, as in the following:

```
private System.Windows.Forms.Label label1;
this.label1 = new System.Windows.Forms.Label();
```

As when you created `Button` objects in Chapter 10, it is almost always more convenient to use the Visual Studio IDE to design `Form`s than it is to write the code statements. Figure 11-2

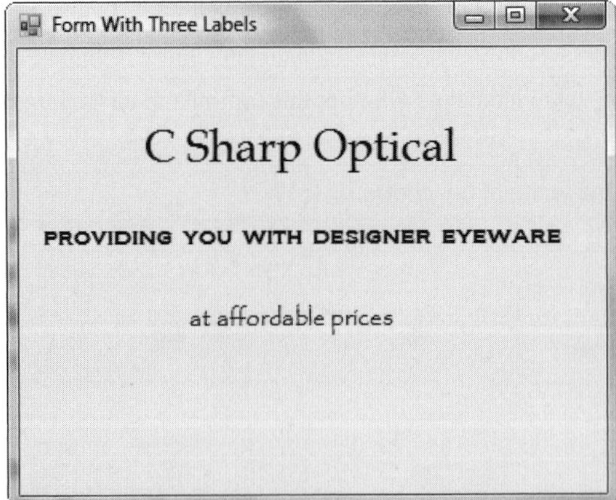

Figure 11-2 `Form` generated by `FormWithThreeLabels` program

shows a `Form` created in the IDE. Three `Labels` have been dragged onto a `Form`. The `Text` property of the `Form` has been set to "Form With Three Labels", and the `Text` property of each `Label` has been set. Additionally, a different `Font` has been selected for each `Label`.

Within the Form1.Designer.cs file in Visual Studio, three lines of code are generated as follows:

```
private System.Windows.Forms.Label label1;
private System.Windows.Forms.Label label2;
private System.Windows.Forms.Label label3;
```

These lines declare the three `Labels` just as you could have by typing the statements yourself.

To create this `Form`, the programmer only had to drag three objects and type four `strings`—one for the `Form` caption and three for the contents of the `Labels`. Then the programmer selected a font for each `Label` from a drop-down list in the Properties window. These actions generate all the code in Figure 11-3. (You must expand the code to see it. To do so, you can click the + in the **method node** to the left of the gray box that contains Windows Form Designer generated code, or you can double-click the gray box.) More than 30 statements are generated. By using the Visual Studio Designer, you save lots of time and eliminate many chances for error.

When you hover your mouse over the gray box, you can preview the collapsed code.

```
private void InitializeComponent()
{
    this.label1 = new System.Windows.Forms.Label();
    this.label2 = new System.Windows.Forms.Label();
    this.label3 = new System.Windows.Forms.Label();
    this.SuspendLayout();
    //
    // label1
    //
    this.label1.AutoSize = true;
    this.label1.Font = new System.Drawing.Font
       ("Book Antiqua", 20.25F,
       System.Drawing.FontStyle.Regular,
       System.Drawing.GraphicsUnit.Point, ((byte)(0)));
    this.label1.Location = new
       System.Drawing.Point(72, 42);
    this.label1.Name = "label1";
    this.label1.Size = new System.Drawing.Size(207, 32);
    this.label1.TabIndex = 0;
    this.label1.Text = "C Sharp Optical";
    //
    // label2
    //
```

Figure 11-3 `InitializeComponent()` method for `FormWithThreeLabels` (*continued*)

```
    this.label2.AutoSize = true;
    this.label2.Font = new System.Drawing.Font
       ("Biondi", 11.25F,
       System.Drawing.FontStyle.Regular,
       System.Drawing.GraphicsUnit.Point, ((byte)(0)));
    this.label2.Location = new
       System.Drawing.Point(12, 101);
    this.label2.Name = "label2";
    this.label2.Size = new System.Drawing.Size(326, 18);
    this.label2.TabIndex = 1;
    this.label2.Text =
       "providing you with designer eyeware";
    //
    // label3
    //
    this.label3.AutoSize = true;
    this.label3.Font = new System.Drawing.Font
       ("Papyrus", 11.25F,
       System.Drawing.FontStyle.Regular,
       System.Drawing.GraphicsUnit.Point, ((byte)(0)));
    this.label3.Location = new
       System.Drawing.Point(101, 148);
    this.label3.Name = "label3";
    this.label3.Size = new System.Drawing.Size(136, 24);
    this.label3.TabIndex = 2;
    this.label3.Text = "at affordable prices";
    //
    // Form1
    //
    this.AutoScaleDimensions = new
       System.Drawing.SizeF(6F, 13F);
    this.AutoScaleMode =
       System.Windows.Forms.AutoScaleMode.Font;
    this.ClientSize = new
       System.Drawing.Size(360, 264);
    this.Controls.Add(this.label3);
    this.Controls.Add(this.label2);
    this.Controls.Add(this.label1);
    this.Name = "Form1";
    this.Text = "Form With Three Labels";
    this.ResumeLayout(false);
    this.PerformLayout();

}
```

NOTE In Figure 11-3, every instance of `this` means "this `Form`."

Figure 11-3 (*continued*)

» **NOTE** So much code is automatically generated by Visual Studio that it can be hard to find what you want. To locate a line of code, click Edit on the main menu in the IDE, point to Find and Replace, click Quick Find, type a key phrase to search for, and click the Find Next button. (Instead of using the menu, you also can press Ctrl+F to open the Find dialog box.)

» **NOTE** When you view code in the IDE, some lines will be longer than those in Figure 11-3. Many code statements in this book have been split into multiple lines to fit the size of the page.

Do not be intimidated by the amount of code generated in Figure 11-3. You can easily understand most of it.

- After the `InitializeComponent()` method header and opening brace, the next three statements call the `Label` constructor for each `Label`.
- `SuspendLayout()` is a method that prevents conflicts when you are placing `Controls` on a form. Its counterparts are `ResumeLayout()` and `PerformLayout()`, which appear at the bottom of the method. If you remove these method calls from small applications, you won't notice the difference. However, in large applications, suspending the layout logic while you adjust the appearance of components improves performance.
- Comments serve to separate the `label1` code from other code in the method. Following the `label1` comment lines, seven statements set properties of the `Label`. For example, you can see that the `Font`, `Location`, `Size`, and `Text` have been assigned values based on the programmer's choices in the IDE.
- The property statements for `label2` and `label3` are similar to those for `label1`. The `TabIndex` for `label1` is 0 by default, the `TabIndex` for `label2` is 1, and so on. The `TabIndex` values determine the order in which `Controls` receive focus when the user presses the Tab key. This property is typically more useful for selectable items like `Buttons`.
- The `InitializeComponent()` method ends with statements that set the properties of the `Form`, such as its drawing size and text. You can also see the statements that add the three `Labels` to the `Form` using the `Add()` method.

» **NOTE** Although the property settings for the `Labels` refer to the label identifiers (for example, `this.label1.Name` or `this.label2.Font`), the property settings for the `Form` itself use only the reference `this`.

If you wanted to add a fourth label to the form while designing it, you *could* code a statement to declare it, code another statement to call its constructor, write all the statements to set all the properties, and insert a new `Add()` method call into the code for the `Form`. However, you should not design programs in this way. Instead, you should return to the Design view of the `Form` in the IDE, drag a new `Label` onto the form, and make changes in the Properties window. It is far easier this way, and you are less likely to generate errors.

» **NOTE** In this chapter, you will learn about several additional `Controls`. When designing a `Form`, you usually will use the drag-and-drop design features in the IDE instead of typing code statements. However, this chapter also teaches you about the code behind these actions so you can troubleshoot problems in projects and write usable statements when necessary.

»TWO TRUTHS AND A LIE: CREATING A `Form` WITH `Label`S

1. By using the Visual Studio Designer, you save lots of time and eliminate many chances for error.
2. When you use the Visual Studio IDE to drag a `Label` onto a `Form`, no constructor call is needed for the `Label`.
3. You can use the Visual Studio IDE to set properties for a `Label` such as `Font`, `Location`, `Size`, and `Text`.

The false statement is #2. When you use the Visual Studio IDE to drag a `Label` onto a `Form`, you do not have to write a constructor call, but one is generated for you.

SETTING A `Label`'S `Font`

You use the **`Font`** class to change the appearance of printed text on your `Form`s. When designing a `Label` or other `Control` on a `Form`, it is easiest to select a `Font` from the Properties list. After you place a `Control` on a `Form` in the IDE, you can select the ellipsis (three dots) that follows the current `Font` property name in the Properties list. (See Figure 11-4.) This selection displays a `Font` window in which you can choose a `Font` name, size, style, and other effects. (See Figure 11-5.)

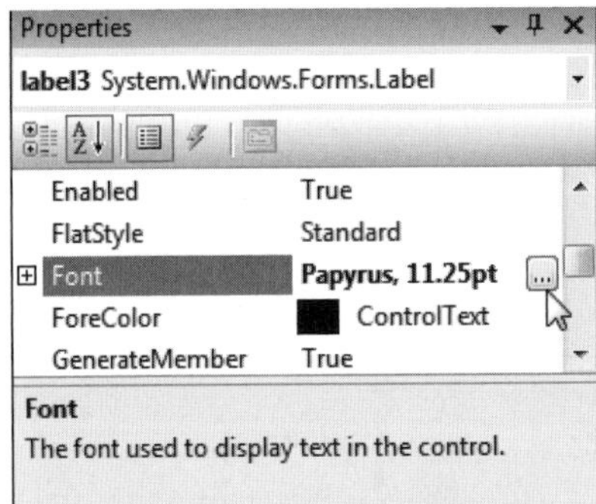

Figure 11-4 Clicking the ellipsis following the `Font` property

However, if you wanted to change a `Font` later in a program—for example, after a user clicks a button—you might want to create your own instance of the `Font` class. As another example, suppose you want to create multiple controls that use the same `Font`. In that case, it makes sense to declare a named instance of the `Font` class. For example, you can declare the following `Font`:

```
System.Drawing.Font myFont = new
   System.Drawing.Font("Courier New", 16f);
```

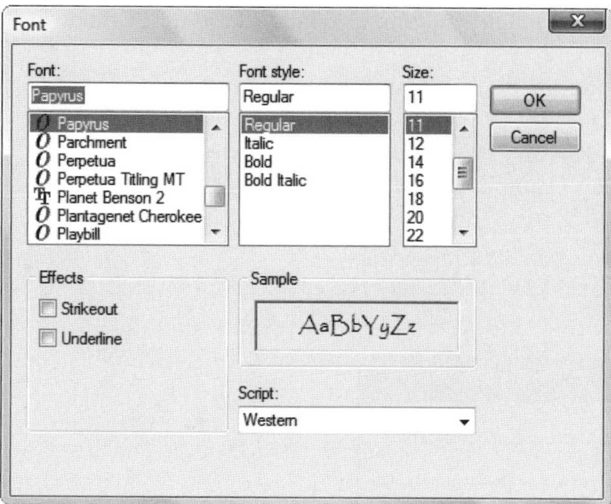

Figure 11-5 The `Font` window

Then, in the three statements that set the `Font` in the `InitializeComponent()` method in Figure 11-3, you can code the following:

```
this.label1.Font = myFont;
this.label2.Font = myFont;
this.label3.Font = myFont;
```

All three labels will display the same font: size 16 Courier New. If you want to change the font size or style later, you change it only in the one location where it is defined.

> **NOTE**
> If you want to change the properties of several objects at once in the IDE, you can drag your mouse around them to create a temporary group, and then change the property for all of them with one entry in the Properties list.

The `Font` class includes a number of overloaded constructors. For example, you can create a `Font` using two arguments (a type and a size) as follows:

```
System.Drawing.Font myFavoriteFont = new
     System.Drawing.Font("Courier New", 12.5F);
```

The string you pass to the `Font` constructor is the name of the font. If you use a font name that does not exist in your system, the `Font` defaults to Microsoft Sans Serif. The second value is a `float` that represents the font size. Notice that you must use an *F* (or an *f*) following the `Font` size value constant when it contains a decimal point to ensure that the constant will be recognized as a `float` and not a `double`. The `Font` constructor parameter list contains a `float` for size; using a `double` will generate a compiler error indicating that the `double` cannot be converted to a `float`. (If you use an `int` as the font size, you do not need the *f*, because the `int` will automatically be cast to a `float`, but a numeric constant such as 12.5 is a `double` by default.) An alternative would be to instantiate a `float` constant or variable, as in the following example, and use its name in the argument to the `Font` constructor:

> **NOTE**
> In Chapter 2, you learned to use an `f` following a floating-point constant to indicate the `float` type.

```
const float PREFERRED_SIZE = 12.5f;
```

You also can create a Font using three arguments, adding a FontStyle, as in the following example:

```
Font aFancyFont = new Font("Arial", 24, FontStyle.Italic);
```

Table 11-3 lists the available FontStyles. You can combine multiple styles using the pipe (|), which is also called the logical OR. For example, the following code creates a Font that is bold and underlined:

```
Font boldAndUnderlined = new Font("Helvetica",
   10, FontStyle.Bold | FontStyle.Underline);
```

Member Name	Description
Bold	Bold text
Italic	Italic text
Regular	Normal text
Strikeout	Text with a line through the middle
Underline	Underlined text

Table 11-3 FontStyle enumeration

Once you have defined a Font, you can set a Label's Font with a statement like the following:

```
this.label1.Font = myFavoriteFont;
```

Alternatively, you can create and assign an anonymous Font in one step. In other words, you do not provide an identifier for the Font, as in this example:

```
this.label1.Font = new
   System.DrawingFont("Courier New", 12.5F);
```

»NOTE If you don't provide an identifier for a Font, you can't reuse it. You will have to create it again to use it with additional Controls.

»TWO TRUTHS AND A LIE: SETTING A Label'S Font

1. You use the Font class to change the appearance of printed text on Controls in your Forms.
2. When designing a Label or other Control on a Form, you must select a Font from the Properties list in the IDE.
3. The Font class includes several overloaded constructors.

The false statement is #2. When designing a Label or other Control on a Form, it is easiest to select a Font from the Properties list, but you also can create your own instance of the Font class.

USING A LinkLabel

A **LinkLabel** is similar to a Label; it is a child of Label. Therefore, you can use it like a Label, but it provides the additional capability to link the user to other sources, such as Web pages or files. Table 11-4 summarizes the properties and lists the default event method for a LinkLabel. The **default event** for a Control is:

- » The method whose shell is automatically created when you double-click the Control while designing a project in the IDE
- » The method that you are most likely to alter when you use the Control
- » The event that users most likely expect to generate when they encounter the Control in a working application

With many Controls, including a LinkLabel, a mouse click by the user triggers the default event. When designing a program, you can double-click a Control in the IDE to generate a method shell, and then write any necessary statements within the shell.

Property or Method	Description
ActiveLinkColor	The color of the link when it is clicked
LinkColor	The original color of links before they have been visited; usually blue by default
LinkVisited	If true, the link's color is changed to the VisitedLinkColor
VisitedLinkColor	The color of a link after it has been visited; usually purple by default
LinkClicked()	Default event that is generated when the link is clicked by the user

Table 11-4 Commonly used LinkLabel properties and default event

»NOTE The default event for many Controls, such as Buttons and LinkLabels, occurs when the user clicks the Control. However, the default event for a Form is the Load() method. In other words, if you double-click a Form in the IDE, you generate this method. In it, you can place statements that execute as soon as a Form is loaded.

When you create a LinkLabel, it appears as underlined text. The text is blue by default, but you can change the color in the LinkLabel Properties list in the IDE. When you pass the mouse pointer over a LinkLabel, the pointer changes to a hand; you have seen similar behavior while using hyperlinks in Web pages. When a user clicks a LinkLabel, it generates a click event, just as clicking a Button does. When a click event is fired from a LinkLabel, a LinkClicked() method is executed, similar to how clicking a Button can execute a Clicked() method.

»NOTE You can create a program so that a user generates an event by clicking many types of objects. For example, for a Label named label1, you could write statements in a label1_Click() method. However, users do not usually expect to click Labels, but they do expect to click LinkLabels.

> **NOTE**
> When you double-click a `Label`, the automatically generated method name ends with `Click()`, but when you double-click a `LinkLabel`, the corresponding method ends with `Clicked()`.

Figure 11-6 shows a `Form` onto which two `LinkLabels` have been dragged from the Toolbox in the IDE. The `Text` properties of the `LinkLabels` have been changed to "Course Technology Website" and "Read Our Policy".

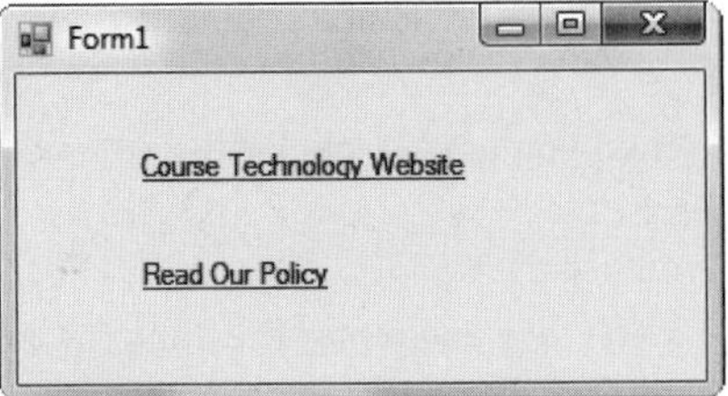

Figure 11-6 A `Form` with two `LinkLabels`

If you double-click a `LinkLabel` in the IDE, a method shell is created for you in the format `xxx_LinkClicked()`, where `xxx` is the value of the `Name` property assigned to the `LinkLabel`. (This corresponds to what happens when you double-click a `Button` in the IDE.) For example, Figure 11-7 shows the two generated methods for the `Form` in Figure 11-6 when the default `LinkLabel` identifiers `linkLabel1` and `linkLabel2` are used. In Figure 11-7, all the code was automatically generated except for the two shaded lines. The programmer added those lines to indicate which actions should occur when a user clicks the corresponding `LinkLabel` in a running application.

```
public partial class Form1 : Form
{
   public Form1()
   {
      InitializeComponent();
   }

   private void linkLabel1_LinkClicked(object sender,
     LinkLabelLinkClickedEventArgs e)
   {
      System.Diagnostics.Process.Start("IExplore",
         "http://www.course.com");
   }

   private void linkLabel2_LinkClicked(object sender,
      LinkLabelLinkClickedEventArgs e)
   {
      System.Diagnostics.Process.Start
         (@"C:\C#\Chapter.11\Policy.txt");
   }
}
```

Figure 11-7 Two `LinkClicked()` methods

In each of the `LinkClicked()` methods in Figure 11-7, the programmer has added a call to `System.Diagnostics.Process.Start()`. This method allows you to run other programs from within an application. The `Start()` method has two overloaded versions:

» When you use one `string` argument, you open the named file.

» When you use two arguments, you open an application and provide its needed arguments.

In the `linkLabel1_LinkClicked()` method, the two arguments open Internet Explorer ("`IExplore`") and pass it the address of the Course Technology Web site. If an Internet connection is active, control transfers to the Web site.

In the `linkLabel2_LinkClicked()` method, only one argument is provided. It opens a file stored on the local disk. Figure 11-8 shows the text file that opens when the user clicks the link. By default, Notepad opens to display the policy because Notepad is the default application for a file with a .txt extension. Alternatively, you could code the following, which explicitly names Notepad as the application:

```
System.Diagnostics.Process.Start("Notepad",
    @"C:\C#\Chapter.11\Policy.txt");
```

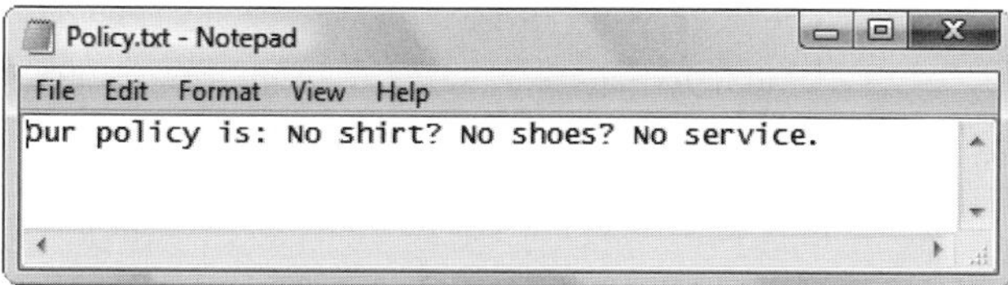

Figure 11-8 Text file opened by `linkLabel2_LinkClicked()` method

»NOTE In the `linkLabel2_LinkClicked()` method, an at sign (@) appears in front of the filename to be opened. This symbol indicates that all characters in the string should be interpreted literally. Therefore, the backslashes in the path are not interpreted as escape sequence characters.

The `LinkVisited` property can be set to `true` when you determine that a user has clicked a link, as shown in Figure 11-9. This setting indicates that the link should be displayed in a different color so the user can see the link has been visited. By default, the visited link color is purple, but you can change this setting in the Properties list for the `LinkLabel`.

```
private void linkLabel1_LinkClicked(object sender,
    LinkLabelLinkClickedEventArgs e)
{
    System.Diagnostics.Process.Start("IExplore",
        "http://www.course.com");
    linkLabel1.LinkVisited = true;
}
```

Figure 11-9 Setting the `LinkVisited` property

»TWO TRUTHS AND A LIE: USING A `LinkLabel`

1. A `LinkLabel` is similar to a child class of `Label` and it provides the additional capability to link the user to other sources.
2. The default event for a `Control` is the method whose shell is automatically created when you double-click the `Control` while designing a project in the IDE. Users most likely expect to generate this event when they encounter the `Control` in a working application.
3. When you create a `LinkLabel`, it appears as italicized underlined text, and when you pass the mouse pointer over a `LinkLabel`, the pointer changes to an hourglass.

The false statement is #3. When you create a `LinkLabel`, it appears as underlined text, and when you pass the mouse pointer over a `LinkLabel`, the pointer changes to a hand.

ADDING COLOR TO A `Form`

The **`Color`** class contains a wide variety of predefined `Colors` that you can use with your `Controls` (see Table 11-5).

» NOTE C# also allows you to create custom colors. If no color in Table 11-5 suits your needs, search for "custom color" in the Visual Studio Help to obtain more information.

AliceBlue	Chocolate	DarkOrchid	Fuchsia
AntiqueWhite	Coral	DarkRed	Gainsboro
Aqua	CornflowerBlue	DarkSalmon	GhostWhite
Aquamarine	Cornsilk	DarkSeaGreen	Gold
Azure	Crimson	DarkSlateBlue	Goldenrod
Beige	Cyan	DarkSlateGray	Gray
Bisque	DarkBlue	DarkTurquoise	Green
Black	DarkCyan	DarkViolet	GreenYellow
BlanchedAlmond	DarkGoldenrod	DeepPink	Honeydew
Blue	DarkGray	DeepSkyBlue	HotPink
BlueViolet	DarkGreen	DimGray	IndianRed
Brown	DarkKhaki	DodgerBlue	Indigo
BurlyWood	DarkMagenta	Firebrick	Ivory
CadetBlue	DarkOliveGreen	FloralWhite	Khaki
Chartreuse	DarkOrange	ForestGreen	Lavender

Table 11-5 `Color` properties (*continued*)

LavenderBlush	MediumAquamarine	PaleGoldenrod	SkyBlue
LawnGreen	MediumBlue	PaleGreen	SlateBlue
LemonChiffon	MediumOrchid	PaleTurquoise	SlateGray
LightBlue	MediumPurple	PaleVioletRed	Snow
LightCoral	MediumSeaGreen	PapayaWhip	SpringGreen
LightCyan	MediumSlateBlue	PeachPuff	SteelBlue
LightGoldenrodYellow	MediumSpringGreen	Peru	Tan
LightGray	MediumTurquoise	Pink	Teal
LightGreen	MediumVioletRed	Plum	Thistle
LightPink	MidnightBlue	PowderBlue	Tomato
LightSalmon	MintCream	Purple	Transparent
LightSeaGreen	MistyRose	Red	Turquoise
LightSkyBlue	Moccasin	RosyBrown	Violet
LightSlateGray	NavajoWhite	RoyalBlue	Wheat
LightSteelBlue	Navy	SaddleBrown	White
LightYellow	OldLace	Salmon	WhiteSmoke
Lime	Olive	SandyBrown	Yellow
LimeGreen	OliveDrab	SeaGreen	YellowGreen
Linen	Orange	SeaShell	
Magenta	OrangeRed	Sienna	
Maroon	Orchid	Silver	

Table 11-5 (*continued*)

When you are designing a `Form`, you can choose colors from a list next to the `BackColor` and `ForeColor` properties in the IDE's Properties list. The statements created will be similar to the following:

```
this.label1.BackColor = System.Drawing.Color.Blue;
this.label1.ForeColor = System.Drawing.Color.Gold;
```

NOTE If you add `using System.Drawing;` at the top of your file, you can eliminate the references in the preceding lines and refer to the colors simply as `Color.Blue` and `Color.Gold`.

NOTE For professional-looking results when you prepare a resume or most other business documents, business executives recommend that you only use one or two fonts and colors, even though your word-processing program allows many such selections. The same is true when you design interactive GUI applications. Although many fonts and colors are available, you probably should stick with a few choices in a single project.

»TWO TRUTHS AND A LIE: ADDING COLOR TO A `Form`

1. Because the choice of colors in C# is limited, you are required to create custom colors for many GUI applications.
2. When you are designing a `Form`, color choices appear in a list next to the `BackColor` and `ForeColor` properties in the IDE's Properties list.
3. The complete name of the color pink in C# is `System.Drawing.Color.Pink`.

The false statement is #1. The `Color` class contains a wide variety of predefined `Colors` that you can use with your `Controls`.

USING `CheckBox` AND `RadioButton` OBJECTS

In Chapter 10, you placed `Button` objects on a `Form`. The `Button` class derives from the `ButtonBase` class. The `ButtonBase` class has two other descendants: `CheckBox` and `RadioButton`.

`CheckBox` objects are GUI widgets the user can click to select or deselect an option. When a `Form` contains multiple `CheckBox`es, any number of them can be checked or unchecked at the same time. **`RadioButtons`** are similar to `CheckBox`es, except that when they are placed on a `Form`, only one `RadioButton` can be selected at a time—selecting any `RadioButton` automatically deselects the others. Table 11-6 contains commonly used `CheckBox` properties and the default event for which a method shell is generated when you double-click a `CheckBox` in the IDE. Table 11-7 contains the properties and default event for `RadioButtons`.

Property or Method	Description
`Checked`	Indicates whether the `CheckBox` is checked
`CheckState`	Indicates whether the `CheckBox` is checked, with a value for the `CheckState` enumeration (`Checked`, `Unchecked`, or `Indeterminate`)
`Text`	The text displayed to the right of the `CheckBox`
`CheckedChanged()`	Default event that is generated when the `Checked` property changes

Table 11-6 Commonly used `CheckBox` properties and default event

»NOTE If you precede a letter in the `Text` property value of a `ButtonBase` object with an ampersand (&), that letter acts as an access key. For example, if a `Button`'s text is defined as `&Press`, then typing Alt + P has the same effect as clicking the `Button`. Access keys are also called hot keys.

Property or Method	Description
Checked	Indicates whether the RadioButton is checked
Text	The text displayed to the right of the RadioButton
CheckedChanged()	Default event that is generated when the Checked property changes

Table 11-7 Commonly used RadioButton properties and default event

»NOTE You can place multiple groups of RadioButtons on a Form by using a GroupBox or Panel. For example, if you place several GroupBox Controls on a Form and you place several RadioButtons in each GroupBox, then one RadioButton can be selected from each GroupBox at any point in time; in other words, each GroupBox operates independently. You will learn more about GroupBoxes and Panels later in this chapter.

Figure 11-10 shows an example of a Form that contains several Labels, four CheckBox objects, and three RadioButton objects. It makes sense for the pizza topping choices to be displayed using CheckBoxes because a user might select multiple toppings. However, options for delivery, pick-up, and dining in the restaurant are mutually exclusive, so they are presented using RadioButton objects.

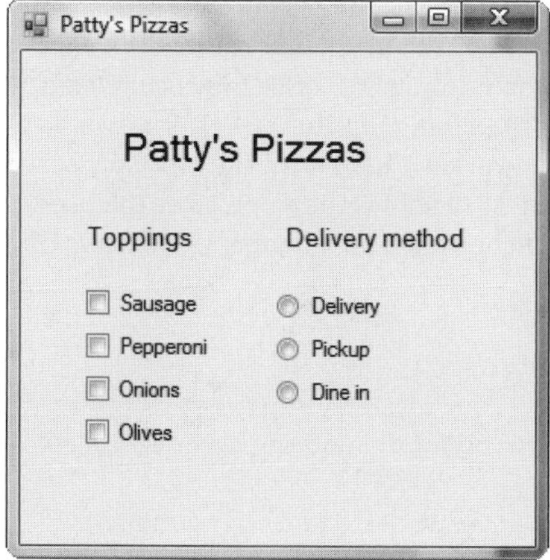

Figure 11-10 A Form with Labels, CheckBoxes, and RadioButtons

When you add CheckBox and RadioButton objects to a form, they automatically are named using the same conventions you have seen with Buttons and Labels. That is, the first CheckBox is named checkBox1 by default, the second is named checkBox2, and so on. Using the Properties list, you can assign more meaningful names such as sausageCheckBox and pepperoniCheckBox. Naming objects appropriately makes your code more understandable to others, and makes your programming job easier.

Both CheckBox and RadioButton objects have a Checked property whose value is true or false. For example, if you create a CheckBox named sausageCheckBox and you want to add $1.00 to a pizzaPrice value when the user checks the box, you can write the following:

```
if(sausageCheckBox.Checked)
    pizzaPrice = pizzaPrice + 1.00;
```

Both CheckBox and RadioButton objects also have a CheckedChanged() method that is called when a user clicks any CheckBox or RadioButton.

Suppose the total price of a pizza should be altered based on a user's selections. In this example, the base price for a pizza is $12.00, and $1.25 is added for each selected topping. You can declare constants for the BASE_PRICE and TOPPING_PRICE of a pizza and declare a variable that is initialized to the pizza base price as follows:

```
private const double BASE_PRICE = 12.00;
private const double TOPPING_PRICE = 1.25;
private double price = BASE_PRICE;
```

Figure 11-11 shows some of the code you would add to the Form.cs file for the application. The sausageCheckBox_CheckedChanged() method changes the pizza price. The shaded statements in the method were written by a programmer; the unshaded statements were generated by the IDE. If a change occurs because the sausageCheckBox was checked, then the TOPPING_PRICE is added to the price. If the change to the checkBox was to uncheck it, the TOPPING_PRICE is subtracted from the price. Either way, the Text property of a Label is changed to reflect the new price. Figure 11-12 shows the Form after the user has checked a box, checked another box, and then unchecked a box. Figure 11-13 shows the entire Form.cs file.

```
private void sausageCheckBox_CheckedChanged(object sender, EventArgs e)
{
    if (sausageCheckBox.Checked)
        price += TOPPING_PRICE;
    else
        price -= TOPPING_PRICE;
    totalLabel.Text = "Total is " + price.ToString("C");
}
```

Figure 11-11 The sausageCheckBox_CheckedChanged() method

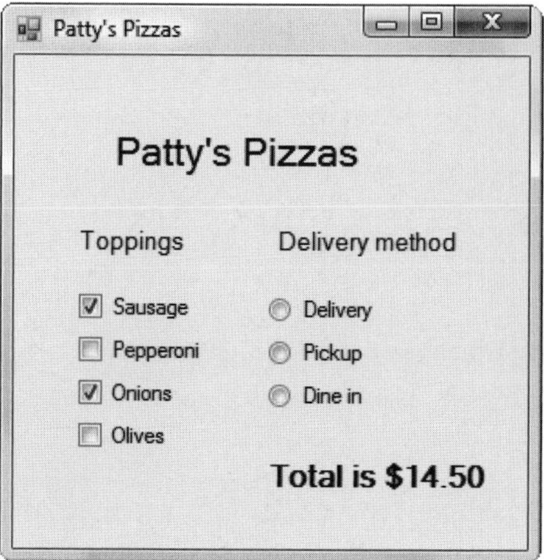

Figure 11-12 Typical execution of `PattysPizza` program after code is added for `CheckBox`es

```
using System;
using System.Collections.Generic;
using System.ComponentModel;
using System.Data;
using System.Drawing;
using System.Linq;
using System.Text;
using System.Windows.Forms;

namespace PattysPizza
{
     public partial class Form1 : Form
     {
          private const double BASE_PRICE = 12.00;
          private const double TOPPING_PRICE = 1.25;
          private double price = BASE_PRICE;

          public Form1()
          {
               InitializeComponent();
          }
```

Figure 11-13 The Form1.cs file of the `PattysPizza` application showing `CheckBox CheckedChanged` methods (*continued*)

```
        private void sausageCheckBox_CheckedChanged(object sender, EventArgs e)
        {
            if (sausageCheckBox.Checked)
                price += TOPPING_PRICE;
            else
                price -= TOPPING_PRICE;
            totalLabel.Text = "Total is " + price.ToString("C");
        }

        private void pepperoniCheckBox_CheckedChanged(object sender, EventArgs e)
        {
            if (pepperoniCheckBox.Checked)
                price += TOPPING_PRICE;
            else
                price -= TOPPING_PRICE;
            totalLabel.Text = "Total is " + price.ToString("C");
        }

        private void onionCheckBox_CheckedChanged(object sender, EventArgs e)
        {
            if (onionCheckBox.Checked)
                price += TOPPING_PRICE;
            else
                price -= TOPPING_PRICE;
            totalLabel.Text = "Total is " + price.ToString("C");
        }

        private void oliveCheckBox_CheckedChanged(object sender, EventArgs e)
        {
            if (oliveCheckBox.Checked)
                price += TOPPING_PRICE;
            else
                price -= TOPPING_PRICE;
            totalLabel.Text = "Total is " + price.ToString("C");
        }
    }
}
```

Figure 11-13 (*continued*)

In a similar fashion, you can add appropriate code for `RadioButton` objects. For example, assume that a $2.00 delivery charge is in effect, but there is no extra charge for customers who pick up a pizza or dine in. The code for `deliverRadioButton_CheckedChanged()` appears in Figure 11-14. When the user selects the `deliverRadioButton`, $2.00 is added to the total. When the user selects either of the other `RadioButton`s, the `deliverRadioButton` becomes unchecked, and the $2.00 charge is removed from the total.

```
private void deliverRadioButton_CheckedChanged(object sender, EventArgs e)
{
    const double DELIVERY_CHARGE = 2.00;
    if (deliverRadioButton.Checked)
        price += DELIVERY_CHARGE;
    else
        price -= DELIVERY_CHARGE;
    totalLabel.Text = "Total is " + price.ToString("C");
}
```

Figure 11-14 The `deliverRadioButton_CheckedChanged()` method

»TWO TRUTHS AND A LIE: USING CheckBox AND RadioButton OBJECTS

1. CheckBox objects are GUI widgets that the user can click to select or deselect an option; when a Form contains multiple CheckBoxes, any number of them can be checked or unchecked at the same time.
2. RadioButtons are similar to CheckBoxes, except that when they are placed on a Form, only one RadioButton can be selected at a time—selecting any RadioButton automatically deselects the others.
3. The default event for a CheckBox is CheckBoxChanged() and the default event for a RadioButton is RadioButtonChanged().

The false statement is #3. The default event for both CheckBox and RadioButton objects is CheckedChanged().

»NOTE When an application starts, sometimes you want a CheckBox or RadioButton to be selected by default. If so, you can set the CheckBox or RadioButton's Checked property to true.

ADDING A PictureBox TO A Form

A **PictureBox** is a Control in which you can display graphics from a bitmap, icon, JPEG, GIF, or other image file type. Just as with a Button or a Label, you can easily drag a PictureBox Control onto a Form in the Visual Studio IDE. Table 11-8 shows the common properties and default event for a PictureBox.

Property or Method	Description
Image	Sets the image that appears in the PictureBox
SizeMode	Controls the size and position of the image in the PictureBox; values are Normal, StretchImage (which resizes the image to fit the PictureBox), AutoSize (which resizes the PictureBox to fit the image), and CenterImage (which centers the image in the PictureBox)
Click()	Default event that is generated when the user clicks the PictureBox

Table 11-8 Commonly used PictureBox properties and default event

Figure 11-15 shows a new project in the IDE. The following tasks have been completed:

- A project was started.
- The `Form Text` property was changed to "Save Money".
- The `Form BackColor` property was changed to white.
- A `Label` was dragged onto the `Form`, and its `Text` and `Font` were changed.
- A `PictureBox` was dragged onto the `Form`.

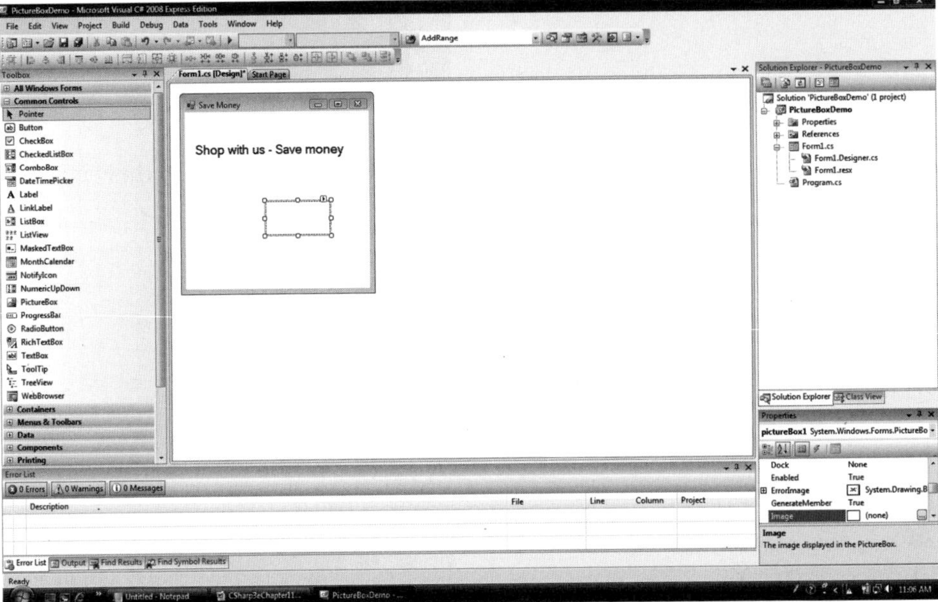

Figure 11-15 The IDE with a `Form` that contains a `PictureBox`

In Figure 11-15, in the Properties list at the right of the screen, the `Image` property is set to *none*. If you click the button with the ellipsis, a Select Resource window appears, as shown on the left in Figure 11-16. When you click the Import button, you can browse for stored images. When you select one, you see a preview in the Select Resource window, as shown on the right in Figure 11-16.

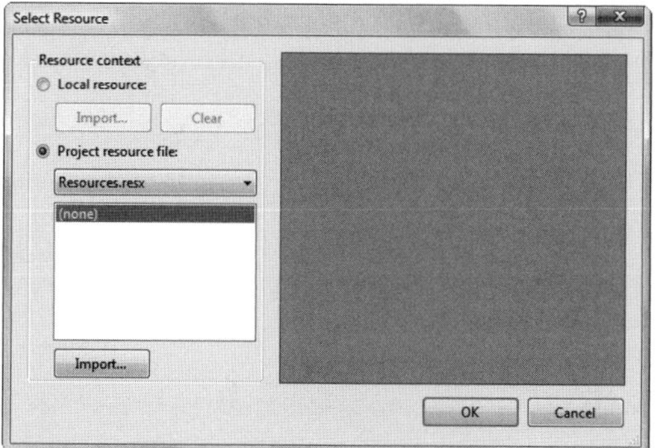

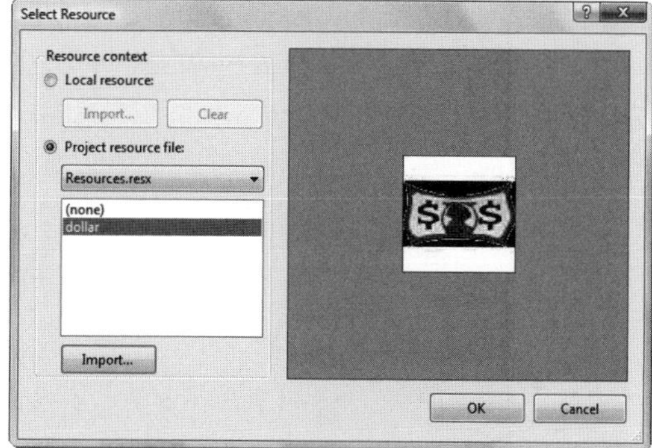

Figure 11-16 Select Resource window before and after image is selected

After you click OK, the image appears in the `PictureBox`, as in Figure 11-17. In the Solution Explorer on the right side of the IDE, notice that the dollar.jpg file has been added to the project. (You can resize the `PictureBox` so the image displays clearly.)

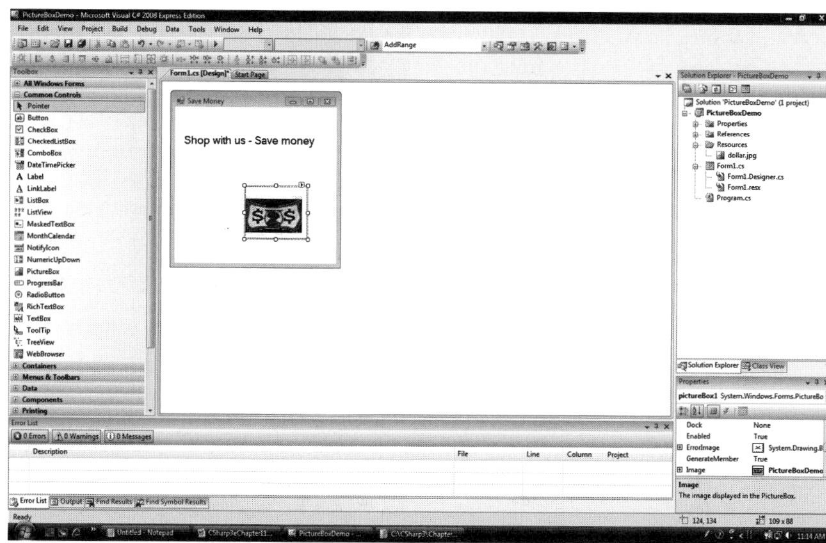

Figure 11-17 The `SaveMoney` project with an inserted image

If you examine the generated code, you can find the statements that instantiate a `PictureBox` (named `pictureBox1` by default) and statements that set its properties, such as `Size` and `Location`.

»TWO TRUTHS AND A LIE: ADDING A `PictureBox` TO A `Form`

1. A `PictureBox` is a `Control` in which you can display graphics from a bitmap, icon, JPEG, GIF, or other image file type.
2. The default event for a `PictureBox` is `LoadImage()`.
3. The `Image` property of a `PictureBox` holds the name of a file where a picture is stored.

The false statement is #2. The default event for a `PictureBox` is `Click()`.

ADDING `ListBox`, `CheckedListBox`, AND `ComboBox` `Control`S TO A `Form`

`Button`s, `RadioButton`s, and `CheckBox`es represent a GUI family because they all descend from the `ButtonBase` class and they all share certain characteristics. Similarly, `ListBox`, `ComboBox`, and `CheckedListBox` objects descend from the same family—they all are list-type widgets that descend from `ListControl`. Of course, they are also `Control`s and so inherit properties such as `Text` and `BackColor` from the `Control` class. Other properties are more specific to list-type objects. Table 11-9 describes some commonly used `ListBox` properties.

Property or Method	Description
`Items`	The collection of items in the `ListBox`; frequently, these are `string`s, but they can also be other types of objects
`MultiColumn`	Indicates whether display can be in multiple columns
`SelectedIndex`	Returns the index of the selected item. It no item has been selected, the value is -1. Otherwise, it is a value from 0 through $n - 1$, where n is the number of items in the `ListBox`.
`SelectedIndices`	Returns a collection of all the selected indices (when `SelectionMode` is more than `One`)
`SelectedItem`	Returns a reference to the selected item
`SelectedItems`	Returns a collection of the selected items (when `SelectionMode` is more than `One`)
`SelectionMode`	Determines how many items can be selected (see Table 11-10)
`Sorted`	Sorts the items when set to `true`
`SelectedIndexChanged()`	Default event that is generated when the selected index changes

Table 11-9 Commonly used `ListBox` properties and default event

Figure 11-18 shows a typical ListBox on a Form. The **ListBox** Control enables you to display a list of items that the user can select by clicking. After you drag a ListBox onto a Form, you can select its Items property and type a list into a String Collection Editor, as shown on the right in Figure 11-18.

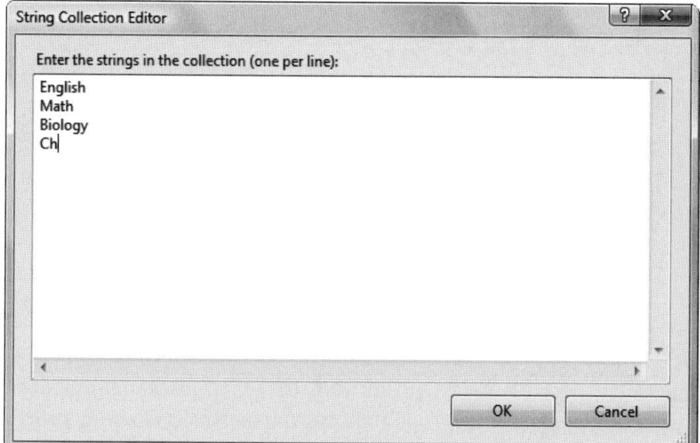

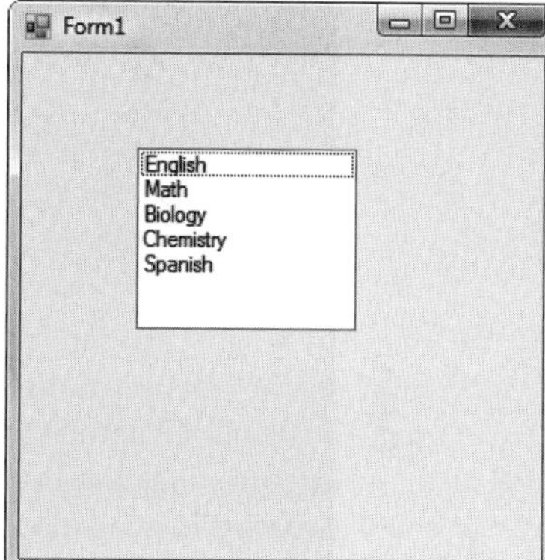

Figure 11-18 The String Collection Editor filling a ListBox and the completed ListBox on a Form

When you fill the String Collection Editor with the strings in Figure 11-18, the following code is generated in the InitializeComponent() method:

```
this.listBox1.Items.AddRange(new object[] {
          "English",
          "Math",
          "Biology",
          "Chemistry",
          "Spanish",
          ""});
```

With a ListBox, you allow the user to make a single selection or multiple selections by setting the SelectionMode property appropriately. For example, when the SelectionMode property is set to One, the user can make only a single selection from the ListBox. When the SelectionMode is set to MultiExtended, pressing Shift and clicking the mouse or pressing Shift and one of the arrow keys (up, down, left, or right) extends the selection to span from the previously selected item to the current item. Pressing Ctrl and clicking the mouse selects or deselects an item in the list. Table 11-10 lists the possible SelectionMode values.

NOTE When the SelectionMode property is set to SelectionMode.MultiSimple, click the mouse or press the spacebar to select or deselect an item in the list.

Member Name	Description
`MultiExtended`	Multiple items can be selected, and the user can press the Shift, Ctrl, and arrow keys to make selections
`MultiSimple`	Multiple items can be selected
`None`	No items can be selected
`One`	Only one item can be selected

Table 11-10 `SelectionMode` enumeration list

For example, within a `Form`'s `Load()` method (the one that executes when a `Form` is first loaded), you could add the following:

```
this.listBox1.SelectionMode =
   System.Windows.Forms.SelectionMode.MultiExtended;
```

As the example in Figure 11-19 shows, when you size a `ListBox` so that all the items cannot be displayed at the same time, a scroll bar is provided automatically on the side. The `ListBox` also provides the Boolean `MultiColumn` property, which you can set to display items in columns instead of a straight vertical list. This approach allows the control to display more items and avoids the need for the user to scroll down to an item. See Figure 11-20.

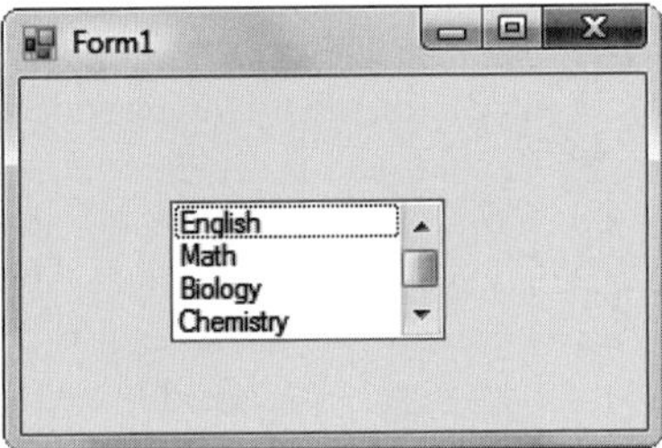

Figure 11-19 A `ListBox` with a scroll bar

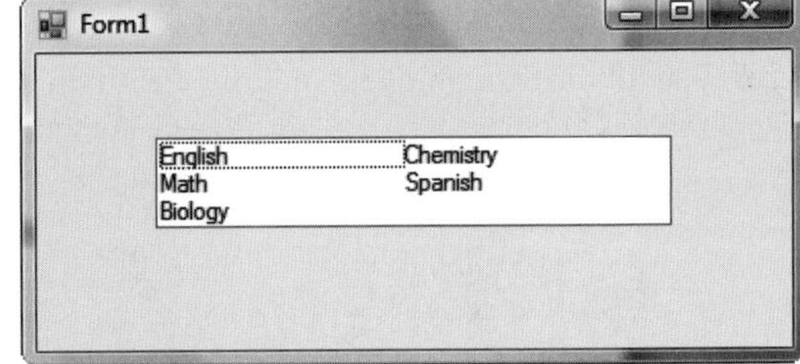

Figure 11-20 A multicolumn `ListBox`

The `SelectedItem` property of a `ListBox` contains the value of the item a user has selected. For example, if you create a `Label` with the `Text` property "You selected: ", you can modify the label's `Text` property in the `majorListBox_SelectedIndexChanged()` method with a statement such as the following:

```
private void majorListBox_SelectedIndexChanged
    (object sender, EventArgs e)
{
    majorLabel.Text += majorListBox1.SelectedItem;
}
```

The `SelectedItem` is appended to the label. Figure 11-21 shows a typical result.

NOTE With this code, the user's selection is appended to the text. If the user continues to make selections, the `Text` for `label2` will continue to grow longer. Depending on your application, you might prefer to replace the `Text` for the label instead of adding to it.

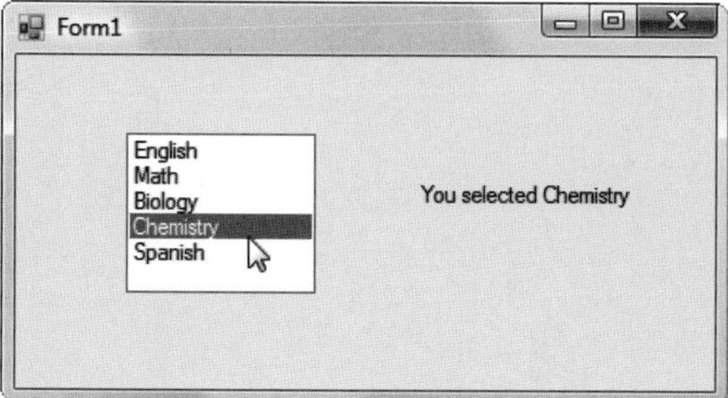

Figure 11-21 `ListBoxDemo` application after user has chosen *Chemistry*

The `Items.Count` property of a `ListBox` object holds the number of items in the `ListBox`. The `GetSelected()` method accepts an integer argument representing the array position of an item in the list. The method returns `true` if an item is selected and `false` if it is not. Therefore, code like the following could be used to count the number of selections a user makes from `listbox1`:

```
int count = 0;
for(int x = 0; x < majorListBox.Items.Count; ++x)
    if(majorListBox.GetSelected(x))
        ++count;
```

NOTE In Chapter 5 you learned that the first position in an array is position 0.

The `SetSelected()` method can be used to set a `ListBox` item to be automatically selected by default. For example, the following statement causes the first item in `majorListBox` to be the selected one:

```
majorListBox.SetSelected(0, true);
```

A **`ComboBox`** is similar to a `ListBox`, except that it displays an additional editing field to allow the user to select from the list or to enter new text. The default `ComboBox` displays an editing field with a hidden list box. The application in Figure 11-22 contains a `ComboBox` for selecting an airline. A **`CheckedListBox`** is also similar to a `ListBox`, with check boxes appearing to the left of each desired item. The application in Figure 11-22 uses a `CheckedListBox` for flight options.

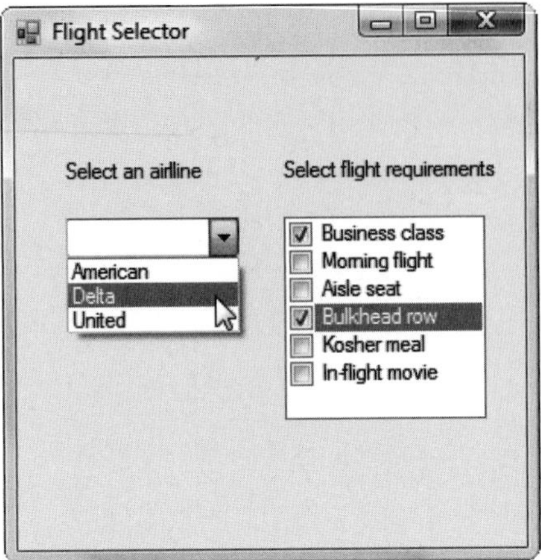

Figure 11-22 `ComboBoxAndCheckedListBoxDemo` application after user has made some selections

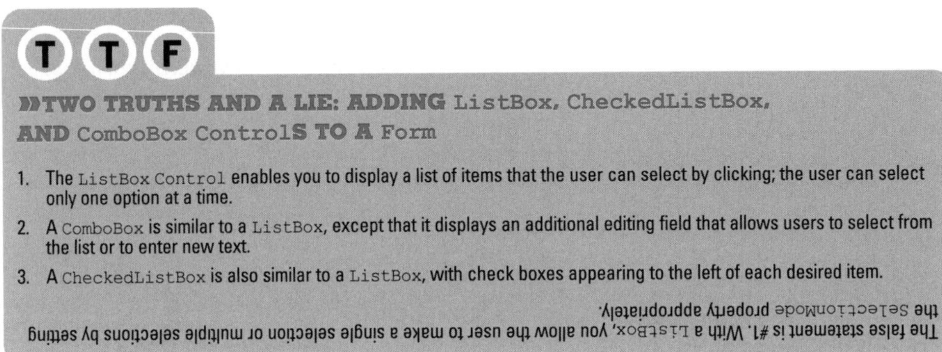

»TWO TRUTHS AND A LIE: ADDING `ListBox`, `CheckedListBox`, AND `ComboBox` `Control`S TO A `Form`

1. The `ListBox Control` enables you to display a list of items that the user can select by clicking; the user can select only one option at a time.
2. A `ComboBox` is similar to a `ListBox`, except that it displays an additional editing field that allows users to select from the list or to enter new text.
3. A `CheckedListBox` is also similar to a `ListBox`, with check boxes appearing to the left of each desired item.

The false statement is #1. With a `ListBox`, you allow the user to make a single selection or multiple selections by setting the `SelectionMode` property appropriately.

ADDING `MonthCalendar` AND `DateTimePicker` `Control`S TO A `Form`

The **`MonthCalendar`** and **`DateTimePicker`** `Controls` allow you to retrieve date and time information. Figure 11-23 shows a `MonthCalendar` that has been placed on a `Form`. The current date is contained in a rectangle by default, and the date that the user clicked is shaded. `Controls` at the top of the calendar allow the user to go forward or back one month at a time. Table 11-11 describes common `MonthCalendar` properties and the default event.

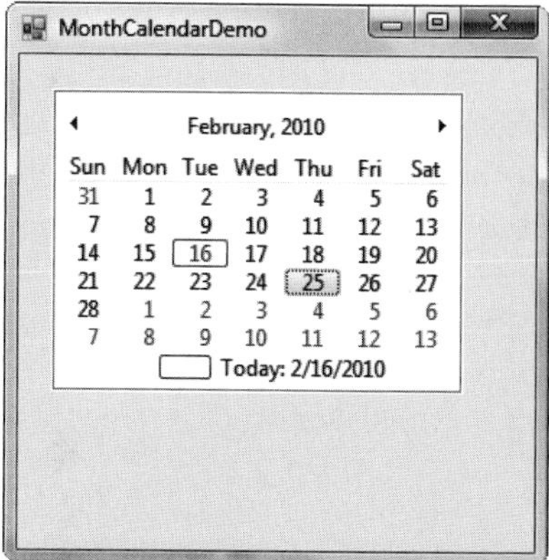

Figure 11-23 Typical execution of `MonthCalendarDemo`

Property or Method	Description
`MaxDate`	Sets the last day that can be selected (the default is 12/31/9998)
`MaxSelectionCount`	Sets the maximum number of dates that can be selected at once (the default is 7)
`MinDate`	Sets the first day that can be selected (the default is 1/1/1753)
`MonthlyBoldedDates`	An array of dates that appear in boldface in the calendar; for example, holidays
`SelectionEnd`	The last of a range of dates selected by the user
`SelectionRange`	The dates selected by the user
`SelectionStart`	The first of a range of dates selected by the user
`ShowToday`	If `true`, the date displays in text at the bottom of the calendar
`ShowTodayCircle`	If `true`, today's date is circled (the "circle" appears as a square)
`DateChanged()`	Default event that is generated when the user selects a date

Table 11-11 Commonly used `MonthCalendar` properties and default event

NOTE If you set the `MinDate` value to the `MonthCalendar`'s `TodayDate` property, the user cannot select a date before today. For example, you cannot make appointments or schedule deliveries to happen in the past, so you might code the following:

```
monthCalendar1.MinDate = monthCalendar1.TodayDate;
```

Conversely, you might want to prevent users from selecting a date in the future—for example, if the user is entering the date he placed an outstanding order. In that case, you could code a statement similar to the following:

```
monthCalendar1.MaxDate = monthCalendar1.TodayDate;
```

You can use several useful methods with the `SelectionStart` and `SelectionEnd` properties of `MonthCalendar`, including the following:

- `ToShortDateString()`, which displays the date in the format 2/16/2010
- `ToLongDateString()`, which displays the date in the format Tuesday, February 16, 2010
- `AddDays()`, which takes a `double` argument and adds a specified number of days to the date
- `AddMonths()`, which takes an `int` argument and adds a specified number of months to the date
- `AddYears()`, which takes an `int` argument and adds a specified number of years to the date

NOTE The format in which dates are displayed depends on the operating system's regional settings. For example, using United Kingdom settings, the short string format would use the day first, followed by the month, as in 16/02/2010. The examples in the preceding list assume United States settings.

NOTE The `AddDays()` method accepts a `double` argument because you can add fractional days to `SelectionStart` and `SelectionEnd`.

NOTE `SelectionStart` and `SelectionEnd` are structures of the `DateTime` type. Chapter 13 contains additional information about using `DateTime` objects to determine when files were created, modified, or accessed.

Many business and financial applications use `AddDays()`, `AddMonths()`, and `AddYears()` to calculate dates for events, such as payment for a bill (perhaps due in 10 days from an order) or scheduling a salesperson's callback to a customer (perhaps two months after initial contact). The default event for `MonthCalendar` is `DateChanged()`. For example, Figure 11-24 shows a method that executes when the user clicks a `MonthCalendar` named `cal`. A `string` is created from the literal text "You selected " and the start of the user's selection is converted to a short `string`. The message is placed on a `Label` that has been named `messageLabel`. Figure 11-25 shows the output when the user selects February 26, 2010. The date that is 10 days in the future is correctly calculated as March 8.

```
private void cal_DateChanged(object sender, DateRangeEventArgs e)
{
    const int DAYS_TO_ADD = 10;
    string newDate = "You selected " +
      calendar.SelectionStart.ToShortDateString();
    messageLabel.Text = newDate + "\nTen days from now is " +
      calendar.SelectionStart.AddDays(DAYS_TO_ADD).ToShortDateString();
}
```

Figure 11-24 `MonthCalendarDemo` application `cal_DateChanged()` method

Figure 11-25 Typical execution of `MonthCalendarDemo`

The `DateTimePicker Control` displays a month calendar when the down arrow is selected. For example, Figure 11-26 shows a `DateTimePicker` before and after the user clicks the down arrow.

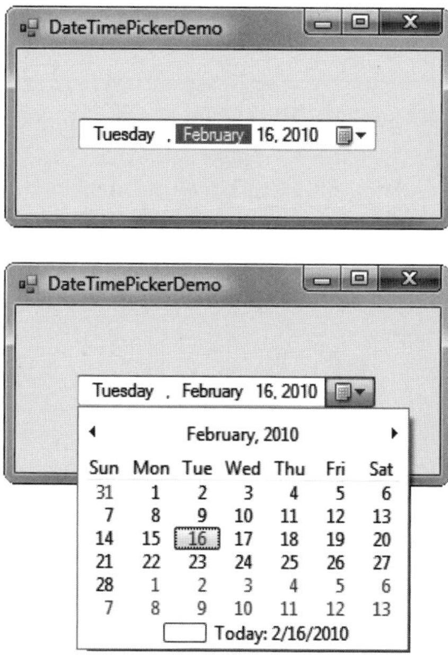

Figure 11-26 The `DateTimePicker Control`

When you use the CustomFormat property, the date displayed in a DateTimePicker Control is more customizable than the one in a MonthCalendar. Table 11-12 describes some commonly used DateTimePicker properties and the default event.

Property or Method	Description
CalendarForeColor	Sets the calendar text color
CalendarMonthBackground	Sets the calendar background color
CustomFormat	A string value that uses codes to set a custom date and time format. For example, to display the date and time as 02/16/2010 12:00 PM - Friday, set this property to "MM'/'dd'/'yyyy hh':'mm tt - dddd". See the C# documentation for a complete set of format string characters.
Format	Sets the format for the date or time. Options are Long (for example, Tuesday, February 16, 2010), Short (2/16/2010), and Time (for example, 3:15:01 PM). You can also create a CustomFormat.
Value	The data selected by the user
ValueChanged()	Default event that is generated when the Value property changes

Table 11-12 Commonly used DateTimePicker properties and default event

»TWO TRUTHS AND A LIE: ADDING MonthCalendar AND DateTimePicker ControlS TO A Form

1. The MonthCalendar and DateTimePicker Controls allow you to retrieve date and time information.
2. The default event for MonthCalendar is DateChanged().
3. The DateTimePicker Control displays a small clock when you click it.

The false statement is #3. The DateTimePicker Control displays a month calendar when the down arrow is selected.

WORKING WITH A Form'S LAYOUT

When you place Controls on a Form in the IDE, you can drag them to any location to achieve the effect you want.

When you drag multiple Controls onto a Form, blue **snap lines** appear and help you align new Controls with others already in place. Figure 11-27 shows two snap lines that you can use to align a second label below the first one. Snap lines also appear when you place a control closer to the edge of a container than is recommended.

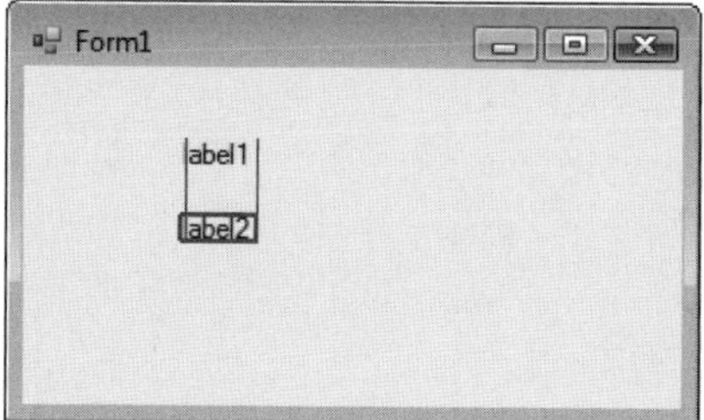

Figure 11-27 Snap lines in the Visual Studio Designer

You also can use the Location property in a Control's Properties list to specify a location. With either technique, code like the following is generated:

```
this.label1.Location = new System.Drawing.Point(23, 19);
```

Several other properties can help you to manage the appearance of a Form (or other ContainerControl). For example, setting the **Anchor property** causes a Control to remain at a fixed distance from the side of a container when the user resizes it. Figure 11-28 shows the Properties window for a Label that has been placed on a Form. The Anchor property has a drop-down window that lets you select or deselect the sides to which the label should be anchored. For most Controls, the default setting for Anchor is Top, Left.

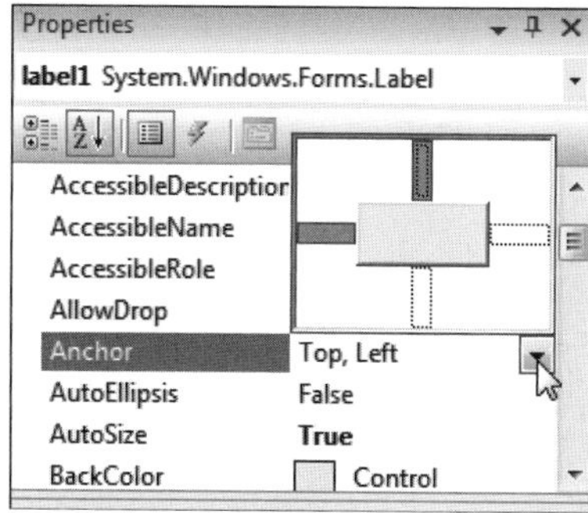

Figure 11-28 Selecting an Anchor property

Figure 11-29 shows a Form with two Labels. On the Form, label1 has been anchored to the top left and label2 has been anchored to the bottom right. The left side of the figure shows the Form as it first appears to the user, and the right side shows the Form after the user has resized it. Notice that in the resized Form, label1 is still the same distance from the top left as it originally was, and `label2` is still the same distance from the bottom right as it originally was. Anchoring is useful when users expect a specific control to always be in the same general location in a container.

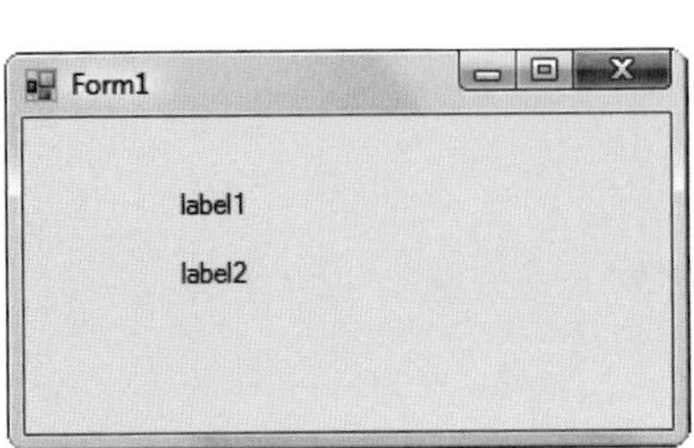

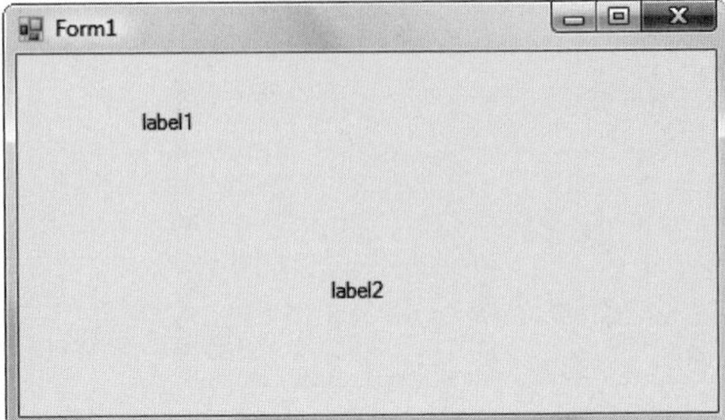

Figure 11-29 A `Form` with two `Label`s anchored to opposite corners

Setting the **Dock property** attaches a `Control` to the side of a container so that the `Control` stretches when the container's size is adjusted. Figure 11-30 shows the drop-down `Dock` Properties window for a `Button`. You can select any region in the window. Figure 11-31 shows a `Button` docked to the bottom of a `Form` before and after the `Form` has been resized.

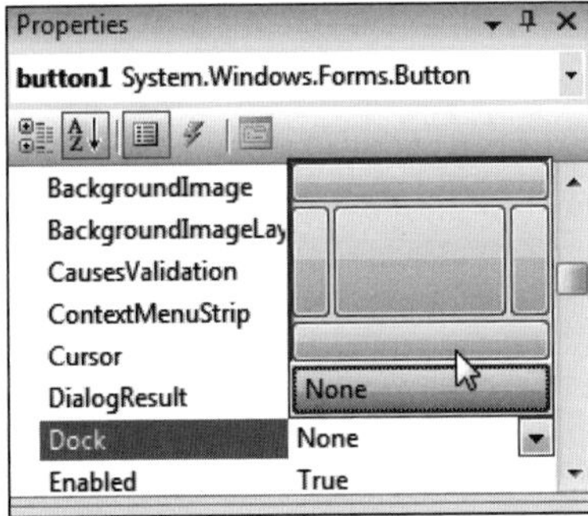

Figure 11-30 The `Dock` Properties window

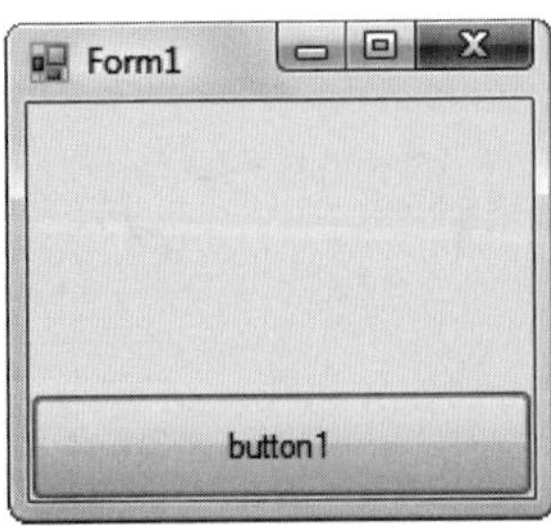

Figure 11-31 A `Form` with a docked `Button`

A `Form` has a **Padding property** that specifies the distance between docked `Controls` and the edges of the `Form`. The `Padding` property has four values—one for each side of the `Form` (left, top, right, and bottom). They are set to 0 by default. Figure 11-32 shows the docked button from Figure 11-31 when the padding values have been set to 0, 0, 30, and 10. The `Button` is three times further from the right edge of the `Form` than it is from the bottom.

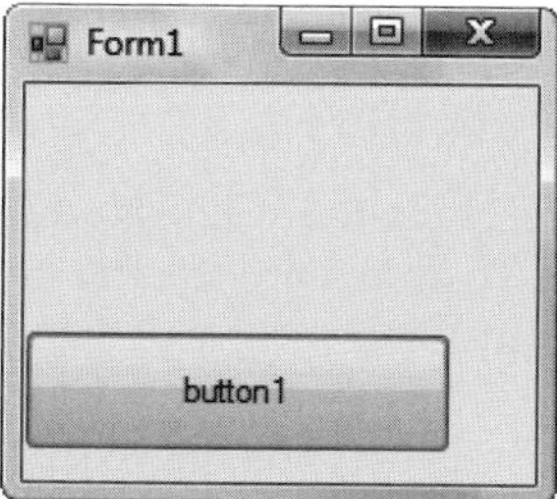

Figure 11-32 A docked button on a `Form` with padding

A `Form` also has a **`MinimumSize` property** and a **`MaximumSize` property**. Each has two values—`Width` and `Height`. If you set these properties, the user cannot make the `Form` smaller or larger than you have specified. If you do not want the user to be able to adjust a `Form`'s size at all, set the `MinimumSize` and `MaximumSize` properties to be equal.

UNDERSTANDING GROUPBOXES AND PANELS

Many types of `ContainerControls` are available to hold `Controls`. For example, you can use a **`GroupBox`** or **`Panel`** to group related `Controls` on a `Form`. When you move a `GroupBox` or `Panel`, all its `Controls` are moved as a group. To create either of these `Controls`, you drag it from the Toolbox in the IDE, and then drag the `Controls` you want on top of it. `GroupBox`es can display a caption, but `Panels` cannot. `Panels` can include a scroll bar that the user can manipulate to view `Controls`; `GroupBox`es do not have scroll bars. You can anchor or dock `Controls` inside a `GroupBox` or `Panel`, and you can anchor or dock a `GroupBox` or `Panel` inside a `Form`. Doing this provides `Control` groups that easily can be arranged.

»TWO TRUTHS AND A LIE: WORKING WITH A `Form`'S LAYOUT

1. Setting the `Anchor` property causes a `Control` to remain at a fixed distance from the side of a container when the user resizes it.
2. Setting the `Dock` property attaches a `Control` to the side of a container so that the `Control`'s size does not change when the container's size is adjusted.
3. A `Form` has a `Padding` property that specifies the distance between docked `Controls` and the edges of the `Form`.

The false statement is #2. Setting the `Dock` property attaches a `Control` to the side of a container so that the `Control` stretches when the container's size is adjusted.

ADDING A `MenuStrip` TO A `Form`

Most programs you use in a Windows environment contain a **menu strip,** which is a horizontal list of general options that appears under the title bar of a `Form` or `Window`. When you click an item in a menu strip, you might initiate an action. More frequently, you see a list box that contains more specific options. Each of these might initiate an action, or it might lead to another menu. For example, the Visual Studio IDE contains a horizontal main menu strip that begins with the options File, Edit, and View. You have used word-processing, spreadsheet, and even game programs with similar menus.

>> **NOTE** If you do not see a `MenuStrip` in your Toolbox, click the Menus & Toolbars group to expose it.

You can add a **`MenuStrip`** `Control` object to any `Form` you create. Using the Visual Studio IDE, you can add a `MenuStrip` to a `Form` by dragging it from the Toolbox onto the `Form`. This creates a menu bar horizontally across the top of the `Form`, just below the title bar. Figure 11-33 shows a `MenuStrip` dragged onto a `Form`. The strip extends across the width of the `Form` and contains a "Type Here" text box. When you click the text box, you can enter a menu item. New text boxes appear below and to the right of the first one. Each time you add a menu item, new boxes are created so you can see where your next options will go.

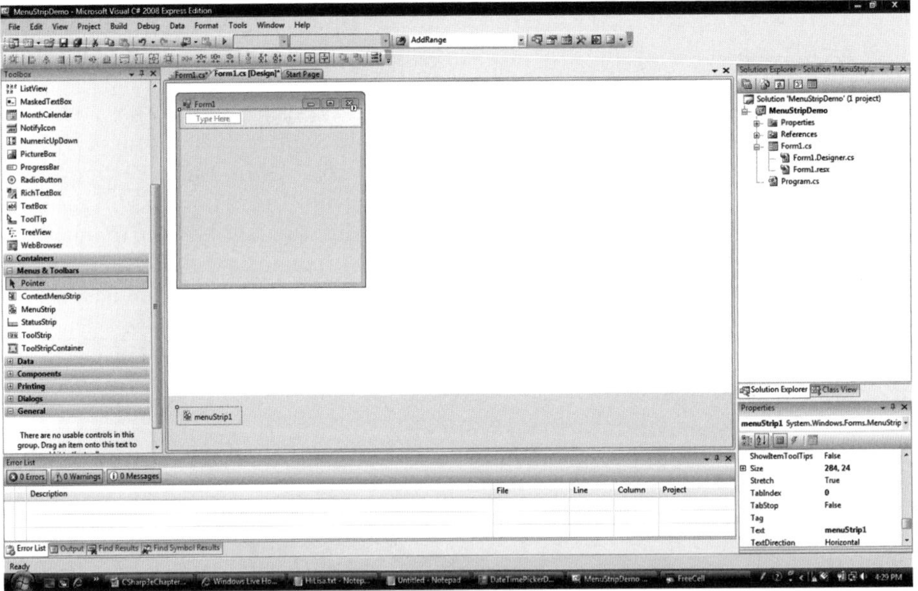

Figure 11-33 `Form` with `MenuStrip`

>> **NOTE** You can click the `MenuStrip` icon at the bottom of the design screen to view and change the properties for the `MenuStrip`. For example, you might want to change the `Font` or `BackColor` for the `MenuStrip`.

Figure 11-34 shows a `MenuStrip` in which the programmer has typed *Font*, and beneath it, *Large* and *Small*. New boxes are available to the right of Font and beneath Small. Figure 11-35 shows that the programmer continued by entering *Color* and three choices beneath it.

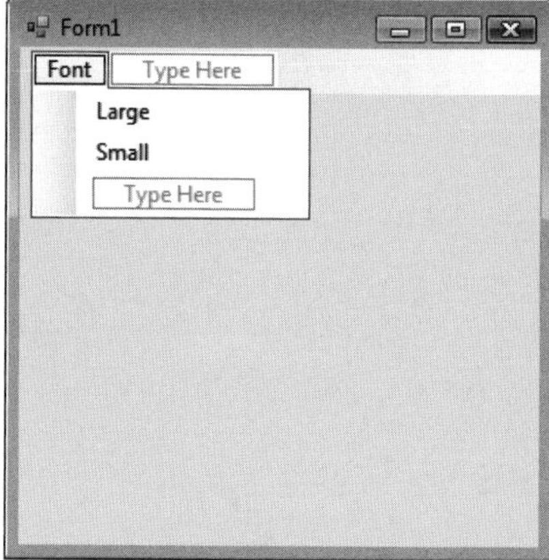

Figure 11-34 `Form` that contains `MenuStrip` with a few entries

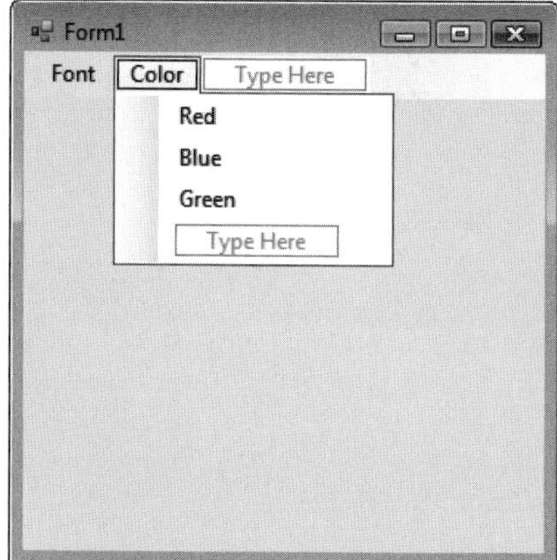

Figure 11-35 `Form` that contains `MenuStrip` with more entries

»NOTE If possible, your main menu selections should be single words. That way, a user will not mistakenly think that a single menu item represents multiple items.

»NOTE If you create each main menu item with an ampersand (&) in front of a unique letter, then the user can press Alt and the letter to activate the menu choice, besides clicking it with the mouse.

When you double-click an entry in the `MenuStrip`, a `Click()` method is generated. For example, if you click Large in the menu shown in Figure 11-36, the method generated is `largeToolStripMenuItem_Click()`, as follows:

```
private void largeToolStripMenuItem_Click
    (object sender, EventArgs e)
{
}
```

As with all the other controls you have learned about, you can write any code statements you like within the method. For example, suppose a `Label` named `helloLabel` has been dragged onto the `Form`. If choosing the Large menu option should result in a larger font for the label, you might code the method as follows:

```
private void largeToolStripMenuItem_Click
   (object sender, EventArgs e)
{
    helloLabel.Font = new Font("Courier New", 34);
}
```

With the addition of this method, the `Form` operates as shown in Figure 11-36. If the `Label` appears in a small font and the user clicks the Large menu option, the font changes.

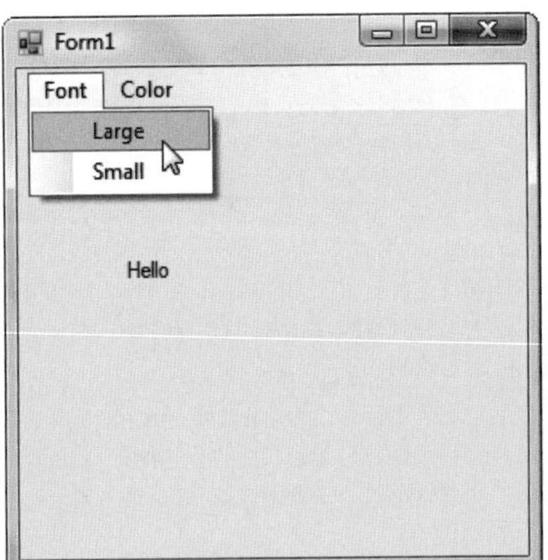

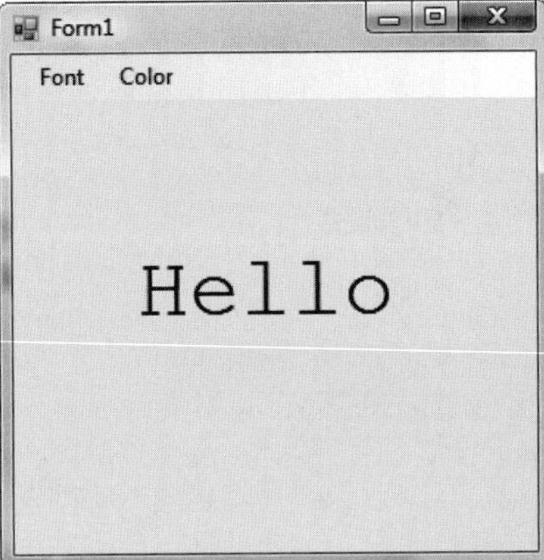

Figure 11-36 Executing the `MenuStripDemo` program

»NOTE Users expect menu options to appear in conventional order. For example, users expect the far-left option on the main menu to be File, and they expect the Exit option to appear under File. Similarly, if an application contains a Help option, users expect to find it at the right side of the main menu. You should follow these conventions when designing your own main menus.

»NOTE You can work with the other menu items in this program in an exercise at the end of this chapter.

»TWO TRUTHS AND A LIE: ADDING A `MenuStrip` TO A `Form`

1. When you click an item in a menu strip, the most common result is to initiate an action.
2. When you drag a `MenuStrip Control` object onto a `Form` using the Visual Studio IDE, the `MenuStrip` is added horizontally across the top of the `Form`, just below the title bar.
3. The default event for `MenuStrip` is `Click()`.

The false statement is #1. When you click an item in a menu strip, you might initiate an action. More frequently, you see a list box that contains more specific options.

USING OTHER `Controls`

If you examine the Visual Studio IDE or search through the Visual Studio documentation, you will find many other `Controls` that are not covered in this chapter. If you click Project on the main menu and click Add New Item, you can add extra `Forms`, `Files`, `Controls`, and other elements to your project. New controls and containers will be developed in the future, and you might even design new controls of your own. Still, all controls will contain properties and methods, and your solid foundation in C# will prepare you to use new controls effectively.

YOU DO IT

ADDING `Labels` TO A `Form` AND CHANGING THEIR PROPERTIES

In the next steps, you will begin to create an application for Bailey's Bed and Breakfast. The main `Form` allows the user to select one of two suites and discover the amenities and price associated with each choice. You will start by placing two `Labels` on a `Form` and setting several of their properties.

> **NOTE** The screen images in the next steps represent a typical Visual Studio environment. Based on options you selected in your installation, your screen might look different.

To create a `Form` with `Labels`:

1. Open Microsoft Visual Studio. You might be able to use a desktop shortcut, or you might click the **Start button**, point to **All Programs**, and click the version of C# you have installed (for example, **Microsoft Visual C# Express Edition**).
2. Click **File** on the menu bar and click **New Project**. A New Project window appears. In the window under Templates, click **Windows Forms Application**. Near the bottom of the New Project window, click in the **Name** text box and replace the default name with **BedAndBreakfast**. See Figure 11-37.

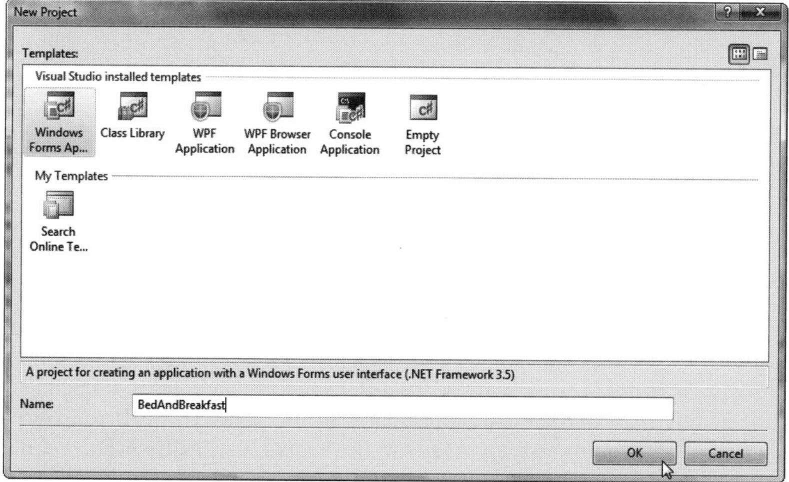

Figure 11-37 The New Project window for the `BedAndBreakfast` application

3. Click **OK**. The design screen appears. The blank `Form` in the center of the screen has an empty title bar. Click the `Form`. The lower-right corner of the screen contains a Properties window that lists the `Form`'s properties. (If you do not see the Properties window, you can click **View** on the main menu and then click **Properties Window**. Another option is to press **Ctrl+W**, followed by **P**.)
4. In the Properties list, click the **`Name`** property and change the `Name` of the `Form` to **BaileysForm**. Click the **`Text`** property and change it to **Bailey's Bed and Breakfast.** Press **Enter**; the title of the `Form` in the center of the screen changes to *Bailey's Bed and Breakfast*. (See Figure 11-38.)

Figure 11-38 `Form` with revised `Text` property

5. On the left side of the design screen, the Toolbox contains a list of components that can be added to a `Form`, including `Buttons`, `CheckBoxes`, `Labels`, and many others. Click **`Label`** and drag a `Label` onto the `Form`. When you release your mouse button, the `Label` appears on the `Form` and contains the default text "label1". On the right side of the screen under Properties, make sure the list box shows that you are viewing the properties for `label1`. If not, click `label1` on the `Form` on the design screen.

»NOTE If you do not see the Toolbox, click the **Toolbox tab** at the left side of the screen and pin it to the screen by clicking the pushpin. Alternatively, you can select **View** from the main menu and then click **Toolbox**.

6. Change the `Name` of `label1` to **`welcomeLabel`** and change the `Text` property to **Welcome to Bailey's**, then press **Enter**; the text of the `Label` on the `Form` changes. Drag and resize the `Label` so it is close to the position of the `Label` in Figure 11-39. (If you prefer to set the `Label`'s `Location` property manually in the Properties list, the `Location` should be **60, 30**.)

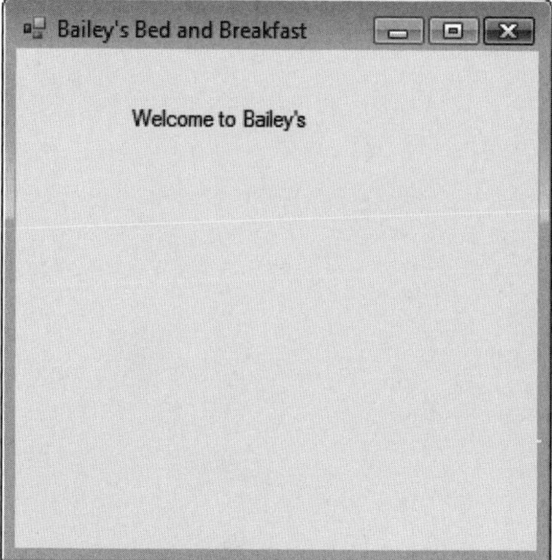

Figure 11-39 A `Label` placed on the `Form` in the `BedAndBreakfast` project

7. Make sure the Properties list still shows the properties for `welcomeLabel`; if not, click the `Label` on the design screen. Locate the `Font` property in the Properties list. Currently, it lists the default font: Microsoft Sans Serif, 8.25 pt. Notice the ellipsis (three dots) at the right of the `Font` property name. (You might have to click in the Property to see the button.) Click the ellipsis to display the `Font` dialog box. Make selections to change the font to **Microsoft Sans Serif**, **18 point**, and **Italic**. Click **OK**. When you enlarge the `Font` for the `Label`, it is too close to the right edge of the `Form`. Drag it to change its `Location` property to approximately **30, 25**, or type the new `Location` value in the Properties window.

8. Drag a second `Label` onto the `Form` beneath the first one, and then set its `Name` property to `rateLabel` and its `Text` property to **Check our rates**. Change its `Location` to approximately **80, 80** and its `Font` to **Microsoft Sans Serif, 12 point, Regular**.

9. Save the project using one of the following methods: Click **File** on the menu bar and then click **Save All**, click the **Save All** button (which resembles a stack of diskettes), or press **Ctrl+Shift+S**. The project name (BedAndBreakfast) should already appear in the dialog box. You can browse for the location where you want to save the project. For example, you can choose the Chapter.11 folder on your Student Disk.

10. Click **Debug** on the menu bar and then click **Start Without Debugging**, or press **Ctrl+F5**. The `Form` appears, as shown in Figure 11-40.

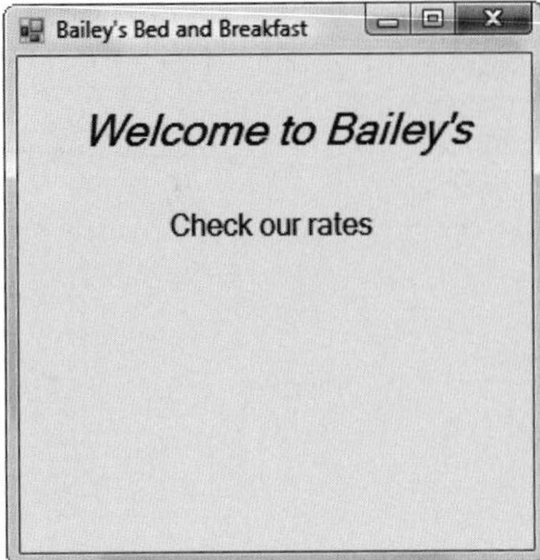

Figure 11-40 The `BedAndBreakfast Form` with two `Labels`

11. Dismiss the `Form` by clicking the **Close** button in its upper-right corner.

EXAMINING THE CODE GENERATED BY THE IDE

In the next steps, you will examine the code generated by the IDE for at least two reasons:

- » To gain an understanding of the types of statements created by the IDE.
- » To lose any intimidation you might have about the code generated. You will recognize many of the C# statements from what you have already learned in this book.

To examine the generated code:

1. Click **View** on the menu bar and then click **Code** (or press **F7**) to view the code. As shown in Figure 11-41, you see several `using` statements, the `BedAndBreakfast` namespace header, the `BaileysForm` class header, and the constructor for `Form1` that calls the `InitializeComponent()` method.

```
BedAndBreakfast.BaileysForm                    BaileysForm()
using System;
using System.Collections.Generic;
using System.ComponentModel;
using System.Data;
using System.Drawing;
using System.Linq;
using System.Text;
using System.Windows.Forms;

namespace BedAndBreakfast
{
    public partial class BaileysForm : Form
    {
        public BaileysForm()
        {
            InitializeComponent();
        }
    }
}
```

Figure 11-41 The Form1.cs code

2. In the Solution Explorer at the right side of the screen, double-click the **Form1.Designer.cs** filename. Scroll to the gray rectangle that contains **Windows Form Designer generated code** and click the node to its left to expose the hidden code. (You can drag the bottom border of the code window to expose more of the code or you can scroll to see all of it.) As Figure 11-42 shows, `welcomeLabel`, `rateLabel`, and `BaileysForm` objects have been declared and assigned the attributes you provided for them.

```
BedAndBreakfast.BaileysForm                    InitializeComponent()
        private void InitializeComponent()
        {
            this.welcomeLabel = new System.Windows.Forms.Label();
            this.rateLabel = new System.Windows.Forms.Label();
            this.SuspendLayout();
            //
            // welcomeLabel
            //
            this.welcomeLabel.AutoSize = true;
            this.welcomeLabel.Font = new System.Drawing.Font("Microsoft Sans Serif", 18F, System.Drawing.
            this.welcomeLabel.Location = new System.Drawing.Point(30, 25);
            this.welcomeLabel.Name = "welcomeLabel";
            this.welcomeLabel.Size = new System.Drawing.Size(229, 29);
            this.welcomeLabel.TabIndex = 0;
            this.welcomeLabel.Text = "Welcome to Bailey\'s";
            //
            // rateLabel
            //
            this.rateLabel.AutoSize = true;
            this.rateLabel.Font = new System.Drawing.Font("Microsoft Sans Serif", 12F, System.Drawing.Fon
            this.rateLabel.Location = new System.Drawing.Point(80, 80);
            this.rateLabel.Name = "rateLabel";
            this.rateLabel.Size = new System.Drawing.Size(121, 20);
            this.rateLabel.TabIndex = 1;
            this.rateLabel.Text = "Check our rates";
            //
            // BaileysForm
            //
            this.AutoScaleDimensions = new System.Drawing.SizeF(6F, 13F);
            this.AutoScaleMode = System.Windows.Forms.AutoScaleMode.Font;
            this.BackColor = System.Drawing.Color.Yellow;
            this.ClientSize = new System.Drawing.Size(284, 264);
            this.Controls.Add(this.mealButton);
            this.Controls.Add(this.lincolnBox);
            this.Controls.Add(this.belleAireBox);
            this.Controls.Add(this.rateLabel);
```

Figure 11-42 Part of the Form1.Designer.cs code

3. In the Solution Explorer, double-click the **Program.cs** filename to view the `Main()` method for the application. The method contains just three statements; each is a method call. Click the **Form1.cs [Design] tab** to return to the Design view for the `Form`.

4. Next, change the `BackColor` property of the Bailey's Bed and Breakfast `Form`. Click the **`Form`** or click the list box of components at the top of the Properties window and select **BaileysForm**. In the Properties list, click the **`BackColor`** property to see its list of choices. Choose the **Custom** tab and select **Yellow** in the third row of available colors. Click the **`Form`**, notice the color change, and then view the code in the Form1.Designer.cs file. Locate the statement that changes the `BackColor` of the `Form` to `Yellow`. As you continue to design `Forms`, periodically check the code to confirm your changes and better learn C#.

5. Save the project.
6. If you want to take a break at this point, close Visual Studio.

ADDING CheckBoxES TO A Form

In the next steps, you will add two CheckBoxes to the BedAndBreakfast Form. These controls allow the user to select an available room and view information about it.

To add CheckBoxes to a Form:

1. Open the BedAndBreakfast project in Visual Studio, if it is not still open on your screen.
2. In the Design view of the Bed And Breakfast project in the Visual Studio IDE, drag a CheckBox onto the Form below the "Check our rates" Label. (See Figure 11-43 for its approximate placement.)
3. Change the Text property of the CheckBox to **BelleAire Suite**. Change the Name of the property to **belleAireBox**. Drag a second CheckBox onto the Form beneath the first one. Change its Text property to **Lincoln Room** and its Name to **lincolnBox**.

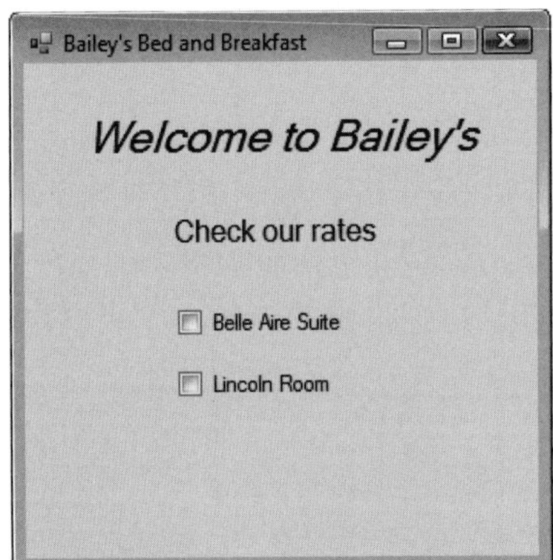

Figure 11-43 BedAndBreakfast Form with two CheckBoxes

4. Next, you will create two new Forms: one that appears when the user selects the BelleAire CheckBox and one that appears when the user selects the Lincoln CheckBox. Click **Project** on the menu bar, then click **Add New Item**. In the Add New Item window, click **Windows Form**. In the Name text box at the bottom of the window, type **BelleAireForm**. See Figure 11-44.

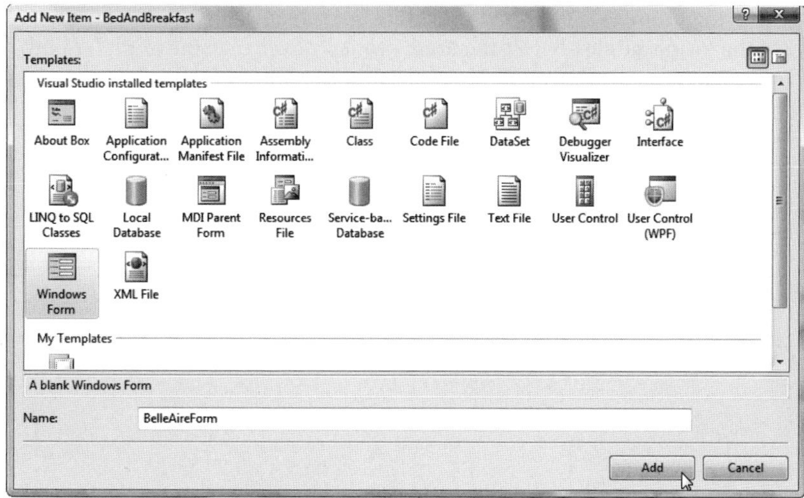

Figure 11-44 The Add New Item window

5. Click the **Add** button. A new `Form` is added to the project, and its title bar contains *BelleAireForm*. Save the project (and continue to do so periodically).
6. Change the `BackColor` property of the `Form` to `Yellow` to match the `welcomeForm`.
7. Drag a `Label` onto the `Form`, using Figure 11-45 as a guide to approximate its placement. Change the `Name` of the `Label` to **`belleAireDescriptionLabel`**. Change the `Text` property of the `Label` to contain the following: **The BelleAire Suite has two bedrooms, two baths and a private balcony**. Click the arrow on the text property to type the long label message on two lines. Adjust the size of the `Label` if necessary to resemble Figure 11-45. Drag a second `Label` onto the `Form`, name it **`belleAirePriceLabel`**, and type the price as the `Text` property: **$199.95 per night**.

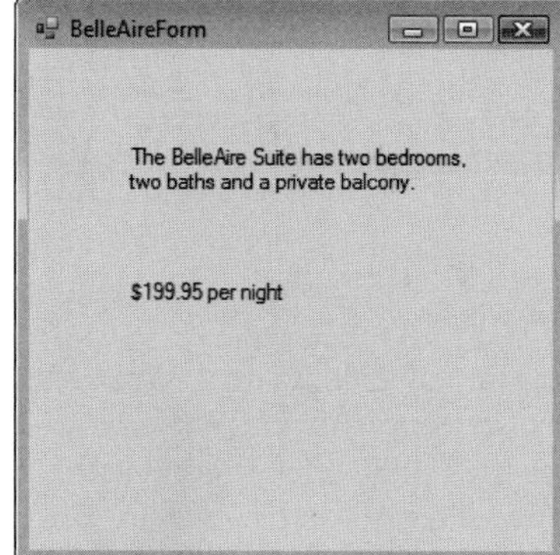

Figure 11-45 `BelleAireForm` with two `Labels`

8. Select the **Pointer** tool from the Toolbox at the left of the screen. Drag it to encompass both `Labels`. In the Properties list, select the **`Font`** property to change the `Font` for both `Controls` at once. Choose a pleasing `Font`. Figure 11-46 shows **10-point Regular Papyrus**; you might choose a different font. Adjust the positions of the `Labels` if necessary to achieve a pleasing effect.

Figure 11-46 `Font` changed for the `Labels`

9. In the Solution Explorer at the right side of the screen, double-click **Form1.cs**. Alternatively, click the **Form1** tab at the top of the Designer screen. Double-click the **BelleAire Suite `CheckBox`**. The program code (the method shell for the default event of a `CheckBox`) appears in the IDE main window. Within the `belleAireBox_CheckedChanged()` method, add an `if` statement that determines whether the `BelleAire` `CheckBox` is checked. If it is checked, create a new instance of `BelleAireForm` and display it.

```
private void belleAireBox_CheckedChanged(object sender,
   EventArgs e)
{
     if (belleAireBox.Checked)
     {
          BelleAireForm belleAireForm = new BelleAireForm();
          belleAireForm.ShowDialog();
     }
}
```

10. Save and then execute the program by selecting **Debug** from the main menu, then **Start Without Debugging**. The main Bed and Breakfast `Form` appears. Click the **BelleAire Suite `CheckBox`**. The BelleAire `Form` appears. Dismiss the `Form`. Click the **Lincoln Room `CheckBox`**. Nothing happens because you have not yet written event code for this `CheckBox`. When you click the **BelleAire Suite `CheckBox`** again, the BelleAire form reappears. Dismiss the BelleAire `Form`.

NOTE If you inadvertently click a component for which you did not mean to generate an action, you cannot simply delete the automatically created method. For now, leave the empty method in your application. You will learn how to eliminate the unwanted method in Chapter 12.

11. When you dismiss the BelleAire `Form`, the BelleAire `CheckBox` remains checked. To see it appear as unchecked after its `Form` is dismissed, dismiss the program's main form (Bailey's Bed and Breakfast) and add a third statement within the `if` block in the `CheckedChanged()` message as follows:

    ```
    belleAireBox.Checked = false;
    ```

    That way, whenever the `CheckedChanged()` method executes because the `belleAireBox` was checked, it will become unchecked.
12. Save the project, then execute it again. When you select the BelleAire `CheckBox`, view the `Form`, and dismiss it, the `CheckBox` appears unchecked and is ready to check again. Dismiss the BedAndBreakfast `Form`.
13. Click **Project** on the menu bar and then click **Add New Item**. Click **Windows Form** and enter its `Name`: **`LincolnForm`**. When the new `Form` appears, change its `Name` property to **`LincolnForm`** and its `Text` property to **Lincoln Room**. Then add two `Labels` to the `Form` and provide appropriate `Name` properties for them. Change the `Text` on the first `Label` to: **Return to the 1850s in this lovely room with private bath**. The second should be: **$110.00 per night**. Change the `Form`'s `BackColor` property to **White**. Change the `Font` to match the `Font` on the BelleAire `Form`. See Figure 11-47.

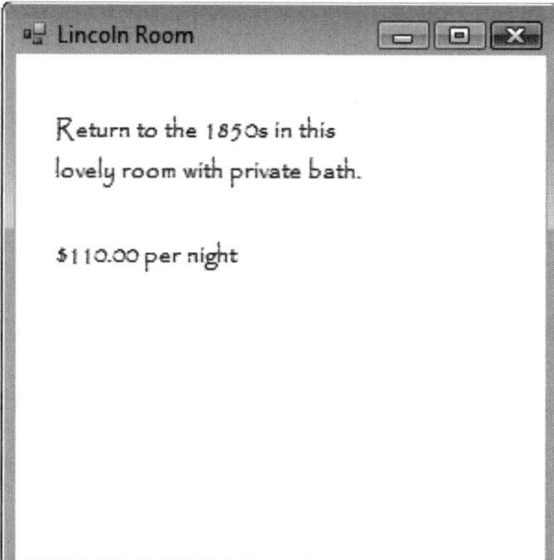

Figure 11-47 The `LincolnForm`

14. From the Toolbox, drag a `PictureBox` onto the `Form`. Select its **`Image`** property. A dialog box allows you to browse for an image. Find the AbeLincoln file on your Student Disk and select **Import**. Adjust the size of the `Form` and the sizes and positions of the labels and picture box so that everything looks attractive on the `Form`. See Figure 11-48.

Figure 11-48 `LincolnForm` with `Image` in `PictureBox`

NOTE The AbeLincoln file was obtained at *www.free-graphics.com*. You can visit the site and download other images to use in your own applications. You should also search the Web for "free clip art" and similar phrases.

15. In the Solution Explorer, double-click **`Form1.cs`** or click the **Form1.cs[Design] tab** at the top of the design screen. On the Bed and Breakfast `Form`, double-click the Lincoln Room `CheckBox`, and add the following `if` statement to the `lincolnBox_CheckedChanged()` method:

```
private void lincolnBox_CheckedChanged(object sender,
   EventArgs e)
{
     if (lincolnBox.Checked)
     {
          LincolnForm lincolnForm = new LincolnForm();
          lincolnForm.ShowDialog();
          lincolnBox.Checked = false;
     }
}
```

16. Save the project and then execute it. When the Bed and Breakfast `Form` appears, click either `CheckBox`—the appropriate informational `Form` appears. Close it and then click the other `CheckBox`. Again, the appropriate `Form` appears.
17. Close all forms. If you are taking a break, exit Visual Studio.

ADDING RadioButtons TO A Form

Next you will add more Controls to the Bed And Breakfast Form. You generally use RadioButtons when a user must select from mutually exclusive options.

To add RadioButtons to the project:

1. Open the BedAndBreakfast project if it is not still open. In the Design view of the main Form, add a Button to the Form, using Figure 11-49 as a general guide to locations. Change the Button's Name property to **mealButton** and the Button's Text to **Click for meal options**.

Figure 11-49 BedAndBreakfast Form with an added Button

2. From the main menu, select **Project**, click **Add New Item**, and click **Windows Form**. Name the Form **BreakfastOptionForm** and click **Add**. On the new Form, make the following changes:

   - Drag a Label onto the Form. Name it appropriately and set its Text to **Select your breakfast option**.
   - Drag three RadioButtons onto the Form. Set their respective Text properties to **Continental**, **Full**, and **Deluxe**. Set their respective Names to **contBreakfastButton**, **fullBreakfastButton**, and **deluxeBreakfastButton**.
   - Drag a Label onto the Form, then set its Text to **Price:** and its Name to **priceLabel**. Make its Font property a little larger than the Font for the other Form components.

See Figure 11-50 for approximate placement of all these Controls.

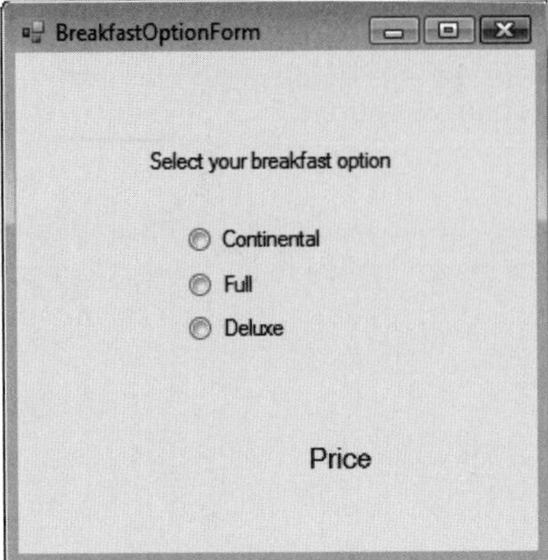

Figure 11-50 Developing the `BreakfastOptionForm`

3. Double-click the title bar of the `BreakfastOptionForm`. You generate a method named `BreakfastOptionForm_Load()`. Within this method, you can type statements that execute each time the `Form` is created. Add the following statements within the `BreakfastOptionForm` class, which declare three constants representing prices for different breakfast options. Within the `BreakfastOptionForm_Load()` method, set the `priceLabel Text` to the lowest price by default when the `Form` loads.

```
public partial class BreakfastOptionForm : Form
{
    private const double CONT_BREAKFAST_PRICE = 6.00;
    private const double FULL_BREAKFAST_PRICE = 9.95;
    private const double DELUXE_BREAKFAST_PRICE = 16.50;
    public BreakfastOptionForm()
    {
        InitializeComponent();
    }

    private void BreakfastOptionForm_Load
      (object sender, EventArgs e)
    {
        priceLabel.Text = "Price: " +
           CONT_BREAKFAST_PRICE .ToString("C");
    }
}
```

4. Return to the Design view for the BreakfastOption `Form` and double-click the **Continental breakfast** `RadioButton`. When you see the generated `CheckedChanged()` method, add a statement that sets `priceLabel` to the continental breakfast price when the user makes that selection.

```
private void contBreakfastButton _CheckedChanged
      (object sender, EventArgs e)
{
      priceLabel.Text = "Price: " +
         CONT_BREAKFAST_PRICE.ToString("C");
}
```

5. Return to the Design view for the `BreakfastOptionForm`, double-click the **Full breakfast** `RadioButton`, and add a statement to the generated method that sets the `priceLabel` to the full breakfast price when the user makes that selection.

```
private void fullBreakfastButton_CheckedChanged
      (object sender, EventArgs e)
{
      priceLabel.Text = "Price: " +
         FULL_BREAKFAST_PRICE.ToString("C");
}
```

6. Return to the Design view for the `BreakfastOptionForm`, double-click the **Deluxe breakfast** `RadioButton`, and add a statement to the generated method that sets the `priceLabel` to the deluxe breakfast price when the user makes that selection.

```
private void deluxeBreakfastButton_CheckedChanged
      (object sender, EventArgs e)
{
      priceLabel.Text = "Price: " +
         DELUXE_BREAKFAST_PRICE.ToString("C");
}
```

7. In the Solution Explorer, double-click the **Form1.cs file** to view the original `Form`. Double-click the **Click for meal options** `Button`; when the `Click()` method is generated, add the following code so that the `BreakfastOptionForm` is loaded when a user clicks the `Button`:

```
private void mealButton_Click(object sender,
   EventArgs e)
{
   BreakfastOptionForm breakfastForm = new
      BreakfastOptionForm();
   breakfastForm.ShowDialog();
}
```

8. Save the project and execute it. When the `BedAndBreakfast Form` appears, confirm that the BelleAire Suite and Lincoln Room `CheckBox`es still work correctly, displaying their information `Form`s when they are clicked. Then click the **Click for meal options** `Button`. By default, the Continental breakfast option is chosen, as shown in Figure 11-51, so the price is $6.00. Click the other `RadioButton` options to confirm that each correctly changes the breakfast price.

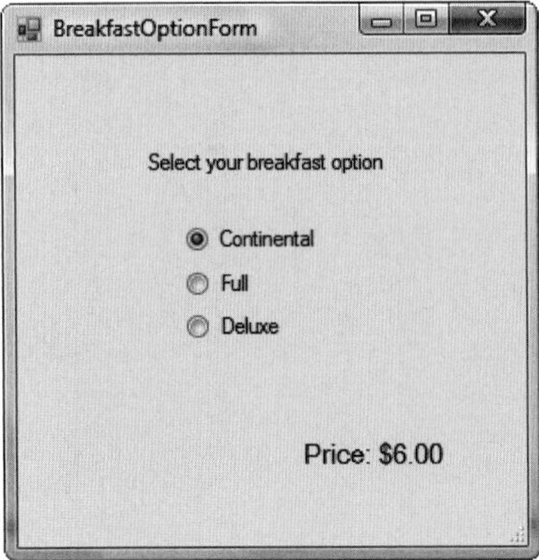

Figure 11-51 The `BreakfastOptionForm` with Continental breakfast `RadioButton` selected

9. Dismiss all the `Forms` and close Visual Studio.

CHAPTER SUMMARY

- The `Control` class provides definitions for GUI objects such as `Forms` and `Buttons`. There are 26 direct descendants of `Control` and additional descendants of those classes. Each `Control` has more than 80 `public` properties and 20 `protected` ones. For example, each `Control` has a `Font` and a `ForeColor` that dictate how its text is displayed, and each `Control` has a `Width` and `Height`.
- A `Label` is one of the simplest GUI `Control` objects you can place on a `Form`. The `Label` class descends directly from `Control`. Typically, you use a `Label` to provide descriptive text for another `Control` object or to display other text information on a `Form`. You can create a `Label` by writing code or by using the Visual Studio IDE.
- You use the `Font` class to change the appearance of printed text on your `Forms`. When designing a `Label` or other `Control` on a `Form`, it is easiest to select a `Font` from the Properties list. The `Font` class includes a number of overloaded constructors.
- A `LinkLabel` is similar to a `Label`; it is a child of `Label`, but it provides the additional capability to link the user to other sources, such as Web pages or files.
- The `Color` class contains a wide variety of predefined `Colors` that you can use with your `Controls`.
- `CheckBox` objects are GUI widgets the user can click to select or deselect an option. When a `Form` contains multiple `CheckBoxes`, any number of them can be checked or unchecked at the same time. `RadioButtons` are similar to `CheckBoxes`, except that when they are placed on a `Form`, only one `RadioButton` can be selected at a time—selecting any `RadioButton` automatically deselects the others. `CheckBox` and `RadioButton` objects both have a `Checked` property whose value is `true` or `false`.

- A PictureBox is a Control in which you can display graphics from a bitmap, icon, JPEG, GIF, or other image file type. Just as with a Button or a Label, you can easily add a PictureBox by dragging its Control onto the Form in the Visual Studio IDE.
- ListBox, ComboBox, and CheckedListBox objects descend from ListControl. The ListBox Control enables you to display a list of items that the user can select by clicking. With a ListBox, you allow the user to make a single selection or multiple selections by setting the SelectionMode property appropriately. A ComboBox is similar to a ListBox, except that it displays an additional editing field to allow the user to select from the list or to enter new text. A CheckedListBox is also similar to a ListBox, with check boxes appearing to the left of each desired item.
- The MonthCalendar and DateTimePicker Controls allow you to retrieve date and time information.
- When you place Controls on a Form in the IDE, you can drag them to any location to achieve the effect you want. When you drag multiple Controls onto a Form, blue snap lines appear and help you align new Controls with others already in place. You also can use the Location property in the Properties list to specify a location. Anchor, Dock, and Padding properties help you determine a Control's size and position in the Form. A Form also has a MinimumSize property and a MaximumSize property. Each has two values—Width and Height. Many types of ContainerControls are available to hold Controls. For example, you can use a GroupBox or Panel to group related Controls on a Form. When you move a GroupBox or Panel, all its Controls are moved as a group.
- Most programs you use in a Windows environment contain a menu strip, which is a horizontal list of general options that appears under the title bar of a Form or Window. When you click an item in a menu strip, you might initiate an action. More frequently, you see a list box that contains more specific options. Each of these might initiate an action, or it might lead to another menu. You can add a MenuStrip Control object to any Form you create.
- If you examine the Visual Studio IDE or search through the Visual Studio documentation, you will find many other Controls you can use. If you click Project on the main menu and click Add New Item, you can add extra Forms, Files, Controls, and other elements to a project.

KEY TERMS

Widgets are interactive controls such as labels, scroll bars, check boxes, and radio buttons.

The **Control** class provides the definitions for GUI objects.

The **Component** class provides containment and cleanup for other objects.

A **Label** is a Control object that typically provides descriptive text for another Control object or displays other text information on a Form.

In Visual Studio, a **method node** is a small box that appears to the left of code; you use it to expand or collapse code.

The **Font** class is used to change the appearance of printed text on Forms.

A **LinkLabel** is similar to a Label, but it provides the additional capability to link the user to other sources, such as Web pages or files.

The **default event** for a Control is the one generated when you double-click it while designing it in the IDE. It is the method you are most likely to alter when you use the Control, as well as the event that users most likely expect to generate when they encounter the Control in a working application.

The **Color** class contains a wide variety of predefined colors to use with Controls.

CheckBox objects are GUI widgets the user can click to select or deselect an option. When a Form contains multiple CheckBoxes, any number of them can be checked or unchecked at the same time.

RadioButtons are similar to CheckBoxes, except that when they are placed on a Form, only one RadioButton can be selected at a time—selecting any RadioButton automatically deselects the others.

A **PictureBox** is a Control in which you can display graphics from a bitmap, icon, JPEG, GIF, or other image file type.

The **ListBox** Control enables you to display a list of items that the user can select by clicking.

A **ComboBox** is similar to a ListBox, except that it displays an additional editing field that allows a user to select from the list or enter new text.

A **CheckedListBox** is also similar to a ListBox, with check boxes appearing to the left of each desired item.

The **MonthCalendar** and **DateTimePicker** Controls allow you to retrieve date and time information.

Snap lines appear in a design environment to help you align new Controls with others already in place.

Setting the **Anchor property** causes a Control to remain at a fixed distance from the side of a container when the user resizes it.

Setting the **Dock property** attaches a Control to the side of a container so that the Control stretches when the container's size is adjusted.

A Form has a **Padding property** that specifies the distance between docked Controls and the edges of the Form.

A Form also has a **MinimumSize property** and a **MaximumSize property**. Each has two values—Width and Height.

A **GroupBox** or **Panel** can be used to group related Controls on a Form.

A **menu strip** is a horizontal list of general options that appears under the title bar of a Form or Window. When you click an item in a menu strip, you might initiate an action. More frequently, you see a list box that contains more specific options.

You can add a **MenuStrip** Control object to any Form you create.

REVIEW QUESTIONS

1. `Label`s, `Button`s, and `CheckBoxes` are all ________.
   a. GUI objects
   b. `Controls`
   c. widgets
   d. all of these

2. All `Control` objects descend from ________.
   a. `Form`
   b. `Component`
   c. `ButtonBase`
   d. all of these

3. Which of the following is most like a `RadioButton`?
   a. `ListControl`
   b. `CheckedListBox`
   c. `PictureBox`
   d. `Button`

4. Which of the following is not a commonly used `Control` property?
   a. `BackColor`
   b. `Language`
   c. `Location`
   d. `Size`

5. The `Control` you frequently use to provide descriptive text for another `Control` object is a ________.
   a. `Form`
   b. `Label`
   c. `CheckBox`
   d. `MessageBox`

6. Which of the following creates a `Label` named `firstLabel`?
   a. `firstLabel = new firstLabel();`
   b. `Label = new firstLabel();`
   c. `Label firstLabel = new Label();`
   d. `Label firstLabel = Label();`

7. The property that determines what the user reads on a `Label` is the ________ property.
   a. `Text`
   b. `Label`
   c. `Phrase`
   d. `Setting`

8. Which of the following correctly creates a `Font`?
   a. `Font myFont = new Font("Arial", 14F, FontStyle.Bold);`
   b. `Font myFont = new Font("Courier", 13.6);`
   c. `myFont = Font new Font("TimesRoman", FontStyle.Italic);`
   d. `Font myFont = Font(20, "Helvetica", Underlined);`

9. The default event for a `Control` is the one that ________.
   a. occurs automatically whether a user manipulates the `Control` or not
   b. is generated when you double-click the `Control` while designing it in the IDE
   c. requires no parameters
   d. occurs when a user clicks the `Control` with a mouse

10. Assume you have created a `Label` named `myLabel`. Which of the following sets `myLabel`'s background color to green?
    a. `myLabel = BackColor.System.Drawing.Color.Green;`
    b. `myLabel.BackColor = System.Drawing.Color.Green;`
    c. `myLabel.Green = System.DrawingColor;`
    d. `myLabel.Background = new Color.Green;`

11. A difference between `CheckBox` and `RadioButton` objects is ________.
    a. `RadioButton`s descend from `ButtonBase`; `CheckBox`es do not
    b. only one `RadioButton` can be selected at a time
    c. only one `CheckBox` can appear on a `Form` at a time
    d. `RadioButton`s cannot be placed in a `GroupBox`; `CheckBox`es can

12. The `Checked` property of a `RadioButton` can hold the values ________.
    a. `true` and `false`
    b. `Checked` and `Unchecked`
    c. 0 and 1
    d. `Yes`, `No`, and `Undetermined`

13. The `Control` in which you can display a bitmap or JPEG image is a(n) ________.
    a. `DisplayModule`
    b. `ImageHolder`
    c. `BitmapControl`
    d. `PictureBox`

14. `ListBox`, `ComboBox`, and `CheckedListBox` objects descend from the same family: ________.
    a. `ListControl`
    b. `List`
    c. `ButtonBase`
    d. `ListBase`

15. Which of the following properties is associated with a `ListBox` but not a `Button`?
    a. `BackColor`
    b. `SelectedItem`
    c. `Location`
    d. `IsSelected`

16. With a `ListBox` you can allow the user to choose ________.
    a. only a single option
    b. multiple selections
    c. either of these
    d. none of these

17. You can add items to a `ListBox` by using the ________ method.
    a. `Add()`
    b. `Append()`
    c. `List()`
    d. `AddRange()`

18. A `ListBox`'s `SelectedItem` property contains ________.
    a. the position of the currently selected item
    b. the value of the currently selected item
    c. a Boolean value indicating whether an item is currently selected
    d. a count of the number of currently selected items

19. When you create a `ListBox`, by default its `SelectionMode` is ________.
    a. `Simple`
    b. `MultiExtended`
    c. `One`
    d. `false`

20. A horizontal list of general options that appears under the title bar of a `Form` or `Window` is a ________.
    a. task bar
    b. subtitle bar
    c. menu strip
    d. list box

EXERCISES

1. Create a `Form` that contains two `Button`s, one labeled Stop and one labeled Go. Add a `Label` telling the user to click a button. When the user clicks Stop, change the `BackColor` of the `Form` to `Red`; when the user clicks Go, change the `BackColor` of the `Form` to `Green`. Save the project as **StopGo**.

2. Create a `Form` that contains at least five `Button` objects, each labeled with a color. When the user clicks a `Button`, change the `BackColor` of the `Form` appropriately. Save the project as **FiveColors**.

3. Create a `Form` that contains at least five `RadioButton` objects, each labeled with a color. When the user clicks a `RadioButton`, change the `BackColor` of the `Form` appropriately. Save the project as **FiveColors2**.

4. Create a `Form` for a video store that contains a `ListBox` with the titles of at least eight videos available to rent. Provide directions that tell users they can choose as many videos as they want by holding down the Ctrl key while making selections. When the user clicks a `Button` to indicate the choices are final, display the total rental price, which is $2.50 per video. If the user selects or deselects items and clicks the button again, make sure the total is updated correctly. Save the project as **Video**.

5. Create a `Form` with two `ListBoxes`—one contains at least four `Font` names and the other contains at least four `Font` sizes. Let the first item in each list be the default selection if the user fails to make a selection. Allow only one selection per `ListBox`. After the user clicks a `Button`, display "Hello" in the selected `Font` and size. Save the project as **FontSelector**.

6. Create a `Form` for a car rental company. Allow the user to choose a car style (compact, standard, or luxury) and a number of days (1 through 7). After the user makes selections, display the total rental charge, which is $19.95 per day for a compact car, $24.95 per day for a standard car, and $39 per day for a luxury car. Use the `Controls` that you think are best for each function. Label items appropriately and use fonts and colors to achieve an attractive design. Save the project as **CarRental**.

7. Create a `Form` for a restaurant. Allow the user to choose one item from at least three options in each of the following categories—appetizer, entrée, and dessert. Assign a different price to each selection and display the total when the user clicks a `Button`. Use the `Controls` that you think are best for each function. Label items appropriately and use fonts and colors to achieve an attractive design. Save the project as **Restaurant**.

8. Create a `Form` for an automobile dealer. Include options for at least three car models. After users make a selection, proceed to a new `Form` that contains information about the selected model. Use the `Controls` that you decide are best for each function. Label items on the `Form` appropriately and use fonts and colors to achieve an attractive design. Save the project as **CarDealer**.

9. Create a spreadsheet and then include a few numbers in it that represent an annual budget. Create a `Form` that includes two `LinkLabels`. One opens the spreadsheet for viewing, and the other visits your favorite Web site. Include `Labels` on the `Form` to explain each link. Save the project as **AnnualBudget**.

10. Create a `Form` for Nina's Cookie Source. Allow the user to select from at least three types of cookies, each with a different price per dozen. Allow the user to select 1/2, 1, 2, or 3 dozen cookies. Adjust the final displayed price as the user chooses cookie types and quantities. Also allow the user to select an order date from a `MonthCalendar`. Assuming that shipping takes three days, display the estimated arrival date for the order. Include as many labels as necessary so the user understands how to use the `Form`. Save the project as **NinasCookieSource**.

11. Using the `MenuStripDemo` project on your Student Disk (see Figure 11-36), add appropriate functionality to the currently unprogrammed menu options (Small in the Font menu and the three options in the Color menu). Add at least three other menu options to the program, either vertically, horizontally, or both. Save the modified project as **MenuStripDemo2**.

DEBUGGING EXERCISES

Each of the following projects in the Chapter.11 folder on your Student Disk has syntax and/or logical errors. In each case, determine the problem and fix the program. After you correct the errors, save each project using the same name preceded with *Fixed*. For example, DebugEleven1 will become FixedDebugEleven1.

> **NOTE**
> Immediately save the four project folders with their new names before starting to correct their errors.

a. DebugEleven1

b. DebugEleven2

c. DebugEleven3

d. DebugEleven4

UP FOR DISCUSSION

1. Making exciting, entertaining, professional-looking GUI applications becomes easier once you learn to include graphics images, as you did when you learned about `PictureBox` objects in this chapter. You can copy graphics images from many locations on the Web. Should there be any restrictions on what graphics you use? Does it make a difference if you are writing programs for your own enjoyment, as opposed to putting them on the Web where others can see them? Should restrictions be different for using photographs versus using drawings? Does it matter if the photographs contain recognizable people? Would you impose any restrictions on images posted to your organization's Web site?
2. Should you be allowed to store computer games on your computer at work? If so, should you be allowed to play the games at work? If so, should there be any restrictions on when you can play them?
3. Suppose you discover a way to breach security in a Web site so that visitors might access information that belongs to the company. Should you be allowed to publish your findings? Should you notify the organization? Should the organization pay you a reward for discovering the breach? If they do, would this encourage you to search for more potential security violations? Suppose the newly available information on the Web site is relatively innocuous—for example, office telephone numbers of company executives. Suppose it is not—for example, home telephone numbers for the same executives. Does this make a difference?

CHAPTER TWELVE

12

HANDLING EVENTS

In this chapter you will:

Learn about event handling
Learn about delegates
Create composed delegates
Declare your own events and handlers
Use the built-in `EventHandler`
Handle `Control` component events
Handle mouse events
Handle keyboard events
Manage multiple `Controls`
Learn how to continue your exploration of `Controls` and events

Throughout this book, you have learned how to create C# programs that perform a variety of tasks. In the last few chapters, you expanded your repertoire from creating functional but dull-looking command-line applications to creating attractive and interactive GUI programs.

The aspect of Windows widgets that makes them useful is their ability to cause events when a user interacts with them. In the last two chapters, you have seen `Controls` that respond to a user-initiated event—for example, a mouse click. In those chapters, you provided actions for `Controls`' default events. In this chapter, you will expand your understanding of the event-handling process. You will learn more about the object that triggers an event and the object that captures and responds to that event. You also will learn about delegates—objects that act as intermediaries in transferring messages from senders to receivers. You will create delegates and manage interactive events. You will learn to manage multiple events for a single `Control` and to manage multiple `Controls` for a project.

EVENT HANDLING

In C#, an event occurs when something interesting happens to an object. When you create a class, you decide exactly what is considered "interesting." For example, when you create a `Form`, you might decide to respond to a user clicking a `Button` but ignore a user who clicks a `Label`—clicking the `Label` is just not "interesting" to the `Form`.

You use an event to notify a client program when something happens to a class object the program is using. Events are used frequently in GUI programs—for example, you notify a program when the user clicks a `Button` or chooses an option from a `ListBox`. In addition, you can use events with ordinary classes that do not represent GUI controls. When an object's client might want to know about any changes that occur in the object, events enable the object to signal the client.

In Chapter 10, you learned that when a user interacts with a GUI object, an event is generated that causes the program to perform a task. GUI programs are **event driven**—an event such as a button click "drives" the program to perform a task. Programmers also say that a button click **raises an event**, **fires an event**, or **triggers an event**. A method that performs a task in response to an event is an **event handler**.

For example, Figure 12-1 shows a `Form` that contains a `Label` and a `Button`. The following changes are the only ones that have been made to the default `Form` in the IDE:

» The `Size` property has been adjusted to 500, 120.

» A `Label` has been dragged onto the `Form`, its `Name` property has been set to `helloLabel`, its `Text` property has been set to "Hello", and its `Font` has been increased to 9.75.

» A `Button` has been dragged onto the `Form`, its `Name` property has been set to `changeButton`, and its `Text` property has been set to "Change Label".

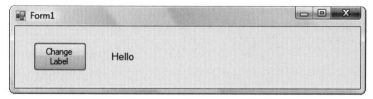

Figure 12-1 A `Form` with a `Label` and a `Button`

If you double-click the button on the form in the IDE, you generate the following empty method in the program code:

```
private void changeButton_Click(object sender, EventArgs e)
{
}
```

The `changeButton_Click()` method is an event handler. Conventionally, event handlers are named using the identifier of the `Control` (in this case, `changeButton`), an underscore, and the name of the event type (in this case, `Click`). You can create your own methods to handle events and provide any names for them, but the names should follow these conventions.

Suppose that when a user clicks the button, you want the text on the label to change from "Hello" to "Goodbye". You can write the following code within the event handler:

```
private void changeButton_Click(object sender, EventArgs e)
{
    helloLabel.Text = "Goodbye";
}
```

Then, when you run the application and click the button, the output appears as shown in Figure 12-2.

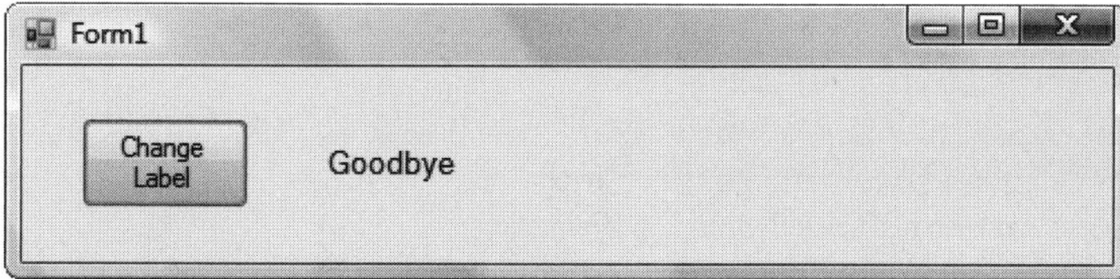

Figure 12-2 Output of `EventDemo` application after user clicks button

The event-handler method is also known as an **event receiver**. The control that generates an event is an **event sender**. The first parameter in the list for the event receiver method is an object named sender; it is a reference to the object that generated the event. For example, if you code the event handler as follows, the output appears as in Figure 12-3.

```
private void changeButton_Click(object sender, EventArgs e)
{
   helloLabel.Text = sender.ToString();
}
```

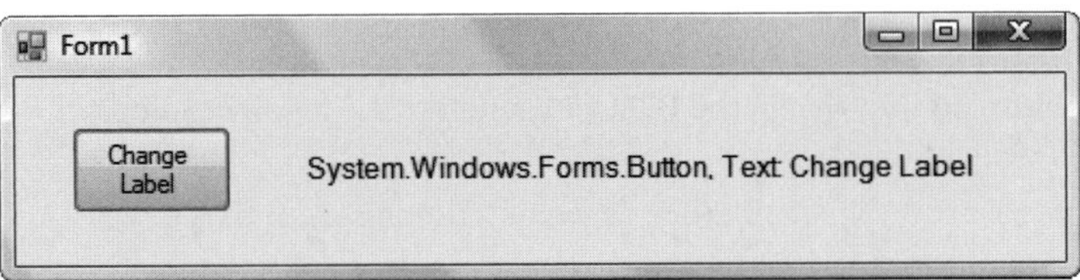

Figure 12-3 EventDemo application modified to display sender information

The label in Figure 12-3 shows that the sender of the event is an instance of System.Windows.Forms.Button, whose Text property is "Change Label".

The second parameter in the event-handler parameter list is a reference to an event arguments object of type EventArgs; in this method, the EventArgs argument is named e. **EventArgs** is a C# class designed for holding event information. If you change the code in the event handler to the following, then run the program and click the button, you see the output in Figure 12-4:

```
private void changeButton_Click(object sender, EventArgs e)
{
   helloLabel.Text = e.ToString();
}
```

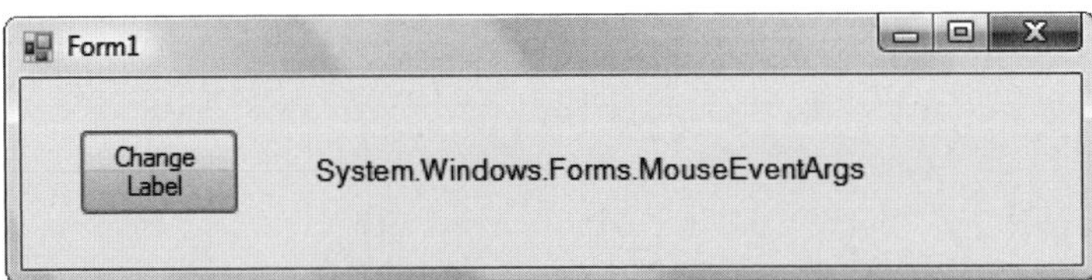

Figure 12-4 EventDemo application modified to display EventArgs information

In Figure 12-4, you can see that the e object is a MouseEventArgs object. That makes sense, because the user used the mouse to click the Button.

As you learned in Chapter 10, you can examine all the code generated for the application that creates the Form shown in Figure 12-4. When you open the Designer.cs file in the IDE and expand the Windows Form Designer generated code, you see comments as well as statements

```
//
// changeButton
//
this.changeButton.Location = new System.Drawing.Point(21, 33);
this.changeButton.Name = "changeButton";
this.changeButton.Size = new System.Drawing.Size(75, 23);
this.changeButton.TabIndex = 1;
this.changeButton.Text = "Change Label";
this.changeButton.UseVisualStyleBackColor = true;
this.changeButton.Click += new
   System.EventHandler(this.changeButton_Click);
```

Figure 12-5 Code involving `changeButton` generated by Visual Studio

>> **NOTE** The code generated in Design mode in the IDE is not meant to be altered by typing. You should modify `Control` properties through the Properties window in the IDE, not by typing in the Designer.cs file.

that set the `Controls`' properties. For example, the code generated for `changeButton` appears in Figure 12-5. You can recognize that such features as the button's `Location`, `Name`, and `Size` have been set.

The most unusual statement in the section of `changeButton` code is shaded in Figure 12-5; this statement concerns the **`Click` event**, which is generated when `changeButton` is clicked by a user. This statement is necessary because `changeButton` does not automatically "know" what method will handle its events—C# and all other .NET languages allow you to choose your own names for event-handling methods for events generated by GUI objects. In other words, there is no requirement that the event-handling method be named `changeButton_Click()`. You *could* create your program so that when the user clicks the button, the event-handling method is named `calculatePayroll()`, `changeLabel()`, or any other identifier for a method you could then write. Of course, you do not want to make such a change; it is clearest if the method that executes when `changeButton` is clicked is named `changeButton_Click()`. However, that convention is not required by the compiler, so the shaded statement in Figure 12-5 is necessary to identify the method that will handle the `Click` event. The shaded statement indicates that, for this program, the method named `changeButton_Click()` is the receiver for `changeButton`'s `Click` event. Programmers say the shaded method creates a delegate, or more specifically, a composed delegate. You will learn about these terms in the next two sections of this chapter.

>> **NOTE** Connecting an event to its resulting actions is called **event wiring**.

>> **TWO TRUTHS AND A LIE: EVENT HANDLING**

1. An action such as a key press or button click raises an event.
2. A method that performs a task in response to an event is an event handler.
3. The control that generates an event is an event receiver.

The false statement is #3. The control that generates an event is an event sender.

UNDERSTANDING DELEGATES

A **delegate** is an object that contains a reference to a method; object-oriented programmers would say that a delegate encapsulates a method. In government, a delegate is a representative that you authorize to make choices for you. For example, you select a delegate to a presidential nominating convention. When human delegates arrive at a convention, they are free to make choices based on current conditions. Similarly, C# delegates provide a way for a program to take alternative courses when running. When you write a method, you don't always know which actions will occur, so you give your delegates authority to run the correct methods.

>> **NOTE** In Chapter 1, you learned that encapsulation is a basic feature of object-oriented programming. Recall that encapsulation is the technique of packaging an object's attributes and methods into a cohesive unit that can then be used as an undivided entity.

After you have instantiated a C# delegate, you can pass this object to a method, which then can call the method referenced within the delegate. In other words, a delegate provides a way to pass a reference to a method as an argument to another method. For example, if `del` is a delegate that contains a reference to the method `M1()`, you can pass `del` to a new method named `MyMethod()`. Alternatively, you could create a delegate named `del` that contains a reference to a method named `M2()` and then pass this version to `MyMethod()`. When you write `MyMethod()`, you don't have to know whether it will call `M1()` or `M2()`; you only need to know that it will call whatever method is referenced within `del`.

>> **NOTE** A C# delegate is similar to a function pointer in C++. A function pointer is a variable that holds a method's memory address. In the C++ programming language, you pass a method's address to another method using a pointer variable. Java does not allow function pointers because they are dangerous—if the program alters the address, you might inadvertently execute the wrong method. C# provides a compromise between the dangers of C++ pointers and the Java ban on passing functions. Delegates allow flexible method calls but remain secure because you cannot alter the method addresses.

You declare a delegate using the keyword `delegate`, followed by an ordinary method declaration that includes a return type, method name, and argument list. For example, by entering the following statement, you can declare a delegate named `GreetingDelegate()`, which accepts a `string` argument and returns nothing:

```
delegate void GreetingDelegate(string s);
```

The `GreetingDelegate` can encapsulate any method as long as it has a `void` return type and a single `string` parameter. Any delegate can encapsulate any method that has the same return type and parameter list as the delegate. If you declare the delegate and then write a method with the same return type and parameter list, you can assign an instance of the delegate to represent it. For example, the following `Hello()` method is a `void` method that takes a `string` parameter:

```
public static void Hello(string s)
{
   Console.WriteLine("Hello, {0}!", s);
}
```

Because the Hello() method matches the GreetingDelegate definition, you can assign a reference to the Hello() method to a new instance of GreetingDelegate, as follows:

```
GreetingDelegate myDel = new GreetingDelegate(Hello);
```

Once the reference to the Hello() method is encapsulated in the delegate myDel, each of the following statements will result in the same output: "Hello, Kim!":

```
Hello("Kim");
myDel("Kim");
```

In this example, the ability to use the delegate myDel does not seem to provide any benefits over using a regular method call to Hello(). If you have a program in which you pass the delegate to a method, however, the method becomes more flexible; you gain the ability to send a reference to an appropriate method you want to execute at the time.

For example, Figure 12-6 shows a Greeting class that contains Hello() and Goodbye() methods. The Main() method declares two delegates named firstDel and secondDel.

```
using System;
delegate void GreetingDelegate(string s);
class Greeting
{
   public static void Hello(string s)
   {
      Console.WriteLine("Hello, {0}!", s);
   }
   public static void Goodbye(string s)
   {
      Console.WriteLine("Goodbye, {0}!", s);
   }
   public static void Main()
   {
      GreetingDelegate firstDel, secondDel;
      firstDel = new GreetingDelegate(Hello);
      secondDel = new GreetingDelegate(Goodbye);
      GreetMethod(firstDel, "Cathy");
      GreetMethod(secondDel, "Bob");
   }
   public static void GreetMethod
     (GreetingDelegate gd, string name)
   {
      Console.WriteLine("The greeting is:");
      gd(name);
   }
}
```

Figure 12-6 The Greeting program

One is instantiated using the `Hello()` method, and the other is instantiated using the `Goodbye()` method. When the `Main()` method calls `GreetMethod()` two times, it passes a different method and string each time. Figure 12-7 shows the output.

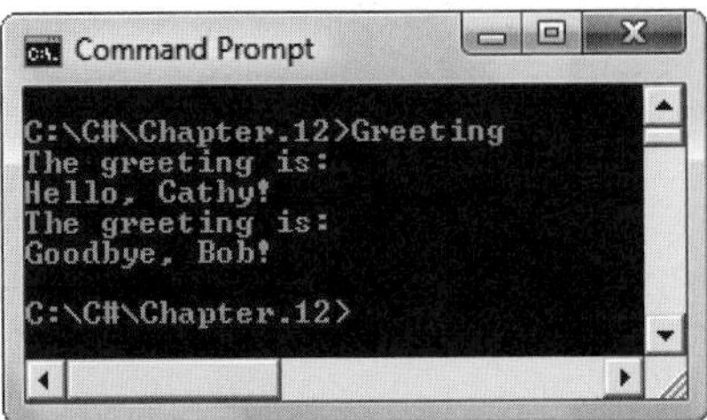

Figure 12-7 Output of the `Greeting` program

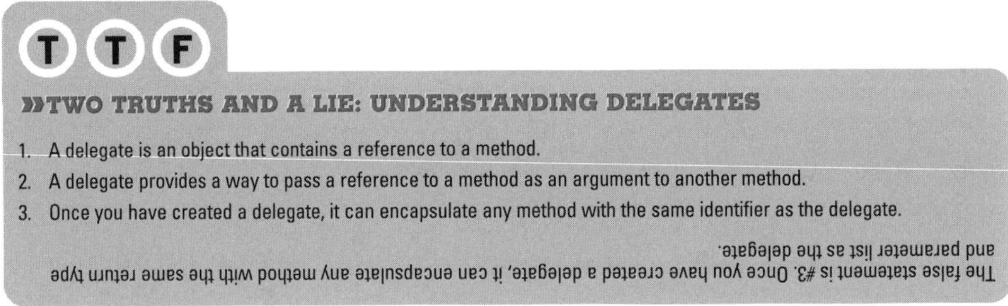

T T F

»TWO TRUTHS AND A LIE: UNDERSTANDING DELEGATES

1. A delegate is an object that contains a reference to a method.
2. A delegate provides a way to pass a reference to a method as an argument to another method.
3. Once you have created a delegate, it can encapsulate any method with the same identifier as the delegate.

The false statement is #3. Once you have created a delegate, it can encapsulate any method with the same return type and parameter list as the delegate.

CREATING COMPOSED DELEGATES

»NOTE A composed delegate is a collection of delegates. The += and −= operators add and remove items from the collection.

You can assign one delegate to another using the = operator. You also can use the + and += operators to combine delegates into a **composed delegate** that calls the delegates from which it is built. As an example, assume that you declare three delegates named `del1`, `del2`, and `del3`, and that you assign a reference to the method `M1()` to `del1` and a reference to method `M2()` to `del2`. When the statement `del3 = del1 + del2;` executes, `del3` becomes a delegate that executes both `M1()` and `M2()`, in that order. Only delegates with the same parameter list can be composed, and the delegates used must have a `void` return type. Additionally, you can use the − and −= operators to remove a delegate from a composed delegate.

Figure 12-8 shows a program that contains a composed delegate. This program contains only two changes from the `Greeting` program in Figure 12-6—the class name (`Greeting2`) and the shaded statement that creates the composed delegate. The delegate `firstDel` now executes two methods, `Hello()` and `Goodbye()`, whereas `secondDel` still executes only `Goodbye()`. Figure 12-9 shows the output; “Cathy” is used with two methods, but “Bob” is used with only one.

```
using System;
delegate void GreetingDelegate(string s);
class Greeting2
{
   public static void Hello(string s)
   {
      Console.WriteLine("Hello, {0}!", s);
   }
   public static void Goodbye(string s)
   {
      Console.WriteLine("Goodbye, {0}!", s);
   }
   public static void Main()
   {
      GreetingDelegate firstDel, secondDel;
      firstDel = new GreetingDelegate(Hello);
      secondDel = new GreetingDelegate(Goodbye);
      firstDel += secondDel;
      GreetMethod(firstDel, "Cathy");
      GreetMethod(secondDel, "Bob");
   }
   public static void GreetMethod
     (GreetingDelegate gd, string name)
   {
      Console.WriteLine("The greeting is:");
      gd(name);
   }
}
```

Figure 12-8 The `Greeting2` program

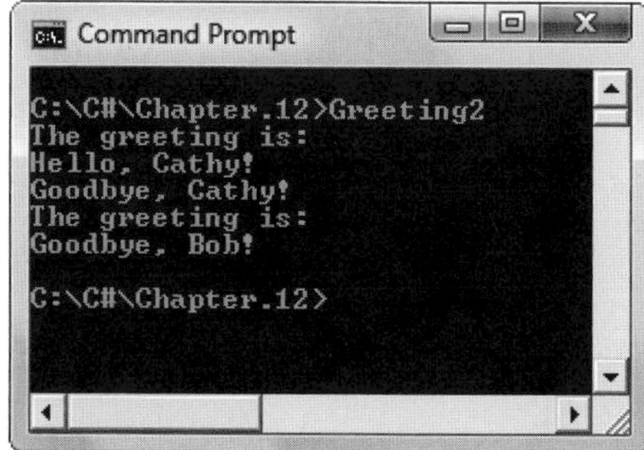

Figure 12-9 Output of the `Greeting2` program

»TWO TRUTHS AND A LIE: CREATING COMPOSED DELEGATES

1. A composed delegate can be created using the += operator; it calls the delegates from which it is built.
2. Only delegates with a `void` parameter list can be composed, and the delegates used must have no return type.
3. You can use the – and –= operators to remove a delegate from a composed delegate.

The false statement is #2. Only delegates with the same parameter list can be composed, and the delegates used must have a `void` return type.

DECLARING YOUR OWN EVENTS AND HANDLERS

To declare your own event, you use a delegate. An event provides a way for a class's clients to dictate methods that should execute when an event occurs. The clients identify methods to execute by providing delegates. When an event occurs, any delegate that a client has given or passed to the event is invoked. Just like the event handlers automatically created in the IDE, each of your own event handler `delegate`s requires two arguments—the object where the event was initiated (the sender) and an `EventArgs` argument. You can create an `EventArgs` object that contains event information, or you can use the `EventArgs` class static field named `Empty`, which represents an event that contains no event data. In other words, using the `Empty` field simply tells the client that an event has occurred, without specifying details. For example, you can declare a `delegate` event handler named `ChangedEventHandler`, as follows:

```
public delegate void ChangedEventHandler
    (object sender, EventArgs e);
```

The identifier `ChangedEventHandler` can be any legal identifier you choose. This delegate defines the set of arguments that will be passed to the method that handles the event. It can be used in a program that handles events.

» NOTE The value of `Empty` is a read-only instance of `EventArgs`. You can pass it to a method that accepts an `EventArgs` parameter.

For example, Figure 12-10 contains a simple `Student` class that is similar to many classes you already have created. The `Student` class contains just two data fields and will generate an event when the data in either field changes.

The `Student` class in Figure 12-10 contains fields that will hold an ID number and grade point average (GPA) for a `Student`. The first shaded statement in the

```
public class Student
{
   private int idNum;
   private double gpa;
   public event ChangedEventHandler Changed;
   public int IdNum
   {
      get
      {
         return idNum;
      }
      set
      {
         idNum = value;
         OnChanged(EventArgs.Empty);
      }
   }
   public double Gpa
   {
      get
      {
         return gpa;
      }
      set
      {
         gpa = value;
         OnChanged(EventArgs.Empty);
      }
   }
   public void OnChanged(EventArgs e)
   {
      Changed(this, e);
   }
}
```

Figure 12-10 The `Student` class

figure defines a third `Student` class attribute—an event named `Changed`. The declaration for an event looks like a field, but instead of being an `int` or a `double`, it is a `ChangedEventHandler`.

The `Student` class event (`Changed`) looks like an ordinary field. However, you cannot assign values to the event as easily as you can to ordinary data fields. You can take only two actions on an event: you can compose a new delegate onto it using the += operator, and you can remove a delegate from it using the -= operator. For example, to add

NOTE Events usually are declared as `public`, but you can use any accessibility modifier.

StudentChanged to the Changed event of a Student object named stu, you would write the following:

```
stu.Changed += new ChangedEventHandler(StudentChanged);
```

In the Student class, each set accessor assigns a value to the appropriate class instance field. However, when either the idNum or the gpa changes, the method in the Student class named OnChanged() is also called, using EventArgs.Empty as the argument. The OnChanged() method calls Changed() using two arguments—a reference to the Student object that was changed and the empty EventArgs object. Calling Changed() is also known as **invoking the event**.

NOTE If no client has wired a delegate to the event, the Changed field will be null, rather than referring to the delegate that should be called when the event is invoked. Therefore, programmers often check for null before invoking the event, as in the following example:

```
if(Changed != null)
   Changed(this, e);
```

For simplicity, the example in Figure 12-10 does not bother checking for null.

Figure 12-11 shows an EventListener class that listens for Student events. This class contains a Student object that is assigned a value using the parameter to the EventListener class constructor. The StudentChanged() method is added to the Student's event delegate using the += operator. The StudentChanged() method displays a message and Student data.

```
class EventListener
{
   private Student stu;
   public EventListener(Student student)
   {
      stu = student;
      stu.Changed += new ChangedEventHandler
         (StudentChanged);
   }
   private void StudentChanged(object sender, EventArgs e)
   {
      Console.WriteLine("The student has changed.");
      Console.WriteLine("   ID# {0}  GPA {1}",
         stu.IdNum, stu.Gpa);
   }
}
```

Figure 12-11 The EventListener class

Figure 12-12 shows a program that demonstrates the Student and EventListener classes. The program contains a single Main() method, which declares one Student and registers the program to listen for events from the Student class. Then three assignments are made.

```
using System;
class DemoStudentEvent
{
   public static void Main()
   {
      Student oneStu = new Student();
      EventListener listener = new EventListener(oneStu);
      oneStu.IdNum = 2345;
      oneStu.IdNum = 4567;
      oneStu.Gpa = 3.2;
   }
}
```

Figure 12-12 The `DemoStudentEvent` program

Because this program is registered to listen for events from the `Student`, each change in a data field triggers an event. That is, each assignment not only changes the value of the data field, it also executes the `StudentChanged()` method that displays two lines of explanation. In Figure 12-13, the program output shows that an event occurs three times—once when the ID becomes 2345 (and the GPA is still 0), again when the ID becomes 4567 (and the GPA still has not changed), and a third time when the GPA becomes 3.2.

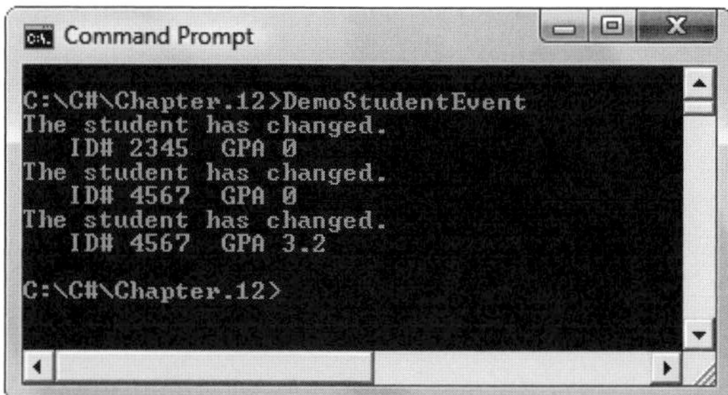

Figure 12-13 Output of the `DemoStudentEvent` program

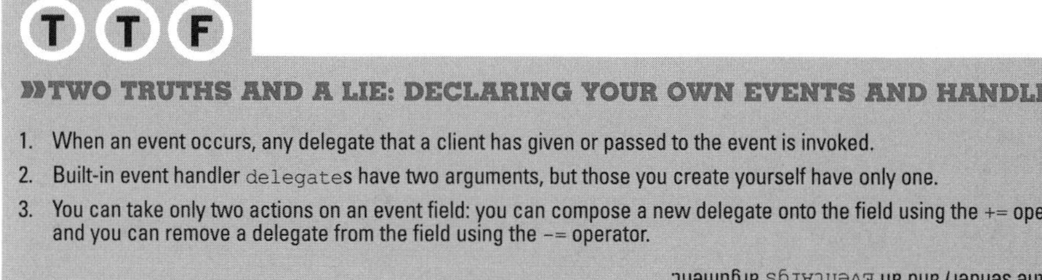

»TWO TRUTHS AND A LIE: DECLARING YOUR OWN EVENTS AND HANDLERS

1. When an event occurs, any delegate that a client has given or passed to the event is invoked.
2. Built-in event handler `delegate`s have two arguments, but those you create yourself have only one.
3. You can take only two actions on an event field: you can compose a new delegate onto the field using the += operator, and you can remove a delegate from the field using the -= operator.

The false statement is #2. Every event handler `delegate` requires two arguments—the object where the event was initiated (the sender) and an `EventArgs` argument.

USING THE BUILT-IN `EventHandler`

The C# language allows you to create events using any delegate type. However, the .NET Framework provides guidelines you should follow if you are developing a class that others will use. These guidelines indicate that the delegate type for an event should take exactly two parameters: a parameter indicating the source of the event, and an `EventArgs` parameter that encapsulates any additional information about the event. For events that do not use additional information, the .NET Framework has already defined an appropriate delegate type named **`EventHandler`**.

Figure 12-14 shows all the code necessary to demonstrate an `EventHandler`. Note the following changes from the classes used in the `DemoStudentEvent` program:

- No delegate named `ChangedEventHandler` is declared.
- In the first statement with shading in the `Student` class, the event is associated with the built-in delegate `EventHandler`.
- In the second statement with shading, which appears in the `EventListener` class, the delegate composition uses `EventHandler`.

```
using System;
public class Student
{
   private int idNum;
   private double gpa;
   public event EventHandler Changed;
   public int IdNum
   {
      get
      {
         return idNum;
      }
      set
      {
         idNum = value;
         OnChanged(EventArgs.Empty);
      }
   }
   public double Gpa
   {
      get
      {
         return gpa;
      }
```

Figure 12-14 The `Student`, `EventListener`, and `DemoStudentEvent2` classes (*continued*)

```
        set
        {
           gpa = value;
           OnChanged(EventArgs.Empty);
        }
     }
     public void OnChanged(EventArgs e)
     {
        Changed(this, e);
     }
}
class EventListener
{
     private Student stu;
     public EventListener(Student student)
     {
        stu = student;
        stu.Changed += new EventHandler(StudentChanged);
     }
     private void StudentChanged(object sender, EventArgs e)
     {
        Console.WriteLine("The student has changed.");
        Console.WriteLine("   ID# {0}   GPA {1}",
          stu.IdNum, stu.Gpa);
     }
}
class DemoStudentEvent2
{
     public static void Main()
     {
        Student oneStu = new Student();
        EventListener listener = new EventListener(oneStu);
        oneStu.IdNum = 2345;
        oneStu.IdNum = 4567;
        oneStu.Gpa = 3.2;
     }
}
```

Figure 12-14 (*continued*)

When you compile and execute the program in Figure 12-14, the output is identical to that in Figure 12-13.

»TWO TRUTHS AND A LIE: USING THE BUILT-IN `EventHandler`

1. The .NET Framework guidelines indicate that the delegate type for an event should take exactly two parameters.
2. The `EventArgs` parameter for an event handler holds the source of an event.
3. For events that do not require custom code for information about the event, the .NET Framework has already defined an appropriate type named `EventHandler`.

The false statement is #2. An object that is the first parameter to an event handler holds the source of the event. The `EventArgs` parameter for an event handler (the second parameter) encapsulates information about an event.

HANDLING `Control` COMPONENT EVENTS

Handling events requires understanding several difficult concepts. Fortunately, you most frequently will want to handle events in GUI environments when the user will manipulate `Controls`, and the good news is that these events have already been defined for you. When you want to handle events generated by GUI `Controls`, you use the same techniques as when you handle events that are not generated by `Controls`. The major difference is that when you create your own classes, like `Student`, you must define both the data fields and events you want to manage; but existing `Control` components, like `Buttons` and `ListBoxes`, already contain fields and `public` properties, like `Text`, as well as events with names, like `Click`. Table 12-1 lists just some of the more commonly used `Control` events.

»NOTE You can consult the Visual Studio Help feature to discover additional `Control` events as well as more specific events assigned to individual `Control` child classes.

You have already used the IDE to create some event-handling methods. These methods have been the default events generated when you double-click a `Control` in the IDE. For example, in Chapter 10 you created a `Click()` method for a `Button`, and in Chapter 11 you created a `LinkClicked()` method for a `LinkLabel`. A `Form` can contain any number of `Controls` that might have events associated with them. Additionally, a single `Control` might be able to raise any number of events. For example, besides creating a `Button`'s default `Click` event, you might want to define various actions when the user's mouse rolls over the button. Table 12-1 lists only a few of the many events available with `Controls`; any `Control` could conceivably raise many of those events.

Event	Description
BackColorChanged	Occurs when the value of the BackColor property has changed
Click	Occurs when a control is clicked
ControlAdded	Occurs when a new control is added
ControlRemoved	Occurs when a control is removed
CursorChanged	Occurs when the Cursor property value has changed
DragDrop	Occurs when a drag-and-drop operation is completed
DragEnter	Occurs when an object is dragged into a control's bounds
DragLeave	Occurs when an object has been dragged into and out of a control's bounds
DragOver	Occurs when an object has been dragged over a control's bounds
EnabledChanged	Occurs when the Enabled property value has changed
Enter	Occurs when a control is entered
FontChanged	Occurs when the Font property value has changed
ForeColorChanged	Occurs when the ForeColor property value has changed
GotFocus	Occurs when a control receives focus
HelpRequested	Occurs when a user requests help for a control
KeyDown	Occurs when a key is pressed while a control has focus
KeyPress	Occurs when a key is pressed while a control has focus
KeyUp	Occurs when a key is released while a control has focus
Leave	Occurs when a control is left
LocationChanged	Occurs when the Location property value has changed
LostFocus	Occurs when a control loses focus
MouseDown	Occurs when the mouse pointer hovers over a control and a mouse button is pressed
MouseEnter	Occurs when the mouse pointer enters a control
MouseHover	Occurs when the mouse pointer hovers over a control
MouseLeave	Occurs when the mouse pointer leaves a control
MouseMove	Occurs when the mouse pointer moves over a control
MouseUp	Occurs when the mouse pointer hovers over a control and a mouse button is released
MouseWheel	Occurs when the mouse wheel moves while a control has focus
Move	Occurs when a control is moved
Resize	Occurs when a control is resized
TextChanged	Occurs when the Text property value has changed
VisibleChanged	Occurs when the Visible property value has changed

Table 12-1 Some Control class public instance events

Suppose you want to create a project that takes a different set of actions when the mouse is over a `Button` than when the mouse is clicked. Figure 12-15 shows a project that has been started in the IDE. The following actions have been taken:

- A `Button` was dragged onto the `Form` and its `Text` was set to "Click me".
- A `Label` was added to the `Form`, its `Text` was set to "Hello", and its `Font` was increased.

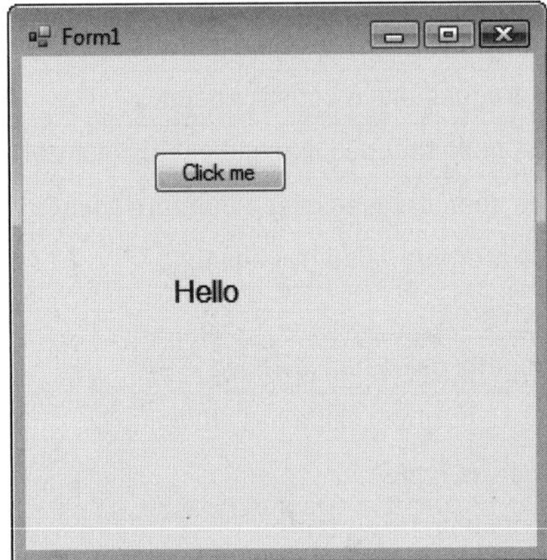

Figure 12-15 Start of `OneButtonTwoEvents` project in the IDE

When you double-click the `Button` on the `Form` in the IDE, you generate the shell of a `Click()` method into which you can type a command to change the `Label`'s text and its color, as follows:

```
private void button1_Click(object sender, EventArgs e)
{
   label1.Text = "Button was clicked";
   label1.BackColor = Color.CornflowerBlue;
}
```

NOTE `Color.CornflowerBlue` is one of C#'s predefined `Color` properties. A complete list appears in Table 11-5 in Chapter 11.

With the `Button` selected on the design `Form`, you can click the Events icon in the Properties window at the right side of the screen. The Events icon looks like a lightning bolt. Figure 12-16 shows that the Properties window displays events instead of properties and that the `Click` event has an associated method.

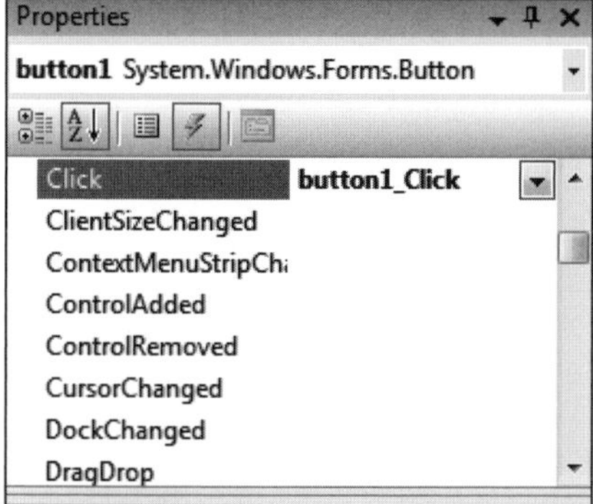

Figure 12-16 Properties window displaying events

If you scroll through the `Events` listed in the Properties window, you can see a wide variety of `Event` choices. If you scroll down to `MouseEnter` and double-click, you can see the code for an event handler as follows:

```
private void button1_MouseEnter(object sender, EventArgs e)
{
}
```

NOTE When you are viewing events in the Properties window, you can return to the list of properties by clicking the Properties icon. This icon is to the immediate left of the Events icon.

You can type any statements you want within this method. For example:

```
private void button1_MouseEnter(object sender, EventArgs e)
{
    label1.Text = "Go ahead";
    button1.BackColor = Color.Red;
}
```

When you run the program with the two new methods, two different events can occur:

- When you enter the button with the mouse (that is, pass the mouse over it), the `Label`'s `Text` changes to "Go ahead" and the button turns red, as shown on the left in Figure 12-17.
- After the button is clicked, the `Label`'s `Text` changes again and the `Label` becomes blue, as shown on the right in Figure 12-17.

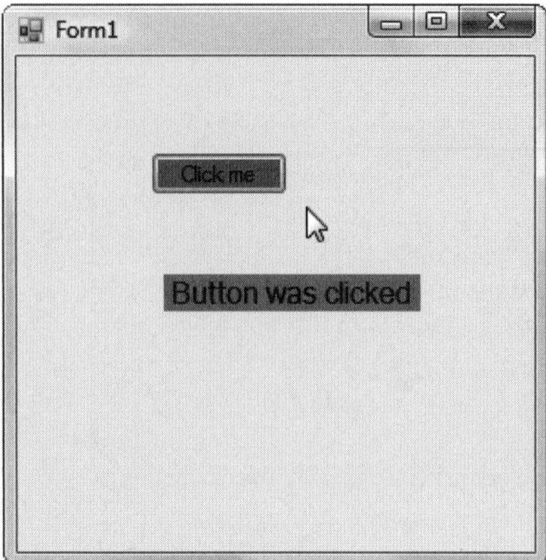

Figure 12-17 `OneButtonTwoEvents` program when mouse enters button and after button is clicked

If you examine the code generated by the Windows Form Designer, you will find the following two statements:

```
this.button1.Click += new System.EventHandler(this.button1_Click);
this.button1.MouseEnter += new System.EventHandler
   (this.button1_MouseEnter);
```

These `EventHandler` statements are similar to those in the `Student` class in Figure 12-14. The `Click` and `MouseEnter` delegates have been set to handle events appropriately for this application. You could have used the IDE to create these events just by selecting them from the Properties list and writing the action statements you want. The IDE saves you time by automatically entering the needed statement correctly. However, by knowing how to manually create a GUI program that contains events, you gain a greater understanding of how event handling works. This knowledge helps you troubleshoot problems and helps you create your own new events and handlers when necessary.

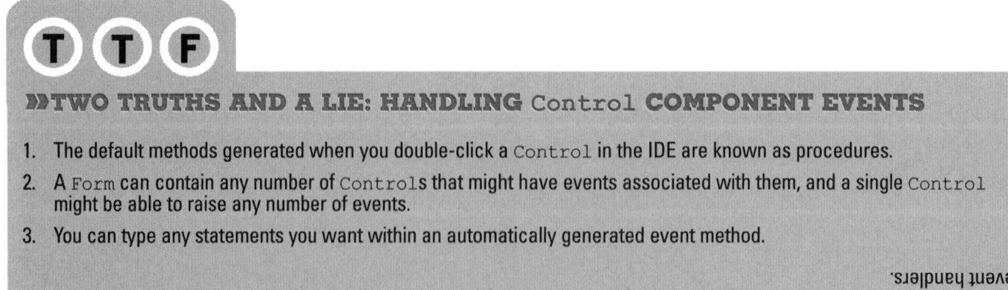

»TWO TRUTHS AND A LIE: HANDLING `Control` COMPONENT EVENTS

1. The default methods generated when you double-click a `Control` in the IDE are known as procedures.
2. A `Form` can contain any number of `Control`s that might have events associated with them, and a single `Control` might be able to raise any number of events.
3. You can type any statements you want within an automatically generated event method.

The false statement is #1. The default methods generated when you double-click a `Control` in the IDE are known as event handlers.

HANDLING MOUSE EVENTS

Mouse events include all the actions a user takes with a mouse, including clicking, pointing, and dragging. Mouse events can be handled for any `Control` through an object of the class `MouseEventArgs`. The delegate used to create mouse event handlers is `MouseEventHandler`. Every mouse event-handling method must have two parameters: an object representing the sender and an object representing the event. Depending on the event, the type of the second parameter is `EventArgs` or `MouseEventArgs`. Table 12-2 describes several common mouse events, and Table 12-3 lists some properties of the `MouseEventArgs` class.

»NOTE The `MouseEventArgs` class descends from `EventArgs`.

Mouse Event	Description	Event Argument Type
`MouseClick`	Occurs when the user clicks the mouse within the `Control`'s boundaries	`MouseEventArgs`
`MouseDoubleClick`	Occurs when the user double-clicks the mouse within the `Control`'s boundaries	`MouseEventArgs`
`MouseEnter`	Occurs when the mouse cursor enters the `Control`'s boundaries	`EventArgs`
`MouseLeave`	Occurs when the mouse cursor leaves the `Control`'s boundaries	`EventArgs`
`MouseDown`	Occurs when a mouse button is pressed while the mouse is within the `Control`'s boundaries	`MouseEventArgs`
`MouseHover`	Occurs when the mouse cursor is within the `Control`'s boundaries	`MouseEventArgs`
`MouseMove`	Occurs when the mouse is moved while within the `Control`'s boundaries	`MouseEventArgs`
`MouseUp`	Occurs when a mouse button is released while the mouse is within the `Control`'s boundaries	`MouseEventArgs`

Table 12-2 Common mouse events

»NOTE A `MouseDown` event can occur without a corresponding `MouseUp` if the user presses the mouse but switches focus to another control or application before releasing the mouse button.

MouseEventArgs Property	Description
Button	Specifies which mouse button triggered the event; the value can be Left, Right, Middle, or none
Clicks	Specifies the number of times the mouse was clicked
X	The x-coordinate where the event occurred on the control that generated the event
Y	The y-coordinate where the event occurred on the control that generated the event

Table 12-3 Properties of the MouseEventArgs class

> **NOTE** MouseClick and Click are separate events. The Click event takes an EventArgs parameter, but MouseClick takes a MouseEventArgs parameter. For example, if you define a Click event, you do not have the MouseEventArgs class properties.

Each part of Figure 12-18 contains a Form with a single Label named clickLocationLabel that changes as the user continues to click the mouse on it. The figure shows how the Label changes in response to a series of user clicks. Initially, the Label is empty (that is, the default Text property has been deleted and not replaced), but the following code was added to the Form.cs file:

```
private void Form1_MouseClick(object sender, MouseEventArgs e)
{
   clickLocationLabel.Text += "\nClicked at " + e.X +
      ", " + e.Y;
}
```

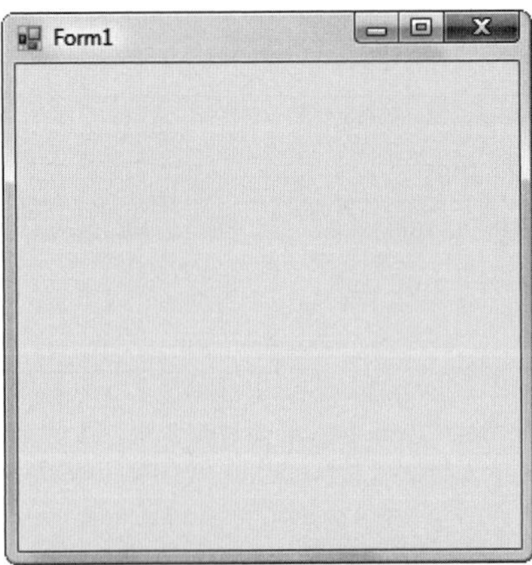

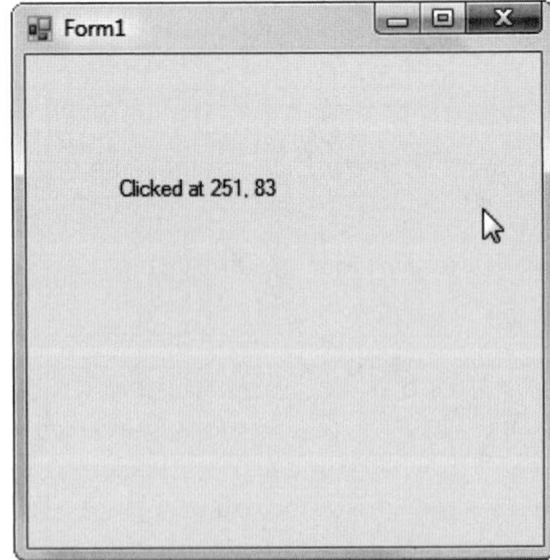

Figure 12-18 A Form that responds to clicks (*continued*)

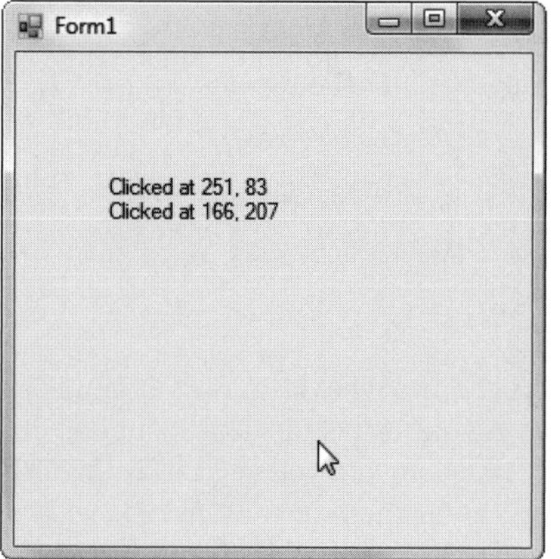

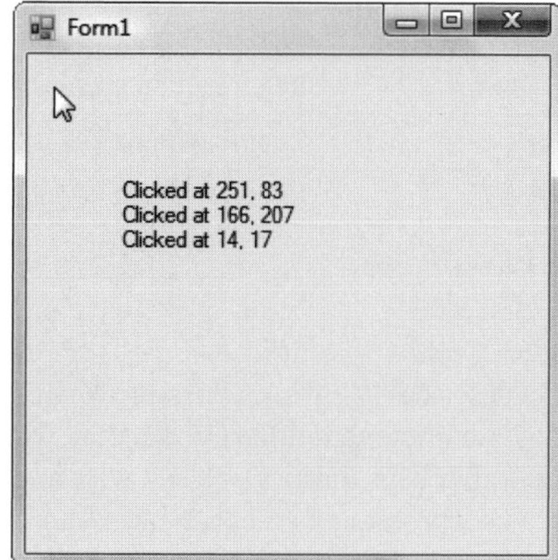

Figure 12-18 (*continued*)

Every time the mouse is clicked on the `Form`, the `Label` is appended with the words "Clicked at" on a new line and the x- and y-coordinate position where the click occurred on the `Form`.

When the programmer selects the `MouseClick()` event for `Form1` from the Event list in the IDE, the following code is generated in the Designer.cs file. This code instantiates the `MouseClick` delegate.

```
this.MouseClick += new System.Windows.Forms.MouseEventHandler
    (this.Form1_MouseClick);
```

»TWO TRUTHS AND A LIE: HANDLING MOUSE EVENTS

1. The delegate used to create mouse event handlers is `MouseEventHandler`.
2. Depending on the event, the type of the second parameter to a mouse-handling method is `EventArgs` or `MouseEventArgs`.
3. Commonly used mouse events include `ClickMouse()`, `DoubleClickMouse()`, and `MoveMouse()`.

The false statement is #3. `ClickMouse()`, `DoubleClickMouse()`, and `MoveMouse()` are not mouse events. Commonly used mouse events include `MouseClick()`, `MouseDoubleClick()`, and `MouseMove()`.

HANDLING KEYBOARD EVENTS

Keyboard events, also known as **key events**, occur when a user presses and releases keyboard keys. Table 12-4 lists some common keyboard events. Similar to the way mouse events work, every keyboard event-handling method must have two parameters: an object representing the sender and an object representing the event. Depending on the event, the delegate used to create the keyboard event handler is either `KeyEventHandler` or `KeyPressEventHandler`, and the type of the second parameter is `KeyEventArgs` or `KeyPressEventArgs`.

Keyboard Event	Description	Event Argument Type
`KeyDown`	Occurs when a key is first pressed	`KeyEventArgs`
`KeyUp`	Occurs when a key is released	`KeyEventArgs`
`KeyPress`	Occurs when a key is pressed	`KeyPressEventArgs`

Table 12-4 Keyboard events

Table 12-5 describes `KeyEventArgs` properties, and Table 12-6 describes `KeyPressEventArgs` properties. An important difference is that `KeyEventArgs` objects include data about helper keys or modifier keys that are pressed with another key. For example, if you need to distinguish between a user pressing *A* and pressing *Alt+A* in your application, then you must use a keyboard event that uses an argument of type `KeyEventArgs`.

Property	Description
`Alt`	Indicates whether the Alt key was pressed
`Control`	Indicates whether the Control (Ctrl) key was pressed
`Shift`	Indicates whether the Shift key was pressed
`KeyCode`	Returns the code for the key
`KeyData`	Returns the key code along with any modifier key
`KeyValue`	Returns a numeric representation of the key (this number is known as the Windows virtual key code)

Table 12-5 Some properties of `KeyEventArgs` class

Property	Description
`KeyChar`	Returns the ASCII character for the key pressed

Table 12-6 A property of `KeyPressEventArgs` class

For example, suppose you create a `Form` with an empty `Label`, like the first `Form` in the series in Figure 12-18. From the Properties window for the `Form`, you can double-click the `KeyUp` event to generate the shell for a method named `Form1KeyUp()`. Suppose you then insert the statements into the method in the Form1.cs file, as shown in Figure 12-19. When the user runs the program and presses and releases a keyboard key, the `Label` is filled with information about the key. Figure 12-20 shows four executions of this modified program. During the first execution, the user typed *a*. You can see on the form that the `KeyCode` is “A” (not “a”), but you also can see that the user did not press the Shift key.

```
private void Form1_KeyUp(object sender,
   KeyEventArgs e)
{
   label1.Text += "Key Code " + e.KeyCode;
   label1.Text += "\nAlt " + e.Alt;
   label1.Text += "\nShift " + e.Shift;
   label1.Text += "\nControl " + e.Control;
   label1.Text += "\nKey Data " + e.KeyData;
   label1.Text += "\nKey Value " + e.KeyValue;
}
```

Figure 12-19 `KeyUp()` method

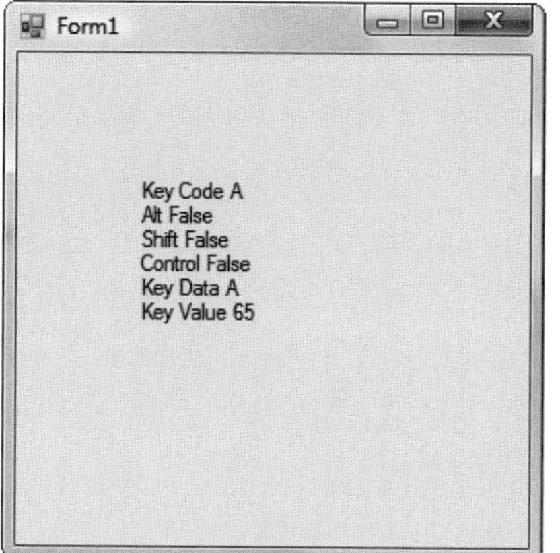

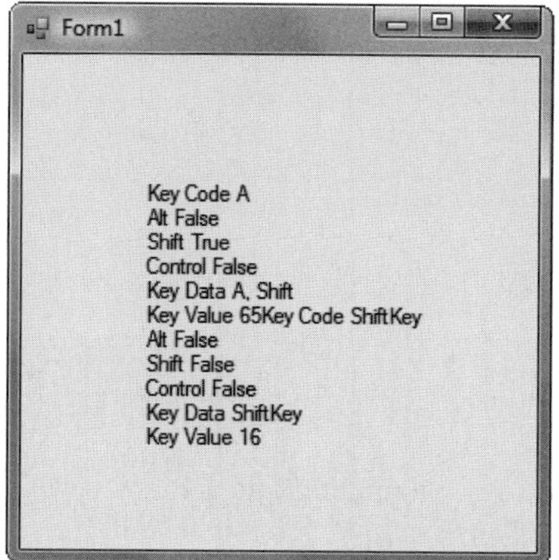

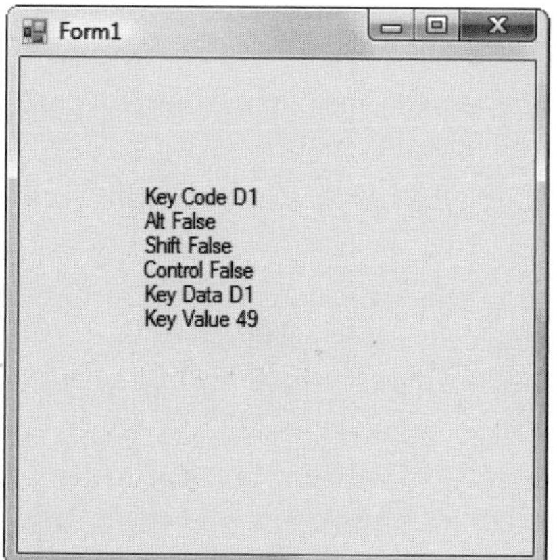

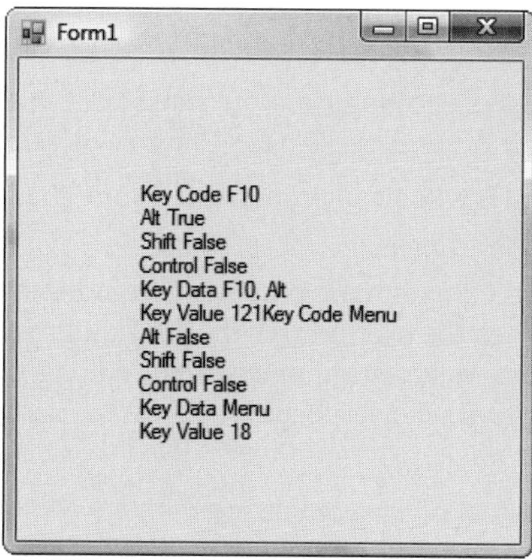

Figure 12-20 Four executions of `KeyDemo` program

In the second execution in Figure 12-20, the user held down Shift, pressed *a*, and then released the Shift key. This causes two separate `KeyUp` events. The first has `KeyCode` "A" with Shift `true`, and the second has `KeyCode ShiftKey`. Notice that the `Key` values generated after typing *a*, *A*, and Shift are all different.

In the third execution in Figure 12-20, the user pressed the number 1, whose code is D1. In the final execution, the user pressed Alt+F10 and released the F10 key first. When you view the Form1.Designer.cs file for the `KeyDemo` program, you see the following automatically created statement, which defines the composed delegate:

```
this.KeyUp += new System.Windows.Forms.KeyEventHandler
    (this.Form1_KeyUp);
```

»TWO TRUTHS AND A LIE: HANDLING KEYBOARD EVENTS

1. Keyboard events, also known as key events, occur when a user presses and releases keyboard keys.
2. Unlike mouse events, every keyboard event-handling method must be parameterless.
3. Depending on the event, the delegate used to create the keyboard event handler is either `KeyEventHandler` or `KeyPressEventHandler`.

The false statement is #2. Like mouse events, every keyboard event-handling method must have two parameters: an object representing the sender and an object representing the event.

MANAGING MULTIPLE CONTROLS

When `Forms` contain multiple `Controls`, you often want several actions to have a single consequence. For example, you might want the same action to occur whether the user clicks a button or presses the Enter key, or you might want multiple buttons to generate the same event when they are clicked.

DEFINING FOCUS

When users encounter multiple GUI `Controls` on a `Form`, usually one `Control` has **focus**. That is, if the user presses the Enter key, the `Control` will raise an event.

`TabStop` is a Boolean property of a `Control` that identifies whether the `Control` will serve as a stopping place in a sequence of Tab key presses.

`TabIndex` is a numeric property that indicates the order in which the `Control` will receive focus when the user presses the Tab key. Programmers typically use small numbers for `TabIndex` values, beginning with 0. When a `Control` has the lowest `TabIndex` of a `Form`'s `Controls`, it receives focus when the `Form` is initialized.

»NOTE Setting two or more `Controls`' `TabIndex` values to 0 does not cause an error. Only one `Control` will receive focus, however.

Figure 12-21 shows a `Form` that contains three `Buttons` and a `Label`. The `Button` labeled "1" has focus because the `TabStop` value has been set to `true` for each of the `Buttons`, and they have been assigned `TabIndex` values in ascending order. When the application starts, the first `Button` has focus; whether the user clicks that button or presses Enter, the message appears as shown on the second view of the `Form` in the figure. In the third part of the figure, the user has pressed Tab and Enter to select `button2`, so it has focus and the `Label`'s `Text` property has changed. Alternatively, the user could have clicked `button2` to achieve the same result. The user could then select either of the other `Buttons` by clicking them as usual, or by pressing Tab until the desired button has focus and then pressing Enter.

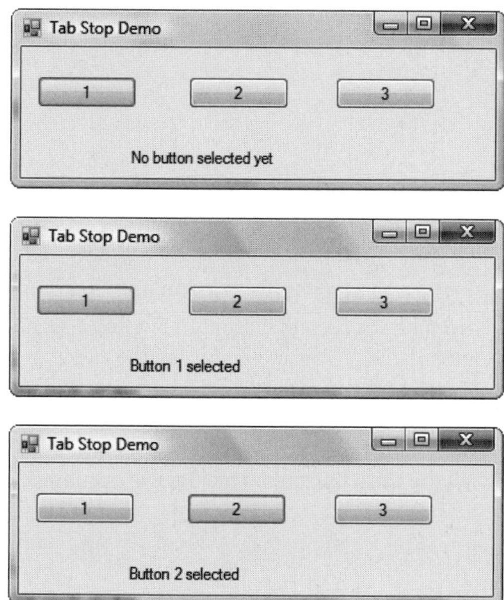

Figure 12-21 The `TabStopDemo` application

In the application that generates the results shown in Figure 12-21, each button was associated with a `Click()` event such as the following:

```
private void button1_Click(object sender, EventArgs e)
{
    buttonInfoLabel.Text = "Button 1 selected";
}
```

HANDLING MULTIPLE EVENTS WITH A SINGLE HANDLER

When a `Form` contains multiple `Controls`, you can create a separate event handler for each `Control`. However, you can also associate the same event handler with multiple `Controls`. For example, Figure 12-22 shows a `Form` that contains three `Buttons` and a `Label`. The buttons have been labeled "A", "B", and "3'. Suppose you want to display one message when the user clicks a letter button and a different message when the user clicks a number button. In the IDE, you can double-click the first `Button` and create an associated method such as the following:

```
private void button1_Click(object sender, EventArgs e)
{
   buttonInfoLabel.Text += "You clicked a letter button";
}
```

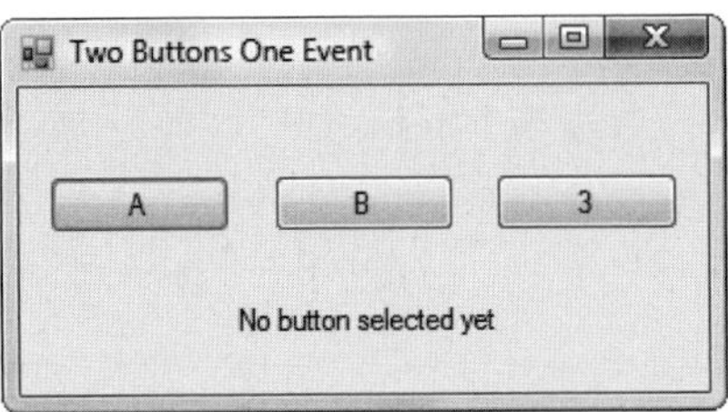

Figure 12-22 `Form` displayed by `TwoButtonsOneEvent` program

If you click the second button so its properties are displayed in the IDE's Properties list, you can click the Events icon to see a list of events associated with the second button. In Figure 12-23, no `Click` event has been chosen yet, but a list box is available. This list contains all the existing events that have the correct signature to be the event handler for the event. The list shows that the `button1_Click()` handler can also handle a `button2_Click` event, so you can select it. When you run the program, clicking either button produces the output shown in Figure 12-24. When you run the program and click the third button, no message is displayed.

> **NOTE** If you run the application in Figure 12-24 and click a letter button, the label changes. If you subsequently click the "3" button, nothing happens because no event has been associated with the third button, so the `Label`'s `Text` property remains "You clicked a letter button." Most likely, you would want to associate an event with the "3" button to modify the `Label`'s `Text` to "You clicked a number button".

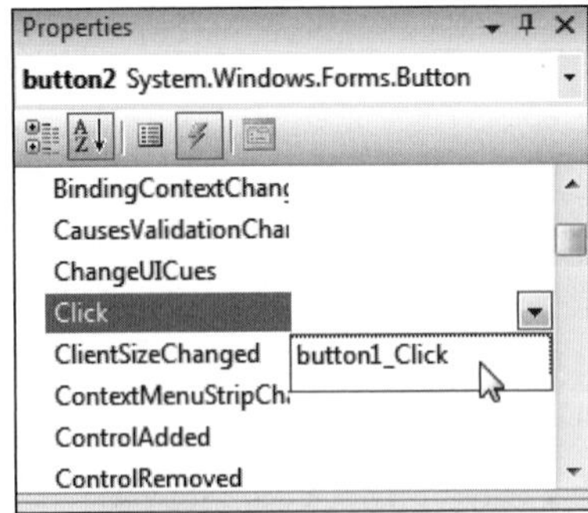

Figure 12-23 `Event` properties for `button2`

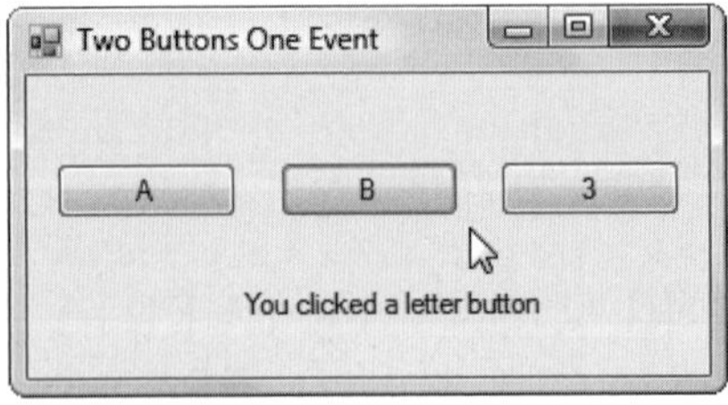

Figure 12-24 Output of `TwoButtonsOneEvent` program after either letter button is clicked

»NOTE When two or more `Controls` generate the same event, many programmers prefer to generalize the event method name. For example, if `button1` and `button2` call the same method when clicked, it makes sense to name the event method `button_Click()` instead of `button1_Click()`.

»NOTE Perhaps you have shopped online at a site that offers multiple ways to "buy now." For example, you might click a grocery cart icon, choose "Buy now" from a menu, or click a button. If you want to encourage a user's behavior, it makes sense to provide multiple ways to accommodate it.

»TWO TRUTHS AND A LIE: MANAGING MULTIPLE `Controls`

1. The `Control TabStop` property can be set to true or false; it identifies whether the `Control` will serve as a stopping place in a sequence of Tab key presses.
2. On a `Form` with multiple `Controls`, one `Control` must have a `TabIndex` value of 0.
3. When a `Form` contains multiple `Controls`, you can associate the same event with all of them.

The false statement is #2. `TabIndex` is a numeric property that indicates the order in which the `Control` will receive focus when the user presses the Tab key. Programmers typically use small numbers for `TabIndex` values, beginning with 0. However, you might choose not to use any `TabIndex` values, or if you do, you might choose not to start with 0.

CONTINUING TO LEARN ABOUT `Controls` AND EVENTS

If you examine the Visual Studio IDE, you will discover many additional `Controls` that contain hundreds of properties and events. No single book or programming course can demonstrate all of them for you. However, if you understand good programming principles and the syntax and structure of C# programs, learning about each new C# feature becomes progressively easier. When you encounter a new control in the IDE, you probably can use it without understanding all the code generated in the background, but when you do understand the background, your knowledge of C# is more complete.

Continue to explore the Help facility in the Visual Studio IDE. Particularly, read the brief tutorials there. Also, you should search the Internet for C# discussion groups. C# is a new, dynamic language, and programmers pose many questions to each other online. Reading these discussions can provide you with valuable information and suggest new approaches to resolving problems.

»TWO TRUTHS AND A LIE: CONTINUING TO LEARN ABOUT `Controls` AND EVENTS

1. Now that you have completed this chapter, you are aware of all the available C# `Controls` in the Visual Studio IDE.
2. When you encounter a new control in the IDE, you probably can use it without understanding all the code generated in the background.
3. C# is a new, dynamic language, and programmers pose many questions to each other about C# online.

The false statement is #1. If you examine the Visual Studio IDE, you will discover many additional `Controls` that contain hundreds of properties and events.

YOU DO IT

CREATING DELEGATES

To demonstrate how delegates work, you will create two delegate instances in the next steps and assign different method references to them.

To demonstrate delegates:

1. Open a new file in your text editor. Type the necessary `using` statement, then create a delegate that encapsulates a `void` method that accepts a `double` argument:

```
using System;
delegate void DiscountDelegate(ref double saleAmount);
```

2. Begin creating a `Discount` class that contains a `StandardDiscount()` method. The method accepts a reference parameter that represents an amount of a sale. If the sale amount is at least $1000.00, a discount of 5% is calculated and subtracted from the sale amount; if the sale amount is not at least $1000, nothing is subtracted.

```
class Discount
{
   public static void StandardDiscount
      (ref double saleAmount)
   {
      const double DISCOUNT_RATE = 0.05;
      const double CUTOFF = 1000.00;
      double discount;
      if(saleAmount >= CUTOFF)
         discount = saleAmount * DISCOUNT_RATE;
      else
         discount = 0;
      saleAmount -= discount;
   }
```

3. Add a `PreferredDiscount()` method. The method also accepts a reference parameter that represents the amount of a sale and calculates a discount of 10% on every sale.

```
public static void PreferredDiscount(ref double saleAmount)
{
   const double SPECIAL_DISCOUNT = 0.10;
   double discount = saleAmount * SPECIAL_DISCOUNT;
   saleAmount -= discount;
}
```

4. Start a `Main()` method that declares variables whose values will be supplied by the user—a sale amount and a code. Declare two `DiscountDelegate` objects named `firstDel` and `secondDel`. Assign a reference to the `StandardDiscount()` method to one `DiscountDelegate` object and a reference to the `PreferredDiscount()` method to the other `DiscountDelegate` object.

```
public static void Main()
{
    double saleAmount;
    char code;
    DiscountDelegate firstDel, secondDel;
    firstDel = new DiscountDelegate(StandardDiscount);
    secondDel = new DiscountDelegate(PreferredDiscount);
```

5. Continue the `Main()` method with prompts to the user to enter a sale amount and a code indicating whether the standard or preferred discount should apply. Then, depending on the code, use the appropriate delegate to calculate the correct new value for `saleAmount`. Display the value and add closing curly braces for the `Main()` method and the class.

```
        Console.Write("Enter amount of sale ");
        saleAmount = Convert.ToDouble(Console.ReadLine());
        Console.Write("Enter S for standard discount, " +
           "or P for preferred discount ");
        code = Convert.ToChar(Console.ReadLine());
        if(code == 'S')
           firstDel(ref saleAmount);
        else
           secondDel(ref saleAmount);
        Console.WriteLine("New sale amount is {0}",
           saleAmount.ToString("C2"));
    }
}
```

6. Save the file as **DiscountDelegateDemo.cs**, then compile and execute it. Figure 12-25 shows the results when the program is executed several times.

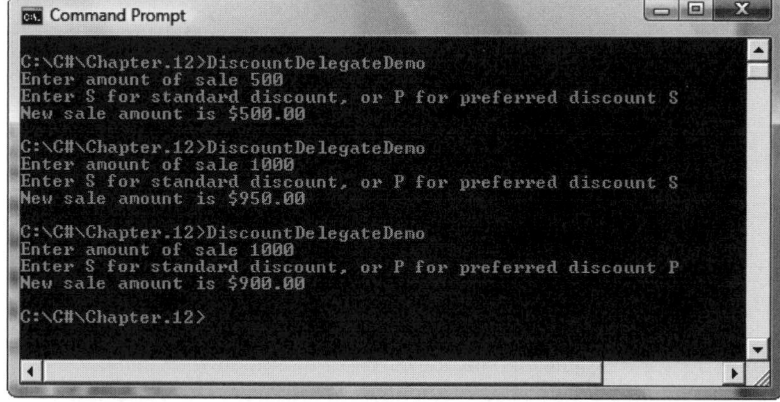

Figure 12-25 Sample executions of `DiscountDelegateDemo` program

CREATING A COMPOSED DELEGATE

When you compose delegates, you can invoke multiple method calls using a single statement. In the next steps, you will create a composed delegate to demonstrate how composition works.

To create a composed delegate:

1. Open the **DiscountDelegateDemo.cs** file in your text editor. Immediately save it as **DiscountDelegateDemo2.cs**.

2. Within the `Main()` method, add a third `DiscountDelegate` object to the statement that declares the two existing versions, as follows:

```
DiscountDelegate firstDel, secondDel, thirdDel;
```

3. After the statements that assign values to the existing `DiscountDelegate` objects, add statements that assign the `firstDel` object to `thirdDel` and then add `secondDel` to it through composition.

```
thirdDel = firstDel;
thirdDel += secondDel;
```

4. Change the prompt for the code, as follows, to reflect three options. The standard and preferred discounts remain the same, but the extreme discount (supposedly for special customers) provides both types of discounts, first subtracting 5% for any sale equal to or greater than $1000, and then providing a discount of 10% more.

```
Console.Write("Enter S for standard discount, " +
   "P for preferred discount, " +
   "\nor X for eXtreme discount ");
```

5. Change the `if` statement so that if the user does not enter *S* or *P*, then the extreme discount applies.

```
if(code == 'S')
   firstDel(ref saleAmount);
else
   if(code == 'P')
      secondDel(ref saleAmount);
   else
      thirdDel(ref saleAmount);
```

6. Save the program, then compile and execute it. For reference, Figure 12-26 shows the complete program. Figure 12-27 shows the output when the program is executed several times. When the user enters a sale amount of $1000 and an *S*, a 5% discount is applied. When the user enters a *P* for the same amount, a 10% discount is applied. When the user enters *X* with the same amount, a 5% discount is applied, followed by a 10% discount, which produces a net result of a 14.5% discount.

```
using System;
delegate void DiscountDelegate(ref double saleAmount);
class Discount
{
   public static void StandardDiscount(ref double saleAmount)
   {
      const double DISCOUNT_RATE = 0.05;
      const double CUTOFF = 1000.00;
      double discount;
      if(saleAmount >= CUTOFF)
         discount = saleAmount * DISCOUNT_RATE;
      else
         discount = 0;
      saleAmount -= discount;
   }
   public static void PreferredDiscount(ref double saleAmount)
   {
      const double SPECIAL_DISCOUNT = 0.10;
      double discount = saleAmount * SPECIAL_DISCOUNT;
      saleAmount -= discount;
   }
   public static void Main()
   {
      double saleAmount;
      char code;
      DiscountDelegate firstDel, secondDel, thirdDel;
      firstDel = new DiscountDelegate(StandardDiscount);
      secondDel = new DiscountDelegate(PreferredDiscount);
      thirdDel = firstDel;
      thirdDel += secondDel;
      Console.Write("Enter amount of sale ");
      saleAmount = Convert.ToDouble(Console.ReadLine());
      Console.Write("Enter S for standard discount, " +
         "P for preferred discount, " +
         "\nor X for eXtreme discount ");
      code = Convert.ToChar(Console.ReadLine());
      if(code == 'S')
         firstDel(ref saleAmount);
      else
         if(code == 'P')
            secondDel(ref saleAmount);
         else
            thirdDel(ref saleAmount);
      Console.WriteLine("New sale amount is {0}",
         saleAmount.ToString("C2"));
   }
}
```

Figure 12-26 DiscountDelegateDemo2 **program**

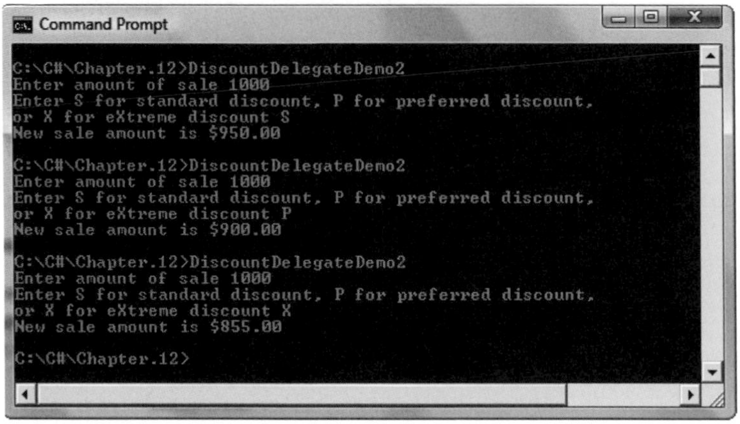

```
C:\C#\Chapter.12>DiscountDelegateDemo2
Enter amount of sale 1000
Enter S for standard discount, P for preferred discount,
or X for eXtreme discount S
New sale amount is $950.00

C:\C#\Chapter.12>DiscountDelegateDemo2
Enter amount of sale 1000
Enter S for standard discount, P for preferred discount,
or X for eXtreme discount P
New sale amount is $900.00

C:\C#\Chapter.12>DiscountDelegateDemo2
Enter amount of sale 1000
Enter S for standard discount, P for preferred discount,
or X for eXtreme discount X
New sale amount is $855.00

C:\C#\Chapter.12>
```

Figure 12-27 Three executions of `DiscountDelegateDemo2` program

NOTE For `static` methods, like `StandardDiscount` and `PreferredDiscount`, a `delegate` object encapsulates the method to be called. When creating a class that contains instance methods, you create `delegate` objects that encapsulate both an instance of the class and a method of the instance. You will create this type of `delegate` in the next section.

CREATING A DELEGATE THAT ENCAPSULATES INSTANCE METHODS

In the next set of steps, you will create a simple `BankAccount` class that is similar to many classes you already have created. The `BankAccount` class will contain just two data fields—an account number and a balance. It also will contain methods to make withdrawals and deposits. An event will be generated after any withdrawal or deposit.

To create the `BankAccount` class:

1. Open a new file in your text editor. Type the `using System;` statement, then begin a class named `BankAccount`. The class contains an account number, a balance, and an event that executes when an account's balance is adjusted.

```
using System;
public class BankAccount
{
   private int acctNum;
   private double balance;
   public event EventHandler BalanceAdjusted;
```

2. Add a constructor that accepts an account number parameter and initializes the balance to 0.

```
public BankAccount(int acct)
{
   acctNum = acct;
   balance = 0;
}
```

3. Add read-only properties for both the account number and the account balance.

```
public int AcctNum
{
    get
    {
        return acctNum;
    }
}
public double Balance
{
    get
    {
        return balance;
    }
}
```

4. Add two methods. One makes account deposits by adding the parameter to the account balance, and the other makes withdrawals by subtracting the parameter value from the bank balance. Each uses the `OnBalanceAdjusted` event handler that reacts to all deposit and withdrawal events by displaying the new balance.

```
public void MakeDeposit(double amt)
{
    balance += amt;
    OnBalanceAdjusted(EventArgs.Empty);
}
public void MakeWithdrawal(double amt)
{
    balance -= amt;
    OnBalanceAdjusted(EventArgs.Empty);
}
```

5. Add the `OnBalanceAdjusted()` method that accepts an `EventArgs` parameter and calls `BalanceAdjusted`, passing it a reference to the current `BankAccount` object that was adjusted and to the `EventArgs` object. Include a closing curly brace for the class.

```
  public void OnBalanceAdjusted(EventArgs e)
  {
    BalanceAdjusted(this, e);
  }
}
```

NOTE Earlier in the chapter, you learned that calling a method such as `OnBalanceAdjusted()` is also known as invoking the event.

6. Save the file as **DemoBankEvent.cs**.

CREATING AN EVENT LISTENER

When you write an application that declares a BankAccount, you might want the client program to listen for BankAccount events. To do so, you create an EventListener class.

To create an EventListener class:

1. After the closing curly brace of the BankAccount class, type the following EventListener class that contains a BankAccount object. When the EventListener constructor executes, the BankAccount field is initialized with the constructor parameter. Using the += operator, add the BankAccountBalanceAdjusted() method to the event delegate. Next, write the BankAccountBalanceAdjusted() method to display a message and information about the BankAccount.

```
class EventListener
{
   private BankAccount acct;
   public EventListener(BankAccount account)
   {
      acct = account;
      acct.BalanceAdjusted += new EventHandler
         (BankAccountBalanceAdjusted);
   }
   private void BankAccountBalanceAdjusted(object sender,
      EventArgs e)
   {
      Console.WriteLine
         ("The account balance has been adjusted.");
      Console.WriteLine("   Account# {0}  balance {1}",
         acct.AcctNum, acct.Balance.ToString("C2"));
   }
}
```

2. Create a class to test the BankAccount and EventListener classes. Below the closing curly brace for the EventListener class, start a DemoBankAccountEvent class that contains a Main() method. Declare an integer to hold the number of transactions that will occur in the demonstration program. Also declare two variables: one can hold a code that indicates whether a transaction is a deposit or withdrawal, and one is the amount of the transaction.

```
class DemoBankAccountEvent
{
   public static void Main()
   {
      const int TRANSACTIONS = 5;
      char code;
      double amt;
```

3. Declare a BankAccount object that is assigned an arbitrary account number and declare an EventListener object so this program is registered to listen for events from the BankAccount. Each change in the BankAccount balance will not only

change the balance data field, it will execute the `BankAccountBalanceAdjusted()` method that displays two lines of explanation.

```
BankAccount acct = new BankAccount(334455);
EventListener listener = new EventListener (acct);
```

4. Add a loop that executes five times (the value of `TRANSACTIONS`). On each iteration, prompt the user to indicate whether the current transaction is a deposit or withdrawal and to enter the transaction amount. Call the `MakeDeposit()` or `MakeWithdrawal()` method accordingly. At the end of the `for` loop, add a closing curly brace for the `Main()` method and another one for the class.

```
        for(int x = 0; x < TRANSACTIONS; ++x)
        {
           Console.Write
               ("Enter D for deposit or W for withdrawal ");
           code = Convert.ToChar(Console.ReadLine());
           Console.Write("Enter dollar amount ");
           amt = Convert.ToDouble(Console.ReadLine());
           if(code == 'D')
              acct.MakeDeposit(amt);
           else
               acct.MakeWithdrawal(amt);
        }
    }
}
```

5. Save the file, then compile and execute it. For reference, Figure 12-28 shows a typical execution in which five transactions modify the account. The output shows that an event occurs five times—twice for deposits and three times for withdrawals.

USING `TabStop` AND `TabIndex`

In the next steps, you will create a `Form` in the Visual Studio IDE and add four `Buttons` so you can demonstrate how to manipulate the `TabStop` and `TabIndex` properties.

To demonstrate `TabStop` and `TabIndex`:

1. Open the Visual Studio IDE and start a new project. Define it to be a **Windows Forms Application** named **ManyButtons**.
2. Change the `Text` property of `Form1` to **Many Buttons**.
3. Drag four `Buttons` onto the `Form` and place them so that they are similar to the layout shown in Figure 12-29. Change the `Name` properties of the buttons to `redButton`, `whiteButton`, `blueButton`, and `favoriteButton`. Change the `Text` on the `Buttons` to **Red**, **White**, **Blue**, and **My Favorite Color**, respectively. Adjust the size of the last button so its longer `Text` is fully displayed.
4. Examine the Properties list for the Red button. The `TabStop` property has been set to `True`, and the `TabIndex` is 0. Examine the properties for the White, Blue, and My Favorite Color buttons. The IDE has set their `TabIndex` values to 1, 2, and 3, respectively.

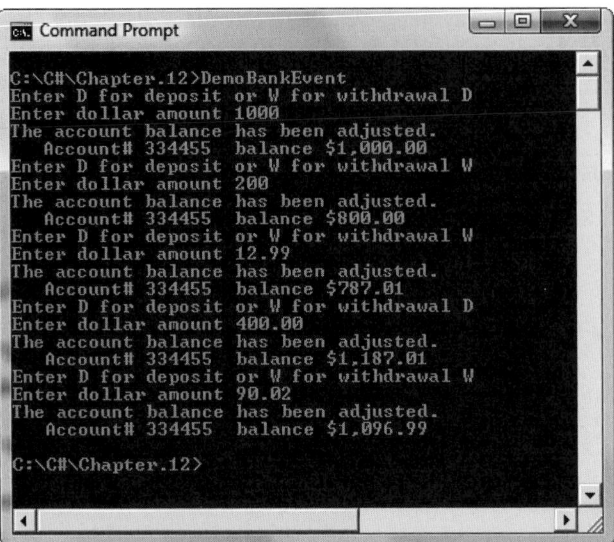

Figure 12-28 Typical execution of `DemoBankEvent` program

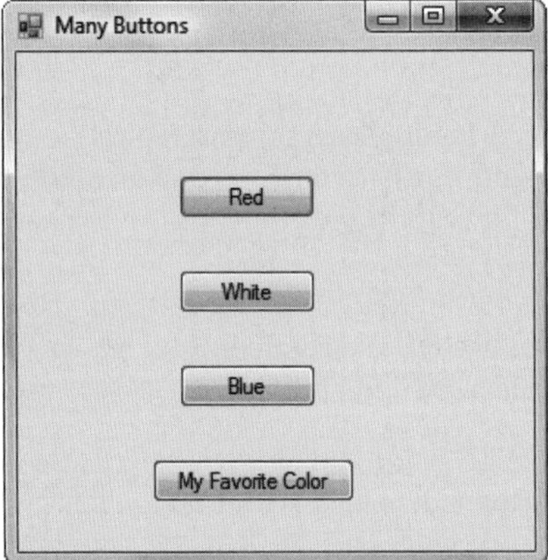

Figure 12-29 Four `Button`s on the Many Buttons `Form`

5. Click the **Save All** button and then run the program. When the `Form` appears, the Red button has focus. Press the **Tab** key, and notice that focus changes to the White button. When you press **Tab** again, focus changes to the Blue button. Press **Tab** several more times and observe that the focus rotates among the four `Button`s.
6. Dismiss the `Form`.

7. Change the TabIndex property of the Blue button to **0**, and change the TabIndex of the Red button to **2**. (The TabIndex of the White button remains 1 and the TabIndex of the My Favorite Color button remains 3.) Save the program again and then run it. This time, the Blue button begins with focus. When you press Tab, the order in which the Buttons receive focus is Blue, then White, then Red, then My Favorite Color. (Clicking the Buttons or pressing Enter raises no event because you have not assigned events to the Buttons.)
8. Dismiss the Form. Select the White button and change its TabStop property to **False**. Save the program and then execute it. This time, the Blue button has focus when the Form appears. When you press **Tab**, focus alternates among the Blue, Red, and My Favorite Color buttons, bypassing the White button, which is no longer part of the tabbing sequence.
9. Change the White button's TabStop value back to True. Change the TabIndex property for the Red button back to **0** and the TabIndex property for the Blue button back to **2**. Click the **Save All** button.

ASSOCIATING ONE METHOD WITH MULTIPLE EVENTS

In the next steps, you will add three methods to the Many Buttons Form and cause one of the methods to execute each time the user clicks one of the four Buttons.

To associate methods with the application's events:

1. If it is not still open, open the **Many Buttons** project in the Visual Studio IDE. Drag a Label onto the Form and place it at the approximate location of the Label in Figure 12-30. Change the Label's Text property to **Click a button** and change its Font to **12**.

Figure 12-30 Many Buttons Form with Label

2. Double-click the **Red** button on the `Form` to view the code for the shell of a `button1_Click()` method. Between the method's curly braces, insert a statement that will change the `Form`'s background color to red as follows:

```
this.BackColor = Color.Red;
```

»NOTE At first glance, you might think `this` refers to the `Button` that is clicked. However, if you examine the `redButton_Click()` code in the Form1.cs file in the IDE, you will discover that the method is part of the `Form1` class. Therefore, `this.BackColor` refers to the `Form`'s `BackColor` property.

3. Select the **Form1.cs [Design]** tab and then double-click the **White** button. Add the following code to the `whiteButton_Click()` method that is generated:

```
this.BackColor = Color.White;
```

4. On the `Form`, double-click the **Blue** button. In its `Click()` method, add the following statement:

```
this.BackColor = Color.Blue;
```

5. On the form, click the **My Favorite Color** button. In its Properties list, click the **Events** button (the lightning bolt). Select the **`Click`** event. From the list box next to the `Click` event, select one of the three events to correspond to your favorite color of the three.
6. Click the **Save All** button and then execute the program. As you click `Buttons`, the `Form`'s background color changes appropriately.
7. Dismiss the form and exit Visual Studio.

CHAPTER SUMMARY

- You use an event to notify a client program when something happens to a class object the program is using. GUI programs are event driven—an event such as a button click "drives" the program to perform a task. Programmers also say a button click raises an event, fires an event, or triggers an event. A method that performs a task in response to an event is an event handler. The `Click` event is the event generated when a button is clicked.
- A delegate is an object that contains a reference to a method. C# delegates provide a way for a program to take alternative courses when running; a delegate provides a way to pass a reference to a method as an argument to another method.
- You can assign one delegate to another using the = operator. You also can use the + and += operators to combine delegates into a composed delegate that calls the delegates from which it is built.
- To declare your own event, you use a delegate. An event provides a way for a class's clients to dictate methods that should execute when an event occurs. The clients identify

methods to execute by providing delegates. When an event occurs, any delegate that a client has given or passed to the event is invoked.

» The .NET Framework provides guidelines you should follow if you are developing a class that others will use. These guidelines indicate that the delegate type for an event should take exactly two parameters: a parameter indicating the source of the event, and an `EventArgs` parameter that encapsulates any additional information about the event. For events that do not use additional information, the .NET Framework has already defined an appropriate type named `EventHandler`.

» When you use existing `Control` components like `Buttons` and `ListBoxes`, they contain fields and `public` properties like `Text`, as well as events with names like `Click`. A `Form` can contain any number of `Controls` that might have events associated with them. Additionally, a single control might be able to raise any number of events.

» Mouse events include all the actions a user takes with a mouse, including clicking, pointing, and dragging. Mouse events can be handled for any `Control` through an object of the class `MouseEventArgs`. The delegate used to create mouse event handlers is `MouseEventHandler`. Every mouse event-handling method must have two parameters: an object representing the sender and an object representing the event. Depending on the event, the type of the second parameter is `EventArgs` or `MouseEventArgs`.

» Keyboard events, also known as key events, occur when a user presses and releases keyboard keys. Every keyboard event-handling method must have two parameters: an object representing the sender and an object representing the event. Depending on the event, the type of the second parameter is `KeyEventArgs` or `KeyPressEventArgs`.

» When users encounter multiple GUI `Controls` on a `Form`, usually one `Control` has focus. That is, if the user presses Enter, the `Control` will raise an event. When a `Form` contains multiple `Controls`, you can create a separate event for each `Control`. However, you can also associate the same event with multiple `Controls`.

» When you encounter a new control in the IDE, you probably can use it without understanding all the code generated in the background. However, when you do understand the background, your knowledge of C# is more complete.

KEY TERMS

Event-driven programs contain code that causes an event such as a button click to drive the program to perform a task.

A button click **raises an event**, **fires an event**, or **triggers an event**.

An **event handler** is a method that performs a task in response to an event.

An **event receiver** is another name for an event handler.

An **event sender** is the control that generates an event.

`EventArgs` is a C# class designed for holding event information.

The **`Click` event** is the event generated when a `Control` is clicked.

Event wiring is the act of connecting an event to its resulting actions.

A **delegate** is an object that contains a reference to a method.

A **composed delegate** calls the delegates from which it is built.

Invoking the event occurs when you call an event method.

`EventHandler` is an appropriate type for events that do not use any information besides the source of the event and the `EventArgs` parameter.

Key events are keyboard events that occur when a user presses and releases keyboard keys.

When a `Control` has **focus** and the user presses Enter, the `Control` will raise an event.

REVIEW QUESTIONS

1. A delegate is an object that contains a reference to a(n) ________ .

   a. object
   b. class
   c. method
   d. `Control`

2. C# delegates provide a way for a program to ________ .

   a. take alternative courses when running
   b. include multiple methods
   c. include methods from other classes
   d. include multiple `Control`s that use the same method

3. Which of the following correctly declares a `delegate` type?

   a. `void aDelegate(int num);`
   b. `delegate void aDelegate(num);`
   c. `delegate void aDelegate(int num);`
   d. `delegate aDelegate(int num);`

4. If you have declared a `delegate` instance, you can assign it a reference to a method as long as the method has the same ________ as the `delegate`.

   a. return type
   b. identifier
   c. parameter list
   d. two of the above

5. You can combine two delegates to create a(n) ________ delegate.

   a. assembled
   b. classified
   c. artificial
   d. composed

6. To combine two delegates using the + operator, the `delegate` objects must ________ .
   a. have the same parameter list
   b. have the same return type
   c. both of these
   d. neither of these

7. In C#, a(n) ________ occurs when something interesting happens to an object.
   a. delegate
   b. event
   c. notification
   d. instantiation

8. In C#, an event provides a way for a class to allow clients to provide ________ .
   a. GUI objects that other classes can use
   b. delegates to methods
   c. arguments to other classes
   d. widgets to `Forms`

9. An event handler `delegate` requires ________ arguments.
   a. zero
   b. one
   c. two
   d. any number greater than zero

10. Using an event handler, the sender is the ________ .
    a. delegate associated with the event
    b. method called by the event
    c. object where the event was initiated
    d. class containing the method that the event invokes

11. The `EventArgs` class contains a static field named ________ .
    a. `Empty`
    b. `Text`
    c. `Location`
    d. `Source`

12. When creating events, you can use a predefined delegate type named ________ that is automatically provided by the .NET Framework.
    a. `EventArgs`
    b. `EventHandler`
    c. `EventType`
    d. `Event`

13. Which of the following is not a predefined `Control` event?
    a. `MouseEnter`
    b. `Click`
    c. `Destroy`
    d. `TextChanged`

14. A single `Control` can raise ________ event(s).

    a. one
    b. two
    c. five
    d. any number of

15. When you create `Forms` with `Controls` that raise events, an advantage to creating the code by hand over using the Visual Studio IDE is ________ .

    a. you are less likely to make typing errors
    b. you save a lot of repetitious typing
    c. you are less likely to forget to set a property
    d. you gain a clearer understanding of the C# language

16. When a `Form` contains three `Controls` and one has focus, you can raise an event by ________ .

    a. clicking any `Control`
    b. pressing Enter
    c. either of these
    d. none of these

17. The `TabStop` property of a `Control` is a(n) ________ .

    a. integer value indicating the tab order
    b. Boolean value indicating whether the `Control` has a position in the tab sequence
    c. string value indicating the name of the method executed when the `Control` raises an event
    d. `delegate` name indicating the event raised when the user tabs to the `Control`

18. The `TabIndex` property of a `Control` is a(n) ________ .

    a. integer value indicating the tab order
    b. Boolean value indicating whether the `Control` has a position in the tab sequence
    c. string value indicating the name of the method executed when the `Control` raises an event
    d. `delegate` name indicating the event raised when the user tabs to the `Control`

19. The `Control` that causes an event is the ________ argument to an event method.

    a. first
    b. second
    c. third
    d. fourth

20. Which of the following is true?

    a. You can generate a single event from multiple `Controls`.
    b. You can generate multiple events from a single `Control`.
    c. Both of the above are true.
    d. None of the above are true.

EXERCISES

1. Create a `Form` that contains three `Label`s that hold famous quotes of your choice. When the program starts, the background color of the `Form` and each `Label` should be black. When the user passes a mouse over a `Label`, change its `BackColor` to white, revealing the text of the quote. Save the project as **DisplayQuotes**.

2. Create a `Form` with a list of three `LinkLabel`s that link to any three Web sites you choose. When a user clicks a `LinkLabel`, link to that site. When a user's mouse hovers over a `LinkLabel`, display a brief message that explains the site's purpose. After a user clicks a link, move the most recently selected link to the top of the list and move the other two links down, making sure to retain the correct explanation with each link. Save the project as **RecentlyVisitedSites**.

3. Create a `Form` with a `ListBox` that lists at least four sports teams of your choice. When the user places the mouse over the `ListBox`, display a `Label` that contains single-game ticket prices for each team. The `Label` disappears when the user's mouse leaves the `ListBox` area. When the user clicks a team name in the `ListBox`, display another `Label` that contains the correct ticket price. Also change the `BackColor` of the `Form` to the selected team's color. Save the project as **TeamSelector**.

4. Locate an animated .gif file on the Web or use the one stored in the Chapter.12 folder on your Student Disk. Create a `Form` that contains a `PictureBox`. Display three different messages on a `Label`—one when the user's mouse is over the `PictureBox`, one when the mouse is not over the `PictureBox`, and one when the user clicks the `PictureBox`. Save the project as **Animated**.

5. The Sunshine Subdivision allows users to select siding for their new homes, but they allow only specific trim colors with each siding color. Create a `Form` for Sunshine Subdivision that allows a user to choose one of three siding colors from a `ListBox`—white, gray, or blue. When the user selects a siding color, the program should display a second `ListBox` that contains only the following choices:

   » White siding—black, red, green, or dark blue trim

   » Gray siding—black or white trim

   » Blue siding—white or dark blue trim

   After the user selects a trim color, the program should display a congratulatory message on a `Label` indicating that the choice is a good one. The trim `ListBox` also becomes invisible. If the user makes a new selection from the siding `ListBox`, the congratulatory message is invisible until the user selects a complementary trim.

   Hint: You can remove the entire contents of a `ListBox` using the `Items.Clear()` method, as in `this.listBox2.Items.Clear();`.

   Save the project as **SunshineSubdivision**.

6. Create a `Form` that contains a guessing game with five `RadioButtons` numbered 1 through 5. Randomly choose one of the `RadioButtons` as the winning button. When the user clicks a `RadioButton`, display a message indicating whether the user is right.

   Add a `Label` to the `Form` that provides a hint. When the user's mouse hovers over the label, notify the user of one `RadioButton` that is incorrect. After the user makes a selection, disable all the `RadioButtons`. Save the project as **GuessANumber**.

»NOTE You can create a random number that is at least `min` but less than `max` using the following statements:

```
Random RandomClass = new Random();
int randomNumber;
randomNumber = RandomClass.Next(min, max);
```

7. Create a `Form` that contains two randomly generated arrays, each containing 100 numbers. Include two `Buttons` labeled "1" and "2". Starting with position 0 in each array, ask the user to guess which of the two arrays contains the higher number and to click one of the two buttons to indicate the guess. After each button click, the program displays the values of the two compared numbers, as well as running counts of the number of correct and incorrect guesses. After the user makes a guess, disable the `Buttons` while the user views the results. After clicking a Next `Button`, the user can make another guess using the next two array values. If the user makes more than 100 guesses, the program should reset the array subscript to 0 so the comparisons start over, but continue to keep a running score. Save the project as **PickLarger**.

DEBUGGING EXERCISES

»NOTE Immediately save the two project folders with their new names before starting to correct their errors.

Each of the following files or projects in the Chapter.12 folder on your Student Disk has syntax and/or logical errors. In each case, determine the problem and fix the program. After you correct the errors, save each file or project using the same filename preceded with *Fixed*. For example, the file DebugTwelve1.cs will become FixedDebugTwelve1.cs and the project folder for DebugTwelve3 will become FixedDebugTwelve3.

a. DebugTwelve1.cs

b. DebugTwelve2.cs

c. DebugTwelve3.cs

d. DebugTwelve4.cs

UP FOR DISCUSSION

1. Programming is a job that can be done from a remote location. For example, as a professional programmer, you might be able to work from home. Does this appeal to you? What are the advantages and disadvantages? If you have other programmers working for you, would you allow them to work from home? Would you require any "face time"—that is, time in the office with you or other workers?
2. Programming is a job that can be done from a remote location. For example, your organization might contact programmers who live in another country where wages are considerably lower than in the United States. Do you have any objections to employers using these workers? If so, what are they? If not, what objections might others have?
3. Suppose your organization hires programmers to work in another country. Suppose you also discover that working conditions there are not the same as in your country. For example, the buildings in which the workers do their jobs might not be subject to the same standards for ventilation and fire codes as the building where you work. Is your company under any obligation to change the working conditions?
4. Would you ever participate in a computer dating site? Would you go on a date with someone you met over the Web? What precautions would you take before such a date?

CHAPTER THIRTEEN

13

FILES AND STREAMS

In this chapter you will:

- Understand computer files and how they are stored
- Use the `File` and `Directory` classes
- Understand data organization within a file
- Understand streams
- Write to a sequential access text file
- Read from a sequential access text file
- Search a sequential file
- Understand serialization and deserialization

In the early chapters of this book, you learned that storing values in variables provides programs with flexibility—a program that uses variables to replace constants can manipulate different values each time the program executes. However, when data values in a program are stored in variables, they are lost when the program ends. To retain data values for future use, you must store them in files. In this chapter, you will learn to create and manage files in C#.

UNDERSTANDING COMPUTER FILES AND HOW THEY ARE STORED

When data items are stored in a computer system, they can be stored for varying periods of time—temporarily or permanently.

Temporary storage is usually called computer memory or **random access memory** (RAM). When you write a C# program that stores a value in a variable, you are using temporary storage; the value you store is lost when the program ends or the computer loses power. This type of storage is **volatile**.

Permanent storage, on the other hand, is not lost when a computer loses power; it is **nonvolatile**. When you write a program and save it to a disk, you are using permanent storage.

NOTE When discussing computer storage, *temporary* and *permanent* refer to volatility, not length of time. For example, a *temporary* variable might exist for several hours in a large program or one that the user forgets to end, but a *permanent* piece of data might be saved and then deleted within a few seconds.

A **computer file** is a collection of information stored on a nonvolatile device in a computer system. Files exist on **permanent storage devices**, such as hard disks, floppy disks, Zip disks, USB drives, reels or cassettes of magnetic tape, and optical disks, which include CDs and DVDs. Some files are **data files** that contain facts and figures, such as a payroll file that contains employee numbers, names, and salaries; some files are **program files** or **application files** that store software instructions. (You have created many such files throughout this book.) Other files can store graphics, text, or operating system instructions (such as the files with an .exe extension that your compiler has created for every .cs project you compile). Although their contents vary, files have many common characteristics—each file occupies space on a section of a storage device, and each has a name and a specific time of creation.

When you use data, you never directly use the copy that is stored in a file. Instead, you use a copy that is in memory. Especially when data items are stored on a hard disk, their location might not be clear to you—data just seems to be "in the computer." However, when you work with stored data, you must transfer a copy from the storage device into memory. When you store data in a computer file on a persistent storage device, you **write to the file**. This means you copy data from RAM to the file. When you copy data from a file on a storage device into RAM, you **read from the file**.

NOTE Because you can erase data from files, some programmers prefer the term ***persistent** storage* to permanent storage. In other words, you can remove data from a file stored on a device such as a disk drive, so it is not technically permanent. However, the data remains in the file even when the computer loses power, so, unlike RAM, the data persists, or perseveres.

Computer files are the electronic equivalent of paper documents stored in file cabinets. In a physical file cabinet, the easiest way to store a document is to toss it into a drawer without a folder. When storing computer files, this is the equivalent of placing a file in the main or **root directory** of your storage device. However, for better organization, most office clerks place documents in folders; most computer users also organize their files into **folders** or **directories**. Users also can place folders within folders to form a hierarchy. The combination of the disk drive plus the complete hierarchy of directories in which a file resides is its **path**. For example, in the Windows operating system, the following line would be the complete path for a file named Data.txt on the C drive in a folder named Chapter.13 within the C# folder:

```
C:\C#\Chapter.13\Data.txt
```

NOTE The terms *directory* and *folder* are used synonymously to mean an entity that is used to organize files. *Directory* is the more general term; the term *folder* came into use in graphical systems. For example, Microsoft began calling directories *folders* with the introduction of Windows 95.

C# provides built-in classes named `File` and `Directory` that contain methods to help you manipulate files and their directories, respectively.

TWO TRUTHS AND A LIE: UNDERSTANDING COMPUTER FILES AND HOW THEY ARE STORED

1. Temporary storage is nonvolatile and permanent storage is volatile.
2. When you write to a file, you copy data from RAM to a permanent storage device.
3. Most computer users organize their files into directories; the complete hierarchy of directories in which a file resides is its path.

The false statement is #1. Temporary storage is volatile and permanent storage is nonvolatile.

USING THE `File` AND `Directory` CLASSES

The **`File` class** contains methods that allow you to access information about files. Some of the methods are listed in Table 13-1.

Method	Description
`Create()`	Creates a file
`CreateText()`	Creates a text file
`Delete()`	Deletes a file
`Exists()`	Returns `true` if the specified file exists
`GetCreationTime()`	Returns a `DateTime` object specifying when a file was created
`GetLastAccessTime()`	Returns a `DateTime` object specifying when a file was last accessed
`GetLastWriteTime()`	Returns a `DateTime` object specifying when a file was last modified
`Move()`	Moves a file to the specified location

Table 13-1 Selected `File` class methods

NOTE `DateTime` is a structure that contains data about a date and time. In Chapter 11, you used the date data from `DateTime` structures with `MonthCalendar` and `DateTimePicker` GUI objects. `DateTime` values can be expressed using Coordinated Universal Time (UTC), which is the internationally recognized name for Greenwich Mean Time (GMT). By default, `DateTime` values are expressed using the local time set on your computer. The property `DateTime.Now` returns the current local time. The property `DateTime.UtcNow` returns the current UTC time.

The `File` class is contained in the `System.IO` namespace. So, to use the `File` class, you can use its fully qualified name, `System.IO.File`, or you can add the statement `using System.IO;` at the top of your file. Figure 13-1 shows a program that includes the `using` statement and demonstrates several of the `File` class methods. The program prompts the user for a filename and then tests the file's existence. If the file exists, the last creation time, write time, and access time are displayed. If the file does not exist, a message is displayed. Figure 13-2 shows two executions of the program. In the first execution, the user enters a filename that is not found. In the second execution, the file is found and the three significant dates are displayed.

NOTE The `System.IO.FileInfo` class also allows you to access information about a file. See the Microsoft documentation at *http://msdn2.microsoft.com* for more information.

```
using System;
using System.IO;
public class FileStatistics
{
   public static void Main()
   {
      string fileName;
      Console.Write("Enter a filename ");
      fileName = Console.ReadLine();
      if(File.Exists(fileName))
      {
         Console.WriteLine("File exists");
         Console.WriteLine("File was created " +
            File.GetCreationTime(fileName));
         Console.WriteLine("File was last accessed " +
            File.GetLastAccessTime(fileName));
         Console.WriteLine("File was last written to " +
            File.GetLastWriteTime(fileName));
      }
      else
      {
         Console.WriteLine("File does not exist");
      }
   }
}
```

Figure 13-1 The `FileStatistics` program

>> **NOTE**
In the `FileStatistics` program in Figure 13-1, the file must be in the same directory as the program that is running.

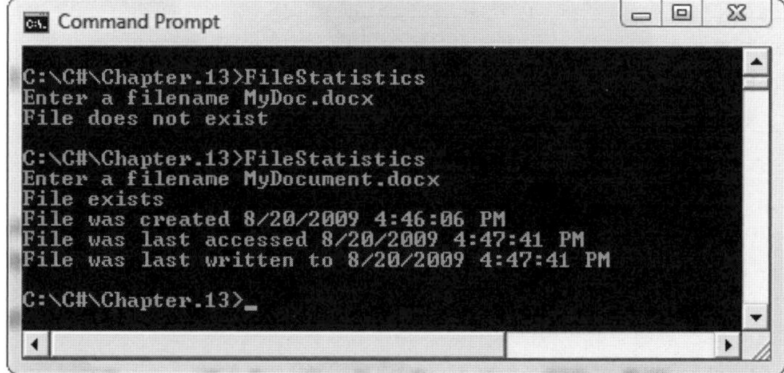

Figure 13-2 Two typical executions of the `FileStatistics` program

The **`Directory` class** provides you with information about directories or folders. Table 13-2 lists some available methods in the `Directory` class.

Figure 13-3 contains a program that prompts a user for a directory and then displays a list of the files stored within it. Figure 13-4 shows two typical executions of the program.

Method	Description
`CreateDirectory()`	Creates a directory
`Delete()`	Deletes a directory
`Exists()`	Returns `true` if the specified directory exists
`GetCreationTime()`	Returns a `DateTime` object specifying when a directory was created
`GetDirectories()`	Returns a `string` array that contains the names of the subdirectories in the specified directory
`GetFiles()`	Returns a `string` array that contains the names of the files in the specified directory
`GetLastAccessTime()`	Returns a `DateTime` object specifying when a directory was last accessed
`GetLastWriteTime()`	Returns a `DateTime` object specifying when a directory was last modified
`Move()`	Moves a directory to the specified location

Table 13-2 Selected `Directory` class methods

```
using System;
using System.IO;
public class DirectoryInformation
{
   public static void Main()
   {
      string directoryName;
      string[] listOfFiles;
      Console.Write("Enter a folder ");
      directoryName = Console.ReadLine();
      if(Directory.Exists(directoryName))
      {
         Console.WriteLine("Directory exists");
         listOfFiles = Directory.GetFiles(directoryName);
         for(int x = 0; x < listOfFiles.Length; ++x)
           Console.WriteLine(listOfFiles[x]);
      }
      else
      {
         Console.WriteLine("Directory does not exist");
      }
   }
}
```

Figure 13-3 The `DirectoryInformation` program

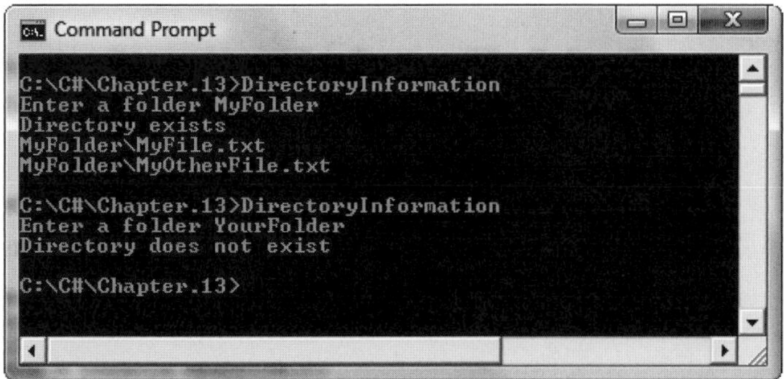

Figure 13-4 Two typical executions of the `DirectoryInformation` program

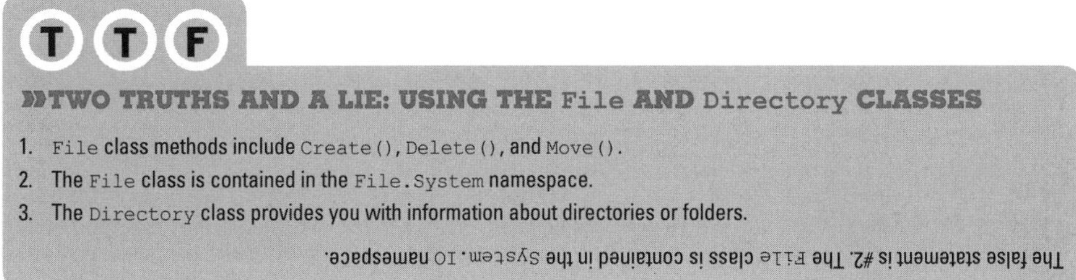

»TWO TRUTHS AND A LIE: USING THE `File` AND `Directory` CLASSES

1. `File` class methods include `Create()`, `Delete()`, and `Move()`.
2. The `File` class is contained in the `File.System` namespace.
3. The `Directory` class provides you with information about directories or folders.

The false statement is #2. The `File` class is contained in the `System.IO` namespace.

UNDERSTANDING DATA ORGANIZATION WITHIN A FILE

Most businesses generate and use large quantities of data every day. You can store data in variables within a program, but this type of storage is temporary. When the application ends, the variables no longer exist, and the data is lost. Variables are stored in the computer's main or primary memory (RAM). When you need to retain data for any significant amount of time, you must save the data on a permanent, secondary storage device.

Businesses store data in a relationship known as the **data hierarchy**, as shown in Figure 13-5. The smallest useful piece of data to most people is the character. A **character** is any one of the letters, numbers, or other special symbols (such as punctuation marks) that comprise data. Characters are made up of bits (the zeros and ones that represent computer circuitry), but people who use data do not care whether the internal representation for an 'A' is 01000001 or 10111110; rather, they are concerned with the meaning of 'A'—for example, it might represent a grade in a course, a person's initial, or a company code.

»NOTE C# uses Unicode to represent its characters. You first learned about Unicode in Chapter 1.

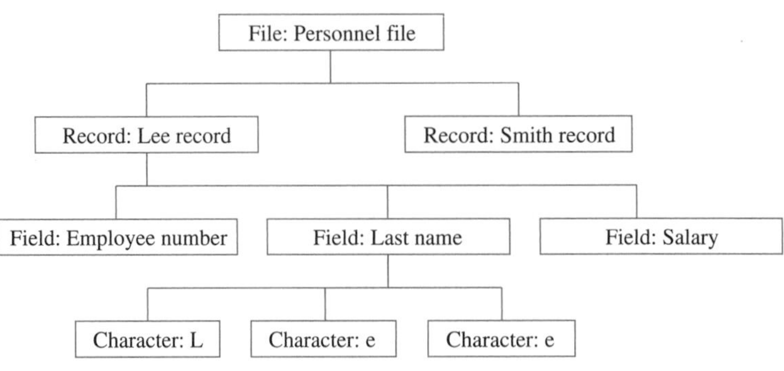

Figure 13-5 Data hierarchy

»NOTE In computer terminology, a character can be any group of bits, and it does not necessarily represent a letter or number. Some of these do not correspond to characters in natural language; for example, some "characters" produce a sound or control your display. You also have used the '\n' character to start a new line.

»NOTE You can think of a character as a unit of information instead of data with a particular appearance. For example, the mathematical character *pi* (π) and the Greek letter *pi* look the same, but have two different Unicode values.

»NOTE The set of all the characters used to represent data on a particular computer is that computer's **character set**.

When businesses use data, they group characters into fields. A **field** is a character or group of characters that has some meaning. For example, the characters *T*, *o*, and *m* might represent your first name. Other data fields might represent items such as last name, Social Security number, zip code, and salary.

»NOTE The field used to uniquely identify each record in a sequential file is the **key field**. Frequently, records are sorted based on the key field.

Fields are grouped together to form records. A **record** is a collection of fields that contain data about an entity. For example, a person's first and last names, Social Security number, zip code, and salary represent that person's record. When programming in C#, you have created many classes, such as an `Employee` class or a `Student` class. You can think of the data typically stored in each of these classes as a record. These classes contain individual variables that represent data fields. A business's data records usually represent a person, item, sales transaction, or some other concrete object or event.

»NOTE When records are not used in sequence, the file is used as a random access file, which means that records can be accessed in any order.

Records are grouped to create files. **Data files** consist of related records, such as a company's personnel file that contains one record for each company employee. Some files have only a few records; perhaps your professor maintains a file for your class with 25 records—one record for each student. Other files contain thousands or even millions of records. For example, a large insurance company maintains a file of policyholders, and a mail-order catalog company maintains a file of available items. A data file is a **sequential access file** when each record is read in order of its position in the file. Usually, the records are stored in order based on the value in some field; for example, employees might be stored in Social Security number order, or inventory items might be stored in item number order.

Before an application can use a data file, it must open the file. A C# application **opens a file** by creating an object and associating a stream of bytes with that object. When you finish using a file, the program should **close the file**—that is, make the file no longer available to your application. If you fail to close an input file (a file from which you are reading data), there usually are no serious consequences; the data still exists in the file. However, if you fail to close an output file (a file to which you are writing data), the data might become inaccessible. You should always close every file you open, and you should close the file as soon as you no longer need it. When you leave a file open for no reason, you use computer resources and your computer's performance suffers. Also, particularly within a network, another program might be waiting to use the file.

>> **NOTE** Frequently, business data is stored in databases. You will learn about databases in Chapter 14.

>> **NOTE** If you fail to close an input file for which only one client is allowed access at a time, then there could be consequences for another application.

»TWO TRUTHS AND A LIE: UNDERSTANDING DATA ORGANIZATION WITHIN A FILE

1. A field is a character or group of characters that has some meaning.
2. A record is a collection of data files that contain information about an entity.
3. A data file that is used as a sequential access file frequently contains records stored in order based on the value in some field.

The false statement is #2. A record is a collection of fields that contain data about an entity. Data files consist of related records.

UNDERSTANDING STREAMS

Whereas people view files as a series of records, with each record containing data fields, C# views files as just a series of bytes. When you perform an input operation in an application, you can picture bytes flowing into your program from an input device through a **stream**, which functions as a pipeline or channel. When you perform output, some bytes flow out of your application through another stream to an output device, as shown in Figure 13-6. A stream is an object, and like all objects, streams have data and methods. The methods allow you to perform actions such as opening, closing, and flushing (clearing) the stream.

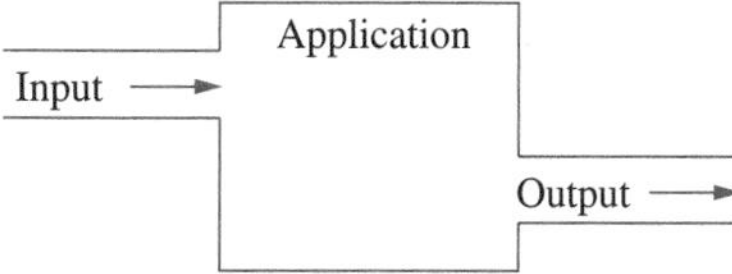

Figure 13-6 File streams

When a file is opened, an object is created and a stream is associated with that object. When a C# program executes, three stream objects are created:

» `Console.In` refers to the standard input stream object, which accepts data from the keyboard.

» `Console.Out` refers to the standard output stream object, which allows a program to produce output on the screen.

» `Console.Error` refers to the standard error stream object, which allows a program to write error messages to the screen.

You have been using `Console.Out` and its `WriteLine()` and `Write()` methods throughout this book. However, you may have forgotten about the `Out` reference because in Chapter 1 you learned to eliminate it by including `using System;` at the top of your program files. Likewise, you have used `Console.In` with the `ReadLine()` and `Read()` methods.

Most streams flow in only one direction; each stream is either an input or output stream. You might open several streams at once within an application. For example, an application that reads a data disk and separates valid records from invalid ones might require three streams. The data arrives via an input stream, and as the program checks the data for invalid values, one output stream writes some records to a file of valid records, and another output stream writes other records to a file of invalid records.

Many file processing classes are available to you, including:

» `StreamReader` for text input from a file

» `StreamWriter` for text output to a file

» `FileStream` (which is used alone and with both `StreamReader` and `StreamWriter`) for both input from and output to a file

»NOTE `StreamReader` and `StreamWriter` inherit from `TextReader` and `TextWriter`, respectively. `Console.In` and `Console.Out` are properties of `TextReader` and `TextWriter`, respectively.

When you write a program that stores data in a file, you create a `FileStream` object. Table 13-3 lists some `FileStream` properties.

Property	Description
`CanRead`	Gets a value indicating whether current `FileStream` supports reading
`CanSeek`	Gets a value indicating whether current `FileStream` supports seeking
`CanWrite`	Gets a value indicating whether current `FileStream` supports writing
`Length`	Gets the length of the `FileStream` in bytes
`Name`	Gets the name of the `FileStream`
`Position`	Gets or sets the current position of the `FileStream`

Table 13-3 Selected `FileStream` properties

The FileStream class has 15 overloaded constructors. One that is used frequently includes the filename (or complete path), mode, and type of access. For example, you might construct a FileStream object using the following statement:

```
FileStream outFile = new FileStream("SomeText.txt",
   FileMode.Create, FileAccess.Write);
```

NOTE Another of FileStream's overloaded constructors requires only a filename and mode. If you use this version and the mode is set to Append, then the default access is Write; otherwise, the access is set to ReadWrite.

In this example, the filename is "SomeText.txt" and the mode is Create, which means a new file will be created even if one with the same name already exists. Also, the access is Write, which means you can write data to the file, but not read from it. Table 13-4 describes the available file modes and Table 13-5 describes the access types.

NOTE Programmers say FileStream **exposes** a stream around a file.

Member	Description
Append	Opens the file if it exists and seeks the end of the file to append new data
Create	Creates a new file; if the file already exists, it is overwritten
CreateNew	Creates a new file; if the file already exists, an IOException is thrown
Open	Opens an existing file; if the file does not exist, a System.IO.FileNotFoundException is thrown
OpenOrCreate	Opens an existing file; if the file does not exist, it is created
Truncate	Opens an existing file; once opened, the file is truncated so its size is zero bytes

Table 13-4 FileMode enumeration

Member	Description
Read	Data can be read from the file.
ReadWrite	Data can be read from and written to the file.
Write	Data can be written to the file.

Table 13-5 FileAccess enumeration

When you create a FileStream object, you associate the object with a StreamWriter. Then you use WriteLine() or Write() with the StreamWriter object in much the same way you use it with Console.Out. For example, Figure 13-7 shows an application in which a FileStream object named outFile is created, then associated with a StreamWriter named writer in the first shaded line. The writer object then uses WriteLine() to send a string to the FileStream file instead of sending it to the Console. Figure 13-8 shows a typical execution of the program, and Figure 13-9 shows the file as it appears in Notepad.

```
using System;
using System.IO;
public class WriteSomeText
{
   public static void Main()
   {
      FileStream outFile = new
         FileStream("SomeText.txt", FileMode.Create,
            FileAccess.Write);
      StreamWriter writer = new StreamWriter(outFile);
      Console.Write("Enter some text >> ");
      string text = Console.ReadLine();
      writer.WriteLine(text);
      // Error occurs if the next two statements are reversed
      writer.Close();
      outFile.Close();
   }
}
```

Figure 13-7 `WriteSomeText` program

NOTE Although the `WriteSomeText` application uses `Console.ReadLine()` to accept user input, you could also create a GUI `Form` to accept input. You will create an application that writes to and reads from files using a GUI environment in the "You Do It" exercises at the end of this chapter.

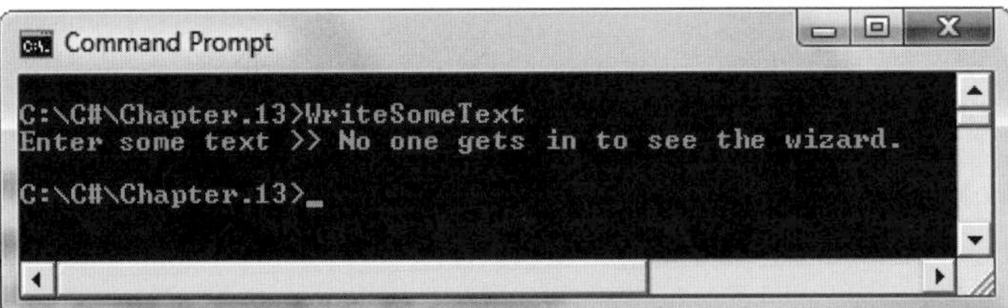

Figure 13-8 Typical execution of `WriteSomeText` program

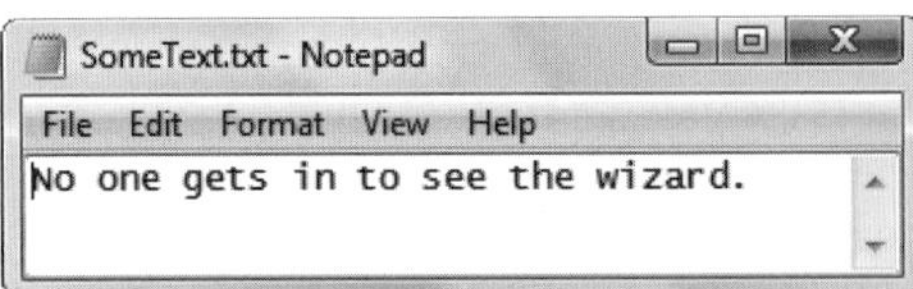

Figure 13-9 File created by `WriteSomeText` program

»NOTE In Chapter 9, you learned about exception handling with `try` and `catch` blocks. In most applications that use files, you will want to place all the statements that open, write to, read from, and close files in a `try` block and then catch any `IOException`s that are thrown. Exception handling is eliminated from many examples in this chapter so that you can concentrate on the details of handling files without extra statements. In the "You Do It" section at the end of this chapter, you will add exception handling to an application.

»NOTE The classes `BinaryReader` and `BinaryWriter` exist for working with binary files. **Binary files** can store any of the 256 combinations of bits in any byte instead of just those combinations that form readable text. For example, photographs and music are stored in binary files.

»NOTE The classes `XmlTextReader` and `XmlTextWriter` exist for working with XML files. **XML** is an abbreviation of eXtensible Markup Language, which is a standard for exchanging data over the Internet.

»TWO TRUTHS AND A LIE: UNDERSTANDING STREAMS

1. When a file is opened in C#, an object is created and a stream is associated with that object.
2. Most streams flow in only one direction; each stream is either an input or output stream.
3. You can open one stream at a time within a C# application.

The false statement is #3. You might open several streams at once within an application.

WRITING TO A SEQUENTIAL ACCESS TEXT FILE

Although people think of data files as consisting of records that contain fields, C# uses files only as streams of bytes. Therefore, when you write a program to store a data file, you must dictate the form in which the program will handle the file.

For example, suppose you want to store `Employee` data in a file. Assume an `Employee` contains an ID number, a name, and a salary. You could write stand-alone data for each of the three types to a file, or you could create an `Employee` class that is similar to many you have seen throughout this book. Figure 13-10 shows a typical `Employee` class that contains three fields and properties for each.

```
public class Employee
{
   private int empNum;
   private string name;
   private double salary;
   public int EmpNum {get; set;}
   public string Name {get; set;}
   public double Salary {get; set;}
}
```

Figure 13-10 An `Employee` class

NOTE In Chapter 7, you learned that the concise form of `{get; set;}` is new to C# 3.0. If you want to use the `Employee` class with an earlier version of C#, you must explicitly code implementations for the methods.

To store `Employee` data to a persistent storage device, you declare a `FileStream` object. For example:

```
FileStream outFile = new FileStream(FILENAME,
   FileMode.Create, FileAccess.Write);
```

The object is then associated with a `StreamWriter` object. For example:

```
StreamWriter writer = new StreamWriter(outFile);
```

After the `outFile` is associated with the `writer` object, `Employee` data can be written to the `writer` object using the `WriteLine()` method. When you write `Employee` data to a file, the fields should be separated by a delimiter. A **delimiter** is a character used to specify the boundary between data items in text files. Without a delimiter, the process of separating and interpreting data fields on a storage device is more difficult. For example, suppose you define a delimiter as follows:

```
const string DELIM = ",";
```

NOTE A comma is a commonly used delimiter, but a delimiter can be any character that is not needed as part of the data in a file. A file that contains comma-separated values is often called a **CSV file**. When commas are needed as part of the data, sometimes either the Tab character, the pipe character (|), or a comma within quotes is used as a delimiter.

Then, when you write data to a file, you can separate the fields with a comma using a statement such as the following:

```
writer.WriteLine(emp.EmpNum + DELIM + emp.Name + DELIM + emp.Salary);
```

NOTE Because `WriteLine()` is used for writing data to the file, the carriage return becomes the *record delimiter.*

NOTE A block of text within a string that represents an entity or field is a **token**.

Figure 13-11 contains a complete program that opens a file and continuously prompts the user for `Employee` data. When all three fields have been entered for an employee, the fields are written to the file, separated by commas. When the user enters the sentinel value 999 for an `Employee` ID number, the data entry loop ends and the file is closed. Figure 13-12 shows a typical execution and Figure 13-13 shows the contents of the sequential data file that is created.

```
using System;
using System.IO;
public class WriteSequentialFile
{
   public static void Main()
   {
      const int END = 999;
      const string DELIM = ",";
      const string FILENAME = "EmployeeData.txt";
      Employee emp = new Employee();
      FileStream outFile = new FileStream(FILENAME,
         FileMode.Create, FileAccess.Write);
      StreamWriter writer = new StreamWriter(outFile);
      Console.Write("Enter employee number or " + END + " to quit ");
      emp.EmpNum = Convert.ToInt32(Console.ReadLine());
      while(emp.EmpNum != END)
      {
         Console.Write("Enter last name ");
         emp.Name = Console.ReadLine();
         Console.Write("Enter salary ");
         emp.Salary = Convert.ToDouble(Console.ReadLine());
         writer.WriteLine(emp.EmpNum + DELIM + emp.Name +
            DELIM + emp.Salary);
         Console.Write("Enter next employee number or " +
            END + " to quit ");
         emp.EmpNum = Convert.ToInt32(Console.ReadLine());
      }
      writer.Close();
      outFile.Close();
   }
}
```

Figure 13-11 `WriteSequentialFile` **class**

NOTE In the `WriteSequentialFile` class, the delimiter is defined to be a `string` instead of a `char` to force the composed argument to `WriteLine()` to be a `string`. If the first data field sent to `WriteLine()` was a `string`, then `DELIM` could have been declared as a `char`.

NOTE In the `WriteSequentialFile` program in Figure 13-11, the constant `END` is defined to be 999 so it can be used to check for the sentinel value. You first learned to use named constants in Chapter 2. Defining a named constant eliminates using a magic number in a program. The term **magic number** refers to the bad programming practice of hard-coding numbers (unnamed, literal constants) in code without explanation. In most cases, this makes programs harder to read, understand, and maintain.

```
Command Prompt
C:\C#\Chapter.13>WriteSequentialFile
Enter employee number or 999 to quit 324
Enter last name LaFreniere
Enter salary 35.55
Enter next employee number or 999 to quit 512
Enter last name Fortune
Enter salary 21.85
Enter next employee number or 999 to quit 802
Enter last name Cox
Enter salary 19.35
Enter next employee number or 999 to quit 999

C:\C#\Chapter.13>
```

Figure 13-12 Typical execution of `WriteSequentialFile` program

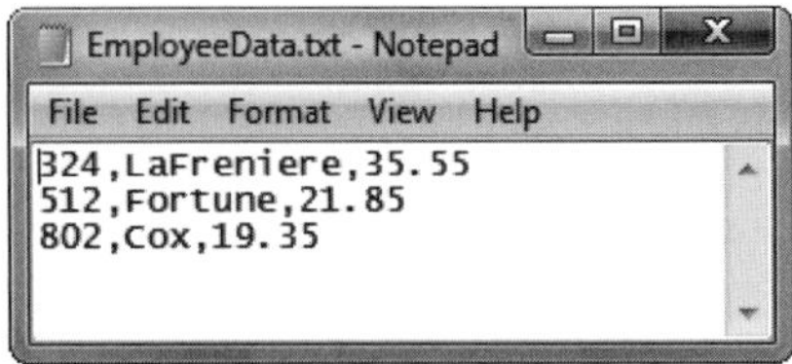

Figure 13-13 Contents of file created by `WriteSequentialFile` program

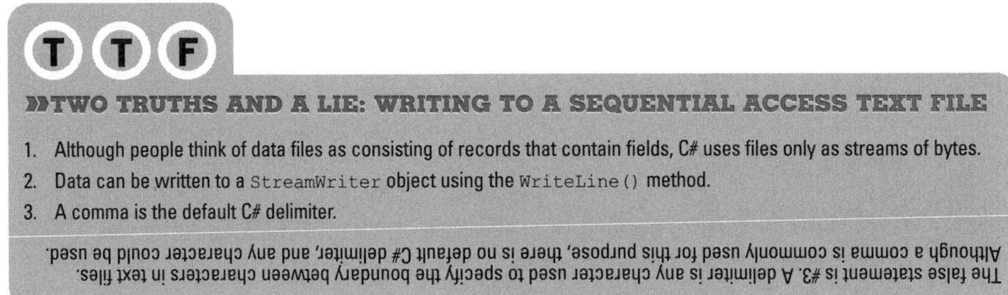
T T F

»TWO TRUTHS AND A LIE: WRITING TO A SEQUENTIAL ACCESS TEXT FILE

1. Although people think of data files as consisting of records that contain fields, C# uses files only as streams of bytes.
2. Data can be written to a `StreamWriter` object using the `WriteLine()` method.
3. A comma is the default C# delimiter.

The false statement is #3. A delimiter is any character used to specify the boundary between characters in text files. Although a comma is commonly used for this purpose, there is no default C# delimiter, and any character could be used.

READING FROM A SEQUENTIAL ACCESS TEXT FILE

A program that reads from a sequential access data file contains many similar components to one that writes to a file. For example, a `FileStream` object is created, as in a program that writes a file. However, the access must be `FileAccess.Read` (or `ReadWrite`), as in the following statement:

```
FileStream inFile = new FileStream(FILENAME,
   FileMode.Open, FileAccess.Read);
```

Then, as when data is being written, the `FileStream` object is associated with a `StreamReader` object, as in the following statement:

```
StreamReader reader = new StreamReader(inFile);
```

»NOTE Using `ReadLine()` assumes that a carriage return is the record delimiter, which is true, for example, if the records were created using `WriteLine()`.

After the `StreamReader` has been defined, the `ReadLine()` method can be used to retrieve one line at a time from the data file. For example, the following statement gets one line of data from the file and stores it in a string named `recordIn`:

```
string recordIn = reader.ReadLine();
```

If the value of `recordIn` is `null`, then no more data exists in the file. Therefore, a loop that begins `while(recordIn != null)` can be used to control the data entry loop.

After a record (line of data) is read in, the `Split()` method can be used to separate the data fields into an array of strings. The `Split()` method takes a character parameter and separates a string into substrings at each occurrence of the character delimiter. For example, the following code splits `recordIn` into the `fields` array at each `DELIM` occurrence. Then the three array elements can be stored as an `int`, `string`, and `double`, respectively.

```
string[] fields;
fields = recordIn.Split(DELIM);
emp.EmpNum = Convert.ToInt32(fields[0]);
emp.Name = fields[1];
emp.Salary = Convert.ToDouble(fields[2]);
```

Figure 13-14 contains a complete `ReadSequentialFile` application that uses the data file created in Figure 13-12. The records stored in the EmployeeData.txt file are read in

```
using System;
using System.IO;
public class ReadSequentialFile
{
   public static void Main()
   {
      const char DELIM = ',';
      const string FILENAME = "EmployeeData.txt";
      Employee emp = new Employee();
      FileStream inFile = new FileStream(FILENAME,
         FileMode.Open, FileAccess.Read);
      StreamReader reader = new StreamReader(inFile);
      string recordIn;
      string[] fields;
      Console.WriteLine("\n{0,-5}{1,-12}{2,8}\n",
         "Num", "Name", "Salary");
      recordIn = reader.ReadLine();
      while(recordIn != null)
      {
         fields = recordIn.Split(DELIM);
         emp.EmpNum = Convert.ToInt32(fields[0]);
         emp.Name = fields[1];
         emp.Salary = Convert.ToDouble(fields[2]);
         Console.WriteLine("{0,-5}{1,-12}{2,8}",
            emp.EmpNum, emp.Name, emp.Salary.ToString("C"));
         recordIn = reader.ReadLine();
      }
      reader.Close();
      inFile.Close();
   }
}
```

Figure 13-14 `ReadSequentialFile` program

one at a time, split into their `Employee` record components, and displayed. Figure 13-15 shows the output.

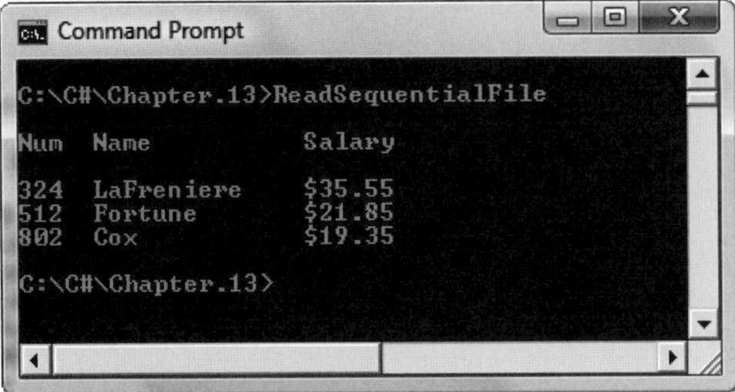

Figure 13-15 Output of `ReadSequentialFile` program

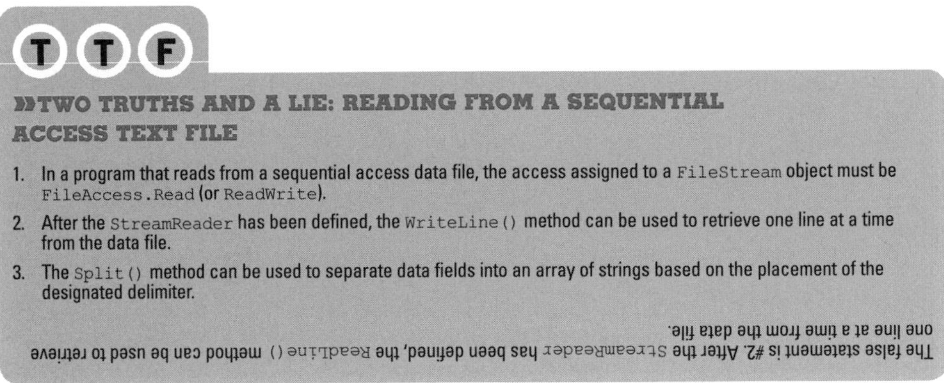

T T F

»TWO TRUTHS AND A LIE: READING FROM A SEQUENTIAL ACCESS TEXT FILE

1. In a program that reads from a sequential access data file, the access assigned to a `FileStream` object must be `FileAccess.Read` (or `ReadWrite`).
2. After the `StreamReader` has been defined, the `WriteLine()` method can be used to retrieve one line at a time from the data file.
3. The `Split()` method can be used to separate data fields into an array of strings based on the placement of the designated delimiter.

The false statement is #2. After the `StreamReader` has been defined, the `ReadLine()` method can be used to retrieve one line at a time from the data file.

SEARCHING A SEQUENTIAL FILE

When you read data from a sequential file, as in the `ReadSequentialFile` program in Figure 13-14, the program starts at the beginning of the file and reads each record in turn until all the records have been read. Subsequent records are read in order because a file's **file position pointer** holds the byte number of the next byte to be read. For example, if each record in a file is 32 bytes long, then the file position pointer holds 0, 32, 64, and so on in sequence during the execution of the program.

Sometimes it is necessary to process a file multiple times from the beginning during a program's execution. For example, suppose you want to continue to prompt a user for a minimum salary and then search through a file for `Employee`s who make at least that salary.

You can compare the user's entered minimum with each salary in the data file and list those employees who meet the requirement. However, after one list is produced, the file pointer is at the end of the file and no more records can be read. To reread the file, you could close it and reopen it, but that requires unnecessary overhead. Instead, you can just reposition the file pointer using the `Seek()` method and the `SeekOrigin` enumeration. For example, the following statement repositions the pointer of a file named `inFile` to 0 bytes away from the `Begin` position of the file:

```
inFile.Seek(0, SeekOrigin.Begin);
```

Table 13-6 lists the values in the `SeekOrigin` enumeration that you can use.

Member	Description
`Begin`	Specifies the beginning of a stream
`Current`	Specifies the current position of a stream
`End`	Specifies the end of a stream

Table 13-6 The `SeekOrigin` enumeration

Figure 13-16 contains a program that repeatedly searches a file to produce lists of employees who meet a minimum salary requirement. The shaded portions of the program represent differences from the `ReadSequentialFile` application in Figure 13-14. In this program, each time the user enters a minimum salary that does not equal 999, the file position pointer is set to the beginning of the file, and then each record is read and compared to the minimum. Figure 13-17 shows a typical execution of the program.

```
using System;
using System.IO;
public class FindEmployees
{
   public static void Main()
   {
      const char DELIM = ',';
      const int END = 999;
      const string FILENAME = "EmployeeData.txt";
      Employee emp = new Employee();
      FileStream inFile = new FileStream(FILENAME,
         FileMode.Open, FileAccess.Read);
      StreamReader reader = new StreamReader(inFile);
      string recordIn;
      string[] fields;
      double minSalary;
```

Figure 13-16 `FindEmployees` program (*continued*)

```
        Console.Write("Enter minimum salary to find or " +
           END + " to quit ");
        minSalary = Convert.ToDouble(Console.ReadLine());
        while(minSalary != END)
        {
           Console.WriteLine("\n{0,-5}{1,-12}{2,8}\n",
              "Num", "Name", "Salary");
           inFile.Seek(0, SeekOrigin.Begin);
           recordIn = reader.ReadLine();
           while(recordIn != null)
           {
              fields = recordIn.Split(DELIM);
              emp.EmpNum = Convert.ToInt32(fields[0]);
              emp.Name = fields[1];
              emp.Salary = Convert.ToDouble(fields[2]);
              if(emp.Salary >= minSalary)
                 Console.WriteLine("{0,-5}{1,-12}{2,8}",
                    emp.EmpNum, emp.Name,
                       emp.Salary.ToString("C"));
              recordIn = reader.ReadLine();
           }
           Console.Write("\nEnter minimum salary to find or " +
              END + " to quit ");
           minSalary = Convert.ToDouble(Console.ReadLine());
        }
        reader.Close();  // Error occurs if
        inFile.Close(); //  these two statements are reversed
     }
}
```

Figure 13-16 (*continued*)

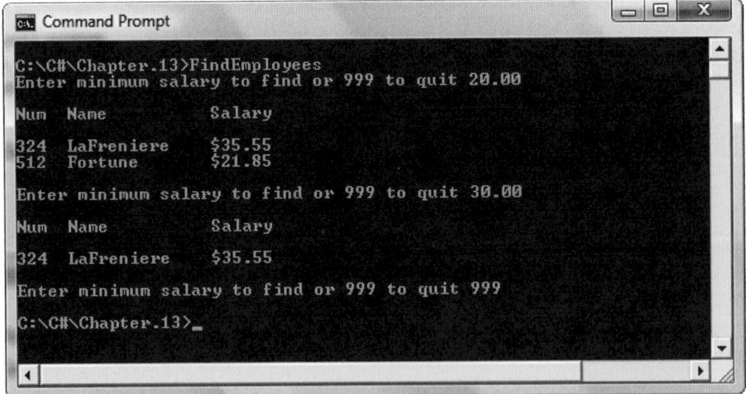

Figure 13-17 Typical execution of `FindEmployees` program

»NOTE The program in Figure 13-16 is intended to demonstrate using the `Seek()` method. In a business setting, you might prefer not to leave a file open in one application if other users might be waiting for it. As an alternative, you could load all the records into an array and then search the array for desired records.

»NOTE When you seek beyond the length of the file, you do not cause an error. Instead, the file size grows. In Microsoft Windows NT and later, any data added to the end of a file is set to zero. In Microsoft Windows 98 or earlier, any data added to the end of the file is not set to zero. This means that previously deleted data might become visible to the stream.

»TWO TRUTHS AND A LIE: SEARCHING A SEQUENTIAL FILE

1. When you read data from a sequential file, the program starts at the beginning of the file and reads each record in turn until all the records have been read.
2. When you read from a sequential file, its file position pointer holds the number of the record to be read.
3. To reread a file, you can close it and reopen it, or you can reposition the file pointer to the beginning of the file.

The false statement is #2. When you read from a sequential file, its file position pointer holds the byte number of the next byte to be read.

UNDERSTANDING SERIALIZATION AND DESERIALIZATION

Writing to a text file allows you to store data for later use. However, there are two disadvantages to writing to a text file:

- Data in a text file is easily readable in a text editor such as Notepad. Although this feature is useful to developers when they test programs, it is not a very secure way to store data.
- When a record in a data file contains many fields, it is cumbersome to convert each field to text and combine the fields with delimiters before storing the record on a disk. Similarly, when you read a text file, it is somewhat unwieldy to eliminate the delimiters, split the text into tokens, and convert each token to the proper data type. It would be more convenient to write an entire object to a file at once.

C# provides a technique called serialization that can be used for writing objects to and reading objects from data files. **Serialization** is the process of converting objects into streams of bytes. **Deserialization** is the reverse process; it converts streams of bytes back into objects.

To create a class that can be serialized, you mark it with the `[Serializable]` attribute, as shown in the shaded statement in Figure 13-18. The `Employee` class in the figure is identical to the one in Figure 13-10 except for the `[Serializable]` attribute.

In a class marked with the `[Serializable]` attribute, every instance variable must also be serializable. By default, all C# simple data types are serializable, including `string`s. However, if your class contains fields that are more complex data types, you must check the declaration of those classes to ensure they are serializable. By default, array objects are serializable.

» **NOTE** Attributes provide a method of associating information with C# code. They are always contained in square brackets. The C# documentation at *http://msdn2.microsoft.com* provides more details.

```
[Serializable]
public class Employee
{
   private int empNum;
   private string name;
   private double salary;
   public int EmpNum {get; set;}
   public string Name {get; set;}
   public double Salary {get; set;}
}
```

Figure 13-18 Serializable `Employee` class

However, if the array contains references to other objects, such as `Dates` or `Students`, those objects must be serializable.

» **NOTE** If you want to be able to write class objects to a file, you can implement the `ISerializable` interface instead of marking a class with the `[Serializable]` attribute. When you use this approach, you must write a method named `GetObjectData()`. Marking the class with the attribute is the simpler format.

Two namespaces are included in programs that employ serialization:

- `System.Runtime.Serialization.Formatters.Binary;`
- `System.Runtime.Serialization;`

When you create a program that writes objects to files, you declare an instance of the `BinaryFormatter` class with a statement such as the following:

```
BinaryFormatter bFormatter = new BinaryFormatter();
```

Then, after you fill a class object with data, you can write it to an output file named `outFile` with a statement such as the following:

```
bFormatter.Serialize(outFile, objectFilledWithData);
```

The `Serialize()` method takes two arguments—the name of the file and a complete object that might contain any number of data fields. The entire object is written to the data file with this single statement.

Similarly, when you read an object from a data file, you use a statement like the following:

```
objectInstance = (TypeOfObject)bFormatter.Deserialize(inFile);
```

This statement uses the `Deserialize()` method with a `BinaryFormatter` object to read in one object from the file. The object is cast to the appropriate type and can be assigned to an instance of the object. Then you can access individual fields. An entire object is read with this single statement, no matter how many data fields it contains.

Figure 13-19 shows a program that writes `Employee` class objects to a file and later reads them in. After the `FileStream` is declared for an output file, a `BinaryFormatter` is declared in the first shaded statement. The user enters an ID number, name, and salary for an `Employee`, and the completed object is written to a file in the second shaded statement. When the user enters 999, the output file is closed.

```
using System;
using System.IO;
using System.Runtime.Serialization.Formatters.Binary;
using System.Runtime.Serialization;
public class SerializableDemonstration
{
   public static void Main()
   {
      const int END = 999;
      const string FILENAME = "Data.ser";
      Employee emp = new Employee();
      FileStream outFile = new FileStream(FILENAME,
         FileMode.Create, FileAccess.Write);
      BinaryFormatter bFormatter = new BinaryFormatter();
      Console.Write("Enter employee number or " + END +
         " to quit ");
      emp.EmpNum = Convert.ToInt32(Console.ReadLine());
      while(emp.EmpNum != END)
      {
         Console.Write("Enter last name ");
         emp.Name = Console.ReadLine();
         Console.Write("Enter salary ");
         emp.Salary = Convert.ToDouble(Console.ReadLine());
         bFormatter.Serialize(outFile, emp);
         Console.Write("Enter employee number or " + END +
            " to quit ");
         emp.EmpNum = Convert.ToInt32(Console.ReadLine());
      }
      outFile.Close();
      FileStream inFile = new FileStream(FILENAME,
         FileMode.Open, FileAccess.Read);
      Console.WriteLine("\n{0,-5}{1,-12}{2,8}\n",
         "Num", "Name", "Salary");
      while(inFile.Position < inFile.Length)
      {
         emp = (Employee)bFormatter.Deserialize(inFile);
         Console.WriteLine("{0,-5}{1,-12}{2,8}",
            emp.EmpNum, emp.Name, emp.Salary.ToString("C"));
      }
      inFile.Close();
   }
}
```

Figure 13-19 `SerializableDemonstration` program

After the output file closes in the `SerializableDemonstration` program in Figure 13-19, it is reopened for reading. A loop is executed while the `Position` property of the input file is less than its `Length` property. In other words, the loop executes while there is more data in the file. The last shaded statement in the figure deserializes data from the file and casts it to an `Employee` object, where the individual fields can be accessed. Figure 13-20 shows a typical execution of the program.

```
C:\C#\Chapter.13>SerializableDemonstration
Enter employee number or 999 to quit 218
Enter last name Mack
Enter salary 23.98
Enter employee number or 999 to quit 479
Enter last name Alberts
Enter salary 12.55
Enter employee number or 999 to quit 560
Enter last name Samson
Enter salary 40.00
Enter employee number or 999 to quit 812
Enter last name Johnson
Enter salary 30.10
Enter employee number or 999 to quit 999

Num  Name          Salary

218  Mack          $23.98
479  Alberts       $12.55
560  Samson        $40.00
812  Johnson       $30.10

C:\C#\Chapter.13>
```

Figure 13-20 Typical execution of `SerializableDemonstration` program

The file created by the `SerializableDemonstration` program is not as easy to read as the text file created by the `WriteSequentialFile` program earlier in the chapter (in Figure 13-13). Figure 13-21 shows the file contents displayed in Notepad. If you examine the file carefully, you can discern the string names and some `Employee` class information, but the rest of the file is not easy to read.

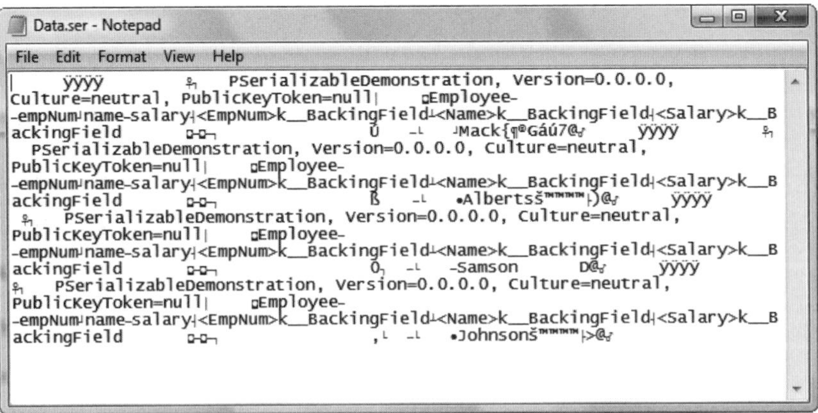

Figure 13-21 Data file created using `SerializableDemonstration` program

»TWO TRUTHS AND A LIE: UNDERSTANDING SERIALIZATION AND DESERIALIZATION

1. An advantage of writing data to a text file is that the data is easily readable in a text editor such as Notepad.
2. Serialization is the process of converting objects into streams of bytes and deserialization is the reverse process; it converts streams of bytes back into objects.
3. By default, all C# classes are serializable.

The false statement is #3. By default, all C# simple data types are serializable, including `string`s. However, if your class contains fields that are more complex data types, you must check the declaration of those classes to ensure they are serializable.

YOU DO IT

CREATING A FILE

In the next steps, you will create a file that contains a list of names.

To create a file:

1. Open a new file in your editor and write the first lines needed for a program that creates a file of names.

```
using System;
using System.IO;
public class CreateNameFile
{
```

2. Start a `Main()` method that declares a `FileStream` you can use to create a file named Names.txt that is open for writing. Also create a `StreamWriter` to which you associate the file.

```
public static void Main()
{
   FileStream file = new FileStream("Names.txt",
      FileMode.Create, FileAccess.Write);
   StreamWriter writer = new StreamWriter(file);
```

3. Add an array of names as follows. Each name is 10 characters long.

```
string[] names =  {"Anthony    ",
                   "Belle      ",
                   "Carolyn    ",
                   "David      ",
                   "Edwin      ",
                   "Frannie    ",
                   "Gina       ",
                   "Hannah     ",
                   "Inez       ",
                   "Juan       "};
```

»NOTE Add spaces to make each new name the same length so that they can demonstrate the `Seek()` method in a later exercise.

4. Declare a variable to use as an array subscript, then write each name to the output file.

```
int x;
for(x = 0; x < names.Length; ++x)
   writer.WriteLine(names[x]);
```

5. Close the `StreamWriter` and the `FileStream`. Also add two closing curly braces—one for the `Main()` method and one for the class.

```
      writer.Close();
      file.Close();
   }
}
```

6. Save the file as **CreateNameFile.cs**. Compile and execute it. Using My Computer or Windows Explorer, open the newly created **Names.txt** file in a text editor. The file contents appear in Figure 13-22.

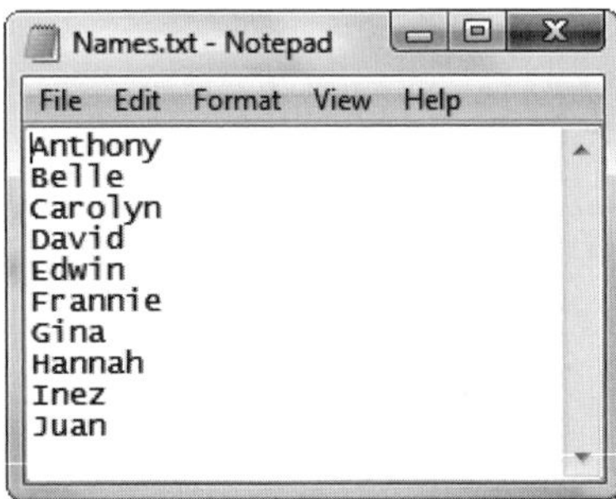

Figure 13-22 File created by `CreateNameFile` program

READING FROM A FILE

In the next steps, you will read the text from the file created by the `CreateNameFile` program.

To read text from a file:

1. Start a new file in your text editor as follows:

```
using System;
using System.IO;
public class ReadNameFile
{
```

2. Start a `Main()` method that declares a `FileStream` that uses the same filename as the one created by the `CreateNameFile` program. Declare the file mode to be `Open` and the access to be `Read`. Declare a `StreamReader` with which to associate the file. Also declare an integer that counts the names read and a `string` that holds the names.

```
public static void Main()
{
   FileStream file = new FileStream("Names.txt",
      FileMode.Open, FileAccess.Read);
   StreamReader reader = new StreamReader(file);
   int count = 1;
   string name;
```

3. Display a heading and read the first line from the file. While a name is not `null`, display a count and a name, and increment the count.

```
Console.WriteLine("Displaying all names");
name = reader.ReadLine();
while(name != null)
{
   Console.WriteLine("" + count + "  " + name);
   name = reader.ReadLine();
   ++count;
}
```

4. Close the `StreamReader` and the `File`, and add closing curly braces for the method and the class.

```
         reader.Close();
         file.Close();
      }
}
```

5. Save the file as **ReadNameFile.cs**. Compile and execute it. The output appears in Figure 13-23.

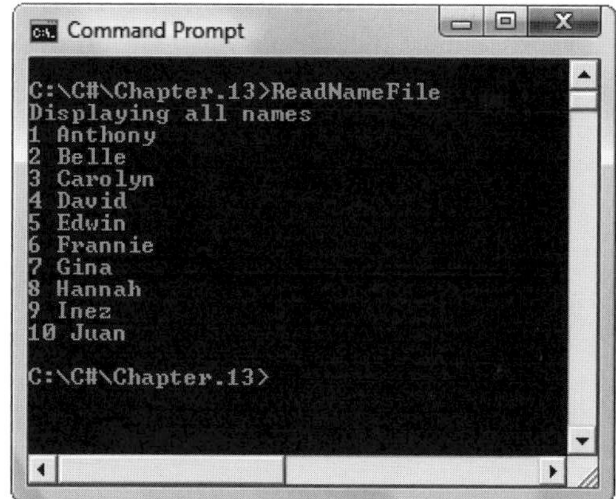

Figure 13-23 Output produced by `ReadNameFile` program

USING THE `Seek()` METHOD

In the next steps, you will use the `Seek()` method to reposition a file pointer so you can access a file from any location. The user will be prompted to enter a number representing a starting point to list the names in the Names.txt file. Names from that point forward will be listed, and then the user will be prompted for another selection.

To demonstrate the `Seek()` method:

1. Open a new file in your editor and start a program that will demonstrate how to access certain names from the Names.txt file. You created this file in the `CreateNameFile` application.

```
using System;
using System.IO;
public class AccessSomeNames
{
   public static void Main()
   {
      FileStream file = new FileStream("Names.txt",
         FileMode.Open, FileAccess.Read);
      StreamReader reader = new StreamReader(file);
```

2. Declare a constant named END that represents an input value that allows the user to exit the program. Then declare other variables that the program will use.

```
const int END = 999;
int count = 0;
int num;
int size;
string name;
```

3. Read a line from the input file. While names are available, continue to read and count them. Then compute the size of each name by dividing the file length by the number of strings stored in it.

```
name = reader.ReadLine();
while(name != null)
{
   ++count;
   name = reader.ReadLine();
}
size = (int)file.Length / count;
```

4. Prompt the user for the number of the first record to read, and read the value from the `Console`.

```
Console.Write("\nWith which number do you want to start? ");
num = Convert.ToInt32(Console.ReadLine());
```

5. As long as the user does not enter the sentinel END value, display the number and then use the `Seek()` method to position the file pointer at the correct file location. Because users enter numbers starting with 1, you calculate the file position by first subtracting 1 from the user's entry. For example, when a user enters 1 as the number of the first record to view, the file should start at position 0. The calculated record number is then multiplied by the size of each name in the file. For example, if each name is 12 bytes long, then the calculated starting position should be 0, 12, 24, 36, or some other multiple of the record size. Read and write the name at the calculated location. Then, in a loop, read and write all the remaining names until the end of the file. Finally, prompt the user for the next starting value for a new list and inform the user how to quit the application.

```
while(num != END)
{
   Console.WriteLine("Starting with name " + num +": ");
   file.Seek((num - 1) * size, SeekOrigin.Begin);
   name = reader.ReadLine();
   Console.WriteLine("   " + name);
   while(name != null)
   {
      name = reader.ReadLine();
      Console.WriteLine("   " + name);
   }
   Console.Write("\nWith which number do you " +
      "want to start? (Enter " + END + " to quit) ");
   num = Convert.ToInt32(Console.ReadLine());
}
```

6. Close the `StreamReader` and `File` objects and add closing braces for the method and the class.

```
      reader.Close();
      file.Close();
   }
}
```

7. Save the file as **AccessSomeNames.cs**. Compile and execute it. Figure 13-24 shows a typical execution during which the user displays three sets of names starting at a different point each time.

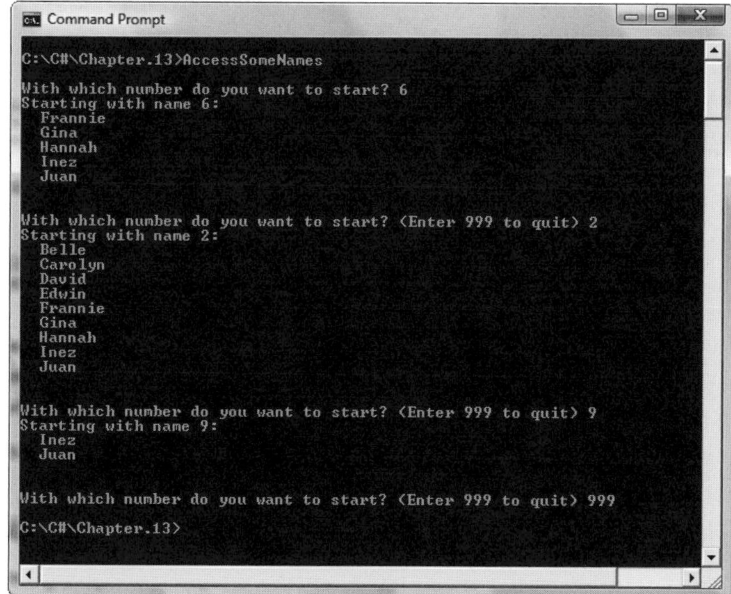

Figure 13-24 Typical execution of `AccessSomeNames` program

CREATING A FILE IN A GUI ENVIRONMENT

The file writing and reading examples in this chapter have used console applications so that you could concentrate on the features of files in the simplest environment. However, you can write and read files in GUI environments as well. In the next steps, you will create two applications. The first allows a user to enter invoice records using a `Form` and to store them in a file. The second application allows a user to view stored records using a `Form`.

To write a GUI application that creates a file:

1. Open the Visual Studio IDE and start a new Windows Forms Application project named **EnterInvoices**.
2. Create a `Form` like the one shown in Figure 13-25 by making the following changes:
   - » Change the `Text` property of the `Form` to **Invoice Data**.
   - » Drag a `Label` onto the `Form` and change its `Text` property to **Enter invoice data**. Increase the `Label`'s `Font` to **12**.
   - » Drag three more `Labels` onto the `Form` and change their `Text` properties to **Invoice number**, **Last name**, and **Amount**, respectively.
   - » Drag three `TextBoxes` onto the `Form` next to the three descriptive `Labels`. Change the `Name` properties of the three `TextBoxes` to **`invoiceBox`**, **`nameBox`**, and **`amountBox`**, respectively.
   - » Drag a `Button` onto the `Form`, change its `Name` to **`enterButton`**, and change its `Text` to **Enter record**. If necessary, resize **`enterButton`** so that all of its text is visible.

Figure 13-25 Designing the `EnterInvoices Form`

3. View the code for the `Form`. At the start of the class, before the `Form1()` constructor, add the shaded code shown in Figure 13-26. The new code contains statements that perform the following:
   - » Declare a delimiter that will be used to separate records in the output file.
   - » Declare a path and filename. You can change the path if you want to store the file in a different location on your system.
   - » Declare variables for the number, name, and amount of each invoice.
   - » Open the file and associate it with a `StreamWriter`.

```
namespace EnterInvoices
{
    public partial class Form1 : Form
    {
        const string DELIM = ",";
        const string FILENAME =
           @"C:\C#\Chapter.13\Invoices.txt";
        int num;
        string name;
        double amount;
        static FileStream outFile = new
           FileStream(FILENAME, FileMode.Create,
           FileAccess.Write);
        StreamWriter writer = new StreamWriter(outFile);
        public Form1()
        {
            InitializeComponent();
        }
```

Figure 13-26 Partial code for `EnterInvoices` program with typed statements shaded

»NOTE In Chapter 11, you learned that placing an at sign (@) in front of a filename indicates that all characters in the string should be interpreted literally. This means that the backslashes in the path will not be interpreted as escape sequence characters.

4. At the top of the file, with the other `using` statements, add the following so that the `FileStream` can be declared:

   `using System.IO;`

5. Click **Save All** (and continue to do so periodically as you work). Return to Design view and double-click the **Enter record** button. As shown in the shaded portions of Figure 13-27, add statements within the method to accept data from each of the three `TextBox`es and convert each field to the appropriate type. Then write each field to a text file, separated by delimiting commas. Finally, clear the `TextBox` fields to be ready for the user to enter a new set of data.

```
private void enterButton_Click(object sender, EventArgs e)
{
    num = Convert.ToInt32(invoiceBox.Text);
    name = nameBox.Text;
    amount = Convert.ToDouble(amountBox.Text);
    writer.WriteLine(num + DELIM + name + DELIM + amount);
    invoiceBox.Clear();
    nameBox.Clear();
    amountBox.Clear();
}
```

Figure 13-27 Code for `enterButton_Click()` method of `EnterInvoices` program

6. Locate the `Dispose()` method, which executes when the user clicks the Close button to dismiss the `Form`. A quick way to locate the method in the Visual Studio IDE is to select **Edit** from the main menu, click **Find and Replace**, click **Quick Find**, and type **Dispose** in the Find What: box. (The Look in: setting can be either Entire Solution or Current Project.) The method appears on the screen. Add two statements to close `writer` and `outFile`, as shown in the shaded statements in Figure 13-28.

```
protected override void Dispose(bool disposing)
 {
     writer.Close();
     outFile.Close();
     if (disposing && (components != null))
     {
        components.Dispose();
     }
     base.Dispose(disposing);
 }
```

Figure 13-28 The `Dispose()` method in the `EnterInvoices` program

7. Click **Save All**. Execute the program. When the `Form` appears, enter data in each `TextBox` and then click the **Enter record** button when you finish. The `TextBoxes` clear in preparation for you to enter another record. Enter at least three records before dismissing the `Form`. Figure 13-29 shows data entry in progress.

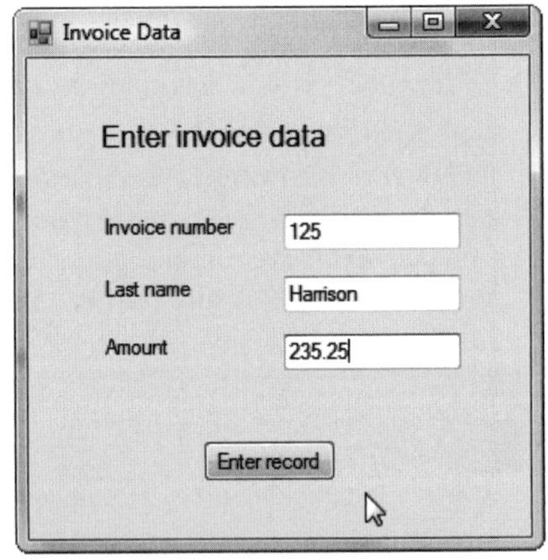

Figure 13-29 Entering data in the `EnterInvoices` application

READING DATA FROM A FILE INTO A `Form`

In the next steps, you will create a `Form` that you can use to read records from a `File`.

To read data into a `Form`:

1. Open a new Windows project in Visual Studio and name it **ViewInvoices**.
2. Create a `Form` like the one shown in Figure 13-30 by making the following changes:

- Change the `Text` of `Form1` to **Invoice Data**.
- Add four `Labels` with the text, font, and approximate locations shown in Figure 13-30. (You can click the down arrow next to the `Text` property of a component and then type multiple lines of text.)
- Add a `Button` with the `Text` **View records**.
- Add three `TextBoxes`. Name them `invoiceBox`, `nameBox`, and `amountBox`, respectively.

Figure 13-30 The `ViewInvoices` `Form`

3. In the IDE, double-click the **View records** `Button` to view the code.
4. Add the shaded statements in 13-31. They include:
   - A `using System.IO` statement
   - Constants for the file delimiter character and the filename
   - A `string` into which records can be read and an array of `strings` into which to separate the string read in
   - A `FileStream` and `StreamReader` to handle the input file
   - Within the `button1_Click()` method, statements to read in a line from the file and split it into three components

NOTE If you used a different path for the Invoices.txt file in the `EnterInvoices` program, then change this file's path accordingly.

```
using System;
using System.Collections.Generic;
using System.ComponentModel;
using System.Data;
using System.Drawing;
using System.Text;
using System.Windows.Forms;
using System.IO;
```

Figure 13-31 Partial code for the `ViewInvoices` application (*continued*)

```
namespace ViewInvoices
{
    public partial class Form1 : Form
    {
        const char DELIM = ',';
        const string FILENAME = @"C:\C#\Chapter.13\Invoices.txt";
        string recordIn;
        string[] fields;
        static FileStream file = new FileStream(FILENAME,
           FileMode.Open, FileAccess.Read);
        StreamReader reader = new StreamReader(file);
        public Form1()
        {
            InitializeComponent();
        }

        private void button1_Click(object sender, EventArgs e)
        {
            recordIn = reader.ReadLine();
            fields = recordIn.Split(DELIM);
            invoiceBox.Text = fields[0];
            nameBox.Text = fields[1];
            amountBox.Text = fields[2];
        }
    }
}
```

Figure 13-31 (*continued*)

5. Add two `Close()` statements to the `Dispose()` method in the Form1Designer.cs file, as shown in Figure 13-32.

```
protected override void Dispose(bool disposing)
{
    reader.Close();
    file.Close();
    if (disposing && (components != null))
    {
         components.Dispose();
    }
    base.Dispose(disposing);
}
```

Figure 13-32 The `Dispose()` method for the `ViewInvoices` program

6. Save the project and then execute it. When the `Form` appears, click the `Button` to view records. You see the data for the first record you entered when you ran the `EnterInvoices` application; your `Form` should look like the one in Figure 13-33. Click the `Button` again to display the next record.

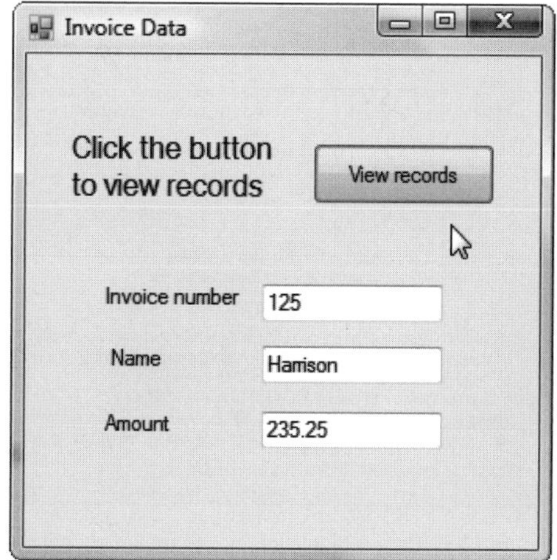

Figure 13-33 Typical execution of `ViewInvoices` program

7. Continue to click the `Button` to view each record. After you view the last record you entered, click the `Button` again. An unhandled exception is generated, as shown in Figure 13-34, because you attempted to read data past the end of the input file.

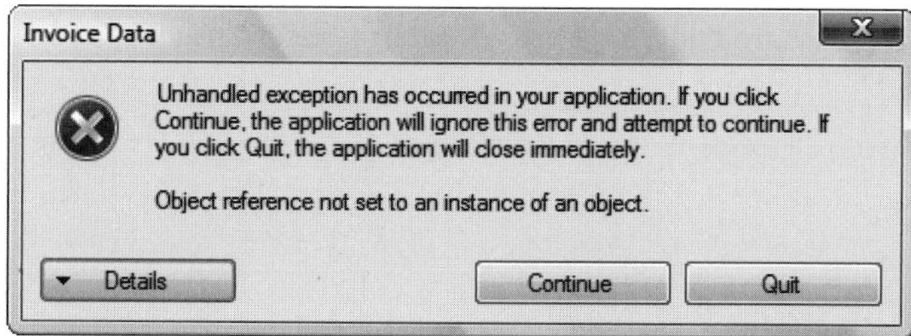

Figure 13-34 Error message window displayed after user attempts to read past the end of the file

8. Click the **Details** button in the `UnhandledException` window to view details of the error. Figure 13-35 shows that a `System.NullReferenceException` was thrown and not handled.

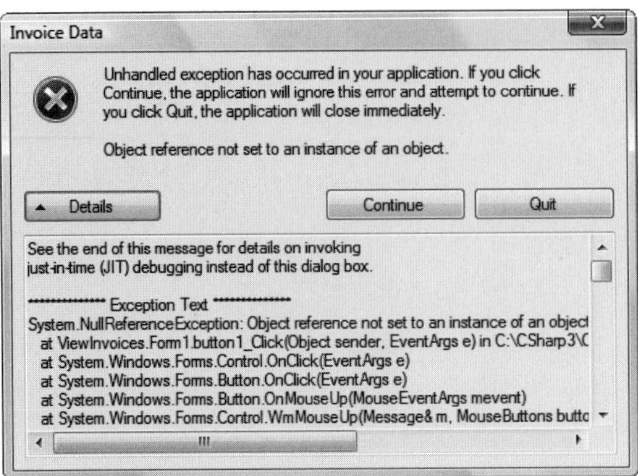

Figure 13-35 Details displayed by unhandled exception window

9. Click **Quit** to close the unhandled exception window.
10. To remedy the unhandled `NullReferenceException` problem, you could take any number of actions. Depending on the application, you might want to do one or more of the following:
    - » Display a message.
    - » Disallow any more button clicks.
    - » End the program.
    - » Reposition the file pointer to the file's beginning so the user can view the records again.

    For this example, you will take the first two actions: display a message and disallow further button clicks. Return to Visual Studio and locate the code for the `button1_Click()` method. Add a `try...catch` block, as shown in Figure 13-36. Place all the record-handling code

```
private void button1_Click(object sender, EventArgs e)
{
    try
    {
        recordIn = reader.ReadLine();
        fields = recordIn.Split(DELIM);
        invoiceBox.Text = fields[0];
        nameBox.Text = fields[1];
        amountBox.Text = fields[2];
    }
    catch (NullReferenceException)
    {
        label1.Text = "You have viewed\nall the records";
        button1.Enabled = false;
    }
}
```

Figure 13-36 The `button1_Click()` method modified to handle an exception

» **NOTE** You learned about exception handling and `try...catch` pairs in Chapter 9.

in a `try` block, and if a `NullReferenceException` is thrown, change the `Text` in `label1` and disable the View records `Button`.

11. Save the project and then execute it. This time, after you have viewed all the available records, an appropriate message is displayed and the button is disabled, as shown in Figure 13-37.

Figure 13-37 `ViewInvoices Form` after user has viewed last record

12. Dismiss the `Form`. Close Visual Studio.

CHAPTER SUMMARY

» Temporary storage is usually called computer memory or random access memory (RAM). This type of storage is volatile. Permanent storage, on the other hand, is nonvolatile. A computer file is a collection of information stored on a nonvolatile device in a computer system. Files exist on permanent storage devices. When you store data in a computer file on a persistent storage device, you write to the file. When you copy data from a file on a storage device into RAM, you read from the file. Computer users organize their files into folders or directories.

» The `File` class contains methods that allow you to access information about files. The `Directory` class provides you with information about directories or folders.

» A character can be any one of the letters, numbers, or other special symbols (such as punctuation marks) that comprise data. A field is a group of characters that has some meaning. Fields are grouped together to form records. A record is a collection of fields that contain data about an entity. Records are grouped to create files. A data file is a sequential access file when each record is read in order of its position in the file. Usually, the records are stored in order based on the value in some field. Before an application can use a data file, it must open the file by creating an object and associating a stream of bytes with that object. When you close a file, it is no longer available to your application.

» C# views files as a series of bytes that flow into a program from an input device or out of a program to an output device through an object called a stream, which functions as a pipeline or channel. When a C# program executes, three stream objects are created: `Console.In`, `Console.Out`, and `Console.Error`. When you write a program that stores data in a file, you create a `FileStream` object.

- Data can be written to a `StreamWriter` object using the `WriteLine()` method. Fields should be separated by a delimiter, which is a character used to specify the boundary between data items in text files.
- Data can be read from a `StreamReader` object using the `ReadLine()` method. The return value is a string. If the value of the returned string is `null`, then no more data exists in the file. After a record (line of data) is read in, the `Split()` method can be used to separate the data fields into an array of strings. The `Split()` method takes a character parameter and separates a string into substrings at each occurrence of the character delimiter.
- When you read data from a sequential file, subsequent records are read in order because a file's position pointer holds the byte number of the next byte to be read. To reread a file, you could close it and reopen it, or you can just reposition the file pointer using the `Seek()` method and the `SeekOrigin` enumeration.
- Serialization is the process of converting objects into streams of bytes. Deserialization is the reverse process; it converts streams of bytes back into objects. To create a class that can be serialized, you mark it with the `[Serializable]` attribute. An entire object can be written to or read from a data file with a single statement.

KEY TERMS

Random access memory (RAM) is temporary storage in a computer.

Volatile storage is the type that is lost when power is lost.

Nonvolatile storage is permanent storage; it is not lost when a computer loses power.

A **computer file** is a collection of information stored on a nonvolatile device in a computer system.

Permanent storage devices, such as hard disks, floppy disks, Zip disks, USB drives, reels or cassettes of magnetic tape, and optical disks, are used to store files.

Data files contain facts and figures.

Program files or **application files** store software instructions.

When you store data in a computer file on a permanent storage device, you **write to the file**.

When you copy data from a file on a storage device into RAM, you **read from the file**.

Persistent storage is nonvolatile storage.

The **root directory** is the main directory of a storage device.

Folders or **directories** are structures used to organize files on a storage device.

A **path** is composed of the disk drive in which a file resides plus the complete hierarchy of directories.

The **`File` class** contains methods that allow you to access information about files.

The **`Directory` class** provides information about directories or folders.

The **data hierarchy** is the relationship of characters, fields, records, and files.

A **character** is any one of the letters, numbers, or other special symbols (such as punctuation marks) that comprise data.

A computer's **character set** is the group of all the characters used to represent data on a particular computer.

A **field** is a character or group of characters that has some meaning.

A **record** is a collection of fields that contain data about an entity.

Data files consist of related records.

A **sequential access file** is a data file in which each record is read in order based on its position in the file; usually the records are stored in order based on the value in some field.

The **key field** is the field used to control the order of records in a sequential file.

Opening a file involves creating an object and associating a stream of bytes with it.

Closing a file means it is no longer available to an application.

A **stream** is a pipeline or channel through which bytes are input from and output to a file.

Programmers say `FileStream` **exposes** a stream around a file.

Binary files are files that can store any of the 256 combinations of bits in any byte instead of just those combinations that form readable text.

XML is an abbreviation of eXtensible Markup Language, which is a standard for exchanging data over the Internet.

A **delimiter** is a character used to specify the boundary between characters in text files.

A **CSV file** is one that contains comma-separated values.

A **token** is a block of text within a string that represents an entity or field.

The term **magic number** refers to the bad programming practice of hard-coding numbers in code without explanation.

A file's **file position pointer** holds the byte number of the next byte to be read.

Serialization is the process of converting objects into streams of bytes.

Deserialization is the process of converting streams of bytes back into objects.

REVIEW QUESTIONS

1. Random access memory is ___________.
   a. persistent
   b. volatile
   c. permanent
   d. sequential

2. A collection of facts and figures stored on a nonvolatile device in a computer system is a(n) ___________.
   a. data file
   b. application file
   c. operating system
   d. memory map

3. Which of the following is not permanent storage?
   a. RAM
   b. a hard disk
   c. a USB drive
   d. all of these

4. When you store data in a computer file on a persistent storage device, you are ________.
   a. reading
   b. directing
   c. writing
   d. rooting

5. Which of the following is not a `File` class method?
   a. `Create()`
   b. `Delete()`
   c. `Exists()`
   d. `End()`

6. In the data hierarchy, a group of characters that has some meaning, such as a last name or ID number, is a ________.
   a. byte
   b. field
   c. file
   d. record

7. When each record in a file is stored in order based on the value in some field, the file is a(n) ________ file.
   a. random access
   b. application
   c. formatted
   d. sequential

8. When you open a file, you create an object and associate a ________ of bytes with it.
   a. path
   b. folder
   c. stream
   d. directory

9. Which of the following is not part of a `FileStream` constructor?
   a. the file size
   b. the file mode
   c. the filename
   d. the type of access

10. When a file's mode is `Create`, a new file will be created ________.
    a. even if one with the same name already exists
    b. only if one with the same name does not already exist
    c. only if one with the same name already exists
    d. only if the access is `Read`

11. Which of the following is not a `FileStream` property?
    a. `CanRead`
    b. `CanExist`
    c. `CanSeek`
    d. `CanWrite`

12. Which of the following is not a file `Access` enumeration?
    a. `Read`
    b. `Write`
    c. `WriteRead`
    d. `ReadWrite`

13. A character used to specify the boundary between data items in text files is a __________.
    a. sentinel
    b. stopgap
    c. delimiter
    d. margin

14. Which character can be used to specify a boundary between characters in text files?
    a. a comma
    b. a semicolon
    c. either of these
    d. neither of these

15. After a `StreamReader` has been defined and associated with a file, the `ReadLine()` method can be used to __________.
    a. retrieve one line at a time from the file
    b. retrieve one character at a time from the file
    c. store one line at a time in a file
    d. split a `string` into tokens

16. The argument to the `Split()` method is __________.
    a. `void`
    b. the number of fields into which to split a record
    c. the character that identifies a new field in a `string`
    d. a `string` that can be split into tokens

17. The `Split()` method stores its results in __________.
    a. a `string`
    b. an array of `strings`
    c. an appropriate data type for each token
    d. an array of bytes

18. A file's __________ holds the byte number of the next byte to be read.
    a. index indicator
    b. position pointer
    c. header file
    d. key field

19. The process of converting objects into streams of bytes is __________.
    a. extrication
    b. splitting
    c. mapping
    d. serialization

20. Which of the following is serializable?
    a. an `int`
    b. an array of `ints`
    c. a `string`
    d. all of the above

EXERCISES

1. Create a program that allows a user to continually enter directory names until the user types "end". If the directory name exists, display a list of the files in it; otherwise, display a message indicating the directory does not exist. If the directory exists and files are listed, prompt the user to enter one of the filenames. If the file exists, display its creation date and time; otherwise, display a message indicating the file does not exist. Save the program as **TestFileAndDirectory.cs**. Create as many test directories and files as necessary to test your program. Figure 13-38 shows a typical execution.

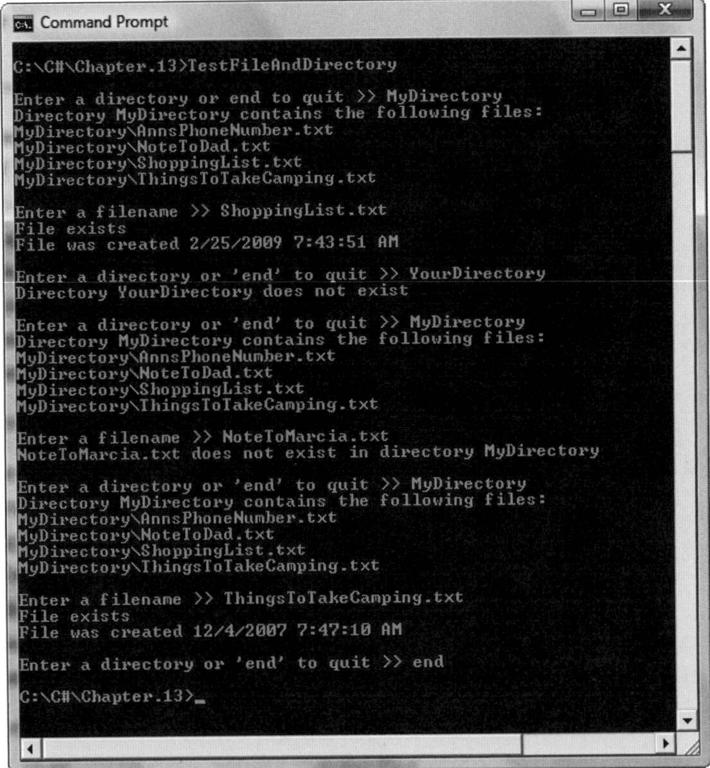

Figure 13-38 Typical execution of `TestFileAndDirectory` program

2. Create a file that contains your favorite movie quote. Use a text editor such as Notepad and save the file as **Quote.txt**. Copy the file contents and paste them into a word-processing program such as Word. Save the file as **Quote.doc**. Write an application that displays the sizes of the two files as well as the ratio of their sizes to each other. To discover a file's

size, you can create a `System.IO.FileInfo` object using a statement such as the following, where `FILE_NAME` is a string that contains the name of the file:

```
FileInfo wordInfo = new FileInfo(FILE_NAME);
```

Save the file as **FileComparison.cs.**

3. Using Visual Studio, create a `Form` like the one shown in Figure 13-39. Specify a directory on your system, and when the `Form` loads, list the files it contains in a `CheckedListBox`. Allow the user to click a file's check box and display the file's creation date and time. (Each time the user checks a new filename, display its creation date in place of the original selection.) Save the project as **TestFileAndDirectory2**. Create as many files as necessary to test your program. Figure 13-39 shows a typical execution.

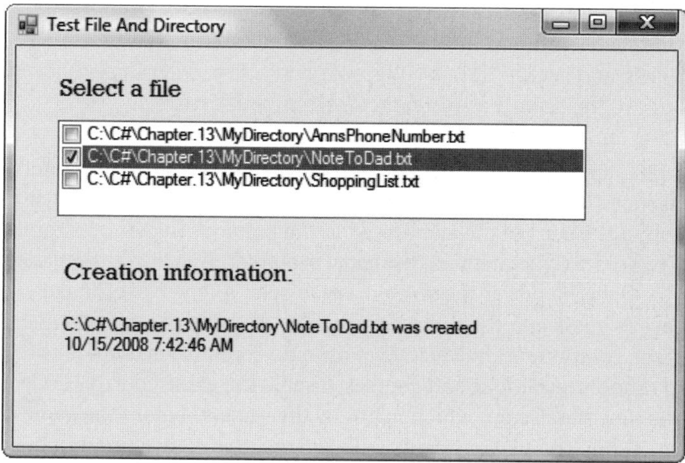

Figure 13-39 Typical execution of `TestFileAndDirectory2` program

4. a. Create a `Friend` class in which you can store your friends' first and last names, phone numbers, and the month and day of your friends' birthdays. Write a program that prompts you to enter friends' data and saves each record to a file. Save the program as **WriteFriendRecords.cs.**

   b. Create a program that reads the file created in Exercise 4a and displays each friend's data to the screen. Save the programs as **ReadFriendRecords.cs.**

   c. Create a program that prompts you for a birth month, reads the file created in Exercise 4a, and displays data for each friend who has a birthday in the specified month. Save the programs as **FriendBirthdayReminder.cs.**

5. a. In the Visual Studio IDE, design a `Form` that allows a user to select options for the background color and size and to give the `Form` a title. The `Form` should look like the one shown in Figure 13-40. Change each feature of the `Form` as the user makes selections. After the user clicks the "Save form settings" `Button`, save the color, size, and title as strings to a file and disable the button. Save the project as **CustomizeAForm**.

   b. In the Visual Studio IDE, design a `Form` like the one in Figure 13-40, except include a `Button` to retrieve the `Form` settings. When the user clicks the "Retrieve form settings" `Button`, read the settings from the file saved in the `CustomizeAForm` project, and set the `Form`'s color, size, and title to the values that were saved previously. Save the project as **RetrieveCustomizedForm**.

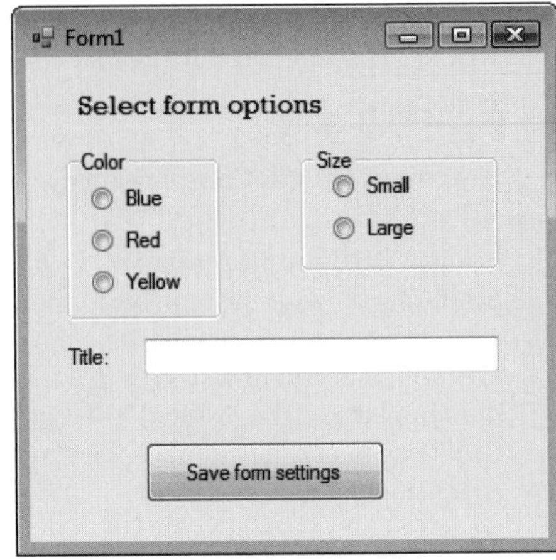

Figure 13-40 Form in `CustomizeAForm` project

6. Using the Visual Studio IDE, create a `Form` that contains a game in which the computer randomly selects one of three letters (A, B, or C) 10 times, and the user tries to guess which letter was selected. At the start of the game, read in the previous high score from a data file. (Create this file to hold "0" the first time the game is played.) Display the previous high score on the `Form` to show the player the score to try to beat. As the player makes each guess, show the player's guess and the computer's choice, and award a point if the player correctly guesses the computer's choice. Keep a running count of the number of correct guesses. After 10 random selections and guesses, disable the game controls and create a file that holds the new high score, which might be the same as before the game or a new higher number. When the player begins a new game, the high score will be displayed on the `Form` as the new score to beat. Save the project as **HighScore**.

DEBUGGING EXERCISES

Each of the following files in the Chapter.13 folder on your Student Disk has syntax and/or logical errors. In each case, determine the problem and fix the program. After you correct the errors, save each file using the same filename preceded with *Fixed*. For example, save DebugThirteen1.cs as **FixedDebugThirteen1.cs**.

a. DebugThirteen1.cs

b. DebugThirteen2.cs

c. DebugThirteen3.cs

d. DebugThirteen4.cs

UP FOR DISCUSSION

1. In Exercise 2 earlier in this chapter, what did you discover about the size difference between files that hold the same contents but were created using different software (such as Word and Notepad)? Why do you think the file sizes are so different, even though the files contain the same data?
2. Suppose your employer asks you to write a program that lists all the company's employees, their salaries, and their ages. You are provided with the company personnel file to use as input. You decide to take the file home so you can create the program over the weekend. Is this acceptable? What if the file contained only employees' names and departments, but not more sensitive data such as salaries and ages?

CHAPTERFOURTEEN

14

USING LINQ TO ACCESS DATA IN C# PROGRAMS

In this chapter you will:

Understand relational database fundamentals
Create databases and table descriptions
Be able to identify primary keys
Understand database structure notation
Create SQL queries
Create an Access database
Understand implicitly typed variables
Understand LINQ
Retrieve data from an Access database in C#
Use LINQ queries with an Access database table
Use LINQ operators to sort and group data

Businesses run by using data. Most businesses would be damaged severely if their data was lost—for example, customers could not be contacted, employees could not be paid, and orders could not be shipped. Well-run businesses do not just possess a lot of data; the data must be organized to be useful. When a business's data is structured in a useful manner, the business can improve its performance. For example, salespeople can discover which customers prefer which products or services, and administrators can discover which employees are the most productive. Businesses can determine which products and services produce the most profit and which should be dropped. Relational databases provide a means to accomplish all these tasks.

» NOTE
LINQ is pronounced "link".

In this chapter you will learn about databases. You also will learn about LINQ, which is a Visual Studio tool for accessing data stored in databases and other collections, and you will learn how to incorporate LINQ into your C# programs. This chapter is only a brief introduction to these topics. You can buy entire books on database construction and theory, and other books on every detail of LINQ. This chapter covers only the fundamentals of each topic so you can begin to appreciate how your C# programs have the potential to satisfy important business data needs.

UNDERSTANDING RELATIONAL DATABASE FUNDAMENTALS

» NOTE
The term *data hierarchy* was introduced in Chapter 13 when you learned about files.

When you store data items for use within computer systems, they are often stored in what is known as a data hierarchy, where the smallest usable unit of data is the character, often a letter or number. Characters are grouped together to form fields, such as `firstName`, `lastName`, and `socialSecurityNumber`. Related fields are often grouped together to form records—groups of fields that go together because they represent attributes of some entity, such as an employee, a customer, an inventory item, or a bank account. Files are composed of related records; for example, a file might contain a record for each employee in a company or each account at a bank.

Most organizations store many files that contain the data they need to operate their businesses. For example, businesses often need to maintain files that contain data about employees, customers, inventory items, and orders. Many organizations use database software to organize the information in these files. A **database** holds a file, or more frequently, a group of files that an organization needs to support its applications. In a database, the files often are called **tables** because you can arrange their contents in rows and columns. Real-life examples of database-like tables abound. For example, consider the listings in a telephone book. Each listing in a city directory might contain four columns, as shown in Figure 14-1—last name, first name, street address, and phone number. Although your local phone directory might not store its data in the rigid columnar format shown in the figure, it could. You can see that each column represents a field and that each row represents one record. You can picture a table within a database in the same way.

Last Name	First Name	Address	Phone
Abbott	William	123 Oak Lane	490-8920
Ackerman	Kimberly	467 Elm Drive	787-2781
Adams	Stanley	8120 Pine Street	787-0129
Adams	Violet	347 Oak Lane	490-8912
Adams	William	12 Second Street	490-3667

Figure 14-1 A telephone book table

NOTE In Chapter 6, you learned that arrays also are sometimes referred to as tables. Arrays (stored in memory) and tables (stored in databases) are similar in that both contain rows and columns. When an array has multiple columns, all must have the same data type. The same is not true for tables stored in databases.

Figure 14-1 includes five records, each representing a unique person. It is relatively easy to scan this short list of names to find a person's phone number; of course, telephone books contain many more records. Some telephone book users, such as telemarketers or even the phone company, might prefer to use a book in which the records are organized in telephone-number order. Others, such as door-to-door salespeople, might prefer a telephone book in which the records are organized in street-address order. Most people, however, prefer a telephone book in which the records are organized as shown, in alphabetical order by last name. It is most convenient for different users when computerized databases can sort records in various orders based on the contents of different columns.

Unless you are reading a telephone book for a very small town, a last name alone often is not sufficient to identify a person. In the example in Figure 14-1, three people have the last name of Adams. For these records, you need to examine the first name before you can determine the correct phone number. In a large city, many people might have the same first and last names; in that case, you might also need to examine the street address to identify a person. As with the telephone book, most computerized database tables require a way to identify each record uniquely, even if it means using multiple columns. A value that uniquely identifies a record is called a **primary key**, or a **key** for short. Key fields often are defined as a single column, but as with the telephone book, keys can be constructed from multiple columns. A key constructed from multiple columns is a **compound key**, also known as a **composite key**.

Telephone books are republished periodically because changes have occurred—new people have moved into the city and become telephone customers, and others have left, canceled service, or changed phone numbers. With computerized database tables, you also need to add, delete, and modify records, although usually far more frequently than phone books are published.

As with telephone books, computerized database tables frequently contain thousands of records, or rows, and each row might contain entries in dozens of columns. Handling and organizing all the data contained in an organization's tables requires sophisticated software.

Database management software, also known as a **database management system (DBMS)**, is a set of programs that allows users to:

- » Create table descriptions.
- » Identify keys.
- » Add, delete, and update records within a table.
- » Arrange records within a table so they are sorted by different fields.
- » Write questions that select specific records from a table for viewing.
- » Write questions that combine information from multiple tables. This is possible because the database management software establishes and maintains relationships between the columns in the tables. A group of database tables from which you can make these connections is a **relational database**.
- » Create reports that allow users to easily interpret your data, and create forms that allow users to view and enter data using an easy-to-manage interactive screen.
- » Keep data secure by employing sophisticated security measures.

If you have used different word-processing or spreadsheet programs, you know that each version works a little differently, although each carries out the same types of tasks. Like other computer programs, each database management software package operates differently; however, with each, you need to perform the same types of tasks.

»TWO TRUTHS AND A LIE: UNDERSTANDING RELATIONAL DATABASE FUNDAMENTALS

1. Files are composed of related records, and records are composed of fields.
2. In a database, files often are called tables because you can arrange their contents in rows and columns.
3. Key fields always are defined as a single table column.

The false statement is #3. Key fields often are defined as a single table column, but keys can be constructed from multiple columns. A key constructed from multiple columns is a compound or composite key.

CREATING DATABASES AND TABLE DESCRIPTIONS

Creating a useful database requires a lot of planning and analysis. You must decide what data will be stored, how that data will be divided between tables, and how the tables will interrelate. Before you create any tables, you must create the database itself. With most database software packages, creating the database that will hold the tables requires nothing more than providing a name for the database and indicating the physical location, perhaps a hard disk drive, where the database will be stored. When you save a table, one convention recommends that you use a name that begins with the prefix “tbl”—for example, `tblCustomers`. Your databases often become filled with a variety of objects—tables, forms that users can use for data entry, reports that organize the data for viewing, queries that select subsets of data for viewing, and so on. Using naming conventions, such as beginning each table name with a prefix that identifies it as a table, helps you to keep track of the various objects in your system.

»NOTE When you save a table description, many database management programs suggest a default, generic name such as `Table1`. Usually, a more descriptive name is more useful to you as you continue to create objects.

»NOTE Beginning table names with the `tbl` prefix is part of the **Leszynski naming convention** (LNC). This convention is most popular with Microsoft Access users and Visual Basic programmers. This format is just a convention, and is not required by any database. Your instructor or supervisor might approve of a different convention.

Before you can enter any data into a database table, you must design the table. At minimum, this involves two tasks:

- You must decide what columns your table needs, and provide names for them.
- You must provide a data type for each column.

For example, assume you are designing a customer database table. Figure 14-2 shows some column names and data types you might use.

Column	Data Type
`customerID`	Text
`lastName`	Text
`firstName`	Text
`streetAddress`	Text
`balanceOwed`	Numeric

Figure 14-2 Customer table description

»NOTE A table description closely resembles the list of variables that you have used with every program throughout this book.

»NOTE It is important to think carefully about the original design of a database. After the database has been created and data has been entered, it could be difficult and time consuming to make changes.

The table description in Figure 14-2 uses just two data types—text and numeric. Text columns can hold any type of characters—letters or digits. Numeric columns can hold numbers only. Depending on the database management software you use, you might have many more sophisticated data types at your disposal. For example, some database software divides the numeric data type into several subcategories such as integers (whole number only) and double-precision numbers (numbers that contain decimals). Other options might include special categories for currency numbers (representing dollars and cents), dates, and Boolean columns (representing true or false). At the least, all database software recognizes the distinction between text and numeric data.

»NOTE Throughout this book, you have been aware of the distinction that computers make between text and numeric data. Because of the way computers handle data, every type of software observes this distinction. Throughout this book, the term "string" has been used to describe text fields. The term "text" is used in this chapter only because popular database packages use it.

»NOTE Unassigned variables within computer programs might be empty (containing a null value), or might contain unknown or garbage values. Similarly, columns in database tables might also contain null or unknown values. When a field in a database contains a null value, it does not mean that the field holds a 0 or a space; it means that no data has been entered for the field at all. Although "null" and "empty" are used synonymously by many database developers, the terms have slightly different meanings to some programming professionals such as Visual Basic programmers.

The table description in Figure 14-2 uses one-word column names and camel casing, in the same way that variable names have been defined throughout this book. Many database software packages do not require that data column names be single words without embedded spaces, but many database table designers prefer single-word names because they resemble variable names in programs. In addition, when you write programs that access a database table, the single-word field names can be used "as is," without special syntax to indicate the names that represent a single field. As a further advantage, when you use a single word to label each database column, it is easier to understand whether just one column is being referenced, or several.

The `customerID` column in Figure 14-2 is defined as a text field or text column. If `customerID` numbers are composed entirely of digits, this column could also be defined as numeric. Some database designers feel that key fields should usually be numeric. However, some database designers feel that columns should be defined as numeric only if they need to be—that is, only if they might be used in arithmetic calculations. The description in Figure 14-2 follows this convention by declaring `customerID` to be a text column, but it would also be reasonable to declare it as a numeric column.

»NOTE Among database designers, there is controversy about the best data type for key fields. As you continue to study database creation, you will learn more about the relevant issues and be able to establish your own opinions about them.

Many database management software packages allow you to add a narrative description of each data column of a table. This allows you to make comments that become part of the table. These comments do not affect the way the table operates; they simply serve as documentation for those who are reading a table description. For example, you might want to make a note that `customerID` should consist of five digits, or that `balanceOwed` should not exceed a given limit. Some software allows you to specify that values for a certain column are required—the user cannot create a record without providing data for these columns. In addition, you might be able to indicate value limits for a column—high and low numbers between which the column contents must fall.

»TWO TRUTHS AND A LIE: CREATING DATABASES AND TABLE DESCRIPTIONS

1. Databases are often filled with multiple objects such as tables, forms, and queries.
2. Designing a table involves deciding how many rows your table needs and filling them with appropriate data.
3. Many database table designers prefer single-word column names because they resemble variable names in programs, because the names can be easily used in programs, and because people can more easily understand whether one or several columns are being referenced.

The false statement is # 2. Designing a table involves deciding what columns your table needs, providing names for them, and providing a data type for each column.

IDENTIFYING PRIMARY KEYS

In most tables you create for a database, you want to identify a column, or possibly a combination of columns, as the table's key column or field, also called the primary key. The primary key in a table is the column that makes each record different from all others. For example, in the customer table in Figure 14-2, the logical choice for a primary key is the `customerID` column—each customer record that is entered into the customer table has a unique value in this column. Many customers might have the same first name or last name (or both), and multiple customers also might have the same street address or balance due. However, each customer possesses a unique ID number.

»NOTE In some database software packages, such as Microsoft Access, you indicate a primary key simply by selecting a column name and clicking a button that is labeled with a key icon.

Other typical examples of primary keys include:

- » A student ID number in a table that contains college student information
- » A part number in a table that contains inventory items
- » A Social Security number in a table that contains employee information

»NOTE A primary key should be immutable, meaning that a value does not change during normal operation.

In each of these examples, the primary key uniquely identifies the row. For example, each student has a unique ID number assigned by the college. Other columns in a student table would not be adequate keys—many students have the same last name, first name, hometown, or major.

»NOTE Even if a database table contains only one employee named Smith, for example, or only one employee with the job title of Salesperson, those fields are still not good primary key candidates because more Smiths and salespeople could be added later. Analyzing existing data is not a foolproof way to select a good key; you must also consider likely future data.

»NOTE It is no coincidence that each of the preceding examples of a key is a number, such as a student ID number or item number. Often, assigning a number to each row in a table is the simplest and most efficient method of obtaining a useful key. However, it is possible that a table's key could be a text field.

»NOTE Sometimes, several columns could serve as the key. For example, if an employee record contains both a company-assigned employee ID and a Social Security number, then both columns are candidate keys. After you choose a primary key from among candidate keys, the remaining candidate keys become alternate keys.

The primary key is important for several reasons:

- You can configure your database software to prevent multiple records from containing the same value in this column, thus avoiding data-entry errors.
- You might want to sort your records in this order before displaying or printing them.
- You use this column when setting up relationships between this table and others that will become part of the same database.

In addition, you need to understand the concept of the primary key when you normalize a database. **Normalization** is the process of designing and creating a set of database tables that satisfies users' needs and avoids many potential problems such as data redundancies and anomalies. **Data redundancy** is the unnecessary repetition of data. An **anomaly** is an irregularity in a database's design that causes problems and inconveniences. To keep the examples in this chapter simple, only single database tables are used. However, as you grow proficient in database use and constructions, you will want to create databases with relationships between multiple tables, which requires a more thorough understanding of normalization.

»NOTE As an example of data redundancy, consider a table of names and addresses in which many addresses are in the same zip code. Instead of storing the same city and state name with each record, it is more efficient to store only the zip code with each record, and then to associate the table with another table that contains a list of zip codes and the corresponding cities and states.

»NOTE There are many types of anomalies. For example, an anomaly occurs when the same data is stored in multiple locations. For example, if a database contains a table of items in stock and their prices, and another table contains customer orders, including items and prices, then any price changes must be made in multiple locations, increasing the chance for error.

Usually, after you have identified the necessary fields and their data types and identified the primary key, you are ready to save your table description and begin to enter data.

»TWO TRUTHS AND A LIE: IDENTIFYING PRIMARY KEYS

1. The primary key in a table is the record that appears first in a sorted list.
2. Normalization is the process of designing and creating a set of database tables that satisfies users' needs and avoids many potential problems.
3. Data redundancy is the unnecessary repetition of data.

The false statement is #1. The primary key in a table is the column that makes each record different from all others.

UNDERSTANDING DATABASE STRUCTURE NOTATION

A shorthand way to describe a table is to use the table name followed by parentheses that contain all the field names, with the primary key underlined. Thus, when a table is named `tblStudents` and contains columns named `idNumber`, `lastName`, `firstName`, and `gradePointAverage`, and `idNumber` is the key, you can reference the table using the following notation:

```
tblStudents(idNumber, lastName, firstName, gradePointAverage)
```

Although this shorthand notation does not provide information about data types or range limits on values, it does provide a quick overview of the table's structure.

>> **NOTE** Some database designers insert an asterisk after the key instead of underlining it.

>> **NOTE** The key does not have to be the first attribute listed in a table reference, but frequently it is.

>> TWO TRUTHS AND A LIE: UNDERSTANDING DATABASE STRUCTURE NOTATION

1. A shorthand way to describe a table is to use the table name followed by parentheses that contain all the field names.
2. Typically, when you describe a table using database structure notation, the primary key is underlined.
3. Database structure notation provides you with information about column names, their data types, and their range limits.

The false statement is #3. Although this shorthand notation does not provide information about data types or range limits on values, it does provide a quick overview of the structure of a table.

CREATING SQL QUERIES

Data tables often contain hundreds or thousands of rows; making sense out of that much information is a daunting task. Frequently, you want to cull subsets of data from a table you have created. For example, you might want to view only those customers with an address in a specific state, only inventory items whose quantity in stock has fallen below the normal reorder point, or only employees who participate in an insurance plan. Besides limiting records, you might also want to limit the columns that you view. For example, student records might contain dozens of fields, but a school administrator might only be interested in looking at names and grade point averages (GPAs). The questions that cause the database software to extract the appropriate records from a table and specify the fields to be viewed are called queries; a **query** is simply a request using syntax that the database software can understand.

Depending on the software you use, you might create a query by filling in blanks (using a language called **query by example**) or by writing statements similar to those in many programming languages. The most common language that database administrators use to access data in their tables is **Structured Query Language**, or **SQL**. The basic form of the SQL command that retrieves selected records from a table is **SELECT-FROM-WHERE**. The SELECT-FROM-WHERE SQL statement:

- *Selects* the columns you want to view
- *From* a specific table
- *Where* one or more conditions are met

NOTE "SQL" frequently is pronounced "sequel"; however, several SQL product Web sites insist that the official pronunciation is "S-Q-L." Similarly, some people pronounce GUI as "gooey" and others insist that it should be "G-U-I." In general, a preferred pronunciation evolves in an organization. The **TLA**, which is a three-letter abbreviation for *three-letter abbreviation*, is the most popular type of abbreviation in technical terminology.

For example, suppose a customer table named `tblCustomer` contains data about your business customers and that the structure of the table is `tblCustomer(custId, lastName, state)`. Then, a statement such as:

```
SELECT custId, lastName FROM tblCustomer WHERE state = "WI"
```

NOTE Conventionally, SQL keywords such as `SELECT` appear entirely in uppercase; this book follows that convention.

would display a new table that contains two columns—`custId` and `lastName`—and only as many rows as needed to hold customers whose state column contains "WI". Besides using = to mean "equal to," you can use the comparison conditions > (greater than), < (less than), >= (greater than or equal to), and <= (less than or equal to). As you have already learned from working with programming variables throughout this book, text field values are always contained within quotes, whereas numeric values are not.

NOTE In database management systems, a particular way of looking at a database is sometimes called a **view**. Typically, a view arranges records in some order and makes only certain fields visible. The different views provided by database software are virtual; that is, they do not affect the physical organization of the database.

To select all fields for each record in a table, you can use the asterisk as a wildcard; a **wildcard** is a symbol that means "any" or "all." For example, `SELECT * FROM tblCustomer WHERE state = " WI "` would select all columns for every customer whose state is "WI", not just specifically named columns. To select all customers from a table, you can omit the `WHERE` clause in a `SELECT-FROM-WHERE` statement. In other words, `SELECT * FROM tblCustomer` selects all columns for all customers. You learned about making selections in computer programs much earlier in this book, and you have probably noticed that `SELECT-FROM-WHERE` statements serve the same purpose as programming decisions. As with decision statements in programs, SQL allows you to create compound conditions using `AND` or `OR` operators. In addition, you can precede any condition with a `NOT` operator to achieve a negative result. In summary, Figure 14-3 shows a database table named `tblInventory` with the following structure:

```
tblInventory(itemNumber, description, quantityInStock, price)
```

The table contains five records. Figure 14-4 lists several typical SQL `SELECT` statements you might use with `tblInventory`, and explains each.

itemNumber	description	quantityInStock	price
144	Pkg 12 party plates	250	$14.99
231	Helium balloons	180	$2.50
267	Paper streamers	68	$1.89
312	Disposable tablecloth	20	$6.99
383	Pkg 20 napkins	315	$2.39

Figure 14-3 The `tblInventory` table

SQL Statement	Explanation
`SELECT itemNumber, price FROM tblInventory`	Shows only the item number and price for all five records.
`SELECT * FROM tblInventory WHERE price > 5.00`	Shows all fields from only those records in which price is greater than $5.00—items 144 and 312.
`SELECT itemNumber FROM tblInventory WHERE quantityInStock > 200 AND price > 10.00`	Shows item number 144—the only record that has a quantity greater than 200 as well as a price greater than $10.00.
`SELECT description, price FROM tblInventory WHERE description = "Pkg 20 napkins" OR itemNumber < 200`	Shows the description and price fields for the package of 12 party plates and the package of 20 napkins. Each selected record only needs to satisfy one of the two criteria.
`SELECT itemNumber FROM tblInventory WHERE NOT price < 14.00`	Shows the item number for the only record in which the price is not less than $14.00—item 144.

Figure 14-4 Sample SQL statements and explanations

»TWO TRUTHS AND A LIE: CREATING SQL QUERIES

1. A query is a question that causes database software to extract appropriate fields and records from a table.
2. The most common language that database administrators use to access data in their tables is Structured Query Language, or SQL.
3. The basic form of the SQL command that retrieves selected records from a table is `RETRIEVE-FROM-SELECTION`.

The false statement is # 3. The basic form of the SQL command that retrieves selected records from a table is `SELECT-FROM-WHERE`.

CREATING AN ACCESS DATABASE

»NOTE Access was the name of an earlier failed Microsoft communications program. The corporation reused the name when it developed its database software in 1992.

Microsoft Office Access is a relational database that is part of some versions of the Microsoft Office 2007 system. It combines the relational Microsoft Jet Database Engine with a GUI user interface and other tools. Access is not the only database on the market, but it is convenient for many users because it comes packaged with some versions of Microsoft Office. Using Access correctly and efficiently can take some time to learn; at most colleges, you can take at least a two-semester course to learn Access thoroughly. This section introduces you to Access as an example of a typical database.

»NOTE Other popular database packages include Microsoft SQL, MySQL, Borland Paradox, FileMaker Pro, Lotus Approach, Oracle XE, and Sun StarBase.

Figure 14-5 shows the environment in which a database table is designed in Access. Suppose Cartman College wants to keep track of some student data in a database. To keep the example simple, suppose the college wants to store only an ID number, first and last names, and a GPA for each student. In Access, a database developer can type field names for the data that will be stored and can assign an appropriate data type for each. In Figure 14-5, a `tblStudents` table is defined, including fields for `ID`, `LastName`, `FirstName`, and `GradePointAverage`.

»NOTE In the "You Do It" section at the end of this chapter, you can walk through the specific steps to create your own database.

»NOTE When you open the Cartman College database file that is provided with your Student files, if you do not immediately see the Design View as shown in Figure 14-5, you can click the Home tab, click the down arrow under View, and click Design View.

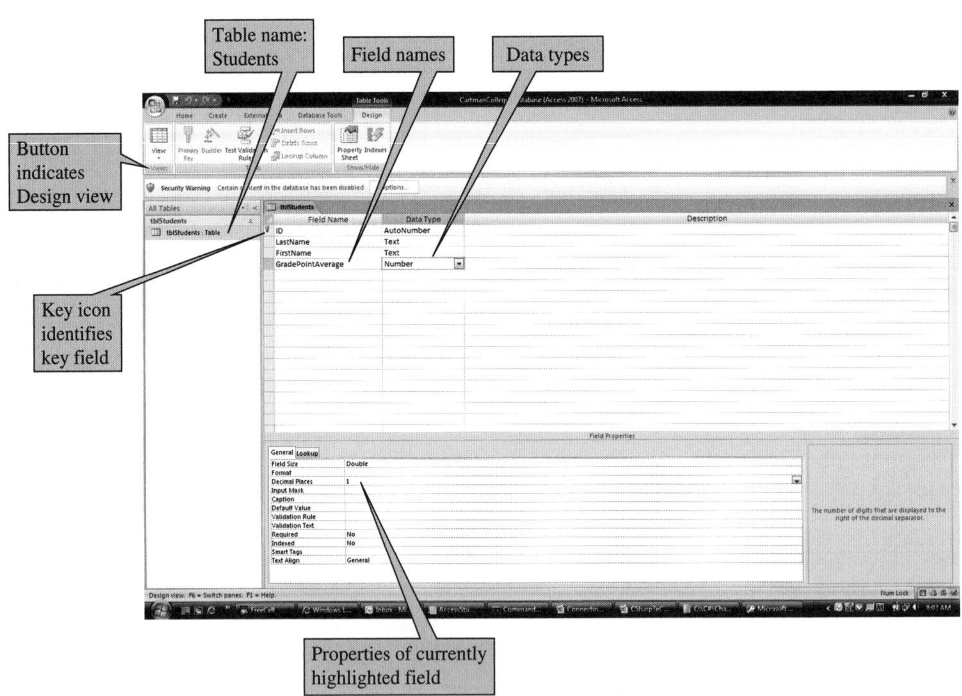

Figure 14-5 The Design view of the `tblStudents` table in Access

»NOTE Figure 14-5 shows that the ID field type was chosen to be `AutoNumber`, which means Access will automatically assign consecutive numbers to each new record as it is entered.

After a table's design has been completed, a user can enter data into the table. Figure 14-6 shows the `tblStudents` table in Access's Datasheet view, in which a user can type data like it would be typed into a spreadsheet. The column headings in the datasheet are provided automatically based on the names that were selected in the Design view.

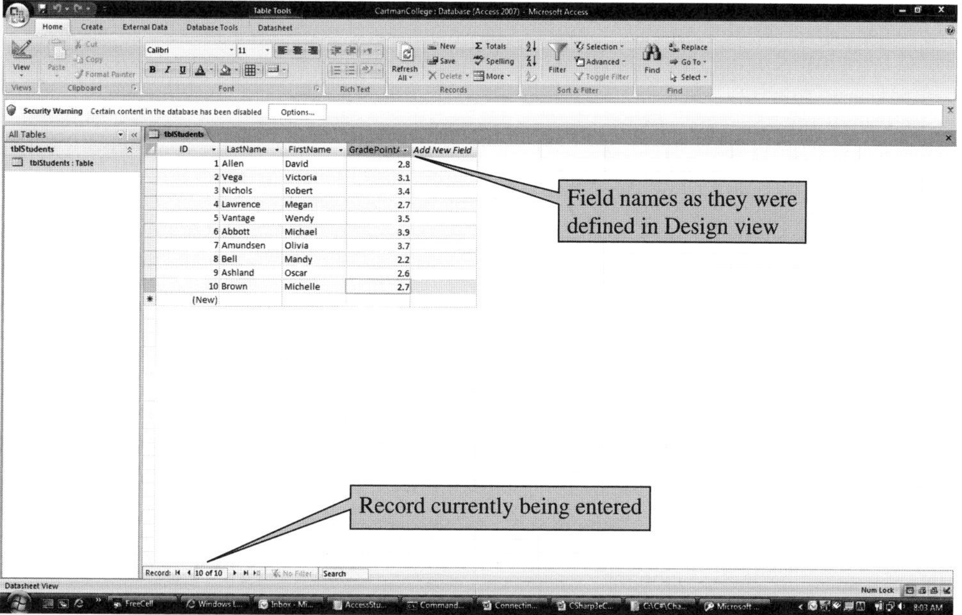

Figure 14-6 The Datasheet view of the `tblStudents` table in Access

In a database actually used by a college, many more fields would be stored for each student and additional tables would be created for courses, faculty, and so on. However, this small database provides enough data to demonstrate using C# to access the stored data.

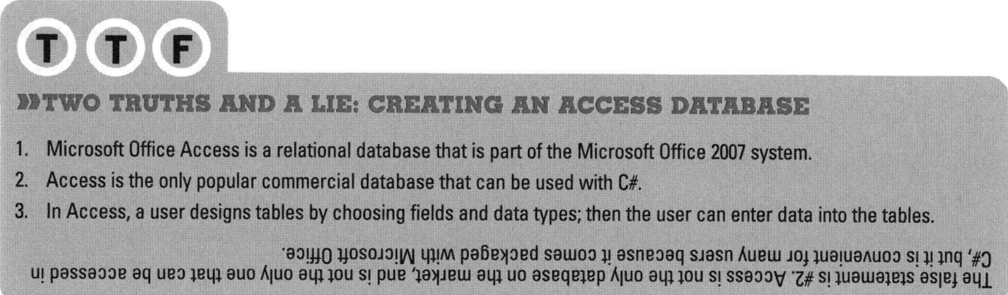

T T F

»TWO TRUTHS AND A LIE: CREATING AN ACCESS DATABASE

1. Microsoft Office Access is a relational database that is part of the Microsoft Office 2007 system.
2. Access is the only popular commercial database that can be used with C#.
3. In Access, a user designs tables by choosing fields and data types; then the user can enter data into the tables.

The false statement is #2. Access is not the only database on the market, and is not the only one that can be used in C#, but it is convenient for many users because it comes packaged with Microsoft Office.

UNDERSTANDING IMPLICITLY TYPED VARIABLES

Implicitly typed variables are a new feature in C# 3. An **implicitly typed variable** has a data type that is inferred from the expression used to initialize the variable. To create an implicitly typed variable, you use a variable declaration with **`var`** as the data type. When you use an implicitly typed variable, the C# compiler decides on a data type for you. This process is called **type inference**. When you use an implicitly typed variable, an object's set of allowed properties and methods is not fixed when the code is written but is determined when the program executes.

»NOTE Using `var` to create implicitly typed variables is also called **duck typing** because it fits the phrase, "If it walks like a duck and quacks like a duck, I would call it a duck." The phrase is attributed to an American writer and poet, James Whitcomb Riley, who lived from 1849 to 1916.

For example, in the following statement, `money` is implicitly typed as a `double` because the value assigned to the variable is a `double`:

```
var money = 1.99;
```

Because `money` is a `double`, you can, for example, perform arithmetic with it. If the declaration had been `var money = "a dollar ninety-nine";`, then `money` would be a string and you could not perform arithmetic with it. The statement `var money = 1.99;` has exactly the same meaning as the following:

```
double money = 1.99;
```

»NOTE Although each of these uses of `var` is a valid C# statement, you should not use `var` simply to avoid declaring a data type for an item. The `var` keyword should be used only in specific situations, such as with LINQ statements.

Other examples of assigning values to implicitly typed variables include the following:

- `var age = 30;` has the same meaning as `int age = 30;`
- `var name = "Roxy";` has the same meaning as `string name = "Roxy";`
- `var book = new Book();` has the same meaning as `Book book = new Book();`
- `var emp = new Employee(101, "Smith", 15.00);` has the same meaning as `Employee emp = new Employee(101, "Smith", 15.00);`

In Chapter 5 you learned to use the `foreach` statement to process array elements. For example, the following code displays each `double` in the `payRate` array:

```
double[] payRate = {6.00, 7.35, 8.12, 12.45, 22.22};
foreach(double money in payRate)
   Console.WriteLine("{0}", money.ToString("C"));
```

In this example, `money` is declared as a `double` and is used as the **iteration variable**—the variable that is used to hold each successive value in the array. Alternatively, you can declare the iteration variable in a `foreach` statement to be an implicitly typed local variable. In this case, the iteration variable's type is inferred from the collection type it uses. For example, the same results can be achieved with the following:

```
double[] payRate = {6.00, 7.35, 8.12, 12.45, 22.22};
foreach(var money in payRate)
   Console.WriteLine("{0}", money.ToString("C"));
```

In this example, `money` is implied to be a `double` because `payRate` is an array of `doubles`. In Figure 14-7, the implicitly typed variable `n` is an `int` because `numbers` is an `int` array. Figure 14-8 shows the program's output.

```
using System;
public class ImplicitVariableDemo
{
   public static void Main()
   {
      int[] numbers = { 6, 4, 2, 1, 8, 3, 7, 5, 2, 0 };
      Console.WriteLine("Numbers List");
      foreach (var n in numbers)
         Console.WriteLine(n);
   }
}
```

Figure 14-7 The `ImplicitVariableDemo` class

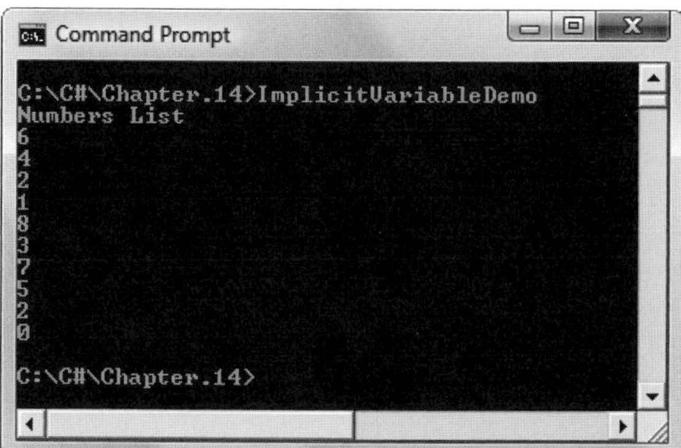

Figure 14-8 Output of the `ImplicitVariableDemo` program

When you declare a variable, usually you want to assign a data type. One advantage of a modern programming language like C# is that it is **strongly typed**. When a language is strongly typed, severe restrictions are placed on what data types can be mixed. Strong typing prevents certain errors—for example, the loss of data that might occur if you inadvertently assigned a double to an integer. However, you will use implicitly typed variables frequently in LINQ statements, which you will use to access data stored in a database.

> **NOTE** Unlike C#, Visual Basic is considered to be a weakly typed language. If you run a VB program in Visual Studio 2008, you have the option of declaring `Option Strict`, which means that types will be checked.

»TWO TRUTHS AND A LIE: UNDERSTANDING IMPLICITLY TYPED VARIABLES

1. An implicitly typed variable has a data type that is inferred from the expression used to initialize the variable.
2. To create an implicitly typed variable, you use a variable declaration with `implicit` as the data type.
3. When you use an implicitly typed variable, the C# compiler decides on a data type for you.

The false statement is #2. To create an implicitly typed variable, you use a variable declaration with `var` as the data type.

UNDERSTANDING LINQ

As you have studied C#, you have become comfortable with the ideas of objects and classes. However, businesses operate using data that frequently is stored in relational databases. Applications that tried to bridge the gap between modern languages and traditional databases have been difficult to build and maintain. To reduce the complexity of accessing and integrating data that is stored in databases and other collections, Microsoft Corporation developed the **LINQ** (Language INtegrated Query) Project to provide queries that can be used in C# and Visual Basic.

In older versions of C#, you could access database data by passing an SQL string to a database object (and you still *can* do so in C# 3.0). For example, if you want to select all the fields in records in a table named `tblStudents` for which the field `GradePointAverage` was greater than 3.0, you could create a string such as "`SELECT * from tblStudents WHERE GradePointAverage > 3.00`" and pass it to an object of type `OleDbCommand`, which is a built-in type used to access databases. (The "Ole" stands for "Object linking and embedding.") You also would be required to type a few other statements that performed tasks like establishing a connection to the database and opening the database, and the select command would then select all the fields for all the records in the table that met the GPA criterion. The drawback to using a string command is that C# does not provide any syntax checking for characters stored within a string. For example, if you misspelled `SELECT` or `GradePointAverage`, the compiler would not issue an error message, but the program would fail when you executed it. Obviously, this feature is good when you want to store people's names or addresses, but it is a shortcoming when you want to issue a correct command.

LINQ was created to help solve these problems. LINQ provides a set of general-purpose standard operators that allow queries to be constructed using syntax that is easy to understand. This syntax is similar to SQL's, and the compiler can check it for errors. The operators defined in LINQ can be used to query arrays, enumerable classes, XML, relational databases, and other sources. This chapter concentrates on arrays and databases, but the LINQ queries you learn can be used with many types of data.

Some keywords in the LINQ vocabulary include the following:

- » **`select`** indicates what to select
- » **`from`** indicates the collection or sequence from which data will be drawn
- » **`where`** indicates conditions for selecting records

It is no accident that these are the same words you learned about in the discussion of SQL earlier in this chapter.

Figure 14-9 shows an example of LINQ in action. In the first shaded section, an implicitly typed collection, `highNums`, is constructed from each variable `x` in the `numbers` array where the value of `x` is greater than 3. The `foreach` loop uses the sequence which is a subset of the original array to display all the records that meet the selection criteria—that is, all the integers greater than 3. Figure 14-10 shows the output.

> **NOTE**
> The operator `where` is a **restriction operator**, or one that places a restriction on which data is added to a collection. The operator `select` is a **projection operator**, or one that projects, or sends off, specific data from a collection.

```
using System;
using System.Linq;
public class LinqDemo1
{
   public static void Main()
   {
      int[] numbers = { 6, 4, 2, 1, 8, 3, 7, 5, 2, 0 };
      const int CUTOFF = 3;
      var highNums =
            from x in numbers
            where x > CUTOFF
            select x;

      Console.WriteLine("Numbers > " + CUTOFF);
      foreach (var n in highNums)
      {
            Console.WriteLine(n);
      }
   }
}
```

Figure 14-9 `LinqDemo1` program

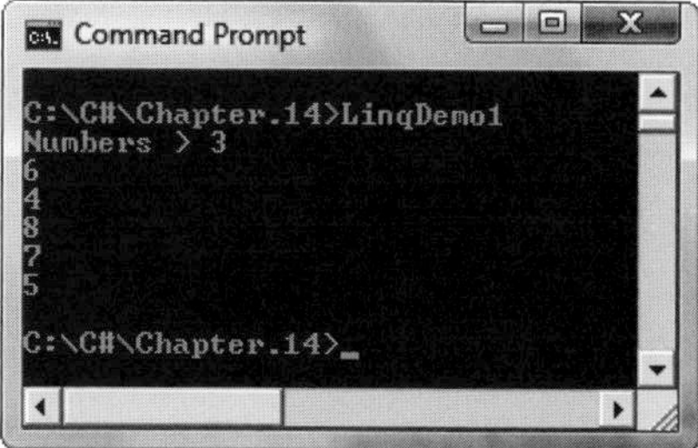

Figure 14-10 Output of the `LinqDemo1` application

You can use LINQ with more complicated sequences, such as a list of objects. Figure 14-11 shows a `Student` class that is similar to many you have seen throughout this book. The class contains three fields, a constructor that requires three parameters, and auto-implemented properties for each field. Figure 14-12 provides an example of how LINQ can select specific `Students` from an array. Figure 14-13 shows this output.

```
public class Student
{
   private int idNumber;
   private string name;
   private double gradePointAverage;
   public Student(int num, string name, double avg)
   {
      IdNumber = num;
      Name = name;
      GradePointAverage = avg;
   }
   public int IdNumber {get; set;}
   public string Name {get; set;}
   public double GradePointAverage {get; set;}
}
```

Figure 14-11 `Student` class

```
using System;
using System.Linq;
public class LinqDemo2
{
   public static void Main()
   {
      Student[] stus = {  new Student(1,  "Jones",    3.1),
                          new Student(2,  "Kimball",  2.9),
                          new Student(5,  "Oliver",   2.6),
                          new Student(6,  "Mitchell", 3.0),
                          new Student(8,  "Lee",      4.0),
                          new Student(10, "Cooper",   3.5) };
      const double CUTOFF = 3.0;
      var goodStudents =
         from s in stus
         where s.GradePointAverage > CUTOFF
         select s;

      Console.WriteLine("Students with GPA > " + CUTOFF);
      foreach (var s in goodStudents)
      {
         Console.WriteLine("{0,3} {1,-8} {2,5}", s.IdNumber,
            s.Name, s.GradePointAverage.ToString("F1"));
      }
   }
}
```

Figure 14-12 `LinqDemo2` program

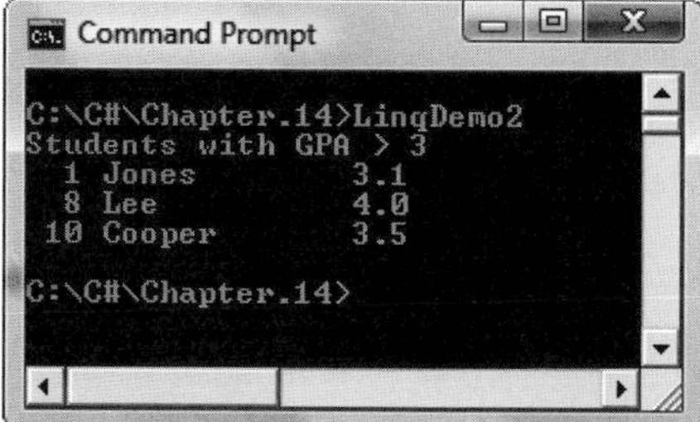

Figure 14-13 Output of the `LinqDemo2` program

Although LINQ statements work well to select specific records from an array, you could have used traditional C# statements to achieve the same results. However, few businesses can operate with all their data hard coded and stored in arrays within programs. The true power of LINQ becomes available when you can access an external database.

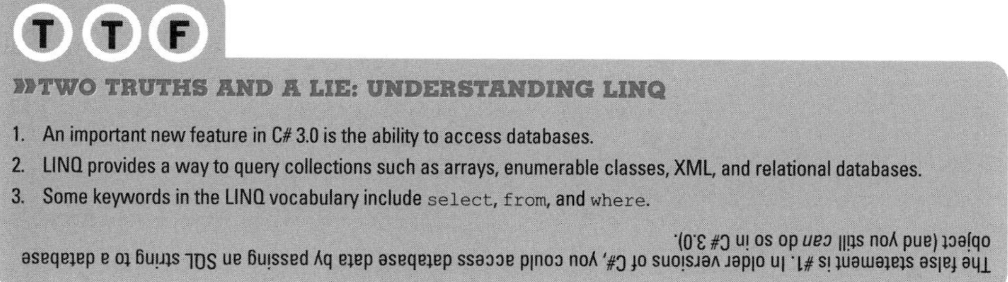

»TWO TRUTHS AND A LIE: UNDERSTANDING LINQ

1. An important new feature in C# 3.0 is the ability to access databases.
2. LINQ provides a way to query collections such as arrays, enumerable classes, XML, and relational databases.
3. Some keywords in the LINQ vocabulary include `select`, `from`, and `where`.

The false statement is #1. In older versions of C#, you could access database data by passing an SQL string to a database object (and you still *can* do so in C# 3.0).

RETRIEVING DATA FROM AN ACCESS DATABASE IN C#

As with many features of C#, you can write code to access a database table by hand, but you save time and reduce the chance for error by using the built-in tools of the Visual Studio IDE.

Adding a database to a Windows Forms project requires making only a few menu selections and browsing for a stored database. (In the "You Do It" section later in this chapter, you can walk through instructions that add a database to your project.) To add a database table to a Windows Forms project, you must perform two sets of tasks:

» From a project's main menu, you choose Data and then Add a New Data Source. Next, you browse for the database and answer a few questions.

» Then you drag a table onto your form. The table's data is bound to the form and you are supplied with a grid in which you can view the data. The grid is an instance of the `DataGridView` class.

Figure 14-14 shows a new Windows Forms project named `StudentsDemo` in which only these two steps have been taken. The Cartman College database depicted in Figures 14-5 and 14-6 earlier in this chapter has been added to the project. You can see the data grid on the `Form`. At the right of the screen, the Solution Explorer contains the `CartmanCollege` database. In the Data Sources window at the lower right, you can see that the `cartmanCollegeDataSet` contains just one table, named `tblStudents`. The bottom of the screen displays icons for several objects that were added to the project automatically when the data source was added and the table was dragged onto the form. These include:

- `cartmanCollegeDataSet`
- `tblStudentsBindingSource`
- `tblStudentsTableAdapter`
- `tblAdapterManager`
- `tblStudentsBindingNavigator`

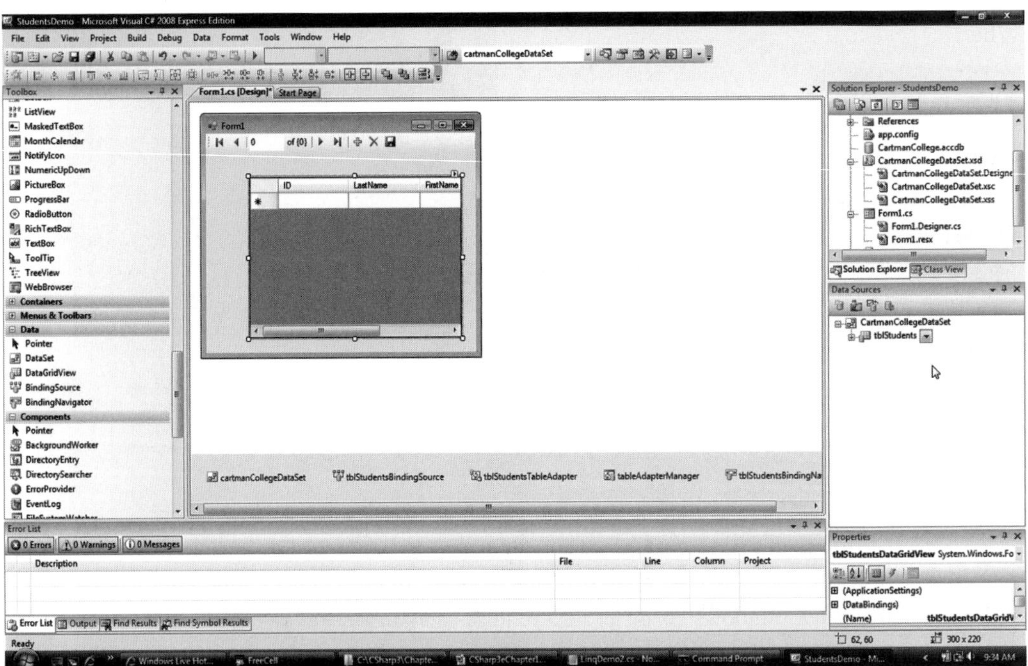

Figure 14-14 A project to which a data source has been added and in which a table has been dragged onto the `Form`

When you view the code behind the `Form` in Figure 14-14, you can see that one comment and one statement have been added to the `Form1_Load()` method, the method that executes when a Windows application starts and the main form is initialized. Figure 14-15 shows the method.

```
private void Form1_Load(object sender, EventArgs e)
{
    // TODO: This line of code loads data
    // into the 'cartmanCollegeDataSet.tblStudents' table.
    // You can move, or remove it, as needed.

    this.tblStudentsTableAdapter.Fill
      (this.cartmanCollegeDataSet.tblStudents);
}
```

Figure 14-15 `Form1_Load()` method with automatically generated code after `CartmanCollege` database is added to the `Form`

>>**NOTE** The line breaks in Figure 14-15 have been altered from the way they appear in Visual Studio to better fit this page.

The comment in the `Form1_Load()` method indicates that you can move the `Fill()` method statement or delete it. The `Fill()` method fills the table adapter with the data from `tblStudents` in the `cartmanCollegeDataSet`.

When you execute the program that contains the method in Figure 14-15, the data from `tblStudents` in the database is loaded into the `Form`, as shown in Figure 14-16. The grid that holds the data is not wide enough to display all the fields in each record, but if you compare the figure to Figure 14-6, you should be able to confirm that the exposed data comes from the database.

>>**NOTE** If you search the code for the project, you will find 18 references to `cartmanCollegeDataSet`. All this code was automatically generated when you added the data to the project and added the table to the `Form`, saving you many chances for error.

Form1

1 of 10

ID	LastName	FirstNa
1	Allen	David
2	Vega	Victoria
3	Nichols	Robert
4	Lawrence	Megan
5	Vantage	Wendy
6	Abbott	Michael
7	Amundsen	Olivia
8	Bell	Mandy

Figure 14-16 A `Form` that contains loaded data

You could return to Design view and increase the size of both the form and the grid to make the display easier to read. Figure 14-17 shows the larger view in which you can see all the data. In Figure 14-17, notice the controls that are provided for you automatically at the top of the `Form`. You can use these controls to navigate through the records, add a new record, delete the current record, and save the changes. When you exit the program and restart it, changes to the data will have been retained.

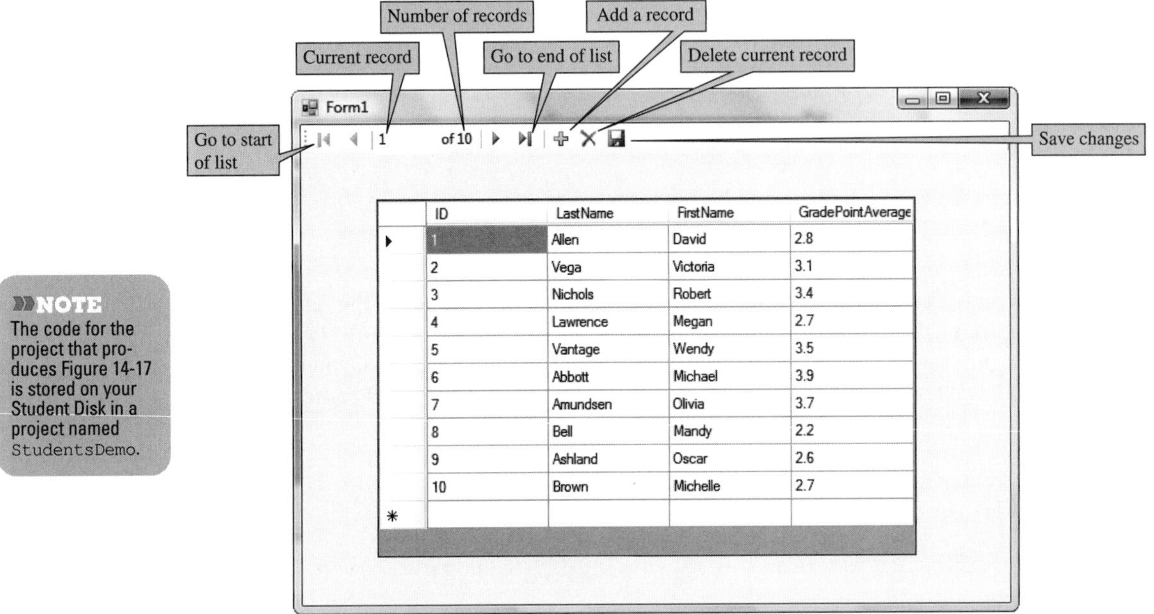

Figure 14-17 A larger `Form` that contains loaded data

»NOTE The code for the project that produces Figure 14-17 is stored on your Student Disk in a project named `StudentsDemo`.

You do not have to load the data into the viewing grid when the `Form` loads. For example, you could add a button to the `Form` and move the `Fill()` statement to the button's `Click()` method. Then, when the `Form` loads, no data would be visible, but after the user clicks the button, the data fills the table.

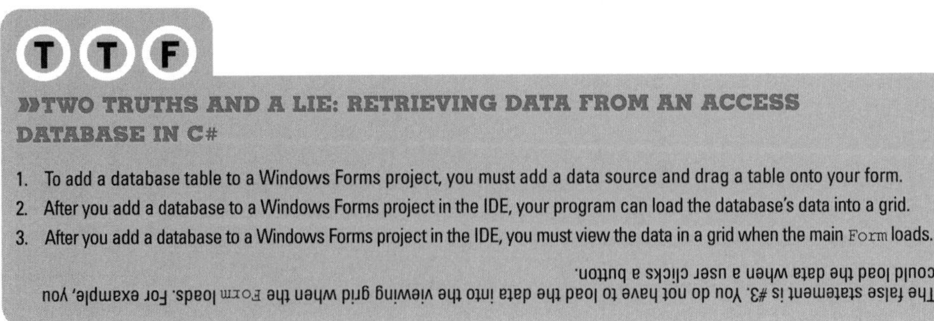

T T F

»TWO TRUTHS AND A LIE: RETRIEVING DATA FROM AN ACCESS DATABASE IN C#

1. To add a database table to a Windows Forms project, you must add a data source and drag a table onto your form.
2. After you add a database to a Windows Forms project in the IDE, your program can load the database's data into a grid.
3. After you add a database to a Windows Forms project in the IDE, you must view the data in a grid when the main `Form` loads.

The false statement is #3. You do not have to load the data into the viewing grid when the `Form` loads. For example, you could load the data when a user clicks a button.

USING LINQ QUERIES WITH AN ACCESS DATABASE TABLE

You are not required to use the data grid to view database records. You also are not required to view all the records in the database table or to view all the fields for each record. Instead, you can use a LINQ query to select a collection of data from a table when specific criteria are met. For example, Figure 14-18 shows a `button1_Click()` method that could be used to fill a list box with only the last names of students who have a GPA greater than 3.0. The shaded code in the figure is a copy of the shaded code used with the array in Figure 14-12. Instead of using `Console.WriteLine()` to display students, this method adds them to a `ListBox` named `listBox1`.

```
private void button1_Click(object sender, EventArgs e)
{
     const double CUTOFF = 3.0;
     this.tblStudentsTableAdapter.Fill
       (this.cartmanCollegeDataSet.tblStudents);
     var goodStudents =
          from s in this.cartmanCollegeDataSet.tblStudents
          where s.GradePointAverage > CUTOFF
          select s;
     foreach (var s in goodStudents)
          listBox1.Items.Add(s.LastName);
}
```

Figure 14-18 The `button1_Click()` method that uses a `ListBox` to display the last names of students with high GPAs

»NOTE The method in Figure 14-18 is part of the project named `StudentsDemo2`, which is available on your Student Disk.

»NOTE In a completed project, you would want to change the `Name` properties of `button1` and `listBox1` to better reflect their purposes. However, this example was created with the fewest possible changes to a project so you could more quickly replicate the results for yourself.

»NOTE The `from-where-select` combination is a single statement. Conventionally, its parts are written on separate lines for clarity, but that is not required. However, be careful not to use a semicolon until the entire statement is complete.

In the example in Figure 14-18, `goodStudents` is an implicitly typed collection of students with high GPAs. In this case, `goodStudents` is the following type (where `StudentsDemo2` is the name of the current project):

```
System.Data.EnumerableRowCollection<StudentsDemo2.cartmanCollegeDataSet.
tblStudentsRow>
```

This means that `goodStudents` is a collection of rows from the `tblStudents` database table. However, it is easier to use `var` and to have the type inferred than to use this lengthy type name.

Assume that you start a C# Windows Forms project and take the following steps:

» Add the `CartmanCollege` database `tblStudents` table to the project.
» Delete the automatically added grid from the `Form`.
» Drag a button onto the `Form` and change its `Text` property.
» Drag a `ListBox` onto the `Form`.
» Add the `button1_Click()` method from Figure 14-18.

Figure 14-19 shows the results when you execute the program and click the button. Although 10 student records are stored in the table, the figure lists only the last names of the five students who have GPA values over 3.0. You can confirm that these are the correct students by referring back to the complete listing in Figure 14-6.

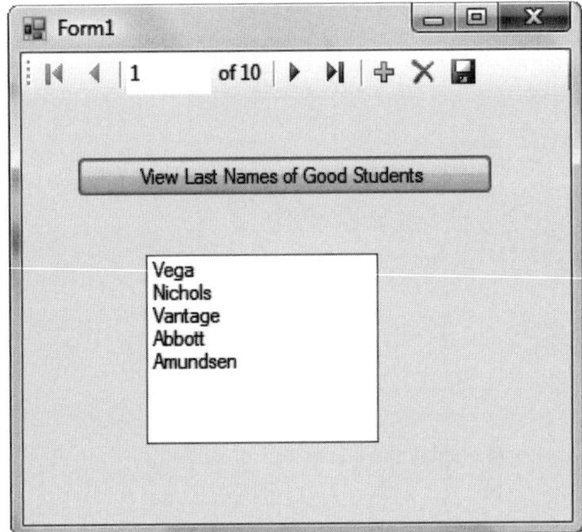

Figure 14-19 Execution of the program containing the method in Figure 14-18

In the method in Figure 14-18, `goodStudents` is a collection of student records gathered from the `tblStudents` table in the `CartmanCollege` database, as indicated in the `from` clause. The `where` clause specifies the condition for selection—a GPA greater than `CUTOFF`. The `select` clause indicates what to select—a record. The `foreach` statement that follows the shaded portion of the method selects each record in the collection, and adds its `LastName` field to the `ListBox`.

As an alternative to the code in Figure 14-18, instead of creating a collection of records, you could create a collection of last names. Figure 14-20 shows an example in which only last names are selected to be added to the collection (see the first shaded expression in the figure). That is, in this example `goodStudents` is a collection of `string`s, and not a collection of records. When each `s` is added to the `ListBox` in the second expression, it is a `string` that is added. In other words, in this example, you do not write `s.LastName` because each `s` *is* a last name. The results are identical to those shown in Figure 14-19.

```
var goodStudents =
     from s in this.cartmanCollegeDataSet.tblStudents
     where s.GradePointAverage > CUTOFF
     select s.LastName;
foreach (var s in goodStudents)
     listBox1.Items.Add(s);
```

Figure 14-20 Collecting strings from a database table

Figure 14-21 contains a `button1_Click()` method from a different application in which a constant GPA cutoff is not used. Instead, the user can enter a cutoff GPA value into a `TextBox` that has been named `gpaTextBox` (see the first shaded expression). In this example, a student's GPA must be greater than the user-supplied value to qualify for the list. The last name, a comma, and the first name of each qualifying student (see the last shaded expression in Figure 14-21) are shown in the `ListBox`. Figure 14-22 shows the output.

```
private void button1_Click(object sender, EventArgs e)
{
     double minGpa = Convert.ToDouble(gpaTextBox.Text);
     this.tblStudentsTableAdapter.Fill
        (this.cartmanCollegeDataSet.tblStudents);
     var goodStudents =
          from s in this.cartmanCollegeDataSet.tblStudents
          where s.GradePointAverage > minGpa
          select s;
     foreach (var s in goodStudents)
          listBox1.Items.Add(s.LastName + ", " + s.FirstName);
}
```

Figure 14-21 The `button1_Click()` method that displays students with a minimum GPA entered by the user

»NOTE The method in Figure 14-21 is part of the project named `StudentsDemo3`, which is available on your Student Disk. In the example in Figure 14-21, instead of using a `button1_Click()` method, you might prefer to add the code to a `gpaTextBox_TextChanged()` method so that it executes each time the user enters a new value as a minimum GPA instead of when the user clicks a button. You might also prefer to add some error checking in case the user enters a non-numeric value. Error checking was omitted from this example to keep it short.

When you execute an application that contains the method in Figure 14-21, the list of items in `listBox1` is appended each time the user clicks `button1`. In other words, if a user clicks the button twice without changing the selection criterion, the `ListBox` contains a second set of the same records. To prevent the list from growing and to see only the students who meet the current criteria, add the following statement near the beginning of the `Click()` method:

```
listBox1.Items.Clear();
```

With the inclusion of this statement, `listBox1` is emptied before each new group is added to it.

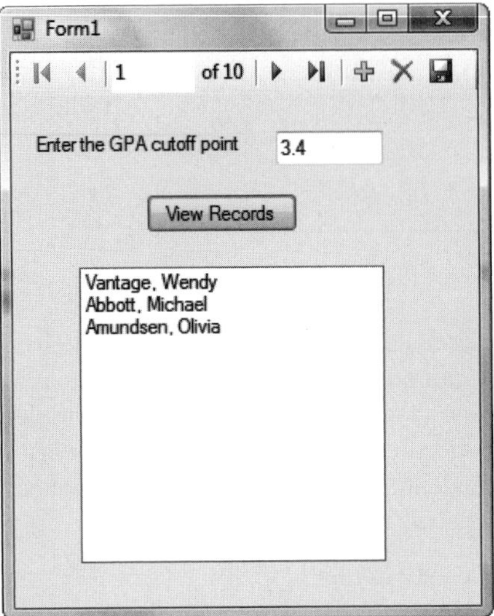

Figure 14-22 Typical execution of an application containing the `button1_Click()` method in Figure 14-21

Many other options are available when you use LINQ expressions. For example, you can use AND and OR expressions in your LINQ statements. The following code selects all students with GPAs between 2.5 and 3.0:

```
var someStudents =
     from s in this.cartmanCollegeDataSet.tblStudents
     where s.GradePointAverage > 2.5 && s.GradePointAverage < 3.0
     select s;
```

With text values, you can use `StartsWith()`, `EndsWith()`, and `Contains()`. For example, the following code selects all students whose first name starts with "M":

```
var someStudents =
     from s in this.cartmanCollegeDataSet.tblStudents
     where s.FirstName.StartsWith("M")
     select s;
```

You can use several **aggregate operators**, or operators that produce statistics for groups of data. The aggregate operators include `Average()`, `Count()`, `Sum()`, `Max()`, and `Min()`. For example, the method in Figure 14-23 assembles a collection of `GradePointAverage` values named `gpas`. Then several aggregate operators are applied to the collection and the results are assigned to `Labels`. Figure 14-24 shows the output when this method is used with `tblStudents`. You can confirm the accuracy of these statistics by referring to the complete data set in Figure 14-6.

```
private void button1_Click(object sender, EventArgs e)
{
   var gpas =
      from s in this.cartmanCollegeDataSet.tblStudents
         select s.GradePointAverage;
   countLabel.Text = "Count is " + gpas.Count();
   minLabel.Text = "Lowest GPA is " + gpas.Min();
   maxLabel.Text = "Highest GPA is " + gpas.Max();
   avgLabel.Text = "Average of all GPAs is " + gpas.Average();
}
```

Figure 14-23 Method that uses some aggregate operators

»NOTE The method in Figure 14-23 is part of the project named `StudentsDemo4`, which is available on your Student Disk.

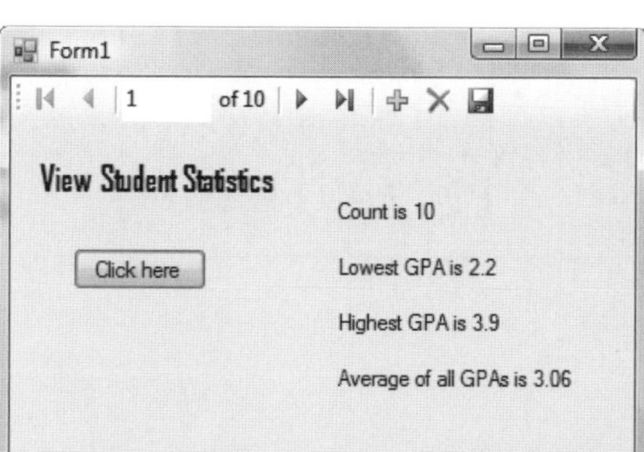

Figure 14-24 Output of program that uses the method in Figure 14-23

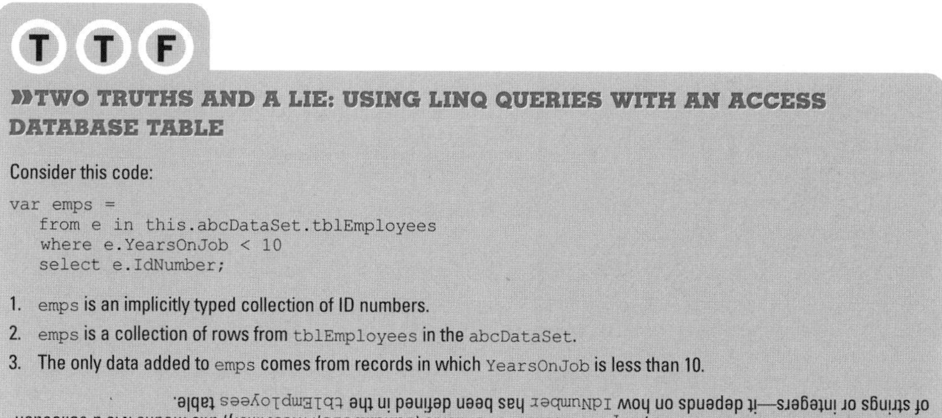

T T F

»TWO TRUTHS AND A LIE: USING LINQ QUERIES WITH AN ACCESS DATABASE TABLE

Consider this code:

```
var emps =
   from e in this.abcDataSet.tblEmployees
   where e.YearsOnJob < 10
   select e.IdNumber;
```

1. `emps` is an implicitly typed collection of ID numbers.
2. `emps` is a collection of rows from `tblEmployees` in the `abcDataSet`.
3. The only data added to `emps` comes from records in which `YearsOnJob` is less than 10.

The false statement is #2. In this code, `emps` is a collection of fields (`IdNumbers`). Most likely, this means it is a collection of strings or integers—it depends on how `IdNumber` has been defined in the `tblEmployees` table.

USING LINQ OPERATORS TO SORT AND GROUP DATA

You can use the **orderby operator** to sort a collection of data based on a field or fields. For example, the method in Figure 14-25 produces the output in Figure 14-26. The shaded statement causes the list of students to be ordered by GPA.

»NOTE The method in Figure 14-25 is part of the project named StudentsDemo5, which is available on your Student Disk.

```
private void button1_Click(object sender, EventArgs e)
{
   listBox1.Items.Add("GPA   LastName");
   var students =
      from s in this.cartmanCollegeDataSet.tblStudents
         orderby s.GradePointAverage
         select s;
   foreach (var s in students)
      listBox1.Items.Add(" " + s.GradePointAverage + "    " +
         s.LastName);
}
```

Figure 14-25 Method that uses orderby

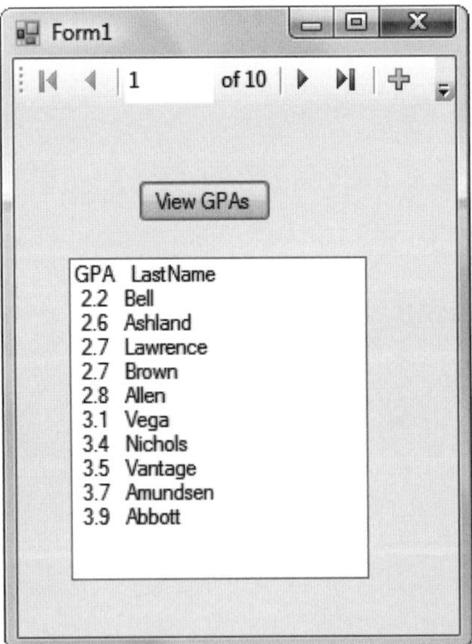

Figure 14-26 Output of project that uses the method in Figure 14-25

The default order for sorting is ascending; that is, from lowest to highest. You can explicitly indicate an ascending sort by using the following phrase:

```
orderby s.GradePointAverage ascending
```

To view the students in the reverse order, from the highest GPA to the lowest, you would write the following:

```
orderby s.GradePointAverage descending
```

You can use compound conditions for ordering. For example, the following would sort students by last name, and then by first name when last names are the same:

```
orderby s.LastName, s.FirstName
```

Data items also can be grouped; the **group operator** groups data by specified criteria. For example, Figure 14-27 shows a `Click()` method that groups students by the integer part of the `GradePointAverage` field. In other words, all students with GPAs between 2 and 3 are in one group, and students with GPAs between 3 and 4 are in another group. (Additional groups would be formed if students had higher or lower GPAs.) The example in Figure 14-27 uses nested `foreach` loops. In the outer loop, which executes one time for each group, the group `Key` is displayed as a heading. The `Key` is not required to be the key field in the database table, although it might be; the `Key` is the value used to determine the groups, which in this case is determined by the integer part of the GPA. In the inner `foreach` loop in Figure 14-27, the GPA and last name for each record in the group are added to the `ListBox`. Figure 14-28 shows the results.

```
private void button1_Click(object sender, EventArgs e)
{
   var stus = from s in cartmanCollegeDataSet.tblStudents
      group s by (int)s.GradePointAverage;

   foreach (var groupByGpa in stus)
   {
      listBox1.Items.Add("GPA:  " + groupByGpa.Key);
      foreach (var s in groupByGpa)
        listBox1.Items.Add("   " + s.GradePointAverage +
           "  " + s.LastName);
   }
}
```

Figure 14-27 A method that groups records

»NOTE The method in Figure 14-27 is part of the project named `StudentsDemo6`, which is available on your Student Disk.

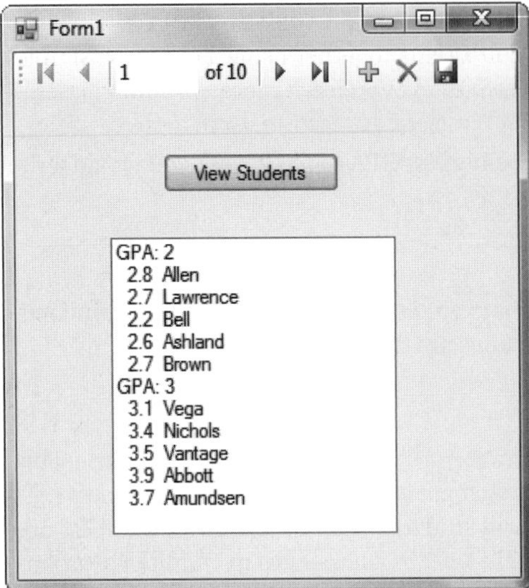

Figure 14-28 Output of application that contains the method in Figure 14-27

When you use the `group` operator, the number of possible values in the criterion determines the number of possible groups. For example, if a company has five departments and you group employees with an expression such as the following, you form five groups:

```
group e by e.Department
```

However, if you use a Boolean expression in the `by` clause, then only two groups are possible because the `by` expression has only two possible values—true or false:

```
group e by e.Department == 1
```

That is, every `e` is part of the group for which `e.Department == 1` is true, or the group for which `e.Department == 1` is false.

A query body must end with a `select` clause or a `group` clause. Therefore, if you combine `orderby` and `group`, `orderby` must come first. For example, to view the students in each GPA category in alphabetical order by last name, you would write the following:

```
var stus = from s in cartmanCollegeDataSet.tblStudents
    orderby s.LastName
    group s by (int)s.GradePointAverage;
```

Many more LINQ operations are available than can be covered in this chapter. More than 50 operators are available, and they can be combined in practically an infinite number of ways. For example, you can insert and delete records from a database. Additionally, a key feature of normalized relational databases is the ability to make relationships between tables. LINQ allows you to join multiple object collections together using a relatively simple syntax that is familiar to those who already know SQL. As you learn more about databases, C#, and LINQ, you will discover many possibilities and learn to create useful applications that access data and provide business clients with powerful ways to view and use their information.

»NOTE For more good ideas on working with LINQ, see "101 LINQ Samples" at *http://msdn2.microsoft.com/en-us/vcsharp/aa336746.aspx*.

»TWO TRUTHS AND A LIE: USING LINQ OPERATORS TO SORT AND GROUP DATA

Consider the following code:

```
var emps =
   from e in this.abcDataSet.tblEmployees
      orderby e.LastName
      group e by e.Department;
```

1. In the collection `emps`, Brown in Department 1 would come before Adams in Department 3.
2. In the collection `emps`, Graham in Department 4 would come before Lee in Department 7.
3. In the collection `emps`, Kimball in Department 5 would come before Thompson in Department 3.

The false statement is #3. Each lower-numbered department group would precede any higher-numbered group. Within the groups, the employees would be in alphabetical order.

YOU DO IT

ADDING A DATASET TO A PROJECT

In the next steps, you will add a previously created database table to a C# project and retrieve data from the table so you can display it in a `Form`.

To add a dataset to a project:

1. Your Student Disk contains a Microsoft Office Access Database file named **HonestRalphsUsedCars**. If Access is installed on your computer, open the database file by double-clicking its name. When Access opens, double-click `tblCars : Table` under All Tables. (See Figure 14-29.) Examine the data in the table. The fields are `ID`, `ModelYear`, `Make`, `Price`, and `Color`. Ten records have been entered into the table.

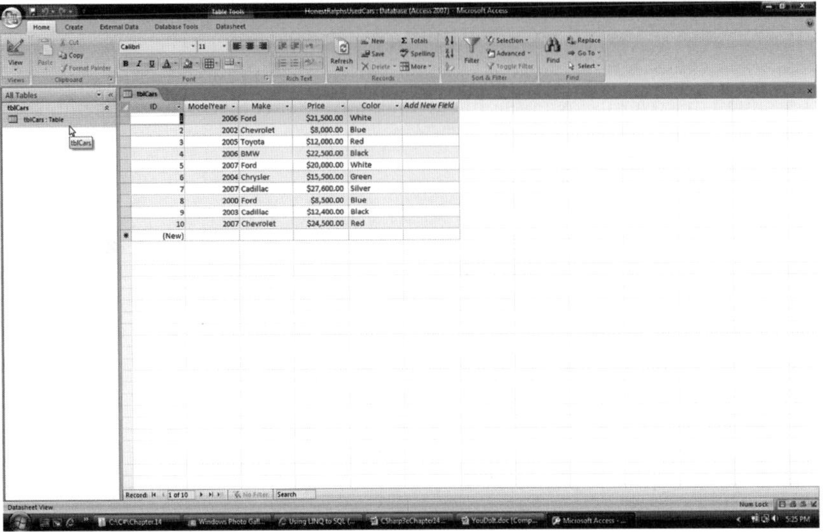

Figure 14-29 HonestRalphsUsedCars `tblCars` table in Access

2. Close Access. Open Visual Studio and start a new Windows Forms Application named `AccessCars`. Change the `Text` property of the `Form` to **Honest Ralph's Used Cars**.

3. In the main menu at the top of the screen, click **Data**. From the drop-down list, click **Add New Data Source** to start the Data Source Configuration Wizard. In the Choose a Data Source Type window, select **Database** and then click **Next**. See Figure 14-30.

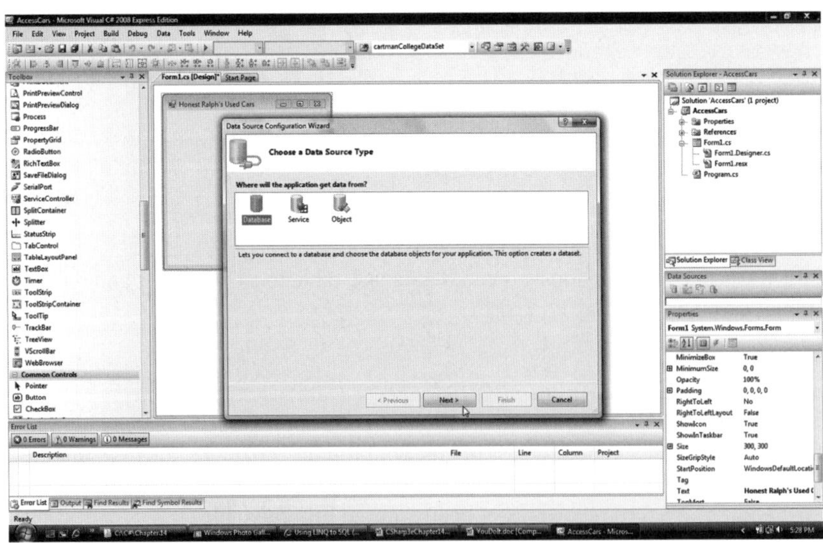

Figure 14-30 The Data Source Configuration Wizard

4. In the Choose Your Data Connection window, click **New Connection**. In the Add Connection dialog box, select **Microsoft Access Database file** as the Data Source, and then click Browse to find the file to use. Select **HonestRalphsUsedCars.accdb** from the folder where the file is stored. Then click **Next**. A dialog box appears and asks if you want to add the file to your project. See Figure 14-31. Click **Yes**.

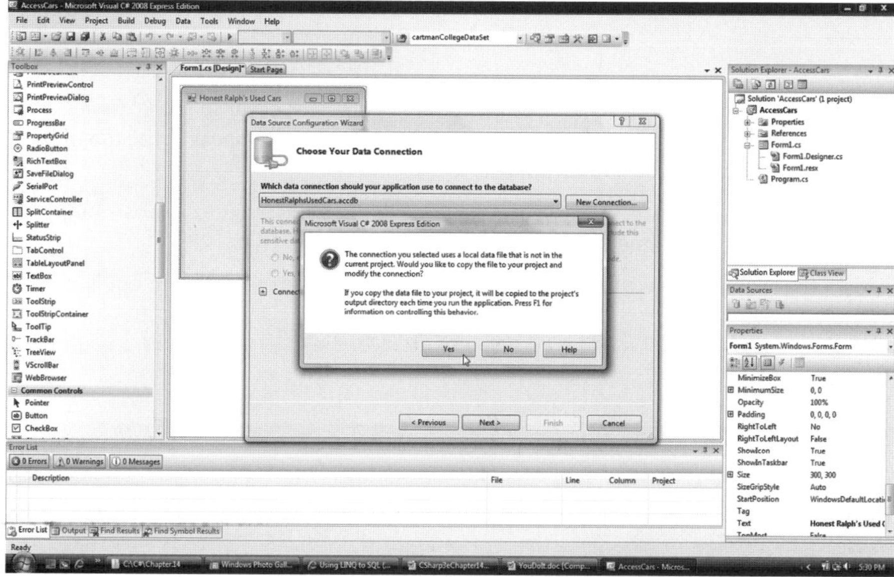

Figure 14-31 Dialog box asking to add a data file to a project

5. In the Data Source Connection window, click **Next**. In the next window that appears, select **Tables**. Then click the **Finish** button.

6. In the Solution Explorer, confirm that the `HonestRalphsUsedCars` database has been added to the project. See Figure 14-32.

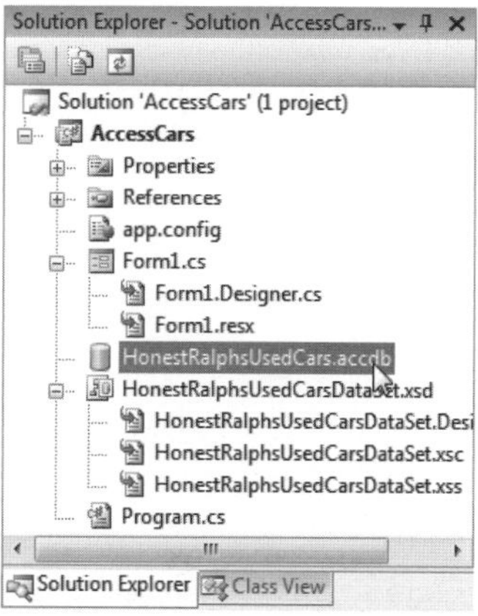

Figure 14-32 Database added to project

7. From Visual Studio's main menu, click **Data** and then click **Show Data Sources**. A Data Sources window should appear under the Solution Explorer. (Drag its borders if it is too narrow to read the contents.) See Figure 14-33.

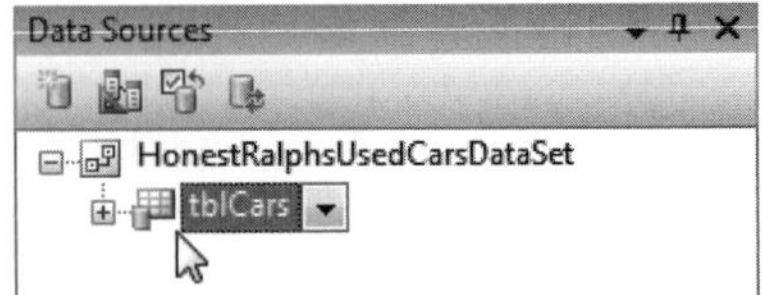

Figure 14-33 The Data Sources window

8. Drag `tblCars` onto the `Form` in the Designer. Several changes occur in the `Form`: a large data grid appears and several icons for scrolling through records appear at the top of the `Form`. Additionally, five new objects appear:

   `honestRalphsUsedCarsDataSet`, `tblCarsBindingSource`, `tblCarsTableAdapter`, `tableAdapterManager`, and `tblCarsBindingNavigator`

   Together, these objects make the connection between the database and your application. See Figure 14-34.

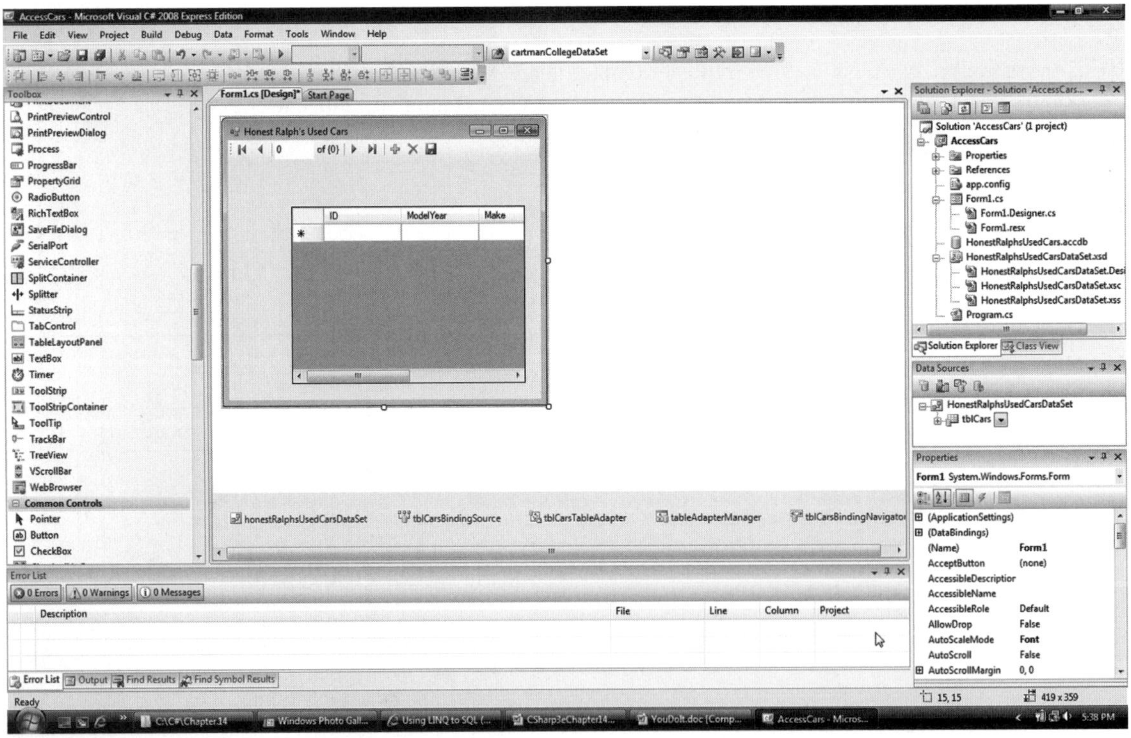

Figure 14-34 The `Form` after `tblCars` has been dragged onto it

9. Save the project, then click **Debug** from the main menu and click **Start without Debugging**. The data appears in the table grid, as shown in Figure 14-35.

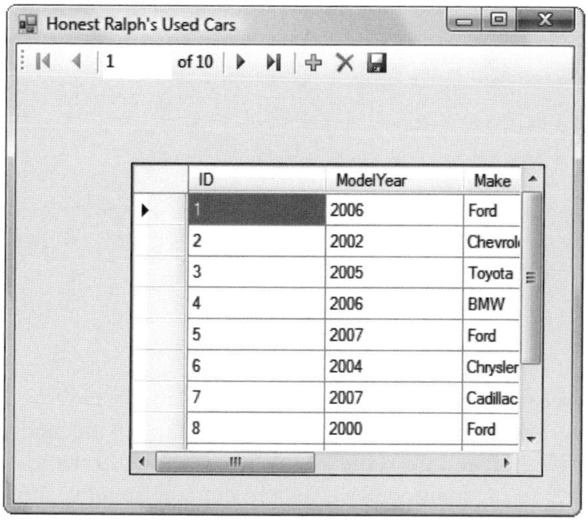

Honest Ralph's Used Cars

1 of 10

ID	ModelYear	Make
1	2006	Ford
2	2002	Chevrol
3	2005	Toyota
4	2006	BMW
5	2007	Ford
6	2004	Chrysler
7	2007	Cadillac
8	2000	Ford

Figure 14-35 Ralph's Used Cars data as it appears in the grid

10. Dismiss the `Form`. In Design view, reposition the grid and widen both the table and the grid to see all the records' fields. Save the project, then click **Debug** and **Start without Debugging**. The data appears in the table grid, as shown in Figure 14-36. Use the scroll bar to view the hidden records at the bottom of the list. Use the arrows at the top of the form to navigate through the records.

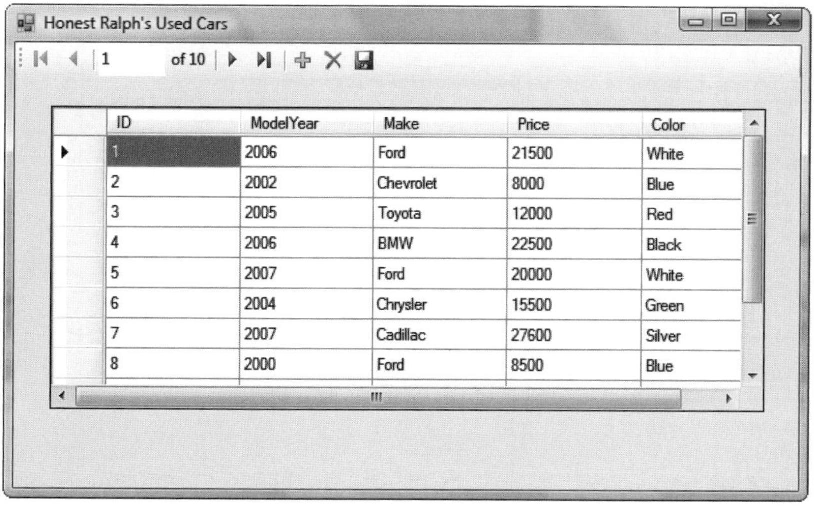

Honest Ralph's Used Cars

1 of 10

ID	ModelYear	Make	Price	Color
1	2006	Ford	21500	White
2	2002	Chevrolet	8000	Blue
3	2005	Toyota	12000	Red
4	2006	BMW	22500	Black
5	2007	Ford	20000	White
6	2004	Chrysler	15500	Green
7	2007	Cadillac	27600	Silver
8	2000	Ford	8500	Blue

Figure 14-36 Ralph's Used Cars data as it appears in a wider grid

11. Dismiss the `Form`. In the IDE, double-click the `Form` title bar. The `Form1_Load()` method appears as follows. (Note that the comment has been divided into three comments and the `Fill()` method has been divided into two lines so the code fits better on this page.)

```
private void Form1_Load(object sender, EventArgs e)
{
    // TODO: This line of code loads data into the
    // 'honestRalphsUsedCarsDataSet.tblCars' table.
    // You can move, or remove it, as needed.

    this.tblCarsTableAdapter.Fill
        (this.honestRalphsUsedCarsDataSet.tblCars);
}
```

12. Return to Design view. Drag a `Button` onto the `Form`, as shown in Figure 14-37. Change its `Name` property to **`recordsButton`** and its `Text` property to **Retrieve Records**. Double-click the `Button` to generate a `recordsButton_Click()` method and view its code. Cut the `Fill()` method call from the `Form1_Load()` method and paste it into the `recordsButton_Click()` method. Save the project and then execute the program again. This time the grid is empty. When you click the button, the grid fills with data.

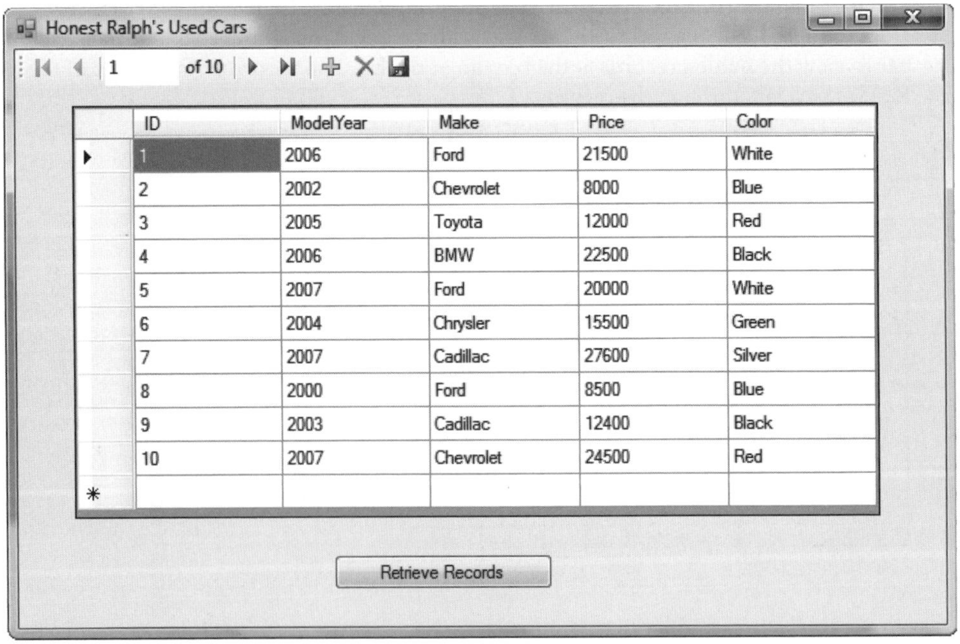

Honest Ralph's Used Cars

1 of 10

ID	ModelYear	Make	Price	Color
1	2006	Ford	21500	White
2	2002	Chevrolet	8000	Blue
3	2005	Toyota	12000	Red
4	2006	BMW	22500	Black
5	2007	Ford	20000	White
6	2004	Chrysler	15500	Green
7	2007	Cadillac	27600	Silver
8	2000	Ford	8500	Blue
9	2003	Cadillac	12400	Black
10	2007	Chevrolet	24500	Red

Retrieve Records

Figure 14-37 Ralph's Used Cars data accessed after user clicks a button

QUERYING A DATASET

In the next steps, you will write LINQ queries that demonstrate how to access subsets of the data stored in the `tblCars` table.

To query a dataset:

1. In Visual Studio, in the `AccessCars` project, go to Form1.cs[Design] view. Delete the data grid from the `Form`. Drag a `Label` and a `ListBox` onto the `Form`, as shown in Figure 14-38. Change the `Label`'s `Text` to **Inexpensive Cars**. Change the `ListBox`'s name to **`inexpensiveCarsBox`**. Reduce the width of the `Form` appropriately.

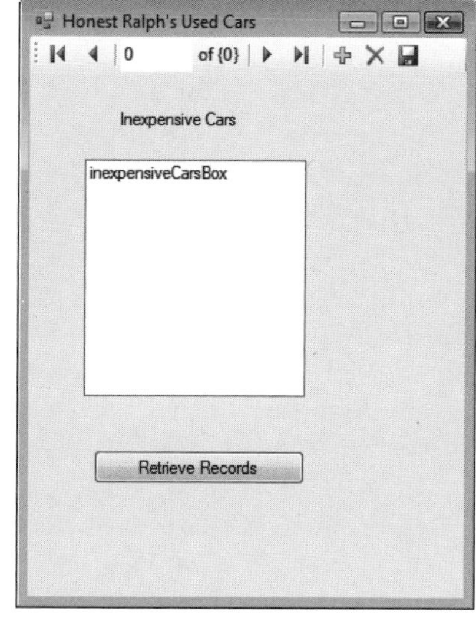

Figure 14-38 Adding a `Label` and `ListBox` to the `AccessCars` project

2. Double-click the button on the `Form` and revise the `recordsButton_Click()` method, as shown in the shaded portions of Figure 14-39. The LINQ code selects all the records in the table in which `Price` is less than $20,000 and then adds the ID number, model year, and make of those cars to the `ListBox`.

```
private void recordsButton_Click(object sender, EventArgs e)
{
   const int HIGHPRICE = 20000;
   this.tblCarsTableAdapter.Fill
       (this.honestRalphsUsedCarsDataSet.tblCars);
   var inexpensiveCars =
      from c in this.honestRalphsUsedCarsDataSet.tblCars
      where c.Price < HIGHPRICE
      select c;
   foreach (var c in inexpensiveCars)
      inexpensiveCarsBox.Items.Add
         (c.ID + " - " + c.ModelYear + " " + c.Make);
}
```

Figure 14-39 The `recordsButton_Click()` method

3. Execute the project. When the `Form` appears, click the `Button`. The output looks like Figure 14-40. Five cars appear in the list.
4. Dismiss the `Form`.

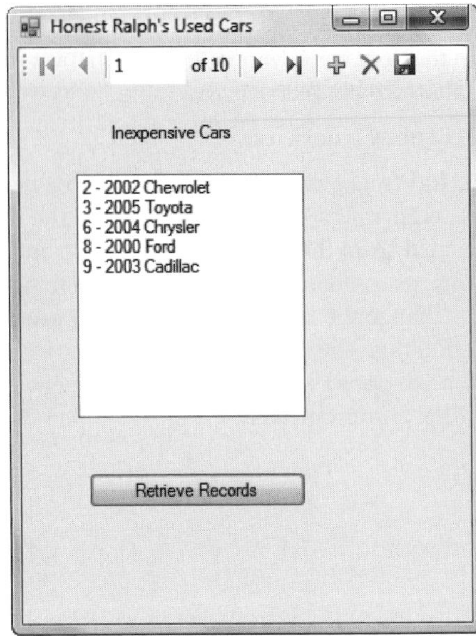

Figure 14-40 Execution of `AccessCars` project

ALLOWING THE USER TO PROVIDE SELECTION CRITERIA

In the next steps, you will provide a `TextBox` to make the application more flexible. Instead of listing cars priced under $20,000, the user will be able to enter a cutoff price.

To provide selection criteria for the user:

1. In the Form1.cs Design view, rearrange the existing components and add a new `Label` and `TextBox`, as shown in Figure 14-41. Name the `TextBox` **`priceTextBox`**.

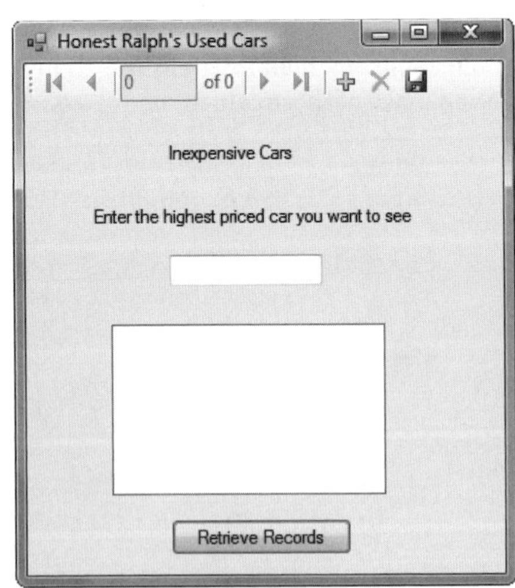

Figure 14-41 Form with `Label` and `TextBox` for data entry

2. Modify the `recordsButton_Click()` method, as shown in the shaded sections of Figure 14-42. Delete the declaration of the constant `HIGHPRICE` and replace it with a statement that accepts entered text from the `TextBox` and converts it to an `int`. Change the selection criterion from less than the constant `HIGHPRICE` to less than or equal to the value entered by the user. Also, add the price to the output in the `ListBox`, which will make it easier for you to confirm that the correct cars were selected for the `inexpensiveCars` collection.

```
private void recordsButton_Click(object sender, EventArgs e)
{
     int highprice = Convert.ToInt32(priceTextBox.Text);
     this.tblCarsTableAdapter.Fill
         (this.honestRalphsUsedCarsDataSet.tblCars);
     var inexpensiveCars =
         from c in this.honestRalphsUsedCarsDataSet.tblCars
         where c.Price <= highprice
         select c;
     foreach (var c in inexpensiveCars)
         inexpensiveCarsBox.Items.Add
             (c.ID + " - " + c.ModelYear + " " + c.Make +
                " $" + c.Price);
}
```

Figure 14-42 The `recordsButton_Click()` method that allows user data entry

3. Save and execute the program. Depending on the value you type into the `TextBox`, the output will look similar to Figure 14-43.

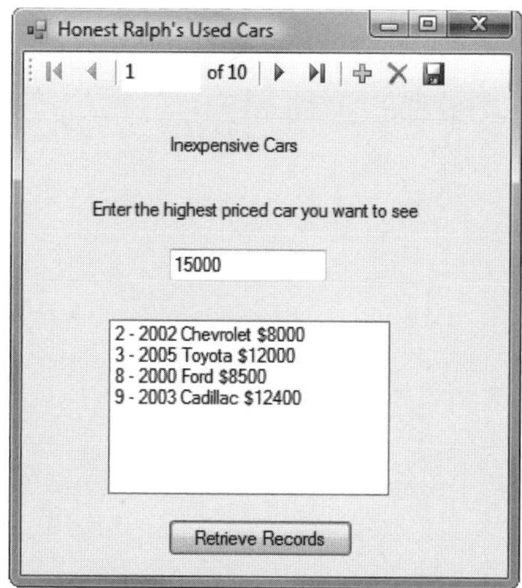

Figure 14-43 Typical execution of application that contains the method in Figure 14-42

4. If you click the button more than once in the current project, the `ListBox` list is appended rather than replaced. To remedy the problem, dismiss the `Form` and return to the code. Add the following statement near the beginning of the `recordsButton_Click()` method, before any items are added to the `inexpensiveCarsBox`:

```
inexpensiveCarsBox.Items.Clear();
```

5. Save and run the application again. If you enter different values and click the `Button` multiple times, now the list of cars is replaced with each new selection.
6. Dismiss the `Form` and run the application again, entering a low value such as $3500 for the maximum price in the search. When you click the `Button`, the `ListBox` is empty, as it should be, because no cars in the table are priced below that value. However, providing no feedback can confuse or frustrate a user, who might think the application is not working properly. To remedy the problem, you can add a message that appears when no cars meet the search criteria. Just before the closing curly brace of the `recordsButton_Click()` method, add the following:

```
if (inexpensiveCars.Count() == 0)
{
   inexpensiveCarsBox.Items.Add("Sorry - there are no cars");
   inexpensiveCarsBox.Items.Add
      ("less than or equal to $" + highprice);
}
```

This code uses the `Count()` aggregate operator to determine the number of records in the `inexpensiveCars` collection. When the count is 0, the user sees an appropriate message.

7. Save and execute the program. When the entered price is too low, the user sees a message confirming that the program works, but that no records meet the search criterion. See Figure 14-44.

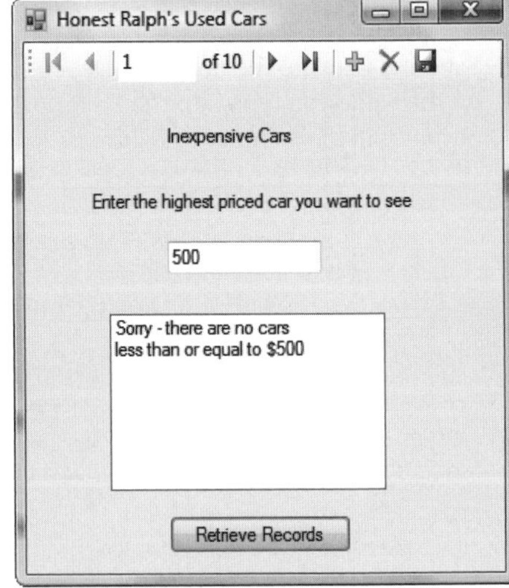

Figure 14-44 Output of `AccessCars` application when no cars meet the selection criterion

GROUPING DATA

In the next steps, you will group output records to make them easier for users to view and inspect.

1. Open a new Visual Studio C# project named **CarsGroupByMake**.
2. As shown in Figure 14-45, change the `Form`'s `Text` property to **Honest Ralph's Used Cars**. Add a `Button` to the `Form`, change its `Name` to **`carsButton`**, and change its `Text` property to **View Cars**. Add a `ListBox` to the `Form` and change its name to **`carsList`**.

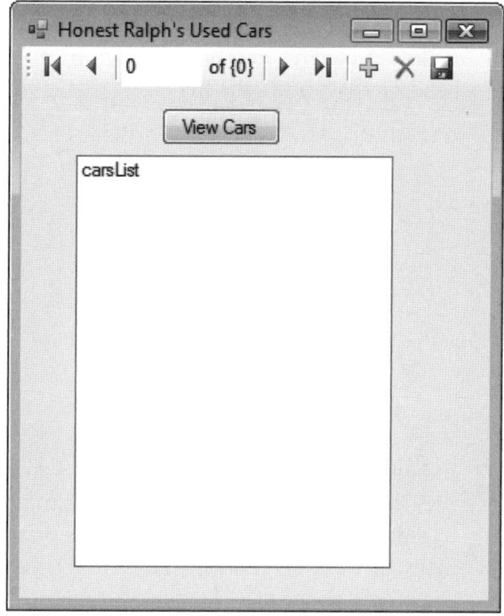

Figure 14-45 Form design for `CarsGroupByMake` project

3. Add `HonestRalphsUsedCars.accdb` to the project, drag the `tblCars` table onto the `Form`, and delete the automatically supplied grid from the `Form`.
4. Double-click the `Button` and add the following LINQ query within the automatically generated `Click()` method:

```
var cars =
     from c in this.honestRalphsUsedCarsDataSet.tblCars
     group c by c.Make;
```

   This statement groups the cars by the value in each `Make` field.

5. Following the LINQ query, add a nested `foreach` loop that displays a car make for each group, then lists the year and price for each car within each group.

```
foreach(var group in cars)
{
   carsList.Items.Add("Make: " + group.Key);
   foreach(var c in group)
      carsList.Items.Add("     " + c.ModelYear + " $" + c.Price);
}
```

6. Save and execute the project. Click the `Button` on the `Form`. The output appears as in Figure 14-46. The year and price for each of the 10 cars in the table is displayed. Each car is grouped with others of the same make, and each group is preceded by a heading that shows the make.

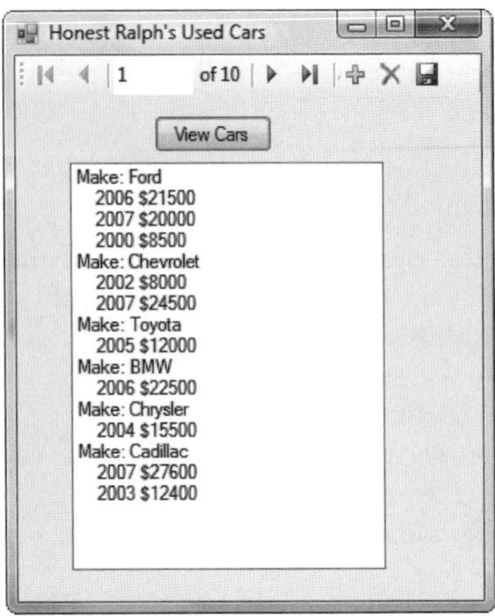

Figure 14-46 Output of `CarsGroupByMake` project

7. In Figure 14-46, the order in which cars are listed in each group is inconsistent. For example, the Chevrolets are listed from oldest to newest but the Cadillacs are listed from newest to oldest. To consistently display the cars in each group in order from newest to oldest, insert an `orderby` clause in the LINQ query as follows:

```
var cars =
     from c in this.honestRalphsUsedCarsDataSet.tblCars
     orderby c.ModelYear descending
     group c by c.Make;
```

8. Save the project and execute it again. When you click the `Button`, the output appears as shown in Figure 14-47. The cars are listed in order by model year within each group.

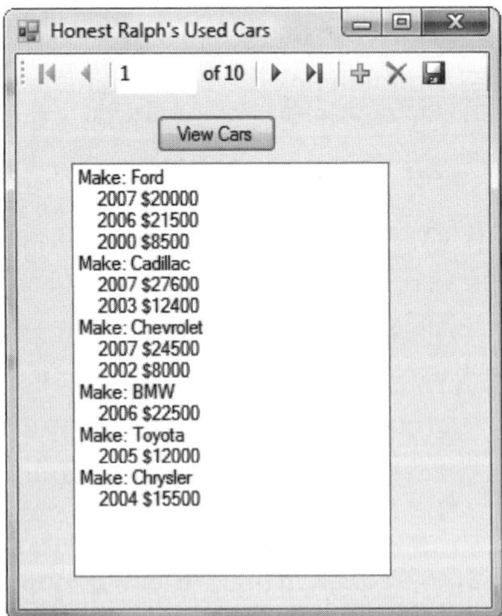

Figure 14-47 Output of `CarsGroupByMake` project ordered by `ModelYear`

9. The output in Figure 14-47 contains only 10 cars in only six different groupings by make. However, if there were more cars, it might be difficult to locate a specific car. To show the `Make` groups in alphabetical order, add a condition to the sort order specified in the LINQ query, as follows:

```
var cars =
     from c in this.honestRalphsUsedCarsDataSet.tblCars
     orderby c.Make, c.ModelYear descending
     group c by c.Make;
```

10. Save and execute the program. When you click the `Button` on the `Form`, the output appears as shown in Figure 14-48. Each make is listed in alphabetical order and each car is listed in descending model-year order within its `Make` group.

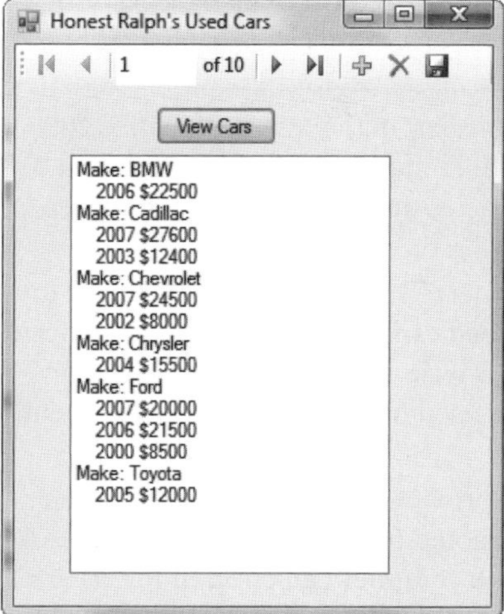

Figure 14-48 Output of `CarsGroupByMake` project ordered by `ModelYear` within alphabetized `Make`

11. Dismiss the `Form` and exit Visual Studio.

CHAPTER SUMMARY

» A database holds a group of files that an organization needs to support its applications. In a database, the files often are called tables because you can arrange their contents in rows and columns. A value that uniquely identifies a record is called a primary key, or a key for short. Database management software, or a database management system, is a set of programs that allows users to create table descriptions, identify keys, add, delete, and update records within a table, arrange records within a table so they are sorted by different fields, write questions that select specific records from a table for viewing, and perform other tasks.

- Creating a useful database requires a lot of planning and analysis. You must decide what data will be stored, how that data will be divided between tables, and how the tables will interrelate. For each table you must decide what columns are needed, provide names for them, and enter data.
- In most tables you create for a database, you want to identify a column, or possibly a combination of columns, as the table's key column or field (also called the primary key). The primary key in a table is the column that makes each record different from all others.
- A shorthand way to describe a table is to use the table name followed by parentheses that contain all the field names, with the primary key underlined.
- Queries are questions that cause database software to extract the appropriate records from a table and specify the fields to be viewed. The most common language that database administrators use to access data in their tables is Structured Query Language, or SQL. The basic form of the SQL command that retrieves selected records from a table is SELECT-FROM-WHERE.
- Microsoft Office Access is a relational database that is part of the Microsoft Office 2007 system. In Access, a database developer can type field names for the data that will be stored and can assign an appropriate data type for each. After a table's design has been completed, a user can enter data into the table.
- An implicitly typed variable has a data type that is inferred from the expression used to initialize the variable. When you use an implicitly typed variable, an object's set of allowed properties and methods is not fixed when the code is written, but is determined when the program executes. Implicitly typed variables are used frequently in LINQ statements, which access data stored in a database.
- The LINQ (Language INtegrated Query) Project provides a set of general-purpose standard operators that allow queries to be constructed using syntax that is easy to understand. This syntax is similar to SQL's, and the compiler can check it for errors. The operators defined in LINQ can be used to query arrays, enumerable classes, XML, relational databases, and other sources. Some keywords in the LINQ vocabulary include `select`, `from`, and `where`.
- To add a database table to a Windows Forms project, you must perform two sets of tasks. From a project's main menu, you choose Data and then Add a New Data Source. Next, you browse for the database and answer a few questions. Then you drag a table onto your form. The table's data is bound to the form and you are supplied with a grid in which you can view the data.
- You can use a LINQ query to select a collection of data from a table when specific criteria are met. You can use AND and OR expressions to limit criteria in your LINQ statements. With text values, you can use `StartsWith()`, `EndsWith()`, and `Contains()`. You can use several aggregate operators, or operators that produce statistics for groups of data, including `Average()`, `Count()`, `Sum()`, `Max()`, and `Min()`.
- You can use the `orderby` operator to sort a collection of data based on a field or fields. Data items also can be grouped. A query body must end with a `select` clause or a `group` clause.

KEY TERMS

A **database** holds a group of files that an organization needs to support its applications.

Tables are database files. They are called *tables* because their contents are arranged in rows and columns.

A **primary key**, or **key** for short, is a value that uniquely identifies a record.

A **compound key** or **composite key** is constructed from multiple columns.

Database management software, also known as a **database management system (DBMS)**, is a set of programs that allows users to create table descriptions, identify keys, add, delete, and update records within a table, arrange records within a table so they are sorted by different fields, write questions that select specific records from a table for viewing, write questions that combine information from multiple tables, create reports, and keep data secure.

A **relational database** is one in which you can establish and maintain relationships between columns in the tables.

The **Leszynski naming convention** (LNC) is a convention for naming database elements that is most popular with Microsoft Access users and Visual Basic programmers.

Normalization is the process of designing and creating a set of database tables that satisfies users' needs and avoids many potential problems such as data redundancies and anomalies.

Data redundancy is the unnecessary repetition of data.

An **anomaly** is an irregularity in a database's design that causes problems and inconveniences.

A **query** is a request to retrieve information from a database using syntax that the database software can understand.

Query by example is a language that allows you to query relational databases by filling in blanks.

Structured Query Language, or **SQL**, is the most common language that database administrators use to access data in their tables.

SELECT-FROM-WHERE is the basic form of the SQL command that retrieves selected records from a table.

TLA is a three-letter abbreviation for *three-letter abbreviation*; it is the most popular type of abbreviation in technical terminology.

A **view** is a particular way of looking at a database in database management systems.

A **wildcard** is a symbol that means "any" or "all."

Microsoft Office Access is a relational database that is part of the Microsoft Office 2007 system.

An **implicitly typed variable** has a data type that is inferred from the expression used to initialize the variable.

The `var` data type creates an implicitly typed variable.

Type inference is the process of implicitly typing a variable; it is also called **duck typing**.

An **iteration variable** is used to hold each successive value in an array.

When a language is **strongly typed**, severe restrictions are placed on what data types can be mixed.

The **LINQ** (Language INtegrated Query) Project provides a set of general-purpose standard operators that allow queries to be constructed in C# using syntax that is easy to understand. This syntax is similar to SQL's, and the compiler can check it for errors.

The LINQ keyword `select` indicates what to select from a collection.

The LINQ keyword `from` indicates the collection or sequence from which data will be drawn.

The LINQ keyword `where` indicates conditions for selecting records.

A **restriction operator** places a restriction on which data is added to a collection.

A **projection operator** is one that projects, or sends off, specific data from a collection.

Aggregate operators are operators that produce statistics for groups of data.

The **`orderby` operator** sorts a collection of data based on a field or fields.

The **`group` operator** groups data by specified criteria.

REVIEW QUESTIONS

1. A database's files often are called ________.

   a. records
   b. tables
   c. catalogs
   d. registers

2. A value that uniquely identifies a record is a(n) ________.

   a. source
   b. ID
   c. key
   d. prime

3. Database management software is a set of programs that allows users to do all of the following except ________.

   a. add, delete, and update records within a table
   b. sort records in a table
   c. verify that all entered data is correct
   d. write queries

4. When you design a database table, you must do all of the following except ________.

   a. decide how many columns the table needs
   b. decide how many rows the table needs
   c. provide names for the columns
   d. provide a data type for each column

5. Which of the following would not be a good candidate for a primary key?
   a. The number of seats on a bus in a table that stores data about a city's fleet of buses
   b. A bus pass number in a table of a city's bus service customers
   c. A bus driver's ID number in a table that stores data about bus drivers
   d. A bus route number in a table that stores bus route data

6. Normalization ________.
   a. is the process of entering data into database tables
   b. is a design process that reduces redundancy and anomalies in databases
   c. is a flaw in database design that results in the repetition of data
   d. is a flaw in database design that causes anomalies

7. Which of the following do you know based on this database notation?

```
tblProducts(itemNum, description, price, quantity)
```

   a. The table name is `Products`.
   b. `itemNum` is the key field.
   c. No two descriptions hold the same value.
   d. `price` is a numeric field.

8. A question asked using syntax that database software can understand is a(n) ________.
   a. query
   b. anomaly
   c. request
   d. redundancy

9. The basic form of the SQL command that retrieves selected records from a table is ________.
   a. QUERY-BY-EXAMPLE
   b. SELECT-FROM-WHERE
   c. RETRIEVE-FROM-SOURCE
   d. STRUCTURED-QUERY-LIST

10. Based on the following SQL statement, you know that ________ will be displayed.

```
SELECT itemNum, price FROM tblProducts WHERE quantity <= 0
```

   a. two rows
   b. two columns
   c. more than two columns
   d. more than two rows

11. Microsoft Office Access is ________.
   a. a spreadsheet as well as a database
   b. no longer used by professional information specialists
   c. part of Visual Studio
   d. a typical database program

12. Which of the following is not true of implicitly typed variables?

    a. Their data types are inferred from the expression used to initialize the variable.

    b. They are declared using `var` as the data type.

    c. They use a process called type inference.

    d. They use a process called static typing.

13. Which of the following is true?

    a. `var product = new Product();` has the same meaning as `Product product = new Product();`

    b. `var x = 3;` has the same meaning as `double x = 3.0;`

    c. `var a = 17;` has the same meaning as `var b = 17;`

    d. `var Item();` has the same meaning as `var item = Item();`

14. C# is __________.

    a. strongly typed, like Visual Basic

    b. strongly typed, unlike Visual Basic

    c. weakly typed, like Visual Basic

    d. weakly typed, unlike Visual Basic

15. In __________ you can access database data.

    a. C# 3.0

    c. both of the above

    d. older versions of C#

    d. none of the above

16. The operators defined in LINQ can be used to query __________.

    a. arrays

    c. both of these

    b. relational databases

    d. none of the above

17. Consider the following code. In this example, `nums` is __________.

```
var nums =
     from n in numbers
     where n > 5
     select n;
```

    a. an array of integers

    c. an implicitly typed collection

    b. a database

    d. a single record in the collection numbers

18. Consider the following code. In this example, `numbers` is __________.

```
var nums =
     from n in numbers
     where n > 5
     select n;
```

a. an array of integers
b. a record in a database
c. a database
d. an implicitly typed collection

19. Consider the following code. In this example, x is ________.

```
var cheapProducts =
     from p in this.abcCompany.tblProducts
     where p.Price < MAX
     select p.Description;
foreach(var x in cheapProducts)
     listBox1.Items.Add(x);
```

a. a row in `tblProducts`
b. a column in `tblProducts`
c. a price
d. a description

20. Which of the following is not true of LINQ?
a. `Average()` is an aggregate operator.
b. `Max()` is an aggregate operator.
c. You can use the `orderby` operator to sort data.
d. You can use the `groupby` operator to group data.

EXERCISES

1. Create a program that holds an array of 10 integers. Prompt the user for and accept a value for each integer. Use LINQ statements to sort the integers in descending order and display them. Save the program as **LinqIntegersDemo.cs**.

2. Create a program that holds an array of eight integers. Prompt the user for and accept a value for each integer. Use LINQ statements to group the integers into two groups (even and odd), and then display each group. Figure 14-49 shows a typical execution. Save the program as **EvenAndOdd.cs**.

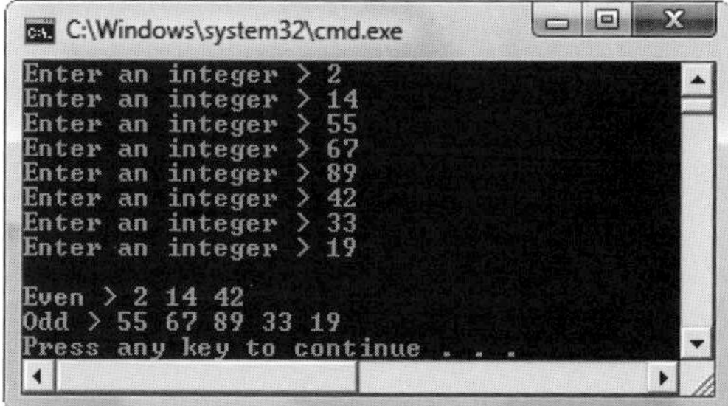

Figure 14-49 Typical execution of `EvenAndOdd` program

3. Create a program that contains an array of 12 strings. Prompt the user to enter a minimum string length and use LINQ statements to display all the strings that are at least as long as the value entered by the user. If no strings meet the criterion, display an appropriate message. Save the program as **LongWords.cs**.

4. Create a program that contains an array of 20 words of your choice. Use LINQ statements to display separate lists: One shows words that begin with letters in the first half of the alphabet (A through M), and the other list shows words that begin with letters in the second half (N through Z). Display a count of the number of words in each group. Save the program as **SplitAlphabet.cs**.

5. Create a `Book` class that contains `Title`, `Author`, and `Price` properties and a constructor that requires data for all three. Create a program that declares an array of at least eight `Book`s. Prompt the user for an author. Display all the books written by that author, or an appropriate message if no such books exist. Save the program as **BookQuery.cs**.

6. Create a `Book` class that contains `Title`, `Author`, and `Price` properties and a constructor that requires data for all three. Create a program that declares an array of at least eight `Book`s. Display the `Book` titles alphabetically by title and grouped by author. For an example, see Figure 14-50. Save the program as **BookQuery2.cs**.

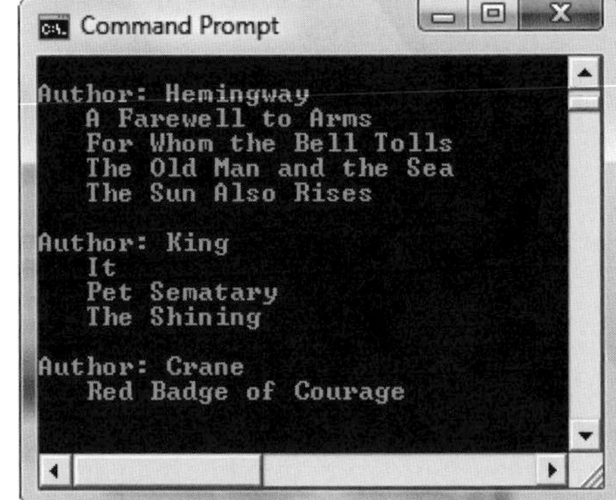

Figure 14-50 Typical execution of `BookQuery` program

7. Create an application that displays statistics about a database table when a user clicks various buttons. Use the HonestRalphsUsedCars database in the Student Files folder of your Student Disk, and display a count of the records, the most expensive car, and the least expensive car. Figure 14-51 shows the program before the user has clicked any buttons and after the user has clicked two of the buttons. Save the project as **CarStatistics**.

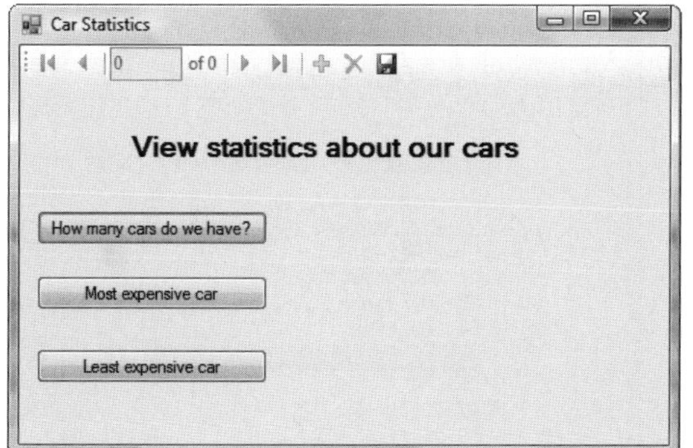

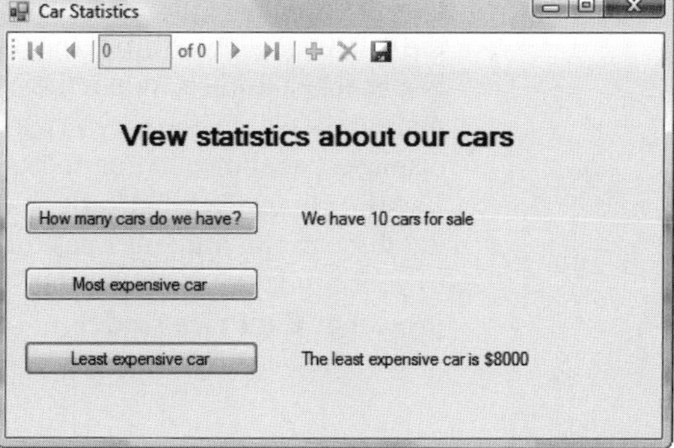

Figure 14-51 Typical execution of `CarStatistics` program before the user clicks any buttons and after the user has clicked two buttons

8. Create an application that allows a user to display cars of different makes. Use the HonestRalphsUsedCars database in the Student Files folder of your Student Disk. Your application should contain four check boxes labeled "Ford", "Chevrolet", "Cadillac", and "All". The user should be able to click any combination of check boxes to see the color, year, make, and price for each car with the desired make. For example, when the user clicks "Cadillac" and "Chevrolet", as in Figure 14-52, only those cars are displayed. Make sure that when the user changes selections, only the newly appropriate cars are visible. Save the project as **CarFinderByMake**.

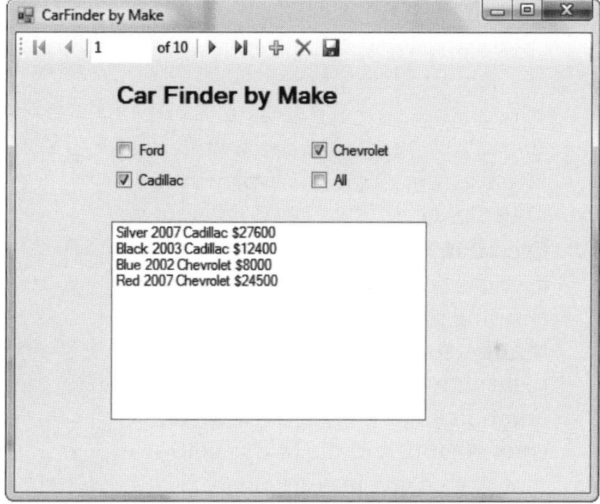

Figure 14-52 Execution of `CarFinderByMake` project

9. Create an application in which all of the cars in a database are displayed in a checked list box. When the user makes a selection, the car's price is displayed, as shown in Figure 14-53. Use the HonestRalphsUsedCars database in the Student Files folder of your Student Disk. Save the project as **CarPriceFinder**.

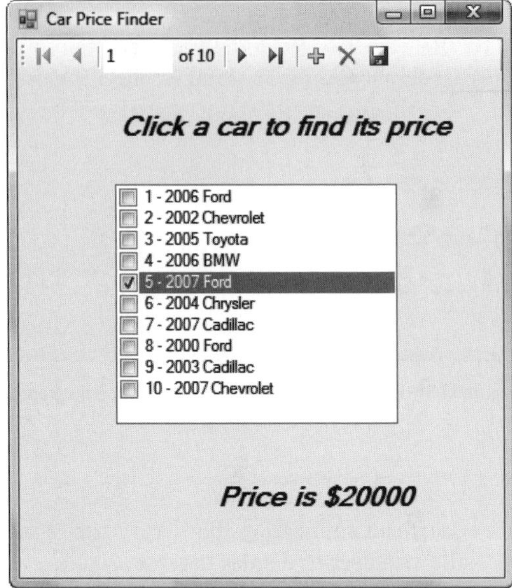

Figure 14-53 Execution of `CarPriceFinder` project

10. Create an application in which the user can select movies to view by entering part of the title or part of the director's name. The user clicks a radio button to choose which type of criterion is used. Then the user can enter all or part of the title's name or director's name into a `TextBox`. Allow the user to find matches regardless of case. See Figure 14-54 for a typical execution. Use the Movies database in the Student Files folder of your Student Disk. Save the project as **MovieFinder**.

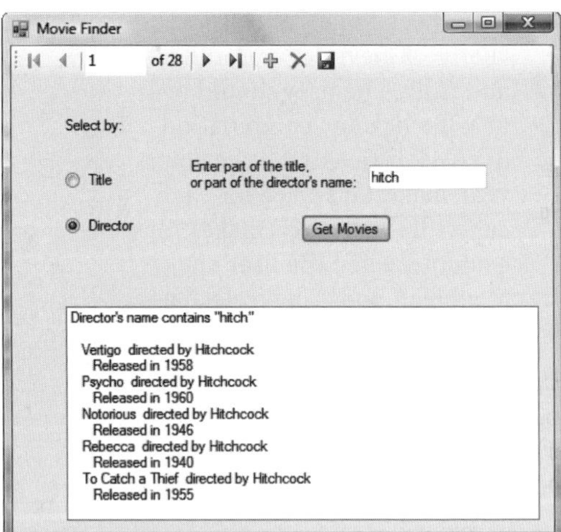

Figure 14-54 Typical execution of `MovieFinder` project

11. Create an application in which the user can enter a year to split a list of movies into those released before the indicated year and those released in the indicated year or afterward. Labels above each list should reflect the user's chosen cutoff year. Each list should be in order by release year. See Figure 14-55 for a typical execution. Use the Movies database in the Student Files folder of your Student Disk. Save the project as **MovieFinder2**.

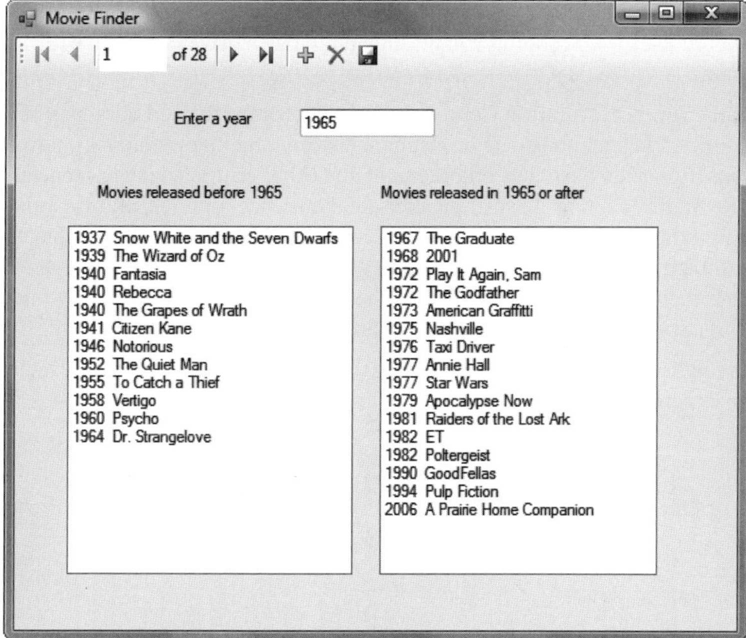

Figure 14-55 Typical execution of `MovieFinder2` project

DEBUGGING EXERCISES

Each of the following files in the Chapter.14 folder on your Student Disk has syntax and/or logical errors. In each case, determine the problem and fix the program. After you correct the errors, save each file using the same filename preceded with *Fixed*. For example, save DebugFourteen1.cs as **FixedDebugFourteen1.cs**.

a. DebugFourteen1.cs

b. DebugFourteen2.cs

c. DebugFourteen3.cs

d. DebugFourteen4.cs

UP FOR DISCUSSION

1. In this chapter, a phone book was mentioned as an example of a database you use frequently. Name some other examples.
2. Suppose you have authority to browse your company's database. The company keeps information on each employee's past jobs, health insurance claims, and any criminal records. Also suppose that you want to ask one of your co-workers out on a date. Should you use the database to obtain information about the person? If so, are there any limits on the data you should use? If not, should you be allowed to pay a private detective to discover similar data?
3. The FBI's National Crime Information Center (NCIC) is a computerized database of criminal justice information, including data on criminal histories, fugitives, stolen property, and missing persons. It is available to law enforcement and other criminal justice agencies 24 hours a day. Inevitably, such large systems contain some inaccuracies, and various studies have indicated that perhaps less than half the records in this database are complete, accurate, and unambiguous. Do you approve of this system or object to it? Would you change your mind if there were no inaccuracies? Is there a level of inaccuracy you would find acceptable to realize the benefits such a system provides?
4. What type of data might be useful to a community in the wake of a natural disaster? Who should pay for the expense of gathering, storing, and maintaining this data?

CHAPTER FIFTEEN

15

MULTITHREADING

In this chapter you will:

- Understand threads and multithreading
- Learn about a `Thread`'s life cycle
- Understand `Thread` properties
- Work with the limitations of parameterless `ThreadStart` delegates
- Understand `Thread` priorities
- Understand unsynchronized `Thread`s and how to synchronize them

Modern computer systems frequently need to perform concurrent tasks. In the early days of personal computing, you had to close one application before starting the next one. For example, you could not view spreadsheet data while typing a memo using your word-processing program. Such limitations seem very antiquated now. For example, when you download a video, you often want to be able to watch the beginning of it while the rest is still downloading. Such a system runs multiple threads of execution to perform the separate tasks during the same time period. In this chapter, you will learn how multithreading works to perform concurrent tasks.

UNDERSTANDING THREADS AND MULTITHREADING

A **thread** is the flow of execution of one set of program statements. When you execute a program statement by statement, from beginning to end, you are following a thread. Each of the programs you have written while working through this book has had a single thread; this means that at any one time, C# was executing only a single program statement.

»NOTE The term *thread* is short for *thread of execution.*

Single-thread programs contain statements that execute in very rapid sequence, but only one statement executes at a time. When a computer contains a single central processing unit (CPU, or processor), it can execute only one computer instruction at a time, regardless of its processor speed. When you use a computer with multiple CPUs, the computer can execute multiple instructions simultaneously.

C# allows you to launch, or start, multiple threads, no matter which type of processing system you use. Using multiple threads of execution is known as **multithreading**. As already noted, if you use a computer system that contains more than one CPU (such as a very large mainframe or supercomputer, or even a PC with a dual-core processor), multiple threads can execute simultaneously. Figure 15-1 illustrates how multithreading executes in a multiprocessor system. Three threads (named T1, T2, and T3 in the figure) all run at the same time, each using its own processor. In the figure, all three threads start and end at the same time. In any particular system, some threads might be complete sooner than others because they contain fewer tasks or tasks that can be carried out more quickly.

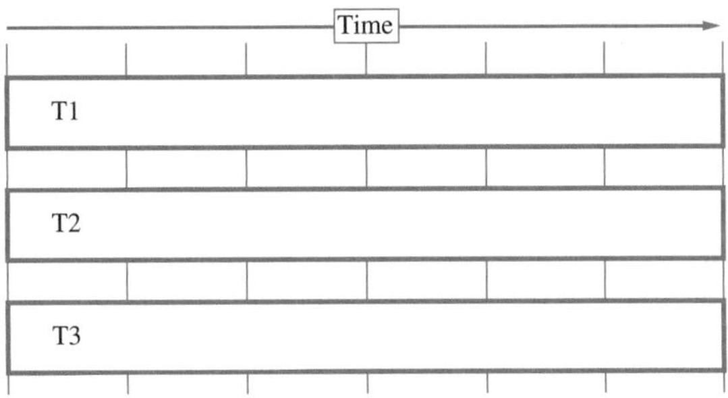

Figure 15-1 Executing multiple threads in a multiprocessing system

If you use a computer with a single processor, the multiple threads share the CPU's time, as shown in Figure 15-2. The CPU devotes a small amount of time to one task, and then devotes a small amount of time to another task. The CPU never actually performs two tasks at the same instant. Instead, it performs a piece of one task, and then a piece of another task. The CPU performs so quickly that each task seems to execute without interruption. The tasks execute **concurrently**, or during the same time period.

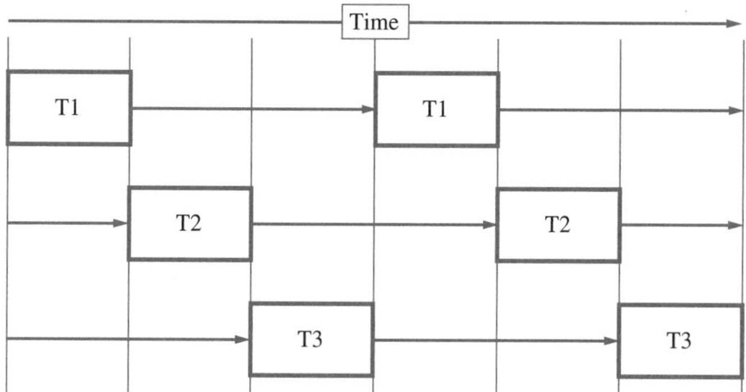

Figure 15-2 Executing multiple threads in a single-processor processing system

NOTE Programmers say that concurrent tasks execute **in parallel**. When you examine Figure 15-2, you can understand the use of this term.

In Figure 15-2, you can see that over time, the processor executes part of the first thread (T1). Then T1 must wait while the processor devotes some time to the second thread (T2), and then to the third thread (T3). Eventually, T1 runs for a while again, and then the other threads get more processing time. The intervals might not always be equal, as shown in Figure 15-2, but each thread gets a slice of the processor's time.

The concept of sharing processor time is known as **timeslicing**. With timeslicing, each thread receives a small segment of processor time, called a **quantum**. A thread can execute for this brief period, but at the end of the quantum, the processor can be assigned to a new thread.

Perhaps you have seen an expert chess player participate in chess games with several opponents at once. The chess player makes a move on the first playing board, and then moves to the second board against a second opponent while the first opponent analyzes his next move. The master can move to the third board, make a move, and return to the first board before the first opponent is even ready to respond. To the first opponent, it might seem as though the expert player is devoting all of her time to him. Because the expert is so fast, she can play other opponents in the first opponent's "downtime." Executing multiple threads on a single CPU works in a similar way. The CPU transfers its attention from thread to thread so quickly that the tasks don't even "miss" the CPU's attention.

You use multithreading to improve the performance of your programs. Multithreaded programs often run faster, but more important, they are more user friendly. With a multithreaded program, your user can continue to click buttons while your program is reading a data file. With multithreading, an animated figure can perform on one part of the screen while the user makes menu selections on another part of the screen. When you use the Internet, multithreading increases in importance. For example, you can begin to read a long text file or listen to an audio file while it is still downloading. Web users are likely to abandon a site if downloading a file takes too long. When you use multithreading to perform concurrent tasks, you are more likely to retain visitors to your Web site—this is particularly important if your site sells a product or service.

>> **NOTE** Programmers sometimes use the terms "thread of execution" or "execution context" to describe a thread. They also describe a thread as a lightweight process because it is not a full-blown program. Rather, a thread must run within the context of a full, heavyweight program.

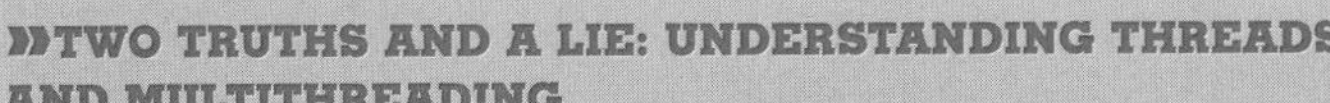

>>TWO TRUTHS AND A LIE: UNDERSTANDING THREADS AND MULTITHREADING

1. Single-thread programs contain statements that execute in very rapid sequence, but only one statement executes at a time.
2. On modern computers with a single CPU, any number of threads can execute simultaneously.
3. With timeslicing, each executing thread receives a small segment of processor time, called a quantum.

The false statement is #2. If you use a computer system that contains more than one CPU, multiple threads can execute simultaneously, but only one thread is executing at any moment on a single CPU, although threads can execute concurrently.

LEARNING ABOUT A THREAD'S LIFE CYCLE

>> **NOTE** "Started" is not a `Thread` state. In other words, it is not one of the defined `ThreadState` enumerations in the C# documentation. However, "started" describes many threads.

Technically, every program you have created is a thread. You can use the **`Thread` class** to create additional threads. A `Thread` object can be in one of several states during its life, including `Unstarted`, `Running`, and `Stopped`.

Figure 15-3 shows the relationship of many thread states, and Table 15-1 summarizes how they operate. Continue to refer to Figure 15-3 and Table 15-1 as you read through this section.

>> **NOTE** Figure 15-3 does not show the `Background` state. Later in this chapter, you will learn that any thread might be running in the background as well as being in one of the other states.

Figure 15-3 `Thread` states

Thread state	Description
`Unstarted`	The `Thread.Start()` method has not yet been invoked on the thread
`Running`	The thread has been started, it is not blocked, and there is no pending abort request
`StopRequested`	The thread has been requested to stop
`SuspendRequested`	The thread is being requested to suspend
`Background`	The thread is being executed in the background
`Stopped`	The thread has stopped
`WaitSleepJoin`	The thread is blocked
`Suspended`	The thread has been suspended
`AbortRequested`	The `Thread Abort()` method has been invoked on the thread, but the thread is not yet dead
`Aborted`	The thread state includes `AbortRequested` and the thread is dead, but its state has not yet been changed to `Stopped`

Table 15-1 The execution states of a `Thread`

A program that instantiates a `Thread` object passes a `ThreadStart` delegate to the object's constructor. A **`ThreadStart` delegate** acts as a reference to a method that the `Thread` executes. The delegate is initialized with a parameterless `void` method. When you create a `Thread`, it is in the `Unstarted` state. For example, the following statement instantiates a `Thread` named `myThread`:

```
Thread myThread = new Thread(WriteB);
```

NOTE You learned about delegates in Chapter 12. They are objects that act as intermediaries in transferring messages from senders to receivers.

In this statement, `WriteB` is the name of a method with return type `void` and no parameters. When you use the method's name as a parameter to `Thread`, you do not include parentheses. For example, `WriteB()` might be defined as follows:

```
public static void WriteB()
{
    Console.WriteLine("B");
}
```

Alternatively, you can create a `ThreadStart` object and assign it as the delegate as follows:

```
ThreadStart ts = new ThreadStart(WriteB);
Thread t = new Thread(ts);
```

Creating a `ThreadStart` object and then passing it to the `Thread` constructor is necessary in some other programming languages and in older versions of C#. However, in newer versions of C#, you do not need to create a `ThreadStart` object explicitly.

THE UNSTARTED, RUNNING, AND STOPPED STATES

»NOTE Threads created within the common language runtime are initially in the Unstarted state, but external threads that come into the runtime are already in the Running state.

A Thread that has been created remains Unstarted until a program calls the Thread's Start() method. The Start() method places the Thread in the Running state and returns control to the program. The name of the Running state is misleading. A better description for a started Thread is *runnable*, which means that the Thread *can* run. A Running Thread might not actually be running or executing at the moment because the CPU might be busy elsewhere. Just as your runnable automobile might not be running at the moment and cannot pass through an intersection until the traffic light allows it, a runnable Thread cannot run until the CPU allocates some time to it. When the operating system assigns a processor to a thread, it is **dispatching the thread**. A Thread that is Running has the capability of executing concurrently with other Threads; at any moment the CPU might be running a different Thread. When processor time is assigned to the Thread, the method that was specified as the ThreadStart delegate starts to execute.

»NOTE You can also use a ParameterizedThreadStart delegate to which you can pass a method that requires arguments. For more information, visit *msdn2.microsoft.com.*

Figure 15-4 shows a program that demonstrates a running thread. To use a Thread in a program, you include the statement using System.Threading; at the top of the file. Within the Main() method of the Thread1 class, a Thread named t is declared. The ThreadStart delegate WriteB is passed to the constructor. Before the shaded statement, the Thread named t is Unstarted; in the shaded statement, the Thread becomes Started. The Main() method runs in its own thread, writing "A" 200 times, and the Thread named t runs separately, writing "B" 200 times.

```
using System;
using System.Threading;
class Thread1
{
   const int TIMES = 200;
   public static void Main()
   {
      Thread t = new Thread(WriteB);
      t.Start();
      for(int x = 0; x < TIMES; ++x)
         Console.Write("A ");
   }
   public static void WriteB()
   {
      for(int x = 0; x < TIMES; ++x)
         Console.Write ("B ");
   }
}
```

Figure 15-4 The Thread1 class

Figure 15-5 shows two executions of the program. Notice that in the first execution, "A" prints 15 times before "B" prints for the first time, but in the second execution, "A" prints 28 times before "B" is written. If you ran the program additional times, each output might appear differently. Depending on available resources, the operating system might alternate between "A" and "B", or execute several repetitions of one thread in a row, followed by several repetitions of the other one. Each `Thread` completes its 200 repetitions, but you have no guarantee as to the exact pattern of execution; your only guarantee is that the threads execute concurrently.

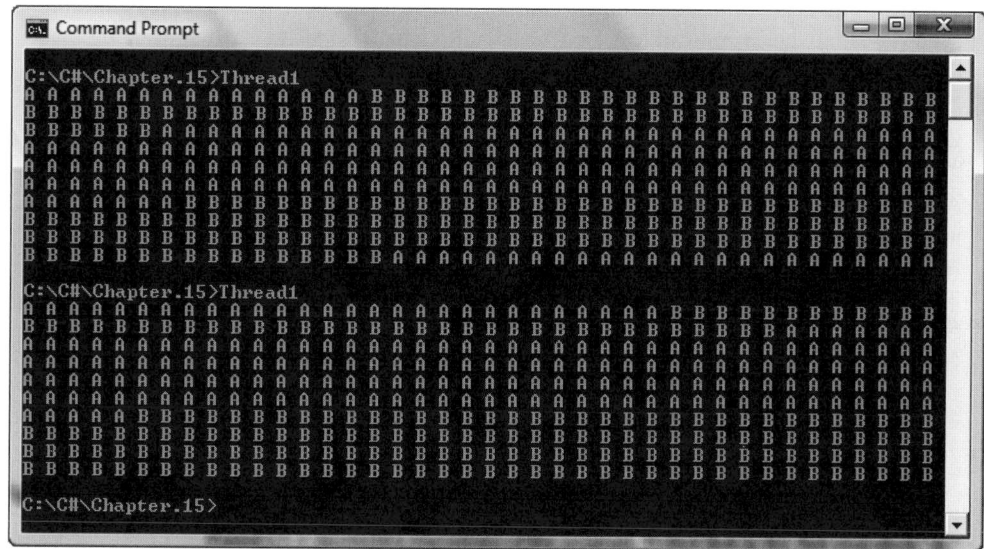

Figure 15-5 Two executions of the `Thread1` class

A `Running Thread` enters the `Stopped` state when its `ThreadStart` delegate terminates, which normally means the `Thread` has completed its task. In the program in Figure 15-4, the `Thread` named `t` enters the `Stopped` state when "B" has been written 200 times. A `Thread` can also be stopped by calling the `Abort()` method, which throws a `ThreadAbortException`. When a `Thread` is in the `Stopped` state and there are no references to it in the program, the system's garbage collector can remove the `Thread` object from memory. **Garbage collection** is automatic memory management; the garbage collector frees up memory occupied by objects that a program no longer needs.

> **NOTE** If you call a `Thread` method that the `Thread`'s present state does not allow, C# automatically throws a `ThreadStateException`. For example, you cannot call the `Resume()` method for a `Thread` that is new and has not been started, and you cannot call the `Start()` method for a `Thread` that has already been started and then suspended.

BLOCKED THREADS

A `Thread` is blocked when it cannot use a processor even if one becomes available. For example, when a thread issues an input or output (I/O) request, it becomes blocked until the operating system can complete the request. When the request is complete, the thread returns to the

Running state. As another example, a thread sometimes becomes blocked during synchronization. A thread that is being synchronized requires a lock on an object, and if a lock is not available, the thread is blocked. You will learn about synchronization later in this chapter.

THE WAITSLEEPJOIN STATE

When a thread encounters a statement that it cannot execute yet because some condition is not satisfied, the thread can call Wait(), which is a method of the Monitor class. (You will learn more about the Monitor class later in this chapter.) The thread then enters the WaitSleepJoin state. When another thread calls Pulse() or PulseAll(), the thread becomes Running again. The Pulse() method returns the next waiting Thread to the Running state; the PulseAll() method returns all waiting Threads to the Running state.

A Thread can also enter the WaitSleepJoin state by calling the Sleep() method using an argument that represents a number of milliseconds. When the sleep time expires, the Thread returns to the Running state. For example, Figure 15-6 shows a Thread2 class in which the Main() method instantiates and starts three threads. Within the delegate method for each thread, a random value of up to 6,000 milliseconds (6 seconds) is generated using the Random.Next() method, and it is passed to the Sleep() method. Figure 15-7 shows the results of three executions. The threads start and stop in different orders, partially depending on the time they sleep and on the processing time allocated to each thread behind the scenes.

```
using System;
using System.Threading;
class Thread2
{
   static Random time = new Random();
   static int milliseconds;
   const int LIMIT = 6000;
   public static void Main()
   {
      Thread t1 = new Thread(Method1);
      Thread t2 = new Thread(Method2);
      Thread t3 = new Thread(Method3);
      t1.Start();
      t2.Start();
      t3.Start();
   }
   public static void Method1()
   {
      milliseconds = time.Next(LIMIT);
      Console.WriteLine("Method 1 will sleep for {0} milliseconds",
         milliseconds);
      Thread.Sleep(milliseconds);
      Console.WriteLine("Method 1 ended");
   }
```

Figure 15-6 The Thread2 class (*continued*)

```
    public static void Method2()
    {
       milliseconds = time.Next(LIMIT);
       Console.WriteLine("Method 2 will sleep for {0} milliseconds",
          milliseconds);
       Thread.Sleep(milliseconds);
       Console.WriteLine("Method 2 ended");
    }
    public static void Method3()
    {
       milliseconds = time.Next(LIMIT);
       Console.WriteLine("Method 3 will sleep for {0} milliseconds",
          milliseconds);
       Thread.Sleep(milliseconds);
       Console.WriteLine("Method 3 ended");
    }
}
```

Figure 15-6 (*continued*)

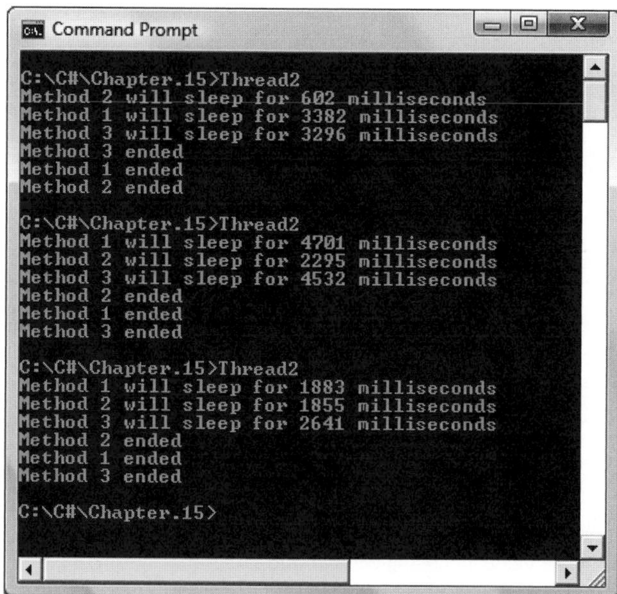

Figure 15-7 Three executions of the `Thread2` program

If a thread enters the `WaitSleepJoin` state via the `Wait()` or `Sleep()` method, the `Thread` can be returned to the `Running` state by calling the `Thread`'s `Interrupt()` method from another program thread. The interrupted thread throws a `ThreadInterruptionException` when its `Interrupt()` method is called.

If a thread cannot finish until another thread does, the one that can't continue can call the other thread's `Join()` method. The two threads are then joined, meaning that the thread that couldn't continue leaves the `WaitSleepJoin` state and enters the `Running` state when the other thread finishes.

THE `SUSPENDED` STATE

When a running thread's `Suspend()` method is called, the thread enters the `Suspended` state. When another thread calls the suspended thread's `Resume()` method, the thread's state returns to `Running`. The methods `Suspend()` and `Resume()` are deprecated, and you should not use them. (You will receive a compiler warning if you do.) The term **deprecated** is applied to programming language features that have been superseded by newer techniques and should not be used. Deprecated methods remain in the current version of a language to provide backward compatibility so that older programs will work with the newer version of the software. Later in this chapter, you will learn the currently approved method for suspending and resuming a thread using `Monitor` class methods.

»TWO TRUTHS AND A LIE: LEARNING ABOUT A `Thread's` LIFE CYCLE

1. A particular `Thread` might never be `Suspended` or `Aborted`.
2. A `Thread` is always `Running` before it is `Aborted`.
3. A `Thread` is always `Suspended` before it is `Stopped`.

The false statement is #3. A `Stopped` `Thread` might never have been `Suspended`.

UNDERSTANDING `THREAD` PROPERTIES

Each `Thread` contains a number of useful properties. Selected properties are listed in Table 15-2.

»NOTE You will learn about priorities later in this chapter.

Property	Description
`CurrentThread`	Gets the `Thread` that is currently running
`IsAlive`	Gets the live status of the `Thread`; returns `false` if the `Thread` is `Unstarted` or `Stopped`; otherwise returns `true`
`IsBackground`	Gets or sets a value indicating whether the `Thread` is a background `Thread`
`Name`	Gets or sets the name of the current `Thread`
`Priority`	Gets or sets the scheduling priority of a `Thread`
`ThreadState`	Gets a value indicating a `Thread`'s state

Table 15-2 Selected `Thread` properties

The properties in Table 15-2 can be useful in helping you to manipulate Threads. For example, suppose you write a program in which you start a Thread named myThread. Further suppose you have a task that you want the Main() method thread to perform only after myThread is complete. You can write a loop such as the following:

```
while(myThread.IsAlive);
//Perform final Main() method tasks
```

The while loop in the code has an empty body. The Main() method thread will continue to loop until myThread comes to completion; then the Main() method thread can perform its final tasks.

As another example of the usefulness of the properties, suppose you create two Threads named myThread and yourThread. You can assign a name to each Thread, as in the following:

```
myThread.Name = "Mine";
yourThread.Name = "Yours";
```

Then, suppose both Threads use the same method. Within the method, you can use a statement such as the following to understand which thread is executing the method:

```
Console.WriteLine("The {0} thread is running", Thread.CurrentThread.Name);
```

UNDERSTANDING THE BACKGROUND STATE

A thread can reside in the Background state at the same time it resides in any of the other states. A thread in the **Background state** runs when time becomes available because no threads in the foreground state need CPU time. You can place a thread in the Background state by setting its IsBackground property to true. A process must wait for all foreground threads (threads not in the Background state) to finish executing and enter the Stopped state before the process can end. If the only threads remaining in a process are background threads, each thread is terminated and the process ends.

For example, the program in Figure 15-8 declares two threads and sets one's IsBackground property to true in the shaded statement. Both threads are started, and because each thread sleeps during its execution, both threads have an opportunity to run and they finish to completion. Figure 15-9 shows the output.

```
using System;
using System.Threading;
class TestBackgroundThread
{
   public static void Main()
   {
      Thread foregroundThread = new Thread(LoopFore);
      Thread backgroundThread = new Thread(LoopBack);
      backgroundThread.IsBackground = true;
      foregroundThread.Start();
      backgroundThread.Start();
   }
```

Figure 15-8 The TestBackgroundThread class (*continued*)

```
    public static void LoopFore()
    {
       for(int x = 0; x < 5; ++x)
       {
          Console.WriteLine("Foreground count: {0}", x);
          Thread.Sleep(300);
       }
       Console.WriteLine("Foreground loop finished.");
    }
    public static void LoopBack()
    {
       for(int x = 0; x < 5; ++x)
       {
          Console.WriteLine("Background count: {0}", x);
          Thread.Sleep(300);
       }
       Console.WriteLine("Background loop finished.");
    }
}
```

Figure 15-8 (*continued*)

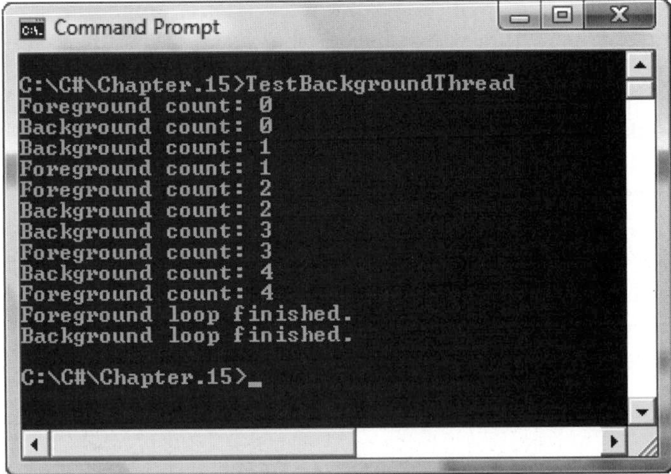

Figure 15-9 Output of the `TestBackgroundThread` program

The application in Figure 15-10 contains only two small changes from the one in Figure 15-8:

» The class name is changed to `TestBackgroundThread2`.

» The number of loops in the `LoopBack()` method (the delegate to the `backgroundThread` object) is increased.

```
using System;
using System.Threading;
class TestBackgroundThread2
{
   public static void Main()
   {
      Thread foregroundThread = new Thread(LoopFore);
      Thread backgroundThread = new Thread(LoopBack);
      backgroundThread.IsBackground = true;
      foregroundThread.Start();
      backgroundThread.Start();
   }
   public static void LoopFore()
   {
      for(int x = 0; x < 5; ++x)
      {
         Console.WriteLine("Foreground count: {0}", x);
         Thread.Sleep(300);
      }
      Console.WriteLine("Foreground loop finished.");
   }
   public static void LoopBack()
   {
      for(int x = 0; x < 100; ++x)
      {
         Console.WriteLine("Background count: {0}", x);
         Thread.Sleep(300);
      }
      Console.WriteLine("Background loop finished.");
   }
}
```

Figure 15-10 The `TestBackgroundThread2` class

»NOTE When you run the program in Figure 15-10 multiple times, sometimes the last (fifth) loop in the background thread will execute, and sometimes it will not, depending on how the CPU allocated resources at the time.

Figure 15-11 shows the output of the `TestBackgroundThread2` program. When the foreground thread finishes, the background thread is terminated even though its method had many more loops to perform.

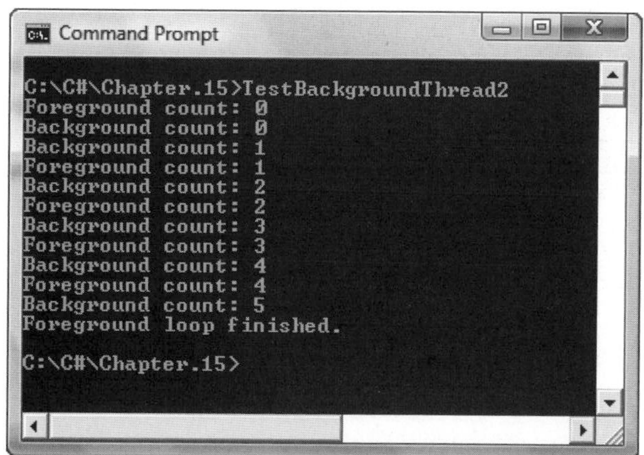

Figure 15-11 Output of the `TestBackgroundThread2` program

»TWO TRUTHS AND A LIE: UNDERSTANDING Thread PROPERTIES

1. The Thread property CurrentThread makes a Thread become the currently running Thread.
2. The Thread property IsAlive returns true or false, indicating whether the Thread is alive.
3. The Thread property Name allows you to assign a name to a Thread.

The false statement is #1. The Thread property CurrentThread gets the currently running Thread.

WORKING WITH THE LIMITATIONS OF PARAMETERLESS ThreadStart DELEGATES

In Figures 15-8 and 15-10, the methods LoopFore() and LoopBack() are very similar. The only differences are in the number of repetitions in each loop and the description displayed in each WriteLine() statement. It would be convenient to write a single method that accepts the repetition value and the name of the currently executing thread to a single method, but a ThreadStart delegate method must be parameterless. You can solve this problem by encapsulating the ThreadStart method in its own class.

For example, Figure 15-12 shows an application in which a nonstatic class named ThreadTest is created. The class contains fields that can hold the name of a Thread and a number of loop repetitions. The class constructor accepts values for both of these and assigns them to the fields. In the Main() method, two instances of this class are created, and then each Thread is instantiated using one of the two ThreadTest object's Loop() methods. The result is identical to the output shown in Figure 15-11 because each Thread uses its own version of the Loop() method as its ThreadStart delegate.

```
using System;
using System.Threading;
class TestBackgroundThread3
{
   public static void Main()
   {
      ThreadTest foreTest = new ThreadTest("Foreground", 5);
      ThreadTest backTest = new ThreadTest("Background", 100);
      Thread foregroundThread = new Thread(foreTest.Loop);
      Thread backgroundThread = new Thread(backTest.Loop);
      backgroundThread.IsBackground = true;
      foregroundThread.Start();
      backgroundThread.Start();
   }
```

Figure 15-12 The TestBackgroundThread3 class (*continued*)

```
    public class ThreadTest
    {
       String name;
       int repetitions;
       public ThreadTest(string name, int reps)
       {
          this.name = name;
          repetitions = reps;
       }
       public void Loop()
       {
           for(int x = 0; x < repetitions; ++x)
           {
              Console.WriteLine("{0} count: {1}", name, x);
              Thread.Sleep(300);
           }
           Console.WriteLine("{0} loop finished.", name);
       }
    }
}
```

Figure 15-12 (*continued*)

`ThreadTest` is an example of a **wrapper class**—a class that you wrap around data or methods to give them added functionality.

»NOTE In other OO languages, such as Java, you can extend the `Thread` class to create a child. In C#, `Thread` is a **sealed class**, meaning you cannot extend it. An abstract class also cannot be extended, but when a class is sealed rather than abstract, you can create instances.

»TWO TRUTHS AND A LIE: WORKING WITH THE LIMITATIONS OF PARAMETERLESS `ThreadStart` DELEGATES

1. A `ThreadStart` delegate method can, at most, accept one parameter of type `Delegate`.
2. You can encapsulate a `ThreadStart` method in its own class.
3. A wrapper class is a class that you wrap around data or methods to give them added functionality.

The false statement is #1. A `ThreadStart` delegate method must be parameterless.

THREAD PRIORITIES

Every `Thread` has a `Priority` property. A **priority** is a rank of preferential access to an operating system's resources. `Threads` with the same priority are called **peers**. The priorities in C# are defined in the **`ThreadPriority` enumeration**. The `ThreadPriority` values are:

- » `ThreadPriority.Lowest`
- » `ThreadPriority.BelowNormal`
- » `ThreadPriority.Normal`
- » `ThreadPriority.AboveNormal`
- » `ThreadPriority.Highest`

NOTE In Chapter 10, you learned that an enumeration is a list of values in which names are substituted for numeric values. Even though `ThreadPriority.Lowest` and all the other values stand for numbers, you cannot use a constant number when setting a priority—you must use one of the named `ThreadPriority` values.

When you do not assign a value to a `Thread`'s `Priority`, its `Priority` is `ThreadPriority.Normal` by default. Thread priorities are relative values. That is, they represent differences only in comparison to the priorities of other threads. For example, two `BelowNormal` priority `Threads` are just as equal to each other as two `AboveNormal` priority `Threads` are to each other.

NOTE The priority of a thread does not affect the thread's state; the state of the thread must be `Running` before it can be scheduled.

Thread scheduling is the process by which an operating system allocates processor time to each running thread. The thread scheduler usually keeps the highest-priority thread running. If there is more than one thread with the highest priority, the scheduler ensures that each receives a quantum in rotation (often called round-robin fashion). Lower-priority `Threads` usually run only when higher-priority `Threads` are not runnable (such as when they are finished, suspended, or asleep).

In general, when `ThreadA` has a higher priority than `ThreadB`, `ThreadA` will run and `ThreadB` will wait. However, sometimes C# will choose to run `ThreadB` to avoid starvation. **Starvation** occurs when a `Thread` cannot make any progress because of the priorities of other `Threads`. The result of starvation can be similar to creating an infinite loop—the program runs continuously without completing because one or more threads never get the opportunity to execute.

NOTE The ultimate form of starvation is called deadlock. **Deadlock** occurs when two `Threads` must wait for each other to do something before either can progress.

Consider the `DemoMessageThreadPriorities` class in Figure 15-13. It is similar to the `TestBackgroundThread3` class in Figure 15-12, in that it declares a class to hold `Thread` information and a parameterless method named `Loop()` that can be used as a `ThreadStart` delegate. The `Main()` method declares three `Threads` named `a`, `b`, and `c`. The `a` `Thread` is assigned the lowest priority, the `c` `Thread` is assigned the highest priority, and the `b` `Thread` has normal priority by default. All three `Threads` are started.

```
using System;
using System.Threading;
class DemoMessageThreadPriorities
{
   public static void Main()
   {
      MessageThread msg1 = new MessageThread("AAA");
      MessageThread msg2 = new MessageThread("BBB");
      MessageThread msg3 = new MessageThread("CCC");
      Thread a = new Thread(msg1.Loop);
      Thread b = new Thread(msg2.Loop);
      Thread c = new Thread(msg3.Loop);
      a.Priority = ThreadPriority.Lowest;
      c.Priority = ThreadPriority.Highest;
      a.Start();
      b.Start();
      c.Start();
   }
```

Figure 15-13 The `DemoMessageThreadPriorities` program (*continued*)

```
    public class MessageThread
    {
       private const int TIMES = 100;
       private String message;
       public MessageThread(String msg)
       {
          message = msg;
       }
       public void Loop()
       {
          for(int x = 0; x < TIMES; ++x)
             Console.Write(" " + message + " ");
       }
}
```

Figure 15-13 (*continued*)

Figure 15-14 shows the output in two executions of the application. The messages are interspersed, and in a different order in each execution, but in both cases, the 100 high-priority "CCC" messages are all displayed before the normal-priority "BBB" messages finish. In both executions, the low-priority "AAA" messages finish last.

NOTE
Operating systems are not required to honor the priority of a thread.

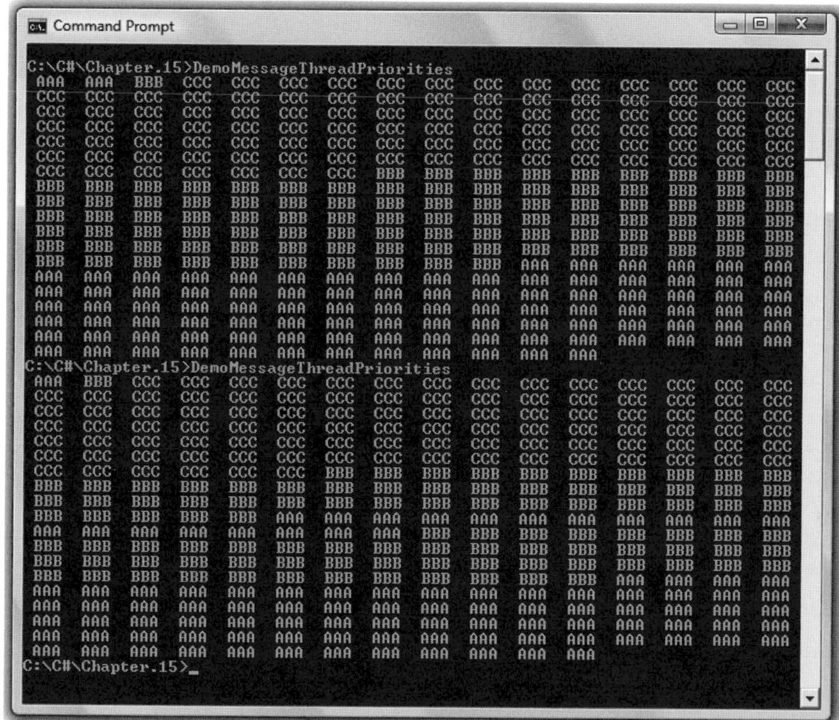

Figure 15-14 Two executions of the `DemoMessageThreadPriorities` program

»TWO TRUTHS AND A LIE: THREAD PRIORITIES

1. A priority is a rank, in terms of preferential access to the operating system's resources; `Thread`s with the same priority are called peers.
2. Thread scheduling is the process by which an operating system allocates processor time to each running thread.
3. Only one thread at a time can have the highest-priority value—otherwise, the scheduler throws an exception.

The false statement is #3. If there is more than one thread with the highest priority, the scheduler ensures that each receives a quantum in rotation (often called round-robin fashion).

UNDERSTANDING UNSYNCHRONIZED AND SYNCHRONIZED THREADS

Sometimes multiple threads need to use a shared object. For example, consider an `InventoryItem` class like the one shown in Figure 15-15. The class contains fields that hold the description of an inventory item and the number of items currently in stock.

```
class InventoryItem
{
   private String description;
   private int quantity;
   public InventoryItem(String desc, int quan)
   {
      Description = desc;
      Quantity = quan;
   }
   public String Description {get; set;}
   public int Quantity {get; set;}
}
```

Figure 15-15 The `InventoryItem` class

Suppose that two threads are both allowed to retrieve and set the value of `quantity` when items are ordered. Because both threads can alter the contents of a shared object, the results can be unpredictable. For example, consider the following scenario, in which two threads are assigned the tasks of filling customer orders of `Inventory` objects:

1. A first thread accesses `quantity`. Assume that the original value of `quantity` is 1.
2. Another thread accesses the same value, which is still 1.
3. The first thread fills a customer order and subtracts 1 from `quantity`, leaving 0.
4. The second thread, which has already accessed the `quantity` value as 1, fills a different customer's order and subtracts 1 from the quantity, making its value –1.

5. The `Inventory` object now has –1 in the `quantity` field, but two items have been ordered, even though only one originally existed. There will be confusion in the warehouse, problems in the accounting department, and one unsatisfied customer, because two orders were supposed to be filled for one item each, but only one item is in stock.

Similar problems could occur if two threads are allowed to schedule a meeting on your calendar after determining that 10:30 on Tuesday is an available time slot, or two threads update your bank account balance with automatic payroll deposits from two part-time jobs you hold. Unless shared objects are managed correctly, errors and unpredictable results can occur. To manage threads and prevent this sort of inconsistency, you can give exclusive use of a shared object to one `Thread` at a time. In other words, one thread has access to an object while all the other threads are kept waiting. When the thread with exclusive access completes its tasks, only then is another thread allowed to access the object. This process of mutual exclusion is called **thread synchronization**.

» **NOTE** The flaw in a system in which the results of a process are critically dependent on the timing of other processes is called a **race hazard**. The term *race hazard* comes from the notion of two processes racing with each other to influence the output first.

The **`Monitor` class** provides the means to lock objects to implement synchronized access to shared data. **Locking an object** means that only one thread can access it.

The `Monitor` class maintains the following for each synchronized object:

» A reference to the thread that currently holds the lock

» A reference to a **ready queue** that contains the threads that are ready to obtain the lock

» A reference to a **waiting queue** that contains the threads waiting for notification of a change in the state of the locked object

A `Thread` can call the `Monitor` method `Enter()` to acquire a lock on the data in that object. While an object is locked, all other threads that attempt to acquire a lock are blocked. When a thread that locks an object no longer needs it, the thread calls the `Monitor` method `Exit()` to release the lock. Then, if there is a `Thread` that was blocked previously, it can acquire a lock on the object.

Additionally, C# provides an easier-to-use, more intuitive way to lock an object. You can place the keyword `lock` before a block of code as follows:

```
lock(reference)
{
    // code that requires synchronization
}
```

Using `lock()` is simply a shortcut for using the `Monitor` class `Enter()` and `Exit()` methods. The `lock` keyword is an example of **syntactic sugar**, which refers to any programming construct that makes programs easier to read and write. You should use `lock()` in your own programs, but understand that it replaces `Monitor.Enter()` and `Monitor.Exit()` in case you see that syntax in programs written by others.

UNDERSTANDING THE PROBLEMS WITH UNSYNCHRONIZED THREADS

Figure 15-16 contains an `Order` class that is a wrapper for the `PlaceOrder()` method. The class constructor accepts an order number. The `PlaceOrder()` method processes an order for a single item, and performs the following tasks:

- » Displays the order number being processed
- » Displays the current quantity in stock before filling the order
- » Announces whether the order can or cannot be filled; if it can, the method subtracts 1 from the quantity in stock
- » Displays the updated quantity

```
public class Order
{
   private int orderNum;
   public Order(int num)
   {
      orderNum = num;
   }
   public void PlaceOrder()
   {
      Console.WriteLine("Processing order {0}", orderNum);
      Console.WriteLine("   Order {0} - Number left: {1}",
         orderNum, InventoryApp.item.Quantity);
      if(InventoryApp.item.Quantity <= 0)
         Console.WriteLine
            ("   Order {0} - Order cannot be filled", orderNum);
      else
      {
         Console.WriteLine
            ("   Order {0} - Order will be filled", orderNum);
         --InventoryApp.item.Quantity;
      }
      Console.WriteLine("   After Order {0} - Number left: {1}",
         orderNum, InventoryApp.item.Quantity);
   }
}
```

» DON'T DO IT

There are potential problems in altering a shared item.

Figure 15-16 The `Order` class

Figure 15-17 declares the `InventoryApp` class that holds the `InventoryItem` and starts the threads. An `InventoryItem` is declared globally; it represents two shirts in stock. In a full-blown application, you might have an array of items, or more likely, a file with many stored items, and the quantities of each available item would most likely be much larger. However, to keep this example simple, assume that just one type of item is available, and that there are just two of them. The `Main()` method declares three `Orders` with different order numbers, and three Threads that each place an order for an item. (Such a scenario could occur at a call center with three telephone operators who might each accept a call from different customers wanting to place orders.)

```
using System;
using System.Threading;
class InventoryApp
{
   public static InventoryItem item = new InventoryItem("shirt", 2);
   public static void Main()
   {
      Order first = new Order(111);
      Order second = new Order(222);
      Order third = new Order(333);
      Thread firstOrder = new Thread(first.PlaceOrder);
      Thread secondOrder = new Thread(second.PlaceOrder);
      Thread thirdOrder = new Thread(third.PlaceOrder);
      firstOrder.Start();
      secondOrder.Start();
      thirdOrder.Start();
   }
}
```

Figure 15-17 The InventoryApp program

»NOTE In a full-blown inventory application, many more activities would be performed when an order is filled. For example, an order might be printed to pull an item from the warehouse, a customer bill might be printed or an e-mail notification might be sent to the customer, or a credit card balance might be checked.

»NOTE For convenience, the classes in Figures 15-15, 15-16, and 15-17 are stored in a single file named InventoryApp.cs on your Student Disk.

Figure 15-18 shows two typical program executions. It demonstrates how threads work unpredictably when they are not synchronized. The first execution in Figure 15-18 shows the following:

- » Order 111 begins processing.
- » Order 222 begins processing.
- » Order 333 processing begins.
- » Order 333 determines that two items are in stock, notifies the customer that the order will be filled, and displays a message that one item is left.
- » Order 222 has accessed inventory before Order 333 was complete, so Order 222 "thinks" that two items are left. The customer is notified that the order will be filled, and the next message correctly indicates that after Order 222, there are no items left.
- » Order 111 has accessed inventory before either Order 222 or 333 was filled, so the customer is told that two items are left, but then the customer is told the order cannot be filled. After Order 111, there are no items left.

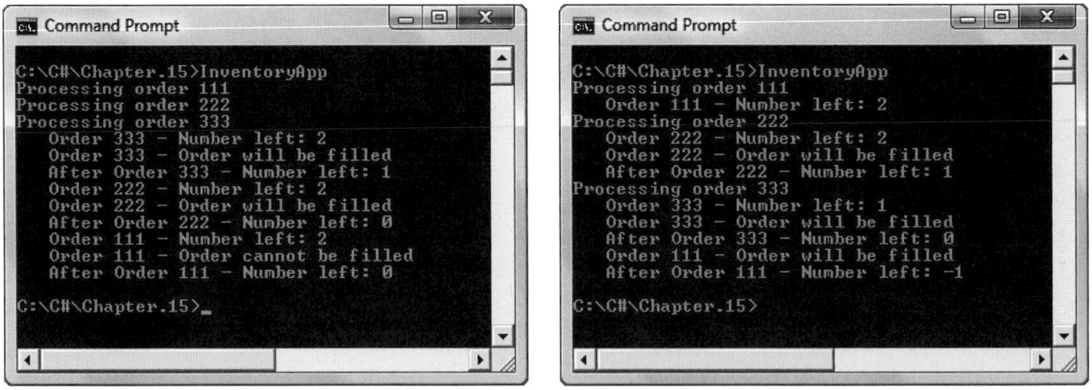

```
Command Prompt

C:\C#\Chapter.15>InventoryApp
Processing order 111
Processing order 222
Processing order 333
   Order 333 - Number left: 2
   Order 333 - Order will be filled
   After Order 333 - Number left: 1
   Order 222 - Number left: 2
   Order 222 - Order will be filled
   After Order 222 - Number left: 0
   Order 111 - Number left: 2
   Order 111 - Order cannot be filled
   After Order 111 - Number left: 0

C:\C#\Chapter.15>_
```

```
Command Prompt

C:\C#\Chapter.15>InventoryApp
Processing order 111
   Order 111 - Number left: 2
Processing order 222
   Order 222 - Number left: 2
   Order 222 - Order will be filled
   After Order 222 - Number left: 1
Processing order 333
   Order 333 - Number left: 1
   Order 333 - Order will be filled
   After Order 333 - Number left: 0
   Order 111 - Order will be filled
   After Order 111 - Number left: -1

C:\C#\Chapter.15>
```

Figure 15-18 Two executions of the `InventoryApp` program

In this first execution, although the inventory quantity value was briefly incorrect during the order process, it does end up with the correct value. However, one customer was incorrectly notified about stock availability.

In the second execution in Figure 15-18, the outcome is worse. Because the processor allocates time differently during this program run, the following occurs:

- Order 111 begins processing, and determines that two items are available.
- Order 222 starts processing, determines that two items are available, fills the order, and reduces inventory to 1.
- Order 333 starts processing, determines that one item is left, and fills the order, reducing inventory to 0.
- Order 111 indicates that the order can be filled (because when it accessed inventory, the quantity available was still 2), incorrectly notifies the customer that the order will be filled, and then reduces the inventory to a negative value.

In this second scenario, three customers believe their orders will be filled, one is disappointed (or angry, vowing never to deal with the company again!), and the inventory records hold an invalid quantity.

If you ran this application several more times, you would discover that the `PlaceOrder()` statements are displayed in a variety of sequences, and that some of the statements are almost always inaccurate.

SYNCHRONIZING THREADS

If you run the `InventoryApp` program multiple times, different events will occur in different sequences; sometimes the results will be dire, and sometimes they will not. The situation can be easily remedied by locking the `InventoryItem` object until each thread finishes its ordering process.

Figure 15-19 shows a modified `PlaceOrder()` method in which the minor changes from the original version have been shaded. The phrase `lock(item)` and an opening brace have been inserted before the statements that process an order, and a closing brace has been inserted after them. As each order is processed, a lock is placed on the `InventoryItem`. That way, each order can access the quantity, determine whether the order can be placed, and update the quantity without interference from other threads. Figure 15-20 shows how the program executes. No matter how many times you run the application, each thread will be allowed to complete its execution and use the `InventoryItem` without interference from any other threads.

```
public void PlaceOrder()
{
    lock(InventoryApp.item)
    {
        Console.WriteLine("Processing order {0}", orderNum);
        Console.WriteLine("   Order {0} - Number left: {1}",
           orderNum, InventoryApp.item.Quantity);
        if(InventoryApp.item.Quantity <= 0)
           Console.WriteLine("   Order {0} - Order cannot be filled", orderNum);
        else
        {
           Console.WriteLine("   Order {0} - Order will be filled", orderNum);
           --InventoryApp.item.Quantity;
        }
        Console.WriteLine("   After Order {0} - Number left: {1}",
           orderNum, InventoryApp.item.Quantity);
    }
}
```

Figure 15-19 The modified `PlaceOrder()` method that uses a lock

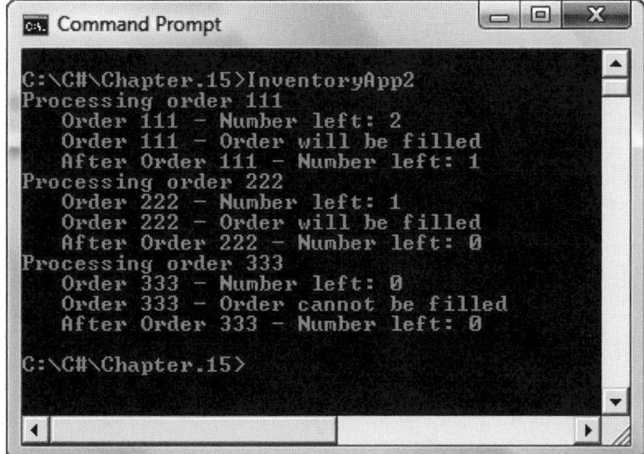

Figure 15-20 Typical execution of the `InventoryApp2` program

NOTE
The modified `PlaceOrder()` method is stored on your Student Disk in a complete application named InventoryApp2.cs.

»TWO TRUTHS AND A LIE: UNDERSTANDING UNSYNCHRONIZED AND SYNCHRONIZED THREADS

1. Because multiple threads can alter the contents of a shared object, the results can be unpredictable unless you give exclusive use of the shared object to one thread at a time.
2. Thread synchronization is the technique of making sure one thread is finished running before any other threads can run.
3. Locking an object means that only one thread can access it; to lock an object, you can use the `Monitor` class `Enter()` and `Exit()` methods, or the shortcut `lock` keyword and a `lock` block.

The false statement is #2. Thread synchronization is the process of excluding all but one thread from an object to avoid timing errors.

YOU DO IT

CREATING A THREAD

In the next steps, you will create a `Thread` so that you can observe how your thread and the main program thread share the resources of the CPU.

To create a Thread:

1. Open a new file in your text editor and type the `using` statements the program needs.

```
using System;
using System.Threading;
```

2. Start the `HelloGoodbye` class by typing the class header and declaring a constant for the number of repetitions that will be performed in the class.

```
class HelloGoodbye
{
   const int TIMES = 40;
```

3. Add a `Main()` method that instantiates a `Thread` using a method named `Goodbye()` as the `ThreadStart` delegate, then start the thread. End the `Main()` method by displaying "Hello " 40 times.

```
   public static void Main()
   {
      Thread t = new Thread(Goodbye);
      t.Start();
      for(int x = 0; x < TIMES; ++x)
         Console.Write("Hello ");
   }
```

4. Add the `Goodbye()` method that acts as the `ThreadStart` delegate for the thread declared in `Main()`. The method displays "Goodbye " 40 times. Add a closing curly brace for the class.

```
      public static void Goodbye()
      {
         for(int x = 0; x < TIMES; ++x)
            Console.Write ("Goodbye ");
      }
   }
```

5. Save the file as **HelloGoodbye.cs**. Compile and execute it a few times. Figure 15-21 shows two typical executions. The executions are similar, but not identical. Run the program a few more times and observe the results.

Figure 15-21 Two typical executions of the `HelloGoodbye` program

6. Change the value of the `TIMES` constant to 400. Compile and run the program several more times. You will probably notice even more variation in the allocation of CPU time to the two threads.

DEMONSTRATING PROBLEMS WITH UNSYNCHRONIZED THREADS

In the next steps, you will create a bank application to show the effect when multiple threads are allowed to withdraw random amounts from a bank account, both when the withdrawal process is locked and when it is not. You will assume that a bank account has a starting balance of $500 and that up to 10 different owners of the account can make withdrawals of up to $200 each. In real life, the various owners might be at different bank branches or ATMs, completely unaware that their account co-owners are making withdrawals at the same time. In such a situation, it is easy to overdraw the account.

To demonstrate the effect of a lock:

1. Open a new file in your text editor and enter the first few lines of a `BankAccount` class. The class contains a field that holds the account balance, and a variable to hold a random number.

```
using System;
using System.Threading;
class BankAccount
{
   double balance;
   Random r = new Random();
```

2. Add a constructor that accepts a parameter for the initial bank balance and assigns it to the balance field.

```
   public BankAccount(double bal)
   {
      balance = bal;
   }
```

3. Create the `Withdraw()` method, which accepts an amount to withdraw. If the bank balance is less than 0, an exception is thrown. Otherwise, the starting balance, withdrawal amount, and new balance after the withdrawal are all displayed.

```
   void Withdraw(double amount)
   {
      if(balance < 0)
      {
         throw new Exception("Balance is negative");
      }
      if(balance >= amount)
      {
         Console.WriteLine("Original balance:    " + balance);
         Console.WriteLine("    Withdraw: " + amount);
         balance -= amount;
         Console.WriteLine("    New balance: " + balance);
      }
   }
```

4. Add the `TransactionLoop()` method, which calls the `Withdraw()` method 100 times, withdrawing a random amount between $1 and $200 each time. After this method, add a closing curly brace for the `BankAccount` class. The value 100 is used in this example to ensure that the balance falls to 0 even if very small numbers are selected for all withdrawals.

```
    public void TransactionLoop()
    {
        const int MAX_WITHDRAWAL = 200;
        for(int x = 0; x < 100; ++x)
        {
            Withdraw(r.Next(1, MAX_WITHDRAWAL));
        }
    }
}
```

5. Next, add a class to test the `BankAccount` class. The class name is `TestBankAccount` and it contains a single `Main()` method. Declare a constant for the starting balance and a constant for the number of account owners who can make withdrawals. Then declare an array that can hold a `Thread` for each owner. Instantiate a bank account with the starting balance. In a loop, place a new `Thread` in each element of the array, using the `TransactionLoop()` method as the `ThreadStart` delegate. Then, in a second loop, start each of the `Thread`s.

```
class TestBankAccount
{
    public static void Main()
    {
        const double STARTING_BAL = 500;
        const int OWNERS = 10;
        Thread[] threads = new Thread[OWNERS];
        BankAccount acc = new BankAccount(STARTING_BAL);
        int x;
        for(x = 0; x < OWNERS; ++x)
        {
            Thread t = new Thread(new ThreadStart(acc.TransactionLoop));
            threads[x] = t;
        }
        for(x = 0; x < OWNERS; ++x)
        {
            threads[x].Start();
        }
    }
}
```

6. Save the file as **BankAccount.cs**. Compile and execute the program. Figure 15-22 shows a typical execution. Depending on your operating system, you might be notified that BankAccount.exe has stopped working, and you will be asked to click a button to close the program. You may safely do so.

```
Command Prompt

C:\C#\Chapter.15>BankAccount
Original balance:   500
   Withdraw: 17
Original balance:   500
   Withdraw: 58
   New balance: 425
Original balance:   425
   Withdraw: 93
Original balance:   500
   Withdraw: 87
   New balance: 245
Original balance:   245
   Withdraw: 117
   New balance: 128
Original balance:   128
   Withdraw: 112
   New balance: 16
Original balance:   16
   Withdraw: 8
   New balance: 8
Original balance:   8
   Withdraw: 3
   New balance: 5
Original balance:   5
   Withdraw: 1
   New balance: 4
   New balance: 483
Original balance:   4
   Withdraw: 3
   New balance: 1
   New balance: 332
Original balance:   1
   Withdraw: 1
   New balance: 0
Original balance:   4
   Withdraw: 1
   New balance: -1

Unhandled Exception: Unhandled Exception:Unhandled Exception:  Unhandled Excepti
on: Unhandled Exception:System.Exception: Balance is negative
   at BankAccount.Withdraw(Double amount)
   at BankAccount.TransactionLoop()
   at System.Threading.ThreadHelper.ThreadStart_Context(Object state)
   at System.Threading.ExecutionContext.Run(ExecutionContext executionContext, C
ontextCallback callback, Object state)
   at System.Threading.ThreadHelper.ThreadStart() Unhandled Exception: System.Ex
ception: Balance is negative
   at BankAccount.Withdraw(Double amount)
   at BankAccount.TransactionLoop()
   at System.Threading.ThreadHelper.ThreadStart_Context(Object state)
   at System.Threading.ExecutionContext.Run(ExecutionContext executionContext, C
ontextCallback callback, Object state)
   at System.Threading.ThreadHelper.ThreadStart()

Unhandled Exception:
C:\C#\Chapter.15>
```

Figure 15-22 A typical execution of the `BankAccount` program

The output in Figure 15-22 obviously shows that the `BankAccount` program is not working very well. For example:

- The original balance is $500.
- A $17 withdrawal is requested.
- A second thread shows the original balance of $500.
- A $58 withdrawal is requested.
- The new balance is now $425, which is $17 plus $58 less than the original balance.
- A third transaction withdraws $93, but then a fourth transaction shows the balance back at $500. If you examine the transactions down the list, you see that the balance goes up and down willy-nilly because earlier threads display final balances after later threads have already finished. Finally, when the balance falls below 0, the unhandled exception is thrown. In the second line of the exception message, you can see the "Balance is negative" statement.

The problems with this program can be corrected with very few additions.

SYNCHRONIZING THE BANK ACCOUNT APPLICATION BY LOCKING THE WITHDRAWAL PROCESS

Next, you will make minor adjustments to the `BankAccount` program to lock the withdrawal process so that only one account owner can make a withdrawal at a time.

To improve the `BankAccount` program:

1. Open the **BankAccount.cs** file in your text editor. Immediately save it as **BankAccount2.cs**.
2. Change the class name to `BankAccount2`. Also change the constructor name and the two references to `BankAccount` in the `Main()` method so that they match.
3. Within the `Withdraw()` method, add a lock around the withdrawal process. Add the following as the first two lines in the method after the opening curly brace:

   ```
   lock(this)
   {
   ```

   The `this` refers to the current `BankAccount` object.
4. As the last line within the `Withdraw()` method, just before the closing curly brace, add another closing curly brace that ends the block of statements that are locked. In other words, the following statements are enclosed in the `lock` block:

   ```
       if(balance < 0)
       {
          throw new Exception("Balance is negative");
       }
       if(balance >= amount)
       {
          Console.WriteLine("Original balance:    " + balance);
          Console.WriteLine("    Withdraw: " + amount);
          balance -= amount;
          Console.WriteLine("    New balance: " + balance);
       }
   ```

5. If you want, you can indent the statements within the `lock()` block to improve the appearance of the code. This step is not necessary to produce a functioning program.

6. Save the file, then compile and execute it. Figure 15-23 shows a typical execution. Each withdrawal and new balance makes sense because only one account owner can make a withdrawal at a time. From the moment one thread accesses the previous balance, until the moment the withdrawal process is complete, no other threads can interfere. When the balance reaches 0, no more withdrawals are allowed.

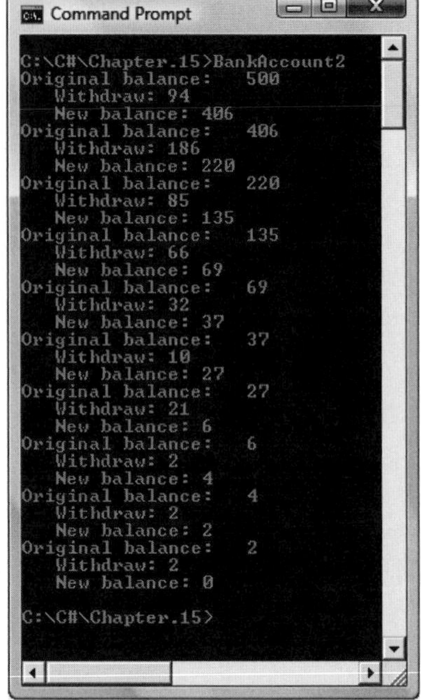

Figure 15-23 Typical execution of the `BankAccount2` program

CHAPTER SUMMARY

» A thread is the flow of execution of one set of program statements. C# allows you to launch, or start, multiple threads that execute concurrently, whether you use a single-processor or multiprocessor machine. Using multiple threads of execution is known as multithreading. The concept of sharing processor time is known as time-slicing. Multithreaded programs often run faster, but more important, they are more user friendly.

» A `Thread` object can be in one of several states during its life, including `Unstarted`, `Running`, and `Stopped`. A program that instantiates a `Thread` object passes a `ThreadStart` delegate to the object's constructor; the delegate is initialized with a parameterless `void` method.

» `Threads` have a number of useful properties that provide information about them. A thread can reside in the `Background` state at the same time it resides in any of the other states; you can place a thread in the `Background` state by setting its `IsBackground` property to `true`. A process must wait for all foreground threads to finish executing and enter the `Stopped` state before the process can end.

» You can create a wrapper class to facilitate working with the limitation of parameterless delegate methods used by `Threads`.

- Every `Thread` has a priority, or rank, in terms of preferential access to an operating system's resources. There are five `ThreadPriority` values. Thread scheduling is the process by which an operating system allocates processor time to each running thread; the thread scheduler keeps the highest-priority thread running, but allocates time to lower-priority `Threads` to prevent starvation.
- Sometimes multiple threads need to use a shared object. Thread synchronization prevents problems caused by sharing objects. The `Monitor` class provides the means to lock objects to implement synchronized access to shared data. Locking an object means that only one thread can access it.

KEY TERMS

A **thread** is the flow of execution of one set of program statements.

Multithreading is the process of using multiple threads of execution in a program.

When tasks execute **concurrently**, they execute during the same time period.

When tasks execute **in parallel**, they execute concurrently.

Timeslicing is the concept of sharing processor time.

A **quantum** is the small segment of processor time each thread receives to execute.

The **`Thread` class** is used to create threads in addition to an application's main thread.

A **`ThreadStart` delegate** is a method that a `Thread` executes.

When the operating system assigns a processor to a thread, it is **dispatching the thread**.

Garbage collection is automatic memory management; the garbage collector frees up memory occupied by objects that a program no longer needs.

Deprecated features of programming languages have been superseded by newer techniques and should not be used.

A thread in the **`Background` state** runs when time becomes available because no threads in the foreground state need CPU time.

A **wrapper class** is a class that you wrap around data or methods to give them added functionality.

A **sealed class** cannot be extended.

A **priority** is a rank of preferential access to an operating system's resources.

Peers are `Threads` with the same priority.

The **`ThreadPriority` enumeration** defines the priorities in C#.

Thread scheduling is the process by which an operating system allocates processor time to each running thread.

Starvation occurs when a `Thread` cannot make any progress because of the priorities of other `Threads`.

Deadlock occurs when two `Threads` must wait for each other to do something before either can progress.

Thread synchronization is the process of excluding all but one thread from an object to avoid timing errors when accessing data.

A **race hazard** is a flaw in a system in which the results of a process are critically dependent on the timing of other processes.

The **`Monitor` class** provides the means to lock objects to implement synchronized access to shared data.

Locking an object means that only one thread can access it.

The **ready queue** contains the threads that are ready to obtain a lock.

The **waiting queue** contains the threads that are waiting for notification of a change in the state of the locked object.

Syntactic sugar refers to any programming construct that makes programs easier to read and write.

REVIEW QUESTIONS

1. A thread is the ________ one set of program statements.

   a. amount of memory occupied by

   b. flow of execution of

   c. machine language code for

   d. area of memory occupied by

2. A modern computer with a single CPU can execute ________ statement(s) at a time.

   a. one
   c. at least several dozen

   b. two
   d. at least several thousand

3. If you use a computer with a single processor, you can execute ________ concurrently.

   a. only one thread

   b. several threads

   c. any number of threads

   d. You cannot execute multiple threads on a single-processor computer.

4. You achieve ________ by starting more than one `Thread` object.

   a. polythreading
   c. multithreading

   b. bithreading
   d. buffered threading

5. With timeslicing, each thread receives a small segment of processor time, called a ________.
   a. millisecond
   b. quark
   c. slice
   d. quantum

6. Which of the following states is not possible for a `Thread`?
   a. `Altered`
   b. `WaitSleepJoin`
   c. `Suspended`
   d. `Unstarted`

7. A thread can be in ________ at a given point in time.
   a. one state
   b. two states
   c. 10 states
   d. any number of states

8. A `ThreadStart` delegate is initialized with ________.
   a. a `Thread` object
   b. a parameterless `void` method
   c. an array of `Thread` states
   d. nothing

9. A `Running Thread` might not actually be running because ________.
   a. it might be `Stopped`
   b. it might be blocked
   c. the CPU might be busy with another `Thread`
   d. it might not have been assigned a `ThreadStart` delegate

10. The `Sleep()` method accepts an argument measured in ________.
   a. nanoseconds
   b. milliseconds
   c. seconds
   d. minutes

11. You write a ________ class to surround a method so you can add usable data.
   a. package
   b. cover
   c. transparent
   d. wrapper

12. A `Thread`'s rank in terms of preferential access to the operating system's resources is its ________.
   a. priority
   b. prerogative
   c. supremacy
   d. license

13. If you do not assign a priority to a `Thread` object, it assumes a priority of ________ by default.

    a. `Average`

    b. `Normal`

    c. `Usual`

    d. `Lowest`

14. Two `Threads` with the same priority are ________ .

    a. peers

    b. cohorts

    c. not allowed to be instantiated in the same method

    d. not allowed in the same application

15. C# sometimes chooses to run a low-priority `Thread` to avoid ________ .

    a. construction

    b. death

    c. sedation

    d. starvation

16. If the only threads remaining in a process are background threads, then ________ .

    a. one background thread gets promoted to a foreground thread

    b. all background threads get promoted to foreground threads

    c. each thread is terminated and the process ends

    d. each background thread finishes in sequence

17. The process of excluding a thread from processing while another thread uses a resource is ________ .

    a. thread synchronization

    b. boxing and unboxing

    c. wrapping

    d. thread management

18. Only one thread can access an object when it is ________ .

    a. running

    b. secure

    c. locked

    d. local to the delegate method

19. The phrase that describes a programming language's syntactic add-ons that make programs easier to write and understand is ________ .

    a. painless programming

    b. wrapping

    c. locking

    d. syntactic sugar

20. Using ________ is simply a shortcut for using both the `Monitor` class `Enter()` and `Exit()` methods.

    a. `monitor()`
    b. `lock()`
    c. `freeze()`
    d. `start()` and `stop()`

EXERCISES

1. Create a program that holds two `Threads`. One `Thread` uses a method that displays "Loves me", and the other displays "Loves me not". Each method should sleep a random amount of time of up to five seconds before displaying its message. Start the two `Threads`; the final message is the answer to your question! Save the file as **LovesMe.cs**.

2. a. Create a wrapper class named `WriteClass` that contains a field that holds a `String`. The class constructor accepts a friend's name and assigns it to the `String`. The `WriteName()` method displays a single space 1,000 times before displaying the friend's name once. Write a program that instantiates three `Threads` to which you pass your first name and the first names of two friends. Start the `Threads` and observe which `Thread` wins the race—that is, finishes first. (When you run the program several times, a different `Friend` will win by different margins, which are represented by the spaces between the names.) Save the file as **Friends.cs**.

   b. Modify the `Friends` program so that after the three names are displayed, the program announces the winner, which was the name in the `Thread` that finished first. Save the file as **Friends2.cs**.

3. Create an application that simulates a horse race. Assign three horses to three threads that each run a method for a random amount of time, up to five seconds. Ask the user to bet on a horse, start the threads, declare the winner (the thread that finishes first), and notify the player whether the bet was correct. Save the program as **HorseRace.cs**.

4. Create an application that simulates making appointments at a doctor's office. Assume there are seven appointment slots in a day, at 9, 10, and 11 a.m. and at 1, 2, 3, and 4 p.m. Also assume there are 20 patients numbered 101–120 who attempt to make an appointment during the day. Have each of 20 patient threads request one of the time slots randomly. Assign the patient to the time slot if it is available and display an appropriate message if the time slot is not available. Make sure you have placed a lock on the schedule for the duration of each patient's request. At the end of the 20 requests, display a schedule of the day's appointments. (Due to the nature of random numbers, some time slots during the day might not be filled.) Figure 15-24 shows a typical execution. Save the file as **AppointmentSystem.cs**.

```
C:\C#\Chapter.15>AppointmentSystem
Making appt for patient 101 at 4 pm
   4 pm appointment made for patient #101
Making appt for patient 102 at 4 pm
   Attempt to make appointment failed - time slot already taken
Making appt for patient 104 at 9 am
   9 am appointment made for patient #104
Making appt for patient 105 at 10 am
   10 am appointment made for patient #105
Making appt for patient 106 at 2 pm
   2 pm appointment made for patient #106
Making appt for patient 103 at 1 pm
   1 pm appointment made for patient #103
Making appt for patient 107 at 3 pm
   3 pm appointment made for patient #107
Making appt for patient 108 at 2 pm
   Attempt to make appointment failed - time slot already taken
Making appt for patient 109 at 3 pm
   Attempt to make appointment failed - time slot already taken
Making appt for patient 110 at 11 am
   11 am appointment made for patient #110
Making appt for patient 111 at 1 pm
   Attempt to make appointment failed - time slot already taken
Making appt for patient 112 at 10 am
   Attempt to make appointment failed - time slot already taken
Making appt for patient 113 at 3 pm
   Attempt to make appointment failed - time slot already taken
Making appt for patient 114 at 2 pm
   Attempt to make appointment failed - time slot already taken
Making appt for patient 115 at 3 pm
   Attempt to make appointment failed - time slot already taken
Making appt for patient 116 at 11 am
   Attempt to make appointment failed - time slot already taken
Making appt for patient 117 at 2 pm
   Attempt to make appointment failed - time slot already taken
Making appt for patient 118 at 3 pm
   Attempt to make appointment failed - time slot already taken
Making appt for patient 119 at 9 am
   Attempt to make appointment failed - time slot already taken
Making appt for patient 120 at 1 pm
   Attempt to make appointment failed - time slot already taken

Schedule for the day
    9 am   Patient # 104
   10 am   Patient # 105
   11 am   Patient # 110
    1 pm   Patient # 103
    2 pm   Patient # 106
    3 pm   Patient # 107
    4 pm   Patient # 101

C:\C#\Chapter.15>_
```

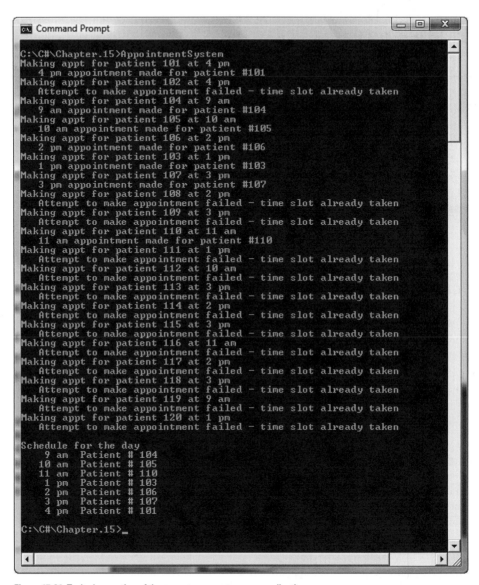

Figure 15-24 Typical execution of the `AppointmentSystem` application

5. Create an application that simulates the management of a credit card account. Assume there are two cardholders, John and Mary, who share an account. Their credit limit is $2,000. Each can make up to five transactions a week, but no transaction can be more than half the credit limit. Allow each cardholder to make random charges that are accepted if credit is available, but denied if not enough credit is left. Figure 15-25 shows a typical execution. Save the file as **CreditCard.cs**.

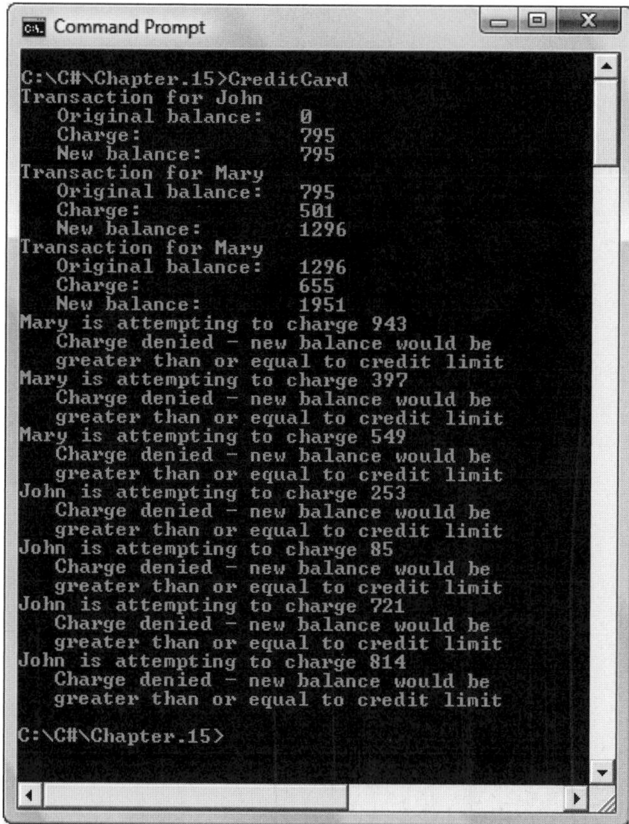

Figure 15-25 Typical execution of the `CreditCard` application

DEBUGGING EXERCISES

Each of the following files in the Chapter.15 folder on your Student Disk has syntax and/or logical errors. In each case, determine the problem and fix the program. After you correct the errors, save each file using the same filename preceded with *Fixed*. For example, save DebugFifteen1.cs as **FixedDebugFifteen1.cs**.

a. DebugFifteen1.cs

b. DebugFifteen2.cs

c. DebugFifteen3.cs

d. DebugFifteen4.cs

UP FOR DISCUSSION

1. After reading this chapter, you might realize that you have experienced a lock on some data you were using. Describe such a situation and explain why the lock was a benefit to you.
2. Think of a nonprogramming analogy of a lock that is used in everyday life.

CHAPTER SIXTEEN

16

GRAPHICS AND MULTIMEDIA

In this chapter you will:

- Understand drawing basics
- Use `Point` and `Pen` objects and the `DrawLine()` method
- Understand the `OnPaint()` method
- Understand graphics contexts and `Graphics` objects
- Create custom colors
- Use `Brush` objects
- Create shapes and simple animation
- Add images to applications
- Use the IDE to create an interactive `Graphics` application
- Add a Windows Media Player to an application

Twenty or 30 years ago, computer users worked with text that was typed from a keyboard and displayed on a black-and-white monitor. Modern computer users expect shapes, colors, images, music, and video clips to be part of their computer experiences. C# provides many techniques for you to add eye-catching (and ear-catching) features to your applications. This chapter starts you on the path to creating appealing and artistic projects.

UNDERSTANDING DRAWING BASICS

Applications can be more interesting to users when they contain drawings and pictures. In Microsoft Windows, you can use the **Graphics Device Interface Plus (GDI+)** Application Programming Interface (API) to paint and work with graphic objects on components such as windows and forms. GDI+ is a set of classes that allows applications to use graphics and formatted text on both video displays and printers. GDI+ sits between the program and the hardware and transfers data from one to the other; GDI+ interacts with device drivers on behalf of applications. In other words, GDI+ insulates the application from the graphics hardware so that programmers can create applications that work correctly on different devices.

> **NOTE** As you might have guessed, an earlier version of GDI+ was called GDI. GDI was a low-to-middle level of programming API, where you needed to know about the display devices on which graphics were rendered. GDI+ is a higher level of programming model, in which you do not need to know such details.

GDI+ is defined in the `Drawing` namespace and its five subnamespaces. All drawing code resides in one of the following namespaces:

- `System.Drawing`
- `System.Drawing.Design`
- `System.Drawing.Printing`
- `System.Drawing.Imaging`
- `System.Drawing.Drawing2D`
- `System.Drawing.Text`

The `System.Drawing` namespace provides the basic functionality for GDI+. It contains the definition of basic drawing classes and structures with "artistic" names such as `Brush` and `Pen`. Figure 16-1 shows the relationship of some of the `System.Drawing` classes and structures.

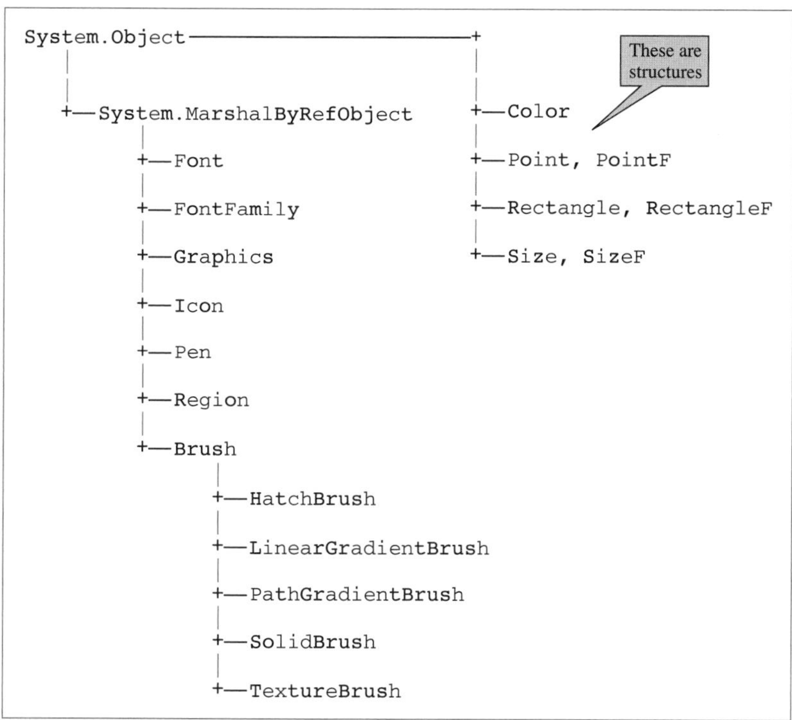

Figure 16-1 Selected `System.Drawing` classes and structures

The **`Graphics` class** contains methods you can use to draw strings, lines, and shapes on a control. Usually you use a `Pen` object (to make outlines) or `Brush` object (to make solid objects) to create the desired shape. The four structures (and three derivations of them) in the `System.Drawing` namespace appear to the right in Figure 16-1. They are `Color`, `Point`, `PointF`, `Rectangle`, `RectangleF`, `Size`, and `SizeF`. At least `Point`, `Size`, and `Color` are used in nearly every `Form` you create. Table 16-1 summarizes the attributes of these structures.

Structure	Description
`Color`	Represents a color
`Point`, `PointF`	Represents x- and y-coordinates; the `PointF` structure allows floating-point values as the coordinates
`Rectangle`, `RectangleF`	Represents a rectangle defined by two `Point` pairs—upper left and lower right; the `RectangleF` structure allows floating-point values as coordinates
`Size`, `SizeF`	Represents the size of a rectangular region, defined by width and height; the `SizeF` structure allows floating-point values as width and height

Table 16-1 Description of selected `System.Drawing` structures

»NOTE In Chapter 11, you saw the `Color` and `Size` structures in action. You selected colors from a component's properties list in the IDE, and set components' sizes by dragging their borders with your mouse. For example, you created programs that contained statements like the following:

```
this.label1.BackColor = System.Drawing.Color.Blue;
this.label1.Size = System.Drawing.Size(100, 40);
```

»TWO TRUTHS AND A LIE: UNDERSTANDING DRAWING BASICS

1. GDI+ is a set of classes that allows applications to use graphics and formatted text on both video displays and printers.
2. GDI+ is defined in the `Drawing` namespace and its five subnamespaces.
3. The `Pen` class contains methods you can use to draw strings, lines, and shapes on a control.

The false statement is #3. The `Graphics` class contains methods you can use to draw strings, lines, and shapes on a control.

THE `Point` STRUCTURE, THE `Pen` OBJECT, AND THE `DrawLine()` METHOD

Programmers position text and shapes on a screen by using coordinates. A window or frame consists of a number of horizontal and vertical pixels on the screen. A **pixel** is a picture element, or one tiny dot on a monitor. Any component you place on the screen has a horizontal, or **x-axis**, position as well as a vertical, or **y-axis**, position. The upper-left corner of any display is position 0, 0. The first, or **x-coordinate**, value increases as you travel from left to right across the window. The second, or **y-coordinate**, value increases as you travel from top to bottom. Figure 16-2 illustrates the screen coordinate positions.

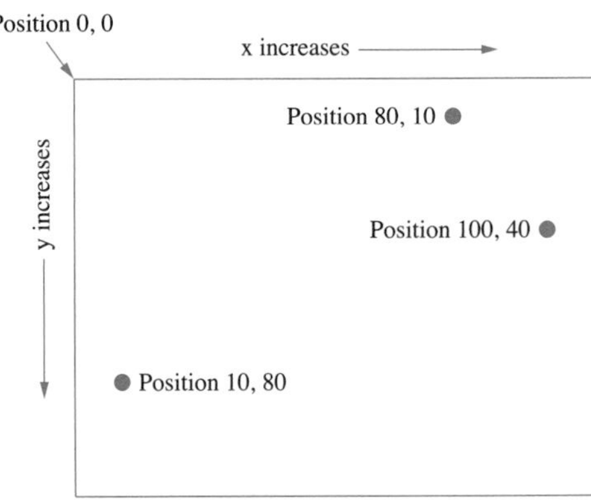

Figure 16-2 Screen coordinate positions

»NOTE The coordinate system used for graphics differs from the one used by mathematicians. When you plot algebraic equations, the y-coordinate value increases while going upward from a baseline. However, in computer graphics, the y-coordinate value increases as it goes down.

»NOTE The density of pixels varies depending on the monitor used and the resolution at which it is set. Graphics, therefore, might appear different to different users.

You can create a **`Point` object** to refer to a single screen position. The `Point` structure contains x- and y-coordinates. You can declare a `Point` using the parameterless version of its constructor, or you can provide x- and y-coordinates in that order. For example, you can refer to a point at position (30, 60) by declaring and creating the following:

```
Point myPoint = new Point(30, 60);
```

After you have created a `Point`, you can change either its `X` or `Y` property using an assignment statement, as in the following:

```
myPoint.X = 10;
myPoint.Y = 200;
```

The **`Pen` class** provides a tool for drawing lines, curves, and outlines. You can create a `Pen` with a specific color, as in the following statement:

```
Pen myPen = new Pen(Color.Red);
```

The `myPen` object draws with a default thickness of 1.

You can change the color of the `Pen` by assigning a different value to the `Pen`'s `Color` property as follows:

```
myPen.Color = Color.Orange;
```

You can change the width of the drawing line by setting the `myPen` object's `Width` property as follows:

```
myPen.Width = 5;
```

Alternatively, you can use an overloaded `Pen` constructor to specify a wider drawing width, as in either of the following:

```
Pen yourPen = new Pen(Color.Green, 5.0F);
Pen herPen = new Pen(Color.Green, 2);
```

The second argument to an overloaded `Pen` constructor is a `float`, so you can pass an integer and it will be promoted to a `float`. Table 16-2 lists some useful properties of the `Pen` class.

Property	Description
`Color`	Gets or sets the color of the `Pen`
`DashCap`	Gets or sets the cap style used at the end of the dashes that make up a dashed line drawn with the `Pen`; `DashCap` styles include `Round`, `Square`, and `Flat`
`DashStyle`	Gets or sets the dash style used for dashed lines drawn with the `Pen`; `DashStyle`s include `Dash`, `DashDot`, `DashDotDot`, `Dot`, and `Solid`
`EndCap`	Gets or sets the cap style at the end of lines drawn with the `Pen`; `EndCap`s include `Round`, `Square`, and `Flat`
`StartCap`	Gets or sets the cap style at the start of lines drawn with the `Pen`; `StartCap`s include `Round`, `Square`, and `Flat`
`Width`	Gets or sets the width of a line drawn with the `Pen`

Table 16-2 Selected `Pen` class properties

When you have created a `Pen` object, you can draw lines. The **`DrawLine()` method** draws a line on the screen. You use the `DrawLine()` method with a `Graphics` object. In the next section, you will learn about accessing `Graphics` objects. For now, assume you have created one named `g`. Then, you can draw a line from `point1` to `point2` using the following statements:

```
Pen pen = new Pen(Color.Black);
Point point1 = new Point(40, 20);
Point point2 = new Point(80, 100);
g.DrawLine(pen, point1, point2);
```

These statements create a `Pen` object, set its drawing color, create two `Point` objects, and then use all three objects to draw a line. Figure 16-3 shows the line. It angles down and to the right, because the `point1` coordinates (40, 20) are higher than and to the left of the `point2` coordinates (80, 100).

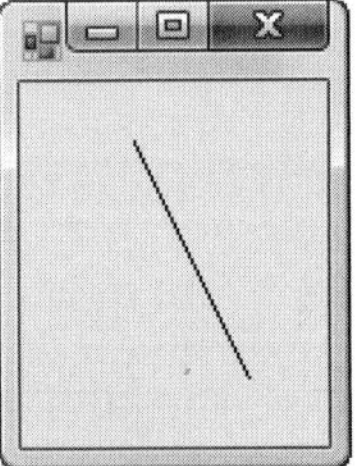

Figure 16-3 The line created from 40, 20 to 80, 100

You can draw the same line using four point coordinates following the `Pen` argument to `DrawLine()`. The following statement draws the line in Figure 16-3 in the same way as the one that uses two `Point` objects:

```
g.DrawLine(pen, 40, 20, 80, 100);
```

Whenever you encounter a `Point` object in a method definition, you can almost always assume that you can substitute two integer values that represent x- and y-coordinates. Similarly, when you encounter a pair of x- and y-coordinates, assume you can substitute a `Point` object. In the future, when you design your own `Graphics` classes, you should overload your methods to accept either type of argument because other programmers will expect it.

»TWO TRUTHS AND A LIE: THE `Point` STRUCTURE, THE `Pen` OBJECT, AND THE `DrawLine()` METHOD

1. Any component you place on the screen has a horizontal, or x-axis, position as well as a vertical, or y-axis, position.
2. The `Point` object defined as `new Point(300, 10)` would be near the lower left of a 350 × 350 `Frame`.
3. You can declare a `Pen`'s `Color` and `Width` when you instantiate it or later in the program.

The false statement is #2. The `Point` object defined as `new Point(300, 10)` would be near the upper right of a 350 × 350 `Frame`.

LEARNING ABOUT THE `OnPaint()` METHOD

When you run a C# program that contains graphics, such as the `Frame` applications in Chapters 10, 11, and 12, the display surface must be frequently redisplayed, or rerendered. Redisplaying a surface is also called **painting**. In C#, programmers say that when painting is required, a **`Paint` event** is triggered. Many painting events are automatically triggered while a program is running. For example, a `Frame` must be painted when it is first made visible, or if it is resized or damaged. A component becomes damaged, for example, when another component that previously covered part of it has been moved, revealing a portion that was not visible.

When automatic painting occurs, a component's `OnPaint()` method is invoked; that method triggers the component's `Paint` event. The header for the `OnPaint()` method is:

```
protected override void OnPaint(PaintEventArgs e)
```

You can override the `OnPaint()` method in your programs when you want specific actions to take place when components must be rendered, or when you want to use the `PaintEventArgs` parameter to the method, as explained in the next section of this chapter.

For example, Figure 16-4 shows a `PaintDemo` class that extends `Form`. The `PaintDemo` constructor contains just one statement that sets a `Size` for the `Form`, and the `Main()` method contains just one statement that runs the application. The only statement in the `OnPaint()` method displays a message at the command prompt. Nowhere in the class is the `OnPaint()` method explicitly called. However, when you run the application in Figure 16-4, you can see from the output in Figure 16-5 that the method must be called automatically because it produces output.

```
using System;
using System.Windows.Forms;
using System.Drawing;
public class PaintDemo : Form
{
   public PaintDemo()
   {
      this.Size = new System.Drawing.Size(120, 160);
   }
   protected override void OnPaint(PaintEventArgs e)
   {
      Console.WriteLine("In paint method");
   }
   public static void Main()
   {
      Application.Run(new PaintDemo());
   }
}
```

Figure 16-4 The `PaintDemo` class

>> **NOTE** In the constructor of the `PaintDemo` class, the keyword `this` is not required with the `Size` property. With or without the keyword, the property is that of "this" current object.

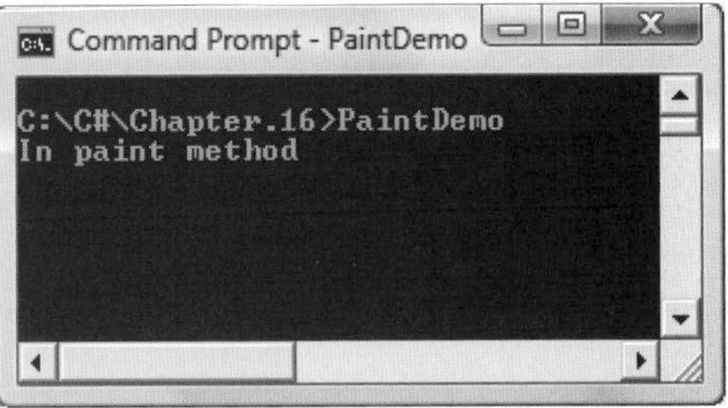

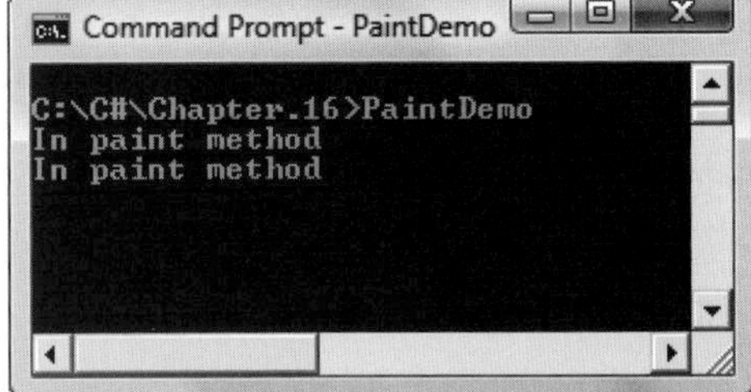

Figure 16-5 Execution of the `PaintDemo` class when it starts and after a user minimizes and restores the `Frame`

Figure 16-5 shows a typical execution of the `PaintDemo` program. When the program starts, the command prompt shown on the left side of the figure indicates that the `OnPaint()` method is called. After the user minimizes and restores the `Frame`, the command prompt appears as shown on the right of the figure—the `OnPaint()` method has executed again. If the user changes the size of the `Frame` by dragging one of its borders, the `OnPaint()` method executes repeatedly to reflect many rerenderings of the `Frame`.

>> **NOTE** When you resize a `Frame` by dragging its border, many hundreds of calls to `OnPaint()` might be made. If a second request to repaint the frame occurs before C# can carry out the first request, only the last request executes.

»TWO TRUTHS AND A LIE: LEARNING ABOUT THE `OnPaint()` METHOD

1. A program must explicitly call the `OnPaint()` method when a `Frame` is resized or damaged.
2. The `OnPaint()` method triggers the component's `Paint` event; the method takes a `PaintEventArgs` parameter.
3. You can override the `OnPaint()` method in your programs when you want specific actions to take place when components must be rendered, or when you want to use the `PaintEventArgs` parameter to the method.

The false statement is #1. Many painting events are automatically triggered while a program is running, including when a `Frame` is first made visible, or if it is resized or damaged.

UNDERSTANDING GRAPHICS CONTEXTS AND GRAPHICS OBJECTS

A C# **graphics context** is a collection of attributes that determines how graphics operations affect components. A **`Graphics` object** manages a graphics context by controlling how much information is drawn. `Graphics` objects contain methods for drawing, manipulating fonts and color, and other graphics-related actions.

Every `Control` (that is, every class that derives from `Control`, including `Form`) inherits the `OnPaint()` method, which performs most graphics operations. As you saw in the program in Figure 16-4, the arguments to the `OnPaint()` method include a `PaintEventArgs` object. You can use this object to obtain a `Graphics` object for the current `Form`. Every time `OnPaint()` is called, you must obtain a new `Graphics` object, because the properties of the graphics context that the `Graphics` object represents could have changed since the last call.

When you override the `OnPaint()` method with the following header, the `PaintEventArgs` parameter is named `e`:

```
protected override void OnPaint(PaintEventArgs e)
```

Then, you can extract the `Graphics` object from `e` with a statement such as the following:

```
Graphics g = e.Graphics;
```

After you have obtained the `Graphics` object `g`, you can use it with methods to draw on the `Form`. Figure 16-6 shows a complete application. The class `GraphicsDemo1` extends `Form`. The constructor sets the size of the form. The `OnPaint()` method gets a `Graphics` object from the `PaintEventArgs` parameter, declares a `Pen` (that is black and thicker than the default pen), declares two `Points`, and then draws a line. Figure 16-7 shows the result.

```
using System;
using System.Windows.Forms;
using System.Drawing;
public class GraphicsDemo1 : Form
{
   public GraphicsDemo1()
   {
      this.Size = new System.Drawing.Size(120, 160);
   }
   protected override void OnPaint(PaintEventArgs e)
   {
      Graphics g = e.Graphics;
      Pen pen = new Pen(Color.Black, 3);
      Point pt1 = new Point(80, 40);
      Point pt2 = new Point(20, 100);
      g.DrawLine(pen, pt1, pt2);
   }
   public static void Main()
   {
      Application.Run(new GraphicsDemo1());
   }
}
```

Figure 16-6 The `GraphicsDemo1` class

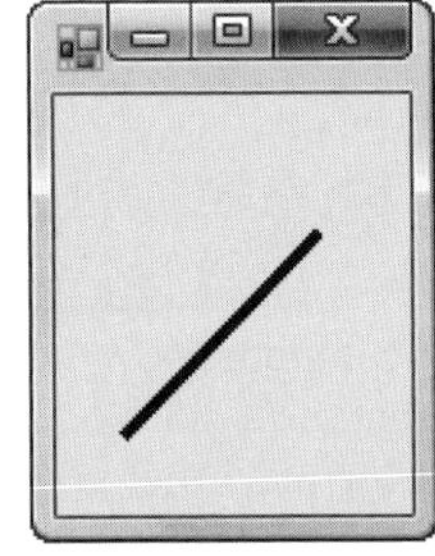

Figure 16-7 Output of the `GraphicsDemo1` application

> **NOTE**
> Notice how the line in Figure 16-7 extends from the upper-right area of the `Frame` (position 80, 40) to the lower-left area (position 20, 100).

Instead of overriding the `OnPaint()` method, programmers can add an event handler for the `Form`'s `Paint` event with a method that has a header such as the following:

```
private void PaintMethod(object sender, PaintEventArgs e)
```

In this example, `PaintMethod()` is a programmer-chosen name; it could be any legal method name. Although the method you create can contain any legal statements, it must be of type `void`, and it requires two arguments of type `object` and `PaintEventArgs`, respectively. You can add this method to the `Form`'s `Paint` event to create a composed delegate with the following statement:

> **NOTE**
> You learned to use the += sign to create composed delegates in Chapter 12.

```
this.Paint += new PaintEventHandler(PaintMethod);
```

In the statement, `this` refers to this `Form`—the class in which the statement is placed. Figure 16-8 shows a class that uses this technique.

```
using System;
using System.Windows.Forms;
using System.Drawing;

public class GraphicsDemo2 : Form
{
    public GraphicsDemo2()
    {
        this.Size = new System.Drawing.Size(120, 160);
        this.Paint += new PaintEventHandler(PaintMethod);
    }

    private void PaintMethod(object sender, PaintEventArgs e)
    {
        Graphics g = e.Graphics;
        Pen pen = new Pen(Color.Black, 3);
        Point pt1 = new Point(80, 40);
        Point pt2 = new Point(20, 100);
        g.DrawLine(pen, pt1, pt2);
    }
    public static void Main()
    {
        Application.Run(new GraphicsDemo2());
    }
}
```

Figure 16-8 The `GraphicsDemo2` class

In the constructor for `GraphicsDemo2`, the size of the frame is set, and the shaded statement shows that a composed delegate is created using the `PaintMethod()` method. This means that when painting is required, the built-in `OnPaint()` method will execute along with the programmer-written `PaintMethod()` method. The statements within the `PaintMethod()` method in the `GraphicsDemo2` class are identical to the statements in the `OnPaint()` method in the `GraphicsDemo1` class, and the output is identical to that shown in Figure 16-7.

The `OnPaint()` method almost always executes in a program because it is called automatically; programmers seldom call the `OnPaint()` method directly, because drawing graphics is an event-driven process. Usually, an event, such as a user minimizing a `Form`, forces a call to the `OnPaint()` method that belongs to that `Form`. Similarly, when any `Control` (such as a `Label` or `Button`) is displayed, that `Control`'s `OnPaint()` method is called.

You can force a call to `OnPaint()` by calling a `Control`'s `Invalidate()` method. This method refreshes a `Control` and implicitly repaints all its graphical components.

NOTE The `Control` class has several overloaded versions of `Invalidate()` so that you can only update a portion of a `Control`. For example, you can use a `Rectangle` parameter to `Invalidate()` so that only a small rectangular portion of a `Control` is repainted instead of the entire visible surface.

`Controls` such as `Labels` and `Buttons` do not have their own graphics contexts. However, you can create a graphics context for a `Control`. For example, the following statement creates a `Graphics` object for a `Label` named `label1`:

```
Graphics gr1 = label1.CreateGraphics();
```

Then, you can use the `gr1` object with the methods provided in the `Graphics` class to draw on the `Label`. Later in this chapter, when you learn to use `Graphics` within `Forms` generated through the Visual Studio IDE, you will use this technique to obtain a `Graphics` object.

»TWO TRUTHS AND A LIE: UNDERSTANDING GRAPHICS CONTEXTS AND `Graphics` OBJECTS

1. You can use the `OnPaint()` method's `PaintEventArgs` object to obtain a `Graphics` object for the current `Form`.
2. When you create an event-handler method to handle painting tasks, the method must be of type `Graphics`, and it requires an argument of type `Pen` or `Brush`.
3. You can force a call to `OnPaint()` by calling a `Control`'s `Invalidate()` method; this method refreshes a `Control` and implicitly repaints all its graphical components.

The false statement is #2. When you create an event-handler method to handle painting tasks, the method must be of type `void`, and it requires two arguments of type `object` and `PaintEventArgs`, respectively.

CREATING CUSTOM COLORS

In Chapter 11, you learned that C# provides over 140 predefined colors in the `Color` structure. Besides standard colors such as `Color.Black`, `Color.Red`, and `Color.Blue`, the `Color` structure provides picturesque values such as `LightSkyBlue`, `MediumSeaGreen`, and `Thistle`. Besides the predefined colors, you can create nearly 17 million custom colors from a combination of four components: alpha, red, green, and blue. These components are called **ARGB values**. All four ARGB components are bytes that hold a value from 0 to 255. The `A`, or alpha, value determines the **opacity**, or degree of transparency, of the color. The value 0 represents a transparent color and 255 represents one that is completely opaque. The values between 0 and 255 result in a blending of the color with any background color so the result looks semitransparent. The `R`, `G`, and `B` values represent the amount of red, green, and blue in the color, respectively. For example, the color whose ARGB value is 255, 255, 0, 0 is opaque and pure red, and the color whose ARGB value is 150, 0, 100, 100 is semitransparent and green-blue.

To create a custom color, you use the `FromArgb()` method. If you call it using three arguments, they represent `R`, `G`, and `B` values, and the `A` value is 255 by default, creating an opaque color. If you call it using four arguments, they represent `A`, `R`, `G`, and `B` values. Each of the values must be between 0 and 255, inclusive.

Figure 16-9 shows an application that displays many, but not nearly all, of the colors you can create using the `FromArgb()` method. The shaded statement makes new colors in a loop, using every twentieth value for the `R`, `G`, and `B` parameters. A short horizontal line, 10 pixels long, is drawn in each color combination. After each set of blue components has reached the end of its cycle, the x-coordinate is returned to 0 and the y-coordinate increases by 3. Figure 16-10 shows the output; you cannot appreciate the full effect in this book because it is printed in only two colors, but you can see that a rainbow effect is achieved by subtly altering the `r`, `g`, and `b` components of the color on each cycle through the loop.

```
using System;
using System.Windows.Forms;
using System.Drawing;

public class ColorDemo : Form
{
   public ColorDemo()
   {
      this.Size = new System.Drawing.Size(150, 560);
   }
   protected override void OnPaint(PaintEventArgs e)
   {
      int x = 0, y = 0;
      int r, g, b;
      const int STEP = 20;
      const int LIMIT = 255;
      Graphics gr = e.Graphics;
      for(r = 0; r <= LIMIT; r += STEP)
         for(g = 0; g <= LIMIT; g += STEP)
         {
            for(b = 0; b <= LIMIT; b += STEP)
            {
               Color color = Color.FromArgb(r, g, b);
               Pen pen = new Pen(color, 3);
               Point pt1 = new Point(x, y);
               Point pt2 = new Point(x += 10, y);
               gr.DrawLine(pen, pt1, pt2);
            }
            x = 0;
            y += 3;
         }
   }
   public static void Main()
   {
      Application.Run(new ColorDemo());
   }
}
```

Figure 16-9 The `ColorDemo` class

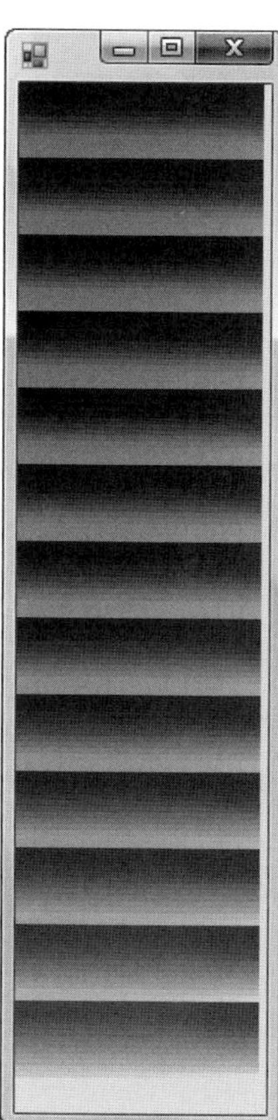

Figure 16-10 Execution of the `ColorDemo` program

»TWO TRUTHS AND A LIE: CREATING CUSTOM COLORS

1. Besides C#'s predefined colors, you can create millions of custom colors.
2. A custom color's components are called ARGB values; all four ARGB components are bytes that hold a value from 0 to 255.
3. The `A`, or automatic, ARGB value determines whether the red, green, and blue components of a color are assigned the same intensity.

The false statement is #3. The `A`, or alpha, ARGB value determines the opacity, or degree of transparency, of the color.

USING `Brush` OBJECTS

`Pen` objects are used to draw lines, but **`Brush` objects** are used to color the inside of graphical shapes. In other words, you create solid or filled objects using a `Brush`. `Brush` is an abstract class; you cannot instantiate a `Brush`. Instead, you instantiate one of the classes that derives from `Brush`: `SolidBrush`, `HatchBrush`, `TextureBrush`, `LinearGradientBrush`, and `PathGradientBrush`. Table 16-3 describes these child classes of `Brush`. You cannot extend these classes.

`Brush` Class Descendent	Description
`SolidBrush`	Paints a solid color
`HatchBrush`	Similar to `SolidBrush`, but you can select from a set of preset patterns instead of painting with a solid color
`TextureBrush`	Paints with a texture, such as an image
`LinearGradientBrush`	Paints two colors blended along a gradient
`PathGradientBrush`	Paints using a complex gradient of blended colors, based on a unique path defined by the programmer

Table 16-3 `Brush` child classes

The `SolidBrush` class is the easiest to use. For example, you can create a blue `SolidBrush` with the following declaration:

```
SolidBrush blueSolid = new SolidBrush(Color.Blue);
```

Then, you can fill a shape using the brush. In the next section, you will learn the details of how to create different shapes. One of the simplest methods is `FillRectangle()`, which creates a filled rectangle. It requires five parameters: a brush, the x- and y-coordinates of the upper-left corner of the rectangle, and the width and height of the rectangle. Figure 16-11 shows a program that creates a `SolidBrush` object and uses it to fill a rectangle. Figure 16-12 shows the output.

```
using System;
using System.Windows.Forms;
using System.Drawing;

public class SolidBrushDemo : Form
{
   public SolidBrushDemo()
   {
      this.Size = new System.Drawing.Size(120, 160);
   }
   protected override void OnPaint(PaintEventArgs e)
   {
      int x = 30;
      int y = 40;
      int width = 50;
      int height = 60;
      Graphics g = e.Graphics;
      SolidBrush brush = new SolidBrush(Color.Blue);
      g.FillRectangle(brush, x, y, width, height);
   }
   public static void Main()
   {
      Application.Run(new SolidBrushDemo());
   }
}
```

Figure 16-11 The `SolidBrushDemo` class

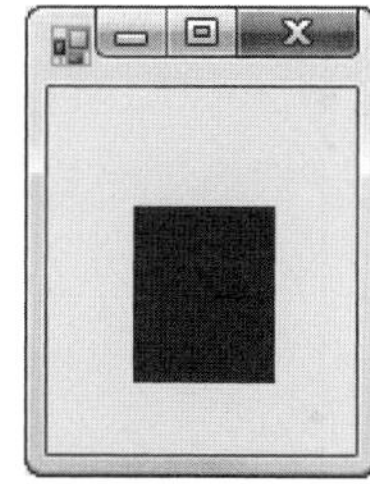

Figure 16-12 Output of the `SolidBrushDemo` program

The `HatchBrush` constructor requires a style and two colors. The styles available to use with a `HatchBrush` include `Horizontal`, `Vertical`, `ForwardDiagonal`, `BackwardDiagonal`, `LargeGrid`, `DiagonalCross`, `Plaid`, `LargeCheckerboard`, `DashedHorizontal`, `ZigZag`, and `Percent05`. Figure 16-13 shows a program that creates four different brushes, which in turn use four different `HatchStyles` to create four black-and-white filled rectangles. Notice in the first shaded line that you must include the `Drawing2D` class to use the `HatchStyles`. In the second shaded line, a `HatchBrush` is created using one of the styles.

```
using System;
using System.Windows.Forms;
using System.Drawing;
using System.Drawing.Drawing2D;
public class HatchBrushDemo : Form
{
   public HatchBrushDemo()
   {
      this.Size = new System.Drawing.Size(190, 100);
   }
   protected override void OnPaint(PaintEventArgs e)
   {
      int x = 10;
      int y = 10;
      int width = 30;
      int height = 30;
      const int GAP = 40;
      Graphics g = e.Graphics;
      HatchBrush brush1 = new
         HatchBrush(HatchStyle.Horizontal,
          Color.Black, Color.White);
      g.FillRectangle(brush1, x, y, width, height);
      x += GAP;
      HatchBrush brush2 = new
         HatchBrush(HatchStyle.Vertical,
         Color.Black, Color.White);
      g.FillRectangle(brush2, x, y, width, height);
      x += GAP;
      HatchBrush brush3 = new
         HatchBrush(HatchStyle.LargeCheckerBoard,
         Color.Black, Color.White);
      g.FillRectangle(brush3, x, y, width, height);
      x += GAP;
      HatchBrush brush4 = new
         HatchBrush(HatchStyle.ZigZag,
         Color.Black, Color.White);
      g.FillRectangle(brush4, x, y, width, height);
   }
   public static void Main()
   {
      Application.Run(new HatchBrushDemo());
   }
}
```

Figure 16-13 The `HatchBrushDemo` class

In the `HatchBrushDemo` class, a rectangle is drawn with the first `HatchBrush` object, and then the x-coordinate is increased before the next brush is used to create a rectangle using a different style. Figure 16-14 shows the output.

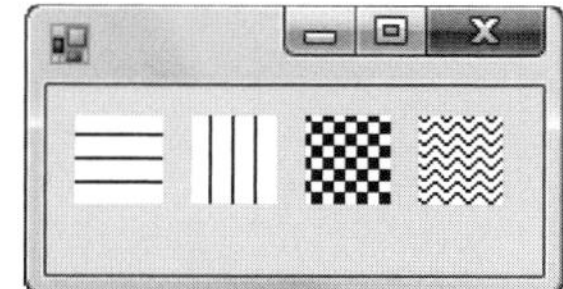

Figure 16-14 Output of the `HatchBrushDemo` program

You can create a `Pen` object from a `Brush` object. The new `Pen` object will have the same display attributes as the brush. For example, in the following code, `pen1` has the characteristics of `brush1` and a default thickness of 1, and `pen2` has the characteristics of `brush1` and a thickness of 4.

```
SolidBrush brush1 = new SolidBrush(Color.Red);
Pen pen1 = new Pen(brush1);
Pen pen2 = new Pen(brush1, 4);
```

»TWO TRUTHS AND A LIE: USING `Brush` OBJECTS

1. As opposed to `Pens`, `Brush` objects are used to create filled objects.
2. To instantiate a red brush, you can code the following:

   ```
   Brush redBrush = new Brush(Color.Red);
   ```

3. `HatchBrush` styles include `Plaid`, `LargeCheckerboard`, and `ZigZag`.

The false statement is #2. You cannot instantiate a `Brush`. Instead, you instantiate one of the classes that derives from `Brush`: `SolidBrush`, `HatchBrush`, `TextureBrush`, `LinearGradientBrush`, and `PathGradientBrush`.

CREATING SHAPES AND SIMPLE ANIMATION

The `Graphics` class contains many methods for drawing lines and shapes; you have already seen a few of them in programs earlier in this chapter. The two groups of methods are as follows:

- » Methods that draw hollow shapes, such as rectangles and ovals. These method names typically begin with `Draw` and require a `Pen` as the first argument.
- » Methods that create filled shapes. These method names typically begin with `Fill` and require a `Brush` as the first argument.

Table 16-4 describes some common shapes you can create, and some of their constructors.

Method	Description
`DrawLine(Pen p, int x1, int y1, int x2, int y2)` `DrawLine(Pen p, Point p1, Point p2)`	Draws a line from coordinates (`x1`, `y1`) to (`x2`, `y2`), or, in an overloaded version using `Point`s, from `p1` to `p2`
`DrawRectangle(Pen p, int x, int y, int width, int height)`	Draws a rectangle of the specified width and height with the upper-left corner at point (`x`, `y`)
`FillRectangle(Brush b, int x, int y, int width, int height)`	Draws a solid rectangle of the specified width and height with the upper-left corner at point (`x`, `y`)
`DrawEllipse(Pen p, int x, int y, int width, int height)` `DrawEllipse(Pen p, Rectangle r)`	Draws an ellipse that fills a rectangle of the specified width and height; the upper-left corner of the unseen, bounding rectangle is at point (`x`, `y`). In the second version, the ellipse is drawn to fill the `Rectangle`.
`FillEllipse(Brush b, int x, int y, int width, int height)` `FillEllipse(Brush b, Rectangle r)`	Draws a solid ellipse of the specified width and height; the upper-left corner of the unseen, bounding rectangle is at point (`x`, `y`). In the second version, the ellipse is drawn to fill the `Rectangle`.
`DrawArc(Pen p, int x, int y, int width, int height, int startAngle, int sweepAngle)`	Draws an arc beginning from `startAngle` and sweeping `sweepAngle` degrees as part of an ellipse defined by `x`, `y`, `width`, and `height`
`DrawPie(Pen p, int x, int y, int width, int height, int startAngle, int sweepAngle)`	Draws a pie section of an ellipse that fills a rectangle of the specified width and height; the upper-left corner of the unseen, bounding rectangle is at point (`x`, `y`)
`FillPie(Brush b, int x, int y, int width, int height, int startAngle, int sweepAngle)`	Draws a solid pie section of an ellipse that fills a rectangle of the specified width and height; the upper-left corner of the unseen, bounding rectangle is at point (`x`, `y`)
`DrawLines(Pen p, Point[])`	Draws a series of lines that connect an array of `Point`s (unlike with `DrawPolygon()`, the figure is not necessarily closed)
`DrawPolygon(Pen p, Point[])`	Draws a polygon that connects an array of `Point`s; if the last and first points differ, they are connected to close the polygon
`FillPolygon(Brush b, Point[])`	Draws a solid polygon that connects an array of `Point`s; if the last and first points differ, they are connected to close the polygon

Table 16-4 Commonly used drawing methods

»NOTE Many of the methods in Table 16-4 have additional overloaded versions. In particular, many have versions that accept floating-point values for the parameters instead of integers. Also, in general, if a method takes four parameters representing x- and y-coordinates, width, and height, you should expect that an overloaded version of the method also exists, and that it accepts a `Rectangle` object.

UNDERSTANDING ELLIPSES

An **ellipse** is an oval shape. Technically, it is a curve for which every point is the same total distance from two fixed points called **foci**. In the program in Figure 16-15, the shaded statements draw an ellipse and a rectangle using the same x- and y-coordinates and the same width and height.

```
using System;
using System.Windows.Forms;
using System.Drawing;
using System.Drawing.Drawing2D;
public class EllipseDemo : Form
{
   public EllipseDemo()
   {
      this.Size = new System.Drawing.Size(100, 140);
   }
   protected override void OnPaint(PaintEventArgs e)
   {
      int x = 10;
      int y = 10;
      int width = 80;
      int height = 60;
      Graphics g = e.Graphics;
      SolidBrush brush = new SolidBrush(Color.Black);
      Pen pen = new Pen(Color.Blue, 2);
      g.FillEllipse(brush, x, y, width, height);
      g.DrawRectangle(pen, x, y, width, height);
   }
   public static void Main()
   {
      Application.Run(new EllipseDemo());
   }
}
```

Figure 16-15 The `EllipseDemo` class

The output of the `EllipseDemo` class in Figure 16-16 shows that when you draw an ellipse, it touches all the sides of a rectangle with the same dimensions. When you just draw an ellipse without a rectangle, of course, you do not see the rectangle that creates the bounds.

Figure 16-16 Execution of the `EllipseDemo` program

»NOTE When you draw an ellipse with the same width and height, it is a circle.

UNDERSTANDING ARCS

An **arc** is a portion of an ellipse. An arc has a starting angle measured in degrees; there are 360 degrees in a circle. Figure 16-17 shows how arc angles are measured.

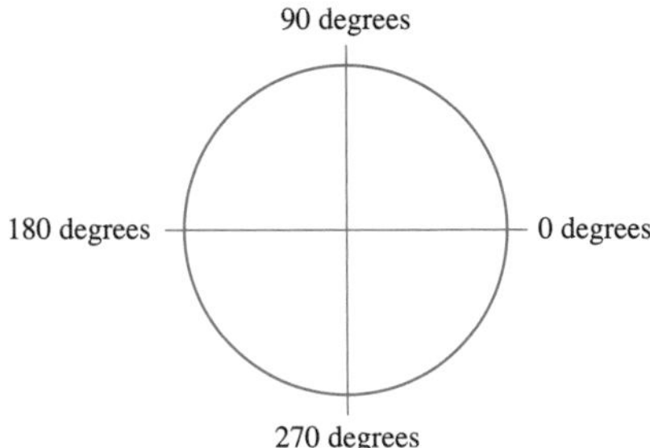

Figure 16-17 Arc positions

The zero-degree position for any arc is the three o'clock position. The other 359-degree positions increase as you move counterclockwise around an imaginary circle, so 90 degrees is at the top of the circle in the 12 o'clock position, 180 degrees is opposite the starting position at nine o'clock, and 270 degrees is at the bottom of the circle in the six o'clock position.

The **sweep angle** is the number of degrees over which you want to draw the arc, traveling counterclockwise from the starting position. For example, you can draw a half circle by indicating an arc angle of 180 degrees, or a quarter circle by indicating an arc angle of 90 degrees. If you want to travel clockwise from the starting position, you express the degrees as a negative number. Just as when you draw a line, you can take one of two approaches when drawing an arc: Either start at point A and travel to point B, or start at point B and travel to point A. For example, to create an arc object using a `Graphics` object named `g` that looks like the top half of a circle, the following statements produce identical results:

```
g.DrawArc(x, y, w, h, 0, 180);
g.DrawArc(x, y, w, h, 180, -180);
```

The first statement starts an arc at the three o'clock position and travels 180 degrees counterclockwise to the nine o'clock position. The second statement starts at nine o'clock and travels clockwise to three o'clock.

The `DrawPie()` and `FillPie()` methods are used to create variations on arcs. Each produces an arc, but also shows the radius lines that extend from the arc's endpoints to the radius of the imaginary circle that encompasses the arc. Figure 16-18 shows a program that draws two filled arcs created with the `FillPie()` method.

NOTE If you create an arc with a 360-degree sweep, you create a circle. If you create an arc with a sweep greater than 360 degrees, no error occurs; you still see a complete circle.

```
using System;
using System.Windows.Forms;
using System.Drawing;
using System.Drawing.Drawing2D;
public class ArcDemo : Form
{
   public ArcDemo()
   {
      this.Size = new System.Drawing.Size(160, 140);
   }
   protected override void OnPaint(PaintEventArgs e)
   {
      int x = 10;
      int y = 10;
      int width = 80;
      int height = 60;
      Graphics g = e.Graphics;
      SolidBrush brush = new SolidBrush(Color.Black);
      g.FillPie(brush, x, y, width, height, 45, 270);
      g.FillPie(brush, x + 30, y, width, height, 45, -90);
   }
   public static void Main()
   {
       Application.Run(new ArcDemo());
   }
}
```

Figure 16-18 The ArcDemo class

> **NOTE**
> Don't forget that when you use any of the arc methods, you can substitute a Rectangle for the four parameters that define the arc's bounds.

In the first shaded statement in the ArcDemo class, a pie shape is drawn from a 45-degree starting position counterclockwise 270 degrees, or three-quarters of a circle, ending at the 315-degree position. In the second shaded statement, a pie shape is drawn from the same 45-degree starting position using a negative value for the sweep. Because the sweep value is negative, the sweep goes clockwise instead of counterclockwise. The –90 value creates a quarter-circle arc that starts at approximately the two o'clock position and extends downward to the 4 o'clock position. Figure 16-19 shows the two pie shapes that the program produces.

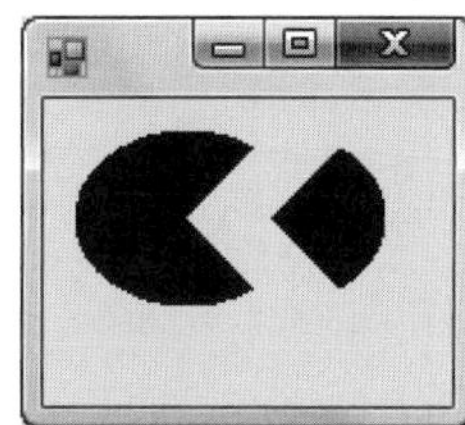

Figure 16-19 Output of the ArcDemo program

»NOTE
Technically, a rectangle is a polygon; you could draw a rectangle with the `DrawPolygon()` method.

»NOTE
Although their names are very similar, the `DrawLine()` and `DrawLines()` methods accomplish different tasks.

UNDERSTANDING POLYGONS

A **polygon** is a multisided shape. The `DrawLines()` method allows you to draw a series of connected lines, but the shape is not necessarily closed. In contrast, when you use the `DrawPolygon()` or `FillPolygon()` method, the shape is closed. If the start point and last point are different when you use `DrawPolygon()` or `FillPolygon()`, the endpoints are connected, so that a closed shape is produced. Each of these methods uses an array of `Point` objects to produce its outline.

For example, Figure 16-20 shows a program that creates a form, sets its size, and sets the background color to dark blue. The `OnPaint()` method declares an array of `Point` objects, and two `int` arrays that hold a series of x- and y-point values. These integer values are then loaded into the `Point` array.

```
using System;
using System.Windows.Forms;
using System.Drawing;
using System.Drawing.Drawing2D;
public class PolygonDemo : Form
{
   public PolygonDemo()
   {
      this.Size = new System.Drawing.Size(160, 160);
      this.BackColor = Color.DarkBlue;
   }
   protected override void OnPaint(PaintEventArgs e)
   {
      const int SIZE = 11;
      Point[] points = new Point[SIZE];
      int[] xPoints = {42, 52, 72, 52,  60, 40, 15,  28, 9,  32, 42};
      int[] yPoints = {38, 62, 68, 80, 105, 85, 102, 75, 58, 60, 38};
      for(int x = 0; x < SIZE; ++x)
         points[x] = new Point(xPoints[x], yPoints[x]);
      Graphics g = e.Graphics;
      HatchBrush brush = new HatchBrush(HatchStyle.Percent05,
         Color.Black, Color.White);
      g.FillPolygon(brush, points);
   }
   public static void Main()
   {
      Application.Run(new PolygonDemo());
   }
}
```

Figure 16-20 The `PolygonDemo` class

In the `PolygonDemo` class in Figure 16-20, the `Point` array is created, and then the `Graphics` object is retrieved, a brush is created, and the shaded statement draws the polygon with the brush. Figure 16-21 shows the output—an enclosed star, painted with tiny dots because the brush uses the `Percent05` `HatchStyle`.

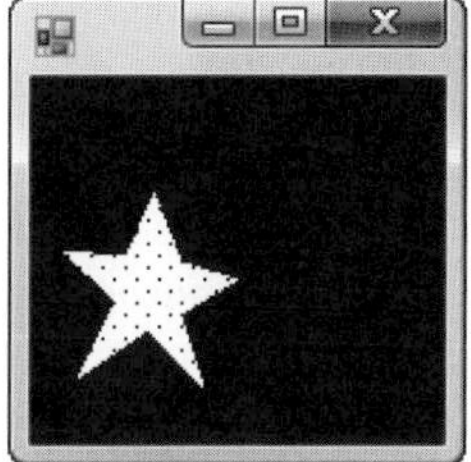

Figure 16-21 Output of the `PolygonDemo` program

CREATING SIMPLE ANIMATION

After you learn to create shapes and understand how their x- and y-coordinates position them on the screen, you can create animated effects. **Animation** is the process of displaying slightly altered images, one at a time, to give the illusion of motion. To create simple animation on a `Frame` in C#, you might draw a shape (or set of shapes) at specific screen coordinates, and then pause execution for a few milliseconds. Then, you can redraw the shape in the `Frame`'s background color to make it seem to disappear. Next, you can draw the shape in a slightly different position using the original drawing color. The new placement of the shape gives a viewer the illusion that the shape has moved. In the You Do It section at the end of this chapter, you will create a `Frame` that employs animation.

»TWO TRUTHS AND A LIE: CREATING SHAPES AND SIMPLE ANIMATION

1. Methods that draw hollow shapes typically begin with `Draw` and require a `Pen` as the first argument.
2. Methods that create filled shapes typically begin with `Fill` and require a `Brush` as the first argument.
3. An arc's zero-degree position is at the 12 o'clock position; the other 359-degree positions increase as you move clockwise around an imaginary circle.

The false statement is #3. The zero-degree position for any arc is the three o'clock position. The other 359-degree positions increase as you move counterclockwise around an imaginary circle.

ADDING IMAGES TO APPLICATIONS

Multimedia describes the use of sound, images, graphics, and video in computer programs. Most computers sold today are "multimedia ready"—that is, they have CD-RW and DVD drives, audio boards, and video capabilities. C# provides extensive multimedia tools that can add interest and excitement to your applications.

>> NOTE
Lossless data compression is a set of rules that allows an exact replica of data to be reconstructed from a compressed version. If you have ever worked with a .zip file, you have worked with lossless data compression.

An **image** is a likeness of a person or thing. Images abound on the Internet in all shapes, colors, and sizes. Some image formats supported by C# include the following:

- **Graphics Interchange Format (GIF)**, which can contain a maximum of 256 different colors.
- **Joint Photographic Experts Group (JPEG)**, which is commonly used to store photographs, and is a more sophisticated way to represent a color image.
- **Portable Network Graphics (PNG)**, which is more flexible than the GIF format and stores images in a lossless form. (PNG was originally designed to be a portable image storage format for computer-originated images.)

For example, Figure 16-22 shows a file named Hello.png.

Figure 16-22 The Hello.png file

You can use the **Image class** to create an Image from an image file, as in the following statement:

```
Image image = Image.FromFile("Hello.png");
```

If the image file is not stored in the same folder as the program, you can use a complete pathname to identify the image, as in the following:

```
Image image = Image.FromFile("C:\\MyPictures\\Hello.png");
```

>> NOTE Recall that you use two slashes in a literal filename because the single slash is the escape sequence character. As an alternative, you can precede the string that holds the filename with an at-sign, as in the following:

```
Image image = Image.FromFile(@"C:\MyPictures\Hello.png");
```

This style of string is called an **@-quoted string**; escape sequences are not processed within it.

You can use the DrawImage() method of the Graphics class to place an image on a Form. One version of DrawImage() takes five parameters—the image, the two coordinates of the upper-left corner of the image, and the width and height. For example, the following statement places an Image named image at position 20, 20 in a rectangle 100 pixels wide by 100 pixels tall.

```
g.DrawImage(image, 20, 20, 100, 100);
```

Alternatively, you can use a Rectangle object to place the image on a Form, and use the image and its rectangle to draw the image, as in the following statements:

```
Rectangle r = new Rectangle(20, 20, 100, 100);
g.DrawImage(image, r);
```

Figure 16-23 shows an application that displays the Hello.png file. The program creates a `Form`, sets its background color to dark blue, and displays the stored image in a rectangle starting at position 20, 20 in a square that is 100 pixels wide by 100 pixels tall. Figure 16-24 shows the output.

```
using System;
using System.Windows.Forms;
using System.Drawing;
using System.Drawing.Drawing2D;
public class ImageDemo1 : Form
{
   public ImageDemo1()
   {
      this.Size = new System.Drawing.Size(160, 180);
      this.BackColor = Color.DarkBlue;
   }
   protected override void OnPaint(PaintEventArgs e)
   {
      Graphics g = e.Graphics;
      Rectangle r = new Rectangle(20, 20, 100, 100);
      Image image = Image.FromFile("Hello.png");
      g.DrawImage(image, r);
   }
   public static void Main()
   {
      Application.Run(new ImageDemo1());
   }
}
```

Figure 16-23 The `ImageDemo1` class

Figure 16-24 Output of the `ImageDemo1` program

By changing the size of the rectangle in the `ImageDemo1` class, you can create different effects. For example, when you change the `Rectangle` declaration from a size of 100 by 100 to a size of 40 by 40, Figure 16-25 shows the output.

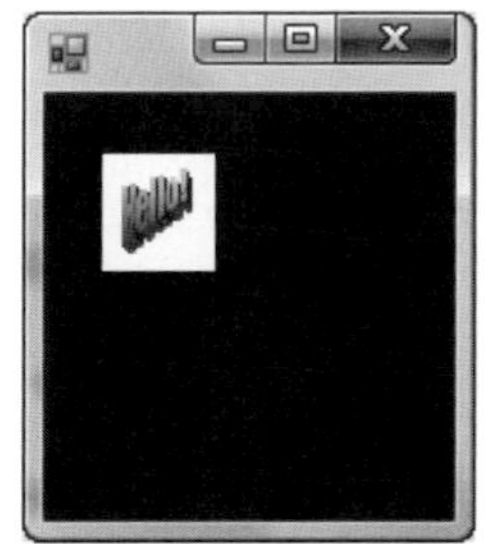

Figure 16-25 Output of the `ImageDemo1` program when the rectangle size is reduced to 40 by 40

»NOTE The code that produces Figure 16-25 is stored on your Student Disk in a file named ImageDemo2.cs.

»NOTE
The code that produces Figure 16-26 is stored on your Student Disk in a file named ImageDemo3.cs.

You can also stretch or distort an image figure. Suppose you define the `Rectangle` object in the `ImageDemo1` program as follows:

```
Rectangle r = new Rectangle(20, 20, 100, 20);
```

The output appears in Figure 16-26.

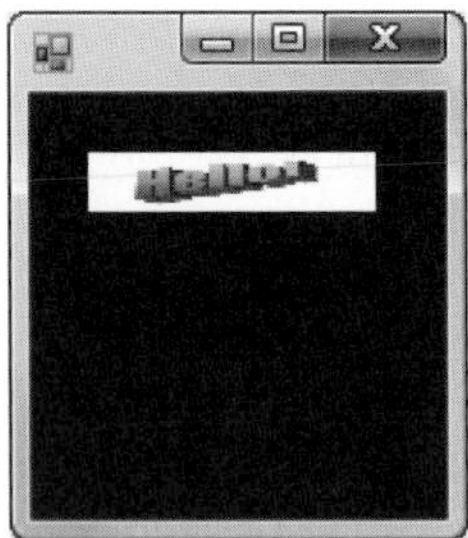

Figure 16-26 Output of the `ImageDemo1` program when the rectangle size is changed to 100 by 20

»TWO TRUTHS AND A LIE: ADDING IMAGES TO APPLICATIONS

1. Multimedia describes the use of sound, images, graphics, and video in computer programs; most computers sold today are multimedia ready.
2. GIF, JPEG, and PNG are image formats supported by C#.
3. You can create an `Image` object by passing a filename to the `Image` constructor.

The false statement is #3. You use the `Image.FromFile()` statement to get an `Image`.

CREATING AN INTERACTIVE GRAPHICS APPLICATION USING THE IDE

Professional programmers seldom create `Forms` using a text editor, as in the previous examples in this chapter. Starting in Chapter 10, you learned that the Visual Studio IDE provides a wealth of tools to help you design `Forms`. Now that you understand graphics, it is easy to add `Graphics` methods to `Forms` you create using the IDE. In particular, creating `Forms` that use other `Controls` as well becomes a simpler task.

For example, suppose you want to add the Hello image from Figure 16-26 and earlier figures to a `Form`, and you want to make the image appear only when the user clicks a button. You can start a new project, select Windows Forms Application, and assign the name `DemoImageApplication`. When the `Form` appears in the IDE, you can drag a button to location 100, 40 and change the button's text to "Show Image", as shown in Figure 16-27.

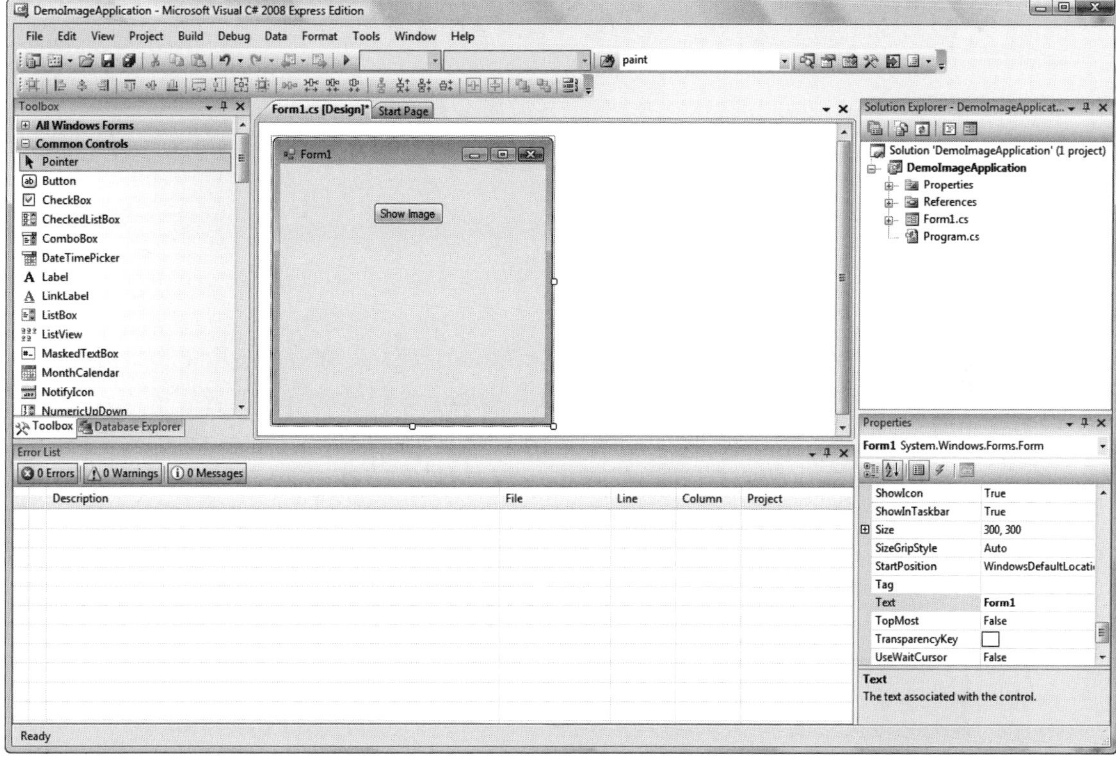

Figure 16-27 Starting the `DemoImageApplication` in the Visual Studio IDE

When you double-click the button in the IDE, the code that includes the `button1_Click()` method appears on the screen. You can then add the statements needed to display the Hello image when the user clicks the button. The unshaded statements in Figure 16-28 are automatically generated by the IDE; the shaded statements are added by the programmer.

```
using System;
using System.Collections.Generic;
using System.ComponentModel;
using System.Data;
using System.Drawing;
using System.Linq;
using System.Text;
using System.Windows.Forms;

namespace DemoImageApplication
{
    public partial class Form1 : Form
    {
        private Image image = Image.FromFile("C:\\C#\\Chapter.16\\Hello.png");
        private Graphics g;
        private int x = 90;
        private int y = 80;
        private int width = 100;
        private int height = 100;
        public Form1()
        {
            InitializeComponent();
            g = this.CreateGraphics();
        }
        private void button1_Click(object sender, EventArgs e)
        {
            g.DrawImage(image, x, y, width, height);
        }
    }
}
```

Figure 16-28 Automatically generated and programmer-supplied statements in the `DemoImageApplication` program

All of the shaded statements in Figure 16-28 should be familiar to you. They perform the following tasks:

- An `Image` object is created from the Hello.png file.
- A `Graphics` object is declared.
- Variables are established for the x- and y-coordinates where the image will appear on the `Form`, and for the width and height of the image. Of course, unnamed constants could be used instead of named variables to position the image on the form.
- Within the `Form`'s constructor, the `Graphics` object `g` is created.
- Within the `Click()` method for the button, the image is drawn.

Figure 16-29 shows the application when it starts and after the user clicks the button; the image is displayed as expected.

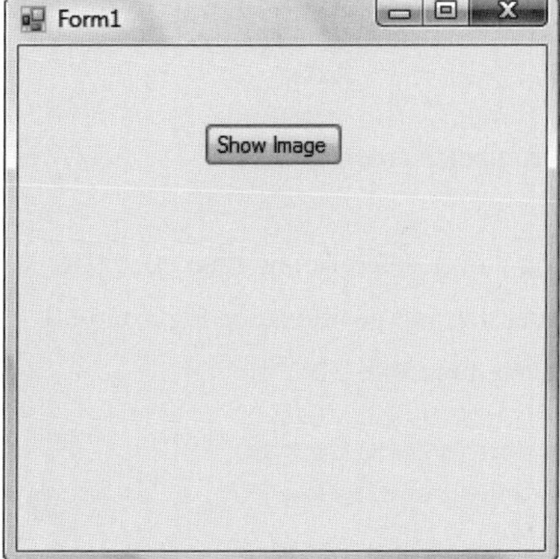

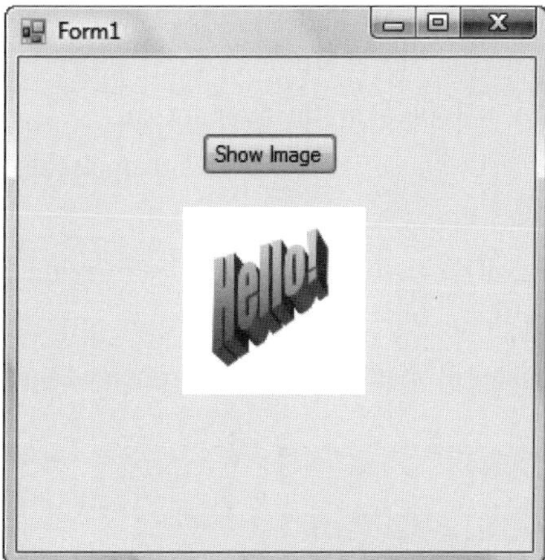

Figure 16-29 Execution of the `DemoImageApplication` program

In a similar way, you could use the `Graphics` object to create any of the shapes discussed earlier in this chapter, or you could move the `Graphics` instructions to other methods.

»TWO TRUTHS AND A LIE: CREATING AN INTERACTIVE GRAPHICS APPLICATION USING THE IDE

1. Professional programmers seldom create `Form`s using a text editor; C# programmers usually use the Visual Studio IDE.
2. A disadvantage to using the IDE is that you cannot add your own statements to the methods it generates.
3. An advantage to using the IDE is that much of the code is generated for you automatically.

The false statement is #2. You can add C# statements to the code generated by the IDE.

ADDING A WINDOWS MEDIA PLAYER TO AN APPLICATION

C# programs can play audio clips on computers that have speakers and a sound card (which includes most computers sold today). You can use the Windows Media Player to retrieve and play sound files that use various formats, including the Windows Wave file format (.wav), Sun Audio file format (.au), and Music and Instrument Digital Interface file format (.midi or .mid). You can also play videos that are stored in such formats as Motion Pictures Experts Group (.mpeg) and Audio-Video Interleave (.avi).

The Windows Media Player control is in the Toolbox in the IDE. However, unless another programmer has used it in your IDE, it is probably not in the list of available controls.

To retrieve and use the Windows Media Player control, you must perform the following steps in the Visual Studio IDE:

1. Select Tools from the main menu.
2. Select Choose Toolbox Items to open the Choose Toolbox Items dialog box.
3. Click the COM Components tab.
4. Scroll down the alphabetical list to Windows Media Player, select it, and then click **OK**.
5. Click the `Form`. The Media Player appears. Adjust its size and position. See Figure 16-30.
6. Under Properties, click the Property Pages button. See Figure 16-31.

Figure 16-30 The Media Player on a `Form`

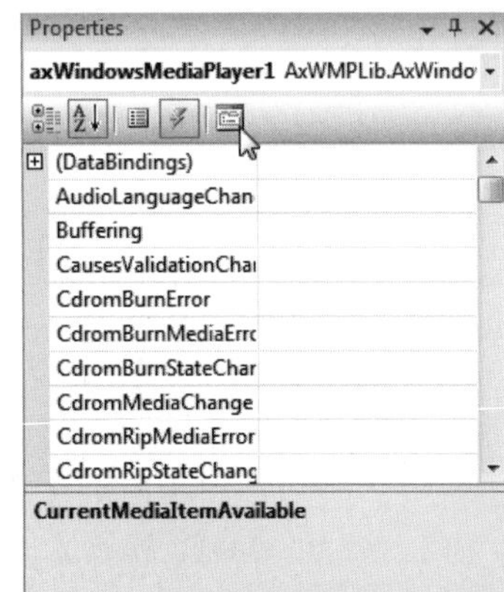

Figure 16-31 Selecting Properties Pages

NOTE The program shown in development in Figures 16-30 through 16-32 is saved on your Student Disk as `MusicApplication`. The business.mid file that plays a tune is stored there, too.

7. The Windows Media Player Properties dialog box opens. Browse for a file to play. See Figure 16-32. Select OK.
8. Run the application. When the `Form` opens, the file starts to play. You can pause, rewind, seek, and perform all the operations you have seen with other media players.

Figure 16-32 The Media Player Properties dialog box

As an alternative to using the Properties Pages to browse for a file, you can assign a file directly to the object created when you add the Windows Media Player to the `Form`. The object's default name is `axWindowsMediaPlayer1`. If you do not change the `Name` property for this object, the statement that assigns a file named business.mid might be:

```
axWindowsMediaPlayer1.URL = "C:\\C#\\Chapter.16\\business.mid";
```

Of course, your path might be different. As you might guess from the property name URL, you could also assign a Web address to the property.

»TWO TRUTHS AND A LIE: ADDING A WINDOWS MEDIA PLAYER TO AN APPLICATION

1. C# programs can play audio clips on specialized devices such as iPods, but not on most personal computers.
2. You can use the Windows Media Player to retrieve and play sound files that use various sound formats, including .wav and .midi.
3. The Windows Media Player control can be retrieved from the Toolbox in the IDE; you can add it if it is not already there.

The false statement is #1. Most computers sold today have speakers and a sound card and can play audio clips.

YOU DO IT

CREATING A FRAME THAT CONTAINS COLORS AND SHAPES

In the next steps, you will create a `Frame` that displays a variety of colors using two different shapes. While creating the program, you will manipulate the x- and y-coordinates of screen graphics. The output will provide you with an idea of the variety of colors you can create in your C# programs.

To create a `Frame` that contains colors and shapes:

1. Open a new file in your text editor, and type the first few statements needed for the `ColorsAndShapes` class that derives from `Form`:

```
using System;
using System.Windows.Forms;
using System.Drawing;
public class ColorsAndShapes : Form
{
```

2. Declare the variables and constants that the class will use, including a constant that defines the increase of the x- and y-coordinates at which each new column or row starts (`INC`), the frame's width and height (`FRAMEWIDTH` and `FRAMEHEIGHT`), the maximum

x-coordinate at which shapes will be drawn (MAXDRAW), and variables that define the drawing shapes and the brush used to paint them.

```
const int INC = 30;
const int FRAMEWIDTH = 440;
const int FRAMEHEIGHT = FRAMEWIDTH + 150;
const int MAXDRAW = FRAMEWIDTH - INC * 2;
Rectangle rec = new Rectangle(0, 0, 20, 20);
SolidBrush brush = new SolidBrush(Color.Black);
```

3. Create the class constructor, which sets the size of the frame:

```
public ColorsAndShapes()
{
    this.Size = new System.Drawing.Size(FRAMEWIDTH, FRAMEHEIGHT);
}
```

4. Start the OnPaint() method that overrides the parent class version by declaring integers that will hold the red, green, and blue components of colors. Add constants to indicate the increase in each red, green, and blue component in each successive image. The value 60 was chosen arbitrarily; increasing the red, green, and blue values by only 1 or 2 would create too many colors, many of which would be indistinguishable from each other.

```
protected override void OnPaint(PaintEventArgs e)
{
    int r, g, b;
    const int STEP = 60;
    const int LIMIT = 255;
    Graphics gr = e.Graphics;
```

5. Continue the OnPaint() method with three nested loops that, respectively, vary the red, green, and blue components that will be applied to a color. Set the color using the FromArgb() method, and assign it to the brush object. Draw a circle, increase the x-coordinate of the drawing, draw a square, and increase the x-coordinate again. If the x-coordinate is near the end of the row, set the x-coordinate back to 0 and increase the y-coordinate to start a new row. Add a closing curly brace for the method.

```
    for(r = 0; r <= LIMIT; r += STEP)
        for(g = 0; g <= LIMIT; g += STEP)
        {
            for(b = 0; b <= LIMIT; b += STEP)
            {
                Color color = Color.FromArgb(r, g, b);
                brush.Color = color;
                gr.FillEllipse(brush, rec);
                rec.X += INC;
                gr.FillRectangle(brush, rec);
                rec.X += INC;
```

```
                if(rec.X >= MAXDRAW)
                {
                    rec.X = 0;
                    rec.Y += INC;
                }
            }
        }
    }
```

6. Add a `Main()` method that displays the `Frame`, and add a closing curly brace for the class:

```
    public static void Main()
    {
        Application.Run(new ColorsAndShapes());
    }
}
```

7. Save the file as **ColorsAndShapes.cs**. Compile and execute it. Figure 16-33 shows the output, which will look more interesting on your screen than in this two-color book.

8. Experiment with the application by changing the step values for the red, green, and blue color values, and the values by which the x- and y-coordinates are increased during each loop cycle.

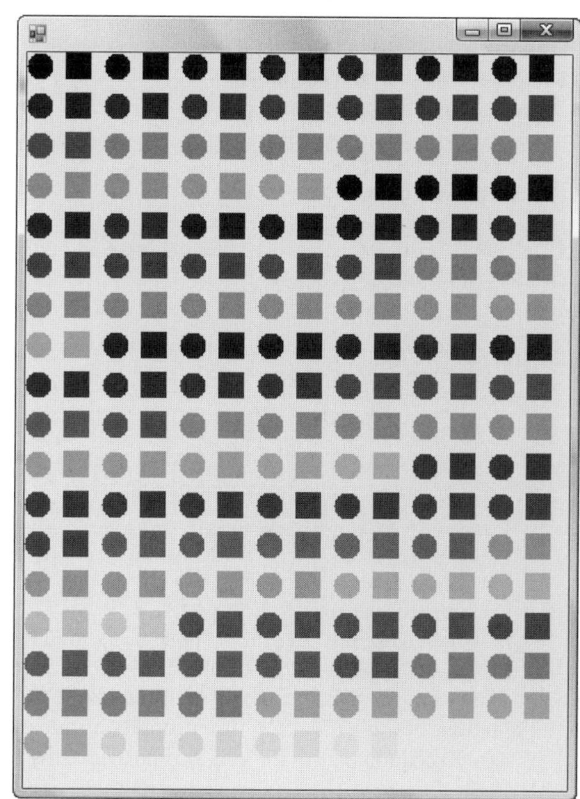

Figure 16-33 Execution of the `ColorsAndShapes` program

CREATING SIMPLE ANIMATION

In the next steps, you will create a simple animation of a small rectangle traveling across the screen.

To create an application with animation:

1. Open a new file in your text editor and enter the first few lines of a program that will show a traveling rectangle:

```
using System;
using System.Windows.Forms;
using System.Drawing;
using System.Threading;
public class Traveling : Form
{
```

2. Declare the constants and variables the program will use. The `time`, `milliseconds`, and `TIMELIMIT` values will control the timing of the movement in the program. The `SIZE`, `MARKER`, and `GAP` constants control the screen and rectangle size and the distance between the rectangles.

```
static Random time = new Random();
static int milliseconds;
const int TIMELIMIT = 50;
const int SIZE = 350;
const int MARKER = 16;
const int GAP = 8;
```

3. Add the constructor to set the `Frame`'s size and color:

```
    public Traveling()
    {
        this.Size = new System.Drawing.Size(SIZE, SIZE);
        this.BackColor = Color.White;
    }
```

4. Start the `OnPaint()` method by declaring variables for the x- and y-coordinates, getting a `Graphics` object, and instantiating a brush:

```
    protected override void OnPaint(PaintEventArgs e)
    {
        int x = 0, y = 0;
        Graphics gr = e.Graphics;
        SolidBrush brush = new SolidBrush(Color.Black);
```

5. Start a nested loop. Painting will continue while the y-coordinate of the image is less than the height of the `Frame`. An inner loop continues while x is less than the width of the `Frame`. Execution pauses for a short time to give the viewer's eyes a chance to see the image. Without the pause, the actions would happen so quickly that the user would not be able to discern them. Then, use a white brush to paint a small rectangle in the `Frame`'s background color, increase the x-coordinate slightly, and paint a small rectangle with the same

dimensions in a slightly new position. Because the x-coordinate of the shape continuously increases, the shape appears to move from left to right across the screen.

```
while (y <= SIZE)
{
    while(x <= SIZE)
    {
        milliseconds = time.Next(TIMELIMIT);
        Thread.Sleep(milliseconds);
        brush.Color = Color.White;
        gr.FillRectangle(brush, x, y, MARKER, MARKER);
        x += GAP;
        brush.Color = Color.Black;
        gr.FillEllipse(brush, x, y, MARKER, MARKER);
    }
```

6. After the x-coordinate reaches the frame's width, increase the y-coordinate so that the next set of shapes will be slightly lower on the `Frame`. Create a second loop that makes the shapes appear to travel from right to left across the screen.

```
y += GAP;
while(x >= -GAP)
{
    milliseconds = time.Next(TIMELIMIT);
    Thread.Sleep(milliseconds);
    brush.Color = Color.White;
    gr.FillRectangle(brush, x, y, MARKER, MARKER);
    x -= GAP;
    brush.Color = Color.Black;
    gr.FillEllipse(brush, x, y, MARKER, MARKER);
}
y += GAP;
```

7. Add a closing curly brace for the outer `while` loop, and another for the `OnPaint()` method.
8. Add a `Main()` method for the program and a closing brace for the class:

```
    public static void Main()
    {
        Application.Run(new Traveling());
    }
}
```

9. Save the file as **Traveling.cs**. Compile and execute the program. You see a small shape move from left to right across the screen, move down slightly, and go from right to left. The crisscross motion continues until the shape reaches the bottom of the `Frame`. Close the `Frame`.
10. Experiment with the `Traveling` class by increasing or decreasing the pause time or the gap between drawn shapes. Also change the `Frame`'s background color and observe the effects.

CREATING AN APPLICATION WITH AN IMAGE AND SOUND

In the next steps, you will create an application that contains an image and sound as part of an advertisement for the Primrose School of Music.

To create an application that contains an image and sound:

1. Locate the **beethoven.png** and **beethoven5.mid** files in the Chapter.16 folder of your Student Disk. One file contains an image of Ludwig van Beethoven and the other contains part of a piece of music he composed.
2. Open Visual Studio and start a new Windows Forms Application named **MusicSchool**. Change the `Text` property of the `Form` to **Primrose School of Music**.
3. Drag a `Button` near the top center of the `Form`. Change its `Text` property to **Check us out**. Change the `Font` property to **Broadway, Regular, 10**. Adjust the size of the button to see all the text.
4. Drag a `Label` and position it below the `Button`. Change its `Text` property to **Become a superstar** and change its `Font` property to **Broadway, Bold, 12**. Set its `Visible` property to **`false`**. You will make the `Label` visible when the user clicks the button.
5. Examine your Toolbox. If it contains the Windows Media Player Control, drag it onto your `Form`. Otherwise, select **Tools** from the main menu, and select **Choose Toolbox Items**. This displays the Choose Toolbox Items dialog box. Click the **COM Components** tab, scroll down the alphabetical list to **Windows Media Player**, and select it. Click **OK**, and then click the `Form`. The Media Player appears.
6. Adjust the size and position of the Windows Media Player Control. See Figure 16-34 for guidance. Set its `Visible` property to **`false`**.

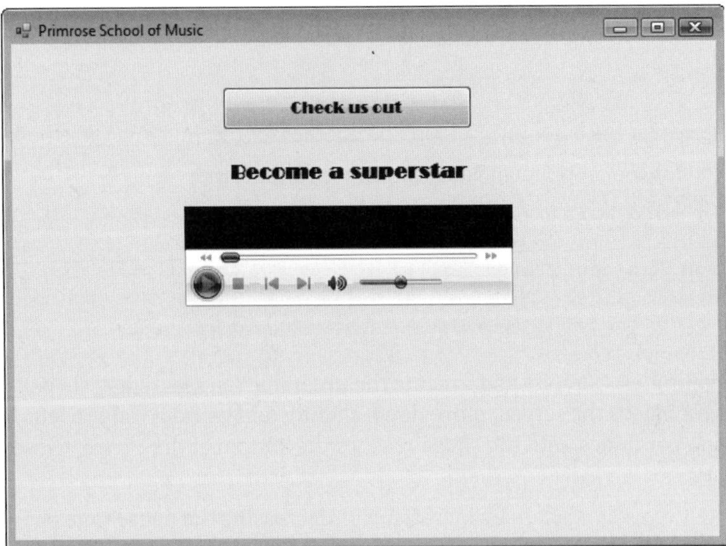

Figure 16-34 Creating the `MusicSchool` project

7. Click the **Windows Media Player** on the `Form`, and then click the **Property Pages** button in its property list. Browse for the **beethoven5.mid** file on your Student Disk. Select it, click **Open**, and then click **OK**.

8. Drag a `Label` to the lower-left portion of the `Form`. Change its `Text` property to the following:

   Learn an instrument.

   Learn composition.

   World-renowned faculty.

   Reasonable prices.

   Call 1-800-555-1776.

   Change the `Font` of the `Label` to **Century 12**. Set its `Visible` property to **`false`**.

9. Double-click the button to expose the `button1_Click()` method and the rest of the code that goes with the `Form`. In the `Form1` class, before the constructor, add the following declarations. Change the reference to the beethoven.png file if you have stored it in a different location:

```
private Image image =
   Image.FromFile("C:\\C#\\Chapter.16\\beethoven.png");
private Graphics g;
```

10. Within the constructor, after the `InitializeComponent()` statement, add the following to get the graphics context for the `Form`:

```
g = this.CreateGraphics();
```

11. Add the following statements within the `button1_Click()` method to display the previously invisible components and to add the image of Beethoven to the `Form`:

```
label1.Visible = true;
label2.Visible = true;
axWindowsMediaPlayer1.Visible = true;
g.DrawImage(image, 300, 220, 150, 150);
```

12. Save the project, and then execute it. When the `Form` appears, it contains only a button. Click the button to display the two labels, the media player, and the image. Figure 16-35 shows the program during execution.

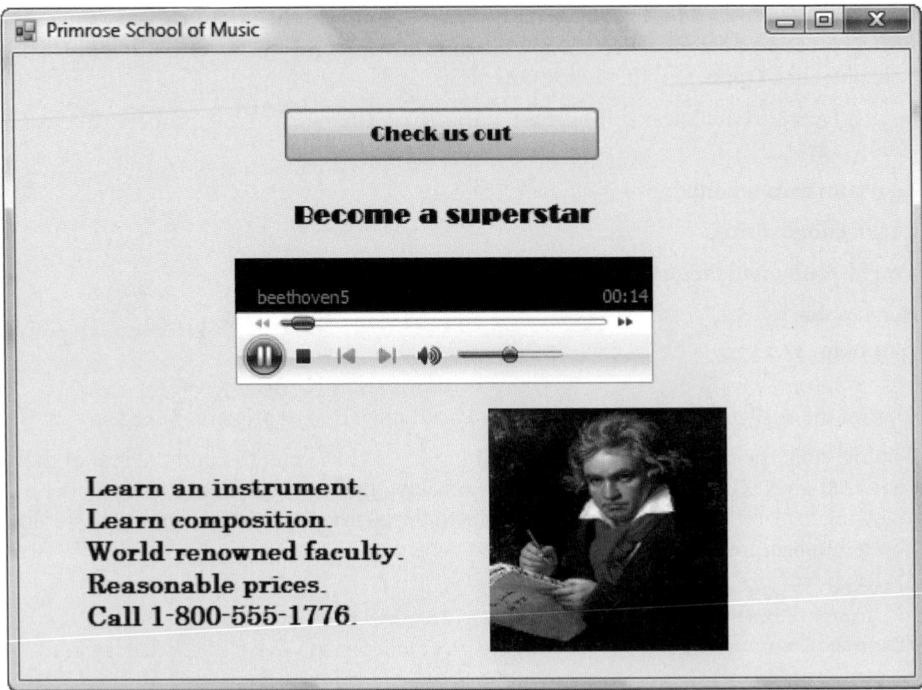

Figure 16-35 The `MusicSchool` application

13. Experiment with the media player by pausing and restarting the music, and by seeking a new position. When you are done, exit Visual Studio.

CHAPTER SUMMARY

» In Microsoft Windows, you can use the Graphics Device Interface Plus (GDI+) Application Programming Interface (API) to paint and work with graphic objects on components such as windows and forms. The `System.Drawing` namespace in GDI+ provides the basic GDI+ functionality. The `Graphics` class contains methods you can use to draw strings, lines, and shapes on a control. Usually you use a `Pen` object (to make outlines) or `Brush` object (to make solid objects) to create the desired shape.

» Programmers position text and shapes on a screen by using x- and y-coordinates. You can create a `Point` object to refer to a single screen position. The `Pen` class provides a tool for drawing lines, curves, and outlines. The `DrawLine()` method draws a line on the screen.

» When painting a surface is required, a `Paint` event is triggered. A component's `OnPaint()` method is invoked when painting must occur. You can override the `OnPaint()` method in your programs when you want specific actions to take place when components must be rendered or when you want to use the `PaintEventArgs` parameter to the method.

- A C# graphics context is a collection of attributes that determines how graphics operations affect components. A `Graphics` object manages a graphics context by controlling how much information is drawn. `Graphics` objects contain methods for drawing, manipulating fonts and color, and other graphics-related actions. You can extract the `Graphics` object from the `PaintEventArgs` parameter to the `OnPaint()` method. After you have obtained the `Graphics` object, you can use it with methods to draw on the `Form`. Instead of overriding the `OnPaint()` method, programmers can add an event handler for the `Form`'s `Paint` event. The `OnPaint()` method is usually called automatically, but you can force a call to `OnPaint()` by calling a `Control`'s `Invalidate()` method.
- Besides the predefined colors in C#, you can create nearly 17 million custom colors from a combination of four components: alpha, red, blue, and green.
- `Brush` objects are used to color the inside of graphical shapes. You can instantiate one of the classes that derives from `Brush`: `SolidBrush`, `HatchBrush`, `TextureBrush`, `LinearGradientBrush`, and `PathGradientBrush`.
- The `Graphics` class contains many methods for drawing lines and shapes. Some methods draw hollow shapes, such as rectangles and ovals. These method names typically begin with `Draw` and require a `Pen` as the first argument. Other methods create filled shapes. These method names typically begin with `Fill` and require a `Brush` as the first argument.
- Multimedia describes the use of sound, images, graphics, and video in computer programs. You can use the `Image` class to create an `Image` from an image file.
- The Visual Studio IDE provides a wealth of tools to help you design `Forms`. It is easy to add `Graphics` methods to `Forms` you create using the IDE.
- C# programs can play audio clips on computers that have speakers and a sound card. You can use the Windows Media Player to retrieve and play sound files that use various sound formats.

KEY TERMS

The **Graphics Device Interface Plus (GDI+)** Application Programming Interface (API) is a set of classes that allows applications to use graphics and formatted text both on video displays and printers.

The **`Graphics` class** contains methods you can use to draw strings, lines, and shapes on a control.

A **pixel** is a picture element, or one tiny dot on a monitor.

The **x-axis** is the imaginary horizontal line that determines screen position.

The **y-axis** is the imaginary vertical line that determines screen position.

The **x-coordinate** is the first value in a screen position; its value increases as you travel from left to right across a window.

The **y-coordinate** is the second value in a screen position; its value increases as you travel from top to bottom in a window.

A **`Point` object** refers to a single screen position; it contains x- and y-coordinates.

The **`Pen` class** provides a tool for drawing lines, curves, and outlines.

The **`DrawLine()` method** draws a line on the screen.

Painting is the act of displaying or redisplaying a surface.

A **`Paint` event** is triggered when painting is required.

A **graphics context** is a collection of attributes that determines how graphics operations affect components.

A **`Graphics` object** manages a graphics context by controlling how much information is drawn.

The **ARGB values** of a color are its alpha, red, green, and blue components.

Opacity is the degree of transparency of a color.

`Brush` objects are used to color the inside of graphical shapes.

An **ellipse** is an oval shape.

Foci are two fixed points on an ellipse; every other point on an ellipse is the same distance from these foci.

An **arc** is a portion of an ellipse.

The **sweep angle** is the number of degrees over which an arc is drawn.

A **polygon** is a multisided shape.

Animation is the process of displaying slightly altered images, one at a time, to give the illusion of motion.

Multimedia describes the use of sound, images, graphics, and video in computer programs.

An **image** is a likeness of a person or thing.

Graphics Interchange Format (GIF) is an image format that can contain a maximum of 256 different colors.

Joint Photographic Experts Group (JPEG) is an image format that is commonly used to store photographs. JPEG is a sophisticated way to represent a color image.

Portable Network Graphics (PNG) is an image format that is more flexible than the GIF format and stores images in a lossless form.

Lossless data compression is a set of rules that allows an exact replica of data to be reconstructed from a compressed version.

The **`Image` class** holds images.

An **@-quoted string** is a string preceded with an @ sign and within which escape sequences are not processed.

REVIEW QUESTIONS

1. Which of the following is not true of the GDI+ API?

   a. It allows the programmer to paint and work with graphic objects.

   b. It is a set of classes that allows applications to use graphics and formatted text on both video displays and printers.

   c. It interacts with device drivers on behalf of applications.

   d. All of its code resides in a single namespace.

2. Which of the following `Graphics` objects is used to draw lines?

   a. `Pencil`

   b. `Pen`

   c. `Brush`

   d. all of the above

3. The horizontal position of a component is placed at its ________ coordinate.

   a. h

   b. w

   c. x

   d. y

4. The class that defines objects that refer to a single screen position is ________.

   a. `Point`

   b. `Position`

   c. `XY`

   d. `Coordinate`

5. Which of the following does not declare a `Pen` object?

   a. `Pen a = new Pen(Color.Blue);`

   b. `Pen b = new Pen(3.2F, Color.Red);`

   c. `Pen c = new Pen(Color.Green, 3);`

   d. `Pen d = new Pen(Color.Yellow, 3.4F);`

6. Assuming a `Graphics` object has been correctly instantiated as `g`, and that a `Pen` object has been correctly instantiated as `pen`, which of the following creates a line that slants down and to the right?

   a. `g.DrawLine(pen, 0, 20, 80, 60);`

   b. `g.DrawLine(pen, 20, 40, 80, 10);`

   c. `g.DrawLine(pen, 0, 50, 100, 30);`

   d. `g.DrawLine(pen, 30, 80, 50, 20);`

7. A `Frame` must be painted ________.

   a. when it is first made visible

   b. if it is resized

   c. if it is damaged

   d. all of the above

8. A component's `OnPaint()` method ________.
   a. must be called explicitly
   b. must be overridden by every program that paints
   c. triggers a `Paint` event
   d. must be declared to return a `Brush` or `Pen` object

9. If you write an `OnPaint()` method to override the parent class version, you must ________.
   a. declare a `Graphics` object within it
   b. include a `PaintEventArgs` parameter
   c. not draw lines or shapes from within the method
   d. declare the method to be `public`

10. Which of the following could be the header for a method in a `Form`'s `Paint` event?
    a. `private void MyPainter(PaintEventArgs e)`
    b. `private int MyPainter(object sender, PaintEventArgs e)`
    c. `private void MyPainter(object sender, PaintEventArgs e)`
    d. `public void MyPainter(object sender)`

11. Which of the following statements within a `Frame`'s constructor creates a composed delegate that adds a method named `MyPainter()` to the `Form`'s `Paint` event?
    a. `this.Paint += new PaintEventHandler(PaintMethod);`
    b. `this.Paint += new PaintEventHandler(PaintMethod());`
    c. `this.Paint = new PaintEventHandler(PaintMethod);`
    d. `this.Paint = new PaintEventHandler(PaintMethod());`

12. Which of the following is not true of colors in C#?
    a. More than 140 colors are predefined with descriptive names.
    b. You can create nearly 17 million custom colors from a combination of four components: alpha, red, blue, and green.
    c. Each of the four values, `A`, `R`, `G`, and `B`, can range from 0 to 100%.
    d. The `A`, or alpha, value determines the opacity of the color.

13. Of the following color combinations passed to the `FromArgb()` method, which would look the most green?
    a. 0, 200, 20
    b. 220, 0, 220
    c. 100, 100, 50
    d. 2, 4, 6

14. Which of the following is not true of the `Brush` class?

    a. `Brush`es are used to color the inside of graphical shapes rather than to draw lines.

    b. `Brush` is an abstract class; you cannot instantiate a `Brush`.

    c. `SolidBrush` and `HatchBrush` can be extended to create brushes that use special effects.

    d. The `SolidBrush` constructor takes a `Color` argument; the `HatchBrush` constructor takes a style and two colors.

15. In C#, methods that draw hollow shapes __________ .

    a. typically begin with `Hollow`

    b. use a `Pen`

    c. typically begin with `Fill`

    d. use a descendent of `Brush`

16. In C#, methods that create filled shapes __________ .

    a. use a descendent of `Pen`

    b. typically begin with `Fill`

    c. typically use a `Crayon`

    d. begin with `Solid`

17. Which of the following creates a circle?

    a. `drawEllipse(pen, 20, 40, 60, 80)`

    b. `drawEllipse(pen, 40, 40, 80, 60)`

    c. `drawEllipse(pen, 20, 20, 40, 80)`

    d. `drawEllipse(pen, 20, 80, 60, 60)`

18. The 12 o'clock position in an arc is at the __________ degree position.

    a. 0

    b. 90

    c. 180

    d. 270

19. Which of the following is not true of how multimedia features are used in C#?

    a. Multimedia describes the use of sound, images, graphics, and video in computer programs.

    b. Multimedia functions are not automatically supported by most computers sold today, but they probably will be in the future.

    c. In C#, you can use the `Image` class to create an `Image` from an image file.

    d. You can use the `DrawImage()` method of the `Graphics` class to place an image on a `Form`.

20. The Windows Media Player can retrieve and play sound files in all the following formats except __________ .

    a. Windows Wave file format (.wav)

    b. Sun Audio file format (.au)

    c. Computer Music Group (.cmg)

    d. Music and Instrument Digital Interface file format (.midi or .mid)

EXERCISES

1. Write an application that displays 15 nested circles like the ones shown in Figure 16-36. You may use only one `DrawEllipse()` statement in your program. (*Hint:* Draw the ellipses in a loop.) Save the file as **NestedCircles.cs**.

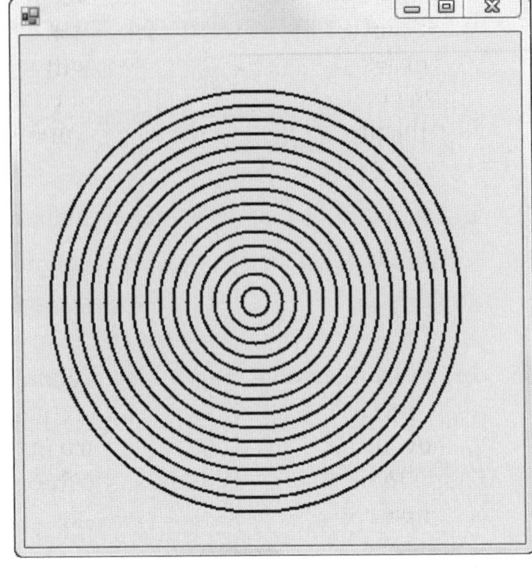

Figure 16-36 Execution of the `NestedCircles` program

2. a. Write an application that displays eight nested rectangles like the ones shown in Figure 16-37. You may use only one `DrawRectangle()` statement in your program. Save the file as **NestedBoxes.cs**.

   b. Modify the NestedBoxes program so that the boxes appear on screen one at a time with a slight pause between them. Save the file as **NestedBoxes2.cs**.

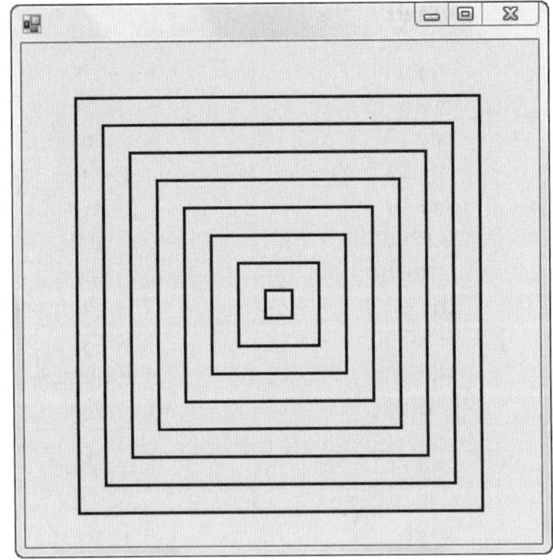

Figure 16-37 Execution of the `NestedBoxes` program

3. Create a `Form` that contains three `NumericUpDown` controls with which a user can select values ranging from 0 to 255. These values represent red, green, and blue components of a color. After the user makes selections and clicks a button, display a filled circle using the selected color combination. Save the project as **ColorMixer**. Figure 16-38 shows a typical execution.

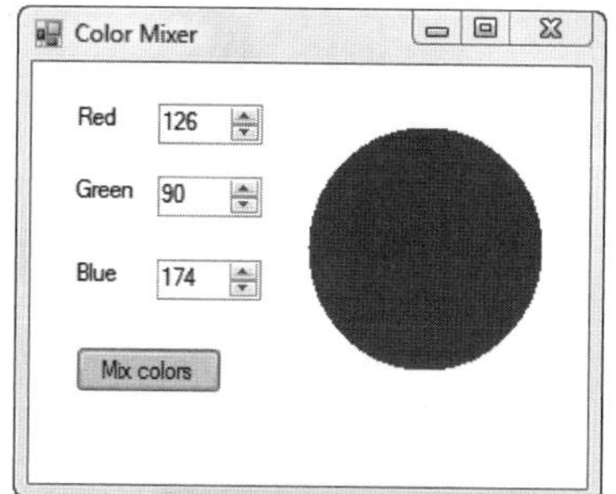

Figure 16-38 Typical execution of the `ColorMixer` project

4. Create a `Form` that shows a city skyline at night. At random time intervals, add a flake of snow or have a window light turn on. Figure 16-39 shows a typical `Form` after it is complete. Save the file as **CityNight.cs**.

5. Create a `Form` on which a ball travels from the upper-left corner to the lower-right corner and then back again. Save the file as **DiagonalBall.cs**.

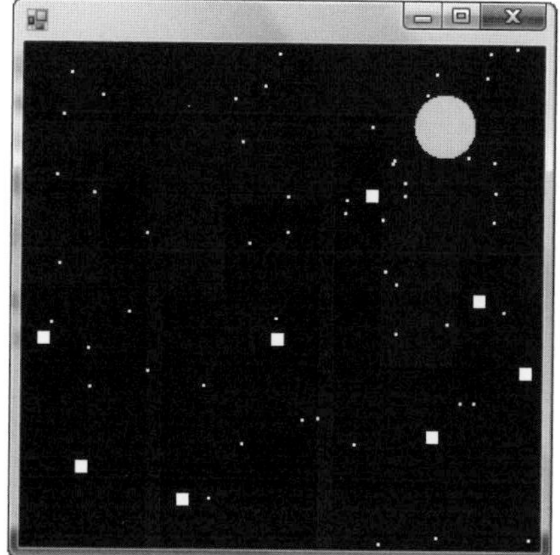

Figure 16-39 Typical execution of the `CityNight` program

6. Create an application that contains a `Form` with a `Button`. The `Button` text is "Show the face". When the user clicks the button, a happy face appears, and the button text changes to "Make me sad". You create the face with ellipses and arcs. When the user clicks the button again, a sad face appears, and the button text changes to "Make me happy". The user can switch the face from happy to sad and back again repeatedly. (*Hint:* Instead of redrawing the entire face when the user clicks the button, you can redraw the mouth in the background color to "erase" it, and then draw the new mouth configuration.) Save the project as **Face**.

7. Create a `Form` that displays a photo album of at least three pictures. When the user clicks a button, display the next picture in sequence. After the user reaches the last picture, start over with the first picture. Use pictures of your choice that you find on the Web or download some from your own camera. Save the project as **PhotoAlbum**.

8. Create an application that allows the user to choose any of at least three genres of music from a checked list box. When the user makes a choice, change the background color of the form to a color of your choice, and start playing the appropriate type of music. You can search the Web for free downloadable music files, or you can use some of the files included on your Student Disk. Save the project as **MusicChoice**.

DEBUGGING EXERCISES

Each of the following files in the Chapter.16 folder on your Student Disk has syntax and/or logical errors. In each case, determine the problem and fix the program. After you correct the errors, save each file using the same filename preceded with *Fixed*. For example, save DebugSixteen1.cs as **FixedDebugSixteen1.cs**.

a. DebugSixteen1.cs

b. DebugSixteen2.cs

c. DebugSixteen3.cs

d. DebugSixteen4.cs

Figure 16-40 shows the desired results when the four Debug files are repaired.

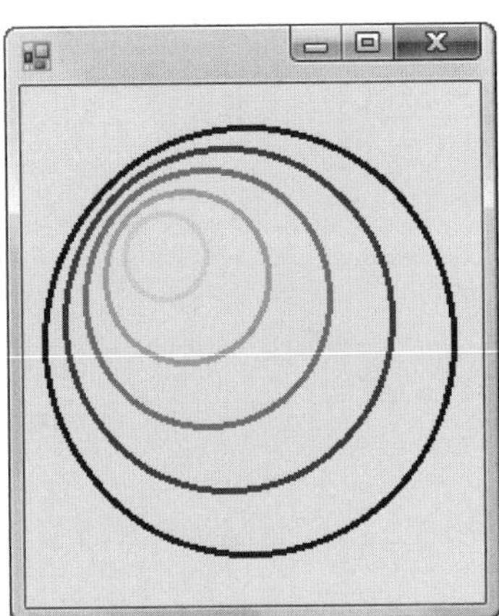

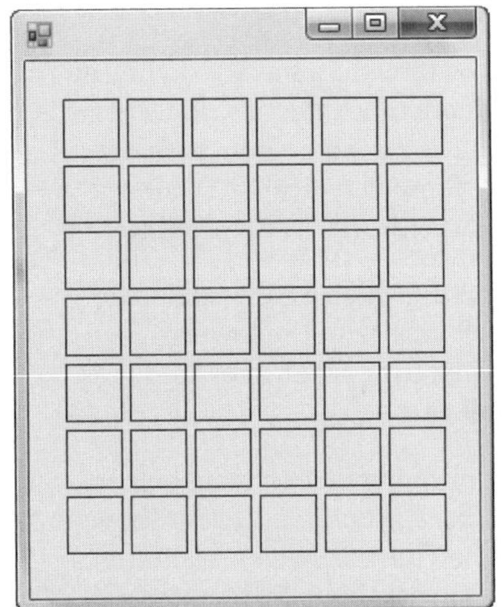

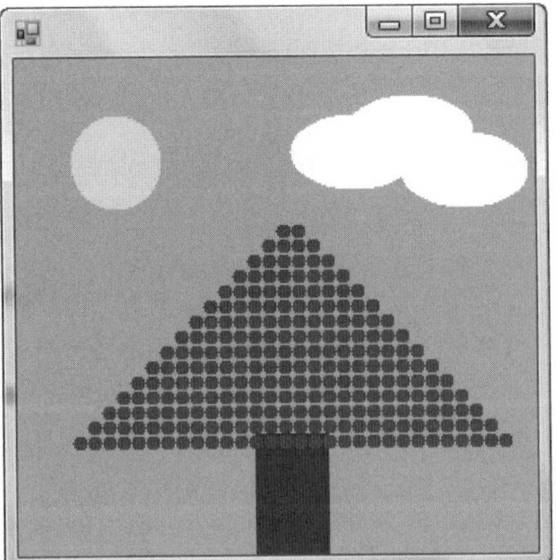

Figure 16-40 Output of the four `FixedDebug` files

UP FOR DISCUSSION

1. Making exciting and professional-looking programs becomes easier once you learn to include graphics images. You can copy graphics images from many locations on the Web. Should there be any restrictions on what graphics you use? Does it make a difference if you are writing programs for your own enjoyment as opposed to putting them on the Web where others can see them? Is using photographs different from using drawings? Does it matter if the photographs contain recognizable people? Would you impose any restrictions on images posted to your organization's Web site?
2. Suppose you are hired to produce a Web site that includes original art and music. Who do you think should be paid the most—the programmer, the artist, or the composer? Why?

CHAPTER SEVENTEEN

17

MANIPULATING DATA WITH XML, XAML, AND WPF

In this chapter you will:

Learn about XML
Format XML documents with XSL
Create and read an XML file using C#
Learn about XAML and WPF
Use WPF in Visual Studio
Learn about WPF controls and layouts
Learn about data binding

The most valuable asset of many businesses is not a piece of equipment or parcel of real estate; instead, it is the data a business uses to keep track of its products, customers, suppliers, employees, and budgets. In Chapter 14, you were introduced to databases and how to couple C# programs with the data stored there. In this chapter, you will be introduced to additional ways to manage data using XML, XAML, and the Windows Presentation Foundation (WPF).

UNDERSTANDING XML

The **Extensible Markup Language (XML)** is a specification for creating markup languages. **Markup** refers to the sequence of characters and symbols that you can insert into text to indicate how a file should look when it is printed or displayed on a computer screen. XML describes data in a way that is easily interpreted by humans. It is **extensible** because users can extend it by defining their own language elements. For example, authors of mathematical, financial, technical, and musical documents each might want to define new elements to format particular text element types that are not shared by authors in other fields. The markup indicators used in XML are **tags**.

NOTE XML is similar to **Hypertext Markup Language (HTML)**. However, XML was designed to transport and store data, with a focus on what data is. HTML, on the other hand, was designed to display data, with a focus on how data looks. HTML has predefined tags like <h1>. In XML, the user creates his own tags.

Consider a book that is an anthology of short stories written by various authors. Each author's content would be very different, but an editor can mark up each author's finished story so that the chapters have a consistent appearance in the final book. For example, each story's title might appear in Arial 16-point font, while the story bodies might all appear in 12-point font. When the editor inserts different codes in the manuscripts near each element, the printer who composes the pages can make similar elements have a uniform appearance.

XML documents can describe printed material, such as chapter elements in a short story anthology, but they also can describe many other types of objects. XML documents contain data and **elements** that specify the document's structure. For example, Figure 17-1 is an XML document that describes an employee.

```
<employee>
   <lastName>Beaumont</lastName>
   <address>12 Pine Court</address>
   <hourlyPay>21.25</hourlyPay>
</employee>
```

Figure 17-1 An XML document that defines an employee

NOTE The file in Figure 17-1 is stored on your Student Disk as employee.xml.

XML documents delimit their elements with **start tags** that begin with a left angle bracket (<), and **end tags** that start with a left angle bracket and a forward slash. Both start and end tags use a right angle bracket to close. In Figure 17-1, `<employee>`, `<lastName>`, `<address>`, and `<hourlyPay>` are start tags, and `</lastName>`, `</address>`, `</hourlyPay>`, and `</employee>` are end tags. An element's start and end tags surround a piece of data, such as Beaumont, 12 Pine Court, and 21.25. The structure of an XML document is a **tree** consisting of a main or **root element** (`employee` in Figure 17-1) and branches (`lastName`, `address`, and `hourlyPay` in Figure 17-1). Every XML document has exactly one root element.

NOTE The hard drive in your computer is organized as a tree. There is a root directory (most often named C:) and folders that extend from it that act like branches.

In Figure 17-1, the tags for `lastName`, `address`, and `hourlyPay` are nested within the `employee` root element. The end tag for every element must correspond to the most recent start tag. This structuring of XML documents is just like the way you manage the curly braces in nested `if` and `while` statements in C# programs.

XML allows you to assign meaning to data. "Beaumont" as a string of characters might mean anything—for example, a school, a street, or a city. By defining it as the `lastName` of an `employee`, a program that uses this data can recognize it as such. If, for example, a program on the Web uses this data, it might provide the user with related information, such as the derivation of the name or photos of famous people with the same name. Similarly, because "12 Pine Court" is recognized as an address, a program might provide an aerial view of the location, or directions to drive there.

The identifiers you assign in XML, such as `lastName`, must follow these rules:

- Names can contain letters, numbers, and other characters.
- Names must not start with a number or punctuation.
- Names must not start with "`xml`".
- Names cannot contain spaces.

Because you know how to create identifiers for variables in C#, these naming rules seem quite standard and logical.

When you create an XML document, you store it in a file with an .xml extension. You can view an XML document in almost any text editor or Web browser. For example, Figure 17-2 shows the employee.xml document displayed in Microsoft Internet Explorer.

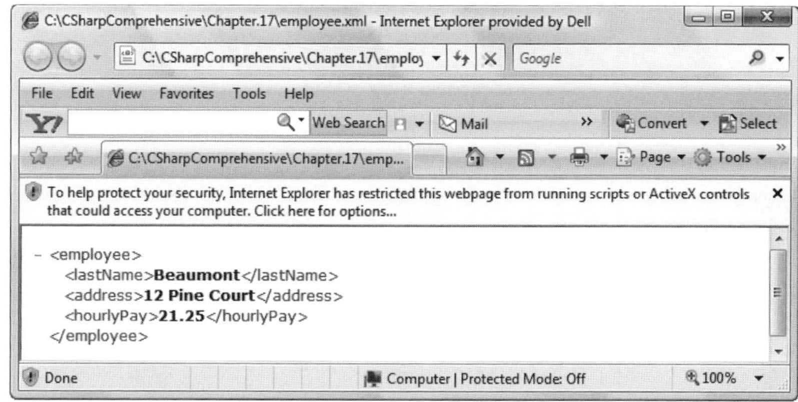

Figure 17-2 The employee.xml document in Internet Explorer

In Figure 17-2, you see a node (small minus sign) to the left of the `<employee>` tag. Internet Explorer places a minus sign in front of every container element in an XML document to indicate that the contents are currently expanded, or viewable. You have seen the same notation in program code in the Visual Studio IDE. Normally, you would expect to click this minus sign to collapse the contents, but by default, Internet Explorer does not allow this operation.

Figure 17-3 shows how you can allow Internet Explorer to collapse container elements. When you click the security warning that appears in the information bar at the top of Internet Explorer's window, you can select the Allow Blocked Content option. You receive a warning message. Because you know your code is safe, you can click Yes. Then, you can collapse the `<employee>` container, as shown in the last part of Figure 17-3.

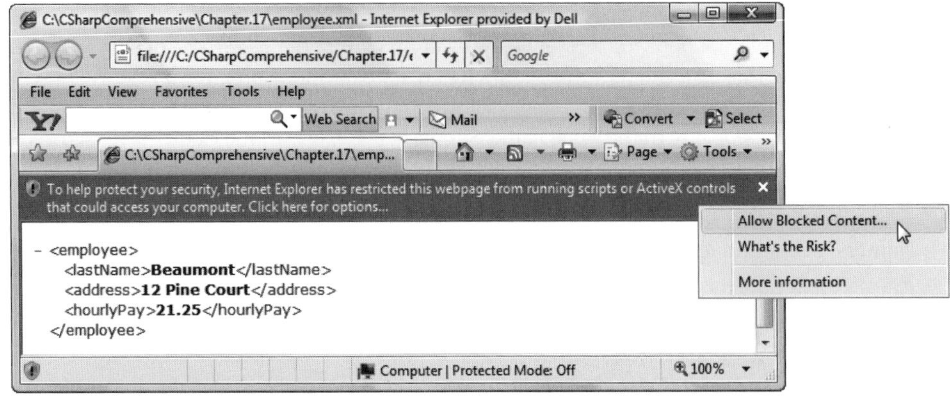

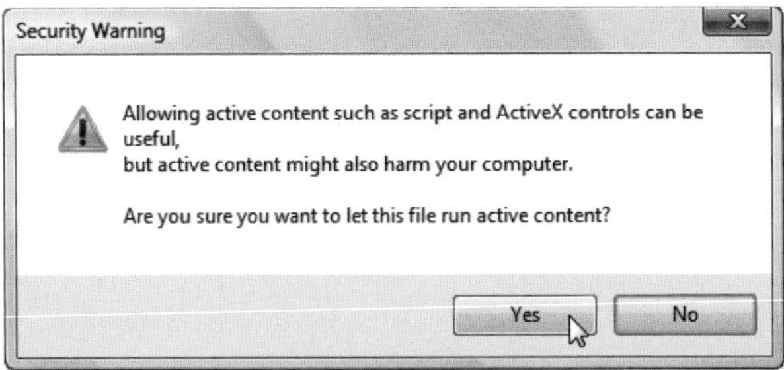

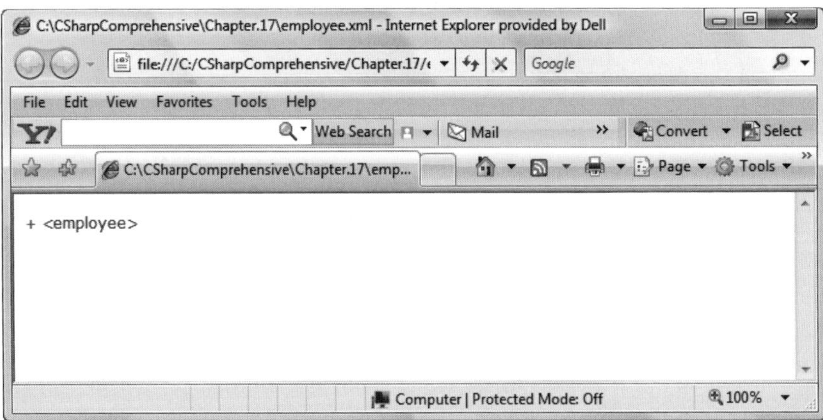

Figure 17-3 Steps to collapsing a node in Internet Explorer

>> **NOTE**
> XML is case sensitive; so, for example, you cannot specify a version by starting with `<?XML` or `<?Xml`.

XML elements can contain attributes. An **attribute** provides additional information about an element (just like C# properties). Frequently, this information is important to the software that will use the XML data. An attribute must appear in single or double quotes. For example, you can include a **version attribute** that specifies the XML version used by the document. Figure 17-4 shows the attribute version in the first line. An attribute version statement starts with <?xml version and ends with ?>. The actual attribute, "1.0", appears in quotes. If you declare a version attribute, it must be the first line in the XML document.

```
<?xml version = "1.0"?>
<!-- This is the employee description -->
<employee>
   <name>
      <lastName>Beaumont</lastName>
      <firstName>James</firstName>
      <middleInitial>M</middleInitial>
   </name>
<address>
      <street>12 Pine Court</street>
      <city>Wild Rose</city>
      <zip>54984</zip>
</address>
   <hourlyPay>21.25</hourlyPay>
</employee>
<!--End of employee description -->
```

Figure 17-4 A more detailed employee XML document

>> **NOTE** The file in Figure 17-4 is stored on your Student Disk as employee2.xml.

You can place comments anywhere within an XML document. Comments must begin with a left angle bracket, an exclamation point, and two dashes (<!--), and they must end with two dashes and a right angle bracket (-->). You can place any text you want within a comment, except two adjoining dashes. The second line in Figure 17-4 is a comment, as is the last line in the figure.

XML documents can contain any number of nesting levels for their elements. You are not required to indent the elements that are contained within others, as shown in Figure 17-4. If you provide no indentation, it is created for you when you open the document in Internet Explorer, and the collapsible nodes are created in the correct places. Although not required, appropriate indentation makes your document easier to understand. Of course, this is another concept you already appreciate after having written C# programs.

>>TWO TRUTHS AND A LIE: UNDERSTANDING XML

1. XML is considered to be extensible because it was extended from HTML.
2. XML documents contain data and elements that specify the document's structure; XML documents delimit their elements with tags.
3. When you create an XML document, you store it in a file with an .xml extension; you can view an XML document in almost any text editor or Web browser.

The false statement is #1. XML is considered to be extensible because users can extend it by defining their own language elements.

FORMATTING XML WITH XSL

XML documents do not contain formatting information. An application that uses an XML document must determine how to display data. For example, a desktop computer might display the same data differently than a wireless phone does. **XSL Transformations (XSLT)** is a standard for transforming XML documents into other formats. You can use XSLT to create **stylesheets** that specify how to render data stored in an XML document. For example, you can indicate that elements surrounded by specific tags will be displayed in different fonts and colors. You can also select only specific element types to display, or display the elements in sorted order. Programmers use the following phrase to describe the transformation process: "XSLT transforms an XML source tree into an XML result tree."

Most popular browsers support XSLT, including Mozilla, Firefox, Opera version 9 and up, and Internet Explorer version 6 and up.

For example, suppose you have an XML file like the one in Figure 17-5. The file describes four employees. To keep this example simple, each employee has just two attributes—a name and an hourly pay rate. Comments have also been omitted to keep the example simple.

```
<?xml version = "1.0"?>
<?xml-stylesheet type="text/xsl" href="employeeStyle.xsl"?>
<employeeList>
   <employee>
      <name>Beaumont</name>
      <hourlyPay>21.25</hourlyPay>
   </employee>
   <employee>
      <name>Cunningham</name>
      <hourlyPay>15.50</hourlyPay>
   </employee>
   <employee>
      <name>Darnell</name>
      <hourlyPay>18.95</hourlyPay>
   </employee>
   <employee>
      <name>Edwards</name>
      <hourlyPay>14.50</hourlyPay>
   </employee>
</employeeList>
```

Figure 17-5 The employeeList.xml file

The shaded statement in the file links the `employeeList` data to a stylesheet named employeeStyle.xsl that will describe how to display the data. You could create additional stylesheets that display the data in different ways, and substitute their names in this statement.

Figure 17-6 shows a stylesheet that describes the template for transforming the `employeeList` data into an attractive format. An XML stylesheet is an XML document, so it begins with the same version declaration used in the data file. Every stylesheet must also include a declaration similar to the shaded one in Figure 17-6. You can substitute the transform version for the stylesheet version—their meaning in this context is identical. The www address points to the official **World Wide Web Consortium (W3C)** XSLT namespace. The W3C is a coalition that develops specifications, guidelines, software, and tools to standardize information and communication on the Web. If you use this namespace, you must also include the attribute version="1.0".

```
<?xml version = "1.0"?>
<xsl:stylesheet version="1.0"
   xmlns:xsl="http://www.w3.org/1999/XSL/Transform">
<xsl:template match="/">
   <html>
      <h1>Employees</h1>
      <table border="3">
      <tr bgcolor="lightblue">
         <th>Last name</th>
         <th>Pay rate</th>
      </tr>
      <xsl:for-each select="employeeList/employee">
      <tr>
         <td>
            <xsl:value-of select="name" />
         </td>
         <td>
            <xsl:value-of select="hourlyPay" />
         </td>
      </tr>
      </xsl:for-each>
      </table>
   </html>
</xsl:template>
</xsl:stylesheet>
```

Figure 17-6 The employeeStyle.xsl stylesheet document

The fourth line in Figure 17-6 is the `<xsl:template>` element. It describes the **`match` attribute** that is used to associate a template with an XML element. The `match` attribute defines which nodes in the XML document will be subject to the stylesheet rules. The attribute represented by the forward slash ("/") means that the template is defined for the entire document.

The fifth line declares that what follows is HTML code. HTML is very similar to XML, but it contains predefined tags for screen elements like headings and well-formatted tables. Some commonly used HTML tags include the following:

- `<h1>`, `<h2>`, and so on through `<h6>`, which describe headings of increasingly smaller font sizes.
- `<table>`, which defines a table. The border attribute sets the table border's width; in this case it is "3".
- `<tr>`, which sets table row attributes. In Figure 17-6, the background color attribute for the first table row is set to "lightblue". No color is set for the subsequent table rows.
- `<th>`, which sets table heading values.

You can see each of these elements in the employeeStyle.xsl document in Figure 17-6. They define a screen that contains the fairly large heading "Employees" and a table that contains a light blue headline row and displays the labels "Last name" and "Pay rate". Notice that as each attribute is defined, its start tag is paired with an end tag.

NOTE The color `lightblue` is one of approximately 140 predefined colors available in HTML. Basically, if you know the name of a C# color, as listed in Chapter 11, you know the name of the same color in HTML. HTML, however, uses all lowercase identifiers. As in C#, you also can create custom colors using red, green, and blue components.

The real work of the stylesheet document in Figure 17-6 is contained in the following lines:

```
<xsl:for-each select="employeeList/employee">
<tr>
   <td>
      <xsl:value-of select="name" />
   </td>
   <td>
      <xsl:value-of select="hourlyPay" />
   </td>
</tr>
</xsl:for-each>
```

NOTE You used C#'s `foreach` statement in Chapter 5 to process array elements and in Chapter 14 to work with database values.

The **`for-each` statement** selects attributes of `employee`s from the `employeeList`. For each `employee`, the name and hourly pay values are inserted into a table row. Because you already understand C# `foreach` statements and SQL, the logic of the stylesheet document is not hard to understand. Of course, many more HTML tags are available for formatting Web pages; you can find many books and Web resources that describe them all.

When the employeeList.xml document in Figure 17-5 is loaded into Internet Explorer with the shaded statement missing, the results look like Figure 17-7. When you add the statement back into the document, it links the stylesheet to the XML document, and the results look like Figure 17-8. The data appears below a large "Employees" heading in a nicely formatted table with a light blue heading row.

NOTE If you remove the following tag pair from the employeeStyle.xsl document, you see only the first employee's data in the table instead of all of them:

```
<xsl:for-each select="employeeList/employee">
</xsl:for-each>
```

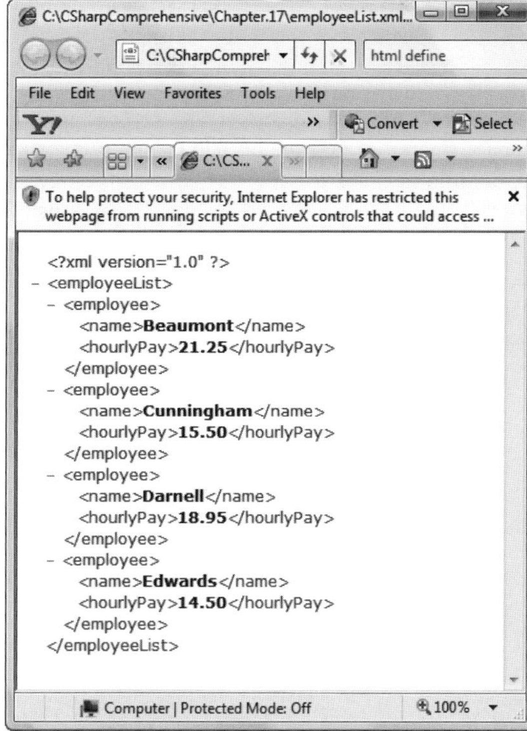

Figure 17-7 The employeeList.xml document in Internet Explorer without a link to the stylesheet

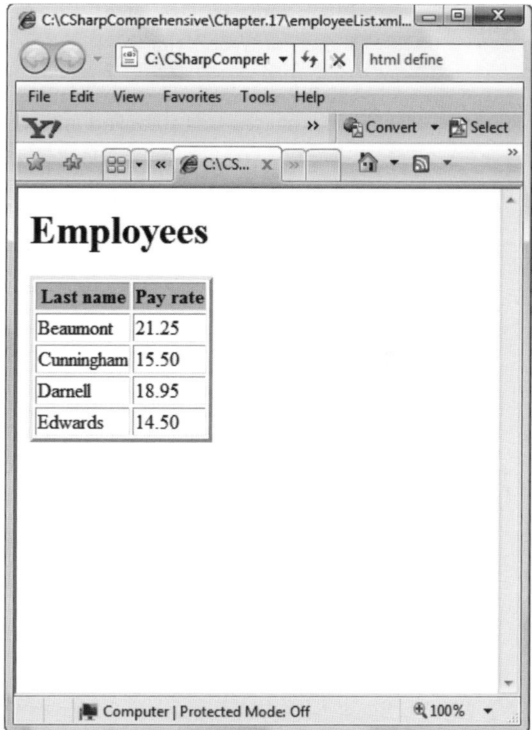

Figure 17-8 The employeeList.xml document in Internet Explorer when linked to the stylesheet

You can also filter what is displayed from the XML file by adding **filter operators** to a stylesheet to define criteria in the `select` attribute in `for-each` statements. Filter operators work like `if` statements in C#. For example, you might write the following to select only employees whose `hourlyPay` value is greater than 16.00:

```
<xsl:for-each select="employeeList/employee[hourlyPay &gt; 16.00]">
```

»NOTE The file that produces Figure 17-9 is stored on your Student Disk as employeeStyle2.xml.

Figure 17-9 shows the output when this statement is substituted for the existing `for-each` statement in the employeeStyle.xsl stylesheet.

The legal filter operators are:

- = (equal)
- != (not equal)
- < (less than)
- > (greater than)

Employees

Last name	Pay rate
Beaumont	21.25
Darnell	18.95

Figure 17-9 Selecting employees with hourly pay greater than 16.00

Notice that the less-than and greater-than operators begin with an ampersand and end with a semicolon. The greater-than (>) and less-than (<) operators that you used in C# are not used because they would be misinterpreted as tag delimiters.

»NOTE Because the XML documents in this chapter are short, you can write and modify them without too much trouble using a simple text editor like Notepad. However, if you need to use XML extensively, you might want to acquire a professional XML editor. Professional editors color-code your syntax, notify you of errors and inconsistencies, and automatically add a closing tag when you write an opening tag.

»TWO TRUTHS AND A LIE: FORMATTING XML WITH XSL

1. XSL Transformations (XSLT) can be used to create stylesheets that specify how to render data stored in an XML document.
2. W3C is a standard for formatting XML documents.
3. A `for-each` statement in an XSLT stylesheet selects attributes from an XML document to display; XSLT filter operators are similar to `if` statements in C#.

The false statement is #2. W3C is a coalition that develops specifications, guidelines, software, and tools to standardize information and communication on the Web.

CREATING AND READING AN XML FILE USING C#

The employeeList.xml file in Figure 17-5 contains only four employees, and each has only two data fields. A business might have hundreds of employees, and might maintain dozens of pieces of data for each of them. Creating a more realistic XML data file in a text editor would be a time-consuming and inefficient task. Fortunately, you have several options for generating XML files automatically. One way is to write an interactive C# program that accepts data from a user and generates an XML file from the data.

For example, Figure 17-10 contains a simple `Product` class that can store product information for a company. The class contains two data fields that hold a product ID and price, and two properties. The class is similar to many you have seen in this book.

```
public class Product
{
   private int id;
   private double price;
   public int Id {get; set;}
   public double Price {get; set;}
}
```

Figure 17-10 The `Product` class

Figure 17-11 contains a program that declares an array of five `Product`s and, in the first shaded statement, declares an `XmlSerializer` that can be used to write the data to an XML file. The **`XmlSerializer` class** serializes and deserializes objects to and from XML documents. **XML serialization** is the process of converting an object's public properties and fields to XML. **XML deserialization** re-creates objects from XML. The argument to the `XmlSerializer` constructor is the value returned by getting the data type for the `Product` array.

>> NOTE
In Chapter 13, you learned that serialization is the process of converting objects into streams of bytes. In that chapter, you used the `Serialize()` method to write objects to files.

```
using System;
public class CreateXML
{
   public static void Main()
   {
      const int MAX = 5;
      Product[] prod = new Product[MAX];
      System.IO.StreamWriter prodFile =
         new System.IO.StreamWriter("Products.xml");
      System.Xml.Serialization.XmlSerializer writer =
            new System.Xml.Serialization.XmlSerializer(
            prod.GetType());
      for(int x = 0; x < MAX; ++x)
      {
         prod[x] = new Product();
         Console.Write
            ("Enter a product ID number ");
         prod[x].Id  = Convert.ToInt32(Console.ReadLine());
         Console.Write("Enter the price ");
         prod[x].Price = Convert.ToDouble(Console.ReadLine());
      }
      writer.Serialize(prodFile, prod);
      prodFile.Close();
   }
}
```

Figure 17-11 The `CreateXML` class

>> NOTE
In the program shown in Figure 17-11, the Products.xml file is created in the same folder as the program. You could change the reference to a different path if you wanted it stored elsewhere.

NOTE To use the code in Figure 17-11 in a professional application, you would want to handle several possible exceptions. For example, if the file Products.xml already exists and is read-only, or the disk is too full to accommodate the new file, an `IOException` is thrown. If the pathname is too long, a `PathTooLongException` is thrown. Exception handling is omitted from this example to keep it simple.

In the `for` loop in the `CreateXML` program, each `Product` is created, and the user is prompted for values for the ID and price. After the array is filled, the XML file is created using the second shaded statement in the figure.

Figure 17-12 shows a typical program execution, and Figure 17-13 shows the generated file when it is opened in Notepad.

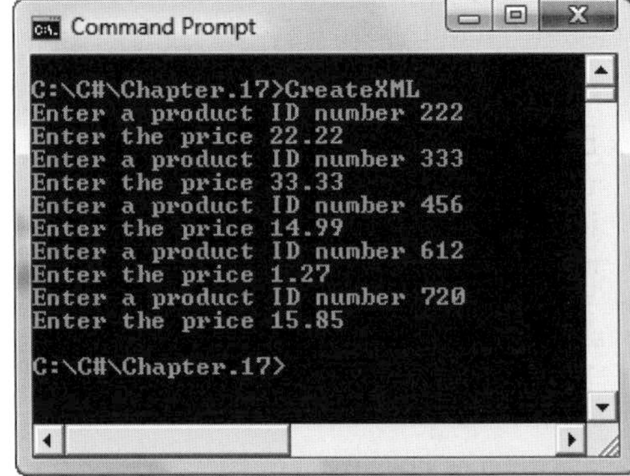

Figure 17-12 Typical execution of the `CreateXML` program

Products.xml - Notepad

File Edit Format View Help

```
<?xml version="1.0" encoding="utf-8"?>
<ArrayOfProduct xmlns:xsi="http://www.w3.org/2001/XMLSchema-instance"
xmlns:xsd="http://www.w3.org/2001/XMLSchema">
  <Product>
    <Id>222</Id>
    <Price>22.22</Price>
  </Product>
  <Product>
    <Id>333</Id>
    <Price>33.33</Price>
  </Product>
  <Product>
    <Id>456</Id>
    <Price>14.99</Price>
  </Product>
  <Product>
    <Id>612</Id>
    <Price>1.27</Price>
  </Product>
  <Product>
    <Id>720</Id>
    <Price>15.85</Price>
  </Product>
</ArrayOfProduct>
```

Figure 17-13 The Products.xml file created in the execution in Figure 17-12

In the Products.xml file in Figure 17-13, notice that the root element tags are `<ArrayOfProduct>` and `</ArrayOfProduct>`, that each `Product` has its own set of tags, and that each field also has its own set of tags. Also notice that the `xml version` code and the reference to *www.w3.org*

were generated automatically. Creating an XML file with C# is far more convenient than typing an XML file into a text editor.

»NOTE Another option to generate an XML data file is to enter data into a database program, read it into a C# program, and create the XML file there. Still another option is to enter data into a database program, such as Microsoft Access, and use an add-in that comes with the program, or use one that you can purchase from a third party or download from the Web. The add-in program converts the database file to XML automatically without going through your C# program.

READING AN XML FILE USING C#

You can serialize an XML file, and you can also deserialize one, or convert it back into an object. You can read from an XML file in C# using the `Deserialize()` method. Figure 17-14 contains a `ReadXML` program. After an array of `Product`s is declared and the `reader` and `file` are identified, the `Deserialize()` method is used in the shaded statement to deserialize the file and cast the returned objects into the array of `Product`s.

```
using System;
public class ReadXML
{
    public static void Main()
    {
        const int MAX = 5;
        Product[] prod = new Product[MAX];
        System.Xml.Serialization.XmlSerializer reader = new
           System.Xml.Serialization.XmlSerializer(prod.GetType());
        System.IO.StreamReader file=
           new System.IO.StreamReader("Products.xml");
        prod = (Product[]) reader.Deserialize(file);
        Console.WriteLine("ID     Price");
        for(int x = 0; x < MAX; ++x)
           Console.WriteLine("{0}    {1, 5}", prod[x].Id, prod[x].Price);
    }
}
```

Figure 17-14 The `ReadXML` program

Figure 17-15 shows the results when the `ReadXML` program is used with the file created in Figure 17-13. The records that were stored in the Products.xml file are stored in the array and displayed in a `for` loop. The extraneous XML statements are discarded, and only the significant tagged data is brought into the program.

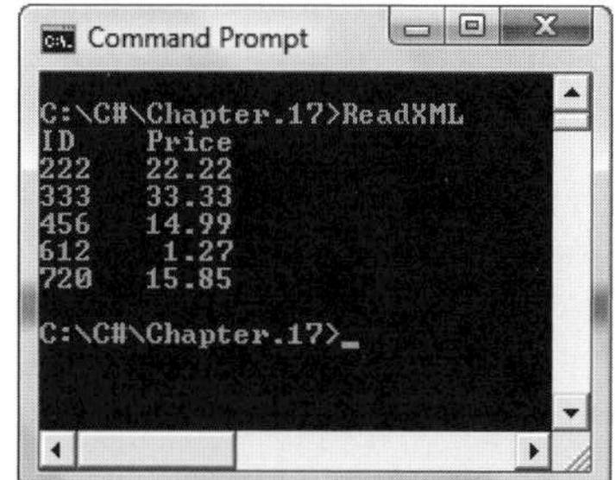

Figure 17-15 Output of the `ReadXML` program

»TWO TRUTHS AND A LIE: CREATING AND READING AN XML FILE USING C#

1. You can generate XML files from within a C# program.
2. XML serialization is the process of converting an object's public properties and fields to XML.
3. XML deserialization is the process of creating XML stylesheets from C# objects.

The false statement is #3. XML deserialization is the process of re-creating objects from XML.

UNDERSTANDING XAML AND WPF

»NOTE The C# programming language derived from C. Because XAML derives from XML, some developers have jokingly referred to it as XML#.

»NOTE XAML originally stood for Extensible Avalon Markup Language because *Avalon* was the code name for the Windows Presentation Foundation when it was in development.

Extensible Application Markup Language (XAML, pronounced *zammel*) represents a new generation of markup languages. It was created by Microsoft, is a direct descendent of HTML and XML, and is also used to initialize structured values and objects. You can say XAML is the "new XML" for .NET.

Windows Presentation Foundation (WPF) is a presentation system that allows you to build impressive and eye-catching Windows client applications. WPF is included in the Microsoft .NET Framework, and you can build applications with it using any .NET language, such as C# or Visual Basic. With WPF, you can create both stand-alone and browser-hosted applications. Professional applications built using WPF include Yahoo! Messenger, the New York Times Reader, and Microsoft Expression Design.

WPF is designed to take advantage of modern graphics hardware. WPF includes a wide-ranging set of application development features, including the following:

- » XAML
- » Controls
- » 2-D and 3-D graphics
- » Animation
- » Documents
- » Media
- » Text
- » Typography

In this chapter, you learn about XAML and `Controls`. In Chapter 18, you will learn about graphics, animation, and other WPF features. All the programming techniques you have learned in C#, including instantiating classes, setting objects' properties, calling methods, and handling events, are used in WPF. Additionally, WPF includes some new programming constructs.

The most important advantage provided to developers by WPF is the ability to develop an application using both markup and traditional programming code. Designers (who do not necessarily have programming skills) can use XAML markup to implement the appearance of an application, while programmers (who might not have design skills) can use a programming language to implement the application's behavior. The programming language statements that provide functionality for a design are called **code-behind**. Separating appearance and code-behind can have several benefits:

- » Development time and costs are reduced because designers can work on an application's appearance simultaneously with programmers who are creating the application's logic and behavior.
- » Maintenance time and costs are reduced because appearance issues handled by the markup are not tightly coupled with the logic behind the program. In other words, appearance and behavior are separate.
- » Multiple design tools can be used to implement and share XAML markup. For example, designers can use Microsoft Expression Blend, which is a design tool for creating graphical interfaces, while programmers and developers can use Visual Studio. Both teams can share XAML markup.

Additionally, with WPF, globalization is simplified. **Globalization** is the process of making programs useful and appropriate for cultures worldwide. WPF helps you take other cultures into consideration when you design programs so that they work correctly when their text is translated into another language. For example, WPF helps you write a program that works even if the language reads from right to left instead of left to right, or if a displayed message requires more words and more space than when displayed in its original language. WPF also makes it easy to indicate which language dictionary is used to check words, and to correctly display numbers and dates the way people in different locales most easily understand them.

»TWO TRUTHS AND A LIE: UNDERSTANDING XAML AND WPF

1. Extensible Application Markup Language is a direct descendent of C# and is used to create graphic objects that applications can display.
2. Windows Presentation Foundation (WPF) is a presentation system that allows you to build Windows client applications. An important advantage provided by WPF is the ability to develop an application using both markup and traditional programming code.
3. WPF facilitates globalization, the process of making programs useful and appropriate for cultures worldwide.

The false statement is #1. Extensible Application Markup Language is a direct descendent of HTML and XML, and is used to initialize structured values and objects.

USING WPF IN VISUAL STUDIO

When you open a new project in Visual Studio 2008, one of the options is to create a WPF project (see Figure 17-16). The default name for your first WPF project is `WpfApplication1`, but you usually change the default name, just as you do for Windows Forms applications and console applications.

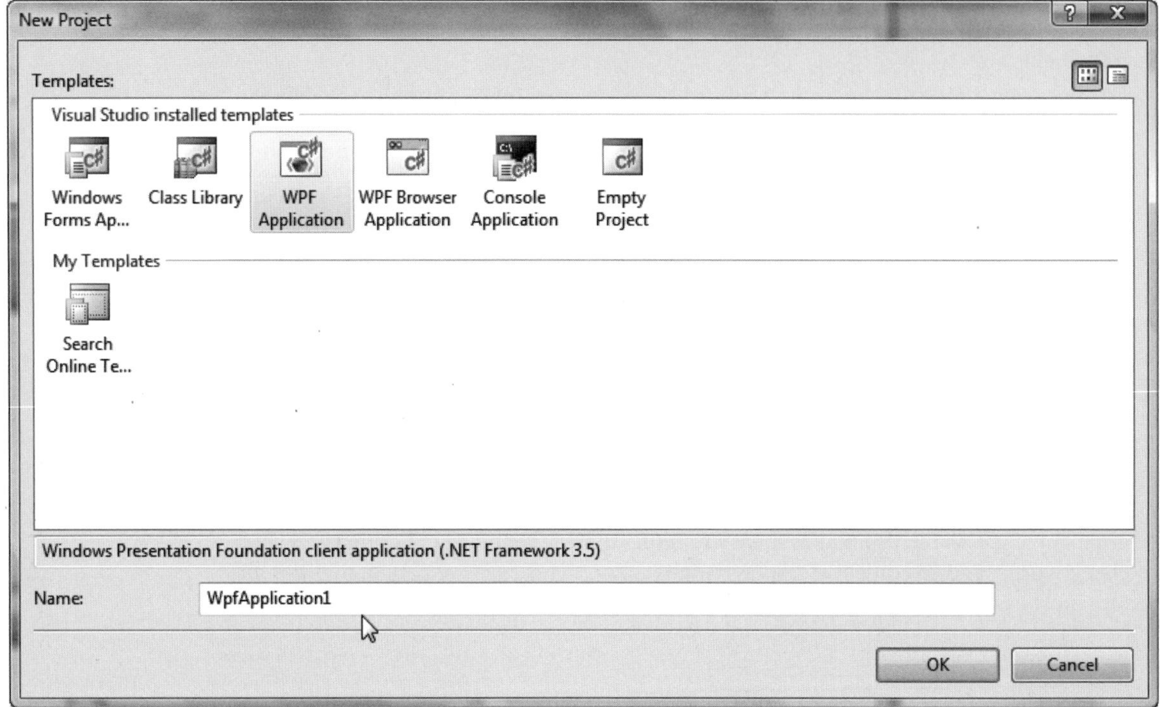

Figure 17-16 The New Project window in Visual Studio

The design environment that appears after you name your application is similar to the design screen in the Visual Studio IDE when you develop a Windows Forms application. Figure 17-17 shows the environment. The menu selections, Toolbox, design screen, Solution Explorer, and Properties window are all familiar. The most significant difference is the XAML code that appears in the center of the screen.

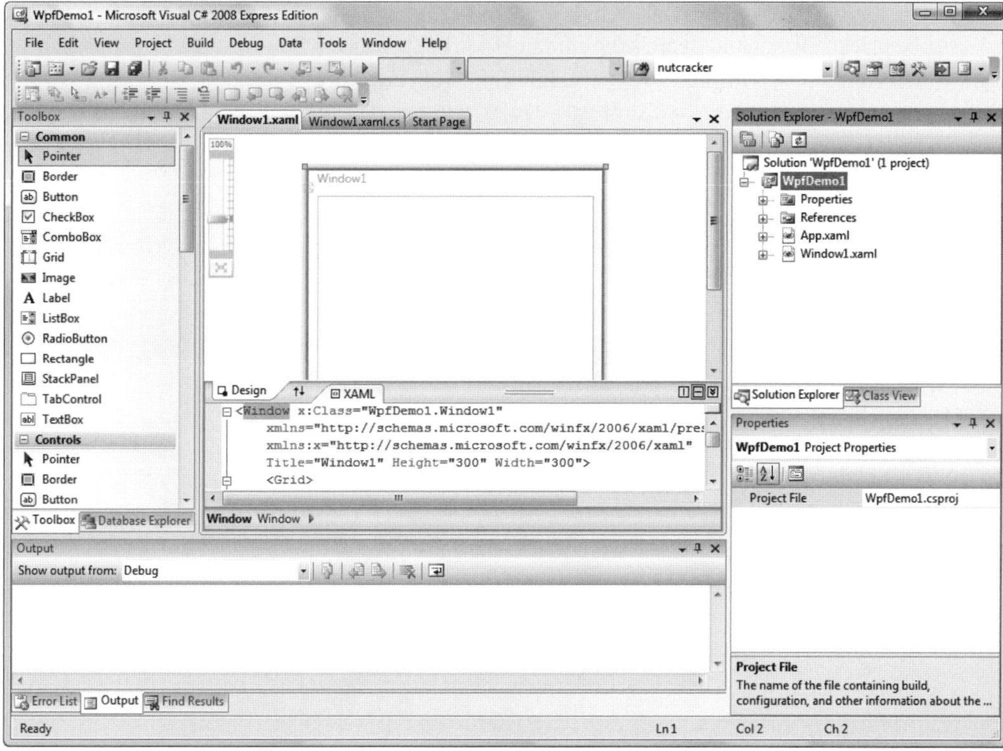

Figure 17-17 The Visual Studio IDE

The automatically generated XAML code for the window might not be completely visible (it is not in Figure 17-17). You can resize the viewing area by dragging on a border, and you can scroll up or down to view more of the code. Figure 17-18 contains the XAML code. The code is fairly simple to interpret: It creates a window with the title "Window1" whose width and height are each 300 pixels. In the IDE, you can click Debug on the main menu, then click Start Without Debugging, and a 300 × 300 window will be displayed.

```
<Window x:Class="WpfDemo1.Window1"
   xmlns="http://schemas.microsoft.com/winfx/2006/xaml/presentation"
   xmlns:x="http://schemas.microsoft.com/winfx/2006/xaml"
   Title="Window1" Height="300" Width="300">
   <Grid>

   </Grid>
</Window>
```

Figure 17-18 Automatically generated `Window` for the `WpfDemo1` project

The shaded <Grid> and </Grid> tags in Figure 17-18 define a panel on which components can be placed. By default, Grid is the container for WPF projects. You can take two approaches to add components to the Grid:

- You can type code between the Grid tags.
- You can drag components onto the Form and automatically generate code.

You can use the Visual Studio designer in exactly the same ways you have used it with a Form. For example, you can drag a Button from the Toolbox onto the Form, as shown in Figure 17-19. The XAML code is automatically updated, as shown in Figure 17-20. The shaded tag defines a Button with Height, Margin, Name, and Vertical Alignment attributes, as indicated by the code. The Button's text (or data), which is defined after the other attributes and before the closing </Button> tag, is Button.

Figure 17-19 A Button on a Form

> **NOTE**
> The x:Class attribute in the first line of Figure 17-20 is what associates the XAML markup with the code-behind that resides in the WpfDemo1 class.

```
<Window x:Class="WpfDemo1.Window1"
   xmlns="http://schemas.microsoft.com/winfx/2006/xaml/presentation"
   xmlns:x="http://schemas.microsoft.com/winfx/2006/xaml"
   Title="Window1" Height="300" Width="300">
   <Grid>
      <Button Height="23" Margin="100,52,104,0"
      Name="button1" VerticalAlignment="Top">Button</Button>
   </Grid>
</Window>
```

Figure 17-20 The XAML code that defines the Button in Figure 17-19

To create the same button, you could have simply typed the code instead of dragging a button onto the Form. Similarly, you can alter any of the attributes by typing new values, and the image of the button in the IDE changes accordingly. Most importantly, a designer using a different tool could have created the XAML button code and then imported it into your C# application, and the image shown in Figure 17-19 would be drawn for you.

After the simple design in Figure 17-19 is created in the IDE, you can double-click the button to see the button1_Click() method, just as you can do in a Windows Forms application, and you can write any legal C# code there. For example, depending on the application, clicking the button might calculate a paycheck or save a file.

»TWO TRUTHS AND A LIE: USING WPF IN VISUAL STUDIO

1. When you open a new project in Visual Studio 2008, one of the options is to create a WPF project.
2. Although WPF projects were not designed to contain XAML, you can select a menu option to allow XAML code.
3. When you use the Visual Studio designer, you can drag controls onto a window or type code for them.

The false statement is #2. WPF projects automatically contain XAML code.

USING WPF CONTROLS AND LAYOUTS

WPF has approximately 60 built-in controls. You can think of them as belonging to 11 groups as follows:

- » Buttons: `Button` and `RepeatButton`
- » Dialog boxes: `OpenFileDialog`, `PrintDialog`, and `SaveFileDialog`
- » Digital ink: `InkCanvas` and `InkPresenter`
- » Documents: `DocumentViewer`, `FlowDocumentPageViewer`, `FlowDocumentReader`, `FlowDocumentScrollViewer`, and `StickyNoteControl`
- » Input: `TextBox`, `RichTextBox`, and `PasswordBox`
- » Layout: `Border`, `BulletDecorator`, `Canvas`, `DockPanel`, `Expander`, `Grid`, `GridView`, `GridSplitter`, `GroupBox`, `Panel`, `ResizeGrip`, `Separator`, `ScrollBar`, `ScrollViewer`, `StackPanel`, `Thumb`, `Viewbox`, `VirtualizingStackPanel`, `Window`, and `WrapPanel`
- » Media: `Image`, `MediaElement`, and `SoundPlayerAction`
- » Menus: `ContextMenu`, `Menu`, and `ToolBar`
- » Navigation: `Frame`, `Hyperlink`, `Page`, `NavigationWindow`, and `TabControl`
- » Selection: `CheckBox`, `ComboBox`, `ListBox`, `TreeView`, `RadioButton`, and `Slider`
- » User information: `AccessText`, `Label`, `Popup`, `ProgressBar`, `StatusBar`, `TextBlock`, and `ToolTip`

You are familiar with the basic functionality of many of these controls because you have used their `Form` counterparts earlier in this book.

WPF includes several layout controls. When you create a user interface, you arrange your controls by location and size to form a layout. When designing an application that will be distributed over the Web or used by clients on a variety of hardware devices, you must create a layout that can adapt to changes in window size and display settings. Rather than forcing you to write the code to adapt a layout in these circumstances, WPF provides an extensible layout system for you.

WPF applications support relative positioning, which increases the ability of an application to adapt correctly to changing window and display conditions. **Relative positioning** involves placing components in positions that depend on the borders of their containers and the placement of other components. The concept is the opposite of **absolute positioning**, in which you place components at specific points; for example, 50, 100. In addition, the layout system manages the **negotiation** between controls to determine the most appropriate layout. Just as with people, negotiation implies give-and-take in access to space and resources. A container's controls are called its **child controls**, and the container is called a parent. The negotiation between controls is a two-step process: First, a control tells its parent what location and size it requires; second, the parent tells the child control what space it can have.

» **NOTE**
This chapter uses `Grid` and `DockPanel` layouts to give you an idea of the range of WPF layout designs. In Chapter 18, you will learn more about the `Grid` layout and other layouts.

The layouts used in WPF are:

- `Canvas`: Child controls provide their own layout.
- `DockPanel`: Child controls are aligned to the edges of the panel.
- `Grid`: Child controls are positioned by rows and columns.
- `StackPanel`: Child controls are stacked either vertically or horizontally.
- `VirtualizingStackPanel`: Child controls are virtualized and arranged on a single line that is either horizontally or vertically oriented. Virtualizing is the process of generating only currently visible elements, thus saving processor time and memory.
- `WrapPanel`: Child controls are positioned in left-to-right order and wrapped to the next line when there are more controls on the current line than space allows.

» **NOTE**
A property such as `DockPanel.Dock` that is implemented by a parent control for use by child controls is called an **attached property**.

For example, Figure 17-21 shows code placed between the `<Grid>` tags in a WPF application that demonstrates a `DockPanel`. In the XAML code, three `TextBox` objects with various background colors are docked to the top, bottom, and left of a `DockPanel`. A fourth shaded `TextBox` (the `LightCoral` one) is allowed to flexibly fill the remaining space. The `DockPanel` allows the child `TextBox` controls to tell it how to arrange them. To do this, the `DockPanel` `Dock` property is set by each child (each `TextBox`) so the child can specify a `Dock` location.

```
<Grid>
   <DockPanel>
      <TextBox Background="Yellow" DockPanel.Dock="Top">
          This is the top</TextBox>
      <TextBox Background="Yellow" DockPanel.Dock="Bottom">
          This is the bottom</TextBox>
      <TextBox Background="Honeydew" DockPanel.Dock="Left">
          This is left</TextBox>
      <TextBox Background="LightCoral">
          This always fills the space left over.</TextBox>
   </DockPanel>
</Grid>
```

Figure 17-21 XAML code that creates docked `TextBox`es

Figure 17-22 shows the resulting window when the program first executes, and Figure 17-23 shows the window after the user has adjusted the window size using a mouse. The docked areas remain attached to correct sides of the window, and the undocked panel adjusts as needed.

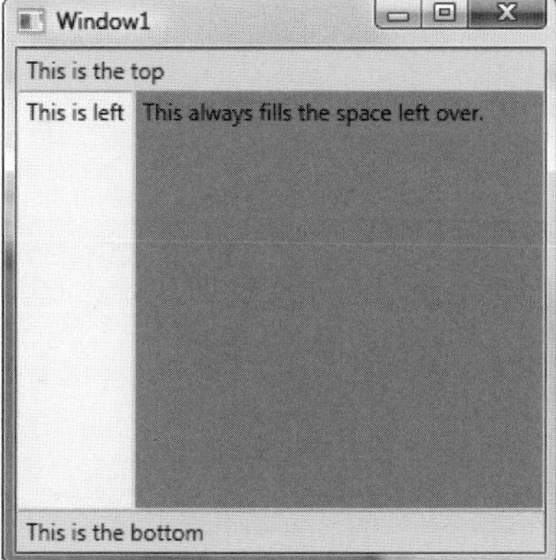

Figure 17-22 The window displayed by the code in Figure 17-21

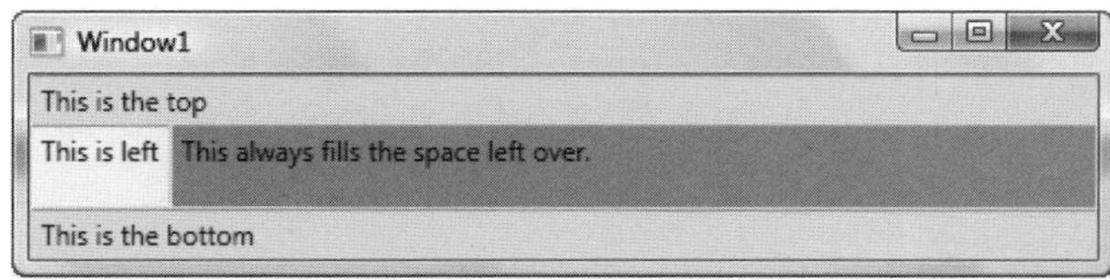

Figure 17-23 The window displayed by the code in Figure 17-21 after the user alters the size

»NOTE If you drag `TextBox` objects onto the `Window` in the IDE instead of creating them using the code in Figure 17-21, your output might not resemble Figure 17-22 unless you delete the automatically generated `Height`, `Width`, and `Margin` settings.

»NOTE The project that creates the windows displayed in Figures 17-22 and 17-23 is in the WpfDemo2 folder on your Student Disk.

Figure 17-24 shows the code between the `<Grid>` tags with a newly added `TextBox` in the shaded statement. This `TextBox` is docked to the right side of the containing `Grid`, so now `TextBox`es are anchored to all four sides, and the area left over for the last `TextBox` is in the center of the `Grid`. Figure 17-25 shows the application when it first executes, and Figure 17-26 shows the application after the user has significantly reduced the `Window`'s size.

```
<Grid>
   <DockPanel>
      <TextBox Background="Yellow" DockPanel.Dock="Top">
          This is the top</TextBox>
      <TextBox Background="Yellow" DockPanel.Dock="Bottom">
          This is the bottom</TextBox>
      <TextBox Background="Honeydew" DockPanel.Dock="Left">
          This is left</TextBox>
      <TextBox Background="Honeydew" DockPanel.Dock="Right">
          This is right</TextBox>
      <TextBox Background="LightCoral">
          This always fills the space left over.</TextBox>
   </DockPanel>
</Grid>
```

Figure 17-24 XAML code that docks five `TextBox` objects

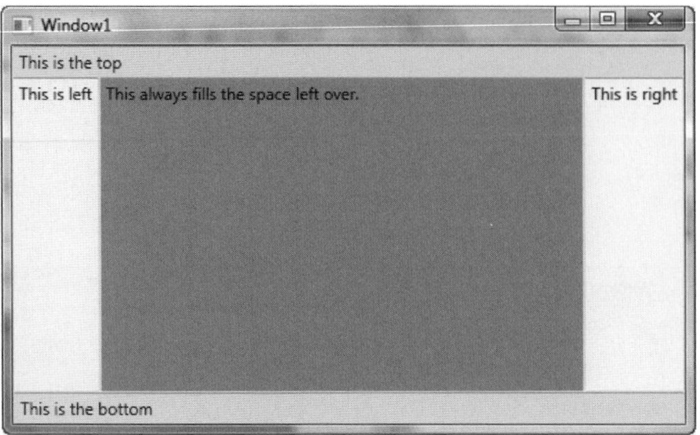

Figure 17-25 The window displayed by the code in Figure 17-24

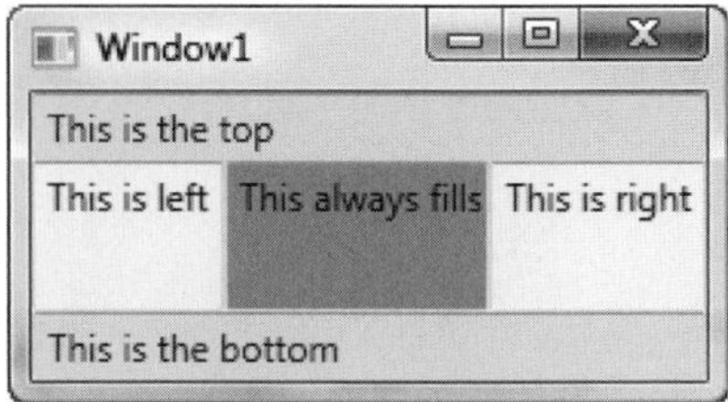

Figure 17-26 The window displayed by the code in Figure 17-24 after the user alters the size

»NOTE The project that creates the windows displayed in Figures 17-25 and 17-26 is in the WpfDemo3 folder on your Student Disk.

»TWO TRUTHS AND A LIE: USING WPF CONTROLS AND LAYOUTS

1. WPF has more than 50 built-in controls, including buttons, dialog boxes, layouts, and menus.
2. WPF applications support relative positioning, which involves placing components in positions that depend on the border of their containers and the placement of other components.
3. With absolute positioning, a system negotiates appropriate positions of parent controls in a child container.

The false statement is #3. With relative positioning, a system negotiates positions of child controls in a parent container. With absolute positioning, specific positions are predetermined.

AN INTRODUCTION TO DATA BINDING

The most important business applications are likely to use data. Many user interface applications provide users with the means to view data, and possibly to edit it. For example, Internet stores need to display their inventory and allow users to make selections from it. For WPF applications, the work of storing and accessing data can be provided through data entry, accessing files, and accessing databases. The role of WPF is to display data in controls and, if an application is allowed to edit data, to store changes back into the object from which the data came.

»NOTE You have probably heard the term *engine* used in the more specific term *search engine*, which is software used to find information on the Internet.

To simplify application development, WPF provides a **data binding engine** to perform these steps automatically. (An **engine** is software that is the "working part" of a program, as opposed to the parts that affect appearance.) The core unit of the data binding engine is the **`Binding` class**, whose job is to bind a control (also called the **binding target**) to a data object (also called the **binding source**). This relationship is illustrated in Figure 17-27.

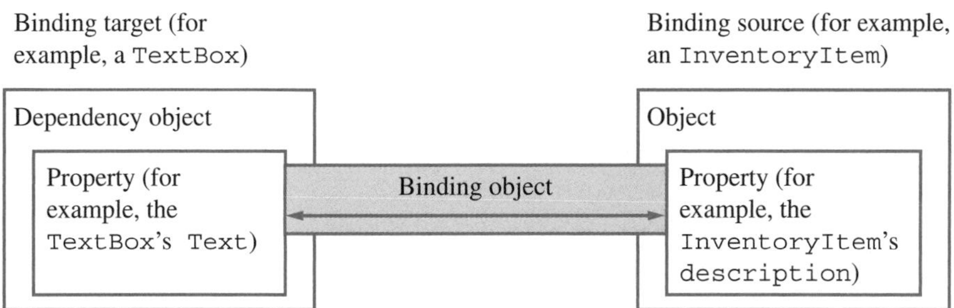

Figure 17-27 The relationship between a binding target and its source

NOTE As Figure 17-27 shows, data binding is essentially a bridge between a binding target and a binding source.

For example, assume you have defined an `InventoryItem` class, as shown in Figure 17-28. Each `InventoryItem` has two fields, `description` and `price`, which each have a property with `get` and `set` accessors.

```
class InventoryItem
{
   string description;
   double price;
   public InventoryItem(string des, double pr)
   {
      Description = des;
      Price = pr;
   }
   public string Description {get; set;}
   public double Price {get; set;}
}
```

Figure 17-28 The `InventoryItem` class

Figure 17-29 shows the XAML code that binds two `TextBox` objects to the `Description` and `Price` properties of an `InventoryItem` object stored in the `DataContext` property of the window. (In Figure 17-30, you will see how the `DataContext` property is set.) The code in Figure 17-29 was generated by starting a WPF project in Visual Studio, dragging two `Labels`, a `Button`, and three `TextBoxes` onto the `Grid`, assigning values to the `Content` properties of the `Labels` and `Button`, and then typing the two shaded additions to the code. As an alternative, you could have typed all of the XAML code instead of designing it visually.

```
<Window x:Class="WpfApplication1.Window1"
   xmlns="http://schemas.microsoft.com/winfx/2006/xaml/presentation"
   xmlns:x="http://schemas.microsoft.com/winfx/2006/xaml"
   Title="Window1" Height="300" Width="300">
   <Grid>
      <TextBox Height="28" Margin="126,39,51,0"
         Name="textBox1" VerticalAlignment="Top"
         Text="{Binding Path=Description}"/>
      <TextBox Height="28" Margin="126,87,51,0"
         Name="textBox2" VerticalAlignment="Top"
         Text="{Binding Path=Price}"/>
      <Label Height="28" Margin="24,39,0,0"
         Name="label1" VerticalAlignment="Top"
         HorizontalAlignment="Left" Width="75">
         Description</Label>
      <Label Height="28" Margin="43,87,0,0"
         Name="label2" VerticalAlignment="Top"
         HorizontalAlignment="Left" Width="47">
         Price</Label>
      <Button Height="23" HorizontalAlignment="Left"
         Margin="34,0,0,73" Name="button1"
         VerticalAlignment="Bottom" Width="75">View updates</Button>
      <TextBox Height="23" Margin="34,0,59,26"
         Name="textBox3" VerticalAlignment="Bottom" />
   </Grid>
</Window>
```

Figure 17-29 The XAML code that binds `TextBox` objects to `InventoryItem` data

The code for the `Window1` partial class appears in Figure 17-30. A single `InventoryItem` named `item` is declared. Within the `Window1` constructor, after the automatically generated call to the `InitializeComponent()` method, the item is stored in the `DataContext` property of the `Window` (`this`), which makes it available to the `TextBox`es.

»NOTE The complete application that includes Figures 17-28, 17-29, and 17-30 is stored on your Student Disk as `DataBindingDemo`.

```
public partial class Window1 : Window
{
   InventoryItem item = new InventoryItem("Sweatshirt", 39.99);
   public Window1()
   {
      InitializeComponent();
      this.DataContext = item;
   }
}
```

Figure 17-30 The `Window1` class

When you run the project that binds the TextBoxes and the InventoryItem properties, the result looks like Figure 17-31.

Figure 17-31 Output of the DataBindingDemo project before the button is clicked

The output in Figure 17-31 is rather bland. Of course, you would add labels, color, and perhaps an image in a professional application. These details were omitted from this example so you could concentrate on data binding.

In Figure 17-31, you can see the InventoryItem's values in the first two TextBoxes. You might not think this is remarkable until you realize two things about the code:

- No data was retrieved using a get accessor with the InventoryItem object.
- No data was assigned to either of the TextBoxes.

In other words, the program contains no statement such as the following:

```
textBox1.Text = item.Description;
```

The TextBox and InventoryItem are related because they are bound.

Not only can the TextBoxes in the application be altered by the InventoryItem, but the InventoryItem can also be altered by the TextBoxes. When a user changes either of the two TextBoxes, the original data is altered. You can prove this by adding a button1_Click() method to the application, as shown in Figure 17-32. When the user clicks the application's Button, the current values of the InventoryItem are displayed in the third text box.

```
private void button1_Click(object sender, RoutedEventArgs e)
{
   textBox3.Text = "Current data: " +
      item.Description + " $" + item.Price;
}
```

Figure 17-32 The button1_Click() method in the DataBindingDemo project

NOTE When you write a Click() method for a Button in a Windows Forms project, the method contains an EventArgs parameter. The button1_Click() method in Figure 17-32 contains a RoutedEventArgs parameter instead of an EventArgs parameter. When you double-click a button on a Window, you are developing in WPF; the automatically generated Click() method contains a RoutedEventArgs parameter. A **routed event** is a WPF construct; it is a type of event that can invoke handlers on multiple listeners in an element tree, rather than just on the object that raised the event.

Figure 17-33 shows a typical execution of the project after the user has typed new values for the item's description and price and clicked the `Button`. The third `TextBox` displays the new values. It's important to understand that the values shown in the third `TextBox` are not being retrieved from the first two `TextBox`es; instead, they are being retrieved from `item` itself. No assignment was ever made to `item`, such as:

```
item.Description = textBox1.Description;
```

The state of the `item` object has been altered only because it was bound to `textBox1` and `textBox2`, and a user made changes there.

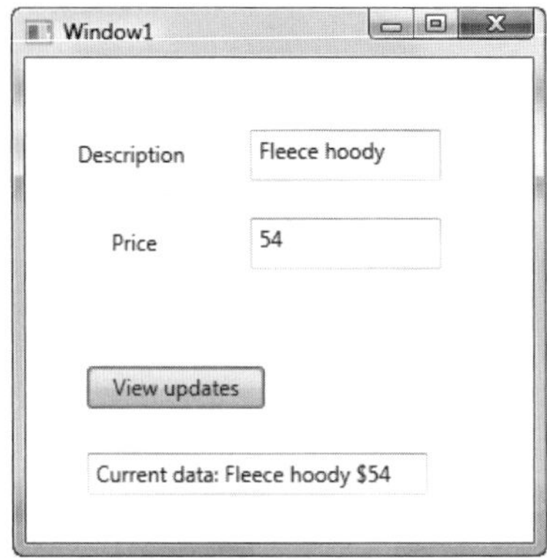

Figure 17-33 Typical execution of the `DataBindingDemo` project

> **NOTE** WPF also provides **one-time binding**. In this scenario, the source provides values for the target just once to initialize it, but no further changes cause any effects.

The example in the `DataBindingDemo` project uses **two-way binding**. That is, a change in the source causes a change in the target, and any change in the target causes a change in the source. You also can implement **one-way binding** in either direction. For example, you might want a control to change source data, but not the other way around. You might want to update a `TextBox` to display current weather conditions from the National Weather Service, but you do not want a user to be able to type in a `TextBox` and alter the Service's data.

The timing of the change to a source depends on the trigger event that causes the change. Different dependency properties have different `UpdateSourceTrigger` values. When you use a `Control` such as a `CheckBox`, `ComboBox`, or `RadioButton` to alter data, the source value is updated when the property changes; for example, when a user clicks the check box. However, when you use a `Text` property to update a source, as you do with the `TextBox`es in the `DataBindingDemo`, then the value of the `UpdateSourceTrigger` is `LostFocus`. That means the value of the source is changed only when the `TextBox` loses focus instead of every time the property changes. This makes sense when you consider that if the source was updated with every keystroke in a `TextBox`, a lot of unnecessary, intermediate changes would be made. Performance would be diminished, and the user would not be able to backspace or correct typing errors before committing to changes.

> **NOTE** The WPF data binding engine provides additional methods that enable you to sort, filter, and group data. See the C# documentation at *www.msdn.microsoft.com* for more details.

»TWO TRUTHS AND A LIE: AN INTRODUCTION TO DATA BINDING

1. WPF provides a data binding engine that retrieves data from and stores data in objects.
2. In data binding, a control is called a binding source and a data object is the binding target.
3. With two-way binding, a change in the source causes a change in the target, and any change in the target causes a change in the source; you also can implement one-way binding in either direction.

The false statement is #2. In data binding, a control is called a binding target and a data object is the binding source.

YOU DO IT

CREATING A WPF APPLICATION THAT STORES STUDENT DATA

In the next steps, you will create an interactive data-entry application in Visual Studio to store student data for the Patton School. You will create a WPF project and write XAML code as well as code-behind. First, you will create a `Student` class that can hold student data.

To create a `Student` class:

1. Open a new file in your text editor and type the following `Student` class. It contains three properties that get and set three implied fields that hold a student's last name, first name, and grade point average.

```
using System;
public class Student
{
   public String LastName {get; set;}
   public String FirstName {get; set;}
   public double Gpa {get; set;}
}
```

2. Save the file as **Student.cs**.

To create an interactive data-entry application for the Patton School:

1. Open Microsoft Visual Studio. You might be able to use a desktop shortcut, or you might click the **Start** button, point to **All Programs**, and click the version of C# you have installed (for example, **Microsoft Visual C# Express Edition**).

2. Click **File** on the menu bar and click **New Project**. A New Project window appears. In the window under Templates, click **WPF Application**. Near the bottom of the New Project window, click in the **Name** text box and replace the default name with **CreateStudentRecords**. See Figure 17-34.

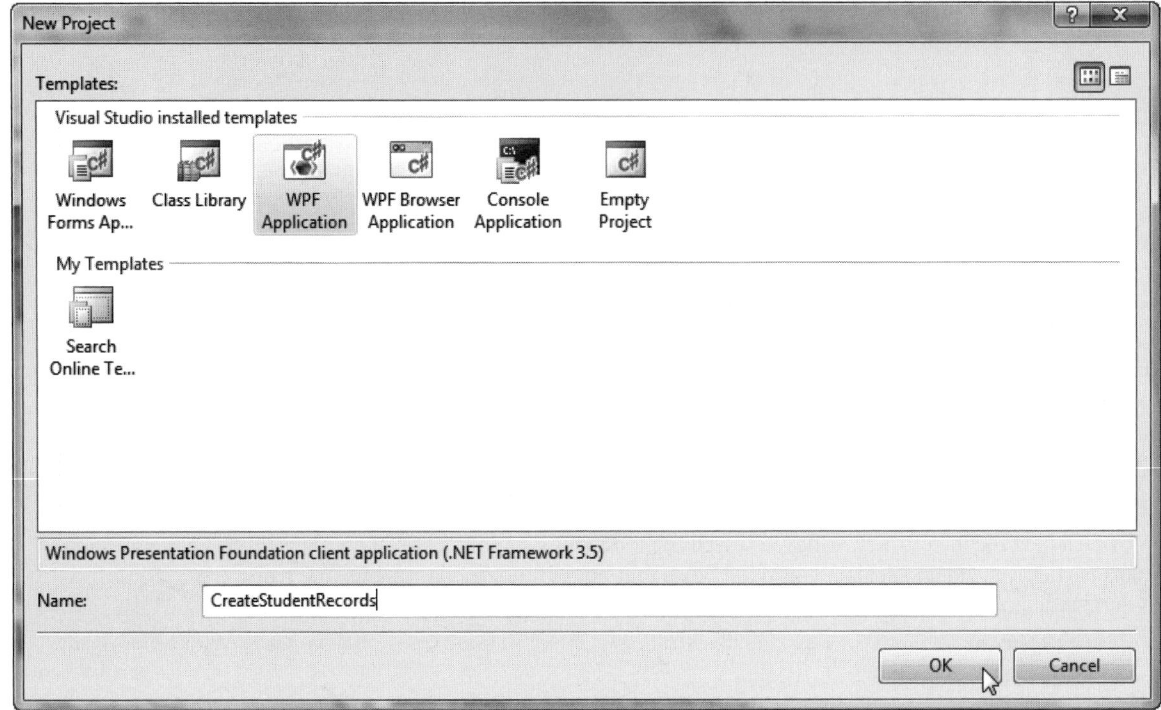

Figure 17-34 Starting the `CreateStudentRecords` project

3. Click **OK**. The design screen appears. A blank `Window1` appears in the center of the screen, and some automatically generated XAML code appears in the tab below it, as shown in Figure 17-35.

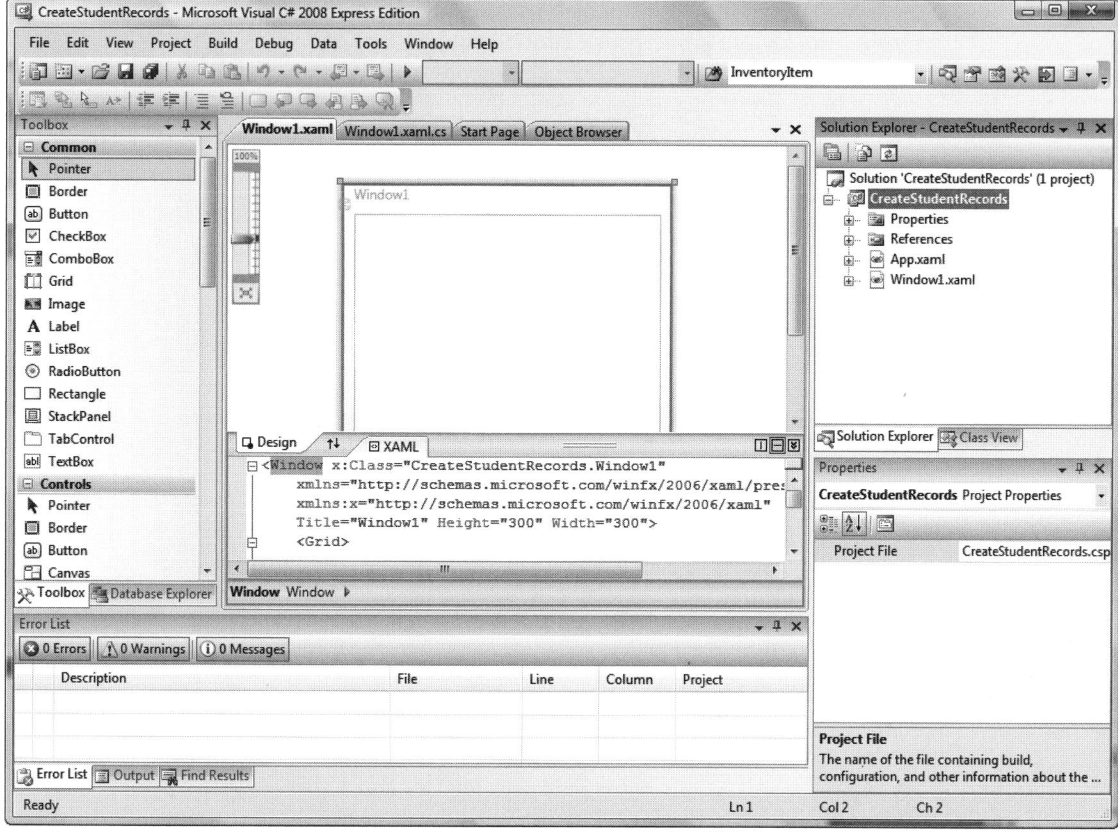

Figure 17-35 The design screen for the `CreateStudentRecords` project

4. On the main menu, click **Project**, click **Add Existing Item**, browse for the **Student.cs** file you just created and saved, and add it to the project by double-clicking it. Examine the Solution Explorer window at the right side of the IDE and verify that the file has been added to the project.

5. In the designer, add a `Label` to the `Window` and change its `Content` property to **Patton School Student Records**. Change the `FontSize` property to **16**. Adjust the `Label` size manually so the content fits. Use Figure 17-36 as a guide. Change the `Label`'s `Background` property to **`WhiteSmoke`** and its `Foreground` property to **`Chocolate`**.
6. Add the three `Labels` shown in Figure 17-36 and change their `Content` properties to **First name**, **Last name**, and **Grade point average**, respectively. Add a `TextBox` for each data item. Finally, add a `Button` and change its `Content` to **Enter student**.

Figure 17-36 Components on the design screen in the `CreateStudentRecords` project

7. Take a moment to examine the XAML code generated by your actions. Make adjustments if you want. For example, if you manually created one `Label` to have a `Height` property of "30", and another to have a `Height` property of "34", you can delete one of the values and type a new one for consistency. Adjusting the code can often be more precise than trying to drag component borders to exact dimensions.
8. Double-click the `Button` on the design screen to expose the `button1_Click()` method and the other code behind the application. Add the following code after the opening brace of the partial class `Window1`. The code declares a constant for the maximum number of students to be stored and a variable to use a subscript with a `Student` array. It declares an array of eight `Student` objects and declares a file and `XmlSerializer` so that `Student` data can be saved. In the second-to-last line of code, change the file path to indicate where you want to store the output file on your computer.

```
const int MAX = 8;
int x;
Student[] stu = new Student[MAX];
System.IO.StreamWriter stuFile =
   new System.IO.StreamWriter("C:\\C#\\Chapter.17\\Students.xml");
System.Xml.Serialization.XmlSerializer writer;
```

9. After the automatically generated call to `InitializeComponent()`, but before the closing curly brace for the `Window1` constructor, add the following code to initialize `writer`, place eight objects in the `Student` array, and reset the subscript variable to 0:

```
writer =
   new System.Xml.Serialization.XmlSerializer(
   stu.GetType());
for (x = 0; x < MAX; ++x)
   stu[x] = new Student();
x = 0;
```

10. Within the `button1_Click()` method, add the following `if` statement. If the user has not yet entered eight records, get the data from the three `TextBox`es, add 1 to the counter, and clear the `TextBox`es. If the user has entered eight records, write the array to the output file and close it. Then, clear the `TextBox`es and disable the `Button`.

```
if (x < MAX)
{
    stu[x].FirstName = textBox1.Text;
    stu[x].LastName = textBox2.Text;
    stu[x].Gpa = Convert.ToDouble(textBox3.Text);
    ++x;
    textBox1.Text = "";
    textBox2.Text = "";
    textBox3.Text = "";
}
else
{
    writer.Serialize(stuFile, stu);
    stuFile.Close();
    textBox1.Text = "";
    textBox2.Text = "";
    textBox3.Text = "";
    button1.IsEnabled = false;
}
```

11. Save the project and then execute the program. The displayed window looks like the one in Figure 17-37. Enter data for a student, and then click the **Enter student** button. When the `TextBox`es clear, enter data for a new student. After you have entered data for eight students, the button is no longer clickable. Close the `Window` to end the application.

Figure 17-37 Typical execution of the `CreateStudentRecords` project

12. Locate the **Students.xml** file on your computer and open it in a text editor. Verify that the file data represents the values you typed in the interactive program. Figure 17-38 shows the first part of a typical file when it is opened in Notepad.

```
Students.xml - Notepad
File  Edit  Format  View  Help
<?xml version="1.0" encoding="utf-8"?>
<ArrayOfStudent xmlns:xsi="http://www.w3.org/2001/XMLSchema-instance"
xmlns:xsd="http://www.w3.org/2001/XMLSchema">
  <Student>
    <LastName>Vega</LastName>
    <FirstName>Carlos</FirstName>
    <Gpa>3.1</Gpa>
  </Student>
  <Student>
    <LastName>Reynolds</LastName>
    <FirstName>Diane</FirstName>
    <Gpa>2.2</Gpa>
  </Student>
  <Student>
    <LastName>Ortega</LastName>
    <FirstName>Joshua</FirstName>
    <Gpa>2.5</Gpa>
  </Student>
```

Figure 17-38 First part of Students.xml in Notepad

CREATING A STYLESHEET TO USE WITH AN XML FILE

In the next steps, you will create a stylesheet that can be used to attractively display the Students.xml file created in the last steps.

To create a stylesheet for the Students.xml file:

1. Open a new file in your text editor. Enter the following tags that will surround the stylesheet instructions, including the `xml version`, `stylesheet`, and `template` attributes. Include the end tags that correspond to the opening tags for the stylesheet and template. The rest of the document that you enter in the following steps will be placed between these opening and closing tags.

```
<?xml version = "1.0"?>
<xsl:stylesheet version="1.0"
   xmlns:xsl="http://www.w3.org/1999/XSL/Transform">
<xsl:template match="/">

</xsl:template>
</xsl:stylesheet>
```

More code will go here.

NOTE
Many people who write XML documents automatically include a closing tag every time they write an opening tag. That way, they are less likely to make the mistake of omitting one.

2. Between the `template` tags, add an `html` tag, two headings, and a `table` tag that includes a `border` attribute. Add closing tags for `table` and `html`. The rest of the tags for the table will be placed between these opening and closing tags.

```
<html>
   <h2>Patton School</h2>
   <h3>Student List</h3>
   <table border="4">
                            More code will go here.
   </table>
</html>
```

3. Following the tag that defines the table border, add color and column heading information for the first table row as follows:

```
<tr bgcolor="red">
   <th>First name</th>
   <th>Last name</th>
   <th>GPA</th>
</tr>
```

4. Add the instructions for each subsequent table row. Each cell will be pink and contain one of the elements from the Students.xml file—first name, last name, and grade point average.

```
<xsl:for-each select="ArrayOfStudent/Student">
   <tr bgcolor= "pink">
      <td>
         <xsl:value-of select="FirstName" />
      </td>
      <td>
         <xsl:value-of select="LastName" />
      </td>
      <td>
         <xsl:value-of select="Gpa" />
      </td>
   </tr>
</xsl:for-each>
```

5. Save the file as **StudentStylesheet.xsl**. Take a moment to compare your file with the complete version in Figure 17-39.

```
<?xml version = "1.0"?>
<xsl:stylesheet version="1.0"
   xmlns:xsl="http://www.w3.org/1999/XSL/Transform">
<xsl:template match="/">
   <html>
      <h2>Patton School</h2>
      <h3>Student List</h3>
      <table border="4">
      <tr bgcolor="red">
         <th>First name</th>
         <th>Last name</th>
         <th>GPA</th>
      </tr>
      <xsl:for-each select="ArrayOfStudent/Student">
      <tr bgcolor= "pink">
         <td>
            <xsl:value-of select="FirstName" />
         </td>
         <td>
            <xsl:value-of select="LastName" />
         </td>
         <td>
            <xsl:value-of select="Gpa" />
         </td>
      </tr>
      </xsl:for-each>
      </table>
   </html>
</xsl:template>
</xsl:stylesheet>
```

Figure 17-39 The StudentStylesheet.xsl file

6. Open the **Students.xml** file that you created in the `CreateStudentRecords` project in the last set of steps. Insert the following code as the second line in the document just after the version attribute. This links the file to the stylesheet:

```
<?xml-stylesheet type="text/xsl" href="StudentStylesheet.xsl"?>
```

7. Save the **Students.xml** file. Then, locate the file and double-click it to open it in your default browser. Alternatively, you can open a browser, browse for the Students.xml file, and load it. Figure 17-40 shows how a typical file is displayed.
8. Search the Web to discover how to alter the stylesheet to sort the students in the table into alphabetical order by last name. Create a new stylesheet that sorts records and test it with the Students.xml file. Save the new stylesheet as **StudentStylesheet2.xsl**.

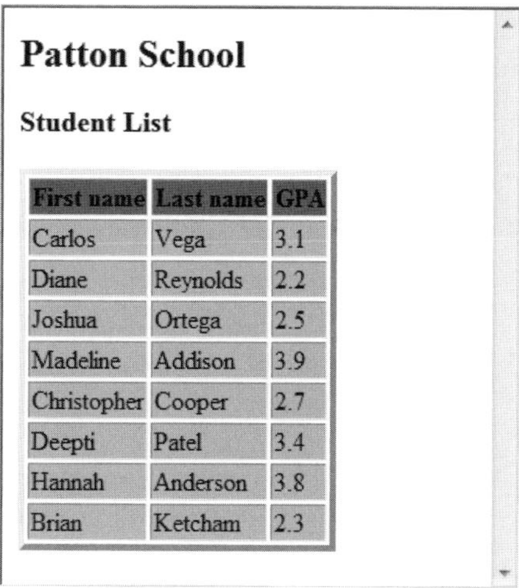

Patton School

Student List

First name	Last name	GPA
Carlos	Vega	3.1
Diane	Reynolds	2.2
Joshua	Ortega	2.5
Madeline	Addison	3.9
Christopher	Cooper	2.7
Deepti	Patel	3.4
Hannah	Anderson	3.8
Brian	Ketcham	2.3

Figure 17-40 The Students.xml file in Internet Explorer

9. If you have a spreadsheet installed on your computer, open the program, and open the **Students.xml** file in it. For example, Figure 17-41 shows the Students.xml file in Microsoft Excel when the option to include a stylesheet is not selected. If you are familiar with spreadsheet manipulation, confirm that you can sort the data, create formulas that use it, and perform other spreadsheet tasks just as you would with manually entered data.

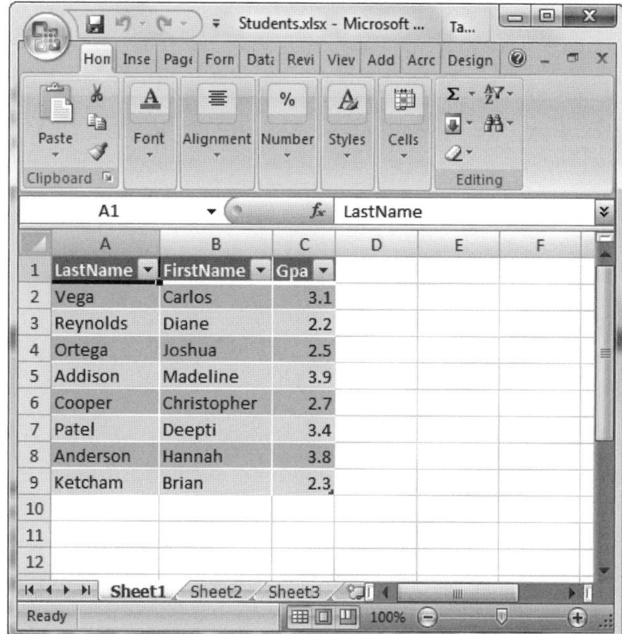

	A	B	C
1	LastName	FirstName	Gpa
2	Vega	Carlos	3.1
3	Reynolds	Diane	2.2
4	Ortega	Joshua	2.5
5	Addison	Madeline	3.9
6	Cooper	Christopher	2.7
7	Patel	Deepti	3.4
8	Anderson	Hannah	3.8
9	Ketcham	Brian	2.3

Figure 17-41 The Students.xml file in Excel

CREATING A C# APPLICATION THAT USES AN XML FILE

In the next steps, you will write a C# application that uses the Students.xml file created by the `CreateStudentRecords` application. As you will see, you can use the data saved in the XML file just like you would use data entered interactively or retrieved from another type of data file.

To create a C# application that uses the Students.xml file:

1. Open Visual Studio, and open a new WPF project named **ReadStudentRecords**.
2. Design a user interface similar to the one in Figure 17-42. The `Window` title has been changed to **Patton School**, a `Label`, `Button`, and `TextBox` have been dragged onto the `Window`, and the `Content` property of the `Label` and `Button` have been changed. The `Window`'s background color has been changed to a light color. Figure 17-43 shows the XAML code that is generated by these changes.

Figure 17-42 The Patton School `Window`

```
<Window x:Class="ReadStudentRecords.Window1"
   xmlns="http://schemas.microsoft.com/winfx/2006/xaml/presentation"
   xmlns:x="http://schemas.microsoft.com/winfx/2006/xaml"
   Title="Patton School" Height="300" Width="300">
   <Grid Background="Linen">
      <Label Height="28" Margin="18,18,17,0" Name="label1"
         VerticalAlignment="Top" FontSize="16">
         Patton School Student Records</Label>
      <TextBox Margin="45,109,45,16" Name="textBox1" />
      <Button Height="29" Margin="99,61,105,0" Name="button1"
         VerticalAlignment="Top">Get records</Button>
   </Grid>
</Window>
```

Figure 17-43 XAML code generated by designing the `Window` in Figure 17-42

3. From the main menu in the IDE, select **Project**, then **Add Existing Item**, and then browse for and select the **Students.xml** file you created by using the `CreateStudentRecords` application. Examine the Solution Explorer window at the right side of the IDE and verify that the file has been added to the project.

4. In the design window, double-click the `Button` to expose the `button1_Click()` method and the other code behind the application.
5. After the `Window1` class's opening brace, but before the definition of the constructor, add the following code. An array of `Student` objects is declared and the `stuFile` is defined.

```
const int MAX = 8;
Student[] stu = new Student[MAX];
System.IO.StreamReader stuFile =
   new System.IO.StreamReader("C:\\C#\\Chapter.17\\Students.xml");
System.Xml.Serialization.XmlSerializer reader;
```

6. Within the `Window1` constructor, after the call to `InitializeComponent()`, add the following statement that initializes the reader and deserializes the file, storing the records in the `stu` array:

```
reader = new
   System.Xml.Serialization.XmlSerializer(stu.GetType());
stu = (Student[])reader.Deserialize(stuFile);
```

7. Within the `button1_Click()` method, declare a `String` that can be used to compose a line of data. Then, in a loop, compose a series of `String`s that contain student data and add each to the `TextBox`.

```
String line;
for(int x = 0; x < MAX; ++x)
{
   line = stu[x].FirstName + "  " +
   stu[x].LastName + "  " + stu[x].Gpa + "\n";
   textBox1.AppendText(line);
}
```

8. Save the project, then execute the program. Click the **Get records** button. Figure 17-44 shows the output that uses a typical set of data.
9. Close Visual Studio.

Figure 17-44 Output of the `ReadStudentRecords` application

CHAPTER SUMMARY

- » The Extensible Markup Language (XML) is a specification for creating markup languages. Users can extend XML by defining their own language elements. The markup indicators used in XML are tags. XML documents contain data and elements that specify the document's structure; the elements are delimited with start and end tags.
- » XML documents do not contain formatting information. XSL Transformations (XSLT) is a standard for transforming XML documents into other formats. You can use XSLT to create stylesheets that specify how to render data stored in an XML document.
- » You can generate XML files through a C# program. The `XmlSerializer` class serializes and deserializes objects to and from XML documents. XML serialization is the process of converting an object's public properties and fields to XML for storage or transport. XML deserialization re-creates objects in their original states from XML.
- » Extensible Application Markup Language (XAML) is a markup language created by Microsoft for .NET, and it is a direct descendent of HTML and XML. Windows Presentation Foundation (WPF) is a presentation system that allows you to build impressive and eye-catching Windows client applications. WPF is included in the Microsoft .NET Framework, and you can build applications with it using any .NET language. WPF is designed to take advantage of modern graphics hardware, and includes a wide-ranging set of application development features. The most important advantage provided to developers by WPF is the ability to develop an application using both markup and traditional programming code.
- » When you open a new project in Visual Studio 2008, one of the options is to create a WPF project. The most significant difference from the IDE you use when creating a Windows `Form` is the XAML code that appears in the center of the screen. By default, `Grid` is the container for WPF projects. You can take two approaches to add components to the `Grid`: You can type code between the `Grid` tags, or you can drag components onto the `Form` and automatically generate code.
- » WPF has approximately 60 built-in controls, including buttons, input controls, and selection controls. WPF also includes several layout controls to provide an extensible layout system for you. WPF applications support relative positioning, which increases the ability of an application to adapt correctly to changing window and display conditions.
- » The role of WPF is to display data in controls and, if an application is allowed to edit data, to store changes back into the file from which the data came. To simplify application development, WPF provides a data binding engine to perform these steps automatically.

KEY TERMS

The **Extensible Markup Language (XML)** is a specification for creating markup languages.

Markup refers to the sequence of characters and symbols that you can insert into text to indicate how a file should look when it is printed or displayed on a computer screen.

Extensible describes a language that can be extended by users defining their own language elements.

Tags are the markup indicators used in XML and XAML.

Hypertext Markup Language (HTML) is a markup language designed to display data.

Elements specify an XML document's structure.

Start tags delimit XML document elements; they begin with a left angle bracket (<).

End tags delimit XML document elements; they start with a left angle bracket and a forward slash.

The metaphor of a **tree** describes the structure of an XML document.

The **root element** is the main element in an XML document tree.

An **attribute** provides additional information about an element in an XML document.

A **version attribute** in an XML document specifies the XML version used by the document.

XSL Transformations (XSLT) is a standard for transforming XML documents into other formats.

Stylesheets specify how to render data stored in an XML document.

The **World Wide Web Consortium (W3C)** is a coalition that develops specifications, guidelines, software, and tools to standardize information and communication on the Web.

A **`match` attribute** in an XML file associates a template with an XML element.

The **`for-each` statement** in an XML document selects attributes.

Filter operators define criteria in the `select` attribute in `for-each` statements in XML documents.

The **`XmlSerializer` class** serializes and deserializes objects to and from XML documents.

XML serialization is the process of converting an object's public properties and fields to XML for storage or transport.

XML deserialization re-creates objects in their original states from XML.

Extensible Application Markup Language (XAML, pronounced *zammel*) is a markup language created by Microsoft for .NET.

Windows Presentation Foundation (WPF) is a presentation system that allows you to build impressive and eye-catching Windows client applications. WPF is included in the Microsoft .NET Framework, and you can build applications with it using any .NET language, such as C# or Visual Basic.

Code-behind is the set of programming language statements that provide functionality for a design.

Globalization is the process of making programs useful and appropriate for cultures worldwide.

Relative positioning involves placing components in positions that depend on the borders of their containers and the placement of other components.

Absolute positioning involves placing components at specific points.

Negotiation is the process of determining the most appropriate layout based on the needs of components.

Child controls are the controls contained by a parent.

An **attached property** is implemented by a parent control for use by child controls.

A **data binding engine** is software that connects data and controls.

An **engine** is software that is the "working part" of a program, as opposed to the parts that affect appearance.

The **`Binding` class** binds controls to data.

The **binding target** is the control in a binding scenario.

The **binding source** is the data object in a binding scenario.

A **routed event** is a WPF construct; it is a type of event that can invoke handlers on multiple listeners in an element tree, rather than just on the object that raised the event.

Two-way binding exists when a change in a source causes a change in the target, and any change in the target causes a change in the source.

One-way binding exists when a change in a source causes a change in the target, or a change in the target causes a change in the source.

One-time binding exists when a source provides values for the target just once to initialize it, but no further changes cause any effects.

REVIEW QUESTIONS

1. A __________ is a sequence of characters and symbols that you can insert into text to indicate how a file should look when it is printed or displayed on a computer screen.

   a. template   c. format
   b. markup   d. display diagram

2. Which of the following is a legal XML element?

   a. `<age>25</age>`   c. `<idNum>3454</IDNum>`
   b. `<salary>12.50<salary>`   d. `<phone>555-1234<\phone>`

3. The identifiers you assign in HTML and XML __________.

   a. can start with a letter   c. can start with "xml"
   b. can start with a number   d. all of the above

4. All XML document attributes __________.

   a. start with a question mark (?)   c. appear in quotes
   b. are numeric   d. all of the above

5. You can use XSLT to create ________ that specify how to render data stored in an XML document.

   a. XAML documents   c. HTML documents

   b. browsers   d. stylesheets

6. Assume you have an XML document named books and its root element is book. Which of the following selects all books?

   a. <xsl:for-each "books/book">

   b. <xsl:for-each select="book/books">

   c. <xsl:for-each select="books/book">

   d. <xsl:for-each select=books/book>

7. Assume you have an XML document named books and its root element is book. Which of the following selects books with a publication date prior to 2009?

   a. <xsl:for-each select="book/books[pubDate < 2009]">

   b. <xsl:for-each select="books/book[pubDate < 2009]">

   c. <xsl:for-each select="books/book[pubDate < 2009]">

   d. both b and c

8. The process of converting an object's public properties and fields to XML for storage or transport is XML ________ .

   a. transportation   c. deserialization

   b. conversion   d. serialization

9. The descendent of XML used for .NET is ________ .

   a. HTML   c. XML2

   b. XAML   d. XML++

10. WPF is a ________ .

    a. programming language   c. presentation system

    b. markup language   d. GUI

11. An advantage of using WPF is that it allows an application's logic developers ________ .

    a. to avoid using classes and properties

    b. to work fairly independently from designers

    c. to design a program's logic using GUI tools

    d. to write code and compile it simultaneously

12. The programming language statements that provide functionality for a design are called ________.

    a. code-behind
    b. hidden implementation
    c. structured programming
    d. polymorphism

13. The process of making programs useful and appropriate for cultures worldwide is ________.

    a. culturalization
    b. globalization
    c. inclusion
    d. universalization

14. When you open a new WPF project in Visual Studio 2008, ________.

    a. you can design a window using drag-and-drop tools from the Toolbox
    b. some XAML code is already written
    c. both of the above
    d. none of the above

15. A `Grid` is ________.

    a. a panel on which components can be placed
    b. a section of C# code that is collapsible
    c. another name for a `Window`
    d. all of the above

16. Which of the following does not represent a group of built-in WPF controls?

    a. `TextBox` and `PasswordBox`
    b. `ContextMenu`, `Menu`, and `ToolBar`
    c. `Button` and `RepeatButton`
    d. `Radio`, `Player`, and `Speaker`

17. Placing components on a window so that they adapt to display conditions relies on ________ positioning.

    a. fixed
    b. absolute
    c. relative
    d. negative

18. In WPF, the __________ manages the negotiation between controls to determine the most appropriate layout.

    a. XAML
    b. layout manager
    c. operating system
    d. user

19. Which of the following is not a WPF layout?

    a. `Grid`
    b. `Canvas`
    c. `DockPanel`
    d. `Portrait`

20. Connecting a control to a data source is called data __________.

    a. binding
    b. overloading
    c. tying
    d. exclusion

EXERCISES

1. a. Create an XML file that holds information about albums in your music collection. Include at least five albums, and store a title, artist, and release year for each. Save the file as **musicList.xml**.

   b. Create an XSLT stylesheet that displays the musicList.xml data in a nicely formatted table. Use at least two colors in your table. Save the stylesheet as **musicStyle.xsl**.

   c. Create an interactive C# program in which the user can enter titles, artists, and years for five albums in the user's music collection. Then create an XML document from the data. Save the project as **CreateAlbumXML.cs**.

   d. Modify the XML file output of the `CreateAlbumXML` program so that it refers to a stylesheet named musicStyle2.xsl. Modify the musicStyle.xsl stylesheet to accommodate the XML file produced by the `CreateAlbumXML` program, but retain the same appearance and colors. Save the new stylesheet as **musicStyle2.xsl**.

   e. Create a C# program that reads the XML file output of the `CreateAlbumXML` program and displays the data. Save the file as **ReadAlbumXML.cs**.

2. a. Create an interactive C# program in which the user can enter names and phone numbers for up to 40 friends, and create an XML document from the data. Save the project as **CreateFriendListXML.cs**.

   b. Write a C# program that reads the XML file created in Exercise 2a and displays the list of friends and phone numbers. (Remember that the `CreateFriendListXML` program might store information for up to 40 friends. Note that when you deserialize an XML file into an array of objects, the stored array becomes only as large as needed to accommodate the file.) Save the program as **ReadFriendListXML.cs**.

3. a. Create an interactive project that allows a user to store data about five favorite movies. Store at least three pieces of data for each movie, such as the title, director, and release year. Figure 17-45 shows a typical execution of a typical project. Save the movies to an XML file. Save the project as **CreateMovieRecords**.

   b. Create a project that allows a user to click a button to view the list of movies, directors, and years created in Exercise 3a. Save the project as **ViewMovies**.

Figure 17-45 Execution of the `CreateMovieRecords` project

DEBUGGING EXERCISES

Each of the following files in the Chapter.17 folder on your Student Disk has syntax and/or logical errors. In each case, determine the problem and fix the program. After you correct the errors, save each file using the same filename preceded with *Fixed*. For example, save DebugSeventeen1.xml as **FixedDebugSeventeen1.xml**.

a. DebugSeventeen1.xml
b. DebugSeventeen2.xsl
c. DebugSeventeen3.cs
d. DebugSeventeen4.cs

UP FOR DISCUSSION

1. WPF attempts to separate the programming aspects of an application from the design aspects. In theory, programmers and artists might work on separate teams with limited interaction. Of which team would you rather be a member?
2. Developers have promoted WPF's separation of code from design as one of its major features, and this chapter presented some advantages to this approach. What are some disadvantages of this separation? What are other disadvantages of WPF?

CHAPTER EIGHTEEN

18

WPF GRAPHICS

In this chapter you will:

- Understand `Shape` basics
- Create lines, rectangles, ellipses, and polygons
- Understand `Brushes` and color
- Paint an area with gradients and images
- Understand layouts
- Understand `Shape` events
- Create animation

The Windows Presentation Foundation (WPF) provides advanced drawing and animation features that make it easier for developers to build interesting user interfaces and entertaining content. This chapter introduces some of the graphical features of WPF.

UNDERSTANDING `Shape` BASICS

WPF provides a `Shape` class that is the base class for objects such as `Line`, `Ellipse`, `Path`, `Polygon`, `Polyline`, and `Rectangle`. All `Shape` objects share the following common properties:

- `Stroke`, which describes how the outline of the shape is rendered
- `StrokeThickness`, which describes the thickness of the shape's outline
- `Fill`, which describes how the interior of the shape is painted
- Data-independent properties that specify, depending on the shape, coordinates or vertices, which are measured in device-independent pixels

`Shape` objects can be used inside `Panel`s (which includes `Grid`s, `Canvas`es, `DockPanel`s, and several others) and most `Control`s.

In Chapter 17, you learned that when you start a new WPF project in Visual Studio, a `Window` is automatically generated for you. Figure 18-1 shows the default XAML code for the automatically created window. In Chapter 17, you learned you could place `Control`s such as `Button`s and `TextBox`es on the `Grid` by writing XAML statements between the `Grid` tags. Similarly, you can write XAML statements that draw shapes on the `Grid`.

```
<Window x:Class="LineDemo1.Window1"
    xmlns="http://schemas.microsoft.com/winfx/2006/xaml/presentation"
    xmlns:x="http://schemas.microsoft.com/winfx/2006/xaml"
    Title="Window1" Height="300" Width="300">
    <Grid>

    </Grid>
</Window>
```

You can add code here to create drawings on the `Grid`.

Figure 18-1 Automatically generated XAML code in WPF and where to place drawing code

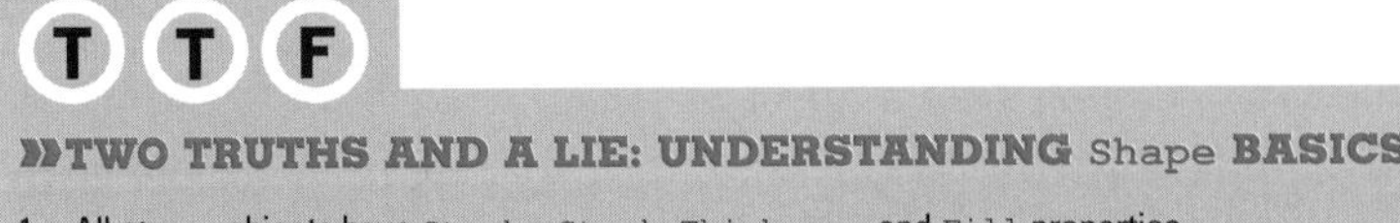

»TWO TRUTHS AND A LIE: UNDERSTANDING `Shape` BASICS

1. All `Shape` objects have `Stroke`, `StrokeThickness`, and `Fill` properties.
2. `Shape` objects can be used inside `Panel`s (which includes `Grid`s, `Canvas`es, `DockPanel`s, and several others) and most `Control`s.
3. When you start a new WPF project in Visual Studio, the default `Panel` created is a `Canvas`.

The false statement is #3. When you start a new WPF project in Visual Studio, the default `Panel` created is a `Grid`.

CREATING LINES, RECTANGLES, ELLIPSES, AND POLYGONS

You can use the `Line` class to draw a line between two points. The names of the point coordinates are `X1`, `Y1` and `X2`, `Y2`. For example, Figure 18-2 shows the XAML code that draws a `Line` from position 10, 10 to position 100, 50, so it slants gently down and to the right. The line is black and fairly thick.

```
<Line
    X1="10" Y1="10"
    X2="100" Y2="50"
    Stroke="Black"
    StrokeThickness="5" />
```

Figure 18-2 XAML code that creates the `Line` in Figure 18-3

» NOTE
You do not need to place the `X1` and `Y1 Line` attribute definitions on the same line, as shown in Figure 18-2. Placing short assignments on the same line saves space, but providing each with its own line might make finding a specific attribute easier. You can list the attributes in any order.

Figure 18-3 shows the line as it is being created in the IDE. You can see a portion of code that creates the `Line` in the XAML window. You could alter the code there, or you could use the Properties window at the right of the screen to type new values for `X1`, `Y1`, `X2`, `Y2`, `Stroke`, or `StrokeThickness`. Whether you use the Properties window or the XAML code area to make changes, changes are immediately reflected in the visual representation in the design area. For example, Figure 18-4 shows how the line changes when the developer types a new value for the `Y2` coordinate.

» NOTE
Many examples in this chapter use `Black` or other dark colors for drawing because black objects are clearer to see in this two-color book. When you write your own applications, you can experiment with a wider variety of available colors.

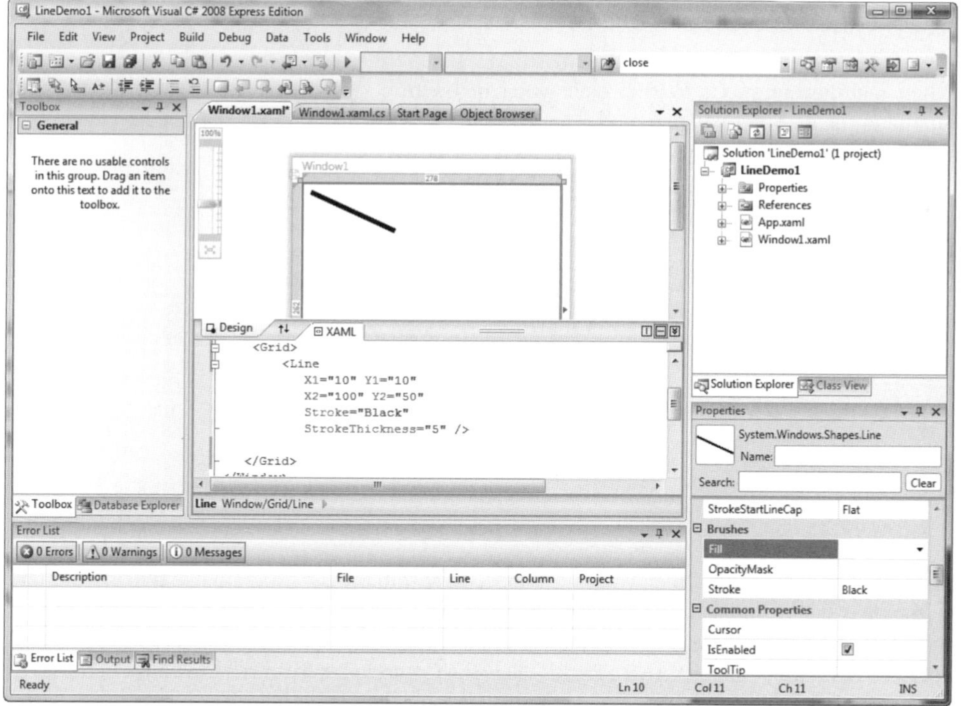

Figure 18-3 `Line` created by code in Figure 18-2

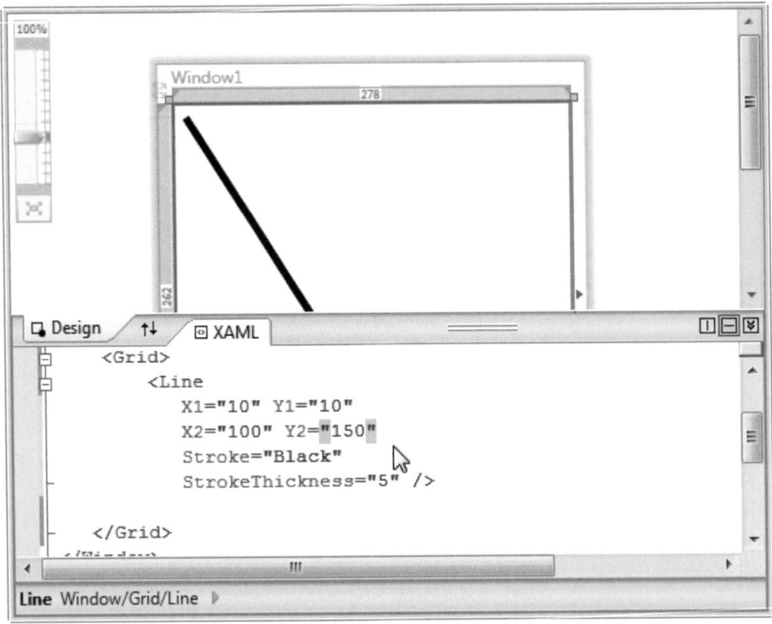

Figure 18-4 The `Line` created with `Y2` set to 150 as the program is in development

» NOTE
You can learn a lot about the options available with shapes and controls by taking time to scroll through the properties windows that support them.

When you open a new C# WPF project, you can assign a name to the automatically created `Grid` by adding an identifier in the Properties window, as shown in Figure 18-5, or by adding a `Name` attribute to the XAML code for the `Grid` as follows:

```
<Grid Name="grid1">
```

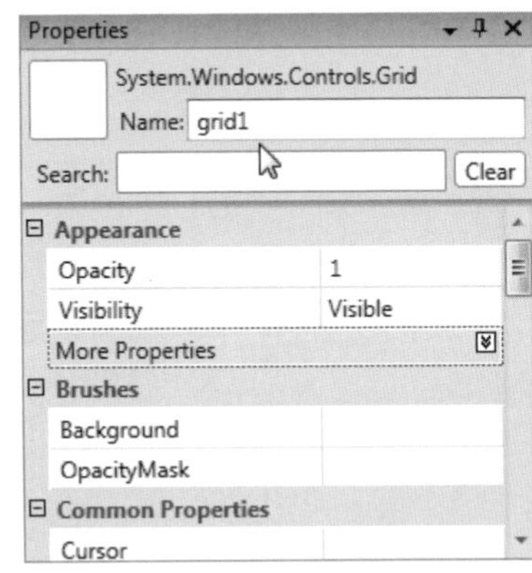

Figure 18-5 Adding an identifier for the automatically created `Grid` in a WPF project

After the `Grid` has an identifier, you can write code within the C# program like the one shown on the right side of Figure 18-6. (The left side shows the XAML code so you can compare the C# code with the XAML code.) In other words, you can create a `Line` using C# statements; you do not need to create it using XAML. In this case, the C# code is written in the constructor for `Window1`, but you could write it in other methods as well. For example, if you want the line to appear when the user clicks a `Button`, you could place the line-drawing code in a `Click()` method.

XAML code	C# code

`<Grid Name="grid1">`
`<Line`
`Name="aLine"`
`X1="200"`
`Y1="10"`
`X2="10"`
`Y2="240"`
`Stroke="Black"`
`StrokeThickness="4"`
`/>`
`</Grid>`
	`public Window1()`
	`{`
	`InitializeComponent();`
	`Line aLine = new Line();`
	`aLine.X1 = 200;`
	`aLine.Y1 = 10;`
	`aLine.X2 = 10;`
	`aLine.Y2 = 240;`
	`aLine.Stroke = Brushes.Black;`
	`aLine.StrokeThickness = 4;`
	`grid1.Children.Add(aLine);`
	`}`

Figure 18-6 XAML code and alternate C# code that created the line in Figure 18-7

»NOTE If you place both sets of code in Figure 18-6 into a project, the XAML code executes first. Then the constructor code places a new line on top of the first line, completely obscuring it.

»NOTE The code in Figure 18-6 is stored on your Student Disk as LineDemo2.xaml and LineDemo2.cs. You can copy and paste either set of statements into a WPF project to observe the output and experiment with the settings.

»NOTE The `Brushes` class used in Figure 18-6 requires that your program includes the following statement: `using System.Windows.Media;`. Alternatively, you could fully qualify `Brushes` as `System.Windows.Media.Brushes`. You will learn about `Brushes` later in this chapter.

Figure 18-7 shows the line generated by either the XAML code or C# code in Figure 18-6.

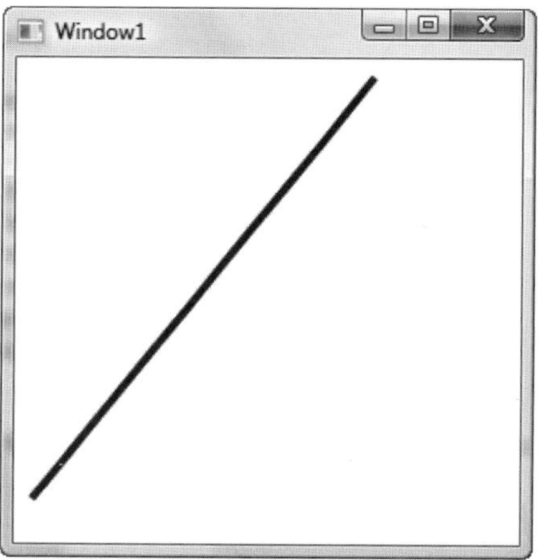

Figure 18-7 `Line` generated by code in Figure 18-6

»NOTE Like an `Ellipse`, a line has a `Fill` attribute, but setting it makes no difference in the `Line`'s appearance.

CREATING AN ELLIPSE

You can create an `Ellipse` in WPF by defining the shape's `Width` and `Height` properties. You also can choose a color as a `Fill` attribute. Figure 18-8 shows both XAML and C# code; either could be used in a WPF project to create the `Ellipse` in Figure 18-9.

NOTE The code in Figure 18-8 is stored on your Student Disk in files named EllipseDemo1.xaml and EllipseDemo1.cs. The C# code assumes that you have modified the automatically generated XAML code to assign the identifier `grid1` to the `Grid`.

XAML code	C# code

`<Ellipse`
`   Height="100"`
`   Width="200"`
`   StrokeThickness="3"`
`   Stroke="Black"`
`   Fill="Chartreuse"`
`/>`
	`Ellipse anEllipse = new Ellipse();`
	`anEllipse.Width = 200;`
	`anEllipse.Height = 100;`
	`anEllipse.StrokeThickness = 3;`
	`anEllipse.Stroke = Brushes.Black;`
	`anEllipse.Fill = Brushes.Chartreuse;`
	`grid1.Children.Add(anEllipse);`

Figure 18-8 Code that creates the `Ellipse` in Figure 18-9

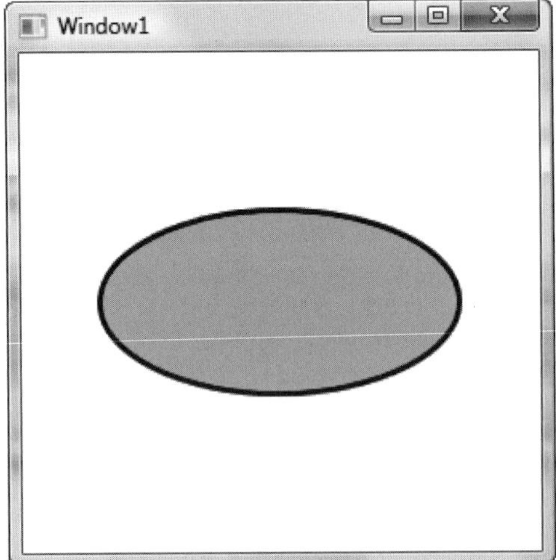

Figure 18-9 `Ellipse` created by code in Figure 18-8

CREATING A RECTANGLE

Like an `Ellipse`, a `Rectangle` requires a `Width` and `Height`. Figure 18-10 shows the XAML and C# code that create the rectangle in Figure 18-11.

XAML code	C# code

`<Rectangle`
`   Width="200"`
`   Height="120"`
`   StrokeThickness="3"`
`   Stroke="Black"`
`   Fill="Yellow"`
`/>`
	`Rectangle aRectangle = new Rectangle();`
	`aRectangle.Width = 200;`
	`aRectangle.Height = 100;`
	`aRectangle.StrokeThickness = 3;`
	`aRectangle.Stroke = Brushes.Black;`
	`aRectangle.Fill = Brushes.Yellow;`
	`grid1.Children.Add(aRectangle);`

Figure 18-10 Code that creates the `Rectangle` in Figure 18-11

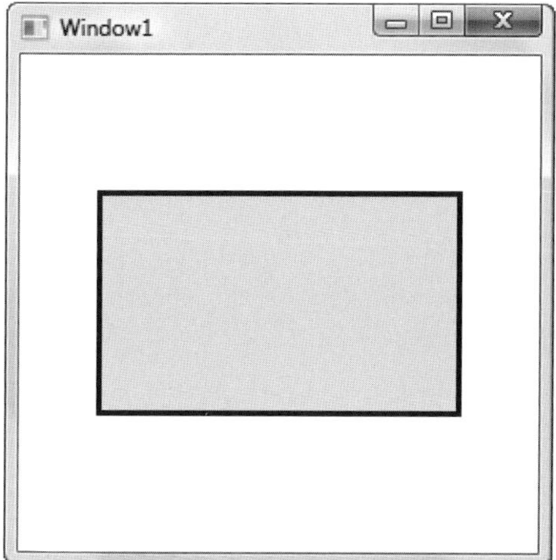

Figure 18-11 `Rectangle` created by the code in Figure 18-10

CREATING A POLYGON

You can create a `Polygon` by defining a set of points. When you create a `Polygon`, a line is drawn automatically to join the first and last points and create a closed shape. (If you do not want a closed shape, you can create a `Polyline` instead.) In XAML, the points of a `Polygon` element are a list of comma-separated pairs. As with the other shapes, `Stroke`, `StrokeThickness`, and `Fill` are optional. As you can see from Figure 18-12, creating a `Polygon` in C# is more complicated. You can create an array of `Point` objects and assign x- and y-coordinate values to them. Then you create a `PointCollection`, which is the object assigned to the `Points` property of a `Polygon`. Whether you use the XAML code or the C# code in Figure 18-12, the finished product looks like Figure 18-13. The figure labels the three points of the `Polygon`.

XAML code

```
<Polygon
   Points="60,60 220,120 130,200"
   Stroke="Black"
   StrokeThickness="3"
   Fill="Yellow"
/>
```

C# code

```
Polygon aPolygon = new Polygon();
Point[] pointList = new Point[3];
int[] xpts = {60, 220, 130};
int[] ypts = {60, 120, 200};
for(int x = 0; x < pointList.Length; ++x)
   pointList[x] = new Point(xpts[x], ypts[x]);
aPolygon.Stroke = Brushes.Black;
aPolygon.StrokeThickness = 3;
aPolygon.Fill = Brushes.Yellow;
PointCollection aPointCollection = new
   PointCollection(pointList);
aPolygon.Points = aPointCollection;
grid1.Children.Add(aPolygon);
```

Figure 18-12 Code that draws the `Polygon` in Figure 18-13

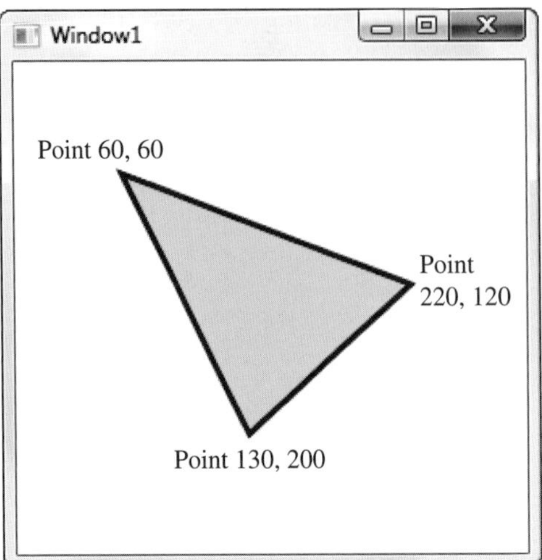

Figure 18-13 The `Polygon` drawn by the code in Figure 18-12

»TWO TRUTHS AND A LIE: CREATING LINES, RECTANGLES, ELLIPSES, AND POLYGONS

1. You can use the `Connect` class to draw a line between two points; the coordinates of the points are named `a`, `b` and `x`, `y`.
2. You can create `Ellipse`s and `Rectangle`s in WPF by defining their `Width` and `Height` properties.
3. When you create a `Polygon`, you create a set of points and a line is drawn to join them.

The false statement is #1. You can use the `Line` class to draw a line between two points; the coordinates of the points are named `X1`, `Y1` and `X2`, `Y2`.

UNDERSTANDING BRUSHES AND COLOR

In the C# code in Figure 18-12, you see the following statements:

```
aPolygon.Stroke = Brushes.Black;
aPolygon.Fill = Brushes.Yellow;
```

The `Brushes` class contains named values that represent colors and that correspond to the ones you learned about in Chapters 11 and 16; for example, `Pink`, `Green`, and `Blue`.

In the XAML code in Figure 18-12, you see the following statements:

```
Stroke="Black"
StrokeThickness="3"
Fill="Yellow"
```

In the XAML code, the `Brushes` class is implied. You could substitute the following with no difference in the outcome:

```
Stroke="Brushes.Black"
Fill="Brushes.Yellow"
```

In XAML, you can create a custom color for the `Fill` or `Stroke` attributes of a `Shape` by using a hexadecimal value such as the following:

```
Fill="#FF00FF00"
```

The octothorpe (#) indicates a hexadecimal value in which each position ranges from 0 through 9 and A through F (which represent 10 through 15 in hexadecimal). The next four pairs of hexadecimal digits represent, in order, the opacity, the red component of the color, the green component, and the blue component. The pairs range in value from 00 through FF, so "#FF00FF00" is completely opaque green, with no red or blue components to the color. If you wanted to make a green ellipse, you would probably prefer to code the following instead of using the hexadecimal notation:

```
Fill="Green";
```

However, the option of using more precise hexadecimal values provides great flexibility.

> **NOTE**
> The value "#FF000000" is opaque black, and "#FFFFFFFF" is opaque white.

You also can use decimal numbers to represent the opacity and red, green, and blue components of a color. Decimal numbers are easier for many people to use than their hexadecimal counterparts because they represent the numbering system we use on a daily basis. Figure 18-14 shows the XAML and C# code that create a small `Ellipse` that is purple (some red, and some blue), and Figure 18-15 shows the output. In Chapter 16, you learned that the `A`, or alpha, value of a color determines its opacity, and that the `R`, `G`, and `B` values represent the amount of red, green, and blue in the color, respectively. When you use XAML to assign a color, you assign string values to its `A`, `R`, `G`, and `B` properties; when you use C# code, you pass integers to the `FromArgb()` method.

XAML code

```
<Ellipse
   Width="30"
   Height="30">
   <Ellipse.Fill>
      <SolidColorBrush>
        <SolidColorBrush.Color>
           <Color A="255" R="200" G="0"
                B="200" />
        </SolidColorBrush.Color>
      </SolidColorBrush>
   </Ellipse.Fill>
</Ellipse>
```

C# code

```
Ellipse anEllipse = new Ellipse();
anEllipse.Width = 30;
anEllipse.Height = 30;
SolidColorBrush aSolidColorBrush = new
    SolidColorBrush();
aSolidColorBrush.Color =
    Color.FromArgb(255, 200, 0, 200);
anEllipse.Fill = aSolidColorBrush;
```

Figure 18-14 Code that creates the `Ellipse` in Figure 18-15

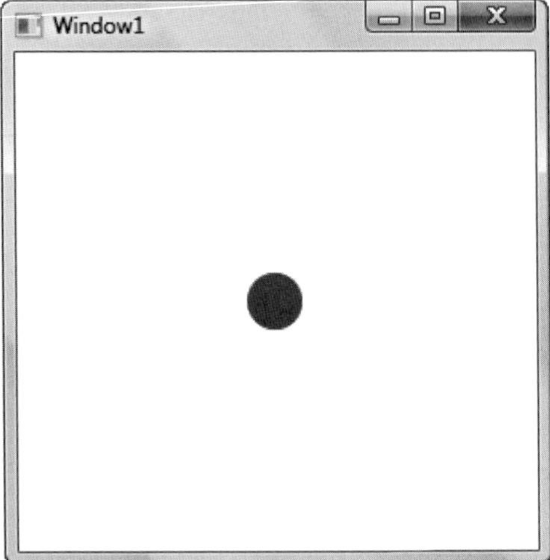

Figure 18-15 `Ellipse` created by code in Figure 18-14

Unlike `Width` and `Height`, the `Fill` property value is not a string. Therefore, in the XAML code in Figure 18-14, **property element syntax** is used to assign a value to the `Fill` property. Many properties in XAML are simple strings, but when they are not, you use property element syntax, which starts with the type name of the class, a dot, and the property, all within a pair of angle brackets; for example, `<Ellipse.Fill>`. Then, an object is defined, such as a `SolidColorBrush`. The property assignment ends with a closing tag, such as `</Ellipse.Fill>`. In Figure 18-14, property element syntax also is used for the `SolidColorBrush.Color` assignment.

`Controls` can be painted in the same way that shapes can. As you have seen, you can make many visual enhancements to your programs either in the XAML code or in the C# code-behind. For example, to make a `Button` with a red background, you can use any of the following techniques:

- Using XAML, choose a predefined solid color brush by name. For example:

  ```
  <Button Background="Red">Click here</Button>
  ```

- Using XAML, choose a color by specifying the amounts of red, green, and blue to combine into a single solid color. For example:

  ```
  <Button Background="#FFFF0000">Click here</Button>
  ```

- In XAML, use property tag syntax to describe a `SolidColorBrush` using a predefined color name. For example:

  ```
  <Button>
    <Button.Background>
      <SolidColorBrush Color="Red" />
    </Button.Background>Click here
  </Button>
  ```

» In XAML, use property tag syntax to describe a `SolidColorBrush` using hexadecimal notation for the color.

```
<Button>
  <Button.Background>
    <SolidColorBrush Color="#FFFF0000" />
  </Button.Background>Click here
</Button>
```

» In C# code, declare a `Button`, and in the Properties window, select `Red` for the `Background` property.

» In C# code, declare a `Button` and use the `Brushes` class `Red` value as follows:

```
button1.Background=Brushes.Red;
```

» In C#, declare a `Button`, declare a `SolidColorBrush`, use the `FromArgb()` method to define the color, and in the code set the `Background` property as follows:

```
SolidColorBrush aSolidColorBrush = new
   SolidColorBrush();
aSolidColorBrush.Color = Color.FromArgb(255, 255, 0, 0);
button1.Background = aSolidColorBrush;
```

» In C#, declare a `Button`, declare a `SolidColorBrush`, use the `FromRgb()` method (which assumes 255 for the `A` value), and in the code set the `Background` property as follows:

```
SolidColorBrush aSolidColorBrush = new SolidColorBrush();
aSolidColorBrush.Color = Color.FromRgb(255, 0, 0);
button1.Background = aSolidColorBrush;
```

Probably there are many other ways to create a red `Button`. Most likely, you will employ a variety of techniques as you create projects. For example, when you design your own small applications, it is often easiest to select Properties from the Properties list in the IDE and click a color choice. If you are part of a design team for a larger application, you might write XAML code for all the visual aspects of a project. If you are part of the programming team that develops the logic for the application, you might use C# statements, especially to create changes in attributes of `Controls` and `Shapes` during a program's execution.

»TWO TRUTHS AND A LIE: UNDERSTANDING `Brushes` AND COLOR

1. In WPF, the `Brushes` class contains drawing tools such as `Rollers` and `InkPens`.
2. You can use decimal numbers to represent the opacity and red, green, and blue components of a color, both in XAML code and in C# code.
3. In WPF, `Shapes` and `Controls` both can be painted with colors and shapes.

The false statement is #1. The `Brushes` class contains named values that represent colors.

PAINTING AN AREA WITH GRADIENTS AND IMAGES

A gradient brush creates interesting paint effects by blending colors continuously along a line called the **gradient axis**. Using a gradient brush gives shapes and controls a three-dimensional feel and can give the impression of light and shadow. You specify the gradient's colors and their location along the gradient axis using `GradientStop` objects. A `LinearGradientBrush` uses a default gradient axis that runs on a diagonal from upper left to lower right. A `RadialGradientBrush` uses an axis that extends outward from the center of an object.

LINEAR GRADIENTS

»NOTE
You can change the coordinate system of a bounding box by altering an object's `MappingMode` property.

Figure 18-16 contains code that creates a `LinearGradientBrush`, which is used to paint an `Ellipse`. In both the XAML code and C# code, you can see that start and end points are declared. By default, the upper-left and lower-right corners of an object's **bounding box** (the imaginary box that surrounds an object) are defined as 0, 0 and 1, 1, respectively. You can paint part of an object by using a fractional value for one or both of the start and end points. In the code in Figure 18-16, the complete object is painted. Figure 18-17 shows the output.

XAML code

```
<Ellipse
   Name="anEllipse"
   Height="200"
   Width="200">
   <Ellipse.Fill>
     <LinearGradientBrush
        StartPoint="0,0"
        EndPoint="1,1">
       <GradientStop
          Color="Black"
          Offset="0.0" />
       <GradientStop
          Color="White"
          Offset="0.33" />
       <GradientStop
          Color="Black"
          Offset="0.67" />
     </LinearGradientBrush>
   </Ellipse.Fill>
</Ellipse>
```

C# code

```
Ellipse anEllipse =
   new Ellipse ();
anEllipse.Height = 200;
anEllipse.Width = 200;
LinearGradientBrush aBrush = new
   LinearGradientBrush();
aBrush.StartPoint = new Point(0,0);
aBrush.EndPoint = new Point(1,1);
aBrush.GradientStops.Add(
    new GradientStop(Colors.Black, 0.0));
aBrush.GradientStops.Add(
    new GradientStop(Colors.White, 0.33));
aBrush.GradientStops.Add(
    new GradientStop(Colors.Black, 0.67));
anEllipse.Fill = aBrush;
```

Figure 18-16 Code that creates the output in Figure 18-17

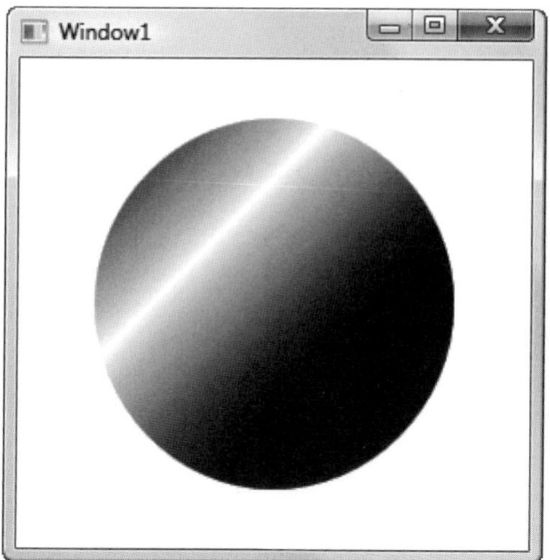

Figure 18-17 Figure created by the code in Figure 18-16

When you use a gradient brush, you define `GradientStops` that provide information about the points at which one color changes to another. You provide a color and an offset for each `GradientStop`. The `Offset` property is a `double` that can range from 0.0 to 1.0; in other words, it represents a percentage of the area that is painted. The color of each point in a painted area gradually changes from the color specified with the lower offset value to the one specified with the higher offset value. Figure 18-18 shows the location of the gradient stops in the output in Figure 18-17. The gradient axis is a diagonal line that passes through the figure. The stops are at positions 0.0, 0.33, and 0.67.

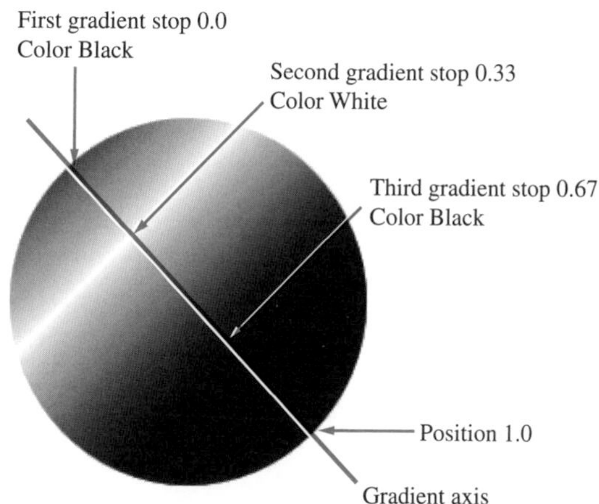

Figure 18-18 Analysis of the gradient stops

The first gradient stop specifies the color `Black` at an offset of 0.0. The second gradient stop specifies the color `White` at an offset of 0.33. The points between these two stops gradually change from `Black` to `White` as your eye moves from left to right down the gradient axis. The third gradient stop specifies the color `Black` at an offset of 0.67. The points between the second and third gradient stops gradually change from `White` back to `Black`. Because no offset values greater than 0.67 were specified, the figure remains `Black` from stop 0.67 to position 1.0.

ALTERING THE GRADIENT AXIS

You can alter the gradient axis when you use a gradient brush that is not an upper-left to lower-right diagonal. For example, you can make the axis vertical or horizontal by altering the brush's start and end points. By default, the linear gradient brush's `StartPoint` is 0, 0 and the `EndPoint` is 1, 1. Figure 18-19 shows how to create a horizontal gradient by specifying the brush's `StartPoint` at 0, 0.5 and its `EndPoint` at 1, 0.5. In other words, the y-value for the start and end axes are halfway down the painting area. Figure 18-20 shows the result when nothing is changed from Figure 18-16 except for the `LinearGradientBrush` start and end points. With a horizontal gradient, the shading emanates from an imaginary horizontal line that crosses the filled area. In other words, the colors are the same above and below a horizontal line at each point from left to right across the image. The effect of a horizontal gradient is to produce a series of vertical lines, each with a slightly different color.

XAML code	C# code

`<LinearGradientBrush`
`    StartPoint="0,0.5"`
`    EndPoint="1,0.5"`
`>`
	`LinearGradientBrush aHorizontalGradient =`
	`    new LinearGradientBrush();`
	`aHorizontalGradient.StartPoint = new Point(0,0.5);`
	`aHorizontalGradient.EndPoint = new Point(1,0.5);`

Figure 18-19 Setting start and end points to make a horizontal gradient

NOTE You can define the start and end points of a `LinearGradientBrush` to be more than 1 or less than 0 to achieve interesting effects.

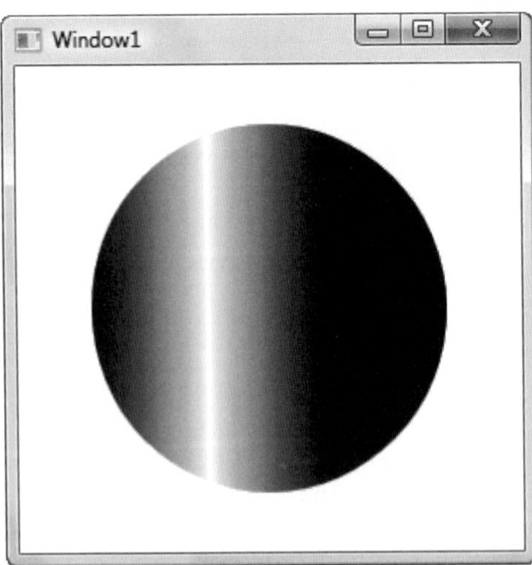

Figure 18-20 Output when code in Figure 18-16 is modified to hold new values for the start and end points of the `LinearGradientBrush`

RADIAL GRADIENTS

The axis of a `RadialGradientBrush` is a circle; its colors radiate outward from the origin. Figure 18-21 contains code that creates a `Rectangle` painted with a `RadialGradientBrush`. The origin is set at 0, 0.5, and `Black` and `White` stops are set as they were for the `LinearGradientBrush` examples. Figure 18-22 shows the result.

XAML code

```
<Rectangle
   Name="aRectangle"
   Width="200"
   Height="200" >
   <Rectangle.Fill>
      <RadialGradientBrush
         GradientOrigin="0,0.5"
         Center="0.5,0.5"
         RadiusX="1"
         RadiusY="1">
      <GradientStop
         Color="Black"
         Offset="0"
      />
      <GradientStop
         Color="White"
         Offset="0.33"
      />
      <GradientStop
         Color="Black"
         Offset="0.67"
      />
      </RadialGradientBrush>
   </Rectangle.Fill>
</Rectangle>
```

C# code

```
Rectangle aRectangle = new Rectangle ();
aRectangle.Width = 200;
aRectangle.Height = 200;
RadialGradientBrush aRadialGradientBrush =
   new RadialGradientBrush();
aRadialGradientBrush.GradientOrigin =
   new Point(0,0.5);
aRadialGradientBrush.Center =
   new Point(0.5,0.5);
aRadialGradientBrush.RadiusX = 1;
aRadialGradientBrush.RadiusY = 1;
aRadialGradientBrush.GradientStops.Add(new
   GradientStop(Colors.Black, 0.0));
aRadialGradientBrush.GradientStops.Add(new
   GradientStop(Colors.White, 0.33));
aRadialGradientBrush.GradientStops.Add(new
   GradientStop(Colors.Black, 0.67));
aRectangle.Fill = aRadialGradientBrush;
```

Figure 18-21 Code that creates the rectangle in Figure 18-22

Figure 18-22 The rectangle created by the code in Figure 18-21

You can achieve amazing effects by making very small alterations to gradient brush settings. For example, Figure 18-23 shows the output of the same program in Figure 18-21, with only the minor change of setting the `GradientOrigin` to 0, 0.

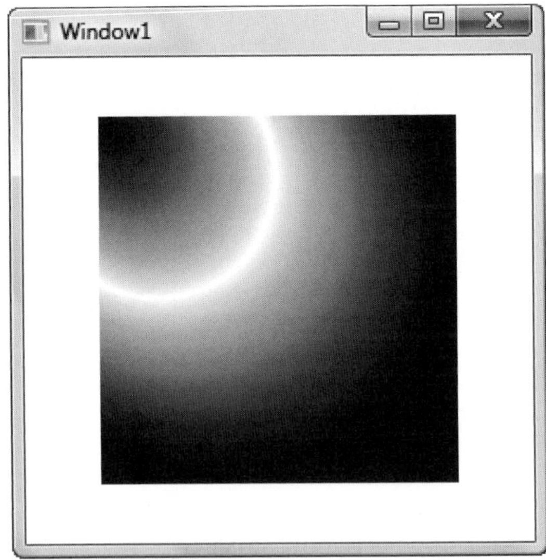

Figure 18-23 Output produced when origin is changed to 0, 0

USING AN ImageBrush

You can use an `ImageBrush` to refer to a stored file to load an image into a WPF application. Figure 18-24 shows code that accesses a stored .jpg file, and Figure 18-25 shows the result.

XAML code

```
<Grid Background="ForestGreen">
   <Rectangle
      Width="200"
      Height="175">
      <Rectangle.Fill>
         <ImageBrush ImageSource=
         "C:\C#\Chapter.18\puppy.jpg"
         />
      </Rectangle.Fill>
   </Rectangle>
</Grid>
```

C# code

```
Grid aGrid = new Grid();
aGrid.Background = Brushes.ForestGreen;
Rectangle aRectangle = new Rectangle();
aRectangle.Width = 200;
aRectangle.Height = 175;
ImageBrush aBrush = new ImageBrush();
aBrush.ImageSource = new
   BitmapImage(new
      Uri("C:\\C#\\Chapter.18\\puppy.jpg"));
aRectangle.Fill = aBrush;
aGrid.Children.Add(aRectangle);
```

Figure 18-24 Code that creates the output in Figure 18-25

Figure 18-25 Output created by the code in Figure 18-24

>>**NOTE**
A Uniform Resource Indicator is also known as a Uniform Resource Identifier.

>>**NOTE**
By default, an `ImageBrush` object fills the area being painted, possibly distorting the image. You can change the `Stretch` property of the image from `Fill` (the default value) to alter this behavior.

An `ImageBrush` uses an `ImageSource` to paint an area. The most common type of `ImageSource` used is a `BitmapImage`. In the C# code in Figure 18-24, you can see that a `BitmapImage` is used to set the `ImageSource` property of the `ImageBrush`. The `BitmapImage` object is initialized with a `Uri` object whose constructor accepts the name of an image file. A `Uri` object is a Uniform Resource Indicator, which defines an object on your computer, network, or the Internet. After the `ImageBrush` is created, it is applied to the object to be painted—in this case, a rectangle. In the XAML code, the process is simpler; you just set the `ImageSource` property of the `ImageBrush` with the path of the image you want to display.

»TWO TRUTHS AND A LIE: PAINTING AN AREA WITH GRADIENTS AND IMAGES

1. Using a gradient brush gives shapes and controls a three-dimensional feel and can give the impression of light and shadow.
2. A `LinearGradientBrush` uses a default gradient axis that runs on a diagonal from upper right to lower left.
3. A `RadialGradientBrush` uses an axis that extends outward from the center of an object.

The false statement is #2. A `LinearGradientBrush` uses a default gradient axis that runs on a diagonal from upper left to lower right.

»NOTE In Chapter 17, you learned that a container's controls are its *child controls*.

»NOTE You were introduced to layout in Chapter 17 when you learned about `DockPanel`.

UNDERSTANDING LAYOUTS

Layout describes the arrangement of the collection of children that reside on a parent container. In WPF, layout includes measuring all the components that will be placed on a `Panel` (or one of its descendents) and negotiating the space each receives.

`Panel` is the base class for all elements that provide layout support in WPF. WPF includes several built-in `Panel`-derived elements that enable you to create many complex layouts. Table 18-1 describes the available `Panels`.

Panel	Description
`Canvas`	Defines an area in which you can explicitly position child elements
`DockPanel`	Defines an area in which you can arrange child elements relative to each other horizontally or vertically
`Grid`	Defines a flexible grid area that contains rows and columns
`StackPanel`	Arranges child elements into a single line that can be horizontally or vertically oriented
`VirtualizingPanel`	Provides a framework for `Panel` elements that saves memory and processor time by generating only currently visible elements (this is an abstract class)
`WrapPanel`	Positions child elements in sequential position from left to right, breaking content to the next line when necessary

Table 18-1 WPF `Panels`

WORKING WITH GRID LAYOUT

By default, every WPF project you have opened in Visual Studio has started with a `Window` that uses a `Grid` layout. However, the `Grids` you have seen do not appear to be grids because they do not contain any grid lines; also, by default, these `Grids` have contained only one row and one column.

Figure 18-26 shows XAML code you can use to define rows and columns in a grid, and to see the grid lines that separate those rows and columns. The `ShowGridLines` attribute of the `Grid` is set to `True`, and four rows and three columns are defined. The code in Figure 18-26 adds a `Button` to row 0, column 0 of the grid; an `Ellipse` to row 1, column 0; and a `Label` to row 1, column 1. Figure 18-27 shows the results.

```
<Grid ShowGridLines="True">
     <Grid.RowDefinitions>
          <RowDefinition></RowDefinition>
          <RowDefinition></RowDefinition>
          <RowDefinition></RowDefinition>
          <RowDefinition></RowDefinition>
     </Grid.RowDefinitions>
     <Grid.ColumnDefinitions>
          <ColumnDefinition></ColumnDefinition>
          <ColumnDefinition></ColumnDefinition>
          <ColumnDefinition></ColumnDefinition>
     </Grid.ColumnDefinitions>
     <Button Grid.Row="0" Grid.Column="0" Width="100">
          Button 1</Button>
     <Ellipse Grid.Row="1" Grid.Column="0" Fill="Blue"/>
     <Label Grid.Row="1" Grid.Column="1"
          Background="Azure">Label 1</Label>
</Grid>
```

Figure 18-26 XAML code that demonstrates grid lines and positions

»NOTE
As with the other examples in this chapter, the same output produced by the XAML code in Figure 18-26 could be produced using C# code. The C# code is omitted here because XAML is used more frequently than code for layout design, because the width of the XAML code sample would make it difficult to show the C# code next to it, and because by now, you should be fairly confident in translating XAML to C#.

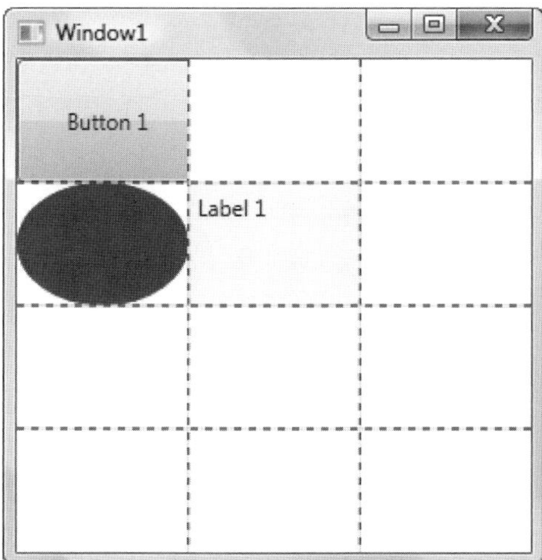

Figure 18-27 Output created by code in Figure 18-26

In Figure 18-27, you can see that the two `Controls` and the `Shape` placed on the grid are given their size from the available size of their cells in the grid. You can still specify a size for a child if you want. For example, Figure 18-28 shows the output when the `Ellipse Height` attribute is set to 30, and then to 80.

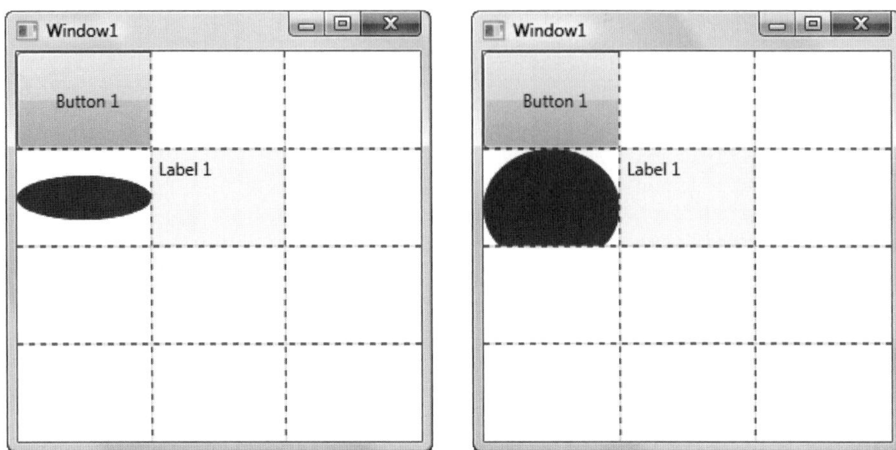

Figure 18-28 Two `Height` settings for the `Ellipse` in the grid

When you resize a window that uses a `Grid` layout, child objects stretch to retain their relative positions. For example, Figure 18-29 shows the grid when a user has made it narrower, then wider.

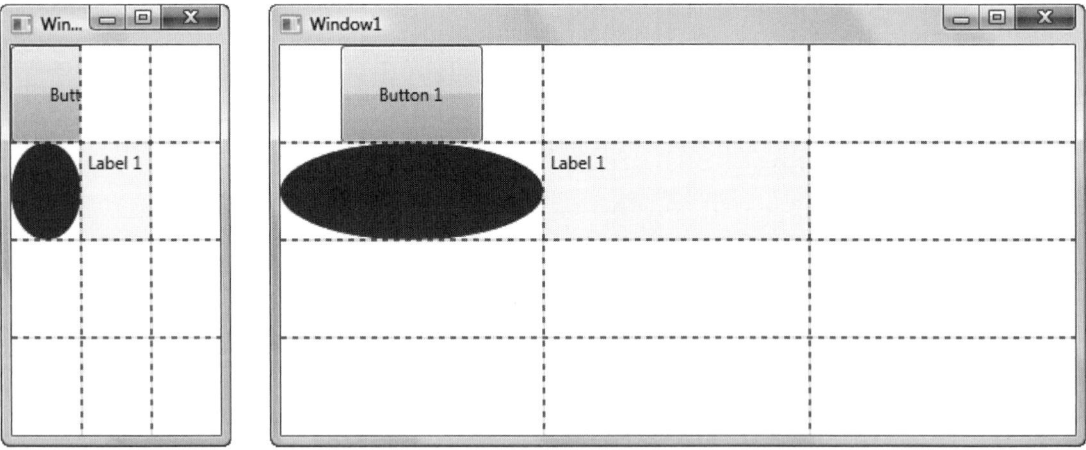

Figure 18-29 The `Grid` in Figure 18-27 resized by a user two times

WORKING WITH CANVAS LAYOUT

The Canvas layout is the simplest of the layouts. Unlike child elements in a Grid, child elements of Canvas are never resized; they are positioned at their designated coordinates.

Figure 18-30 shows the code that creates a Canvas that holds three rectangles. The first (gray) rectangle is size 100 by 100 and is placed at position 0, 0 on the Canvas. The second (black) rectangle is at position 50, 50, so it overlaps and appears to be on top of the lower-right portion of the first rectangle. The last rectangle is light gray and much smaller. It starts at position 30, 30, so it appears to cover part of both the first two rectangles. Figure 18-31 shows the output.

```
<Canvas Height="300" Width="300">
   <Rectangle Height="100" Width="100" Canvas.Top="0"
       Canvas.Left="0" Fill="Gray"/>
   <Rectangle Height="100" Width="100" Canvas.Top="50"
       Canvas.Left="50" Fill="Black"/>
   <Rectangle Height="40" Width="40" Canvas.Top="30"
       Canvas.Left="30" Fill="LightGray"/>
</Canvas>
```

Figure 18-30 XAML code that creates a Canvas that holds three rectangles

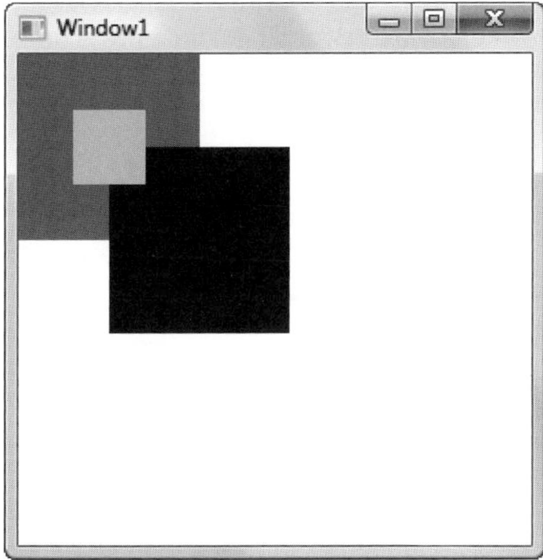

Figure 18-31 Output of code in Figure 18-30

When you adjust the size of a Canvas, shapes are not distorted as they are with the Grid. Figure 18-32 shows the Canvas in Figure 18-31 when it is resized.

Figure 18-32 The `Canvas` in Figure 18-31 resized two times

» NOTE
The `ZIndex` property is so named because x and y represent horizontal and vertical dimensions; z is the third, front-to-back dimension.

The `ZIndex` property for a `Canvas` defines how overlapping elements appear. The higher the `ZIndex` value, the more likely the element is to appear in the foreground. For example, Figure 18-33 shows the code for a `Canvas` that contains three rectangles. The first, at position 10, 10, is given the highest `ZIndex`, so in the output in Figure 18-34, it appears in front of the other rectangles. The second rectangle, at position 40, 40, has the lowest `ZIndex` value, so it appears at the back. The third rectangle, at 80, 80, appears in the middle.

```
<Canvas>
    <Rectangle Canvas.ZIndex="3" Width="100" Height="100"
       Canvas.Top="10" Canvas.Left="10" Stroke="Black"
       StrokeThickness="5" Fill="White"/>
    <Rectangle Canvas.ZIndex="1" Width="100" Height="100"
       Canvas.Top="40" Canvas.Left="40" Stroke="Black"
       StrokeThickness="5" Fill="White"/>
    <Rectangle Canvas.ZIndex="2" Width="100" Height="100"
       Canvas.Top="80" Canvas.Left="80" Stroke="Black"
       StrokeThickness="5" Fill="White"/>
</Canvas>
```

Figure 18-33 XAML code that creates a `Canvas` that holds overlapping rectangles

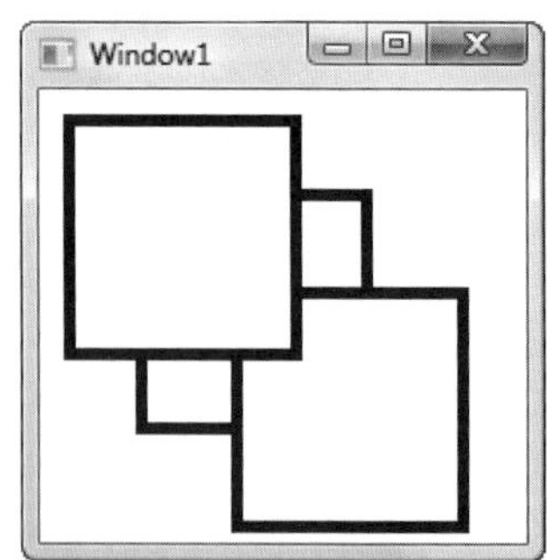

Figure 18-34 Output of the code in Figure 18-33

WORKING WITH StackPanel LAYOUT

As its name implies, `StackPanel` allows you to stack components. Figure 18-35 shows several children created in order as follows:

- A black rectangle with a height of 40 and no specified width
- A button with a width of 50
- A button with no specified width
- Another black rectangle
- A third button
- A small ellipse
- A fourth button

Figure 18-36 shows how the children appear on the `StackPanel`.

```
<StackPanel>
   <Rectangle Height="40" Fill = "Black"/>
   <Button Width="50">Button 1</Button>
   <Button>Button 2</Button>
   <Rectangle Height="40" Width="100" Fill = "Black"/>
   <Button>Button 3</Button>
   <Ellipse Height="30" Width="30" Fill = "Black"/>
   <Button>Button 4</Button>
</StackPanel>
```

Figure 18-35 Code that creates the `StackPanel` shown in Figure 18-36

In a `StackPanel`, if a child control has no specified width, the control stretches to fill the available space; however, if the width of a child control is specified, the control is centered. By default, children are stacked vertically in a `StackPanel`; you can change the `Orientation` property from `Vertical` to `Horizontal`.

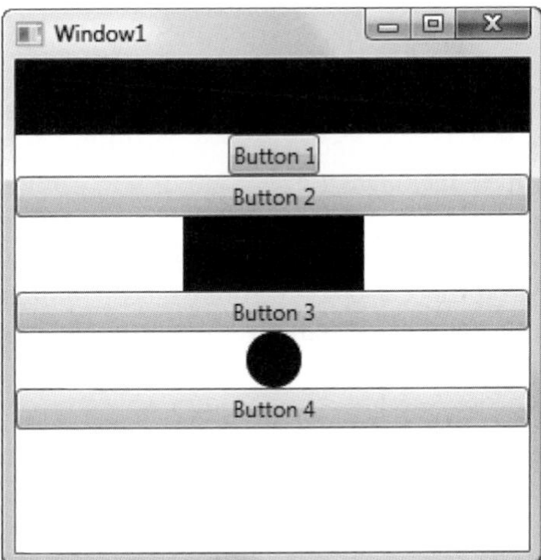

Figure 18-36 `StackPanel` created by code in Figure 18-35

WORKING WITH WRAPPANEL LAYOUT

When you use a `WrapPanel`, children are placed from left to right in rows across the panel surface as long as they fit. When a child does not fit, its position is wrapped around to the next row. Figure 18-37 shows the definition of a `WrapPanel` with `Width` 150 that contains five buttons. Only two buttons fit across each of the first two rows, so the wrapping places the five buttons in three rows. Figure 18-38 shows the output. Because the background color of the `WrapPanel` differs from the `Window` color, you can see where the button objects fit on the `WrapPanel`.

```
<WrapPanel Background="Red" Width="150" Height="100">
    <Button>Button 1</Button>
    <Button>Button 2</Button>
    <Button>This is Button 3</Button>
    <Button>Button 4</Button>
    <Button>Button 5</Button>
</WrapPanel>
```

Figure 18-37 Code that creates the `WrapPanel` in Figure 18-38

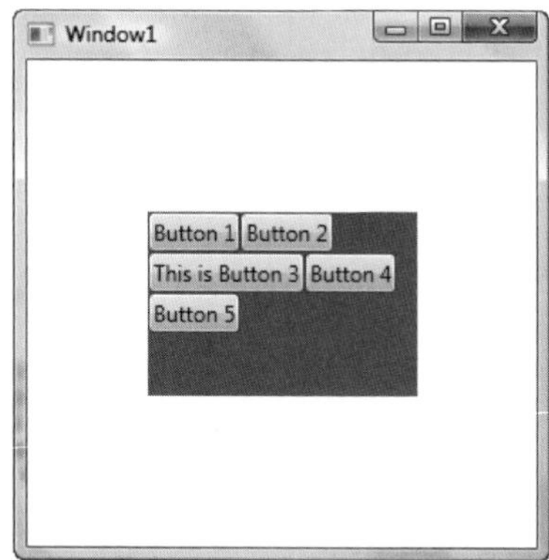

Figure 18-38 `WrapPanel` created by code in Figure 18-37

NESTING LAYOUTS

You can create an infinite number of layout possibilities by nesting layouts within others. For example, Figure 18-39 contains the code for a `Grid` that has three rows and three columns. Cell 0, 0 in the grid contains a nested `Grid`, which also has three rows and three columns, and an ellipse that fills row 1, column 0 of the inner grid. Row 0, column 1 of the main `Grid Panel` holds a `StackPanel`, and three `Ellipses` are stacked there. Row 0, column 1 and row 1, column 0 of the main grid simply contain `Ellipses`. Row 1, column 1 contains a `WrapPanel` with a blue background, and the four white ellipses stored there are laid out horizontally and allowed to wrap. Figure 18-40 shows the execution of the code. In the figure, the beginning of the definition of each major component is shaded.

```
<Grid ShowGridLines="True">
   <Grid.RowDefinitions>
      <RowDefinition></RowDefinition>
      <RowDefinition></RowDefinition>
      <RowDefinition></RowDefinition>
   </Grid.RowDefinitions>
   <Grid.ColumnDefinitions>
      <ColumnDefinition></ColumnDefinition>
      <ColumnDefinition></ColumnDefinition>
      <ColumnDefinition></ColumnDefinition>
   </Grid.ColumnDefinitions>
   <Grid Grid.Row="0" Grid.Column="0">
      <Grid.RowDefinitions>
         <RowDefinition></RowDefinition>
         <RowDefinition></RowDefinition>
         <RowDefinition></RowDefinition>
      </Grid.RowDefinitions>
      <Grid.ColumnDefinitions>
         <ColumnDefinition></ColumnDefinition>
         <ColumnDefinition></ColumnDefinition>
         <ColumnDefinition></ColumnDefinition>
      </Grid.ColumnDefinitions>
      <Ellipse Grid.Row="1" Grid.Column="0" Fill="Blue"/>
   </Grid>
   <StackPanel Grid.Row="0" Grid.Column="1">
      <Ellipse Width="30" Height="30" Fill="Black"/>
      <Ellipse Width="30" Height="30" Fill="Black"/>
      <Ellipse Width="30" Height="30" Fill="Black"/>
   </StackPanel>
   <Ellipse Grid.Row="0" Grid.Column="2" Fill="Blue"/>
   <Ellipse Grid.Row="1" Grid.Column="0" Fill="Blue"/>
   <WrapPanel Grid.Row ="1" Grid.Column="1" Background="Blue">
      <Ellipse Width="30" Height="30" Fill="White"/>
      <Ellipse Width="30" Height="30" Fill="White"/>
      <Ellipse Width="30" Height="30" Fill="White"/>
      <Ellipse Width="30" Height="30" Fill="White"/>
   </WrapPanel>
</Grid>
```

Definition of the outer Grid starts here.

This (and the next 12 lines) defines the Grid that is nested in row 0, column 0 of the outer grid.

This defines the StackPanel that is nested in row 0, column 1 of the outer Grid.

These two Ellipses occupy row 0, column 2 and row 1, column 0 of the outer Grid.

This defines the WrapPanel that is nested in row 1, column 1 of the outer Grid.

Figure 18-39 XAML code that creates nested layout in Figure 18-40

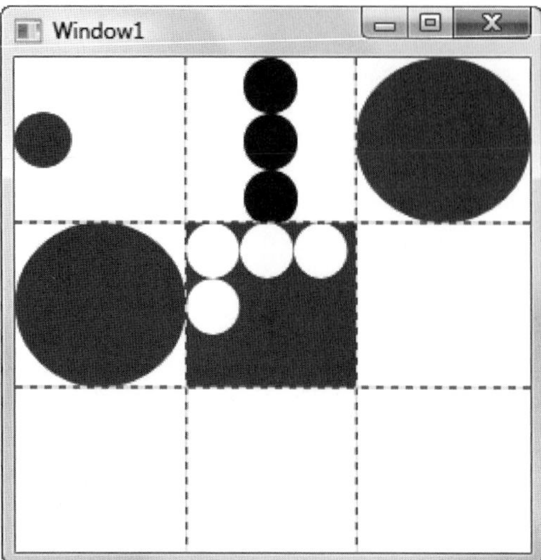

Figure 18-40 Nested layout created by code in Figure 18-39

The code in Figure 18-39 is lengthy, so you might want to take a few minutes to verify that you understand why each section of the grid in Figure 18-40 looks like it does. More options are available for each of the layouts discussed in this section, and more layouts are available as well, so the combinations you create can suit the needs of virtually any application you develop.

»TWO TRUTHS AND A LIE: UNDERSTANDING LAYOUTS

1. `Panel` is the base class for all elements that provide layout support in WPF.
2. `DockPanel` is a `Panel` that allows you to arrange child elements relative to others vertically or horizontally.
3. `StackPanel` is a `Panel` that positions child elements in sequential position from left to right, breaking content to the next line when necessary.

The false statement is #3. `StackPanel` arranges children in a single line. `WrapPanel` positions child elements in sequential position from left to right, breaking content to the next line when necessary.

SHAPE EVENTS

In WPF, `Shape`s are active objects; that is, they can perform much like controls. For example, you can make shapes respond to events such as mouse clicks and keyboard commands. Consider the XAML code in Figure 18-41. It defines a small `BlueViolet Ellipse` on a grid. Two new attributes have been added—`MouseEnter` and `MouseLeave` events. Each is associated with a handler method.

```
<Grid Name="aGrid">
   <Ellipse
      Name="anEllipse"
      Fill="BlueViolet"
      Height="50"
      Width="50"
      MouseEnter="anEllipse_MouseEnter"
      MouseLeave="anEllipse_MouseLeave">
   </Ellipse>
</Grid>
```

Figure 18-41 Code that creates an `Ellipse` associated with two events

»NOTE In Visual Studio, when you write the XAML code and type `MouseEnter=`, a drop-down menu offers `<New Event Handler>`. When you click that choice, the event-handling method is automatically named for you, and the header and curly braces for the method are placed in the C# code.

Figure 18-42 contains the C# code that accompanies and supports the XAML code in Figure 18-41. Two methods have been added to the `Window1` class. The `anEllipse_MouseEnter()` method increases the size of the `Ellipse`. The `anEllipse_MouseLeave()` method reduces the size. Figure 18-43 shows the program in action. When the program starts, the `Ellipse` is small, but each time the user's mouse enters the area covered by the `Ellipse`, it grows in size.

```
public partial class Window1 : Window
{
   public Window1()
   {
      InitializeComponent();
   }
   private void anEllipse_MouseEnter(object sender, MouseEventArgs e)
   {
      anEllipse.Height = 200;
      anEllipse.Width = 200;
   }
   private void anEllipse_MouseLeave(object sender, MouseEventArgs e)
   {
      anEllipse.Height = 30;
      anEllipse.Width = 30;
   }
}
```

Figure 18-42 C# code that provides actions for an `Ellipse`'s events

»NOTE The project that contains the code in Figures 18-41 and 18-42 is stored on your Student Disk as `EllipseActionDemo`.

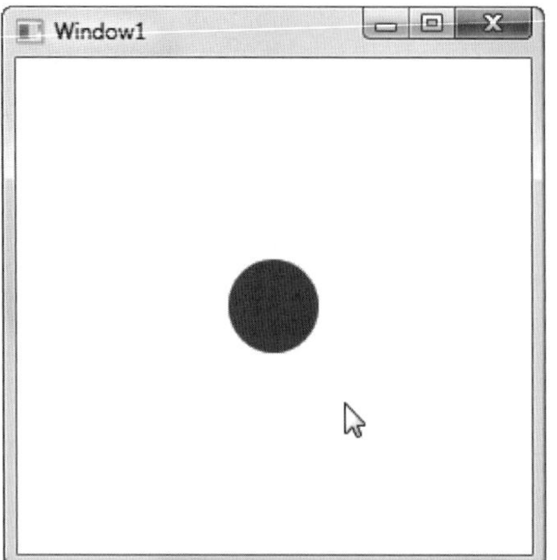

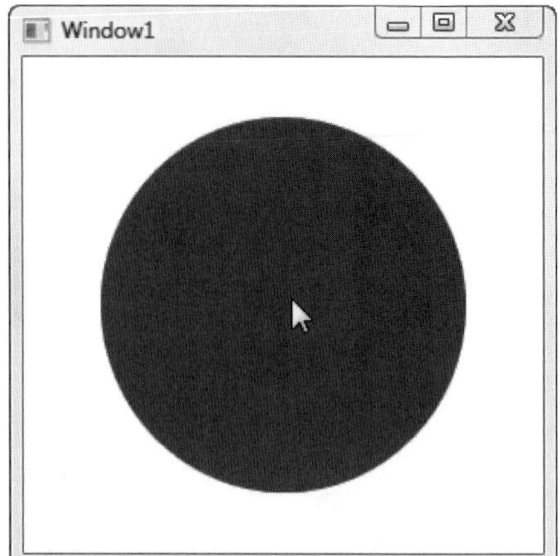

Figure 18-43 Execution of the `EllipseActionDemo` project

Besides `MouseEnter` and `MouseLeave`, other mouse events that you can add to your XAML code include `MouseDown`, `MouseLeftButtonDown`, `MouseLeftButtonUp`, `MouseMove`, `MouseRightButtonDown`, `MouseRightButtonUp`, `MouseUp`, and `MouseWheel`. Keyboard events include `KeyDown` and `KeyUp`.

»TWO TRUTHS AND A LIE: `Shape` EVENTS

1. In WPF, `Shape`s are static objects that can be made to respond to mouse and keyboard events when you associate them with `Control`s.
2. Mouse events that you can add to XAML code include `MouseDown` and `MouseMove`.
3. Keyboard events that you can add to XAML code include `KeyDown` and `KeyUp`.

The false statement is #1. In WPF, `Shape`s are active objects that respond to mouse and keyboard events.

CREATING ANIMATION

Animation is an illusion created by cycling through a series of images, each slightly different from the previous one. For example, artists who create animated movies draw many images, each slightly different from the previous one, and display them in rapid sequence to give the illusion of movement. Similarly, with older programming languages, if you wanted to achieve animation, you were required to create a series of images, and display them in sequence. WPF provides tools that help you time the **transitions** of animated images from an original appearance to a final one, without requiring you to create every image that falls between them.

For example, suppose you want to create the illusion of a flipping coin. If you create an ellipse that starts as a circle and continues to become flatter until it is just a line, it appears to be a coin that changes from a full front view to a side view. Figure 18-44 shows a sequence of images. As you watch the screen, an `Ellipse`'s height transitions from its original height down to 0 in a few seconds.

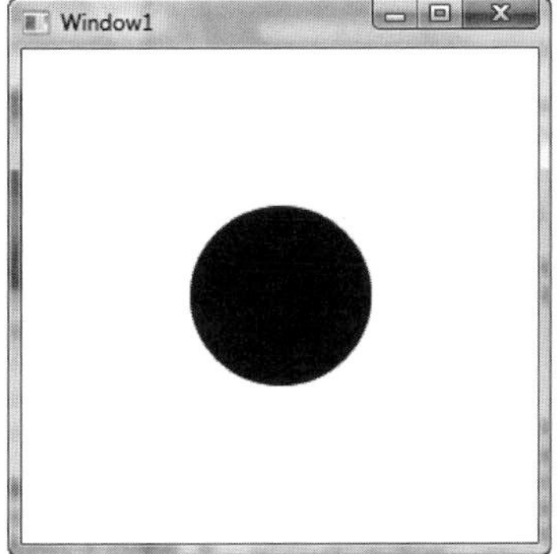

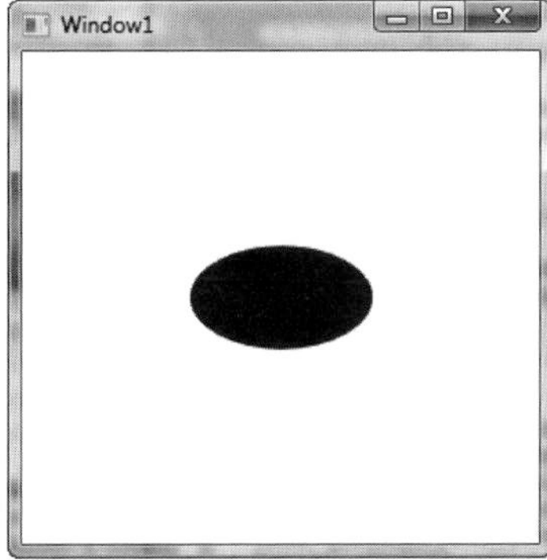

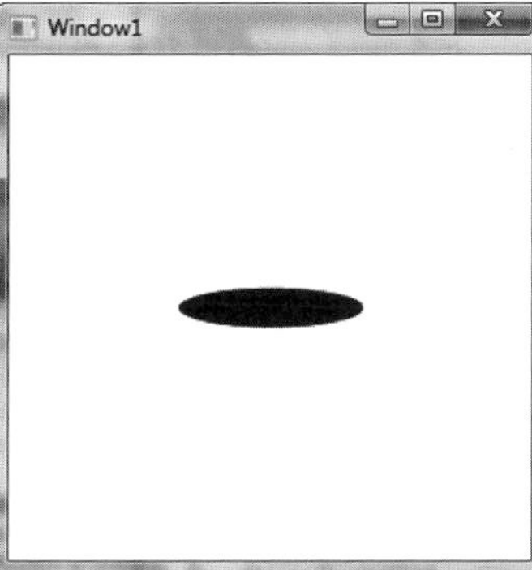

Figure 18-44 Execution of the `FlippingEllipse` project

You start to create the flipping coin demonstration program by creating an `Ellipse`, as shown in Figure 18-45.

```
<Grid>
   <Ellipse
      Name="flippingEllipse"
      Width="100"
      Height="100"
      Fill="Black">
                                More code will go here.
   </Ellipse>
</Grid>
```

Figure 18-45 Defining an `Ellipse` in a `Grid`

You add a `Triggers` collection to the object you want to animate. The collection can contain an `EventTrigger` that names an event that starts animation. For example, the animation might begin when the user releases a clicked button; if so, you would write the following `EventTrigger` code:

```
<EventTrigger RoutedEvent="Ellipse.MouseUp">
```

To begin an animation as soon as the animated object is loaded, you can declare the `EventTrigger RoutedEvent` to be the `Loaded` event, as shown in the shaded code in Figure 18-46.

> **NOTE**
> A `RoutedEvent` is a type of event that can evoke handler methods on multiple listeners rather than just on the object that raised the event.

```
<Grid>
   <Ellipse
      Name="flippingEllipse"
      Width="100"
      Height="100"
      Fill="Black">
      <Ellipse.Triggers>
          <EventTrigger RoutedEvent="Ellipse.Loaded">
                                        More code will go here.
          </EventTrigger>
      </Ellipse.Triggers>
   </Ellipse>
</Grid>
```

Figure 18-46 Defining the `Ellipse`'s `Triggers` collection

In moviemaking, a **storyboard** is a series of drawings that depicts the general plot outline of the movie. One way to create animation in WPF is to create a `Storyboard` object. A `Storyboard` is a type of container that provides timelines for animation. To apply an animation to an object, you can create a `Storyboard` and use the `TargetName` and `TargetProperty` attributes to specify which object and which of its properties to animate. For example, if you want the height of the `flippingEllipse` object to be the property that is altered when the ellipse is loaded, enter the following code.

```
Storyboard.TargetName="flippingEllipse"
Storyboard.TargetProperty="Height"
```

Several types of animations are available for a `Storyboard` to use. Commonly used animations include the following:

- `DoubleAnimation` to vary a numeric property of an object. For example, to vary the `Height`, `Width`, `Top`, `Left`, `Bottom`, `Right`, `StrokeThickness`, or `Opacity` property of an object, you use a `DoubleAnimation`.
- `ColorAnimation` to vary the color of an object. For example, to animate a shape to vary between `Blue` and `Red`, displaying a transition that uses each color value between the two extremes, you use a `ColorAnimation`.
- `PointAnimation` to vary the value of a `Point` attribute of an object; for example, a point that defines a polygon.

Because the height of the `Ellipse` must change to give the illusion of a flipping coin, and because the `Height` property of an `Ellipse` is a `double`, you need to use an animation that produces `double` values. Therefore, you use a `DoubleAnimation` to create a transition between two `double`s.

You can set several DoubleAnimation attributes to various values to achieve a variety of effects. For example:

» To specify a starting value for a DoubleAnimation transition, you set its From attribute. To specify its ending value, you set its To attribute. For example, to vary the height of the ellipse from 100 to 0, you code the following:

```
From="100" To="0"
```

You can also specify a By attribute that indicates a value to add to the starting value.

» To specify how long a transition takes, you use the Duration attribute. The duration is set in hours, minutes, and seconds. For example, to set a transition duration of 4 seconds, you code the following:

```
Duration="0:0:4"
```

If you do not code a value for Duration, it assumes a default value of 1 second.

» To specify a waiting period after the trigger event occurs and before the animation should begin, you code a Begin attribute. By default, the value of Begin is "0:0:0".

» To make an element's transition perform in both directions, you set its AutoReverse property to True. For example, to cause the ellipse height to go from 200 to 0, and then immediately from 0 to 200 again when the duration is complete, you code the following:

```
AutoReverse="True"
```

By default, AutoReverse is False.

» To make an animation repeat indefinitely, you set its RepeatBehavior to "Forever". To specify the number of times the animation should repeat, you use a numeric value followed by "x". For example, to repeat an animation two times, you code the following:

```
RepeatBehavior="2x"
```

To repeat an animation for a specified amount of time, you can designate the time span. For example, to repeat an animation for one minute, you code the following:

```
RepeatBehavior="0:1:0"
```

If you do not set a RepeatBehavior value, the animation plays one time.

Figure 18-47 shows the complete code that animates an Ellipse, varying its height from 100 to 0 and back again, taking four seconds for each transition, and repeating forever. The new code is shaded.

» NOTE
The By attribute is a step value. You learned the term *step value* in Chapter 4.

»NOTE
The complete project that contains the code shown in Figure 18-47 is stored on your Student Disk as FlippingEllipse.

»NOTE
You do not need to set the `Height` property for the `Ellipse` in the fifth line of code in Figure 18-47 because the `Height` is varied from 200 to 0 in the animation. That initial assignment could be omitted from the code with no difference in the outcome.

```
<Grid>
   <Ellipse
      Name="flippingEllipse"
      Width="100"
      Height="100"
      Fill="Black">
      <Ellipse.Triggers>
         <EventTrigger RoutedEvent="Ellipse.Loaded">
            <BeginStoryboard>
               <Storyboard>
                  <DoubleAnimation
                     Storyboard.TargetName="flippingEllipse"
                     Storyboard.TargetProperty="Height"
                     From="100"
                     To="0"
                     Duration="0:0:4"
                     AutoReverse="True"
                     RepeatBehavior="Forever" />
               </Storyboard>
            </BeginStoryboard>
         </EventTrigger>
      </Ellipse.Triggers>
   </Ellipse>
</Grid>
```

Figure 18-47 Code that creates a flipping ellipse

»TWO TRUTHS AND A LIE: CREATING ANIMATION

1. WPF provides tools that help you time the transitions of animated images from an original appearance to a final one, without requiring you to create every image that falls between them.
2. You add a `Triggers` collection to the object you want to animate. The collection can contain an `EventTrigger` that names an event that starts animation.
3. To apply an animation to an object in WPF, you create a series of separate images and access them in sequence using an `ImageBrush`.

The false statement is #3. To apply an animation to an object, you can create a `Storyboard` and use the `TargetName` and `TargetProperty` attributes to specify which object and which of its properties to animate.

YOU DO IT

CREATING IDENTICAL SHAPES USING XAML AND C#

In the next steps, you will create a `Rectangle Shape` using XAML. Then you will create the same `Rectangle` using C#. When you develop projects, you will frequently have the choice of which tool to use.

To create a `Rectangle` using XAML:

1. Open a new WPF project in Visual Studio and name it **MyRectangle**, as shown in Figure 18-48.

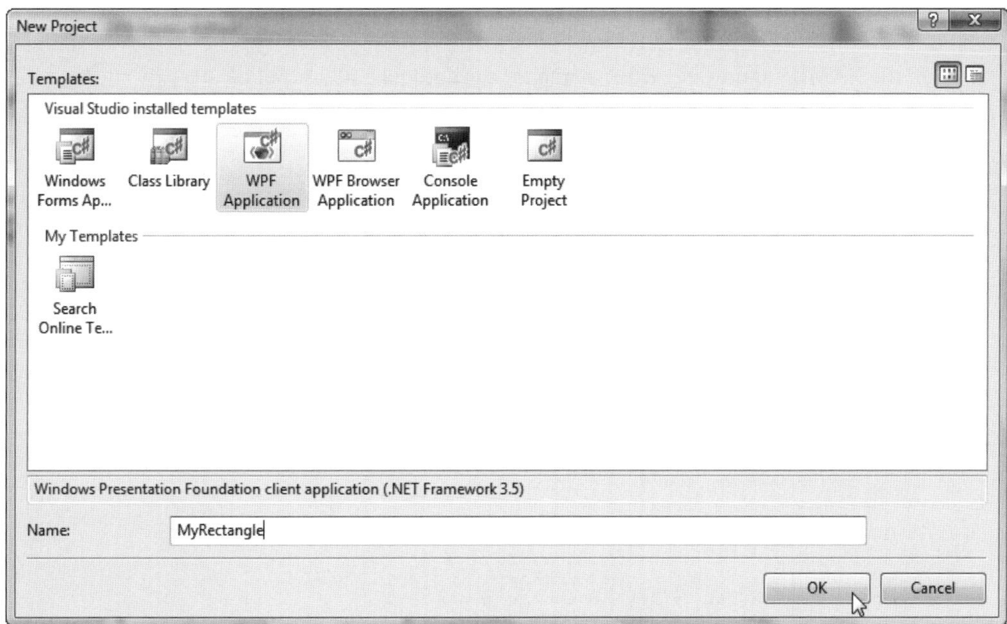

Figure 18-48 Opening the `MyRectangle` project in Visual Studio

2. In the XAML code area, locate the `<Grid>` and `</Grid>` tags. Within the `<Grid>` tag, designate a background color as follows:

```
<Grid Background="Yellow">
```

3. Between the `<Grid>` tags, add the following code that creates a rectangle:

```
<Rectangle
   Width="80"
   Height="120"
   StrokeThickness="3"
   Stroke="Black"
   Fill="Red"
/>
```

4. Execute the program. You see a red rectangle on a yellow background like the one in Figure 18-49.

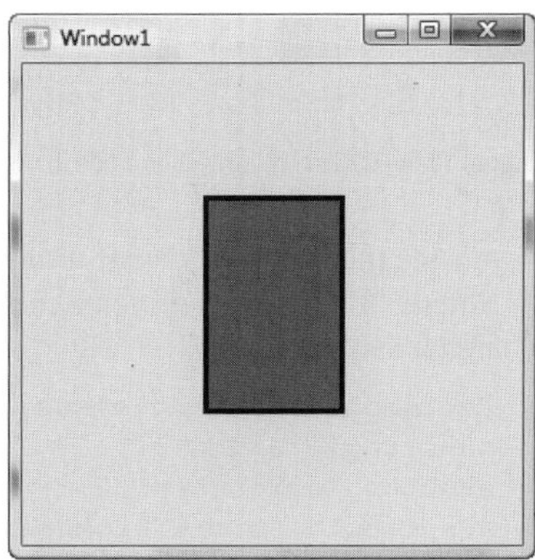

Figure 18-49 Output of the `MyRectangle` project

5. Experiment by changing the `Grid`'s background color and, in turn, each of the rectangle's attributes. Observe the results.
6. Dismiss the window and save the project.

To create a `Rectangle` using C#:

1. Open a new WPF project in Visual Studio and name it **MyRectangle2**.
2. In the XAML window, provide a name for the automatically supplied `Grid` by adding a name attribute to the `<Grid>` tag as follows:

```
<Grid Name="myGrid">
```

3. Click the `Window` in the design screen. Then, from the main menu, choose **View** and then **Code**. (Alternatively, you could press F7.) See Figure 18-50.

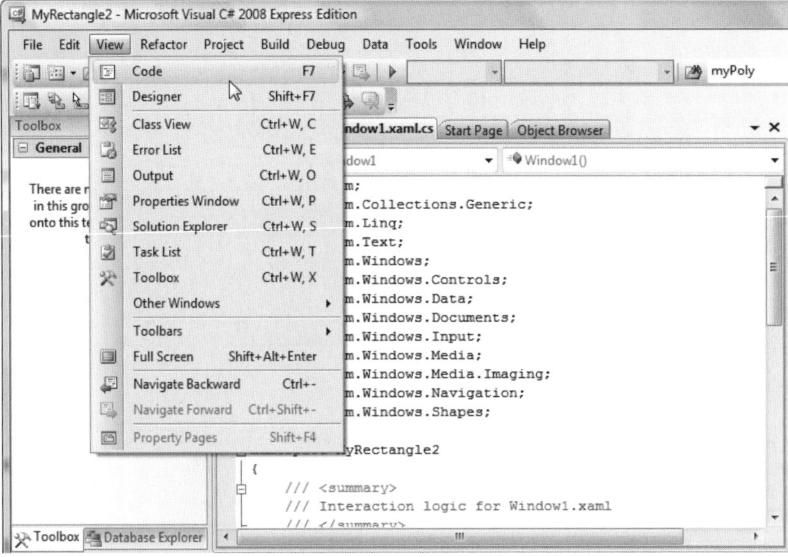

Figure 18-50 Selecting View, then Code in Visual Studio

4. Locate the `Window1` constructor, and after the `InitializeComponent()` method call, add the following statements that create a rectangle just like the one created using XAML in the last set of steps:

```
Rectangle aRectangle=new Rectangle();
aRectangle.Width=80;
aRectangle.Height=120;
aRectangle.StrokeThickness=3;
aRectangle.Stroke=Brushes.Black;
aRectangle.Fill=Brushes.Red;
myGrid.Background=Brushes.Yellow;
myGrid.Children.Add(aRectangle);
```

5. Execute the program. You see a red rectangle on a yellow background, exactly like the rectangle in Figure 18-49.
6. Experiment by changing the Grid's background color and, in turn, each of the rectangle's attributes. Observe the results.
7. Dismiss the window and save the project.

ANIMATING A SHAPE IN WPF

In the next steps, you will provide animation for a Shape in WPF. You will create a Window that displays a small yellow circle. When a user places a mouse over the circle, the small circle grows to become a large red circle, looking something like a sunrise. You will use two types of animation: A DoubleAnimation will control the dimensions of the Ellipse and a ColorAnimation will control the color transition.

To animate a shape in WPF:

1. Start a new WPF project in Visual Studio and name it **Sunrise**.
2. In the XAML code, between the <Grid> tags, enter the following code to define an Ellipse. The Ellipse must be given a name because its dimensions will be used as targets for part of the animation. The Ellipse is small (30 × 30) and is filled with a SolidColorBrush. The Brush must be given a name because its color will be used as part of the animation.

```
<Ellipse Name="anEllipse"
   Width="30"
   Height="30">
   <Ellipse.Fill>
      <SolidColorBrush x:Name="aSolidColorBrush"
         Color="Yellow"
      />
   </Ellipse.Fill>
```

NOTE The Name attribute of the SolidColorBrush is preceded by x: because, in WPF, some attributes (Name, Key, and Uid) of SolidColorBrush must be given a prefix. You will learn more about these attributes as you study C#. For now, just understand that you must precede the Brush's Name property with x:.

3. Add the Triggers collection that will initiate the animation when a user's mouse enters the area covered by the Ellipse. Then begin the Storyboard.

```
<Ellipse.Triggers>
   <EventTrigger RoutedEvent="Ellipse.MouseEnter">
      <BeginStoryboard>
         <Storyboard>
```

4. Create a `DoubleAnimation` that varies the width of the `Ellipse` from 50 to 200 for two seconds.

```
<DoubleAnimation
   Storyboard.TargetName="anEllipse"
   Storyboard.TargetProperty="Width"
   From="50"
   To="200"
   Duration="0:0:2"
/>
```

5. Create a second `DoubleAnimation` that varies the height of the `Ellipse` from 50 to 200 for two seconds.

```
<DoubleAnimation
   Storyboard.TargetName="anEllipse"
   Storyboard.TargetProperty="Height"
   From="50"
   To="200"
   Duration="0:0:2"
/>
```

6. Create a `ColorAnimation` that varies the color of the `Ellipse` from yellow to red for two seconds.

```
<ColorAnimation
   Storyboard.TargetName="aSolidColorBrush"
   Storyboard.TargetProperty="Color"
   From="Yellow"
   To="Red"
   Duration="0:0:2"
/>
```

7. Add the end tags for each element of the XAML code that was started:

```
                  </Storyboard>
               </BeginStoryboard>
            </EventTrigger>
        </Ellipse.Triggers>
    </Ellipse>
```

8. Save the project and execute it. The application displays a small yellow circle. When you place your mouse over it, it grows to a large red circle. Experiment using the mouse with the application, especially holding it near the border of the ellipse. Experiment with altering some of the attributes in the XAML code and observe the effects.
9. Dismiss the window and close Visual Studio.

CHAPTER SUMMARY

- WPF provides a `Shape` class that is the base class for objects such as `Line`, `Ellipse`, `Path`, `Polygon`, `Polyline`, and `Rectangle`. All `Shape` objects have `Stroke`, `StrokeThickness`, and `Fill` properties. `Shape` objects can be used inside `Panel`s.
- You can use the `Line`, `Ellipse`, `Rectangle`, `Polygon`, and `Polyline` classes to create shapes. You can use XAML or C# code to define any of these.
- The `Brushes` class contains named values that correspond to colors. You can use these colors to designate the `Fill` or `Stroke` attributes of a `Shape` or to designate the colors in a `Control`. Alternatively, you can use hexadecimal or decimal values to create custom colors.
- A gradient brush creates interesting paint effects by blending colors continuously along a gradient axis. Using a gradient brush gives shapes and controls a three-dimensional feel and can give the impression of light and shadow. A `LinearGradientBrush` causes colors to gradually change along a straight line; a `RadialGradientBrush` causes a color change that emanates from the center of a circle. You can use an `ImageBrush` to refer to a stored file to load an image into a WPF application.
- Layout describes the arrangement of the collection of children that reside on a parent container. In WPF, layout includes measuring all the components that will be placed on a `Panel` (or one of its descendents) and negotiating the space each receives. `Panel` is the base class for all elements that provide layout support in WPF; its descendents include `Canvas`, `DockPanel`, `Grid`, `StackPanel`, `VirtualizingPanel`, and `WrapPanel`. You can create an infinite number of layout possibilities by nesting layouts within others.
- In WPF, `Shape`s are active objects that can respond to events such as mouse clicks and keyboard commands.
- WPF provides tools that assist you in setting the limits for and timing the transitions of animated images.

KEY TERMS

Property element syntax is the XAML syntax used to assign nonstring values to object properties.

A **gradient axis** is a line along which colors are blended using a gradient brush.

A **bounding box** is an imaginary box that surrounds an object.

Layout describes the arrangement of the collection of children that reside on a parent container.

Animation is an illusion created by cycling through a series of images, each slightly different from the previous one.

A **transition** encompasses the changes that occur for the duration of an animation.

A **storyboard** is a series of drawings that depicts the general plot outline of a movie or animation.

REVIEW QUESTIONS

1. All `Shape` objects have a ________ property.

   a. `Stroke`
   b. `Color`
   c. `Text`
   d. all of the above

2. `Shape` objects can be used inside ________.

   a. `Controls`
   b. `Panels`
   c. all of the above
   d. none of the above

3. Which of the following set of coordinates would create a horizontal `Line`?

   a. `X1="20" Y1="50" X1="20" Y1="150"`
   b. `X1="20" Y1="20" X1="150" Y1="150"`
   c. `X1="20" Y1="50" X1="150" Y1="150"`
   d. `X1="20" Y1="150" X1="150" Y1="150"`

4. You can place WPF C# drawing code in a ________.

   a. `Window`'s constructor
   b. `Button`'s `Click()` method
   c. method you write named `myDrawingCode()`
   d. all of the above

5. Suppose you have created an `Ellipse` named `myEllipse`. Which of the following paints it red in C# code?

   a. `myEllipse.Fill=Red;`
   b. `myEllipse.Fill="Red";`
   c. `myEllipse.Fill=Brushes.Red;`
   d. `myEllipse.Fill(Brushes.Red);`

6. Suppose you have created a `Rectangle` named `myRectangle`. Which of the following XAML statements makes its outline blue?

   a. `Outline="Blue"`
   b. `Stroke="Blue"`
   c. `Fill="Blue"`
   d. `Line="Blue"`

7. Which of the following XAML statements defines the points that draw a rectangular `Polygon`?

   a. `Points="20,20 20,50 20,100 100,100"`
   b. `Points="20,20 120,20 120,100"`
   c. `Points="20,20 120,20 20,100 120,100"`
   d. `Points="20,20 100,100"`

8. In WPF, when you use C# code to create a `Polygon`, you create __________, which is assigned to the `Polygon`'s `Points` property.
   a. `PointCollection`
   b. an array of `Point` objects
   c. an array of `PointCollection` objects
   d. none of the above

9. A gradient brush blends continuously along a line called the __________.
   a. color radius
   b. slope selector
   c. gradient axis
   d. diagonal demarcation

10. The imaginary box that surrounds an object is its __________.
    a. erasable edge
    b. bounding box
    c. invisible fence
    d. artistic limitation

11. When you use a gradient brush, you provide __________ for each `GradientStop`.
    a. point and thickness
    b. color and offset
    c. diameter and paint type
    d. size and range

12. The reason you would alter the `StartPoint` or `EndPoint` of a `LinearGradientBrush` is to __________.
    a. limit the percentage of the area to be painted
    b. limit the opacity of the brush
    c. add or delete `GradientStops`
    d. alter the slope of the gradient axis

13. The axis of a `RadialGradientBrush` is __________.
    a. a circle
    b. a line that slopes down as it moves to the right
    c. a line that slopes upward as it moves to the right
    d. defined by the user

14. You use an `ImageBrush` to __________.
    a. paint detailed or complicated images
    b. refer to a stored file
    c. render an image that looks as though it is a photograph
    d. create animated graphics

15. Which of the following is not a WPF `Panel`?
    a. `Image`
    b. `Grid`
    c. `Canvas`
    d. `StackPanel`

16. When you open a WPF project in Visual Studio, the default layout is ________.
    a. a `Grid` with four rows and four columns
    b. a `StackPanel` with one `Panel`
    c. a `WrapPanel`
    d. none of the above

17. `Canvas` children ________.
    a. are resized when the `Canvas` is stretched
    b. are positioned at designated coordinates
    c. both of the above
    d. none of the above

18. WPF allows you to ________.
    a. provide an event for a `Shape`
    b. provide an event for a `Control`
    c. time transitions in animations
    d. all of the above

19. The collection you add to an animated object that defines the event that will start an animation is ________.
    a. `Prompts`
    b. `Triggers`
    c. `Routes`
    d. `Start`

20. A ________ is a series of drawings that depicts the general plot outline of a movie.
    a. storyboard
    b. script
    c. image dictionary
    d. libretto

EXERCISES

For each of the following exercises, your instructor might request the XAML code, the C# code, or both. Filenames for the saved assignments are suggested without extensions; use the appropriate extensions following your filenames.

1. Create a screen that displays a gradient using at least four different colors. When the user clicks a button, change the screen to all one color. Save the project as **ChangeToSolidColor**.

2. Create a checkerboard with eight rows and eight columns of alternating black and white squares like the one in Figure 18-51. Save the project as **Checkerboard**.

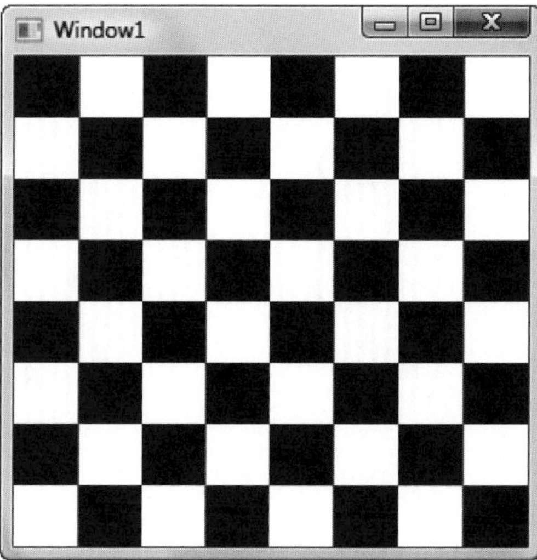

Figure 18-51 Output of `Checkerboard` project

3. Create an application that alternates displaying two different radial gradient patterns that use different colors when the user clicks a button. Save the project as **GradientColor**.

4. Create a window on which an image is placed behind a dark rectangle. Continuously reduce the width of the rectangle to expose the image, and then increase the width to hide it again. Figure 18-52 shows a typical execution in progress. Save the project as **SlidingDoor**.

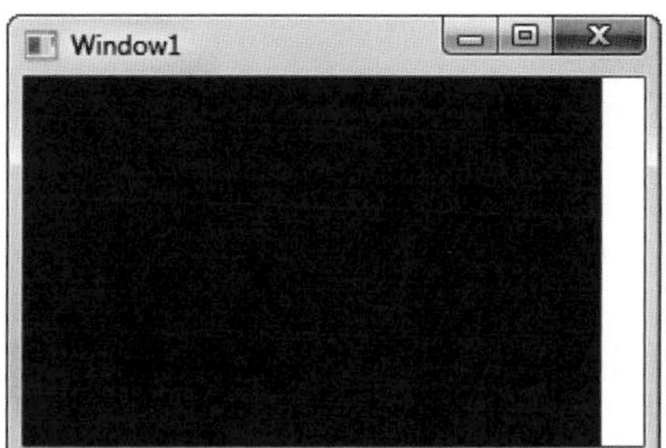

Figure 18-52 Typical execution of `SlidingDoor` project

5. Create an `Ellipse` that continuously fades from solid black to invisible by transitioning its `Opacity` property. Save the project as **FadingEllipse**.

6. Create an animated stoplight. The lights should have the standard vertical arrangement of red on top, yellow in the middle, and green on the bottom. Animate the stoplight so that the green light displays for a few seconds, fades away, and the yellow light displays for a shorter time. Then, as the yellow light fades, display the red light. When the animation ends, continue to show the red light. Save the project as **Stoplight**.

7. Using a single loop in which you vary coordinates, draw lines to produce the design in Figure 18-53. Save the project as **Bowtie**.

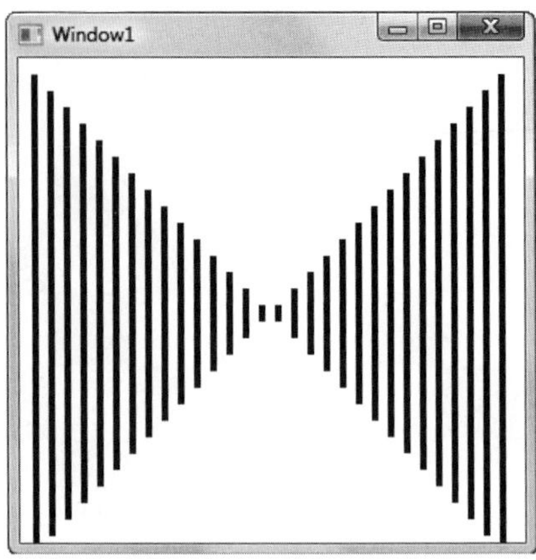

Figure 18-53 Output of `Bowtie` project

DEBUGGING EXERCISES

Each of the following projects in the Chapter.18 folder on your Student Disk has syntax and/or logical errors. In each case, make a copy of the folder and rename it using the prefix *Fixed*. For example, save the DebugEighteen1 project as **FixedDebugEighteen1**. In each case, determine the problems and fix the projects so that they work correctly.

a. DebugEighteen1
b. DebugEighteen2
c. DebugEighteen3
d. DebugEighteen4

UP FOR DISCUSSION

1. In this chapter, you learned that if you create a shape using XAML code and then create an identical shape in C# in the `Window` constructor, the XAML code executes first. How could you prove this?
2. In this chapter, you learned that you almost always have the choice to create a graphic in XAML or C# code when you work in WPF. Which do you prefer? Why?

CHAPTER NINETEEN

19

DYNAMIC DATA STRUCTURES

In this chapter you will:

Learn about `struct`s, boxing, and unboxing
Understand self-referential classes
Understand linked lists
Understand stacks
Understand queues
Understand trees

Data structures are collections of data in memory that are organized to perform specific tasks. In Chapter 5, you learned about arrays, which are examples of fixed data structures, so named because they have specific sizes. Dynamic data structures grow and shrink appropriately while a program executes. In this chapter, you will learn about several types of dynamic data structures: linked lists, stacks, queues, and binary trees.

UNDERSTANDING `STRUCTS`, BOXING, AND UNBOXING

»NOTE There are other differences between `struct`s and classes. For example, `struct`s do not support inheritance and they do not have destructors.

A **`struct`** is a C# data type that is similar to a class. However, a class is a reference type, whereas a `struct` is a value type. The main significance of this difference is that when you assign a `struct` object to another one, a copy is made, but when you assign a class object to another one, the address of the first object is assigned to the second reference. A `struct` is typically used to encapsulate small groups of related values. For example, you have worked with the `Color struct`, which holds names of colors you can use in C# applications. Like classes, `struct`s can have properties and methods. As you learned in Chapter 2, each simple, intrinsic data type in C# has a corresponding `struct` in the `System` namespace that declares the simple type. Table 19-1 reviews the simple types and their `System` types.

Type	`System` type	Bytes	Description
`byte`	Byte	1	Unsigned byte
`sbyte`	Sbyte	1	Signed byte
`short`	Int16	2	Signed short
`ushort`	UInt16	2	Unsigned short
`int`	Int32	4	Signed integer
`uint`	UInt32	4	Unsigned integer
`long`	Int64	8	Signed long integer
`ulong`	UInt64	8	Unsigned long integer
`float`	Single	4	Floating-point
`double`	Double	8	Double-precision floating-point
`decimal`	Decimal	16	Fixed precision number
`string`	String	NA	Unicode string
`char`	Char	2	Unicode character
`bool`	Boolean	1	Boolean value

Table 19-1 C# data types

When you want to use a simple data type for a variable in a program, you usually declare the variable as its simple type and not its `System` type (for example, as an `int` and not as an `Int32`). Using the simple data type is easier and more conventional. However, one situation in which you need to know that the `System` type exists is when you want to use a value type as a descendent of the `object` class. In this chapter, you will learn about structures that use `object` references, so when you want to use these structures with a simple data type, you can use the `System` version of the simple data type that is easily converted to an `object`. To use a simple type variable as an object, you do not need to declare the simple variable explicitly using its `System` name; the `System` name is used automatically. When you assign a simple data type (a value type) to an `object` class reference, the process is called **boxing**. For example, you can box an integer using code like the following:

```
int x = 2;
object anObject = x;
```

In this case, `x` is implicitly boxed as an object. Alternatively, you can perform boxing explicitly by naming the resulting type in parentheses, as in the following example:

```
int x = 2;
object anObject = (object) x;
```

Whether you box a variable implicitly or explicitly, the result is the same.

Unboxing is the process of converting an object reference into a simple type. When you unbox an object, you must do so explicitly, as in the following:

```
int x = (int)anObject;
```

>>NOTE If you try to unbox a value and store it in a variable that is an incorrect type, an `InvalidCastException` is thrown.

>>TWO TRUTHS AND A LIE: UNDERSTANDING `structs`, BOXING, AND UNBOXING

1. A class is a reference type, so when you assign a class object to another one, a copy is made.
2. Like classes, `structs` can have properties and methods.
3. Boxing is the process of assigning a value type to an object reference.

The false statement is #1. A class is a reference type, so when you assign a class object to another one, only the reference is assigned. When you assign a `struct` to another one, a copy is made.

UNDERSTANDING SELF-REFERENTIAL CLASSES

A **self-referential class** contains a reference to an object of the same type. For example, suppose you set up an emergency telephone number list for students so that when a class meeting is canceled, the instructor notifies the student with the lowest ID number on the class roster, and each student notifies the next one. The class might look like the one in Figure 19-1.

Each `Student` has `idNumber`, `name`, and `phoneNumber` fields, as well as a shaded statement that contains another `Student` who represents the next `Student` on the class list. Each `Student` also has a `ToString()` method that overrides the `Object` class version; it constructs and returns a string of student data.

```
public class Student
{
   private int idNumber;
   private string name;
   private string phoneNumber;
   private Student nextStudent;
   public int IdNumber {get; set;}
   public string Name {get; set;}
   public string PhoneNumber {get; set;}
   public Student NextStudent {get; set;}
   public override string ToString()
   {
      return ("Student #" + IdNumber + " " + Name + " " +  PhoneNumber);
   }
}
```

Figure 19-1 A self-referential `Student` class

Self-referential objects can be linked to make useful structures. For example, Figure 19-2 illustrates the data that might be stored in several `Student` objects and how the objects are linked to create a list. Each `Student` in the list in Figure 19-2 contains a reference (called `nextStudent`) that indicates, or points to, the next `Student` to notify. The last `Student` does not have to notify any other `Student`, so the last `Student`'s `nextStudent` reference is `null`.

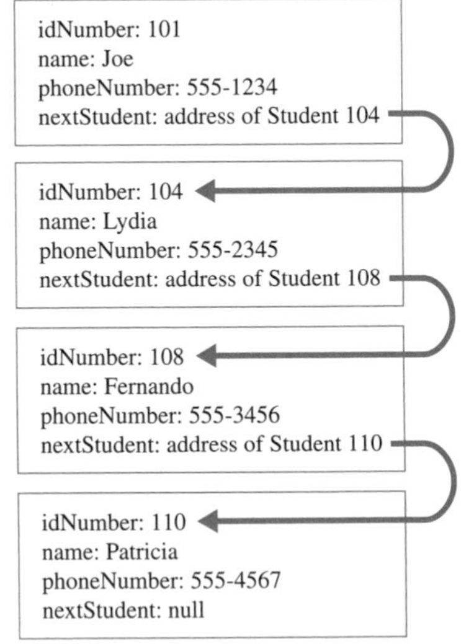

Figure 19-2 `Student` objects linked together

Instead of using a list like the one in Figure 19-2, you could store a list of `Students` in an array. A major disadvantage to using an array is that it has a fixed size. Therefore, if you decide to store `Students` in an array, you are faced with the following dilemma:

- You can define an array with just enough room to hold the current list, but you will run out of room if more objects must be added.
- You can define the array to be much larger than currently needed, but you waste memory, and if enough new objects are added, you still might run out of room.

When you maintain a sequence of self-referential objects instead of using an array to store them, you run out of room only when the computer's memory is physically exhausted.

Another advantage to using a list is that it is easier to insert new objects than it is with an array. Consider the list of `Students` in Figure 19-2. If the `Students` were stored in an array and a new `Student` with `idNumber` 106 joined the class, you would have to handle the new student in one of the following ways:

- If the original array was declared to contain only four `Students`, a new array would have to be declared and all the existing `Students` would have to be copied to the new array, adding the new `Student` in the correct slot.
- If the original array had been made larger in anticipation of possible new `Students`, there would be enough room for the new `Student`. (On the other hand, space would be wasted until the new `Student` joined the class.) The correct location for the new `Student` would have to be determined based on ID number, the `Students` in the array after that point would each have to be moved down one element, and the new `Student` could be inserted into the correct array element.

In either of these scenarios, `Student` objects would have to be copied. If the objects were large or numerous, or both, the process could be quite time consuming.

On the other hand, if the `Student` list is maintained using self-referential objects, you need to do only the following when a new `Student` 106 joins the class:

- Change the `Student` reference of `Student` 104 so it points to the new `Student` 106.
- Make sure the `Student` reference for the new `Student` 106 holds the `Student` who follows logically—`Student` 108.

Figure 19-3 illustrates the process. When you use the list of self-referential objects, no objects need to be copied from one memory location to another; instead, just two assignments are made to maintain the logical order of the list.

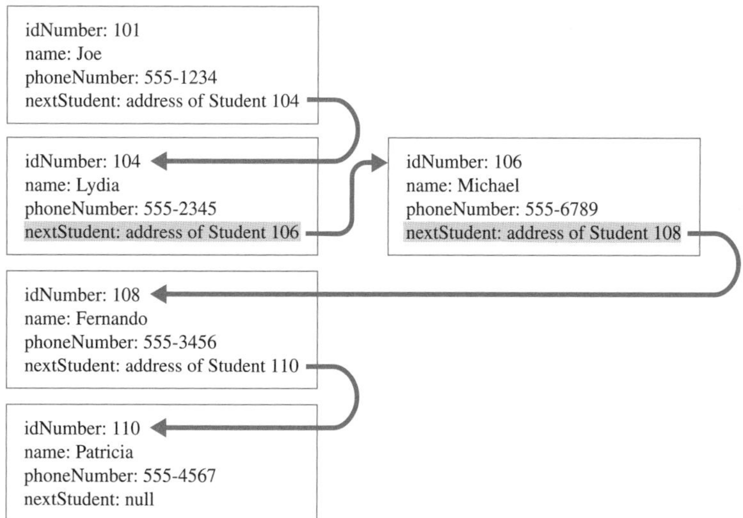

Figure 19-3 Inserting a new object into an existing list

>> **NOTE** If you use the `new` operator to allocate memory and not enough is available, the operator throws an `OutOfMemoryException`.

When arrays are stored in memory, each element resides in memory contiguous to the next one. Therefore, when you use a loop to vary a subscript as you traverse an array, access is very fast. When you store objects in a list with self-referential members, access is slower because objects are not stored in adjacent memory locations. You cannot go directly to an object as you can when you use an array; instead you must start with the first object in the list, obtain its reference to the next object, obtain its reference to the next object, and so on. Therefore, it is often more efficient to use an array of objects when you know how many objects you will have, or when the array will always be processed sequentially, but you might prefer to use a list of self-referential objects when you cannot predict the number of objects.

>>TWO TRUTHS AND A LIE: UNDERSTANDING SELF-REFERENTIAL CLASSES

1. A self-referential class contains a reference to an object of the same type.
2. When you maintain a sequence of self-referential objects instead of using an array to store them, you run out of room only when you run out of computer memory.
3. When you use an array instead of maintaining a sequence of self-referential objects, it is easier to insert new objects into the list.

The false statement is #3. When you use an array instead of maintaining a sequence of self-referential objects, it is more difficult to insert new objects into the list.

CREATING AND USING LINKED LISTS

A **linked list** is a sequence of objects that are connected by references. Each object in a linked list is a **node**. The data in Figures 19-2 and 19-3 represent a linked list.

When you use a linked list in a program, you typically use the first object, and then you use its link to access the succeeding object. After you use the second object, you use its link to access the next object, and so on. You typically continue to process objects until the link that belongs to the last object is `null`.

Suppose you have a linked list with just one `Student` in it. That `Student` has an ID number, name, phone number, and a `nextStudent` link that is set to `null`. The method in Figure 19-4 could be used to display the linked list. The method receives a `Student` parameter named `current`. As long as the `current Student` is not `null`, the `Student` data is displayed. Then the value of `current` is changed to become a reference to the next `Student` on the list. When just one `Student` is listed, the value of `current` becomes `null` after the first `Student` is displayed, and the loop ends.

```
public static void DisplayList(Student current)
{
   while(current != null)
   {
      Console.WriteLine(current.ToString());
      current = current.NextStudent;
   }
}
```

Figure 19-4 The `DisplayList()` method

Next, assume there are two `Students` in a linked list. When the first is passed to the `DisplayList()` method, the `Student`'s data is displayed, and `current` becomes the address pointed to by its `nextStudent` reference—that is, the address of the second `Student`. The reference is not `null`, so the second `Student`'s data is displayed, and the value of `current` becomes the second `Student`'s `nextStudent` reference, which is `null`. No matter how many `Students` are in the linked list, the `DisplayList()` method correctly displays each one in order.

It is important to understand the technique of setting a variable reference like `current` to the next object in sequence in a list, because the technique is useful for traversing any list that is connected by references. It works because when you finish processing any current object in a list, the new current object becomes the next one in order.

CREATING A LINKED LIST

Assume you have data for one `Student` who is the first `Student` in a linked list. The single `Student` has a `nextStudent` value of `null`. To add a subsequent `Student` to the list, you must allocate memory for the new `Student` and change the first `Student`'s `nextStudent` value to become a reference to the newly created `Student`. **Dynamic memory allocation** is the allotment of new memory during a program's execution. When you want to insert a new object in a linked list, a new memory location must be assigned for it. You use the `new` operator to allocate memory.

> **NOTE**
> You have been using the `new` operator to allocate memory for new object instantiations throughout this book.

The basic logic to adding a second student to the existing linked list is as follows:

1. Allocate memory for the new `Student`.
2. Get the data for the new `Student`.
3. Set the first `Student`'s `nextStudent` value to refer to the new `Student`.
4. Set the second `Student`'s `nextStudent` value to `null` because the second `Student` is now at the end of the list.

Figure 19-5 shows how a new `Student` (ID 108) is appended to a linked list that previously contained just one node.

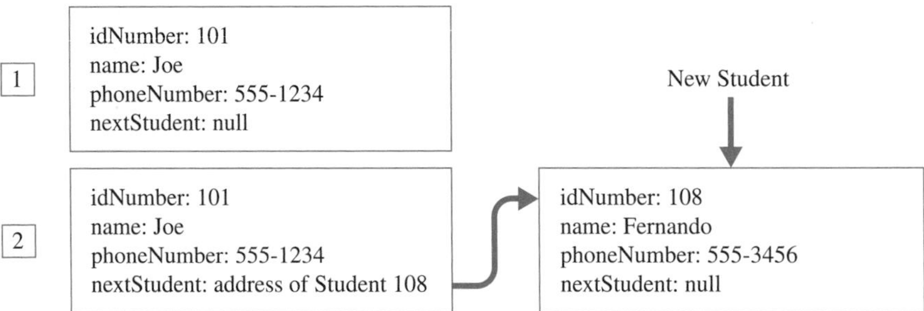

Figure 19-5 Adding a second `Student` to a linked list

> **NOTE** In the Exercises section at the end of this chapter, you will create an application in which the first student is not required to have the lowest ID number. That application is more practical than this one. To help you follow the logic more easily, this example assumes that the first student entered should always remain first in the list.

Now suppose you want to add a third `Student` to the list. This example assumes that the first `Student` has the lowest ID number, but the third `Student` might have an ID number that falls between the first two or after the second `Student`'s ID. So, adding the third `Student` proceeds as follows:

1. Allocate memory for the new, third `Student`.
2. Get the data for the new `Student`.
3. If the new, third `Student`'s ID number is greater than the first `Student`'s but less than the second `Student`'s, set the first `Student`'s `nextStudent` value to refer to the third `Student` and the new, third `Student`'s `nextStudent` value to refer to the second `Student`. For example, if `Students` 101 and 108 are already in the list and you add 104, the process looks like Figure 19-6. The first `Student`'s `nextStudent` value and the new `Student`'s `nextStudent` value must be set (see the shading in the figure), but the `Student` who was added second remains unchanged.

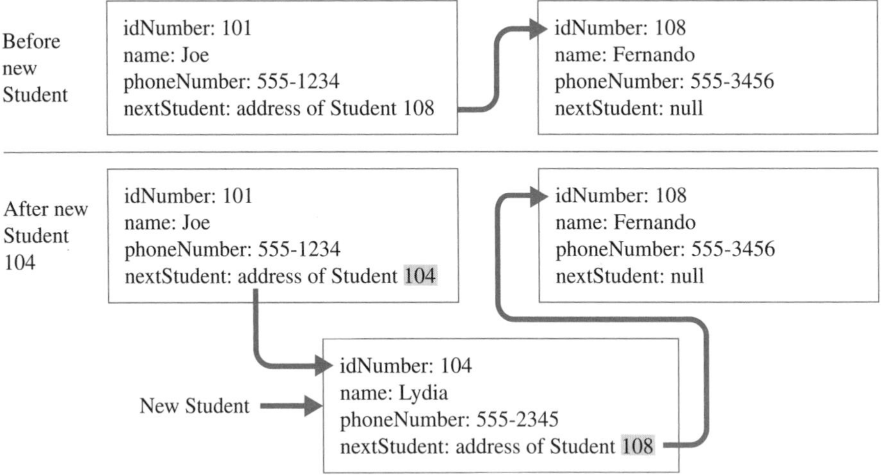

Figure 19-6 Inserting a new `Student` into a list

4. If the new, third `Student`'s ID number is greater than that of both the first and second `Students`, set the second `Student`'s `nextStudent` value to refer to the new, third `Student` and set the new, third `Student`'s `nextStudent` value to `null`. For example, if the new `Student`'s ID number is 110, the process looks like Figure 19-7. The `nextStudent` value for the `Student` who was added second must be changed, but the `Student` who was placed in the list first remains unchanged.

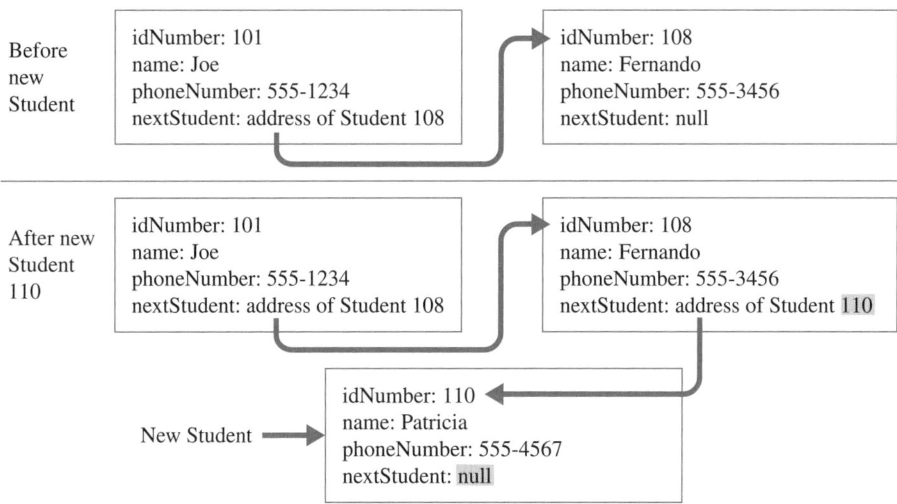

Figure 19-7 Adding a new `Student` at the end of a list

As more `Students` are entered into the list, more comparisons must be made, but the process is really not more complicated. For each new `Student` that you want to add, take the following steps:

1. Allocate memory for the new `Student`.
2. Get the data for the new `Student`.
3. Declare a variable named `current` and hold a reference to the first `Student` there.
4. While the new `Student`'s ID number is greater than the current `Student`'s ID number, save the current `Student`'s reference in a variable named `previous`, then alter `current` so it holds `current`'s `nextStudent` value, and then check again.
5. When the new `Student`'s ID number is not greater than the current `Student`'s ID number, it means that the new `Student` falls between the `previous Student` and the `current Student`. So, set the `previous Student`'s `nextStudent` value to the new `Student`, and set the new `Student`'s `nextStudent` value to the current `Student`.

The code for a program that adds new `Students` to a linked list is presented in Figure 19-8. The first shaded portion supplies the logic that places a `Student` in the correct position within the list. The logic of the first shaded section can be summarized as follows:

» While the end of the list is not reached, and while the new `Student`'s ID number is greater than the current `Student`'s number, save the current `Student` in `previous`, and make the `current Student` become the next `Student`. When the shaded loop ends, the correct position for the new `Student` is known—it is between `previous` and `current`.

The logic of the second shaded portion of the code, after the correct position is located, can be summarized in one sentence:

» Set the new `Student`'s `nextStudent` value to point where the `previous Student` used to point, and set the `previous Student`'s `nextStudent` value to point to the new `Student`.

```
using System;
public class AddStudentsToLinkedList
{
   public static void Main()
   {
      Student firstStudent = new Student();
      firstStudent = EnterStudentData(101);
      firstStudent.NextStudent = null;
      const int QUIT = 999;
      int newId;
      Student previous = null;
      Student current;
      Console.Write("Enter student ID number or {0} to quit ", QUIT);
      newId = Convert.ToInt32(Console.ReadLine());
      while(newId != QUIT)
      {
         current = firstStudent;
         while(current != null && newId > current.IdNumber)
         {
            previous = current;
            current = current.NextStudent;
         }
         Student newStudent = new Student();
         newStudent = EnterStudentData(newId);
         newStudent.NextStudent = previous.NextStudent;
         previous.NextStudent = newStudent;
         DisplayList(firstStudent);
         Console.Write("Enter student ID number or {0} to quit ",
            QUIT);
         newId = Convert.ToInt32(Console.ReadLine());
      }
   }
```

Figure 19-8 The `AddStudentsToLinkedList` application (*continued*)

```
    public static Student EnterStudentData(int newId)
    {
        Student temp = new Student();
        temp.IdNumber = newId;
        Console.Write("Enter name for Student {0} ", newId);
        temp.Name = Console.ReadLine();
        Console.Write("Enter phone number ");
        temp.PhoneNumber = Console.ReadLine();
        return temp;
    }
    public static void DisplayList(Student current)
    {
        while(current != null)
        {
            Console.WriteLine(current.ToString());
            current = current.NextStudent;
        }
    }
}
```

Figure 19-8 (*continued*)

Figure 19-9 shows a typical execution of the program. After the user is prompted for data for `Student` 101, the user is continually prompted for more `Students`. Each new `Student` is inserted into the correct list position, and the existing list is displayed.

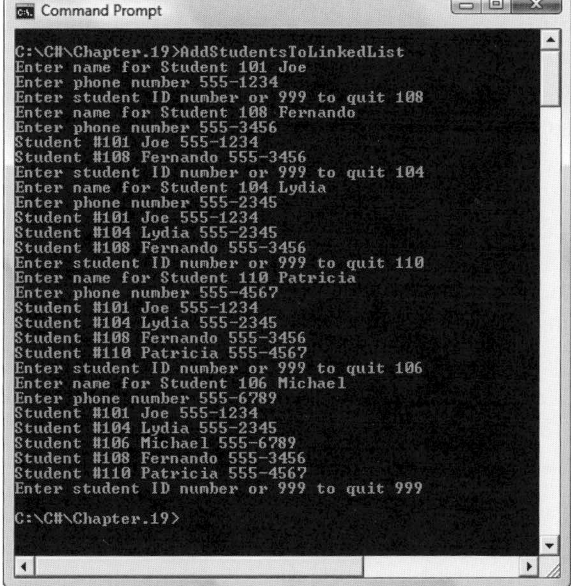

Figure 19-9 Typical execution of the `AddStudentsToLinkedList` application

NOTE
To keep this example simple, it assumes that the first student entered always remains the one with the lowest ID number. In a professional application, you would either want to modify this feature of the example (as you will in the Exercises section at the end of this chapter) or provide exception-handling code for the potential mistake.

MORE SOPHISTICATED LINKED LISTS

The linked list discussed in the previous section is a **singly linked list**. The list begins with a reference to the first node, and each node contains a reference to a single next node. The list ends when a node's link is `null`.

You can also create a **circular, singly linked list** in which the last node holds a reference to the first node, as shown in the diagram in Figure 19-10. This list provides a closed circle.

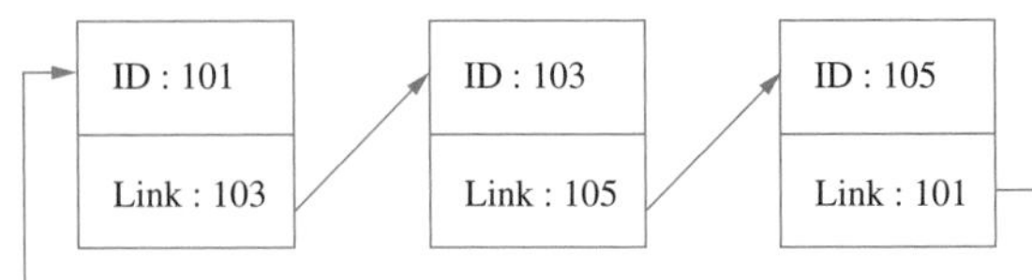

Figure 19-10 A circular, singly linked list

>> **NOTE**
> C# contains a class named `LinkedList<T>` that provides linked list functionality for any object type. To understand this class, you must first learn about generics, which are covered in the next chapter.

You can design class elements to be part of a doubly linked list. In a **doubly linked list**, each node contains two references: one to the next element and one to the previous element. With a doubly linked list, you can look for objects in either direction. For example, when searching for a `Student` with a relatively high ID number, it would be better to start a search from the end of the list and travel backward. Figure 19-11 shows how a doubly linked list looks in memory.

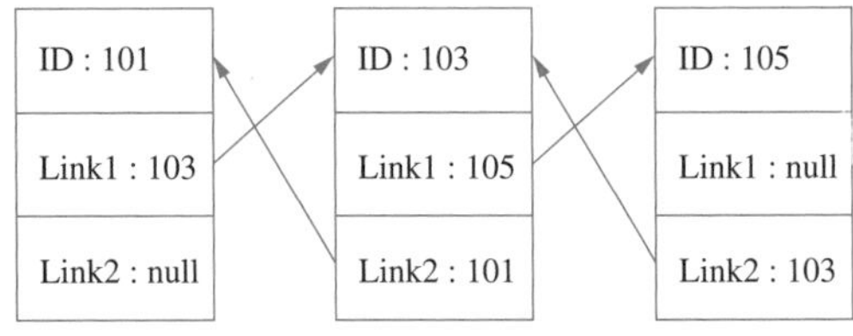

Figure 19-11 A doubly linked list

>> **NOTE**
> Linked lists were developed in 1955 and 1956 by Allen Newell, Cliff Shaw, and Herbert Simon at RAND Corporation. They were the primary data structure of Information Processing Language (IPL), which has been used to develop artificial intelligence programs such as the Logic Theory machine, the General Problem Solver, and a chess program.

You also can create a **circular, doubly linked list** in which the first node's previous reference points to the last object in the list, and the last node's next reference points to the first object in the list.

USING A LINKED LIST

After you have placed objects in a linked list, you might want to store them in a data file, or you might want to search through the list to find a specific object. However, linked lists alone are of limited use. Their primary use is in enabling you to better understand two other structures: stacks and queues.

>>TWO TRUTHS AND A LIE: CREATING AND USING LINKED LISTS

1. Each object in a linked list is a node; you typically continue to traverse linked list objects until the link that belongs to the last node is `null`.
2. Typically, when you insert a new object into a linked list, the only action required is the reassignment of a single reference.
3. Linked lists can be singly linked or doubly linked, and might be circular.

The false statement is #2. Typically, when you insert a new object into a linked list, the only actions required are the reassignments of two references.

USING STACKS

A **stack** is a specialized form of linked list in which nodes are added or removed only from the top of the list. For this reason, a stack is referred to as a **last-in first-out (LIFO)** data structure. With a stack, you do not need to manipulate the object-connecting links; they are maintained for you as you add or remove list objects.

The primary operations to manipulate a stack are push, pop, and peek. When you add a new node to the top of a stack, you **push** it; when you remove a data item from the top of a stack, you **pop** it. When you examine the item at the top of a stack without removing it, you **peek** at it.

>> **NOTE**
> Perhaps you have seen dishes in a spring-loaded stack in a cafeteria. The last dish is added to the top of the stack by pushing it onto the stack. The last dish added is the first one popped off the top by the next cafeteria customer.

You have witnessed a stack in action when you have called nested methods in C# programs. For example, if you write a program in which method A calls method B, the memory address to which the logic should return when method B is done is stored in a stack. If method B calls method C before returning, the memory address in B to which C should return is pushed onto the stack "on top of" the first return address. When method C ends, the last return address pushed onto the stack (the address within method B) is popped off and used. When method B ends, the next address in the stack is popped off and used to return to method A.

You could write an application that employs a stack by creating a linked list and allowing additions or removals only at the top of the list. Consider the linked list of `Students` implemented in the example earlier in this chapter. When you add a new `Student` to the list, you want this new, last `Student` to be at the start of the list. You would make the new `Student` become `firstStudent`, and you would set its link to the `Student` who used to be `firstStudent`. However, there is no need to write your own stack logic to accomplish this chain of events because C#'s `System.Collections` namespace includes a `Stack` class. Table 19-2 lists some useful methods and a property of the `Stack` class.

>> **NOTE**
> In Chapter 9, you learned how `Exceptions` are traced through the method call stack.

Method or property	Description
`Clear()`	Removes all objects from the `Stack`
`Contains()`	Determines whether an element is in the `Stack`
`Peek()`	Returns the object at the top of the `Stack` without removing it
`Pop()`	Returns and removes the object at the top of the `Stack`
`Push()`	Inserts an object at the top of the `Stack`
`Count`	Gets the number of elements in the `Stack`

Table 19-2 Useful `Stack` class methods and a property

The `Stack` class is designed to stack `Objects`. Therefore, it can hold any type of object (because all C# classes derive from `Object`), and the types can even be mixed. For example, Figure 19-12 shows a `StackDemo` class. The statement `using System.Collections;`

is added because that namespace contains the `Stack` class. A `Stack` is created and then a `Student` is created using the class defined in Figure 19-1. Then, five values of diverse types are pushed onto the stack—two integers, a `double`, a string, and a `Student`. The program displays a count of the objects, then pops each one in turn and displays it.

```
using System;
using System.Collections;
public class StackDemo
{
   public static void Main()
   {
      Stack aStack = new Stack();
      Student aStudent = new Student();
      aStudent.IdNumber = 333;
      aStudent.Name = "Brooke";
      aStudent.PhoneNumber = "555-9191";
      aStack.Push(19);
      aStack.Push(6.8);
      aStack.Push("Hello");
      aStack.Push(aStudent);
      aStack.Push(100);
      int times = aStack.Count;
      Console.WriteLine("Number of items: {0}", aStack.Count);
      for(int x = 0; x < times; ++x)
         Console.WriteLine("{0}   {1}   ", x, aStack.Pop());
   }
}
```

Figure 19-12 The `StackDemo` program

Each of the simple data types (the integers and `double`) that are pushed onto the stack are implicitly boxed to become their reference types. Therefore, they have a `ToString()` method that is called automatically when they are written in the `WriteLine()` statement in the loop at the end of the program. The string and `Student` values are objects, so they are references and do not need to be boxed. When the `Student` object is displayed in the loop at the end of the program, its `ToString()` method that overrides the `Object` class version is used to produce the formatted display. Figure 19-13 shows the output of the program. The objects are popped from the stack in reverse order of their entry.

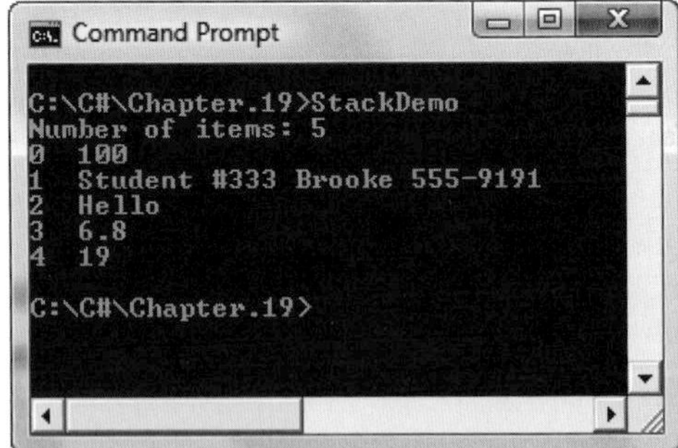

Figure 19-13 Output of the `StackDemo` application

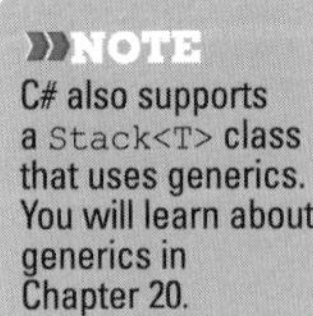
»NOTE
C# also supports a `Stack<T>` class that uses generics. You will learn about generics in Chapter 20.

»TWO TRUTHS AND A LIE: USING STACKS

1. A stack is a FIFO structure.
2. When you use a stack, the object-connecting links are maintained automatically as you add or remove list objects.
3. When you add a new node to the top of a stack, you push it; when you remove a data item from the top of a stack, you pop it.

The false statement is #1. A stack is a LIFO structure.

USING QUEUES

A **queue** is a form of linked list in which nodes are inserted at the end but removed from the beginning. In other words, a queue is a **first-in first-out (FIFO)** data structure. When you stand in line for a concert, you are in a queue; the first person in line is the first one to leave the line to enter the auditorium. When you insert an object into a queue, you **enqueue** it; the queue method is `Enqueue()`. When you remove an object from a queue, you **dequeue** it; the corresponding method is `Dequeue()`. Table 19-3 shows some useful methods and a property of the `Queue` class that you can use to create queues.

Method or property	Description
`Clear()`	Removes all objects from the `Queue`
`Contains()`	Determines whether an element is in the `Queue`
`Peek()`	Returns the object at the top of the `Queue` without removing it
`Dequeue()`	Returns and removes the object at the front of the `Queue`
`Enqueue()`	Inserts an object at the end of the `Queue`
`Count`	Gets the number of elements in the `Queue`

Table 19-3 Useful `Queue` class methods and a property

Queues have many uses in computer systems. For example, many computers on a network might share a printer. When you send a job to the printer, it gets a place in a queue; other jobs that arrived prior to yours will be processed first.

Figure 19-14 shows a program that demonstrates a `Queue` of different objects. Figure 19-15 displays the output. Notice that the first object enqueued is the first object dequeued.

```
using System;
using System.Collections;
public class QueueDemo
{
   public static void Main()
   {
      Queue aQueue = new Queue();
      Student aStudent = new Student();
      aStudent.IdNumber = 333;
      aStudent.Name = "Brooke";
      aStudent.PhoneNumber = "555-9191";
      aQueue.Enqueue(19);
      aQueue.Enqueue(6.8);
      aQueue.Enqueue("Hello");
      aQueue.Enqueue(aStudent);
      aQueue.Enqueue(100);
      int times = aQueue.Count;
      Console.WriteLine("Number of items: {0}", aQueue.Count);
      for(int x = 0; x < times; ++x)
         Console.WriteLine("{0}  {1}  ",  x, aQueue.Dequeue());
   }
}
```

Figure 19-14 The `QueueDemo` class

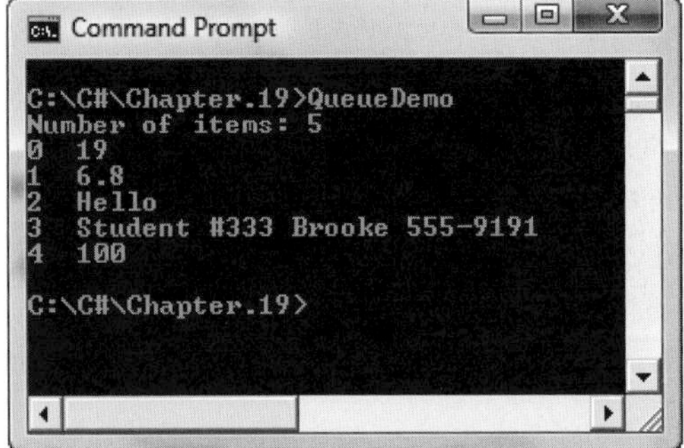

Figure 19-15 Output of the `QueueDemo` class

»NOTE C# also supports a `Queue<T>` class that uses generics. You will learn about generics in Chapter 20.

»TWO TRUTHS AND A LIE: USING QUEUES

1. A queue is a FIFO structure.
2. The queue insert method is `Enqueue()` and the removal method is `Dequeue()`.
3. The `Queue Peek()` method removes an item from the bottom of the `Queue`.

The false statement is #3. The `Queue Peek()` method returns the first item from the top of a `Queue` without removing it.

USING TREES

Linked lists, stacks, and queues are **linear data structures**; that is, each node follows another in a line. A **tree** is a **nonlinear data structure** in which each node contains multiple self-referential links that branch to diverse paths; in other words, the logical paths follow multiple lines. You can picture a tree structure as an inverted "real" tree; its root is at the top, and **branches** extend downward. A node that has no further branches is a **leaf**. Although each tree node can contain any number of links, the most commonly used tree is a **binary tree**, in which each node contains two links. Each link in the root node of a binary tree refers to a **left child** or a **right child**. Figure 19-16 shows a binary tree.

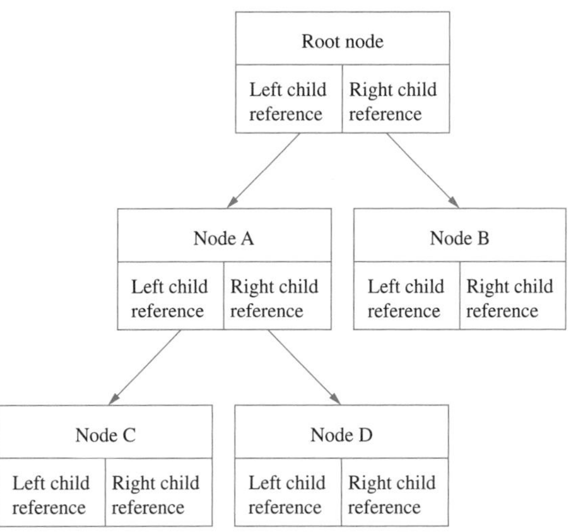

Figure 19-16 A binary tree

In the tree in Figure 19-16, the root node has a left child, Node A, and a right child, Node B. Node A also has left and right children—Nodes C and D, respectively. Nodes B, C, and D are leaves.

NOTE In Chapter 17, you learned that the metaphor of a tree also describes the structure of an XML document.

Programmers sometimes create binary trees in their programs because searching them is very fast. For example, consider the two structures of integers illustrated in Figure 19-17. These two illustrations represent two possible strategies when you play a game with a friend who says, "I am thinking of a number between 1 and 10. Guess what it is." Each time you guess an incorrect number, your friend will say "higher" or "lower" and give you another chance. In the diagrams in Figure 19-17, each node contains a possible number guess, and each link shows the path to the next guess depending on whether the clue giver says "higher" (H) or "lower" (L). If you use the guessing strategy on the left, the clue giver never says "lower."

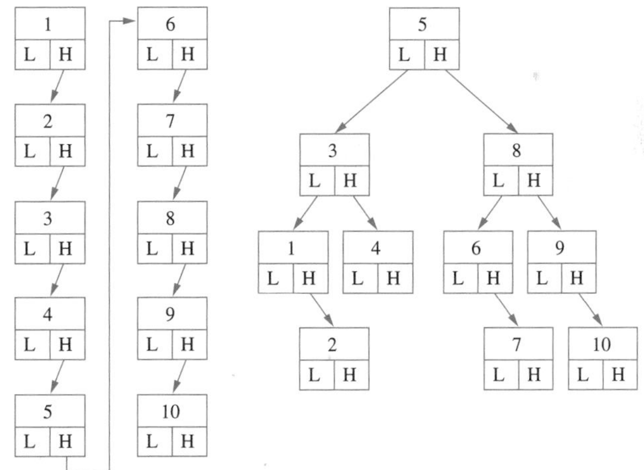

Figure 19-17 A linear tree and a binary tree that represent number-guessing strategies

NOTE Note that there are many more guessing strategies than those shown in Figure 19-17. For example, a player might start with 3. Figure 19-17 just shows one very inefficient sequence of guesses and one very efficient one.

Suppose the clue giver starts a game by thinking of 7. If you guess numbers in a linear fashion, as shown on the left side of Figure 19-17, you will need seven guesses to get the right answer. In other words, you will guess "1" and the clue giver will say "higher"; then you will guess "2" and the clue giver will say "higher" again, and so on.

Next, suppose you use the binary tree logic shown on the right side of Figure 19-17. You guess "5," the clue giver says "higher," you guess "8," the clue giver says "lower," you guess "6," the clue giver says "higher," and you finally guess "7." It took only four guesses, instead of seven, to get the right answer. In fact, for every number that the clue giver might select as the target number, except 1 and 2, you will always need fewer guesses using the binary tree method than the sequential method.

» NOTE In the You Do It exercises later in this chapter, you will create a program that proves the superiority of the binary tree search.

In business programs, you might use a binary tree to store any type of object. For example, you might store inventory items based on product numbers. When the program needs to find the price and description of an item, the program will usually find the data faster by making a series of decisions that follow a binary tree than by searching in a sequential fashion.

You can also use a dynamically created binary tree to simulate rudimentary artificial intelligence. Suppose you want to create a guessing game in which the player thinks of an animal and the computer tries to guess the animal. When the game begins, the computer "knows" just one question to ask ("Does the animal you are thinking of have legs?") and just two possible answers ("dog" and "fish"). Figure 19-18 shows two game executions.

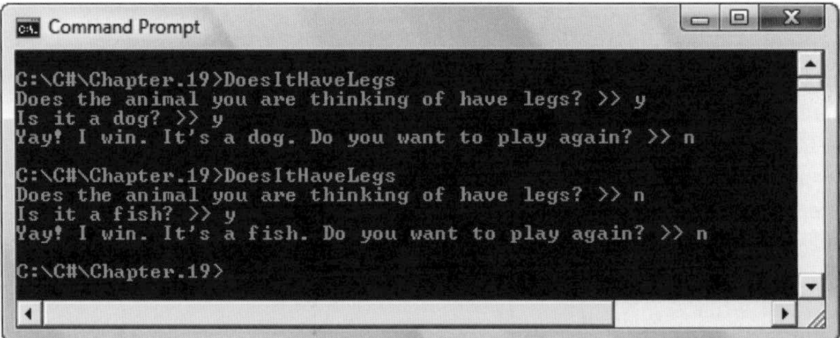

Figure 19-18 Two executions of the `DoesItHaveLegs` game

In both games in Figure 19-18, the computer guessed the player's secret animal. However, when the player chooses a different secret animal, the computer loses. Using a binary tree, you can make the computer continually become "smarter" by providing it with new information. If the player finishes a game and the computer has not guessed the correct animal, the player can "teach" the computer how to become more specific with its questions. For example, a typical game session might proceed as shown in Figure 19-19.

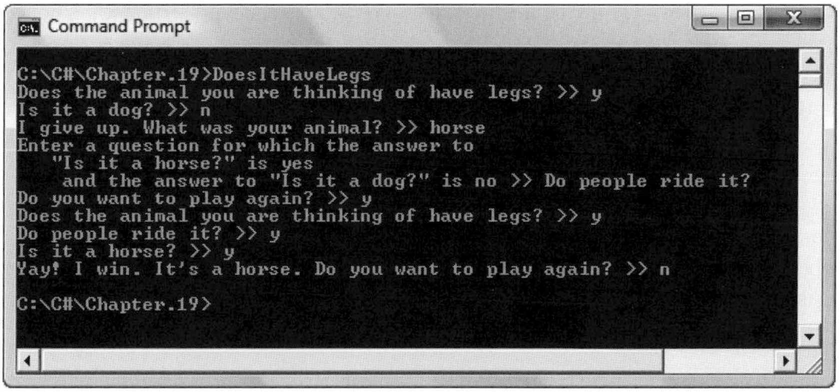

```
C:\C#\Chapter.19>DoesItHaveLegs
Does the animal you are thinking of have legs? >> y
Is it a dog? >> n
I give up. What was your animal? >> horse
Enter a question for which the answer to
   "Is it a horse?" is yes
    and the answer to "Is it a dog?" is no >> Do people ride it?
Do you want to play again? >> y
Does the animal you are thinking of have legs? >> y
Do people ride it? >> y
Is it a horse? >> y
Yay! I win. It's a horse. Do you want to play again? >> n

C:\C#\Chapter.19>
```

Figure 19-19 Typical execution of the `DoesItHaveLegs` program

As you can see in Figure 19-19, when the computer cannot guess the animal, it "gives up" and asks you to name the new animal. The computer also learns to differentiate between the animal it guesses and your secret choice by having you supply an appropriate yes-or-no question. When the computer guesses "dog" but your secret animal is "horse," you might enter an appropriate distinguishing question such as, "Do people ride it?" By teaching the computer one difference between "dog" and "horse," the computer knows more during the next game. For example, the next time you indicate that your secret animal has legs, the computer can ask an additional differentiating question such as "Do people ride it?" The computer can also make a more refined guess based on your answer—"Is it a horse?" or "Is it a dog?"

To use the `DoesItHaveLegs` program, you can define a `Node` class, as coded on the left side of Figure 19-20 and diagrammed on the right side. Each `Node` has a `Question`, an `Answer`, and two references: the `YesNode` and the `NoNode`. The reference links are used to point to the next two question-and-answer pairs—one or the other will be displayed depending on whether the answer to the current question is yes or no.

```
class Node
{
   public Node YesNode {get; set;}
   public string Question {get; set;}
   public string Answer {get; set;}
   public Node NoNode {get; set;}
}
```

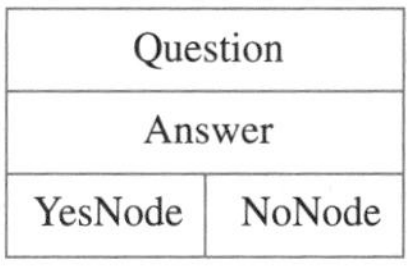

Question	
Answer	
YesNode	NoNode

Figure 19-20 The `Node` class

»NOTE In the `Node` class in Figure 19-20, the fields were not defined because they are not used in the class's methods. As you learned in Chapter 7, when you create auto-implemented properties like those shown in Figure 19-20, you do not need to explicitly declare the corresponding implied fields.

As the game progresses and new `Node` objects are inserted into a binary tree, each `Node` is one of two types:

» A question node is one that contains a question but no answer. This type of node is never the final `Node` in a branch. When this type of node is encountered, more questions should be asked. For example, the node that contains the "legs?" question is a question node.

» An answer node is one that contains an answer, but no question. It is the final node in a branch (in other words, it is a leaf). When this type of node is encountered, the computer must make a guess about the animal. For example, the nodes that contain "dog" and "fish" are answer nodes.

To write the DoesItHaveLegs guessing game program, you can create three nodes, as shown in Figure 19-21. First, a root node for the binary tree is created, and its question is set to "Does the animal you are thinking of have legs?" This node is a question node, so no answer is assigned for the root node. As is the case with all references that you define in classes, the unassigned Answer value is null by default.

```
Node root = new Node();
root.Question = "Does the animal you are thinking of have legs? >> ";
Node firstNo = new Node();
firstNo.Answer = "fish";
Node firstYes = new Node();
firstYes.Answer = "dog";
root.NoNode = firstNo;
root.YesNode = firstYes;
```

Figure 19-21 Defining start-up nodes for the DoesItHaveLegs guessing game

Besides the root node, two additional start-up Nodes are created in Figure 19-21. These are answer nodes. The firstNo Node is the Node that will be accessed if the player indicates the secret animal does *not* have legs; the computer's guess will be "fish." Similarly, the firstYes Node is the Node that will be accessed if the player indicates the secret animal *does* have legs; the computer's guess will be "dog." Because firstNo and firstYes hold animal Answer values, they do not hold Question values. By default, their Question values are null.

In Figure 19-21, the root Node's NoNode reference is set to point to the firstNo object, and the root Node's YesNode reference is set to point to the firstYes object. Figure 19-22 shows a diagram of the relationships created by the code in Figure 19-21.

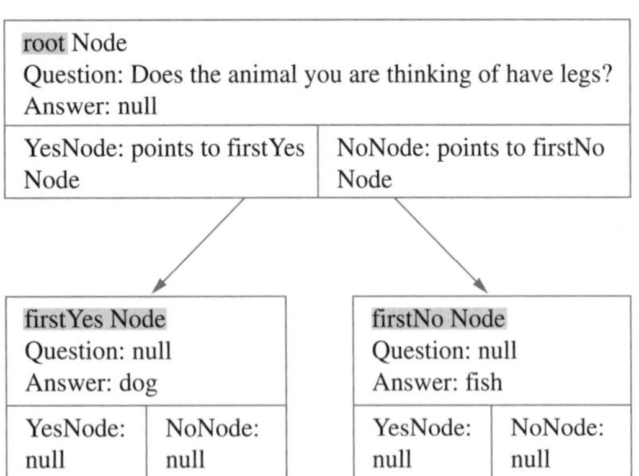

Figure 19-22 The root node, firstYes Node, and firstNo Node for the DoesItHaveLegs program

When a user begins to play the DoesItHaveLegs game, a current node is set to the root Node, the current Node is accessed, and its "legs" question is displayed. Because this question node has an `Answer` value of `null`, it is the last question in the series. In other words, the answer the computer will guess is stored either in the node pointed to by the current question's `YesNode` reference or in its `NoNode` reference.

When the player answers the "legs" question, the value of `current` is updated. If the player's answer to the "legs" question is yes, the `current` node becomes the `YesNode` associated with the "legs" question. If the player's answer is no, the `current` node becomes the `NoNode` associated with the "legs" question. Figure 19-23 shows the loop that contains this decision. While the `current` node is a question node, questions continue to be displayed. The loop ends when an answer node is encountered. For example, in the first round of the game, after the "legs" question, an answer node ("dog" or "fish") is encountered immediately.

```
current = root;
while(current.Answer == null)
{
   Console.Write("{0} >> ", current.Question);
   answer = Console.ReadLine();
   if(answer=="y")
      current = current.YesNode;
   else
      current = current.NoNode;
}
Console.Write("Is it a {0}? >> ", current.Answer);
answer = Console.ReadLine();
if(answer == "y")
   Console.Write("Yay! I win. It's a {0}. ", current.Answer);
else
   // Code that executes when computer's animal guess is incorrect
   // It prompts for a differentiating question
   // and assigns values to the current object's YesNode
   // and NoNode pointers
```

Figure 19-23 Decision that updates `current` node

When an answer node is encountered, the loop in Figure 19-23 ends and the computer displays a question in the form "Is it a __?", using the type of animal stored in the `current` object's `Answer` node. For example, when the player responds "y" to the "legs" question, the computer asks, "Is it a dog?"

If the player indicates that the computer has guessed the correct animal (by entering "y"), the game ends, and the user can choose to play again. However, if the computer has guessed the wrong animal, the computer prompts the player for a question that differentiates the user's animal from the `current` object's `Answer`.

For example, when the computer asks "Is it a dog?", but the player's secret animal was "horse," the computer prompts the player to enter a question that differentiates a horse from a dog. The question might be "Can you ride it?" or "Does it eat hay?" or "Does it most often live in a stable?"

Suppose the player indicates that the differentiating question should be "Can you ride it?" The results look like Figure 19-24. The `current Node` (the top shaded `Node` in the figure) held the `Answer` "dog" (which caused the "Is it a dog?" question), so "dog" becomes the `Answer` in a new `Node`, and the `current` object's `NoNode` is set to point to the new `Node`. The player's secret animal, "horse," is placed in the `Answer` of another new `Node`, and that `Node`'s reference is assigned to the current object's `YesNode`. (Each of these new `Node`s has no `Question` value assigned; they are answer nodes.) The current `Node` is no longer an answer node; it is no longer a final leaf on a branch of the tree. Instead, it becomes a question node. Its `Question` becomes the horse-dog differentiating question ("Do people ride it?"), and its `Answer` becomes `null`. Figure 19-25 shows the code that carries out the construction and assignment of the new `Node`s.

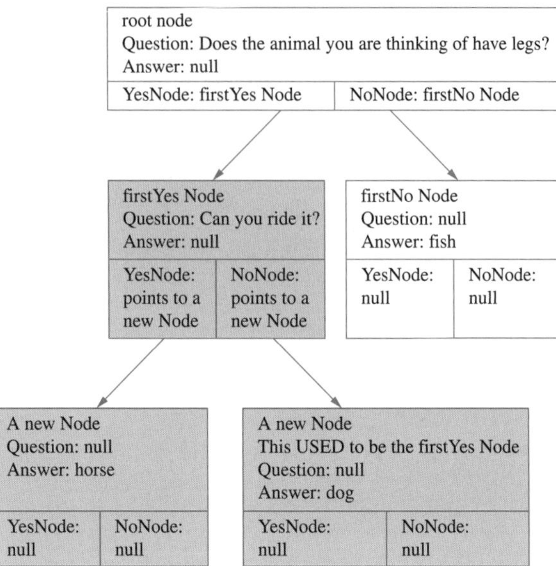

Figure 19-24 The tree after the user enters a differentiating question for horse and dog

```
Node newYesNode = new Node();
Node newNoNode = new Node();
Console.Write("I give up. What was your animal? >> ");
usersAnimal = Console.ReadLine();
Console.WriteLine("Enter a question for which the answer to");
Console.WriteLine("   \"Is it a {0}?\" is yes", usersAnimal);
Console.Write("    and the answer to \"Is it a {0}?\" is no >> ",
   current.Answer);
usersQuestion = Console.ReadLine();
newNoNode.Answer = current.Answer;
current.NoNode = newNoNode;
current.Question = usersQuestion;
current.Answer = null;
current.YesNode = newYesNode;
newYesNode.Answer = usersAnimal;
```

Figure 19-25 Assigning values to the tree's nodes after the computer makes an incorrect guess

If the player wants to continue the game, the process starts over. The player thinks of an animal, such as "gerbil." The `current Node` is set to restart the game using the first question "Does the animal you are thinking of have legs?" When the player answers "y", `current` is set to its own `YesNode` reference, and the player will be asked "Do people ride it?" When the player answers "n", `current` is set to its own `NoNode` reference, and the player is asked "Is it a dog?" When the player responds "n", the player is asked to provide the secret animal and a question that differentiates a gerbil and a dog. Figure 19-26 shows the complete program, and Figure 19-27 shows an extended game.

```
using System;
class DoesItHaveLegs
{
   public static void Main()
   {
      Node root = new Node();
      root.Question = "Does the animal you are thinking of have legs? >> ";
      Node firstNo = new Node();
      firstNo.Answer = "fish";
      Node firstYes = new Node();
      firstYes.Answer = "dog";
      root.NoNode = firstNo;
      root.YesNode = firstYes;
      Node current;
      bool wantsToPlay = true;
      string answer;
      string usersAnimal;
      string usersQuestion;
      while(wantsToPlay)
      {
         current = root;
         while(current.Answer == null)
         {
            Console.Write("{0} >> ", current.Question);
            answer = Console.ReadLine();
            if(answer=="y")
               current = current.YesNode;
            else
               current = current.NoNode;
         }
         Console.Write("Is it a {0}? >> ", current.Answer);
         answer = Console.ReadLine();
         if(answer == "y")
            Console.Write("Yay! I win. It's a {0}. ", current.Answer);
```

Figure 19-26 The `DoesItHaveLegs` program (*continued*)

```
            else
            {
               Node newYesNode = new Node();
               Node newNoNode = new Node();
               Console.Write("I give up. What was your animal? >> ");
               usersAnimal = Console.ReadLine();
               Console.WriteLine("Enter a question for which the answer to");
               Console.WriteLine("    \"Is it a {0}?\" is yes", usersAnimal);
               Console.Write("     and the answer to \"Is it a {0}?\" is no >> ",
                  current.Answer);
               usersQuestion = Console.ReadLine();
               newNoNode.Answer = current.Answer;
               current.NoNode = newNoNode;
               current.Question = usersQuestion;
               current.Answer = null;
               current.YesNode = newYesNode;
               newYesNode.Answer = usersAnimal;
            }
            Console.Write("Do you want to play again? >> ");
            answer = Console.ReadLine();
            if(answer != "y")
               wantsToPlay = false;
         }
      }
   }
```

Figure 19-26 (*continued*)

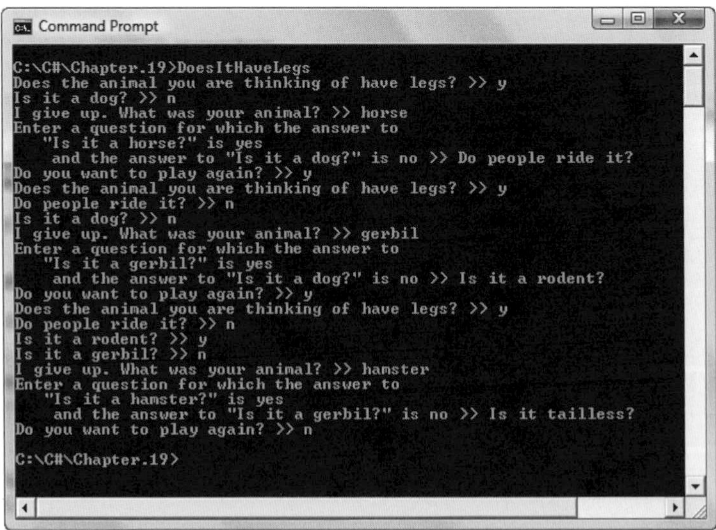

Figure 19-27 Long game session of `DoesItHaveLegs`

The tree stored within the `DoesItHaveLegs` program can continue to grow until no more computer memory is left for new nodes. With each animal that the computer fails to guess, it learns a new differentiating question to add to the logical tree. You could write a game program similar to "Does it have legs?" without using a self-referential class in a binary tree, but understanding these topics makes the logic much simpler to comprehend.

»TWO TRUTHS AND A LIE: USING TREES

1. Linked lists, stacks, and queues are nonlinear data structures.
2. In a tree, each node contains multiple self-referential links that branch to diverse paths.
3. Each link in a node of a binary tree refers to a left child and a right child.

The false statement is #1. A tree is a nonlinear data structure, but linked lists, stacks, and queues are linear data structures.

YOU DO IT

CREATING A SIMULATION USING A QUEUE

In a bank, customers waiting in line for a teller operate as a queue; that is, the first person in line is the first one to leave the line after being served. In the next steps, you will create a simulation for a bank. The bank officials want to know how long customers must wait in line before a teller serves them.

To create an application that simulates a waiting line:

1. Open a new file in your text editor and type the first few lines of a class that will simulate waiting time in a queue.

```
using System;
using System.Collections;
public class WaitingTime
{
   public static void Main()
   {
      Queue aQueue = new Queue();
```

2. The simulation requires some assumptions. Assume that you want the simulation to run for 10 minutes of a teller's open-window time. Assume that a random number of customers from none to four might join the waiting line in any minute, and that it takes a teller one minute to serve a customer. Also assume that after the simulation period finishes, the line waiting for the teller will be closed, but any customers already in line will be served. Declare some constants and variables for these factors. The variable `customerBeingServed` will hold the minute during which a customer enters the line; this variable can be subtracted from the current minute when the customer is served to calculate `timeWaited`.

Each customer's `timeWaited` value is added to `totalTime` so that an average waiting time can be calculated at the end of the simulation.

```
const int MINUTES = 10;
const int CUSTS = 4;
Random RandomClass = new Random();
int random;
int minute;
int customerBeingServed;
int timeWaited;
double totalTime = 0;
```

3. Execute a loop for the number of minutes designated for the simulation. Within the loop, obtain a random number of customers entering the line in that minute. Send the queue, the number of customers, and the minute the customer enters the line to a method that adds customers to the line.

```
for(minute = 1; minute < MINUTES; ++minute)
{
   random = RandomClass.Next(0, CUSTS);
   AddCustomersToQueue(aQueue, random, minute);
```

4. Continuing within the `for` loop, display the current minute. Then, if at least one customer is in the queue, remove the customer's minute of entry from the queue and calculate the time waited. Display the waiting time and add it to a total so an average can be calculated at the end of the simulation.

```
Console.WriteLine("Minute {0}", minute);
if(aQueue.Count != 0)
{
   customerBeingServed = (int)aQueue.Dequeue();
   timeWaited = minute - customerBeingServed;
   Console.WriteLine("   Customer being served waited {0} minutes",
      timeWaited);
   totalTime += timeWaited;
}
```

5. Display the number of customers left in line, and end the `for` loop with a curly brace.

```
   Console.WriteLine("   Customers in line: {0}", aQueue.Count);
}
```

6. At the end of the simulation, display the number of customers left in line. Assume that the line is then closed, but that the remaining customers will be served. While the queue's `Count` property remains greater than 0, remove a customer from the line, calculate the waiting customer's time in line, display it, add it to the total time, and increase the time

needed after the line has closed. When the queue is empty, calculate and display the average waiting time for the customers who were served. Add a closing curly brace for the `Main()` method.

```
    Console.WriteLine("At end of simulation");
    Console.WriteLine("there are {0} customers in line", aQueue.Count);
    while(aQueue.Count != 0)
    {
       customerBeingServed = (int)aQueue.Dequeue();
       timeWaited = minute - customerBeingServed;
       Console.WriteLine("   Customer being served waited {0} minutes",
          timeWaited);
       totalTime += timeWaited;
       minute++;
    }
    totalTime += aQueue.Count;
    Console.WriteLine("Average customer waited {0} minutes",
       totalTime / minute);
}
```

7. Write the `AddCustomersToQueue()` method. It enqueues as many customers as indicated by the randomly generated number. The minute the customer entered the line is stored in the queue so that it can be retrieved later and subtracted from the current time. The difference will indicate how long the customer waited. Also display a message that indicates the number of customers added during the current minute so that you can better follow the output of the simulation. After the closing brace for the method, add a closing brace for the class.

```
    public static void AddCustomersToQueue(Queue aQ, int ran,
       int minute)
    {
       for(int x = 0; x < ran; ++x)
          aQ.Enqueue(minute);
       Console.WriteLine("   {0} customers added to line", ran);
    }
}
```

8. Save the file as **WaitingTime.cs**. Compile and execute the program several times. A typical execution looks like Figure 19-28. Experiment with the values for the duration of the simulation and the number of customers entering the line. Observe the results.

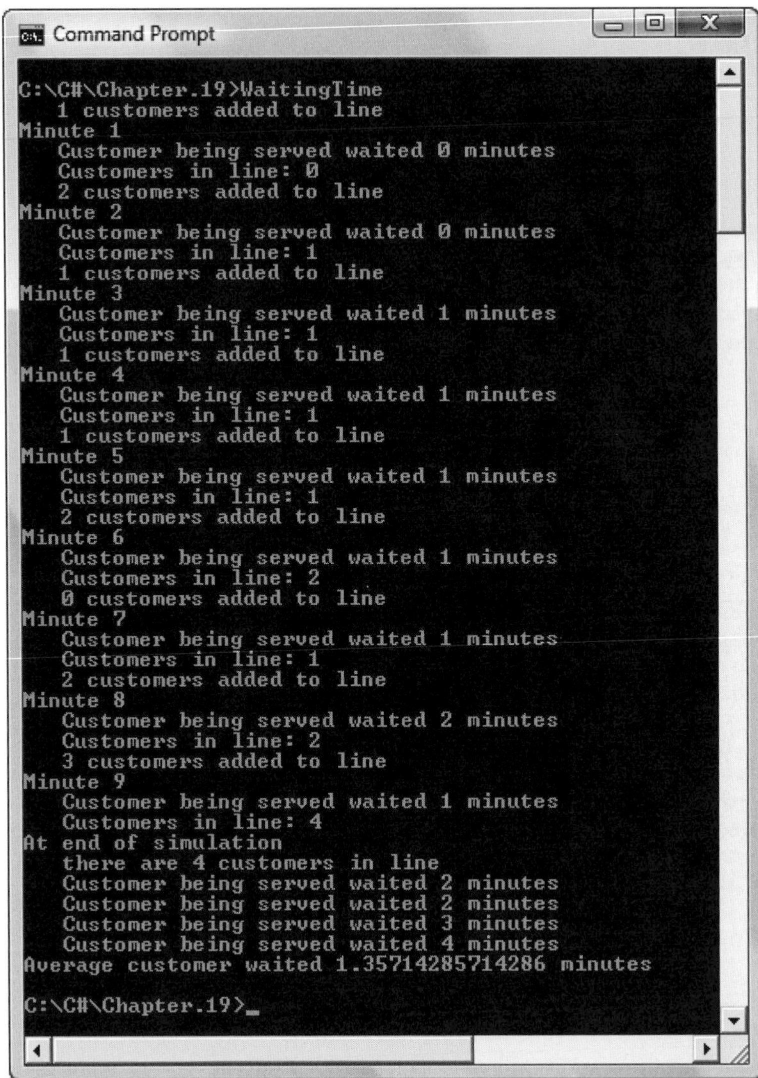

Figure 19-28 Typical execution of the `WaitingTime` application

COMPARING BINARY TREE AND SEQUENTIAL SEARCHES

In the next steps, you will prove that searching a binary tree is faster than searching a sequential list by running random trials with each structure type. First, you will create a `NumberNode` class to provide a self-referential object for both list types, and then you will write a program that creates two list types and compares the average number of attempts it takes to find a randomly generated number in each list.

To create a `NumberNode` class:

1. Open a new file in your text editor and create a `NumberNode` class as follows:

```
using System;
class NumberNode
{
   public NumberNode LowerNode {get; set;}
   public int Number {get; set;}
   public NumberNode HigherNode {get; set;}
   public NumberNode(int n, NumberNode left, NumberNode right)
   {
      Number = n;
      LowerNode = left;
      HigherNode = right;
   }
}
```

   The class contains properties that hold an integer `Number` and links to both a higher and lower node of the same type. The constructor requires all three values as parameters.

2. Start the `TreeVsList` class that creates the tree illustrated in Figure 19-29. Create nodes for `NumberNode`s 2, 7, and 10, as shown at the bottom of the figure. Each of these nodes contains a number and is a leaf. That is, none of these nodes link to any further nodes.

```
public class TreeVsList
{
   public static void Main()
   {
      NumberNode bnode2 = new NumberNode(2, null, null);
      NumberNode bnode7 = new NumberNode(7, null, null);
      NumberNode bnode10 = new NumberNode(10, null, null);
```

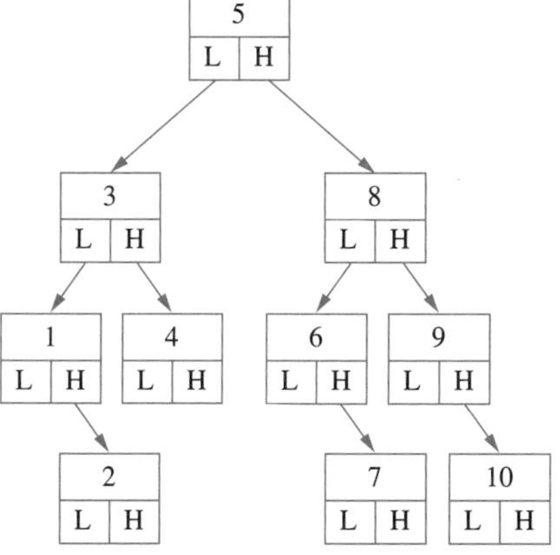

Figure 19-29 The tree for the guessing game

3. Create the next level of `NumberNode`s for nodes 1, 4, 6, and 9.

```
NumberNode bnode1 = new NumberNode(1, null, bnode2);
NumberNode bnode4 = new NumberNode(4, null, null);
NumberNode bnode6 = new NumberNode(6, null, bnode7);
NumberNode bnode9 = new NumberNode(9, null, bnode10);
```

4. Create the last three nodes for numbers 3, 8, and 5.

```
NumberNode bnode3 = new NumberNode(3, bnode1, bnode4);
NumberNode bnode8 = new NumberNode(8, bnode6, bnode9);
NumberNode bnode5 = new NumberNode(5, bnode3, bnode8);
```

5. Send the starting node for the binary tree and a string that represents the list type to a method you will write named `MakeGuesses()`, as follows:

```
MakeGuesses(bnode5, "binary tree");
```

6. Next, for comparison, create a sequential guessing list as shown in Figure 19-30.

```
NumberNode snode10 = new NumberNode(10, null, null);
NumberNode snode9 = new NumberNode(9, null, snode10);
NumberNode snode8 = new NumberNode(8, null, snode9);
NumberNode snode7 = new NumberNode(7, null, snode8);
NumberNode snode6 = new NumberNode(6, null, snode7);
NumberNode snode5 = new NumberNode(5, null, snode6);
NumberNode snode4 = new NumberNode(4, null, snode5);
NumberNode snode3 = new NumberNode(3, null, snode4);
NumberNode snode2 = new NumberNode(2, null, snode3);
NumberNode snode1 = new NumberNode(1, null, snode2);
```

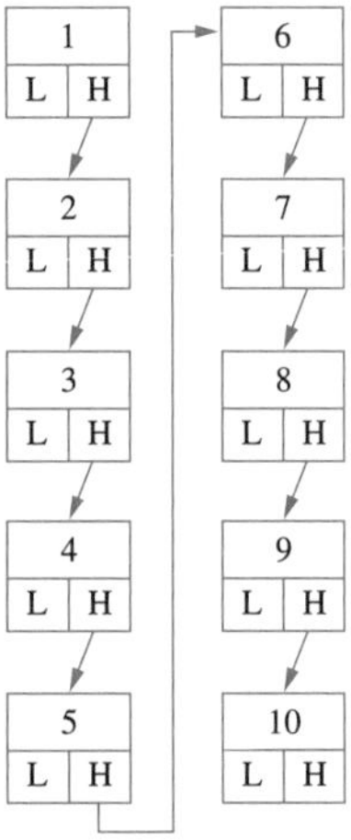

Figure 19-30 A sequential list for the guessing game

7. Add a call to the `MakeGuesses()` method, send it the starting node for the sequential tree, and send a description. Then end the `Main()` method with a closing brace.

```
    MakeGuesses(snode1, "sequential tree");
}
```

8. Start the `MakeGuesses()` method as follows. The method accepts a starting node and a string. Declare the variables and constants you will need to create a random number. This number will be 10 or less and used for 1,000 guesses. Also declare variables to hold the number of guesses needed in each round, the total number of guesses in 1,000 trials, and the average number of guesses it takes to find each randomly selected value.

```
public static void MakeGuesses(NumberNode curr, string listType)
{
   Random RandomClass = new Random();
   int randomNumber;
   const int MAX = 10;
   const int TIMES = 1000;
   int guesses;
   int totalGuesses = 0;
   double average;
```

9. Add a loop that executes 1,000 times. Within the loop, generate a random number and then find it in the list. To find a number, you set a current reference to the first object in the list, set the `guesses` to 1, and while the number is not found, add 1 to the number of guesses made and upgrade the current `NumberNode` to the next level. When the random number is found, add the number of guesses needed to the total number of guesses made for all 1,000 trials.

```
for(int x = 0; x < TIMES; ++x)
{
   randomNumber = RandomClass.Next(1, MAX);
   NumberNode current = curr;
   guesses = 1;
   while(randomNumber != current.Number)
   {
      ++guesses;
      if(randomNumber < current.Number)
         current = current.LowerNode;
      else
         current = current.HigherNode;
   }
   totalGuesses += guesses;
}
```

10. Compute the average number of guesses for the list type, display the results, and add closing braces for the method and the class.

```
      average = (double)totalGuesses / TIMES;
      Console.WriteLine("Using a {0}, the random number", listType);
      Console.WriteLine("   was guessed on average in {0} guesses",
         average);
   }
}
```

11. Save the file as **TreeVsList.cs**. Compile and execute it several times. Figure 19-31 shows three typical executions. Although the number of average guesses varies based on the specific random numbers generated in each trial, the outcome is fairly consistent. It takes fewer than three guesses on average to reach a match for the random number using the binary tree list, but it takes about five guesses to reach the random number using the sequential list.

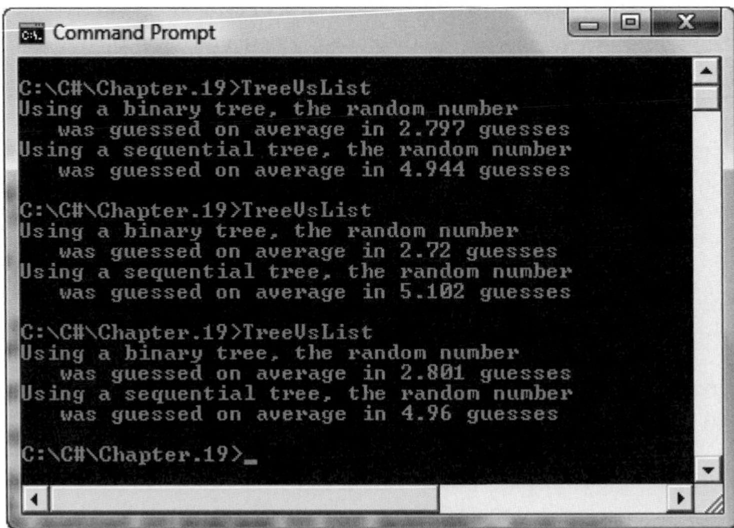

Figure 19-31 Three executions of the `TreeVsList` program

CHAPTER SUMMARY

» A class is a reference type and a `struct` is a value type. Each simple, intrinsic data type, such as `int`, has a corresponding `struct` in the `System` namespace that declares the simple type. Boxing is the process of assigning a value type to an `object` class reference; unboxing is the process of converting an object reference into a simple type.

» A self-referential class contains a reference to an object of the same type. Self-referential objects can be linked to make useful structures. When you maintain a sequence of self-referential objects instead of using an array to store them, you run out of room only when the computer's memory is physically exhausted; it is also easier to insert new objects into a list than into an array.

» A linked list is a sequence of objects that are connected by references. Each object in a linked list is a node. When you use a linked list in a program, you typically use references in each object to access the succeeding object. The technique of setting a variable reference is useful for traversing any list that is connected by references.

» Dynamic memory allocation is the allotment of new memory during a program's execution. When you want to insert a new object in a linked list, a new memory location must be assigned for the object using the `new` operator. A linked list might be singly linked, doubly linked, or circular. Understanding linked lists is useful to help you understand stacks and queues.

» A stack is a specialized form of linked list in which nodes are added or removed only from the top of the list; it is a last-in first-out (LIFO) data structure. The primary operations to manipulate a stack are push, pop, and peek.

- A queue is a form of linked list in which nodes are inserted at the end but removed from the beginning; it is a first-in first-out (FIFO) data structure. The queue insert operation is enqueue and the removal operation is dequeue.
- A tree is a data structure in which each node contains multiple self-referential links. The node at the top of the structure is the root, and branches extend downward. A node that has no further branches is a leaf. A binary tree is one in which each node contains two links. Each link in the root node of a binary tree refers to a left child and a right child. Binary trees are sometimes built in computer programs because searching them is very fast.

KEY TERMS

A **`struct`** is a C# data type that is similar to a class; a `struct` is typically used to encapsulate small groups of related values.

Boxing is the process of assigning a value's data type to an `object` reference.

Unboxing is the process of converting an `object` reference into a simple type.

A **self-referential class** contains a reference to an object of the same type.

A **linked list** is a sequence of objects that are connected by references.

A **node** is an object in a linked list.

Dynamic memory allocation is the allotment of new memory during a program's execution.

A **singly linked list** begins with a reference to the first node, and each node contains a reference to a single next node; the list ends when a node's link is `null`.

A **circular, singly linked list** begins with a reference to the first node; each node contains a reference to a single next node, and the last node holds a reference to the first node.

In a **doubly linked list**, each node contains two references: one to the next element and one to the previous element.

In a **circular, doubly linked list**, each node contains two references: one to the next element and one to the previous element. Also, the first node's previous reference points to the last object in the list and the last node's next reference points to the first object in the list.

A **stack** is a specialized form of linked list in which nodes are added or removed only from the top of the list.

In a **last-in first-out (LIFO)** data structure, the last item added is the first item removed.

To **push** an object is to add a new node to the top of a stack.

To **pop** an object is to remove it from a stack.

To **peek** at an object is to examine it without removing it from a list, stack, or queue.

A **queue** is a form of linked list in which nodes are inserted at the end but removed from the beginning.

In a **first-in first-out (FIFO)** data structure, the first item added is the first one removed.

Enqueue is the queue insert operation.

Dequeue is the queue removal operation.

Linear data structures are those in which each node is linked to another in a line.

A **tree** is a nonlinear data structure in which each node contains multiple self-referential links.

In a **nonlinear data structure**, each node contains multiple self-referential links that branch to diverse paths.

Branches are the paths of a tree structure created by its logical links.

A **leaf** is a node that has no further branches.

In a **binary tree** structure, each node contains two links.

A **left child** is one of the nodes to which a parent node in a binary tree links.

A **right child** is one of the nodes to which a parent node in a binary tree links.

REVIEW QUESTIONS

1. Which of the following is true of `struct`s and classes?

   a. A `struct` is a reference type, but a class is a value type.

   b. When you assign one `struct` to another, a copy is made.

   c. You can inherit from a `struct`, but not from a class.

   d. There are classes in the `System` namespace, but not `struct`s.

2. Assume that you have declared a variable as `double money = 12.34;` and an `object` as `object1`. Which of the following would perform boxing?

   a. `object1 = (double) money;`

   b. `object1 = money;`

   c. `object1 = (object)money;`

   d. all of the above

3. Assume that you have declared a variable as `double money = 43.21;` and an `object` as `object2`. Which of the following would perform unboxing?

   a. `money = (double)object2;`

   b. `money = (object)object2;`

   c. `object2 = (double)money;`

   d. `object2 = money;`

4. A class that contains a reference to an object of the same type is __________.

   a. a `struct`

   b. an unboxed class

   c. a self-referential class

   d. illegal in C#

5. Which of the following is an advantage to using an array to store a list instead of using a list of self-referential objects?
   a. An array has no fixed size, so it is more flexible.
   b. With an array, you never run out of room.
   c. With an array, you can easily insert new objects without making copies of them.
   d. It is more efficient to process array objects sequentially.

6. Which of the following is most likely to waste storage space?
   a. an array in an application when you do not know in advance how many objects will be stored
   b. an array in an application when you know in advance how many objects will be stored
   c. a list of self-referential objects when you do not know in advance how many objects will be stored
   d. a list of self-referential objects when you know in advance how many objects will be stored

7. Assume that you have a list of self-referential objects stored in numeric order based on a key field. When you insert a new object into the list, what must you do?
   a. Copy two objects.
   b. Change two references.
   c. Copy an object and change one reference.
   d. Copy an object and change two references.

8. Each object in a linked list is a __________ .
   a. nuance
   b. reference
   c. node
   d. branch

9. When you use a linked list in a program, you typically __________ .
   a. maintain a reference to the first object
   b. use each object's link to access the next object
   c. both of the above
   d. none of the above

10. Most links in nodes in functional linked lists __________ .
    a. hold a reference to an object of the same type
    b. hold `null`
    c. are value types
    d. are reference types of a parent class of the current type

11. The allotment of new memory during a program's execution is __________ memory allocation.
    a. static
    b. object-oriented
    c. dynamic
    d. vigorous

12. The basic logic to adding a second object to a linked list that already contains a first object includes which of the following steps?

    a. Allocate memory for the new second object.

    b. Set the new second object's link to point to the first object.

    c. Set the first object's link to `null`.

    d. all of the above

13. In which of the following linked lists does each node have one reference that points to the next node, and the last node's reference points to the first node?

    a. noncircular, singly linked list
    b. circular, singly linked list
    c. noncircular, doubly linked list
    d. circular, doubly linked list

14. Which of the following is a specialized form of linked list in which nodes are added or removed only from the top?

    a. pile
    b. heap
    c. stack
    d. queue

15. A __________ is a FIFO structure.

    a. stack
    b. queue
    c. both of the above
    d. none of the above

16. The queue-related term that is closest in meaning to push is __________.

    a. peek
    b. pop
    c. dequeue
    d. enqueue

17. The queue-related term that is closest in meaning to pop is __________.

    a. peek
    b. push
    c. dequeue
    d. enqueue

18. A tree in which each node has just two children is a __________.

    a. branched tree
    b. binary tree
    c. queue
    d. stack

19. In a tree structure, a node with no branches extending from it is a __________.

    a. leaf
    b. nodette
    c. root
    d. folio

20. Which of the following is a major advantage to using a tree structure, but not an advantage to using a linked list?

    a. You can store references in a tree.

    b. You can mix the data types stored in a tree.

    c. Searching a tree for a specified object is very fast.

    d. Tree memory is dynamically allocated.

EXERCISES

1. Employees are frequently hired and fired on a LIFO basis; in other words, the employee hired last is the first one to be dismissed when layoffs are required. Create an `Employee` class that contains data for a last name and pay rate, and include a `ToString()` method to return a string that contains employee data. Write an application that contains a `Stack` in which to store employee objects. Prompt the user to enter employee data in chronological order by hire date; any number of employees can be entered until the user types a sentinel value. Then ask the user how many employees need to be dismissed. If the user enters a number that is greater than the number of employees in the list, display an error message. Otherwise, display the data for employees who must be dismissed. Save the application as **HireAndFire.cs**.

2. a. Open the `AddStudentsToLinkedList` program stored on your Student Disk and displayed in Figure 19-8 in this chapter. Modify the program so that when a user enters an ID number for a new student that is lower than any existing ID number, the new `Student` is still inserted into the correct position in the list and the program continues to function as expected. Save the file as **AddStudentsToLinkedList2.cs**.

    b. Modify the `AddStudentsToLinkedList2` program created in Exercise 2a so that no duplicate `Student` ID numbers are allowed. Save the file as **AddStudentsToLinkedList3.cs**.

3. You can access your computer's current system time using the `DateTime` class and the `Now` property. For example, the following statement stores the current system time in a variable named `time`:

    ```
    DateTime time = DateTime.Now;
    ```

    You can subtract `DateTime` objects to find their difference, and you can use the `TotalMilliseconds` property of the resulting `DateTime` object to convert the time difference to milliseconds.

    Create a program that includes an array of 20 integers. Load the integers into a stack. Display the integers from the array in reverse order and display the integers as they are popped from the stack. Calculate and display the difference in the amount of time needed for those operations. Save the application as **ArrayVsStackTime.cs**. Execute the program several times and notice the values that are displayed.

4. Create a simulation for a grocery store. Assume that the store has two checkout queues, that any number of customers from none to seven might be ready to check out while one customer is being served, and that it takes two minutes to check a customer out. Assume that each customer will always choose the shortest queue available. Display a record of customer activity in each queue for a 30-minute period. Display a message any time the clerks for both queues are idle. At the end of the program, display the average customer wait time. Save the file as **CheckOutLine.cs**.

5. Write a program that accepts a string from a user and determines whether it is a palindrome. A palindrome is a string that reads the same forward or backward. For example, the words "did," "eye," and "racecar" are palindromes. To determine whether a string is a palindrome, insert all the characters from the first half of the string into a stack (ignoring the middle character in strings with an odd number of letters), and all the characters from the second half into a queue (again, ignoring a middle character if there is one). If each character removed from the stack matches each character removed from the queue in order, the result is a palindrome. Save the file as **PalindromeTester.cs**.

DEBUGGING EXERCISES

Each of the following files in the Chapter.19 folder on your Student Disk has syntax and/or logical errors. In each case, determine the problem and fix the program. After you correct the errors, save each file using the same filename preceded with *Fixed*. For example, save DebugNineteen1.cs as **FixedDebugNineteen1.cs**.

a. DebugNineteen1.cs

b. DebugNineteen2.cs

c. DebugNineteen3.cs

d. DebugNineteen4.cs

UP FOR DISCUSSION

1. An exercise in this chapter mentioned that employees are frequently hired and laid off on a LIFO basis. Describe some other everyday situations in which LIFO is used.
2. Describe some everyday situations in which tree structures are used.

CHAPTER TWENTY

20

GENERICS

In this chapter you will:

Understand the usefulness of generics
Create generic methods
Understand the compiler's role in creating generic methods
Use multiple type parameters
Overload generic methods
Understand the need for type constraints and how to use them
Create generic classes
Use built-in generic classes

Object-oriented programming provides many benefits compared to traditional procedural programming. You have already used concepts such as inheritance and polymorphism that make a programmer's task easier. In this chapter, you will learn how to create generics. Understanding generics will make some future programming tasks easier because you will learn some techniques that promote code reusability. Generics allow you to define type-safe data structures without being committed to use specific data types with them.

UNDERSTANDING THE USEFULNESS OF GENERICS

You learned to use variables when you first learned about C#. The concepts involved in the use of variables are basic to all programming languages, and the use of variable names makes programming manageable. If a program should process 1000 employee records, you don't need 1000 different variable names to hold the salaries. When you can label a computer memory location with a variable name such as `employeeSalary`, the variable can contain any number of unique values, one at a time, during each execution of the program that declares it.

Similarly, creating methods within programs is a helpful feature because methods can hold a single set of instructions that can operate on any values passed to them (as long as the values are of the correct type). A method that has the header `void compute(int aNum)` can receive any integer value, whether it is an unnamed constant (such as 15 or –2), a value stored in another integer variable, or a value in a named constant in the calling method. You can call the `compute()` method dozens of times from various locations in a program, and it can receive dozens of different integer values. Each integer value, however, will have the identifier `aNum` within the `compute()` method.

In your C# programs, you have created many methods with a variety of types in their parameter lists. Not only have you used scalar types such as `int`, `double`, and `char` in method parameter lists, you have also passed programmer-created class objects, such as `Student`s or `InventoryItem`s. In each case, the C# compiler determined the method's parameter types when the method was compiled. In your programs to this point, once a method was created, its parameter types remained fixed.

In Chapter 19, you learned about some data structures that manipulate `object` references. For example, `Stack`s and `Queue`s hold `object` references, allowing any data type to be stored. This can be an advantage because once you learn to use `Stack` and `Queue` structures, you can use them to hold `int`s, `double`s, `string`s, `Student`s, `InventoryItem`s, or any other data type. If the creators of C# had not made `Stack`s and `Queue`s to hold `object`s, they could have made many specific structures with names such as `IntegerStack`, `DoubleStack`, and so on, and you would have had to write your own code to manipulate `StudentStack`s or `InventoryItemStack`s.

There are some inconveniences to using structures that hold `object`s. For example, when a `Student` or `InventoryItem` object is removed from a `Stack` or a `Queue`, you usually need to downcast it from an `object` so that you can use the methods that are part of the appropriate class. Similarly, when a primitive type such as an `int` or `double` is added to a `Stack` or `Queue`, it must be boxed, and when it is removed it must be unboxed before it can be used. Both downcasting and unboxing require extra processing time. Additionally, when all the items in a structure are cast as `objects`, there is no compile-time safety. **Compile-time safety** is the compiler feature that provides for detecting mismatches of data types when a program is compiled.

Generics provide a compromise between the flexibility of creating methods and classes that can handle any object type and the safety of checking for correct data types. When you understand generics, you can create classes and methods that work with any data type but that still provide compile-time type checking. In other words, generic classes and methods are flexible, reusable, and type safe without compromising a program's performance.

»TWO TRUTHS AND A LIE: UNDERSTANDING THE USEFULNESS OF GENERICS

1. Generic classes and methods are more flexible than nongeneric ones.
2. Generic classes and methods do not provide type safety, but nongeneric ones do.
3. Generic classes and methods are easier to reuse than nongeneric ones.

The false statement is #2. Generic classes and methods provide type safety while nongeneric ones do not.

CREATING GENERIC METHODS

You have learned that you can overload a method to accept different parameter lists. Overloading is a form of polymorphism—using a consistent message that acts appropriately with different objects. For example, you might want to create several methods named `Reverse()`. A `Reverse()` method might change the sign of a number if a numeric variable is passed to it, reverse the order of characters in a string if a string is passed to it, set a code to make a `PhoneCall` object a collect call if a `PhoneCall` is passed to it, or issue a refund to a customer if a `Customer` class object is passed to it. Because "Reverse" makes sense in each of these instances, and because such diverse tasks are needed for the four cases of `Reverse()`, overloading is a useful and appropriate tool. When the method name is the same, but the program logic is different depending on the argument sent to the method, the ability to overload methods is a valuable asset.

»NOTE Recall that overloading a method involves writing two or more methods with the same name but different parameter lists. You first overloaded methods in Chapter 6.

Sometimes the tasks required are not so diverse, however, and overloading methods requires a lot of unnecessary, tedious coding. When the programming logic is the same, writing multiple overloaded methods becomes wearisome. For example, assume you need a simple method named `DisplayData()` that displays data in a standardized format using the word "Data" and a colon preceding each data item. Figure 20-1 shows three overloaded versions of the `DisplayData()` method. Each has a different parameter list so you can call the method with an `int`, `double`, or `Student` argument.

```
static void DisplayData(int data)
{
   Console.WriteLine("Data: {0}", data);
}
static void DisplayData(double data)
{
   Console.WriteLine("Data: {0}", data);
}
static void DisplayData(Student data)
{
   Console.WriteLine("Data: {0}", data);
}
```

Figure 20-1 Three overloaded versions of `DisplayData()`

The three method bodies in Figure 20-1 differ only in the shaded parameter type used in each method, so it would be convenient to write just one method with a variable name standing in for the type, as in Figure 20-2. Such a method is a **generic method** because it works with multiple data types. A generic method uses a **parameterized type**—a data type that is determined by a parameter. The code in Figure 20-2 shows a generic method with a shaded `variableType` where the type belongs. Although it demonstrates a good idea, the method in Figure 20-2 doesn't quite work in C#. To make it work, you need to include a type parameter list.

»NOTE Later in this chapter, you will learn that generic classes also employ parameterized data types.

```
static void DisplayData(variableType data)
{
   Console.WriteLine("Data: {0}", data);
}
```

»DON'T DO IT You need to replace `variableType` with a type parameter list before this example will compile.

Figure 20-2 Proposed, but incomplete, `variableType` method

A **type parameter list** is a list of generic data types contained between angle brackets that follows a generic method's name. (If multiple generic types are used by a method, their names are separated by commas.) Each type parameter in the list is represented by an identifier that is used in place of actual type names. For example, Figure 20-3 shows a working `DisplayData()` method that includes a shaded type parameter list. The type parameter list indicates that the identifier `T` can stand for any data type. Therefore, when `T` is used between the parentheses in the method's parameter list to describe `data`, it might be an `int`, `double`, `Student`, or any other data type. The only requirement is that the data type passed to the method works with all the statements coded within the method. In this case, because `data` is displayed as part of a string, any data type will work because every data type either inherits the `ToString()` method from the `object` class or contains its own overriding version.

```
static void DisplayData<T>(T data)
{
   Console.WriteLine("Data: {0}", data);
}
```

Figure 20-3 Generic `DisplayData()` method

The generic data type identifier for a generic method can be any legal C# identifier. However, by convention, it is usually a single uppercase letter. Many programmers use `T` to stand for "type."

Figure 20-4 shows a `Student` class. Each `Student` contains an ID number and name, values for which are both required by the constructor. The `ToString()` method is overloaded so that `Students` produce useful output in a `WriteLine()` method call.

```
public class Student
{
   public int IdNumber {get; set;}
   public string Name {get; set;}
   public Student(int id, string name)
   {
      IdNumber = id;
      Name = name;
   }
   public override string ToString()
   {
      return("Student #" + IdNumber + " " + Name);
   }
}
```

Figure 20-4 The `Student` class

Figure 20-5 contains a program that demonstrates that an `int`, a `double`, and a `Student` can all use the same generic `DisplayData()` method. Figure 20-6 shows the output.

```
using System;
public class GenericMethodDemo
{
   public static void Main()
   {
      int x = 14;
      double y = 1.732;
      Student stu = new Student(882,"Boris");
      DisplayData(x);
      DisplayData(y);
      DisplayData(stu);
   }
   static void DisplayData<T>(T data)
   {
      Console.WriteLine("Data: {0}", data);
   }
}
```

Figure 20-5 The `GenericMethodDemo` class

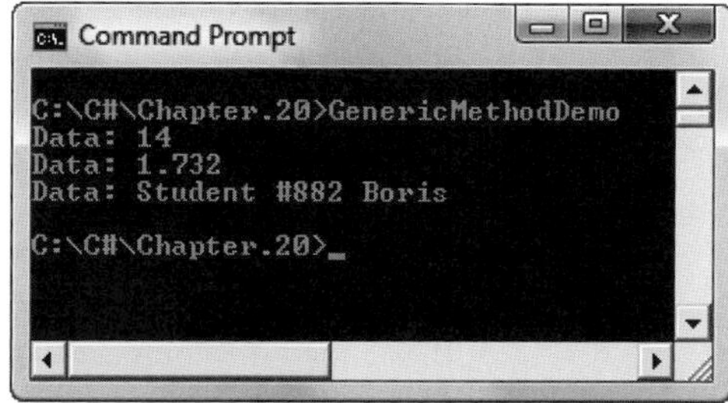

Figure 20-6 Output of the `GenericMethodDemo` program

Creating the generic `DisplayData()` method in the `GenericMethodDemo` program in Figure 20-5 provides several advantages:

- Your work is reduced because you do not have to code a separate method for each data type.
- You eliminate the possibility that some data types will be displayed in an invalid format due to typographical errors. For example, consider how easy it would be to incorrectly insert an extra space into the display of one data type if you had to code several versions of the `DisplayData()` method.
- When the method must be revised, perhaps because your organization decides to replace the colon with a dash, only one revision must be made, reducing the amount of work and eliminating the chance of introducing inconsistencies.

»TWO TRUTHS AND A LIE: CREATING GENERIC METHODS

1. A generic method uses a parameterized type, which is a data type that is determined by a parameter.
2. A type parameter list is a list of data types contained between the parentheses in a method header.
3. An advantage to creating generic methods is that it is easier to revise a single generic method than multiple overloaded versions of the method.

The false statement is #2. A type parameter list is a list of generic data types contained between angle brackets that follows a generic method's name.

UNDERSTANDING THE COMPILER'S ROLE IN CREATING GENERIC METHODS

In Chapter 1, you learned how to compile and execute your first C# programs. There you learned that after you write and save a program, two more steps must be performed before you can produce output:

1. You must compile the program you wrote (called the source code) into intermediate language (IL).
2. The C# just in time (JIT) compiler must translate the intermediate code into executable code.

»NOTE Executable code for a specific processor is also called *native code.*

In other words, when you compile a C# program, your source code is translated into intermediate language, and the JIT compiler converts IL instructions into executable code at the last moment.

In C#, when the compiler encounters a call to a nongeneric method like the ones you have created throughout this book, it searches for a method with the correct parameter type among all the overloaded method versions and displays an error message if it cannot find a match. When the compiler encounters a call to a generic method, it uses the argument type in the call to determine the generic type in the method. This process is called **type inferencing** because the type used in the method is inferred from the method call.

When you compile generic C# code, the compiler turns it into IL in the same way it does for any other method. However, when the method is generic, the IL contains only placeholders for the actual data types that will be used when a call to the method is made. The placeholder is altered during program execution when method calls are made as follows:

- If a call to a generic method specifies a value type, such as an `int`, as the argument, the JIT compiler replaces the generic type parameters in the IL with the specific value type and compiles it to executable code. If, later in the program, the compiler is asked to compile the generic method with a type it has already compiled, it returns a reference to that code; it does not create the code again or make extra copies of the same method.
- If a call to a generic method specifies a reference type, such as a `Student`, the JIT compiler replaces the generic parameters in the IL with `object`, and that code is reused for further calls that include a reference as the parameter.

NOTE
You might think that it makes perfect sense for the compiler not to re-create method versions it has already created. However, this is a new feature in .NET and was not true in some older programming languages.

For example, when the compiler encounters the method call `DisplayData(x);`, the generated method is:

```
static void DisplayData(int data)
{
    Console.WriteLine("Data: {0}", data);
}
```

However, when the compiler encounters the method call `DisplayData(stu);`, the generated method is:

```
static void DisplayData(object data)
{
    Console.WriteLine("Data: {0}", data);
}
```

Of course, you could have written your own `DisplayData()` method to accept an `object` parameter instead of allowing the compiler to create the method based on the argument in your method call. However, using a generic method with a generic type and allowing the compiler to generate the method eliminates the boxing that would be necessary with simple data types if the only version of your method accepted an `object` reference. Additionally, you can use explicit type arguments to indicate the exact type that should be used when you call a generic method. To do so, you insert a type name between angle brackets following the method name and in front of the parentheses that contain the argument list. For example, assuming `num` is an `int`, the following two method calls operate in an identical fashion:

```
DisplayData(num);
DisplayData<int>(num);
```

Using the second version, in which the data type is explicitly specified, provides documentation; it also makes the compiler check the data type and flag an incorrect argument.

»TWO TRUTHS AND A LIE: UNDERSTANDING THE COMPILER'S ROLE IN CREATING GENERIC METHODS

1. When you compile a C# program that calls a nongeneric method, the program searches for a method with the correct parameter type among all the existing overloaded method versions.
2. When you compile a C# program that calls a generic method, the program uses the argument type in the call to determine the generic type in the method.
3. If you compile a C# program that calls a generic method multiple times, and the method specifies a reference type, the JIT compiler creates individual method versions for each type.

The false statement is #3. If you compile a C# program that calls a generic method, and the method specifies a reference type, the JIT compiler replaces the generic parameters with `object`, and that code is reused for further calls that include a reference as the parameter. When you call a generic method using a value type, individual type-specific versions of the method are created.

USING MULTIPLE TYPE PARAMETERS

Type parameters can be used to declare any of the following in a method:

- » One or more parameter types
- » The return type
- » One or more local variable types

For example, Figure 20-7 shows a method that displays every element in a passed array and returns the first element in the array. The method uses the identifier `T` in five shaded locations:

- » As the type parameter in angle brackets following the method name
- » As the return type for the method
- » As the parameter type for the array that is passed to the method
- » As the type used in the `foreach()` statement
- » As the type of the locally declared variable named `firstElement`

»NOTE If you have trouble deciding where to use the generic type when you write a generic method, first write and test the method using a built-in type such as `int` or `double`. When your method works correctly with the built-in type, replace the appropriate type names with the generic type.

```
public static T DisplayArrayAndReturnFirstElement<T>(T[] array)
{
   foreach(T arrayElement in array)
      Console.Write(arrayElement + " ");
   Console.WriteLine();
   T firstElement = array[0];
   return firstElement;
}
```

Figure 20-7 A method that uses a type parameter in multiple locations

Figure 20-8 shows a `Main()` method that demonstrates that the method in Figure 20-7 works with arrays of diverse types that each hold a different number of elements. Figure 20-9 shows the output.

```
public static void Main()
{
   int[] intArray = {3, 6, 9};
   double[] doubleArray = {4.5, 7.8, 12.2, 15.9};
   string[] stringArray = {"Andy", "Betsy", "Connie",
      "David", "Elaine", "Francis"};
   int firstInt;
   double firstDouble;
   string firstString;
   firstInt = DisplayArrayAndReturnFirstElement(intArray);
   firstDouble = DisplayArrayAndReturnFirstElement(doubleArray);
   firstString = DisplayArrayAndReturnFirstElement(stringArray);
   Console.WriteLine("The first elements were {0}, {1}, and {2}",
      firstInt, firstDouble, firstString);
}
```

Figure 20-8 `Main()` method that demonstrates using a method with multiple generic references

NOTE The methods in Figures 20-7 and 20-8 are contained in a program named MultipleGenericReferencesDemo.cs on your Student Disk.

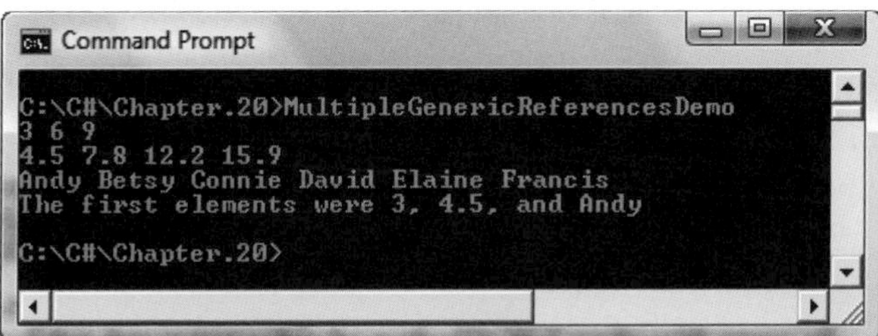

Figure 20-9 Output of the method in Figure 20-8

NOTE You probably would not want to use a generic method such as `DisplayArrayAndReturnFirstElement()` with many diverse types in a single professional program. The advantage to creating a generic method is that it can be used in different programs—one that handles `int`s, another that handles `string`s, and so on.

You can only declare a type parameter (such as `T`) once in the type parameter list, but the type parameter can appear any number of times in the method's parameter list. For example, the following is a valid method header:

```
public static void DisplayThreeItems<T>(T first, T second, T third)
```

When you call this method, it requires three parameters of any type, as long as they are all the same type (or can be promoted to the same type).

You also can declare multiple type parameters to stand for different types in the same method. For example, Figure 20-10 shows a method that uses two generic types named `T` and `U`. In this method, `T` and `U` can stand for any two types, whether they are the same or different.

```
public static void DisplayDiverseTypes<T, U>(T first, U second)
{
   Console.WriteLine("First is {0}, and second is {1}",
      first, second);
}
```

Figure 20-10 The `DisplayDiverseTypes()` method

Figure 20-11 contains a `Main()` method that declares a `Student` using the `Student` class defined in Figure 20-4 earlier in this chapter. Then the method calls `DisplayDiverseTypes()` five times using various combinations of `int`, `double`, `string`, and `Student`. In each case, the method functions correctly, as shown in the output in Figure 20-12.

```
public static void Main()
{
   Student stu = new Student(512, "Marco");
   DisplayDiverseTypes(12, "Hello");
   DisplayDiverseTypes("Goodbye", 34.91);
   DisplayDiverseTypes(stu, 14);
   DisplayDiverseTypes(99.9, stu);
   DisplayDiverseTypes(123.45, 678.12);
}
```

Figure 20-11 `Main()` method that calls `DisplayDiverseTypes()` five times

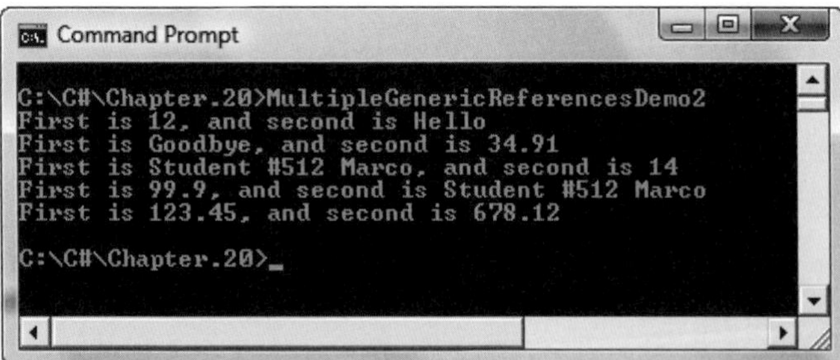

Figure 20-12 Output of the method in Figure 20-11

NOTE The methods in Figures 20-10 and 20-11 are contained in a program named MultipleGenericReferencesDemo2.cs on your Student Disk.

»TWO TRUTHS AND A LIE: USING MULTIPLE TYPE PARAMETERS

1. A type parameter is used for a method's first parameter; other parameters and the return type must be specified nongenerically.
2. You can only declare a type parameter once in the type parameter list, but the type parameter can appear any number of times in the method's parameter list.
3. You can declare multiple type parameters to stand for different types in the same method.

The false statement is #1. A type parameter can be used for a method's return type and for any number of local variables.

OVERLOADING GENERIC METHODS

Like other methods, generic methods can be overloaded. Figure 20-13 contains overloaded `Display()` methods. The first version accepts one parameter and the second version accepts two. Figure 20-14 shows the output.

```
using System;
public class OverloadedDemo
{
   public static void Main()
   {
      Student stu = new Student(123, "Carmen");
      Student stu2 = new Student(234, "Robin");
      Display(stu);
      Display(stu, stu2);
      Display(45);
      Display(56, 67);
   }
   public static void Display<T>(T first)
   {
      Console.WriteLine("First is {0}; there is no second", first);
   }
   public static void Display<T>(T first, T second)
   {
      Console.WriteLine("First is {0}, and second is {1}",
         first, second);
   }
}
```

Figure 20-13 The `OverloadedDemo` class

```
C:\C#\Chapter.20>OverloadedDemo
First is Student #123 Carmen; there is no second
First is Student #123 Carmen, and second is Student #234 Robin
First is 45; there is no second
First is 56, and second is 67

C:\C#\Chapter.20>
```

Figure 20-14 Output of the `OverloadedDemo` program

When you create more than one generic method in a program, you can reuse the type parameter names. For example, it is fine to have two methods that both use `T` as a generic parameter type. However, it is also fine to use different identifiers for the types in different methods.

NOTE You learned about ambiguous method calls in Chapter 6.

When you overload generic methods, you risk creating ambiguous method calls, just as you do when you overload nongeneric methods. For example, the following two method headers could not coexist in a program:

```
public static void Display<T>(T first, T second)
public static void Display<T, U>(T first, U second)
```

If you call `Display()` with two integer arguments, for example, neither version of `Display()` is a better match than the other. The call would be ambiguous between the following methods:

```
Display<int>(int, int)
Display<int, int>(int, int)
```

However, you can overload a generic method with a nongeneric one, even if they have the same number of parameters. For example, you could include the following two method declarations in a program:

```
public static void Display(int first, int second)
public static void Display<T>(T first, T second)
```

NOTE A program on your Student Disk named OverloadedDemo2.cs proves that a call to `Display()` that uses two integers as arguments uses the first version method. Other calls use the second version.

When you call the `Display()` method using two integer arguments, the first version is a better match because it explicitly defines the needed arguments as `int`s; when you call `Display()` with any other type of arguments, the second version is a better match.

»TWO TRUTHS AND A LIE: OVERLOADING GENERIC METHODS

1. Generic methods can be overloaded as long as you use different type parameter names in each version.
2. When you overload generic methods, you risk creating ambiguous method calls, just as you do when you overload nongeneric messages.
3. You can overload a generic method with a nongeneric one, even if they have the same number of parameters.

The false statement is #1. When you overload generic methods, you can use the same type parameter names in different versions.

UNDERSTANDING THE NEED FOR TYPE CONSTRAINTS AND HOW TO USE THEM

Suppose you want to create a generic method named `FindLargest()` that finds the largest of three values. You might first code the integer version, as shown in Figure 20-15. The method accepts three integer parameters. If the first is larger than the second, the first is stored in a variable named `largest`; otherwise, the second one is stored there. Then, if the third parameter is larger than `largest`, its value replaces the value stored in `largest`.

```
public static int FindLargest(int val1, int val2, int val3)
{
   int largest;
   if(val1 > val2)
      largest = val1;
   else
      largest = val2;
   if(val3 > largest)
      largest = val3;
   return largest;
}
```

Figure 20-15 `FindLargest()` method that compares three `int`s

After you test the `FindLargest()` method by writing a program that calls it using three integer arguments and verifying that the largest value is displayed, you might want to generalize the method to accept any parameter type. You could replace all the instances of `int` with a generic type, as shown in Figure 20-16. Although this approach seems reasonable, the method in Figure 20-16 does not compile. Figure 20-17 shows the compiler error messages.

```
public static T FindLargest<T>(T val1, T val2, T val3)
{
   T largest;
   if(val1 > val2)
      largest = val1;
   else
      largest = val2;
   if(val3 > largest)
      largest = val3;
   return largest;
}
```

»DON'T DO IT

This program does not compile because it requires a type constraint.

Figure 20-16 Incorrectly parameterized `FindLargest()` method

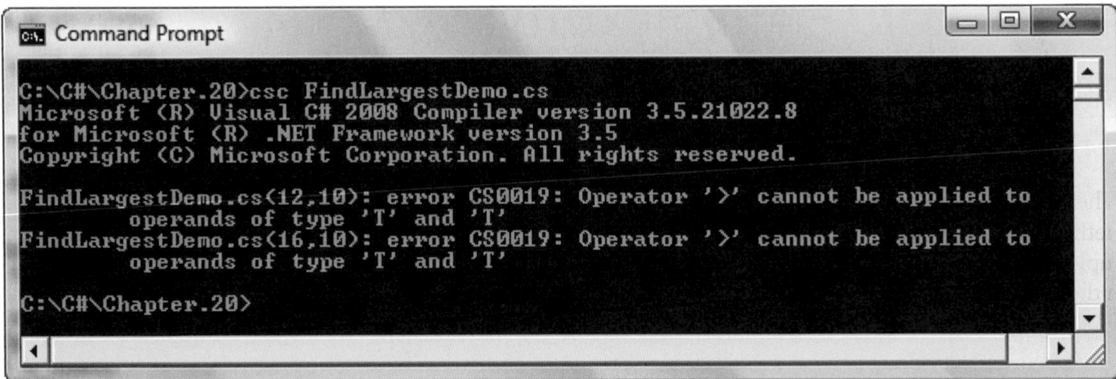

Command Prompt
C:\C#\Chapter.20>csc FindLargestDemo.cs
Microsoft (R) Visual C# 2008 Compiler version 3.5.21022.8
for Microsoft (R) .NET Framework version 3.5
Copyright (C) Microsoft Corporation. All rights reserved.
FindLargestDemo.cs(12,10): error CS0019: Operator '>' cannot be applied to
operands of type 'T' and 'T'
FindLargestDemo.cs(16,10): error CS0019: Operator '>' cannot be applied to
operands of type 'T' and 'T'
C:\C#\Chapter.20>

Figure 20-17 Error messages generated by method in Figure 20-16

The error messages in Figure 20-17 indicate that the greater-than operator cannot be applied to objects of type `T`. In reality, if `T` stood for `int` or `double` or another numeric type, the operator could be applied, but the compiler does not assume you will only use data types for which > is a defined operation. Unless every operation in the method can be performed on any data type, the method will not compile.

IMPLEMENTING `IComparable` AND USING `CompareTo()`

To be able to write a generic `FindLargest()` method, you avoid the use of the greater-than sign in the code. An alternate way to compare two objects of any data type is to use the `CompareTo()` method to compare objects. In Chapter 8, you learned that when a class implements an interface, the class must contain its own specific versions of the methods defined within the interface. In other words, implementing an interface provides a guarantee that a class will contain specific methods. When a class implements the `IComparable<T>` interface, it must contain a `CompareTo()` method. The structures that correspond to the simple data types, such as `Int32` and `Double`, all implement this interface. For example, two integers, `x` and `y`, can be compared using the following expression:

```
x.CompareTo(y)
```

NOTE You first learned about the `CompareTo()` method in Chapter 2 and the `IComparable` interface in Chapter 7. You wrote your own interfaces in Chapter 8.

In this expression, `x` and `y` can use the `CompareTo()` method because they are implicitly promoted to their structure type (`Int32`), and that type implements the `IComparable<T>` interface. The `CompareTo()` method returns the following:

- 0 when `x` and `y` are equal
- A negative number when `x` is less than `y`
- A positive number when `x` is greater than `y`

When you create a class that implements `IComparable<T>`, you must declare a `CompareTo()` method that follows the same model. For example, Figure 20-18 contains a `Student` class that implements `IComparable`. This class differs from the earlier `Student` class (in Figure 20-4) in the shaded areas:

- The `IComparable` interface is listed in the class header. It indicates that a `Student` will be comparable to another `Student`.
- The `CompareTo()` method is implemented to return 0, 1, or –1 depending on whether the `Student` object used to invoke the method has an `IdNumber` equal to, greater than, or less than the `Student` that will be used as an argument to the `CompareTo()` method. Comparing `Students` based on their ID numbers is the programmer's choice; when you create a student class, you might decide `Students` should be compared on the basis of their names, or some other field that `Student` objects contain. For the generic method to work, it does not matter how `Students` are compared; it only matters that they are compared using a `CompareTo()` method that follows the usual format.

```
public class Student : IComparable<Student>
{
   public int IdNumber {get; set;}
   public string Name {get; set;}
   public Student(int id, string name)
   {
      IdNumber = id;
      Name = name;
   }
   public override string ToString()
   {
      return("Student #" + IdNumber + " " + Name);
   }
   public int CompareTo(Student stu)
   {
      int returnVal;
      if(IdNumber == stu.IdNumber)
         returnVal = 0;
      else
         if(IdNumber > stu.IdNumber)
            returnVal = 1;
         else
            returnVal = -1;
      return returnVal;
   }
}
```

Figure 20-18 The `Student` class with a `CompareTo()` method

The generic method that can compare objects using the `CompareTo()` method instead of the greater-than sign can be written as shown in Figure 20-19. In the shaded sections, the greater-than comparisons have been replaced by `CompareTo()` method calls. However, the method in Figure 20-19 is still not complete.

```
public static T FindLargest<T>(T val1, T val2, T val3)
{
   T largest;
   if(val1.CompareTo(val2) > 0)
      largest = val1;
   else
      largest = val2;
   if(val3.CompareTo(largest) > 0)
      largest = val3;
   return largest;
}
```

»DON'T DO IT

This generic method does not work because it is not constrained yet.

Figure 20-19 `FindLargest()` method that uses the `CompareTo()` method

ADDING A TYPE CONSTRAINT

Although the `Student` class in Figure 20-18 that implements `CompareTo()` could use the `FindLargest()` method in Figure 20-19, the compiler still has no guarantee that a program will not try to pass in some other object type that is not supported by a `CompareTo()` method. When you want to use a generic method in which objects are compared using `CompareTo()`, such as the `FindLargest()` method in Figure 20-19, you must restrict the types allowed as method parameters; you must use a type constraint to avoid the error messages in Figure 20-17. A **type constraint** is a clause that restricts the type of argument that can be supplied to a generic parameter. For example, you can require that `T` be only a value type or only a reference type, or you can require that `T` be a specific class or a type that implements `IComparable`. If a client program tries to use a constrained method with a type that is forbidden by the constraint, a compiler error is issued. You specify a type constraint using the keyword `where` followed by a colon and the constraint type. Table 20-1 lists the allowed constraints.

Constraint Type	Syntax	Description
Value type constraint	`where T: struct`	The type argument must be a value type.
Reference type constraint	`where T: class`	The type argument must be a reference type.
Class constraint	`where T:` *class name*	The type argument must be from the specified class or one of its descendents.
Interface constraint	`where T:` *interface name*	The type argument must implement the specified interface.
Naked type constraint	`where T: U`	The type argument supplied for `T` must be or derive from the argument supplied for `U`.
Constructor constraint	`where T: new()`	The type argument must have a public parameterless constructor. (This allows the simple data types.) This constraint indicates that the generic code can use the `new` operator to create objects of the type represented by the type parameter.

Table 20-1 Type constraints

For example, if a generic method contains one or more calls to the `CompareTo()` method, only classes that implement `IComparable` should be used by the method because only those classes are guaranteed to implement `CompareTo()`. The generic method should contain an interface constraint and look like the one in Figure 20-20. The shaded `where` clause specifies the type constraint for `T`. In other words, this method requires any arguments to implement `IComparable`. Arguments that can be used as types for `T` include types where the `CompareTo()` method has already been written for you (such as for `int`s and `string`s) and arguments for classes you have designed yourself and in which you have created an appropriate `CompareTo()` method (like the `Student` class in Figure 20-18).

»NOTE When no type constraint is specified for a method, the default type constraint is the `object` class.

```
public static T FindLargest<T>(T val1, T val2, T val3)
   where T : IComparable<T>
{
   T largest;
   if(val1.CompareTo(val2) > 0)
      largest = val1;
   else
      largest = val2;
   if(val3.CompareTo(largest) > 0)
      largest = val3;
   return largest;
}
```

Figure 20-20 The generic `FindLargest()` method with an interface constraint

Figure 20-21 shows a program that demonstrates how `FindLargest()` can be called using any three values of the same type as long as those values are supported by the `IComparable` interface. Figure 20-22 shows the output. The largest `int` is the one with the highest numeric value, the largest `string` is the one that has the highest lexicographical value, and the largest `Student` is the one with the highest numeric ID number.

```
using System;
public class FindLargestDemo
{
   public static void Main()
   {
      int largestInt = FindLargest(3, 9, 5);
      string largestString = FindLargest("Nicole", "Larry", "Richard");
      Student stu1 = new Student(567, "Joe");
      Student stu2 = new Student(345, "Viola");
      Student stu3 = new Student(212, "Kim");
      Student largestStudent = FindLargest(stu1, stu2, stu3);
      Console.WriteLine("Largest int is {0}", largestInt);
      Console.WriteLine("Largest string is {0}", largestString);
      Console.WriteLine("Largest student is {0}", largestStudent);
   }
   public static T FindLargest<T>(T val1, T val2, T val3)
      where T : IComparable<T>
   {
      T largest;
      if(val1.CompareTo(val2) > 0)
         largest = val1;
      else
         largest = val2;
      if(val3.CompareTo(largest) > 0)
         largest = val3;
      return largest;
   }
}
```

Figure 20-21 The `FindLargestDemo` program (*continued*)

```
public class Student : IComparable<Student>
{
   public int IdNumber {get; set;}
   public string Name {get; set;}
   public Student(int id, string name)
   {
      IdNumber = id;
      Name = name;
   }
   public override string ToString()
   {
      return("Student #" + IdNumber + " " + Name);
   }
   public int CompareTo(Student stu)
   {
      int returnVal;
      if(IdNumber == stu.IdNumber)
         returnVal = 0;
      else
         if(IdNumber > stu.IdNumber)
            returnVal = 1;
         else
            returnVal = -1;
      return returnVal;
   }
}
```

Figure 20-21 (*continued*)

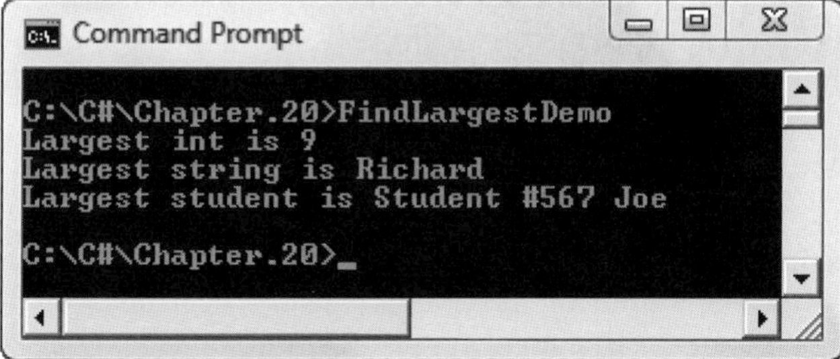

Figure 20-22 Output of the `FindLargestDemo` program

You can apply multiple constraints to a type parameter using a comma-separated list in the `where` clause. When you use a class constraint, reference type constraint, or value type constraint, you can use only one of the three for each parameter type. When you do use one of these, it must be the first constraint listed. If there is a constructor constraint, it must be last in the list. You also can apply constraints to multiple parameters. For example, the following provides a valid declaration:

```
static void aMethod<T, U>(T param1, U param2)
   where T : struct where U: Student, new()
```

In this example, the `T` parameter must be a value (`struct`) type, the `U` parameter must be a `Student` or a child of `Student`, and the type must have a default constructor.

Although many programmers always use `T` as their first choice for a generic type identifier, others recommend that if there is a constraint for a generic type, the type name should be more descriptive—for example, when the type must implement `IComparable`, they might name it `TComparable`.

»TWO TRUTHS AND A LIE: UNDERSTANDING THE NEED FOR TYPE CONSTRAINTS AND HOW TO USE THEM

1. A properly overloaded `CompareTo()` method returns 0 when two values are equal, a negative number when the first value used is less than the argument, and a positive value when the first value is greater than the argument.
2. A type constraint is a clause that restricts the type of argument that can be supplied to a generic parameter.
3. You can apply any number of constraints to a type parameter in any order.

The false statement is #3. You can apply multiple constraints to a type parameter using a comma-separated list, but there are rules for the order of the constraints. When you use a class constraint, reference type constraint, or value type constraint, you can use only one of the three for each parameter type. When you do use one of these, it must be the first constraint listed. If there is a constructor constraint, it must be last in the list.

CREATING GENERIC CLASSES

A **generic class** describes a class that is not specific to a data type. For example, you can understand how arrays, stacks, queues, and linked lists operate, no matter what data types they hold. All these structures are perfect candidates for generic classes. After you create a generic class, you can write code that uses it by indicating a type to use in place of the class's generic type parameter.

A declaration for a generic class includes a type parameter list in angle brackets after the class name. You also can include constraints on its type parameters. Typically, you create a generic class by starting with an existing nongeneric class, and then changing types into type parameters one at a time until you reach a point where the class seems most usable with a wide variety of data types.

For example, suppose you often need to display integer arrays forward and backward. You might create a class like the one in Figure 20-23. The class contains an integer array, a constructor that accepts an array as a parameter, and two methods—one that displays the array from the first element to the last, and another that displays the array from the last element to the first.

```
public class MyList
{
   int[] array;
   public MyList(int[] arr)
   {
      array = arr;
   }
   public void Forward()
   {
      foreach(int element in array)
         Console.Write(element + " ");
      Console.WriteLine();
   }
   public void Backward()
   {
      int x;
      for(x = array.Length -1 ; x >= 0; --x)
         Console.Write(array[x] + " ");
      Console.WriteLine();
   }
}
```

Figure 20-23 The `MyList` class—a nongeneric class

Figure 20-24 contains a short demonstration program that uses the `MyList` class. The program declares an array of five integers and declares a `MyList` object using the array as the constructor argument. The program then displays the list forward and backward. Figure 20-25 shows the output.

```
using System;
public class MyListDemoInt
{
   public static void Main()
   {
      int[] integers = {2, 6, 19, 45, 77};
      MyList list = new MyList(integers);
      list.Forward();
      list.Backward();
   }
}
```

Figure 20-24 The `MyListDemoInt` program

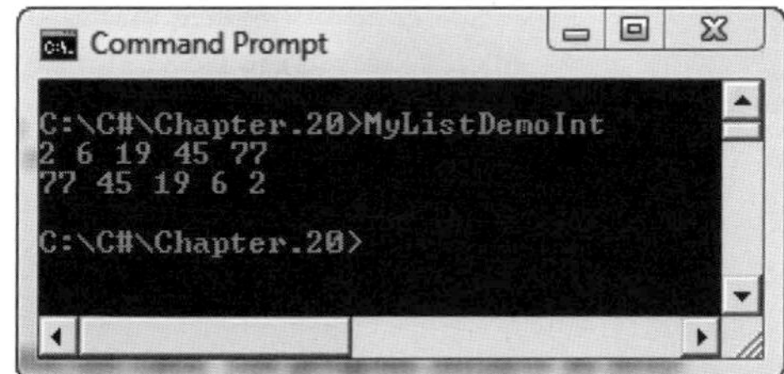

Figure 20-25 Output of `MyListDemoInt` program

Suppose you decide that displaying arrays of objects forward and backward would be useful with many kinds of data types. You could revise the int-processing MyList class to make it a generic list class, as shown in Figure 20-26. You would add a generic parameter following the class name, as shown in the first shaded portion of the figure. When referring to the class verbally, instead of calling the class "MyList," many programmers would now say "MyList of T." Of course, you could use any identifier for the parameterized type, but as with generic methods, a single uppercase letter is a traditional generic type name. Then you would replace every appropriate instance of int with the generic parameter T. In the class shown in Figure 20-26, this means that three replacements are needed—in the data type for the array held within the class, in the constructor parameter list, and in the foreach statement in the Forward() method.

```
public class MyList<T>
{
   T[] array;
   public MyList(T[] arr)
   {
      array = arr;
   }
   public void Forward()
   {
      foreach(T element in array)
         Console.Write(element + " ");
      Console.WriteLine();
   }
   public void Backward()
   {
      int x;
      for(x = array.Length -1 ; x >= 0; --x)
         Console.Write(array[x] + " ");
      Console.WriteLine();
   }
}
```

Notice that the instance of int in the Backward() method is not parameterized. This variable is used as an array subscript and should remain an int no matter what types of objects are stored in the array.

Figure 20-26 The generic MyList<T> class

With the changes to the parameters shown in Figure 20-26, you can write a client program like the one shown in Figure 20-27. The demonstration program creates an array of four integers, assigns it to a MyList object, and calls both display methods. Then the program declares an array of six strings and two Students and does the same. Figure 20-28 shows the output. Each data type is handled successfully by the generic MyList class, producing two lines of output for each data type.

```
using System;
public class MyListDemoGeneric
{
   public static void Main()
   {
      int[] arr = {3, 4, 7, 12};
      MyList<int> list = new MyList<int>(arr);
      list.Forward();
      list.Backward();

      string[] strings = {"you", "say", "goodbye", "I", "say", "hello"};
      MyList<string> list2 = new MyList<string>(strings);
      list2.Forward();
      list2.Backward();

      Student[] stu = new Student[2];
      stu[0] = new Student(222, "Nancy");
      stu[1] = new Student(333, "Cooper");

      MyList<Student> list3 = new MyList<Student>(stu);
      list3.Forward();
      list3.Backward();
   }
}
```

Figure 20-27 The `MyListDemoGeneric` class

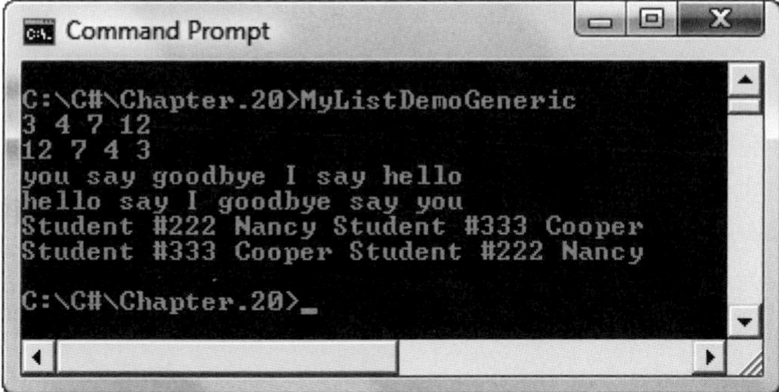

Figure 20-28 Output of the `MyListDemoGeneric` program

»TWO TRUTHS AND A LIE: CREATING GENERIC CLASSES

1. A generic class is a class that contains only generic data and methods.
2. A declaration for a generic class includes a type parameter list in angle brackets after the class name.
3. As with generic methods, you can include constraints on a generic class's type parameters.

The false statement is #1. A generic class is a class that is not specific to a data type. It might contain any combination of generic and nongeneric data and methods.

USING BUILT-IN GENERIC CLASSES

Manipulating lists of various object types is a common programming task. For that reason, the C# library already contains a `List<T>` class that is more powerful than the `MyList` class in Figure 20-26. It is contained in the `System.Collections.Generic` namespace; that namespace contains several classes that allow you to create strongly typed collections of data, including lists, linked lists, stacks, and queues. When you write professional programs, you most likely will want to use the supplied classes instead of reinventing the wheel by creating your own versions.

The `List<T>` class allows you to use an index to access individual elements, so it operates like an array. The class contains nearly 40 useful methods, including ones to search and sort the contained list. Table 20-2 shows the properties of the `List` collection and Table 20-3 shows some of the methods you might want to employ.

Property	Description
`Capacity`	Gets or sets the number of elements the `List` can hold without resizing. As soon as you add one element to the `List`, the `Capacity` is 4. Whenever you add more elements than the current `Capacity` allows, the capacity automatically doubles.
`Count`	Gets the number of elements in the `List`. This value is always less than or equal to `Capacity`.
`Item`	Gets or sets the element at the specified index.

Table 20-2 Properties of `List<T>`

Method Name	Description
`Add()`	Adds an object to the end of the `List`
`BinarySearch()`	Locates a specific item in the `List`
`Clear()`	Removes all `List` elements
`Contains()`	Determines whether an element is in the `List`
`Find()`	Searches for an element that matches specified conditions and returns the first occurrence
`FindAll()`	Searches for elements that match specified conditions and returns them all as a `List`
`ForEach()`	Performs the specified action on each `List` element
`Insert()`	Inserts an element into the list at the specified index
`Remove()`	Removes the first occurrence of an object from the `List`
`RemoveAll()`	Removes all the occurrences of objects that match specified conditions
`RemoveAt()`	Removes an element at the specified index
`Reverse()`	Reverses the order of `List` elements
`Sort()`	Sorts the elements in the `List`
`TrimExcess()`	Sets the `Capacity` to the actual number of elements in the `List`

Table 20-3 Selected methods of `List<T>`

»NOTE The conditions mentioned in the descriptions of methods such as `Find()` and `FindAll()` are determined by a **predicate method**, also called a **predicate delegate** or simply a **predicate**. A predicate is a Boolean method that defines a set of criteria and determines whether the specified object meets those criteria. In the You Do It section at the end of this chapter, you will create a predicate method and use it in a `FindAll()` method call.

Figure 20-29 contains a demonstration of some of the `List<T>` methods. The program starts by creating an empty `List`, displaying its initial `Capacity` (zero), and adding three strings to the `List`. Then those three names are displayed, and, as you can see in the first part of the output in Figure 20-30, the `Capacity` of the `List` is 4 when the `Count` is 3.

```
using System;
using System.Collections.Generic;
public class CollectionsListDemo
{
   public static void Main()
   {
      List<string> names = new List<string>();
      Console.WriteLine("Capacity at start: {0}", names.Capacity);
      names.Add("Belle");
      names.Add("Carl");
      names.Add("Dylan");
      foreach(string name in names)
      {
         Console.Write(name + " ");
      }
      Console.WriteLine();
      Console.WriteLine("Capacity after three names added: {0}", names.Capacity);
      Console.WriteLine("Count after three names added: {0}", names.Count);
      Console.WriteLine("Contains Carl: {0}",
         names.Contains("Carl"));
      Console.WriteLine("Contains Emily: {0}",
         names.Contains("Emily"));
      names.Insert(1, "Bruno");
      names.Insert(4, "Eugene");
      names.Insert(4, "Ellen");
      foreach(string name in names)
      {
         Console.Write(name + " ");
      }
      Console.WriteLine();
      names.Remove("Belle");
      foreach(string name in names)
      {
         Console.Write(name + " ");
      }
      Console.WriteLine();
      Console.WriteLine("Before trim capacity: {0}", names.Capacity);
      names.TrimExcess();
      Console.WriteLine("After trim capacity: {0}", names.Capacity);
      names.Clear();
      Console.WriteLine("After clear capacity: {0}", names.Capacity);
      Console.WriteLine("After clear count: {0}", names.Count);
   }
}
```

Figure 20-29 The `CollectionsListDemo` class

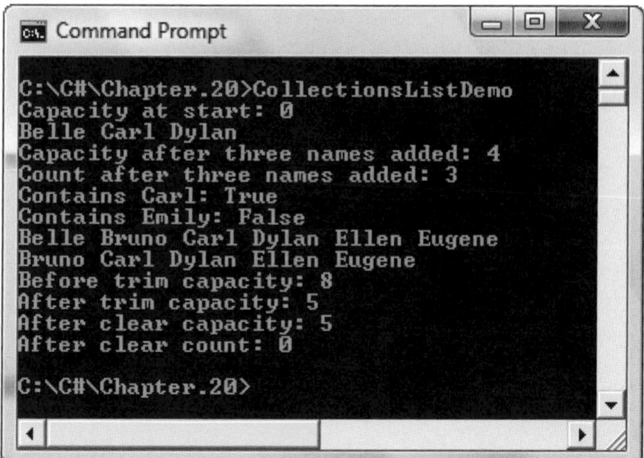

Figure 20-30 Output of the CollectionsListDemo program

The program tests for the inclusion of two names, "Carl" and "Emily", and displays true and false, respectively. Three new names are inserted into the list at specified locations, the revised List is displayed, then a name is removed from the list, and the names are displayed again. The List Capacity is now 8, but the Count is just 5.

The program uses the Trim() method to reduce the capacity to match the Count, eliminating unnecessary elements, so the Count is reduced to 5. Finally, the List is cleared. It retains its last Capacity of 5, but its Count becomes 0.

You could write code to perform all the actions demonstrated in the CollectionsListDemo program using an array. However, understanding the List<T> class provides several advantages:

- The code is already written for you.
- Adding and removing items is faster than with an array.
- Once you learn about the List<T> methods, you need to remember only one group of method names that will operate reliably and consistently on a collection of any data type.

Besides List<T>, other generic classes in the Collections namespace include SortedList, LinkedList, Dictionary, SortedDictionary, Collection, KeyedCollection, ReadOnlyCollection, Queue, and Stack. You can search online for help with specific generic collections. When appropriate, you should use generic collections because you gain the immediate benefit of type safety. In addition, although some generic collection types have nongeneric counterparts (like Queue and Stack), the generic versions usually perform better when the collection elements are value types because with generics there is no need to box the elements.

»TWO TRUTHS AND A LIE: USING BUILT-IN GENERIC CLASSES

1. The `List<T>` class resides in the `System.Collections.Generic` namespace.
2. The `List<T>` class is more difficult to use than an array because you cannot directly access elements using an index.
3. The `List<T>` class contains nearly 40 useful methods, including ones to search and sort the contained list.

The false statement is #2. The `List<T>` class allows you to use an index to access individual elements, so it operates like an array.

YOU DO IT

CREATING AND DEMONSTRATING A GENERIC METHOD

In the following steps, you will create a small generic method and demonstrate that it can work with several different data types as parameters.

To create and demonstrate a generic method:

1. Open a new file in your text editor and type a simple `Student` class as follows. You will use this class to generate an object to help demonstrate that a generic method can work with both objects and simple data types. This `Student` class is identical to the one that appeared in Figure 20-4. If you prefer, you can simply copy the class from the file on your Student Disk.

```
public class Student
{
   public int IdNumber {get; set;}
   public string Name {get; set;}
   public Student(int id, string name)
   {
      IdNumber = id;
      Name = name;
   }
   public override string ToString()
   {
      return("Student #" + IdNumber + " " + Name);
   }
}
```

2. In the same file, above the `Student` class, start a demonstration program that will provide information about a variety of objects.

```
using System;
public class InformationDemo
{
   public static void Main()
   {
```

3. Declare an `int`, a `double`, a `string`, and a `Student`.

```
int x = 24;
double amt = 23.89;
string word = "banana";
Student stu = new Student(123, "Carmen");
```

4. In turn, pass each object to an `Information()` method, then add a closing curly brace for the `Main()` method.

```
   Information(x);
   Information(amt);
   Information(word);
   Information(stu);
}
```

5. Add the `Information()` method as follows. The method displays the automatically converted `ToString()` value of an item and the type of the item.

```
public static void Information<T>(T item)
{
   Console.WriteLine("{0} is a {1}", item, item.GetType());
}
```

6. Save the file as **InformationDemo.cs**. Compile and execute it. Figure 20-31 shows the output, in which the `Information()` method works correctly with the different data types.

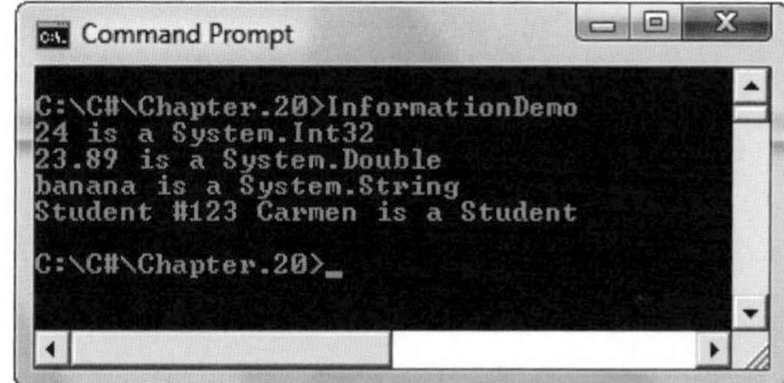

Figure 20-31 Output of the `InformationDemo` program

BUILDING AND SEARCHING A LIST<T>

In the next steps, you will build a `List<T>` of integers, then use the `FindAll()` method to generate a sublist that meets a specific criterion. Later, you will minimally modify the program to make it useful with a different data type.

To write a program that builds and searches a `List<T>`:

1. Open a new file in your text editor and start a file that will build a `List<T>` of integers and allow you to search for specific values.

```
using System;
using System.Collections.Generic;
public class BuildAndSearchListWithInt
{
```

2. To begin the `Main()` method, create two generic `List<T>` objects. One will hold the list of integers you create, and the other will hold a sublist of those integers that fall below a specified value.

```
public static void Main()
{
   List<int>items = new List<int>();
   List<int>sublist = new List<int>();
```

3. Declare a `string` that will hold a value that designates the user's desire to continue the program after each data entry, then prompt the user and accept a value for that string.

```
string continueString = "y";
Console.Write("Do you want to add an item? y or n >> ");
continueString = Console.ReadLine();
```

4. Create a loop that adds integers to the list for as long as the user wants to continue. The data entry is accomplished in a separate method named `DataEntry()` that returns an item that is added to the list.

```
while(!continueString.Equals("n"))
{
   int item;
   item = DataEntry();
   items.Add(item);
   Console.Write("Do you want to add an item? y or n >> ");
   continueString = Console.ReadLine();
}
```

5. Display a line of asterisks to provide visual separation for the parts of the output, and then display the list and a count of the items in the list.

```
Console.WriteLine("************************");
foreach(int item in items)
{
   Console.WriteLine("    " + item);
}
Console.WriteLine("Count: {0}", items.Count);
```

6. Populate the sublist with all items returned by the `FindAll()` method. The `FindAll()` method uses a predicate method name (`LowerThan2000`) as its argument. A predicate method is a method that accepts an object of the appropriate data type and returns a `bool`. You will write the predicate method in Step 8; here, you just use its name, without parentheses, as the argument to `FindAll()`. After the call to `FindAll()`, display another row of asterisks and then display a heading. Next, in a loop, display the sublist of items that are less than the value 2000. Display a count of the sublist items, and then add a closing curly brace for the `Main()` method.

```
        Console.WriteLine("**********************");
        sublist = items.FindAll(LowerThan2000);
        Console.WriteLine("Items under 2000");
        foreach(int item in sublist)
        {
           Console.WriteLine("    " + item);
        }
        Console.WriteLine("Count: {0}", sublist.Count);
    }
```

7. Following the `Main()` method, add the method that accepts an integer value from the user and returns it.

```
    public static int DataEntry()
    {
        int num;
        Console.Write ("Enter an integer >> ");
        num = Convert.ToInt32(Console.ReadLine());
        return num;
    }
```

8. Create the predicate method. Predicates are required to return a `bool`. The `LowerThan2000()` method returns `true` for each list item that is less than 2000; otherwise, it returns `false`. Add a closing curly brace for the class.

»NOTE You probably prefer to create a method more flexible than `LowerThan2000()`—one that can accept any value as the cutoff point for inclusion in the sublist. You will make this modification later in these exercises.

```
        public static bool LowerThan2000(int num)
        {
           bool result = false;
           if(num < 2000)
              result = true;
           return result;
        }
    }
```

9. Save the file as **BuildAndSearchListWithInt.cs**. Compile and execute the program. Figure 20-32 shows a typical execution in which the user enters several values, and then values below 2000 are displayed.

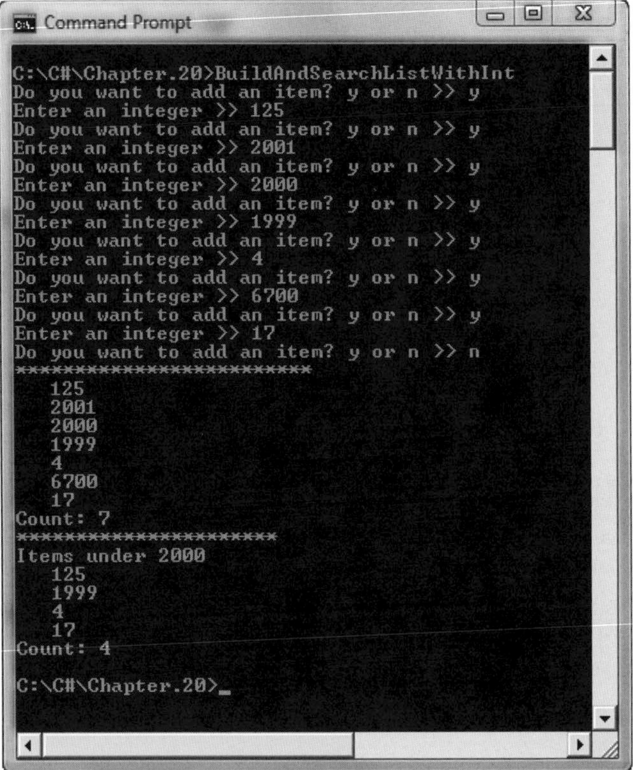

Figure 20-32 Typical execution of `BuildAndSearchListWithInt` program

CREATING AN OBJECT TO USE IN A List<T>

Next, you will create a `Car` class to demonstrate creating a `List<T>` of `Cars`.

To create a class to support objects to use in a `List<T>`:

1. Open a new file in your text editor and start a `Car` class that contains properties for `Make`, `Model`, and `Price`.

```
public class Car
{
   public string Make {get; set;}
   public string Model {get; set;}
   public double Price {get; set;}
```

2. Create two constructors for the `Car` class. One is a default constructor, and the other requires values for all three `Car` data fields.

```
public Car() : this("", "", 0)
{
}
```

```
public Car(string make, string model, double price)
{
    Make = make;
    Model = model;
    Price = price;
}
```

> **NOTE** You learned the code-saving technique of calling one constructor from another using the `this` reference in Chapter 7.

3. Create a `ToString()` method for the `Car` class so that it overrides the `object` class version and returns useful `Car` information.

```
public override string ToString()
{
    return(Make + " " + Model + " $" + Price);
}
```

4. Create a `DataEntry()` method for the `Car` class. It prompts the user for and accepts data for each `Car` field. Then add a closing curly brace for the `Car` class.

```
    public void DataEntry()
    {
        Console.Write("Enter the make >> ");
        Make = Console.ReadLine();
        Console.Write("Enter the model >> ");
        Model = Console.ReadLine();
        Console.Write("Enter the price >> ");
        Price = Convert.ToDouble(Console.ReadLine());
    }
}
```

5. Save the file as **Car.cs**.

MODIFYING THE BUILD AND SEARCH PROGRAM TO USE A LIST<T> OF OBJECTS

Next, you will make minor alterations to the `BuildAndSearchListWithInt` program so it can use your own `Car` objects instead of integers. This will help you to understand that the `List<T>` class can work with all data types.

To modify the `BuildAndSearchListWithInt` program so that it can use `Car` objects:

1. Open the **BuildAndSearchListWithInt.cs** file in your text editor. Make the shaded changes shown in Figure 20-33. The changes are very minor. The references to `int` are changed to `Car`, the `DataEntry()` method is called differently because it is a member of the `Car` class, and the comparison in the predicate method uses a `Car`'s price to make the under-2000 comparison.

```
using System;
using System.Collections.Generic;
public class BuildAndSearchListWithCar
{
   public static void Main()
   {
      List<Car>items = new List<Car>();
      List<Car>sublist = new List<Car>();
      string continueString = "y";
      Console.Write("Do you want to add an item? y or n >> ");
      continueString = Console.ReadLine();
      while(!continueString.Equals("n"))
      {
         Car item = new Car();
         item.DataEntry();
         items.Add(item);
         Console.Write("Do you want to add an item? y or n >> ");
         continueString = Console.ReadLine();
      }
      Console.WriteLine("************************");
      foreach(Car item in items)
      {
         Console.WriteLine("    " + item);
      }
      Console.WriteLine("Count: {0}", items.Count);
      Console.WriteLine("*********************");
      sublist = items.FindAll(LowerThan2000);
            Console.WriteLine("Items under 2000");
      foreach(Car item in sublist)
      {
         Console.WriteLine("    " + item);
      }
      Console.WriteLine("Count: {0}", sublist.Count);

   }
   public static bool LowerThan2000(Car car)
   {
      bool result = false;
      if(car.Price < 2000)
         result = true;
      return result;
   }
}
```

Figure 20-33 The `BuildAndSearchListWithCar` program

2. Save the file as **BuildAndSearchListWithCar.cs**, and then compile and execute it. Enter data for as many cars as you want, and then examine the output. Figure 20-34 shows a typical execution. The program operates much like the integer version you created earlier. Because you had already written usable code to display, count, and find items in an integer list, transferring those capabilities to a Car list was simple.

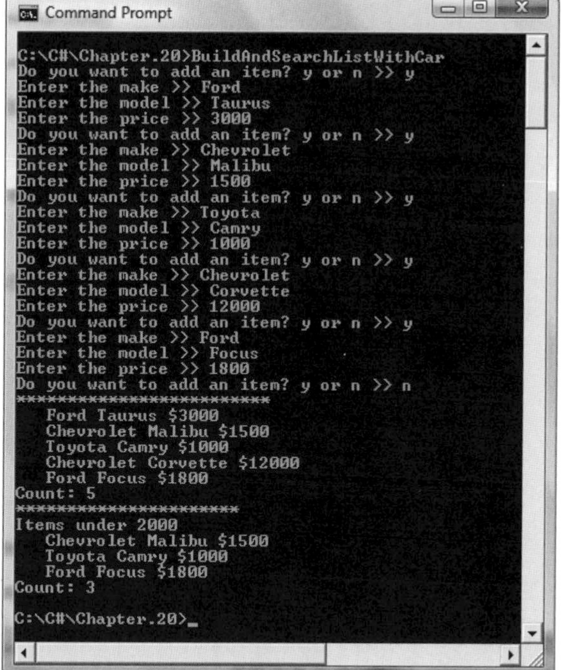

Figure 20-34 Typical execution of the BuildAndSearchListWithCar program

CREATING A MORE USEFUL PREDICATE

Writing a method that determines whether a value is less than 2000 is not very flexible. Certainly, by this point in your programming experience you can see the advantage to creating a method that compares List<T> elements with any value requested by the user, not just 2000. The problem is that predicate methods cannot accept parameters other than the one that holds an object of the T data type used in the List<T>, so you cannot pass a cutoff value into the predicate method. There are at least two possible solutions to this problem:

- You could prompt the user for a maximum value within the predicate method. That way, no value would need to be passed into the method. However, the calling method could not know about or be able to display the value because the predicate method must return a bool and could not return the user's entered value.
- You could declare a maximum value variable in the containing class as a class variable. Then all the class's methods would have access to it, and you could prompt the user for a value in the Main() method but use it as a cutoff point for sublist inclusion in the predicate method. This is the approach you will take in the following steps.

To modify the build and search program so that the sublist inclusion cutoff is a variable:

1. Open the **BuildAndSearchListWithCar.cs** file in your text editor. Immediately save it as **BuildAndSearchListWithCar2.cs**.
2. Change the class name to **BuildAndSearchListWithCar2**.
3. Following the class header and before the `Main()` method header, add a declaration for `max`:

```
static double max;
```

4. Following the line that displays the second set of asterisks in the program, add these lines to prompt for and receive the maximum value for the search:

```
Console.Write("Enter a maximum value for the search >> ");
max = Convert.ToDouble(Console.ReadLine());
```

5. Revise the call to `FindAll()` to call a method named `LowerThan()` instead of `LowerThan2000()`:

```
sublist = items.FindAll(LowerThan);
```

6. Modify the statement that displays "Items under 2000" to the following more flexible version:

```
Console.WriteLine("Items under {0}", max);
```

7. Change the header of the `LowerThan2000()` method so that the method name is just `LowerThan()`:

```
public static bool LowerThan(Car car)
```

8. Within the method, change the `if` statement to use a variable instead of the constant 2000:

```
if(car.Price < max)
```

9. Either add the text of the Car.cs file to the end of the BuildAndSearchListWithCar2.cs program file or add an import statement to include it in the program. Save and compile the **BuildAndSearchListWithCar2.cs** file and execute the program. Figure 20-35 shows a typical execution in which you can enter any cutoff value for the `FindAll()` search.

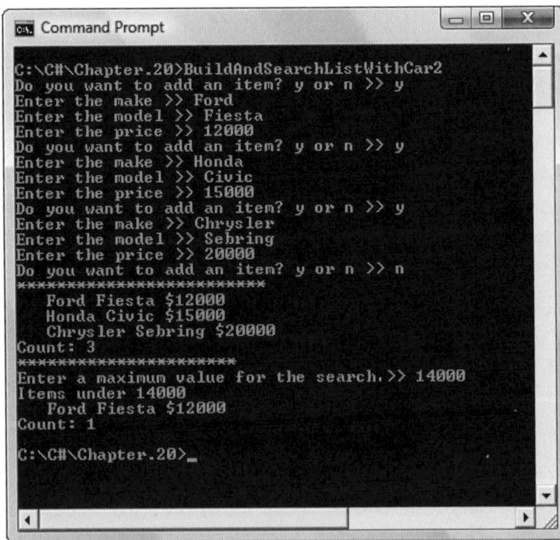

Figure 20-35 Typical execution of the `BuildAndSearchListWithCar2` program

CHAPTER SUMMARY

- Using structures that hold objects is convenient, but they perform poorly because casting, downcasting, boxing, and unboxing are required. Additionally, compile-time safety is not provided. Generics provide a compromise between the flexibility of creating structures that can handle any object type and the safety of checking for correct data types.
- When the programming logic within methods is the same, writing multiple overloaded versions is inefficient. Instead, you can write a generic method that works with any data type. To create a generic method, you include a type parameter list, which is a list of generic data types contained between angle brackets that follows a generic method's name. The only requirement is that the data type passed to the method works with all the statements coded within the method.
- When the compiler encounters a call to a generic method, it uses type inferencing to determine the generic type in the method from the argument type. When you compile generic C# code, the compiler turns it into IL, which contains placeholders for the actual data types that will be used when a method call is made. This eliminates the boxing that would be necessary with simple data types if the only version of your method accepted an `object` reference. When you call a generic method, you can use explicit type arguments to indicate the exact type that should be used; insert a type name within angle brackets between the method name and the parentheses that contain the argument list.
- Generic type parameters can be used to declare parameter types, the return type, and local variable types within a method. You can only declare a type parameter once in the type parameter list, but the type parameter can appear any number of times in the method's parameter list. You can also declare multiple type parameters to stand for different types in the same method.
- Like other methods, generic methods can be overloaded. When you create more than one generic method in a program, you can reuse the type parameter names. When you overload generic methods, you risk creating ambiguous method calls, just as you do when you overload nongeneric methods. You can overload a generic method with a nongeneric one, even if they have the same number of parameters.
- Unless every operation in a generic method can be performed on any data type, the method will not compile. When a class implements an interface, it is guaranteed that specific methods are included. A type constraint is a clause that restricts the type of argument that can be supplied to a generic parameter. You can apply multiple constraints to a type parameter using a comma-separated list.
- A generic class describes a class that is not specific to a data type. A declaration for a generic class includes a type parameter list in angle brackets after the class name. You can also include constraints on its type parameters.
- The C# library contains a `List<T>` class in the `System.Collections.Generic` namespace; that namespace contains several classes that allow you to create strongly typed collections of data. The `List<T>` class allows you to use an index to access individual elements, so that it operates like an array. The class contains nearly 40 useful methods, including ones to search and sort the contained list.

KEY TERMS

Compile-time safety is the compiler feature that provides for detecting mismatches of data types when a program is compiled.

Generics provide a compromise between the flexibility of creating structures that can handle any object type and the safety of checking for correct data types.

A **generic method** can work with multiple data types by using a type parameter list.

A **parameterized type** is a data type that is determined by a parameter.

A **type parameter list** is a list of generic data types contained between angle brackets that follows the name of each generic method and generic class.

Type inferencing occurs when a compiler uses the argument type in a call to a generic method to determine the method's generic type.

A **type constraint** is a clause that restricts the type of argument that can be supplied to a generic parameter.

A **generic class** describes a class that is not specific to a data type.

A **predicate method**, also called a **predicate delegate** or a **predicate**, is a Boolean method that defines a set of criteria and determines whether the specified object meets those criteria.

REVIEW QUESTIONS

1. Advantages to creating generic classes and methods include all of the following except __________.

   a. flexibility
   b. reusability
   c. compile-time safety
   d. All of the above are advantages to creating generic classes.

2. A generic method works with any data type that __________.

   a. is listed in its header
   b. is listed in its parameter list
   c. can be used by all the operations within the method
   d. descends from `object`

3. A type parameter list is __________.

   a. contained between angle brackets following a generic method's name
   b. contained between parentheses in a generic method's header
   c. placed in front of a generic method's name
   d. placed in a `using` statement at the top of a program file

4. When multiple generic types are used by a method, their names __________.

   a. must be `T` and `U`
   b. are separated by commas
   c. are separated by semicolons
   d. are separated by separate sets of angle brackets

5. Which of the following is not an advantage to creating a generic method instead of a nongeneric one?
   a. The amount of coding required is reduced.
   b. Diverse data types are handled consistently.
   c. The code within generic methods executes faster.
   d. You reduce the work needed when revisions are required.

6. Which of the following statements accurately describes the way the C# compiler operates?
   a. The JIT compiler converts source code into executable statements.
   b. The C# compiler converts source code to IL, and the JIT compiler converts IL into executable code.
   c. The C# compiler converts executable code back to source code when program execution is complete.
   d. The JIT compiler converts IL into source code and the C# compiler converts source code into executable statements.

7. What is the significance of the term JIT?
   a. It means that executable code is not created until the last possible moment after data types have been determined.
   b. It is a small program component.
   c. It means that generic parameters can be interpreted and used by the compiler.
   d. It means that generic methods execute more efficiently than nongeneric ones.

8. When a generic method uses type inferencing, ___________.
   a. all types in a method are determined from the types used in the method call
   b. parameterized types in a method are determined from the types used in the method call
   c. all types in the method are determined from the calling method's return type
   d. parameterized types in the method are determined from the method's type parameter list

9. If a call to a generic method specifies a value type as the argument, the JIT compiler replaces the generic type parameters with ___________.
   a. the specific value type
   b. a generic value type
   c. an `object` type
   d. a reference

10. If a call to a method specifies a reference type, the JIT compiler replaces the generic parameters with ___________.
   a. the specific type
   b. a generic value type
   c. an `object` type
   d. a reference

11. Assuming `money` is a `double`, which of the following method calls is identical to `CalculateInterest(money);`?

    a. `CalculateInterest<>(double);`

    b. `CalculateInterest(<double>);`

    c. `CalculateInterest<double>(<money>);`

    d. `CalculateInterest<double>(money);`

12. Type parameters can be used to declare ________.

    a. a generic method's parameter types

    b. a generic method's return type

    c. a local variable within a generic method

    d. all of the above

13. Which of the following is true about type parameters?

    a. You can only declare a type parameter once in a type parameter list.

    b. A type parameter can appear only once in a generic method's parameter list.

    c. Both of these are true.

    d. None of these are true.

14. Assume that `x` is an `int` and `s` is a `string`. Based on the following method header, which call to the method is invalid?

    ```
    public static void ProduceReport<T, U>(T count, U title)
    ```

    a. `ProduceReport(x, s);`

    b. `ProduceReport(s, x);`

    c. `ProduceReport(x, x);`

    d. All the calls are valid.

15. Which of the following method headers correctly overloads the following one?

    ```
    public static int MethodA<T, U>(T var1, U var2)
    ```

    a. `public static int MethodA<T, U, V>`
    `(T var1, U var2, V var3)`

    b. `public static int MethodA<T, U>(U var1, T var2)`

    c. `public static T MethodA<T, U>(T var1, U var2)`

    d. all of the above

16. Which of the following method headers correctly overloads this one?

    ```
    public static void MethodB<T>(T var)
    ```

    a. `public static T MethodB<T>(T var)`

    b. `public static void MethodB<U>(U var)`

    c. `public static void MethodB(double var)`

    d. all of the above

17. Which of the following is not true of type constraints?
    a. A type constraint is a clause that restricts the type of argument that can be supplied to a generic parameter.
    b. If a client program tries to use a constrained method with a type that is forbidden by the constraint, a compiler error is issued.
    c. You specify a type constraint using the keyword `constraint` followed by a colon and the constraint type.
    d. You can apply multiple constraints to a type parameter using a comma-separated list.

18. A generic class __________.
    a. describes a class that is not specific to a data type
    b. must include at least one generic method
    c. must include only generic methods
    d. all of the above

19. C#'s `List<T>` class includes all the following properties except __________.
    a. `Capacity`
    b. `Count`
    c. `Length`
    d. `Item`

20. C#'s `List<T>` class includes all the following methods except __________.
    a. `Subtract()`
    b. `FindAll()`
    c. `Reverse()`
    d. `Sort()`

EXERCISES

1. Write a generic method that accepts three parameters of the same type and displays them in order. For numeric data, "in order" means in numeric order. For other classes, you can define "in order" appropriately. Test your method using at least four different data types, including at least one for which you implement a `CompareTo()` method. Save the program as **OrderThree.cs**.

2. a. Create a `Book` class that holds a title and author of a book. Include a constructor that requires values for both data fields. Also include `Equals()` and `ToString()` methods that override the object class version. The `Equals()` method returns `true` when two `Book` objects have the same title and author.
   b. Create two generic methods that each accept an array and an individual object of the same type. Name the first method `EliminateDuplicates()`. When this method is passed an array, it searches the array and replaces any duplicate items with a default or elimination value represented by the second parameter. For example, when you pass the method a `Book` array, an appropriate elimination replacement value might be a `Book` for which the title and author are both set

to an empty string. When you pass the method an `int` array, an appropriate elimination replacement value might be 0. Name the second method `Display()`. When `Display()` is passed an array, it displays each element except any represented by the value used as the elimination value.

c. Write a program that demonstrates that both the `EliminateDuplicates()` and `Display()` methods work correctly with arrays of at least three different types (including `Book`), with arrays of different sizes, and with arrays that hold different numbers of duplicates. For each array type, display all the members, eliminate the duplicates, and display all the members again. Save the program as **EliminateDuplicatesDemo.cs**. Figure 20-36 shows a typical execution.

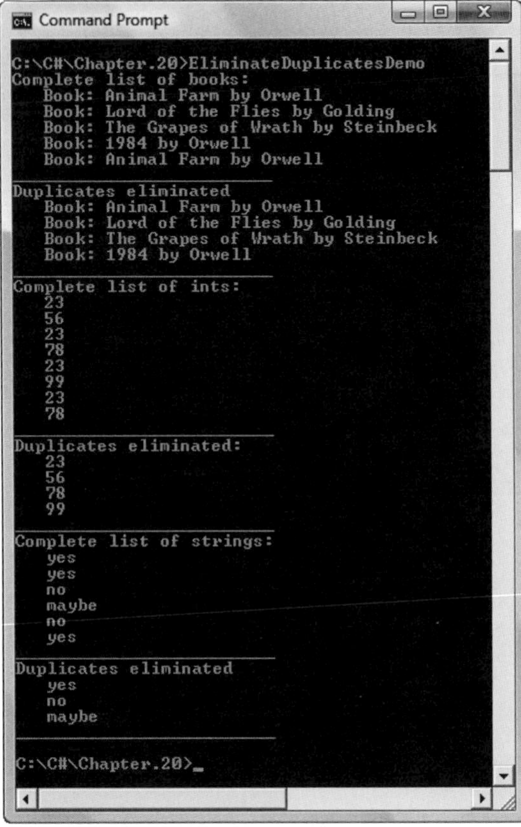

Figure 20-36 Typical execution of `EliminateDuplicatesDemo` program

3. Write a generic method that displays an object surrounded by a box constructed from asterisks. Write a demonstration program that shows that the method works correctly with at least five different data types, at least one of which must be a class you develop. Save the program as **FancyBox.cs**.

4. Write a program that generates 50 random numbers between 0 and 50 and store them in a `List<T>` object. Display the numbers, then compute and display their average. Determine the most frequently occurring value by extracting a series of sublists from the original list and compare their sizes. Display the value that occurs most frequently, then redisplay the list with asterisks next to the most frequent value so that the user can easily see its positions. Figure 20-37 shows a typical execution. Save the program as **RandomNumbers.cs**.

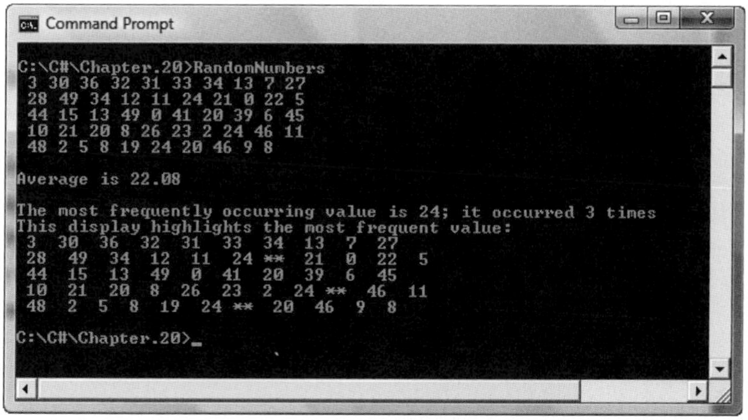

```
Command Prompt
C:\C#\Chapter.20>RandomNumbers
 3 30 36 32 31 33 34 13 7 27
 28 49 34 12 11 24 21 0 22 5
 44 15 13 49 0 41 20 39 6 45
 10 21 20 8 26 23 2 24 46 11
 48 2 5 8 19 24 20 46 9 8

Average is 22.08

The most frequently occurring value is 24; it occurred 3 times
This display highlights the most frequent value:
 3  30  36  32  31  33  34  13  7  27
 28  49  34  12  11  24 **  21  0  22  5
 44  15  13  49  0  41  20  39  6  45
 10  21  20  8  26  23  2  24 **  46  11
 48  2  5  8  19  24 **  20  46  9  8

C:\C#\Chapter.20>_
```

Figure 20-37 Typical execution of the `RandomNumbers` program

5. Create an `Item` class that holds an ID number, description, and price for an inventory item. The class implements `IComparable` to compare `Items` by their ID numbers. Create an application that allows you to add, find and display, or remove any item from a `List<T>` of items as long as the user wants to continue. Display appropriate error messages when the user tries to find or remove an item that does not exist. After the user adds any items, sort the list by ID number. After each user-initiated request, display the complete list and a current count of items in the list. Save the program as **InventoryManagement.cs**.

DEBUGGING EXERCISES

Each of the following files in the Chapter.20 folder on your Student Disk has syntax and/or logical errors. In each case, determine the problem and fix the program. After you correct the errors, save each file using the same filename preceded with *Fixed*. For example, save DebugTwenty1.cs as **FixedDebugTwenty1.cs**.

a. DebugTwenty1.cs
b. DebugTwenty2.cs
c. DebugTwenty3.cs
d. DebugTwenty4.cs

UP FOR DISCUSSION

1. In this chapter, you learned that when you call a generic method using a value type as the argument, the JIT compiler replaces the generic type parameters in the IL with the specific value type and compiles it to executable code. This creates a different compiled method version for each simple data type used. The advantage is that boxing and unboxing are eliminated. Are there any disadvantages to this approach?
2. From the programmer's point of view, what are the disadvantages to using generics?
3. Develop a real-life analogy for boxing and unboxing.

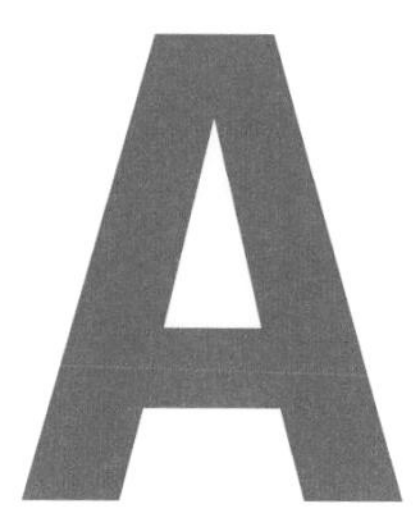

OPERATOR PRECEDENCE AND ASSOCIATIVITY

When an expression contains multiple operators, their **precedence** controls the order in which the individual operators are evaluated. For example, multiplication has a higher precedence than addition, so the expression 2 + 3 * 4 evaluates as 14 because the value of 3 * 4 is calculated before adding 2. Table A-1 summarizes all operators in order of precedence from highest to lowest.

When you use two operators with the same precedence, the **associativity** of the operators controls the order in which the operations are performed:

- Except for the assignment and conditional operators, all binary operators (those that take two arguments) are **left-associative**, meaning that operations are performed from left to right. For example, 5 + 6 + 7 is evaluated first as 5 + 6, or 11; then 7 is added, bringing the value to 18.
- The assignment operators and the conditional operator (?:) are **right-associative**, meaning that operations are performed from right to left. For example, x = y = z is evaluated as y = z first, and then x is set to the result.
- All unary operators (those that take one argument) are right-associative. If b is 5, the value of –++b is determined by evaluating ++b first (6), then taking its negative value (–6).

<table>
<tr><th>Category</th><th>Operators</th><th>Associativity</th></tr>
<tr><td>Primary</td><td>x.y f(x) a[x] x++ x-- new typeof checked unchecked</td><td>left</td></tr>
<tr><td>Unary</td><td>+ - ! ~ ++x --x (T)x</td><td>right</td></tr>
<tr><td>Multiplicative</td><td>* / %</td><td>left</td></tr>
<tr><td>Additive</td><td>+ -</td><td>left</td></tr>
<tr><td>Shift</td><td><< >></td><td>right</td></tr>
<tr><td>Relational</td><td>< > <= >= is as</td><td>left</td></tr>
<tr><td>Equality</td><td>== !=</td><td>left</td></tr>
<tr><td>Logical AND</td><td>&</td><td>left</td></tr>
<tr><td>Logical XOR</td><td>^</td><td>left</td></tr>
<tr><td>Logical OR</td><td>|</td><td>left</td></tr>
<tr><td>Conditional AND</td><td>&&</td><td>left</td></tr>
<tr><td>Conditional OR</td><td>||</td><td>left</td></tr>
<tr><td>Conditional</td><td>?:</td><td>right</td></tr>
<tr><td>Assignment</td><td>= *= /= %= += = <<= >>= &= ^= |=</td><td>right</td></tr>
</table>

Table A-1 Operator precedence

You can control precedence and associativity by using parentheses. For example, a + b * c first multiplies b by c and then adds the result to a. The expression (a + b) * c, however, forces the sum of a and b to be calculated first; then the result is multiplied by c.

KEY TERMS

The **precedence** of operators controls the order in which individual operators are evaluated in an expression.

The **associativity** of operators controls the order in which operations of equal precedence are performed in an expression.

With **left-associative** operators, operations are performed from left to right.

With **right-associative** operators, operations are performed from right to left.

B

CREATING A MULTIFILE ASSEMBLY

When you write a program that contains a `Main()` method and other methods, you can contain all the methods in a single file, as shown in the program in Figure B-1.

```
using System;
public class ProgramThatCallsAMethod
{
   public static void Main()
   {
      DisplayMessage();
   }
   public static void DisplayMessage()
   {
      Console.WriteLine("Hello");
   }
}
```

Figure B-1 A class that contains a `Main()` method and a `DisplayMessage()` method

>> **NOTE**
> You first learned about namespaces when you used the `System` namespace in Chapter 1. A namespace is a scheme that provides a way to group similar classes.

Instead of including the `DisplayMessage()` method in the `ProgramThatCallsAMethod` class, as shown in Figure B-1, you might want to write the method in its own class. That way, it can more easily be used by any application. To be able to use `DisplayMessage()` from its own class, you can create a multifile assembly. In the Microsoft .NET Framework, an **assembly** is a partially compiled code library; a **multifile assembly** is one composed from multiple files. As you become more proficient using C#, you will find additional reasons to create multifile assemblies besides including methods stored in separate files. Probably the most common reason is to combine modules written in different languages, such as Visual C++ or Visual Basic. To create a multifile assembly, you need to create a namespace and use some additional command-line options when you compile your program.

Suppose you want to include the `DisplayMessage()` method in its own class. Figure B-2 shows how the class should be constructed. The `DisplayMessage()` method has been copied from Figure B-1, and the shaded statements have been added.

```
namespace MessageNamespace
{
    using System;
    class Message
    {
        public static void DisplayMessage()
        {
            Console.WriteLine("Hello");
        }
    }
}
```

Figure B-2 The `MessageNamespace` namespace, stored in a file named DisplayMessage.cs

A namespace is created, using any identifier you choose. In Figure B-2, the name is `MessageNamespace`. Normally, you do not include *Namespace* within the name of a namespace; a more conventional name would be *Message*. This example uses *MessageNamespace* to help you remember that the name refers to a namespace rather than a class or a file. The `using System;` command is used in the DisplayMessage.cs file because the method uses `Console.WriteLine()`. The `DisplayMessage()` method is enclosed in its own class. The class might have any legal C# identifier; in this case, it is named `Message`.

When the file in Figure B-2 is saved as DisplayMessage.cs and compiled using the `csc` command, an error message is issued, as shown in Figure B-3. The message indicates that the file does not have a `Main()` method and cannot be compiled as a regular program. Your intention is not to have the class act as a stand-alone program; rather, you want the class to contain a method that other programs can use. To compile the class file, you must use a command that tells the compiler to create a **netmodule file**—that is, a file that contains modules to be used as part of another program rather than one that contains an executable program.

When you compile the program that contains the `Main()` method for the multifile assembly, you must include a command that adds the netmodule to the `Main()` program.

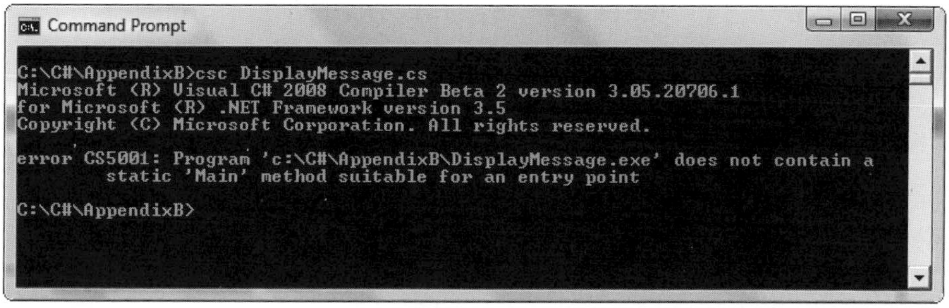

```
C:\C#\AppendixB>csc DisplayMessage.cs
Microsoft (R) Visual C# 2008 Compiler Beta 2 version 3.05.20706.1
for Microsoft (R) .NET Framework version 3.5
Copyright (C) Microsoft Corporation. All rights reserved.

error CS5001: Program 'c:\C#\AppendixB\DisplayMessage.exe' does not contain a
        static 'Main' method suitable for an entry point

C:\C#\AppendixB>
```

Figure B-3 Error message issued when DisplayMessage.cs is compiled using the `csc` command

To compile the DisplayMessage.cs file as a netmodule, use the following command:

```
csc /t:module DisplayMessage.cs
```

This command creates a file named DisplayMessage.netmodule. The file can now be used by a client program. For example, Figure B-4 shows a class named `Test`. Because the shaded statement `using MessageNamespace;` is included at the top of the file, the program has access to the methods stored in the `MessageNamespace` namespace. The method there can be called with the class-dot-method command `Message.DisplayMessage()`, as shown in the second shaded line.

```
using MessageNamespace;
public class Test
{
   public static void Main()
   {
      Message.DisplayMessage();
   }
}
```

Figure B-4 The `Test` class

After the client program in Figure B-4 is stored in a file named Test.cs, you can use the `addmodule` command to associate the netmodule file with the program.

```
csc Test.cs /addmodule:DisplayMessage.netmodule
```

Figure B-5 shows the command that compiles the program and the subsequent execution. The output "Hello" comes from the `DisplayMessage()` method within the `MessageNamespace` namespace.

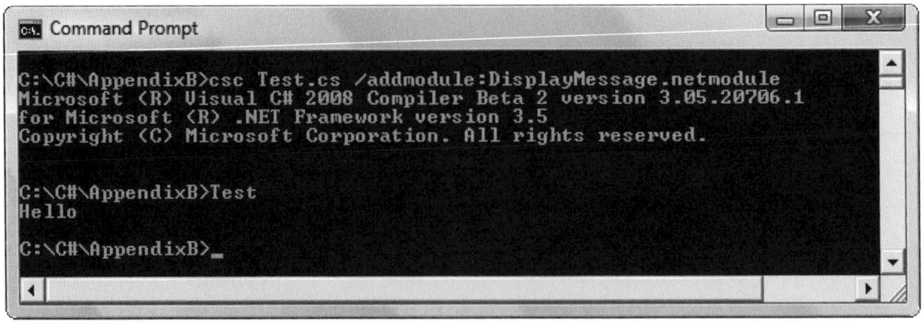

```
C:\C#\AppendixB>csc Test.cs /addmodule:DisplayMessage.netmodule
Microsoft (R) Visual C# 2008 Compiler Beta 2 version 3.05.20706.1
for Microsoft (R) .NET Framework version 3.5
Copyright (C) Microsoft Corporation. All rights reserved.


C:\C#\AppendixB>Test
Hello

C:\C#\AppendixB>_
```

Figure B-5 Compiling and executing Test.cs

KEY TERMS

An **assembly** is a partially compiled code library.

A **multifile assembly** is an assembly composed from multiple files.

A **netmodule file** contains modules to be used as part of another program rather than containing an executable program.

APPENDIX C

C

USING THE IDE EDITOR

The Visual C# Code Editor is like a word processor for writing source code. Just as a word-processing program provides support for spelling and grammar, the C# Code Editor helps ensure that your C# syntax is free of spelling and grammar errors. This support can be grouped into five main categories:

- IntelliSense
- Refactoring
- Code snippets
- Wavy underlines
- Readability aids

INTELLISENSE

IntelliSense is Microsoft's name for the set of features designed to minimize the time you spend looking for help and to help you enter code more accurately and efficiently. The IntelliSense features provide basic information about C# language keywords, .NET Framework types, and method signatures as you type them in the editor.

The information is displayed in ToolTips, list boxes, and Smart Tags. Features of IntelliSense include:

- » Providing completion lists
- » Providing quick information
- » Listing members
- » Providing parameter information
- » Adding `using` statements

PROVIDING COMPLETION LISTS

As you enter source code in the editor, IntelliSense displays a list box that contains all the C# keywords, .NET Framework classes, and names you have defined in your program that fit the current circumstances. For example, Figure C-1 shows a list box that makes suggestions based on what the programmer has typed in the Code Editor. If you find a match in the list box for the name you intend to type, you can select the item. Alternatively, you can press the Tab key to have IntelliSense finish entering the name or keyword for you.

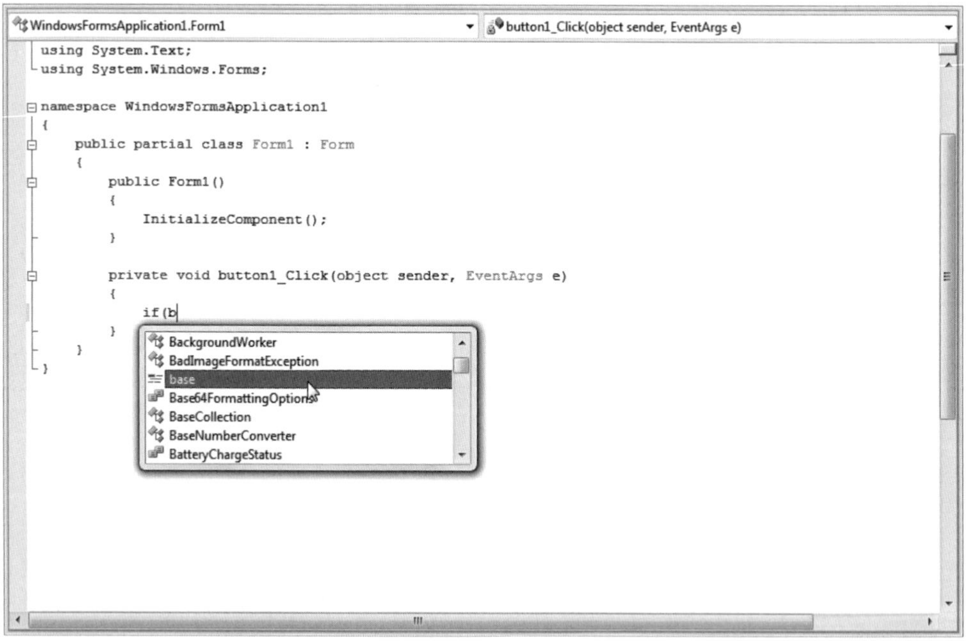

Figure C-1 A list displayed by IntelliSense

PROVIDING QUICK INFORMATION

When you hover the cursor over a .NET Framework type, IntelliSense displays a Quick Info ToolTip that contains basic documentation about that type.

LISTING MEMBERS

When you enter a .NET Framework type or an identifier of a specific type into the Code Editor, and then type the dot operator (.), IntelliSense displays a list box that contains the members of that type. When you make a selection and then press the Tab key, IntelliSense enters the member's name. For example, Figure C-2 shows the list displayed when the user types button1, which is an identifier of type Button. When you don't know what method or property you want for an object, typing its identifier and a dot can direct you to the appropriate choice. This technique sometimes teaches you about features you did not even realize were available.

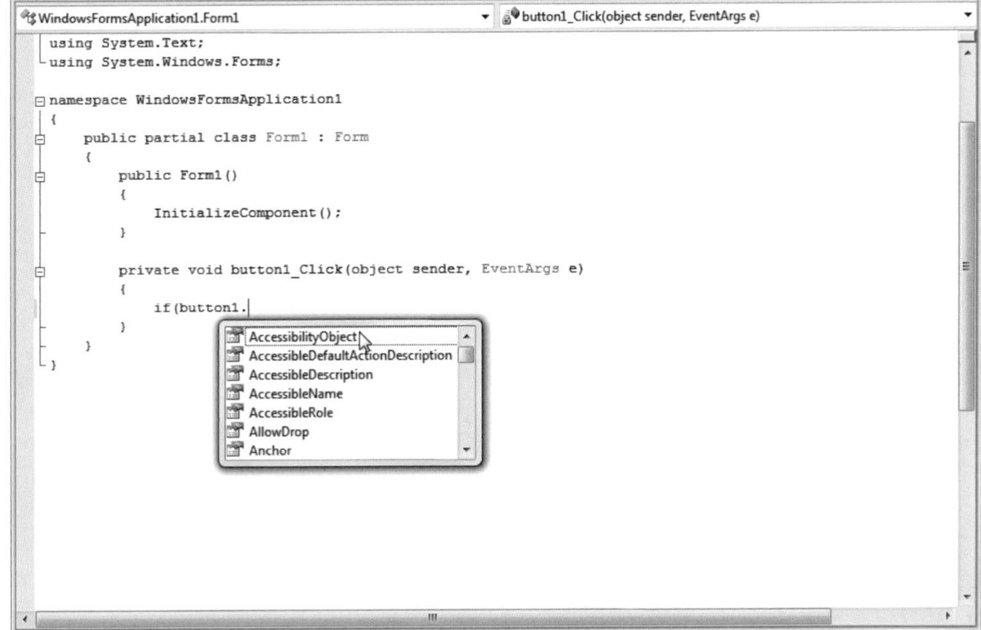

Figure C-2 List displayed after programmer types an object and a dot

PROVIDING PARAMETER INFORMATION

When you enter a method name in the Code Editor and then type an opening parenthesis, IntelliSense displays a Parameter Info ToolTip that shows the method's parameter list. If the method is overloaded, multiple method signatures are displayed and you can scroll through them.

ADDING `using` STATEMENTS

If you attempt to create an instance of a .NET Framework class without a sufficiently qualified name, IntelliSense displays a Smart Tag after the unresolved identifier. When you click the Smart Tag, IntelliSense displays a list of `using` statements to help you resolve the identifier. When you select one from the list, IntelliSense adds the directive to the top of your source code file, and you can continue coding at your current location.

REFACTORING

As a project grows during development, you sometimes need to make changes to make it more readable, better organized, or more portable. For example, you might want to divide methods into smaller methods, change the number or types of a method's parameters, or rename identifiers. **Refactoring** is the process of rewriting a computer program to improve its structure, readability, or performance without changing its function. The IDE's refactoring tool is accessible by right-clicking in the Code Editor. The tool helps you restructure code much more conveniently and thoroughly than traditional approaches, such as searching and replacing every instance of a variable name. For more information, see the C# documentation.

CODE SNIPPETS

Code snippets are small units of commonly used C# source code that you can enter accurately and quickly with only a couple of keystrokes. To access the code snippet menu, right-click in the Code Editor. You can browse from the many snippets provided with Visual C#, and you can also create your own.

WAVY UNDERLINES

Wavy underlines give you instant feedback about errors in your code as you type. A red wavy underline identifies a syntax error, such as a missing semicolon or mismatched braces. A green wavy underline identifies a potential compiler warning, and blue identifies an Edit and Continue issue. In Figure C-3, two wavy underlines appear because the code in the last statement is not yet complete.

```
using System.Text;
using System.Windows.Forms;

namespace WindowsFormsApplication1
{
    public partial class Form1 : Form
    {
        public Form1()
        {
            InitializeComponent();
        }

        private void button1_Click(object sender, EventArgs e)
        {
            if(button1.Text
        }
    }
}
```

Figure C-3 Wavy underlines in Code Editor

READABILITY AIDS

The editor assigns different colors to various categories of identifiers in a C# source code file to make the code easier to read. For example, C# keywords are bright blue, classes are blue-green, and comments are green.

KEY TERMS

IntelliSense is Microsoft's name for the set of features designed to minimize the time you spend looking for help and to help you enter code more accurately and efficiently.

Refactoring is the process of rewriting a computer program to improve its structure, readability, or performance without changing its function.

Code snippets are small units of commonly used C# source code that you can enter accurately and quickly with only a couple of keystrokes.

GLOSSARY

@-quoted string—a string preceded with an @ sign and within which escape sequences are not processed.

A

absolute positioning—the technique of placing components at specific points.

abstract class—a class from which you cannot create concrete objects, but from which you can inherit. Contrast with *concrete*.

abstract method—a method that contains no statements; any class derived from a class that contains an abstract method must override the abstract method by providing a body (an implementation) for it.

accessibility—describes limits set for a method as to whether and how other methods can use it.

access modifier—a keyword that defines the circumstances under which a method or class can be accessed; `public` access is the most liberal type of access.

accessors—methods in properties that specify how a class's fields are accessed. See *get accessors* and *set accessors*.

accumulated—describes totals added into a final sum by processing individual records one at a time in a loop.

actual parameters—arguments within a method call.

add and assign operator (+=)—an operator that adds the operand on the right to the operand on the left and assigns it to the operand on the left in one step.

aggregate operators—in LINQ, operators that produce statistics for groups of data.

alias—an alternative name or pseudonym.

ambiguous—describes overloaded methods between which the compiler cannot distinguish.

ancestors—all the superclasses from which a subclass is derived.

`Anchor` property—an attribute that causes a `Control` to remain at a fixed distance from the side of a container when the user resizes it.

AND operator—determines whether two expressions are both true; it is written using two ampersands (&&). Also called the *conditional AND operator*. Contrast with *Boolean logical AND*.

animation—the process of displaying slightly altered images, one at a time, to give the illusion of motion.

anomaly—an irregularity in a database's design that causes problems and inconveniences.

application files—files that store software instructions; program files. Contrast with *data files*.

arc—a portion of an ellipse.

ARGB values—values of a color that represent its alpha, red, green, and blue components.

argument—the expression passed to a method.

array—a list of data items that all have the same data type and the same name, but are distinguished from each other by a subscript or index.

array element—one object in an array.

assignment—a statement that provides a variable with a value.

assignment operator—the equal sign (=); any value to the right of the assignment operator is assigned to, or taken on by, the variable to the left.

associativity—specifies the order in which a sequence of operations with the same precedence are evaluated.

attached property—a property implemented by a parent control for use by child controls.

attributes—the characteristics of an object. In an XML document, a property that provides additional information about an element.

auto-implemented property—a property in which the code within the accessors is created automatically and the only action in the set accessor is to assign a value to the associated field. The only action in the get accessor is to return the associated field value.

B

`Background` state—a condition of a thread that runs when time becomes available because no threads in the foreground state need CPU time.

`base`—a keyword that refers to the superclass of the class in which you use it.

base 16—a mathematical system that uses 16 symbols to represent numbers; hexadecimal.

base class—a class that is used as a basis for inheritance.

binary files—files that can store any of the 256 combinations of bits in any byte instead of just those combinations that form readable text.

binary operators—operators that use two arguments: one value to the left of the operator and another value to the right of it.

`BinarySearch()` method—a member of the `System.Array` class that finds a requested value in a sorted array.

binary tree—a tree structure in which each node contains two links.

`Binding` class—a class that binds controls to data.

binding source—the data object in a binding scenario.

binding target—the control in a binding scenario.

black box—any device that you can use without knowing how it works internally.

block—a collection of one or more statements contained within a pair of curly braces.

block comments—comments that start with a forward slash and an asterisk (/*) and end with an asterisk and a forward slash (*/). Block comments can appear on a line by themselves, on a line before executable code, or after executable code. They can also extend across as many lines as needed. Compare with *line comments.*

`bool`—a data type that holds a Boolean value.

Boolean logical AND—an operator that determines whether two expressions are both true; it is written using a single ampersand (&). Unlike the conditional AND operator, it does not use short-circuit evaluation.

Boolean logical inclusive OR—an operator that determines whether at least one of two conditions is true; it is written using a single pipe (|). Unlike the conditional OR operator, it does not use short-circuit evaluation.

Boolean variable—a variable that can hold only one of two values—true or false.

bounding box—an imaginary box that surrounds an object.

boxing—the process of assigning a value type to an `object` reference.

branches—the paths of a tree structure created by its logical links.

`break`—a keyword that optionally terminates a `switch` structure at the end of each case.

`Brush` objects—objects used to color the inside of graphical shapes.

`Button`—a GUI object that you can click to cause some action.

`byte`—an integral data type that can hold an unsigned numeric value from 0 to 155.

C# programming language—a computer programming language developed as an object-oriented and component-oriented language. It exists as part of Visual Studio 2008, a package used for developing applications for the Windows family of operating systems.

call—to invoke a method.

called—describes a method that has been invoked.

called method—a method that has been invoked by another method.

calling method—a method that calls another method.

call stack—the memory location where the computer stores the list of locations to which the system must return after method calls.

camel casing—a style of creating identifiers in which the first letter is not capitalized, but each new word is. Contrast with *Pascal casing*.

`case`—a keyword in a `switch` structure that is followed by one of the possible values that might equal the `switch` expression.

case label—identifies a course of action in a `switch` structure.

`catch` block—a block of code that can catch one type of `Exception`.

`char`—an integral data type that can store a character such as 'A', '4', or '$'.

character—any one of the letters, numbers, or other special symbols (such as punctuation marks) that compose data.

character set—the group of all the characters used to represent data on a particular computer.

`CheckBox`—a GUI widget that a user can click to select or deselect an option. When a `Form` contains multiple `CheckBoxes`, any number of them can be checked or unchecked at the same time.

check digit—a digit calculated from a formula and appended to a number to help verify the accuracy of the other digits in the number.

`CheckedListBox`—a `Control` similar to a `ListBox`, with check boxes appearing to the left of each desired item.

child class—a derived class; a subclass; a class that has inherited from a base class.

child controls—the controls contained by a parent.

circular, doubly linked list—a list in which each node contains two references—one to the next element and one to the previous element—and in which the first node's previous reference points to the last object in the list and the last node's next reference points to the first object in the list. Compare with *circular, singly linked list* and *doubly linked list*.

circular, singly linked list—a list that begins with a reference to the first node, and in which each node contains a reference to a single next node and the last node holds a reference to the first node. Compare with *doubly linked list* and *singly linked list*.

class—a category of objects or a type of object.

class access modifier—describes access to a class.

class client—a program or class that instantiates objects of another prewritten class. Also called a *class user*.

class definition—the first class line that describes a class; it contains an optional access modifier, the keyword `class`, and any legal identifier for the name of the class.

class header—the first class line that describes a class; it contains an optional access modifier, the keyword `class`, and any legal identifier for the name of the class.

class user—a program or class that instantiates objects of another prewritten class. Also called a *class client*.

`Click` event—the action fired and the event generated when a `Control` is clicked in a GUI environment.

client—a method that uses another method.

closing a file—the process of making a file no longer available to an application.

code-behind—describes the set of programming language statements that provide functionality for a design.

code bloat—a term that describes unnecessarily long or repetitive program statements.

Code Editor—the portion of the Visual Studio IDE in which you can write or view code statements.

`Color`—a class that contains a wide variety of predefined colors to use with `Control`s.

`ComboBox`—a `Control` similar to a `ListBox`, except that it displays an additional editing field that allows a user to select from the list or enter new text.

command line—the line on which you type a command in a system that uses a text interface.

command prompt—a request for input that appears at the beginning of the command line.

comment out—to turn a statement into a comment so that the compiler will not execute its command.

`Compare()`—a method that compares two values. In the `String` class, it is a method that requires two `string` arguments; when it returns 0, the two `string`s are equivalent; when it returns a positive number, the first `string` is greater than the second; and when it returns a negative value, the first `string` is less than the second.

`CompareTo()`—a method that compares objects. In the `String` class, it is a method used with a `string` and a dot before the method name, with another `string` as an argument. When the method returns 0, the two `string`s are equivalent; when it returns a positive number, the first `string` is greater than the second; and when it returns a negative value, the first `string` is less than the second. In the `IComparable` interface, `CompareTo()` is a method that compares one object to another and returns an integer.

comparison operator(= =)—an operator that compares two items; an expression that contains a comparison operator has a Boolean value.

compiler—a computer program that translates high-level language statements into machine code.

compile-time safety—the compiler feature that provides for detecting mismatches of data types when a program is compiled.

`Component`—a class that provides containment and cleanup for other objects.

composed delegate—a delegate that calls the delegates from which it is built.

composite key—a key constructed from multiple columns; a compound key.

composition—the technique of using an object within another object.

compound key—a key constructed from multiple columns; a composite key.

computer file—a collection of information stored on a nonvolatile device in a computer system.

concatenate—to join strings together in a chain.

concrete—nonabstract; describes classes from which objects can be instantiated.

concurrently—during the same time period.

conditional AND operator—determines whether two expressions are both true; it is written using two ampersands (&&). Also called the *AND operator*. Contrast with *Boolean logical AND*.

conditional operator—a ternary operator that is used as an abbreviated version of the `if-else` statement; it requires three expressions separated by a question mark and a colon.

conditional OR operator—determines whether at least one of two conditions is true; it is written using two pipes (||). Also called the *OR operator*. Contrast with *Boolean logical inclusive OR*.

`Console.ReadLine()`—a method that accepts user input from the keyboard.

constant—describes a data item when it cannot be changed after a program is compiled—in other words, when it cannot vary.

constructor—a method that instantiates (creates an instance of) an object.

constructor initializer—a clause that indicates another instance of a class constructor should be executed before any statements in the current constructor body.

contextual keywords—identifiers that act like keywords in specific circumstances.

`Control`—a class that provides the definitions for GUI components such as text fields, buttons, and check boxes that users can manipulate to interact with a program.

counted loop—a definite loop.

CSV file—a file that contains comma-separated values.

culture—a set of rules that determines how culturally dependent values such as money and dates are formatted.

D

database—a collection of files that an organization needs to support its applications.

database management software or **database management system (DBMS)**—a set of programs that allows users to create table descriptions, identify keys, add, delete, and update records within a table, arrange records within a table so that they are sorted by different fields, write questions that select specific records from a table for viewing, write questions that combine information from multiple tables, create reports, and keep data secure.

data binding engine—software that connects data and controls.

data files—files that contain facts and figures; persistent collections of related records. Contrast with *program files* and *application files*.

data hierarchy—the relationship of characters, fields, records, and files.

data redundancy—the unnecessary repetition of data.

data type—a description of the format and size of a data item as well as the operations that can be performed on it.

`DateTimePicker`—a `Control` that retrieves date and time information.

dead code—describes code statements that can never execute under any circumstances because the program logic "can't get there." Also see *unreachable*.

deadlock—the state that occurs when two `Threads` must wait for each other to do something before either can progress.

debugging—the process of removing all syntax and logical errors from a program.

`decimal`—a floating-point data type that has a greater precision and a smaller range than a `float` or `double`, which makes it suitable for financial and monetary calculations.

decision structure—a unit of program logic that involves choosing between alternative courses of action based on some value.

decrementing—the act of decreasing the value of a variable, often by 1.

decrement operator (--)—an operator that reduces a variable's value by 1; there is a prefix and a postfix version.

`default`—a keyword that optionally is used prior to any action that should occur if the test expression in a case structure does not match any case.

default constructor—a constructor that requires no parameters; the automatically supplied parameterless constructor for a class is a default constructor, but you can also create a default constructor.

default event—for a `Control`, the event or method generated when you double-click it while designing it in the IDE. It is the method you are most likely to alter when you use the `Control`, as well as the event that users most likely expect to generate when they encounter the `Control` in a working application.

default value of an object—the value initialized with a default constructor.

definite loop—a loop in which the number of iterations is predetermined. Also called a *counted loop*. Contrast with *indefinite loop*.

delegate—an object that contains a reference to a method.

delimiter—a character used to specify the boundary between characters in text files.

deprecated—describes features of programming languages that have been superseded by newer techniques and that should not be used.

dequeue—the queue removal operation. Contrast with *enqueue*.

derived class—a subclass; a class that has inherited from a base class.

deserialization—the process of converting streams of bytes back into objects.

destructor—a method that contains the actions performed when an instance of a class is destroyed.

`DialogResult`—an enumeration that contains a user's potential `MessageBox` button selections.

directories—structures used to organize files on a storage device; folders.

`Directory` **class**—a class that provides information about directories or folders.

dismiss—to get rid of a component, frequently by pressing its Close button, but in some cases by making some other selection.

dispatching the thread—the assignment of a processor to a thread by the operating system.

`Dock` **property**—an attribute that attaches a `Control` to the side of a container so that the `Control` stretches when the container's size is adjusted.

`do` **loop**—a type of posttest loop; a loop that is tested at the bottom of the loop after one repetition has occurred.

`double`—a data type that can hold a floating-point number with 15 or 16 significant digits of accuracy.

doubly linked list—a list in which each node contains two references—one to the next element and one to the previous element. Contrast with *singly linked list*.

`DrawLine()` **method**—a graphics method that draws a line on the screen.

dual-alternative decisions—decisions that have two possible outcomes.

duck typing—the process of implicitly typing a variable.

dynamic memory allocation—the allotment of new memory during a program's execution.

E

elements—components that specify an XML document's structure.

ellipse—an oval shape.

empty body—a block that has no statements in it.

encapsulation—the technique of packaging an object's attributes and methods into a cohesive unit that can be used as an undivided entity.

end tags—XML document element delimiters; they start with a left angle bracket and a forward slash.

engine—software that is the "working part" of a program, as opposed to the parts that affect appearance.

enqueue—the queue insert operation. Contrast with *dequeue*.

`enum`—an enumeration; a programmer-defined type that declares a set of constants.

enumeration—a list of values in which names are substituted for numeric values.

`Equals()`—a method that determines equivalency; in the `String` class, it is the method that determines if two `string`s have the same value; it requires two `string` arguments that you place within its parentheses, separated by a comma.

error list tab—a portion of the Visual Studio IDE that displays compiler errors.

escape sequence—a single character composed of two symbols beginning with a backslash that represents a nonprinting character such as a tab.

event—an object generated when a user interacts with a GUI object, causing the program to perform a task.

`EventArgs`—a C# class designed for holding event information.

event-driven—describes programs that contain code that causes an event such as a button click to drive the program to perform a task.

`EventHandler`—a class for events that do not use any information besides the source of the event and the `EventArgs` parameter.

event handler—a method that performs a task in response to an event; an event receiver.

event receiver—a method that performs a task in response to an event; an event handler.

event sender—the control that generates an event.

event wiring—the act of connecting an event to its resulting actions.

exception—an error condition or unexpected behavior in an executing program.

exception handling—the set of object-oriented techniques used to manage unexpected errors.

explicit cast—purposefully assigns a value to a different data type; it involves placing the desired result type in parentheses followed by the variable or constant to be cast.

explicitly—purposefully. Contrast with *implicitly*.

exposes—a term used to associate a `FileStream` with a file.

extended class—a derived class; a child class; a subclass; a class that has inherited from a base class.

extensible—describes a language that can be extended by users defining their own language elements.

Extensible Application Markup Language (**XAML,** pronounced *zammel*)—a markup language created by Microsoft for .NET.

Extensible Markup Language (**XML**)—a specification for creating markup languages.

extension methods—static methods that act like instance methods. You can write extension methods to add to any type.

F

fault-tolerant—describes applications that are designed so that they continue to operate, possibly at a reduced level, when some part of the system fails.

field—in a class, an instance variable. In a file or database, a character or group of characters that has some meaning.

`File` class—a class that contains methods that allow you to access information about files.

file position pointer—a variable that holds the byte number of the next byte to be read from a file.

filter operators—operators that define criteria in the `select` attribute in `for-each` statements in XML documents.

`finally` block—a block of code that optionally follows a `try` block; the code within one executes whether the `try` block identifies any `Exception`s or not.

fires an event—causes an event to occur. Also see *raises an event* and *triggers an event*.

first-in first-out (FIFO)—describes a data structure in which the first item added is the first one removed. Contrast with *last-in first-out*.

`float`—a data type that can hold a floating-point number with as many as seven significant digits of accuracy.

floating-point—describes a number that contains decimal positions.

flowchart—a tool that helps programmers plan a program's logic by writing program steps in diagram form, as a series of shapes connected by arrows.

foci—two fixed points on an ellipse; every other point on an ellipse is the same distance from these foci.

focus—refers to the "ready" state of a GUI component, in which its action is executed if the user presses the Enter key. When a component has focus, the user's attention is drawn to it visually.

folders—structures used to organize files on a storage device; directories.

`Font`—a class used to change the appearance of printed text on `Forms`.

`for` loop—a loop that contains the starting value for the loop control variable, the test condition that controls loop entry, and the expression that alters the loop control variable, all in one statement.

`for-each` statement—a statement in an XML document that selects attributes.

`foreach` statement—a C# statement used to cycle through every array element without using a subscript.

Form Designer—a portion of the Visual Studio IDE in which you visually design applications.

formal parameter—a parameter within a method header that accepts a value.

format specifier—one of nine built-in format characters in a format string that defines the most commonly used numeric format types.

format string—a string of characters that contains one or more placeholders for variable values.

`Forms`—a GUI interface for collecting, displaying, and delivering information.

fragile—describes classes that depend on field names from parent classes because they are prone to errors—that is, they are easy to "break."

`from`—a LINQ keyword that indicates the collection or sequence from which data will be drawn.

G

garbage—an unknown memory value.

garbage collection—a feature of automatic memory management; the garbage collector frees up memory occupied by objects that a program no longer needs.

generic class—describes a class that is not specific to a data type.

generic method—a method that can work with multiple data types by using a type parameter list.

generics—a programming feature that provides a compromise between the flexibility of creating structures that can handle any object type and the safety of checking for correct data types.

get accessors—methods in properties that allow retrieval of a field value by using a property name.

getter—another term for a class property's get accessor.

globalization—the process of making programs useful and appropriate for cultures worldwide.

governing type—in a `switch` statement, the type that is established by the `switch` expression. The governing type can be `sbyte`, `byte`, `short`, `ushort`, `int`, `uint`, `long`, `ulong`, `char`, `string`, or `enum`.

gradient axis—a line along which colors are blended using a gradient brush.

graphical user interface (GUI)—an interface that employs graphical images that the user manipulates. GUI objects include the buttons, check boxes, and toolbars that you are used to controlling with a mouse when you interact with Windows-type programs.

`Graphics` class—a class that contains methods you can use to draw strings, lines, and shapes on a control.

graphics context—a collection of attributes that determines how graphics operations affect components.

Graphics Device Interface Plus (GDI+)—an application programming interface that allows applications to use graphics and formatted text both on video displays and printers.

Graphics Interchange Format (GIF)—an image format that can contain a maximum of 256 different colors.

`Graphics` **object**—an object that manages a graphics context by controlling how much information is drawn.

`group` **operator**—in LINQ, the operator that groups data by specified criteria.

`GroupBox`—a `Control` that can be used to group other `Controls` on a `Form`; similar to a `Panel`, but it has a `Title` property.

H

has-a relationship—the relationship created using composition, so called because one class "has an" instance of another.

hash code—a number that should uniquely identify an object.

hexadecimal—a mathematical system that uses 16 symbols to represent numbers; base 16.

hides—overrides so as to make invisible.

high-level programming language—allows you to use a vocabulary of reasonable terms such as "read," "write," or "add" instead of the sequence of on/off switches that perform these tasks.

Hypertext Markup Language (HTML)—a markup language designed to display data.

I

`IComparable` **interface**—an interface that contains the definition for the `CompareTo()` method.

identifier—the name of a program component such as a variable, class, or method.

`if-else` **statement**—a statement that performs a dual-alternative decision.

`if` **statement**—a program statement used to make a single-alternative decision.

image—a likeness of a person or thing.

`Image` **class**—a class that holds images.

immutable—unchangeable.

implementation hiding—the technique of keeping the details of a method's operations hidden.

implicit cast—the automatic transformation that occurs when a value is assigned to a type with higher precedence.

implicit conversion—the conversion that occurs when a type is automatically changed to another upon assignment.

implicit parameter—an undeclared parameter that gets its value automatically.

implicit reference conversion—a type of conversion that occurs when a derived class object is assigned to its ancestor's data type.

implicitly—automatically. Contrast with *explicitly*.

implicitly typed variable—a variable that has a data type that is inferred from the expression used to initialize the variable.

incrementing—the act of increasing the value of a variable, often by 1.

indefinite loop—a loop in which the number of iterations is not predetermined. Contrast with *definite loop*.

index—an integer contained within square brackets that indicates the position of one of an array's elements. Also see *subscript*.

infinite loop—a loop that (theoretically) never ends.

information hiding—a feature found in all object-oriented languages, in which a class's data is private and changed or manipulated only by its own methods.

inheritance—the ability to extend a class so as to create a more specific class that contains all the attributes and methods of a more general class; the extended class usually contains new attributes or methods as well. Inheritance also refers to the application of your knowledge of a general category to more specific objects.

initialization—an assignment made when a variable is declared.

initializer list—the list of values provided for an array.

inner loop—the loop in a pair of nested loops that is entirely contained within another loop.

in parallel—describes tasks that execute concurrently.

instance—an object; one specific occurrence of a class. Often used as "instance of a class."

instance methods—methods that are used with object instantiations.

instance variables—data components of a class that exist separately for each instantiation. Also called *fields*.

instantiation—a created object.

`int`—an integral data type that can hold a signed numeric value in four bytes.

integers—whole numbers.

integral data types—data types that store whole numbers; the nine integral types are `byte`, `sbyte`, `short`, `ushort`, `int`, `uint`, `long`, `ulong`, and `char`.

interactive program—a program that allows user input.

interface—a collection of abstract methods (and perhaps other members) that can be used by any class as long as the class provides a definition to override the interface's abstract definitions. An interface is also the interaction between a method and an object.

intermediate language (IL)—the language into which source code statements are compiled.

internal—a class access modifier that means access is limited to the assembly to which the class belongs.

internal access—a level of method accessibility that limits method access to the containing program.

intrinsic types—basic, built-in data types; C# provides 14 intrinsic types.

invoked—describes a method that has been called.

invokes—to call a method.

invoking object—the object referenced by `this` in an instance method.

invoking the event—calling an event method.

is-a relationships—object-class relationships.

iteration—one execution of any loop.

iteration variable—a temporary variable that holds each array value in turn in a `foreach` statement.

jagged array—a one-dimensional array in which each element is another array.

Joint Photographic Experts Group (JPEG)—an image format that is commonly used to store photographs. JPEG is a sophisticated way to represent a color image.

jump statement—a statement that causes program logic to "jump" out of the normal flow in a control structure. Jump statements include `break` and `continue`.

just in time (JIT)—the C# compiler that translates intermediate code into executable code.

key—a value that uniquely identifies a record.

key events—keyboard events that occur when a user presses and releases keyboard keys.

key field—the field used to control the order of records in a sequential file.

keywords—predefined and reserved identifiers that have special meaning to the compiler.

`Label`—a `Control` object that typically provides descriptive text for another `Control` object or displays other text information on a `Form`.

last-in first-out (LIFO)—describes a data structure in which the last item added is the first item removed. Contrast with *first-in first-out*.

layout—the arrangement of the collection of children that reside on a parent container.

leaf—a node in a tree structure that has no further branches.

left child—one of the nodes to which a parent node in a binary tree links. Also see *right child.*

`Length` property—a member of the `System.Array` class that automatically holds an array's length.

Leszynski naming convention (LNC)—a convention for naming database elements that is most popular with Microsoft Access users and Visual Basic programmers.

lexically—alphabetically.

line comments—comments that start with two forward slashes (//) and continue to the end of the current line. Line comments can appear on a line by themselves, or at the end of a line following executable code. Compare with *block comments.*

linear data structures—structures in which each node is linked to another in a line.

linked list—a sequence of objects that are connected by references.

`LinkLabel`—a `Control` that is similar to a `Label`, but provides the additional capability to link the user to other sources, such as Web pages or files.

LINQ (Language INtegrated Query)—provides a set of general-purpose standard query operators that allow queries to be constructed in C#. LINQ uses easy-to-understand syntax that is similar to SQL and that the compiler can check for errors.

`ListBox`—a `Control` that enables you to display a list of items that the user can select by clicking.

literal constant—a value that is taken literally at each use.

literal string—a series of characters that is used exactly as entered.

local variable—a variable that is declared in the current method.

locking an object—the act of excluding all but one thread from access to the object.

logic—the sequence of statements and methods that produce the desired results in a computer program.

`long`—an integral data type that can hold a signed numeric value in eight bytes.

loop—a structure that allows repeated execution of a block of statements.

loop body—the block of statements executed in a loop.

loop control variable—a variable that determines whether loop execution will continue on each iteration.

lossless data compression—a set of rules that allows an exact replica of data to be reconstructed from a compressed version.

M

machine language—the most basic circuitry-level language.

magic number—a hard-coded number.

main menu—in the Visual Studio IDE, the list of choices that run horizontally across the top of the screen; it includes a File menu from which you open, close, and save projects.

markup—the sequence of characters and symbols that you can insert into text to indicate how a file should look when it is printed or displayed on a computer screen.

`match` attribute—an attribute in an XML file that associates a template with an XML element.

matrix—a name frequently used by mathematicians when referring to an array. Also see *table.*

`MaximumSize` property—an attribute of a `Form` that has two values—`Width` and `Height`.

menu strip—a horizontal list of general options that appears under the title bar of a `Form` or `Window`.

`MenuStrip`—a control that creates a menu strip.

`MessageBox`—a GUI object that can contain text, buttons, and icons that inform and instruct a user.

method—an encapsulated series of statements that carry out a task.

method body—the block of statements that carry out a method's work; all the instructions contained within a pair of curly braces ({ }) following a method header.

method declaration—a method header or definition; it precedes a method and includes a `return` type, identifier, and an optional parameter list.

method definition—a method header or declaration; it precedes a method and includes a `return` type, identifier, and an optional parameter list.

method header—the first line of a method; it includes the method name and information about what will pass into and be returned from a method.

method node—in Visual Studio, a small box that appears to the left of code; you use it to expand or collapse code.

method's type—a method's `return` type.

Microsoft Office Access—a relational database that is part of the 2007 Microsoft Office system.

`MinimumSize` property—an attribute of a `Form` that has two values—`Width` and `Height`.

mission critical—describes any process that is crucial to an organization.

modal dialog box—a dialog box that prevents a program from further progress until the user dismisses it.

`Monitor` class—a class that provides the means to lock objects to implement synchronized access to shared data.

`MonthCalendar`—a `Control` that retrieves date and time information.

multidimensional arrays—arrays that require multiple subscripts to access the array elements.

multifile assembly—a group of files containing methods that work together to create an application.

multimedia—describes the use of sound, images, graphics, and video in computer programs.

multiple inheritance—the ability to inherit from more than one class.

multithreading—the process of using multiple threads of execution in a program.

N

named constant—an identifier whose contents cannot change.

namespace—a scheme that provides a way to group similar classes.

negotiation—the process of determining the most appropriate layout based on the needs of components.

nested `if`—a statement in which one decision structure is contained within another.

nested method calls—method calls placed inside other method calls.

`new`—a keyword used to create objects; also known as the `new` operator.

node—in the Visual Studio IDE, a box that appears on a vertical tree to the left of a list or a section of code and that can be expanded or condensed. Also, an object in a linked list.

nonlinear data structure—a structure in which each node contains multiple self-referential links that branch to diverse paths.

nonstatic—describes a method that requires an object reference.

nonvolatile—the type of computer storage that is permanent; it is not lost when a computer loses power.

normalization—the process of designing and creating a set of database tables that satisfies the users' needs and avoids many potential problems such as data redundancies and anomalies.

NOT operator (!)—negates the result of any Boolean expression.

`object` (or `Object`)—a class type in the `System` namespace that is the ultimate base class for all other types.

object initializer—a clause that allows you to assign values to any accessible members or properties of a class at the time of instantiation without calling a constructor with parameters.

object-oriented programming—a programming technique that features objects, classes, encapsulation, interfaces, polymorphism, and inheritance.

objects—program elements that are instances of a class.

one-dimensional array—an array whose elements you can access using a single subscript. Also see *single-dimensional array*.

one-time binding—binding that exists when a source provides values for the target just once to initialize it, but no further changes cause any effects.

one-way binding—binding that exists when a change in a source causes a change in the target, or a change in the target causes a change in the source. Contrast with *two-way binding*.

opacity—the degree of transparency of a color.

opening a file—the process of creating an object and associating a stream of bytes with it.

operands—the values that operators use in expressions.

operator precedence—rules that determine the order in which parts of a mathematical expression are evaluated. Also called *order of operation*.

OR operator—determines whether at least one of two conditions is true; it is written using two pipes (||). Also called the *conditional OR operator*. Contrast with *Boolean logical inclusive OR*.

`orderby` operator—in LINQ, the operator that sorts a collection of data based on a field or fields.

order of operation—rules that determine the order in which parts of a mathematical expression are evaluated. Also called *operator precedence*.

outer loop—the loop in a pair of nested loops that contains another loop.

out of scope—describes a variable that is not usable because it has ceased to exist.

output parameter—a parameter to a method that receives the argument's address; it is not required to have an initial value. Contrast with *value parameter* and *reference parameter*.

output tab—a portion of the Visual Studio IDE that displays compiler errors.

overloading—using one term to indicate diverse meanings. When you overload a C# method, you write multiple methods with the same name but different parameter lists.

`override`—a keyword used in method headers when you create a derived class that inherits an abstract method from a parent.

override—the action that occurs when a method takes precedence over another method, hiding the original version.

P

`Padding` property—an attribute of a `Form` that specifies the distance between docked `Controls` and the edges of the `Form`.

`Paint` event—an event that is triggered when painting is required.

painting—the act of displaying or redisplaying a surface.

`Panel`—a `Control` that can be used to group other `Controls` on a `Form`; similar to a `GroupBox`, but it does not have a `Title` property.

parallel array—an array that has the same number of elements as another array and holds corresponding data.

parameter—an object or reference that is declared in a method definition; that is, where the method instructions are written.

parameter array—a local array declared within a method header.

parameterized type—a data type that is determined by a parameter in a generic method.

parameterless constructor—a constructor that takes no parameters; one that is called using no arguments.

`params`—a keyword used to declare a local array in a method so the method can receive any number of arguments.

parent class—a base class; a superclass; a class that is used as a basis for inheritance.

Pascal casing—a style of creating identifiers in which the first letter of all new words in a variable name, even the first one, is capitalized. Contrast with *camel casing*.

passed by reference—describes how data is passed to a method when the method receives the memory address of the argument passed to it.

path—the disk drive in which a file resides plus the complete hierarchy of directories.

peek—to examine an object without removing it from a list, stack, or queue.

peers—`Thread`s with the same priority.

`Pen` **class**—a class that provides a tool for drawing lines, curves, and outlines.

permanent storage devices—hardware such as hard disks, floppy disks, Zip disks, USB drives, reels or cassettes of magnetic tape, and compact discs, which are used to store files.

persistent—describes storage that is nonvolatile.

`PictureBox`—a `Control` in which you can display graphics from a bitmap, icon, JPEG, GIF, or other image file type.

pixel—a picture element, or one tiny dot on a monitor.

placeholder—in a format string, it consists of a pair of curly braces containing a number that indicates the desired variable's position in a list that follows the string.

`Point` **object**—describes a single screen position; it contains x- and y-coordinates.

polygon—a multisided shape.

polymorphism—the ability to create methods that act appropriately depending on the context.

pop—to remove an object from a stack. Contrast with *push*.

Portable Network Graphics (PNG)—an image format that is more flexible than the GIF format and stores images in a lossless form.

postfix increment operator (++)—an operator placed after a variable that evaluates the variable and then adds 1 to it.

posttest loop—a loop in which the loop control variable is tested after the loop body executes. Contrast with *pretest loop*.

precision specifier—controls the number of significant digits or zeros to the right of the decimal point in a format string.

predicate method—a Boolean method that defines a set of criteria and determines whether the specified object meets those criteria. Also called a *predicate delegate* or a *predicate*.

prefix increment operator (++)—an operator placed before a variable that increases the variable's value by 1 and then evaluates it.

preprocessor—a program that executes before the compiler and looks for preprocessor directives for instructions on how to modify code.

preprocessor directives—statements that always start with a pound sign (#) and are instructions to the preprocessor to modify the code in some way.

pretest loop—a loop in which the loop control variable is tested before the loop body executes. Contrast with *posttest loop*.

primary key—a value that uniquely identifies a record; the term is often used in databases.

primitive data—simple data, such as a number.

priority—a rank of preferential access to an operating system's resources.

`private`—an access modifier that indicates other classes may not use the method or variable that it modifies. When used as a class access modifier, it means access is limited to another class to which the class belongs.

private access—a level of method accessibility that limits method access to the containing class.

procedural program—a program created by writing a series of steps or operations to manipulate values.

procedures—compartmentalized program units that accomplish tasks. Also see *methods*.

program—a set of instructions that you write to tell a computer what to do.

program comments—nonexecuting statements that document a program.

program files—files that store software instructions; application files. Contrast with *data files*.

projection operator—in LINQ, an operator that projects, or sends off, specific data from a collection.

prompt—an instruction to the user to enter data.

Properties window—a portion of the Visual Studio IDE that allows you to configure properties and events on controls in your user interface.

property—a member of a class that provides access to a field of a class; properties define how fields will be set and retrieved. The value of an object.

property element syntax—the XAML syntax used to assign nonstring values to object properties.

`protected`—a keyword that provides an intermediate level of security between `public` and `private` access. A `protected` data field or method can be used within its own class or in any classes extended from that class, but it cannot be used by "outside" classes. As a class access modifier, it means access to the class is limited to the class and to any classes derived from the class.

`protected` access—a level of method accessibility that limits method access to the containing class or types derived from the containing class.

`protected` internal access—a level of method accessibility that limits method access to the containing program, containing class, or types derived from the containing class.

pseudocode—a tool that helps programmers plan a program's logic by writing plain English statements.

`public`—an access modifier that indicates other classes may use the method or variable that it modifies. As a class access modifier, it means access to the class is not limited.

`public` access—a level of method accessibility that allows unlimited access to a method.

push—to add a new node to the top of a stack. Contrast with *pop*.

Q

quantum—the small segment of processor time each thread receives to execute.

query—a question asked to retrieve information from a database using the syntax that the database software can understand.

query by example—a language that allows you to query relational databases by filling in blanks.

queue—a form of linked list in which nodes are inserted at the end but removed from the beginning. Contrast with *stack*.

R

race hazard—a flaw in a system in which the results of a process are critically dependent on the timing of other processes.

`RadioButtons`—GUI widgets, similar to `CheckBox`es, except that when they are placed on a `Form`, only one `RadioButton` can be selected at a time—selecting any `RadioButton` automatically deselects the others.

raises an event—causes an event to occur. Also see *fires an event* and *triggers an event*.

random access memory (RAM)—temporary storage in a computer.

range check—a series of statements that determine whether a value falls within a specified range.

range match—a process that determines whether a value falls between a pair of limiting values.

read from the file—to copy data from a file on a storage device into RAM.

read-only property—a property that has only a get accessor, and not a set accessor.

ready queue—a list of the threads that are ready to obtain a lock.

record—a collection of fields that contain data about an entity.

rectangular array—an array in which each row has the same number of columns.

recursive—describes a method that calls itself.

reference equality—a type of equality that occurs when two reference type objects refer to the same object.

reference parameter—a parameter to a method that receives the argument's address; it is required to have an initial value. Contrast with *value parameter* and *output parameter*.

reference type—a data type that holds a memory address. Contrast with *value types*.

relational database—a database in which you can establish and maintain relationships between columns in the tables.

relative positioning—the technique of placing components in positions that depend on the borders of their containers and the placement of other components.

restriction operator—in LINQ, an operator that places a restriction on which data is added to a collection.

rethrowing the `Exception`—the act of throwing a caught `Exception` instead of handling it.

`return` statement—a method statement that causes a value to be sent back from a method to its calling method.

`return` type—the data type of the value a method will return to any other method that calls it.

`Reverse()` method—a member of the `System.Array` class that reverses the order of items in an array.

right child—one of the nodes to which a parent node in a binary tree links. Also see *left child*.

robustness—describes the degree to which a system is resilient to stress, maintaining correct functioning even in the presence of errors.

root directory—the main directory of a storage device.

root element—the main element in an XML document tree.

routed event—a WPF construct and a type of event that can invoke handlers on multiple listeners in an element tree, rather than just on the object that raised the event.

S

`sbyte`—an integral data type that can hold a signed numeric value from –128 to 127.

scientific notation—a numeric expression format that includes an *E* (for exponent) that specifies a number of implied decimal places.

scope—the area where a variable or constant is known and can be used.

`sealed`—a keyword that describes a class that cannot be extended.

`select`—a LINQ keyword that indicates what to select from a collection.

SELECT-FROM-WHERE—the basic form of the SQL command that retrieves selected records from a table.

self-documenting—describes a program element that is self-explanatory.

self-referential class—a class that contains a reference to an object of the same type.

semantic errors—the type of logical errors that occur when you use a correct word in the wrong context.

sentinel value—a value that a user must supply to stop a loop.

sequence structure—a unit of program logic in which one step follows another unconditionally.

sequential access file—a data file in which each record is read in order based on its position in the file; usually the records are stored in order based on the value in some field.

serialization—the process of converting objects into streams of bytes.

set accessors—methods in properties that allow use of the assignment operator with a property name.

setter—another term for a class property's set accessor.

`short`—an integral data type that can hold a signed numeric value in two bytes.

short-circuit evaluation—the C# feature in which parts of an AND or OR expression are evaluated only as far as necessary to determine whether the entire expression is true or false.

side effect—an unintended consequence of an operation.

signature—a method's name and parameter list.

significant digits—specifies the mathematical accuracy of the value.

single-dimensional array—an array whose elements you can access using a single subscript. Also see *one-dimensional array*.

singly linked list—a list that begins with a reference to the first node, and in which each node contains a reference to a single next node; the list ends when a node's link is `null`. Contrast with *doubly linked list*.

snap lines—lines that appear in a design environment to help you align new `Controls` with others already in place.

Solution Explorer—a portion of the Visual Studio IDE that allows you to view and manage project files and settings.

`Sort()` method—a member of the `System.Array` class that arranges array items in ascending order.

source code—the statements you write when you create a program.

stack—a specialized form of linked list in which nodes are added or removed only from the top of the list. Contrast with *queue*.

standard numeric format strings—strings of characters expressed within double quotation marks that indicate a format for output.

start tags—XML document element delimiters; they begin with a left angle bracket (<).

`StartsWith()`—a `String` method that returns `true` if the object `string` starts with the characters contained in the argument `string`.

starvation—a state that occurs when a `Thread` cannot make any progress because of the priorities of other `Threads`.

state of an object—the collective value of all an object's attributes at any point in time.

`static`—a keyword that indicates that a method will be executed through a class and not by an object.

step value—the amount by which a loop control variable is altered on each iteration, especially in a `for` loop.

storyboard—a series of drawings that depicts the general plot outline of a movie or animation.

stream—a pipeline or channel through which bytes are input from and output to a file.

string—a data type that can hold a series of characters.

strongly typed—describes a language in which severe restrictions are placed on what data types can be mixed.

`struct`—a C# data type that is similar to a class that is typically used to encapsulate small groups of related values.

Structured Query Language (SQL)—the most common language that database administrators use to access data in their tables.

stylesheets—documents that specify how to render data stored in an XML document.

subclass—a derived class; a child class; a class that has inherited from a base class.

subscript—an integer contained within square brackets that indicates the position of one of an array's elements. Also see *index*.

superclass—a base class; a parent class; a class that is the basis for inheritance.

sweep angle—the number of degrees over which an arc is drawn.

`switch`—a keyword that starts a `switch` structure.

`switch` expression—a condition in a `switch` statement enclosed in parentheses.

`switch` structure—tests a single variable against a series of exact matches.

syntactic sugar—describes any programming construct that makes programs easier to read and write.

syntax—the set of grammar rules in a programming language.

syntax error—an error that occurs when a programming language is used incorrectly.

`System.Array`—a built-in class that defines fields and methods that belong to every array.

`System` namespace—a scheme built into the C# compiler that holds commonly used classes.

T

table—a name frequently used by mathematicians when referring to an array. Also see *matrix*.

tables—database files, so called because their contents are arranged in rows and columns.

tags—the markup indicators used in XML and XAML.

ternary—describes an operator that requires three arguments.

`this` reference—the reference to an object that is implicitly passed to an instance method of its class.

thread—the flow of execution of one set of program statements.

`Thread` class—a class used to create threads in addition to an application's main thread.

`ThreadPriority` enumeration—a defined list of thread priorities in C#.

thread scheduling—the process by which an operating system allocates processor time to each running thread.

thread synchronization—the process of excluding all but one thread from an object to avoid timing errors when accessing data.

`ThreadStart` delegate—a method that a `Thread` executes.

timeslicing—the concept of sharing processor time.

TLA—a three-letter abbreviation for *three-letter abbreviation*; it is the most popular type of abbreviation in technical terminology.

token—a block of text within a string that represents an entity or field.

Toolbox tab—a portion of the Visual Studio IDE that contains controls you can drag onto a `Form` so that you can develop programs visually, using a mouse.

transition—the changes that occur for the duration of an animation.

transitive—inheriting all the members of one's ancestors.

tree—a nonlinear data structure in which each node contains multiple self-referential links. Also, a metaphor used to describe the structure of an XML document.

triggers an event—causes an event to occur. Also see *fires an event* and *raises an event*.

`try` block—a block that contains code that might create exceptions you want to handle.

two-dimensional arrays—multidimensional arrays that have two or more columns of values for each row.

two-way binding—binding that exists when a change in a source causes a change in the target, and any change in the target causes a change in the source. Contrast with *one-way binding*.

type constraint—a clause that restricts the type of argument that can be supplied to a generic parameter in a generic method or class.

type inferencing—the act performed by a compiler when it uses the argument type in a call to a generic method to determine the method's generic type.

type parameter list—a list of generic data types contained between angle brackets that follows the name of each generic method and generic class.

type precedence—a hierarchy of data types used to determine the unifying type in arithmetic expressions containing dissimilar data types.

U

`uint`—an integral data type that can hold an unsigned numeric value in four bytes.

`ulong`—an integral data type that can hold an unsigned numeric value in eight bytes.

unary operators—operators used with one operand.

unboxing—the process of converting an `object` reference into a simple type.

Unicode—a 16-bit coding scheme for characters.

Unified Modeling Language (UML) diagrams—graphical tools that programmers and analysts use to describe systems.

unifying type—the type chosen for an arithmetic result when operands are of dissimilar types.

unreachable—describes code statements that can never execute under any circumstances because the program logic "can't get there." Also see *dead code*.

`ushort`—an integral data type that can hold an unsigned numeric value in two bytes.

`using` clause, or **`using` directive**—code that declares a namespace.

value parameter—a parameter to a method that receives a copy of the value passed to it. Contrast with *reference parameter* and *output parameter*.

value types—data types that hold a value; they are predefined types such as `int`, `double`, and `char`. Contrast with *reference type*.

`var`—a data type that creates an implicitly typed variable.

variable—a named location in computer memory that can hold different values at different points in time.

variable declaration—the statement that names a variable; it includes the data type that the variable will store, an identifier that is the variable's name, an optional assignment operator and assigned value when you want a variable to contain an initial value, and an ending semicolon.

verbatim identifier—an identifier with an @ prefix.

version attribute—in an XML document, the attribute that specifies the XML version used by the document.

virtual method—a method whose behavior is determined by the implementation in a child class.

visible—describes a class member that has not been hidden.

`void`—a keyword that indicates that a method does not return any value when called.

volatile—the type of computer storage that is lost when power is lost.

W

waiting queue—a list of the threads that are waiting for notification of a change in the state of a locked object.

`where`—a LINQ keyword that indicates conditions for selecting records.

`while` loop—a structure that executes a body of statements continuously while some condition continues to be true; it uses the keyword `while`.

whitespace—any combination of spaces, tabs, and carriage returns (blank lines) in a program.

widgets—interactive controls such as labels, scroll bars, check boxes, and radio buttons.

wildcard—a symbol that means "any" or "all."

Windows Presentation Foundation (WPF)—a presentation system included in the Microsoft .NET Framework that helps you build Windows client applications.

World Wide Web Consortium (W3C)—a coalition that develops specifications, guidelines, software, and tools to standardize information and communication on the Web.

wrapper class—a class that you wrap around data or methods to give them added functionality.

`WriteLine()` method—a method that displays a line of output on the screen, positions the cursor on the next line, and waits for additional output.

`Write()` method—a method that displays a line of output on the screen, but the cursor does not advance to a new line; it remains on the same line as the output.

write to the file—to store data in a computer file on a permanent storage device.

x-axis—the imaginary horizontal line that determines screen position.

x-coordinate—the first value in a screen position; its value increases as you travel from left to right across a window.

XML—an abbreviation of eXtensible Markup Language, which is a standard for exchanging data over the Internet.

XML deserialization—the process of re-creating objects in their original states from XML.

XML-documentation format comments—comments that use a special set of tags within angle brackets to create documentation within a program.

XML serialization—the process of converting an object's public properties and fields to XML for storage or transport.

`XmlSerializer` class—A class that serializes and deserializes objects to and from XML documents.

XSL Transformations (XSLT)—a standard for transforming XML documents into other formats.

y-axis—the imaginary vertical line that determines screen position.

y-coordinate—the second value in a screen position; its value increases as you travel from top to bottom in a window.

INDEX

Note: Page numbers in boldface indicate pages where key terms are defined.

E

H

I

T

Z